STANDARD GUIDE

GOLDEN AGE
COMICS

2006

ALEX G. MALLOY AND STUART W. WELLS

CH

©2006 Alex G. Malloy & Stuart W. Wells III
Published by

**kp books**
*An Imprint of F+W Publications*

**700 East State Street • Iola, WI 54990-0001
715-445-2214 • 888-457-2873**

Our toll-free number to place an order or obtain
a free catalog is (800) 258-0929.

Library of Congress Catalog Number: 2005922947
ISBN: 0-89689-181-X
Designed by Stuart W. Wells III
Edited by Kristine Manty
Printed in China

| A-1 Comics N# | Batman 3-D #1 | Canteen Kate #1 |

# CONTENTS

| Xmas Comics, 2nd Series #7 | Yellowjacket Comics #8 | Zorro #15 |

# Preface 2005

## By Alex G. Malloy & Stuart W. Wells III

The Golden Age of comic books started in the late 1930s, just at the onset of World War II. Much of the rest of the current popular culture, including color movies, television, and paperback books, also started at virtually the same moment. Graphical story-telling worked beautifully for most of the genres then popular in pulp magazines, movies, and cartoons, including westerns, mysteries, sci-fi and war stories, but the real innovation was the super-hero story. Vision seekers, comic publishers, artists, writers and creators conceived this new American genre.

The popularity of comics in the market place exploded in World War II and continued through the post war era. Collecting of Golden Age Comics started early, and has not stopped over the subsequent 60+ years. The best early comics have been recognized as fine art, and collectors now seeking Golden Age comics are paying astonishing prices.

We can thank the creators for establishing, fine tuning and producing the Super-hero, Science Fiction, the War Hero, Funny Animal (such as Disney and Looney Tunes), Horror, Drama and Romantic Adventure, and for bringing classic literature to the populace in Classic Comics. Current hot publishers include Timely, especially titles like *Jumbo* and *Planet Comics*, DC, early Fiction House, Centaur, Lev Gleason, and MLJ Magazines. EC is ever popular, with its titles benefiting from a strong crossover collector base of fans interested in top artists, horror and science fiction stories, and, of course, *MAD* magazine. The early Baby Boomers are now the primary group that buy Golden Age comics.

The paper shortages in 1944-45, due to World War II, resulted in smaller print runs for most comics. The issues from this period should see new price increases when the collectors realize this. Romance comics also have the potential of further increases in value. They are far scarcer than their super-hero counterparts, especially in high grade. Atlas-Marvel love romances and teenage romances are good examples. Millie the Model and related titles are currently in strong demand.

Work by the best artists continues to be highly sought. The covers of Alex Schomburg from World War II are very hot. Other popular early artists include Lou Fine, Simon & Kirby, Bill Everett, Leonard B. Cole, Bernie Krigstein, Bob Powell, Will Eisner and George Tuska. Post war era artists such as Wally Wood, Carl Barks, Walt Kelly, Bill Ward, Alex Toth, Matt Baker, Frank Frazetta, Joe Orlando, Johnny Craig, Jack Davis, Graham Ingles, Al Williamson, and Bill Elder are also in demand.

As with any collectible, the three key words are condition, condition, and condition. With the advent of CGC, the third party grading guide, sales of Golden Age comics have risen to impressive heights, mirroring the exceptional price increases in the U. S. coin market when coins were encapsulated and graded by independent experts some years ago. The new collector can venture into buying and selling with confidence. Investors have entered the market, bringing new big money into the collecting realm. High grade comics are harder and harder to locate. Collectors also seek so called "pedigree comics," especially those from the Mile High collection, as well as ones from the Allentown, San Francisco, Larson, Bethlehem, Boston, White Mountain and Gaines collections.

This book follows the listing system and format we devised in the early days of "Comic Values Monthly" (started in 1986) and *Comics Values Annual* (now in its 13$^{th}$ edition). Comics are covered in numerical order, with keys to artists, happenings, character appearances, etc. Prices in this guide are for strict standards like CGC grading, not like the grading standards of comics in the '80s and '90s.

Special thanks is extended to Paul Kennedy and Don Gulbrandsen at KP Books for saying 'Go' to this project. Great appreciation to Ed Jaster, director of acquisitions at Heritage Comics, and Ben Samuels for writing the introduction. Lastly, special thanks to Heritage Comics for its market report, and letting us use many of its fine comic cover illustrations.

Alex G. Malloy and Stuart W. Wells III

**The fearless creators of this book also produce *Comics Values Annual*. Look for a copy of the 2005 edition, now in print, or a copy of the 2006 edition, coming soon to a comic shop or book store near you.**

# GOLDEN AGE MARKET REPORT

## by Ed Jaster and Ben Samuels

Heritage Comics Auctions

The Golden Age comic market looks as strong as ever. At the top of the heap are the usual suspects: key issues from mainstream superhero titles featuring characters like Batman, Superman, Captain America, the Human Torch, Wonder Woman, Flash, and the Spectre — and the higher the grade, the better! The sale of *Marvel Comics* #1 (Denver pedigree) CGC VF+ 8.5 off-white pages for $172,500 in August 2005, and the sale of *Detective Comics* #38 (Allentown pedigree) CGC NM 9.4 off-white pages for $126,500 in May 2005, shows that there is plenty of competition for these high-end comics.

Key Archie-related comics are still in much demand, and can be very challenging to locate. Early Archie appearances in *Pep*, *Archie* #1, and *Jughead* #1 are as good as money in the bank. The early Disney Four Color key issues are also showing very healthy demand. File copies and bound volumes are proving to be especially popular.

Classic EC horror and science fiction titles are still holding strong, and demand is as strong as ever for *MAD* comics and the first

*Marvel Comics #1, © Marvel Comics Group, and Detective Comics #38, © DC Comics, Inc.*

few magazine issues. The market for some Quality titles like *Police*, *Plastic Man*, *Military*, and *Modern Comics* still show that current Overstreet values are somewhat inflated, but we see this as an opportunity for buyers to get good deals on books with fantastic work by artists like Jack Cole, Will Eisner, and Lou Fine.

The Mile High pedigree of Edgar Church still commands a healthy premium among collectors, but for many collectors a comic's CGC grade will trump the provenance of many "lesser" pedigrees. Another market segment that deserves note are comics with restoration, which seem to making a comeback as collectors re-adjust their attitudes and realize that a nice-looking book with restoration, at a reasonable price, can be a great addition to most collections!

Overall, the market for Golden Age comics looks very stable, and for the "best of the best," prices continue to rise with no limit in sight. High-grade, key Golden Age books are harder and harder to come by, as they find homes in permanent collections. Collectors of high-grade books know what they want, and they're willing to pay for it. The competition for the really nice books is very fierce, especially for key issues. There's no arguing with the fundamental economics of the hobby; as long as demand outweighs supply, prices will continue to rise.

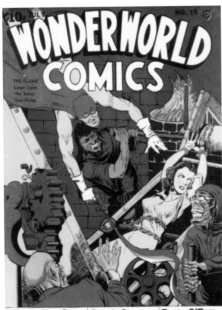

*Wonderworld Comics #15, © Fox Features Syndicate, cover by Lou Fine*
*& Police Comics #57, © Quality Comics Group, cover by Jack Cole.*

*Marvel Mystery Comics #46, $2,700*
*Marvel Timely 1943.*

*Captain America #3, $17,000*
*Marvel Timely 1941.*

## Covers by Alex Schomburg

*Sub-Mariner #11, $4,500*
*Marvel Timely 1943.*

*The Fighting Yank #11, $1,500*
*Nedor 1945.*

Exciting Comics #62, $1,000,
Nedor 1948.

Startling Comics #50, $1,100,
Better Publications 1948.

## Covers by "Xela" (Alex Schomburg)

Thrilling Comics #70, $900,
Better Publications 1948.

Wonder Comics #15, $1,700,
Better Publications 1947.

*Seven Seas Comics #4, $1,200*
*Universal Phoenix 1947.*

*The Saint #4, $800*
*Avon 1948.*

## Covers by Matt Baker

*Phantom Lady #16, $3,200*
*Fox Features Syndicate 1948.*

*Flyin' Jenny #2, $350*
*Pentagon Publishing 1947.*

Blue Beetle #52, $1,700,
Fox Features Syndicate 1948.

Dagar Desert Hawk #15, $1,000,
Fox Features Syndicate 1948.

## Covers by Jack Kamen

Brenda Starr #14 (#2), $5,000,
Four Star Publications 1948.

All Top Comics #10, $1,500,
Fox Features Syndicate 1948.

Dark Mysteries #1, $1,500
Master Publications 1951.

Judy Canova #23 (#1), $350
Fox Features Syndicate 1950.

# Covers by Wally Wood

My Experience #19, $400
Fox Features Syndicate 1949.

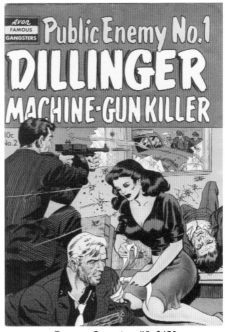

Famous Gangsters #2, $450
Avon 1951.

*Jumbo Comics #73, $350,*
*Fiction House 1945.*

*Rangers Comics #31, $400,*
*Fiction House 1946.*

## Covers by Joe Doolin

*Planet Comics #51, $1,200,*
*Fiction House 1948.*

*Planet Comics #41, $1,500,*
*Fiction House 1946.*

*Zoot #11, $900, Fox Features
Syndicate 1947, cover by Jack Kamen.*

*Wings Comics #91, $900,
Fiction House 1948, cover by Bob Lubbers.*

## Untie Me You Fiends!

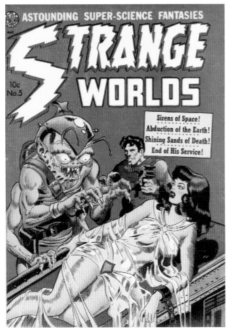

*Strange Worlds #5, $2,400,
Avon 1951, cover by Wally Wood.*

*Adventure Comics #39, $3,000,
DC Comics 1939.*

*Planet Comics #46, $1,500,*
*Fiction House 1947, cover by Joe Doolin.*

*Seven Seas #6, $1,000, Universal Phoenix*
*Feature 1947, cover by Matt Baker.*

## Girls to the Rescue!

*Black Cat #15, $375,*
*Harvey Publications 1949, cover by Lee Elias.*

*Miss Fury #5, $1,300,*
*Marvel Timely 1945, cover by Alex Schomburg.*

Blonde Phantom #14, $1,500,
Marvel Timely 1947, cover by Syd Shores.

Fight Comics #41, $1,000,
Fiction House 1945, cover by Joe Doolin.

## Wheel of Doom!

Mister Mystery #6, $800,
Aragon Magazines 1952, cover by Mortellaro.

Rangers Comics #25, $450,
Fiction House 1945, cover by Lee Elias.

Heroic Comics #3, $750,
Eastern Color 1940, cover by Bill Everett.

Captain Marvel Adventures #21, $1,700, Fawcett
1942, cover by C. C. Beck.

## Heroes to the Rescue!

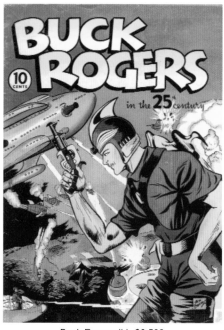

Strange Adventures #12 , $1,000,
DC Comics 1951, cover by Gil Kane.

Buck Rogers #1, $6,500,
Eastern Color 1940, cover by Dick Calkins.

*Junior #15, $1,000, Fox Features Syndicate 1948, cover by Al Feldstein.*

*Al Capp's Wolf Gal #1, $500, Toby Press 1951, cover by Al Capp.*

## Here's Looking at You, Kid!

*Sunny America's Sweetheart #11, $2,000, Fox Features 1947, cover by Al Feldstein.*

*Torchy #4, #1,400, Quality Publications 1950, cover by Gill Fox.*

Son of Sinbad #1, $500, St. John
Publications 1950, cover by Joe Kubert.

MAD Magazine #4, $2,500,
EC Comics 1953, cover by Harvey Kurtzman.

## Famous Artists

Two-Fisted Annual 1953 (#2), $1,400,
EC Comics 1953, cover by Jack Davis.

Tales From the Crypt #32, $1,500,
EC Comics 1952, cover by Jack Davis.

*Blue Beetle #54, $1,800,*
*Fox Features Syndicate 1948.*

*Moon Girl and the Prince #1, $1,400,*
*EC Comics 1947, cover by Johnny Craig.*

## Famous Artists

*Love Diary #1, $400,*
*Quality Comics 1949, cover by Bill Ward.*

*Zoot Comics #16, $650, Fox Features*
*Syndicate 1948, cover by Victor Fox.*

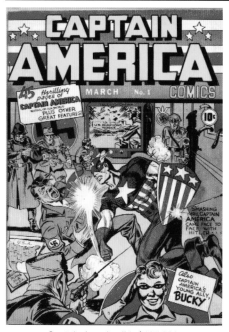

Captain America #1, $135,000,
Marvel Timely 1941, cover by Jack Kirby.

Whiz Comics #30, $1,400,
Fawcett Publications 1942, cover by C. C. Beck.

## Famous Artists

National Comics #7, $3,500,
Quality Publications 1941, cover by Lou Fine.

Walt Disney Comics and Stories #167, $150,
Dell Publications 1954, cover by Carl Barks.

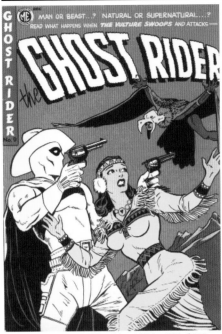

*A-1 Comics #69 (The Ghost Rider #9), $600,*
*Magazine Ent. 1952, cover by Dick Ayers.*

*A-1 Comics #47 (Thunda #1), $2,200, Magazine*
*Ent. 1952, cover by Frank Frazetta.*

## Famous Artists

*Captain America Comics #66, $3,300,*
*Marvel Timely 1948, cover by Syd Shores.*

*Sub-Mariner Comics #23, $2,200,*
*Marvel Timely 1947, cover by Syd Shores.*

Walt Disney's Comics and Stories #109, $275.,
Dell Publ. 1950, cover by Carl Barks.

The Marvel Family #37, $350, Fawcett
Publications 1949, cover by C. C. Beck.

## Famous Artists

Target Comics #5, $9,000,
Novelty Press 1940, cover by Bill Everett.

Donald Duck #26, $800,
Dell Publishing 1952, cover by Carl Barks.

Pogo Possum #10, $450,
Dell Publishing Co. 1952, cover by Walt Kelly.

Animal Fables #7, $1,200,
EC Comics 1947, cover by Al Fago.

## Famous Artists

Holiday #7, $275,
Star 1952, cover by L. B. Cole.

Walt Disney's Comics and Stories #22, $750,
Dell 1942, cover by Carl Buettner.

# GRADING GUIDE

In David Brin's science fiction–fantasy novel, *The Practice Effect*, things improve with use. You start with a crudely made tool and keep using it until it becomes a fine instrument. If our world worked that way, you could read your Golden Age comics as often as you liked and they would just get better looking each time. Unfortunately, our world does not work that way, and reading your comics (along with just about everything else) causes comics to deteriorate.

Even if you could protect your comics from external light, heat, cold, moisture, pressure and everything else, you couldn't protect them from their own paper. Most comic books were printed on pulp paper, which has a high acid content. This means that the paper slowly turns brittle with age, no matter what you do to it, short of special museum-style preservation.

Very old, well-preserved comics are coveted collector's items. In most cases, people did not save their comic books for future generations. They read them and discarded them. Comic books were considered harmless ephemera for children. When these children outgrew their comics, their parents often threw them away. If everybody kept all of their comics, comics would not be valuable because everybody would have them scattered about the house!

The value of any comic depends on scarcity, popularity and condition. Scarcity increases with age and popularity depends on the whim of the public — only condition automatically decreases with age. Newer comics are generally available in near-mint condition, so newer comics in lesser condition have little collector potential. However, older comics are scarce, so they are still collectible in less than near-mint condition, but the value is obviously less. This is a basic tenet of all collectibles. A car is more valuable with its original paint. A baseball card is more valuable if it has not been marred by bicycle spokes. Coke bottles, stamps, coins, and toys in good condition are all more valuable than their abused counterparts. Comic books are no exception.

New comic book collectors should learn how to assess the prospective value of a comic in order to protect themselves from being fleeced by unscrupulous dealers or hucksters. Yet, a majority of dealers, especially store owners, can be considered reliable judges of comic grade. Because comic retail may be their primary source of income, certain dealers are particularly adept at noticing comic book imperfections, especially in issues they intend to purchase. As such, hobbyists and collectors must understand that dealers need to make a minimum profit on their investments. Buying collectible comics entails certain risks. Therefore, dealers must scrutinize a comic to determine if the particular book will stand a chance of resale. Well-preserved comics are invariably more desirable to dealers because they are more desirable to collectors.

There are eight standard comic grades: mint, near mint, very fine, fine, very good, good, fair, and poor. Clearly, these eight grades could be split into even finer categories when haggling over an exceptionally rare or coveted Golden Age comic. In most cases, however, comic books can be evaluated using these eight standard grades. The values listed in this book are all for comics in "Near Mint" condition. The grading/price chart given at the back of this book should be used to adjust this price for comics in different grades.

For many Golden Age comic issues, there are no known mint condition examples, but most issues have a few near mint copies in the hands of collectors. Many of these come from a few "pedigree" sources like the famous mile-high collection. There are, however, some issues where no known example is in near mint condition. To be consistent, the value listed

---

in this price guide is still for a "near mint" copy, even if no such copy exists. The grading/price chart in the back will still yield a price for the lesser grades that actually exist. And, who knows, maybe there is another treasure trove of old comics somewhere — maybe you'll even be the one who finds it!

## Mint (CGC 9.5 or above)

Finding old comics in mint condition is almost impossible because of inferior storage techniques and materials. In the early days of collecting, few people anticipated that the very boxes and bags in which they stored their comics were contributing to decay. Acid from bags, backing boards, and boxes eat away at many comics.. Mint condition comics usually fetch prices higher than price guide listings. Mint comics can sell for 120% or more of the listed price.

Mint comics are perfect comics and allow no room for imperfections. Pages and covers must be free of discoloration, wear, and wrinkles. A mint comic is one that looks like it just rolled off the press. Staples and spine must meet perfectly without cover "rollover." The cover must be crisp, bright, and trimmed perfectly. The staples must not be rusted and the cover should not have any visible creases. The interior pages of a mint comic are equally crisp and new. A mint comic must not show any signs of age or decay. Because of the paper stock used on many older comics, acid and oxygen cause interior pages to yellow and flake.

## Near Mint (CGC 9.4)

A near mint comic and a mint comic are close siblings, with their differences slight, even to an experienced eye. Most of the new comics on the shelf of the local comic shop are in near mint condition. These are comics that have been handled gingerly to preserve the original luster of the book. Near mint comics are bright, clean copies with no major or minor defects. Slight stress lines near the staples and perhaps a very minor printing defect are permissible. Corners must still be sharp and devoid of creases. Interior pages of newsprint stock should show almost no discernible yellowing. Near mint comics usually trade for 100% of the listed price, with just a small discount for slightly lower grades.

## Very Fine (CGC 8.0)

A very fine comic is one that is routinely found on the shelves and back issue bins of most good direct market comic shops. This grade comic has few defects, none of them major. Stress around the staples of a very fine comic are visible but not yet radical enough to create wrinkles. Both the cover and interior pages should still be crisp and sharp, devoid of flaking and creases. Interior pages may be slightly yellowed from age.

Most high-quality older comics graded as very fine can obtain 80-90% of listed prices. More, if the comic is the highest-graded comic known to exist.

## Fine (CGC 6.0)

Fine comics are often issues that may have been stored carefully under a bed or on a shelf by a meticulous collector. This grade of comic is also very desirable because it shows little wear and retains much of its original sharpness. The cover may be slightly off center from rollover. The cover retains less of its original gloss and may even possess a chip or wrinkle. The comers should be sharp but may also have a slight crease. Yellowing begins to creep into the interior pages of a comic graded as fine.

Fine comics are respectable additions to collections and sell for about 40-60% of the listed price.

## Very Good (CGC 4.0)

A very good comic may have been an issue passed around or read frequently. This grade is the common condition of older books. Its cover will probably have lost some luster and may have two or three creases around the staples or edges. The corners of the book may begin to show the beginnings of minor rounding and chipping, but it is by no means a damaged or defaced comic. Comics in very good condition sell for about 30-40% of listed price.

## Good (CGC 2.0)

A good comic is one that has been well read and is beginning to show its age. Although both front and back covers are still attached, a good grade comic may have a number of serious wrinkles and chips. The corners and edges of this grade comic may show clear signs of rounding and flaking. There should be no major tears in a good comic nor should any pages be clipped out or missing. Interior pages may be fairly yellowed and brittle. Good comics sell for about 15-25% of the listed price.

## Fair (CGC 1.0)

A fair comic is one that has definitely seen better days and has considerably limited resale value for most collectors. This comic may be soiled and damaged on the cover and interior. Fair comics should be completely intact and may only be useful as a reading copy, or a comic to lend to friends. Fair comics sell for about 10-20% of the listed price.

## Poor

Comics in poor condition are generally unsuitable for collecting or reading because they range from damaged to unrecognizable. Poor comics may have been water damaged, attacked by a small child, or worse, perhaps, gnawed on by the family pet! Interior and exterior pages may be cut apart or missing entirely. A poor comic sells for about 5-15% of the listed price.

## Sniffing Out Grades

Despite everything that is mentioned about comic grading, the process remains relative to the situation. A comic that seems to be in very good condition may actually be a restored copy. A restored copy is generally considered to be in between the grade it was previous to restoration and the grade it has become. Many collectors avoid restored comics entirely.

Each collector builds his collection around what he believes is important. Some want every issue of a particular series or company. Others want every issue of a favorite artist or writer. Because of this, many collectors will purchase lower-grade comics to fill out a series or to try out a new series. Mint and near mint comics are usually much more desirable to hardcore collectors. Hobbyists and readers may find the effort and cost of collecting only high-grade comics financially prohibitive.

Getting artists or writers to autograph comics has also become a source of major dispute. Some collectors enjoy signed comics and others consider those very comics defaced! The current trends indicate that most collectors do enjoy signed comics. A signature does not usually change the grade of the comic.

As mentioned, comic grading is a subjective process that must be agreed upon by the buyer and seller. Buyers will often be quick to note minor defects in order to negotiate a better price. Sellers are sometimes selectively blind to their comic's defects.

| | | | |
|---|---|---|---|
| Abel, Jack . . . JA | Dresser, Larry . . . LDr | Kelly, Walt . . . WK | Rubano, Aldo . . . ARu |
| Addeo, Stephen . . . StA | Drucker, Mort . . . MD | Kiefer, Henry C. . . . HcK | Sahle, Harry . . . HSa |
| Alcala, Alfredo . . . AA | Duursema, Jan . . . JD | Kildale, Malcolm . . . MKd | Sale, Tim . . . TSe |
| Anderson, Murphy . . . MA | Eisner, Will . . . WE | Kinsler, Everett R. . . . EK | Saltares, Javier . . . JS |
| Andriola, Alfred . . . AIA | Elder, Bill . . . BE | Kirby, Jack . . . JK | Saunders, Norm . . . NS |
| Andru, Ross . . . RA | Elias, Lee . . . LEl | Krenkel, Roy . . . RKu | Schaffenberger, Kurt . . . KS |
| Ashe, Edd . . . EA | Evans, George . . . GE | Krigstein, Bernie . . . BK | Schomburg, Alex . . . ASh |
| Avison, Al . . . AAv | Evans, Ray . . . REv | Kubert, Joe . . . JKu | Schrotter, Gustav . . . GS |
| Ayers, Dick . . . DAy | Everett, Bill . . . BEv | Kurtzman, Harvey . . . HK | Sekowsky, Mike . . . MSy |
| Bailey, Bernard . . . BBa | Fabry, Glenn . . . GF | Lamme, Bob . . . BbL | Severin, John . . . JSe |
| Bailey, M . . . MBi | Fago, Al . . . AFa | LaRocque, Greg . . . GrL | Sherman, Jim . . . JSh |
| Baker, Kyle . . . KB | Feldstein, Al . . . AF | Larsen, Erik . . . EL | Shores, Syd . . . SSh |
| Baker, Matt . . . MB | Fine, Lou . . . LF | Lavery, Jim . . . JLv | Shuster, Joe . . . JoS |
| Barks, Carl . . . CB | Finnocchiaro, Sal . . . SF | Lawrence, Terral . . . TLw | Siegel & Shuster . . . S&S |
| Barry, Dan . . . DBa | Fiske, J . . . JFe | Leonard, Lank . . . LLe | Silvestri, Mark . . . MS |
| Battlefield, Dennis . . . DB | Flemming, Homer . . . HFl | Livingstone, Rolland . RLv | Sim, Dave . . . DS |
| Battlefield, Ken . . . KBa | Flessel, Creig . . . CF | Lubbers, Bob . . . BLb | Simon & Kirby . . . S&K |
| Beck, C. C. . . . CCB | Forte, John . . . JF | Maneely, Joe . . . JMn | Simon, Allen . . . ASm |
| Berg, Dave . . . DBe | Foster, Hal . . . HF | Manning, Russ . . . RsM | Simon, Joe . . . JSm |
| Berger, Charles . . . ChB | Fox, Gill . . . GFx | Maxwell, Stanley . . . StM | Sinnott, Joe . . . JSt |
| Biggs, Geoffrey . . . GB | Fox, Matt . . . MF | Mayer, Sheldon . . . ShM | Smith, Fran . . . FSm |
| Binder, Jack . . . JaB | Frazetta, Frank . . . FF | McCann, Gerald . . . GMc | Sparling, Jack . . . JkS |
| Bingham, Jerry . . . JBi | Frese, George . . . GFs | McWilliams, Al . . . AMc | Spector, Irving . . . IS |
| Biro, Charles . . . CBi | Froehlich, August . . . AgF | Meagher, Fred . . . FMe | Starr, Leonard . . . LSt |
| Blum, Alex . . . AB | Fujitani(Fuje), Bob . . . BF | Meskin, Mort . . . MMe | Stein, Marvin . . . MvS |
| Bolle, Frank . . . FBe | Giacoia, Frank . . . FrG | Messmer, Otto . . . OM | Streeter, Lin . . . LnS |
| Boring, Wayne . . . WB | Giordano, Dick . . . DG | Miller, Steve . . . SM | Swan, Curt . . . CS |
| Bossart, William . . . WmB | Glanzman, Sam . . . SG | Moe, C. S. . . . CSM | Tallarico, Tony . . . TyT |
| Braithwaite, Doug. . . DBw | Goldberg, Rube . . . RuG | Moldoff, Sheldon . . . SMo | Tartaglione, John . . . JTg |
| Brewster, Ann . . . ABr | Gottfredson, Floyd . . . FG | Mooney, Jim . . . JM | Thompson, Bud . . . BTh |
| Briefer, Dick . . . DBr | Gould, Chester . . . ChG | Morales, Lou . . . LM | Thorne, Frank . . . FT |
| Brodsky, Allyn . . . AyB | Grandmetti, Jerry . . . JGr | Moreira, Ruben . . . RMo | Torres, Angelo . . . AT |
| Burgos, Carl . . . CBu | Griffiths, Harley . . . HyG | Morisi, Pete . . . PMo | Toth, Alex . . . ATh |
| Burnley, Jack . . . JBu | Guardineer, Fred . . . FGu | Morrow, Gray . . . GM | Trapain, Sal . . . ST |
| Burns, Robert . . . RBu | Guinan, Paul . . . PGn | Mortimer, Win . . . WMo | Tuska, George . . . GT |
| Buscema, John . . . JB | Gulacy, Paul . . . PG | Moskowitz, Seymour . SMz | Ulmer, Al . . . AU |
| Cady, Harrison . . . HCa | Gustavson, Paul . . . PGv | Nodel, Norman . . . NN | Van Buren, Raeburn . . RvB |
| Cameron, Don . . . DCn | Harmon, Jim . . . JHa | Noonan, Dan . . . DNo | Vincent, A. . . . AVi |
| Cameron, Lou . . . LC | Harrison, Simon . . . SHn | Nostrand, Howard . . . HN | Waldinger, Morris . . . MsW |
| Campbell, Stan . . . StC | Hart, Ernest . . . EhH | Novick, Irv . . . IN | Waldman, Ed . . . EW |
| Cardy, Nick . . . NC | Hearnes, David . . . DvH | Orlando, Joe . . . JO | Ward, Bill . . . BWa |
| Carlson, George . . . GCn | Hearne, Jack . . . JH | Oskner, Bob . . . BO | Warren, Jack A. . . . JW |
| Castrillo, Anthony . . . ACa | Heath, Russ . . . RH | Oughton, Thomas . . . TO | Webb, Robert . . . RWb |
| Chestney, Lillian . . . LCh | Hebbard, Robert . . . RtH | Palais, Rudy . . . RP | Whiteman, Ezra . . . EzW |
| Citron, Sam . . . SmC | Heck, Don . . . DH | Paul, Frank R. . . . FP | Whitman, Bill . . . BWh |
| Colan, Gene . . . GC | Hibbard, E.E. . . . EHi | Payne, Pop . . . PP | Whitney, Ogden . . . OW |
| Cole, Jack . . . JCo | Hicks, Arnold . . . AdH | Perlin, Don . . . DP | Wiacek, Bob . . . BWi |
| Cole, Leonard B. . . . LbC | Hing, T. F. . . . TFH | Plastino, Al . . . APl | Wildey, Doug . . . DW |
| Colletta, Vince . . . ViC | Hogarth, Burne . . . BHg | Polseno, Jo . . . JP | Williams, J.H. . . . JWi |
| Collins, Mike . . . MC | Hughes, Adam . . . AH | Powell, Bob . . . BP | Williamson, Al . . . AW |
| Colon, Ernie . . . EC | Hultgren, Ken . . . KHu | Premaini, Bruno . . . BPr | Willingham, Bill . . . BWg |
| Cooper, Sam . . . SCp | Infantino, Carmine . . . CI | Prezio, Victor . . . VP | Wilson, Gahan . . . GW |
| Costanza, Peter . . . PrC | Ingles, Graham . . . GrI | Quinlan, Charles . . . CQ | Woggin, Bill . . . BWo |
| Craig, Johnny . . . JCr | Iorio, Medio . . . MI | Raboy, Mac . . . MRa | Wolverton, Basil . . . BW |
| Crandall, Reed . . . RC | Isherwood, Geoff . . . GI | Ramsey, Ray . . . RR | Wood, Bob . . . BoW |
| Cuidera, Chuck . . . CCu | Jaffee, Al . . . AJ | Rasmussen, H . . . HR | Wood, Wally . . . WW |
| Davis, Bob . . . BD | Jenney, Robert . . . RJ | Raymond, Alex . . . AR | Woodbridge, George . GWb |
| Davis, Jack . . . JDa | Johnson, Walter . . . WJo | Rico, Don . . . DRi | Woodring, Jim . . . JWo |
| Del Bourgo, Maurice . MDb | Kaluta, Mike . . . MK | Robinson, James . . . JeR | Zansky, Louis . . . LZ |
| Dillin, Dick . . . DD | Kamen, Jack . . . JKa | Roea, Doug . . . DgR | |
| Disbrow, Jay . . . JyD | Kane, Bob . . . BKa | Rogers, Boody . . . BRo | |
| Ditko, Steve . . . SD | Kane, Gil . . . GK | Romita, John . . . JR | |
| Dougherty, H. . . . HD | Katz, Jack . . . JKz | Ross, David . . . DR | |

## GENERAL ABBREVIATIONS FOR COMICS LISTINGS

| | | | | |
|---|---|---|---|---|
| Adaptation . . . Adapt. | Cover . . . (c) | King Size . . . K-Size | Retold . . . rtd. |
| Appearance of . . . A: | Crossover with . . x-over | Leaving of . . . L: | Return/Revival of . . . R: |
| Anniversary . . . Anniv. | Death/Destruction of . D: | New Costume . . . N: | Story, or, Written by . (s) |
| Annual . . . Ann.# | Edition . . . Ed. | No Issue Number . . N# | Special . . . Spec. |
| Art & Cover . . . (a&c) | Ending of . . . E: | Origin of . . . O: | Team-up . . . T.U. |
| Artist . . . (a) | Features . . . F: | Painted Cover . . . P(c) | Versus . . . V: or vs. |
| Back-Up Story . . . BU: | Giant Size . . . G-Size | Part . . . pt. or Pt. | Wedding of . . . W: |
| Beginning of . . . B: | Identity Revealed . . . IR: | Photo cover . . . Ph(c) | With . . . w/ |
| Birth of . . . b: | Introduction of . . . I: | Preview . . . Prev. | Without . . . w/o |
| Cameo Appearance . . C: | Joins of . . . J: | Reprinted issue . . . rep. | |

| Abbr. | Name | Abbr. | Name | Abbr. | Name | Abbr. | Name |
|---|---|---|---|---|---|---|---|
| AA | Alfredo Alcala | DBw | Doug Braithwaite | JBu | Jack Burnley | MSy | Mike Sekowsky |
| AAv | Al Avison | DCn | Don Cameron | JCo | Jack Cole | MvS | Marvin Stein |
| AB | Alex Blum | DD | Dick Dillin | JCr | Johnny Craig | NC | Nick Cardy |
| ABr | Ann Brewster | DG | Dick Giordano | JD | Jan Duursema | NN | Norman Nodel |
| ACa | Anthony Castrillo | DgR | Doug Roea | JDa | Jack Davis | NS | Norm Saunders |
| AdH | Arnold Hicks | DH | Don Heck | JeR | James Robinson | OM | Otto Messmer |
| AF | Al Feldstein | DNo | Dan Noonan | JF | John Forte | OW | Ogden Whitney |
| AFa | Al Fago | DP | Don Perlin | JFe | J. Fiske | PG | Paul Gulacy |
| AgF | August Froehlich | DR | Ross, David | JGr | Jerry Grandmetti | PGn | Paul Guinan |
| AH | Adam Hughes | DRi | Don Rico | JH | Jack Hearne | PGv | Paul Gustavson |
| AIA | Alfred Andriola | DS | Dave Sim | JHa | Jim Harmon | PMo | Pete Morisi |
| AJ | Al Jaffee | DvH | David Hearnes | JK | Jack Kirby | PP | Pop Payne |
| AMc | Al McWilliams | DW | Doug Wildey | JKa | Jack Kamen | PrC | Peter Costanza |
| API | Al Plastino | EA | Edd Ashe | JkS | Jack Sparling | RA | Ross Andru |
| AR | Alex Raymond | EC | Ernie Colon | JKu | Joe Kubert | RBu | Robert Burns |
| ARu | Aldo Rubano | EhH | Ernest Hart | JKz | Jack Katz | RC | Reed Crandall |
| ASh | Alex Schomburg | EHi | E.E. Hibbard | JLv | Jim Lavery | REv | Ray Evans |
| ASm | Allen Simon | EK | Everett R. Kinsler | JM | Jim Mooney | RH | Russ Heath |
| AT | Angelo Torres | EL | Erik Larsen | JMn | Joe Maneely | RJ | Robert Jenney |
| ATh | Alex Toth | EW | Ed Waldman | JO | Joe Orlando | RKu | Roy Krenkel |
| AU | Al Ulmer | EzW | Ezra Whiteman | JoS | Joe Shuster | RLv | Rolland Livingstone |
| AVi | A. Vincent | FBe | Frank Bolle | JP | Jo Polseno | RMo | Ruben Moreira |
| AW | Al Williamson | FF | Frank Frazetta | JR | John Romita | RP | Rudy Palais |
| AyB | Allyn Brodsky | FG | Floyd Gottfredson | JRo | Jerry Robinson | RR | Ray Ramsey |
| BBa | Bernard Bailey | FGu | Fred Guardineer | JS | Javier Saltares | RsM | Russ Manning |
| BbL | Bob Lamme | FMe | Fred Meagher | JSe | John Severin | RtH | Robert Hebbard |
| BD | Bob Davis | FP | Frank R. Paul | JSh | Jim Sherman | RuG | Rube Goldberg |
| BE | Bill Elder | FrG | Frank Giacoia | JSm | Joe Simon | RvB | Raeburn Van Buren |
| BEv | Bill Everett | FSm | Fran Smith | JSt | Joe Sinnott | RWb | Robert Webb |
| BF | Bob Fujitani(Fuje) | FT | Frank Thorne | JTg | John Tartaglione | S&K | Simon & Kirby |
| BHg | Burne Hogarth | GB | Geoffrey Biggs | JW | Jack A Warren | S&S | Siegel & Shuster |
| BK | Bernie Krigstein | GC | Gene Colan | JWi | J.H. Williams | SCp | Sam Cooper |
| BKa | Bob Kane | GCn | George Carlson | JWo | Jim Woodring | SD | Steve Ditko |
| BLb | Bob Lubbers | GE | George Evans | JyD | Jay Disbrow | SF | Sal Finnocchiaro |
| BO | Bob Oskner | GF | Glenn Fabry | KB | Kyle Baker | SG | Sam Glanzman |
| BoW | Bob Wood | GFs | George Frese | KBa | Ken Battlefield | ShM | Sheldon Mayer |
| BP | Bob Powell | GFx | Gill Fox | KHu | Ken Hultgren | SHn | Simon Harrison |
| BPr | Bruno Premaini | GI | Geoff Isherwood | KS | Kurt Schaffenberger | SmC | Sam Citron |
| BRo | Boody Rogers | GK | Gil Kane | LbC | Leonard B. Cole | SM | Steve Miller |
| BTh | Bud Thompson | GM | Gray Morrow | LC | Lou Cameron | SMo | Sheldon Moldoff |
| BW | Basil Wolverton | GMc | Gerald McCann | LCh | Lillian Chestney | SMz | Seymour Moskowitz |
| BWa | Bill Ward | Grl | Graham Ingles | LDr | Larry Dresser | SSh | Syd Shores |
| BWg | Bill Willingham | GrL | Greg LaRocque | LEl | Lee Elias | ST | Sal Trapain |
| BWh | Bill Whitman | GS | Gustav Schrotter | LF | Lou Fine | StA | Stephen Addeo |
| BWi | Bob Wiacek | GT | George Tuska | LLe | Lank Leonard | StC | Stan Campbell |
| BWo | Bill Woggin | GW | Gahan Wilson | LM | Lou Morales | StM | Stanley Maxwell |
| CB | Carl Barks | GWb | George Woodbridge | LnS | Lin Streeter | TFH | T. F. Hing |
| CBi | Charles Biro | HCa | Harrison Cady | LSt | Leonard Starr | TLw | Terral Lawrence |
| CBu | Carl Burgos | HcK | Henry C. Kiefer | LZ | Louis Zansky | TO | Thomas Oughton |
| CCB | C. C. Beck | HD | H. Dougherty | MA | Murphy Anderson | TSe | Tim Sale |
| CCu | Chuck Cuidera | HF | Hal Foster | MB | Matt Baker | TyT | Tony Tallarico |
| CF | Creig Flessel | HFl | Homer Flemming | MBi | M. Bailey | ViC | Vince Colleta |
| ChB | Charles Berger | HK | Harvey Kurtzman | MC | Mike Collins | VP | Victor Prezio |
| ChG | Chester Gould | HN | Howard Nostrand | MD | Mort Drucker | WB | Wayne Boring |
| CI | Carmine Infantino | HR | H. Rasmussen | MDb | Maurice Del Bourgo | WE | Will Eisner |
| CQ | Charles Quinlan | HSa | Harry Sahle | MF | Matt Fox | WJo | Walter Johnson |
| CS | Curt Swan | HyG | Harley Griffiths | MI | Medio Iorio | WK | Walt Kelly |
| CSM | C. S. Moe | IN | Irv Novick | MK | Mike Kaluta | WmB | William Bossart |
| DAy | Dick Ayers | IS | Irving Spector | MKd | Malcolm Kildale | WMo | Win Mortimer |
| DB | Dennis Battlefield | JA | Jack Abel | MMe | Mort Meskin | WW | Wally Wood |
| DBa | Dan Barry | JaB | Jack Binder | MRa | Mac Raboy | | |
| DBe | Dave Berg | JB | John Buscema | MS | Mark Silvestri | | |
| DBr | Dick Briefer | JBi | Jerry Bingham | MsW | Morris Waldinger | | |

## GENERAL ABBREVIATIONS FOR COMICS LISTINGS

|  |  |  |  |  |  |  |  |
|---|---|---|---|---|---|---|---|
| A: | Appearance of | (c) | Cover | L: | Leaving of | rtd. | Retold |
| (a) | Artist | D: | Death/Destruction of | N: | New Costume | (s) | Story, or Written by |
| Adapt. | Adaptation | Ed. | Edition | N# | No Issue Number | Spec. | Special |
| Anniv. | Anniversary | E: | Ending of | O: | Origin of | T.U. | Team-up |
| Ann.# | Annual | F: | Features | P(c) | Painted Cover | V: or vs. | Versus |
| (a&c) | Art & Cover | G-Size | Giant Size | Ph(c) | Photo cover | W: | Wedding of |
| B: | Beginning of | I: | Introduction of | Prev. | Preview | w/ | With |
| b: | Birth of | IR: | Identity Revealed | pt. or Pt. | Part | w/o | Without |
| BU: | Back-Up Story | J: | Joins of | rep. | Reprinted issue | x-over | Crossover with |
| C: | Cameo Appearance | K-Size | King Size | R: | Return/Revival of | | |

## A-1 COMICS

### Magazine Enterprises, 1944

N# F:Kerry Drake,BU:Johnny
Devildog & Streamer Kelly . . 300.00
1 A:Dotty Driple,Mr. EX,Bush
Berry and Lew Loyal . . . . . . 150.00
2 A: Texas Slim & Dirty Dalton,
The Corsair,Teddy Rich, Dotty
Dripple,Inca Dinca,Tommy Tinker
Little Mexico and Tugboat . . . 100.00
3 same . . . . . . . . . . . . . . . . . 100.00
4 same . . . . . . . . . . . . . . . . . 100.00
5 same . . . . . . . . . . . . . . . . . 100.00
6 same . . . . . . . . . . . . . . . . . 100.00
7 same . . . . . . . . . . . . . . . . . 100.00
8 same . . . . . . . . . . . . . . . . . 100.00
9 Texas Slim Issue . . . . . . . . . . 125.00
10 Same characters as
issues #2–#8 . . . . . . . . . . . . 100.00
11 Teena . . . . . . . . . . . . . . . . . 150.00
12 Teena . . . . . . . . . . . . . . . . . 100.00
13 JCr,Guns of Fact and Fiction,
narcotics & junkies featured . 400.00
14 Tim Holt #1. . . . . . . . . . . . . 1,100.00
15 Teena . . . . . . . . . . . . . . . . . 100.00
16 Vacation Comics . . . . . . . . . . . 75.00
17 Tim Holt #2, E:"A-1" on cover . 500.00
18 Jimmy Durante, Ph(c). . . . . . . 650.00
19 Tim Holt #3 . . . . . . . . . . . . . . 400.00
20 Jimmy Durante Ph(c) . . . . . . 600.00
21 OW,Joan of Arc movie adapt. . 400.00
22 Dick Powell (1949) . . . . . . . . 350.00
23 Cowboys N' Indians #6. . . . . . 175.00
24 FF(c),LbC,Trail Colt #1 . . . . . 600.00
25 Fibber McGee & Molly (1949). 125.00
26 LbC, Trail Colt #2 . . . . . . . . . 500.00
27 GhostRider#1,O:GhostRider 1,500.00
28 Christmas (Koko & Kola #6) . . . 75.00
29 FF(c), Ghost Rider #2 . . . . . 1,100.00
30 BP, Jet Powers #1 . . . . . . . . 600.00
31 FF,Ghost Rider #3,O:Ghost
Rider . . . . . . . . . . . . . . . . 1, 100.00
32 AW,GE,Jet Powers #2 . . . . . . 550.00
33 Muggsy Mouse #1 . . . . . . . . 100.00
34 FF(c),Ghost Rider #4. . . . . . 1,100.00
35 AW,Jet Powers#3 . . . . . . . . . 550.00
36 Muggsy Mouse #2 . . . . . . . . 125.00
37 FF(c),Ghost Rider #5. . . . . . 1,100.00
38 AW,WW,Jet Powers#4, Drugs 900.00

39 Muggsy Mouse #3 . . . . . . . . 100.00
40 Dogface Dooley #1. . . . . . . . 100.00
41 Cowboys 'N' Indians #7 . . . . 100.00
42 BP,Best of the West #1. . . . . 700.00
43 Dogface Dooley#2 . . . . . . . . . 75.00
44 Ghost Rider #6 . . . . . . . . . . . 500.00
45 American Air Forces #5 . . . . . 200.00
46 Best of the West #4 . . . . . . . . 650.00
47 FF,Thunda #1. . . . . . . . . . . 2,200.00
48 Cowboys N' Indians #8. . . . . 150.00
49 Dogface Dooley #3. . . . . . . . . 75.00
50 BP,Danger is Their
Business #11 . . . . . . . . . . . . 200.00
51 Ghost Rider #7 . . . . . . . . . . . 500.00
52 Best of the West #3 . . . . . . . . 400.00
53 Dogface Dooley #4. . . . . . . . . 75.00
54 BP,American Air Forces #6. . . 100.00
55 BP,U.S. Marines #5. . . . . . . . 100.00
56 BP,Thunda #2. . . . . . . . . . . . 350.00
57 Ghost Rider #8, Drugs . . . . . 600.00
58 American Air Forces #7 . . . . . 100.00
59 Best of the West #4 . . . . . . . . 350.00
60 The U.S. Marines #6. . . . . . . 100.00
61 Space Ace #5 . . . . . . . . . . . 900.00
62 Starr Flagg #5 . . . . . . . . . . . 600.00
63 FF,Manhunt #13 . . . . . . . . . 550.00
64 Dogface Dooley #5. . . . . . . . . 75.00
65 BP,American Air Forces #8. . . 100.00
66 Best of the West #5 . . . . . . . . 350.00
67 American Air Forces #9 . . . . . 100.00
68 U.S. Marines #7 . . . . . . . . . . 100.00
69 Ghost Rider #9, Drugs . . . . . 600.00
70 Best of the West #6 . . . . . . . . 350.00
71 Ghost Rider #10 . . . . . . . . . . 500.00
72 U.S. Marines #8 . . . . . . . . . . 100.00
73 BP,Thunda #3. . . . . . . . . . . . 300.00
74 BP,American Air Forces #10. . 100.00
75 Ghost Rider #11 . . . . . . . . . . 400.00
76 Best of the West #7 . . . . . . . . 250.00
77 LbC,Grl,Manhunt #14 . . . . . . 450.00
78 BP,Thunda #4. . . . . . . . . . . . 300.00
79 American Air Forces #11. . . . 100.00
80 Ghost Rider #12, Bondage(c). 500.00
81 Best of the West #8 . . . . . . . . 200.00
82 BP,Cave Girl #11. . . . . . . . . . 700.00
83 BP,Thunda #5. . . . . . . . . . . . 250.00
84 Ghost Rider #13 . . . . . . . . . . 400.00
85 Best of the West #9 . . . . . . . . 200.00
86 BP,Thunda #6. . . . . . . . . . . . 250.00

87 Best of the West #10 . . . . . . 200.00
88 Bobby Benson's B-Bar-B #29. 150.00
89 BP,Home Run #3,Stan Musial. 275.00
90 Red Hawk #11 . . . . . . . . . . . 200.00
91 BP,American Air Forces #12. . 100.00
92 Dream Book of Romance #5 . 175.00
93 BP,Great Western #8 . . . . . . 300.00
94 FF,White Indian #11 . . . . . . . 350.00
95 BP,Muggsy Mouse #4. . . . . . . 75.00
96 BP,Cave Girl #12 . . . . . . . . . 500.00
97 Best of the West #11 . . . . . . 200.00
98 Undercover Girl #6 . . . . . . . . 600.00
99 Muggsy Mouse #5 . . . . . . . . . 75.00
100 Badmen of the West #1 . . . . 325.00
101 FF,White Indian #12 . . . . . . 325.00
101(a) BP(c),FGu, Dream Book of
Romance #6, Marlon Brando 300.00
103 BP,Best of the West #12. . . . 200.00
104 FF,White Indian #13 . . . . . . 325.00
105 Great Western #9 . . . . . . . . 200.00
106 BP,Dream Book of Love #1 . 200.00
107 Hot Dog #1 . . . . . . . . . . . . . 125.00
108 BP,LbC,Red Fox #15 . . . . . . 350.00
109 BP,Dream Book of Romance 150.00
110 Dream Book of Romance #8 150.00
111 BP,I'm a Cop #1 . . . . . . . . . 200.00
112 Ghost Rider #14 . . . . . . . . . 400.00
113 BP,Great Western #10 . . . . . 175.00
114 Dream Book of Love #2 . . . . 150.00
115 Hot Dog #2 . . . . . . . . . . . . . 100.00
116 BP,Cave Girl #13. . . . . . . . . 500.00
117 White Indian #14 . . . . . . . . . 175.00
118 BP(c),Starr Flagg–
Undercover Girl #7 . . . . . . . 550.00
119 Straight Arrow's Fury #1 . . . 225.00
120 Badmen of the West #2 . . . . 250.00
121 Mysteries of the
Scotland Yard #1 . . . . . . . . 250.00
122 Black Phantom #1. . . . . . . . 550.00
123 Dream Book of Love #3 . . . . 125.00
124 Hot Dog #3 . . . . . . . . . . . . . 100.00
125 BP,Cave Girl #14 . . . . . . . . . 500.00
126 BP,I'm a Cop #2. . . . . . . . . . 150.00
127 BP,Great Western . . . . . . . . 200.00
128 BP,I'm a Cop #3 . . . . . . . . . 150.00
129 The Avenger #1 . . . . . . . . . . 600.00
130 BP,Strongman #1 . . . . . . . . 325.00
131 BP,The Avenger #2 . . . . . . . 450.00
132 Strongman #2 . . . . . . . . . . . 300.00

*A-1 Comics #27*
*© Magazine Enterprises*

*A-1 Comics #56*
*© Magazine Enterprises*

*A-1 Comics #61*
*© Magazine Enterprises*

*Ace #2*
© David McKay Publications

*Aces High #4*
© EC Publications

*Action Comics #17*
© DC Comics

133 BP,The Avenger #3 . . . . . . . 450.00
134 Strongman #3 . . . . . . . . . . . 300.00
135 White Indian #15. . . . . . . . . 175.00
136 Hot Dog #4 . . . . . . . . . . . . 100.00
137 BP,Africa #1 . . . . . . . . . . . . 350.00
138 BP,Avenger #4 . . . . . . . . . . 450.00
139 BP,Strongman #4, 1955 . . . . 300.00

## ABBIE AN' SLATS

**United Features Syndicate,
March–Aug., 1948**

1 RvB(c) . . . . . . . . . . . . . . . . . 250.00
2 RvB(c) . . . . . . . . . . . . . . . . . 175.00
3 RvB(c) . . . . . . . . . . . . . . . . . 150.00
4 Aug., 1948 . . . . . . . . . . . . . . 150.00
N# 1940,Earlier Issue . . . . . . . . 600.00
N# . . . . . . . . . . . . . . . . . . . . . 500.00

## ABBOTT AND COSTELLO

**St. John Publishing Co.,
Feb., 1948**

1 PP(c), Waltz Time . . . . . . . . . 800.00
2 Jungle Girl and Snake(c). . . . . 450.00
3 Outer Space (c) . . . . . . . . . . . 300.00
4 MD, Circus (c) . . . . . . . . . . . . 250.00
5 MD,Bull Fighting (c) . . . . . . . . 250.00
6 MD,Harem (c) . . . . . . . . . . . . 250.00
7 MD,Opera (c). . . . . . . . . . . . . 250.00
8 MD,Pirates (c) . . . . . . . . . . . . 250.00
9 MD,Polar Bear (c) . . . . . . . . . 250.00
10 MD,PP(c),Son of Sinbad tale . 300.00
11 MD. . . . . . . . . . . . . . . . . . . 200.00
12 PP(c), Movie issue . . . . . . . . 250.00
13 Fire fighters (c) . . . . . . . . . . . 200.00
14 Bomb (c) . . . . . . . . . . . . . . . 200.00
15 Bubble Bath (c). . . . . . . . . . . 200.00
16 thru 29 MD . . . . . . . . . . . . . @175.00
30 thru 39 MD . . . . . . . . . . . . . @150.00
40 MD,Sept., 1956. . . . . . . . . . . 150.00
3-D #1, Nov., 1953. . . . . . . . . . . 500.00

## ACE COMICS

**David McKay Publications,
April, 1937**

1 JM, F:Katzenjammer Kids . . 5,000.00
2 JM, A:Blondie . . . . . . . . . . . 1,500.00
3 JM, A:Believe It Or Not . . . . 1,000.00
4 JM, F:Katzenjammer Kids . . 1,000.00
5 JM, A:Believe It Or Not. . . . . 1,000.00
6 JM, A:Blondie. . . . . . . . . . . . . 750.00
7 JM, A:Believe It Or Not . . . . . . 750.00
8 JM, A:Jungle Jim . . . . . . . . . . 750.00
9 JM, A:Blondie. . . . . . . . . . . . . 750.00

10 JM, F:Katzenjammer Kids. . . . 700.00
11 I:The Phantom series. . . . . . 1,200.00
12 A:Blondie, Jungle Jim . . . . . . 600.00
13 A:Ripley's Believe It Or Not . . 500.00
14 A:Blondie, Jungle Jim . . . . . . 500.00
15 A:Blondie. . . . . . . . . . . . . . . 475.00
16 F:Katzenjammer Kids . . . . . . 475.00
17 A:Blondie. . . . . . . . . . . . . . . 475.00
18 A:Ripley's Believe It Or Not . . 475.00
19 F:Katzenjammer Kids . . . . . . 475.00
20 A:Jungle Jim . . . . . . . . . . . . 475.00
21 A:Blondie. . . . . . . . . . . . . . . 450.00
22 A:Jungle Jim . . . . . . . . . . . . 450.00
23 F:Katzenjammer Kids . . . . . . 450.00
24 A:Blondie. . . . . . . . . . . . . . . 450.00
25 . . . . . . . . . . . . . . . . . . . . . 450.00
26 O:Prince Valiant . . . . . . . . . 1,500.00
27 thru 36. . . . . . . . . . . . . . . . @450.00
37 Krazy Kat Ends. . . . . . . . . . . 350.00
38 thru 40. . . . . . . . . . . . . . . . @350.00
41 thru 59. . . . . . . . . . . . . . . . @300.00
60 thru 69. . . . . . . . . . . . . . . . @250.00
70 thru 89. . . . . . . . . . . . . . . . @150.00
90 thru 99. . . . . . . . . . . . . . . . @125.00
100 . . . . . . . . . . . . . . . . . . . . 150.00
101 thru 109. . . . . . . . . . . . . . @125.00
110 thru 119 . . . . . . . . . . . . . . @100.00
120 thru 143. . . . . . . . . . . . . . @100.00
144 Phantom covers begin . . . . . 125.00
145 thru 150. . . . . . . . . . . . . . @100.00
151 Oct.–Nov., 1949 . . . . . . . . . 125.00

## ACES HIGH

**E.C. Comics, March–April, 1955**

1 GE(a&c),JDa,WW,BK . . . . . . 500.00
2 GE(a&c),JDa,WW,BK . . . . . . 300.00
3 GE(a&c),JDa,WW,BK . . . . . . 250.00
4 GE(a&c),JDa,WW,BK . . . . . . 250.00
5 GE(c),JDa,WW,BK. . . . . . . . 250.00

## ACTION

**DC Comics, June, 1938**

1 JoS,I&O:Superman;Rescues Evelyn
   Curry from electric chair . 500,000.00
2 JoS,V:Emil Norvell . . . . . . . 60,000.00
3 JoS,V:Thorton Blakely . . . . 40,000.00
4 JoS,V:Coach Randall . . . . . 25,000.00
5 JoS,Emergency of
   Vallegho Dam . . . . . . . . . 25,000.00
6 JoS,I:Jimmy Olsen,
   V:Nick Williams. . . . . . . . . 25,000.00
7 JoS,V:Derek Niles. . . . . . . . 50,000.00
8 JoS,V:Gimpy . . . . . . . . . . . 15,000.00
9 JoS,A:Det.Captain Reilly . . 15,000.00

10 JoS,Superman fights
   for prison reform . . . . . . . 30,000.00
11 JoS,Disguised as
   Homer Ramsey . . . . . . . . 7,500.00
12 JoS,Crusade against
   reckless drivers . . . . . . . . 8,000.00
13 JoS,I:Ultra Humanite . . . . . 15,000.00
14 JoS,BKa,V:Ultra Humanite,
   B:Clip Carson . . . . . . . . . 8,000.00
15 JoS,BKa,Superman in
   Kidtown. . . . . . . . . . . . . . 15,000.00
16 JoS,BKa,Crusade against
   Gambling . . . . . . . . . . . . 8,000.00
17 JoS,BKa,V:Ultra Humanite. 12,000.00
18 JoS,BKa,V:Mr.Hamilton
   O:Three Aces . . . . . . . . . 8,000.00
19 JoS,BKa,V:Ultra Humanite
   B:Superman (c) . . . . . . . . 12,000.00
20 JoS,BKa,V:Ultra Humanite. 10,000.00
21 JoS,BKa,V:Ultra Humanite. 10,000.00
22 JoS,BKa,War between Toran
   and Galonia . . . . . . . . . . 10,000.00
23 JoS,BKa,SMo,I:Lex Luthor 16,000.00
24 JoS,BKa,BBa,SMo,FGu,Meets
   Peter Carnahan . . . . . . . . 10,000.00
25 JoS,BKa,BBa,SMo,
   V:Medini . . . . . . . . . . . . . 10,000.00
26 JoS,BKa,V:ClarenceCobalt 10,000.00
27 JoS,BKa,V:Mr & Mrs.Tweed 6,000.00
28 JoS,BKa,JBu,V:Strongarm
   Bandit . . . . . . . . . . . . . . . 6,000.00
29 JoS,BKa,V:Martin. . . . . . . . 7,000.00
30 JoS,BKa,V:Zolar . . . . . . . . 6,000.00
31 JoS,BKa,JBu,V:Baron
   Munsdorf . . . . . . . . . . . . . 4,000.00
32 JoS,BKa,JBu,I:Krypto Ray Gun
   V:Mr.Preston . . . . . . . . . . 4,000.00
33 JoS,BKa,JBu,V:Brett Hall,
   O:Mr. America. . . . . . . . . . 4,000.00
34 JoS,BKa,V:Jim Laurg. . . . . 4,000.00
35 JoS,BKa,V:Brock Walter . . . 4,000.00
36 JoS,BKa,V:StuartPemberton 4,000.00
37 JoS,BKa,V:Commissioner
   Kennedy, O:Congo Bill . . . 3,900.00
38 JoS,BKa,V:Harold Morton . . 3,900.00
39 JoS,BKa,Meets Britt Bryson 3,900.00
40 JoS,BKa,Meets Nancy
   Thorgenson . . . . . . . . . . . 3,900.00
41 JoS,BKa,V:Ralph Cowan,
   E:Clip Carson . . . . . . . . . 3,500.00
42 V:Lex Luthor,I&O:Vigilante. . 5,000.00
43 V:Dutch O'Leary,Nazi(c) . . . 3,500.00
44 V:Prof. Steffens,Nazi(c) . . . 3,500.00
45 V:Count Von Henzel,
   I:Stuff,Nazi(c). . . . . . . . . . 3,500.00
46 V:The Domino . . . . . . . . . . 3,500.00

Ac

*Action Comics #56*
© DC Comics

*Action Comics #112*
© DC Comics

*Action Comics #160*
© DC Comics

47 V:Lex Luthor—1st app. w/super
   powers,I:Powerstone . . . . . 5,000.00
48 V:The Top. . . . . . . . . . . . . . 3,200.00
49 I:Puzzler. . . . . . . . . . . . . . . 3,200.00
50 Meets Stan Doborak . . . . . . 3,200.00
51 I:Prankster. . . . . . . . . . . . . 4,000.00
52 V:Emperor of America . . . . . 4,500.00
53 JBu,V:Night-Owl. . . . . . . . . 3,500.00
54 JBu,Meets Stanley
   Finchcomb . . . . . . . . . . . . 3,500.00
55 JBu,V:Cartoonist Al Hatt . . . 3,500.00
56 V:Emil Loring . . . . . . . . . . . 3,500.00
57 V:Prankster . . . . . . . . . . . . 3,500.00
58 JBu,V:Adonis . . . . . . . . . . . 3,500.00
59 I:Susie Thompkins,Lois
   Lane's niece . . . . . . . . . . . 3,500.00
60 JBu,Lois Lane-Superwoman 3,500.00
61 JBu,Meets Craig Shaw . . . . 3,500.00
62 JBu,V:Admiral Von Storff . . . 3,500.00
63 JBu,V:Professor Praline. . . . 3,500.00
64 I:Toyman . . . . . . . . . . . . . . 3,500.00
65 JBu,V:Truman Treadwell . . . 3,500.00
66 JBu,V:Mr.Annister . . . . . . . . 3,500.00
67 JBu,Superman School for
   Officer's Training . . . . . . . . 3,500.00
68 A:Susie Thompkins . . . . . . . 3,500.00
69 V:Prankster . . . . . . . . . . . . 3,500.00
70 JBu,V:Thinker . . . . . . . . . . . 3,500.00
71 Superman Valentine's
   Day Special . . . . . . . . . . . 3,000.00
72 V:Mr. Sniggle . . . . . . . . . . . 3,000.00
73 V:Lucius Spruce . . . . . . . . . 3,000.00
74 Meets Adelbert Dribble . . . . 3,000.00
75 V:Johnny Aesop . . . . . . . . . 3,000.00
76 A Voyage with Destiny . . . . 3,000.00
77 V:Prankster . . . . . . . . . . . . 3,000.00
78 The Chef of Bohemia. . . . . . 3,000.00
79 JBu,A:J. Wilbur Wolfingham 3,000.00
80 A:Mr. Mxyzptlk (2nd App). . . 3,500.00
81 Meets John Nicholas . . . . . . 3,000.00
82 JBu,V:Water Sprite. . . . . . . . 3,000.00
83 I:Hocus and Pocus. . . . . . . . 3,000.00
84 JBu,V:Dapper Gang. . . . . . . 3,000.00
85 JBu,V:Toyman . . . . . . . . . . . 3,000.00
86 JBu,V:Wizard of Wokit . . . . . 3,000.00
87 V:Truck Hijackers. . . . . . . . . 3,000.00
88 A:Hocus and Pocus . . . . . . . 3,000.00
89 V:Slippery Andy . . . . . . . . . 3,000.00
90 JBu,V:Horace Rikker and the
   Amphi-Bandits . . . . . . . . . 3,000.00
91 JBu,V:Davey Jones. . . . . . . . . 900.00
92 JBu,V:Nowmie Norman. . . . . . 900.00
93 Superman Christmas story . . . 900.00
94 JBu,V:Bullwar 'Bull' Rylie . . . . 900.00
95 V:Prankster . . . . . . . . . . . . . . 900.00
96 V:Mr. Twister . . . . . . . . . . . . . 900.00

97 A:Hocus and Pocus . . . . . . . 900.00
98 V:Mr. Mxyzptlk, A:Susie
   Thompkins . . . . . . . . . . . 3,500.00
99 V:Keith Langwell . . . . . . . . . . 900.00
100 I:InspectorErskineHawkins. 1,300.00
101 V:Specs Dour,A-Bomb(c). . 1,900.00
102 V:Mr. Mxyzptlk . . . . . . . . . 1,400.00
103 V:Emperor Quexo . . . . . . . 1,400.00
104 V:Prankster . . . . . . . . . . . 1,400.00
105 Superman Christmas story 1,400.00
106 Clark Kent becomes Baron
   Edgestream . . . . . . . . . . . 1,400.00
107 JBu,A:J.Wilbur Wolfingham 1,400.00
108 JBu,V:Vince Vincent . . . . . 1,400.00
109 V:Prankster . . . . . . . . . . . 1,400.00
110 A:Susie Thompkins . . . . . . . 800.00
111 Cameras in the Clouds . . . . 800.00
112 V:Mr. Mxyzptlk . . . . . . . . . 1,400.00
113 Just an Ordinary Guy. . . . . 1,400.00
114 V:Mike Chesney. . . . . . . . . 1,400.00
115 Meets Arthur Parrish . . . . . 1,400.00
116 A:J. Wilbur Wolfingham . . . 1,400.00
117 Superman Christmas story 1,400.00
118 Execution of Clark Kent . . . 1,400.00
119 Meets Jim Banning . . . . . . 1,400.00
120 V:Mike Foss . . . . . . . . . . . 1,400.00
121 V:William Sharp . . . . . . . . 1,400.00
122 V:Charley Carson. . . . . . . . 1,400.00
123 V:Skid Russell . . . . . . . . . 1,400.00
124 Superman becomes
   radioactive . . . . . . . . . . . 1,200.00
125 V:Lex Luthor . . . . . . . . . . . . 750.00
126 V:Chameleon . . . . . . . . . . 1,200.00
127 JKu,Superman on Truth or
   Consequences . . . . . . . . . 2,100.00
128 V:'Aces' Deucey . . . . . . . . 2,000.00
129 Meets Gob-Gob . . . . . . . . 2,000.00
130 V:Captain Kidder . . . . . . . . 2,000.00
131 V:Lex Luthor. . . . . . . . . . . 2,000.00
132 Superman meets George
   Washington. . . . . . . . . . . . 2,000.00
133 V:Emma Blotz . . . . . . . . . . 2,000.00
134 V:Paul Strong . . . . . . . . . . 2,000.00
135 V:John Morton . . . . . . . . . 2,000.00
136 Superman Show-Off! . . . . . 2,000.00
137 Meets Percival Winter . . . . 2,000.00
138 Meets Herbert Hinkle. . . . . 2,000.00
139 Clark Kent...Daredevil!. . . . 2,000.00
140 Superman becomes Hermit 2,000.00
141 V:Lex Luthor. . . . . . . . . . . 2,000.00
142 V:Dan the Dip . . . . . . . . . . 2,000.00
143 Dates Nikki Larve. . . . . . . . 2,000.00
144 O:Clark Kent reporting for
   Daily Planet . . . . . . . . . . . 2,000.00
145 Meets Merton Gloop . . . . . 2,000.00
146 V:Luthor . . . . . . . . . . . . . . 2,000.00

147 V:'Cheeks' Ross. . . . . . . . . 2,000.00
148 Superman, Indian Chief. . . 2,000.00
149 The Courtship on Krypton!. 2,000.00
150 V:Morko . . . . . . . . . . . . . . 2,000.00
151 V:Mr.Mxyzptlk,Lex Luthor
   and Prankster. . . . . . . . . . 2,000.00
152 I:Metropolis Shutterbug
   Society . . . . . . . . . . . . . . 2,100.00
153 V:Kingpin . . . . . . . . . . . . . 2,000.00
154 V:Harry Reed . . . . . . . . . . 2,000.00
155 V:Andrew Arvin . . . . . . . . . 2,000.00
156 Lois Lane becomes Super-
   woman,V:Lex Luthor. . . . . . 1,800.00
157 V:Joe Striker. . . . . . . . . . . 1,800.00
158 V:Kane Korrell
   O:Superman (retold). . . . . 2,500.00
159 Meets Oswald Whimple. . . 1,800.00
160 I:Minerva Kent . . . . . . . . . 1,800.00
161 Meets Antara . . . . . . . . . . 1,800.00
162 V:'IT!' . . . . . . . . . . . . . . . 1,800.00
163 Meets Susan Semple. . . . . 1,800.00
164 Meets Stefan Andriessen. . 1,800.00
165 V:Crime Czar. . . . . . . . . . . 1,800.00
166 V:Lex Luthor. . . . . . . . . . . 1,800.00
167 V:Prof. Nero . . . . . . . . . . . 1,800.00
168 O:Olaf. . . . . . . . . . . . . . . . 1,800.00
169 Caveman Clark Kent!. . . . . 1,800.00
170 V:Mad Artist of Metropolis . 1,800.00
171 The Secrets of Superman . 1,800.00
172 Lois Lane..Witch! . . . . . . . 1,800.00
173 V:Dragon Lang. . . . . . . . . 1,800.00
174 V:Miracle Twine Gang . . . . 1,800.00
175 V:John Vinden . . . . . . . . . 1,800.00
176 V:Billion Dollar Gang . . . . . 1,800.00
177 V:General . . . . . . . . . . . . . 1,800.00
178 V:Prof. Sands. . . . . . . . . . 1,800.00
179 Superman in Mapleville . . . 1,800.00
180 V:Syndicate of Five . . . . . . 1,800.00
181 V:Diamond Dave Delaney . 1,200.00
182 Return from Planet Krypton 1,200.00
183 V:Lex Luthor. . . . . . . . . . . 1,200.00
184 Meets Donald Whitmore . . 1,200.00
185 V:Issah Pendleton . . . . . . . 1,200.00
186 The Haunted Superman . . 1,200.00
187 V:Silver. . . . . . . . . . . . . . . 1,200.00
188 V:Cushions Raymond gang 1,200.00
189 Meets Mr.& Mrs. Vandeveir 1,200.00
190 V:Mr. Mxyzptlk . . . . . . . . . 1,200.00
191 V:Vic Vordan . . . . . . . . . . 1,200.00
192 Meets Vic Vordan. . . . . . . 1,200.00
193 V:Beetles Brogan. . . . . . . . 1,200.00
194 V:Maln . . . . . . . . . . . . . . . 1,200.00
195 V:Tiger Woman . . . . . . . . . 1,200.00
196 Superman becomes Mental
   Man. . . . . . . . . . . . . . . . . 1,200.00
197 V:Stanley Stark. . . . . . . . . 1,200.00

All comics prices listed are for *Near Mint* condition. **Page 33**

**Ac**

*Action Comics #209*
© DC Comics

*Action Comics #271*
© DC Comics

*Adventure Comics #33*
© DC Comics

| | | |
|---|---|---|
| 198 The Six Lives of Lois Lane | 1,200.00 | |
| 199 V:Lex Luthor | 1,200.00 | |
| 200 V:Morwatha | 1,200.00 | |
| 201 'V:Benny the Brute | 1,200.00 | |
| 202 Lois Lane's X-Ray Vision | 1,000.00 | |
| 203 Meets Pietro Paresca | 1,000.00 | |
| 204 Meets Sam Spulby | 1,000.00 | |
| 205 Sergeant Superman | 1,000.00 | |
| 206 Imaginary story F:L.Lane | 1,000.00 | |
| 207 Four Superman Medals! | 1,000.00 | |
| 208 V:Mr. Mxyzptlk | 1,000.00 | |
| 209 V:'Doc' Winters | 1,000.00 | |
| 210 V:Lex,I:Superman Land | 1,000.00 | |
| 211 Superman Spectaculars | 1,000.00 | |
| 212 V:Thorne Varden | 1,000.00 | |
| 213 V:Paul Paxton | 1,000.00 | |
| 214 Superman,Sup.Destroyer! | 1,000.00 | |
| 215 I:Superman of 2956 | 1,000.00 | |
| 216 A:Jor-El | 1,000.00 | |
| 217 Meets Mr&Mrs.Roger Bliss | 1,000.00 | |
| 218 I:Super-Ape from Krypton | 1,000.00 | |
| 219 V:Art Shaler | 1,000.00 | |
| 220 Interplanetary Olympics | 1,000.00 | |
| 221 V:Jay Vorrell | 800.00 | |
| 222 The Duplicate Superman | 800.00 | |
| 223 A:Jor-El | 800.00 | |
| 224 I:Superman Island | 800.00 | |
| 225 The Death of Superman | 800.00 | |
| 226 V:Lex Luthor | 800.00 | |
| 227 Man with Triple X-Ray Eyes | 800.00 | |
| 228 A:Superman Museum | 800.00 | |
| 229 V:Dr. John Haley | 800.00 | |
| 230 V:Bart Wellins | 800.00 | |
| 231 Sir Jimmy Olsen, Knight of Metropolis | 800.00 | |
| 232 Meets Johnny Kirk | 800.00 | |
| 233 V:Torm | 800.00 | |
| 234 Meets Golto | 800.00 | |
| 235 B:Congo Bill, B:Tommy Superman | 800.00 | |
| 236 A:Lex Luthor | 800.00 | |
| 237 V:Nebula Gang | 800.00 | |
| 238 I:King Krypton, the Gorilla | 800.00 | |
| 239 Superman's New Face | 800.00 | |
| 240 V:Superman Sphinx | 800.00 | |
| 241 WB,A:Batman,Fortress of Solitude (Fort Superman) | 700.00 | |
| 242 I&O:Brainiac | 5,000.00 | |
| 243 Lady and the Lion | 700.00 | |
| 244 CS,A:Vul-Kor,Lya-La | 700.00 | |
| 245 WB,V:Kak-Kul | 700.00 | |
| 246 WB,A:Krypton Island | 700.00 | |
| 247 WB,Superman Lost Parents | 700.00 | |
| 248 B&I:Congorilla | 700.00 | |
| 249 A:Lex Luthor | 700.00 | |
| 250 WB,The Eye of Metropolis | 700.00 | |

| | | |
|---|---|---|
| 251 E:Tommy Tomorrow | 700.00 | |
| 252 I&O:Supergirl | 5,000.00 | |
| 253 B:Supergirl | 1,300.00 | |
| 254 I:Adult Bizarro | 1,000.00 | |
| 255 I:Bizarro Lois | 800.00 | |
| 256 Superman of the Future | 500.00 | |
| 257 WB,JM,V:Lex Luthor | 500.00 | |
| 258 A:Cosmic Man | 500.00 | |
| 259 A:Lex Luthor,Superboy | 500.00 | |
| 260 A:Mighty Maid | 500.00 | |
| 261 I:Streaky,E:Congorilla | 500.00 | |
| 262 A:Bizarro | 500.00 | |
| 263 O:Bizarro World | 600.00 | |
| 264 V:Bizarro | 500.00 | |
| 265 A:Hyper-Man | 500.00 | |
| 266 A:Streaky,Krypto | 500.00 | |
| 267 JM,3rd A:Legion,I:Invisible Kid | 1,200.00 | |
| 268 WB,A:Hercules | 400.00 | |
| 269 A:Jerro | 400.00 | |
| 270 CS,JM,A:Batman | 500.00 | |
| 271 A:Lex Luthor | 400.00 | |
| 272 A:Aquaman | 400.00 | |
| 273 A:Mr.Mxyzptlk | 400.00 | |
| 274 A:Superwoman | 400.00 | |
| 275 WB,JM,V:Braimiac | 400.00 | |
| 276 JM,6th A:Legion,I:Brainiac 5, Triplicate Girl,Bouncing Boy | 700.00 | |
| 277 CS,JM,V:Lex Luthor | 300.00 | |
| 278 CS,Perry White Becomes Master Man | 300.00 | |
| 279 JM,V:Hercules,Samson | 300.00 | |
| 280 CS,JM,V:Braniac, A:Congorilla | 300.00 | |
| 281 JM,A:Krypto | 300.00 | |
| 282 JM,V:Mxyzptlk | 300.00 | |
| 283 CS,JM,A:Legion of Super Outlaws | 400.00 | |
| 284 A:Krypto,Jerro | 300.00 | |
| 285 JM,Supergirl Existence Revealed, C:Legion (12th app.) | 400.00 | |
| 286 CS,JM,V:Lex Luthor | 250.00 | |
| 287 JM,A:Legion | 250.00 | |
| 288 JM,A:Mon-El | 250.00 | |
| 289 JM,A:Adult Legion | 250.00 | |
| 290 JM,C:Phantom Girl | 250.00 | |
| 291 JM,V:Mxyzptlk | 250.00 | |
| 292 JM,I:Superhorse | 250.00 | |
| 293 JM,O:Comet-Superhorse | 300.00 | |
| 294 JM,V:Lex Luthor | 250.00 | |
| 295 CS,JM,O:Lex Luthor | 250.00 | |
| 296 V:Super Ants | 250.00 | |
| 297 CS,JM,A:Mon-El | 250.00 | |
| 298 CS,JM,V:Lex Luthor | 250.00 | |
| 299 O:Superman Robots | 250.00 | |
| 300 JM,A:Mxyzptlk | 300.00 | |

## REAL ADVENTURE COMICS
**Gillmor Magazines, Apr. 1955**

| | |
|---|---|
| 1 | 100.00 |

**Becomes:**

## ACTION ADVENTURE
**Gillmor Magazines, June–Oct., 1955**

| | |
|---|---|
| 2 | 100.00 |
| 3 | 100.00 |
| 4 | 100.00 |

## ACTUAL CONFESSIONS
## See: LOVE ADVENTURES

## ACTUAL ROMANCES
**Marvel, Oct., 1949**

| | |
|---|---|
| 1 | 150.00 |
| 2 Photo Cover | 100.00 |

## ADVENTURE COMICS
**DC Comics, Nov., 1938–83**
**[Prev: New Adventure Comics]**

| | |
|---|---|
| 32 CF(c) | 7,000.00 |
| 33 CF(c),BKa | 4,000.00 |
| 34 FGu(c) | 4,000.00 |
| 35 FGu(c) | 4,000.00 |
| 36 Giant Snake(c) | 4,000.00 |
| 37 CF,Rampaging Elephant(c) | 4,000.00 |
| 38 Tiger(c) | 4,000.00 |
| 39 Male Bondage(c) | 3,000.00 |
| 40 CF(c),1st app. Sandman | 90,000.00 |
| 41 Killer Shark(c) | 15,000.00 |
| 42 CF,Sandman(c) | 30,000.00 |
| 43 CF(c) | 9,000.00 |
| 44 CF,FGu,Sandman(c) | 15,000.00 |
| 45 FGu(c) | 9,000.00 |
| 46 CF,Sandman(c) | 14,000.00 |
| 47 Sandman (c) | 14,000.00 |
| 48 1st app.& B:Hourman | 60,000.00 |
| 49 SMo(c),BKa,CF | 6,000.00 |
| 50 Hourman(c) | 6,000.00 |
| 51 BBa(c),Sandman(c) | 9,000.00 |
| 52 BBa(c),Hourman(c) | 5,500.00 |
| 53 BBa(c),1st app. Minuteman | 5,500.00 |
| 54 BBa(c),Hourman(c) | 5,500.00 |
| 55 BBa(c),same | 5,500.00 |
| 56 BBa(c),same | 5,500.00 |
| 57 BBa(c),same | 5,500.00 |
| 58 BBa(c),same | 5,500.00 |
| 59 BBa(c),same | 5,500.00 |

**Ac**

Adventure Comics #57
© DC Comics

Adventure Comics #138
© DC Comics

Adventure Comics #161
© DC Comics

60 Sandman(c) . . . . . . . . . . . . 4,800.00
61 CF(c),JBu,Starman(c) . . . . 25,000.00
62 JBu(c),JBu,Starman(c) . . . . . 7,000.00
63 JBu(c),JBu,same . . . . . . . . 5,000.00
64 JBu(c),JBu,same . . . . . . . . 5,000.00
65 JBu(c),JBu,same . . . . . . . . 5,000.00
66 JBu(c),JBu,O:Shining Knight,
    Starman(c) . . . . . . . . . . . . 5,500.00
67 JBu(c),JBu,O:Mist . . . . . . . 5,000.00
68 JBu(c),JBu,same . . . . . . . . 5,000.00
69 JBu(c),JBu,1st app. Sandy,
    Starman(c) . . . . . . . . . . . . 5,000.00
70 JBu(c),JBu,Starman(c). . . . . 5,000.00
71 JBu(c),JBu,same . . . . . . . . 5,000.00
72 JBu(c),S&K,JBu,Sandman. 30,000.00
73 S&K(c),S&K,I:Manhunter . . 31,000.00
74 S&K(c),S&K,You Can't Escape
    Your Fate-The Sandman . . 5,000.00
75 S&K(c),S&K,Sandman and
    Sandy Battle Thor. . . . . . . 5,000.00
76 S&K(c),Sandman(c),S&K. . . 5,000.00
77 S&K,(c),S&K,same. . . . . . . 5,000.00
78 S&K(c),S&K,same . . . . . . . 5,000.00
79 S&K(c),S&K,Manhunter . . . 12,000.00
80 S&K(c),Sandman(c),S&K. . . 5,000.00
81 S&K(c),MMe,S&K,same. . . . 3,000.00
82 S&K(c),S&K,Sandman
    X-Mas story . . . . . . . . . . . 3,000.00
83 S&K(c),S&K,Sandman
    Boxing(c),E:Hourman . . . . . 3,000.00
84 S&K(c),S&K . . . . . . . . . . . 3,000.00
85 S&K(c),S&K,Sandman in
    The Amazing Dreams of
    Gentleman Jack . . . . . . . . . 3,000.00
86 S&K(c),Sandman(c). . . . . . . 3,000.00
87 S&K(c),same . . . . . . . . . . . 3,000.00
88 S&K(c),same . . . . . . . . . . . 3,000.00
89 S&K(c),same . . . . . . . . . . . 3,000.00
90 S&K(c),same . . . . . . . . . . . 3,000.00
91 S&K(c),JK . . . . . . . . . . . . . 3,000.00
92 S&K(c) . . . . . . . . . . . . . . . 2,000.00
93 S&K(c),Sandman in Sleep
    for Sale . . . . . . . . . . . . . . . 2,000.00
94 S&K(c),Sandman(c). . . . . . . 2,000.00
95 S&K(c),same . . . . . . . . . . . 2,000.00
96 S&K(c),same . . . . . . . . . . . 2,000.00
97 S&K(c),same . . . . . . . . . . . 2,000.00
98 JK(c),Sandman in Hero
    of Dreams. . . . . . . . . . . . . 2,000.00
99 JK(c). . . . . . . . . . . . . . . . . 2,000.00
100 JK(c&a) . . . . . . . . . . . . . . 2,000.00
101 S&K(c) . . . . . . . . . . . . . . 2,000.00
102 S&K(c) . . . . . . . . . . . . . . 2,000.00
103 B:Superboy stories,(c),BU:
    Johnny Quick,Aquaman,Shining
    Knight,Green Arrow . . . . . 5,000.00

104 S&S,ToyTown USA . . . . . . 1,900.00
105 S&S,Palace of Fantasy . . . 1,500.00
106 S&S,Weather Hurricane . . 1,500.00
107 S&S,The Sky is the Limit . . 1,500.00
108 S&S,Proof of the Proverbs 1,500.00
109 S&S,You Can't Lose . . . . . 1,500.00
110 S&S,The Farmer Takes
    it Easy . . . . . . . . . . . . . . . 1,500.00
111 S&S,The Whiz Quiz Club . . 1,500.00
112 S&S,Super Safety First . . . 1,500.00
113 S&S,The 33rd Christmas . . 1,400.00
114 S&S,Superboy Spells
    Danger . . . . . . . . . . . . . . . 1,400.00
115 S&S,The Adventure of
    Jaguar Boy . . . . . . . . . . . . 1,400.00
116 S&S,JBu,Superboy Toy
    Tester . . . . . . . . . . . . . . . . 1,400.00
117 S&S,JBu,Miracle Plane . . . 1,400.00
118 S&S,JBu,The Quiz Biz
    Broadcast . . . . . . . . . . . . . 1,400.00
119 WMo,JBu,Superboy
    Meets Girls . . . . . . . . . . . . 1,400.00
120 S&S,JBu,A:Perry White;
    I:Ringmaster . . . . . . . . . . . 1,500.00
121 S&S,Great Hobby Contest. 1,600.00
122 S&S,Superboy-Super-
    Magician . . . . . . . . . . . . . . 1,800.00
123 S&S,Lesson For a Bully. . . 1,600.00
124 S&S,Barbed Wire Boys
    Town . . . . . . . . . . . . . . . . . 1,200.00
125 S&S,The Weight Before
    Christmas . . . . . . . . . . . . . 1,200.00
126 S&S,Superboy:Crime
    Fighting Poet . . . . . . . . . . . 1,200.00
127 MMe,O:Shining Knight;
    Super Bellboy . . . . . . . . . . 1,200.00
128 WMo,How Clark Kent Met
    Lois Lane . . . . . . . . . . . . . . 1,200.00
129 WMo,Pupils of the Past . . . 1,200.00
130 WMo,Superboy Super
    Salesman . . . . . . . . . . . . . 1,200.00
131 WMo,The Million Dollar
    Athlete . . . . . . . . . . . . . . . . 1,200.00
132 WMo,Superboy Super
    Cowboy. . . . . . . . . . . . . . . 1,200.00
133 WMo,Superboy's Report
    Card . . . . . . . . . . . . . . . . . 1,200.00
134 WMo,Silver Gloves Sellout 1,200.00
135 WMo,The Most Amazing
    of All Boys . . . . . . . . . . . . 1,200.00
136 WMo,My Pal Superboy . . . 1,200.00
137 WMo,Treasure of Tondimo. 1,200.00
138 WMo,Around the World in
    Eighty Minutes . . . . . . . . . 1,200.00
139 WMo,Telegraph Boy . . . . . 1,200.00
140 Journey to the Moon . . . . . 1,200.00

141 WMo,When Superboy Lost
    His Powers . . . . . . . . . . . . 1,200.00
142 WMo,The Man Who Walked
    With Trouble . . . . . . . . . . . 1,200.00
143 WMo,Superboy Savings Bank,
    A:Wooden Head Jones . . . 1,200.00
144 WMo,The Way to Stop
    Superboy . . . . . . . . . . . . . 1,200.00
145 WMo,Holiday Hijackers . . . 1,200.00
146 The Substitute Superboy . . 1,200.00
147 Clark Kent,Orphan. . . . . . . 1,200.00
148 Superboy Meets Mummies 1,200.00
149 Fake Superboys. . . . . . . . . 1,200.00
150 FF,Superboy's Initiation . . . 1,100.00
151 FF,No Hunting(c). . . . . . . . . 850.00
152 Superboy Hunts For a Job. 1,000.00
153 FF,Clark Kent,Boy Hobo . . 1,100.00
154 The Carnival Boat Crimes . 1,000.00
155 FF,Superboy-Hollywood
    Actor . . . . . . . . . . . . . . . . 1,100.00
156 The Flying Peril . . . . . . . . 1,000.00
157 FF,The Worst Boy in
    Smallville . . . . . . . . . . . . . 1,100.00
158 The Impossible Task . . . . . 1,000.00
159 FF,Superboy Millionaire? . . 1,100.00
160 Superboy's Phoney Father . . 950.00
161 FF. . . . . . . . . . . . . . . . . . . 1,100.00
162 Super-Coach of
    Smallville High!. . . . . . . . . 1,000.00
163 FF,Superboy's Phoney
    Father. . . . . . . . . . . . . . . . 1,100.00
164 Discovers the Secret of
    a Lost Indian Tribe!. . . . . . 1,000.00
165 Superboy's School for
    Stunt Men! . . . . . . . . . . . . 1,000.00
166 Town That Stole Superboy. 1,000.00
167 Lana Lang, Super-Girl! . . . 1,100.00
168 The Boy Who Out Smarted
    Superboy . . . . . . . . . . . . . 1,000.00
169 Clark Kent's Private Butler. 1,000.00
170 Lana Lang's Big Crush . . . . 900.00
171 Superboy's Toughest Tasks . 900.00
172 Laws that Backfired . . . . . . 900.00
173 Superboy's School of
    Hard Knocks . . . . . . . . . . . 900.00
174 The New Lana Lang! . . . . . 900.00
175 Duel of the Superboys . . . . 900.00
176 Superboy's New Parents! . . 900.00
177 Hot-Rod Chariot Race! . . . . 900.00
178 Boy in the Lead Mask. . . . . 900.00
179 World's Whackiest
    Inventors . . . . . . . . . . . . . . 900.00
180 Grand Prize o/t Underworld . 900.00
181 Mask for a Hero . . . . . . . . . 900.00
182 Super Hick from Smallville . . 800.00
183 Superboy and Cleopatra. . . . 800.00

All comics prices listed are for *Near Mint* condition.                     **Page 35**

*Adventure Comics #195*
© DC Comics

*Adventure Comics #250*
© DC Comics

*Adventure Into Mystery #1*
© Marvel Comics Group

184 Shutterbugs of Smallville . . . 800.00
185 The Mythical Monster . . . . . . 800.00
186. . . . . . . . . . . . . . . . . . . . . . . 800.00
187 25th Century Superboy. . . . . 800.00
188 Bull Fighter from
     Smallville. . . . . . . . . . . . . . . 800.00
189 Girl of Steel(Lana Lang) . . . . 800.00
190 The Two Clark Lents . . . . . . 800.00
191 . . . . . . . . . . . . . . . . . . . . . . . 800.00
192 Coronation of Queen
     Lana Lang. . . . . . . . . . . . . . . 800.00
193 Superboy's Lost Costume. . . 800.00
194 Super-Charged Superboy. . . 800.00
195 Lana Lang's Romance
     on Mars! . . . . . . . . . . . . . . . . 800.00
196 Superboy vs. King Gorilla . . . 800.00
197 V:Juvenile Gangs . . . . . . . . . 800.00
198 Super-Carnival from Space . . 800.00
199 Superboy meets Superlad . . 800.00
200 Superboy and the Apes! . . 1,000.00
201 Safari in Smallville! . . . . . . . . 750.00
202 Superboy City, U.S.A. . . . . . . 750.00
203 Uncle Superboy! . . . . . . . . . . 750.00
204 Super-Brat of Smallville . . . . 750.00
205 Journey of the Second
     Superboy! . . . . . . . . . . . . . . . 750.00
206 The Impossible Creatures. . . 750.00
207 Smallville's Worst Athlete . . . 750.00
208 Rip Van Winkle of
     Smallville? . . . . . . . . . . . . . . . 750.00
209 Superboy Week! . . . . . . . . . . 750.00
210 I:Krypto,The Superdog
     from Krypton. . . . . . . . . . . 8,000.00
211 Superboy's Amazing Dream! 600.00
212 Superboy's Robot Twin. . . . . 600.00
213 Junior Jury of Smallville!. . . . 600.00
214 A:Krypto . . . . . . . . . . . . . . . 1,100.00
215 Super-Hobby of Superboy . . 500.00
216 The Wizard City . . . . . . . . . . 500.00
217 Farewell to Smallville . . . . . . 500.00
218 Two World's of Superboy . . . 500.00
219 Rip Van Wrinkle of
     Smallville. . . . . . . . . . . . . . . . 500.00
220 Greatest Show on Earth
     A:Krypto. . . . . . . . . . . . . . . . 600.00
221 The Babe of Steel. . . . . . . . . 500.00
222 Superboy's Repeat
     Performance . . . . . . . . . . . . . 500.00
223 Hercules Junior. . . . . . . . . . . 500.00
224 Pa Kent Superman . . . . . . . . 500.00
225 Bird with Super-Powers . . . . 500.00
226 Superboy's Super Rival! . . . . 500.00
227 Good Samaritan of
     Smallville. . . . . . . . . . . . . . . . 500.00
228 Clark Kent's Body Guard . . . 500.00
229 . . . . . . . . . . . . . . . . . . . . . . . 500.00

230 Secret o/t Flying Horse . . . . . 450.00
231 Super-Feats of Super-Baby . 450.00
232 House where Superboy
     was Born . . . . . . . . . . . . . . . 450.00
233 Joe Smith, Man of Steel . . . . 450.00
234 1,001 Rides of Superboy . . . 450.00
235 Confessions of Superboy . . . 450.00
236 Clark Kent's Super-Dad . . . . 450.00
237 Robot War of Smallville . . . . 450.00
238 Secret Past of
     Superboy's Father. . . . . . . . . 450.00
239 Super-Tricks of
     the Dog of Steel. . . . . . . . . . 450.00
240 Super Teacher from Krypton. 450.00
241 Super-Outlaw of Smallville . . 450.00
242 The Kid From Krypton . . . . . 450.00
243 Super Toys from Krypton . . . 450.00
244 Poorest Family in Smallville . 450.00
245 The Mystery of Monster X . . 450.00
246 Girl Who Trapped Superboy . 450.00
247 I&O:Legion . . . . . . . . . . . . 10,000.00
248 Green Arrow . . . . . . . . . . . . . 400.00
249 CS,Green Arrow . . . . . . . . . . 400.00
250 JK,Green Arrow . . . . . . . . . . 400.00
251 JK,Green Arrow . . . . . . . . . . 400.00
252 JK,Green Arrow . . . . . . . . . . 400.00
253 JK,1st Superboy &
     Robin T.U. . . . . . . . . . . . . . . 600.00
254 JK,Green Arrow . . . . . . . . . . 400.00
255 JK,Green Arrow . . . . . . . . . . 400.00
256 JK,O:Green Arrow . . . . . . . 1,200.00
257 CS,LEI,A:Hercules,Samson . 350.00
258 LEI,Aquaman,Superboy . . . 350.00
259 I:Crimson Archer. . . . . . . . . . 350.00
260 1st S.A. O:Aquaman . . . . . 1,400.00
261 GA,A:Lois Lane. . . . . . . . . . . 300.00
262 O:Speedy . . . . . . . . . . . . . . . 300.00
263 GA,Aquaman,Superboy . . . . 300.00
264 GA,A:Robin Hood . . . . . . . . 300.00
265 GA,Aquaman,Superboy . . . . 300.00
266 GA,I:Aquagirl. . . . . . . . . . . . . 300.00
267 N:Legion(2nd app.) . . . . . . 1,800.00
268 I:Aquaboy . . . . . . . . . . . . . . . 300.00
269 I:Aqualad,E:Green Arrow . . . 450.00
270 2nd A:Aqualad,B:Congorilla . 300.00
271 O:Lex Luthor rtd . . . . . . . . . . 450.00
272 I:Human Flying Fish . . . . . . . 300.00
273 Aquaman,Superboy . . . . . . . 300.00
274 Aquaman,Superboy . . . . . . . 300.00
275 O:Superman/Batman
     T.U. rtd . . . . . . . . . . . . . . . . . 400.00
276 Superboy,3rd A:Metallo. . . . 300.00
277 Aquaman,Superboy . . . . . . . 300.00
278 Aquaman,Superboy . . . . . . . 300.00
279 CS,Aquaman,Superboy . . . . 300.00
280 CS,A:Lori Lemaris. . . . . . . . . 300.00

281 Aquaman,Superboy
     E:Congorilla. . . . . . . . . . . . . 300.00
282 5th A:Legion,I:Starboy. . . . . 400.00
283 I:Phantom Zone . . . . . . . . . . 400.00
284 CS,JM,Aquaman,Superboy . 250.00
285 WB,B:Bizarro World . . . . . . . 350.00
286 I:Bizarro Mxyzptlk . . . . . . . . 350.00
287 I:Dev-Em,Bizarro Perry White,
     Jimmy Olsen . . . . . . . . . . . . 250.00
288 A:Dev-Em . . . . . . . . . . . . . . . 250.00
289 Superboy. . . . . . . . . . . . . . . . 250.00
290 8th A:Legion,O&J:Sunboy,
     I:Brainiac 5 . . . . . . . . . . . . . . 400.00
291 A:Lex Luthor . . . . . . . . . . . . . 250.00
292 Superboy,I:Bizarro Lucy Lane,
     Lana Lang . . . . . . . . . . . . . . . 250.00
293 CS,O&I:Marv-El,I:Bizarro
     Luthor . . . . . . . . . . . . . . . . . . 350.00
294 I:Bizarro M.Monroe,JFK . . . . 300.00
295 I:Bizarro Titano . . . . . . . . . . . 250.00
296 A:Ben Franklin,George
     Washington . . . . . . . . . . . . . 250.00
297 Lana Lang Superboy Sister . 250.00
298 The Fat Superboy. . . . . . . . . 250.00
299 I:Gold Kryptonite . . . . . . . . . 250.00
300 B:Legion,I:Mon-El,
     E:Bizarro World . . . . . . . . . 1,000.00

## ADVENTURE INTO MYSTERY
### Marvel Atlas, 1956–57

1 BP,BEv(c),Future Tense . . . . . 500.00
2 Man on the 13th Floor . . . . . . 300.00
3 Next Stop Eternity . . . . . . . . . . 300.00
4 BP,AW, The Hex . . . . . . . . . . . 300.00
5 JO,BEv,The People Who
   Weren't . . . . . . . . . . . . . . . . . . 300.00
6 The Wax Man . . . . . . . . . . . . . 300.00
7 AT,BEv(c). . . . . . . . . . . . . . . . . 300.00
8 AT,JWo,TSe . . . . . . . . . . . . . . 300.00

## ADVENTURE IS MY CAREER
### Street & Smith Publ., 1944
n# U.S.Coast Guard Academy. . . 300.00

## ADVENTURES
### St. John Publishing Co., Nov. 1949–Feb. 1950
1 Adventures in Romance . . . . . 350.00
2 Spectacular Adventures . . . . . 500.00

Adventures in 3-D #1
© Harvey Publ.

Adventures into the Unknown #39
© American Comics Group

Adventures Into Weird Worlds #6
© Marvel Comics Group

## ADVENTURES FOR BOYS
**Bailey Enterprises, Dec. 1954**
n# . . . . . . . . . . . . . . . . . . . . . . . 100.00

## ADVENTURES IN 3-D
**Harvey Publications,
Nov. 1953–Jan 1954**
1 with glasses . . . . . . . . . . . . . . 350.00
1a rep. O'Dells Adventures
  in 3-D . . . . . . . . . . . . . . . . . 300.00
2 with glasses . . . . . . . . . . . . . . 300.00

## ADVENTURES INTO DARKNESS
**Standard Publications,
Aug., 1952**
5 JK(c), ATh . . . . . . . . . . . . . . . 700.00
6 GT, JK . . . . . . . . . . . . . . . . . . 500.00
7 JK(c) . . . . . . . . . . . . . . . . . . . 500.00
8 ATh . . . . . . . . . . . . . . . . . . . . 500.00
9 JK,ATh . . . . . . . . . . . . . . . . . . 500.00
10 JK,ATh,MSy . . . . . . . . . . . . 450.00
11 JK,ATh,MSy . . . . . . . . . . . . 450.00
12 JK,ATh,MSy . . . . . . . . . . . . 450.00
13 Cannibalism feature . . . . . . . . 600.00
14 . . . . . . . . . . . . . . . . . . . . . . . 350.00

## ADVENTURES INTO TERROR
**See: JOKER COMICS**

## ADVENTURES INTO THE UNKNOWN!
**American Comics Group,
Fall 1948**
1 FGu, Haunted House (c) . . . 5,000.00
2 Haunted Island (c) . . . . . . . 2,000.00
3 AF, Sarcophagus (c) . . . . . . 2,000.00
4 Monsters (c) . . . . . . . . . . . . . . 950.00
5 Monsters (c) . . . . . . . . . . . . . . 950.00
6 Giant Hands (c) . . . . . . . . . . . 900.00
7 Skeleton Pirate (c) . . . . . . . . . 900.00
8 Horror . . . . . . . . . . . . . . . . . . . 900.00
9 Snow Monster . . . . . . . . . . . . 900.00
10 Red Bats . . . . . . . . . . . . . . . . 900.00
11 Death Shadow . . . . . . . . . . . 900.00
12 OW(c) . . . . . . . . . . . . . . . . . . 900.00
13 OW(c),Dinosaur . . . . . . . . . . 500.00
14 OW(c),Cave . . . . . . . . . . . . . 500.00
15 Red Demons . . . . . . . . . . . . . 500.00

16 OW(c) . . . . . . . . . . . . . . . . . . 400.00
17 OW(c),The Thing Type . . . . . . 600.00
18 OW(c),Wolves . . . . . . . . . . . . 500.00
19 OW(c),Graveyard . . . . . . . . . . 500.00
20 OW(c),Graveyard . . . . . . . . . . 500.00
21 OW(c),Bats and Dracula . . . . . 400.00
22 Death . . . . . . . . . . . . . . . . . . 400.00
23 OW(c),Bats . . . . . . . . . . . . . . 400.00
24 Swamp Monster . . . . . . . . . . . 400.00
25 . . . . . . . . . . . . . . . . . . . . . . . 400.00
26 DW(s) . . . . . . . . . . . . . . . . . . 400.00
27 AW,RKu,OW(c) . . . . . . . . . . . 400.00
28 thru 37 . . . . . . . . . . . . . . . @400.00
38 A-Bomb . . . . . . . . . . . . . . . . . 600.00
39 thru 49 . . . . . . . . . . . . . . . @500.00
50 Giant fly (c) . . . . . . . . . . . . . . 500.00
51 H. Lazarus . . . . . . . . . . . . . . . 500.00
52 H. Lazarus, 3-D-ish . . . . . . . . 500.00
53 thru 55 . . . . . . . . . . . . . . . @500.00
56 H. Lazarus . . . . . . . . . . . . . . . 500.00
57 SMo,OW(c) . . . . . . . . . . . . . . 500.00
58 H. Lazarus . . . . . . . . . . . . . . . 500.00
59 3-D-ish . . . . . . . . . . . . . . . . . 400.00
60 . . . . . . . . . . . . . . . . . . . . . . . 300.00
61 OW,Rocket ship (c) . . . . . . . . 300.00
62 thru 69 . . . . . . . . . . . . . . . @250.00
70 thru 79 . . . . . . . . . . . . . . . @250.00
80 thru 90 . . . . . . . . . . . . . . . @200.00
91 AW . . . . . . . . . . . . . . . . . . . . 250.00
92 thru 95 . . . . . . . . . . . . . . . @150.00
96 AW . . . . . . . . . . . . . . . . . . . . 225.00
97 thru 99 . . . . . . . . . . . . . . . @150.00
100 JB . . . . . . . . . . . . . . . . . . . . 200.00
101 thru 106 . . . . . . . . . . . . . . @150.00
107 AW . . . . . . . . . . . . . . . . . . . 225.00
108 thru 115 . . . . . . . . . . . . . . @150.00
116 AW,AT . . . . . . . . . . . . . . . . 225.00
117 thru 127 . . . . . . . . . . . . . . @150.00
128 AW,Forbidden Worlds . . . . . . 150.00
129 thru 151 . . . . . . . . . . . . . . @150.00
152 JCr . . . . . . . . . . . . . . . . . . . 150.00
153 A:Magic Agent . . . . . . . . . . . 150.00
154 O:Nemesis . . . . . . . . . . . . . . 200.00
155 Nemesis . . . . . . . . . . . . . . . 125.00
156 A:Magic Agent . . . . . . . . . . . 125.00
157 thru 167 . . . . . . . . . . . . . . @125.00
168 JB,SD, Nemesis . . . . . . . . . . 125.00
169 Nemesis vs. Hitler . . . . . . . . 150.00
170 thru 174, Aug., 1967 . . . . . @125.00

## ADVENTURES INTO WEIRD WORLDS
**Marvel, Jan., 1952–June, 1954**
1 RH,GT,The Walking Death . . 1,400.00

2 GT,JMn,Thing in the Bottle . . . 600.00
3 JMn,The Thing That Waited . . 500.00
4 BEv,RH,TheVillageGraveyard . 500.00
5 BEv,I Crawl Thru Graves . . . . 500.00
6 The Ghost Still Walks . . . . . . 500.00
7 OW,Monsters In Disguise . . . . 500.00
8 DAy,Nightmares . . . . . . . . . . 500.00
9 Do Not Feed . . . . . . . . . . . . . 500.00
10 BEv,Down In The Cellar . . . . . 500.00
11 JMn,Phantom . . . . . . . . . . . . 450.00
12 GT,Lost In the Graveyard . . . . 450.00
13 JeR,DRi,Where Dead Men
  Walk . . . . . . . . . . . . . . . . 450.00
14 A Shriek In the Night . . . . . . . 450.00
15 GT,Terror In Our Town . . . . . . 450.00
16 The Kiss of Death . . . . . . . . . 450.00
17 RH,He Walks With A Ghost . . 450.00
18 Ivan & Petroff . . . . . . . . . . . . 450.00
19 It Happened One Night . . . . . . 450.00
20 JMn,The Doubting Thomas . . . 450.00
21 JF,What Happened In
  the Cave,Hitler . . . . . . . . . . 500.00
22 JMn,RH,Vampire's Partner . . . 450.00
23 JMn,The Kiss of Death . . . . . 300.00
24 JF,Halfway Home . . . . . . . . . 300.00
25 BEv,JSt,The Mad Mamba . . . . 300.00
26 DAy,Good-Bye Earth . . . . . . . 300.00
27 The Dwarf of Horror Moor . . . 600.00
28 DW,Monsters From the Grave 500.00
29 Bone Dry . . . . . . . . . . . . . . . 250.00
30 JSt,The Impatient Ghost . . . . 250.00

## ADVENTURES IN WONDERLAND
**Lev Gleason Publications,
April, 1955**
1 . . . . . . . . . . . . . . . . . . . . . . . 200.00
2 . . . . . . . . . . . . . . . . . . . . . . . 150.00
3 and 4 . . . . . . . . . . . . . . . . @125.00
5 Christmas . . . . . . . . . . . . . . . 150.00

## THE ADVENTURES OF ALAN LADD
**DC Comics, 1949–51**
1 Ph(c) . . . . . . . . . . . . . . . . . 1,500.00
2 Ph(c) . . . . . . . . . . . . . . . . . . . 900.00
3 Ph(c) . . . . . . . . . . . . . . . . . . . 550.00
4 Ph(c) . . . . . . . . . . . . . . . . . . . 550.00
5 Ph(c),inc.Destination Danger . 500.00
6 Ph(c) . . . . . . . . . . . . . . . . . . . 500.00
7 RMo(c&a) . . . . . . . . . . . . . . . 500.00
8 Grand Duchess takes over . . . 500.00
9 Deadlien in Rapula . . . . . . . . 500.00

---

All comics prices listed are for *Near Mint* condition.        **Page 37**

Adventures of Bob Hope #11
© DC Comics

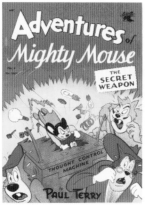

Adventures of Mighty Mouse #4
© St. John Publishing Co.

Adventures of Rex, The Wonderdog
#18 © DC Comics

## ADVENTURES OF ALICE
**Civil Service Publ., 1945–46**
| | |
|---|---|
| 1 In Wonderland | 300.00 |
| 2 Through the Looking Glass | 200.00 |
| 3 Monkey Island | 200.00 |

## THE ADVENTURES OF BOB HOPE
**DC Comics, 1951**
| | |
|---|---|
| 1 Ph(c) | 3,000.00 |
| 2 Ph(c) | 1,500.00 |
| 3 Ph(c) | 1,000.00 |
| 4 Ph(c) | 1,000.00 |
| 5 thru 10 | @750.00 |
| 11 thru 20 | @600.00 |
| 21 thru 40 | @400.00 |
| 41 thru 60 | @300.00 |
| 61 thru 90 | @150.00 |
| 91 thru 93 | @125.00 |
| 94 C:Aquaman | 150.00 |
| 95 1st Superhip | 150.00 |
| 96 thru 105 | @125.00 |
| 106 thru 109 NA | @200.00 |

## ADVENTURES OF DEAN MARTIN AND JERRY LEWIS
**DC Comics, 1952–57**
| | |
|---|---|
| 1 | 2,700.00 |
| 2 | 1,000.00 |
| 3 | 750.00 |
| 4 | 750.00 |
| 5 | 750.00 |
| 6 thru 10 | @750.00 |
| 11 thru 20 | @500.00 |
| 21 thru 40 | @300.00 |
| Becomes: | |

## ADVENTURES OF JERRY LEWIS
**DC Comics, 1957**
| | |
|---|---|
| 41 thru 55 | @250.00 |
| 56 thru 69 | @200.00 |
| 70 thru 87 | @150.00 |
| 88 A:Bob Hope | 150.00 |

## THE ADVENTURES OF HOMER COBB
**Say/Bart Prod., Sept. 1947**
| | |
|---|---|
| 1 | 500.00 |

## ADVENTURES OF HOMER GHOST
**Marvel Atlas, June–Aug., 1957**
| | |
|---|---|
| 1 | 250.00 |
| 2 | 250.00 |

## ADVENTURES OF LITTLE ORPHAN ANNIE COMICS
**Giveaway 1940–42**
| | |
|---|---|
| N#(1) | 600.00 |
| N#(2) | 500.00 |
| N#(3) | 500.00 |

## MIGHTY MOUSE ADVENTURES
**St. John Publishing Co., Nov., 1951**
| | |
|---|---|
| 1 Mighty Mouse Adventures | 400.00 |
| Becomes: | |

## ADVENTURES OF MIGHTY MOUSE
**St. John Publishing Co., Nov., 1951**
| | |
|---|---|
| 2 Menace of the Deep | 400.00 |
| 3 Storm Clouds of Mystery | 300.00 |
| 4 Thought Control Machine | 300.00 |
| 5 Jungle Peril | 300.00 |
| 6 'The Vine of Destruction' | 250.00 |
| 7 Space Ship(c) | 250.00 |
| 8 Charging Alien(c) | 250.00 |
| 9 Meteor(c) | 200.00 |
| 10 'Revolt at the Zoo' | 200.00 |
| 11 Jungle(c) | 200.00 |
| 12 A:Freezing Terror | 200.00 |
| 13 A:Visitor from Outer Space | 200.00 |
| 14 V:Cat | 200.00 |
| 15 | 200.00 |
| 16 | 200.00 |
| 17 | 200.00 |
| 18 May, 1955 | 200.00 |

## ADVENTURES OF MIGHTY MOUSE
See: TERRY-TUNES COMICS

## ADVENTURES OF OZZIE AND HARRIET
**DC Comics, 1949–50**
| | |
|---|---|
| 1 Ph(c) | 1,500.00 |
| 2 | 900.00 |
| 3 thru 5 | @750.00 |

## ADVENTURES OF PATORUZU
**Green Publishing Co., 1946**
| | |
|---|---|
| N# | 125.00 |

## ADVENTURES OF PINKY LEE
**Marvel Atlas, July, 1955**
| | |
|---|---|
| 1 | 400.00 |
| 2 | 300.00 |
| 3 thru 5 | @275.00 |

## THE ADVENTURES OF PIPSQUEAK
**Archie Publications Sept. 1959–July 1960**
| | |
|---|---|
| 34 | 125.00 |
| 35 thru 39 | @100.00 |

## ADVENTURES OF REX, THE WONDER DOG
**DC Comics, 1952–59**
| | |
|---|---|
| 1 ATh | 2,000.00 |
| 2 ATh | 1,000.00 |
| 3 ATh | 900.00 |
| 4 | 800.00 |
| 5 | 800.00 |
| 6 thru 10 | @600.00 |
| 11 Atom Bomb | 700.00 |
| 12 thru 20 | @400.00 |
| 21 thru 46 | @300.00 |

## ADVENTURES OF ROBIN HOOD
See: ROBIN HOOD

## THE ADVENTURES OF BIG BOY
**Marvel Timely Comics, 1956**
| | |
|---|---|
| 1 | 1,500.00 |

---

All comics prices listed are for *Near Mint* condition.

Adventures of the Big Boy #15
© Marvel Comics Group

Aggie Mack #2
© Four Star Comics

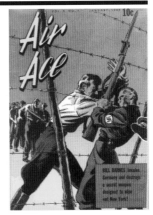

Air Ace Vol2, #1
© Street & Smith

2 . . . . . . . . . . . . . . . . . . . . . . . . . . . 900.00
3 . . . . . . . . . . . . . . . . . . . . . . . . . . . 500.00
**Becomes:**

## ADVENTURES OF THE BIG BOY
**Marvel Timely Comics, 1956**
4 . . . . . . . . . . . . . . . . . . . . . . . . . . 450.00
5 . . . . . . . . . . . . . . . . . . . . . . . . . . 400.00
6 . . . . . . . . . . . . . . . . . . . . . . . . . . 300.00
7 . . . . . . . . . . . . . . . . . . . . . . . . . . 300.00
8 . . . . . . . . . . . . . . . . . . . . . . . . . . 300.00
9 . . . . . . . . . . . . . . . . . . . . . . . . . . 300.00
10 . . . . . . . . . . . . . . . . . . . . . . . . . 300.00
11 thru 20 . . . . . . . . . . . . . . . . @200.00
21 thru 30 . . . . . . . . . . . . . . . . @125.00
31 thru 40 . . . . . . . . . . . . . . . . @75.00
41 thru 50 . . . . . . . . . . . . . . . . @60.00
51 thru 60 . . . . . . . . . . . . . . . . @50.00
61 thru 70 . . . . . . . . . . . . . . . . @50.00

## ADVENTURES OF THE DOVER BOYS
**Close-up/Archie 1950**
1 . . . . . . . . . . . . . . . . . . . . . . . . . . 150.00
2 . . . . . . . . . . . . . . . . . . . . . . . . . . 150.00

## ADVENTURES OF THE FLY
**Archie Publications/ Radio Comics, 1959–65**
1 JSm/JK,O:Fly,I:SpiderSpry
  A:Lancelot Strong/Shield . . 1,000.00
2 JSm/JK,DAy,AW . . . . . . . . . . . 600.00
3 JDa, O:Fly . . . . . . . . . . . . . . . 500.00
4 V:Dazzler NA panel . . . . . . . . . 300.00
5 A:Spider Spry . . . . . . . . . . . . . 200.00
6 V:Moon Men . . . . . . . . . . . . . . 200.00
7 A:Black Hood . . . . . . . . . . . . . 225.00
8 A:Lancelot Strong/Shield . . . . 225.00
9 A:Lancelot Strong/Shield
  I:Cat Girl . . . . . . . . . . . . . . . . . 200.00
10 A:Spider Spry . . . . . . . . . . . . 200.00
11 V:Rock Men . . . . . . . . . . . . . . 125.00
12 V:Brute Invaders . . . . . . . . . . 125.00
13 I:Kim Brand . . . . . . . . . . . . . . 125.00
14 I:Fly-Girl(Kim Brand) . . . . . . . 150.00
15 A:Spider . . . . . . . . . . . . . . . . 125.00
16 A:Fly-Girl . . . . . . . . . . . . . . . . 125.00
17 A:Fly-Girl . . . . . . . . . . . . . . . . 125.00
18 A:Fly-Girl . . . . . . . . . . . . . . . . 125.00
19 A:Fly-Girl . . . . . . . . . . . . . . . . 125.00
20 O:Fly-Girl . . . . . . . . . . . . . . . . 150.00

21 A:Fly-Girl . . . . . . . . . . . . . . . . 100.00
22 A:Fly-Girl . . . . . . . . . . . . . . . . 100.00
23 A:Fly-Girl,Jaguar . . . . . . . . . . 100.00
24 A:Fly-Girl . . . . . . . . . . . . . . . . 100.00
25 A:Fly-Girl . . . . . . . . . . . . . . . . 100.00
26 A:Fly-Girl,Black Hood . . . . . . 100.00
27 A:Fly-Girl,Black Hood . . . . . . 100.00
28 A:Black Hood . . . . . . . . . . . . . 100.00
29 A:Fly-Girl,Black Hood . . . . . . 100.00
30 A:Fly-Girl,R:Comet . . . . . . . . 150.00
31 A:Black Hood, Shield, Comet . 150.00

## AFTER DARK
**Sterling Comics, May–Sept. 1955**
6 . . . . . . . . . . . . . . . . . . . . . . . . . . 125.00
7 . . . . . . . . . . . . . . . . . . . . . . . . . . 100.00
8 . . . . . . . . . . . . . . . . . . . . . . . . . . 100.00

## AGGIE MACK
**Four Star Comics/ Superior Comics, Jan., 1948**
1 AF,HR(c),Johnny Prep . . . . . . 600.00
2 JK(c) . . . . . . . . . . . . . . . . . . . . 300.00
3 AF,JK(c) . . . . . . . . . . . . . . . . . . 300.00
4 AF, Johnny Prep . . . . . . . . . . . 400.00
5 AF,JK(c) . . . . . . . . . . . . . . . . . . 300.00
6 AF,JK(c) . . . . . . . . . . . . . . . . . . 275.00
7 AF,Burt Lancaster on cover . . . 325.00
8 AF,JK(c), Aug., 1949 . . . . . . . . 275.00

## BILL BARNES
**Street & Smith Publ.,July, 1940**
1 (Bill Barnes Comics) . . . . . . 1,500.00
**Becomes:**

## BILL BARNES, AMERICA'S AIR ACE
**Street & Smith Publ., 1940**
2 Second Battle Valley Forge . . . 750.00
3 A:Aviation Cadets . . . . . . . . . . 500.00
4 Shotdown(c) . . . . . . . . . . . . . . 500.00
5 A:Air Warden, Danny Hawk . . . 500.00
6 A:Danny Hawk,RocketRodney. 400.00
7 How to defeat the Japanese . . 400.00
8 Ghost Ship . . . . . . . . . . . . . . . 400.00
9 Flying Tigers, John Wayne . . . 425.00
10 I:Roane Waring . . . . . . . . . . . 400.00
11 Flying Tigers . . . . . . . . . . . . . 400.00
12 War Workers . . . . . . . . . . . . . 400.00
**Becomes:**

## AIR ACE
**Street & Smith Publ., Jan., 1944**
2-1 Invades Germany . . . . . . . . 600.00
2-2 Jungle Warfare . . . . . . . . . . 450.00
2-3 A:The Four Musketeers . . . . 200.00
2-4 A:Russell Swann . . . . . . . . . 200.00
2-5 A:The Four Musketeers . . . . 200.00
2-6 Raft(c) . . . . . . . . . . . . . . . . . 200.00
2-7 BP, What's New In Science . 200.00
2-8 XP-59 . . . . . . . . . . . . . . . . . 200.00
2-9 The Northrop P-61 . . . . . . . . 200.00
2-10 NCG-14 . . . . . . . . . . . . . . . 200.00
2-11 Whip Launch . . . . . . . . . . . 200.00
2-12 PP(c) . . . . . . . . . . . . . . . . . 200.00
3-1 . . . . . . . . . . . . . . . . . . . . . . 150.00
3-2 Atom and Its Future . . . . . . . 150.00
3-3 Flying in the Future . . . . . . . . 150.00
3-4 How Fast Can We Fly . . . . . 150.00
3-5 REv(c) . . . . . . . . . . . . . . . . . 150.00
3-6 V:Wolves . . . . . . . . . . . . . . . 150.00
3-7 BP(c), Vortex of Atom Bomb 400.00
3-8 BP,Feb.–March, 1947 . . . . . . 175.00

## AIRBOY
## See: AIR FIGHTERS COMICS

## AIR FIGHTERS COMICS
**Hillman Periodicals, Nov., 1941**
1 I:Black Commander
  (only App) . . . . . . . . . . . . . 5,000.00
2 O:Airboy A:Sky Wolf . . . . . . 7,000.00
3 O:Sky Wolf and Heap . . . . . . 4,000.00
4 A:Black Angel, Iron Ace . . . . 3,500.00
5 A:Sky Wolf and Iron Ace . . . . 2,500.00
6 Airboy's Bird Plane . . . . . . . . 2,700.00
7 Airboy Battles Kultur . . . . . . . 2,500.00
8 A:Skinny McGinty . . . . . . . . . 2,200.00
9 A:Black Prince, Hatchet Man 2,200.00
10 I:The Stinger . . . . . . . . . . . . 2,200.00
11 Kida(c) . . . . . . . . . . . . . . . . . 2,200.00
12 A:Misery . . . . . . . . . . . . . . . . 2,200.00
2-1 A:Flying Dutchman . . . . . . . 2,400.00
2-2 I:Valkyrie . . . . . . . . . . . . . . . 2,700.00
2-3 Story Panels (c) . . . . . . . . . 1,000.00
2-4 V:Japanese . . . . . . . . . . . . . 1,000.00
2-5 Air Boy in Tokyo . . . . . . . . . 1,000.00
2-6 'Dance of Death' . . . . . . . . . 1,000.00
2-7 A:Valkyrie . . . . . . . . . . . . . . 1,000.00
2-8 Airboy Battles Japanese . . . 1,000.00
2-9 Airboy Battles Japanese . . . 1,000.00
2-10 O:Skywolf . . . . . . . . . . . . . 1,200.00
**Becomes:**

**Ai**

Airboy Comics Vol. 4 #5
© Hillman Periodicals

Airboy Comics Vol. 10 #4
© Hillman Periodicals

Al Capp's Wolf Gal #2
© Toby Press

## AIRBOY COMICS

**Hillman Periodicals, Dec., 1945**

2-11 . . . . . . . . . . . . . . . . . . . 1,200.00
2-12 A:Valykrie . . . . . . . . . . . . 800.00
3-1 . . . . . . . . . . . . . . . . . . . . 600.00
3-2 . . . . . . . . . . . . . . . . . . . . 600.00
3-3 Never published
3-4 I:The Heap . . . . . . . . . . . . 500.00
3-5 Airboy . . . . . . . . . . . . . . . 500.00
3-6 A:Valykrie . . . . . . . . . . . . 500.00
3-7 AMc,Witch Hunt . . . . . . . . . 500.00
3-8 A:Condor. . . . . . . . . . . . . . 550.00
3-9 O:The Heap . . . . . . . . . . . . 550.00
3-10 . . . . . . . . . . . . . . . . . . . 500.00
3-11 . . . . . . . . . . . . . . . . . . . 500.00
3-12 Airboy missing . . . . . . . . . 650.00
4-1 Elephant in chains (c). . . . . . 600.00
4-2 I:Rackman . . . . . . . . . . . . . 450.00
4-3 Airboy profits on name . . . . . 450.00
4-4 S&K . . . . . . . . . . . . . . . . . 500.00
4-5 S&K,The American Miracle . 450.00
4-6 S&K,A:Heap and
   Flying Fool. . . . . . . . . . . . . 450.00
4-7 S&K . . . . . . . . . . . . . . . . . 450.00
4-8 S&K,Girlfriend captured . . . . 450.00
4-9 S&K,Airboy in Quick Sand . . 450.00
4-10 S&K,A:Valkyrie . . . . . . . . . 450.00
4-11 S&K,A:Frenchy . . . . . . . . . 450.00
4-12 FBe . . . . . . . . . . . . . . . . 500.00
5-1 LSt . . . . . . . . . . . . . . . . . 400.00
5-2 I:Wild Horse of Calabra . . . . 400.00
5-3 . . . . . . . . . . . . . . . . . . . . 400.00
5-4 CI . . . . . . . . . . . . . . . . . . 400.00
5-5 Skull on cover. . . . . . . . . . . 400.00
5-6. . . . . . . . . . . . . . . . . . . . 400.00
5-7. . . . . . . . . . . . . . . . . . . . 400.00
5-8 Bondage (c) . . . . . . . . . . . 400.00
5-9 Zoi,Row . . . . . . . . . . . . . . 400.00
5-10 A:Valykrie,O:The Heap . . . 450.00
5-11 Airboy vs. The Rats. . . . . . 400.00
5-12 BK,Rat Army captures
   Airboy . . . . . . . . . . . . . . . 400.00
6-1 . . . . . . . . . . . . . . . . . . . . 400.00
6-2. . . . . . . . . . . . . . . . . . . . 400.00
6-3. . . . . . . . . . . . . . . . . . . . 400.00
6-4 Airboy boxes . . . . . . . . . . . 500.00
6-5 A:The Ice People . . . . . . . . 400.00
6-6 . . . . . . . . . . . . . . . . . . . . 400.00
6-7 Airboy vs. Chemical Giant . 400.00
6-8 O:The Heap . . . . . . . . . . . . 400.00
6-9 . . . . . . . . . . . . . . . . . . . . 400.00
6-10 . . . . . . . . . . . . . . . . . . . 400.00
6-11 . . . . . . . . . . . . . . . . . . . 400.00
6-12 . . . . . . . . . . . . . . . . . . . 400.00
7-1 . . . . . . . . . . . . . . . . . . . . 400.00

7-2 BP. . . . . . . . . . . . . . . . . . . 400.00
7-3 BP. . . . . . . . . . . . . . . . . . . 500.00
7-4 I:Monsters of the Ice. . . . . . 400.00
7-5 V:Monsters of the Ice . . . . . 400.00
7-6 . . . . . . . . . . . . . . . . . . . . 400.00
7-7 Mystery of the Sargasso
   Sea . . . . . . . . . . . . . . . . . 400.00
7-8 A:Centaur . . . . . . . . . . . . . 400.00
7-9 I:Men of the StarlightRobot. . 400.00
7-10 O:The Heap . . . . . . . . . . . 400.00
7-11 . . . . . . . . . . . . . . . . . . . 400.00
7-12 Airboy visits India . . . . . . . 400.00
8-1 BP,A:Outcast and Polo
   Bandits. . . . . . . . . . . . . . . 400.00
8-2 BP,Suicide Dive (c). . . . . . . 400.00
8-3 BK, I:The Living Fuse . . . . . 400.00
8-4 A:Death Merchants of
   the Air . . . . . . . . . . . . . . . 400.00
8-5 A:Great Plane from Nowhere 400.00
8-6 . . . . . . . . . . . . . . . . . . . . 400.00
8-7 . . . . . . . . . . . . . . . . . . . . 400.00
8-8 . . . . . . . . . . . . . . . . . . . . 400.00
8-9 . . . . . . . . . . . . . . . . . . . . 400.00
8-10 A:Mystery Walkers . . . . . . 400.00
8-11 . . . . . . . . . . . . . . . . . . . 400.00
8-12 . . . . . . . . . . . . . . . . . . . 450.00
9-1 . . . . . . . . . . . . . . . . . . . . 350.00
9-2 A:Valykrie . . . . . . . . . . . . . 300.00
9-3 A:Heap (c). . . . . . . . . . . . . 300.00
9-4 A:Water Beast, Frog Headed
   Riders . . . . . . . . . . . . . . . 350.00
9-5 A:Heap vs.Man of Moonlight 300.00
9-6 Heap (c) . . . . . . . . . . . . . . 300.00
9-7 Heap (c) . . . . . . . . . . . . . . 300.00
9-8 Heap (c) . . . . . . . . . . . . . . 350.00
9-9 . . . . . . . . . . . . . . . . . . . . 350.00
9-10 Space (c) . . . . . . . . . . . . 350.00
9-11 . . . . . . . . . . . . . . . . . . . 350.00
9-12 Heap (c) . . . . . . . . . . . . . 350.00
10-1 Heap (c) . . . . . . . . . . . . . 350.00
10-2 Ships on Space . . . . . . . . 300.00
10-3. . . . . . . . . . . . . . . . . . . 350.00
10-4 May, 1953 . . . . . . . . . . . . 350.00

## ALARMING TALES

**Harvey Publications, 1957–58**

1 JK,JK(c) . . . . . . . . . . . . . . . 400.00
2 JK,JK(c) . . . . . . . . . . . . . . . 300.00
3 JK. . . . . . . . . . . . . . . . . . . . 275.00
4 JK,BP. . . . . . . . . . . . . . . . . 275.00
5 JK,AW . . . . . . . . . . . . . . . . 275.00
6 JK . . . . . . . . . . . . . . . . . . . 275.00

## AL CAPP'S DOGPATCH COMICS

**Toby Press, June, 1949**

1 . . . . . . . . . . . . . . . . . . . . . 350.00
2 A:Daisy. . . . . . . . . . . . . . . . 250.00
3 . . . . . . . . . . . . . . . . . . . . . 225.00
4 Dec., 1949 . . . . . . . . . . . . . 225.00

## AL CAPP'S SHMOO

**Toby Press, July, 1949**

1 100 Trillion Schmoos . . . . . . . 550.00
2 Super Shmoo(c). . . . . . . . . . . 400.00
3 . . . . . . . . . . . . . . . . . . . . . 400.00
4 . . . . . . . . . . . . . . . . . . . . . 400.00
5 April, 1950 . . . . . . . . . . . . . . 400.00

## AL CAPP'S WOLF GAL

**Toby Press, 1951**

1 Pin-Up . . . . . . . . . . . . . . . . . 500.00
2 1952. . . . . . . . . . . . . . . . . . 450.00

## ALGIE

**Timor Publ. Co., Dec. 1953**

1 Teen-age . . . . . . . . . . . . . . . 125.00
1a reprint. . . . . . . . . . . . . . . . 125.00
2 . . . . . . . . . . . . . . . . . . . . . 100.00
3 . . . . . . . . . . . . . . . . . . . . . 100.00

## ALICE

**Ziff-Davis Publ. Co., 1952**

10 New Adventures in
   Wonderland . . . . . . . . . . . . 400.00
11 (#2) . . . . . . . . . . . . . . . . . 350.00

## ALL-AMERICAN COMICS

**DC Comics, 1939–48**

1 B:Hop Harrigan,Scribbly,Mutt&Jeff,
   Red,White&Blue,Bobby Thatcher,
   Skippy,Daiseybelle,Mystery Men
   of Mars,Toonerville . . . . . . 10,000.00
2 B:Ripley's Believe It or Not . . 5,000.00
3 Hop Harrigan (c). . . . . . . . . 3,500.00
4 Flag(c). . . . . . . . . . . . . . . . 3,500.00
5 B:The American Way . . . . . . 3,500.00
6 ShM(c),Fredric Marchin in
   The American Way . . . . . . 3,000.00
7 E:Bobby Thatcher,C.H.
   Claudy's A Thousand Years
   in a Minute . . . . . . . . . . . . 3,000.00
8 B:Ultra Man. . . . . . . . . . . . . 5,500.00

*All-American Comics #24*
© DC Comics

*All-American Comics #65*
© DC Comics

*All-American Western #117*
© DC Comics

AI

9 A:Ultra Man . . . . . . . . . . . . . . 3,000.00
10 ShM(c),E:The American Way,
   Santa-X-Mas(c) . . . . . . . . . 3,000.00
11 Ultra Man(c) . . . . . . . . . . . . . 3,000.00
12 E:Toonerville Folks . . . . . . . . 2,500.00
13 The Infra Red Des'Royers . . 2,500.00
14 Ultra Man . . . . . . . . . . . . . . . 2,500.00
15 E:Tippie and Reg'lar Fellars  3,000.00
16 O&1st App:Green Lantern,
   B:Lantern(c) . . . . . . . . . 220,000.00
17 SMo(c) . . . . . . . . . . . . . . . . 30,000.00
18 SMo(c) . . . . . . . . . . . . . . . . 25,000.00
19 SMo(c),O&I: Atom, E:Ultra
   Man . . . . . . . . . . . . . . . . . . 30,000.00
20 I:Atom's Costume,Hunkle
   becomes Red Tornado . . . 10,000.00
21 E:Wiley of West Point
   & Skippy . . . . . . . . . . . . . . 6,000.00
22 SMo(c),F:Green Lantern . . . 5,800.00
23 E:Daieybelle . . . . . . . . . . . . 6,000.00
24 E:Ripley's Believe It or Not . 8,000.00
25 O&I:Dr. Mid-Nite . . . . . . . . 20,000.00
26 O&I:Sargon the Sorcerer . . . 7,000.00
27 I:Doiby Dickles . . . . . . . . . . 7,000.00
28 F:Green Lantern . . . . . . . . . 3,000.00
29 ShM(c) . . . . . . . . . . . . . . . . 3,000.00
30 ShM(c) . . . . . . . . . . . . . . . . 3,000.00
31 Adventures of the Underfed
   Orphans . . . . . . . . . . . . . . 3,000.00
32 . . . . . . . . . . . . . . . . . . . . . . 2,500.00
33 . . . . . . . . . . . . . . . . . . . . . . 2,500.00
34 . . . . . . . . . . . . . . . . . . . . . . 2,500.00
35 Doiby discovers Lantern's ID 2,500.00
36 Auto Racing (c) . . . . . . . . . . 2,500.00
37 . . . . . . . . . . . . . . . . . . . . . . 2,500.00
38 ShM,V:A Modern Napoleon . 2,500.00
39 . . . . . . . . . . . . . . . . . . . . . . 2,500.00
40 Doiby Dickles idol(c) . . . . . . 2,500.00
41 . . . . . . . . . . . . . . . . . . . . . . 2,000.00
42 ShM . . . . . . . . . . . . . . . . . . 2,000.00
43 . . . . . . . . . . . . . . . . . . . . . . 2,000.00
44 I Accuse the Green Lantern! 2,000.00
45 . . . . . . . . . . . . . . . . . . . . . . 2,000.00
46 Riddle of Dickles Manor . . . 2,000.00
47 Hop Harrigan meets the
   Enemy,(c) . . . . . . . . . . . . . 2,000.00
48 . . . . . . . . . . . . . . . . . . . . . . 2,000.00
49 Doiby Dickles Cab . . . . . . . . 2,000.00
50 E:Sargon . . . . . . . . . . . . . . . 2,000.00
51 Murder Under the Stars . . . . 1,500.00
52 . . . . . . . . . . . . . . . . . . . . . . 1,500.00
53 Green Lantern delivers
   the Mail . . . . . . . . . . . . . . . 1,500.00
54 . . . . . . . . . . . . . . . . . . . . . . 1,500.00
55 The Riddle of the
   Runaway Trolley . . . . . . . . 1,500.00

56 V:Elegant Esmond . . . . . . . 1,500.00
57 V:The Melancholy Men . . . . 1,500.00
58 . . . . . . . . . . . . . . . . . . . . . . 1,500.00
59 The Story of the Man Who
   Couldn't Tell The Truth . . . . 1,500.00
60 . . . . . . . . . . . . . . . . . . . . . . 1,500.00
61 O:Soloman Grundy,Fighters
   Never Quit . . . . . . . . . . . . . 9,000.00
62 Da Distrik Attorney . . . . . . . . 1,300.00
63 . . . . . . . . . . . . . . . . . . . . . . 1,300.00
64 A Bag of Assorted Nuts! . . . . 1,300.00
65 The Man Who Lost
   Wednesday . . . . . . . . . . . . 1,300.00
66 The Soles of Manhattan! . . . 1,300.00
67 V:King Shark . . . . . . . . . . . . 1,300.00
68 F:Napoleon & Joe Safeen . . 1,300.00
69 Backwards Man! . . . . . . . . . 1,300.00
70 JKu,I:Maximillian O'Leary,
   V:Colley, the Leprechaun . . 1,300.00
71 E:Red,White&Blue,The
   Human Bomb . . . . . . . . . . . 1,200.00
72 B:Black Pirate . . . . . . . . . . . 1,200.00
73 B:Winkey,Blinky&Noddy,
   Mountain Music Mayhem . . 1,200.00
74 . . . . . . . . . . . . . . . . . . . . . . 1,200.00
75 . . . . . . . . . . . . . . . . . . . . . . 1,200.00
76 Spring Time for Doiby . . . . . 1,200.00
77 Hop Harrigan(c) . . . . . . . . . . 1,200.00
78 . . . . . . . . . . . . . . . . . . . . . . 1,200.00
79 Mutt & Jeff . . . . . . . . . . . . . . 1,200.00
80 . . . . . . . . . . . . . . . . . . . . . . 1,200.00
81 . . . . . . . . . . . . . . . . . . . . . . 1,200.00
82 . . . . . . . . . . . . . . . . . . . . . . 1,200.00
83 Mutt & Jeff . . . . . . . . . . . . . . 1,200.00
84 The Adventure of the Man
   with Two Faces . . . . . . . . . . 1,200.00
85 . . . . . . . . . . . . . . . . . . . . . . 1,200.00
86 V:Crime of the Month Club . 1,200.00
87 The Strange Case of
   Professor Nobody . . . . . . . . 1,200.00
88 Canvas of Crime . . . . . . . . . 1,200.00
89 O:Harlequin . . . . . . . . . . . . . 1,700.00
90 O:Icicle . . . . . . . . . . . . . . . . . 1,700.00
91 Wedding of the Harlequin . . 1,700.00
92 The Icicle goes South . . . . . 1,700.00
93 Double Crossing Decoy . . . . 1,700.00
94 A:Harlequin . . . . . . . . . . . . . 1,700.00
95 The Unmasking of the
   Harlequin . . . . . . . . . . . . . . 1,700.00
96 ATh(c),Solve the Mystery
   of the Emerald Necklaces! . 1,700.00
97 ATh(c),The Country Fair
   Crimes . . . . . . . . . . . . . . . . 1,700.00
98 ATh,ATh(c),End of Sports! . . 1,700.00
99 ATh,ATh(c),E:Hop Harrigan . 1,700.00
100 ATh,I:Johnny Thunder . . . . 3,000.00

101 ATh,ATh(c),E:Mutt & Jeff . . 2,500.00
102 ATh,ATh(c),E:GrnLantern . . 7,000.00
**Becomes:**

## ALL-AMERICAN
## WESTERN
### DC Comics, 1948–52

103 A:Johnny Thunder,The City
   Without Guns, All Johnny
   Thunder stories . . . . . . . . . 1,400.00
104 ATh(c),Unseen Allies . . . . . . 800.00
105 ATh(c),Hidden Guns . . . . . . . 700.00
106 ATh(c),Snow Mountain
   Ambush . . . . . . . . . . . . . . . . 700.00
107 ATh(c),Cheyenne Justice . . . 700.00
108 ATh(c),Vengeance of
   the Silver Bullet . . . . . . . . . . 400.00
109 ATh(c),Secret of
   Crazy River . . . . . . . . . . . . . 400.00
110 ATh(c),Ambush at
   Scarecrow Hills . . . . . . . . . . 400.00
111 ATh(c),Gun-Shy Sheriff . . . . 400.00
112 ATh(c),Double Danger . . . . . 400.00
113 ATh(c),Johnny Thunder
   Indian Chief . . . . . . . . . . . . . 400.00
114 ATh(c),The End of
   Johnny Thunder . . . . . . . . . . 400.00
115 ATh(c),Cheyenne Mystery . . 400.00
116 ATh(c),Buffalo Raiders
   of the Mesa . . . . . . . . . . . . . 400.00
117 ATh,V:Black Lightnin . . . . . 300.00
118 ATh(c),Challenge of
   the Aztecs . . . . . . . . . . . . . . 300.00
119 GK(c),The Vanishing
   Gold Mine . . . . . . . . . . . . . . 300.00
120 GK(c),Ambush at
   Painted Mountain . . . . . . . . . 300.00
121 ATh(c),The Unmasking of
   Johnny Thunder . . . . . . . . . . 300.00
122 ATh(c),The Real
   Johnny Thunder . . . . . . . . . . 300.00
123 GK(c),Johnny Thunder's
   Strange Rival . . . . . . . . . . . . 300.00
124 ATh(c),The Iron Horse's
   Last Run . . . . . . . . . . . . . . . 300.00
125 ATh(c),Johnny Thunder's
   Last Roundup . . . . . . . . . . . 300.00
126 ATh(c),Phantoms of the
   Desert . . . . . . . . . . . . . . . . . 300.00
**Becomes:**

## ALL-AMERICAN
## MEN OF WAR
### DC Comics, 1952–66

127 (0) . . . . . . . . . . . . . . . . . . . 2,000.00

**AI**

*All-American Men of War #8*
© DC Comics

*All-American Men of War #57*
© DC Comics

*All-American Men of War #88*
© DC Comics

128 (1) IN, . . . . . . . . . . . . . . . 1,200.00
2 JGr(c),Killer Bait. . . . . . . . . . . 900.00
3 Pied Piper of Pyong-Yang . . . . 800.00
4 JGr(c),The Hills of Hate. . . . . . 800.00
5 One Second to Zero . . . . . . . . 800.00
6 IN(c),Jungle Killers. . . . . . . . . . 700.00
7 IN(c),Beach to Hold . . . . . . . . . 700.00
8 IN(c),Sgt. Storm Cloud. . . . . . . 700.00
9 . . . . . . . . . . . . . . . . . . . . . . . 700.00
10 . . . . . . . . . . . . . . . . . . . . . . . 700.00
11 JGr(c),Dragon's Teeth . . . . . . . 700.00
12 . . . . . . . . . . . . . . . . . . . . . . . 600.00
13 JGr(c),Lost Patrol . . . . . . . . . . 600.00
14 IN(c),Pigeon Boss. . . . . . . . . . 600.00
15 JGr(c),Flying Roadblock . . . . . 600.00
16 JGr(c),The Flying Jeep . . . . . . 600.00
17 JGr(c),Booby Trap Ridge . . . . . 600.00
18 JKu(c),The Ballad of
  Battling Bells . . . . . . . . . . . . 600.00
19 IN(c),IN,Torpedo Track . . . . . 500.00
20 JGr(c),JKu,Lifenet to
  Beach Road. . . . . . . . . . . . . 500.00
21 JGr(c),IN,RH,The
  Coldest War. . . . . . . . . . . . . 500.00
22 JGr(c),IN,JKu,Snipers Nest . . 500.00
23 JGr(c),The Silent War . . . . . . . 500.00
24 JGr(c),The Thin Line. . . . . . . . 500.00
25 JGr(c),IN,For Rent-One
  Foxhole . . . . . . . . . . . . . . . . 500.00
26 Dial W-A-R . . . . . . . . . . . . . . 500.00
27 JGr(c),RH,Fighting Pigeon . . . 500.00
28 JGr(c),RA,JKu,Medal
  for A Dog . . . . . . . . . . . . . . . 500.00
29 IN(c),JKu,Battle Bridges . . . . 500.00
30 JGr(c),RH,Frogman Hunt . . . . 500.00
31 JGr(c),Battle Seat. . . . . . . . . . 400.00
32 JGr(c),IN,Battle Station . . . . . 400.00
33 JGr(c),IN,Sky Ambush . . . . . . 400.00
34 JGr(c),JKu,No Man's Alley . . . 400.00
35 JGr(c),IN, Battle Call. . . . . . . . 400.00
36 JGr(c),JKu,Battle Window. . . . 400.00
37 JGr(c),JKu,The Big Stretch . . . 400.00
38 JGr(c),RH,JKu,The
  Floating Sentinel . . . . . . . . . 400.00
39 JGr(c),JKu,The Four Faces
  of Sgt. Fay. . . . . . . . . . . . . . . 400.00
40 JGr(c),IN,Walking Helmet . . . . 400.00
41 JKu(c),RH,JKu,The 50-50 War 300.00
42 JGr(c),JKu,Battle Arm . . . . . . 300.00
43 JGr(c),JKu,Command Post. . . 300.00
44 JKu(c),The Flying Frogman . . 300.00
45 JGr(c),RH,Combat Waterboy . 300.00
46 JGr(c),IN,RH,Tank Busters . . . 300.00
47 JGr(c),JKu,MD,Battle Freight . 300.00
48 JGr(c),JKu,MD,Roadblock . . . 300.00
49 JGr(c),Walking Target . . . . . . 300.00

50 IN,RH,Bodyguard For A Sub. . 300.00
51 JGr(c),RH,Bomber's Moon . . . 250.00
52 JKu(c),RH,MD,Back
  Seat Driver . . . . . . . . . . . . . 250.00
53 JKu(c),JKu,Night Attack . . . . . 250.00
54 JKu(c),IN,Diary of a
  Fighter Pilot. . . . . . . . . . . . . 250.00
55 JKu(c),RH,Split-Second Target 250.00
56 JKu,IN,RH,Frogman Jinx . . . . 250.00
57 Pick-Up for Easy Co. . . . . . . . 250.00
58 JKu(c),RH,MD,A Piece of Sky 250.00
59 JGr(c),JKu,The Hand of War . 250.00
60 JGr(c),The Time Table . . . . . . 250.00
61 JGr(c),IN,MD,Blind Target. . . . 250.00
62 JGr(c),RH,RA,No(c) . . . . . . . . 250.00
63 JGr(c),JKu,Frogman Carrier . . 250.00
64 JKu(c),JKu,RH,The Other
  Man's War . . . . . . . . . . . . . . 250.00
65 JGr(c),JKu,MD,Same
  Old Sarge . . . . . . . . . . . . . . 250.00
66 JGr(c),The Walking Fort . . . . . 250.00
67 JGr(c),RH,A:Gunner&Sarge,
  The Cover Man . . . . . . . . . . . 700.00
68 JKu(c),Gunner&Sarge,
  The Man & The Gun . . . . . . . 300.00
69 JKu(c),A:Tank Killer,
  Bazooka Hill . . . . . . . . . . . . 300.00
70 JKu(c),IN,Pigeon
  Without Wings . . . . . . . . . . . 250.00
71 JGr(c),A:Tank Killer,Target
  For An Ammo Boy . . . . . . . . . 200.00
72 JGr(c),A:Tank Killer,T.N.T.
  Broom . . . . . . . . . . . . . . . . . 200.00
73 JGr(c),JKu,No Detour . . . . . . . 200.00
74 The Minute Commandos . . . . 200.00
75 JKu(c),Sink That Flattop . . . . 200.00
76 JKu(c),A:Tank Killer,
  Just One More Tank . . . . . . . 200.00
77 JKu(c),IN,MD,Big Fish–
  little Fish . . . . . . . . . . . . . . . . 200.00
78 JGr(c),Tin Hat for an
  Iron Man . . . . . . . . . . . . . . . . 200.00
79 JKu(c),RA,Showdown Soldier. 200.00
80 JGr(c),RA,The Medal Men . . . 200.00
81 JGr(c),IN,Ghost Ship of
  Two Wars. . . . . . . . . . . . . . . 150.00
82 IN(c),B:Johnny Cloud,
  The Flying Chief . . . . . . . . . . 300.00
83 IN(c),Fighting Blind . . . . . . . . 250.00
84 IN(c),Death Dive . . . . . . . . . . 150.00
85 RH(c),Battle Eagle . . . . . . . . 150.00
86 JKu(c),Top-Gun Ace . . . . . . . 150.00
87 JGr(c),Broken Ace . . . . . . . . . 150.00
88 JGr(c),The Ace of Vengeance 150.00
89 JGr(c),The Star Jockey. . . . . . 150.00
90 JGr(c),Wingmate of Doom . . . 125.00

91 RH(c),Two Missions To Doom 125.00
92 JGr(c),The Battle Hawk . . . . . 125.00
93 RH(c),The Silent Rider . . . . . . 125.00
94 RH(c),Be Brave-Be Silent. . . . 125.00
95 RH(c),Second Sight
  For a Pilot . . . . . . . . . . . . . . 125.00
96 RH(c),The Last Flight
  of Lt. Moon . . . . . . . . . . . . . . 125.00
97 IN(c),A Target Called Johnny . 125.00
98 The Time-Bomb Ace . . . . . . . 125.00
99 IN(c),The Empty Cockpit. . . . . 125.00
100 RH(c),Battle o/t Sky Chiefs . . 125.00
101 RH(c),Death Ship of
  Three Wars . . . . . . . . . . . . . 100.00
102 JKu(c),Blind Eagle-Hungry
  Hawk . . . . . . . . . . . . . . . . . . 100.00
103 IN(c),Battle Ship-
  Battle Heart . . . . . . . . . . . . . 100.00
104 JKu(c),The Last Target . . . . . 100.00
105 IN(c),Killer Horse-Ship . . . . . 100.00
106 IN(c),Death Song For
  A Battle Hawk . . . . . . . . . . . . 100.00
107 IN(c),Flame in the Sky . . . . . 100.00
108 IN(c),Death-Dive of the Aces 100.00
109 IN(c),The Killer Slot. . . . . . . . 100.00
110 RH(c),The Co-Pilot was
  Death. . . . . . . . . . . . . . . . . . 100.00
111 RH(c),E:Johnny Cloud, Tag–
  You're Dead. . . . . . . . . . . . . 100.00
112 RH(c),B:Balloon Buster,Lt.
  Steve Savage-Balloon Buster 100.00
113 JKu(c),The Ace of
  Sudden Death . . . . . . . . . . . 100.00
114 JKu(c),The Ace Who
  Died Twice. . . . . . . . . . . . . . 100.00
115 IN(c),A:Johnny Cloud,
  Deliver One Enemy Ace-
  Handle With Care . . . . . . . . . 100.00
116 JKu(c),A:Baloon Buster,
  Circle of Death. . . . . . . . . . . 100.00
117 Sept.–Oct., 1966. . . . . . . . . . 100.00

## ALLEY OOP
### Standard Comics,
### Sept. 1947–Oct. 1949

10 . . . . . . . . . . . . . . . . . . . . . . . 350.00
11 . . . . . . . . . . . . . . . . . . . . . . . 300.00
12 . . . . . . . . . . . . . . . . . . . . . . . 300.00
13 . . . . . . . . . . . . . . . . . . . . . . . 300.00
14 . . . . . . . . . . . . . . . . . . . . . . . 300.00
15 . . . . . . . . . . . . . . . . . . . . . . . 300.00
16 . . . . . . . . . . . . . . . . . . . . . . . 300.00
17 . . . . . . . . . . . . . . . . . . . . . . . 300.00
18 . . . . . . . . . . . . . . . . . . . . . . . 300.00

*All-Famous Crime #9 (#2)*
© Star Publications

*All-Flash #32*
© DC Comics

*All Good Comics #1*
© Fox Publications

## (The Adventures of )
## ALLEY OOP
**Argo Publications, 1955–56**

| | |
|---|---|
| 1 | 200.00 |
| 2 | 150.00 |
| 3 | 150.00 |

## ALL-FAMOUS CRIME
**Star Publications, May, 1951**

| | |
|---|---|
| 1 LbC(c) (8) | 350.00 |
| 2 LbC(c) (9) | 500.00 |
| 3 LbC(c) (10) | 325.00 |
| 4 LbC(c) (4) Law Crime | 300.00 |
| 5 LbC(c) (5) | 300.00 |

**Becomes:**

## ALL-FAMOUS
## POLICE CASES
**Feb., 1952**

| | |
|---|---|
| 6 LbC(c) | 325.00 |
| 7 LbC(c) | 300.00 |
| 8 LbC(c) Marijuana | 300.00 |
| 9 LbC(c) | 250.00 |
| 10 thru 15 LbC(c) | @250.00 |
| 16 Sept., 1954 | 250.00 |

## ALL-FLASH
**DC Comics, 1941–47**

| | |
|---|---|
| 1 EHi,O:Flash,I:The Monocle. | 30,000.00 |
| 2 EHi,The Adventure of Roy Revenge | 10,000.00 |
| 3 EHi,The Adventure of Misplaced Faces | 4,000.00 |
| 4 EHi,Tale of the Time Capsule | 4,000.00 |
| 5 EHi,The Case of the Patsy Colt! Last Quarterly | 3,000.00 |
| 6 EHi,The Ray that Changed Men's Souls | 2,700.00 |
| 7 EHi,Adventures of a Writers Fantasy, House of Horrors | 2,700.00 |
| 8 EHi,Formula to Fairyland! | 2,700.00 |
| 9 EHi,Adventure of the Stolen Telescope | 2,700.00 |
| 10 EHi,Case of the Curious Cat | 2,700.00 |
| 11 EHi,Troubles Come in Doubles | 2,500.00 |
| 12 EHi,Tumble INN to Trouble, Becomes Quarterly on orders from War Production Board O:The Thinker | 2,500.00 |
| 13 EHi,I:The King | 2,500.00 |
| 14 EHi,I:Winky,Blinky & Noddy Green Lantern (c) | 2,600.00 |
| 15 EHi,Secrets of a Stranger | 2,500.00 |
| 16 EHi,A:The Sinister | 2,500.00 |
| 17 Tales of the Three Wishes | 2,500.00 |
| 18 A:Winky,Blinky&Noddy B:Mutt & Jeff reprints | 2,500.00 |
| 19 No Rest at the Rest Home | 2,500.00 |
| 20 A:Winky, Blinky & Noddy | 2,500.00 |
| 21 I:Turtle | 2,000.00 |
| 22 The Money Doubler, E:Mutt & Jeff reprints | 2,000.00 |
| 23 The Bad Men of Bar Nothing | 2,000.00 |
| 24 I:Worry Wart,3 Court Clowns Get Caught | 2,000.00 |
| 25 I:Slapsy Simmons, Flash Jitterbugs | 2,000.00 |
| 26 I:The Chef,The Boss,Shrimp Coogan,A:Winky, Blinky & Noddy | 2,000.00 |
| 27 A:The Thinker, Gangplank Gus Story | 2,000.00 |
| 28 A:Shrimp Coogan, Winky, Blinky & Noddy | 2,000.00 |
| 29 The Thousand-Year Old Terror, A:Winky, Blinky & Noddy | 2,500.00 |
| 30 The Vanishing Snowman | 2,000.00 |
| 31 A:Black Hat,Planet of Sport | 2,000.00 |
| 32 I:Fiddler,A:Thinker | 2,500.00 |

## ALL FOR LOVE
**Prize-Feature Publications, 1957–59**

**Vol. 1**

| | |
|---|---|
| 1 | 150.00 |
| 2 thru 6 | @100.00 |

**Vol. 2**

| | |
|---|---|
| 1 thru 6 | @100.00 |

**Vol. 3**

| | |
|---|---|
| 1 thru 4 | @100.00 |

## ALL FUNNY COMICS
**DC Comics, 1943–48**

| | |
|---|---|
| 1 Genius Jones | 750.00 |
| 2 same | 350.00 |
| 3 same | 250.00 |
| 4 same | 250.00 |
| 5 thru 10 | @250.00 |
| 11 Genius Jones | 250.00 |
| 12 same | 250.00 |
| 13 same | 200.00 |
| 14 | 200.00 |
| 15 | 200.00 |
| 16 A:DC Superheroes | 500.00 |
| 17 thru 23 | @200.00 |

## ALL GOOD COMICS
**Fox Publications, 1946**

| | |
|---|---|
| 1 | 400.00 |

## ALL GOOD COMICS
**R. W. Voight/ St. John Publishing, 1949**

| | |
|---|---|
| N# Giant | 1,500.00 |

## ALL GREAT
**Fox Features, 1946**

| | |
|---|---|
| 1 Crazy Horse, etc. | 500.00 |

## ALL GREAT COMICS
## See: DAGAR, DESERT HAWK

## ALL HERO COMICS
**Fawcett Publications, March, 1943**

| | |
|---|---|
| 1 A:Capt. Marvel Jr.,Capt. Midnight,Ibis, Golden Arrow and Spy Smasher | 3,000.00 |

## ALL HUMOR COMICS
**Comic Favorites, Inc. (Quality Comics) Spring 1946**

| | |
|---|---|
| 1 | 350.00 |
| 2 PG Atomic Tot | 200.00 |
| 3 I:Kelly Poole | 150.00 |
| 4 thru 7 | @ 150.00 |
| 8 PG | 150.00 |
| 9 | 150.00 |
| 10 | 150.00 |
| 11 thru 17 | @125.00 |

## ALL LOVE
**Ace Periodicals, May 1949**

| | |
|---|---|
| 26 | 125.00 |
| 27 LbC | 250.00 |
| 28 thru 32 | @100.00 |

## ALL LOVE ROMANCES
## See: SCREAM COMICS

## ALL-NEGRO COMICS
**June,1947**

| | |
|---|---|
| 1 | 9,000.00 |

**AI**

*All-New Comics #13*
© Harvey Publications

*All Select Comics #11*
© Marvel Comics Group

*All-Star Comics #1*
© DC Comics

## ALL-NEW COMICS
### Family Comics
### (Harvey Publ.) Jan., 1943
1 A:Steve Case, Johnny Rebel
  I:Detective Shane . . . . . . . . 5,000.00
2 JKu,O:Scarlet Phantom . . . . 2,000.00
3 Nazi War . . . . . . . . . . . . . . . 1,800.00
4 AdH . . . . . . . . . . . . . . . . . . 1,500.00
5 Flash Gordon . . . . . . . . . . . 1,800.00
6 ASh(c),I:Boy Heroes and
  Red Blazer . . . . . . . . . . . . . 1,800.00
7 JKu,ASh(c),A:Black Cat &
  Zebra . . . . . . . . . . . . . . . . 1,800.00
8 JKu,A:Shock Gibson . . . . . . . 1,800.00
9 JKu,A:Black Cat . . . . . . . . . . 1,800.00
10 ASh(c),JKu,A:Zebra . . . . . . . 1,800.00
11 BP,A:Man in Black, Girl
  Commandos . . . . . . . . . . . 1,800.00
12 JKu . . . . . . . . . . . . . . . . . . 1,500.00
13 Stuntman by S&K,
  A:Green Hornet&(c) . . . . . . 1,600.00
14 BP,A:Green Hornet . . . . . . . 1,200.00
15 Smaller size, Distributed
  by Mail, March–April, 1947. 2,000.00

## ALL PICTURE ALL TRUE
## LOVE STORY
### St. John Publ. Co. 1952
1 MB,Romance on Route 202 . . 600.00
2 MB . . . . . . . . . . . . . . . . . . . . 375.00

## ALL ROMANCES
### Ace Periodicals, 1949–50
1 . . . . . . . . . . . . . . . . . . . . . . . 150.00
2 . . . . . . . . . . . . . . . . . . . . . . . 135.00
3 . . . . . . . . . . . . . . . . . . . . . . . 100.00
4 . . . . . . . . . . . . . . . . . . . . . . . 100.00
5 . . . . . . . . . . . . . . . . . . . . . . . 100.00
6 . . . . . . . . . . . . . . . . . . . . . . . 100.00

## ALL SELECT COMICS
### Marvel Timely, (Daring Comics)
### Fall, 1943
1 ASh(c),B:Capt.America,Sub-Mariner,
  Human Torch;WWII . . . . . 25,000.00
2 ASh(c),A:Red Skull,V:Axis
  Powers . . . . . . . . . . . . . . . 10,000.00
3 ASh(c),B:Whizzer,V:Axis . . . . 7,000.00
4 ASh(c),V: Axis . . . . . . . . . . . 4,500.00
5 ASh(c),E:Sub-Mariner,V:Axis 4,500.00
6 ASh,A:The Destroyer,V:Axis . 3,200.00
7 ASh,MSu,E:Whizzer,V:Axis . . 3,200.00

8 ASh(c),MSu,V:Axis Powers . 3,200.00
9 ASh(c),V:Axis Powers . . . . . . 3,200.00
10 ASh(c),E:Capt.America,Human
  Torch;A:The Destroyer . . . . 3,200.00
11 SSh, I:Blonde Phantom,
  A:Miss America . . . . . . . . . 4,200.00
**Becomes:**

## BLONDE PHANTOM
### Marvel, 1946
12 SSh, B:Miss America;
  The Devil's Playground . . . 2,500.00
13 SSh,B:Sub-Mariner;Horror
  In Hollywood . . . . . . . . . . . 1,600.00
14 SSh,E:Miss America;Horror
  At Haunted Castle . . . . . . . 1,500.00
15 SSh,The Man Who Deserved
  To Die . . . . . . . . . . . . . . . . 1,500.00
16 SSh,A:Capt.America,Bucky;
  Modeled For Murder . . . . . . 2,000.00
17 Torture & Rescue . . . . . . . . 1,600.00
18 SSh,Jealousy,Hate&Cruelty 1,600.00
19 SSh(c),Killer In the Hospital. 1,600.00
20 Blonde Phantom's Big Fall . 1,600.00
21 SSh,Murder At the Carnival . 1,600.00
22 V: Crime Bosses . . . . . . . . . 1,600.00
**Becomes:**

## LOVERS
### Marvel, 1949
23 Love Stories . . . . . . . . . . . . . 350.00
24 My Dearly Beloved . . . . . . . . 200.00
25 The Man I Love . . . . . . . . . . . 200.00
26 thru 29 . . . . . . . . . . . . . . . @150.00
30 MK . . . . . . . . . . . . . . . . . . . . 200.00
31 thru 36 . . . . . . . . . . . . . . . @150.00
37 . . . . . . . . . . . . . . . . . . . . . . . 300.00
38 BK . . . . . . . . . . . . . . . . . . . . 300.00
39 . . . . . . . . . . . . . . . . . . . . . . . 150.00
40 . . . . . . . . . . . . . . . . . . . . . . . 150.00
41 BEv . . . . . . . . . . . . . . . . . . . 200.00
42 thru 65 . . . . . . . . . . . . . . . @150.00
66 . . . . . . . . . . . . . . . . . . . . . . . 125.00
67 ATh . . . . . . . . . . . . . . . . . . . 150.00
68 thru 86 Aug., 1957. . . . . . . @125.00

## REAL SPORTS COMICS
### Hillman Periodicals, 1948
1 BP,Boxing (c) . . . . . . . . . . . . 600.00
**Becomes:**

## ALL SPORTS COMICS
### Hillman Periodicals, 1949
2 BP,BK,Football (c) . . . . . . . . . 550.00
3 Basketball (c) . . . . . . . . . . . . 450.00
**Becomes:**

## ALL-TIME SPORTS
## COMICS
### Hillman Periodicals, 1949
4 Auto Racing (c) . . . . . . . . . . . 350.00
5 BP,Baseball (c), Ty Cobb . . . . 325.00
6 Horse Racing (c) . . . . . . . . . . 300.00
7 BK, Baseball (c), W. Johnson . 300.00

## ALL-STAR COMICS
### DC Comics, 1940–51
1 B:Flash,Hawkman,Hourman,
  Sandman,Spectre,Red White
  & Blue . . . . . . . . . . . . . . . 26,000.00
2 B:Green Lantern and Johnny
  Thunder . . . . . . . . . . . . . . 10,000.00
3 First meeting of Justice Society
  with Flash as Chairman . . 65,000.00
4 First mission of JSA . . . . . . 10,000.00
5 V:Mr. X,I:Hawkgirl . . . . . . . . 8,000.00
6 Flash Leaves . . . . . . . . . . . 5,500.00
7 Green Lantern Becomes Chairman,
  L:Hourman, C:Superman,
  Batman & Flash . . . . . . . . . 6,000.00
8 I:Wonder Women;Starman and
  Dr. Mid-Nite Join,Hawkman
  Becomes Chairman . . . . . 60,000.00
9 JSA in Latin America . . . . . . 6,000.00
10 C:Flash & Green Lantern,
  JSA Time Travel story . . . . 6,000.00
11 Wonder Women joins;
  I:Justice Battalion . . . . . . . . 8,000.00
12 V:Black Dragon society . . . . 5,000.00
13 V:Hitler . . . . . . . . . . . . . . . . 5,000.00
14 JSA in Occupied Europe . . . 5,000.00
15 I:Brain Wave,A:JSA's
  Girl Friends . . . . . . . . . . . . 5,000.00
16 Propaganda/relevance issue 2,400.00
17 V:Brain Wave . . . . . . . . . . . 2,400.00
18 I:King Bee . . . . . . . . . . . . . 2,500.00
19 Hunt for Hawkman . . . . . . . 2,400.00
20 I:Monster . . . . . . . . . . . . . . 2,400.00
21 Time Travel Story . . . . . . . . 2,500.00
22 Sandman and Dr. Fate Leave,
  I:Conscience, Good Fairy . . 2,500.00
23 I:Psycho-Pirate . . . . . . . . . . 2,500.00
24 Propaganda/relevance issue,
  A:Conscience&Wildcat,Mr.Terrific;
  L:Starman & Spectre; Flash
  & Green Lantern Return . . . 2,500.00
25 JSA whodunit issue . . . . . . . 3,000.00
26 V:Metal Men from Jupiter . . . 4,000.00
27 Handicap issue,A:Wildcat . . 4,000.00
28 Ancient curse comes to life . 4,000.00
29 I:Landor from 25th Century . 4,000.00

All comics prices listed are for *Near Mint* condition.

*All Star Western #62*
© DC Comics

*All Surprise #2*
© Marvel Comics Group

*All Top Comics #12*
© Fox Features Syndicate

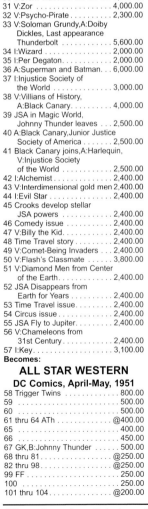

| | |
|---|---|
| 30 V:Brain Wave | 4,000.00 |
| 31 V:Zor | 4,000.00 |
| 32 V:Psycho-Pirate | 2,300.00 |
| 33 V:Soloman Grundy,A:Doiby Dickles, Last appearance Thunderbolt | 5,600.00 |
| 34 I:Wizard | 2,000.00 |
| 35 I:Per Degaton | 2,000.00 |
| 36 A:Superman and Batman | 6,000.00 |
| 37 I:Injustice Society of the World | 3,000.00 |
| 38 V:Villians of History, A:Black Canary | 4,000.00 |
| 39 JSA in Magic World, Johnny Thunder leaves | 2,500.00 |
| 40 A:Black Canary,Junior Justice Society of America | 2,500.00 |
| 41 Black Canary joins,A:Harlequin, V:Injustice Society of the World | 2,500.00 |
| 42 I:Alchemist | 2,400.00 |
| 43 V:Interdimensional gold men | 2,400.00 |
| 44 I:Evil Star | 2,400.00 |
| 45 Crooks develop stellar JSA powers | 2,400.00 |
| 46 Comedy issue | 2,400.00 |
| 47 V:Billy the Kid | 2,400.00 |
| 48 Time Travel story | 2,400.00 |
| 49 V:Comet-Being Invaders | 2,400.00 |
| 50 V:Flash's Classmate | 3,800.00 |
| 51 V:Diamond Men from Center of the Earth | 2,400.00 |
| 52 JSA Disappears from Earth for Years | 2,400.00 |
| 53 Time Travel issue | 2,400.00 |
| 54 Circus issue | 2,400.00 |
| 55 JSA Fly to Jupiter | 2,400.00 |
| 56 V:Chameleons from 31st Century | 2,400.00 |
| 57 I:Key | 3,100.00 |
| Becomes: | |

## ALL STAR WESTERN
**DC Comics, April-May, 1951**

| | |
|---|---|
| 58 Trigger Twins | 800.00 |
| 59 | 500.00 |
| 60 | 500.00 |
| 61 thru 64 ATh | @400.00 |
| 65 | 400.00 |
| 66 | 450.00 |
| 67 GK,B:Johnny Thunder | 500.00 |
| 68 thru 81 | @250.00 |
| 82 thru 98 | @250.00 |
| 99 FF | 250.00 |
| 100 | 250.00 |
| 101 thru 104 | @200.00 |

| | |
|---|---|
| 105 O:JSA, March, 1987 | 200.00 |
| 106 and 107 | @200.00 |
| 108 O:Johnny Thunder | 400.00 |
| 109 thru 116 | @200.00 |
| 117 CI,O:Super-Chief | 250.00 |
| 118 | 200.00 |
| 119 | 200.00 |

## ALL STAR WESTERN
## See: WEIRD WESTERN
## TALES

## ALL SURPRISE
**Marvel Timely, Fall, 1943**

| | |
|---|---|
| 1 (fa),F:Super Rabbit,Gandy, Sourpuss | 400.00 |
| 2 | 200.00 |
| 3 | 150.00 |
| 4 thru 10 | @150.00 |
| 11 HK | 150.00 |
| 12 Winter, 1946 | 150.00 |

## ALL TEEN COMICS
## See: ALL WINNERS
## COMICS

## ALL-TIME
## SPORTS COMICS
## See: ALL SPORTS
## COMICS

## ALL TOP COMICS
**William H. Wise Co., 1944**

| | |
|---|---|
| N# 132pgs.,A:Capt. V,Red Robbins | 500.00 |

## ALL TOP COMICS
**Fox Features Syndicate, Spring 1946**

| | |
|---|---|
| 1 A:Cosmo Cat, Flash Rabbit | 300.00 |
| 2 | 150.00 |
| 3 | 125.00 |
| 4 | 125.00 |
| 5 | 125.00 |
| 6 | 125.00 |
| 7 | 125.00 |
| 7a | 125.00 |
| 8 JKa(c),I:Blue Beetle | 3,600.00 |

| | |
|---|---|
| 9 JKa(c),A:Rulah | 1,800.00 |
| 10 JKa(c),A:Rulah | 1,500.00 |
| 11 A:Rulah,Blue Beetle | 1,600.00 |
| 12 A:Rulah,Jo Jo,Blue Beetle | 1,600.00 |
| 13 A:Rulah | 1,600.00 |
| 14 A:Rulah,Blue Beetle | 2,000.00 |
| 15 A:Rulah | 1,600.00 |
| 16 A:Rulah,Blue Beetle | 1,600.00 |
| 17 A:Rulah,Blue Beetle | 1,600.00 |
| 18 A:Dagar,Jo Jo | 1,000.00 |
| Becomes: | |

## MY EXPERIENCE
**Fox Features Syndicate 1949–50**

| | |
|---|---|
| 19 WW | 400.00 |
| 20 | 125.00 |
| 21 WW | 400.00 |
| 22 WW | 350.00 |
| Becomes: | |

## JUDY CANOVA
**Fox Features Syndicate, May, 1950–Sept., 1950**

| | |
|---|---|
| 23 (1)WW(a&c) | 350.00 |
| 24 (2)WW(a&c) | 350.00 |
| 3 JO,WW(a&c) | 350.00 |

## ALL TOP COMICS
**Green Publ., 1957–59**

| | |
|---|---|
| 6 1957 Patoruzu the Indian | 100.00 |
| 6 1958 Cosmo Cat | 100.00 |
| 6 1959 Atomic Mouse | 100.00 |
| 6 1959 Little Eva | 100.00 |
| 6 Supermouse (c) | 100.00 |

## ALL-TRUE CRIME
## See: OFFICIAL TRUE
## CRIME CASES

## ALL-TRUE
## DETECTIVE CASES
**Avon Periodicals, 1954**

| | |
|---|---|
| 1 WW | 350.00 |
| 2 EK(c),JKa | 250.00 |
| 3 JKa | 250.00 |
| 4 JKa | 300.00 |
| N# (5) JK,JKu | 700.00 |

## ALL TRUE ROMANCE
**Artful/Comic Media, 1951**

| | |
|---|---|
| 1 | 300.00 |

---

All comics prices listed are for *Near Mint* condition. **Page 45**

**AI**

All Winners Comics #8
© Marvel Comics Group

Journey Into Unknown Worlds #14
© Marvel Comics Group

All Western Winners #2
© Marvel Comics Group

2 . . . . . . . . . . . . . . . . . . . . . . . 150.00
3 . . . . . . . . . . . . . . . . . . . . . . . 150.00
4 . . . . . . . . . . . . . . . . . . . . . . . 150.00
5 . . . . . . . . . . . . . . . . . . . . . . . 150.00
6 WW . . . . . . . . . . . . . . . . . . . . 300.00
7 . . . . . . . . . . . . . . . . . . . . . . . 125.00
8 . . . . . . . . . . . . . . . . . . . . . . . 125.00
9 . . . . . . . . . . . . . . . . . . . . . . . 125.00
10 . . . . . . . . . . . . . . . . . . . . . . 125.00
11 thru 13 . . . . . . . . . . . . . . . @100.00
14 Marijuana . . . . . . . . . . . . . . . 125.00
15 thru 27 . . . . . . . . . . . . . . . @100.00
28 LbC . . . . . . . . . . . . . . . . . . . 200.00
29 thru 34 . . . . . . . . . . . . . . . @100.00

## ALL WINNERS COMICS
### Marvel Timely, Summer, 1941
1 S&K,BEv,B:Capt.America & Bucky,
Human Torch & Toro,Sub-Mariner
A:The Angel,Black Marvel 42,000.00
2 S&K,SSh, B:Destroyer,
Whizzer. . . . . . . . . . . . . 10,000.00
3 BEv,Bucky & Toro Captured . 7,000.00
4 BEv,AAv,Battle For Victory
For America . . . . . . . . . . . 7,500.00
5 AAv,V:Nazi Invasion Fleet. . . 5,000.00
6 SSh,AAv,V:Axis Powers,A:
Black Avenger. . . . . . . . . . 6,000.00
7 V:Axis Powers. . . . . . . . . . . 4,500.00
8 V:Axis Powers. . . . . . . . . . . 4,200.00
9 V:Nazi Submarine Fleet . . . . 4,200.00
10 V:Nazi Submarine Fleet. . . . 4,500.00
11 V: Nazis . . . . . . . . . . . . . . . 2,700.00
12 ASh(c),A:Red Skull,E:Destroyer;
Jap P.O.W. Camp. . . . . . . . 3,500.00
13 ASh(c),V:Japanese Fleet . . . 3,000.00
14 ASh(c),V:Japanese Fleet . . . 3,000.00
15 ASh(c),Jap Supply Train . . . 3,000.00
16 ASh(c),In Alaska
V:Gangsters . . . . . . . . . . . 3,000.00
17 V:Gansters;Atomic
Research Department . . . . 3,000.00
18 ASh(c),V:Robbers;Internal
Revenue Department . . . . . 3,200.00
19 ASh(c),SSh,I:All Winners Squad,
Fall, 1946 . . . . . . . . . . . . 10,000.00
21 SSh,AAv,A:All-Winners Squad;
Riddle of Demented Dwarf . 7,500.00
Becomes:

## ALL TEEN COMICS
### Marvel, 1947
20 F:Georgie,Willie,
Mitzi,Patsy Walker . . . . . . . . 200.00
Becomes:

## TEEN COMICS
### Marvel, 1947
21 HK,A:George,Willie,Mitzi,
Patsy Walker, Hey Look . . . . 200.00
22 A:George,Willie,Margie,
Patsy Walker . . . . . . . . . . . 125.00
23 SSh,A:P.Walker,Cindy,George 125.00
24 . . . . . . . . . . . . . . . . . . . . . 150.00
25 thru 27 . . . . . . . . . . . . . . @125.00
28 . . . . . . . . . . . . . . . . . . . . . 150.00
29 . . . . . . . . . . . . . . . . . . . . . 125.00
30 HK,Hey Look. . . . . . . . . . . . 150.00
31 thru 34 . . . . . . . . . . . . . . @125.00
35 May, 1950 . . . . . . . . . . . . . . 125.00
Becomes:

## JOURNEY INTO
## UNKNOWN WORLDS
### Marvel Atlas, Sept., 1950
36(1) RH,End of the Earth. . . . 4,000.00
37(2) BEv,GC,When Worlds
Collide. . . . . . . . . . . . . . . 1,800.00
38(3) GT,Land of Missing Men 1,500.00
4 MSy,RH,Train to Nowhere . . 1,000.00
5 MSy,Trapped in Space . . . . . 1,000.00
6 GC,RH,World Below
the Atlantic . . . . . . . . . . . 1,000.00
7 BW,RH,JMn,House That
Wasn't. . . . . . . . . . . . . . . . 1,500.00
8 RH,JMn,The Stone Thing . . . 1,000.00
9 MSy,JSt,The People Who
Couldn't Exist . . . . . . . . . . 1,000.00
10 The Undertaker . . . . . . . . . 1,000.00
11 BEv,Frankie Was Afraid . . . . . 700.00
12 BK,Last Voice You Hear . . . . . 700.00
13 The Witch Woman . . . . . . . . . 600.00
14 BW,BEv,CondemnedBuilding1,200.00
15 JMn,They Crawl By Night . . 1,200.00
16 JMn,Scared to Death . . . . . . . 600.00
17 BEv,GC,RH,The Ice
Monster Cometh . . . . . . . . . 700.00
18 The Broth Needs Somebody . 700.00
19 MF,GC,The Long Wait . . . . . . 700.00
20 GC,RH,The Race That
Vanished . . . . . . . . . . . . . . . 600.00
21 MF,JMn,JSt,Decapitation . . . . 450.00
22 thru 32. . . . . . . . . . . . . . . @450.00
33 SD,The Man in the Box . . . . . 450.00
34 MK,AT,DAy . . . . . . . . . . . . . . 350.00
35 AT,MD . . . . . . . . . . . . . . . . . 350.00
36 thru 44 . . . . . . . . . . . . . . @400.00
45 AW,SD. . . . . . . . . . . . . . . . . 400.00
46 & 47. . . . . . . . . . . . . . . . . @400.00
48 GW,GM. . . . . . . . . . . . . . . . 400.00
49 JF,JMn. . . . . . . . . . . . . . . . . 400.00

50 JDa,RC . . . . . . . . . . . . . . . . 400.00
51 WW,SD,JSe . . . . . . . . . . . . . 400.00
52 . . . . . . . . . . . . . . . . . . . . . 400.00
53 RC,BP . . . . . . . . . . . . . . . . . 400.00
54 AT,BP . . . . . . . . . . . . . . . . . 400.00
55 AW,RC,BEv. . . . . . . . . . . . . . 400.00
56 BEv . . . . . . . . . . . . . . . . . . . 400.00
57 JO . . . . . . . . . . . . . . . . . . . . 250.00
58 MD,JMn. . . . . . . . . . . . . . . . 250.00
59 AW,Aug., 1957 . . . . . . . . . . . 350.00

## ALL WINNERS COMICS
### Marvel, [2nd Series], Aug., 1948
1 SSh,F:Blonde Phantom,A:Capt.Am.
Sub-Mariner,Human Torch . . . . 5,000.00
Becomes:

## ALL WESTERN
## WINNERS
### Marvel, 1948–49
2 SSh,B,I&O:Black Rider,
B:Two-Gun Kid, Kid-Colt . . 1,200.00
3 Black Rider V: Satan . . . . . . . 600.00
4 Black Rider Unmasked . . . . . . 600.00
Becomes:

## WESTERN WINNERS
### Marvel, 1949
5 I Challenge the Army . . . . . . . 600.00
6 The Mountain Mystery . . . . . . 500.00
7 Ph(c) Randolph Scott . . . . . . . 500.00
Becomes:

## BLACK RIDER
### Marvel, 1950–55
8 Ph(c) of Stan Lee,B:Black Rider;
Valley of Giants . . . . . . . . . . 800.00
9 SSh,JMn,Wrath of the Redskin 500.00
10 O:Black Rider . . . . . . . . . . . . 550.00
11 Redmen on the Warpath. . . . . 300.00
12 GT,The Town That Vanished. . 300.00
13 SSh,The Terrified Tribe. . . . . . 300.00
14 The Tyrant of Texas . . . . . . . . 300.00
15 Revolt of the Redskins . . . . . . 250.00
16 . . . . . . . . . . . . . . . . . . . . . 250.00
17 . . . . . . . . . . . . . . . . . . . . . 250.00
18 . . . . . . . . . . . . . . . . . . . . . 250.00
19 SSh,GT,A:Two-Gun Kid . . . . . 250.00
20 GT . . . . . . . . . . . . . . . . . . . 300.00
21 SSh,GT,A:Two-Gun Kid . . . . . 250.00
22 SSh,DAy(c),A:Two-Gun Kid . . 250.00
23 SSh,A:Two-Gun Kid . . . . . . . . 250.00
24 SSh,JSt. . . . . . . . . . . . . . . . . 250.00
25 SSh,JSt,A:Arrowhead . . . . . . . 250.00
26 SSh,A:Kid-Colt . . . . . . . . . . . 250.00

*All Your Comics #1*
© Fox Features Syndicate

*Amazing Adventures #1*
© Ziff-Davis Publications

*Amazing-Man Comics #8*
© Centaur Publications

27 SSh,JMn(c),A:Kid-Colt . . . . . . 300.00
Becomes:

## WESTERN TALES OF BLACK RIDER
### Marvel, 1955
28 JSe,D:Spider . . . . . . . . . . . . 300.00
29 . . . . . . . . . . . . . . . . . . . . . . 200.00
30 . . . . . . . . . . . . . . . . . . . . . . 200.00
31 . . . . . . . . . . . . . . . . . . . . . . 200.00
Becomes:

## GUNSMOKE WESTERN
### Marvel, 1955–63
32 MD,MB,F:Kid Colt,Billy
   Buckskin . . . . . . . . . . . . . . . 300.00
33 MD . . . . . . . . . . . . . . . . . . . 200.00
34 MB. . . . . . . . . . . . . . . . . . . 175.00
35 GC. . . . . . . . . . . . . . . . . . . . 200.00
36 AW,GC . . . . . . . . . . . . . . . . 200.00
37 JDa . . . . . . . . . . . . . . . . . . . 175.00
38 . . . . . . . . . . . . . . . . . . . . . . 150.00
39 GC. . . . . . . . . . . . . . . . . . . . 150.00
40 AW . . . . . . . . . . . . . . . . . . . 175.00
41 thru 43. . . . . . . . . . . . . . . @125.00
44 AT . . . . . . . . . . . . . . . . . . . 125.00
45 & 46. . . . . . . . . . . . . . . . . @125.00
47 JK . . . . . . . . . . . . . . . . . . . . 150.00
48 & 49. . . . . . . . . . . . . . . . . @125.00
50 JK,RC . . . . . . . . . . . . . . . . . 200.00
51 JK . . . . . . . . . . . . . . . . . . . . 125.00
52 thru 54 . . . . . . . . . . . . . . . @125.00
55 & 56 MB . . . . . . . . . . . . . . @125.00
57 Two Gun Kid . . . . . . . . . . . . 100.00
58 & 59. . . . . . . . . . . . . . . . . @100.00
60 Sam Hawk (Kid Colt) . . . . . . . 125.00
61 RC. . . . . . . . . . . . . . . . . . . . 150.00
62 thru 67 JK . . . . . . . . . . . . . @100.00
68 . . . . . . . . . . . . . . . . . . . . . . 100.00
69 JK . . . . . . . . . . . . . . . . . . . . 100.00
70 . . . . . . . . . . . . . . . . . . . . . . 100.00
71 JK . . . . . . . . . . . . . . . . . . . . 125.00
72 O:Kid Colt . . . . . . . . . . . . . . 125.00
73 JK . . . . . . . . . . . . . . . . . . . . 135.00
74 thru 76. . . . . . . . . . . . . . . @100.00
77 JK,July, 1963 . . . . . . . . . . . . 150.00

## ALL YOUR COMICS
### R.W. Voight, 1944
1 Red Robbins . . . . . . . . . . . . 350.00

## ALL YOUR COMICS
### Fox Features, 1946
1 . . . . . . . . . . . . . . . . . . . . . . 300.00

## AMAZING ADVENTURE FUNNIES
### Centaur Publ,. 1940
1 BEv,The Fantom of the Fair . 4,000.00
2 rep.After Fantoman. . . . . . . . 2,500.00
Becomes:

## FANTOMAN
### Aug., 1940
2 The Fantom of the Fair . . . . . 3,000.00
3 . . . . . . . . . . . . . . . . . . . . . . 2,500.00
4 Red Blaze . . . . . . . . . . . . . . 2,500.00

## AMAZING ADVENTURES
### Ziff-Davis Publ., Co., 1950
1 MA,WW, Asteroid Witch . . . . 1,500.00
2 MA,ASh(c),Masters of Living
   Flame. . . . . . . . . . . . . . . . . . 700.00
3 MA,The Evil Men Do . . . . . . . 700.00
4 Invasion of the Love Robots . . 700.00
5 MA,Secret of the Crater-Men. . 700.00
6 BK,Man Who Killed a World . . 750.00

## AMAZING COMICS
### Marvel Timely, 1944
1 ASh(c),F:Young Allies,Destroyer,
   Whizzer, Sergeant Dix . . . . 4,000.00
Becomes:

## COMPLETE COMICS
2 ASh(c),F:Young Allies,Destroyer,
   Whizzer Sergeant Dix; . . . . 3,200.00

## AMAZING DETECTIVE CASES
### Marvel Atlas, Nov., 1950
3 Detective/Horror Stories . . . . . 350.00
4 Death of a Big Shot . . . . . . . . 200.00
5 . . . . . . . . . . . . . . . . . . . . . . 200.00
6 Danger in the City . . . . . . . . . 200.00
7 . . . . . . . . . . . . . . . . . . . . . . 175.00
8 . . . . . . . . . . . . . . . . . . . . . . 175.00
9 GC, The Man Who Wasn't . . . 175.00
10 GT. . . . . . . . . . . . . . . . . . . . 175.00
11 The Black Shadow . . . . . . . . 350.00
12 MSy,BK, Harrigan's Wake. . . . 350.00
13 BEv,JSt,. . . . . . . . . . . . . . . . 400.00
14 Hands Off; Sept., 1952 . . . . . 350.00

## AMAZING GHOST STORIES
### See: WEIRD HORRORS

## AMAZING-MAN COMICS
### Centaur Publications, Sept., 1939–Feb., 1942
5 BEv,O:Amazing Man. . . . . . 40,000.00
6 BEv,FT,B:The Shark . . . . . . . 8,000.00
7 BEv,I:Magician From Mars . . 6,000.00
8 BEv, Cat-Man as Woman . . . . 5,000.00
9 BEv,FT,A:Eternal Monster. . . 5,000.00
10 BEv,FT . . . . . . . . . . . . . . . . 3,500.00
11 BEv,I:Zardi . . . . . . . . . . . . . 3,500.00
12 SG(c) . . . . . . . . . . . . . . . . . 3,200.00
13 SG(c) . . . . . . . . . . . . . . . . . 3,200.00
14 FT,B:Reef Kinkaid, Dr. Hypo 2,500.00
15 FT,A:Zardi . . . . . . . . . . . . . 2,400.00
16 AAv,Mighty Man's Powers
   Revealed . . . . . . . . . . . . . 2,500.00
17 FT,A:Dr. Hypo . . . . . . . . . . . 2,400.00
18 FT,BLb(a),SG(c). . . . . . . . . . 2,400.00
19 FT,BLb(a),SG(c). . . . . . . . . . 2,400.00
20 FT,BLb(a),SG(c). . . . . . . . . . 2,400.00
21 FT,O:Dash Dartwell . . . . . . . 2,500.00
22 A:Silver Streak, The Voice . . 3,000.00
23 I&O:Tommy the AmazingKid 2,200.00
24 B:King of Darkness,
   Blue Lady . . . . . . . . . . . . . 2,200.00
25 A:Meteor Marvin. . . . . . . . . . 3,200.00
26 A:Meteor Marvin,ElectricRay 3,200.00

## AMAZING MYSTERIES
### Marvel, 1949–50
32 The Isle of No Return . . . . . . 1,500.00
33 The Thing in the Vault. . . . . . . 750.00
34 Photo(c) . . . . . . . . . . . . . . . . 400.00
35 Photo(c) . . . . . . . . . . . . . . . . 400.00

## AMAZING MYSTERY FUNNIES
### Centaur Publications, 1938
1 Skyrocket Steele in Year X . . 8,000.00
2 WE,Skyrocket Steele . . . . . . 4,500.00
3 . . . . . . . . . . . . . . . . . . . . . . 2,700.00
   (#4) WE,bondage (c) . . . . . . . 2,600.00
2-1(#5) . . . . . . . . . . . . . . . . . . 2,400.00
2-2(#6) Drug use. . . . . . . . . . . . 2,000.00
2-3(#7) Air Sub DX . . . . . . . . . . 2,000.00
2-4(#8) Sand Hog . . . . . . . . . . . 2,000.00
2-5(#9) . . . . . . . . . . . . . . . . . . 3,000.00
2-6(#10) . . . . . . . . . . . . . . . . . 2,000.00
2-7(#11) Fantom of Fair, scarce 7,500.00
2-8(#12) Speed Centaur . . . . . . 3,200.00
2-9(#13) . . . . . . . . . . . . . . . . . 2,000.00
2-10(#14) . . . . . . . . . . . . . . . . 2,000.00
2-11(#15)Robot(c). . . . . . . . . . . 2,000.00

*Amazing Mystery Funnies #19*
© *Centaur Publications*

*America's Best Comics #9*
© *Nedor/Standard Publications*

*America's Greatest Comics #4*
© *Fawcett Publications*

2-12(#16) BW,I:Space Patrol . . 4,000.00
3-1(#17) I:Bullet . . . . . . . . . . . 2,000.00
18 Fantom of Fair . . . . . . . . . 2,000.00
19 BW,Space Patrol . . . . . . . . 2,200.00
20 . . . . . . . . . . . . . . . . . . . . . 1,800.00
21 thru 24 BW,Space Patrol . @2,200.00

## AMAZING WILLIE MAYS
### Famous Funnies, 1954
1 Willie Mays(c) . . . . . . . . . . . 1,400.00

## AMERICA IN ACTION
### Dell Publishing Co., 1942
1 . . . . . . . . . . . . . . . . . . . . . . . . 400.00

## THE AMERICAN AIR FORCES
### Flying Cadet Publ., 1944–45
1 War (c) . . . . . . . . . . . . . . . . . . 300.00
2 War (c) . . . . . . . . . . . . . . . . . . 400.00
3 War (c) . . . . . . . . . . . . . . . . . . 400.00
4 War (c) . . . . . . . . . . . . . . . . . . 250.00
Continues in *A-1 Comics*. See #45,
#54, #58, #65, #67, #74, #79, #91

## AMERICAN GRAPHICS
### Henry Stewart, 1954
1 Indian Legends . . . . . . . . . . . . 200.00
2 . . . . . . . . . . . . . . . . . . . . . . . . 150.00

## AMERICAN LIBRARY
### David McKay Publ., 1943
(#1) Thirty Seconds Over
  Tokyo, movie adapt. . . . . . . . 600.00
(#2) Guadalcanal Diary . . . . . . . 500.00
3 Look to the Mountain . . . . . . . 250.00
4 The Case of the Crooked
  Candle (Perry Mason) . . . . . . 250.00
5 Duel in the Sun . . . . . . . . . . . 250.00
6 Wingate's Raiders . . . . . . . . . 250.00

## AMERICA'S BEST COMICS
### Nedor/Better/Standard Publications, Feb., 1942
1 ASh(c),B:Black Terror, Captain Future,
  The Liberator,Doc Strange . 4,500.00
2 O:American Eagle . . . . . . . . 2,000.00
3 B:Pyroman . . . . . . . . . . . . . 1,500.00
4 A:Doc Strange, Jimmy Cole . 1,100.00

5 ASh(c),A:LoneEagle,
  Cap.Future . . . . . . . . . . . . . 1,100.00
6 A:American Crusader . . . . . . 1,100.00
7 ASh(c),A:Hitler,Hirohito . . . . 1,800.00
8 The Liberator ends . . . . . . . . 1,100.00
9 ASh(c),Fighting Yank . . . . . . 1,500.00
10 ASh(c),American Eagle . . . . 1,100.00
11 ASh(c) Hirihito & Tojo(c). . . . 1,500.00
12 Red Cross (c). . . . . . . . . . . . 1,100.00
13 Fighting Yank . . . . . . . . . . . . 1,100.00
14 Last American Eagle app. . . 1,100.00
15 ASh(c),Fighting Yank . . . . . . 1,100.00
16 ASh(c),Fighting Yank . . . . . . 1,100.00
17 ASh(c),Doc Strange
  carries football . . . . . . . . . . 1,100.00
18 Fighting Yank,Bondage(c) . . 1,100.00
19 ASh(c),Fighting Yank . . . . . . 1,100.00
20 ASh(c),vs. the Black Market 1,100.00
21 ASh(c),Infinity (c) . . . . . . . . . 1,100.00
22 A:Captain Future . . . . . . . . . 1,000.00
23 B:Miss Masque . . . . . . . . . . 1,150.00
24 Miss Masque,Bondage (c). . 1,150.00
25 A:Sea Eagle . . . . . . . . . . . . . 750.00
26 A:The Phantom Detective . . . 750.00
27 Pyroman,ASh(c) . . . . . . . . . . 750.00
28 A:Commando Cubs,
  Black Terror . . . . . . . . . . . . . 750.00
29 ASh(c),A:Doc Strange . . . . . . 750.00
30 ASh(c).Xela . . . . . . . . . . . . . 750.00
31 ASh(c),Xela,July, 1949 . . . . . 750.00

## AMERICA'S BIGGEST COMICS BOOK
### William H. Wise, 1944
1 196 pgs. A:Grim Reaper, Zudo,
  Silver Knight, Thunderhoof,
  Jocko and Socko,Barnaby
  Beep,Commando Cubs . . . . . 700.00
**Becomes:**

## AMERICA'S FUNNIEST COMICS
### William H. Wise, 1944
2 Funny Animal . . . . . . . . . . . . . 500.00
N# (3) . . . . . . . . . . . . . . . . . . . . 500.00

## AMERICA'S GREATEST COMICS
### Fawcett Publications, Fall 1941
1 MRa(c),A:Capt. Marvel,
  Bulletman,Spy Smasher and
  Minute Man . . . . . . . . . . . . 6,500.00
2 F:Capt. Marvel . . . . . . . . . . 3,000.00

3 F:Capt. Marvel . . . . . . . . . . 2,500.00
4 B:Commando Yank . . . . . . . 2,000.00
5 Capt.Marvel in 'Lost Lighting' 2,000.00
6 Capt.Marvel fires
  Machine Gun . . . . . . . . . . . 2,000.00
7 A:Balbo the Boy Magician. . . 2,000.00
8 A:Capt.Marvel Jr.,Golden
  Arrow, Summer 1943 . . . . . 2,000.00

## ANCHORS ANDREWS
### St. John Publ. Co. 1953
1 MB,Navy Humor . . . . . . . . . . . 225.00
2 thru 4 . . . . . . . . . . . . . . . . . @75.00

## ANDY COMICS
## See: SCREAM COMICS

## ANDY DEVINE WESTERN
### Fawcett Publ. 1950
1 Photo (c) . . . . . . . . . . . . . . . . 800.00
2 . . . . . . . . . . . . . . . . . . . . . . . . 675.00

## ANGEL
### Dell Publishing Co., Aug., 1954
(1) *see Dell Four Color #576*
2 . . . . . . . . . . . . . . . . . . . . . . . . 100.00
3 thru 16 . . . . . . . . . . . . . . . . . @75.00

## ANIMAL ADVENTURES
### Timor Publ./Accepted Publ. 1953–54
1 Funny Animal . . . . . . . . . . . . . 100.00
1a rep.. . . . . . . . . . . . . . . . . . . . . 90.00
2 . . . . . . . . . . . . . . . . . . . . . . . . . 90.00

## ANIMAL ANTICS
### DC Comics, 1946–49
1 B:Racoon Kids . . . . . . . . . . . . 600.00
2 . . . . . . . . . . . . . . . . . . . . . . . . 300.00
3 thru 10 . . . . . . . . . . . . . . . . @175.00
11 thru 23 . . . . . . . . . . . . . . . @125.00

## ANIMAL COMICS
### Dell Publishing Co., 1942
1 WK,Pogo. . . . . . . . . . . . . . . 1,700.00
2 Uncle Wiggily(c),A:Pogo. . . . 1,000.00
3 Muggin's Mouse(c),A:Pogo . . . 750.00
4 Uncle Wiggily(c). . . . . . . . . . . 500.00
5 Uncle Wiggily(c). . . . . . . . . . . 750.00
6 Uncle Wiggily. . . . . . . . . . . . . 500.00

*Animal Fables #6*
© E.C. Comics

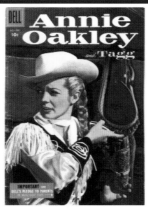

*Annie Oakley & Tagg #4*
© Dell Publishing Co.

*Apache #1*
© Fiction House Magazines

7 Uncle Wiggily . . . . . . . . . . . . . 500.00
8 WK,Pogo . . . . . . . . . . . . . . . . 600.00
9 WK,War Bonds(c),A:Pogo . . . . 600.00
10 WK,Pogo . . . . . . . . . . . . . . . . 600.00
11 WK,Pogo . . . . . . . . . . . . . . . . 400.00
12 WK,Pogo . . . . . . . . . . . . . . . . 400.00
13 WK,Pogo . . . . . . . . . . . . . . . . 400.00
14 WK,Pogo . . . . . . . . . . . . . . . . 400.00
15 WK,Pogo . . . . . . . . . . . . . . . . 400.00
16 Uncle Wiggily . . . . . . . . . . . . 250.00
17 WK,Pogo(c) . . . . . . . . . . . . . . 300.00
18 WK,Pogo(c) . . . . . . . . . . . . . . 300.00
19 WK,Pogo(c) . . . . . . . . . . . . . . 300.00
20 WK,Pogo . . . . . . . . . . . . . . . . 250.00
21 WK,Pogo(c) . . . . . . . . . . . . . . 300.00
22 WK,Pogo . . . . . . . . . . . . . . . . 200.00
23 WK,Pogo . . . . . . . . . . . . . . . . 200.00
24 WK,Pogo(c) . . . . . . . . . . . . . . 200.00
25 WK,Pogo(c) . . . . . . . . . . . . . . 200.00
26 WK,Pogo(c) . . . . . . . . . . . . . . 200.00
27 thru 30 WK,Pogo(c) . . . . . . @200.00

## ANIMAL FABLES
### E.C. Comics, July–Aug., 1946
1 B:Korky Kangaroo,Freddy Firefly
  Petey Pig & Danny Demon . 600.00
2 B:Aesop Fables . . . . . . . . . . . 375.00
3 . . . . . . . . . . . . . . . . . . . . . . . . 300.00
4 . . . . . . . . . . . . . . . . . . . . . . . . 300.00
5 Firefly vs. Red Ants . . . . . . . . 300.00
6 . . . . . . . . . . . . . . . . . . . . . . . . 300.00
7 O:Moon Girls,Nov.–Dec.1947 1,200.00

## ANIMAL FAIR
### Fawcett Publications, March, 1946
1 B:Captain Marvel Bunny,
  Sir Spot . . . . . . . . . . . . . . . . 500.00
2 A:Droopy, Colonel Walrus . . . . 350.00
3 . . . . . . . . . . . . . . . . . . . . . . . . 250.00
4 A:Kid Gloves, Cub Reporter . . 250.00
5 thru 7 . . . . . . . . . . . . . . . . . @200.00
8 thru 10 . . . . . . . . . . . . . . . . @200.00
11 Feb., 1947 . . . . . . . . . . . . . . 200.00

## ANIMATED COMICS
### E.C. Comics, 1948
1 Funny Animal . . . . . . . . . . . . 1,200.00

## ANIMATED MOVIE-TUNES
### Marvel-Margood Publ., 1945
1 Super Rabbit . . . . . . . . . . . . . 300.00
2 Super Rabbit . . . . . . . . . . . . . 300.00

Becomes:
## MOVIE TUNES
### Marvel-Margood Publ., 1946
3 . . . . . . . . . . . . . . . . . . . . . . . . 135.00
Becomes:
## FRANKIE
### Marvel-Margood, 1946–48
4 . . . . . . . . . . . . . . . . . . . . . . . . 200.00
5 . . . . . . . . . . . . . . . . . . . . . . . . 125.00
6 . . . . . . . . . . . . . . . . . . . . . . . . 125.00
7 . . . . . . . . . . . . . . . . . . . . . . . . 125.00
8 . . . . . . . . . . . . . . . . . . . . . . . . 125.00
9 . . . . . . . . . . . . . . . . . . . . . . . . 125.00
10 . . . . . . . . . . . . . . . . . . . . . . . 100.00
11 . . . . . . . . . . . . . . . . . . . . . . . 100.00
Becomes:
## FRANKIE & LANA
### Marvel-Margood, 1949
12 . . . . . . . . . . . . . . . . . . . . . . . 100.00
13 . . . . . . . . . . . . . . . . . . . . . . . 100.00
14 . . . . . . . . . . . . . . . . . . . . . . . 100.00
15 . . . . . . . . . . . . . . . . . . . . . . . 100.00
Becomes:
## FRANKIE FUDDLE
### Marvel-Margood, 1949
16 . . . . . . . . . . . . . . . . . . . . . . . 100.00
17 . . . . . . . . . . . . . . . . . . . . . . . 100.00

## ANNIE OAKLEY
### Marvel Timely, Spring, 1948
1 A:Hedy Devine . . . . . . . . . . . . 750.00
2 CCB,I:Lana,A:Hedy Devine . . 500.00
3 . . . . . . . . . . . . . . . . . . . . . . . . 350.00
4 . . . . . . . . . . . . . . . . . . . . . . . . 350.00
5 . . . . . . . . . . . . . . . . . . . . . . . . 300.00
6 . . . . . . . . . . . . . . . . . . . . . . . . 300.00
7 . . . . . . . . . . . . . . . . . . . . . . . . 300.00
8 . . . . . . . . . . . . . . . . . . . . . . . . 300.00
9 AW, . . . . . . . . . . . . . . . . . . . . 300.00
10 . . . . . . . . . . . . . . . . . . . . . . . 250.00
11 June, 1956 . . . . . . . . . . . . . . 250.00

## ANNIE OAKLEY & TAGG
### Dell Publishing Co., 1953
(1) *see Dell Four Color #438*
(2) *see Dell Four Color #481*
(3) *see Dell Four Color #575*
4 . . . . . . . . . . . . . . . . . . . . . . . . 250.00
5 . . . . . . . . . . . . . . . . . . . . . . . . 200.00
6 thru 10 . . . . . . . . . . . . . . . . @150.00
11 thru 18 . . . . . . . . . . . . . . . . @125.00

## APACHE
### Fiction House Magazines, 1951
1 . . . . . . . . . . . . . . . . . . . . . . . . 300.00

## APACHE KID
### Marvel-Comics, 1950–52
1 (53) . . . . . . . . . . . . . . . . . . . . 500.00
2 . . . . . . . . . . . . . . . . . . . . . . . . 300.00
3 . . . . . . . . . . . . . . . . . . . . . . . . 250.00
4 . . . . . . . . . . . . . . . . . . . . . . . . 250.00
5 . . . . . . . . . . . . . . . . . . . . . . . . 250.00
6 . . . . . . . . . . . . . . . . . . . . . . . . 150.00
7 RH . . . . . . . . . . . . . . . . . . . . . 200.00
8 thru 10 . . . . . . . . . . . . . . . . @150.00
11 RH . . . . . . . . . . . . . . . . . . . . 125.00
12 . . . . . . . . . . . . . . . . . . . . . . . 125.00
13 RH . . . . . . . . . . . . . . . . . . . . 125.00
14 thru 19 . . . . . . . . . . . . . . . @100.00
Becomes:
## WESTERN GUNFIGHTERS
### Marvel Atlas, 1956–57
20 GC,JSe . . . . . . . . . . . . . . . . 150.00
21 RC . . . . . . . . . . . . . . . . . . . . 150.00
22 WW,BP . . . . . . . . . . . . . . . . 250.00
23 AW . . . . . . . . . . . . . . . . . . . . 200.00
24 ATh . . . . . . . . . . . . . . . . . . . . 200.00
25 GM . . . . . . . . . . . . . . . . . . . . 100.00
26 GC . . . . . . . . . . . . . . . . . . . . 100.00
27 GC,JSe . . . . . . . . . . . . . . . . 100.00

## APACHE TRAIL
### America's Best, 1957
1 . . . . . . . . . . . . . . . . . . . . . . . . 125.00
2 GT . . . . . . . . . . . . . . . . . . . . . . 85.00
3 . . . . . . . . . . . . . . . . . . . . . . . . . 75.00
4 . . . . . . . . . . . . . . . . . . . . . . . . . 75.00

## APPROVED COMICS
### St. John Publishing Co., 1954
1 The Hawk . . . . . . . . . . . . . . . . 125.00
2 Invisible Boy . . . . . . . . . . . . . . 200.00
3 Wild Boy of the Congo . . . . . . 100.00
4 Kid Cowboy . . . . . . . . . . . . . . 100.00
5 Flyboy . . . . . . . . . . . . . . . . . . 100.00
6 MB,BK,Daring Adventures . . . . 150.00
7 The Hawk . . . . . . . . . . . . . . . . 100.00
8 BP,Crime on the Run . . . . . . . 125.00
9 MB,Western Bandit Trails . . . . 125.00
10 Dinky Duck . . . . . . . . . . . . . . 100.00
11 MB,Fighting Marines . . . . . . . 150.00
12 Northwest Mounties . . . . . . . . 150.00

*Archie #27*
© Archie Publications

*Archie's Girls Betty and Veronica #26*
© Archie Publications

*Archie's Pal Jughead #4*
© Archie Publications

## ARCHIE COMICS
### MLJ Magazines, Winter, 1942-43

| | |
|---|---|
| 1 I:Jughead & Veronica | 25,000.00 |
| 2 | 5,000.00 |
| 3 | 3,500.00 |
| 4 | 1,800.00 |
| 5 | 1,800.00 |
| 6 Christmas issue | 1,300.00 |
| 7 thru 10 | @1,400.00 |
| 11 thru 15 | @900.00 |
| 16 thru 19 | @800.00 |

### Archie Publications, 1946

| | |
|---|---|
| 20 | 850.00 |
| 21 | 550.00 |
| 22 thru 31 | @525.00 |
| 32 thru 42 | @350.00 |
| 43 thru 50 | @225.00 |
| 51 A:Katy Keene | 175.00 |
| 52 thru 64 | @150.00 |
| 65 thru 70 A:Katy Keene | @150.00 |
| 71 | 100.00 |
| 72 thru 74 A:Katy Keene | @125.00 |
| 75 thru 99 | @100.00 |
| 100 | 100.00 |
| 101 thru 122 | @100.00 |
| 123 UFO,Vampire | 75.00 |
| 124 thru 130 | @75.00 |
| 131 thru 145 | @60.00 |
| 146 thru 182 | @60.00 |
| 183 Caveman Archie | 60.00 |
| 184 | 60.00 |
| 185 I:The Archies Band | 75.00 |
| 186 thru 195 | @50.00 |
| 196 I:Cricket O'Dell | 75.00 |
| 197 thru 200 | @50.00 |
| 201 thru 228 | @50.00 |
| 229 Lost Child | 50.00 |
| 230 thru 260 | @30.00 |
| 261 thru 300 | @30.00 |

## ARCHIE'S GIANT SERIES MAGAZINE
### Archie Publications, 1954

| | |
|---|---|
| 1 | 1,700.00 |
| 2 | 1,000.00 |
| 3 | 700.00 |
| 4 | 650.00 |
| 5 | 650.00 |
| 6 thru 10 | @500.00 |
| 11 thru 20 | @300.00 |
| 21 thru 29 | @175.00 |
| 30 thru 35 | @125.00 |

## ARCHIE'S GIRLS BETTY AND VERONICA
### Archie Publications, 1950

| | |
|---|---|
| 1 | 3,000.00 |
| 2 | 1,500.00 |
| 3 | 650.00 |
| 4 | 600.00 |
| 5 | 600.00 |
| 6 thru 10 | @500.00 |
| 11 thru 15 | @400.00 |
| 16 thru 20 | @350.00 |
| 21 | 275.00 |
| 22 thru 29 | @250.00 |
| 30 thru 40 | @200.00 |
| 41 thru 50 | @175.00 |
| 51 thru 60 | @125.00 |
| 61 thru 70 | @110.00 |
| 71 thru 74 | @100.00 |
| 75 Devil | 200.00 |
| 76 thru 90 | @100.00 |
| 91 thru 99 | @100.00 |
| 100 | 100.00 |

## ARCHIE'S JOKE BOOK MAGAZINE
### Archie Publications, 1953

| | |
|---|---|
| 1 | 1,500.00 |
| 2 | 650.00 |
| 3 | 500.00 |
| 15 thru 19 | @300.00 |
| 20 thru 25 | @175.00 |
| 26 thru 35 | @150.00 |
| 36 thru 40 | @125.00 |
| 41 1st NA art | 300.00 |
| 42 & 43 TV Personalities | @125.00 |
| 44 thru 48 NA | @150.00 |
| 49 thru 60 | @60.00 |

## ARCHIE'S MADHOUSE
### Archie Publications, 1959–69

| | |
|---|---|
| 1 | 350.00 |
| 2 | 175.00 |
| 3 thru 5 | @125.00 |
| 6 thru 10 | @100.00 |
| 11 thru 16 | @75.00 |
| 17 thru 21 | @50.00 |
| 22 I:Sabrina | 350.00 |
| 23 thru 25 Sabrina | @125.00 |
| 26 thru 30 | @50.00 |
| 31 thru 33 Sabrina | @60.00 |
| 34 | 50.00 |
| 35 | 50.00 |
| 36 Salem Cat & Sabrina | 100.00 |

| | |
|---|---|
| 37 Sabrina | 75.00 |
| 38 thru 66 | @50.00 |

## ARCHIE'S MECHANICS
### Archie Publications, 1954

| | |
|---|---|
| 1 | 1,200.00 |
| 2 | 650.00 |
| 3 | 500.00 |

## ARCHIE'S PAL, JUGHEAD
### Archie Publications, 1949

| | |
|---|---|
| 1 | 2,000.00 |
| 2 | 1,000.00 |
| 3 | 600.00 |
| 4 | 550.00 |
| 5 | 550.00 |
| 6 | 400.00 |
| 7 thru 10 | @325.00 |
| 11 thru 15 | @250.00 |
| 16 thru 20 | @175.00 |
| 21 thru 30 | @125.00 |
| 31 thru 39 | @100.00 |
| 40 thru 50 | @100.00 |
| 51 thru 60 | @65.00 |
| 61 thru 70 | @65.00 |
| 71 thru 80 | @45.00 |
| 81 thru 99 | @40.00 |
| 100 | 40.00 |

## ARCHIE'S PALS 'N' GALS
### Archie Publications, 1952–53

| | |
|---|---|
| 1 | 1,100.00 |
| 2 | 550.00 |
| 3 | 350.00 |
| 4 | 225.00 |
| 5 | 225.00 |
| 6 | 200.00 |
| 7 | 200.00 |
| 8 thru 10 | @175.00 |
| 11 thru 15 | @150.00 |
| 16 thru 20 | @125.00 |
| 21 thru 30 | @100.00 |

## ARCHIE'S RIVAL REGGIE
### Archie Publications, 1950

| | |
|---|---|
| 1 | 1,100.00 |
| 2 | 500.00 |
| 3 | 375.00 |

All comics prices listed are for *Near Mint* condition.

*Arrowhead #4*
© Marvel Comics Group

*Astonishing #57*
© Marvel Comics Group

*Atomic Comics #1*
© Green Publishing Co.

| | |
|---|---|
| 4 | 350.00 |
| 5 | 350.00 |
| 6 | 275.00 |
| 7 | 250.00 |
| 8 thru 9 | @250.00 |
| 10 thru 14 A: Katy Keen | @200.00 |
| 15 | 160.00 |
| 16 Aug., 1954 | 175.00 |

## ARIZONA KID
### Marvel Atlas, March, 1951

| | |
|---|---|
| 1 RH,Coming of the Arizons Kid. | 300.00 |
| 2 RH,Code of the Gunman | 150.00 |
| 3 RH(c) | 125.00 |
| 4 PMo | 125.00 |
| 5 PMo | 125.00 |
| 6 PMo,JSt,Jan., 1952 | 125.00 |

## ARMY & NAVY COMICS
## See: SUPERSNIPE
## COMICS

## ARROW, THE
### Centaur Publications,
### Oct., 1940–Oct., 1941

| | |
|---|---|
| 1 B:Arrow, BLb(c). | 6,000.00 |
| 2 BLb(c) | 2,500.00 |
| 3 O:Dash Dartwell,Human Meteor, Rainbow, Bondage(c). | 2,500.00 |

## ARROWHEAD
### Marvel, April, 1954

| | |
|---|---|
| 1 JSt,Indian Warrior Stories | 200.00 |
| 2 JSt | 125.00 |
| 3 JSt | 125.00 |
| 4 JSt,Nov., 1954 | 125.00 |

## MARVEL BOY
### Marvel, Dec., 1950

| | |
|---|---|
| 1 RH,O:Marvel Boy,Lost World | 1,700.00 |
| 2 BEv,The Zero Hour | 1,200.00 |

Becomes:

## ASTONISHING
### Marvel, 1951

| | |
|---|---|
| 3 BEv,Marvel Boy,V:Mr Death . | 1,500.00 |
| 4 BEv,Stan Lee,The Screaming Tomb | 1,100.00 |
| 5 BEv,Horror in the Caves of Doom | 1,100.00 |
| 6 BEv,My Coffin is Waiting E:Marvel Boy | 1,100.00 |

| | |
|---|---|
| 7 JR,JMn,Nightmare | 500.00 |
| 8 RH,Behind the Wall | 500.00 |
| 9 RH(c),The Little Black Box | 500.00 |
| 10 BEv,Walking Dead | 500.00 |
| 11 BF,JSt.Mr Mordeau | 350.00 |
| 12 GC,BEv,Horror Show | 350.00 |
| 13 BK,MSy,Ghouls Gold | 500.00 |
| 14 BK,The Long Jump Down | 500.00 |
| 15 BEv(c),Grounds for Death | 350.00 |
| 16 BEv(c),DAy,SSh,Don't Make a Ghoul of Yourself | 350.00 |
| 17 Who Was the Wilmach Werewolf? | 350.00 |
| 18 BEv(c),JR,Vampire at My Window | 350.00 |
| 19 BK,Back From the Grave | 350.00 |
| 20 GC,Mystery at Midnight | 350.00 |
| 21 Manhunter | 275.00 |
| 22 RH(c),Man Against Werewolf . | 275.00 |
| 23 The Woman in Black | 300.00 |
| 24 JR,The Stone Face | 300.00 |
| 25 RC,I Married a Zombie | 300.00 |
| 26 RH(c),I Died Too Often | 275.00 |
| 27 | 275.00 |
| 28 TLw,No Evidence | 275.00 |
| 29 BEv(c),GC,Decapitation(c) | 275.00 |
| 30 Tentacled eyeball story | 350.00 |
| 31 JMn | 225.00 |
| 32 A Vampire Takes a Wife | 225.00 |
| 33 SMo,JMn | 225.00 |
| 34 JMn,Transformation | 225.00 |
| 35 | 225.00 |
| 36 Pithecanthrope Giant | 225.00 |
| 37 BEv,TLw,Poor Pierre | 225.00 |
| 38 The Man Who Didn't Belong. | 175.00 |
| 39 | 175.00 |
| 40 | 175.00 |
| 41 MD | 175.00 |
| 42 TLw | 175.00 |
| 43 BP,JR | 175.00 |
| 44 RC,BP | 190.00 |
| 45 BK | 190.00 |
| 46 | 190.00 |
| 47 BK,JO,BEv | 190.00 |
| 48 BP | 175.00 |
| 49 BEv | 175.00 |
| 50 DCn | 175.00 |
| 51 | 175.00 |
| 52 GM | 175.00 |
| 53 SD,JF,BEv | 190.00 |
| 54 BEv | 190.00 |
| 55 BEv | 200.00 |
| 56 JMn,JK | 175.00 |
| 57 JR | 200.00 |
| 58 JF,JO | 175.00 |
| 59 TSe,BEv | 175.00 |

| | |
|---|---|
| 60 JF,BEv | 175.00 |
| 61 GM,JO,JR,BEv | 175.00 |
| 62 MD,BEv | 175.00 |
| 63 BEv,August, 1957 | 175.00 |

## ATOM-AGE COMBAT
### St. John Publ. Co., 1952–53

| | |
|---|---|
| 1 Buck Vinson | 1,200.00 |
| 1a rep. (1958) | 350.00 |
| 2 Flying Saucer | 500.00 |
| 3 | 450.00 |
| 4 | 350.00 |
| 5 Flying Saucer | 350.00 |

## ATOM-AGE COMBAT
### Fago Magazines, 1959

| | |
|---|---|
| 2 Nuclear Sub,A-Bomb | 325.00 |
| 3 Space Missile | 225.00 |

## ATOMAN
### Spark Publications, Feb., 1946

| | |
|---|---|
| 1 JRo,MMe,O:Atoman,A:Kid Crusaders | 1,500.00 |
| 2 JRo,MMe | 800.00 |

## ATOMIC BOMB
### Jay Burtis Publ., 1945

| | |
|---|---|
| 1 | 1,500.00 |

## ATOMIC COMICS
### Green Publishing Co., Jan., 1946

| | |
|---|---|
| 1 S&S,A:Radio Squad, Barry O'Neal. | 2,200.00 |
| 2 MB,A:Inspector Dayton, Kid Kane | 1,100.00 |
| 3 MB,A:Zero Ghost Detective | 800.00 |
| 4 JKa(c), July–Aug., 1946 | 800.00 |

## ATOMIC COMICS
### Daniels Publications, 1946 (Reprints)

| | |
|---|---|
| 1 A:Rocketman,Yankee Boy, Bondage (c),rep. | 750.00 |

## ATOMIC MOUSE
### Capital Stories/ Charlton Comics, March, 1953

| | |
|---|---|
| 1 AFa,O:Atomic Mouse | 500.00 |
| 2 AFa,Ice Cream (c) | 150.00 |

# STANDARD GUIDE TO GOLDEN AGE COMICS

**At**

Atomic War! #4
© Ace-Junior Books

Authentic Police Cases #4
© St. John Publ. Co.

Avon One-Shots, An Earthman
on Venus © Avon Periodicals

3 AFa,Genie and Magic
  Carpet (c) . . . . . . . . . . . . . 125.00
4 AFa . . . . . . . . . . . . . . . . . 125.00
5 AFa,A:Timmy the Timid Ghost 125.00
6 thru 10 Funny Animal . . . . . @100.00
11 thru 14 Funny Animal . . @100.00
15 A:Happy the Marvel Bunny . . . 100.00
16 Funny Animal,Giant . . . . . . . . 75.00
17 thru 30 Funny Animal . . . . . @75.00
31 thru 36 Funny Animal . . . . . @75.00
37 A:Atom the Cat . . . . . . . . . . . 75.00
38 thru 40 Funny Animal . . . . . @50.00
41 thru 53 Funny Animal . . . . . @30.00
54 June, 1963 . . . . . . . . . . . . . . 30.00

## ATOMIC RABBIT
**Charlton Comics, 1955–58**
1 . . . . . . . . . . . . . . . . . . . . . . . 350.00
2 . . . . . . . . . . . . . . . . . . . . . . . 150.00
3 . . . . . . . . . . . . . . . . . . . . . . . 100.00
4 . . . . . . . . . . . . . . . . . . . . . . . 100.00
5 . . . . . . . . . . . . . . . . . . . . . . . 100.00
6 . . . . . . . . . . . . . . . . . . . . . . . 100.00
7 . . . . . . . . . . . . . . . . . . . . . . . 100.00
8 . . . . . . . . . . . . . . . . . . . . . . . 100.00
9 . . . . . . . . . . . . . . . . . . . . . . . 100.00
10 . . . . . . . . . . . . . . . . . . . . . . 100.00
11 . . . . . . . . . . . . . . . . . . . . . . 150.00
Becomes:

## ATOMIC BUNNY
12 . . . . . . . . . . . . . . . . . . . . . . 150.00
13 thru 18 . . . . . . . . . . . . . . @100.00
19 Dec., 1959 . . . . . . . . . . . . . 100.00

## ATOMIC THUNDERBOLT, THE
**Regor Company, Feb., 1946**
1 I:Atomic Thunderbolt,
  Mr. Murdo . . . . . . . . . . . . 1,200.00

## ATOMIC WAR!
**Ace-Junior Books, 1952–53**
1 Atomic explosion (c) . . . . . . . 2,000.00
2 . . . . . . . . . . . . . . . . . . . . . 1,600.00
3 A-Bomb . . . . . . . . . . . . . . . 1,600.00
4 . . . . . . . . . . . . . . . . . . . . . 1,600.00

## ATOM THE CAT
## See: BO

## ATTACK
**Youthful Mag./Trojan, 1952**
1 Violence . . . . . . . . . . . . . . . . 500.00
2 . . . . . . . . . . . . . . . . . . . . . . . 250.00
3 Bondage . . . . . . . . . . . . . . . 300.00
4 RKu . . . . . . . . . . . . . . . . . . . 250.00
Becomes:

## ATOMIC ATTACK
**Youthful Magazines, 1953**
5 . . . . . . . . . . . . . . . . . . . . . . . 250.00
6 . . . . . . . . . . . . . . . . . . . . . . . 200.00
7 . . . . . . . . . . . . . . . . . . . . . . . 200.00
8 . . . . . . . . . . . . . . . . . . . . . . . 200.00
5 thru 8 . . . . . . . . . . . . . . . . @ 200.00

## ATTACK
**Charlton Comics, 1958–59**
54 . . . . . . . . . . . . . . . . . . . . . . 150.00
55 thru 60 . . . . . . . . . . . . . . @100.00

## AUTHENTIC POLICE CASES
**St. John Publ. Co., 1948**
1 Hale the Magician . . . . . . . . . 600.00
2 Lady Satan, Johnny Rebel . . . 350.00
3 A:Avenger . . . . . . . . . . . . . . 600.00
4 Masked Black Jack . . . . . . . . 350.00
5 JCo . . . . . . . . . . . . . . . . . . . 350.00
6 JCo,MB(c) . . . . . . . . . . . . . . 650.00
7 thru 10 . . . . . . . . . . . . . . @275.00
11 thru 15 . . . . . . . . . . . . . . @275.00
16 thru 23 . . . . . . . . . . . . . . @175.00
24 thru 28 Giants . . . . . . . . . . @375.00
29 thru 38 . . . . . . . . . . . . . . @150.00

## AVIATION AND MODEL BUILDING
## See: TRUE AVIATION PICTURE STORIES

## AVIATION CADETS
**Street & Smith Publ., 1943**
1 . . . . . . . . . . . . . . . . . . . . . . . 200.00

## AVON ONE-SHOTS
**Avon Periodicals, 1949-1953**
{Listed in Alphabetical Order}
1 Atomic Spy Cases . . . . . . . . . 500.00
N# WW,Attack on Planet Mars . 1,500.00
1 Bachelor's Diary . . . . . . . . . . 450.00
1 Badmen of the West . . . . . . . 450.00
N# Badmen of Tombstone . . . . . 200.00
1 EK,Behind Prison Bars . . . . . 375.00
2 Betty and Her Steady . . . . . . 125.00
N# EK,Blackhawk Indian
  Tomahawk War . . . . . . . . . . 225.00
1 EK,Blazing Sixguns . . . . . . . 200.00
1 EK,Butch Cassidy . . . . . . . . 225.00
N# Chief Crazy Horse . . . . . . . . 235.00
N# FF,AW,EK,Chief Victorio's
  Apache Massacre . . . . . . . . 550.00
N# City of the Living Dead . . . . . 750.00
1 Complete Romance . . . . . . . . 475.00
N# Custer's Last Fight . . . . . . . . 225.00
1 EK(c),Dalton Boys . . . . . . . . . 225.00
N# GT(c),Davy Crockett . . . . . . . 225.00
N# The Dead Who Walk . . . . . . . 800.00
1 Diary of Horror,Bondage(c) . . . 700.00
N# WW,Earth Man on Venus . . 2,000.00
1 Eerie, bondage (c) . . . . . . . 1,200.00
1 EK,Escape from Devil's Island 500.00
N# EK,Fighting Daniel Boone . . . 250.00
N# EK(c),For a Night of Love . . . 375.00
1 WW,Flying Saucers . . . . . . . 1,400.00
N# Flying Saucers . . . . . . . . . . . 700.00
1 Going Steady with Betty . . . . . 150.00
N# Hooded Menace . . . . . . . . . . 800.00
N# EK,King of the Badmen
  of Deadwood . . . . . . . . . . . . 175.00
1 King Solomon's Mines . . . . . . 500.00
N# EK(c),Kit Carson & the
  Blackfeet Warriors . . . . . . . . 100.00
N# EK,Last of the Comanches . . 200.00
N# EK,Masked Bandit . . . . . . . . 200.00
1 WW,Mask of Dr. Fu Manchu. 1,500.00
N# EK,Night of Mystery . . . . . . . 600.00
1 WW,JKu,Outlaws of the
  Wild West . . . . . . . . . . . . . . 400.00
1 JKu,Out of this World . . . . . 1,000.00
N# EK,Pancho Villa . . . . . . . . . . 275.00
1 EK,Phantom Witch Doctor . . . . 700.00
1 Pixie Puzzle Rocket
  to Adventureland . . . . . . . . . 150.00
1 EK,Prison Riot,drugs . . . . . . . 500.00
N# EK,Red Mountain Featuring
  Quantrell's Raiders . . . . . . . . 350.00
N# Reform School Girl . . . . . . . 2,000.00
1 Robotmen of the Lost Planet 1,700.00
N# JO,WW(c),Rocket to
  the Moon . . . . . . . . . . . . . . 1,700.00
N# JKu,Secret Diary of
  Eerie Adventures . . . . . . . . 2,700.00
1 EK,Sheriff Bob Dixon's
  Chuck Wagon . . . . . . . . . . . 175.00
1 Sideshow . . . . . . . . . . . . . . . 400.00

All comics prices listed are for *Near Mint* condition.

*Babe #7*
© *Prize Publications*

*Baffling Mysteries #8*
© *Ace Magazines*

*Bang-Up Comics #2*
© *Progressive Publications*

**Ba**

1 JKu,Sparkling Love . . . . . . . . 275.00
N# Speedy Rabbit . . . . . . . . . . . 100.00
1 EK(c)Teddy Roosevelt &
   His Rough Riders . . . . . . . . 225.00
N# The Underworld Story . . . . . 350.00
N# EK(c),The Unknown Man. . . . 350.00
1 EK,War Dogs of the U.S. Army 175.00
N# EK(c),White Chief of the
   Pawnee Indians. . . . . . . . . . 200.00
N# Women to Love . . . . . . . . . . 700.00

## AWFUL OSCAR
### See: OSCAR

## BABE
**Prize/Headline Feature,
June–July, 1948**
1 BRo . . . . . . . . . . . . . . . . . . . . 300.00
2 BRo . . . . . . . . . . . . . . . . . . . . 175.00
3 BRo . . . . . . . . . . . . . . . . . . . . 150.00
4 thru 9 BRo . . . . . . . . . . . . . @125.00

## BABE RUTH SPORTS COMICS
**Harvey Publications,
April, 1949**
1 BP . . . . . . . . . . . . . . . . . . . . . 500.00
2 BP,Baseball . . . . . . . . . . . . . . 350.00
3 BP,Joe DiMaggio(c) . . . . . . . . 400.00
4 BP,Bob Feller(c). . . . . . . . . . . 325.00
5 BP,Football(c) . . . . . . . . . . . . 325.00
6 BP,Basketball(c). . . . . . . . . . . 325.00
7 BP . . . . . . . . . . . . . . . . . . . . . 250.00
8 BP,Yogi Berra. . . . . . . . . . . . . 325.00
9 BP,Stan Musial(c). . . . . . . . . . 300.00
10 . . . . . . . . . . . . . . . . . . . . . . . 300.00
11 Feb., 1951. . . . . . . . . . . . . . . 250.00

## BABY HUEY, THE BABY GIANT
**Harvey Publications, 1956–80**
1 . . . . . . . . . . . . . . . . . . . . . . . . 800.00
2 . . . . . . . . . . . . . . . . . . . . . . . . 350.00
3 Anti-Pep Pills . . . . . . . . . . . . 250.00
4 . . . . . . . . . . . . . . . . . . . . . . . . 150.00
5 . . . . . . . . . . . . . . . . . . . . . . . . 150.00
6 thru 10 . . . . . . . . . . . . . . . . @100.00
11 thru 20 . . . . . . . . . . . . . . . . @75.00
21 thru 40 . . . . . . . . . . . . . . . . @50.00
41 thru 60 . . . . . . . . . . . . . . . . @35.00
61 thru 79 . . . . . . . . . . . . . . . . @30.00

80 . . . . . . . . . . . . . . . . . . . . . . . . 30.00
81 thru 95 giant size. . . . . . . . @35.00
96 Giant size . . . . . . . . . . . . . . . 30.00
97 Giant size . . . . . . . . . . . . . . . 30.00
98 . . . . . . . . . . . . . . . . . . . . . . . . 20.00
99 . . . . . . . . . . . . . . . . . . . . . . . . 15.00

## BADMEN OF THE WEST
### See: A-1 COMICS

## BADGE OF JUSTICE
### See: CRIME AND JUSTICE

## INDIAN BRAVES
**Ace Periodicals, 1951**
1 Green Arrow. . . . . . . . . . . . . . 150.00
2 . . . . . . . . . . . . . . . . . . . . . . . . . 75.00
3 . . . . . . . . . . . . . . . . . . . . . . . . . 65.00
4 . . . . . . . . . . . . . . . . . . . . . . . . . 65.00
Becomes:

## BAFFLING MYSTERIES
**Periodical House/
Ace Mag., 1951–55**
5 GC,MSy . . . . . . . . . . . . . . . . 450.00
6 MSy . . . . . . . . . . . . . . . . . . . . 325.00
7 . . . . . . . . . . . . . . . . . . . . . . . . 300.00
8 LC . . . . . . . . . . . . . . . . . . . . . 300.00
9 . . . . . . . . . . . . . . . . . . . . . . . . 300.00
10 . . . . . . . . . . . . . . . . . . . . . . . 300.00
11 GC. . . . . . . . . . . . . . . . . . . . 300.00
12 . . . . . . . . . . . . . . . . . . . . . . . 275.00
13 . . . . . . . . . . . . . . . . . . . . . . . 275.00
14 . . . . . . . . . . . . . . . . . . . . . . . 275.00
15 . . . . . . . . . . . . . . . . . . . . . . . 275.00
16 LC . . . . . . . . . . . . . . . . . . . . 275.00
17 LC . . . . . . . . . . . . . . . . . . . . 275.00
18 LC . . . . . . . . . . . . . . . . . . . . 275.00
19 . . . . . . . . . . . . . . . . . . . . . . . 275.00
20 LC,Bondage . . . . . . . . . . . . 350.00
21 LC . . . . . . . . . . . . . . . . . . . . 275.00
22 LC,MSy. . . . . . . . . . . . . . . . 300.00
23 Bondage . . . . . . . . . . . . . . . 300.00
24 reprint . . . . . . . . . . . . . . . . . 200.00
25 reprint . . . . . . . . . . . . . . . . . 200.00
Becomes:

## HEROES OF THE WILD FRONTIER
**Ace Periodicals, 1956**
27 (1) . . . . . . . . . . . . . . . . . . . . 100.00
2 . . . . . . . . . . . . . . . . . . . . . . . . 100.00

## BANG-UP COMICS
**Progressive Publ., 1941**
1 CosmoMan, Lady Fairplay,
   O:Buzz Balmer. . . . . . . . . . 1,700.00
2 Buzz Balmer . . . . . . . . . . . . 1,000.00
3 Buzz Balmer . . . . . . . . . . . . 1,000.00

## BANNER COMICS
**Ace Magazines, Sept., 1941**
3 B:Captain Courageous,
   Lone Warrior. . . . . . . . . . . 1,800.00
4 JM(c),Flag(c) . . . . . . . . . . . 1,500.00
5 . . . . . . . . . . . . . . . . . . . . . . 1,500.00
Becomes:

## CAPTAIN COURAGEOUS COMICS
**March, 1942**
6 I:The Sword . . . . . . . . . . . . 1,500.00

## THE BARKER
**Quality Comics Group, 1946–49**
1 Circus. . . . . . . . . . . . . . . . . . 150.00
2 . . . . . . . . . . . . . . . . . . . . . . . 125.00
3 . . . . . . . . . . . . . . . . . . . . . . . 125.00
4 . . . . . . . . . . . . . . . . . . . . . . . 125.00
5 . . . . . . . . . . . . . . . . . . . . . . . 125.00
6 . . . . . . . . . . . . . . . . . . . . . . . 100.00
7 . . . . . . . . . . . . . . . . . . . . . . . 100.00
8 . . . . . . . . . . . . . . . . . . . . . . . 100.00
9 . . . . . . . . . . . . . . . . . . . . . . . 100.00
10 . . . . . . . . . . . . . . . . . . . . . . 100.00
11 thru 15 . . . . . . . . . . . . . . @ 100.00

## BARNEY BAXTER
**Argo Publ., 1956**
1 . . . . . . . . . . . . . . . . . . . . . . . 125.00
2 . . . . . . . . . . . . . . . . . . . . . . . 125.00

## BARNEY GOOGLE & SNUFFY SMITH
**Toby Press, 1951–52**
1 . . . . . . . . . . . . . . . . . . . . . . . 150.00
2 . . . . . . . . . . . . . . . . . . . . . . . 100.00
3 . . . . . . . . . . . . . . . . . . . . . . . 100.00
4 HK . . . . . . . . . . . . . . . . . . . . 100.00

## BARNYARD COMICS
**Animated Cartoons, June, 1944**
1 (fa) . . . . . . . . . . . . . . . . . . . . 300.00
2 (fa) . . . . . . . . . . . . . . . . . . . . 250.00

---

All comics prices listed are for *Near Mint* condition.

*Barnyard Comics #5*
© *Animated Cartoons*

*Batman #8*
© *DC Comics*

*Batman #61*
© *DC Comics*

3 (fa) . . . . . . . . . . . . . . . . . . . . . 150.00
4 (fa) . . . . . . . . . . . . . . . . . . . . . 150.00
5 (fa) . . . . . . . . . . . . . . . . . . . . . 150.00
6 thru 12 (fa) . . . . . . . . . . . . . @125.00
13 FF(ti) . . . . . . . . . . . . . . . . . . . 150.00
14 FF(ti) . . . . . . . . . . . . . . . . . . . 150.00
15 FF(ti) . . . . . . . . . . . . . . . . . . . 150.00
16 . . . . . . . . . . . . . . . . . . . . . . . . 125.00
17 FF(ti) . . . . . . . . . . . . . . . . . . . 125.00
18 FF,FF(ti) . . . . . . . . . . . . . . . . 150.00
19 FF,FF(ti) . . . . . . . . . . . . . . . . 150.00
20 FF,FF(ti) . . . . . . . . . . . . . . . . 150.00
21 FF(ti) . . . . . . . . . . . . . . . . . . . 125.00
22 FF,FF(ti) . . . . . . . . . . . . . . . . 150.00
23 FF(ti) . . . . . . . . . . . . . . . . . . . 125.00
24 FF,FF(ti) . . . . . . . . . . . . . . . . 150.00
25 FF,FF(ti) . . . . . . . . . . . . . . . . 150.00
26 FF(ti) . . . . . . . . . . . . . . . . . . . 125.00
27 FF(ti) . . . . . . . . . . . . . . . . . . . 125.00
28 . . . . . . . . . . . . . . . . . . . . . . . . 100.00
29 FF(ti) . . . . . . . . . . . . . . . . . . . 125.00
30 and 31 . . . . . . . . . . . . . . . . @100.00
**Becomes:**

## DIZZY DUCK

32 Funny Animal . . . . . . . . . . . . 125.00
33 thru 39 . . . . . . . . . . . . . . . . @100.00

## BASEBALL COMICS

**Will Eisner Productions,
Spring, 1949**
1 WE,A:Rube Rocky . . . . . . . 1,000.00

## BASEBALL HEROS

**Fawcett Publications, 1952**
N# Babe Ruth (c) . . . . . . . . . 1,500.00

## BASEBALL THRILLS

**Ziff-Davis Publ. Co., 1951**
10 Bob Feller Predicts Pennant
 Winners . . . . . . . . . . . . . . . 600.00
2 BP, Yogi Berra story . . . . . . . . 400.00
3 EK, Joe DiMaggio story,
 Summer 1952 . . . . . . . . . . . 450.00

## BASIL

**St. John Publishing, 1953**
1 F:Basil, The Royal Cat . . . . . . . 65.00
2 . . . . . . . . . . . . . . . . . . . . . . . . . 40.00
3 . . . . . . . . . . . . . . . . . . . . . . . . . 20.00
4 . . . . . . . . . . . . . . . . . . . . . . . . . 20.00

## BATMAN

**DC Comics, Spring, 1940**
1 I:Joker,Cat(Catwoman),
 V:Hugo Strange . . . . . . 175,000.00
2 V:Joker/Catwoman team . . 30,000.00
3 V:Catwoman . . . . . . . . . . . 20,000.00
4 V:Joker . . . . . . . . . . . . . . . 15,000.00
5 V:Joker . . . . . . . . . . . . . . . . 9,000.00
6 V:Clock Maker . . . . . . . . . . 6,500.00
7 V:Joker . . . . . . . . . . . . . . . . 6,200.00
8 V:Joker . . . . . . . . . . . . . . . . 6,000.00
9 V:Joker . . . . . . . . . . . . . . . . 6,000.00
10 V:Catwoman . . . . . . . . . . . 6,000.00
11 V:Joker,Penguin . . . . . . . . 11,000.00
12 V:Joker. . . . . . . . . . . . . . . . 5,000.00
13 V:Joker. . . . . . . . . . . . . . . . 5,000.00
14 V:Penguin;Propaganda sty . 5,000.00
15 V:Catwoman . . . . . . . . . . . 5,000.00
16 I:Alfred,V:Joker . . . . . . . . . 8,500.00
17 V:Penguin . . . . . . . . . . . . . 4,000.00
18 V:Tweedledum &
 Tweedledee . . . . . . . . . . . . 4,500.00
19 V:Joker . . . . . . . . . . . . . . . . 5,000.00
20 V:Joker . . . . . . . . . . . . . . . . 4,000.00
21 V:Penguin . . . . . . . . . . . . . 4,000.00
22 V:Catwoman,Cavalier . . . . . 4,000.00
23 V:Joker . . . . . . . . . . . . . . . . 8,000.00
24 I:Carter Nichols, V:Tweedledum
 & Tweedledee . . . . . . . . . . 3,000.00
25 V:Joker/Penguin team . . . . 4,000.00
26 V:Cavalier . . . . . . . . . . . . . 2,700.00
27 V:Penguin . . . . . . . . . . . . . 4,500.00
28 V:Joker. . . . . . . . . . . . . . . . 2,500.00
29 V:Scuttler . . . . . . . . . . . . . . 2,500.00
30 V:Penguin,I:Ally Babble . . . 2,500.00
31 I:Punch and Judy . . . . . . . . 2,000.00
32 O:Robin,V:Joker. . . . . . . . . 2,000.00
33 V:Penguin,Jackall . . . . . . . 2,300.00
34 A:Ally Babble . . . . . . . . . . . 2,000.00
35 V:Catwoman . . . . . . . . . . . 2,000.00
36 V:Penguin,A:King Arthur . . 1,700.00
37 V:Joker. . . . . . . . . . . . . . . . 2,400.00
38 V:Penguin . . . . . . . . . . . . . 4,500.00
39 V:Catwoman,Xmas Story . . 1,700.00
40 V:Joker. . . . . . . . . . . . . . . . 2,500.00
41 V:Penguin . . . . . . . . . . . . . 2,300.00
42 V:Catwoman . . . . . . . . . . . 2,000.00
43 V:Penguin . . . . . . . . . . . . . 2,000.00
44 V:Joker,A:Carter Nichols,Meets
 ancester Silas Wayne. . . . . 2,500.00
45 V:Catwoman . . . . . . . . . . . 1,300.00
46 V:Joker,A:Carter Nichols,
 Leonardo Da Vinci . . . . . . . 1,300.00
47 O:Batman,V:Catwoman . . . . 5,000.00
48 V:Penguin, Bat-Cave story . 1,700.00

49 I:Mad Hatter & Vicki Vale . . . 2,400.00
50 V:Two-Face,A:Vicki Vale . . . 1,400.00
51 V:Penguin . . . . . . . . . . . . . 1,300.00
52 V:Joker. . . . . . . . . . . . . . . . 1,300.00
53 V:Joker. . . . . . . . . . . . . . . . 1,500.00
54 V:The Treasure Hunter . . . . 1,200.00
55 V:Joker. . . . . . . . . . . . . . . . 1,800.00
56 V:Penguin . . . . . . . . . . . . . 1,400.00
57 V:Joker. . . . . . . . . . . . . . . . 1,200.00
58 V:Penguin . . . . . . . . . . . . . 1,400.00
59 I:Deadshot . . . . . . . . . . . . . 1,200.00
60 V:'Shark' Marlin . . . . . . . . . 1,200.00
61 V:Penguin . . . . . . . . . . . . . 1,300.00
62 O:Catwoman,I:Knight
 & Squire . . . . . . . . . . . . . . 2,000.00
63 V:Joker. . . . . . . . . . . . . . . . 1,200.00
64 V:Killer Moth. . . . . . . . . . . . 2,000.00
65 I:Wingman,V:Catwoman . . . 1,200.00
66 V:Joker. . . . . . . . . . . . . . . . 1,000.00
67 V:Joker. . . . . . . . . . . . . . . . 1,000.00
68 V:Two-Face,Alfred story . . . . 850.00
69 I:King of the Cats,
 A:Catwoman . . . . . . . . . . . 1,000.00
70 V:Penguin . . . . . . . . . . . . . . 850.00
71 V:Mr. Cipher . . . . . . . . . . . . . 850.00
72 The Jungle Batman. . . . . . . . 850.00
73 V:Joker,A:Vicki Vale . . . . . . 1,100.00
74 V:Joker . . . . . . . . . . . . . . . . . 850.00
75 I:The Gorilla Boss . . . . . . . . . 850.00
76 V:Penguin . . . . . . . . . . . . . . 850.00
77 The Crime Predictor . . . . . . . 850.00
78 The Manhunter from Mars . . 1,100.00
79 A:Vicki Vale . . . . . . . . . . . . . 850.00
80 V:Joker . . . . . . . . . . . . . . . . . 850.00
81 V:Two-Face. . . . . . . . . . . . . . 850.00
82 The Flying Batman . . . . . . . . 750.00
83 V:'Fish' Frye . . . . . . . . . . . . . 750.00
84 V:Catwoman . . . . . . . . . . . 1,000.00
85 V:Joker . . . . . . . . . . . . . . . . . 750.00
86 V:Joker. . . . . . . . . . . . . . . . . 750.00
87 V:Joker. . . . . . . . . . . . . . . . . 750.00
88 V:Mr. Mystery. . . . . . . . . . . . 750.00
89 I:Aunt Agatha . . . . . . . . . . . . 750.00
90 I:Batboy. . . . . . . . . . . . . . . . . 750.00
91 V:Blinky Grosset . . . . . . . . . . 750.00
92 I:Ace, the Bat-Hound . . . . . . . 750.00
93 The Caveman Batman . . . . . . 700.00
94 Alfred Has Amnesia . . . . . . . 600.00
95 The Bat-Train . . . . . . . . . . . . 600.00
96 Batman's College Days . . . . . 600.00
97 V:Joker. . . . . . . . . . . . . . . . . 600.00
98 A:Carter Nichols,Jules Verne . 600.00
99 V:Penguin,A:Carter Nichols,
 Bat Masterson . . . . . . . . . . 600.00
100 Great Batman Contest. . . . 3,300.00
101 The Great Bat-Cape Hunt. . . 600.00

All comics prices listed are for *Near Mint* condition.

*Batman #128*
© DC Comics

*Battle #11*
© Marvel Comics Group

*Battle Action #1*
© Marvel Comics Group

| | |
|---|---|
| 102 V:Mayne Mallok | 550.00 |
| 103 A:Ace, the Bat-Hound | 550.00 |
| 104 V:Devoe | 550.00 |
| 105 A:Batwoman | 750.00 |
| 106 V:Keene Harper Gang | 600.00 |
| 107 V:Daredevils | 600.00 |
| 108 Bat-Cave Story | 600.00 |
| 109 1,000 Inventions of Batman | 600.00 |
| 110 V:Joker | 550.00 |
| 111 | 450.00 |
| 112 I:Signalman | 450.00 |
| 113 I:Fatman | 450.00 |
| 114 I:Bat Ape | 450.00 |
| 115 | 450.00 |
| 116 | 450.00 |
| 117 | 450.00 |
| 118 | 450.00 |
| 119 | 450.00 |
| 120 | 450.00 |
| 121 I:Mr.Zero (Mr.Freeze) | 600.00 |
| 122 | 300.00 |
| 123 A:Joker | 325.00 |
| 124 Mystery Seed from Space | 300.00 |
| 125 | 300.00 |
| 126 | 300.00 |
| 127 A:Superman & Joker | 325.00 |
| 128 | 300.00 |
| 129 O:Robin (Retold) | 350.00 |
| 130 | 300.00 |
| 131 I:2nd Batman | 250.00 |
| 132 Lair of the Sea-Fox | 250.00 |
| 133 | 250.00 |
| 134 | 250.00 |
| 135 | 250.00 |
| 136 A:Joker, Bat-Mite | 300.00 |
| 137 V:Mr. Marvel,The Brand | 250.00 |
| 138 A:Bat-Mite | 250.00 |
| 139 I:Old Batgirl | 250.00 |
| 140 A:Joker | 250.00 |
| 141 V:Clockmaster | 250.00 |
| 142 Batman Robot Story | 250.00 |
| 143 A:Bathound | 250.00 |
| 144 A:Joker,Bat-Mite,Bat-Girl | 250.00 |
| 145 V:Mr.50,Joker | 300.00 |
| 146 A:Bat-Mite,Joker | 300.00 |
| 147 Batman becomes Bat-Baby | 200.00 |
| 148 A:Joker | 250.00 |
| 149 V:Maestro | 200.00 |
| 150 V:Biff Warner,Jack Pine | 200.00 |
| Ann.#1 CS,O:BatCave | 1,100.00 |
| Ann.#2 | 450.00 |
| Ann.#3 A:Joker | 450.00 |
| Ann.#4 | 200.00 |
| Ann.#5 | 200.00 |
| Ann.#6 | 150.00 |
| Ann.#7 | 150.00 |

## BATTLE
**Marvel Atlas, March, 1951**

| | |
|---|---|
| 1 They called Him a Coward | 350.00 |
| 2 The War Department Secrets | 175.00 |
| 3 The Beast of the Bataan | 125.00 |
| 4 JMn,I:Buck Private O'Toole | 125.00 |
| 5 Death Trap Of Gen. Wu | 125.00 |
| 6 RH, JMn | 125.00 |
| 7 Enemy Sniper | 125.00 |
| 8 A Time to Die | 125.00 |
| 9 RH | 100.00 |
| 10 | 100.00 |
| 11 SC | 100.00 |
| 12 thru 21 | @110.00 |
| 22 | 100.00 |
| 23 BK | 100.00 |
| 24 | 100.00 |
| 25 | 100.00 |
| 26 JR | 100.00 |
| 27 | 100.00 |
| 28 JSe | 100.00 |
| 29 | 100.00 |
| 30 | 100.00 |
| 31 RH,JMn | 100.00 |
| 32 JSe,GT | 100.00 |
| 33 GC,JSe,JSt | 100.00 |
| 34 JSe | 100.00 |
| 35 | 100.00 |
| 36 BEv | 100.00 |
| 37 RA,JSt | 125.00 |
| 38 thru 46 | @100.00 |
| 47 JO | 100.00 |
| 48 | 100.00 |
| 49 JDa | 100.00 |
| 50 BEv | 100.00 |
| 51 | 100.00 |
| 52 GWb | 100.00 |
| 53 BP | 100.00 |
| 54 | 100.00 |
| 55 GC,AS,BP,AW,GWb | 125.00 |
| 56 | 100.00 |
| 57 | 100.00 |
| 58 | 100.00 |
| 59 AT | 100.00 |
| 60 A:Combat Kelly | 100.00 |
| 61 JMn,A:Combat Kelly | 100.00 |
| 62 A:Combat Kelly | 100.00 |
| 63 SD | 125.00 |
| 64 JK | 125.00 |
| 65 JK | 125.00 |
| 66 JSe,JK,JDa | 125.00 |
| 67 JSe,JK,AS,JDa | 125.00 |
| 68 JSe,JK,AW,SD | 125.00 |
| 69 RH,JSe,JK,SW | 135.00 |
| 70 BEv,SD; June, 1960 | 135.00 |

## BATTLE ACTION
**Marvel Atlas, Feb., 1952**

| | |
|---|---|
| 1 | 300.00 |
| 2 | 150.00 |
| 3 JSt,RH | 100.00 |
| 4 | 100.00 |
| 5 | 100.00 |
| 6 JeR | 100.00 |
| 7 JeR | 100.00 |
| 8 RH | 125.00 |
| 9 thru 15 | @100.00 |
| 16 thru 27 | @100.00 |
| 28 GWb | 100.00 |
| 29 | 100.00 |
| 30 GWb,Aug., 1957 | 100.00 |

## BATTLE ATTACK
**Stanmor Publications, 1952–55**

| | |
|---|---|
| 1 War Combat | 150.00 |
| 2 | 100.00 |
| 3 | 100.00 |
| 4 | 100.00 |
| 5 | 100.00 |
| 6 | 100.00 |
| 7 | 100.00 |
| 8 | 100.00 |

## BATTLE BRADY
### See: MEN IN ACTION

## BATTLE CRY
**Stanmor Publications, 1952–55**

| | |
|---|---|
| 1 | 150.00 |
| 2 | 125.00 |
| 3 | 125.00 |
| 4 EC Copy | 125.00 |
| 5 | 125.00 |
| 6 | 100.00 |
| 7 | 100.00 |
| 8 | 100.00 |
| 9 | 100.00 |
| 10 | 100.00 |
| 11 thru 20 | @100.00 |

## BATTLEFIELD
**Marvel Atlas, April, 1952**

| | |
|---|---|
| 1 RH, Slaughter on Suicide Ridge | 250.00 |
| 2 RH | 125.00 |
| 3 Ambush Patrol | 125.00 |
| 4 | 125.00 |
| 5 Into the Jaws of Death | 125.00 |

**Ba**

*Battlefront #34*
*© Marvel Comics Group*

*Best Comics #4*
*© Better Publications*

6 thru 10 . . . . . . . . . . . . . . . . @100.00
11 GC,May, 1953 . . . . . . . . . . . 100.00

## BATTLEFIELD ACTION
### See: DYNAMITE

## BATTLE FIRE
**Stamfor Publications, 1955**
1 War . . . . . . . . . . . . . . . . . . . . 150.00
2 . . . . . . . . . . . . . . . . . . . . . . . 100.00
3 thru 7 . . . . . . . . . . . . . . . . @100.00

## BATTLEFRONT
**Standard Comics, 1952**
5 ATh. . . . . . . . . . . . . . . . . . . . 175.00

## BATTLEFRONT
**Marvel Atlas, June, 1952**
1 JeR,RH(c),Operation Killer . . . 325.00
2 JeR . . . . . . . . . . . . . . . . . . . . 200.00
3 JeR,Spearhead . . . . . . . . . . . 125.00
4 JeR,Death Trap of General
   Chun . . . . . . . . . . . . . . . . . . 125.00
5 JeR,Terror of the Tank Men . . . 125.00
6 A:Combat Kelly . . . . . . . . . . . 125.00
7 A:Combat Kelly . . . . . . . . . . . 125.00
8 A:Combat Kelly . . . . . . . . . . . 125.00
9 A:Combat Kelly . . . . . . . . . . . 125.00
10 A:Combat Kelly . . . . . . . . . . 125.00
11 thru 20 . . . . . . . . . . . . . . @100.00
21 thru 39 . . . . . . . . . . . . . . @100.00
40 AW . . . . . . . . . . . . . . . . . . . 100.00
41 . . . . . . . . . . . . . . . . . . . . . . 100.00
42 AW . . . . . . . . . . . . . . . . . . . 125.00
43 thru 48 Aug.,1957 . . . . . . . @135.00

## BATTLEGROUND
**Marvel Atlas, Sept., 1954**
1 . . . . . . . . . . . . . . . . . . . . . . . 250.00
2 JKz. . . . . . . . . . . . . . . . . . . . 125.00
3 thru 8 . . . . . . . . . . . . . . . . @100.00
9 BK . . . . . . . . . . . . . . . . . . . . 100.00
10 . . . . . . . . . . . . . . . . . . . . . . 100.00
11 AW,GC,GT. . . . . . . . . . . . . . 125.00
12 MD,JSe. . . . . . . . . . . . . . . . 100.00
13 AW . . . . . . . . . . . . . . . . . . . 100.00
14 JD . . . . . . . . . . . . . . . . . . . . 125.00
15 thru 17. . . . . . . . . . . . . . . @100.00
18 AS . . . . . . . . . . . . . . . . . . . 125.00
19 JMn,JSe. . . . . . . . . . . . . . . 100.00
20 Aug., 1957. . . . . . . . . . . . . . 100.00

## BATTLE REPORT
**Excellent Publ./**
**Ajax-Farrell, 1952—53**
1 . . . . . . . . . . . . . . . . . . . . . . . 150.00
2 . . . . . . . . . . . . . . . . . . . . . . . 100.00
3 . . . . . . . . . . . . . . . . . . . . . . . 100.00
4 . . . . . . . . . . . . . . . . . . . . . . . 100.00
5 . . . . . . . . . . . . . . . . . . . . . . . 100.00
6 . . . . . . . . . . . . . . . . . . . . . . . 100.00

## BATTLE SQUADRON
**Stanmor Publications, 1955**
1 . . . . . . . . . . . . . . . . . . . . . . . 125.00
2 . . . . . . . . . . . . . . . . . . . . . . . 100.00
3 Iwo Jima flag . . . . . . . . . . . . 100.00
4 . . . . . . . . . . . . . . . . . . . . . . . 100.00
5 . . . . . . . . . . . . . . . . . . . . . . . 100.00

## BATTLE STORIES
**Fawcett Publications 1952–53**
1 GE . . . . . . . . . . . . . . . . . . . . 175.00
2 . . . . . . . . . . . . . . . . . . . . . . . 100.00
3 . . . . . . . . . . . . . . . . . . . . . . . 100.00
4 . . . . . . . . . . . . . . . . . . . . . . . 100.00
5 . . . . . . . . . . . . . . . . . . . . . . . 100.00
6 thru 11 . . . . . . . . . . . . . . . @100.00

## BEANBAGS
**Approved Comics**
**(Ziff-Davis), 1951–52**
1 . . . . . . . . . . . . . . . . . . . . . . . 125.00
2 . . . . . . . . . . . . . . . . . . . . . . . 125.00

## BEANIE THE MEANIE
**Fago Publications, 1958**
1 thru 3 . . . . . . . . . . . . . . . . . @75.00

## BEANY & CECIL
**Dell Publishing Co., Jan., 1952**
1 . . . . . . . . . . . . . . . . . . . . . . . 250.00
2 . . . . . . . . . . . . . . . . . . . . . . . 150.00
3 . . . . . . . . . . . . . . . . . . . . . . . 150.00
4 . . . . . . . . . . . . . . . . . . . . . . . 150.00
5 . . . . . . . . . . . . . . . . . . . . . . . 150.00

## BEE 29,
## THE BOMBARDIER
**Neal Publications, 1945**
1 Funny Animal. . . . . . . . . . . . . 350.00

## BEN BOWIE & HIS
## MOUNTAIN MEN
**Dell Publishing Co., 1952**
(1) *see Dell Four Color #443*
(2 thru 6) *see Dell Four Color*
7 . . . . . . . . . . . . . . . . . . . . . . . 150.00
8 thru 10 . . . . . . . . . . . . . . . @125.00
11 I:Yellow Hair . . . . . . . . . . . . 100.00
12 thru 17. . . . . . . . . . . . . . . @100.00

## THE BERRYS
**Argo Publications, 1956**
1 . . . . . . . . . . . . . . . . . . . . . . . 100.00

## BEST COMICS
**Better Publications, Nov., 1939**
1 B:Red Mask . . . . . . . . . . . . 2,000.00
2 A:Red Mask, Silly Willie . . . . 1,200.00
3 A:Red Mask . . . . . . . . . . . . 1,200.00
4 Cannibalism story,
   Feb., 1940 . . . . . . . . . . . . 1,500.00

## BEST FROM BOY'S LIFE
**Gilberton Company, 1957**
1 . . . . . . . . . . . . . . . . . . . . . . . 150.00
2 . . . . . . . . . . . . . . . . . . . . . . . 100.00
3 . . . . . . . . . . . . . . . . . . . . . . . 100.00
4 LbC . . . . . . . . . . . . . . . . . . . 125.00
5 . . . . . . . . . . . . . . . . . . . . . . . 100.00

## BEST OF THE WEST
### See: A-1 COMICS

## BEST LOVE
**Marvel-Manvis Publ., 1949**
**(Formerly: Sub-Mariner #32)**
33 JKu . . . . . . . . . . . . . . . . . . . 150.00
34 . . . . . . . . . . . . . . . . . . . . . . 100.00
35 BEv . . . . . . . . . . . . . . . . . . . 125.00
36 BEv . . . . . . . . . . . . . . . . . . . 125.00

## BEST OF DENNIS
## THE MENACE, THE
**Hallden/Fawcett Publ.,**
**Summer, 1959–Spring, 1961**
1 . . . . . . . . . . . . . . . . . . . . . . . 150.00
2 . . . . . . . . . . . . . . . . . . . . . . . 100.00
3 thru 5 . . . . . . . . . . . . . . . . @100.00

*Best Western #58*
© Marvel Comics Group

*Beyond #4*
© Ace Magazines

*Big Shot Comics #13*
© Columbia Comics Group

**Bi**

## BEST ROMANCE
**Visual Editions (Standard Comics), 1952**
5 ATh,Photo(c) . . . . . . . . . . . . . 150.00
6 . . . . . . . . . . . . . . . . . . . . . . . . 100.00
7 Photo(c) . . . . . . . . . . . . . . . . . 100.00

## BEST WESTERN
**Marvel, June, 1949**
58 A:KidColt,BlackRider,Two-Gun
Kid; Million Dollar Train
Robbery . . . . . . . . . . . . . . . . 325.00
59 A:BlackRider,KidColt,Two-Gun
Kid;The Black Rider Strikes. . 300.00
**Becomes:**

## WESTERN OUTLAWS & SHERIFFS
**Marvel, 1949**
60 PH(c),Hawk Gaither . . . . . . . 300.00
61 Ph(c),Pepper Lawson . . . . . . 250.00
62 Murder at Roaring
House Bridge. . . . . . . . . . . . 250.00
63 thru 65 . . . . . . . . . . . . . . . @250.00
66 Hanging. . . . . . . . . . . . . . . . 250.00
67 Cannibalism . . . . . . . . . . . . . 250.00
68 thru 72 . . . . . . . . . . . . . . . @225.00
73 June, 1952 . . . . . . . . . . . . . 225.00

## BEWARE
**See: CAPTAIN SCIENCE**

## BEWARE TERROR TALES
**Fawcett Publications, 1952–53**
1 . . . . . . . . . . . . . . . . . . . . . . . . 900.00
2 . . . . . . . . . . . . . . . . . . . . . . . . 700.00
3 . . . . . . . . . . . . . . . . . . . . . . . . 600.00
4 . . . . . . . . . . . . . . . . . . . . . . . . 600.00
5 . . . . . . . . . . . . . . . . . . . . . . . . 600.00
6 . . . . . . . . . . . . . . . . . . . . . . . . 600.00
7 . . . . . . . . . . . . . . . . . . . . . . . . 550.00
8 . . . . . . . . . . . . . . . . . . . . . . . . 750.00

## THE BEYOND
**Ace Magazines, 1950–55**
1 Werewolf . . . . . . . . . . . . . . . . 650.00
2 . . . . . . . . . . . . . . . . . . . . . . . . 500.00
3 . . . . . . . . . . . . . . . . . . . . . . . . 350.00
4 . . . . . . . . . . . . . . . . . . . . . . . . 350.00
5 . . . . . . . . . . . . . . . . . . . . . . . . 350.00
6 . . . . . . . . . . . . . . . . . . . . . . . . 350.00
7 . . . . . . . . . . . . . . . . . . . . . . . . 350.00

8 . . . . . . . . . . . . . . . . . . . . . . . . 350.00
9 . . . . . . . . . . . . . . . . . . . . . . . . 350.00
10 . . . . . . . . . . . . . . . . . . . . . . . 350.00
11 thru 20 . . . . . . . . . . . . . . . . @300.00
21 thru 30 . . . . . . . . . . . . . . . . @300.00

## BIBLE TALES FOR YOUNG FOLK
**Marvel/Atlas, 1953**
1 . . . . . . . . . . . . . . . . . . . . . . . . 300.00
2 BEv,BK. . . . . . . . . . . . . . . . . . 250.00
3 . . . . . . . . . . . . . . . . . . . . . . . . 175.00
4 JeR . . . . . . . . . . . . . . . . . . . . 200.00
5 . . . . . . . . . . . . . . . . . . . . . . . . 175.00

## BIG ALL-AMERICAN COMIC BOOK
**DC Comics, Dec., 1944**
1 JKu . . . . . . . . . . . . . . . . . . 20,000.00

## BIG BOOK OF FUN COMICS
**DC Comics, Spring, 1936**
1 . . . . . . . . . . . . . . . . . . . . . 25,000.00

## BIG CHIEF WAHOO
**Eastern Color Printing, 1942–43**
1 . . . . . . . . . . . . . . . . . . . . . . . . 500.00
2 BWa(c),Three Ring Circus . . 250.00
3 BWa(c) . . . . . . . . . . . . . . . . . 200.00
4 BWa(c) . . . . . . . . . . . . . . . . . 200.00
5 BWa(c),Wild West Rodeo . . . . 200.00
6 A:Minnie-Ha-Cha . . . . . . . . . . 150.00
7 . . . . . . . . . . . . . . . . . . . . . . . . 125.00
8 . . . . . . . . . . . . . . . . . . . . . . . . 100.00
9 . . . . . . . . . . . . . . . . . . . . . . . . 100.00
10 . . . . . . . . . . . . . . . . . . . . . . . 125.00
11 thru 23 . . . . . . . . . . . . . . . . @100.00

## BIG JON AND SPARKIE
**See: SPARKIE, RADIO PIXIE**

## BIG SHOT COMICS
**Columbia Comics Group, May, 1940**
1 MBI,OW,Skyman,B:The Face,
Joe Palooka, Rocky Ryan . 4,000.00

2 MBi,OW,Marvelo (c) . . . . . . 1,700.00
3 MBi,Skyman (c) . . . . . . . . . 1,500.00
4 MBi,OW,Joe Palooka (c) . . . 1,000.00
5 MBi,Joe Palooka (c) . . . . . . . 800.00
6 MBi,Joe Palooka (c) . . . . . . . 750.00
7 MBi,Elect Joe Palooka
and Skyman . . . . . . . . . . . . 700.00
8 MBi,Joe Palooka and Skyman
dress as Santa . . . . . . . . . . 700.00
9 MBi,Skyman . . . . . . . . . . . . . 700.00
10 MBi,Skyman . . . . . . . . . . . . 700.00
11 MBi . . . . . . . . . . . . . . . . . . . 600.00
12 MBi,OW. . . . . . . . . . . . . . . . 600.00
13 MBi,OW. . . . . . . . . . . . . . . . 600.00
14 MBi,OW,O:Sparky Watts . . . . 600.00
15 MBi,OW,O:The Cloak . . . . . . 800.00
16 MBi,OW. . . . . . . . . . . . . . . . 500.00
17 MBi(c),OW . . . . . . . . . . . . . 500.00
18 MBi,OW. . . . . . . . . . . . . . . . 500.00
19 MBi,OW,The Face (c) . . . . . . 450.00
20 MBi,OW,OW(c),Skyman cov. . 450.00
21 MBi,OW,A:Raja the Arabian
Knight . . . . . . . . . . . . . . . . 450.00
22 MBi,OW,Joe Palooka (c). . . . 450.00
23 MBi,OW,Sparky Watts (c) . . . 400.00
24 MBi,OW,Uncle Sam (c). . . . . 600.00
25 MBi,OW,Hitler,Sparky Watts(c) 500.00
26 MBi,OW,Hitler,Devildog (c) . . 450.00
27 MBi,OW,Skyman (c) . . . . . . . 450.00
28 MBi,OW,Hitler (c) . . . . . . . . . 800.00
29 MBi,OW,I:Captain Yank . . . . . 450.00
30 MBi,OW,Santa (c) . . . . . . . . . 450.00
31 MBi,OW,Sparky Watts (c) . . . . 400.00
32 MBi,OW,B:Vic Jordan
newspaper reps . . . . . . . . . . . 450.00
33 MBi,OW,Sparky Watts (c) . . . . 400.00
34 MBi,OW. . . . . . . . . . . . . . . . 400.00
35 MBi,OW. . . . . . . . . . . . . . . . 400.00
36 MBi,OW,Sparky Watts (c) . . . . 350.00
37 MBi,OW. . . . . . . . . . . . . . . . 350.00
38 MBi,Uncle Slap Happy (c) . . . 350.00
39 MBi,Uncle Slap Happy (c) . . . 350.00
40 MBi,Joe Palooka Happy (c) . . 350.00
41 MBi,Joe Palooka . . . . . . . . . 300.00
42 MBi,Joe Palooka parachutes . 300.00
43 MBi,V:Hitler . . . . . . . . . . . . . 450.00
44 MBi,Slap Happy (c). . . . . . . . 300.00
45 MBi,Slap Happy (c). . . . . . . . 300.00
46 MBi,Uncle Sam (c),V:Hitler . . 450.00
47 MBi,Uncle Slap Happy (c) . . . 300.00
48 MBi . . . . . . . . . . . . . . . . . . . 300.00
49 MBi . . . . . . . . . . . . . . . . . . . 250.00
50 MBi,O:The Face . . . . . . . . . . 250.00
51 MBi . . . . . . . . . . . . . . . . . . . 250.00
52 MBi,E:Vic Jordan (Hitler cov)
newspaper reps . . . . . . . . . . 400.00

Big-3 #7
© Fox Features Syndicate

Big Town #11
© DC Comics

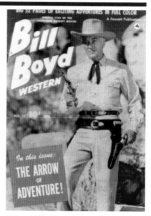

Bill Boyd Western #13
© Fawcett Publications

53 MBi,Uncle Slap Happy (c) . . . 225.00
54 MBi,Uncle Slap Happy (c) . . . 225.00
55 MBi,Happy Easter (c) . . . . . . . 225.00
56 MBi . . . . . . . . . . . . . . . . . . . . . 225.00
57 MBi . . . . . . . . . . . . . . . . . . . . . 225.00
58 MBi . . . . . . . . . . . . . . . . . . . . . 225.00
59 MBi,Slap Happy . . . . . . . . . . . 225.00
60 MBi,Joe Palooka. . . . . . . . . . . 225.00
61 MBi . . . . . . . . . . . . . . . . . . . . . 200.00
62 MBi . . . . . . . . . . . . . . . . . . . . . 200.00
63 MBi . . . . . . . . . . . . . . . . . . . . . 200.00
64 MBi,Slap Happy . . . . . . . . . . . 200.00
65 MBi,Slap Happy . . . . . . . . . . . 200.00
66 MBi,Slap Happy . . . . . . . . . . . 200.00
67 MBi . . . . . . . . . . . . . . . . . . . . . 200.00
68 MBi,Joe Palooka. . . . . . . . . . . 200.00
69 MBi . . . . . . . . . . . . . . . . . . . . . 200.00
70 MBi,OW,Joe Palooka (c) . . . . 200.00
71 MBi,OW. . . . . . . . . . . . . . . . . . 200.00
72 MBi,OW. . . . . . . . . . . . . . . . . . 200.00
73 MBi,OW,The Face (c). . . . . . . 200.00
74 MBi,OW. . . . . . . . . . . . . . . . . . 200.00
75 MBi,OW,Polar Bear Swim
   Club (c) . . . . . . . . . . . . . . . 200.00
76 thru 80 MBi,OW . . . . . . . . @175.00
81 thru 84 MBi,OW . . . . . . . . @175.00
85 MBi,OW,Dixie Dugan (c). . . . 175.00
86 thru 95 MBi,OW . . . . . . . . @150.00
96 MBi,OW,X-Mas (c) . . . . . . . . 150.00
97 thru 99 MBi,OW . . . . . . . . @150.00
100 MBi,OW,Special issue. . . . . . 175.00
101 thru 103 MBi,OW . . . . . . @150.00
104 MBi, Aug., 1949 . . . . . . . . . 175.00

## BIG-3
### Fox Features Syndicate, Fall 1940
1 B:BlueBeetle,Flame,Samson 4,500.00
2 A:BlueBeetle,Flame,Samson 2,000.00
3 same. . . . . . . . . . . . . . . . . . 1,800.00
4 same. . . . . . . . . . . . . . . . . . 1,600.00
5 same. . . . . . . . . . . . . . . . . . 1,600.00
6 E:Samson, bondage (c) . . . . 1,500.00
7 A:V-Man, Jan., 1942 . . . . . . 1,500.00

## THE BIG TOP COMICS
### Toby Press, 1951
1 . . . . . . . . . . . . . . . . . . . . . . . . 135.00
2 . . . . . . . . . . . . . . . . . . . . . . . . 100.00

## BIG TOWN
### DC Comics, 1951–58
1 TV, radio tie-in. . . . . . . . . . . 1,100.00

2 . . . . . . . . . . . . . . . . . . . . . . . . 500.00
3 . . . . . . . . . . . . . . . . . . . . . . . . 350.00
4 . . . . . . . . . . . . . . . . . . . . . . . . 350.00
5 . . . . . . . . . . . . . . . . . . . . . . . . 350.00
6 . . . . . . . . . . . . . . . . . . . . . . . . 350.00
7 . . . . . . . . . . . . . . . . . . . . . . . . 350.00
8 . . . . . . . . . . . . . . . . . . . . . . . . 350.00
9 . . . . . . . . . . . . . . . . . . . . . . . . 350.00
10 . . . . . . . . . . . . . . . . . . . . . . . 350.00
11 thru 20 . . . . . . . . . . . . . . . @300.00
21 thru 30 . . . . . . . . . . . . . . . @250.00
31 thru 40 . . . . . . . . . . . . . . . @150.00
41 thru 50. . . . . . . . . . . . . . . . @125.00

## BILL BARNES, AMERICA'S AIR ACE
### See: AIR ACE

## BILL BATTLE, THE ONE-MAN ARMY
### Fawcett Publications 1952–53
1 . . . . . . . . . . . . . . . . . . . . . . . . 200.00
2 . . . . . . . . . . . . . . . . . . . . . . . . 150.00
3 . . . . . . . . . . . . . . . . . . . . . . . . 150.00
4 . . . . . . . . . . . . . . . . . . . . . . . . 150.00

## BILL BOYD WESTERN
### Fawcett Publications, 1950
1 B:Bill Boyd, Midnite,Ph(c) . . . 800.00
2 P(c) . . . . . . . . . . . . . . . . . . . . . 500.00
3 B:Ph(c). . . . . . . . . . . . . . . . . . . 350.00
4 . . . . . . . . . . . . . . . . . . . . . . . . 300.00
5 . . . . . . . . . . . . . . . . . . . . . . . . 300.00
6 . . . . . . . . . . . . . . . . . . . . . . . . 300.00
7 . . . . . . . . . . . . . . . . . . . . . . . . 250.00
8 . . . . . . . . . . . . . . . . . . . . . . . . 250.00
9 . . . . . . . . . . . . . . . . . . . . . . . . 250.00
10 . . . . . . . . . . . . . . . . . . . . . . . 250.00
11 . . . . . . . . . . . . . . . . . . . . . . . 250.00
12 . . . . . . . . . . . . . . . . . . . . . . . 235.00
13 . . . . . . . . . . . . . . . . . . . . . . . 235.00
14 . . . . . . . . . . . . . . . . . . . . . . . 235.00
15 thru 21. . . . . . . . . . . . . . . @235.00
22 E:Ph(c) . . . . . . . . . . . . . . . . . 235.00
23 June, 1952 . . . . . . . . . . . . . . 250.00

## BILL STERN'S SPORTS BOOK
### Approved Comics, Spring-Summer, 1951
1 Ewell Blackwell . . . . . . . . . . . . 300.00

2 . . . . . . . . . . . . . . . . . . . . . . . . 250.00
2-2 EK Giant. . . . . . . . . . . . . . . 300.00

## BILLY AND BUGGY BEAR
### I.W. Enterprises, 1958
1 Funny animal. . . . . . . . . . . . . 100.00

## BILLY BUCKSKIN WESTERN
### Marvel Atlas, Nov., 1955
1 MD,Tales of the Wild Frontier . 250.00
2 MD,Ambush . . . . . . . . . . . . . . 150.00
3 MD,AW, Thieves in the Night . 200.00
Becomes:

## 2-GUN KID
### Marvel, 1956
4 SD,A: Apache Kid . . . . . . . . . 200.00
Becomes:

## TWO-GUN WESTERN
### Marvel, 1956
5 B:Apache Kid,Doc Holiday,
   Kid Colt Outlaw . . . . . . . . . 250.00
6 . . . . . . . . . . . . . . . . . . . . . . . . 225.00
7 . . . . . . . . . . . . . . . . . . . . . . . . 225.00
8 RC . . . . . . . . . . . . . . . . . . . . . . 200.00
9 AW . . . . . . . . . . . . . . . . . . . . . 200.00
10 . . . . . . . . . . . . . . . . . . . . . . . 200.00
11 AW. . . . . . . . . . . . . . . . . . . . . 225.00
12 Sept., 1957,RC . . . . . . . . . . . 200.00

## BILLY BUNNY
### Excellent Publications, 1954
1 . . . . . . . . . . . . . . . . . . . . . . . . 150.00
2 . . . . . . . . . . . . . . . . . . . . . . . . 100.00
3 . . . . . . . . . . . . . . . . . . . . . . . . 100.00
4 . . . . . . . . . . . . . . . . . . . . . . . . 100.00
Ann. #1 Christmas Frolics . . . . . . 225.00

## BILLY THE KID
### Charlton Publ. Co., 1957
9 . . . . . . . . . . . . . . . . . . . . . . . . 150.00
10 . . . . . . . . . . . . . . . . . . . . . . . 125.00
11 O:Ghost Train . . . . . . . . . . . . 150.00
12 . . . . . . . . . . . . . . . . . . . . . . . 125.00
13 AW,AT . . . . . . . . . . . . . . . . . . 150.00
14 . . . . . . . . . . . . . . . . . . . . . . . 125.00
15 AW,O:Billy the Kid. . . . . . . . . 150.00
16 AW . . . . . . . . . . . . . . . . . . . . 150.00
17 . . . . . . . . . . . . . . . . . . . . . . . 125.00
18 . . . . . . . . . . . . . . . . . . . . . . . 125.00
19 . . . . . . . . . . . . . . . . . . . . . . . 125.00

*Billy the Kid Adventure Magazine #3*
*© Toby Press*

*Black Cat #8*
*© Harvey Publications*

*Black Cobra #1*
*© Ajax Farrell Publications*

**BI**

| | |
|---|---|
| 20 JSe | 150.00 |
| 21 JSe | 150.00 |
| 22 JSe | 150.00 |
| 23 JSe | 150.00 |
| 24 JSe | 150.00 |
| 25 JSe | 150.00 |
| 26 JSe | 150.00 |
| 27 | 100.00 |
| 28 | 100.00 |
| 29 | 100.00 |
| 30 Masked Rider | 125.00 |
| 31 thru 40 | @100.00 |

## BILLY THE KID ADVENTURE MAGAZINE
**Toby Press, Oct., 1950**

| | |
|---|---|
| 1 AW(a&c),FF(a&c) | 500.00 |
| 2 Photo (c) | 200.00 |
| 3 AW,FF | 500.00 |
| 4 | 125.00 |
| 5 | 125.00 |
| 6 FF,Photo (c) | 250.00 |
| 7 Photo (c) | 125.00 |
| 8 | 125.00 |
| 9 HK Pot-Shot Pete | 150.00 |
| 10 | 125.00 |
| 11 | 100.00 |
| 12 | 100.00 |
| 13 HK | 100.00 |
| 14 AW,FF | 150.00 |
| 15 thru 21 | @100.00 |
| 22 AW,FF | 125.00 |
| 23 thru 29 | @100.00 |
| 30 1955 | 100.00 |

## BILLY THE KID AND OSCAR
**Fawcett Publications, 1945–46**

| | |
|---|---|
| 1 Funny animal | 250.00 |
| 2 | 200.00 |
| 3 | 200.00 |

## BILLY WEST
**Visual Editions (Standard Comics), 1949–51**

| | |
|---|---|
| 1 | 200.00 |
| 2 | 150.00 |
| 3 | 100.00 |
| 4 | 100.00 |
| 5 | 100.00 |
| 6 | 100.00 |
| 7 | 100.00 |

| | |
|---|---|
| 8 | 100.00 |
| 9 | 125.00 |

## BINGO COMICS
**Howard Publications, 1945**

| | |
|---|---|
| 1 LbC,Drug | 750.00 |

## BINGO, THE MONKEY DOODLE BOY
**St. John Publishing Co. 1951**

| | |
|---|---|
| 1 | 125.00 |
| 1a rep. (1953) | 100.00 |

## BLACK CAT COMICS
**Harvey Publications (Home Comics), June–July, 1946**

| | |
|---|---|
| 1 JKu | 1,200.00 |
| 2 JKu,JSm(c) | 750.00 |
| 3 JSm(c) | 450.00 |
| 4 B:Red Demon | 450.00 |
| 5 S&K | 550.00 |
| 6 S&K,A:Scarlet Arrow, O:Red Demon | 550.00 |
| 7 S&K | 550.00 |
| 8 S&K,B:Kerry Drake | 500.00 |
| 9 S&K,O:Stuntman | 550.00 |
| 10 JK,JSm | 400.00 |
| 11 | 400.00 |
| 12 'Ghost Town Terror' | 400.00 |
| 13 LEI | 375.00 |
| 14 LEI | 375.00 |
| 15 LEI | 375.00 |
| 16 LEI | 375.00 |
| 17 A:Mary Worth, Invisible Scarlet | 375.00 |
| 18 LEI | 375.00 |
| 19 LEI | 375.00 |
| 20 A:Invisible Scarlet | 375.00 |
| 21 LEI | 375.00 |
| 22 LEI thru 26. | @375.00 |
| 27 X-Mas issue | 350.00 |
| 28 I:Kit,A:Crimson Raider | 350.00 |
| 29 Black Cat bondage (c) | 350.00 |

Becomes:

## BLACK CAT MYSTERY
**Aug., 1951**

| | |
|---|---|
| 30 RP,Black Cat(c) | 500.00 |
| 31 RP | 400.00 |
| 32 BP,RP,Bondage (c) | 450.00 |
| 33 BP,RP,Electrocution (c) | 450.00 |
| 34 BP,RP | 300.00 |

| | |
|---|---|
| 35 BP,RP,OK, Atomic Storm | 500.00 |
| 36 RP | 400.00 |
| 37 RP | 300.00 |
| 38 RP | 300.00 |
| 39 RP | 350.00 |
| 40 RP | 300.00 |
| 41 | 300.00 |
| 42 | 300.00 |
| 43 BP | 300.00 |
| 44 BP,HN,JkS,Oil Burning (c) | 450.00 |
| 45 BP,HN,Classic (c) | 600.00 |
| 46 BP,HN | 300.00 |
| 47 BP,HN | 300.00 |
| 48 BP,HN | 300.00 |
| 49 BP,HN | 300.00 |
| 50 BP,Rotting Face | 1,200.00 |
| 51 BP,HN,MMe | 300.00 |
| 52 BP | 250.00 |
| 53 BP | 250.00 |

Becomes:

## BLACK CAT WESTERN
**Feb., 1955**

| | |
|---|---|
| 54 A:Black Cat & Story | 350.00 |
| 55 A:Black Cat | 250.00 |
| 56 same | 250.00 |

Becomes:

## BLACK CAT MYSTIC
**Sept., 1956**

| | |
|---|---|
| 58 JK,Starts Comic Code | 325.00 |
| 59 KB | 250.00 |
| 60 JK | 275.00 |
| 61 Colorama, HN | 250.00 |
| 62 | 175.00 |
| 63 JK | 200.00 |
| 64 JK | 225.00 |
| 65 April, 1963 | 225.00 |

## BLACK COBRA
**Farrell Publications (Ajax), 1954–55**

| | |
|---|---|
| 1 | 500.00 |
| 2 (6) | 350.00 |
| 3 | 300.00 |

Becomes:

## BRIDES DIARY
**Farrell Publications, 1955**

| | |
|---|---|
| 4 | 150.00 |
| 5 | 100.00 |
| 6 | 100.00 |
| 7 | 100.00 |
| 8 | 100.00 |
| 9 | 125.00 |
| 10 | 125.00 |

All comics prices listed are for *Near Mint* condition.

*Uncle Sam Quarterly #4*
© Quality Comics Group

*Blackhawk #27*
© Comic Magazines

*Blackhawk #72*
© Comic Magazines

## BLACK DIAMOND WESTERN
### See: DESPERADO

## BLACK FURY
### Charlton Comics, 1955
1 . . . . . . . . . . . . . . . . . . . . . . . . 150.00
2 . . . . . . . . . . . . . . . . . . . . . . . . 100.00
3 thru 15 . . . . . . . . . . . . . . . . @100.00
16 thru 18 SD . . . . . . . . . . . . . @150.00
19 and 20 . . . . . . . . . . . . . . . . @75.00
21 thru 56 . . . . . . . . . . . . . . . . @75.00
57 March-April, 1966 . . . . . . . . . . 60.00

## UNCLE SAM QUARTERLY
### Quality Comics Group, Fall, 1941
1 BE,LF(c),JCo,O:Uncle Sam . 6,000.00
2 LF&WE(c),DBe, Ray,
   Black Condor . . . . . . . . . . 3,500.00
3 GT(a&c) . . . . . . . . . . . . . . . 2,700.00
4 GT,GF(c) . . . . . . . . . . . . . . . 2,500.00
5 RC,GT . . . . . . . . . . . . . . . . . 2,700.00
6 GT . . . . . . . . . . . . . . . . . . . . 2,500.00
7 Hitler, Tojo, Mussolini . . . . . . 2,700.00
8 GT . . . . . . . . . . . . . . . . . . . . 2,500.00
**Becomes:**

## BLACKHAWK
### Comic Magazines, Winter, 1944
9 Bait for a Death Trap . . . . . . 6,000.00
10 RC . . . . . . . . . . . . . . . . . . . 1,850.00
11 RC . . . . . . . . . . . . . . . . . . . 1,300.00
12 Flies to thrilling adventure . . 1,200.00
13 Blackhawk Stalks Danger . . 1,200.00
14 BWa . . . . . . . . . . . . . . . . . . 1,300.00
15 Patrols the Universe . . . . . . 1,200.00
16 RC,BWa,Huddles for
   Action . . . . . . . . . . . . . . . . 1,200.00
17 BWa,Prepares for Action . . . 1,500.00
18 RC(a&c),BWa,One for All
   and All for One . . . . . . . . . 1,800.00
19 RC(a&c),BWa,Calls
   for Action . . . . . . . . . . . . . . 2,000.00
20 RC(a&c),BWa,Smashes
   Rugoth the Ruthless God . . 1,700.00
21 BWa,Battles Destiny
   Written in Blood . . . . . . . . . 1,200.00
22 RC(a&c),BWa,Fear battles
   Death and Destruction . . . . 1,200.00
23 RC(a&c),BWa,Batters
   Down Oppression . . . . . . . . 1,200.00
24 RC(a&c),BWa . . . . . . . . . . . 1,200.00

25 RC(a&c),BWa,V:The Evil
   of Mung . . . . . . . . . . . . . . . 1,200.00
26 RC(a&c),V:Menace of a
   Sunken World . . . . . . . . . . . 1,100.00
27 BWa,Destroys a War-Mad
   Munitions Magnate . . . . . . . 1,100.00
28 BWa,Defies Destruction in the
   Battle of the Test Tube . . . . 1,100.00
29 BWa,Tale of the Basilisk
   Supreme Chief . . . . . . . . . . 1,100.00
30 BWa,RC(a&c),The Menace
   of the Meteors . . . . . . . . . . 1,100.00
31 BWa,RC(a&c),JCo,Treachery
   among the Blackhawks . . . 1,000.00
32 BWa,RC(a&c),A:Delya,
   Flying Fish . . . . . . . . . . . . . 1,000.00
33 RC,BWa,A:The Mockers . . . 1,000.00
34 BWa,A:Tana,Mavis . . . . . . . 1,000.00
35 BWa,I:Atlo,Strongest Man
   on Earth . . . . . . . . . . . . . . . 1,000.00
36 RC(a&c),BWa,V:Tarya . . . . . 750.00
37 RC(a&c),BWa,V:Sari,The
   Rajah of Ramastan . . . . . . . . 750.00
38 BWa . . . . . . . . . . . . . . . . . . . 750.00
39 RC(a&c),BWa,V:Lilith . . . . . . . 750.00
40 RC(a&c),BWa,Valley of
   Yesterday . . . . . . . . . . . . . . . 750.00
41 RC(a&c),BWa . . . . . . . . . . . . 700.00
42 RC(a&c),BWa,V:Iron Emperor 700.00
43 RC(a&c),BWa,Terror
   from the Catacombs . . . . . . 700.00
44 RC(a&c),BWa, King of Winds . 700.00
45 BWa,The Island of Death . . . . 700.00
46 RC(a&c),BWa,V:DeathPatrol . 700.00
47 RC(a&c),BWa,War! . . . . . . . . 700.00
48 RC(a&c),BWa,A:Hawks of
   Horror,Port of Missing Ships . 700.00
49 RC(a&c),BWa,A:Valkyrie,
   Waters of Terrible Peace . . . . 700.00
50 RC(a&c),BWa,I:Killer Shark,
   Flying Octopus . . . . . . . . . . 750.00
51 BWa,V:The Whip, Whip of
   Nontelon . . . . . . . . . . . . . . . . 700.00
52 RC(a&c),BWa,Traitor in
   the Ranks . . . . . . . . . . . . . . . 700.00
53 RC(a&c),BWa,V:Golden
   Mummy . . . . . . . . . . . . . . . . 700.00
54 RC(a&c),BWa,V:Dr. Deroski,
   Circles of Suicide . . . . . . . . 700.00
55 RC(a&c),BWa,V:Rocketmen . . 700.00
56 RC(a&c),BWa,V:The Instructor,
   School for Sabotage . . . . . . 700.00
57 RC(a&c),BWa,Paralyzed City
   of Armored Men . . . . . . . . . . 700.00
58 RC(a&c),BWa,V:King Cobra,
   The Spider of Delanza . . . . . 700.00

59 BWa,V:Sea Devil . . . . . . . . . 700.00
60 RC(a&c),BWa,V:Dr. Mole and
   His Devils Squadron . . . . . . . 700.00
61 V:John Smith, Stalin's
   Ambassador of Murder . . . . . 600.00
62 V:General X, Return of
   Genghis Kahn . . . . . . . . . . . 600.00
63 RC(a&c),The Flying
   Buzz-Saws . . . . . . . . . . . . . . 600.00
64 RC(a&c),V:Zoltan Korvas,
   Legion of the Damned . . . . . . 600.00
65 Olaf as a Prisoner in Dungeon
   of Fear . . . . . . . . . . . . . . . . . 600.00
66 RC(a&c),V:The Red
   Executioner, Crawler . . . . . . 600.00
67 RC(a&c),V:Future Fuehrer . . . 600.00
68 V:Killers of the Kremlin . . . . . 500.00
69 V:King of the Iron Men,
   Conference of the Dictators . 500.00
70 V:Killer Shark . . . . . . . . . . . . 500.00
71 V:Von Tepp, The Man Who
   could Defeat Blackhawk
   O:Blackhawk . . . . . . . . . . . . . 550.00
72 V:Death Legion . . . . . . . . . . . 500.00
73 V:Hangman,The Tyrannical
   Freaks . . . . . . . . . . . . . . . . . 400.00
74 Plan of Death . . . . . . . . . . . . 400.00
75 V:The Mad Doctor Baroc,
   The Z Bomb Menace . . . . . . . 400.00
76 The King of Blackhawk Island 400.00
77 V:The Fiendish
   Electronic Brain . . . . . . . . . . 400.00
78 V:The Killer Vulture,
   Phantom Raider . . . . . . . . . . 400.00
79 V:Herman Goering, The
   Human Bomb . . . . . . . . . . . . 400.00
80 V:Fang, the Merciless,
   Dr. Death . . . . . . . . . . . . . . . 400.00
81 A:Killer Shark, The Sea
   Monsters of Killer Shark . . . . 400.00
82 V:Sabo Teur, the Ruthless
   Commie Agent . . . . . . . . . . . 400.00
83 I:Hammmer & Sickle, V:Madam
   Double Cross . . . . . . . . . . . . 400.00
84 V:Death Eye,Dr. Genius,
   The Dreaded Brain Beam . . . 400.00
85 V:The Fiendish Impersonator . 400.00
86 V:The Human Torpedoes . . . . 400.00
87 A:Red Agent Sovietta,V:Sea
   Wolf, Le Sabre,Comics Code 300.00
88 V:Thunder the Indestructible,
   The Phantom Sniper . . . . . . . 300.00
89 V:The Super Communists . . . . 400.00
90 V:The Storm King, Villainess
   Who Smashed the Blackhawk
   Team . . . . . . . . . . . . . . . . . . 400.00

All comics prices listed are for *Near Mint* condition.

**BI**

91 Treason in the Underground . . 400.00
92 V:The World Traitor . . . . . . . . 400.00
93 V:Garg the Destroyer,
   O:Blackhawk . . . . . . . . . . . . . 350.00
94 V:Black Widow, Darkk the
   Destroyer . . . . . . . . . . . . . . . 350.00
95 V:Madam Fury, Queen of the
   Pirates . . . . . . . . . . . . . . . . 350.00
96 Doom in the Deep . . . . . . . . . 350.00
97 Revolt of the Slave Workers . . 300.00
98 Temple of Doom . . . . . . . . . . 300.00
99 The War That Never Ended . . 300.00
100 The Delphian Machine . . . . . 325.00
101 Satan's Paymaster . . . . . . . . 275.00
102 The Doom Cloud . . . . . . . . . 275.00
103 The Super Race . . . . . . . . . 275.00
104 The Jet Menace . . . . . . . . . 275.00
105 The Red Kamikaze Terror . . 275.00
106 The Flying Tank Platoon . . . 275.00
107 The Winged Menace . . . . . . 275.00

**DC Comics, 1957**

108 DD,CCu,DD&CCu(c),The Threat
    from the Abyss A:Blaisie . . . . 650.00
109 DD,CCu,DD&CCu(c),The
    Avalance Kid . . . . . . . . . . . . 250.00
110 DD,CCu,DD&CCu(c),Mystery
    of Tigress Island . . . . . . . . . 250.00
111 DD,CCu,DD&CCu(c),Menace
    of the Machines . . . . . . . . . . 250.00
112 DD,CCu,DD(c),The Doomed
    Dog Fight . . . . . . . . . . . . . . . 250.00
113 DD,CCu,CCu(c),Volunteers
    of Doom . . . . . . . . . . . . . . . . 250.00
114 DD,CCu,DD&CCu(c),Gladiators
    of Blackhawk Island . . . . . . . 250.00
115 DD,CCu,DD&CCu(c),The
    Tyrant's Return . . . . . . . . . . . 250.00
116 DD,CCu,DD&CCu(c),Prisoners
    of the Black Island . . . . . . . . 250.00
117 DD,CCu,DD&CCu(c),Menace
    of the Dragon Boat . . . . . . . . 250.00
118 DD,CCu,DD&SMo(c),FF,The
    Bandit With 1,000 Nets . . . . . 260.00
119 DD,CCu,DD&SMo(c),
    V:Chief Blackhawk . . . . . . . . 200.00
120 DD,CCu,DD&SMo(c),The
    Challenge of the Wizard . . . . 200.00
121 DD,CCu,DD&CCu(c),Secret
    Weapon of the Archer . . . . . . 200.00
122 DD,CCu,DD&CCu(c),The
    Movie That Backfired . . . . . . . 200.00
123 DD,CCu,DD&CCu(c),The
    Underseas Gold Fort . . . . . . . 200.00
124 DD,CCu,DD&CCu(c),Thieves
    With A Thousand Faces . . . . 200.00

125 DD,CCu,DD&CCu(c),Secrets
    o/t Blackhawk Time Capsule . 200.00
126 DD,CCu,DD&CCu(c),Secret
    of the Glass Fort . . . . . . . . . . 200.00
127 DD,CCu,DD&CCu(c),Blackie-
    The Winged Sky Fighter . . . . 200.00
128 DD,CCu,DD&CCu(c),The
    Vengeful Bowman . . . . . . . . . 200.00
129 DD,CCu,DD&CCu(c),The
    Cavemen From 3,000 B.C. . . 200.00
130 DD,CCu,DD&SMo(c),The
    Mystery Missle From Space . 200.00
131 DD,CCu,DD&CCu(c),The
    Return of the Rocketeers . . . 150.00
132 DD,CCu,DD&CCu(c),Raid
    of the Rocketeers . . . . . . . . . 150.00
133 DD,CCu,DD&CCu(c),Human
    Dynamo . . . . . . . . . . . . . . . . 150.00
134 DD,CC,DD&CC(c),The
    Sinister Snowman . . . . . . . . . 150.00
135 DD,CCu,DD&CCu(c),The
    Underworld Supermarket . . . 150.00
136 DD,CCu,DD&CCu(c),The
    Menace of the Smoke-Master 150.00
137 DD,CCu,DD&CCu(c),The
    Weapons That Backfired . . . . 150.00
138 DD,CCu,DD&SMo(c),The
    Menace of the Blob . . . . . . . . 150.00
139 DD,CCu,DD&CCu(c),The
    Secret Blackhawk . . . . . . . . . 150.00
140 DD,CCu,DD&CCu(c),The
    Space Age Marauders . . . . . . 150.00
141 DD,CCu,DD&CCu(c),Crimes
    of the Captive Masterminds . 100.00
142 DD,CCu,DD&CCu(c),Alien
    Blackhawk Chief . . . . . . . . . . 100.00
143 DD,SMo,DD&CCu(c),Lady
    Blackhawk's Rival . . . . . . . . . 100.00
144 DD,CCu,DD&CCu(c),The
    Underworld Sportsmen . . . . . 100.00
145 DD,CCu,DD&CCu(c),The
    Deadly Lensman . . . . . . . . . . 100.00
146 DD,CCu,DD&CCu(c),Black-
    hawk's Fantastic Fables . . . . 100.00
147 DD,SMo,DD&CCu(c),The
    Blackhawk Movie Queen . . . . 100.00
148 DD,CCu,DD&CCu(c),Four
    Dooms For The Blackhawks . 100.00
149 DD,CCu,DD&CCu(c),Masks
    of Doom . . . . . . . . . . . . . . . . 100.00
150 DD,CCu,DD&SMo(c), Black-
    hawk Mascot from Space . . . 100.00
151 DD,CCu,Lost City . . . . . . . . 125.00
152 DD,CCu,DD&SMo(c),Noah's
    Ark From Space . . . . . . . . . . . 100.00

153 DD,CCu,DD&SMo(c),
    Boomerang Master . . . . . . . . 100.00
154 DD,CCu,DD&SMo(c),The
    Beast Time Forgot . . . . . . . . . 100.00
155 DD,CCu,DD&CCu(c),Killer
    Shark's Land Armada . . . . . . 100.00
156 DD,CCu,DD&SMo(c),Peril of
    the Plutonian Raider . . . . . . . 100.00
157 DD,CCu,DD&SMo(c),Secret
    of the Blackhawk Sphinx . . . . 100.00
158 DD,CCu,DD&SMo(c),Bandit
    Birds From Space . . . . . . . . . 100.00
159 DD,CCu,DD&SMo(c),Master
    of the Puppet Men . . . . . . . . . 100.00
160 DD,CCu,DD&CCu(c),The
    Phantom Spy . . . . . . . . . . . . . 100.00
161 DD,SMo,DD&SMo(c),Lady
    Blackhawk's Crime Chief . . . . 100.00
162 DD,CCu,DD&CCu(c),The
    Invisible Blackhawk . . . . . . . . 100.00
163 DD,CCu,DD&SMo(c),
    Fisherman of Crime . . . . . . . . 100.00
164 DD,O:Blackhawk retold . . . . 125.00
165 DD,V:League of Anti
    Blackhawks . . . . . . . . . . . . . . 100.00

## BLACK HOOD
### See: LAUGH COMICS

## BLACK JACK
### Charlton Comics, 1957–59

20 . . . . . . . . . . . . . . . . . . . . . . . . 125.00
21 . . . . . . . . . . . . . . . . . . . . . . . . 100.00
22 . . . . . . . . . . . . . . . . . . . . . . . . 125.00
23 AW,AT . . . . . . . . . . . . . . . . . . . 125.00
24 SD . . . . . . . . . . . . . . . . . . . . . . 135.00
25 SD . . . . . . . . . . . . . . . . . . . . . . 135.00
26 SD . . . . . . . . . . . . . . . . . . . . . . 135.00
27 . . . . . . . . . . . . . . . . . . . . . . . . 100.00
28 SD . . . . . . . . . . . . . . . . . . . . . . 135.00
29 . . . . . . . . . . . . . . . . . . . . . . . . 100.00
30 . . . . . . . . . . . . . . . . . . . . . . . . 100.00

## BLACK KNIGHT, THE
### Toby Press, 1953
1 Bondage . . . . . . . . . . . . . . . . 400.00

## BLACK KNIGHT, THE
### Marvel Atlas, 1955–56
1 JMn,O: Crusader;The Black
  Knight Rides . . . . . . . . . . . 1,500.00
2 JMn,Siege on Camelot . . . . . . 900.00

*Black Magic #1*
© Crestwood Prize Publications

*Blackstone The Magician Detective #1*
© E.C. Comics

*Black Terror #18*
© Better Publications

3 JMn,Black Knight Unmasked . 750.00
4 JMn,Betrayed . . . . . . . . . . . . . 750.00
5 JMn,SSh,The Invincible Tartar. 750.00

## BLACK MAGIC
### Crestwood Publ., 1950–51
1 S&K,MMe . . . . . . . . . . . . . 1,900.00
2 S&K,MMe . . . . . . . . . . . . . 1,000.00
3 S&K,MMe . . . . . . . . . . . . . . 900.00
4 S&K,MMe . . . . . . . . . . . . . . 900.00
5 S&K,MMe . . . . . . . . . . . . . . 900.00
6 S&K,MMe . . . . . . . . . . . . . . 900.00
**Volume 2, 1951**
1 S&K,MMe . . . . . . . . . . . . . . 500.00
2 MMe . . . . . . . . . . . . . . . . . . 400.00
3 . . . . . . . . . . . . . . . . . . . . . . 400.00
4 S&K,MMe . . . . . . . . . . . . . . 500.00
5 S&K,MMe . . . . . . . . . . . . . . 500.00
6 . . . . . . . . . . . . . . . . . . . . . . 400.00
7 S&K,MMe . . . . . . . . . . . . . . 500.00
8 MMe . . . . . . . . . . . . . . . . . . 400.00
9 S&K,MMe . . . . . . . . . . . . . . 500.00
10 . . . . . . . . . . . . . . . . . . . . . 400.00
11 MMe . . . . . . . . . . . . . . . . . 400.00
12 S&K,MMe . . . . . . . . . . . . . 400.00
**Volume 3, 1953**
1 S&K,MMe . . . . . . . . . . . . . . 400.00
2 S&K,MMe,AMc . . . . . . . . . . 400.00
3 S&K . . . . . . . . . . . . . . . . . . 400.00
4 S&K . . . . . . . . . . . . . . . . . . 400.00
5 S&K,MMe . . . . . . . . . . . . . . 400.00
6 S&K,MMe . . . . . . . . . . . . . . 400.00
**Volume 4, 1954**
1 S&K . . . . . . . . . . . . . . . . . . 400.00
2 S&K . . . . . . . . . . . . . . . . . . 400.00
3 S&K,SD(2nd work) . . . . . . . . 800.00
4 S&K,SD,eye damage . . . . . . . 600.00
5 S&K,SD . . . . . . . . . . . . . . . . 400.00
6 S&K,BP . . . . . . . . . . . . . . . . 350.00
**Volume 5, 1956**
1 S&K,MMe . . . . . . . . . . . . . . 200.00
2 S&K,MMe . . . . . . . . . . . . . . 200.00
3 S&K . . . . . . . . . . . . . . . . . . 200.00
4 S&K . . . . . . . . . . . . . . . . . . 200.00
5 S&K . . . . . . . . . . . . . . . . . . 200.00
6 S&K . . . . . . . . . . . . . . . . . . 200.00
**Volume 6, 1957**
1 JO . . . . . . . . . . . . . . . . . . . . 150.00
2 JO(c) . . . . . . . . . . . . . . . . . . 150.00
3 JO(c),GT . . . . . . . . . . . . . . . 150.00
4 JO . . . . . . . . . . . . . . . . . . . . 150.00
5 JO(c) . . . . . . . . . . . . . . . . . . 150.00
6 JO(c) . . . . . . . . . . . . . . . . . . 150.00
**Volume 7, 1958**
1 LSt . . . . . . . . . . . . . . . . . . . . 150.00

2 JO . . . . . . . . . . . . . . . . . . . . 150.00
3 & 4 . . . . . . . . . . . . . . . . . @150.00
5 AT,Hitler(c) . . . . . . . . . . . . . . 140.00
6 BP . . . . . . . . . . . . . . . . . . . . 125.00
**Volume 8, 1961**
1 BP . . . . . . . . . . . . . . . . . . . . 100.00
2 BP,SD . . . . . . . . . . . . . . . . . 100.00
3 thru 5 BP . . . . . . . . . . . . . @100.00

## BLACK RIDER
## See: ALL WINNERS
## COMICS

## BLACK RIDER
## RIDES AGAIN
### Marvel Atlas, Sept., 1957
1 JK,Treachery at Hangman's
Ridge . . . . . . . . . . . . . . . . . 350.00

## BLACKSTONE, MASTER
## MAGICIAN COMICS
### Vital/Street & Smith Publ. 1946
1 . . . . . . . . . . . . . . . . . . . . 1,200.00
2 . . . . . . . . . . . . . . . . . . . . 1,000.00
3 . . . . . . . . . . . . . . . . . . . . 1,000.00

## BLACKSTONE, THE
## MAGICIAN DETECTIVE
### EC Comics, 1947
1 Happy Houlihans . . . . . . . . . . 750.00
**Becomes:**

## BLACKSTONE,
## THE MAGICIAN
### Marvel, May, 1948—Sept., 1948
2 B:Blonde Phantom . . . . . . . . 1,000.00
3 BO(c),bondage (c) . . . . . . . . . 650.00
4 Bondage(c) . . . . . . . . . . . . . . 650.00

## BLACK TERROR
### Better Publications/
### Standard, Winter, 1942-43
1 Bombing (c) . . . . . . . . . . . . . 5,000.00
2 V:Arabs,Bondage(c) . . . . . . . 2,000.00
3 V:Nazis,Bondage(c) . . . . . . . 1,200.00
4 ASh(c),V:Sub Nazis . . . . . . . 1,000.00
5 V:Japanese . . . . . . . . . . . . . 1,000.00
6 Air Battle . . . . . . . . . . . . . . . . 900.00
7 Air Battle,V:Japanese,
A:Ghost . . . . . . . . . . . . . . . . 900.00

8 V:Nazis . . . . . . . . . . . . . . . . . 900.00
9 V:Japanese,Bondage(c) . . . . 1,000.00
10 ASh(c),V:Nazis . . . . . . . . . . . 900.00
11 & 12 . . . . . . . . . . . . . . . . @800.00
13 ASh(c) . . . . . . . . . . . . . . . . . 725.00
14 ASh(c) . . . . . . . . . . . . . . . . . 800.00
15 ASh(c) . . . . . . . . . . . . . . . . . 725.00
16 ASh(c) . . . . . . . . . . . . . . . . . 725.00
17 ASh(c),Bondage(c) . . . . . . . . 800.00
18 ASh(c) . . . . . . . . . . . . . . . . . 700.00
19 & 20 ASh . . . . . . . . . . . . . @700.00
21 ASh(c) . . . . . . . . . . . . . . . . . 800.00
22 FF,ASh . . . . . . . . . . . . . . . . 700.00
23 ASh . . . . . . . . . . . . . . . . . . . 700.00
24 Bondgae(c) . . . . . . . . . . . . . 800.00
25 ASh . . . . . . . . . . . . . . . . . . . 700.00
26 GT,ASh(c) . . . . . . . . . . . . . . 700.00
27 MME,GT,ASh . . . . . . . . . . . . 700.00

## BLAZE CARSON
### Marvel, Sept., 1948
1 SSh(c),Fight,Lawman
or Crawl . . . . . . . . . . . . . . . 300.00
2 Guns Roar on Boot Hill . . . . . . 225.00
3 A:Tex Morgan . . . . . . . . . . . . 225.00
4 SSh,A:Two-Gun Kid . . . . . . . . 225.00
5 A:Tex Taylor . . . . . . . . . . . . . 250.00
**Becomes:**

## REX HART
### Marvel, 1949
6 CCB,Ph(c),B:Rex Hart,
A:Black Rider . . . . . . . . . . . . 300.00
7 Ph(c),Mystery at Bar-2 Ranch  200.00
8 Ph(c),The Hombre Who
Killed His Friends . . . . . . . . 200.00
**Becomes:**

## WHIP WILSON
### Marvel, 1950
9 Ph(c),B:Whip Wilson,O:Bullet;
Duel to the Death . . . . . . . . 800.00
10 Ph(c),Wanted for Murder . . . . 400.00
11 Ph(c) . . . . . . . . . . . . . . . . . . 400.00
**Becomes:**

## GUNHAWK, THE
### Marvel, 1950
12 The Redskin's Revenge . . . . . 350.00
13 GT,The Man Who Murdered
Gunhawk . . . . . . . . . . . . . . 300.00
14 . . . . . . . . . . . . . . . . . . . . . . 250.00
15 . . . . . . . . . . . . . . . . . . . . . . 250.00
16 EC . . . . . . . . . . . . . . . . . . . . 250.00
17 . . . . . . . . . . . . . . . . . . . . . . 250.00
18 JMn,Dec., 1951 . . . . . . . . . . 250.00

*Blazing Comics #3*
*© Enwil Associates*

*Blondie Comics*
*© Harvey Publications*

*Blue Beetle #12*
*© Fox Features Syndicate*

BI

## BLAZE, THE WONDER COLLIE
**Marvel, Oct., 1949**
2 Ph(c),Blaze-Son of Fury . . . . . 300.00
3 Ph(c), Lonely Boy;Feb.,1950 . . 300.00

## BLAZING COMICS
**Enwil Associates/Rural Home, June, 1944**
1 B:Green Turtle, Red Hawk,
  Black Buccaneer . . . . . . . 1,000.00
2 Green Turtle (c) . . . . . . . . . . . 700.00
3 Green Turtle (c) . . . . . . . . . . . 650.00
4 Green Turtle (c) . . . . . . . . . . . 650.00
5 March, 1945 . . . . . . . . . . . . . 650.00
5a Black Buccaneer(c),1955. . . . 400.00
6 Indian-Japanese(c), 1955 . . . . 400.00

## BLAZING WEST
**B & I Publ./American Comics 1948**
1 . . . . . . . . . . . . . . . . . . . . . . . 250.00
2 . . . . . . . . . . . . . . . . . . . . . . . 150.00
3 . . . . . . . . . . . . . . . . . . . . . . . 150.00
4 O&I: Little Lobo . . . . . . . . . . . 125.00
5 . . . . . . . . . . . . . . . . . . . . . . . 100.00
6 . . . . . . . . . . . . . . . . . . . . . . . 100.00
7 . . . . . . . . . . . . . . . . . . . . . . . 100.00
8 . . . . . . . . . . . . . . . . . . . . . . . 100.00
9 . . . . . . . . . . . . . . . . . . . . . . . 100.00
10 . . . . . . . . . . . . . . . . . . . . . . 100.00
11 . . . . . . . . . . . . . . . . . . . . . . 100.00
12 . . . . . . . . . . . . . . . . . . . . . . 100.00
13 . . . . . . . . . . . . . . . . . . . . . . 100.00
14 O&I: The Hooded Horseman . 150.00
15 . . . . . . . . . . . . . . . . . . . . . . 125.00
16 . . . . . . . . . . . . . . . . . . . . . . 125.00
17 . . . . . . . . . . . . . . . . . . . . . . 125.00
18 . . . . . . . . . . . . . . . . . . . . . . 125.00
19 . . . . . . . . . . . . . . . . . . . . . . 125.00
20 . . . . . . . . . . . . . . . . . . . . . . 125.00
Becomes:

## HOODED HORSEMAN
**American Comics, 1952–54**
21 . . . . . . . . . . . . . . . . . . . . . . 250.00
22 . . . . . . . . . . . . . . . . . . . . . . 200.00
23 . . . . . . . . . . . . . . . . . . . . . . 150.00
24 . . . . . . . . . . . . . . . . . . . . . . 150.00
25 . . . . . . . . . . . . . . . . . . . . . . 125.00
26 . . . . . . . . . . . . . . . . . . . . . . 150.00
27 . . . . . . . . . . . . . . . . . . . . . . 135.00

## BLAZING WESTERN
**Timor Publications, 1954**
1 . . . . . . . . . . . . . . . . . . . . . . . 200.00
2 thru 5 . . . . . . . . . . . . . . . . . @100.00

## BLONDE PHANTOM
## See: ALL-SELECT COMICS

## BLONDIE COMICS
**David McKay, Spring, 1947**
1 . . . . . . . . . . . . . . . . . . . . . . . 300.00
2 . . . . . . . . . . . . . . . . . . . . . . . 150.00
3 . . . . . . . . . . . . . . . . . . . . . . . 125.00
4 . . . . . . . . . . . . . . . . . . . . . . . 125.00
5 . . . . . . . . . . . . . . . . . . . . . . . 125.00
6 thru 10 . . . . . . . . . . . . . . . . @100.00
11 thru 15 . . . . . . . . . . . . . . . @100.00
**Harvey Publications, 1950**
16 . . . . . . . . . . . . . . . . . . . . . . 150.00
17 thru 20 . . . . . . . . . . . . . . . @125.00
21 thru 30 . . . . . . . . . . . . . . . @100.00
31 thru 50 . . . . . . . . . . . . . . . @100.00
51 thru 80 . . . . . . . . . . . . . . . @100.00
81 thru 99 . . . . . . . . . . . . . . . @100.00
100 . . . . . . . . . . . . . . . . . . . . . 110.00
101 thru 124 . . . . . . . . . . . . . @100.00
125 Giant, 80-pg. . . . . . . . . . . . 125.00
126 thru 136 . . . . . . . . . . . . . @100.00
137 Giant, 80-pg. . . . . . . . . . . . 125.00
138 thru 139 . . . . . . . . . . . . . @100.00
140 Giant, 80-pg. . . . . . . . . . . . 125.00
141 thru 147 . . . . . . . . . . . . . @100.00
148 Giant, 68-pg. . . . . . . . . . . . 125.00
149 thru 154 . . . . . . . . . . . . . @100.00
155 Giant, 68-pg. . . . . . . . . . . . 125.00
156 . . . . . . . . . . . . . . . . . . . . . 100.00
157 thru 159 Giant, 68-pg. . . . @125.00
160 . . . . . . . . . . . . . . . . . . . . . 100.00
161 thru 163 Giant, 68-pg. . . . @125.00
*See also: DAISY AND HER PUPS*

## BLOOD IS THE HARVEST
**Catechetical Guild 1950**
N# Comunist menace . . . . . . . 2,000.00

## BLUE BEETLE, THE
**Fox Features Syndicate/ Holyoke Publ., Winter 1939**
1 O:Blue Beetle,A:Master
  Magician . . . . . . . . . . . . . . 7,000.00

2 BP,Wonder World . . . . . . . . 2,500.00
3 JSm(c) . . . . . . . . . . . . . . . . 1,600.00
4 Mentions marijuana . . . . . . . 1,500.00
5 GT,A:Zanzibar the Magician 1,300.00
6 B:Dynamite Thor,
  O:Blue Beetle . . . . . . . . . 1,300.00
7 A:Dynamo . . . . . . . . . . . . . 1,200.00
8 E:Thor,A:Dynamo . . . . . . . . 1,200.00
9 BP(c),A:Black Bird,Gorilla . . 1,200.00
10 BP(c),A:Black Bird,
  bondage(c) . . . . . . . . . . . . 1,200.00
11 BP(c),A:Gladiator . . . . . . . . 1,000.00
12 A:Black Fury. . . . . . . . . . . . 1,000.00
13 B:V-Man . . . . . . . . . . . . . . 1,000.00
14 JKu,I:Sparky. . . . . . . . . . . . 1,000.00
15 JKu . . . . . . . . . . . . . . . . . . 1,000.00
16 . . . . . . . . . . . . . . . . . . . . . 1,000.00
17 AyB,A:Mimic. . . . . . . . . . . . 1,000.00
18 JKu,E:V-Man,A:Red Knight . 1,000.00
19 JKu,A:Dascomb Dinsmore. . 1,000.00
20 I&O:Flying Tiger Squadron . 1,000.00
21 . . . . . . . . . . . . . . . . . . . . . . 900.00
22 A:Ali-Baba . . . . . . . . . . . . . . 900.00
23 A:Jimmy DooLittle . . . . . . . . . 900.00
24 I:The Halo . . . . . . . . . . . . . . 900.00
25 . . . . . . . . . . . . . . . . . . . . . . 900.00
26 General Patton story . . . . . . 1,000.00
27 A:Tamoa . . . . . . . . . . . . . . . 900.00
28 . . . . . . . . . . . . . . . . . . . . . . 800.00
29 . . . . . . . . . . . . . . . . . . . . . . 800.00
30 L:Holyoke . . . . . . . . . . . . . . 800.00
31 F:Fox. . . . . . . . . . . . . . . . . . 775.00
32 Hitler (c) . . . . . . . . . . . . . . . 900.00
33 Fight for Freedom . . . . . . . . . 775.00
34 A:Black Terror,Menace of K-4 . 775.00
35 Threat From Saturn . . . . . . . . 775.00
36 The Runaway House . . . . . . . 775.00
37 Inside the House. . . . . . . . . . 775.00
38 Revolt of the Zombies. . . . . . 775.00
39 . . . . . . . . . . . . . . . . . . . . . . 775.00
40 . . . . . . . . . . . . . . . . . . . . . . 775.00
41 A:O'Brine Twins . . . . . . . . . . 750.00
42 . . . . . . . . . . . . . . . . . . . . . . 750.00
43 . . . . . . . . . . . . . . . . . . . . . . 750.00
44 . . . . . . . . . . . . . . . . . . . . . . 750.00
45 . . . . . . . . . . . . . . . . . . . . . . 750.00
46 BP,A:Puppeteer. . . . . . . . . . 750.00
47 JKa,V:Junior Crime Club . . 1,700.00
48 JKa,A:Black Lace. . . . . . . . 1,400.00
49 JKa. . . . . . . . . . . . . . . . . . 1,400.00
50 JKa,The Ambitious Bride . . 1,400.00
51 JKa, Shady Lady . . . . . . . . 1,200.00
52 BP,JKa(c),Bondage (c) . . . 1,700.00
53 JKa,A:Jack "Legs"
  Diamond,Bondage(c) . . . . 1,200.00
54 JKa,The Vanishing Nude . . 1,800.00

**BI**

Blue Bolt #11
© Funnies, Inc.

Blue Bolt #102
© Star Publications

Ghostly Weird Stories #120
© Star Publications

55 JKa . . . . . . . . . . . . . . . . . . 1,100.00
56 JKa,Tri-State Terror . . . . . . . 1,100.00
57 JKa,The Feagle Bros. . . . . . 1,100.00
58 . . . . . . . . . . . . . . . . . . . . . . 200.00
59 . . . . . . . . . . . . . . . . . . . . . . 200.00
60 Aug., 1960 . . . . . . . . . . . . . . 225.00

## BLUE BEETLE
### See: THING!, THE

## BLUE BOLT
**Funnies, Inc./Novelty Press/
Premium Service Co, 1940**
1 JSm,PGv,O:Blue Bolt . . . . . 6,500.00
2 JSm,S&K . . . . . . . . . . . . . . 3,000.00
3 S&K,A:Space Hawk . . . . . . . 2,500.00
4 S&K,BEv(c) . . . . . . . . . . . . . 2,000.00
5 BEv,S&K,B:Sub Zero . . . . . . 2,000.00
6 JK,JSm . . . . . . . . . . . . . . . 1,900.00
7 S&K,BEv . . . . . . . . . . . . . . 1,900.00
8 PGv,S&K(c) . . . . . . . . . . . . 1,900.00
9 . . . . . . . . . . . . . . . . . . . . . 1,700.00
10 PGv,S&K(c) . . . . . . . . . . . . 1,700.00
11 BEv(c) . . . . . . . . . . . . . . . . 1,700.00
12 PGv . . . . . . . . . . . . . . . . . 1,700.00
2-1 BEv(c),PG,O:Dick Cole &
  V:Simba . . . . . . . . . . . . . . . 700.00
2-2 BEv(c),FGu,O:Twister . . . . . 550.00
2-3 PGv,Cole vs Simba . . . . . . . 400.00
2-4 BD . . . . . . . . . . . . . . . . . . 400.00
2-5 I:Freezum . . . . . . . . . . . . . 400.00
2-6 PGv,O:Sgt.Spook, Dick Cole . 350.00
2-7 BD,Lois Blake . . . . . . . . . . . 350.00
2-8 BD . . . . . . . . . . . . . . . . . . 350.00
2-9 JW . . . . . . . . . . . . . . . . . . 350.00
2-10 JW . . . . . . . . . . . . . . . . . 350.00
2-11 JW . . . . . . . . . . . . . . . . . 350.00
2-12 E:Twister . . . . . . . . . . . . . 350.00
3-1 A:115th Infantry . . . . . . . . . 350.00
3-2 A:Phantom Sub . . . . . . . . . 350.00
3-3 . . . . . . . . . . . . . . . . . . . . 350.00
3-4 JW(c) . . . . . . . . . . . . . . . . 250.00
3-5 Jor . . . . . . . . . . . . . . . . . . 250.00
3-6 Jor . . . . . . . . . . . . . . . . . . 250.00
3-7 X-Mas (c) . . . . . . . . . . . . . 250.00
3-8 . . . . . . . . . . . . . . . . . . . . 250.00
3-9 A:Phantom Sub . . . . . . . . . 250.00
3-10 DBa . . . . . . . . . . . . . . . . 250.00
3-11 April Fools (c). . . . . . . . . . . 250.00
3-12 . . . . . . . . . . . . . . . . . . . 250.00
4-1 Hitler,Tojo,Mussolini (c) . . . . 600.00
4-2 Liberty Bell (c) . . . . . . . . . . 200.00
4-3 What are You Doing for Your
  Country . . . . . . . . . . . . . . . 200.00

4-4 I Fly for Vengence . . . . . . . . 200.00
4-5 TFH(c) . . . . . . . . . . . . . . . 200.00
4-6 HcK . . . . . . . . . . . . . . . . . 200.00
4-7 JWi(c) . . . . . . . . . . . . . . . . 200.00
4-8 E:Sub Zero . . . . . . . . . . . . 200.00
4-9 . . . . . . . . . . . . . . . . . . . . 200.00
4-10 . . . . . . . . . . . . . . . . . . . 200.00
4-11 . . . . . . . . . . . . . . . . . . . 200.00
4-12 . . . . . . . . . . . . . . . . . . . 200.00
5-1 thru 5-12. . . . . . . . . . . . . @175.00
6-1 . . . . . . . . . . . . . . . . . . . . 175.00
6-2 War Bonds (c) . . . . . . . . . . 175.00
6-3 . . . . . . . . . . . . . . . . . . . . 175.00
6-4 Racist(c). . . . . . . . . . . . . . 300.00
6-5 Soccer (c) . . . . . . . . . . . . . 175.00
6-6 thru 6-12. . . . . . . . . . . . . @175.00
7-1 thru 7-12. . . . . . . . . . . . . @175.00
8-1 Baseball (c) . . . . . . . . . . . . 175.00
8-2 JHa . . . . . . . . . . . . . . . . . 175.00
8-3 JH . . . . . . . . . . . . . . . . . . 175.00
8-4 JHa . . . . . . . . . . . . . . . . . 175.00
8-5 JH . . . . . . . . . . . . . . . . . . 175.00
8-6 JDo . . . . . . . . . . . . . . . . . 175.00
8-7 LbC(c). . . . . . . . . . . . . . . 350.00
8-8 . . . . . . . . . . . . . . . . . . . . 175.00
8-9 AMc(c) . . . . . . . . . . . . . . . 175.00
8-10 . . . . . . . . . . . . . . . . . . . 175.00
8-11 Basketball (c) . . . . . . . . . . 200.00
8-12 . . . . . . . . . . . . . . . . . . . 175.00
9-1 AMc,Baseball (c) . . . . . . . . 175.00
9-2 AMc . . . . . . . . . . . . . . . . . 175.00
9-3 . . . . . . . . . . . . . . . . . . . . 175.00
9-4 JH . . . . . . . . . . . . . . . . . . 175.00
9-5 JH . . . . . . . . . . . . . . . . . . 175.00
9-6 LbC(c),Football (c) . . . . . . . 300.00
9-7 JH . . . . . . . . . . . . . . . . . . 175.00
9-8 Hockey (c) . . . . . . . . . . . . 185.00
9-9 LbC(c),3-D effect . . . . . . . . 275.00
9-10 . . . . . . . . . . . . . . . . . . . 175.00
9-11 . . . . . . . . . . . . . . . . . . . 175.00
9-12 . . . . . . . . . . . . . . . . . . . 175.00
10-1 Baseball (c),3-D effect. . . . . 200.00
10-2 3-D effect. . . . . . . . . . . . . 200.00
### Star Publications, 1949
102 LbC(c),Chameleon . . . . . . . 550.00
103 LbC(c),same . . . . . . . . . . . 500.00
104 LbC(c),same . . . . . . . . . . . 500.00
105 LbC(c),O:Blue Bolt Space,
  Drug Story . . . . . . . . . . . . . 900.00
106 S&K,LbC(c),A:Space Hawk . 800.00
107 S&K,LbC(c),A:Space Hawk . 800.00
108 S&K,LbC(c),A:Blue Bolt . . . . 800.00
109 BW,LbC(c). . . . . . . . . . . . . 800.00
110 B:Horror (c)s,A:Target . . . . . 800.00
111 Weird Tales of Terror,
  A:Red Rocket . . . . . . . . . . . 800.00

112 JyD . . . . . . . . . . . . . . . . . 700.00
113 BW,JyD,A:Space Hawk . . . . . 700.00
114 LbC(c),JyD . . . . . . . . . . . . 700.00
115 LbC(c),JyD,A:Sgt.Spook . . . . 700.00
116 LbC(c),JyD,A:Jungle Joe . . . 700.00
117 LbC(c),A:Blue Bolt,Jo-Jo. . . . 700.00
118 WW,LbC(c),A:White Spirit . . . 700.00
119 LbC(c) . . . . . . . . . . . . . . . 700.00
**Becomes:**

## GHOSTLY WEIRD
## STORIES
**Star Publications, Sept., 1953**
120 LbC,A:Jo-Jo . . . . . . . . . . . 750.00
121 LbC,A:Jo-Jo . . . . . . . . . . . 700.00
122 LbC,A:The Mask,Sci-Fi. . . . . 750.00
123 LbC,A:Jo-Jo . . . . . . . . . . . 600.00
124 LbC, Sept., 1954. . . . . . . . . 600.00

## BLUE CIRCLE COMICS
**Enwil Associates/
Rural Home, June, 1944**
1 B:Blue Circle,O:Steel Fist . . . . 500.00
2 . . . . . . . . . . . . . . . . . . . . . . 350.00
3 Hitler parody (c) . . . . . . . . . . . 400.00
4 . . . . . . . . . . . . . . . . . . . . . . 300.00
5 E:Steel Fist,A:DriftwoodDavey. 300.00
6 . . . . . . . . . . . . . . . . . . . . . . 300.00

## BLUE RIBBON COMICS
**MLJ Magazines, Nov., 1939**
1 JCo,B:Dan Hastings,
  Richy-Amazing Boy . . . . . . 7,000.00
2 JCo,B:Bob Phantom,
  Silver Fox . . . . . . . . . . . . 3,000.00
3 JCo,A:Phantom,Silver Fox . . 2,500.00
4 O:Fox,Ty Gor,B:Doc Strong,
  Hercules . . . . . . . . . . . . . 2,600.00
5 Gattling Gun (c) . . . . . . . . . 1,500.00
6 Amazing Boy Richy (c) . . . . . 1,400.00
7 A:Fox (c),Corporal Collins
  V:Nazis . . . . . . . . . . . . . . 1,400.00
8 E:Hercules . . . . . . . . . . . . 1,400.00
9 SCp,O&I:Mr. Justice . . . . . . 6,000.00
10 SCp,Mr. Justice . . . . . . . . 2,500.00
11 CBi,MMe,SCp(c) . . . . . . . . 2,500.00
12 SCp,MMe,CBi,E:Doc Strong 2,500.00
13 CBi,IN,MMe,B:Inferno . . . . . 2,500.00
14 MMe,CBi,SCp(c),A:Inferno . 2,200.00
15 A:Inferno,E:Green Falcon . . 2,200.00
16 SCp(c),O:Captain Flag . . . . 3,000.00
17 Captain Flag, V:Black Hand. . 2,200.00
18 SCp(c),Captain Flag . . . . . 2,000.00
19 Captain Flag (c) . . . . . . . . 2,000.00

*Blue Ribbon Comics #12*
© MLJ Magazines

*Bob Colt #1*
© Fawcett Publications

*Bob Swift #5*
© Fawcett Publications

**Bo**

20 Captain Flag V:Nazis (c) . . . 2,200.00
21 Captain Flag V:Death . . . . . 2,000.00
22 Circus (c), March, 1942 . . . . 2,000.00

## BLUE RIBBON COMICS
**St. John Publications,
Feb., 1949**
1 Heckle & Jeckle . . . . . . . . . . 150.00
2 MB(c),Diary Secrets . . . . . . . 250.00
3 MB,MB(c),Heckle & Jeckle . . . 150.00
4 Teen-age Diary Secrets . . . . . 250.00
5 MB,Teen-age Diary Secrets. . . 350.00
6 Dinky Duck . . . . . . . . . . . . . . 100.00

## BO
**Charlton Comics, June, 1955**
1 . . . . . . . . . . . . . . . . . . . . . . . . 100.00
2 . . . . . . . . . . . . . . . . . . . . . . . . 100.00
3 Oct., 1955 . . . . . . . . . . . . . . . 100.00
Becomes:

## TOM CAT
**Charlton Comics, 1956**
4 Funny animal-cat . . . . . . . . . . 100.00
5 . . . . . . . . . . . . . . . . . . . . . . . . . 75.00
6 . . . . . . . . . . . . . . . . . . . . . . . . . 75.00
7 . . . . . . . . . . . . . . . . . . . . . . . . . 75.00
8 . . . . . . . . . . . . . . . . . . . . . . . . . 75.00
Becomes:

## ATOM THE CAT
**Charlton Comics, 1957–58**
9 . . . . . . . . . . . . . . . . . . . . . . . . 100.00
10 . . . . . . . . . . . . . . . . . . . . . . . . 75.00
11 Atomic Mouse . . . . . . . . . . . . 125.00
12 Atomic Mouse . . . . . . . . . . . . 125.00
13 . . . . . . . . . . . . . . . . . . . . . . . . 75.00
14 . . . . . . . . . . . . . . . . . . . . . . . . 75.00
15 . . . . . . . . . . . . . . . . . . . . . . . . 75.00
16 . . . . . . . . . . . . . . . . . . . . . . . . 75.00
17 . . . . . . . . . . . . . . . . . . . . . . . . 75.00

## BOB & BETTY &
## SANTA'S WISHING WELL
**Sears-Roebuck Co., 1941**
N# Giveaway . . . . . . . . . . . . . . . 300.00

## BOBBY BENSON'S
## B-BAR-B RIDERS
**Parkway Publ. Co.
(M.E. Entertainment), 1950**
1 BP, Teen-age cowboy . . . . . . . 750.00

2 BP . . . . . . . . . . . . . . . . . . . . . 300.00
3 BP . . . . . . . . . . . . . . . . . . . . . 250.00
4 BP . . . . . . . . . . . . . . . . . . . . . 250.00
5 BP . . . . . . . . . . . . . . . . . . . . . 250.00
6 BP . . . . . . . . . . . . . . . . . . . . . 250.00
7 BP . . . . . . . . . . . . . . . . . . . . . 250.00
8 BP . . . . . . . . . . . . . . . . . . . . . 250.00
9 BP,FF(c) . . . . . . . . . . . . . . . . . 500.00
10 BP . . . . . . . . . . . . . . . . . . . . . 200.00
11 BP,FF(c) . . . . . . . . . . . . . . . . 500.00
12 BP . . . . . . . . . . . . . . . . . . . . . 150.00
13 DAy,FF(c),A:Ghost Rider . . . . 500.00
14 DAy,A:Ghost Rider,bondage . . 400.00
15 DAy,A:Ghost Rider . . . . . . . . 350.00
16 photo(c) . . . . . . . . . . . . . . . . 200.00
17 . . . . . . . . . . . . . . . . . . . . . . . 150.00
18 . . . . . . . . . . . . . . . . . . . . . . . 150.00
19 . . . . . . . . . . . . . . . . . . . . . . . 150.00

## BOBBY COMICS
**Universal Phoenix
Features, 1946**
1 . . . . . . . . . . . . . . . . . . . . . . . . 200.00

## BOB COLT
**Fawcett Publications,
Nov., 1950**
1 B:Bob Colt,Buck Skin . . . . . . . 600.00
2 Death Round Train . . . . . . . . . 400.00
3 Mysterious Black Knight of the
Prairie . . . . . . . . . . . . . . . . . 300.00
4 Death Goes Downstream . . . . 300.00
5 The Mesa of Mystery . . . . . . . 300.00
6 The Mysterious Visitors . . . . . 300.00
7 Dragon of Disaster . . . . . . . . . 250.00
8 Redman's Revenge . . . . . . . . 250.00
9 Hidden Hacienda . . . . . . . . . . 250.00
10 Fiend from Vulture
Mountain . . . . . . . . . . . . . . . 250.00

## BOB STEELE WESTERN
**Fawcett Publications, 1950–52**
1 Photo(c) . . . . . . . . . . . . . . . . . 800.00
2 Ph(c); Dynamite Death . . . . . . 400.00
3 Ph(c); The Perilous Deadline. . 300.00
4 Ph(c); Six-Gun Menace . . . . . . 300.00
5 Ph(c); Murder on the Hoof. . . . 300.00
6 Ph(c); Range War . . . . . . . . . . 250.00
7 Ph(c); Tall Timber Terror . . . . . 250.00
8 Ph(c); The Race of Death . . . . 250.00
9 Ph(c); Death Rides the Storm . 250.00
10 Ph(c); Draw...Or Die . . . . . . . 250.00

## BOB SWIFT
**Fawcett Publications 1951–52**
1 Boy sportsman . . . . . . . . . . . . 150.00
2 . . . . . . . . . . . . . . . . . . . . . . . . 100.00
3 . . . . . . . . . . . . . . . . . . . . . . . . 100.00
4 . . . . . . . . . . . . . . . . . . . . . . . . 100.00
5 . . . . . . . . . . . . . . . . . . . . . . . . 100.00

## BOLD STORIES
**Kirby Publishing Co., 1950**
1 WW,Near nudity (c) . . . . . . . 2,200.00
2 GI,Cobra's Kiss . . . . . . . . . . 1,500.00
3 WW,Orge of Paris . . . . . . . . 1,500.00
4 Case of the Winking Buddha. . 800.00
5 It Rhymes with Lust . . . . . . . . 800.00
6 Candid Tales, April, 1950 . . . . 800.00

## BOMBER COMICS
**Elliot Publishing Co., 1944**
1 B:Wonder Boy,Kismet,
Eagle Evans . . . . . . . . . 1,500.00
2 Wonder Boy(c) Hitler . . . . . . 1,000.00
3 Wonder Boy-Kismet (c) . . . . . 600.00
4 Hitler,Tojo, Mussolini (c) . . . 1,200.00

## BOOK OF ALL COMICS
**William H. Wise, 1945**
1 A:Green Mask,Puppeteer . . . . 600.00

## BOOK OF COMICS, THE
**William H. Wise, 1945**
N# A:Captain V . . . . . . . . . . . . . 600.00

## BOOTS AND
## HER BUDDIES
**Visual Editions
(Standard Comics), 1948–49**
5 Cowgirl . . . . . . . . . . . . . . . . . 250.00
6 . . . . . . . . . . . . . . . . . . . . . . . . 200.00
7 . . . . . . . . . . . . . . . . . . . . . . . . 225.00
8 . . . . . . . . . . . . . . . . . . . . . . . . 200.00
9 FF . . . . . . . . . . . . . . . . . . . . . 450.00

## BORDER PATROL
**P.L. Publishing Co., 1951**
1 Wild West . . . . . . . . . . . . . . . . 200.00
2 . . . . . . . . . . . . . . . . . . . . . . . . 150.00
3 . . . . . . . . . . . . . . . . . . . . . . . . 150.00

---

All comics prices listed are for *Near Mint* condition.     **Page 65**

*The Bouncer #14*
© Fox Features Syndicate

*Boy Comics #59*
© Lev Gleason Publications

*Boy Commandos #29*
© DC Comics

## THE BOUNCER

**Fox Features Syndicate, 1944**
N# (10). . . . . . . . . . . . . . . . . . . . 500.00
11 O:The Bouncer . . . . . . . . . . . 400.00
12 . . . . . . . . . . . . . . . . . . . . . . . 300.00
13 . . . . . . . . . . . . . . . . . . . . . . . 300.00
14 rep. #(10) . . . . . . . . . . . . . . 300.00

## BOY COMICS

**Comic House, Inc.**
**(Lev Gleason Publ.) April, 1942**
3 O:Crimebuster,Bombshell,Young
   Robin, B:Yankee Longago,
   Swoop Storm . . . . . . . . . . 7,000.00
4 Hitler,Tojo,Mussolini (c) . . . . 2,500.00
5 Crimebuster saves day (c) . 2,000.00
6 O:Iron Jaw & Death of Son,
   B:Little Dynamite . . . . . . . . 5,000.00
7 Hitler,Tojo,Mussolini (c) . . . . 2,000.00
8 D:Iron Jaw . . . . . . . . . . . . . . 2,100.00
9 I:He-She . . . . . . . . . . . . . . . . 2,000.00
10 Iron Jaw returns . . . . . . . . . 2,300.00
11 Iron Jaw falls in love . . . . . . 1,800.00
12 Crimebuster V:Japanese . . . 1,000.00
13 V:New,more terrible
   Iron Jaw . . . . . . . . . . . . . . 1,000.00
14 V:Iron Jaw . . . . . . . . . . . . . . 1,000.00
15 I:Rodent,D:Iron Jaw . . . . . . . 1,200.00
16 Crimebuster V:Knight . . . . . . . 600.00
17 Flag (c),Crimebuster
   V:Moth . . . . . . . . . . . . . . . . . 600.00
18 Smashed car (c) . . . . . . . . . . 550.00
19 Express train (c) . . . . . . . . . . 550.00
20 Coffin (c) . . . . . . . . . . . . . . . . 550.00
21 Boxing (c) . . . . . . . . . . . . . . . 400.00
22 Under Sea (c) . . . . . . . . . . . . 400.00
23 Golf (c) . . . . . . . . . . . . . . . . . 400.00
24 County insane asylum (c). . . . 400.00
25 52 pgs . . . . . . . . . . . . . . . . . . 400.00
26 68 pgs. . . . . . . . . . . . . . . . . . . 400.00
27 Express train (c) . . . . . . . . . . 450.00
28 E:Yankee Longago . . . . . . . . 450.00
29 Prison break (c) . . . . . . . . . . . 450.00
30 O:Crimebuster,Murder (c) . . . 600.00
31 68 pgs . . . . . . . . . . . . . . . . . . 400.00
32 E:Young Robin Hood . . . . . . . 400.00
33 . . . . . . . . . . . . . . . . . . . . . . . . 400.00
34 Suicide (c) & story . . . . . . . . . 350.00
35 . . . . . . . . . . . . . . . . . . . . . . . . 300.00
36 . . . . . . . . . . . . . . . . . . . . . . . . 300.00
37 . . . . . . . . . . . . . . . . . . . . . . . . 300.00
38 . . . . . . . . . . . . . . . . . . . . . . . . 300.00
39 E:Little Dynamite. . . . . . . . . . 300.00
40 . . . . . . . . . . . . . . . . . . . . . . . . 300.00

41 thru 50. . . . . . . . . . . . . . . @275.00
51 thru 56. . . . . . . . . . . . . . . @250.00
57 B:Dilly Duncan . . . . . . . . . . . 275.00
58 . . . . . . . . . . . . . . . . . . . . . . . . 250.00
59 . . . . . . . . . . . . . . . . . . . . . . . . 250.00
60 Iron Jaw returns . . . . . . . . . . 275.00
61 O:Iron Jaw,Crimebuster . . . . 300.00
62 A:Iron Jaw . . . . . . . . . . . . . . . 275.00
63 thru 70 . . . . . . . . . . . . . . . @200.00
71 E:Dilly Duncan . . . . . . . . . . . 200.00
72 . . . . . . . . . . . . . . . . . . . . . . . . 200.00
73 . . . . . . . . . . . . . . . . . . . . . . . . 200.00
74 thru 79. . . . . . . . . . . . . . . @200.00
80 I:Rocky X . . . . . . . . . . . . . . . 150.00
81 thru 88. . . . . . . . . . . . . . . @150.00
89 A:The Claw . . . . . . . . . . . . . . 200.00
90 same . . . . . . . . . . . . . . . . . . . 200.00
91 same . . . . . . . . . . . . . . . . . . . 200.00
92 same . . . . . . . . . . . . . . . . . . . 200.00
93 The Claw(c),A:Rocky X . . . . . 200.00
94 . . . . . . . . . . . . . . . . . . . . . . . . 150.00
95 . . . . . . . . . . . . . . . . . . . . . . . . 150.00
96 . . . . . . . . . . . . . . . . . . . . . . . . 150.00
97 . . . . . . . . . . . . . . . . . . . . . . . . 150.00
98 A:Rocky X . . . . . . . . . . . . . . . 150.00
99 . . . . . . . . . . . . . . . . . . . . . . . . 150.00
100 . . . . . . . . . . . . . . . . . . . . . . . 175.00
101 . . . . . . . . . . . . . . . . . . . . . . . 175.00
102 . . . . . . . . . . . . . . . . . . . . . . . 175.00
103 thru 118. . . . . . . . . . . . . . @175.00
119 March, 1956 . . . . . . . . . . . 175.00

## BOY COMMANDOS

**DC Comics, Winter, 1942–43**
1 S&K,O:Liberty Belle;Sandman
   & Newsboy Legion . . . . . 13,000.00
2 S&K,Hitler(c). . . . . . . . . . . . 4,000.00
3 S&K,WWII(c). . . . . . . . . . . . 1,700.00
4 WWII(c). . . . . . . . . . . . . . . . 1,400.00
5 WWII(c). . . . . . . . . . . . . . . . 1,400.00
6 S&K,WWII(c). . . . . . . . . . . . 1,400.00
7 S&K,WWII(c) . . . . . . . . . . . . . 900.00
8 S&K,WWII(c) . . . . . . . . . . . . . 900.00
9 WWII(c). . . . . . . . . . . . . . . . 1,000.00
10 S&K,WWII(c). . . . . . . . . . . . . 900.00
11 WWII(c). . . . . . . . . . . . . . . . . 900.00
12 WWII(c). . . . . . . . . . . . . . . . . 900.00
13 WWII(c). . . . . . . . . . . . . . . . . 900.00
14 . . . . . . . . . . . . . . . . . . . . . . . . 900.00
15 1st Crazy Quilt . . . . . . . . . . . 800.00
16 . . . . . . . . . . . . . . . . . . . . . . . . 700.00
17 Science Fiction(c) . . . . . . . . . 800.00
18 S&K . . . . . . . . . . . . . . . . . . . . 600.00
19 S&K. . . . . . . . . . . . . . . . . . . . 600.00
20 Science Fiction (c) . . . . . . . . 800.00

21 . . . . . . . . . . . . . . . . . . . . . . . . 500.00
22 Judy Canova. . . . . . . . . . . . . 500.00
23 S&K,S&K,(c) . . . . . . . . . . . . 600.00
24 Superhero . . . . . . . . . . . . . . . 600.00
25 superhero(c) . . . . . . . . . . . . 550.00
26 Science Fiction(c) . . . . . . . . 550.00
27 . . . . . . . . . . . . . . . . . . . . . . . . 600.00
28 . . . . . . . . . . . . . . . . . . . . . . . . 650.00
29 S&K story . . . . . . . . . . . . . . . 600.00
30 Baseball Story. . . . . . . . . . . . 650.00
31 . . . . . . . . . . . . . . . . . . . . . . . . 600.00
32 A:Dale Evans(c) . . . . . . . . . . 650.00
33 . . . . . . . . . . . . . . . . . . . . . . . . 500.00
34 I:Wolf. . . . . . . . . . . . . . . . . . . 500.00
35 . . . . . . . . . . . . . . . . . . . . . . . . 500.00
36 Sci-Fi(c),Nov.–Dec., 1949. . . 600.00

## BOY DETECTIVE

**Avon Periodicals, 1951–52**
1 F:Dan Tayler . . . . . . . . . . . . . 300.00
2 Vice Lords of Crime . . . . . . . . 200.00
3 Spy Menace . . . . . . . . . . . . . . 200.00
4 The Death Trap . . . . . . . . . . . 200.00

## BOY EXPLORERS
## See: TERRY AND
## THE PIRATES

## BOY MEETS GIRL

**Lev Gleason Publ., 1950–52**
1 Romance . . . . . . . . . . . . . . . . 200.00
2 . . . . . . . . . . . . . . . . . . . . . . . . 125.00
3 . . . . . . . . . . . . . . . . . . . . . . . . 100.00
4 . . . . . . . . . . . . . . . . . . . . . . . . 100.00
5 . . . . . . . . . . . . . . . . . . . . . . . . 100.00
6 . . . . . . . . . . . . . . . . . . . . . . . . 100.00
7 . . . . . . . . . . . . . . . . . . . . . . . . 100.00
8 . . . . . . . . . . . . . . . . . . . . . . . . 100.00
9 . . . . . . . . . . . . . . . . . . . . . . . . 100.00
10 . . . . . . . . . . . . . . . . . . . . . . . 100.00
11 thru 24 . . . . . . . . . . . . . . . @ 100.00
**Becomes:**

## BOY LOVES GIRL

**Lev Gleason Publ., 1952–56**
25 Romance. . . . . . . . . . . . . . . . 100.00
26 . . . . . . . . . . . . . . . . . . . . . . . . . 80.00
27 . . . . . . . . . . . . . . . . . . . . . . . . . 80.00
28 . . . . . . . . . . . . . . . . . . . . . . . . . 80.00
29 . . . . . . . . . . . . . . . . . . . . . . . . . 80.00
30 . . . . . . . . . . . . . . . . . . . . . . . . . 80.00
31 thru 57 . . . . . . . . . . . . . . . @80.00

Boys' Ranch #4
© Harvey Publications

Brave and the Bold #34
© DC Comics

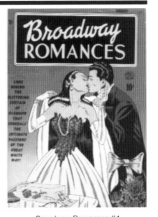

Broadway Romances #1
© Quality Comics

## BOYS' RANCH

**Harvey Publications, 1950–51**
1 S&K,F:Clay Duncan . . . . . . 1,000.00
2 S&K . . . . . . . . . . . . . . . . . . . . . 750.00
3 S&K,MMe. . . . . . . . . . . . . . . . 700.00
4 S&K . . . . . . . . . . . . . . . . . . . . 600.00
5 S&K,MMe. . . . . . . . . . . . . . . . 400.00
6 S&K,MMe. . . . . . . . . . . . . . . . 400.00

## THE BRAIN

**Sussex Publ. Co./Magazine Enterprises, 1956–58**
1 . . . . . . . . . . . . . . . . . . . . . . . . 150.00
2 . . . . . . . . . . . . . . . . . . . . . . . . 100.00
3 . . . . . . . . . . . . . . . . . . . . . . . . 100.00
4 . . . . . . . . . . . . . . . . . . . . . . . . 100.00
5 . . . . . . . . . . . . . . . . . . . . . . . . 100.00
6 . . . . . . . . . . . . . . . . . . . . . . . . 100.00
7 . . . . . . . . . . . . . . . . . . . . . . . . 100.00

## BRAVE AND THE BOLD

**DC Comics, Aug.–Sept., 1955**
1 JKu,RH,IN,I:VikingPrince,Golden
  Gladiator,Silent Knight . . . . 7,000.00
2 F:Viking Prince . . . . . . . . . . . 2,500.00
3 F:Viking Prince . . . . . . . . . . 1,500.00
4 F:Viking Prince . . . . . . . . . . 1,500.00
5 B:Robin Hood . . . . . . . . . . . 1,300.00
6 JKu,F:Robin Hood,E:Golden
  Gladiator . . . . . . . . . . . . . . . . 900.00
7 JKu,F:Robin Hood . . . . . . . . 900.00
8 JKu,F:Robin Hood . . . . . . . . 900.00
9 JKu,F:Robin Hood . . . . . . . . 900.00
10 JKu,F:Robin Hood . . . . . . . 900.00
11 JKu,F:Viking Prince. . . . . . . 700.00
12 JKu,F:Viking Prince . . . . . . 700.00
13 JKu,F:Viking Prince . . . . . . 700.00
14 JKu,F:Viking Prince . . . . . . 650.00
15 JKu,F:Viking Prince . . . . . . 650.00
16 JKu,F:Viking Prince . . . . . . 650.00
17 JKu,F:Viking Prince . . . . . . 650.00
18 JKu,F:Viking Prince . . . . . . 650.00
19 JKu,F:Viking Prince . . . . . . 650.00
20 JKu,F:Viking Prince . . . . . . 650.00
21 JKu,F:Viking Prince . . . . . . 650.00
22 JKu,F:Viking Prince . . . . . . 650.00
23 JKu,O:Viking Prince . . . . . . 900.00
24 JKu,E:Viking Prince,Silent
  Knight . . . . . . . . . . . . . . . . . . 700.00
25 RA,I&B:Suicide Squad . . . . . 850.00
26 F:Suicide Squad . . . . . . . . . . 600.00
27 Creature of Ghost Lake . . . . . 600.00
28 I:Justice League of
  America,O:Snapper Carr . 10,000.00

29 F:Justice League . . . . . . . . 4,200.00
30 F:Justice League . . . . . . . . 3,000.00
31 F:Cave Carson . . . . . . . . . . . 800.00
32 F:Cave Carson . . . . . . . . . . . 500.00
33 F:Cave Carson . . . . . . . . . . . 500.00
34 JKu,I&O:S.A. Hawkman. . . . 4,000.00
35 JKu:F:Hawkman. . . . . . . . . 1,000.00
36 JKu:F:Hawkman. . . . . . . . . 1,000.00
37 F:Suicide Squad . . . . . . . . . . 600.00
38 F:Suicide Squad . . . . . . . . . . 400.00
39 F:Suicide Squad . . . . . . . . . . 400.00
40 JKu,F:Cave Carson . . . . . . . . 300.00
41 F:Cave Carson . . . . . . . . . . . 300.00
42 JKu,F:Hawkman . . . . . . . . . . 600.00
43 JKu,O:Hawkman. . . . . . . . . . 700.00
44 JKu,F:Hawkman. . . . . . . . . . 600.00
45 CI,F:Strange Sports . . . . . . . 200.00
46 CI,F:Strange Sports . . . . . . . 200.00
47 CI,F:Strange Sports . . . . . . . 200.00
48 CI,F:Strange Sports . . . . . . . 200.00
49 CI,F:Strange Sports . . . . . . . 200.00
50 F:GreenArrow & J'onnJ'onzz . 400.00

## BRENDA STARR

**Four Star Comics Corp./ Superior Comics Ltd., Sept., 1947**
13(1) . . . . . . . . . . . . . . . . . . . 3,500.00
14(2) JKa,Bondage (c) . . . . . . 5,000.00
2-3 . . . . . . . . . . . . . . . . . . . . . 3,500.00
2-4 JKa,Operating table (c). . . . 3,500.00
2-5 Swimsuit (c) . . . . . . . . . . . 2,000.00
2-6 . . . . . . . . . . . . . . . . . . . . . 2,000.00
2-7 . . . . . . . . . . . . . . . . . . . . . 2,000.00
2-8 Cosmetic (c) . . . . . . . . . . . 2,000.00
2-9 Giant Starr (c) . . . . . . . . . 2,000.00
2-10 Wedding (c) . . . . . . . . . . 2,000.00
2-11 . . . . . . . . . . . . . . . . . . . . 2,000.00
2-12 . . . . . . . . . . . . . . . . . . . . 2,000.00

## BRICK BRADFORD

**Best Books (Standard Comics) July, 1949**
5 . . . . . . . . . . . . . . . . . . . . . . . 350.00
6 Robot (c) . . . . . . . . . . . . . . . . 500.00
7 ASh(c) . . . . . . . . . . . . . . . . . . 200.00
8 . . . . . . . . . . . . . . . . . . . . . . . 200.00

## BRIDES DIARY
## See: BLACK COBRA

## BRIDES IN LOVE

**Charlton Comics, 1956–65**
1 . . . . . . . . . . . . . . . . . . . . . . . 125.00
2 . . . . . . . . . . . . . . . . . . . . . . . 100.00
3 thru 10 . . . . . . . . . . . . . . . . . @75.00
11 thru 30 . . . . . . . . . . . . . . . . @75.00
31 thru 44 . . . . . . . . . . . . . . . . @60.00
45 . . . . . . . . . . . . . . . . . . . . . . . 50.00

## BRIDES ROMANCES

**Quality Comics, 1953–56**
1 . . . . . . . . . . . . . . . . . . . . . . . 150.00
2 . . . . . . . . . . . . . . . . . . . . . . . 125.00
3 . . . . . . . . . . . . . . . . . . . . . . . 100.00
4 . . . . . . . . . . . . . . . . . . . . . . . 100.00
5 . . . . . . . . . . . . . . . . . . . . . . . 100.00
6 . . . . . . . . . . . . . . . . . . . . . . . 100.00
7 . . . . . . . . . . . . . . . . . . . . . . . 100.00
8 . . . . . . . . . . . . . . . . . . . . . . . 100.00
9 . . . . . . . . . . . . . . . . . . . . . . . 100.00
10 thru 23 . . . . . . . . . . . . . . . @100.00

## BROADWAY ROMANCES

**Quality Comics Group, 1950**
1 PG,BWa(a&c). . . . . . . . . . . . . 600.00
2 BWa,Glittering Desire . . . . . . 400.00
3 BL,Stole My Love. . . . . . . . . . 200.00
4 Enslaved by My Past. . . . . . . 200.00
5 Flame of Passion,Sept.,1950 . 200.00

## BRUCE GENTRY

**Four Star Publ./ Visual Editions/ Superior, Jan., 1948**
1 B:Ray Bailey reprints . . . . . . 900.00
2 Plane crash (c) . . . . . . . . . . . 500.00
3 E:Ray Bailey reprints . . . . . . 500.00
4 Tiger attack (c) . . . . . . . . . . . 400.00
5 . . . . . . . . . . . . . . . . . . . . . . . 400.00
6 Help message (c) . . . . . . . . . 400.00
7 . . . . . . . . . . . . . . . . . . . . . . . 400.00
8 End of Marriage (c),July, 1949 400.00

## BUCCANEERS
## See: KID ETERNITY

## BUCK DUCK

**Marvel Atlas, June, 1953**
1 (fa) stories . . . . . . . . . . . . . . 200.00
2 and 3 . . . . . . . . . . . . . . . . . @100.00
4 Dec., 1953 . . . . . . . . . . . . . . 100.00

---

All comics prices listed are for *Near Mint* condition.

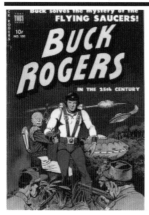

*Buck Rogers #100*
© Toby Press

*Bugs Bunny Christmas Funnies #5*
*(1955)* © Dell Publishing Co.

*Bulletman #6*
© Fawcett Publications

## BUCK JONES
**Dell Publishing Co., 1950**
| | |
|---|---|
| 1 Buck Jones & Horse Silver | 250.00 |
| 2 | 150.00 |
| 3 | 100.00 |
| 4 | 100.00 |
| 5 | 100.00 |
| 6 | 100.00 |
| 7 | 100.00 |
| 8 | 100.00 |

## BUCK ROGERS
**Eastern Color Printing,**
**Winter 1940**
| | |
|---|---|
| 1 Partial Painted(c) | 6,500.00 |
| 2 | 2,400.00 |
| 3 Living Corpse from Crimson Coffin | 2,000.00 |
| 4 One man army of greased lightning | 1,900.00 |
| 5 Sky Roads | 1,700.00 |
| 6 Sept., 1943 | 1,700.00 |

**Toby Press**
| | |
|---|---|
| 100 Flying Saucers | 800.00 |
| 101 | 750.00 |
| 9 MA | 750.00 |

## BUDDIES IN
## THE U.S. ARMY
**Avon Periodicals, 1952–53**
| | |
|---|---|
| 1 Fightin' Guys & Fabulous Gals | 200.00 |
| 2 | 125.00 |

## BUFFALO BILL
**Youthful Magazines, 1950–51**
| | |
|---|---|
| 2 Annie Oakley | 200.00 |
| 3 | 150.00 |
| 4 | 150.00 |
| 5 | 150.00 |
| 6 | 150.00 |
| 7 | 150.00 |
| 8 | 150.00 |
| 9 | 150.00 |

## BUFFALO BILL
## PICTURE STORIES
**Street & Smith Publ. 1949**
| | |
|---|---|
| 1 | 250.00 |
| 2 | 250.00 |

## BUFFALO BILL JR.
**Dell Publishing Co., 1956**
| | |
|---|---|
| 1 | 200.00 |
| 2 | 150.00 |
| 3 | 150.00 |
| 4 | 150.00 |
| 5 | 150.00 |
| 6 | 150.00 |
| 7 thru 13 | @125.00 |

## BUGHOUSE
**Ajax/Farrell, 1954**
| | |
|---|---|
| 1 | 225.00 |
| 2 | 150.00 |
| 3 | 150.00 |
| 4 | 150.00 |

## BUG MOVIES
**Dell Publishing Co., 1931**
| | |
|---|---|
| 1 | 600.00 |

## BUGS BUNNY
## DELL GIANT EDITIONS
**Dell Publishing Co.**
**Christmas**
| | |
|---|---|
| 1 Christmas Funnies (1950) | 350.00 |
| 2 Christmas Funnies (1951) | 300.00 |
| 3 Christmas Funnies (1952) | 250.00 |
| 4 Christmas Funnies (1953) | 200.00 |
| 5 Christmas Funnies (1954) | 200.00 |
| 6 Christmas Party (1955) | 175.00 |
| 7 Christmas Party (1956) | 185.00 |
| 8 Christmas Funnies (1957) | 185.00 |
| 9 Christmas Funnies (1958) | 185.00 |
| 1 County Fair (1957) | 200.00 |

**Halloween**
| | |
|---|---|
| 1 Halloween Parade (1953) | 200.00 |
| 2 Halloween Parade (1954) | 175.00 |
| 3 Trick 'N' Treat Halloween Fun (1955) | 185.00 |
| 4 Trick 'N' Treat Halloween Fun (1956) | 185.00 |

**Vacation**
| | |
|---|---|
| 1 Vacation Funnies (1951) | 325.00 |
| 2 Vacation Funnies (1952) | 275.00 |
| 3 Vacation Funnies (1953) | 250.00 |
| 4 Vacation Funnies (1954) | 200.00 |
| 5 Vacation Funnies (1955) | 200.00 |
| 6 Vacation Funnies (1956) | 175.00 |
| 7 Vacation Funnies (1957) | 175.00 |
| 8 Vacation Funnies (1958) | 175.00 |
| 9 Vacation Funnies (1959) | 175.00 |

## BUGS BUNNY
**Dell Publishing Co., 1942**
**see Four Color for early years**
| | |
|---|---|
| 28 thru 30 | @130.00 |
| 31 thru 50 | @120.00 |
| 51 thru 70 | @100.00 |
| 71 thru 85 | @100.00 |
| 86 Giant-Show Time | 125.00 |
| 87 thru 100 | @100.00 |
| 101 thru 120 | @75.00 |
| 121 thru 140 | @50.00 |
| 141 thru 190 | @50.00 |
| 191 thru 245 | @50.00 |

## BULLETMAN
**Fawcett Publications,**
**Summer, 1941**
| | |
|---|---|
| 1 I:Bulletman & Bulletgirl | 7,000.00 |
| 2 MRa(c) | 3,000.00 |
| 3 MRa(c) | 2,500.00 |
| 4 V:Headless Horror, Guillotine (c) | 2,500.00 |
| 5 Riddle of Dr. Riddle | 2,500.00 |
| 6 V:Japanese | 1,500.00 |
| 7 V:Revenge Syndicate | 1,500.00 |
| 8 V:Mr. Ego | 1,500.00 |
| 9 V:Canine Criminals | 1,500.00 |
| 10 I:Bullet Dog | 1,700.00 |
| 11 V:Fiendish Fiddler | 1,100.00 |
| 12 | 1,000.00 |
| 13 | 1,000.00 |
| 14 V:Death the Comedian | 1,000.00 |
| 15 V:Professor D. | 1,000.00 |
| 16 VanishingElephant,Fall 1946 | 1,000.00 |

## BULLS-EYE
**Charlton Comics, 1954**
| | |
|---|---|
| 1 S&K,Western Scout | 700.00 |
| 2 S&K | 600.00 |
| 3 S&K | 500.00 |
| 4 S&K | 500.00 |
| 5 S&K | 500.00 |
| 6 S&K | 450.00 |
| 7 S&K | 500.00 |

**Becomes:**

## CODY OF THE
## PONY EXPRESS
**Charlton Comics, 1955**
| | |
|---|---|
| 8 F:Buffalo Bill Cody | 125.00 |
| 9 | 100.00 |
| 10 | 100.00 |

**Becomes:**

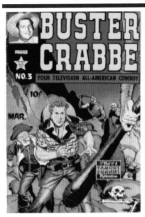

**Ca**

*Buster Crabbe #3*
*© Famous Funnies*

*Buz Sawyer #3*
*© Standard Comics*

*Tex Granger #18*
*© Parents Magzine*

## OUTLAWS OF THE WEST
### Charlton Comics, 1957
| | |
|---|---|
| 11 | 125.00 |
| 12 | 100.00 |
| 13 | 100.00 |
| 14 giant | 150.00 |
| 15 | 100.00 |
| 16 | 100.00 |
| 17 | 100.00 |
| 18 SD | 150.00 |
| 19 thru 40 | @75.00 |

## BULLS-EYE
### See: SCOOP COMICS

## BUSTER BEAR
### Arnold Publications/
### Quality Comics Group, 1953
| | |
|---|---|
| 1 Funny animal | 150.00 |
| 2 | 125.00 |
| 3 | 100.00 |
| 4 | 100.00 |
| 5 | 100.00 |
| 6 | 100.00 |
| 7 | 100.00 |
| 8 | 100.00 |
| 9 | 100.00 |
| 10 | 100.00 |

## BUSTER BROWN COMICS
### Brown Shoe Co., 1945–59
| | |
|---|---|
| 1 | 1,000.00 |
| 2 | 350.00 |
| 3 | 250.00 |
| 4 scarce | 400.00 |
| 5 | 250.00 |
| 6 | 250.00 |
| 7 | 250.00 |
| 8 | 250.00 |
| 9 | 250.00 |
| 10 | 250.00 |
| 11 thru 20 | @100.00 |
| 21 thru 24 | @100.00 |
| 25 RC | 150.00 |
| 26 thru 36 | @100.00 |
| 37 RC | 150.00 |
| 38 | 100.00 |
| 39 | 100.00 |
| 40 RC | 150.00 |
| 41 RC | 150.00 |
| 42 | 100.00 |
| 43 | 100.00 |

## BUSTER BUNNY
### Animated Cartoons
### (Standard)/Pines, 1949
| | |
|---|---|
| 1 FF,Funny animal | 150.00 |
| 2 | 100.00 |
| 3 | 100.00 |
| 4 | 100.00 |
| 5 | 100.00 |
| 6 | 100.00 |
| 7 | 100.00 |
| 8 | 100.00 |
| 9 | 100.00 |
| 10 | 100.00 |
| 11 thru 14 | @100.00 |
| 15 racist(c) | 125.00 |
| 16 | 100.00 |

## BUSTER CRABBE
### Famous Funnies, Nov., 1951
| | |
|---|---|
| 1 The Arrow of Death | 650.00 |
| 2 AW&GE(c) | 700.00 |
| 3 AW&GE(c) | 800.00 |
| 4 FF(c) | 900.00 |
| 5 AW,FF(a&c) | 1,800.00 |
| 6 Sharks (c) | 300.00 |
| 7 FF | 350.00 |
| 8 Gorilla (c) | 300.00 |
| 9 FF | 350.00 |
| 10 | 300.00 |
| 11 Snakes (c) | 250.00 |
| 12 Sept., 1953 | 250.00 |

## BUSTER CRABBE
### Lev Gleason Pub., 1953
| | |
|---|---|
| 1 Ph(c) | 300.00 |
| 2 ATh | 275.00 |
| 3 ATh | 275.00 |
| 4 F. Gordon(c) | 275.00 |

## BUZ SAWYER
### Standard Comics, June, 1948
| | |
|---|---|
| 1 | 300.00 |
| 2 I:Sweeney | 250.00 |
| 3 | 250.00 |
| 4 | 250.00 |
| 5 June, 1949 | 250.00 |

## BUZZY
### DC Comics, 1944–58
| | |
|---|---|
| 1 | 500.00 |
| 2 | 300.00 |
| 3 thru 5 | @250.00 |

| | |
|---|---|
| 6 thru 10 | @150.00 |
| 11 thru 15 | @150.00 |
| 16 thru 25 | @150.00 |
| 26 thru 35 | @125.00 |
| 36 thru 45 | @100.00 |
| 46 thru 77 | @100.00 |

## CALLING ALL BOYS
### Parents Magazine Institute
### Jan., 1946
| | |
|---|---|
| 1 Skiing | 200.00 |
| 2 Roy Rogers Story | 150.00 |
| 3 Peril Out Post | 150.00 |
| 4 Model Airplane | 150.00 |
| 5 Fishing | 150.00 |
| 6 Swimming | 150.00 |
| 7 Baseball | 175.00 |
| 8 School | 150.00 |
| 9 The Miracle Quarterback | 150.00 |
| 10 Gary Cooper (c) | 200.00 |
| 11 Rin-Tin-Tin (c) | 150.00 |
| 12 Bob Hope (c). | 250.00 |
| 13 Bing Cosby (c) | 225.00 |
| 14 J. Edgar Hoover (c) | 150.00 |
| 15 Tex Granger (c). | 125.00 |
| 16 | 125.00 |
| 17 Tex Granger (c), May, 1948 | 125.00 |

**Becomes:**

## TEX GRANGER
### June, 1948
| | |
|---|---|
| 18 Bandits of the Badlands | 125.00 |
| 19 The Seven Secret Cities | 100.00 |
| 20 Davey Crockett's Last Fight | 100.00 |
| 21 Canyon Ambush | 100.00 |
| 22 V:Hooded Terror | 100.00 |
| 23 V:Billy the Kid | 100.00 |
| 24 A:Hector, Sept., 1949 | 100.00 |

## CALLING ALL GIRLS
### Parent Magazine Press, Inc.,
### Sept., 1941
| | |
|---|---|
| 1 | 300.00 |
| 2 Virginia Weidler (c) | 250.00 |
| 3 Shirley Temple (c) | 300.00 |
| 4 Darla Hood (c) | 150.00 |
| 5 Gloria Hood (c) | 150.00 |
| 6 | 150.00 |
| 7 | 150.00 |
| 8 | 150.00 |
| 9 Flag (c) | 150.00 |
| 10 | 150.00 |
| 11 Gary Cooper as Lou Gerrig | 200.00 |
| 12 thru 20 | @125.00 |

---

All comics prices listed are for *Near Mint* condition.

**Ca**

Camera Comics #2
© U.S. Camera Publishing Corp.

Candy #2
© William H. Wise

Captain Aero Comics #25
© Holyoke Publishing Co.

21 thru 39 . . . . . . . . . . . . . . . . @125.00
40 Liz Taylor. . . . . . . . . . . . . . . . 250.00
41 . . . . . . . . . . . . . . . . . . . . . . . . 100.00
42 . . . . . . . . . . . . . . . . . . . . . . . . 100.00
43 Oct., 1945 . . . . . . . . . . . . . . . 100.00

### CALLING ALL KIDS
**Quality Comics, Inc.,**
**Dec./Jan., 1946**
1 Funny Animal stories . . . . . . . 150.00
2 . . . . . . . . . . . . . . . . . . . . . . . . 125.00
3 . . . . . . . . . . . . . . . . . . . . . . . . 100.00
4 . . . . . . . . . . . . . . . . . . . . . . . . 100.00
5 . . . . . . . . . . . . . . . . . . . . . . . . 100.00
6 thru 10 . . . . . . . . . . . . . . . . @100.00
11 thru 25 . . . . . . . . . . . . . . . @100.00
26 Aug., 1949. . . . . . . . . . . . . . 100.00

### CAMERA COMICS
**U.S. Camera Publishing Corp.,**
**July–Sept., 1944**
1 Airfighter,Grey Comet . . . . . . . 350.00
2 How to Set Up a Darkroom . . 300.00
3 Linda Lens V:Nazi (c) . . . . . . . 300.00
4 Linda Lens (c) . . . . . . . . . . . . . 250.00
5 Diving (c) . . . . . . . . . . . . . . . . 250.00
6 Jim Lane (c) . . . . . . . . . . . . . . 250.00
7 Linda Lens (c) . . . . . . . . . . . . . 250.00
8 Linda Lens (c) . . . . . . . . . . . . . 250.00
9 Summer, 1946 . . . . . . . . . . . . 250.00

### CAMP COMICS
**Dell Publishing Co., 1942**
1 Ph(c),WK,A:Bugs Bunny. . . . 1,500.00
2 Ph(c),WK,A:Bugs Bunny. . . . 1,200.00
3 Ph(c),WK . . . . . . . . . . . . . . 1,000.00

### CAMPUS LOVES
**Comic Magazines**
**(Quality Comics Group), 1949**
1 BWa . . . . . . . . . . . . . . . . . . . . 500.00
2 BWa . . . . . . . . . . . . . . . . . . . . 400.00
3 Photo(c) . . . . . . . . . . . . . . . . . 250.00
4 Photo(c) . . . . . . . . . . . . . . . . . 250.00
5 Photo(c) . . . . . . . . . . . . . . . . . 250.00

### CAMPUS ROMANCES
**Avon Periodicals/**
**Realistic Publ., 1949**
1 . . . . . . . . . . . . . . . . . . . . . . . . 350.00
2 . . . . . . . . . . . . . . . . . . . . . . . . 300.00
3 . . . . . . . . . . . . . . . . . . . . . . . . 300.00

### CANDY
**William H. Wise, 1944–45**
1 BW . . . . . . . . . . . . . . . . . . . . . 600.00
1a rep.BW . . . . . . . . . . . . . . . . . 100.00
2 BW . . . . . . . . . . . . . . . . . . . . . 500.00
3 BW . . . . . . . . . . . . . . . . . . . . . 500.00

### CANDY
**Quality Comics Group, 1947–56**
1 JCo,Teen-age . . . . . . . . . . . . 375.00
2 JCo . . . . . . . . . . . . . . . . . . . . 300.00
3 JCo . . . . . . . . . . . . . . . . . . . . 150.00
4 JCo . . . . . . . . . . . . . . . . . . . . 150.00
5 JCo . . . . . . . . . . . . . . . . . . . . 150.00
6 thru 10 JCo . . . . . . . . . . . @150.00
11 thru 20 JCo . . . . . . . . . . . @125.00
21 thru 40 . . . . . . . . . . . . . . . @100.00
41 thru 64 . . . . . . . . . . . . . . . @100.00

### CANNONBALL COMICS
**Rural Home Publ. Co., 1945**
1 Superhero, Crash Kid . . . . . 1,400.00
2 Captive Prince . . . . . . . . . . 1,200.00

### CANTEEN KATE
**St. John Publishing Co., 1952**
1 MB,Sexy babe . . . . . . . . . . . . 800.00
2 MB . . . . . . . . . . . . . . . . . . . . . 600.00
3 MB . . . . . . . . . . . . . . . . . . . . . 700.00

### CAPTAIN AERO COMICS
**Holyoke Publishing Co., 1941**
1 B:Flag-Man&Solar,Master
   of Magic Captain Aero,
   Captain Stone . . . . . . . . . . 4,000.00
2 A:Pals of Freedom . . . . . . . . 1,600.00
3 JKu,B:Alias X,A:Pals of
   Freedom . . . . . . . . . . . . . . 1,600.00
4 JKu,O:Gargoyle,
   Parachute jump . . . . . . . . 1,600.00
5 JKu . . . . . . . . . . . . . . . . . . 1,500.00
6 JKu,Flagman,A:Miss Victory. 1,400.00
7 Alias X . . . . . . . . . . . . . . . . . 900.00
8 O:Red Cross,A:Miss Victory . 900.00
9 A:Miss Victory,Alias X . . . . . . 800.00
10 A:Miss Victory,Red Cross . . . 750.00
11 A:Miss Victory . . . . . . . . . . . 750.00
12 A:Miss Victory . . . . . . . . . . . 750.00
13 A:Miss Victory . . . . . . . . . . . 750.00
14 A:Miss Victory . . . . . . . . . . . 750.00
15 AS(c),A:Miss Liberty . . . . . . 750.00
16 AS(c),Leather Face. . . . . . . . 500.00

17 LbC(c) . . . . . . . . . . . . . . . . . 900.00
21 LbC(c) . . . . . . . . . . . . . . . . . 900.00
22 LbC(c),I:Mighty Mite . . . . . . . 900.00
23 LbC(c) . . . . . . . . . . . . . . . . . 900.00
24 LbC(c) American Planes Dive
   Bomb Japan . . . . . . . . . . 1,200.00
25 LbC(c),Science Fiction(c) . . . . 700.00
26 LbC(c) . . . . . . . . . . . . . . . . 1,500.00

### CAPTAIN AMERICA
### COMICS
**Timely/Atlas, 1941–54**
1 S&K,SSh,JK(c),Hitler(c),I&O:Capt.
   America & Bucky,A:Red Skull,
   B:Hurricane, Tuk . . . . . 135,000.00
2 S&K,RC,AAv,Hitler(c),
   I:Circular Shield;Trapped
   in the Nazi Stronghold . . . 21,000.00
3 ASh(c),S&K,RC,AAv,Stan Lee's
   1st Text,A:Red Skull,
   Bondage(c) . . . . . . . . . . . 17,000.00
4 ASh(c),S&K,AAv,Horror
   Hospital . . . . . . . . . . . . . 12,000.00
5 S&K,AAv,SSh,Ringmaster's
   Wheel of Death . . . . . . . 10,000.00
6 S&K,AAv,SSh,O:Father Time,
   E:Tuk . . . . . . . . . . . . . . . 8,200.00
7 S&K,SSh,A: Red Skull . . . . 10,000.00
8 S&K, The Tomb . . . . . . . . . 7,000.00
9 S&K,RC,V:Black Talon . . . . . 7,000.00
10 S&K,RC,Chamber
   of Horrors . . . . . . . . . . . . . 7,000.00
11 AAv,SSh,E:Hurricane;Feuding
   Mountaineers. . . . . . . . . . . 6,500.00
12 AAv,SSh,B:Imp,E:Father Time;
   Pygmie's Terror. . . . . . . . . 6,000.00
13 AAv,O:Secret Stamp;All Out
   For America . . . . . . . . . . . 6,500.00
14 AAv,V:Japs;Pearl Harbor
   Symbol cover . . . . . . . . . . 6,500.00
15 AAv,Den of Doom . . . . . . . . 6,500.00
16 AAv,A:R.Skull;CapA
   Unmasked . . . . . . . . . . . . 7,000.00
17 AAv,I:Fighting Fool;
   Graveyard. . . . . . . . . . . . . 5,500.00
18 AAv,SSh,V:Japanese . . . . . . 5,500.00
19 AAv,V:Ghouls,
   B:Human Torch. . . . . . . . . 5,000.00
20 AAv,A:Sub-Mariner,V:Nazis . 5,000.00
21 SSh(c),Bucky Captured . . . . 4,500.00
22 SSh(c),V:Japanese . . . . . . . 4,500.00
23 SSh(c),V:Nazis. . . . . . . . . . 4,500.00
24 SSh(c),V:Black
   Dragon Society. . . . . . . . . 4,500.00

---

**Ca**

Captain America #35
© Marvel Comics Group

Captain Atom #3
© Nationwide Publishers

Captain Fearless Comics #2
© Helnit Publishing Co.

25 SSh(c),V:Japs;Drug Story . . 4,500.00
26 SSh(c),SSh,V:Nazi Fleet . . . 4,300.00
27 ASh(c),SSh,AAv,CapAm&Russians
   V:Nazis, E:Secret Stamp . 4,300.00
28 ASh(c),SSh,Nazi Torture
   Chamber. . . . . . . . . . . . . . 4,300.00
29 ASh(c),SSh,V:Nazis;French
   Underground. . . . . . . . . . . 4,300.00
30 SSh(c),Bucky Captured . . . . 4,300.00
31 ASh(c),Bondage(c). . . . . . . 4,000.00
32 SSh(c),V: Japanese Airforce 4,000.00
33 ASh(c),V:Nazis;BrennerPass 4,000.00
34 SSh(c),Bondage(c) . . . . . . . 4,000.00
35 SSh(c),CapA in Japan . . . . . 4,000.00
36 SSh(c),V:Nazis;Hitler(c). . . . 5,500.00
37 SSh(c),SSh,Captain America
   in Berlin, A:Red Skull . . . . . 5,000.00
38 ASh(c),V:Japs;Bondage(c). . 4,200.00
39 ASh(c),SSh,V:Japs;Boulder
   Dam . . . . . . . . . . . . . . . . . 4,200.00
40 SSh(c),V:Japs;Ammo Depot 4,200.00
41 ASh(c),FinalJapaneseWar(c) 4,000.00
42 ASh(c),SSh,V:BankRobbers 4,000.00
43 ASh(c),V:Gangsters . . . . . . . 4,000.00
44 ASh(c),V:Gangsters . . . . . . . 4,000.00
45 ASh(c),V:Bank Robbers . . . . 4,000.00
46 ASh(c),Holocaust(c). . . . . . . 4,500.00
47 ASh(c),Final Nazi War(c) . . . 4,500.00
48 ASh(c),V:Robbers . . . . . . . . 3,500.00
49 ASh(c),V:Saboteurs . . . . . . . 3,500.00
50 ASh(c),V:Gorilla Gang . . . . . 3,600.00
51 ASh(c),V:Gangsters . . . . . . . 3,500.00
52 ASh(c),V:AtomBombThieves 3,500.00
53 ASh(c),V:Burglars . . . . . . . . 3,500.00
54 ASh(c),TV Studio,
   V:Gangsters . . . . . . . . . . . 3,500.00
55 SSh,V:Counterfeiters . . . . . . 3,500.00
56 SSh(c),V:Art Theives . . . . . . 3,500.00
57 SSh,AAv,Symbolic CapA(c). 3,500.00
58 ASh(c),V:Bank Robbers . . . . 3,000.00
59 SSh(c)O:CapA Retold;Private
   Life of Captain America . . . 5,000.00
60 SSh,V:The Human Fly . . . . 3,000.00
61 SSh(c),V:Red Skull;
   Bondage(c). . . . . . . . . . . . 6,000.00
62 SSh(c),Kingdom of Terror . . 3,000.00
63 SSh(c),AAv,I&O:Asbestos Lady;
   The Parrot Strikes. . . . . . . . 3,100.00
64 SSh,Diamonds Spell Doom . 3,200.00
65 SSh,AAv,Friends Turn Foes 3,200.00
66 SSh,O:Golden Girl;Bucky
   Shot . . . . . . . . . . . . . . . . . . 3,300.00
67 SSh,E:Toro(in Human Torch);
   Golden Girl Team-Up . . . . . 3,200.00
68 A:Golden Girl;Riddle of
   the Living Dolls. . . . . . . . . . 3,200.00

69 Weird Tales of the Wee
   Males, A:Sun Girl . . . . . . . . 3,200.00
70 A:Golden Girl,Sub-Mariner,
   Namora;Worlds at War. . . . 3,200.00
71 A:Golden Girl; Trapped . . . . 3,200.00
72 AAv,Murder in the Mind . . . . 3,200.00
73 The Outcast of Time . . . . . . 3,200.00
74 A:Red Skull;Capt.America's
   Weird Tales. . . . . . . . . . . . 10,000.00
75 Thing in the Chest . . . . . . . . 3,200.00
76 JR(c),Capt.America,Commie
   Smasher. . . . . . . . . . . . . . . 3,200.00
77 Capt.A,Commie Smasher . . 2,000.00
78 JR(c),V:Communists . . . . . . 2,000.00

## CAPTAIN AND THE KIDS
### United Features
### Syndicate, 1949

16 Kids humor . . . . . . . . . . . . . . 100.00
17 thru 32. . . . . . . . . . . . . . . . . @100.00
A1. . . . . . . . . . . . . . . . . . . . . . . . 100.00
A2. . . . . . . . . . . . . . . . . . . . . . . . 100.00
A3. . . . . . . . . . . . . . . . . . . . . . . . 100.00

## CAPTAIN ATOM
### Nationwide Publishers, 1951
### Mini-size

1 Scientific adventure . . . . . . . . 500.00
2 . . . . . . . . . . . . . . . . . . . . . . . . 250.00
3 . . . . . . . . . . . . . . . . . . . . . . . . 250.00
4 . . . . . . . . . . . . . . . . . . . . . . . . 250.00
5 . . . . . . . . . . . . . . . . . . . . . . . . 250.00
6 . . . . . . . . . . . . . . . . . . . . . . . . 250.00
7 . . . . . . . . . . . . . . . . . . . . . . . . 250.00

## CAPTAIN BATTLE
### New Friday Publ./
### Magazine Press, Summer, 1941

1 B:Captain Battle,O:Blackout 3,000.00
2 Pirate Ship (c) . . . . . . . . . . . 1,700.00
3 Dungeon (c) . . . . . . . . . . . . . 1,500.00
4 .may not exist
5 V:Japanese, Summer, 1943 . . 900.00

## CAPTAIN BATTLE, Jr.
### Comic House, Fall, 1943

1 Claw V:Ghost, A:Sniffer . . . . 2,500.00
2 Man who didn't believe
   in Ghosts . . . . . . . . . . . . . . 2,000.00

## CAPTAIN COURAGEOUS
## See: BANNER COMICS

## CAPTAIN EASY
### Standard Comics, 1939

N# Swash Buckler . . . . . . . . . . 2,100.00
10 . . . . . . . . . . . . . . . . . . . . . . . . 500.00
11 . . . . . . . . . . . . . . . . . . . . . . . . 300.00
12 . . . . . . . . . . . . . . . . . . . . . . . . 300.00
13 ASh(c). . . . . . . . . . . . . . . . . . . 300.00
14 . . . . . . . . . . . . . . . . . . . . . . . . 300.00
15 . . . . . . . . . . . . . . . . . . . . . . . . 300.00
16 ASh(c). . . . . . . . . . . . . . . . . . . 300.00
17 Sept., 1949 . . . . . . . . . . . . . . 300.00

## CAPTAIN FEARLESS
## COMICS
### Helnit Publishing Co., 1941

1 O:Mr. Miracle,Alias X,Captain
   Fearless Citizen Smith,
   A:Miss Victory . . . . . . . . . . 2,000.00
2 A:Border Patrol, Sept.,1941 . 1,500.00

## CAPTAIN FLASH
### Sterling Comics, Nov., 1954

1 O:Captain Flash . . . . . . . . . . . 500.00
2 V:Black Knight . . . . . . . . . . . . 300.00
3 Beasts from 1,000,000 BC . . . 300.00
4 Flying Saucer Invasion . . . . . . 300.00

## CAPTAIN FLEET
### Approved Comics, Fall, 1952

1 Storm and Mutiny ...Typhoon . 250.00

## CAPTAIN FLIGHT
## COMICS
### Four Star Publications,
### March, 1944–Feb.-March, 1947

N# B:Captain Flight,Ace
   Reynolds, Dash the Avenger,
   ProfessorX . . . . . . . . . . . . . 1,000.00
2 . . . . . . . . . . . . . . . . . . . . . . . . 500.00
3 . . . . . . . . . . . . . . . . . . . . . . . . 500.00
4 B:Rock Raymond Salutes
   America's Wartime Heroines. 500.00
5 Bondage (c),B:Red Rocket
   A:The Grenade . . . . . . . . . 2,000.00
6 Girl tied at the stake . . . . . . . 500.00
7 LbC(c),Dog Fight (c) . . . . . . . 900.00
8 LbC(c),B:Yankee Girl,
   A:Torpedoman . . . . . . . . . . . 900.00
9 LbC(c),Dog Fight (c) . . . . . . . 900.00
10 LbC(c),Bondage (c) . . . . . . . 900.00
11 LbC(c),Future(c). . . . . . . . . 2,000.00

---

All comics prices listed are for *Near Mint* condition.  **Page 71**

**Ca**

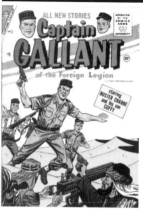

Captain Gallant #3
© Charlton Comics

Captain Marvel Adventures #41
© Fawcett Publications

Captain Marvel Adventures #69
© Fawcett Publications

## CAPTAIN GALLANT
**Charlton Comics, 1955**
1 Ph(c),Buster Crabbe . . . . . . . 200.00
2 . . . . . . . . . . . . . . . . . . . . . . . 150.00
3 . . . . . . . . . . . . . . . . . . . . . . . 150.00
4 Sept., 1956 . . . . . . . . . . . . . . 150.00

## CAPTAIN HOBBY COMICS
**Export Publication Ent., 1948**
1 Adventure. . . . . . . . . . . . . . . 125.00

## CAPTAIN JET
**Four Star Publ., May, 1952**
1 Factory bombing (c). . . . . . . . 300.00
2 Parachute jump (c) . . . . . . . . 200.00
3 Tank bombing (c) . . . . . . . . . 175.00
4 Parachute (c) . . . . . . . . . . . . 175.00
5 . . . . . . . . . . . . . . . . . . . . . . . 175.00

## CAPTAIN KIDD
**See: DAGAR,**
**DESERT HAWK**

## CAPTAIN MARVEL
## ADVENTURES
**Fawcett Publications, 1941**
N# JK, B:Captain Marvel &
Sivana . . . . . . . . . . . . . . . 45,000.00
2 GT,JK(c),Billy Batson (c). . . . 7,000.00
3 JK(c),Thunderbolt (c) . . . . . . 4,000.00
4 Shazam(c) . . . . . . . . . . . . . . 3,000.00
5 V:Nazis . . . . . . . . . . . . . . . . 2,500.00
6 Solomon, Hercules, Atlas, Zeus,
Achilles & Mercury (c) . . . . 2,000.00
7 Ghost of the White Room . . . 2,000.00
8 Forward America. . . . . . . . . . 2,000.00
9 A:Ibac the Monster, Nippo
the Nipponese, Relm of
the Subconscious . . . . . . . . 2,000.00
10 V:Japanese . . . . . . . . . . . . . 2,000.00
11 V:Japanese and Nazis . . . . . 1,500.00
12 Joins the Army . . . . . . . . . . 1,400.00
13 V:Diamond-Eyed Idol of
Doom . . . . . . . . . . . . . . . . . 1,400.00
14 Nippo meets his Nemesis . . 1,400.00
15 Big "Paste the Axis" contest. 1,400.00
16 Uncle Sam (c), Paste
the Axis . . . . . . . . . . . . . . . 1,400.00
17 P(c), Paste the Axis . . . . . . . 1,200.00
18 P(c), O:Mary Marvel. . . . . . . 3,200.00
19 Mary Marvel & Santa (c) . . . 1,500.00

20 Mark of the Black
Swastika . . . . . . . . . . . . . . 5,500.00
21 Hitler (c) . . . . . . . . . . . . . . . 1,700.00
22 B:Mr. Mind serial,
Shipyard Sabotage. . . . . . . 1,200.00
23 A:Steamboat . . . . . . . . . . . . 1,100.00
24 Minneapolis Mystery . . . . . . 1,100.00
25 Sinister Faces (c). . . . . . . . . 1,100.00
26 Flag (c). . . . . . . . . . . . . . . . . 1,100.00
27 Joins Navy . . . . . . . . . . . . . . 900.00
28 Uncle Sam (c). . . . . . . . . . . . 900.00
29 Battle at the China Wall . . . . 900.00
30 Modern Robinson Crusoe . . 900.00
31 Fights his own Conscience. . 900.00
32 V:Mole Men, Dallas. . . . . . . . 900.00
33 Mt. Rushmore parody
(c), Omaha . . . . . . . . . . . . . 800.00
34 Oklahoma City . . . . . . . . . . . 800.00
35 O:Radar the International
Policeman, Indianapolis . . . 700.00
36 Missing face contest,
St. Louis. . . . . . . . . . . . . . . . 700.00
37 V:Block Busting Bubbles,
Cincinnati. . . . . . . . . . . . . . . 700.00
38 V:Chattanooga Ghost,
Rock Garden City . . . . . . . . 700.00
39 V:Mr. Mind's Death Ray,
Pittsburgh . . . . . . . . . . . . . . 700.00
40 V:Ghost of the Tower,Boston . 700.00
41 Runs for President, Dayton . . 600.00
42 Christmas special, St. Paul. . 600.00
43 V:Mr. Mind,I:Uncle Marvel,
Chicago . . . . . . . . . . . . . . . . 600.00
44 OtherWorlds,Washington,D.C. 600.00
45 V:Blood Bank Robbers . . . . . 600.00
46 E: Mr. Mind Serial, Tall
Stories of Jonah Joggins. . . 600.00
47 CCB,Shazam(c) . . . . . . . . . . 550.00
48 Signs Autographs (c) . . . . . . 550.00
49 V: An Unknown Killer . . . . . . 550.00
50 Twisted Powers . . . . . . . . . . 550.00
51 Last of the Batsons. . . . . . . . 500.00
52 O&I:Sivana Jr.,V:Giant
Earth Dreamer. . . . . . . . . . . 500.00
53 Gets promoted . . . . . . . . . . . 500.00
54 Marooned in the Future,
Kansas City . . . . . . . . . . . . . 500.00
55 Endless String, Columbus . . 500.00
56 Goes Crazy, Mobile . . . . . . . 500.00
57 A:Haunted Girl, Rochester . . 500.00
58 V:Sivana . . . . . . . . . . . . . . . . 500.00
59 CCB(c),PrC . . . . . . . . . . . . . . 500.00
60 Man who made Earthquakes . 500.00
61 I&V: Oggar, the Worlds
Mightiest Immortal. . . . . . . . 500.00
62 The Great Harness Race . . . 500.00

63 Stuntman. . . . . . . . . . . . . . . . 500.00
64 CCB(c&a),I:Lester the Imp . . 500.00
65 V:Invaders from Outer Space . 500.00
66 Atomic War (c) . . . . . . . . . . . 500.00
67 Hartford . . . . . . . . . . . . . . . . . 400.00
68 Scenes from the Past,
Baltimore . . . . . . . . . . . . . . . 400.00
69 Gets Knighted . . . . . . . . . . . . 400.00
70 Horror in the Box . . . . . . . . . 400.00
71 Wheel of Death. . . . . . . . . . . 400.00
72 CCB,Empire State Bldg.Ph(c). 400.00
73 Becomes a Petrophile. . . . . . 400.00
74 Who is the 13th Guest . . . . . 400.00
75 V:Astonishing Yeast Menace . 400.00
76 A:Atom Ambassador . . . . . . 400.00
77 The Secret Life . . . . . . . . . . . 400.00
78 O:Mr. Tawny . . . . . . . . . . . . . 450.00
79 O:Atom,A:World's Worst
Actor . . . . . . . . . . . . . . . . . . 400.00
80 Twice told story . . . . . . . . . . 900.00
81 A:Mr. Atom . . . . . . . . . . . . . . 800.00
82 A:Mr. Tawny . . . . . . . . . . . . . 400.00
83 Indian Chief. . . . . . . . . . . . . . 400.00
84 V:Surrealist Imp . . . . . . . . . . 400.00
85 Freedom Train . . . . . . . . . . . 400.00
86 A:Mr. Tawny . . . . . . . . . . . . . 400.00
87 V:Electron Thief . . . . . . . . . . 400.00
88 Billy Batson's Boyhood . . . . . 400.00
89 V:Sivana . . . . . . . . . . . . . . . . 400.00
90 A:Mr. Tawny . . . . . . . . . . . . . 400.00
91 A:Chameleon Stone . . . . . . . 400.00
92 The Land of Limbo . . . . . . . . 400.00
93 Book of all Knowledge . . . . . 400.00
94 Battle of Electricity . . . . . . . . 400.00
95 The Great Ice Cap . . . . . . . . 400.00
96 V:Automatic Weapon . . . . . . 400.00
97 Wiped Out. . . . . . . . . . . . . . . 400.00
98 United Worlds . . . . . . . . . . . . 400.00
99 Rain of Terror . . . . . . . . . . . . 400.00
100 V:Sivana,Plot against
the Universe . . . . . . . . . . . . 750.00
101 Invisibility Trap . . . . . . . . . . 350.00
102 Magic Mix-up . . . . . . . . . . . 350.00
103 Ice Covered World of
1,000,000 AD. . . . . . . . . . . 350.00
104 Mr. Tawny's Masquerade . . 350.00
105 The Dog Catcher . . . . . . . . 350.00
106 V:Menace of the Moon . . . . 350.00
107 V:Space Hunter . . . . . . . . . 350.00
108 V:Terrible Termites . . . . . . . 350.00
109 The Invention Inventor . . . . 350.00
110 CCB(c),V:Sivana . . . . . . . . 350.00
111 The Eighth Sea,V:Vikings . . 350.00
112 Worrybird. . . . . . . . . . . . . . . 350.00
113 Feud with Mr. Tawny . . . . . . 350.00
114 V:The Ogre . . . . . . . . . . . . . 350.00

All comics prices listed are for *Near Mint* condition.

Captain Marvel Jr. #1
© Fawcett Publications

Captain Marvel Jr. #72
© Fawcett Publications

Captain Midnight #27
© Fawcett Publications

**Ca**

115 Mr. Tawny . . . . . . . . . . . . . . 350.00
116 Flying Saucer . . . . . . . . . . . . 400.00
117 Mr. Tawny bondage (c) . . . . 350.00
118 V:Weird Water Man . . . . . . . 350.00
119 Invisibility . . . . . . . . . . . . . . 350.00
120 Voice heard round the world. 350.00
121 Origin retold . . . . . . . . . . . . 350.00
122 Atomic Fire . . . . . . . . . . . . . 350.00
123 Dinosaur Dilemma . . . . . . . . 350.00
124 V:Discarded Instincts . . . . . . 350.00
125 V:Ancient Villain . . . . . . . . . 350.00
126 The Creeping Horror. . . . . . . 350.00
127 Sivana's Voodoo Spell . . . . 350.00
128 . . . . . . . . . . . . . . . . . . . . . 350.00
129 Robot Hunt . . . . . . . . . . . . . 350.00
130 Double Doom . . . . . . . . . . . 350.00
131 Station Whiz gets Atomic
    Powers. . . . . . . . . . . . . . . . 350.00
132 V:Flood . . . . . . . . . . . . . . . . 350.00
133 The Pressure Peril . . . . . . . . 350.00
134 Sivana's Capsule Kingdom. . 350.00
135 Perplexing Past Puzzle. . . . . 325.00
136 Witch of Haven Street. . . . . . 325.00
137 Seven Deadly Sins . . . . . . . . 325.00
138 V:Haunted Horror . . . . . . . . 400.00
139 V:Red Crusher . . . . . . . . . . . 325.00
140 Hand of Horror . . . . . . . . . . . 325.00
141 Man Without a World . . . . . . 325.00
142 The Beauty in Black . . . . . . . 325.00
143 Great Stone Face on Moon . 325.00
144 Stolen Shazam Powers . . . . 325.00
145 The Machines of Murder. . . . 325.00
146 The Unholy Spider . . . . . . . . 325.00
147 Thief From the Past . . . . . . . 325.00
148 V:The World . . . . . . . . . . . . . 325.00
149 Mr. Tawny Hermit . . . . . . . . . 325.00
150 Captain Marvel's Wedding,
    Nov., 1953 . . . . . . . . . . . . . 650.00

## CAPTAIN MARVEL JR.
### Fawcett Publications, 1942
1 MRa(c),O:Captain Marvel, Jr.,
  A:Capt. Nazi . . . . . . . . . . . . 8,000.00
2 MRa(c),O:Capt.Nippon,
  V:Capt. Nazi . . . . . . . . . . . 3,000.00
3 MRa(c),Parade to
  Excitement . . . . . . . . . . . . . 2,000.00
4 MRa(c),V:Invisible Nazi . . . . 1,600.00
5 MRa(c),V:Capt. Nazi . . . . . . 1,500.00
6 MRa(c),Adventure of Sabbac 1,300.00
7 MRa(c),City under the Sea . 1,300.00
8 MRa(c),Dangerous Double . . 1,300.00
9 MRa(c),Independence (c) . . 1,400.00
10 Hitler (c). . . . . . . . . . . . . . . . 1,500.00
11 MRa(c) . . . . . . . . . . . . . . . . 1,100.00

12 MRa(c),Scuttles the Axis
    Isle in the Sky. . . . . . . . . . 1,200.00
13 MRa(c),V:The Axis,Hitler,(c). 1,500.00
14 MRa(c),X-Mas (c), Santa wears
    Capt. Marvel uniform . . . . . 1,000.00
15 MRa(c),V:Capt. Nazi . . . . . . 1,100.00
16 MRa(c),A:Capt. Marvel,
    Sivana, Pogo . . . . . . . . . . . 1,000.00
17 MRa(c),Meets his future self 1,000.00
18 MRa(c),V:Birds of Doom . . . 1,000.00
19 MRa(c),A:Capt. Nazi &
    Capt. Nippon . . . . . . . . . . . 1,000.00
20 MRa(c),Goes on the Warpath 900.00
21 MRa(c),Buy War Stamps . . . . 700.00
22 MRa(c),Rides World's oldest
    steamboat . . . . . . . . . . . . . . 700.00
23 MRa(c) . . . . . . . . . . . . . . . . . 700.00
24 MRa(c),V:Weather Man . . . . . 700.00
25 MRa(c),Flag (c). . . . . . . . . . . 700.00
26 MRa(c),Happy New Year . . . . 700.00
27 MRa(c),Jungle Thrills . . . . . . . 700.00
28 MRa(c),V:Sivana's Crumbling
    Crimes . . . . . . . . . . . . . . . . . 700.00
29 MRa(c),Blazes a Wilderness
    Trail . . . . . . . . . . . . . . . . . . . 700.00
30 MRa(c) . . . . . . . . . . . . . . . . . 700.00
31 MRa(c) . . . . . . . . . . . . . . . . . 500.00
32 Keeper of the Lonely Rock . . . 500.00
33 . . . . . . . . . . . . . . . . . . . . . . . 500.00
34/35 I&O:Sivana Jr. . . . . . . . . 500.00
36 Underworld Tournament . . . . . 500.00
37 FreddyFreeman'sNews-stand. 500.00
38 A:Arabian Knight . . . . . . . . . . 500.00
39 V:Sivana Jr., Headline Stealer 500.00
40 Faces Grave Situation . . . . . . 500.00
41 I:The Acrobat . . . . . . . . . . . . . 400.00
42 V:Sivana Jr. . . . . . . . . . . . . . . 400.00
43 BTh(c),V:Beasts on Broadway 400.00
44 Key to the Mystery . . . . . . . . . 400.00
45 A:Icy Fingers . . . . . . . . . . . . . 400.00
46 BTh(c&a). . . . . . . . . . . . . . . . 400.00
47 BTh(c),V:Giant o/t Beanstalk . 400.00
48 Whale of a Fish Story . . . . . . . 400.00
49 BTh(c),V:Dream Recorder . . . 400.00
50 Wanted: Freddy Freeman . . . . 400.00
51 The Island Riddle . . . . . . . . . . 350.00
52 A:Flying Postman . . . . . . . . . . 350.00
53 Atomic Bomb on the Loose. . . 400.00
54 V:Man with 100 Heads . . . . . . 350.00
55 Pyramid of Eternity . . . . . . . . . 350.00
56 Blue Boy's Black Eye . . . . . . . 350.00
57 MRa(c),Magic Ladder . . . . . . . 350.00
58 BTh(c),Amazing Mirror Maze . 350.00
59 MRa(c) . . . . . . . . . . . . . . . . . . 350.00
60 V:Space Menace . . . . . . . . . . 350.00
61 V:Himself. . . . . . . . . . . . . . . . . 300.00

62 V:Mr. Hydro . . . . . . . . . . . . . . 300.00
63 V:Witch of Winter . . . . . . . . . . 300.00
64 thru 74 . . . . . . . . . . . . . . . . @300.00
75 V:Outlaw of Crooked Creek . . 300.00
76 thru 85 . . . . . . . . . . . . . . . . @300.00
86 Defenders of time . . . . . . . . . 300.00
87 thru 89 . . . . . . . . . . . . . . . . @300.00
90 The Magic Trunk . . . . . . . . . . 300.00
91 thru 99 . . . . . . . . . . . . . . . . @300.00
100 V:Sivana Jr . . . . . . . . . . . . . 300.00
101 thru 106. . . . . . . . . . . . . . @300.00
107 The Horror Dimension . . . . . 400.00
108 thru 118 . . . . . . . . . . . . . . @250.00
119 Condemned to Die, Electric
    Chair, June, 1953 . . . . . . . . 250.00

## CAPTAIN MIDNIGHT
### Fawcett Publications, 1942
1 O:Captain Midnight,
  Capt. Marvel (c) . . . . . . . . . 6,000.00
2 Smashes Jap Juggernaut. . . 2,700.00
3 Battles Phantom Bomber . . . 2,400.00
4 Grapples the Gremlins . . . . . 2,000.00
5 Double Trouble in Tokyo . . . 2,000.00
6 Blasts the Black Mikado . . . 1,500.00
7 Newspaper headline (c) . . . . 1,500.00
8 Flying Torpedoes
  Berlin-Bound . . . . . . . . . . . 1,500.00
9 MRa(c), Subs in Mississippi 1,500.00
10 MRa(c), Flag (c). . . . . . . . . 1,500.00
11 MRa(c), Murder in Mexico . . 1,500.00
12 V:Sinister Angels . . . . . . . . 1,500.00
13 Non-stop around the World . 1,500.00
14 V:King of the Villains . . . . . 1,500.00
15 V:Kimberley Killer. . . . . . . . 1,500.00
16 Hitler's Fortress Breached . . 1,500.00
17 MRa(c), Hello Adolf . . . . . . . 1,500.00
18 Death from the Skies . . . . . . 1,500.00
19 Hour of Doom for the Axis . . 1,500.00
20 Brain & Brawn against Axis . 1,500.00
21 Trades with Japanese . . . . . 1,000.00
22 Plea for War Stamps . . . . . . 1,000.00
23 Japanese Prison (c). . . . . . . 1,000.00
24 Rising Sun Flag (c) . . . . . . . 1,000.00
25 Amusement Park Murder. . . 1,000.00
26 Hotel of Horror . . . . . . . . . . 1,000.00
27 Death Knell for Tyranny . . . . 1,000.00
28 Gliderchuting to Glory . . . . . 1,000.00
29 Bomb over Nippon. . . . . . . . 1,000.00
30 . . . . . . . . . . . . . . . . . . . . . . 1,000.00
31 and 32. . . . . . . . . . . . . . . . @600.00
33 V:Shark . . . . . . . . . . . . . . . . 600.00
34 thru 40. . . . . . . . . . . . . . . . @600.00
41 thru 63. . . . . . . . . . . . . . . . @500.00
64 V:XOG, Ruler of Saturn. . . . . 500.00

**Ca**

Captain Science #4
© Youthful Magazines

Captain Video #2
© Fawcett Publications

Casper The Friendly Ghost #5
© St. John Publishing

65 . . . . . . . . . . . . . . . . . . . . . . . . 500.00
66 V:XOG. . . . . . . . . . . . . . . . . . . 500.00
67 Fall, 1948 . . . . . . . . . . . . . . . 500.00
**Becomes:**

## SWEETHEARTS
### Oct., 1948
68 Robert Mitchum . . . . . . . . . . . 250.00
69 thru 110 . . . . . . . . . . . . . . . . @125.00
111 Ronald Reagan story . . . . . . 175.00
112 thru 118 . . . . . . . . . . . . . . . @125.00
119 WW,Marilyn Monroe . . . . . . . 600.00
120 Atomic Bomb story . . . . . @150.00
121 Liz Taylor. . . . . . . . . . . . . . . 200.00
122 Marjuana,1954 . . . . . . . . . . 150.00

## CAPTAIN ROCKET
### P.L. Publications, 1951
1 Sci-Fi . . . . . . . . . . . . . . . . . . . 550.00

## CAPTAIN SCIENCE
### Youthful Magazines, 1950
1 WW,O:Captain Science,
 V:Monster God of Rogor . . 1,300.00
2 WW,V:Cat Men of Phoebus,
 Space Pirates . . . . . . . . . . . 600.00
3 Ghosts from the Underworld . 600.00
4 WW,Vampires . . . . . . . . . . 1,200.00
5 WW,V:Shark Pirates of
 Pisces . . . . . . . . . . . . . . . 1,200.00
6 WW,V:Invisible Tyrants,
 bondage (c) . . . . . . . . . . . . 700.00
7 WW,Bondage(c) Dec., 1951 . . 700.00
**Becomes:**

## FANTASTIC
### Feb., 1952
8 Isle of Madness . . . . . . . . . . . 500.00
9 Octopus (c) . . . . . . . . . . . . . . 400.00
**Becomes:**

## BEWARE
### June, 1952
10 SHn,Doll of Death. . . . . . . . . 700.00
11 SHn,Horror Head . . . . . . . . . 500.00
12 SHn,Body Snatchers . . . . . . 500.00
**Becomes:**

## CHILLING TALES
### Dec., 1952
13 MF,Screaming Skull . . . . . . 900.00
14 SHn,Smell of Death . . . . . . . 600.00
15 SHn,Curse of the Tomb . . . . 700.00
16 HcK,Mark of the Beast
 Bondage(c) . . . . . . . . . . . . 600.00

17 MFc(c),Wandering Willie,
 Oct.,1953 . . . . . . . . . . . . . . 700.00

## CAPTAIN STEVE SAVAGE
### Avon Periodicals
### [1st Series] 1950
N# WW . . . . . . . . . . . . . . . . . . . 500.00
2 EK(c),The Death Gamble . . . . 300.00
3 EK(c),Crash Landing in
 Manchuria . . . . . . . . . . . . . 250.00
4 EK(c),V:Red Raiders from
 Siang-Po . . . . . . . . . . . . . . 150.00
5 EK(c),Rockets of Death . . . . . 150.00
6 Operation Destruction . . . . . . 150.00
7 EK(c),Flight to Kill . . . . . . . . . 150.00
8 EK(c),V:Red Mystery Jet . . . . 150.00
9 EK(c) . . . . . . . . . . . . . . . . . . . 150.00
10 . . . . . . . . . . . . . . . . . . . . . . . 150.00
11 EK(c) . . . . . . . . . . . . . . . . . . 150.00
12 WW . . . . . . . . . . . . . . . . . . . 225.00
13 . . . . . . . . . . . . . . . . . . . . . . . 150.00
### [2nd Series] Sept./Oct., 1954
5 . . . . . . . . . . . . . . . . . . . . . . . . 150.00
6 WW . . . . . . . . . . . . . . . . . . . . 150.00
7 thru 13 . . . . . . . . . . . . . . . . @150.00

## CAPTAIN TOOTSIE
## & THE SECRET LEGION
### Toby Press, 1950
1 Sci-Fi . . . . . . . . . . . . . . . . . . . 400.00
2 . . . . . . . . . . . . . . . . . . . . . . . . 250.00

## CAPTAIN VIDEO
### Fawcett Publications, 1951
1 GE,Ph(c) From TV series . . . 1,600.00
2 Time When Men Could Not
 Walk . . . . . . . . . . . . . . . . 1,100.00
3 GE,Indestructible Antagonist 1,000.00
4 GE,School of Spies . . . . . . . 1,000.00
5 GE,Missiles of Doom,
 photo (c) . . . . . . . . . . . . . 1,000.00
6 GE,Island of Conquerors,
 Photo (c); Dec., 1951 . . . . . 1,000.00

## CAPTAIN WIZARD
### Rural Home, 1946
1 Impossible Man . . . . . . . . . . . 500.00

## CARNIVAL
## See: SCOOP COMICS

## CARTOON KIDS
### Marvel Atlas, 1957
1 JMn,A:Dexter the Demon, Little
 Zelda,Willie,Wise Guy . . . . . . 200.00

## CASEY–CRIME
## PHOTOGRAPHER
### Marvel, Aug., 1949
1 Ph(c),Girl on the Docks . . . . . . 300.00
2 Ph(c),Staats Cotsworth . . . . . . 250.00
3 Ph(c),He Walked With Danger 250.00
4 Ph(c),Lend Me Your Life . . . . . 250.00
**Becomes:**

## TWO GUN WESTERN
### Marvel, [1st Series], 1950
5 JB,B,I&O:Apache Kid . . . . . . . 300.00
6 JMn,The Outcast . . . . . . . . . . 225.00
7 Human Sacrifice . . . . . . . . . . . 225.00
8 JR,DW,A:Kid Colt,Texas Kid,
 Doc Holiday . . . . . . . . . . . . . 225.00
9 JMn,GM,A:Kid Colt,Marshall
 'Frosty' Bennet Texas Kid . . . 225.00
10 . . . . . . . . . . . . . . . . . . . . . . . 225.00
11 thru 14 JMn,June, 1952 . . . @150.00

## CASPER CAT
### I.W. Enterprises, 1958
1 Funny animal . . . . . . . . . . . . . 100.00

## CASPER, THE
## FRIENDLY GHOST
### St. John Publishing, 1949
1 O:Baby Huey . . . . . . . . . . . . 3,000.00
2 . . . . . . . . . . . . . . . . . . . . . . . 1,500.00
3 . . . . . . . . . . . . . . . . . . . . . . . 1,400.00
4 . . . . . . . . . . . . . . . . . . . . . . . 1,000.00
5 . . . . . . . . . . . . . . . . . . . . . . . 1,000.00
### Harvey Publications
7 Baby Huey . . . . . . . . . . . . . . . 800.00
8 thru 9 Baby Huey . . . . . . . . @500.00
10 I:Spooky . . . . . . . . . . . . . . . . 550.00
11 A:Spooky . . . . . . . . . . . . . . . 300.00
12 thru 18 . . . . . . . . . . . . . . . @300.00
19 I:Nightmare . . . . . . . . . . . . . 400.00
20 I:Wendy the Witch . . . . . . . 2,000.00
21 thru 30 . . . . . . . . . . . . . . . @250.00
31 thru 40 . . . . . . . . . . . . . . . @200.00
41 thru 50 . . . . . . . . . . . . . . . @150.00
51 thru 60 . . . . . . . . . . . . . . . @150.00
61 thru 69 . . . . . . . . . . . . . . . @150.00
70 July, 1958 . . . . . . . . . . . . . . 150.00

All comics prices listed are for *Near Mint* condition.

*Catman Comics #24*
© Holyoke Publishing Co.

*Century of Comics N#*
© Eastern Color Printing

*Challengers of the Unknown #21*
© DC Comics

## CASPER'S GHOSTLAND
**Harvey Publications, Winter, 1958-59**
1 giant . . . . . . . . . . . . . . . . . . . 300.00
2 . . . . . . . . . . . . . . . . . . . . . . 150.00
3 thru 10 . . . . . . . . . . . . . . @125.00
11 thru 20 . . . . . . . . . . . . . . @100.00

## CATHOLIC COMICS
**Catholic Publications, 1946–49**
1 Sports . . . . . . . . . . . . . . . . . 550.00
2 Sports . . . . . . . . . . . . . . . . . 350.00
3 Sports . . . . . . . . . . . . . . . . . 300.00
4 thru 10 . . . . . . . . . . . . . . @300.00
11 thru 20 . . . . . . . . . . . . . @250.00
21 thru 34 . . . . . . . . . . . . . @275.00

## CATMAN COMICS
**Helnit Publ. Co./ Holyoke Publ. Co./ Continental Magazine, 1941**
1 O:Deacon&Sidekick Mickey, Dr. Diamond & Ragman,A:Black Widow, B:Blaze Baylor . . . . 7,500.00
2 Ragman . . . . . . . . . . . . . . 3,000.00
3 B:Pied Piper . . . . . . . . . . . . 2,500.00
4 CQ . . . . . . . . . . . . . . . . . 2,400.00
5 I&O: The Kitten . . . . . . . . . . 1,500.00
6 CQ . . . . . . . . . . . . . . . . . 1,500.00
7 CQ . . . . . . . . . . . . . . . . . 1,500.00
8 JKa, I:Volton . . . . . . . . . . 1,800.00
9 JKa . . . . . . . . . . . . . . . . 1,200.00
10 JKa,O:Blackout, B:Phantom Falcon . . . . . . . 1,200.00
11 JKa,DRi,BF,PzF . . . . . . . . . 1,200.00
12 Volton . . . . . . . . . . . . . . . 1,000.00
13 . . . . . . . . . . . . . . . . . . . 1,500.00
14 CQ . . . . . . . . . . . . . . . . . 1,000.00
15 Rajah of Destruction . . . . . . 1,000.00
16 Bye-Bye Axis, Hitler . . . . . . . 1,500.00
17 Buy Bonds and Stamps . 1,000.00
18 Buy Bonds and Stamps . . . . 1,000.00
19 CQ,Hitler,Tojo &Mussolini(c) 1,500.00
20 CQ,Hitler,Tojo &Mussolini(c) 1,500.00
21 CQ . . . . . . . . . . . . . . . . . 1,000.00
22 CQ . . . . . . . . . . . . . . . . . 1,000.00
23 CQ . . . . . . . . . . . . . . . . . 1,000.00
N# DRiV:Japanese,Bondage(c) 1,000.00
N# V:Demon . . . . . . . . . . . . . 1,000.00
N# LbC(c),A:Leather Face . . . . 1,000.00
27 LbC(c),Flag (c),O:Kitten . . . 1,500.00
28 LbC(c),Horror (c) . . . . . . . . 1,500.00
29 LbC(c),BF,RP . . . . . . . . . . . 1,500.00
30 LbC(c),BF,Bondage(c) . . . . . 1,500.00
31 LbC(c) . . . . . . . . . . . . . . . 1,500.00
32 LbC(c),RP,Aug., 1946 . . . . . 1,500.00

## CAUGHT
**Marvel-Vista Publications, 1956**
1 JSe,Crime . . . . . . . . . . . . . . 350.00
2 MD,JSe . . . . . . . . . . . . . . . 200.00
3 MMe,AI,JSe . . . . . . . . . . . . 200.00
4 MMe,JSe . . . . . . . . . . . . . . 200.00
5 RC,JSe,BK . . . . . . . . . . . . . 200.00

## CAVALIER COMICS
**Sture Ashberg Publ. 1945**
1 Historic adventure . . . . . . . . . 250.00

## CAVE GIRL
## See: A-1 COMICS

## CENTURY OF COMICS
**Eastern Color Printing Co., 1933**
N# . . . . . . . . . . . . . . . . . . . 60,000.00

## CHALLENGER, THE
**Interfaith Publications, 1945**
N# O:The Challenger Club . . . . 750.00
2 JKa . . . . . . . . . . . . . . . . . . 600.00
3 JKa . . . . . . . . . . . . . . . . . . 600.00
4 JKa,BF . . . . . . . . . . . . . . . . 600.00

## CHALLENGERS OF THE UNKNOWN
**DC Comics, 1958**
1 JK&JK(c),The Man Who Tampered With Infinity . . . . 5,000.00
2 JK&JK(c),The Monster Maker . . . . . . . . . . . . . . 1,600.00
3 JK&JK(c),The Secret of the Sorcerer's Mirror . . . . . . . . 1,500.00
4 JK,WW,JK(c),The Wizard of Time . . . . . . . . . . . . . . . . 1,000.00
5 JK,WW&JK(c),The Riddle of the Star-Stone . . . . . . . . . 1,000.00
6 JK,WW,JK(c),Captives of the Space Circus . . . . . . . 1,000.00
7 JK,WW,JK(c),The Isle of No Return . . . . . . . . . . . 1,000.00
8 JK,WW,JK&WW(c),The Prisoners o/t Robot Planet . 1,000.00
9 The Plot To Destroy Earth . . . . 750.00
10 The Four Faces of Doom . . . . 750.00
11 The Creatures From The Forbidden World . . . . . . . . . 600.00
12 The Three Clues To Sorcery . . 600.00
13 The Prisoner of the Tiny Space Ball . . . . . . . . . . . 600.00
14 O: Multi Man . . . . . . . . . . . . 600.00
15 Lady Giant and the Beast . . . . 600.00
16 Prisoners of the Mirage World 500.00
17 The Secret of the Space Capsules . . . . . . . . . . 500.00
18 Menace of Mystery Island . . . 500.00
19 The Alien Who Stole a Planet . 500.00
20 Multi-Man Strikes Back . . . . . 500.00
21 Weird World That Didn't Exist . 500.00
22 The Thing In Challenger Mountain . . . . . . 500.00
23 The Island In The Sky . . . . . . 500.00
24 The Challengers Die At Dawn 200.00
25 Captives of the Alien Hunter . . 200.00
26 Death Crowns The Challenge King . . . . . . . . . . 200.00
27 Master of the Volcano Men . . . 200.00
28 The Riddle of the Faceless Man . . . . . . . . . . 200.00
29 Four Roads to Doomsday . . . . 200.00
30 Multi-Man...Villain Turned Hero . . . . . . . . . . . . . . . . 200.00
31 O:Challengers . . . . . . . . . . . 250.00

## CHALLENGE TO THE WORLD
**Catechetical Guild, 1950**
N# The story of Fatima . . . . . . . 200.00

## CHAMBER OF CHILLS
**Harvey Publications/ Witches Tales, June, 1951**
21 (1) AAv . . . . . . . . . . . . . . . . 900.00
22 (2) AAv . . . . . . . . . . . . . . . . 600.00
23 (3) Eyes Ripped Out . . . . . . . . 600.00
24 (4) LEI,Bondage (c) . . . . . . . . 700.00
5 LEI,Shrunken Skull, Operation Monster . . . . . . . . 700.00
6 LEI,Seven Skulls of Magondi . 600.00
7 LEI,Pit of the Damned . . . . . . 600.00
8 LEI,Formula for Death . . . . . 600.00
9 LEI,Bondage (c) . . . . . . . . . . 500.00
10 LEI,AAv,Cave of Death . . . . . 500.00
11 AAv,Curse of Morgan Kilgane . 400.00
12 AAv,Swamp Monster . . . . . . . 400.00
13 AAv,The Lost Race . . . . . . . . 550.00
14 LEI,Down to Death . . . . . . . . 500.00
15 LEI,AAv,Nightmare of Doom . . 550.00

**Ch**

*Chamber of Clues #28*
© Harvey Publications

*Charlie Chan #3*
© Crestwood Prize

*Cheyenne #8*
© Dell Publishing Co.

16 LEI,Cycle of Horror . . . . . . . . 550.00
17 LEI,Amnesia . . . . . . . . . . . . . 550.00
18 LEI,Hair Cut-Atom Bomb . . . . 600.00
19 LEI,Happy Anniversary . . . . . 500.00
20 Shock is Struck . . . . . . . . . . . 500.00
21 LEI,BP,RP,Decapitation . . . . . . 600.00
22 LEI,Is Death the End? . . . . . . 550.00
23 LEI,BP,RP,Heartline . . . . . . . . 550.00
24 LEI,BP,Bondage(c) . . . . . . . . 600.00
25 LEI, . . . . . . . . . . . . . . . . . . . 400.00
26 LEI,HN,AAv,Captains Return . 400.00
Becomes:

## CHAMBER OF CLUES
**Feb., 1955**
27 BP,A:Kerry Drake . . . . . . . . . 250.00
28 A:Kerry Drake . . . . . . . . . . . . 150.00

## CHAMPION COMICS
**Worth Publishing Co., 1939**
2 B:Champ, Blazing Scarab, Neptina,
 Liberty Lads, Jingleman . . . 3,500.00
3 . . . . . . . . . . . . . . . . . . . . . 2,000.00
4 Bailout(c). . . . . . . . . . . . . . 2,000.00
5 Jungleman(c) . . . . . . . . . . . 2,000.00
6 MNe . . . . . . . . . . . . . . . . . 2,000.00
7 MNe,Human Meteor . . . . . . 2,000.00
8 JK . . . . . . . . . . . . . . . . . . . 3,000.00
9 JK,S&K . . . . . . . . . . . . . . . 3,000.00
10 JK,Bondage (c) . . . . . . . . . 3,000.00
Becomes:

## CHAMP COMICS
**Oct. 1940**
11 Human Meteor . . . . . . . . . . 2,500.00
12 Human Heteor . . . . . . . . . . 2,200.00
13 Dragon's Teeth. . . . . . . . . . 2,000.00
14 Liberty Lads . . . . . . . . . . . . 2,000.00
15 RC,Liberty Lads . . . . . . . . . 2,000.00
16 Liberty Lads . . . . . . . . . . . . 2,000.00
17 Liberty Lads . . . . . . . . . . . . 2,000.00
18 Liberty Lads . . . . . . . . . . . . 2,400.00
19 JSm,A:The Wasp. . . . . . . . . 2,500.00
20 S&K,A:The Green Ghost . . . 2,000.00
21 S&K . . . . . . . . . . . . . . . . . 1,500.00
22 A:White Mask. . . . . . . . . . . 1,500.00
23 Flag (c). . . . . . . . . . . . . . . 1,800.00
24 Hitler,Tojo & Mussolini . . . . 1,600.00
25 . . . . . . . . . . . . . . . . . . . . 1,500.00
26 thru 29 . . . . . . . . . . . . . @1,500.00

## CHARLIE CHAN
**Crestwood, 1948–55**
1 S&K(c),CI,Detective . . . . . . 1,500.00
2 S&K. . . . . . . . . . . . . . . . . . 1,000.00

3 S&K. . . . . . . . . . . . . . . . . . 1,000.00
4 S&K. . . . . . . . . . . . . . . . . . 1,000.00
5 S&K. . . . . . . . . . . . . . . . . . 1,000.00
**Charlton Comics, 1955**
6 S&K . . . . . . . . . . . . . . . . . . . 750.00
7 . . . . . . . . . . . . . . . . . . . . . . 500.00
8 . . . . . . . . . . . . . . . . . . . . . . 500.00
9 . . . . . . . . . . . . . . . . . . . . . . 500.00
Becomes:

## ZAZA THE MYSTIC
**Charlton Comics, 1956**
10 Psychic revelations . . . . . . . . 300.00
11 . . . . . . . . . . . . . . . . . . . . . . 300.00
Becomes:

## THIS MAGAZINE IS HAUNTED
**Charlton Comics, 1957**
12 . . . . . . . . . . . . . . . . . . . . . . 450.00
13 . . . . . . . . . . . . . . . . . . . . . . 650.00
14 The Green Man . . . . . . . . . . 400.00
15 . . . . . . . . . . . . . . . . . . . . . . 350.00
16 . . . . . . . . . . . . . . . . . . . . . . 700.00
Becomes:

## OUTER SPACE
**Charlton Comics, 1958**
17 AS,WW,Sci-Fi . . . . . . . . . . . 300.00
18 SD. . . . . . . . . . . . . . . . . . . . 450.00
19 SD. . . . . . . . . . . . . . . . . . . . 450.00
20 SD. . . . . . . . . . . . . . . . . . . . 450.00
21 SD. . . . . . . . . . . . . . . . . . . . 450.00
22 . . . . . . . . . . . . . . . . . . . . . . 300.00
23 . . . . . . . . . . . . . . . . . . . . . . 300.00
24 SD Machine Men of Mars . . . 300.00
25 . . . . . . . . . . . . . . . . . . . . . . 300.00

## CHARLIE McCARTHY
**Dell Publishing Co., 1947**
1 Ph(c) . . . . . . . . . . . . . . . . . . 300.00
2 . . . . . . . . . . . . . . . . . . . . . . 200.00
3 . . . . . . . . . . . . . . . . . . . . . . 200.00
1 . . . . . . . . . . . . . . . . . . . . . . 200.00
2 . . . . . . . . . . . . . . . . . . . . . . 200.00
3 . . . . . . . . . . . . . . . . . . . . . . 200.00
4 . . . . . . . . . . . . . . . . . . . . . . 200.00
5 . . . . . . . . . . . . . . . . . . . . . . 200.00
6 . . . . . . . . . . . . . . . . . . . . . . 200.00
7 . . . . . . . . . . . . . . . . . . . . . . 200.00
8 . . . . . . . . . . . . . . . . . . . . . . 200.00
9 . . . . . . . . . . . . . . . . . . . . . . 200.00

## CHEYENNE
**Dell Publishing Co., 1956**
1 Ph(c) all . . . . . . . . . . . . . . . . 350.00
2 . . . . . . . . . . . . . . . . . . . . . . 250.00
3 . . . . . . . . . . . . . . . . . . . . . . 200.00
4 thru 12 . . . . . . . . . . . . . . @150.00
13 thru 25 . . . . . . . . . . . . . . @100.00

## CHEYENNE KID
### See: WILD FRONTIER

## CHIEF, THE
**Dell Publishing Co., 1950**
(1) see Dell Four Color #290
2 . . . . . . . . . . . . . . . . . . . . . . 150.00

## CHILDREN'S BIG BOOK
**Dorene Publ. Co., 1945**
N# Humor. . . . . . . . . . . . . . . . . 150.00

## CHILLING TALES
### See: CAPTAIN SCIENCE

## CHIP 'N DALE
**Dell Publishing, 1955–66**
4 . . . . . . . . . . . . . . . . . . . . . . 150.00
5 thru 10 . . . . . . . . . . . . . . @100.00
11 thru 30 . . . . . . . . . . . . . @100.00

## CHOICE COMICS
**Great Comics, 1941**
1 O:Secret Circle . . . . . . . . . . 3,000.00
2 . . . . . . . . . . . . . . . . . . . . . 1,500.00
3 The Lost City . . . . . . . . . . . 2,000.00

## CHRISTMAS CARNIVAL
**Approved Comics (Ziff-Davis)/ St. John Publ., 1955**
N# Santa . . . . . . . . . . . . . . . . . 500.00
2 . . . . . . . . . . . . . . . . . . . . . . 300.00

## CHUCKLE THE GIGGLY BOOK OF COMIC ANIMALS
**R. B. Leffing Well Co., 1944**
1 . . . . . . . . . . . . . . . . . . . . . . 300.00

Cicero's Cat #2
© Dell Publishing Co.

Cisco Kid #17
© Dell Publishing Co.

Claire Voyant #4
© Pentagon Publishing

CI

## CICERO'S CAT
**Dell Publishing Co., 1959**
1 . . . . . . . . . . . . . . . . . . . . . . . 150.00
2 . . . . . . . . . . . . . . . . . . . . . . . 125.00

## CINDERELLA LOVE
**Approved Comics (Ziff-Davis)/
St. John Publ., 1951**
1 (10) Romance . . . . . . . . . . . . 300.00
2 (11) RC . . . . . . . . . . . . . . . . . 200.00
3 (12) . . . . . . . . . . . . . . . . . . . 150.00
4 . . . . . . . . . . . . . . . . . . . . . . . 150.00
5 . . . . . . . . . . . . . . . . . . . . . . . 150.00
6 . . . . . . . . . . . . . . . . . . . . . . . 150.00
7 Ph(c) . . . . . . . . . . . . . . . . . . 150.00
8 . . . . . . . . . . . . . . . . . . . . . . . 150.00
9 EK . . . . . . . . . . . . . . . . . . . . 200.00
10 . . . . . . . . . . . . . . . . . . . . . . 150.00
11 . . . . . . . . . . . . . . . . . . . . . . 125.00
12 . . . . . . . . . . . . . . . . . . . . . . 125.00
13 Ph(c) . . . . . . . . . . . . . . . . . . 125.00
14 MB. . . . . . . . . . . . . . . . . . . . 150.00
15 MB. . . . . . . . . . . . . . . . . . . . 125.00
16 MB(c) . . . . . . . . . . . . . . . . . 150.00
17 . . . . . . . . . . . . . . . . . . . . . . 125.00
18 . . . . . . . . . . . . . . . . . . . . . . 125.00
19 . . . . . . . . . . . . . . . . . . . . . . 125.00
20 . . . . . . . . . . . . . . . . . . . . . . 125.00
21 . . . . . . . . . . . . . . . . . . . . . . 125.00
22 . . . . . . . . . . . . . . . . . . . . . . 125.00
23 . . . . . . . . . . . . . . . . . . . . . . 125.00
24 . . . . . . . . . . . . . . . . . . . . . . 125.00
25 . . . . . . . . . . . . . . . . . . . . . . 125.00
26 MB(c) . . . . . . . . . . . . . . . . . 150.00
27 MB(c) . . . . . . . . . . . . . . . . . 150.00
28 . . . . . . . . . . . . . . . . . . . . . . 125.00
29 MB(c) . . . . . . . . . . . . . . . . . 150.00

## CINDY COMICS
## See: KRAZY COMICS

## CINEMA COMICS
## HERALD
**Paramount/Universal/RKO/
20th Century Fox
Giveaways, 1941–43**
N# Mr. Bug Goes to Town . . . . . 300.00
N# Bedtime Story . . . . . . . . . . . 200.00
N# Lady for a Night,J.Wayne . . . 350.00
N# Reap the Wild Wind . . . . . . . 200.00
N# Thunderbirds . . . . . . . . . . . 150.00
N# They All Kissed Me . . . . . . . 150.00

N# Bombardier . . . . . . . . . . . . . 200.00
N# Crash Dive . . . . . . . . . . . . . 200.00
N# Arabian Nights. . . . . . . . . . . 150.00

## CIRCUS COMICS
**Farm Women's Publ., 1945**
1 Clown, Funny Animal. . . . . . . 300.00
2 . . . . . . . . . . . . . . . . . . . . . . . 200.00

## CIRCUS COMICS
**D.S. Publications, 1948**
1 FF . . . . . . . . . . . . . . . . . . . . . 500.00

## CIRCUS OF FUN COMICS
**A.W. Nugent Publ. Co., 1946**
1 Funny animal . . . . . . . . . . . . 250.00
2 . . . . . . . . . . . . . . . . . . . . . . . 150.00
3 . . . . . . . . . . . . . . . . . . . . . . . 150.00

## CIRCUS THE
## COMIC RIOT
**Globe Syndicate, June, 1938**
1 BKa,WE,BW . . . . . . . . . . . 10,000.00
2 BKa,WE,BW . . . . . . . . . . . 6,000.00
3 BKa,WE,BW, Aug., 1938 . . . 5,000.00

## CISCO KID COMICS
**Bernard Bailey/
Swappers Quarterly, 1944**
1 . . . . . . . . . . . . . . . . . . . . . . . 700.00

## CISCO KID, THE
**Dell Publishing Co.**
(1) See Dell Four Color #292
2 Jan., 1951 . . . . . . . . . . . . . . 550.00
3 thru 5 . . . . . . . . . . . . . . . . . @350.00
6 thru 10 . . . . . . . . . . . . . . . . @300.00
11 thru 20 . . . . . . . . . . . . . . . @250.00
21 thru 36 . . . . . . . . . . . . . . . @200.00
37 thru 41 Ph(c)'s. . . . . . . . . . @375.00

## CLAIRE VOYANT
**Leader Publ./Visual Ed./
Pentagon Publ., 1946-47**
N# . . . . . . . . . . . . . . . . . . . . . 1,100.00
2 JKa(c) . . . . . . . . . . . . . . . . . 800.00
3 Case of the Kidnapped
Bride . . . . . . . . . . . . . . . . . 1,000.00
4 Bondage (c) . . . . . . . . . . . . . 800.00

## CLASSIC COMICS
**(Becomes: CLASSIC
ILLUSTRATED—1947)**
**Elliot Publishing, 1941–42
Gilberton Publications,
1942–60s**

**001-The Three Musketeers
by Alexandre Dumas**
10/41 (——) MKd(a&c),
Original,10¢ (c) Price . . . . . 7,500.00
05/43 (10) MKd(a&c),
No(c)Price; rep . . . . . . . . . . 500.00
11/43 (15) MKd(a&c),Long
Island Independent Ed; . . . . . 300.00
6/44 (18/20) MKd(a&c),
Sunrise Times Edition;rep . . . 200.00
7/44 (21) MKd(a&c),Richmond
Courier Edition;rep . . . . . . . . 175.00
6/46 (28) MKd(a&c);rep . . . . . . . 150.00
4/47 (36) MKd(a&c),
New CILogo;rep . . . . . . . . . . 75.00
6/49 (60) MKd(a&c),CI Logo;rep . . 50.00
10/49 (64) MKd(a&c),CI Logo;rep . 50.00
12/50 (78) MKd(a&c),15¢(c)
Price; CI Logo;rep . . . . . . . . . 30.00
03/52 (93) MKd(a&c),CI Logo;rep . 30.00
11/53 (114) CI Logo;rep . . . . . . . 25.00
09/56 (134) MKd(a&c),New
P(c),CI Logo,64 pgs;rep . . . . . 30.00
03/58 (143) MKd(a&c),P(c),
CI Logo,64 pgs;rep . . . . . . . . 25.00
05/59 (150) GE&RC New Art,
P(c),CILogo;rep . . . . . . . . . . 30.00
03/61 (149) GE&RC,P(c),
CI Logo;rep . . . . . . . . . . . . . 18.00

**002-Ivanhoe
by Sir Walter Scott**
1941 (——) EA,MKd(c),Original . 3,500.00
05/43 (1) EA,MKd(c),word "Presents"
Removed From(c);rep . . . . . 400.00
11/43 (15) EA,MKd(c),Long Island
Independent Edition;rep . . . . 250.00
06/44 (18/20) EA,MKd(c),Sunrise
Times Edition;rep. . . . . . . . . 200.00
07/44 (21) EA,MKd(c),Richmond
Courrier Edition;rep . . . . . . . 175.00
06/46 (28) EA,MKd(c),rep . . . . . . 150.00
07/47 (36) EA,MKd(c),New
CI Logo; rep. . . . . . . . . . . . . 100.00
06/49 (60) EA,MKd(c),CI Logo;rep 50.00
10/49 (64) EA,MKd(c),CI Logo;rep 40.00
12/50 (78) EA,MKd(c),15¢(c)
Price; CI Logo;rep . . . . . . . . 30.00
11/51 (89) EA,MKd(c),CI Logo;rep 25.00

**CI**

*Classic Comics #4*
© *Gilberton Publications*

*Classic Comics #5*
© *Gilberton Publications*

*Classic Comics #9*
© *Gilberton Publications*

04/53 **(106)** EA,MKd(c),CI
Logo;rep . . . . . . . . . . . . . . . 20.00
07/54 **(121)** EA,MKd(c),CI
Logo;rep . . . . . . . . . . . . . . . 30.00
01/57 **(136)** NN New Art,New
P(c),CI Logo;rep . . . . . . . . . . 30.00
01/58 **(142)** NN,P(c),CI Logo;rep. . 18.00
11/59 **(153)** NN,P(c),CI Logo;rep. . 18.00
03/61 **(149)** NN,P(c),CI Logo;rep. . 18.00

**003-The Count of Monte Cristo**
**by Alexandre Dumas**
03/42 **(—)** ASm(a&c),Orig. . . . . 2,200.00
05/43 **(10)** ASm(a&c);rep . . . . . . 400.00
11/43 **(15)** ASm(a&c),Long Island
Independent Edition;rep . . . . 250.00
06/44 **(18/20)** ASm(a&c),
Sunrise Times Edition;rep . . . 225.00
06/44 **(20)** ASm(a&c),Sunrise
Times Edition;rep . . . . . . . . . 200.00
07/44 **(21)** ASm(a&c),Richmond
Courier Edition;rep . . . . . . . . 175.00
06/46 **(28)** ASm(a&c);rep . . . . . . 150.00
04/47 **(36)** ASm(a&c),New
CI Logo; rep. . . . . . . . . . . . . 100.00
06/49 **(60)** ASm(a&c),CI Logo;rep . 60.00
08/49 **(62)** ASm(a&c),CI Logo;rep . 75.00
05/50 **(71)** ASm(a&c),CI Logo;rep . 50.00
09/51 **(87)** ASm(a&c),15¢(c)
Price, CI Logo;rep . . . . . . . . . 30.00
11/53 **(113)** ASm(a&c),CI Logo; rep25.00
11/56 **(—)** LC New Art,New
P(c), CI Logo;rep. . . . . . . . . . 25.00
03/58 **(135)** LC,P(c),CI Logo;rep . . 30.00
11/59 **(153)** LC,P(c),CI Logo;rep . . 18.00
03/61 **(161)** LC,P(c),CI Logo;rep . . 18.00

**004-The Last of the Mohicans**
**by James Fenimore Cooper**
08/42 **(—)** RR(a&c),Original . . 1,800.00
06/43 **(12)** RR(a&c),Price
Balloon Deleted;rep. . . . . . . 400.00
11/43 **(15)** RR(a&c),Long Island
Independent Edition;rep . . . . 250.00
06/44 **(20)** RR(a&c),Long Island
Independent Edition;rep . . . . 225.00
07/44 **(21)** RR(a&c),Queens
Home News Edition;rep. . . . 200.00
06/46 **(28)** RR(a&c);rep . . . . . . . . 150.00
04/47 **(36)** RR(a&c),New
CI Logo; rep. . . . . . . . . . . . . 100.00
06/49 **(60)** RR(a&c),CI Logo;rep . . 50.00
10/49 **(64)** RR(a&c),CI Logo;rep . . 35.00
12/50 **(78)** RR(a&c),15¢(c)
Price,CI Logo rep . . . . . . . . . 35.00
11/51 **(89)** RR(a&c),CI Logo;rep . . 30.00
03/54 **(117)** RR(a&c),CI Logo;rep . 28.00

11/56 **(135)** RR,New P(c),
CI Logo; rep. . . . . . . . . . . . . 28.00
11/57 **(141)** RR,P(c),CI Logo;rep. . 30.00
05/59 **(150)** JSe&StA New Art;
P(c), CI Logo;rep. . . . . . . . . . 35.00
03/61 **(161)** JSe&StA,P(c),CI
Logo; rep . . . . . . . . . . . . . . . 15.00

**005-Moby Dick**
**by Herman Melville**
09/42 **(—)** LZ(a&c),Original . . . 2,400.00
05/43 **(10)** LZ(a&c),Conray Products
Edition, No(c)Price;rep . . . . . 500.00
11/43 **(15)** LZ(a&c),Long Island
Independent Edition;rep . . . . 275.00
06/44 **(18/20)** LZ(a&c),Sunrise
Times Edition;rep. . . . . . . . . 250.00
07/44 **(20)** LZ(a&c),Sunrise
Times Edition;rep. . . . . . . . . 225.00
07/44 **(21)** LZ(a&c),Sunrise
Times Edition;rep. . . . . . . . . 200.00
06/46 **(28)** LZ(a&c);rep . . . . . . . . 150.00
04/47 **(36)** LZ(a&c),New CI
Logo;rep . . . . . . . . . . . . . . . 100.00
06/49 **(60)** LZ(a&c),CI Logo;rep. . 50.00
08/49 **(62)** LZ(a&c),CI Logo;rep. . 55.00
05/50 **(71)** LZ(a&c),CI Logo;rep. . 40.00
09/51 **(87)** LZ(a&c),15¢(c)
Price, CI Logo;rep . . . . . . . . . 30.00
04/54 **(118)** LZ(a&c),CI Logo;rep. . 25.00
03/56 **(131)** NN New Art,New
P(c), CI Logo;rep. . . . . . . . . . 35.00
05/57 **(138)** NN,P(c),CI Logo;rep. . 18.00
01/59 **(148)** NN,P(c),CI Logo;rep. . 18.00
09/60 **(158)** NN,P(c),CI Logo;rep. . 18.00

**006-A Tale of Two Cities**
**by Charles Dickens**
11/42 **(—)** StM(a&c),Original . . 2,000.00
09/43 **(14)** StM(a&c),No(c)
Price; rep. . . . . . . . . . . . . . . 400.00
03/44 **(18)** StM(a&c),Long Island
Independent Edition;rep . . . . 275.00
06/44 **(20)** StM(a&c),Sunrise
Times Edition;rep. . . . . . . . . 235.00
06/46 **(28)** StM(a&c);rep . . . . . . . 150.00
09/48 **(51)** StM(a&c),New CI
Logo; rep. . . . . . . . . . . . . . . 75.00
10/49 **(64)** StM(a&c),CI
Logo;rep . . . . . . . . . . . . . . . 40.00
12/50 **(78)** StM(a&c),15¢(c)
Price, CI Logo; rep . . . . . . . . 30.00
11/51 **(89)** StM(a&c),CI Logo;rep. . 30.00
03/54 **(117)** StM(a&c),CI
Logo; rep . . . . . . . . . . . . . . . 25.00
05/56 **(132)** JO New Art,New
P(c), CI Logo;rep. . . . . . . . . . 35.00

09/57 **(140)** JO,P(c),CI Logo;rep . . 15.00
11/57 **(147)** JO,P(c),CI Logo;rep . . 15.00
09/59 **(152)** JO,P(c),CI Logo;rep . 250.00
11/59 **(153)** JO,P(c),CI Logo;rep . . 18.00
03/61 **(149)** JO,P(c),CI Logo;rep . . 18.00

**007-Robin Hood**
**by Howard Pyle**
12/42 **(—)** LZ(a&c),Original . . . 1,400.00
06/43 **(12)** LZ(a&c),P.D.C.
on(c) Deleted;rep. . . . . . . . . 350.00
03/44 **(18)** LZ(a&c),Long Island
Independent Edition;rep . . . . 225.00
06/44 **(20)** LZ(a&c),Nassau
Bulletin Edition;rep . . . . . . . 250.00
10/44 **(22)** LZ(a&c),Queens
City Times Edition;rep . . . . . 225.00
06/46 **(28)** LZ(a&c),rep . . . . . . . . 150.00
09/48 **(51)** LZ(a&c),New CI
Logo;rep . . . . . . . . . . . . . . . 75.00
06/49 **(60)** LZ(a&c),CI Logo;rep. . . 35.00
10/49 **(64)** LZ(a&c),CI Logo;rep. . . 32.00
12/50 **(78)** LZ(a&c),CI Logo;rep. . . 32.00
07/52 **(97)** LZ(a&c),CI Logo;rep. . . 35.00
03/53 **(106)** LZ(a&c),CI Logo;rep . . 30.00
07/54 **(121)** LZ(a&c),CI Logo;rep . . 30.00
11/55 **(129)** LZ,New P(c),
CI Logo;rep . . . . . . . . . . . . . 35.00
01/57 **(136)** JkS New Art,P(c);rep . 30.00
03/58 **(143)** JkS,P(c),CI Logo;rep . 18.00
11/59 **(153)** JkS,P(c),CI Logo;rep . 15.00
10/61 **(164)** JkS,P(c),CI Logo;rep . 15.00

**008-Arabian Nights**
**by Antoine Galland**
03/43 **(—)** LCh(a&c),Original . . 2,200.00
09/43 **(14)** LCh(a&c);rep . . . . . . . 750.00
01/44 **(17)** LCh(a&c),Long Island
Independent Edition;rep . . . . 750.00
06/44 **(20)** LCh(a&c),Nassau
Bulletin Edition,64 pgs;rep. . . 600.00
06/46 **(28)** LCh(a&c);rep . . . . . . . 400.00
09/48 **(51)** LCh(a&c),New CI
Logo; rep. . . . . . . . . . . . . . . 400.00
10/49 **(64)** LCh(a&c),CI
Logo;rep . . . . . . . . . . . . . . . 300.00
12/50 **(78)** LCh(a&c),CI
Logo;rep . . . . . . . . . . . . . . . 250.00
10/61 **(164)** ChB New Art,P(c),
CI Logo;rep . . . . . . . . . . . . . 225.00

**009-Les Miserables**
**by Victor Hugo**
03/43 **(—)** RLv(a&c),Original . . 1,300.00
09/43 **(14)** RLv(a&c);rep . . . . . . . 400.00
03/44 **(18)** RLv(a&c),Nassau
Bulletin Edition;rep . . . . . . . 275.00

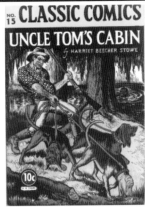

*Classic Comics #11*
© Gilberton Publications

*Classic Comics #12*
© Gilberton Publications

*Classic Comics #15*
© Gilberton Publications

06/44 **(20)** RLv(a&c),Richmond
  Courier Edition;rep . . . . . . . . 250.00
06/46 **(28)** RLv(a&c);rep . . . . . . . 200.00
09/48 **(51)** RLv(a&c),New CI
  Logo; rep . . . . . . . . . . . . . . . 100.00
05/50 **(71)** RLv(a&c),CI
  Logo;rep . . . . . . . . . . . . . . . . 75.00
09/51 **(87)** RLv(a&c),CI Logo,
  15¢(c)Price;rep . . . . . . . . . . . 60.00
03/61 **(161)** NN New Art,GMc
  New P(c), CI Logo;rep . . . . . . 60.00

**010-Robinson Crusoe**
**by Daniel Defoe**
04/43 **(——)** StM(a&c),Original . . 1,100.00
09/43 **(14)** StM(a&c),rep . . . . . . . 400.00
03/44 **(18)** StM(a&c),Nassau Bulletin
  Ed.,'Bill of Rights'Pge.64;rep. 300.00
06/44 **(20)** StM(a&c),Queens
  Home News Edition;rep. . . . . 250.00
??/45 **(23)** StM(a&c),rep . . . . . . . 150.00
06/46 **(28)** StM(a&c),rep . . . . . . . 150.00
09/48 **(51)** StM(a&c),New CI
  Logo; rep . . . . . . . . . . . . . . . 75.00
10/49 **(64)** StM(a&c),CI Logo;rep. . 50.00
12/50 **(78)** StM(a&c),15¢(c)
  Price, CI Logo;rep . . . . . . . . . 35.00
07/52 **(97)** StM(a&c),CI Logo;rep. . 32.00
12/53 **(114)** StM(a&c),CI
  Logo;rep . . . . . . . . . . . . . . . 30.00
01/56 **(130)** StM,New P(c),CI
  Logo; rep . . . . . . . . . . . . . . . 32.00
09/57 **(140)** SmC New Art,P(c),
  CI Logo; rep. . . . . . . . . . . . . 32.00
11/59 **(153)** SmC,P(c),CI Logo;rep 15.00
10/61 **(164)** SmC,P(c),CI Logo;rep 15.00

**011-Don Quixote**
**by Miguel de Cervantes**
**Saavedra**
05/43 **(——)** LZ(a&c),Original . . . 1,300.00
03/44 **(18)** LZ(a&c),Nassau
  Bulletin Edition;rep . . . . . . . . 350.00
07/44 **(21)** LZ(a&c),Queens
  Home News Edition;rep. . . . . 250.00
06/46 **(28)** LZ(a&c);rep . . . . . . . 150.00
08/53 **(110)** LZ,TO New P(c),New
  CI Logo;rep . . . . . . . . . . . . . 50.00
05/60 **(156)** LZ,TO P(c),Pages
  Reduced to 48,CI Logo;rep . . . 30.00

**012-Rip Van Winkle & The**
**Headless Horseman**
**by Washington Irving**
06/43 **(——)** RLv(a&c),Original. 1,200.00
11/43 **(15)** RLv(a&c),Long Island
  Independent Edition;rep . . . . 350.00

06/44 **(20)** RLv(a&c),Long Island
  Independent Edition;rep . . . . 250.00
10/44 **(22)** RLv(a&c),Queens
  City Times Edition;rep . . . . . 225.00
06/46 **(28)** RLv(a&c);rep . . . . . . . 150.00
06/49 **(60)** RLv(a&c),New CI
  Logo;rep . . . . . . . . . . . . . . . 75.00
08/49 **(62)** RLv(a&c),CI
  Logo;rep . . . . . . . . . . . . . . . 45.00
05/50 **(71)** RLv(a&c),CI Logo;rep. . 35.00
11/51 **(89)** RLv(a&c),15¢(c)
  Price, CI Logo;rep . . . . . . . . . 30.00
04/54 **(118)** RLv(a&c),CI
  Logo;rep . . . . . . . . . . . . . . . 32.00
05/56 **(132)** RLv,New P(c),
  CI Logo; rep. . . . . . . . . . . . . 35.00
05/59 **(150)** NN New Art;P(c),
  CI Logo; rep. . . . . . . . . . . . . 35.00
09/60 **(158)** NN,P(c),CI Logo;rep. . 20.00

**013-Dr. Jekyll and Mr. Hyde**
**by Robert Louis Stevenson**
08/43 **(——)** AdH(a&c),Original. . 2,000.00
11/43 **(15)** AdH(a&c),Long Island
  Independent Edition;rep . . . . 500.00
06/44 **(20)** AdH(a&c),Long Island
  Independent Edition;rep . . . . 275.00
06/46 **(28)** AdH(a&c),No(c)
  Price; rep . . . . . . . . . . . . . . . 225.00
06/49 **(60)** AdH,HcK New(c),New CI
  Logo,Pgs.reduced to 48;rep . . 75.00
08/49 **(62)** AdH,HcK(c),CI
  Logo;rep . . . . . . . . . . . . . . . 45.00
05/50 **(71)** AdH,HcK(c),CI
  Logo;rep . . . . . . . . . . . . . . . 40.00
09/51 **(87)** AdH,HcK(c),Erroneous
  Return of Original Date,
  CI Logo;rep . . . . . . . . . . . . . 40.00
10/53 **(112)** LC New Art,New
  P(c), CI Logo;rep. . . . . . . . . . 40.00
11/59 **(153)** LC,P(c),CI Logo;rep . . 20.00
03/61 **(161)** LC,P(c),CI Logo;rep . . 20.00

**014-Westward Ho!**
**by Charles Kingsley**
09/43 **(——)** ASm(a&c),Orig. . . . 3,000.00
11/43 **(15)** ASm(a&c),Long Island
  Independent Edition;rep . . . . 750.00
07/44 **(21)** ASm(a&c);rep. . . . . . . 650.00
06/46 **(28)** ASm(a&c),No(c)
  Price; rep . . . . . . . . . . . . . . . 450.00
11/48 **(53)** ASm(a&c),Pages reduced
  to 48, New CI Logo;rep . . . . . 400.00

**015-Uncle Tom's Cabin**
**by Harriet Beecher Stowe**
11/43 **(——)** RLv(a&c),Original . . 1,000.00

11/43 **(15)** RLv(a&c),Blank
  Price Circle, Long Island
  Independent Ed.;rep . . . . . . . 350.00
07/44 **(21)** RLv(a&c),Nassau
  Bulletin Edition;rep . . . . . . . . 250.00
06/46 **(28)** RLv(a&c),No(c)
  Price; rep . . . . . . . . . . . . . . . 200.00
11/48 **(53)** RLv(a&c),Pages Reduced
  to 48, New CI Logo;rep . . . . . 75.00
05/50 **(71)** RLv(a&c),CI Logo;rep. . 45.00
11/51 **(89)** RLv(a&c),15¢(c)
  Price, CI Logo;rep . . . . . . . . . 45.00
03/54 **(117)** RLv,New P(c),CI
  Logo, Lettering Changes;rep. . 32.00
09/55 **(128)** RLv,P(c),"Picture
  Progress"Promotion,CI
  Logo;rep . . . . . . . . . . . . . . . 22.00
03/57 **(137)** RLv,P(c),CI Logo;rep . 15.00
09/58 **(146)** RLv,P(c),CI Logo;rep . 15.00
01/60 **(154)** RLv,P(c),CI Logo;rep . 15.00
03/61 **(161)** RLv,P(c),CI Logo;rep . 17.00

**016-Gulliver's Travels**
**by Johnathan Swift**
12/43 **(——)** LCh(a&c),Original. 1,200.00
06/44 **(18/20)** LCh(a&c),Queen's
  Home News Edition,No(c)Price;
  rep. . . . . . . . . . . . . . . . . . . 300.00
10/44 **(22)** LCh(a&c),Queen's
  Home News Editon;rep . . . . . 225.00
06/46 **(28)** LCh(a&c);rep . . . . . . . 150.00
06/49 **(60)** LCh(a&c),Pgs. Reduced
  To 48, New CI Logo;rep . . . . . 75.00
08/49 **(62)** LCh(a&c),CI Logo;rep . 45.00
10/49 **(64)** LCh(a&c),CI Logo;rep . 45.00
12/50 **(78)** LCh(a&c),15¢(c)
  Price, CI Logo;rep . . . . . . . . . 35.00
11/51 **(89)** LCh(a&c),Price;rep . . . 30.00
03/60 **(155)** LCh,New P(c),CI
  Logo; rep . . . . . . . . . . . . . . . 35.00

**017-The Deerslayer**
**by James Fenimore Cooper**
01/44 **(——)** LZ(a&c),Original . . 1,000.00
03/44 **(18)** LZ(a&c),No(c)Price;
  rep . . . . . . . . . . . . . . . . . . . 350.00
10/44 **(22)** LZ(a&c),Queen's
  City Times Edition;rep . . . . . 200.00
06/46 **(28)** LZ(a&c);rep . . . . . . . 150.00
06/49 **(60)** LZ(a&c),Pgs. Reduced
  to 48,New CI Logo;rep . . . . . 75.00
10/49 **(64)** LZ(a&c),CI Logo;rep. . . 35.00
07/51 **(85)** LZ(a&c),15¢(c)
  Price, CI Logo;rep . . . . . . . . . 30.00
04/54 **(118)** LZ(a&c),CI Logo;rep. . 28.00
05/56 **(132)** LZ(a&c),CI Logo;rep. . 25.00

---

All comics prices listed are for *Near Mint* condition.      **Page 79**

**CI**

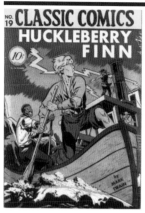

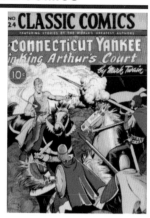

*Classic Comics #19*
© *Gilberton Publications*

*Classic Comics #21*
© *Gilberton Publications*

*Classic Comics #24*
© *Gilberton Publications*

**018-The Hunchback of Notre
Dame
by Victor Hugo**
03/44 (—) ASm(a&c),Original
   Gilberton Edition . . . . . . . . 1,200.00
03/44 (—) ASm(a&c),Original
   Island Publications Edition . 1,000.00
06/44 **(18/20)** ASm(a&c),Queens
   Home News Edition;rep. . . . . 350.00
10/44 **(22)** ASm(a&c),Queens
   City Times Edition;rep . . . . . 250.00
06/46 **(28)** ASm(a&c);rep . . . . . . 225.00
06/49 **(60)** ASm,HcK New(c)8 Pgs.
   Deleted, New CI Logo;rep. . . . 75.00
08/49 **(62)** ASm,HcK(c),CI
   Logo;rep . . . . . . . . . . . . . . . 40.00
12/50 **(78)** ASm,HcK(c),15¢(c)
   Price; CI Logo;rep . . . . . . . . . 35.00
11/51 **(89)** ASm,HcK(c),CI
   Logo;rep . . . . . . . . . . . . . . . 32.00
04/54 **(118)** ASm, HcK(c),CI
   Logo;rep . . . . . . . . . . . . . . . 35.00
09/57 **(140)** ASm,New P(c),CI
   Logo; rep . . . . . . . . . . . . . . . 32.00
09/58 **(146)** ASm,P(c),CI Logo;rep 32.00
09/60 **(158)** GE&RC New Art,GMc
   New P(c),CI Logo;rep . . . . . . . 20.00

**019-Huckleberry Finn
by Mark Twain**
04/44 (—) LZ(a&c),Original
   Gilberton Edition . . . . . . . . . 750.00
04/44 (—) LZ(a&c),Original Island
   Publications Company Ed. . . 800.00
03/44 **(18)** LZ(a&c),Nassau
   Bulletin Editon;rep. . . . . . . . 350.00
10/44 **(22)** LZ(a&c),Queens City
   Times Edition;rep. . . . . . . . . 250.00
06/46 **(28)** LZ(a&c);rep . . . . . . 200.00
06/49 **(60)** LZ(a&c),New CI Logo,
   Pgs.Reduced to 48;rep . . . . . 75.00
08/49 **(62)** LZ(a&c),CI Logo;rep. . 40.00
12/50 **(78)** LZ(a&c),CI Logo;rep. . 35.00
11/51 **(89)** LZ(a&c),CI Logo;rep. . 30.00
03/54 **(117)** LZ(a&c),CI Logo;rep. . 30.00
03/56 **(131)** FrG New Art,New
   P(c), CI Logo; rep . . . . . . . . . 30.00
09/57 **(140)** FrG,P(c),CI Logo;rep . 20.00
05/59 **(150)** FrG,P(c),CI Logo;rep . 20.00
09/60 **(158)** FrG,P(c),CI Logo;rep . 20.00

**020-The Corsican Brothers
by Alexandre Dumas**
06/44 (—) ASm(a&c),Original
   Gilberton Edition . . . . . . . . . 650.00
06/44 (—) ASm(a&c),Original
   Courier Edition. . . . . . . . . . . 550.00

06/44 (—) ASm(a&c),Original Long
   Island Independent Edition . . 550.00
10/44 **(22)** ASm(a&c),Queens
   City Times Edition;rep . . . . . 275.00
06/46 **(28)** ASm(a&c);rep . . . . . . 250.00
06/49 **(60)** ASm(a&c),No(c)Price,
   New CI Logo,Pgs. Reduced
   to 48;rep . . . . . . . . . . . . . . 225.00
08/49 **(62)** ASm(a&c),CI
   Logo;rep . . . . . . . . . . . . . . 165.00
12/50 **(78)** ASm(a&c),15¢(c)
   Price, CI Logo;rep . . . . . . . . 150.00
07/52 **(97)** ASm(a&c),CI
   Logo;rep . . . . . . . . . . . . . . 135.00

**021-Famous Mysteries
by Sir Arthur Conan Doyle
Guy de Maupassant
& Edgar Allan Poe**
07/44 (—) AdH,LZ,ASm(a&c),
   Original Gilberton Edition . . 1,300.00
07/44 (—) AdH,LZ,ASm(a&c),
   Original Island Publications
   Edition; No Date or Indicia 1,350.00
07/44 (—) AdH,LZ,ASm(a&c),
   Original Richmond Courier
   Edition. . . . . . . . . . . . . . . 1,100.00
10/44 **(22)** AdH,LZ,ASm(a&c),
   Nassau Bulletin Edition;rep . . 500.00
09/46 **(30)** AdH,LZ,ASm(a&c);
   rep. . . . . . . . . . . . . . . . . . . 350.00
08/49 **(62)** AdH,LZ,ASm(a&c),
   New CI Logo;rep . . . . . . . . . 300.00
04/50 **(70)** AdH,LZ,ASm(a&c),
   CI Logo;rep . . . . . . . . . . . . 275.00
07/51 **(85)** AdH,LZ,ASm(a&c),
   15¢(c) Price,CI Logo;rep . . . . 250.00
12/53 **(114)** ASm,AdH,LZ,New
   P(c), CI Logo;rep . . . . . . . . . 250.00

**022-The Pathfinder
by James Fenimore Cooper**
10/44 (—) LZ(a&c),Original
   Gilberton Edition . . . . . . . . . 600.00
10/44 (—) LZ(a&c),Original
   Island Publications Edition; . . 500.00
10/44 (—) LZ(a&c),Original
   Queens County Times Edition 450.00
09/46 **(30)** LZ(a&c),No(c)
   Price;rep . . . . . . . . . . . . . . 200.00
06/49 **(60)** LZ(a&c),New CI Logo,
   Pgs.Reduced To 48;rep . . . . . 50.00
08/49 **(62)** LZ(a&c),CI Logo;rep. . 45.00
04/50 **(70)** LZ(a&c),CI Logo;rep . . 35.00
07/51 **(85)** LZ(a&c),15¢(c)
   Price, CI Logo;rep . . . . . . . . . 32.00
04/54 **(118)** LZ(a&c),CI Logo;rep. . 30.00

05/56 **(132)** LZ(a&c),CI Logo;rep. . 30.00
09/58 **(146)** LZ(a&c),CI Logo;rep. . 35.00

**023-Oliver Twist
by Charles Dickens
(First Classic by the Iger shop)**
07/45 (—) AdH(a&c),Original . . . 700.00
09/46 **(30)** AdH(a&c),Price
   Circle is Blank;rep . . . . . . . . 450.00
06/49 **(60)** AdH(a&c),Pgs. Reduced
   To 48, New CI Logo;rep . . . . . 50.00
08/49 **(62)** AdH(a&c),CI
   Logo;rep . . . . . . . . . . . . . . . 45.00
05/50 **(71)** AdH(a&c),CI
   Logo;rep . . . . . . . . . . . . . . . 35.00
07/51 **(85)** AdH(a&c),15¢(c)
   Price CI Logo;rep . . . . . . . . . 32.00
04/52 **(94)** AdH(a&c),CI
   Logo;rep . . . . . . . . . . . . . . . 32.00
04/54 **(118)** AdH(a&c),CI
   Logo;rep . . . . . . . . . . . . . . . 30.00
01/57 **(136)** AdH,New P(c),CI
   Logo; rep . . . . . . . . . . . . . . . 30.00
05/59 **(150)** AdH,P(c),CI Logo;rep. 25.00
1961 **(164)** AdH,P(c),CI Logo;rep . 25.00
10/61 **(164)** GE&RC New Art,P(c),
   CI Logo;rep . . . . . . . . . . . . . 35.00

**024-A Connecticut Yankee in
King Arthur's Court
by Mark Twain**
09/45 (—) JH(a&c),Original . . . . 550.00
09/46 **(30)** JH(a&c),Price Circle
   Blank;rep . . . . . . . . . . . . . . 200.00
06/49 **(60)** JH(a&c),8 Pages
   Deleted,New CI Logo;rep . . . . 50.00
08/49 **(62)** JH(a&c),CI Logo;rep. . 45.00
05/50 **(71)** JH(a&c),CI Logo;rep . . 35.00
09/51 **(87)** JH(a&c),15¢(c) Price
   CI Logo;rep . . . . . . . . . . . . . 30.00
07/54 **(121)** JH(a&c),CI Logo;rep. . 30.00
09/57 **(140)** JkS New Art,New
   P(c),CI Logo;rep . . . . . . . . . . 35.00
11/59 **(153)** JkS,P(c),CI Logo;rep . 18.00
1961 **(164)** JkS,P(c),CI Logo;rep. . 15.00

**025-Two Years Before the Mast
by Richard Henry Dana Jr.**
10/45 (—) RWb,DvH,Original; . . 500.00
09/46 **(30)** RWb,DvH,Price Circle
   Blank;rep . . . . . . . . . . . . . . 200.00
06/49 **(60)** RWb,DvH,8 Pages
   Deleted,New CI Logo;rep . . . . 50.00
08/49 **(62)** RWb,DvH,CI Logo;rep. 45.00
05/50 **(71)** RWb,DvH,CI Logo;rep . 35.00
07/51 **(85)** RWb,DvH,15¢(c) Price
   CI Logo;rep . . . . . . . . . . . . . 30.00

All comics prices listed are for *Near Mint* condition.

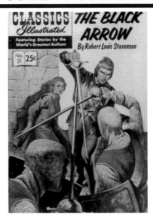

**CI**

Classics Illustrated #26
© Gilberton Publications

Classics Illustrated #31
© Gilberton Publications

Classics Illustrated #33
© Gilberton Publications

12/53 **(114)** RWb,DvH,CI Logo;rep 28.00
05/60 **(156)** RWb,DvH,New P(c),
CI Logo, 3 Pgs. Replaced
By Fillers;rep . . . . . . . . . . . . . 32.00

**026-Frankenstein**
**by Mary Wollstonecraft Shelley**
12/45 **(—)** RWb&ABr(a&c),
Original . . . . . . . . . . . . . . . 1,400.00
09/46 **(30)** RWb&ABr(a&c),
Price Circle Blank;rep . . . . . . 400.00
06/49 **(60)** RWb&ABr(a&c),
New CI Logo;rep . . . . . . . . . . 175.00
08/49 **(62)** RWb&ABr(a&c),
CI Logo;rep . . . . . . . . . . . . . 165.00
05/50 **(71)** RWb&ABr(a&c),
CI Logo;rep . . . . . . . . . . . . . . 75.00
04/51 **(82)** RWb&ABr(a&c),
15¢(c) Price,CI Logo;rep . . . . . 65.00
03/54 **(117)** RWb&ABr(a&c),
CI Logo;rep . . . . . . . . . . . . . . 30.00
09/58 **(146)** RWb&ABr,NS
New P(c), CI Logo; rep . . . . . . 35.00
11/59 **(153)** RWb&ABr,NS
P(c),CI Logo; rep . . . . . . . . . . 50.00
01/61 **(160)** RWb&ABr,NS
P(c),CI Logo; rep . . . . . . . . . . 16.00

**027-The Adventures of Marco**
**Polo**
**by Marco Polo & Donn Byrne**
04/46 **(—)** HFl(a&c);Original . . 550.00
09/46 **(30)** HFl(a&c);rep . . . . . . . 200.00
04/50 **(70)** HFl(a&c),8 Pages Deleted,
No(c) Price,New CI Logo;rep . 45.00
09/51 **(87)** HFl(a&c),15¢(c)
Price,CI Logo;rep . . . . . . . . . 30.00
03/54 **(117)** HFl(a&c),CILogo;rep . 25.00
01/60 **(154)** HFl,New P(c),CI
Logo;rep . . . . . . . . . . . . . . . 25.00
1962 **(165)** HFl,P(c),CI Logo;rep . . 15.00

**028-Michael Strogoff**
**by Jules Verne**
06/46 **(—)** AdH(a&c),Original . . . 500.00
09/48 **(51)** AdH(a&c),8 Pages
Deleted,New CI Logo;rep . . . 150.00
01/54 **(115)** AdH,New P(c),CI
Logo; rep . . . . . . . . . . . . . . . 45.00
03/60 **(155)** AdH,P(c),CI Logo;rep . 18.00

**029-The Prince and the Pauper**
**by Mark Twain**
07/46 **(—)** AdH(a&c),Original . . . 800.00
06/49 **(60)** AdH,New HcK(c),New CI
Logo,8 Pages Deleted;rep. . . 100.00
08/49 **(62)** AdH,HcK(c),CILogo;rep 50.00
05/50 **(71)** AdH,HcK(c),CILogo;rep 35.00

03/52 **(93)** AdH,HcK(c),CILogo;rep 32.00
12/53 **(114)** AdH,HcK(c),CI
Logo;rep . . . . . . . . . . . . . . . 30.00
09/55 **(128)** AdH,New P(c),CI
Logo; rep . . . . . . . . . . . . . . . 30.00
05/57 **(138)** AdH,P(c),CI Logo;rep . 18.00
05/59 **(150)** AdH,P(c),CI Logo;rep . 18.00
1961 **(164)** AdH,P(c),CI Logo;rep . 18.00

**030-The Moonstone**
**by William Wilkie Collins**
09/46 **(—)** DRi(a&c),Original. . . . 550.00
06/49 **(60)** DRi(a&c),8 Pages
Deleted,New CI Logo;rep . . . 100.00
04/50 **(70)** DRi(a&c),CI Logo;rep . . 65.00
03/60 **(155)** DRi,LbC New P(c),
CI Logo;rep . . . . . . . . . . . . . . 90.00
1962 **(165)** DRi,LbC P(c),CI Logo;
rep . . . . . . . . . . . . . . . . . . . 35.00

**031-The Black Arrow**
**by Robert Louis Stevenson**
10/46 **(—)** AdH(a&c),Original . . . 450.00
09/48 **(51)** AdH(a&c),8 Pages
Deleted,New CI Logo;rep . . . . 75.00
10/49 **(64)** AdH(a&c),CI
Logo;rep . . . . . . . . . . . . . . . 35.00
09/51 **(87)** AdH(a&c),15¢(c)
Price;CI Logo;rep . . . . . . . . . 30.00
06/53 **(108)** AdH(a&c),CI
Logo;rep . . . . . . . . . . . . . . . 28.00
03/55 **(125)** AdH(a&c),CI
Logo;rep . . . . . . . . . . . . . . . 27.00
03/56 **(131)** AdH,New P(c),CI
Logo; rep . . . . . . . . . . . . . . . 22.00
09/57 **(140)** AdH,P(c),CI Logo;rep . 20.00
01/59 **(148)** AdH,P(c),CI Logo;rep . 20.00
03/61 **(161)** AdH,P(c),CI Logo;rep . 20.00

**032-Lorna Doone**
**by Richard Doddridge**
**Blackmore**
12/46 **(—)** MB(a&c),Original . . . . 550.00
10/49 **(53/64)** MB(a&c),8 Pages
Deleted,New CI Logo;rep . . . 150.00
07/51 **(85)** MB(a&c),15¢(c)
Price, CI Logo;rep . . . . . . . . . 65.00
04/54 **(118)** MB(a&c),CI Logo;rep . 35.00
05/57 **(138)** MB,New P(c); Old(c)
Becomes New Splash Pge.,CI
Logo;rep . . . . . . . . . . . . . . . 35.00
05/59 **(150)** MB,P(c),CI Logo;rep. . 20.00
1962 **(165)** MB,P(c),CI Logo;rep . . 20.00

**033-The Adventures of**
**Sherlock Holmes**
**by Sir Arthur Conan Doyle**
01/47 **(—)** LZ,HcK(c),Original . 1,750.00

11/48 **(53)** LZ,HcK(c),"A Study in Scarlet"
Deleted,New CI Logo;rep . . . 700.00
05/50 **(71)** LZ,HcK(c),CI Logo;rep 500.00
11/51 **(89)** LZ,HcK(c),15¢(c)
Price,CI Logo;rep . . . . . . . . . 400.00

**034-Mysterious Island**
**by Jules Verne**
02/47 **(—)** RWb&DvH,Original . . 600.00
06/49 **(60)** RWb&DvH,8 Pages
Deleted,New CI Logo;rep . . . . 65.00
08/49 **(62)** RWb&DvH,CI Logo;rep 45.00
05/50 **(71)** RWb&DvH,CI
Logo;rep . . . . . . . . . . . . . . . 65.00
12/50 **(78)** RWb&DvH,15¢(c) Price,
CI Logo;rep . . . . . . . . . . . . . . 35.00
02/52 **(92)** RWb&DvH,CI Logo;rep 35.00
03/54 **(117)** RWb&DvH,CI Logo;
rep . . . . . . . . . . . . . . . . . . . 35.00
09/57 **(140)** RWb&DvH,New P(c),
CI Logo;rep . . . . . . . . . . . . . . 35.00
05/60 **(156)** RWb&DvH,P(c),CI
Logo;rep . . . . . . . . . . . . . . . 20.00
Becomes:

# CLASSICS ILLUSTRATED
**Gilberton Publications,**
**1947–60s**
**035-Last Days of Pompeii**
**by Lord Edward Bulwer Lytton**
03/47 **(—)** HcK(a&c),Original 500.00
03/61 **(161)** JK,New P(c),
15¢(c)Price;rep . . . . . . . . . . . 65.00

**036-Typee**
**by Herman Melville**
04/47 **(—)** EzW(a&c),Original . . . 275.00
10/49 **(64)** EzW(a&c),No(c)price,
8 pages deleted;rep. . . . . . . . 90.00
03/60 **(155)** EzW,GMc New
P(c);rep . . . . . . . . . . . . . . . . 35.00

**037-The Pioneers**
**by James Fenimore Cooper**
05/47 **(37)** RP(a&c),Original . . . . 300.00
08/49 **(62)** RP(a&c),8 Pages
Deleted;rep . . . . . . . . . . . . . . 45.00
04/50 **(70)** RP(a&c);rep . . . . . . . . 35.00
02/52 **(92)** RP(a&c),15¢(c)price;
rep . . . . . . . . . . . . . . . . . . . 35.00
04/54 **(118)** RP(a&c);rep . . . . . . . 30.00
03/56 **(131)** RP(a&c);rep . . . . . . . 30.00
05/56 **(132)** RP(a&c);rep . . . . . . . 30.00
11/59 **(153)** RP(a&c);rep . . . . . . . 25.00

**038-Adventures of Cellini**
**by Benvenuto Cellini**
06/47 **(—)** AgF(a&c),Original . . . 400.00

**CI**

*Classics Illustrated #39*
© *Gilberton Publications*

*Classics Illustrated #44*
© *Gilberton Publications*

*Classics Illustrated #52*
© *Gilberton Publications*

1961 **(164)** NN New Art,New P(c);
rep . . . . . . . . . . . . . . . . . . . . 35.00

**039-Jane Eyre
by Charlotte Bronte**
07/47 (—) HyG(a&c),Original . . . 350.00
06/49 **(60)** HyG(a&c),No(c)Price,
8 pages deleted;rep . . . . . . . . 50.00
08/49 **(62)** HyG(a&c);rep . . . . . . . 45.00
05/50 **(71)** HyG(a&c);rep . . . . . . . 35.00
02/52 **(92)** HyG(a&c),15¢(c)
Price; rep . . . . . . . . . . . . . . . 32.00
04/54 **(118)** HyG(a&c);rep . . . . . . 32.00
01/58 **(142)** HyG,New P(c);rep. . . . 32.00
01/60 **(154)** HyG,P(c);rep. . . . . . . 32.00

**040-Mysteries
(The Pit & the Pendulum,
The Adventures of Hans Pfall,
Fall of the House of Usher)
by Edgar Allan Poe**
08/47 (—) AgF,HyG,HcK(a&c),
Original . . . . . . . . . . . . . . . 1,000.00
08/49 **(62)** AgF,HyG,HcK(a&c),
8 Pages deleted;rep . . . . . . 350.00
09/50 **(75)** AgF,HyG,
HcK(a&c);rep . . . . . . . . . . . 300.00
02/52 **(92)** AgF,HyG,HcK(a&c)
15¢(c) Price;rep . . . . . . . . . . 250.00

**041-Twenty Years After
by Alexandre Dumas**
09/47 (—) RBu(a&c),Original . . . 600.00
08/49 **(62)** RBu,HcK New(c),No(c)
Price, 8 Pages Deleted;rep . . . 65.00
12/50 **(78)** RBu,HcK(c),15¢(c)
Price;rep . . . . . . . . . . . . . . . 45.00
05/60 **(156)** RBu,DgR New P(c);
rep . . . . . . . . . . . . . . . . . . . . 35.00

**042-Swiss Family Robinson
by Johann Wyss**
10/47 **(42)** HcK(a&c),Original. . . . 300.00
08/49 **(62)** HcK(a&c),No(c)price,
8 Pages Deleted,Not Every Issue
Has 'Gift Box' Ad;rep . . . . . . . 75.00
09/50 **(75)** HcK(a&c);rep . . . . . . . 35.00
03/52 **(93)** HcK(a&c);rep . . . . . . . 32.00
03/54 **(117)** HcK(a&c);rep . . . . . . 30.00
03/56 **(131)** HcK,New P(c);rep. . . 28.00
03/57 **(137)** HcK,P(c);rep. . . . . . . 28.00
11/57 **(141)** HcK,P(c);rep. . . . . . . 28.00
09/59 **(152)** NN New art,P(c);rep. . 28.00
09/60 **(158)** NN,P(c);rep . . . . . . . 25.00

**043-Great Expectations
by Charles Dickens**
11/47 (—) HcK(a&c),Original . . 1,400.00

08/49 **(62)** HcK(a&c),No(c)price;
8 pages deleted;rep. . . . . . . 850.00

**044-Mysteries of Paris
by Eugene Sue**
12/47 **(44)** HcK(a&c),Original . . 1,000.00
08/47 **(62)** HcK(a&c),No(c)Price,
8 Pages Deleted,Not Every Issue
Has'Gift Box'Ad;rep . . . . . . . 400.00
12/50 **(78)** HcK(a&c),15¢(c)
Price; rep . . . . . . . . . . . . . . . 350.00

**045-Tom Brown's School Days
by Thomas Hughes**
01/48 **(44)** HFI(a&c),Original,
1st 48 Pge. Issue . . . . . . . . 250.00
10/49 **(64)** HFI(a&c),No(c)
Price;rep . . . . . . . . . . . . . . . 60.00
03/61 **(161)** JTg New Art,GMc
New P(c);rep . . . . . . . . . . . . . 30.00

**046-Kidnapped
by Robert Louis Stevenson**
04/48 **(47)** RWb(a&c),Original . . . 200.00
08/49 **(62)** RWb(a&c),Red Circle
Either Blank or With 10¢;rep . 100.00
12/50 **(78)** RWb(a&c),15¢(c)
Price; rep . . . . . . . . . . . . . . . 35.00
09/51 **(87)** RWb(a&c);rep . . . . . . 32.00
04/54 **(118)** RWb(a&c);rep . . . . . . 30.00
03/56 **(131)** RWb,New P(c);rep . . 30.00
09/57 **(140)** RWb,P(c);rep . . . . . . 18.00
05/59 **(150)** RWb,P(c);rep . . . . . . 18.00
05/60 **(156)** RWb,P(c);rep . . . . . . 18.00
1961 **(164)** RWb,P(c),Reduced Pge.
Wdth;rep . . . . . . . . . . . . . . . . 18.00

**047-Twenty Thousand Leagues
Under the Sea
by Jules Verne**
05/58 **(47)** HcK(a&c),Original. . . . 250.00
10/49 **(64)** HcK(a&c),No(c)
Price; rep . . . . . . . . . . . . . . . 45.00
12/50 **(78)** HcK(a&c),15¢(c)
Price; rep . . . . . . . . . . . . . . . 35.00
04/52 **(94)** HcK(a&c);rep . . . . . . . 35.00
04/54 **(118)** HcK(a&c);rep . . . . . . 30.00
09/55 **(128)** HcK,New P(c);rep. . . 30.00
07/56 **(133)** HcK,P(c);rep. . . . . . . 25.00
09/57 **(140)** HcK,P(c);rep. . . . . . . 18.00
01/59 **(148)** HcK,P(c);rep. . . . . . . 18.00
05/60 **(156)** HcK,P(c);rep. . . . . . . 18.00
62/63 **(165)** HcK,P(c);rep. . . . . . . 18.00
05/48 **(167)** HcK,P(c);rep. . . . . . . 18.00

**048-David Copperfield
by Charles Dickens**
06/48 **(47)** HcK(a&c),Original. . . . 200.00

10/49 **(64)** HcK(a&c),Price Circle
Replaced by Image of Boy
Reading;rep . . . . . . . . . . . . . 45.00
09/51 **(87)** HcK(a&c),15¢(c)
Price; rep . . . . . . . . . . . . . . . 35.00
07/54 **(121)** HcK,New P(c);rep. . . 30.00
10/56 **(130)** HcK,P(c);rep. . . . . . . 18.00
09/57 **(140)** HcK,P(c);rep. . . . . . . 18.00
01/59 **(148)** HcK,P(c);rep. . . . . . . 18.00
05/60 **(156)** HcK,P(c);rep. . . . . . . 18.00

**049-Alice in Wonderland
by Lewis Carroll**
07/48 **(47)** AB(a&c),Original. . . . . 250.00
10/49 **(64)** AB(a&c),No(c)Price;
rep . . . . . . . . . . . . . . . . . . . . 75.00
07/51 **(85)** AB(a&c),15¢(c)Price;
rep . . . . . . . . . . . . . . . . . . . . 50.00
03/60 **(155)** AB,New P(c);rep. . . . 50.00

**050-Adventures of Tom Sawyer
by Mark Twain**
08/48 **(51)** ARu(a&c),Original. . . . 225.00
09/48 **(51)** ARu(a&c),Original. . . . 250.00
10/49 **(64)** ARu(a&c),No(c)
Price; rep . . . . . . . . . . . . . . . 35.00
12/50 **(78)** ARu(a&c),15¢(c)
Price; rep . . . . . . . . . . . . . . . 30.00
04/52 **(94)** ARu(a&c);rep . . . . . . . 30.00
12/53 **(114)** ARu(a&c);rep . . . . . . 30.00
03/54 **(117)** ARu(a&c);rep . . . . . . 25.00
05/56 **(132)** ARu(a&c);rep . . . . . . 25.00
09/57 **(140)** ARu,New P(c);rep. . . 22.00
05/59 **(150)** ARu,P(c);rep. . . . . . . 25.00
10/61 **(164)** New Art,P(c);rep. . . . 15.00

**051-The Spy
by James Fenimore Cooper**
09/48 **(51)** AdH(a&c),Original,
Maroon(c) . . . . . . . . . . . . . . 200.00
09/48 **(51)** AdH(a&c),Original,
Violet(c) . . . . . . . . . . . . . . . . 175.00
11/51 **(89)** AdH(a&c),15¢(c)
Price; rep . . . . . . . . . . . . . . . 35.00
07/54 **(121)** AdH(a&c);rep . . . . . . 30.00
07/57 **(139)** AdH,New P(c);rep. . . 30.00
05/60 **(156)** AdH,P(c);rep. . . . . . . 18.00

**052-The House of the Seven
Gables
by Nathaniel Hawthorne**
10/48 **(53)** HyG(a&c),Original . . . 200.00
11/51 **(89)** HyG(a&c),15¢(c)
Price; rep . . . . . . . . . . . . . . . 35.00
07/54 **(121)** HyG(a&c);rep . . . . . . 30.00
01/58 **(142)** GWb New Art,New
P(c); rep. . . . . . . . . . . . . . . . 35.00
05/60 **(156)** GWb,P(c);rep . . . . . . 18.00

CI

*Classics Illustrated #54*
© Gilberton Publications

*Classics Illustrated #63*
© Gilberton Publications

*Classics Illustrated #68*
© Gilberton Publications

**053-A Christmas Carol
by Charles Dickens**
11/48 **(53)** HcK(a&c),Original.... 250.00
**054-Man in the Iron Mask
by Alexandre Dumas**
12/48 **(55)** AgF,HcK(c),Original .. 200.00
03/52 **(93)** AgF,HcK(c),15¢(c)
Price; rep................ 45.00
09/53 **(111)** AgF,HcK(c);rep ..... 60.00
01/58 **(142)** KBa New Art,New
P(c); rep.............. 35.00
01/60 **(154)** KBa,P(c);rep........ 18.00
**055-Silas Mariner
by George Eliot**
01/49 **(55)** AdH,HcK(c),Original .. 200.00
09/50 **(75)** AdH,HcK(c),Price Circle
Blank,'Coming next'Ad(not
usually in reps.);rep......... 45.00
07/52 **(97)** AdH,HcK(c);rep ...... 32.00
07/54 **(121)** AdH,New P(c);rep.... 30.00
01/56 **(130)** AdH,P(c);rep........ 18.00
09/57 **(140)** AdH,P(c);rep........ 18.00
01/60 **(154)** AdH,P(c);rep........ 18.00
**056-The Toilers of the Sea
by Victor Hugo**
02/49 **(55)** AgF(a&c),Original .... 300.00
01/62 **(165)** AT New Art,New
P(c); rep................ 60.00
**057-The Song of Hiawatha
by Henry Wadsworth
Longfellow**
03/49 **(55)** AB(a&c),Original..... 200.00
09/50 **(75)** AB(a&c),No(c)price,'
Coming Next'Ad(not usually
found in reps.);rep........ 50.00
04/52 **(94)** AB(a&c),15¢(c)
Price;rep ................ 35.00
04/54 **(118)** AB(a&c);rep ....... 32.00
09/56 **(134)** AB,New P(c);rep .... 30.00
07/57 **(139)** AB,P(c);rep........ 18.00
01/60 **(154)** AB,P(c);rep........ 18.00
**058-The Prairie
by James Fenimore Cooper**
04/49 **(60)** RP(a&c),Original .... 200.00
08/49 **(62)** RP(a&c);rep ......... 75.00
12/50 **(78)** RP(a&c),15¢(c) Price
In Double Circle;rep...... 35.00
12/53 **(114)** RP(a&c);rep ....... 30.00
03/56 **(131)** RP(a&c);rep ....... 30.00
05/56 **(132)** RP(a&c);rep ....... 30.00
09/58 **(146)** RP,New P(c);rep..... 30.00
03/60 **(155)** RP,P(c);rep........ 20.00

**059-Wuthering Heights
by Emily Bronte**
05/49 **(60)** HcK(a&c),Original.... 225.00
07/51 **(85)** HcK(a&c),15¢(c)
Price; rep................ 50.00
05/60 **(156)** HcK,GB New P(c);rep 35.00
**060-Black Beauty
by Anna Sewell**
06/49 **(62)** AgF(a&c),Original.... 200.00
08/49 **(62)** AgF(a&c);rep ....... 225.00
07/51 **(85)** AgF(a&c),15¢(c) Price;
rep ................... 40.00
09/60 **(158)** LbC&NN&StA New
Art, LbC New P(c);rep....... 35.00
**061-The Woman in White
by William Wilke Collins**
07/49 **(62)** AB(a&c),Original,
Maroon & Violet(c)s........ 200.00
05/60 **(156)** AB,DgR New P(c);rep 40.00
**062-Western Stories
(The Luck of Roaring Camp &
The Outcasts of Poker Flat)
by Bret Harte**
08/49 **(62)** HcK(a&c),Original.... 200.00
11/51 **(89)** HcK(a&c),15¢(c)
Price; rep................ 40.00
07/54 **(121)** HcK(a&c);rep ....... 32.00
03/57 **(137)** HcK,New P(c);rep.... 30.00
09/59 **(152)** HcK,P(c);rep........ 20.00
10/63 **(167)** HcK,P(c);rep........ 20.00
**063-The Man Without a Country
by Edward Everett Hale**
09/49 **(62)** HcK(a&c),Original.... 200.00
12/50 **(78)** HcK(a&c),15¢(c)Price
In Double Circles;rep....... 40.00
05/60 **(156)** HcK,GMc New P(c);
rep ................... 35.00
01/62 **(165)** AT New Art,GMc P(c),
Added Text Pages;rep....... 32.00
**064-Treasure Island
by Robert Louis Stevenson**
10/49 **(62)** AB(a&c),Original..... 200.00
04/51 **(82)** AB(a&c),15¢(c)
Price;rep ................ 40.00
03/54 **(117)** AB(a&c);rep ....... 32.00
03/56 **(131)** AB,New P(c);rep..... 30.00
05/57 **(138)** AB,P(c);rep........ 18.00
09/58 **(146)** AB,P(c);rep........ 18.00
09/60 **(158)** AB,P(c);rep........ 18.00
**065-Benjamin Franklin
by Benjamin Franklin**
11/49 **(64)** AB,RtH,GS(Iger Shop),
HcK(c),Original .......... 200.00

03/56 **(131)** AB,RtH,GS(Iger Shop),
New P(c) ;rep ............. 35.00
01/60 **(154)** AB,RtH,GS(Iger Shop),
P(c);rep ................ 20.00
**066-The Cloister and the Hearth
by Charles Reade**
12/49 **(67)** HcK(a&c),Original.... 400.00
**067-The Scottish Chiefs
by Jane Porter**
01/50 **(67)** AB(a&c),Original..... 200.00
07/51 **(85)** AB(a&c),15¢(c)
Price;rep ................ 40.00
04/54 **(118)** AB(a&c);rep ....... 35.00
01/57 **(136)** AB,New P(c);rep..... 32.00
01/60 **(154)** AB,P(c);rep........ 20.00
**068-Julius Caesar
by William Shakespeare**
02/50 **(70)** HcK(a&c),Original.... 200.00
07/51 **(85)** HcK(a&c),15¢(c)
Price; rep................ 40.00
06/53 **(108)** HcK(a&c);rep ....... 32.00
05/60 **(156)** HcK,LbC New P(c);rep 35.00
1962 **(165)** GE&RC New Art,
LbC P(c);rep .............. 35.00
**069-Around the World in 80
Days
by Jules Verne**
03/50 **(70)** HcK(a&c),Original.... 200.00
09/51 **(87)** HcK(a&c),15¢(c)
Price; rep................ 45.00
03/55 **(125)** HcK(a&c);rep ....... 32.00
01/57 **(136)** HcK,New P(c);rep..... 32.00
09/58 **(146)** HcK,P(c);rep........ 20.00
09/59 **(152)** HcK,P(c);rep........ 20.00
1961 **(164)** HcK,P(c);rep........ 20.00
**070-The Pilot
by James Fenimore Cooper**
04/50 **(71)** AB(a&c),Original..... 175.00
10/50 **(75)** AB(a&c),15¢(c)
Price;rep ................ 45.00
02/52 **(92)** AB(a&c);rep ....... 32.00
03/55 **(125)** AB(a&c);rep ....... 35.00
05/60 **(156)** AB,GMc New P(c);rep 30.00
**071-The Man Who Laughs
by Victor Hugo**
05/50 **(71)** AB(a&c),Original..... 250.00
01/62 **(165)** NN,NN New P(c);rep 125.00
**072-The Oregon Trail
by Francis Parkman**
06/50 **(73)** HcK(a&c),Original.... 150.00
11/51 **(89)** HcK(a&c),15¢(c)
Price; rep................ 40.00

**CI**

Classics Illustrated #75
© Gilberton Publications

Classics Illustrated #85
© Gilberton Publications

Classics Illustrated #91
© Gilberton Publications

07/54 **(121)** HcK(a&c);rep . . . . . . . 32.00
03/56 **(131)** HcK,New P(c);rep. . . . 30.00
09/57 **(140)** HcK,P(c);rep. . . . . . . . 20.00
05/59 **(150)** HcK,P(c);rep. . . . . . . . 18.00
01/61 **(164)** HcK,P(c);rep. . . . . . . . 18.00

**073-The Black Tulip**
**by Alexandre Dumas**
07/50 **(75)** AB(a&c),Original. . . . . 550.00

**074-Mr. Midshipman Easy**
**by Captain Frederick Marryat**
08/50 **(75)** BbL,Original . . . . . . . 500.00

**075-The Lady of the Lake**
**by Sir Walter Scott**
09/50 **(75)** HcK(a&c),Original. . . . 150.00
07/51 **(85)** HcK(a&c),15¢(c)
  Price;rep . . . . . . . . . . . . . . . . . 40.00
04/54 **(118)** HcK(a&c);rep . . . . . . 35.00
07/57 **(139)** HcK,New P(c);rep. . . . 35.00
01/60 **(154)** HcK,P(c);rep. . . . . . . . 18.00

**076-The Prisoner of Zenda**
**by Anthony Hope Hawkins**
10/50 **(75)** HcK(a&c),Original. . . . 150.00
07/51 **(85)** HcK(a&c),15¢(c) Price;
  rep . . . . . . . . . . . . . . . . . . . . . . 40.00
09/53 **(111)** HcK(a&c);rep . . . . . . 35.00
09/55 **(128)** HcK,New P(c);rep. . . . 35.00
09/59 **(152)** HcK,P(c);rep. . . . . . . . 20.00
1962 **(165)** HcK,P(c);rep . . . . . . . . 18.00

**077-The Illiad**
**by Homer**
11/50 **(78)** AB(a&c),Original . . . . . 175.00
09/51 **(87)** AB(a&c),15¢(c)
  Price;rep . . . . . . . . . . . . . . . . . 40.00
07/54 **(121)** AB(a&c);rep . . . . . . . . 35.00
07/57 **(139)** AB,New P(c);rep. . . . . 35.00
05/59 **(150)** AB,P(c);rep. . . . . . . . . 20.00
1962 **(165)** AB,P(c);rep . . . . . . . . . 18.00

**078-Joan of Arc**
**by Frederick Shiller**
12/50 **(78)** HcK(a&c),Original. . . . 150.00
09/51 **(87)** HcK(a&c),15¢(c)
  Price; rep . . . . . . . . . . . . . . . . . 40.00
11/53 **(113)** HcK(a&c);rep . . . . . . 35.00
09/55 **(128)** HcK,New P(c);rep. . . . 35.00
09/57 **(140)** HcK,P(c);rep. . . . . . . . 20.00
05/59 **(150)** HcK,P(c);rep. . . . . . . . 20.00
11/60 **(159)** HcK,P(c);rep. . . . . . . . 18.00

**079-Cyrano de Bergerac**
**by Edmond Rostand**
01/51 **(78)** AB(a&c),Original,Movie
  Promo Inside Front(c) . . . . . . 175.00
07/51 **(85)** AB(a&c),15¢(c)
  Price;rep . . . . . . . . . . . . . . . . . 40.00

04/54 **(118)** AB(a&c);rep . . . . . . . . 35.00
07/56 **(133)** AB,New P(c);rep. . . . . 35.00
05/60 **(156)** AB,P(c);rep. . . . . . . . . 30.00

**080-White Fang**
**by Jack London**
**(Last Line Drawn (c)**
02/51 **(79)** AB(a&c),Original. . . . . 175.00
09/51 **(87)** AB(a&c);rep . . . . . . . . . 40.00
03/55 **(125)** AB(a&c);rep . . . . . . . . 35.00
05/56 **(132)** AB,New P(c);rep. . . . . 35.00
09/57 **(140)** AB,P(c);rep. . . . . . . . . 20.00
11/59 **(153)** AB,P(c);rep. . . . . . . . . 20.00

**081-The Odyssey**
**by Homer**
**(P(c)s From Now on)**
03/51 **(82)** HyG,AB P(c),Original . 175.00

**082-The Master of Ballantrae**
**by Robert Louis Stevenson**
04/51 **(82)** LDr,AB P(c),Original . . 150.00

**083-The Jungle Book**
**by Rudyard Kipling**
05/51 **(85)** WmB&AB,AB P(c),
  Original . . . . . . . . . . . . . . . . . 150.00
08/53 **(110)** WmB&AB,AB P(c);rep 20.00
03/55 **(125)** WmB&AB,AB P(c);rep 20.00
05/56 **(134)** WmB&AB,AB P(c);rep 20.00
01/58 **(142)** WmB&AB,AB P(c);rep 20.00
05/59 **(150)** WmB&AB,AB P(c);rep 18.00
11/60 **(159)** WmB&AB,AB P(c);rep 18.00

**084-The Gold Bug & Other**
**Stories (Inc. The Telltale Heart**
**& The Cask of Amontillado)**
**by Edgar Allan Poe**
06/51 **(85)** AB,RP,JLv,AB P(c),
  Original . . . . . . . . . . . . . . . . . 200.00

**085-The Sea Wolf**
**by Jack London**
08/51 **(85)** AB,AB P(c),Original . . 150.00
07/54 **(121)** AB,AB P(c);rep . . . . . . 20.00
05/56 **(132)** AB,AB P(c);rep . . . . . . 20.00
11/57 **(141)** AB,AB P(c);rep . . . . . . 20.00
03/61 **(161)** AB,AB P(c);rep . . . . . . 18.00

**086-Under Two Flags**
**by Oiuda**
08/51 **(87)** MDb,AB P(c),Original. 125.00
03/54 **(117)** MDb,AB P(c);rep . . . . 25.00
07/57 **(139)** MDb,AB P(c);rep . . . . 20.00
09/60 **(158)** MDb,AB P(c);rep . . . . 20.00

**087-A Midsummer Nights**
**Dream**
**by William Shakespeare**
09/51 **(87)** AB,AB P(c),Original . . 125.00

03/61 **(161)** AB,AB P(c);rep. . . . . . 20.00

**088-Men of Iron**
**by Howard Pyle**
10/51 **(89)** HD,LDr,GS,Original . . 125.00
01/60 **(154)** HD,LDr,GS,P(c);rep . . 20.00

**089-Crime and Punishment**
**by Fedor Dostoevsky**
11/51 **(89)** RP,AB P(c),Original . . 125.00
09/59 **(152)** RP,AB P(c);rep . . . . . . 25.00

**090-Green Mansions**
**by William Henry Hudson**
12/51 **(89)** AB,AB P(c),Original . . 125.00
01/59 **(148)** AB,New LbC P(c);rep . 30.00
1962 **(165)** AB,LbC P(c);rep . . . . . 18.00

**091-The Call of the Wild**
**by Jack London**
01/52 **(92)** MDb,P(c),Original. . . . 100.00
10/53 **(112)** MDb,P(c);rep . . . . . . . 20.00
03/55 **(125)** MDb,P(c),'PictureProgress'
  Onn. Back(c);rep . . . . . . . . . . 20.00
09/56 **(134)** MDb,P(c);rep . . . . . . . 20.00
03/58 **(143)** MDb,P(c);rep . . . . . . . 18.00
1962 **(165)** MDb,P(c);rep . . . . . . . 18.00

**092-The Courtship of Miles**
**Standish**
**by Henry Wadsworth**
**Longfellow**
02/52 **(92)** AB,AB P(c),Original . . 100.00
1962 **(165)** AB,AB P(c);rep . . . . . . 20.00

**093-Pudd'nhead Wilson**
**by Mark Twain**
03/52 **(94)** HcK,HcK P(c),Original 100.00
1962 **(165)** HcK,GMc New
  P(c);rep . . . . . . . . . . . . . . . . . 25.00

**094-David Balfour**
**by Robert Louis Stevenson**
04/52 **(94)** RP,P(c),Original . . . . . 125.00

**095-All Quiet on the Western**
**Front**
**by Erich Maria Remarque**
05/52 **(96)** MDb,P(c),Original. . . . 200.00
05/52 **(99)** MDb,P(c),Original. . . . . 85.00

**096-Daniel Boone**
**by John Bakeless**
06/52 **(97)** AB,P(c),Original . . . . . 100.00
03/54 **(117)** AB,P(c);rep . . . . . . . . . 20.00
09/55 **(128)** AB,P(c);rep . . . . . . . . . 20.00
05/56 **(132)** AB,P(c);rep . . . . . . . . . 20.00
——— **(134)** AB,P(c),'Story of
  Jesus'on Back);rep . . . . . . . . 20.00
09/60 **(158)** AB,P(c);rep . . . . . . . . . 20.00

CI

*Classics Illustrated #105*
© *Gilberton Publications*

*Classics Illustrated #109*
© *Gilberton Publications*

*Classics Illustrated #120*
© *Gilberton Publications*

**097-King Solomon's Mines**
**by H. Rider Haggard**
07/52 **(96)** HcK,P(c),Original .... 100.00
04/54 **(118)** HcK,P(c);rep . . . . . . . 20.00
03/56 **(131)** HcK,P(c);rep . . . . . . . 20.00
09/51 **(141)** HcK,P(c);rep . . . . . . . 20.00
09/60 **(158)** HcK,P(c);rep . . . . . . . 18.00

**098-The Red Badge of Courage**
**by Stephen Crane**
08/52 **(98)** MDb,GS,P(c),Original. 100.00
04/54 **(118)** MDb,GS,P(c);rep .... 20.00
05/56 **(132)** MDb,GS,P(c);rep .... 20.00
01/58 **(142)** MDb,GS,P(c);rep .... 20.00
09/59 **(152)** MDb,GS,P(c);rep .... 20.00
03/61 **(161)** MDb,GS,P(c);rep .... 20.00

**099-Hamlet**
**by William Shakespeare**
09/52 **(98)** AB,P(c),Original .... 100.00
07/54 **(121)** AB,P(c);rep . . . . . . . 20.00
11/57 **(141)** AB,P(c);rep . . . . . . . 20.00
09/60 **(158)** AB,P(c);rep . . . . . . . 18.00

**100-Mutiny on the Bounty**
**by Charles Nordhoff**
10/52 **(100)** MsW,HcK P(c),Orig.. 100.00
03/54 **(117)** MsW,HcK P(c);rep ... 20.00
05/56 **(132)** MsW,HcK P(c);rep ... 20.00
01/58 **(142)** MsW,HcK P(c);rep ... 20.00
03/60 **(155)** MsW,HcK P(c);rep ... 18.00

**101-William Tell**
**by Frederick Schiller**
11/52 **(101)** MDb,HcK P(c),Orig.. 100.00
04/54 **(118)** MDb,HcK P(c);rep ... 20.00
11/57 **(141)** MDb,HcK P(c);rep ... 20.00
09/60 **(158)** MDb,HcK P(c);rep ... 18.00

**102-The White Company**
**by Sir Arthur Conan Doyle**
12/52 **(101)** AB,P(c),Original .... 150.00
1962 **(165)** AB,P(c);rep . . . . . . . 35.00

**103-Men Against the Sea**
**by Charles Nordhoff**
01/53 **(104)** RP,HcK P(c),Original 100.00
12/53 **(114)** RP,HcK P(c);rep . . . . . 30.00
03/56 **(131)** RP,New P(c);rep..... 35.00
03/59 **(149)** RP,P(c);rep . . . . . . . 30.00
09/60 **(158)** RP,P(c);rep . . . . . . . 38.00

**104-Bring 'Em Back Alive**
**by Frank Buck & Edward**
**Anthony**
02/53 **(105)** HcK,HcK P(c)Original 100.00
04/54 **(118)** HcK,HcK P(c);rep .... 20.00
07/56 **(133)** HcK,HcK P(c);rep .... 20.00
05/59 **(150)** HcK,HcK P(c);rep .... 18.00
09/60 **(158)** HcK,HcK P(c);rep .... 18.00

**105-From the Earth to the**
**Moon**
**by Jules Verne**
03/53 **(106)** AB,P(c),Original .... 100.00
04/54 **(118)** AB,P(c);rep . . . . . . . 20.00
03/56 **(132)** AB,P(c);rep . . . . . . . 20.00
11/57 **(141)** AB,P(c);rep . . . . . . . 20.00
09/58 **(146)** AB,P(c);rep . . . . . . . 20.00
05/60 **(156)** AB,P(c);rep . . . . . . . 20.00

**106-Buffalo Bill**
**by William F. Cody**
04/53 **(107)** MDb,P(c),Original ... 100.00
04/54 **(118)** MDb,P(c);rep . . . . . . . 20.00
03/56 **(132)** MDb,P(c);rep . . . . . . . 20.00
01/58 **(142)** MDb,P(c);rep . . . . . . . 20.00
03/61 **(161)** MDb,P(c);rep . . . . . . . 18.00

**107-King of the Khyber Rifles**
**by Talbot Mundy**
05/53 **(108)** SMz,P(c),Original ... 100.00
04/54 **(118)** SMz,P(c);rep. . . . . . . 20.00
09/58 **(146)** SMz,P(c);rep . . . . . . . 20.00
09/60 **(158)** SMz,P(c);rep . . . . . . . 18.00

**108-Knights of the Round Table**
**by Howard Pyle?**
06/53 **(108)** AB,P(c),Original .... 100.00
06/53 **(109)** AB,P(c),Original .... 70.00
03/54 **(117)** AB,P(c);rep . . . . . . . 20.00
11/59 **(153)** AB,P(c);rep . . . . . . . 18.00
1962 **(165)** AB,P(c);rep . . . . . . . 18.00

**109-Pitcairn's Island**
**by Charles Nordhoff**
07/53 **(110)** RP,P(c),Original .... 100.00
1962 **(165)** RP,P(c);rep . . . . . . . 20.00

**110-A Study in Scarlet**
**by Sir Arthur Conan Doyle**
08/53 **(111)** SMz,P(c),Original ... 200.00
1962 **(165)** SMz,P(c);rep . . . . . . . 100.00

**111-The Talisman**
**by Sir Walter Scott**
09/53 **(112)** HcK,HcK P(c),
 Original . . . . . . . . . . . . . . . . 100.00
1962 **(165)** HcK,HcK P(c);rep .... 20.00

**112-Adventures of Kit Carson**
**by John S. C. Abbott**
10/53 **(113)** RP,P(c),Original .... 100.00
11/55 **(129)** RP,P(c);rep . . . . . . . 20.00
11/57 **(141)** RP,P(c);rep . . . . . . . 20.00
09/59 **(152)** RP,P(c);rep . . . . . . . 18.00
03/61 **(161)** RP,P(c);rep . . . . . . . 18.00

**113-The Forty-Five Guardsmen**
**by Alexandre Dumas**
11/53 **(114)** MDb,P(c),Original ... 150.00

**114-The Red Rover**
**by James Fenimore Cooper**
12/53 **(115)** PrC,JP P(c),Original . 150.00

**115-How I Found Livingston**
**by Sir Henry Stanley**
01/54 **(116)** SF&ST,P(c),Original . 200.00

**116-The Bottle Imp**
**by Robert Louis Stevenson**
02/54 **(117)** LC,P(c),Original .... 200.00

**117-Captains Courageous**
**by Rudyard Kipling**
03/54 **(118)** PrC,P(c),Original ... 200.00

**118-Rob Roy**
**by Sir Walter Scott**
04/54 **(119)** RP,WIP,P(c),Original. 200.00

**119-Solders of Fortune**
**by Richard Harding Davis**
05/54 **(120)** KS,P(c),Original .... 150.00

**120-The Hurricane**
**by Charles Nordhoff**
1954 **(121)** LC,LC P(c),Original .. 150.00

**121-Wild Bill Hickok**
07/54 **(122)** MI,ST,P(c),Original .. 125.00
05/56 **(132)** MI,ST,P(c);rep . . . . . . 20.00
11/57 **(141)** MI,ST,P(c);rep . . . . . . 20.00
01/60 **(154)** MI,ST,P(c);rep . . . . . . 20.00

**122-The Mutineers**
**by Charles Boardman Hawes**
09/54 **(123)** PrC,P(c),Original ... 150.00
01/57 **(136)** PrC,P(c);rep . . . . . . . 20.00
09/58 **(146)** PrC,P(c);rep . . . . . . . 20.00
09/60 **(158)** PrC,P(c);rep . . . . . . . 18.00

**123-Fang and Claw**
**by Frank Buck**
11/54 **(124)** LnS,P(c),Original ... 125.00
07/56 **(133)** LnS,P(c);rep . . . . . . . 20.00
03/58 **(143)** LnS,P(c);rep . . . . . . . 20.00
01/60 **(154)** LnS,P(c);rep . . . . . . . 18.00

**124-The War of the Worlds**
**by H. G. Wells**
01/55 **(125)** LC,LC P(c),Original . 200.00
03/56 **(131)** LC,LC P(c);rep . . . . . . 20.00
11/57 **(141)** LC,LC P(c);rep . . . . . . 20.00
01/59 **(148)** LC,LC P(c);rep . . . . . . 20.00
05/60 **(156)** LC,LC P(c);rep . . . . . . 25.00
1962 **(165)** LC,LC P(c);rep . . . . . . 20.00

**125-The Ox Bow Incident**
**by Walter Van Tilberg Clark**
03/55 **(—)** NN,P(c),Original .... 125.00
03/58 **(143)** NN,P(c);rep . . . . . . . 20.00
09/59 **(152)** NN,P(c);rep . . . . . . . 20.00

All comics prices listed are for *Near Mint* condition.

**CI**

*Classics Illustrated #130*
© Gilberton Publications

*Classics Illustrated #141*
© Gilberton Publications

*Classics Illustrated #156*
© Gilberton Publications

03/61 **(149)** NN,P(c);rep . . . . . . . . 20.00
**126-The Downfall**
**by Emile Zola**
05/55 **(—)** LC,LC P(c),Original,'
Picture Progress'Replaces
Reorder List. . . . . . . . . . . . 125.00
**127-The King of the Mountains**
**by Edmond About**
07/55 **(128)** NN,P(c),Original . . . . 150.00
**128-Macbeth**
**by William Shakespeare**
09/55 **(128)** AB,P(c),Original . . . . 125.00
03/58 **(143)** AB,P(c);rep. . . . . . . . 20.00
09/60 **(158)** AB,P(c);rep. . . . . . . . 20.00
**129-Davy Crockett**
**Author Unknown**
11/55 **(129)** LC,P(c),Original . . . . 200.00
**130-Caesar's Conquests**
**by Julius Caesar**
01/56 **(130)** JO,P(c),Original . . . . 125.00
01/58 **(142)** JO,P(c);rep. . . . . . . . 20.00
09/59 **(152)** JO,P(c);rep. . . . . . . . 20.00
03/61 **(149)** JO,P(c);rep. . . . . . . . 20.00
**131-The Covered Wagon**
**by Emerson Hough**
03/56 **(131)** NN,P(c),Original . . . . 125.00
03/58 **(143)** NN,P(c);rep . . . . . . . 20.00
09/59 **(152)** NN,P(c);rep . . . . . . . 20.00
09/60 **(158)** NN,P(c);rep . . . . . . . 20.00
**132-The Dark Frigate**
**by Charles Boardman Hawes**
05/56 **(132)** EW&RWb,P(c),Orig.. 125.00
05/59 **(150)** EW&RWb,P(c);rep . . . 20.00
**133-The Time Machine**
**by H. G. Wells**
07/56 **(132)** LC,P(c),Original . . . . 175.00
01/58 **(142)** LC,P(c);rep. . . . . . . . 20.00
09/59 **(152)** LC,P(c);rep. . . . . . . . 20.00
09/60 **(158)** LC,P(c);rep. . . . . . . . 20.00
**134-Romeo and Juliet**
**by William Shakespeare**
09/56 **(134)** GE,P(c),Original . . . . 125.00
03/61 **(161)** GE,P(c);rep . . . . . . . 20.00
**135-Waterloo**
**by Emile Erckmann &**
**Alexandre Chatrian**
11/56 **(135)** Grl,AB P(c),Original . 125.00
11/59 **(153)** Grl,AB P(c);rep. . . . . 20.00
**136-Lord Jim**
**by Joseph Conrad**
01/57 **(136)** GE,P(c),Original . . . . 150.00

**137-The Little Savage**
**by Captain Frederick Marryat**
03/57 **(136)** GE,P(c),Original . . . . 125.00
01/59 **(148)** GE,P(c);rep . . . . . . . 20.00
05/60 **(156)** GE,P(c);rep . . . . . . . 20.00
**138-A Journey to the Center**
**of the Earth**
**by Jules Verne**
05/57 **(136)** NN,P(c),Original . . . . 175.00
09/58 **(146)** NN,P(c);rep . . . . . . . 20.00
05/60 **(156)** NN,P(c);rep . . . . . . . 20.00
09/60 **(158)** NN,P(c);rep . . . . . . . 20.00
**139-In the Reign of Terror**
**by George Alfred Henty**
07/57 **(139)** GE,P(c),Original . . . . 125.00
01/60 **(154)** GE,P(c);rep . . . . . . . 20.00
**140-On Jungle Trails**
**by Frank Buck**
09/57 **(140)** NN,P(c),Original . . . . 125.00
05/59 **(150)** NN,P(c);rep . . . . . . . 20.00
01/61 **(160)** NN,P(c);rep . . . . . . . 20.00
**141-Castle Dangerous**
**by Sir Walter Scott**
11/57 **(141)** StC,P(c),Original. . . . 150.00
09/59 **(152)** StC,P(c);rep . . . . . . . 20.00
**142-Abraham Lincoln**
**by Benjamin Thomas**
01/58 **(142)** NN,P(c),Original . . . . 150.00
01/60 **(154)** NN,P(c);rep . . . . . . . 20.00
09/60 **(158)** NN,P(c);rep . . . . . . . 20.00
**143-Kim**
**by Rudyard Kipling**
03/58 **(143)** JO,P(c)Original. . . . . 125.00
**144-The First Men in the Moon**
**by H. G. Wells**
05/58 **(143)** GWb,AW,AT,RKr,
GMC P(c), Original . . . . . . . 175.00
11/59 **(153)** GWb,AW,AT,RKr,
GMC, P(c); rep . . . . . . . . . . 20.00
03/61 **(161)** GWb,AW,AT,RKr,
GMC, P(c); rep . . . . . . . . . . 18.00
**145-The Crisis**
**by Winston Churchill**
07/58 **(143)** GE,P(c),Original . . . . 125.00
05/60 **(156)** GE,P(c);rep . . . . . . . 20.00
**146-With Fire and Sword**
**by Henryk Sienkiewicz**
09/58 **(143)** GWb,P(c),Original . . . 125.00
05/60 **(156)** GWb,P(c);rep . . . . . . 25.00
**147-Ben-Hur**
**by Lew Wallace**
11/58 **(147)** JO,P(c),Original . . . . 125.00

11/59 **(153)** JO,P(c);rep . . . . . . . . 65.00
09/60 **(158)** JO,P(c);rep. . . . . . . . 20.00
**148-The Buckaneer**
**by Lyle Saxon**
01/59 **(148)** GE&RJ,NS P(c),orig. 125.00
—— **(568)** GE&RJ,NS P(c),Juniors
List Only;rep . . . . . . . . . . 20.00
**149-Off on a Comet**
**by Jules Verne**
03/59 **(149)** GMc,P(c),Original. . . 125.00
03/60 **(155)** GMc,P(c);rep . . . . . . 20.00
03/61 **(149)** GMc,P(c);rep . . . . . . 20.00
**150-The Virginian**
**by Owen Winster**
05/59 **(150)** NN,DrG P(c),Original 200.00
1961 **(164)** NN,DrG P(c);rep . . . . 30.00
**151-Won by the Sword**
**by George Alfred Henty**
07/59 **(150)** JTg,P(c),Original . . . 125.00
1961 **(164)** JTg,P(c);rep. . . . . . . . 25.00
**152-Wild Animals I Have**
**Known**
**by Ernest Thompson Seton**
09/59 **(152)** LbC,LbC P(c),
Original . . . . . . . . . . . . . . . 125.00
03/61 **(149)** LbC,LbC P(c),P(c);rep 20.00
**153-The Invisible Man**
**by H. G. Wells**
11/59 **(153)** NN,GB P(c),Original . 150.00
03/61 **(149)** NN,GB P(c);rep . . . . . 20.00
**154-The Conspiracy of Pontiac**
**by Francis Parkman**
01/60 **(154)** GMc,GMc P(c),
Original . . . . . . . . . . . . . . . 125.00
**155-The Lion of the North**
**by George Alfred Henty**
03/60 **(154)** NN,GMc P(c),Original125.00
**156-The Conquest of Mexico**
**by Bernal Diaz Del Castillo**
05/60 **(156)** BPr,BPr P(c),Original 125.00
**157-Lives of the Hunted**
**by Ernest Thompson Seton**
07/60 **(156)** NN,LbC P(c),Original 150.00
**158-The Conspirators**
**by Alexandre Dumas**
09/60 **(156)** GMc,GMc P(c),
Original . . . . . . . . . . . . . . . 150.00
**159-The Octopus**
**by Frank Norris**
11/60 **(159)** GM&GE,LbC P(c),
Original . . . . . . . . . . . . . . . 150.00

Classics Illustrated Giants-Exciting
Mystery Stories © Gilberton Publ.

Classics Illustrated Junior #513
© Gilberton Publications

Classics Illustrated Special
United Nations © Gilberton Publ.

**CI**

**160-The Food of the Gods
by H.G. Wells**
01/61 **(159)** TyT,GMc P(c),
Original . . . . . . . . . . . . . . . 150.00
01/61 **(160)** TyT,GMc P(c),Original;
Same Except For the HRN# . . 60.00

**161-Cleopatra
by H. Rider Haggard**
03/61 **(161)** NN,Pch P(c),Original 125.00

**162-Robur the Conqueror
by Jules Verne**
05/61 **(162)** GM&DPn,CJ P(c),
Original . . . . . . . . . . . . . . . 125.00

**163-Master of the World
by Jules Verne**
07/61 **(163)** GM,P(c),Original. . . . 125.00

**164-The Cossack Chief
by Nicolai Gogol**
1961 **(164)** SyM,P(c),Original . . . 125.00

**165-The Queen's Necklace
by Alexandre Dumas**
01/62 **(164)** GM,P(c),Original. . . . 125.00

**166-Tigers and Traitors
by Jules Verne**
05/62 **(165)** NN,P(c),Original . . . . 150.00

**167-Faust
by Johann Wolfgang von
Goethe**
08/62 **(165)** NN,NN P(c),Original. 200.00

## CLASSICS
## ILLUSTRATED GIANTS
**Gilberton Publications, 1949**
An Illustrated Library of Great
Adventure Stories -(reps. of
Issues 6,7,8,10) . . . . . . . . . 2,000.00
An Illustrated Library of Exciting
Mystery Stories -(reps. of
Issues 30,21,40,13) . . . . . . 2,100.00
An Illustrated Library of Great
Indian Stories -(reps. of
Issues 4,17,22,37) . . . . . . . 2,000.00

## CLASSICS
## ILLUSTRATED JUNIOR
**Gilberton Publications,
Oct., 1953**
501-Snow White and the
Seven Dwarfs . . . . . . . . . . . 150.00
502-The Ugly Duckling . . . . . . . . 100.00

503-Cinderella . . . . . . . . . . . . . . . 75.00
504-The Pied Piper . . . . . . . . . . . 75.00
505-The Sleeping Beauty . . . . . . . 75.00
506-The Three Little Pigs . . . . . . . 75.00
507-Jack and the Beanstalk . . . . . 75.00
508-Goldilocks & the Three Bears. 75.00
509-Beauty and the Beast . . . . . . . 75.00
510-Little Red Riding Hood . . . . . . 75.00
511-Puss-N-Boots . . . . . . . . . . . . 75.00
512-Rumpelstiltskin . . . . . . . . . . . 75.00
513-Pinocchio . . . . . . . . . . . . . . . 75.00
514-The Steadfast Tin Soldier . . . 100.00
515-Johnny Appleseed . . . . . . . . . 75.00
516-Aladdin and His Lamp . . . . . . 75.00
517-The Emperor's New Clothes . 75.00
518-The Golden Goose . . . . . . . . . 75.00
519-Paul Bunyan . . . . . . . . . . . . . 75.00
520-Thumbelina . . . . . . . . . . . . . . 75.00
521-King of the Golden River . . . . 75.00
522-The Nightingale. . . . . . . . . . . . 75.00
523-The Gallant Tailor . . . . . . . . . . 75.00
524-The Wild Swans . . . . . . . . . . . 75.00
525-The Little Mermaid . . . . . . . . . 75.00
526-The Frog Prince . . . . . . . . . . . 75.00
527-The Golden-Haired Giant . . . . 75.00
528-The Penny Prince . . . . . . . . . . 75.00
529-The Magic Servants . . . . . . . . 75.00
530-The Golden Bird . . . . . . . . . . . 75.00
531-Rapunzel. . . . . . . . . . . . . . . . . 75.00
532-The Dancing Princesses. . . . . 75.00
533-The Magic Fountain . . . . . . . . 75.00
534-The Golden Touch . . . . . . . . . 75.00
535-The Wizard of Oz . . . . . . . . . 100.00
536-The Chimney Sweep . . . . . . . 75.00
537-The Three Fairies . . . . . . . . . . 75.00
538-Silly Hans . . . . . . . . . . . . . . . 75.00
539-The Enchanted Fish . . . . . . . . 75.00
540-The Tinder-Box . . . . . . . . . . . . 75.00
541-Snow White and Rose Red . . 75.00
542-The Donkey's Tail . . . . . . . . . . 75.00
543-The House in the Woods . . . . 75.00
544-The Golden Fleece. . . . . . . . . . 75.00
545-The Glass Mountain . . . . . . . . 75.00
546-The Elves and the Shoemaker 75.00
547-The Wishing Table . . . . . . . . . 75.00
548-The Magic Pitcher. . . . . . . . . . 75.00
549-Simple Kate . . . . . . . . . . . . . . 75.00
550-The Singing Donkey . . . . . . . . 75.00
551-The Queen Bee . . . . . . . . . . . 75.00
552-The Three Little Dwarfs . . . . . 75.00
553-King Thrushbeard . . . . . . . . . . 75.00
554-The Enchanted Deer . . . . . . . 75.00
555-The Three Golden Apples. . . . 75.00
556-The Elf Mound . . . . . . . . . . . . 75.00
557-Silly Willy. . . . . . . . . . . . . . . . . 75.00

558-The Magic Dish,LbC(c). . . . . . 75.00
559-The Japanese Lantern,LbC(c) 90.00
560-The Doll Princess,LbC(c) . . . . 90.00
561-Hans Humdrum,LbC(c). . . . . . 75.00
562-The Enchanted Pony,LbC(c) . 90.00
563-The Wishing Well,LbC(c) . . . . 75.00
564-The Salt Mountain,LbC(c). . . . 75.00
565-The Silly Princess,LbC(c) . . . . 75.00
566-Clumsy Hans,LbC(c). . . . . . . . 75.00
567-The Bearskin Soldier,LbC(c). . 75.00
568-The Happy Hedgehog,LbC(c). 75.00
569-The Three Giants . . . . . . . . . . 75.00
570-The Pearl Princess . . . . . . . . . 75.00
571-How Fire Came to the Indians 75.00
572-The Drummer Boy . . . . . . . . . 75.00
573-The Crystal Ball . . . . . . . . . . . 75.00
574-Brightboots . . . . . . . . . . . . . . . 75.00
575-The Fearless Prince . . . . . . . . 75.00
576-The Princess Who Saw
Everything . . . . . . . . . . . . . . . 90.00
577-The Runaway Dumpling . . . . 100.00

## CLASSICS ILLLUSTRATED
## SPECIAL ISSUE
**Gilberton Publications
Dec., 1955–July, 1962**
N# United Nations . . . . . . . . . . . . 400.00
129-The Story of Jesus,Jesus on
Mountain(c) . . . . . . . . . . . . . . 150.00
129a-Three Camels(c). . . . . . . . . . 150.00
129b-Mountain(c),HRN to 161 . . 125.00
129c-Mountain(c) (1968) . . . . . . . 100.00
132A-The Story of America . . . . . 125.00
135A-The Ten Commandments . . . 125.00
138A-Adventures in Science . . . . 125.00
138Aa-HRN to 149 . . . . . . . . . . . . 100.00
138Ab-rep.,12/61 . . . . . . . . . . . . . 100.00
141A-GE,The Rough Rider . . . . . 125.00
144A-RC,GE,Blazing the Trails . . 125.00
147A-RC,GE,Crossing the
Rockies . . . . . . . . . . . . . . . . . 125.00
150A-Grl,Royal Canadian Police. 125.00
153A-GE,Men, Guns, & Cattle. . . 125.00
156A-GE,GM,The Atomic Age. . . 125.00
159A-GE,GM,Rockets, Jets and
Missiles . . . . . . . . . . . . . . . . . 125.00
162A-RC,GE,War Between
the States . . . . . . . . . . . . . . . 165.00
165A-RC/GE,JK,Grl,To the Stars. 125.00
166A-RC/GE,JK,Grl,World War II 150.00
167A-RC/GE,JK,Prehistoric
World . . . . . . . . . . . . . . . . . . . 150.00
167Aa-HRN to 167. . . . . . . . . . . . 110.00

---

All comics prices listed are for *Near Mint* condition.

Clown Comics #3
© Harvey Publications

Clue Comics #15
© Hillman Periodicals

Colossus Comics #1
© Sun Publications

## CLAY CODY, GUNSLINGER
**Better Publications, 1957**
1 Western hero . . . . . . . . . . . . . 100.00

## CLEAN FUN, STARRING 'SHOOGAFOOTS JONES'
**Specialty Book Co., 1945**
N# . . . . . . . . . . . . . . . . . . . . . . 200.00

## CLIMAX!
**Gilmor Magazines, 1955**
1 Mystery . . . . . . . . . . . . . . . . . 200.00
2 . . . . . . . . . . . . . . . . . . . . . . . . 150.00

## CLOAK AND DAGGER
**Approved Comics (Ziff-Davis), Fall, 1952**
1 NS(c),Al Kennedy of the Secret Service . . . . . . . . . . . . . . . . 400.00

## CLOWN COMICS
**Harvey Publications, 1945**
N# . . . . . . . . . . . . . . . . . . . . . . 300.00
2 . . . . . . . . . . . . . . . . . . . . . . . . 200.00
3 . . . . . . . . . . . . . . . . . . . . . . . . 200.00

## CLUBHOUSE RASCALS
**Sussex Publ. Co. 1956**
1 Humor . . . . . . . . . . . . . . . . . . 125.00
2 . . . . . . . . . . . . . . . . . . . . . . . . 100.00

## CLUB "16"
**Famous Funnies, 1948**
1 Teen-age . . . . . . . . . . . . . . . . 140.00
2 thru 4 . . . . . . . . . . . . . . . . . @100.00

## CLUE COMICS
**Hillman Periodicals, 1943**
1 O:Boy King,Nightmare,Micro-Face,
Twilight,Zippo.. . . . . . . . . . . 3,000.00
2 . . . . . . . . . . . . . . . . . . . . . . 2,000.00
3 Boy King V:The Crane . . . . . 1,500.00
4 V:The Crane . . . . . . . . . . . . 1,200.00
5 V:The Crane . . . . . . . . . . . . 1,200.00
6 Hells Kitchen . . . . . . . . . . . . . 750.00
7 V:Dr. Plasma,Torture(c) . . . . . 750.00
8 RP,A:The Gold Mummy King . 700.00
9 I:Paris . . . . . . . . . . . . . . . . . . 700.00
10 O:Gun Master . . . . . . . . . . . . 700.00
11 A:Gun Master . . . . . . . . . . . . 700.00

12 O:Rackman . . . . . . . . . . . . . . 700.00
2-1 S&K,O:Nightro,A:Iron Lady. 1,300.00
2-2 S&K,Bondage(c). . . . . . . . . 1,800.00
2-3 S&K. . . . . . . . . . . . . . . . . . 1,300.00
**Becomes:**

## REAL CLUE CRIME STORIES
**June, 1947**
2-4 DBw,S&K,True Story of
Ma Barker . . . . . . . . . . . . . . 1,300.00
2-5 S&K, Newface surgery(c) . . 1,000.00
2-6 S&K, Breakout (c) . . . . . . . 1,000.00
2-7 S&K, Stick up (c) . . . . . . . . 1,000.00
2-8 Kidnapping (c) . . . . . . . . . . . 250.00
2-9 DBa,Boxing fix (c) . . . . . . . . 250.00
2-10 DBa,Murder (c) . . . . . . . . . . 250.00
2-11 Attempted bankrobbery (c) . 250.00
2-12 Murder (c) . . . . . . . . . . . . . 250.00
3-1 thru 3-12 . . . . . . . . . . . . . . @250.00
4-1 thru 4-12 . . . . . . . . . . . . . . @250.00
5-1 thru 5-12 . . . . . . . . . . . . . . @200.00
6-1 thru 6-12 . . . . . . . . . . . . . . @200.00
6-10 Bondage(c) . . . . . . . . . . . . 250.00
7-1 thru 7-12 . . . . . . . . . . . . . . @175.00
8-1 thru 8-5, May, 1953 . . . . . @175.00

## THE CLUTCHING HAND
**American Comics, 1954**
1 Horror . . . . . . . . . . . . . . . . . . 500.00

## CLYDE BEATTY
**Commodore Productions, 1953**
1 Photo(c) . . . . . . . . . . . . . . . . 400.00

## C-M-O COMICS
**Comic Corp. of America (Centaur), May, 1942**
1 Invisible Terror . . . . . . . . . . 2,500.00
2 Super Ann . . . . . . . . . . . . . . 2,000.00

## COCOMALT BIG BOOK OF COMICS
**Harry A. Chesler, 1938**
1 BoW,PGv,FGu,JCo,(Give away)
Little Nemo . . . . . . . . . . . 4,000.00

## CODY OF THE PONY EXPRESS
### See: BULLS-EYE

## CODY OF THE PONY EXPRESS
**Fox Features Syndicate, 1950**
1 Western . . . . . . . . . . . . . . . . 300.00
2 . . . . . . . . . . . . . . . . . . . . . . 250.00
3 . . . . . . . . . . . . . . . . . . . . . . 250.00

## COLOSSAL FEATURES MAGAZINE
**Fox Features Syndicate, 1950**
1 (33) Cody of the Pony Express 300.00
2 (34) Cody of the Pony Express 300.00
3 Crime . . . . . . . . . . . . . . . . . . 300.00

## COLOSSUS COMICS
**Sun Publications March, 1940**
1 A:Colossus . . . . . . . . . . . . 10,000.00

## COLT .45
**Dell Publishing Co., 1958**
1 Ph(c) all . . . . . . . . . . . . . . . . 300.00
2 . . . . . . . . . . . . . . . . . . . . . . 260.00
3 . . . . . . . . . . . . . . . . . . . . . . 250.00
4 . . . . . . . . . . . . . . . . . . . . . . 250.00
5 . . . . . . . . . . . . . . . . . . . . . . 250.00
6 ATh . . . . . . . . . . . . . . . . . . . 275.00
7 . . . . . . . . . . . . . . . . . . . . . . 250.00
8 . . . . . . . . . . . . . . . . . . . . . . 250.00
9 . . . . . . . . . . . . . . . . . . . . . . 250.00

## COLUMBIA COMICS
**William H. Wise Co., 1944**
1 Joe Palooka,Charlie Chan . . . 450.00

## COMBAT
**Marvel Atlas, June, 1952**
1 JMn,War Stories, Bare
Bayonets . . . . . . . . . . . . . . . 350.00
2 RH, Break Thru,(Dedicated to
US Infantry) . . . . . . . . . . . . . 250.00
3 JMn(c) . . . . . . . . . . . . . . . . . 200.00
4 BK . . . . . . . . . . . . . . . . . . . . 225.00
5 thru 10 . . . . . . . . . . . . . . . @200.00
11 April, 1953 . . . . . . . . . . . . . 250.00

## COMBAT CASEY
### See: WAR COMBAT

**CI**

*Combat Kelly and the Deadly Dozen #12 © Marvel Comics Group*

*Comedy Comics #6 © Marvel Comics Group*

*Comic Cavalcade #6 © DC Comics*

## COMBAT KELLY AND THE DEADLY DOZEN
### Marvel Atlas, Nov., 1951
| | |
|---|---|
| 1 RH,Korean War Stories | 350.00 |
| 2 Big Push | 200.00 |
| 3 The Volunteer | 175.00 |
| 4 JMn,V:Communists | 175.00 |
| 5 JMn,OW,V:Communists | 175.00 |
| 6 V:Communists | 175.00 |
| 7 JMn,V:Communists | 175.00 |
| 8 JMn,Death to the Reds | 175.00 |
| 9 | 175.00 |
| 10 JMn(c) | 175.00 |
| 11 | 150.00 |
| 12 thru 16 | @150.00 |
| 17 A:Combat Casey | 175.00 |
| 18 A:Battle Brady | 125.00 |
| 19 V:Communists | 125.00 |
| 20 V:Communists | 125.00 |
| 21 Transvestite Cover | 75.00 |
| 22 thru 40 | @100.00 |
| 41 thru 44 Aug., 1957 | @100.00 |

## COMEDY COMICS
### Marvel Timely, 1942
| | |
|---|---|
| 9 | 3,600.00 |
| 10 | 2,800.00 |
| 11 | 675.00 |
| 12 | 250.00 |
| 13 Funny animal | 250.00 |
| 14 Super Rabbit | 700.00 |
| 15 | 200.00 |
| 16 | 200.00 |
| 17 | 200.00 |
| 18 | 200.00 |
| 19 | 200.00 |
| 20 | 200.00 |
| 21 thru 32 | @150.00 |
| 33 HK | 200.00 |
| 34 BW | 300.00 |
**Becomes:**

## MARGIE COMICS
### Marvel Comics, 1946
| | |
|---|---|
| 35 thru 39 Glamour Girl | @250.00 |
| 40 | 200.00 |
| 41 thru 49 | @225.00 |
**Becomes:**

## RENO BROWNE
### Marvel Comics, 1950
| | |
|---|---|
| 50 Photo(c); Western babe | 400.00 |
| 51 Photo(c); | 350.00 |
| 52 Photo(c); | 350.00 |

## COMEDY COMICS
### Marvel Animirth 1948–49
| | |
|---|---|
| 1 HK, Romance,F:Hedy, Millie, Tessie | 400.00 |
| 2 | 200.00 |
| 3 | 200.00 |
| 4 HK | 225.00 |
| 5 | 150.00 |
| 6 | 150.00 |
| 7 | 150.00 |
| 8 | 150.00 |
| 9 | 150.00 |
| 10 | 150.00 |

## COMIC ALBUM
### Dell Publishing Co., March-May, 1958
| | |
|---|---|
| 1 Donald Duck | 175.00 |
| 2 Bugs Bunny | 125.00 |
| 3 Donald Duck | 150.00 |
| 4 Tom & Jerry | 125.00 |
| 5 Woody Woodpecker | 125.00 |
| 6 Bugs Bunny | 125.00 |
| 7 Popeye | 150.00 |
| 8 Tom & Jerry | 125.00 |
| 9 Woody Woodpecker | 125.00 |
| 10 Bugs Bunny | 125.00 |
| 11 Popeye | 160.00 |
| 12 Tom & Jerry | 100.00 |
| 13 Woody Woodpecker | 100.00 |
| 14 Bugs Bunny | 100.00 |
| 15 Popeye | 125.00 |
| 16 Flintstones | 150.00 |
| 17 Space Mouse | 125.00 |
| 18 3 Stooges,Ph(c) | 150.00 |

## COMIC BOOKS
### Metropolitan Printing Co. 1950
| | |
|---|---|
| 1 Boots & Saddles | 125.00 |
| 1 Green Lama-The Green Jet | 500.00 |
| 1 My Pal Dizzy | 100.00 |
| 1 Talullah | 150.00 |
| 1 New World | 100.00 |

## COMIC CAPERS
### Marvel Comics, 1944
| | |
|---|---|
| 1 Funny animal, Super Rabbit | 300.00 |
| 2 | 200.00 |
| 3 | 150.00 |
| 4 | 150.00 |
| 5 | 150.00 |
| 6 | 150.00 |

## COMIC CAVALCADE
### DC Comics, 1942–43
| | |
|---|---|
| 1 Green Lantern, Flash, Wildcat, Wonder Woman, Black Pirate | 15,000.00 |
| 2 ShM,B:Mutt & Jeff | 4,000.00 |
| 3 ShM,B:HotHarrigan,Sorcerer | 2,700.00 |
| 4 Gay Ghost, A:Scribby, A:Red Tornado | 2,500.00 |
| 5 Gr.Lantern,Flash,W.Woman | 2,400.00 |
| 6 Flash,W.Woman,Gr.Lantern | 2,000.00 |
| 7 A:Red Tornado, E:Scribby | 2,000.00 |
| 8 Flash,W.Woman,Gr.Lantern | 2,000.00 |
| 9 Flash,W.Woman,Gr.Lantern | 2,000.00 |
| 10 Flash,W.Woman,Gr.Lantern | 2,000.00 |
| 11 Flash,W.Woman,Gr.Lantern | 1,400.00 |
| 12 E:Red, White & Blue | 1,400.00 |
| 13 A:Solomon Grundy | 2,500.00 |
| 14 Flash,W.Woman,Gr.Lantern | 1,400.00 |
| 15 B:Johnny Peril | 1,400.00 |
| 16 Flash,W.Woman,Gr.Lantern | 1,800.00 |
| 17 Flash,W.Woman,Gr.Lantern | 1,500.00 |
| 18 Flash,W.Woman,Gr.Lantern | 1,500.00 |
| 19 Flash,W.Woman,Gr.Lantern | 1,500.00 |
| 20 Flash,W.Woman,Gr.Lantern | 1,500.00 |
| 21 Flash,W.Woman,Gr.Lantern | 1,500.00 |
| 22 A:Atom | 1,500.00 |
| 23 A:Atom | 1,500.00 |
| 24 A:Solomon Grundy | 2,200.00 |
| 25 A:Black Canary | 2,000.00 |
| 26 ATh, E:Mutt & Jeff | 2,000.00 |
| 27 ATh,ATh(c) | 2,000.00 |
| 28 ATh E:Flash, Wonder Woman Green Lantern | 2,000.00 |
| 29 E:Johnny Peril | 1,800.00 |
| 30 RG,B:Fox & Crow | 700.00 |
| 31 thru 39 RG | @500.00 |
| 40 RG,ShM | 300.00 |
| 41 thru 49 RG,ShM | @275.00 |
| 50 thru 62 RG,ShM | @350.00 |
| 63 RG,ShM, July, 1954 | 600.00 |

## COMIC COMICS
### Fawcett Publications, 1946
| | |
|---|---|
| 1 Captain Kidd | 350.00 |
| 2 BW | 400.00 |
| 3 BW | 400.00 |
| 4 BW | 400.00 |
| 5 BW | 400.00 |
| 6 BW | 400.00 |
| 7 BW | 400.00 |
| 8 BW | 400.00 |
| 9 BW | 400.00 |
| 10 BW | 400.00 |

**Co**

*Comics on Parade #5*
*© United Features Syndicate*

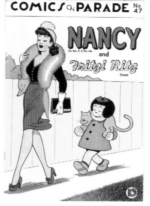

*Comics on Parade #47*
*© United Features Syndicate*

*Commander Battle and the Atomic*
*Submarine #7 © American Comics*

## COMIC LAND
**Fact and Fiction, 1946**
1 Sandusky and the Senator . . . 350.00

## COMICS, THE
**Dell Publishing Co.,**
**March, 1937**
1 I:Tom Mix & Arizona Kid . . . . 3,500.00
2 A:Tom Mix & Tom Beaty . . . . 2,500.00
3 A:Alley Oop . . . . . . . . . . . . 2,000.00
4 same . . . . . . . . . . . . . . . . . 2,000.00
5 same . . . . . . . . . . . . . . . . . 2,000.00
6 thru 11 same . . . . . . . . . . @2,000.00

## THE COMICS CALENDAR
**True Comics Press, 1946**
1 . . . . . . . . . . . . . . . . . . . . . . 750.00

## COMICS DIGEST
**Parents Magazine Institute,**
**1942**
1 True adventure. . . . . . . . . . . . 250.00

## COMICS FOR KIDS
**Marvel Timely, 1945**
1 Funny animal . . . . . . . . . . . . . 300.00
2 . . . . . . . . . . . . . . . . . . . . . . 300.00

## COMICS MAGAZINE
**See: FUNNY PAGES**

## COMICS NOVEL
**Fawcett Publications, 1947**
1 Anarcho Dictator of Death . . . . 500.00

## COMICS ON PARADE
**United Features Syndicate,**
**April, 1938–Feb., 1955**
1 B:Tarzan;Captain and the Kids,
  Little Mary, Mixup,Abbie & Slats,
  Broncho Bill,Li'l Abner . . . . 6,000.00
2 Circus Parade of all . . . . . . . 3,000.00
3 . . . . . . . . . . . . . . . . . . . . . 2,500.00
4 On Rocket. . . . . . . . . . . . . . 2,000.00
5 All at the Store . . . . . . . . . . . 2,000.00
6 All at Picnic. . . . . . . . . . . . . 1,500.00
7 Li'l Abner(c). . . . . . . . . . . . . 1,500.00
8 same . . . . . . . . . . . . . . . . . 1,500.00
9 same . . . . . . . . . . . . . . . . . 1,500.00

10 same . . . . . . . . . . . . . . . . . 1,500.00
11 same . . . . . . . . . . . . . . . . . 1,200.00
12 same . . . . . . . . . . . . . . . . . 1,200.00
13 same . . . . . . . . . . . . . . . . . 1,200.00
14 Abbie n' Slats (c) . . . . . . . . 1,200.00
15 Li'l Abner(c) . . . . . . . . . . . . 1,200.00
16 Abbie n' Slats(c). . . . . . . . . 1,200.00
17 Tarzan,Abbie n' Slats(c). . . . 1,300.00
18 Li'l Abner(c) . . . . . . . . . . . . 1,200.00
19 same . . . . . . . . . . . . . . . . . 1,200.00
20 same . . . . . . . . . . . . . . . . . 1,200.00
21 Li'l Abner(c) . . . . . . . . . . . . 1,000.00
22 Tail Spin Tommy(c). . . . . . . . 1,000.00
23 Abbie n' Slats(c). . . . . . . . . 1,000.00
24 Tail Spin Tommy(c). . . . . . . . 1,000.00
25 Li'l Abner(c) . . . . . . . . . . . . 1,000.00
26 Abbie n' Slats(c). . . . . . . . . 1,000.00
27 Li'l Abner(c) . . . . . . . . . . . . 1,000.00
28 Tail Spin Tommy(c). . . . . . . . 1,000.00
29 Abbie n' Slats(c). . . . . . . . . 1,000.00
30 Li'l Abner(c). . . . . . . . . . . . . . 600.00
31 The Captain & the Kids(c) . . . 400.00
32 Nancy and Fritz Ritz(c) . . . . . 350.00
33 Li'l Abner(c). . . . . . . . . . . . . . 450.00
34 The Captain & the Kids(c) . . . 350.00
35 Nancy and Fritz Ritz(c) . . . . . 350.00
36 Li'l Abner(c). . . . . . . . . . . . . . 450.00
37 The Captain & the Kids(c) . . . 350.00
38 Nancy and Fritz Ritz(c) . . . . . 300.00
39 Li'l Abner(c) . . . . . . . . . . . . . 450.00
40 The Captain & the Kids(c) . . . 350.00
41 Nancy and Fritz Ritz(c) . . . . . 250.00
42 Li'l Abner(c). . . . . . . . . . . . . . 450.00
43 The Captain & the Kids(c) . . . 350.00
44 Nancy and Fritz Ritz(c) . . . . . 250.00
45 Li'l Abner(c). . . . . . . . . . . . . . 350.00
46 The Captain & the Kids(c) . . . 250.00
47 Nancy and Fritz Ritz(c) . . . . . 250.00
48 Li'l Abner(c). . . . . . . . . . . . . . 350.00
49 The Captain & the Kids(c) . . . 250.00
50 Nancy and Fritz Ritz(c) . . . . . 250.00
51 Li'l Abner(c). . . . . . . . . . . . . . 350.00
52 The Captain & the Kids(c) . . . 250.00
53 Nancy and Fritz Ritz(c) . . . . . 250.00
54 Li'l Abner(c). . . . . . . . . . . . . . 350.00
55 Nancy and Fritz Ritz(c) . . . . . 250.00
56 The Captain & the Kids(c) . . . 250.00
57 Nancy and Fritz Ritz(c) . . . . . 250.00
58 Li'l Abner(c). . . . . . . . . . . . . . 350.00
59 The Captain & the Kids(c) . . . 250.00
60 thru 76 Nancy &
  Fritz Ritz(c) . . . . . . . . . . . @200.00
77 Nancy & Sluggo(c) . . . . . . . . 150.00
78 thru 104 Nancy & Sluggo(c) @150.00

## COMICS REVUE
**St. John Publ. Co., 1947**
1 Ella Cinders and Blackie . . . . . 250.00
2 Hap Hopper . . . . . . . . . . . . . . 200.00
3 Iron Vic. . . . . . . . . . . . . . . . . . 200.00
4 Eva Cinders . . . . . . . . . . . . . . 200.00
5 Gordo. . . . . . . . . . . . . . . . . . . 200.00

## COMMANDER BATTLE
## AND THE ATOMIC
## SUBMARINE
**American Comics Group, 1954**
1 3-D(c) . . . . . . . . . . . . . . . . . 1,300.00
2 . . . . . . . . . . . . . . . . . . . . . . . 750.00
3 H-Bomb-3-D type . . . . . . . . . . 800.00
4 . . . . . . . . . . . . . . . . . . . . . . . 750.00
5 . . . . . . . . . . . . . . . . . . . . . . . 750.00
6 . . . . . . . . . . . . . . . . . . . . . . . 750.00
7 . . . . . . . . . . . . . . . . . . . . . . . 750.00

## COMMANDO
## ADVENTURES
**Marvel Atlas, June, 1957**
1 Seek, Find and Destroy . . . . . . 300.00
2 MD, Hit 'em and Hit 'em
  Hard, Aug.,1957 . . . . . . . . . . 150.00

## COMPLETE BOOK OF
## COMICS AND FUNNIES
**William H. Wise & Co., 1945**
1 Wonderman-Magnet . . . . . . . . 700.00

## COMPLETE BOOK OF
## TRUE CRIME COMICS
**William H. Wise & Co., 1945**
1 rep. Crime Does Not Pay . . . 2,000.00

## COMPLETE COMICS
**See: AMAZING COMICS**

## COMPLETE LOVE
## MAGAZINE
**Ace Periodicals, 1951–56**
**(Formerly a pulp magazine)**
1 (26/2 . . . . . . . . . . . . . . . . . . . 150.00
2 (26/3) . . . . . . . . . . . . . . . . . . 100.00
3 thru 8 (27/1–27/6) . . . . . . . . @100.00
9 & 10 (28/1–28/2) . . . . . . . . . . 100.00

Complete Mystery #4
© Marvel Comics Group

Contact Comics #12
© Aviation Press

Cookie #9
© American Comics Group

**Co**

11 thru 16 (29/1–29/6) . . . . . . @100.00
17 thru 22 (30/1–30/6) . . . . . . @100.00
23 thru 28 (31/1–31/6) . . . . . . @100.00
29 thru 32 (32/1–32/4) . . . . . . @100.00

## COMPLETE MYSTERY
### Marvel, Aug., 1948
1 Seven Dead Men . . . . . . . . . . 600.00
2 Jigsaw of Doom . . . . . . . . . . . 450.00
3 Fear in the Night . . . . . . . . . . 450.00
4 A Squealer Dies Fast . . . . . . . 450.00
Becomes:

## TRUE COMPLETE MYSTERY
### Marvel, 1949
5 Rice Mancini,
   The Deadly Dude . . . . . . . . 300.00
6 Ph(c),Frame-up that Failed . . . 250.00
7 Ph(c),Caught . . . . . . . . . . . . . 250.00
8 Ph(c),The Downfall of Mr.
   Anderson,Oct., 1949 . . . . . . 250.00

## CONFESSIONS ILLUSTRATED
### E.C. Comics, 1956
1 WW,JO,JCr,JKa,Adult romance 350.00
2 JCr,RC,JKa,JO . . . . . . . . . . . 300.00

## CONFESSIONS OF LOVE
### Artful Publications, April, 1950
1 . . . . . . . . . . . . . . . . . . . . . . . 300.00
2 July, 1950. . . . . . . . . . . . . . . . 200.00

## CONFESSIONS OF LOVE
### Star Publications, July, 1952
11 AW,LbC(c)Intimate Secrets of
   Daring Romance . . . . . . . . . 250.00
12 AW,LbC(c),I Couldn't Say No 250.00
13 AW,LbC(c),Heart Break . . . . 250.00
14 AW,LbC(c),My Fateful Love . 200.00
4 JyD,AW,LbC(c),The Longing
   Heart . . . . . . . . . . . . . . . . . . 200.00
5 AW,LbC(c),I Wanted Love . . . . 200.00
6 AW,LbC(c),My Jealous Heart. . 200.00
Becomes:

## CONFESSIONS OF ROMANCE
### Nov., 1953
7 LbC(c)Too Good . . . . . . . . . . 250.00

8 AW,LbC(c),I Lied About Love . 200.00
9 WW,AW,LbC(c),I Paid
   Love's Price . . . . . . . . . . . . . 250.00
10 JyD,AW,LbC(c),My Heart Cries
   for Love . . . . . . . . . . . . . . . . 200.00
11 JyD,AW,LbC(c),Intimate
   Confessions, Nov., 1954 . . . . 200.00

## CONFESSIONS OF LOVELORN
### See: LOVELORN

## CONGO BILL
### DC Comics, 1954–56
1 . . . . . . . . . . . . . . . . . . . . . 2,000.00
2 thru 7 . . . . . . . . . . . . . . @1,500.00

## CONQUEROR COMICS
### Albrecht Publications, Winter, 1945
1 . . . . . . . . . . . . . . . . . . . . . . . 250.00

## CONQUEST
### Famous Funnies, 1955
1 Historical adventure . . . . . . . . 100.00

## CONTACT COMICS
### Aviation Press, July, 1944
N# LbC(c),B:Black Venus,
   Golden Eagle. . . . . . . . . . . . 900.00
2 LbC(c),Peace Jet . . . . . . . . . . 700.00
3 LbC(c),LbC,E:Flamingo . . . . . 650.00
4 LbC(c),LbC . . . . . . . . . . . . . . 600.00
5 LbC(c),A:Phantom Flyer . . . . . 650.00
6 LbC(c),HK . . . . . . . . . . . . . . . 750.00
7 LbC(c),Flying Tigers. . . . . . . . 600.00
8 LbC(c),Peace Jet. . . . . . . . . . 600.00
9 LbC(c),LbC,A:Marine Flyers . . 600.00
10 LbC(c),A:Bombers of the AAF 600.00
11 LbC(c),HK,AF,Salutes Naval
   Aviation . . . . . . . . . . . . . . . . 700.00
12 LbC(c),A:Sky Rangers, Air Kids,
   May, 1946. . . . . . . . . . . . . . 1,300.00

## COO COO COMICS
### Nedor/Animated Cartoons (Standard), Oct., 1942
1 O&I:Super Mouse . . . . . . . . . . 500.00
2 . . . . . . . . . . . . . . . . . . . . . . . 250.00
3 . . . . . . . . . . . . . . . . . . . . . . . 200.00
4 . . . . . . . . . . . . . . . . . . . . . . . 225.00

5 . . . . . . . . . . . . . . . . . . . . . . . 225.00
6 thru 10 . . . . . . . . . . . . . . . @150.00
11 thru 33 . . . . . . . . . . . . . . . @150.00
34 thru 40 FF illustration . . . . . @250.00
41 FF . . . . . . . . . . . . . . . . . . . . 400.00
42 FF . . . . . . . . . . . . . . . . . . . . 350.00
43 FF illustration . . . . . . . . . . . . 250.00
44 FF illustration . . . . . . . . . . . . 250.00
45 FF illustration . . . . . . . . . . . . 250.00
46 FF illustration . . . . . . . . . . . . 250.00
47 FF . . . . . . . . . . . . . . . . . . . . 350.00
48 FF illustration . . . . . . . . . . . . 250.00
49 FF illustration . . . . . . . . . . . . 250.00
50 FF illustration . . . . . . . . . . . . 250.00
51 thru 61. . . . . . . . . . . . . . . @125.00
62 April, 1952. . . . . . . . . . . . . . 100.00

## "COOKIE"
### Michel Publ./Regis Publ. (American Comics Group) April, 1946
1 . . . . . . . . . . . . . . . . . . . . . . . 350.00
2 . . . . . . . . . . . . . . . . . . . . . . . 250.00
3 thru 5 . . . . . . . . . . . . . . . . @200.00
6 thru 20 . . . . . . . . . . . . . . . @150.00
21 thru 30 . . . . . . . . . . . . . . @100.00
31 thru 54 . . . . . . . . . . . . . . @100.00
55 Aug., 1955. . . . . . . . . . . . . . 100.00

## COSMO CAT
### Fox Features Syndicate, 1946
1 . . . . . . . . . . . . . . . . . . . . . . . 325.00
2 . . . . . . . . . . . . . . . . . . . . . . . 200.00
3 O:Cosmo Cat . . . . . . . . . . . . 225.00
4 thru 10 . . . . . . . . . . . . . . . @150.00

## COSMO THE MERRY MARTIAN
### Radio Comics/Archie Publ., 1958
1 Funny alien . . . . . . . . . . . . . . 250.00
2 . . . . . . . . . . . . . . . . . . . . . . . 200.00
3 . . . . . . . . . . . . . . . . . . . . . . . 200.00
4 . . . . . . . . . . . . . . . . . . . . . . . 200.00
5 . . . . . . . . . . . . . . . . . . . . . . . 200.00
6 . . . . . . . . . . . . . . . . . . . . . . . 200.00

## COURAGE COMICS
### J. Edward Slavin, 1945
1 . . . . . . . . . . . . . . . . . . . . . . . 250.00
2 Boxing (c). . . . . . . . . . . . . . . 250.00
77 Naval rescue, PT99 (c) . . . . . 250.00

# STANDARD GUIDE TO GOLDEN AGE COMICS

Young Men #25
© Marvel Comics Group

Cowgirl Romances #12
© Fiction House

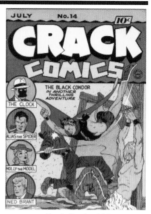

Crack Comics #14
© Comic Magazines

## COWBOY ACTION
## See: WESTERN THRILLERS

## COWBOY COMICS
## See: STAR RANGER

## COWBOY LOVE
**Fawcett Publications, 1949**
1 Photo(c), Western romance. . . 300.00
2 Photo(c). . . . . . . . . . . . . . . . . 100.00
3 Photo(c). . . . . . . . . . . . . . . . . 100.00
4 Photo(c). . . . . . . . . . . . . . . . . 100.00
5 Photo(c). . . . . . . . . . . . . . . . . 100.00
6 Photo(c). . . . . . . . . . . . . . . . . 100.00
7 GE,AW,Photo(c). . . . . . . . . . . 150.00
8 thru 11 Photo(c) . . . . . . . . . @100.00

## COWBOY ROMANCES
**Marvel, Oct., 1949**
1 Ph(c),Outlaw and the Lady . . . 275.00
2 Ph(c),William Holden/Mona
  Freeman,Streets of Laredo . . 250.00
3 Phc,Romance in
  Roaring Valley . . . . . . . . . . . 150.00
**Becomes:**

## YOUNG MEN
**Marvel, 1950**
4 A Kid Names Shorty. . . . . . . . 250.00
5 Jaws of Death . . . . . . . . . . . . 200.00
6 Man-Size . . . . . . . . . . . . . . . . 200.00
7 The Last Laugh . . . . . . . . . . . 200.00
8 Adventure stories continued . . 200.00
9 Draft Dodging story . . . . . . . . 200.00
10 JMn,US Draft Story. . . . . . . . 200.00
11 Adventure stories continued . . 200.00
12 JMn,B:On the Battlefield,
  inc.Spearhead . . . . . . . . . . . 200.00
13 RH,Break-through. . . . . . . . . 200.00
14 GC,RH,Fox Hole. . . . . . . . . . 200.00
15 GC,JMn,Battlefield stories
  cont. . . . . . . . . . . . . . . . . . . 200.00
16 Sniper Patrol. . . . . . . . . . . . . 200.00
17 Battlefield stories cont, . . . . . 200.00
18 BEv,Warlord . . . . . . . . . . . . . 200.00
19 BEv . . . . . . . . . . . . . . . . . . . 200.00
20 BEv,E:On the Battlefield . . . . 200.00
21 B:Flash Foster and his High
  Gear Hot Shots . . . . . . . . . 200.00
22 Screaming Tires . . . . . . . . . . 200.00

23 E:Flash Foster and his High
  Gear Hot Shots . . . . . . . . . 200.00
24 BEv,B:Capt. America,Human
  Torch,Sub-Mariner,O:Capt.
  America,Red Skull . . . . . . 3,600.00
25 BEv,JR, Human Torch,Capt.
  America,Sub-Mariner . . . 1,500.00
26 BEv,Human Torch, Capt.
  America,Sub Mariner . . . . . 1,500.00
27 Bev, Human Torch/Toro
  V:Hypnotist . . . . . . . . . . . 1,400.00
28 E:Human Torch, Capt.America,
  Sub Mariner,June, 1954 . . . 1,400.00

## COWBOYS 'N' INJUNS
**Compix (M.E. Enterprises), 1946-47**
1 Funny Animal Western . . . . . . 300.00
2 thru 5 . . . . . . . . . . . . . . . . @250.00
6 thru 8 See: A-1 Comics, #23,#41,#48

## COWBOY WESTERN/
## COMICS/HEROES
## See: YELLOWJACKET

## COWGIRL ROMANCES
**Fiction House Magazine, 1952**
1 The Range of Singing Guns . . 450.00
2 The Lady of Lawless Range . . 225.00
3 Daughter of the
  Devil's Band. . . . . . . . . . . . . 200.00
4 Bride Wore Buckskin . . . . . . . 200.00
5 Taming of Lone-Star Lou . . . . 200.00
6 Rose of Mustang Mesa . . . . . 175.00
7 Nobody Loves a Gun Man. . . . 175.00
8 Wild Beauty . . . . . . . . . . . . . . 175.00
9 Gun-Feud Sweethearts . . . . . 175.00
10 JKa,AW,No Girl of Stampede
  Valley . . . . . . . . . . . . . . . . . 375.00
11 Love is Where You Find It. . . . 175.00
12 Dec., 1952 . . . . . . . . . . . . . . 175.00

## COWGIRL ROMANCES
## See: DARING MYSTERY

## COW PUNCHER
**Avon Periodicals/ Realistic Publ., Jan., 1947**
1 JKu . . . . . . . . . . . . . . . . . . . . 500.00
2 JKu,JKa(c),Bondage (c) . . . . 400.00
3 AU(c) . . . . . . . . . . . . . . . . . . 350.00

4 . . . . . . . . . . . . . . . . . . . . . . . 350.00
5 . . . . . . . . . . . . . . . . . . . . . . . 350.00
6 WJo(c),Drug story . . . . . . . . . 400.00
7 . . . . . . . . . . . . . . . . . . . . . . . 350.00
1 JKu . . . . . . . . . . . . . . . . . . . . 350.00

## CRACK COMICS
**Comic Magazines (Quality Comics Group) 1940**
1 LF,O:Black Condor,Madame
  Fatal, Red Torpedo, Rock
  Bradden, Space Legion,
  B:The Clock,Wizard Wells . 9,000.00
2 Black Condor (c) . . . . . . . . 4,000.00
3 The Clock (c) . . . . . . . . . . . 3,000.00
4 Black Condor (c) . . . . . . . . 2,700.00
5 LF,The Clock (c) . . . . . . . . 2,000.00
6 PG,Black Condor (c) . . . . . 1,800.00
7 Clock (c) . . . . . . . . . . . . . . 1,800.00
8 Black Condor (c) . . . . . . . . 1,800.00
9 Clock (c) . . . . . . . . . . . . . . 1,800.00
10 Black Condor (c) . . . . . . . . 1,800.00
11 LF,PG,Clock (c) . . . . . . . . 1,500.00
12 LF,PG,Black Condor (c) . . . 1,500.00
13 LF,PG,Clock (c) . . . . . . . . 1,500.00
14 AMc,LF,PG,Clack Condor(c) 1,500.00
15 AMc,LF,PG,Clock (c) . . . . 1,500.00
16 AMc,LF,PG,Black Condor(c) 1,500.00
17 FGu,AMc,LF,PG,Clock (c) . 1,500.00
18 AMc,LF,PG,Black Condor(c) 1,500.00
19 AMc,LF,PG,Clock (c) . . . . 1,500.00
20 AMc,LF,PG,BlackCondor(c) 1,500.00
21 AMc,LF,PG,same . . . . . . . 1,200.00
22 LF,PG,same . . . . . . . . . . . 1,200.00
23 AMc,LF,PG,same . . . . . . . 1,200.00
24 AMc,LF,PG,same . . . . . . . 1,200.00
25 AMc,same . . . . . . . . . . . . 1,000.00
26 AMc,same . . . . . . . . . . . . 1,000.00
27 AMc,I&O:Captain Triumph . 1,800.00
28 Captain Triumph (c). . . . . . 1,000.00
29 A:Spade the Ruthless . . . . 1,000.00
30 I:Biff . . . . . . . . . . . . . . . . . . 800.00
31 Helps Spade Dig His Own
  Grave. . . . . . . . . . . . . . . . . 500.00
32 Newspaper (c) . . . . . . . . . . 500.00
33 V:Men of Darkness . . . . . . . 500.00
34 . . . . . . . . . . . . . . . . . . . . . . 500.00
35 V:The Man Who Conquered
  Flame. . . . . . . . . . . . . . . . . 500.00
36 Good Neighbor Tour . . . . . . 500.00
37 V:The Tyrant of Toar Valley. . 500.00
38 Castle of Shadows . . . . . . . 500.00
39 V:Crime over the City . . . . . 500.00
40 Thrilling Murder Mystery . . . 350.00
41 . . . . . . . . . . . . . . . . . . . . . . 350.00

Crack Western #63
© Comic Magazines

Crackajack Funnies #1
© Dell Publishing Co.

Crash Comics #1
© Tem Publishing Co.

**Cr**

42 All that Glitters is Not Gold . . . 350.00
43 Smashes the Evil Spell of
  Silent . . . . . . . . . . . . . . . . . 350.00
44 V:Silver Tip . . . . . . . . . . . . . . 350.00
45 V:King-The Jack of all Trades. 350.00
46 V:Mr. Weary . . . . . . . . . . . . . 350.00
47 V:Hypnotic Eyes Khor. . . . . . . 400.00
48 Murder in the Sky . . . . . . . . . 400.00
49 . . . . . . . . . . . . . . . . . . . . . . 400.00
50 A Key to Trouble . . . . . . . . . 400.00
51 V:Werewolf . . . . . . . . . . . . . . 400.00
52 V:Porcupine . . . . . . . . . . . . . 400.00
53 V:Man Who Robbed the Dead 400.00
54 Shoulders the Troubles
  of the World . . . . . . . . . . . . . 400.00
55 Brain against Brawn . . . . . . . . 400.00
56 Gossip leads to Murder . . . . . 400.00
57 V:Sitok–Green God of Evil . . . 400.00
58 V:Targets . . . . . . . . . . . . . . . 300.00
59 A Cargo of Mystery . . . . . . . . 300.00
60 Trouble is no Picnic . . . . . . . . 300.00
61 V:Mr. Pointer-Finger of Fear . . 300.00
62 V:The Vanishing Vandals . . . . 300.00
**Becomes:**

## CRACK WESTERN
### Nov., 1949–May, 1951
63 PG, I&O:Two-Gun Lil, B:Frontier
  Marshal,Arizona Ames, . . . . . 350.00
64 RC,Arizona AmesV:Two-
  Legged Coyote . . . . . . . . . . . 225.00
65 RC,Ames Tramples on
  Trouble . . . . . . . . . . . . . . . . 225.00
66 Arizona Ames Arizona Raines,
  Tim Holt,Ph(c) . . . . . . . . . . . 150.00
67 RC, Ph(c),Randolph Scott . . . 225.00
68 Ph(c) . . . . . . . . . . . . . . . . . . 150.00
69 RC. . . . . . . . . . . . . . . . . . . . 150.00
70 O&I:Whip and Diablo . . . . . . 175.00
71 Bob Allen, Marshall,RC(c). . . . 200.00
72 RC,Tim Holt,Ph(c). . . . . . . . . 150.00
73 Tim Holt,Ph(c). . . . . . . . . . . . 100.00
74 RC(c). . . . . . . . . . . . . . . . . . 150.00
75 RC(c). . . . . . . . . . . . . . . . . . 150.00
76 RC(c),Stage Coach to
  Oblivion . . . . . . . . . . . . . . . . 150.00
77 RC(c),Comanche Terror . . . . 150.00
78 RC(c),Killers of Laurel Ridge . 150.00
79 RC(c),Fires of Revenge . . . . . 150.00
80 RC(c),Mexican Massacre . . . 150.00
81 RC(c),Secrets of Terror
  Canyon . . . . . . . . . . . . . . . . 150.00
82 The Killer with a Thousand
  Faces. . . . . . . . . . . . . . . . . . 125.00
83 Rattlesnake Pete's Revenge . 125.00
84 PG(c),Revolt at Broke Creek . 125.00

## CRACKAJACK FUNNIES
### Dell Publishing Co., 1938
1 AMc,A:Dan Dunn,The Nebbs,
  Don Winslow . . . . . . . . . . . 4,000.00
2 AMc,same. . . . . . . . . . . . . . 2,000.00
3 AMc,same. . . . . . . . . . . . . . 1,500.00
4 AMc,same. . . . . . . . . . . . . . 1,200.00
5 AMc,Naked Women(c) . . . . . 1,400.00
6 AMc,same. . . . . . . . . . . . . . 1,100.00
7 AMc,same. . . . . . . . . . . . . . 1,100.00
8 AMc,same. . . . . . . . . . . . . . 1,100.00
9 AMc,A:Red Ryder . . . . . . . . . 2,300.00
10 AMc,A:Red Ryder . . . . . . . . . 900.00
11 AMc,A:Red Ryder . . . . . . . . . 800.00
12 AMc,A:Red Ryder . . . . . . . . . 800.00
13 AMc,A:Red Ryder . . . . . . . . . 800.00
14 AMc,A:Red Ryder . . . . . . . . . 800.00
15 AMc,A:Tarzan . . . . . . . . . . . . 900.00
16 AMc. . . . . . . . . . . . . . . . . . . 750.00
17 AMc. . . . . . . . . . . . . . . . . . . 750.00
18 AMc,A:Stratosphere Jim . . . . 750.00
19 AMc. . . . . . . . . . . . . . . . . . . 750.00
20 AMc. . . . . . . . . . . . . . . . . . . 750.00
21 AMc. . . . . . . . . . . . . . . . . . . 750.00
22 AMc. . . . . . . . . . . . . . . . . . . 750.00
23 AMc,A:Ellery Queen . . . . . . . 750.00
24 AMc. . . . . . . . . . . . . . . . . . . 750.00
25 AMc,I:The Owl . . . . . . . . . . 1,500.00
26 AMc . . . . . . . . . . . . . . . . . 1,000.00
27 AMc . . . . . . . . . . . . . . . . . 1,000.00
28 AMc,A:The Owl . . . . . . . . . 1,000.00
29 AMc,A:Ellery Queen. . . . . . . 1,000.00
30 AMc,A:Tarzan . . . . . . . . . . 1,000.00
31 AMc,A:Tarzan. . . . . . . . . . . 1,000.00
32 AMc,O:Owl Girl . . . . . . . . . 1,100.00
33 AMc,A:Tarzan . . . . . . . . . . . . 900.00
34 AMc,same. . . . . . . . . . . . . . . 900.00
35 AMc,same. . . . . . . . . . . . . . . 900.00
36 AMc,same. . . . . . . . . . . . . . . 900.00
37 AMc. . . . . . . . . . . . . . . . . . . 900.00
38 AMc. . . . . . . . . . . . . . . . . . . 900.00
39 AMc,I:Andy Panada . . . . . . . 1,100.00
40 AMc,A:Owl(c) . . . . . . . . . . . . 750.00
41 AMc. . . . . . . . . . . . . . . . . . . 750.00
42 AMc. . . . . . . . . . . . . . . . . . . 750.00
43 AMc,Terry & The Pirates,
  A:Owl(c). . . . . . . . . . . . . . . . 700.00

## CRACKED
### Major Magazines, 1958
1 AW . . . . . . . . . . . . . . . . . . . 300.00
2 . . . . . . . . . . . . . . . . . . . . . . 250.00
3 . . . . . . . . . . . . . . . . . . . . . . 250.00
4 . . . . . . . . . . . . . . . . . . . . . . 250.00

5 . . . . . . . . . . . . . . . . . . . . . . 250.00
6 . . . . . . . . . . . . . . . . . . . . . . 250.00
7 thru 10 . . . . . . . . . . . . . . . . @200.00
11 thru 20 . . . . . . . . . . . . . . . @150.00

## CRASH COMICS
### Tem Publishing Co., May, 1940
1 S&K,O:Strongman, B:Blue Streak,
  Perfect Human, Shangra . . 6,000.00
2 S&K . . . . . . . . . . . . . . . . . . 3,500.00
3 S&K . . . . . . . . . . . . . . . . . . 2,500.00
4 S&K,O&I:Catman . . . . . . . . 6,000.00
5 S&K, Nov., 1940 . . . . . . . . . 2,500.00

## CRAZY
### Marvel Atlas, Dec., 1953
1 JMn,BEv,satire, Frank N.
  Steins Castle . . . . . . . . . . . . 450.00
2 JMn,BEv,Beast from 1000
  Fathoms. . . . . . . . . . . . . . . . 300.00
3 JMn,BEv,RH,Madame Knock-
  wurst's Whacks Museum. . . . 250.00
4 JMn,BEv,DAv,I Love Lucy
  satire . . . . . . . . . . . . . . . . . . 250.00
5 JMn,BEv,Censorship satire . . . 250.00
6 JMn,BEv,MD,satire . . . . . . . . 300.00
7 JMn,BEv,RH,satire,July, 1954 250.00

## CRIME AND JUSTICE
### Capitol Stories/ Charlton Comics 1951–55
1 . . . . . . . . . . . . . . . . . . . . . . 400.00
2 . . . . . . . . . . . . . . . . . . . . . . 250.00
3 . . . . . . . . . . . . . . . . . . . . . . 200.00
4 . . . . . . . . . . . . . . . . . . . . . . 200.00
5 . . . . . . . . . . . . . . . . . . . . . . 200.00
6 Negligee. . . . . . . . . . . . . . . . 250.00
7 . . . . . . . . . . . . . . . . . . . . . . 200.00
8 . . . . . . . . . . . . . . . . . . . . . . 200.00
9 . . . . . . . . . . . . . . . . . . . . . . 350.00
10 . . . . . . . . . . . . . . . . . . . . . . 175.00
11 thru 14 . . . . . . . . . . . . . . . @250.00
15 Negligee . . . . . . . . . . . . . . . 250.00
16 . . . . . . . . . . . . . . . . . . . . . . 200.00
17 . . . . . . . . . . . . . . . . . . . . . . 200.00
18 SD . . . . . . . . . . . . . . . . . . . 300.00
19 thru 21 . . . . . . . . . . . . . . . @200.00
**Becomes:**

## BADGE OF JUSTICE
### Charlton Comics, 1955
22 (1) . . . . . . . . . . . . . . . . . . . . 200.00
23 (2) . . . . . . . . . . . . . . . . . . . . 150.00

**Cr**

Crime and Punishment #10
© Lev Gleason Publications

Crime Detective Vol. 3 #1
© Hillman Publications

Crime Exposed #2
© Marvel Comics Group

24 (3) . . . . . . . . . . . . . . . . . . . . . . 150.00
25 (4) . . . . . . . . . . . . . . . . . . . . . . 150.00
Revived as:

## CRIME AND JUSTICE
**Charlton Comics, 1955**
23 thru 26 . . . . . . . . . . . . . . . @150.00

## CRIME AND PUNISHMENT
**Lev Gleason Publications, April, 1948**
1 CBi(c),Mr.Crime(c) . . . . . . . . . 450.00
2 CBi(c) . . . . . . . . . . . . . . . . . . . 250.00
3 CBi(c),BF . . . . . . . . . . . . . . . . 275.00
4 CBi(c),BF . . . . . . . . . . . . . . . . 200.00
5 CBi(c) . . . . . . . . . . . . . . . . . . . 200.00
6 thru 10 CBi(c) . . . . . . . . . . . @125.00
11 thru 15 CBi(c) . . . . . . . . . . . @100.00
16 thru 27 CBi(c) . . . . . . . . . . . @100.00
28 thru 38 . . . . . . . . . . . . . . . . . @100.00
39 Drug issue . . . . . . . . . . . . . . . 125.00
40 thru 44 . . . . . . . . . . . . . . . . . @100.00
45 Drug issue . . . . . . . . . . . . . . . 100.00
46 thru 58 . . . . . . . . . . . . . . . . . @100.00
59 . . . . . . . . . . . . . . . . . . . . . . . 350.00
60 thru 65 . . . . . . . . . . . . . . . . . @100.00
66 ATh . . . . . . . . . . . . . . . . . . . . 450.00
67 Drug Storm . . . . . . . . . . . . . . 425.00
68 ATh(c) . . . . . . . . . . . . . . . . . . 350.00
69 Drug issue . . . . . . . . . . . . . . . 125.00
74 Aug., 1955 . . . . . . . . . . . . . . . 100.00

## CRIME CAN'T WIN
### See: KRAZY COMICS

## CRIME CASES COMICS
**Marvel Atlas, 1950–52**
**(Formerly: WILLIE COMICS)**
**(See: IDEAL)**
1 (24) Police . . . . . . . . . . . . . . . 250.00
2 (25) . . . . . . . . . . . . . . . . . . . . 200.00
3 (26) . . . . . . . . . . . . . . . . . . . . 150.00
4 (27) . . . . . . . . . . . . . . . . . . . . 150.00
5 . . . . . . . . . . . . . . . . . . . . . . . 150.00
6 . . . . . . . . . . . . . . . . . . . . . . . 150.00
7 . . . . . . . . . . . . . . . . . . . . . . . 150.00
8 . . . . . . . . . . . . . . . . . . . . . . . 150.00
9 . . . . . . . . . . . . . . . . . . . . . . . 150.00
10 . . . . . . . . . . . . . . . . . . . . . . 150.00
11 . . . . . . . . . . . . . . . . . . . . . . 150.00
12 . . . . . . . . . . . . . . . . . . . . . . 150.00

## CRIME CLINIC
**Approved Publ. (Ziff-Davis), 1951**
1 (10) F:Dr. Tom Rogers . . . . . . . 350.00
2 (11) . . . . . . . . . . . . . . . . . . . . 250.00
3 . . . . . . . . . . . . . . . . . . . . . . . 250.00
4 . . . . . . . . . . . . . . . . . . . . . . . 250.00
5 . . . . . . . . . . . . . . . . . . . . . . . 250.00

## CRIME DETECTOR
**Timor Publications, 1954**
1 . . . . . . . . . . . . . . . . . . . . . . . 300.00
2 . . . . . . . . . . . . . . . . . . . . . . . 250.00
3 . . . . . . . . . . . . . . . . . . . . . . . 225.00
4 . . . . . . . . . . . . . . . . . . . . . . . 225.00
5 . . . . . . . . . . . . . . . . . . . . . . . 250.00

## CRIME DETECTIVE COMICS
**Hillman Publications, March–April, 1948**
1 BF(c),A:Invisible 6 . . . . . . . . . 400.00
2 Jewel Robbery (c) . . . . . . . . . 250.00
3 Stolen Cash (c) . . . . . . . . . . . 200.00
4 Crime Boss Murder (c) . . . . . 200.00
5 BK,Maestro (c) . . . . . . . . . . . 200.00
6 AMc,Gorilla (c) . . . . . . . . . . . 150.00
7 GMc,Wedding (c) . . . . . . . . . 150.00
8 . . . . . . . . . . . . . . . . . . . . . . . 150.00
9 Safe Robbery (c) (a classic) . . 500.00
10 . . . . . . . . . . . . . . . . . . . . . . 150.00
11 BP . . . . . . . . . . . . . . . . . . . . 150.00
12 BK . . . . . . . . . . . . . . . . . . . . 150.00
2-1 Bluebird Captured . . . . . . . . 200.00
2-2 . . . . . . . . . . . . . . . . . . . . . . 150.00
2-3 . . . . . . . . . . . . . . . . . . . . . . 150.00
2-4 BK . . . . . . . . . . . . . . . . . . . 175.00
2-5 . . . . . . . . . . . . . . . . . . . . . . 150.00
2-6 . . . . . . . . . . . . . . . . . . . . . . 150.00
2-7 BK,GMc . . . . . . . . . . . . . . . 175.00
2-8 . . . . . . . . . . . . . . . . . . . . . . 150.00
2-9 . . . . . . . . . . . . . . . . . . . . . . 150.00
2-10 . . . . . . . . . . . . . . . . . . . . . 150.00
2-11 . . . . . . . . . . . . . . . . . . . . . 150.00
2-12 . . . . . . . . . . . . . . . . . . . . . 150.00
3-1 Drug Story . . . . . . . . . . . . . 150.00
3-2 thru 3-7 . . . . . . . . . . . . . . . @150.00
3-8 May/June, 1953 . . . . . . . . . 100.00

## CRIME DOES NOT PAY
### See: SILVER STREAK COMICS

## CRIME EXPOSED
**Marvel Atlas Comics, 1948–52**
1 . . . . . . . . . . . . . . . . . . . . . . . 400.00
2 . . . . . . . . . . . . . . . . . . . . . . . 200.00
3 GT . . . . . . . . . . . . . . . . . . . . . 150.00
4 GT . . . . . . . . . . . . . . . . . . . . . 150.00
5 thru 7 . . . . . . . . . . . . . . . . . . @150.00
8 MMe(c) . . . . . . . . . . . . . . . . . 175.00
9 . . . . . . . . . . . . . . . . . . . . . . . 150.00
10 . . . . . . . . . . . . . . . . . . . . . . 150.00
11 JeR . . . . . . . . . . . . . . . . . . . 175.00
12 BK,JeR . . . . . . . . . . . . . . . . 200.00
13 BK . . . . . . . . . . . . . . . . . . . . 200.00
14 . . . . . . . . . . . . . . . . . . . . . . 125.00

## CRIMEFIGHTERS
**Marvel, April, 1948–Nov., 1949**
1 Police Stories . . . . . . . . . . . . . 350.00
2 Jewelry Robbery . . . . . . . . . . . 200.00
3 The Nine Who Were Doomed, addiction . . . . . . . . . . . . . . . . 225.00
4 Human Beast at Bay . . . . . . . . 150.00
5 V:Gangsters . . . . . . . . . . . . . . 150.00
6 Pickpockets . . . . . . . . . . . . . . 150.00
7 True Cases, Crime Can't Win . 150.00
8 True Cases, Crime Can't Win . 150.00
9 Ph(c),It Happened at Night . . . 150.00
10 Ph(c),Killer at Large . . . . . . . 150.00
Becomes:

## CRIME FIGHTERS ALWAYS WIN
**Marvel Atlas, 1954–1955**
11 JMn,V:Gangsters . . . . . . . . . . 175.00
12 V:Gangsters . . . . . . . . . . . . . 150.00
13 Clay Pidgeon . . . . . . . . . . . . 150.00

## CRIME-FIGHTING DETECTIVE
### See: CRIMINALS ON THE RUN

## CRIME FILES
**Standard Comics, 1952**
5 ATh . . . . . . . . . . . . . . . . . . . . 300.00
6 . . . . . . . . . . . . . . . . . . . . . . . 200.00

## CRIME ILLUSTRATED
**E.C. Comics, Nov.–Dec., 1955**
1 Grl,RC,GE,JO . . . . . . . . . . . . 400.00
2 Grl,RC,JCr,JDa,JO . . . . . . . . 300.00

*Crime(s) Incorporated #1 (12)*
© Fox Features Syndicate

*Crime Mysteries #7*
© Ribage Publishing

*Tales From the Crypt #26*
© E.C. Comics

Cr

## CRIME INCORPORATED

**Fox Features Syndicate, 1950**

**(Formerly: WESTERN THRILLERS; MY PAST CONFESSIONS)**

| | |
|---|---|
| 1 (12) Crimes Incorporated | 300.00 |
| 2 | 225.00 |
| 3 | 225.00 |

## CRIME MUST LOSE!

**Marvel Atlas, 1950**

| | |
|---|---|
| 4 | 300.00 |
| 5 | 200.00 |
| 6 | 200.00 |
| 7 | 200.00 |
| 8 | 200.00 |
| 9 JeR | 225.00 |
| 10 | 200.00 |
| 11 | 200.00 |
| 12 | 200.00 |

## CRIME MUST PAY THE PENALTY

**Ace Magazines, 1948–56**

| | |
|---|---|
| 1 "True cases of actual crimes" | 550.00 |
| 2 Violent | 350.00 |
| 3 | 300.00 |
| 4 | 300.00 |
| 5 | 200.00 |
| 6 | 200.00 |
| 7 | 200.00 |
| 8 Transvestite | 300.00 |
| 9 | 200.00 |
| 10 | 200.00 |
| 11 thru 19 | @200.00 |
| 20 Drugs | 250.00 |
| 21 thru 30 | @200.00 |
| 31 thru 48 | @200.00 |

## CRIME MUST STOP

**Hillman Periodicals, Oct., 1952**

| | |
|---|---|
| 1 BK | 1,000.00 |

## CRIME MYSTERIES

**Ribage Publishing Corp., May, 1952**

| | |
|---|---|
| 1 Transvestism,Bondage(c) | 1,000.00 |
| 2 A:Manhunter, Lance Storm, Drug | 750.00 |
| 3 FF-one page, A:Dr. Foo | 500.00 |

| | |
|---|---|
| 4 A:Queenie Star, BondageStar | 750.00 |
| 5 Claws of the Green Girl | 400.00 |
| 6 | 400.00 |
| 7 Sons of Satan | 400.00 |
| 8 Death Stalks the Crown, Bondage(c) | 400.00 |
| 9 You are the Murderer | 375.00 |
| 10 The Hoax of the Death | 375.00 |
| 11 The Strangler | 375.00 |
| 12 Bondage(c) | 450.00 |
| 13 AT,6 lives for one | 500.00 |
| 14 Painted in Blood | 375.00 |
| 15 Feast of the Dead,Acid Face | 650.00 |

Becomes:

## SECRET MYSTERIES

**Nov., 1954**

| | |
|---|---|
| 16 Hiding Place,Horror | 400.00 |
| 17 The Deadly Diamond,Horror | 300.00 |
| 18 Horror | 350.00 |
| 19 Horror,July, 1955 | 350.00 |

## INTERNATIONAL COMICS

**E.C. Publ. Co., Spring, 1947**

| | |
|---|---|
| 1 KS,I:Manhattan's Files | 1,000.00 |
| 2 KS,A: Van Manhattan & Madelon | 750.00 |
| 3 KS,same | 600.00 |
| 4 KS,same | 600.00 |
| 5 I:International Crime-Busting Patrol | 600.00 |

Becomes:

## INTERNATIONAL CRIME PATROL

**Spring, 1948**

| | |
|---|---|
| 6 A:Moon Girl & The Prince | 1,000.00 |

Becomes:

## CRIME PATROL

**Summer, 1948**

| | |
|---|---|
| 7 SMo,A:Capt. Crime Jr.,Field Marshall of Murder | 1,200.00 |
| 8 JCr,State Prison (c) | 1,000.00 |
| 9 AF,JCr,Bank Robbery | 1,000.00 |
| 10 AF,JCr,Wanted:James Dore | 1,000.00 |
| 11 AF,JCr | 1,000.00 |
| 12 AF,Grl,JCr,Interrogation(c) | 1,000.00 |
| 13 AF,JCr | 1,000.00 |
| 14 AF,JCr,Smugglers (c) | 1,000.00 |
| 15 AF,JCr,Crypt of Terror | 6,000.00 |
| 16 AF,JCr,Crypt of Terror | 3,500.00 |

Becomes:

## CRYPT OF TERROR

**E.C. Comics, April, 1950**

| | |
|---|---|
| 17 JCr(a&c),AF,'Werewolf Strikes Again' | 5,000.00 |
| 18 JCr(a&c),AF,WW,HK 'The Living Corpse' | 3,000.00 |
| 19 JCr(a&c),AF,Grl, 'Voodoo Drums' | 2,900.00 |

Becomes:

## TALES FROM THE CRYPT

**Oct., 1950**

| | |
|---|---|
| 20 JCr(a&c),AF,GI,JKa 'Day of Death' | 3,200.00 |
| 21 AF(a&c),WW,HK,GI,'Cooper Dies in the Electric Chair | 3,000.00 |
| 22 AF, JCr(c) | 2,200.00 |
| 23 AF(a&c),JCr,JDa,Grl 'Locked in a Mausoleum' | 1,500.00 |
| 24 AF(c),WW,JDa,JCr,Grl 'Danger...Quicksand' | 1,500.00 |
| 25 AF(c),WW,JDa,JKa,Grl 'Mataud Waxworks' | 1,500.00 |
| 26 WW(c),JDa,Grl, 'Scared Graveyard' | 1,200.00 |
| 27 JKa, WW(c), Guillotine (c) | 1,200.00 |
| 28 AF(c),JDa,JKa,Grl,JO 'Buried Alive' | 1,200.00 |
| 29 JDa(a&c),JKa,Grl,JO 'Coffin Burier' | 1,200.00 |
| 30 JDa(a&c),JO,JKa,Grl 'Underwater Death' | 1,200.00 |
| 31 JDa(a&c),JKa,Grl,AW 'Hand Chopper' | 1,500.00 |
| 32 JDa(a&c),GE,Grl,'Woman Crushed by Elephant' | 1,500.00 |
| 33 JDa(a&c),GE,JKa,Grl,'Lower Berth',O:Crypt Keeper | 1,500.00 |
| 34 JDa(a&c),JKa,GE,Grl,'Jack the Ripper,'RayBradbury adapt. | 1,200.00 |
| 35 JDa(a&c),JKa,JO,Grl, 'Werewolf' | 1,400.00 |
| 36 JDa(a&c),JKa,GE,Grl, Ray Bradbury adaptation | 900.00 |
| 37 JDa(c),JO,BE | 900.00 |
| 38 JDa(c),BE,RC,Grl,'Axe Man' | 900.00 |
| 39 JDa(a&c),JKa,JO,Grl,'Children in the Graveyard' | 900.00 |
| 40 JDa(a&c),GE,BK,Grl, 'Underwater Monster' | 1,500.00 |
| 41 JDa(a&c),GE,Grl, 'Knife Thrower' | 1,500.00 |
| 42 JDa(c),JO,Vampire (c) | 1,500.00 |
| 43 JDa(c),JO,GE | 1,500.00 |

---

All comics prices listed are for *Near Mint* condition.                    **Page 95**

Cr

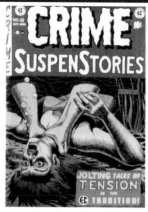

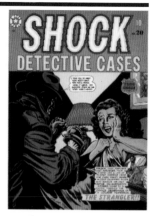

*Crime Reporter #3*
© *St. John Publishing Co.*

*Crime SuspenStories #19*
© *E.C. Comics*

*Shock Detective Cases #20*
© *Star Publications*

44 JO,RC,Guillotine (c)...... 1,400.00
45 JDa(a&c),JKa,BK,GI,'Rat
Takes Over His Life'...... 1,400.00
46 JDa(a&c),GE,JO,GI,Werewolf
man being hunted,Feb.'55 . 1,400.00

## CRIME REPORTER
**St. John Publishing Co.,**
**Aug., 1948**
1 Death Makes a Deadline ... 2,000.00
2 GT,MB(c),Matinee Murders . 2,200.00
3 GT,MB(c),Dec., 1948 ...... 1,800.00

## CRIMES BY WOMEN
**Fox Features Syndicate,**
**June, 1948**
1 Bonnie Parker .......... 2,000.00
2 Vicious Female .......... 1,300.00
3 Prison Break (c) .......... 1,200.00
4 Murder (c) .............. 1,200.00
5 ...................... 1,200.00
6 Girl Fight (c) ............ 1,200.00
7 ........................ 900.00
8 ........................ 900.00
9 ........................ 900.00
10 Girl Fight (c) ........... 800.00
11 ....................... 800.00
12 ....................... 800.00
13 ACME Jewelry Robbery (c) .. 800.00
14 Prison break (c) .......... 800.00
15 Aug., 1951............... 800.00

## CRIME SMASHER
**Fawcett Publications,**
**Summer, 1948**
1 The Unlucky Rabbit's Foot ... 700.00

## CRIME SMASHERS
**Ribage Publishing Corp.,**
**Oct., 1950**
1 Girl Rape............... 1,500.00
2 JKu,A:Sally the Sleuth, Dan
Turner, Girl Friday, Rat Hale . 800.00
3 MFa...................... 600.00
4 Zak(c) ................... 600.00
5 WW ................... 1,000.00
6 ........................ 500.00
7 Bondage (c),Drugs......... 600.00
8 ........................ 500.00
9 Bondage (c)............... 600.00
10 ....................... 500.00
11 ....................... 500.00
12 FF, Eye Injury ........... 600.00

13 ...................... 600.00
14 & 15................... @500.00

## CRIMES ON THE WATERFRONT
**See: FAMOUS GANGSTERS**

## CRIME SUSPENSTORIES
**L.L. Publishing Co.**
**(E.C. Comics), Oct.–Nov., 1950**
1a JCr,Grl ............... 2,700.00
1 JCr,WW,Grl ............. 2,000.00
2 JCr,JKa,Grl ............. 1,500.00
3 JCr,WW,Grl,Poe Story...... 900.00
4 JCr,Gln,Grl,JDa .......... 900.00
5 JCr,JKa,Grl,JDa.......... 900.00
6 JCr,JDa,Grl ............. 600.00
7 JCr,Grl ................. 600.00
8 JCr,Grl ................. 600.00
9 JCr,Grl ................. 600.00
10 JCr,Grl................. 600.00
11 JCr,Grl................. 500.00
12 JCr,Grl................. 500.00
13 JCr,AW ................ 550.00
14 JCr ................... 500.00
15 JCr,Old Witch .......... 500.00
16 JCr,AW ................ 600.00
17 JCr,FF,AW, Ray Bradbury .. 1,300.00
18 JCr,RC,BE............. 550.00
19 JCr,RC,GE,AF(c) ........ 550.00
20 RC,JCr, Hanging (c) ...... 600.00
21 JCr ................... 500.00
22 RC,JO,JCr(c),
Severed head (c)......... 600.00
23 JKa,RC,GE ............. 550.00
24 BK,RC,JO .............. 500.00
25 JKa,(c),RC ............. 600.00
26 JKa,(c),RC,JO........... 700.00
27 JKa,(c),GE,Grl,March, 1955 .. 500.00

## CRIMINALS ON THE RUN
**Premium Group of Comics,**
**Aug., 1948**
4-1 LbC(c) ................ 500.00
4-2 LbC(c), A:Young King Cole . 400.00
4-3 LbC(c), Rip Roaring Action
in Alps .............. 400.00
4-4 LbC(c), Shark (c) ........ 400.00
4-5 AMc ................. 400.00
4-6 LbC,Dr. Doom .......... 400.00

4-7 LbC ................. 900.00
5-1 LbC ................. 350.00
5-2 LbC ................. 350.00
10 LbC ................. 350.00
*Becomes:*

## CRIME-FIGHTING DETECTIVE
**April–May, 1950**
11 LbC, Brodie Gang Captured .. 350.00
12 LbC(c), Jail Break Genius ... 300.00
13 ...................... 250.00
14 LbC(c), A Night of Horror .... 300.00
15 LbC(c)................. 300.00
16 LbC(c), Wanton Murder ..... 300.00
17 LbC(c), The Framer
was Framed............. 300.00
18 LbC(c), A Web of Evil ...... 300.00
19 LbC(c), Lesson of the Law ... 300.00
*Becomes:*

## SHOCK DETECTIVE CASES
**Star Publications, Sept., 1952**
20 LbC(c), The Strangler ...... 400.00
21 LbC(c), Death Ride........ 400.00
*Becomes:*

## SPOOK DETECTIVE CASES
**Jan., 1953**
22 Headless Horror .......... 500.00
*Becomes:*

## SPOOK SUSPENSE AND MYSTERY
23 LbC,Weird Picture of Murder . 350.00
24 LbC(c),Mummy's Case ..... 400.00
25 LbC(c),Horror Beyond Door . 350.00
26 LbC(c),JyD,Face of Death ... 350.00
27 LbC(c),Ship of the Dead .... 350.00
28 LbC(c),JyD,Creeping Death .. 350.00
29 LbC(c),Solo for Death....... 350.00
30 LbC(c),JyD,Nightmare,
Oct.,1954............... 350.00

## CROWN COMICS
**Golfing/McCombs Publ.,**
**Winter 1944**
1 Edgar Allen Poe adapt....... 700.00
2 MB,I:Mickey Magic ........ 500.00
3 MB,Jungle adventure (c) .... 500.00
4 MB(c),A:Voodah........... 550.00
5 MB(c),Jungle Adventure (c) .. 550.00

All comics prices listed are for *Near Mint* condition.

*Crusader From Mars #2*
© Ziff-Davis

*Dagar Desert Hawk #14*
© Fox Features Syndicate

*Dagwood #28*
© Harvey Publications

**Da**

6 MB(c),Jungle Adventure (c) . . 550.00
7 JKa,AF,MB(c),Race Car (c) . . 550.00
8 MB . . . . . . . . . . . . . . . . . . . 500.00
9 . . . . . . . . . . . . . . . . . . . . . . 300.00
10 Plane crash (c),A:Voodah. . . . 300.00
11 LSt,A:Voodah . . . . . . . . . . . . 250.00
12 LSt,AF,Master Marvin . . . . . . 250.00
13 LSt,AF,A:Voodah . . . . . . . . . . 250.00
14 A:Voodah. . . . . . . . . . . . . . . 275.00
15 FBe,A:Voodah. . . . . . . . . . . . 250.00
16 FBe,A:Voodah,Jungle
    Adventure(c) . . . . . . . . . . . 250.00
17 FBe,A:Voodah. . . . . . . . . . . . 250.00
18 FBe,A:Voodah. . . . . . . . . . . . 250.00
19 BP,A:Voodah,July, 1949 . . . . . 250.00

## CRUSADER FROM MARS
### Approved Publ.
### (Ziff-Davis), Jan.–March, 1952
1 Mission Thru Space, Death in
    the Sai . . . . . . . . . . . . . . . 1,300.00
2 Beachhead on Saturn's Ring,
    Bondage(c),Fall, 1952 . . . . 1,000.00

## CRYIN' LION, THE
### William H. Wise Co.,
### Fall, 1944
1 Funny Animal . . . . . . . . . . . . . 500.00
2 A. Hitler . . . . . . . . . . . . . . . . . 300.00
3 Spring, 1945 . . . . . . . . . . . . . 250.00

## CRYPT OF TERROR
### See: CRIME PATROL

## CUPID
### Marvel, Dec., 1949–March, 1950
1 Ph(c),Cora Dod's Amazing
    Decision. . . . . . . . . . . . . . . . 350.00
2 Ph(c),BP,Bettie Page . . . . . . . 500.00

## CURLY KAYOE COMICS
### United Features
### Syndicate, 1946–50
1 Boxing . . . . . . . . . . . . . . . . . 300.00
2 . . . . . . . . . . . . . . . . . . . . . . 250.00
3 . . . . . . . . . . . . . . . . . . . . . . 200.00
4 . . . . . . . . . . . . . . . . . . . . . . 200.00
5 . . . . . . . . . . . . . . . . . . . . . . 200.00
6 . . . . . . . . . . . . . . . . . . . . . . 200.00
7 . . . . . . . . . . . . . . . . . . . . . . 200.00
8 . . . . . . . . . . . . . . . . . . . . . . 200.00
1a United Presents . . . . . (1948) . . 200.00

## CUTIE PIE
### Junior Reader's Guild
### (Lev Gleason), 1955–56
1 . . . . . . . . . . . . . . . . . . . . . . 150.00
2 thru 5 . . . . . . . . . . . . . . . . @100.00

## CYCLONE COMICS
### Bibara Publ. Co., June, 1940
1 O:Tornado Tom . . . . . . . . . . 3,000.00
2 . . . . . . . . . . . . . . . . . . . . . 2,500.00
3 . . . . . . . . . . . . . . . . . . . . . 2,000.00
4 Voltron. . . . . . . . . . . . . . . . 1,500.00
5 A:Mr. Q,Oct., 1940 . . . . . . . 1,600.00

## DAFFY
### Dell Publishing Co.,
### March, 1953
(1) see Dell Four Color #457
(2) see Dell Four Color #536
(3) see Dell Four Color #615
4 thru 7 . . . . . . . . . . . . . . . . @150.00
8 thru 11 . . . . . . . . . . . . . . . . @100.00
12 thru 17 . . . . . . . . . . . . . . . @100.00
Becomes:

## DAFFY DUCK
### July, 1959
18 . . . . . . . . . . . . . . . . . . . . . 100.00
19 . . . . . . . . . . . . . . . . . . . . . 100.00
20 . . . . . . . . . . . . . . . . . . . . . 100.00
21 thru 30 . . . . . . . . . . . . . . . @100.00

## DAFFY TUNES COMICS
### Four Star Publications, 1947
12 Funny Animal . . . . . . . . . . . . 150.00

## ALL GREAT COMICS
### Fox Features Syndicate,
### Oct., 1947
12 A:Brenda Starr . . . . . . . . . . 1,500.00
13 JKa,O:Dagar, Desert Hawk . 1,800.00
Becomes:

## DAGAR, DESERT HAWK
### Feb., 1948
14 JKa,Monster of Mura . . . . . . 1,500.00
15 JKa,Curse of the Lost
    Pharaoh . . . . . . . . . . . . . . 1,000.00
16 JKa,Wretched Antmen . . . . . 900.00
19 Pyramid of Doom . . . . . . . . . 800.00
20 . . . . . . . . . . . . . . . . . . . . . 800.00
21 JKa(c),The Ghost of Fate . . . 850.00

22 . . . . . . . . . . . . . . . . . . . . . 800.00
23 Bondage (c) . . . . . . . . . . . . 850.00
Becomes:

## CAPTAIN KIDD
### June, 1949
24 Blackbeard the Pirate . . . . . . 300.00
25 Sorceress of the Deep . . . . . 300.00
Becomes:

## MY SECRET STORY
### Oct., 1949
26 He Wanted More Than Love. . 300.00
27 My Husband Hated Me . . . . . 250.00
28 I Become a Marked Women . . 250.00
29 My Forbidden Rapture,
    April, 1950 . . . . . . . . . . . . . 250.00

## DAGWOOD
### Harvey Publications, 1950
1 . . . . . . . . . . . . . . . . . . . . . . 300.00
2 . . . . . . . . . . . . . . . . . . . . . . 200.00
3 . . . . . . . . . . . . . . . . . . . . . . 175.00
4 . . . . . . . . . . . . . . . . . . . . . . 175.00
5 . . . . . . . . . . . . . . . . . . . . . . 175.00
6 thru 10 . . . . . . . . . . . . . . . @175.00
11 thru 20 . . . . . . . . . . . . . . . @150.00
21 thru 30 . . . . . . . . . . . . . . . @125.00
31 thru 50 . . . . . . . . . . . . . . . @100.00
51 thru 70 . . . . . . . . . . . . . . . @100.00
71 thru 109 . . . . . . . . . . . . . . . @75.00
110 thru 140 . . . . . . . . . . . . . . @75.00

## DAISY AND HER PUPS
### Harvey Publications,
### 1951–1954
1 (21) F:Blondie & Dagwood's
    dog. . . . . . . . . . . . . . . . . . 150.00
2 (22). . . . . . . . . . . . . . . . . . . 110.00
3 (23). . . . . . . . . . . . . . . . . . . 110.00
4 (24). . . . . . . . . . . . . . . . . . . 110.00
5 (25). . . . . . . . . . . . . . . . . . . 110.00
6 (26). . . . . . . . . . . . . . . . . . . 110.00
7 (27). . . . . . . . . . . . . . . . . . . 110.00
8 . . . . . . . . . . . . . . . . . . . . . . 100.00
9 . . . . . . . . . . . . . . . . . . . . . . 100.00
10 . . . . . . . . . . . . . . . . . . . . . 100.00
11 . . . . . . . . . . . . . . . . . . . . . 100.00
12 . . . . . . . . . . . . . . . . . . . . . 100.00
13 . . . . . . . . . . . . . . . . . . . . . 100.00
14 . . . . . . . . . . . . . . . . . . . . . 100.00
15 . . . . . . . . . . . . . . . . . . . . . 100.00
16 . . . . . . . . . . . . . . . . . . . . . 100.00
17 . . . . . . . . . . . . . . . . . . . . . 100.00
18 . . . . . . . . . . . . . . . . . . . . . 100.00

All comics prices listed are for *Near Mint* condition.

*Dale Evans Comics #4*
© DC Comics

*Nature Boy #5*
© Charlton Comics

*Daredevil #11*
© Lev Gleason

**Da**

## DAISY COMICS

**Eastern Color Printing Co., 1936**

N# . . . . . . . . . . . . . . . . . . . . . 750.00

## DAISY HANDBOOK

**Daisy Manufacturing Co., 1946**

1 Buck Rogers, Red Ryder. . . . . 475.00
2 Capt. Marvel . . . . . . . . . . . . . 475.00
N# (1955) . . . . . . . . . . . . . . . . 400.00

## DALE EVANS COMICS

**DC Comics, 1948–52**

1 Ph(c),ATh,B:Sierra Smith . . . 2,700.00
2 Ph(c),ATh . . . . . . . . . . . . . 1,300.00
3 ATh . . . . . . . . . . . . . . . . . . . 800.00
4 . . . . . . . . . . . . . . . . . . . . . . 425.00
5 . . . . . . . . . . . . . . . . . . . . . . 425.00
6 thru 11 . . . . . . . . . . . . . . @425.00
12 thru 20 . . . . . . . . . . . . . . @325.00
21 thru 24 . . . . . . . . . . . . . . @300.00

## DANDY COMICS

**E.C. Comics 1947–48**

1 Funny Animal . . . . . . . . . . . . 450.00
2 . . . . . . . . . . . . . . . . . . . . . . 325.00
3 thru 7 . . . . . . . . . . . . . . . @250.00

## DANGER

**Comic Media, 1953–54**

1 DH(c&a) . . . . . . . . . . . . . . . . 300.00
2 PMo . . . . . . . . . . . . . . . . . . 150.00
3 PMo . . . . . . . . . . . . . . . . . . 150.00
4 Marijuana (c) & story . . . . . . . 200.00
5 PMo . . . . . . . . . . . . . . . . . . 150.00
6 Drug . . . . . . . . . . . . . . . . . . 175.00
7 . . . . . . . . . . . . . . . . . . . . . 150.00
8 Torture (c) . . . . . . . . . . . . . . 225.00
9 thru 11 . . . . . . . . . . . . . . . . 150.00

**Charlton Comics, 1955**

12 . . . . . . . . . . . . . . . . . . . . . 150.00
13 and 14 . . . . . . . . . . . . . . @125.00
**Becomes:**

## JIM BOWIE

15 thru 19 . . . . . . . . . . . . . . @100.00

## DANGER AND ADVENTURE

See: THIS MAGAZINE IS HAUNTED

## DANGER IS OUR BUSINESS

**Toby Press/ I.W. Enterprises, 1953**

1 AW,FF,Men Who Defy Death
 for a Living . . . . . . . . . . . . . 750.00
2 Death Crowds the Cockpit . . . 300.00
3 Killer Mountain . . . . . . . . . . 250.00
4 . . . . . . . . . . . . . . . . . . . . . 250.00
5 thru 9 . . . . . . . . . . . . . . . @200.00
10 June, 1955 . . . . . . . . . . . . . 250.00

## DANGER TRAIL

**DC Comics, July-Aug., 1950**

1 CI,ATh,I:King For A Day . . . . 1,700.00
2 ATh . . . . . . . . . . . . . . . . . 1,200.00
3 ATh . . . . . . . . . . . . . . . . . 1,400.00
4 ATh . . . . . . . . . . . . . . . . . 1,200.00
5 March-April, 1951 . . . . . . . . 1,200.00

## DAN'L BOONE

**Sussex Publ. Co. 1955–57**

1 F:Dan'l Boone Greatest
 Frontiersman . . . . . . . . . . . 200.00
2 . . . . . . . . . . . . . . . . . . . . . 150.00
3 . . . . . . . . . . . . . . . . . . . . . 100.00
4 . . . . . . . . . . . . . . . . . . . . . 100.00
5 . . . . . . . . . . . . . . . . . . . . . 100.00
6 thru 8 . . . . . . . . . . . . . . . @100.00

## DANNY BLAZE

**Charlton Comics, 1955**

1 . . . . . . . . . . . . . . . . . . . . . 150.00
2 . . . . . . . . . . . . . . . . . . . . . 125.00
**Becomes:**

## NATURE BOY

3 JB,O:Blue Beetle . . . . . . . . . . 300.00
4 . . . . . . . . . . . . . . . . . . . . . 125.00
5 Feb., 1957 . . . . . . . . . . . . . . 100.00

## DAREDEVIL COMICS

**Lev Gleason Publications, July, 1941**

1 Daredevil Battles Hitler, A:Silver
 Streak, Lance Hale, Dickey Dean,
 Cloud Curtis,V:The Claw,
 O:Hitler . . . . . . . . . . . . . 25,000.00
2 I:The Pioneer, Champion of
 American,B:London,Pat
 Patriot,Pirate Prince . . . . . . 5,000.00
3 CBi(c),O:Thirteen . . . . . . . . 3,000.00

4 CBi(c),Death is the Referee . 2,500.00
5 CBi(c),I:Sniffer&Jinx, Claw
 V:Ghost,Lottery of Doom . . 2,000.00
6 CBi(c) . . . . . . . . . . . . . . . 1,700.00
7 CBi(c), What Ghastly Sight Lies
 within the Mysterious Trunk 1,600.00
8 V:Nazis (c), E:Nightro . . . . . 1,500.00
9 V:Double . . . . . . . . . . . . . 1,500.00
10 America will Remember
 Pearl Harbor . . . . . . . . . . 1,500.00
11 Bondage (c), E:Pat
 Patriot, London . . . . . . . . 1,700.00
12 BW,CBi(c), O:The Law . . . . 2,200.00
13 BW,I:Little Wise Guys . . . . 1,700.00
14 BW,CBi(c) . . . . . . . . . . . 1,200.00
15 BW,CBi(c), D:Meatball . . . . 1,400.00
16 BW,CBi(c) . . . . . . . . . . . 1,100.00
17 BW,CBi(c), Into the Valley
 of Death . . . . . . . . . . . . . 1,100.00
18 BW,CBi(c), O:Daredevil,
 double length story . . . . . . 2,000.00
19 BW,CBi(c), Buried Alive . . . . 900.00
20 BW,CBi(c), Boxing (c) . . . . . 900.00
21 CBi(c), Can Little Wise Guys
 Survive Blast of Dynamite? 1,500.00
22 CBi(c) . . . . . . . . . . . . . . . . 750.00
23 CBi(c), I:Pshyco . . . . . . . . . 750.00
24 CBi(c), Punch and Judy
 Murders . . . . . . . . . . . . . . . 750.00
25 CBi(c), Baseball (c) . . . . . . . 750.00
26 CBi(c) . . . . . . . . . . . . . . . . 700.00
27 CBi(c), Bondage (c) . . . . . . . 750.00
28 CBi(c) . . . . . . . . . . . . . . . . 700.00
29 CBi(c) . . . . . . . . . . . . . . . . 700.00
30 CBi(c), Ann Hubbard White
 1922-1943 . . . . . . . . . . . . . 700.00
31 CBi(c), D:The Claw . . . . . . 1,400.00
32 V:Blackmarketeers . . . . . . . 500.00
33 CBi(c) . . . . . . . . . . . . . . . . 500.00
34 CBi(c) . . . . . . . . . . . . . . . . 500.00
35 B:Two Daredevil stories
 every issue . . . . . . . . . . . . . 550.00
36 CBi(c) . . . . . . . . . . . . . . . . 550.00
37 CBi(c) . . . . . . . . . . . . . . . . 550.00
38 CBi(c), O:Daredevil . . . . . . . 800.00
39 CBi(c) . . . . . . . . . . . . . . . . 500.00
40 CBi(c) . . . . . . . . . . . . . . . . 500.00
41 . . . . . . . . . . . . . . . . . . . . 500.00
42 thru 50 CBi(c) . . . . . . . . @500.00
51 CBi(c) . . . . . . . . . . . . . . . . 350.00
52 CBi(c),Football (c) . . . . . . . . 400.00
53 thru 57 . . . . . . . . . . . . . @350.00
58 Football (c) . . . . . . . . . . . . . 400.00
59 . . . . . . . . . . . . . . . . . . . . 350.00
60 . . . . . . . . . . . . . . . . . . . . 350.00
61 thru 68 . . . . . . . . . . . . . @350.00

All comics prices listed are for *Near Mint* condition.

**Da**

Daring Mystery Comics #2
© Marvel Comics Group

Daring Comics #12
© Marvel Comics Group

Dark Mysteries #23
© Merit Publications

69 E:Daredevil . . . . . . . . . . . . . . . 350.00
70 . . . . . . . . . . . . . . . . . . . . . . . . 250.00
71 thru 78 . . . . . . . . . . . . . . . @150.00
79 B:Daredevil . . . . . . . . . . . . . . . 250.00
80 . . . . . . . . . . . . . . . . . . . . . . . . 275.00
81 . . . . . . . . . . . . . . . . . . . . . . . . 150.00
82 . . . . . . . . . . . . . . . . . . . . . . . . 150.00
83 thru 99 . . . . . . . . . . . . . . . . . @150.00
100 . . . . . . . . . . . . . . . . . . . . . . . 175.00
101 thru 133 . . . . . . . . . . . . . . . @150.00
134 Sept., 1956 . . . . . . . . . . . . . 150.00

## DARING CONFESSIONS
## See: YOUTHFUL HEART

## DARING LOVE
### Gilmore Magazines, 1953
1 SD,1st work . . . . . . . . . . . . . . . 800.00
Becomes:
## RADIANT LOVE
### Gilmore Magazines, 1953–54
2 . . . . . . . . . . . . . . . . . . . . . . . . 150.00
3 . . . . . . . . . . . . . . . . . . . . . . . . 125.00
4 . . . . . . . . . . . . . . . . . . . . . . . . 125.00
5 . . . . . . . . . . . . . . . . . . . . . . . . 125.00
6 . . . . . . . . . . . . . . . . . . . . . . . . 125.00

## DARLING LOVE
## See: YOUTHFUL
## ROMANCES

## DARING MYSTERY
## COMICS
### Marvel Timely, Jan., 1940
1 ASh(c),JSm,O:Fiery Mask,
   A:Monako John Steele,Doc Doyle,
   Flash FosterBarney Mullen,
   Sea Rover, Bondage (c). . 50,000.00
2 ASh(c),JSm,O:Phantom Bullet
   A:Zephyr Jones & K4,Laughing
   Mask Mr.E,B:Trojak . . . . . 30,000.00
3 ASh(c),JSm,A:Phantom
   Reporter,Marvex,Breeze
   Barton, B:Purple Mask . . 12,000.00
4 ASh(c),A:G-Man Ace,K4,
   Monako,Marvex,E:Purple
   Mask,B:Whirlwind Carter . 8,000.00
5 ASh(c),JSm,B:Falcon,A:Fiery
   Mask,K4, Little Hercules,
   Bondage(c) . . . . . . . . . . . 8,000.00

6 S&K,O:Marvel Boy,A:Fiery
   Mask, Flying Fame,Dynaman,
   Stuporman,E:Trojak . . . . . 10,000.00
7 ASh(c),S&K,O:Blue Diamond,
   A:The Fin, Challenger,Captain
   Daring, Silver Scorpion,
   Thunderer . . . . . . . . . . . . . . 8,000.00
8 S&K,O:Citizen V,A:Thunderer,
   Fin Silver Scorpion,Captain
   Daring Blue Diamond . . . . . 7,000.00
Becomes:
## DARING COMICS
### Marvel, 1944
9 ASh(c),B:Human Torch,Toro,
   Sub Mariner . . . . . . . . . . . . 3,000.00
10 ASh(c),A:The Angel . . . . . . 2,600.00
11 ASh(c),A:The Destroyer . . . . 2,600.00
12 E:Human Torch,Toro,Sub-
   Mariner, Fall, 1945 . . . . . . . 2,600.00
Becomes:
## JEANIE COMICS
### Marvel, 1947
13 B:Jeanie,Queen of the
   Teens Mitzi,Willie . . . . . . . . . 300.00
14 Baseball(c) . . . . . . . . . . . . . . 250.00
15 Schoolbus(c) . . . . . . . . . . . . . 250.00
16 Swimsuit(c) . . . . . . . . . . . . . . 275.00
17 HK,Fancy Dress Party(c),
   Hey Look . . . . . . . . . . . . . . . 225.00
18 HK,Jeanie's Date(c), Hey
   Look . . . . . . . . . . . . . . . . . . . 200.00
19 Ice-Boat(c),Hey Look . . . . . . 225.00
20 Jukebox(c) . . . . . . . . . . . . . . 200.00
21 . . . . . . . . . . . . . . . . . . . . . . . 200.00
22 HK,Hey Look . . . . . . . . . . . . . 225.00
23 thru 25 . . . . . . . . . . . . . . . . @200.00
26 . . . . . . . . . . . . . . . . . . . . . . . 200.00
27 E:Jeanie,Queen of Teens . . . . 200.00
Becomes:
## COWGIRL ROMANCES
### Marvel, 1950
28 Ph(c),Mona Freeman/MacDonald
   Carey,Copper Canyon . . . . . . 300.00

## DARK MYSTERIES
### Merit Publications,
### June–July, 1951
1 WW(a&c), Curse of the
   Sea Witch . . . . . . . . . . . . . 1,500.00
2 WW(a&c), Vampire Fangs
   of Doom . . . . . . . . . . . . . . 1,200.00
3 Terror of the Unwilling
   Witch . . . . . . . . . . . . . . . . . . 800.00

4 Corpse that Came Alive . . . . 800.00
5 Horror of the Ghostly Crew . . . 650.00
6 If the Noose Fits Wear It! . . . . 650.00
7 Terror of the Cards of Death . . 650.00
8 Terror of the Ghostly Trail . . . . 650.00
9 Witch's Feast at Dawn . . . . . . 650.00
10 Terror of the Burning Witch . . 650.00
11 The River of Blood . . . . . . . . 600.00
12 Horror of the Talking Dead . . 600.00
13 Terror of the Hungry Cats . . . . 600.00
14 Horror of the Fingers of Doom 650.00
15 Terror of the Vampires Teeth . . 550.00
16 Horror of the Walking Dead . . 550.00
17 Terror of the Mask of Death . . 550.00
18 Terror of the Burning Corpse . 550.00
19 The Rack of Terror . . . . . . . . 750.00
20 Burning Executioner . . . . . . . 650.00
21 The Sinister Secret . . . . . . . . 500.00
22 The Hand of Destiny . . . . . . . 500.00
23 The Mardenburg Curse . . . . . 350.00
24 Give A Man Enough Rope,
   July, 1955 . . . . . . . . . . . . . 350.00

## DARK SHADOWS
### Steinway Publications/Ajax
### 1957–58
1 . . . . . . . . . . . . . . . . . . . . . . . 350.00
2 . . . . . . . . . . . . . . . . . . . . . . . 300.00
3 . . . . . . . . . . . . . . . . . . . . . . . 300.00

## DARLING LOVE
### Archie-Close-up Publ., 1949
1 Photo(c) . . . . . . . . . . . . . . . . . 250.00
2 Photo(c) . . . . . . . . . . . . . . . . . 150.00
3 Photo(c) . . . . . . . . . . . . . . . . . 125.00
4 Photo(c) . . . . . . . . . . . . . . . . . 125.00
5 Photo(c) . . . . . . . . . . . . . . . . . 125.00
6 Photo(c) . . . . . . . . . . . . . . . . . 125.00
7 . . . . . . . . . . . . . . . . . . . . . . . 125.00
8 . . . . . . . . . . . . . . . . . . . . . . . 125.00
9 BK . . . . . . . . . . . . . . . . . . . . . . 150.00
10 . . . . . . . . . . . . . . . . . . . . . . . 125.00
11 . . . . . . . . . . . . . . . . . . . . . . . 125.00

## DARLING ROMANCE
### Archie Close-Up Publ., 1949
1 Photo(c) . . . . . . . . . . . . . . . . . 350.00
2 . . . . . . . . . . . . . . . . . . . . . . . 200.00
3 . . . . . . . . . . . . . . . . . . . . . . . 150.00
4 . . . . . . . . . . . . . . . . . . . . . . . 150.00
5 . . . . . . . . . . . . . . . . . . . . . . . 150.00
6 . . . . . . . . . . . . . . . . . . . . . . . 150.00
7 . . . . . . . . . . . . . . . . . . . . . . . 150.00

All comics prices listed are for *Near Mint* condition.

*A Date With Judy #7*
© DC Comics

*A Date With Judy #10*
© DC Comics

*Dear Lonely Heart #1*
© Artful Publications

## DATE WITH DANGER
**Visual Editions**
**(Standard Comics), 1952**
5 Secret Agent . . . . . . . . . . . . . 200.00
6 Atom Bomb . . . . . . . . . . . . . 250.00

## A DATE WITH JUDY
**DC Comics, 1947**
1 Teen-age . . . . . . . . . . . . . . . 500.00
2 . . . . . . . . . . . . . . . . . . . . . 350.00
3 . . . . . . . . . . . . . . . . . . . . . 300.00
4 . . . . . . . . . . . . . . . . . . . . . 300.00
5 . . . . . . . . . . . . . . . . . . . . . 300.00
6 . . . . . . . . . . . . . . . . . . . . . 300.00
7 . . . . . . . . . . . . . . . . . . . . . 300.00
8 . . . . . . . . . . . . . . . . . . . . . 300.00
9 . . . . . . . . . . . . . . . . . . . . . 300.00
10 . . . . . . . . . . . . . . . . . . . . 300.00
11 thru 20 . . . . . . . . . . . . @250.00
21 thru 30 . . . . . . . . . . . . @150.00
31 thru 50 . . . . . . . . . . . . @125.00
51 thru 78 . . . . . . . . . . . . @125.00
79 MD . . . . . . . . . . . . . . . . . 150.00

## A DATE WITH MILLIE
**Marvel Atlas, Oct., 1956**
**[1st Series]**
1 . . . . . . . . . . . . . . . . . . . . . 400.00
2 . . . . . . . . . . . . . . . . . . . . . 250.00
3 thru 7 . . . . . . . . . . . . . . @200.00
**Marvel, [2nd Series], Oct., 1959**
1 . . . . . . . . . . . . . . . . . . . . . 250.00
2 thru 7 . . . . . . . . . . . . . . @200.00

## A DATE WITH PATSY
**Marvel, Sept., 1957**
1 A:Patsy Walker. . . . . . . . . . . 150.00

## DAVY CROCKETT
**Avon Periodicals, 1951**
1 . . . . . . . . . . . . . . . . . . . . . 250.00

## FRONTIER FIGHTER
**Charlton Comics, 1955**
1 JK,Davy Crocket-Buffalo Bill . . 250.00
2 JK. . . . . . . . . . . . . . . . . . . . 150.00
Becomes:

## DAVY CROCKETT
**Charlton Comics, 1956**
3 thru 7 JK. . . . . . . . . . . . . @150.00

8 Jan., 1957 JK. . . . . . . . . . . . 125.00
Becomes:

## KID MONTANA
**Charlton Comics, 1957**
9 . . . . . . . . . . . . . . . . . . . . . 125.00
10 . . . . . . . . . . . . . . . . . . . . 110.00
11 . . . . . . . . . . . . . . . . . . . . 100.00
12 . . . . . . . . . . . . . . . . . . . . 100.00
13 AW . . . . . . . . . . . . . . . . . 100.00
14 thru 20. . . . . . . . . . . . . @100.00
21 thru 35. . . . . . . . . . . . . @75.00
36 thru 49. . . . . . . . . . . . . @75.00
50 March, 1965 . . . . . . . . . . . 75.00

## DC SHOWCASE
**See: SHOWCASE**

## DEAD END
## CRIME STORIES
**Kirby Publishing Co.,**
**April, 1949**
N# BP . . . . . . . . . . . . . . . . . . 750.00

## DEAD-EYE
## WESTERN COMICS
**Hillman Periodicals**
**Nov.–Dec., 1948**
1 BK . . . . . . . . . . . . . . . . . . 300.00
2 . . . . . . . . . . . . . . . . . . . . . 250.00
3 . . . . . . . . . . . . . . . . . . . . . 200.00
4 thru 12 . . . . . . . . . . . . . @150.00
2-1 . . . . . . . . . . . . . . . . . . . 125.00
2-2 . . . . . . . . . . . . . . . . . . . 125.00
2-3 . . . . . . . . . . . . . . . . . . . 150.00
2-4 . . . . . . . . . . . . . . . . . . . 150.00
2-5 thru 2-12 . . . . . . . . . . @125.00
3-1 . . . . . . . . . . . . . . . . . . . 125.00

## DEADWOOD GULCH
**Dell Publishing Co., 1931**
1 . . . . . . . . . . . . . . . . . . . . . 750.00

## DEAR BEATRICE
## FAIRFAX
**Best Books**
**(Standard Comics), Nov., 1950**
5 . . . . . . . . . . . . . . . . . . . . . 300.00
6 thru 9 . . . . . . . . . . . . . . @200.00

## DEAR HEART
**See: LONELY HEART**

## DEAR LONELY HEART
**Artful Publications,**
**March, 1951**
1 . . . . . . . . . . . . . . . . . . . . . 300.00
2 . . . . . . . . . . . . . . . . . . . . . 200.00
3 MB,Jungle Girl. . . . . . . . . . . 350.00
4 . . . . . . . . . . . . . . . . . . . . . 150.00
5 thru 8 . . . . . . . . . . . . . . @125.00

## DEAR LONELY HEARTS
**Comic Media, Aug., 1953**
1 Six Months to Live . . . . . . . . 200.00
2 Date Hungry, Price of Passion  150.00
3 thru 8 . . . . . . . . . . . . . . @200.00

## DEARLY BELOVED
**Approved Comics**
**(Ziff-Davis), Fall, 1952**
1 Ph(c) . . . . . . . . . . . . . . . . . 200.00

## DEATH VALLEY
**Comic Media/**
**Charlton Comics, 1953**
1 Cowboys & Indians . . . . . . . . 200.00
2 DH(c) . . . . . . . . . . . . . . . . . 150.00
3 PMo . . . . . . . . . . . . . . . . . . 125.00
4 . . . . . . . . . . . . . . . . . . . . . 125.00
5 PMo . . . . . . . . . . . . . . . . . . 125.00
6 . . . . . . . . . . . . . . . . . . . . . 125.00
7 . . . . . . . . . . . . . . . . . . . . . 125.00
8 BW. . . . . . . . . . . . . . . . . . . 125.00
9 . . . . . . . . . . . . . . . . . . . . . 125.00
Becomes:

## FRONTIER SCOUT
## DANIEL BOONE
**Charlton Comics**
10 . . . . . . . . . . . . . . . . . . . . 150.00
11 thru 13 . . . . . . . . . . . . @100.00

## DEBBIE DEAN,
## CAREER GIRL
**Civil Service Publishing,**
**April, 1945**
1 . . . . . . . . . . . . . . . . . . . . . 300.00
2 . . . . . . . . . . . . . . . . . . . . . 250.00

*Dell Giant Editions, Lone Ranger Western Treasury #1 © Dell Publ. Co.*

*Dell Giant Comics #37 © Dell Publishing Co.*

*Dennis the Menace #23 © Pines Publications*

## DELLA VISION
### Marvel Atlas, April, 1955
1 The Television Queen . . . . . . 250.00
2 . . . . . . . . . . . . . . . . . . . . . . . . 200.00
3 . . . . . . . . . . . . . . . . . . . . . . . . 200.00
**Becomes:**

## PATTY POWERS
### Marvel, 1955
4 . . . . . . . . . . . . . . . . . . . . . . . . 200.00
5 & 6 . . . . . . . . . . . . . . . . . . . @100.00
7 Oct., 1956 . . . . . . . . . . . . . . . 100.00

## DELL GIANT EDITIONS
### Dell Publishing Co., 1952-58
Abe Lincoln Life Story . . . . . . . . . 175.00
Cadet Gray of West Point . . . . . . 175.00
Golden West Rodeo Treasury . . . 200.00
Life Stories of
American Presidents . . . . . . . 165.00
Lone Ranger Golden West . . . . . . 400.00
Lone Ranger Movie Story . . . . . . 800.00
Lone Ranger Western
Treasury('53) . . . . . . . . . . 400.00
Lone Ranger Western
Treasury('54) . . . . . . . . . . 500.00
Moses & Ten Commandments. . . 150.00
Nancy & Sluggo Travel Time . . . . 200.00
Pogo Parade . . . . . . . . . . . . . . . . 750.00
Raggedy Ann & Andy . . . . . . . . . 350.00
Santa Claus Funnies . . . . . . . . . . 200.00
Tarzan's Jungle Annual #1 . . . . . . 350.00
Tarzan's Jungle Annual #2 . . . . . 225.00
Tarzan's Jungle Annual #3 . . . . . 200.00
Tarzan's Jungle Annual #4 . . . . . 200.00
Tarzan's Jungle Annual #5 . . . . . 200.00
Tarzan's Jungle Annual #6 . . . . . 200.00
Tarzan's Jungle Annual #7 . . . . . 200.00
Treasury of Dogs . . . . . . . . . . . . 175.00
Treasury of Horses . . . . . . . . . . . 175.00
Universal Presents-Dracula-
The Mummy & Other Stories. 500.00
Western Roundup #1 . . . . . . . . . . 600.00
Western Roundup #2 . . . . . . . . . . 350.00
Western Roundup #3 . . . . . . . . . . 275.00
Western Roundup #4 thru #5 . . @250.00
Western Roundup #6 thru #10 . @250.00
Western Roundup #11 thru #17 @225.00
Western Roundup #18 . . . . . . . . . 250.00
Western Roundup #19 thru #25 @180.00
Woody Woodpecker Back
to School #1 (1952) . . . . . . . 300.00
Woody Woodpecker Back
to School #2 (1953) . . . . . . . 250.00

Woody Woodpecker Back
to School #3 (1954) . . . . . . . 250.00
Woody Woodpecker Back
to School #4 (1955) . . . . . . . 250.00
Woody Woodpecker County
Fair #5 (1956) . . . . . . . . . . . 250.00
Woody Woodpecker Back
to School #6 (1957) . . . . . . . 275.00
Woody Woodpecker County
Fair #2 (1958) . . . . . . . . . . . 250.00
**Also See: Bugs Bunny; Marge's Little Lulu; Tom and Jerry, and Walt Disney Dell Giant Editions**

## DELL GIANT COMICS
### Dell Publishing Co., Sept., 1959
21 M.G.M. Tom & Jerry
Picnic Time . . . . . . . . . . . . . 250.00
22 W.Disney's Huey, Dewey & Louie
Back to School (Oct 1959) . . 250.00
23 Marge's Little Lulu &
Tubby Halloween Fun . . . . . . 250.00
24 Woody Woodpeckers
Family Fun. . . . . . . . . . . . . . . 225.00
25 Tarzan's Jungle World . . . . . . 250.00
26 W.Disney's Christmas
Parade,CB . . . . . . . . . . . . . . 600.00
27 W.Disney's Man in
Space (1960) . . . . . . . . . . . . 300.00
28 Bugs Bunny's Winter Fun . . . 250.00
29 Marge's Little Lulu &
Tubby in Hawaii . . . . . . . . . . 300.00
30 W.Disney's DisneylandU.S.A.. 400.00
31 Huckleberry Hound
Summer Fun . . . . . . . . . . . . 300.00
32 Bugs Bunny Beach Party . . . 250.00
33 W.Disney's Daisy Duck &
Uncle Scrooge Picnic Time . . 350.00
34 Nancy&SluggoSummerCamp. 250.00
35 W.Disney's Huey, Dewey &
Louie Back to School . . . . . 400.00
36 Marge's Little Lulu & Witch
Hazel Halloween Fun . . . . . . 275.00
37 Tarzan, King of the Jungle . . . 250.00
38 W.Disney's Uncle Donald and
his Nephews Family Fun . . . 350.00
39 W.Disney's Merry Christmas . . 350.00
40 Woody Woodpecker
Christmas Parade . . . . . . . . . 175.00
41 Yogi Bear's Winter Sports . . . 275.00
42 Marge's Little Lulu &
Tubby in Australia . . . . . . . . 300.00
43 Mighty Mouse in OuterSpace . 500.00

44 Around the World with
Huckleberry & His Friends . . 300.00
45 Nancy&SluggoSummerCamp. 150.00
46 Bugs Bunny Beach Party . . . . 175.00
47 W.Disney's Mickey and
Donald in Vacationland . . . . . 300.00
48 The Flintstones #1
(Bedrock Bedlam) . . . . . . . . . 500.00
49 W.Disney's Huey, Dewey &
Louie Back to School . . . . . . 300.00
50 Marge's Little Lulu &
Witch Hazel Trick 'N' Treat . . 275.00
51 Tarzan, King of the Jungle . . . 200.00
52 W.Disney's Uncle Donald &
his Nephews Dude Ranch . . 300.00
53 W.Disney's Donald Duck
Merry Christmas . . . . . . . . . . 300.00
54 Woody Woodpecker
Christmas Party . . . . . . . . . . 200.00
55 W.Disney's Daisy Duck & Uncle
Scrooge Show Boat (1961) . . 300.00

## DELL JUNIOR TREASURY
### Dell Publishing Co., June, 1955
1 Alice in Wonderland . . . . . . . . 150.00
2 Aladdin . . . . . . . . . . . . . . . . . . . 125.00
3 Gulliver's Travels . . . . . . . . . . . 100.00
4 Adventures of Mr. Frog . . . . . . 125.00
5 Wizard of Oz . . . . . . . . . . . . . . 125.00
6 Heidi . . . . . . . . . . . . . . . . . . . . . 135.00
7 Santa & the Angel . . . . . . . . . . 135.00
8 Raggedy Ann . . . . . . . . . . . . . . 135.00
9 Clementina the Flying Pig . . . . 125.00
10 Adventures of Tom Sawyer . . . 125.00

## DENNIS THE MENACE
### Visual Editions/Literary Ent. (Standard, Pines), Aug., 1953
1 . . . . . . . . . . . . . . . . . . . . . . . 1,200.00
2 . . . . . . . . . . . . . . . . . . . . . . . . . 500.00
3 . . . . . . . . . . . . . . . . . . . . . . . . . 300.00
4 . . . . . . . . . . . . . . . . . . . . . . . . . 300.00
5 thru 10 . . . . . . . . . . . . . . . . @200.00
11 thru 20 . . . . . . . . . . . . . . . @175.00
21 thru 31 . . . . . . . . . . . . . . . @150.00

### Hallden (Fawcett Publications)
32 thru 40 . . . . . . . . . . . . . . . @125.00
41 thru 50 . . . . . . . . . . . . . . . @125.00
51 thru 60 . . . . . . . . . . . . . . . @100.00
61 thru 70 . . . . . . . . . . . . . . . @100.00
71 thru 90 . . . . . . . . . . . . . . . @100.00
91 thru 140 . . . . . . . . . . . . . . . @50.00
141 thru 166 . . . . . . . . . . . . . . @35.00

---

All comics prices listed are for *Near Mint* condition.          **Page 101**

Desperado #1
© Lev Gleason Publications

Detective Comics #7
© DC Comics

Detective Comics #92
© DC Comics

## DENNIS THE MENACE GIANTS
### [VARIOUS SUBTITLES]
**Fawcett, 1955–69**

| | |
|---|---|
| N# Vacation Special | 300.00 |
| N# Christmas | 250.00 |
| 2 thru 10 | @200.00 |
| 11 thru 20 | @150.00 |
| 21 thru 30 | @100.00 |
| 31 thru 40 | @75.00 |
| 41 thru 75 | @75.00 |

## DESPERADO
**Lev Gleason Publications, June, 1948**

| | |
|---|---|
| 1 CBi(c) | 300.00 |
| 2 CBi(c) | 200.00 |
| 3 CBi(c) | 250.00 |
| 4 CBi(c) | 150.00 |
| 5 CBi(c) | 150.00 |
| 6 CBi(c) | 150.00 |
| 7 CBi(c) | 150.00 |
| 8 CBi(c) | 150.00 |
| Becomes: | |

## BLACK DIAMOND WESTERN
**March, 1949**

| | |
|---|---|
| 9 CBi(c) | 300.00 |
| 10 CBi(c) | 200.00 |
| 11 CBi(c) | 150.00 |
| 12 CBi(c) | 150.00 |
| 13 CBi(c) | 150.00 |
| 14 CBi(c) | 150.00 |
| 15 CBi(c) | 150.00 |
| 16 thru 28 BW,Big Bang Buster | @150.00 |
| 29 thru 40 | @175.00 |
| 41 thru 50 | @125.00 |
| 51 thru 52 3-D Luse | @250.00 |
| 53 thru 60 | @100.00 |

## DETECTIVE COMICS
**DC Comics, March, 1937**

| | |
|---|---|
| 1 I:Slam Bradley | 100,000.00 |
| 2 JoS | 35,000.00 |
| 3 JoS | 25,000.00 |
| 4 JoS | 12,000.00 |
| 5 JoS | 10,000.00 |
| 6 JoS | 8,000.00 |
| 7 JoS | 7,500.00 |
| 8 JoS,Mr. Chang(c) | 12,000.00 |
| 9 JoS | 7,500.00 |

| | |
|---|---|
| 10 | 7,500.00 |
| 11 | 6,500.00 |
| 12 | 6,500.00 |
| 13 | 6,500.00 |
| 14 | 6,500.00 |
| 15 | 6,500.00 |
| 16 | 6,500.00 |
| 17 I:Fu Manchu | 6,500.00 |
| 18 Fu Manchu(c) | 10,000.00 |
| 19 | 6,500.00 |
| 20 I:Crimson Avenger | 9,000.00 |
| 21 | 5,000.00 |
| 22 | 6,500.00 |
| 23 | 5,000.00 |
| 24 | 5,000.00 |
| 25 | 5,000.00 |
| 26 | 5,000.00 |
| 27 BK,I:Batman | 475,000.00 |
| 28 BK,V:Frenchy Blake | 45,000.00 |
| 29 BK,I:Doctor Death | 65,000.00 |
| 30 BK,V:Dr. Death | 15,000.00 |
| 31 BK,I:Monk | 65,000.00 |
| 32 BK,V:Monk | 13,000.00 |
| 33 O:Batman,V:Scarlet Horde | 75,000.00 |
| 34 V:Due D'Orterre | 9,000.00 |
| 35 V:Sheldon Lenox | 22,000.00 |
| 36 I:Hugo Strange | 16,000.00 |
| 37 V:Count Grutt, last Batman solo | 15,000.00 |
| 38 I:Robin, the Boy Wonder | 100,000.00 |
| 39 V:Green Dragon | 14,000.00 |
| 40 I:Clayface (Basil Karlo) | 15,000.00 |
| 41 V:Graves | 8,000.00 |
| 42 V:Pierre Antal | 6,500.00 |
| 43 V:Harliss Greer | 6,500.00 |
| 44 Robin Dream Story | 6,500.00 |
| 45 V:Joker | 8,500.00 |
| 46 V:Hugo Strange | 6,000.00 |
| 47 Meets Harvey Midas | 6,000.00 |
| 48 Meets Henry Lewis | 6,000.00 |
| 49 V:Clayface | 6,000.00 |
| 50 V:Three Devils | 6,000.00 |
| 51 V:Mindy Gang | 5,000.00 |
| 52 V:Loo Chung | 5,000.00 |
| 53 V:Toothy Hare Gang | 5,000.00 |
| 54 V:Hook Morgan | 5,000.00 |
| 55 V:Dr. Death | 5,000.00 |
| 56 V:Mad Mack | 5,000.00 |
| 57 Meet Richard Sneed | 5,000.00 |
| 58 I:Penguin | 9,000.00 |
| 59 V:Penguin | 4,000.00 |
| 60 V:Joker,I:Air Wave | 3,500.00 |
| 61 The Three Racketeers | 3,000.00 |
| 62 V:Joker | 5,000.00 |
| 63 I:Mr. Baffle | 3,000.00 |
| 64 I:Boy Commandos,V:Joker | 8,000.00 |

| | |
|---|---|
| 65 Meet Tom Bolton | 6,000.00 |
| 66 I:Two-Face | 8,000.00 |
| 67 V:Penguin | 5,000.00 |
| 68 V:Two-Face | 3,500.00 |
| 69 V:Joker | 3,500.00 |
| 70 Meet the Amazing Carlo | 2,500.00 |
| 71 V:Joker | 2,700.00 |
| 72 V:Larry the Judge | 2,200.00 |
| 73 V:Scarecrow | 2,600.00 |
| 74 I:Tweedledum&Tweedledee | 2,500.00 |
| 75 V:Robber Baron | 2,500.00 |
| 76 V:Joker | 2,800.00 |
| 77 V:Dr. Matthew Thorne | 2,600.00 |
| 78 V:Baron Von Luger | 2,600.00 |
| 79 Destiny's Auction | 2,600.00 |
| 80 V:Two-Face | 2,700.00 |
| 81 I:Cavalier | 1,700.00 |
| 82 V:Blackee Blondeen | 1,700.00 |
| 83 V:Dr. Goodwin | 1,800.00 |
| 84 V:Ivan Krafft | 1,700.00 |
| 85 V:Joker | 2,200.00 |
| 86 V:Gentleman Jim Jewell | 1,700.00 |
| 87 V:Penguin | 1,800.00 |
| 88 V:Big Hearted John | 1,700.00 |
| 89 V:Cavalier | 1,700.00 |
| 90 V:Capt. Ben | 1,700.00 |
| 91 V:Joker | 2,700.00 |
| 92 V:Braing Bulow | 1,600.00 |
| 93 V:Tiger Ragland | 1,600.00 |
| 94 V:Lefty Goran | 1,600.00 |
| 95 V:The Blaze | 1,600.00 |
| 96 F:Alfred | 1,600.00 |
| 97 V:Nick Petri | 1,600.00 |
| 98 Meets Casper Thurbridge | 1,600.00 |
| 99 V:Penguin | 1,600.00 |
| 100 V:Digger | 1,600.00 |
| 101 V:Joe Bart | 1,600.00 |
| 102 V:Joker | 1,600.00 |
| 103 Meet Dean Gray | 1,600.00 |
| 104 V:Fat Frank Gang | 1,600.00 |
| 105 V:Simon Gurlan | 1,600.00 |
| 106 V:Todd Torrey | 1,600.00 |
| 107 V:Bugs Scarpis | 1,600.00 |
| 108 Meet Ed Gregory | 1,600.00 |
| 109 V:Joker | 5,000.00 |
| 110 V:Prof. Moriarty | 2,000.00 |
| 111 Coaltown, USA | 2,000.00 |
| 112 Case Without A Crime | 2,000.00 |
| 113 V:Blackhand | 2,000.00 |
| 114 V:Joker | 2,000.00 |
| 115 V:Basil Grimes | 2,000.00 |
| 116 A:Carter Nichols, Robin Hood | 2,000.00 |
| 117 Steeplejack's Slowdown | 2,000.00 |
| 118 V:Joker | 2,500.00 |
| 119 V:Wiley Derek | 1,500.00 |

All comics prices listed are for *Near Mint* condition.

De

*Detective Comics #122*
© DC Comics

*Detective Comics #167*
© DC Comics

*Detective Comics #233*
© DC Comics

120 V:Penguin . . . . . . . . . . . . 3,000.00
121 F:Commissioner Gordon . . 1,500.00
122 V:Catwoman . . . . . . . . . . 3,000.00
123 V:Shiner . . . . . . . . . . . . . . 1,300.00
124 V:Joker . . . . . . . . . . . . . . . 1,600.00
125 V:Thinker . . . . . . . . . . . . . 1,200.00
126 V:Penguin . . . . . . . . . . . . 1,200.00
127 V:Dr. Agar . . . . . . . . . . . . 1,200.00
128 V:Joker . . . . . . . . . . . . . . . 1,600.00
129 V:Diamond Dan Mob . . . . . 1,500.00
130 . . . . . . . . . . . . . . . . . . . . 1,500.00
131 V:Trigger Joe . . . . . . . . . . 1,500.00
132 V:Human Key . . . . . . . . . . 1,500.00
133 Meets Arthur Loom . . . . . . 1,500.00
134 V:Penguin . . . . . . . . . . . . 1,500.00
135 A:Baron Frankenstein,
      Carter Nichols . . . . . . . . 1,500.00
136 A:Carter Nichols . . . . . . . . 1,500.00
137 V:Joker . . . . . . . . . . . . . . . 1,700.00
138 V:Joker,O:Robotman . . . . . 1,900.00
139 V:Nick Bailey . . . . . . . . . . 1,400.00
140 I:Riddler . . . . . . . . . . . . . . 7,500.00
141 V:Blackie Nason . . . . . . . . 1,400.00
142 V:Riddler . . . . . . . . . . . . . 2,000.00
143 V:Pied Piper . . . . . . . . . . . 1,200.00
144 A:Kay Kyser (radio
      personality) . . . . . . . . . . . 1,200.00
145 V:Yellow Mask Mob . . . . . . 1,200.00
146 V:J.J. Jason . . . . . . . . . . . 1,200.00
147 V:Tiger Shark . . . . . . . . . . 1,200.00
148 V:Prof. Zero . . . . . . . . . . . 1,200.00
149 V:Joker . . . . . . . . . . . . . . . 1,500.00
150 V:Dr. Paul Visio . . . . . . . . 1,200.00
151 I&O:Pow Wow Smith . . . . . 1,400.00
152 V:Goblin . . . . . . . . . . . . . . 1,200.00
153 V:Slits Danton . . . . . . . . . 1,400.00
154 V:Hatch Marlin . . . . . . . . . 1,200.00
155 A:Vicki Vale . . . . . . . . . . . 1,200.00
156 The Batmobile of 1950 . . . 1,200.00
157 V:Bart Gillis . . . . . . . . . . . 1,200.00
158 V:Dr. Doom . . . . . . . . . . . 1,200.00
159 V:T. Worthington Chubb . . . 1,200.00
160 V:Globe-Trotter . . . . . . . . . 1,200.00
161 V:Bill Waters . . . . . . . . . . 1,200.00
162 Batman on Railroad . . . . . . 1,200.00
163 V:Slippery Jim Elgin . . . . . 1,200.00
164 Bat-signal story . . . . . . . . 1,200.00
165 The Strange Costumes
      of Batman . . . . . . . . . . . . 1,200.00
166 Meets John Gillen . . . . . . . 1,200.00
167 A:Carter Nichols, Cleopatra 1,200.00
168 O:Joker . . . . . . . . . . . . . . 7,000.00
169 V:Squint Tolmar . . . . . . . . 1,200.00
170 Batman Teams with Navy
      and Coast Guard . . . . . . . 1,200.00
171 V:Penguin . . . . . . . . . . . . 1,400.00

172 V:Paul Gregorian . . . . . . . 1,100.00
173 V:Killer Moth . . . . . . . . . . . 1,100.00
174 V:Dagger . . . . . . . . . . . . . 1,100.00
175 V:Kangaroo Kiley . . . . . . . 1,100.00
176 V:Mr. Velvet . . . . . . . . . . . 1,100.00
177 Bat-Cave Story . . . . . . . . . 1,000.00
178 V:Baron Swane . . . . . . . . . 1,000.00
179 Mayor Bruce Wayne . . . . . 1,000.00
180 V:Joker . . . . . . . . . . . . . . . 1,000.00
181 V:Human Magnet . . . . . . . . 1,000.00
182 V:Maestro Dorn . . . . . . . . . 1,000.00
183 V:John Cook . . . . . . . . . . . 1,000.00
184 I:Firefly(Garfield Lynns) . . . 1,000.00
185 Secrets of Batman's
      Utility Belt . . . . . . . . . . . . 1,000.00
186 The Flying Bat-Cave . . . . . 1,000.00
187 V:Two-Face . . . . . . . . . . . . 1,000.00
188 V:William Milden . . . . . . . . 1,000.00
189 V:Styx . . . . . . . . . . . . . . . . 1,000.00
190 Meets Dr. Sampson,
      O:Batman . . . . . . . . . . . . 1,200.00
191 V:Executioner . . . . . . . . . . 1,000.00
192 V: Nails Riley . . . . . . . . . . 1,000.00
193 V:Joker . . . . . . . . . . . . . . . 1,000.00
194 V:Sammy Sabre . . . . . . . . 1,000.00
195 Meets Hugo Marmon . . . . . 1,000.00
196 V:Frank Lumardi . . . . . . . . 1,000.00
197 V:Wrecker . . . . . . . . . . . . . 1,000.00
198 Batman in Scotland . . . . . . 1,000.00
199 V:Jack Baker . . . . . . . . . . . 1,000.00
200 V:Brand Keldon . . . . . . . . . 1,000.00
201 Meet Human Target . . . . . . 1,000.00
202 V:Jolly Roger . . . . . . . . . . . 1,000.00
203 V:Catwoman . . . . . . . . . . . 1,000.00
204 V:Odo Neral . . . . . . . . . . . 1,000.00
205 O:Bat-Cave . . . . . . . . . . . . 1,000.00
206 V:Trapper . . . . . . . . . . . . . 1,000.00
207 Meets Merko the Great . . . 1,000.00
208 V:Groff . . . . . . . . . . . . . . . 1,000.00
209 V:Inventor . . . . . . . . . . . . . 1,000.00
210 V:Brain Hobson . . . . . . . . . 1,000.00
211 V:Catwoman . . . . . . . . . . . 1,000.00
212 Meets Jonathan Bard . . . . . 1,000.00
213 O:Mirror-Man . . . . . . . . . . 1,000.00
214 The Batman Encyclopedia . 1,000.00
215 I:Ranger, Legionairy, Gaucho &
      Musketeer,A:Knight & Squire
      (See: World's Finest 89) . . . 900.00
216 A:Brane Taylor . . . . . . . . . . 900.00
217 Meets Barney Barrows . . . . 900.00
218 V:Dr. Richard Marston . . . . 900.00
219 V:Marty Mantee . . . . . . . . . 900.00
220 A:Roger Bacon, historical
      scientist/philosopher . . . . . . 900.00
221 V:Paul King . . . . . . . . . . . . . 900.00
222 V:'Big Jim' Jarrell . . . . . . . . 900.00

223 V:'Blast' Varner . . . . . . . . . . 900.00
224 . . . . . . . . . . . . . . . . . . . . . 900.00
225 I&O:Martian Manhunter
      (J'onn J'onzz) . . . . . . . . . 10,000.00
226 O:Robin's costume,
      A:J'onn J'onzz . . . . . . . . . 2,500.00
227 A:Roy Raymond, J'onn
      J'onzz . . . . . . . . . . . . . . . 1,000.00
228 A:Roy Raymond, J'onn
      J'onzz . . . . . . . . . . . . . . . 1,000.00
229 A:Roy Raymond, J'onn
      J'onzz . . . . . . . . . . . . . . . 1,000.00
230 A:Martian Manhunter,
      I:Mad Hatter . . . . . . . . . . 1,100.00
231 A:Batman,Jr.,Roy Raymond
      J'onn J'onzz . . . . . . . . . . . . 750.00
232 A:J'onn J'onzz . . . . . . . . . . . 750.00
233 I&O:Batwoman . . . . . . . . . 2,400.00
234 V:Jay Caird . . . . . . . . . . . . . 750.00
235 O:Batman's Costume . . . . . 1,100.00
236 V:Wallace Walby . . . . . . . . 1,000.00
237 F:Robin . . . . . . . . . . . . . . . . 750.00
238 V:Checkmate(villain) . . . . . . 750.00
239 Batman robot story . . . . . . . 750.00
240 V:Burt Weaver . . . . . . . . . . . 750.00
241 The Rainbow Batman . . . . . . 750.00
242 Batcave story . . . . . . . . . . . 600.00
243 V:Jay Vanney . . . . . . . . . . . 600.00
244 O:Batarang . . . . . . . . . . . . . 600.00
245 F:Comm.Gordon . . . . . . . . . 600.00
246 . . . . . . . . . . . . . . . . . . . . . 600.00
247 I:Professor Milo . . . . . . . . . . 600.00
248 . . . . . . . . . . . . . . . . . . . . . 600.00
249 V:Collector . . . . . . . . . . . . . 600.00
250 V:John Stannor . . . . . . . . . . 600.00
251 V:Brand Ballard . . . . . . . . . . 600.00
252 Batman in a movie . . . . . . . . 600.00
253 I:Terrible Trio . . . . . . . . . . . . 600.00
254 A:Bathound . . . . . . . . . . . . . 600.00
255 V:Fingers Nolan . . . . . . . . . 600.00
256 Batman outer-space story . . . 600.00
257 Batman sci-fi story . . . . . . . . 600.00
258 Batman robot story . . . . . . . . 600.00
259 I:Calendar Man . . . . . . . . . . 600.00
260 Batman outer space story . . . 600.00
261 I:Dr. Double X . . . . . . . . . . . 400.00
262 V:Jackal-Head . . . . . . . . . . . 400.00
263 V:The Professor . . . . . . . . . . 400.00
264 . . . . . . . . . . . . . . . . . . . . . 400.00
265 O:Batman retold . . . . . . . . . 600.00
266 V:Astro . . . . . . . . . . . . . . . . 400.00
267 I&O:Bat-Mite . . . . . . . . . . . . 600.00
268 V:'Big Joe' Foster . . . . . . . . 400.00
269 V:Director . . . . . . . . . . . . . . 400.00
270 Batman sci-fi story . . . . . . . . 400.00

All comics prices listed are for *Near Mint* condition.

*Detective Picture Stories #5*
© Comics Magazine Co.

*Diary Loves #2*
© Quality Comics Group

*Dick Cole #8*
© Star Publications

**De**

271 V:Crimson Knight,O:Martian
    Manhunter(retold) . . . . . . . . 400.00
272 V:Crystal Creature . . . . . . . . 400.00
273 A:Dragon Society . . . . . . . . 350.00
274 V:Nails Lewin . . . . . . . . . . . 350.00
275 A:Zebra-Man . . . . . . . . . . . 350.00
276 A:Batmite. . . . . . . . . . . . . . 350.00
277 Batman Monster story. . . . . 350.00
278 A:Professor Simms . . . . . . . 350.00
279 Batman robot story . . . . . . . 350.00
280 A:Atomic Man . . . . . . . . . . . 350.00
281 Batman robot story . . . . . . . 300.00
282 Batman sci-fi story . . . . . . . 300.00
283 V:Phantom of Gotham City . . 300.00
284 V:Hal Durgan . . . . . . . . . . . 300.00
285 V:Harbin . . . . . . . . . . . . . . . 300.00
286 A:Batwoman . . . . . . . . . . . . 300.00
287 A:Bathound . . . . . . . . . . . . . 300.00
288 V:Multicreature . . . . . . . . . . 300.00
289 A:Bat-Mite . . . . . . . . . . . . . 300.00
290 Batman's robot story. . . . . . 300.00
291 Batman sci-fi story . . . . . . . 300.00
292 Last Roy Raymond . . . . . . . 300.00
293 A:Aquaman,J'onn J'onzz . . . 300.00
294 V:Elemental Men,
    A:Aquaman . . . . . . . . . . . 300.00
295 A:Aquaman . . . . . . . . . . . . . 300.00
296 A:Aquaman . . . . . . . . . . . . . 300.00
297 A:Aquaman . . . . . . . . . . . . . 300.00
298 I:Clayface(Matt Hagen). . . . 550.00
299 Batman sci-fi stories . . . . . . 300.00
300 I:Mr.Polka-dot,E:Aquaman . . 250.00

### DETECTIVE DAN,
### SECRET OP, 48
**Humor Publ. Co., 1933**
N# 10"x13", 36 pg. b&w . . . . . 25,000.00

### DETECTIVE EYE
**Centaur Publications,
Nov., 1940**
1 B:Air Man, The Eye Sees,
    A:Masked Marvel . . . . . . . 3,500.00
2 O:Don Rance, Mysticape,
    Dec., 1940 . . . . . . . . . . . 2,500.00

### DETECTIVE
### PICTURE STORIES
**Comics Magazine Co.,
Dec., 1936**
1 The Phantom Killer . . . . . . . 7,000.00
2 . . . . . . . . . . . . . . . . . . . . . . 3,500.00

3 . . . . . . . . . . . . . . . . . . . . . 2,500.00
4 WE, Muss Em Up . . . . . . . . 2,200.00
5 Trouble, April, 1937. . . . . . . 2,700.00

### DEVIL-DOG DUGAN
**Marvel Atlas, July, 1956**
1 War Stories . . . . . . . . . . . . . 200.00
2 JSe(c) . . . . . . . . . . . . . . . . . 200.00
3 . . . . . . . . . . . . . . . . . . . . . . . 150.00
**Becomes:**

### TALE OF THE MARINES
4 BP,War Stories . . . . . . . . . . . 150.00
**Becomes:**

### MARINES AT WAR
5 War Stories . . . . . . . . . . . . . . 150.00
6 . . . . . . . . . . . . . . . . . . . . . . . 150.00
7 The Big Push, Aug., 1957 . . . . 150.00

### DEVIL DOGS
**Street & Smith Publ., 1942**
1 U.S. Marines . . . . . . . . . . . . . 600.00

### DEXTER COMICS
**Dearfield Publications,
Summer, 1948–July, 1949**
1 . . . . . . . . . . . . . . . . . . . . . . . 250.00
2 . . . . . . . . . . . . . . . . . . . . . . . 200.00
3 thru 5 . . . . . . . . . . . . . . . . @150.00

### DEXTER THE DEMON
### See: MELVIN THE
### MONSTER

### DIARY CONFESSIONS
### See: TENDER ROMANCE

### DIARY LOVES
**Comic Magazines
(Quality Comics Group)
Sept., 1949**
1 BWa Love Diary . . . . . . . . . . . 250.00
2 BWa . . . . . . . . . . . . . . . . . . . 225.00
3 . . . . . . . . . . . . . . . . . . . . . . . 150.00
4 RC . . . . . . . . . . . . . . . . . . . . . 175.00
5 . . . . . . . . . . . . . . . . . . . . . . . 125.00
6 . . . . . . . . . . . . . . . . . . . . . . . 125.00
7 . . . . . . . . . . . . . . . . . . . . . . . 125.00
8 BWa . . . . . . . . . . . . . . . . . . . 150.00
9 BWa . . . . . . . . . . . . . . . . . . . 150.00

10 BWa . . . . . . . . . . . . . . . . . . . 150.00
11 . . . . . . . . . . . . . . . . . . . . . . . 125.00
12 . . . . . . . . . . . . . . . . . . . . . . . 125.00
13 . . . . . . . . . . . . . . . . . . . . . . . 125.00
14 . . . . . . . . . . . . . . . . . . . . . . . 125.00
15 BWa . . . . . . . . . . . . . . . . . . . 150.00
16 BWa . . . . . . . . . . . . . . . . . . . 150.00
17 thru 20 . . . . . . . . . . . . . . @125.00
21 BWa . . . . . . . . . . . . . . . . . . . 150.00
22 thru 31 . . . . . . . . . . . . . . @100.00
**Becomes:**

### G.I. SWEETHEARTS
**June, 1953**
32 Love Under Fire . . . . . . . . . . 150.00
33 thru 35 . . . . . . . . . . . . . . @125.00
36 Lend Lease Love Affair . . . . . 125.00
37 thru 45 . . . . . . . . . . . . . . @125.00
**Becomes:**

### GIRLS IN LOVE
**Sept., 1955**
46 Somewhere I'll Find You . . . . . 150.00
47 thru 56 . . . . . . . . . . . . . . @125.00
57 MB(a&c), Can Love Really
    Change Him, Dec., 1956. . . . 150.00

### DIARY SECRETS
### See: TEEN-AGE DIARY
### SECRETS

### DICK COLE
**Curtis Publ./
Star Publications,
Dec.–Jan., 1949**
1 LbC(a&c),CS,All sports(c) . . . . 400.00
2 LbC . . . . . . . . . . . . . . . . . . . . 250.00
3 LbC(a&c) . . . . . . . . . . . . . . . . 275.00
4 LbC(a&c),Rowing (c) . . . . . . 275.00
5 LbC(a&c) . . . . . . . . . . . . . . . . 275.00
6 LbC(a&c), Rodeo (c) . . . . . . . 275.00
7 LbC(a&c) . . . . . . . . . . . . . . . . 250.00
8 LbC(a&c), Football (c) . . . . . . 250.00
9 LbC(a&c), Basketball (c) . . . . . 250.00
10 Joe Louis . . . . . . . . . . . . . . . 300.00
**Becomes:**

### SPORTS THRILLS
**Nov., 1950–Nov., 1951**
11 Ted Williams & Ty Cobb . . . . . 450.00
12 LbC, Joe DiMaggio & Phil
    Rizzuto, Boxing (c) . . . . . . . 400.00
13 LbC(c),Basketball (c) . . . . . . 350.00
14 LbC(c),Baseball (c). . . . . . . . 375.00

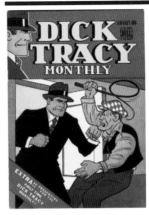

*Dick Tracy Monthly #1*
© Dell Publishing Co.

*Dick Tracy Comics Monthly #38*
© Harvey Publications

*Dick Tracy Comics Monthly #85*
© Harvey Publications

15 LbC(c),Baseball (c) . . . . . . . . 375.00

## DICKIE DARE
**Eastern Color Printing Co.,**
**1941–42**
1 BEv(c),M.Caniff . . . . . . . . . 1,500.00
2 . . . . . . . . . . . . . . . . . . . . . . . . 750.00
3 . . . . . . . . . . . . . . . . . . . . . . . . 750.00
4 H. Scorcery Smith . . . . . . . . . 800.00

## DICK TRACY
## MONTHLY
**Dell Publishing Co.,**
**Jan., 1948**
1 ChG,AAv,Dick Tracy & the Mad
 Doctor'. . . . . . . . . . . . . . . . . 700.00
2 ChG,A:MarySteele,BorisArson 375.00
3 ChG,A:Spaldoni,Big Boy . . . . . 375.00
4 ChG,A:Alderman Zeld . . . . . . 375.00
5 ChG,A:Spaldoni,Mrs.Spaldoni . 350.00
6 ChG,A:Steve the Tramp . . . . . 350.00
7 ChG,A:Boris Arson,Mary
 Steele . . . . . . . . . . . . . . . . 350.00
8 ChG,A:Boris & Zora Arson . . . 350.00
9 ChG,A:Chief Yellowpony . . . . . 350.00
10 ChG,A:Cutie Diamond. . . . . . 350.00
11 ChG,A:Toby Townly,
 Bookie Joe. . . . . . . . . . . . . . 275.00
12 ChG,A:Toby Townly,
 Bookie Joe. . . . . . . . . . . . . . 275.00
13 ChG,A:Toby Townly, Blake . . . 300.00
14 ChG,A:Mayor Waite Wright. . . 250.00
15 ChG,A:Bowman Basil . . . . . . 250.00
16 ChG,A:Maw,'Muscle'
 & 'Cut' Famon . . . . . . . . . . . 250.00
17 ChG,A:Jim Trailer,
 Mary Steele . . . . . . . . . . . . . 250.00
18 ChG,A:Lips Manlis,
 Anthel Jones . . . . . . . . . . . . 250.00
19 I:Sparkle Plenty. . . . . . . . . . 300.00
20 'Black Cat Mystery'. . . . . . . . 275.00
21 'Tracy Meets Number One'. . . 275.00
22 'Tracy and the Alibi Maker' . . 225.00
23 'Dick Tracy Meets Jukebox' . . 225.00
24 'Dick Tracy and Bubbles' . . . . 225.00
**Becomes:**

## DICK TRACY
## COMICS MONTHLY
**Harvey, May, 1950**
25 ChG,A:Flattop . . . . . . . . . . . . 300.00
26 ChG,A:Vitamin Flintheart. . . . . 200.00
27 ChG,'Flattop Escapes Prision' 200.00

28 ChG,'Case o/t Torture
 Chamber'. . . . . . . . . . . . . . . 200.00
29 ChG,A:Brow,Gravel Gertie . . . 250.00
30 ChG,'Blackmail Racket'. . . . . 200.00
31 ChG,A:Snowflake Falls . . . . . 175.00
32 ChG,A:Shaky,Snowflake Falls 175.00
33 ChG,'Strange Case
 of Measles' . . . . . . . . . . . . . 225.00
34 ChG,A:Measles,Paprika . . . . . 200.00
35 ChG,'Case of Stolen $50,000'. 200.00
36 ChG,'Case of the
 Runaway Blonde' . . . . . . . . . 225.00
37 ChG,'Case of Stolen Money'. . 200.00
38 ChG,A:Breathless Mahoney . . 200.00
39 ChG,A:Itchy,B.O.Plenty. . . . . 200.00
40 ChG,'Case of Atomic Killer'. . . 200.00
41 ChG,Pt.1'Murder by Mail' . . . . 175.00
42 ChG,Pt.2'Murder by Mail' . . . . 175.00
43 ChG,'Case of the
 Underworld Brat' . . . . . . . . . 175.00
44 ChG,'Case of the Mouthwash
 Murder' . . . . . . . . . . . . . . . . 175.00
45 ChG,'Case of the Evil Eyes' . . 175.00
46 ChG,'Case of the
 Camera Killers' . . . . . . . . . . 175.00
47 ChG,'Case of the
 Bloodthirsty Blonde'. . . . . . . 175.00
48 ChG,'Case of the
 Murderous Minstrel'. . . . . . . 175.00
49 ChG,Pt.1 'Killer Who Returned
 From the Dead . . . . . . . . . . 175.00
50 ChG,Pt.2 'Killer Who
 Returned From the Dead' . . . 175.00
51 ChG, 'Case of the
 High Tension Hijackers'. . . . . 150.00
52 ChG, 'Case of the
 Pipe-Stem Killer. . . . . . . . . . 150.00
53 ChG,Pt.1 'Dick Tracy Meets
 the Murderous Midget'. . . . . . 150.00
54 ChG,Pt.2 'Dick Tracy Meets
 the Murderous Midget'. . . . . . 150.00
55 ChG,Pt.3 'Dick Tracy Meets
 the Murderous Midget'. . . . . . 150.00
56 ChG,'Case of the
 Teleguard Terror' . . . . . . . . . 150.00
57 ChG,Pt.1 'Case of the
 Ice Cold Killer' . . . . . . . . . . . 175.00
58 ChG,Pt.2 'Case of the
 Ice Cold Killer' . . . . . . . . . . . 150.00
59 ChG,Pt.1 'Case of the
 Million Dollar Murder' . . . . . . 150.00
60 ChG,Pt.2 'Case of the
 Million Dollar Murder' . . . . . . 150.00
61 ChG,'Case of the
 Murderers Mask' . . . . . . . . . 150.00

62 ChG,Pt.1 'Case of the
 White Rat Robbers' . . . . . . . . 150.00
63 ChG,Pt.2 'Case of the
 White Rat Robbers' . . . . . . . . 150.00
64 ChG,Pt.1 'Case of the
 Interrupted Honeymoon' . . . . 150.00
65 ChG,Pt.2 'Case of the
 Interrupted Honeymoon' . . . . 150.00
66 ChG,Pt.1 'Case of the
 Killer's Revenge' . . . . . . . . . 150.00
67 ChG,Pt.2 'Case of the
 Killer's Revenge' . . . . . . . . . 150.00
68 ChG,Pt.1'Case o/t TV Terror' . 150.00
69 ChG,Pt.2'Case o/t TV Terror' . 150.00
70 ChG,Pt.3'Case o/t TV Terror' . 135.00
71 ChG,A:Mrs. Forchune,Opal. . . 135.00
72 ChG,A:Empty Wiliams,Bonny . 135.00
73 ChG,A:Bonny Braids. . . . . . . 135.00
74 ChG,A:Mr. & Mrs.
 Fortson Knox. . . . . . . . . . . . 135.00
75 ChG,A:Crewy Lou, Sphinx . . . 135.00
76 ChG,A:Diet Smith,Brainerd . . 135.00
77 ChG,A:Crewy Lou,
 Bonny Braids. . . . . . . . . . . . 135.00
78 ChG,A:Spinner Records . . . . . 135.00
79 ChG,A:Model Jones,
 Larry Jones . . . . . . . . . . . . . 135.00
80 ChG,A:Tonsils,Dot View . . . . . 135.00
81 ChG,A:Edward Moppet,Tonsils 135.00
82 ChG,A:Dot View,Mr. Crime . . . 135.00
83 ChG,A:RifleRuby,NewsuitNan. 135.00
84 ChG,A:Mr.Crime,NewsuitNan . 135.00
85 ChG,A:NewsuitNan, Mrs.Lava 135.00
86 ChG,A:Mr. Crime,Odds Zonn . 135.00
87 ChG,A:Odds Zonn,Wingy . . . . 135.00
88 ChG,A:Odds Zonn,Wingy . . . . 135.00
89 ChG,Pt.1'Canhead' . . . . . . . . 135.00
90 ChG,Pt.2'Canhead' . . . . . . . . 135.00
91 ChG,Pt.3'Canhead' . . . . . . . . 135.00
92 ChG,Pt.4'Canhead' . . . . . . . . 135.00
93 ChG,Pt.5'Canhead' . . . . . . . . 135.00
94 ChG,Pt.6'Canhead' . . . . . . . . 135.00
95 ChG,A:Mrs. Green,Dewdrop . . 135.00
96 ChG,A:Dewdrop,Sticks . . . . . 135.00
97 ChG,A:Dewdrop,Sticks . . . . . 135.00
98 ChG,A:Open-Mind Monty,
 Sticks . . . . . . . . . . . . . . . . . 135.00
99 ChG,A:Open-Mind Monty,
 Sticks. . . . . . . . . . . . . . . . . . 150.00
100 ChG,A:Half-Pint,Dewdrop . . . 175.00
101 ChG,A:Open-Mind Monty . . . 135.00
102 ChG,A:Rainbow Reiley,
 Wingy. . . . . . . . . . . . . . . . . . 135.00
103 ChG,A:Happy,Rughead. . . . . 135.00
104 ChG,A:Rainbow Reiley,
 Happy . . . . . . . . . . . . . . . . . 135.00

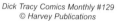

Dick Tracy Comics Monthly #129
© Harvey Publications

Dixie Dugan #6
© Publication Enterprises

Doc Savage Comics #5
© Street & Smith Publications

105 ChG,A:Happy,Rughead . . . . 135.00
106 ChG,A:Fence,Corny,Happy . . 135.00
107 ChG,A:Rainbow Reiley . . . . . 135.00
108 ChG,A:Rughead,Corny,
    Fence . . . . . . . . . . . . . . . . . 135.00
109 ChG,A:Rughead,Mimi,Herky . 135.00
110 ChG,A:Vitamin Flintheart . . . . 135.00
111 ChG,A:Shoulders,Roach . . . . 135.00
112 ChG,A:Brilliant,Diet Smith . . . 135.00
113 ChG,A:Snowflake Falls . . . . . 135.00
114 ChG,A:'Sketch'Paree, . . . . . . 135.00
115 ChG,A:Rod & Nylon Hoze . . . 135.00
116 ChG,A:Empty Williams . . . . . 135.00
117 ChG,A:Spinner Records . . . . 135.00
118 ChG,A:Sleet . . . . . . . . . . . . . 135.00
119 ChG,A:Coffyhead . . . . . . . . . 135.00
120 ChG,'Case Against
    Mumbles Quartet' . . . . . . . . . 135.00
121 ChG,'Case of the Wild Boys'. 135.00
122 ChG,'Case of the
    Poisoned Pellet' . . . . . . . . . . 135.00
123 ChG,'Case of the Deadly
    Treasure Hunt' . . . . . . . . . . . 135.00
124 ChG,'Case of Oodles
    Hears Only Evil' . . . . . . . . . . 135.00
125 ChG,'Case of the Desparate
    Widow' . . . . . . . . . . . . . . . . 135.00
126 ChG,'Case of Oodles'
    Hideout' . . . . . . . . . . . . . . . . 135.00
127 ChG,'Case Against
    Joe Period' . . . . . . . . . . . . . 135.00
128 ChG,'Case Against Juvenile
    Delinquent' . . . . . . . . . . . . . 135.00
129 ChG,'Case of Son of Flattop' 135.00
130 ChG,'Case of Great
    Gang Roundup' . . . . . . . . . . 135.00
131 ChG,'Strange Case of
    Flattop's Conscience' . . . . . . 135.00
132 ChG,'Case of Flattop's
    Big Show' . . . . . . . . . . . . . . 135.00
133 ChG,'Dick Tracy Follows Trail
    of Jewel Thief Gang' . . . . . . . 135.00
134 ChG,'Last Stand of
    Jewel Thieves' . . . . . . . . . . . 135.00
135 ChG,'Case of the
    Rooftop Sniper' . . . . . . . . . . 135.00
136 ChG,'Mystery of the
    Iron Room' . . . . . . . . . . . . . . 135.00
137 ChG,'Law Versus Dick Tracy' 135.00
138 ChG,'Mystery of Mary X' . . . . 135.00
139 ChG,'Yogee the Merciless' . . 135.00
140 ChG,'The Tunnel Trap' . . . . . 135.00
141 ChG,'Case of Wormy &
    His Deadly Wagon' . . . . . . . . 135.00
142 ChG,'Case of the
    Killer's Revenge' . . . . . . . . . 135.00

143 ChG,'Strange Case of
    Measles' . . . . . . . . . . . . . . . 135.00
144 ChG,'Strange Case of
    Shoulders' . . . . . . . . . . . . . . 135.00
145 ChG,'Case of the Fiendish
    Photographers'; April, 1961 . . 135.00

## DICK WINGATE OF THE U.S. NAVY
### Superior Publ./ Toby Press, 1951
N# . . . . . . . . . . . . . . . . . . . . . . 200.00
N# reprint . . . . . . . . . . . . . . . . . 150.00

## DILLY
### Lev Gleason Publications, 1953
1 High School Humor . . . . . . . . 125.00
2 . . . . . . . . . . . . . . . . . . . . . . . . 100.00
3 . . . . . . . . . . . . . . . . . . . . . . . . 100.00

## DIME COMICS
### Newsbook Publ. Corp., 1945
1 LbC,A:Silver Streak . . . . . . . 1,200.00

## DING DONG
### Compix (Magazine Enterprises), 1947
1 (fa) . . . . . . . . . . . . . . . . . . . . 300.00
2 (fa) . . . . . . . . . . . . . . . . . . . . 150.00
3 thru 5 (fa) . . . . . . . . . . . . . . @100.00

## DINKY DUCK
### St. John Publ. Co./Pines, Nov., 1951
1 . . . . . . . . . . . . . . . . . . . . . . . . 150.00
2 . . . . . . . . . . . . . . . . . . . . . . . . 125.00
3 thru 10 . . . . . . . . . . . . . . . . @100.00
11 thru 15 . . . . . . . . . . . . . . . . @100.00
16 thru 18 . . . . . . . . . . . . . . . . @75.00
19 Summer, 1958 . . . . . . . . . . . . 75.00

## DIPPY DUCK
### Marvel Atlas, 1957
1 Funny animal . . . . . . . . . . . . . 100.00

## DIXIE DUGAN
### Columbia Publ./ Publication Enterprises, July, 1942
1 Boxing (c);Joe Palooka . . . . . 500.00

2 . . . . . . . . . . . . . . . . . . . . . . . . 300.00
3 . . . . . . . . . . . . . . . . . . . . . . . . 200.00
4 . . . . . . . . . . . . . . . . . . . . . . . . 150.00
5 . . . . . . . . . . . . . . . . . . . . . . @150.00
6 thru 12 . . . . . . . . . . . . . . . . @100.00
13 1949 . . . . . . . . . . . . . . . . . . 100.00

## DIZZY DAMES
### B&M Distribution Co. (American Comics), Sept.–Oct., 1952
1 . . . . . . . . . . . . . . . . . . . . . . . . 200.00
2 . . . . . . . . . . . . . . . . . . . . . . . . 125.00
3 . . . . . . . . . . . . . . . . . . . . . . . . 100.00
4 . . . . . . . . . . . . . . . . . . . . . . . . 100.00
5 . . . . . . . . . . . . . . . . . . . . . . . . 100.00
6 July–Aug., 1953 . . . . . . . . . . . 100.00

## DIZZY DON COMICS
### Howard Publications/ Dizzy Dean Ent., 1943
1 B&W interior . . . . . . . . . . . . . . 300.00
2 B&W Interior . . . . . . . . . . . . . 200.00
3 B&W Interior . . . . . . . . . . . . . 150.00
4 B&W Interior . . . . . . . . . . . . . 150.00
5 thru 21 . . . . . . . . . . . . . . . . @150.00
22 Oct., 1946 . . . . . . . . . . . . . . 300.00
1a thru 3a . . . . . . . . . . . . . . . @350.00

## DIZZY DUCK
## See: BARNYARD COMICS

## DOC CARTER V.D. COMICS
### Health Publ. Inst., 1949
N# . . . . . . . . . . . . . . . . . . . . . . 350.00
N# . . . . . . . . . . . . . . . . . . . . . . 250.00

## DOC SAVAGE COMICS
### Street & Smith Publ., May, 1940
1 B:Doc Savage, Capt. Fury, Danny
    Garrett, Mark Mallory, Whisperer,
    Capt. Death, Treasure
    Island, A: The Magician . . . 7,500.00
2 O:Ajax,The Sun Man,E:The
    Whisperer . . . . . . . . . . . . . 2,500.00
3 Artic Ice Wastes . . . . . . . . . 1,700.00
4 E:Treasure Island, Saves
    U.S. Navy . . . . . . . . . . . . . 1,400.00
5 O:Astron, the Crocodile
    Queen, Sacred Ruby . . . . . 1,100.00

Di

Do

*Do-Do #1*
© *Nationwide Publishers*

*Doll Man #42*
© *Quality Comics Group*

*Donald and Mickey Merry Christmas*
*N# (#6) © Walt Disney*

6 E: Capt. Fury, O:Red Falcon,
  Murderous Peace Clan .... 850.00
7 V:Zoombas ............ 850.00
8 Finds the Long Lost Treasure . 850.00
9 Smashes Japan's Secret Oil
  Supply .................. 850.00
10 O:Thunder Bolt, The Living
  Dead A:Lord Manhattan .... 850.00
11 V:Giants of Destruction ...... 700.00
12 Saves Merchant Fleet from
  Complete Destruction ...... 700.00
2-1 The Living Evil ........... 700.00
2-2 V:Beggar King ........... 700.00
2-3 ....................... 700.00
2-4 Fight to Death ........... 700.00
2-5 Saves Panama Canal from
  Blood Raider ............. 700.00
2-6 ....................... 700.00
2-7 V:Black Knight ........... 700.00
2-8 Oct., 1943 .............. 700.00

## DR. ANTHONY KING
## HOLLYWOOD LOVE
## DOCTOR
### Harvey, Publ., 1952
1 .......................... 250.00
2 .......................... 200.00
3 .......................... 200.00
4 BP,May, 1954............... 200.00

## DO-DO
### Nationwide Publishers, 1950
1 Funny Animal Circus Humor .. 300.00
2 .......................... 150.00
3 .......................... 150.00
4 .......................... 150.00
5 thru 7 ................. @150.00

## DODO AND THE FROG
### See: FUNNY STUFF

## DOGFACE DOOLEY
### See: A-1 COMICS

## DOLL MAN
### Comic Favorites
### (Quality Comics Group),
### Fall, 1941–Oct., 1953
1 RC,B:Doll Man & Justine
  Wright ............... 5,000.00

2 B:Dragon .............. 1,800.00
3 Five stories ............ 1,500.00
4 Dolls of Death, Wanted:
  The Doll Man .......... 1,300.00
5 RC,Four stories ......... 1,100.00
6 Buy War Stamps (c) ....... 750.00
7 Four stories ............ 750.00
8 BWa,Three stories,A:Torchy . 2,200.00
9 Torchy ................ 750.00
10 RC,V:Murder Marionettes,
  Grim, The Good Sport ... 600.00
11 Shocks Crime Square in the
  Eye ................... 600.00
12 Torchy ................ 600.00
13 RC,Blows Crime Sky High ... 600.00
14 Spotlight on Comics ....... 600.00
15 Faces Danger............. 600.00
16 Torchy ................ 550.00
17 Deals Out Punishment for
  Crime ................. 550.00
18 Redskins Scalp Crime ..... 550.00
19 Fitted for a Cement Coffin ... 550.00
20 Destroys the Black Heart of
  Nemo Black............. 550.00
21 Problem of a Poison Pistol ... 500.00
22 V:Tom Thumb ........... 500.00
23 V:Minstrel, Musician
  of Menace ............. 500.00
24 V:Elixir of Youth........... 500.00
25 V:Thrawn, Lord of Lightning .. 500.00
26 V:Sultan of Satarr &
  Wonderous Runt ........ 500.00
27 Space Conquest .......... 500.00
28 V:The Flame ............ 500.00
29 V:Queen MAB............ 500.00
30 V:Lord Damion ........... 500.00
31 I:Elmo, the Wonder Dog ..... 400.00
32 A:Jeb Rivers ............. 400.00
33 & 34. ................@400.00
35 Prophet of Doom.......... 400.00
36 Death Trap in the Deep ..... 400.00
37 V:The Skull,B:Doll Girl,
  Bondage(c) ............. 550.00
38 The Cult of Death ......... 400.00
39 V:The Death Drug, Narcotics . 400.00
40 Giants of Crime .......... 400.00
41 The Headless Horseman .... 250.00
42 Tale of the Mind Monster ... 250.00
43 The Thing that Kills......... 250.00
44 V:Radioactive Man ........ 250.00
45 What was in the Doom Box? . 250.00
46 Monster from Tomorrow ..... 250.00
47 V:Mad Hypnotist .......... 250.00

## DOLLY
### Approved Comics/
### Ziff-Davis Publ. Co., 1951
1 (10) Adventures in Toy Land .. 125.00

## DOLLY DILL
### Marvel, 1945
1 Newsstand ............... 250.00

## FAMOUS GANG,
## BOOK OF COMICS
### Firestone Tire & Rubber Co.,
### 1942
N# Porky Pig,Bugs Bunny .... 1,200.00
Becomes:

## DONALD AND MICKEY
## MERRY CHRISTMAS
N# (2),CB, 1943........... 1,000.00
N# (3),CB, 1944 ........... 900.00
N# (4),CB, 1945........... 1,400.00
N# (5),CB, 1946........... 1,000.00
N# (6),CB, 1947........... 1,000.00
N# (7),CB, 1948........... 1,000.00
N# (8),CB, 1949 ........... 900.00

## DONALD DUCK
### Whitman
W.Disney's Donald Duck ('35) . 6,000.00
W.Disney's Donald Duck ('36) . 5,000.00
W.Disney's Donald Duck ('38) . 5,000.00

## DONALD DUCK ALBUM
### Dell Publishing Co.,
### May-July, 1959
1 CB(c) .................... 200.00
2 .......................... 150.00

## DONALD DUCK
## GIVEAWAYS
Donald Duck Surprise Party (Icy
  Frost Ice Cream 1948)WK . 4,000.00
Donald Duck (Xmas Giveaway
  1944) ................. 1,500.00
Donald Duck Tells About Kites
  (P.G.&E., Florida 1954).... 4,000.00
Donald Duck Tells About Kites
  (S.C.Edison 1954) ....... 3,500.00
Donald Duck and the Boys
  (Whitman 1948) ......... 1,200.00

---

**Do**

*Donald Duck #30*
© *Walt Disney*

*Don Winslow of the Navy #36*
© *Fawcett Publications*

*Dotty Dripple #22*
© *Harvey Publications*

Donald Ducks Atom Bomb
(Cherrios 1947) . . . . . . . . 1,200.00

## (WALT DISNEY'S)
## DONALD DUCK
**Dell Publishing Co.,**
**Nov., 1952**
(#1-#25) See *Dell Four Color*
26 CB;"Trick or Treat" (1952). . . . 800.00
27 CB(c);"Flying Horse"('53) . . . . 350.00
28 CB(c); Robert the Robot. . . . . 300.00
29 CB(c). . . . . . . . . . . . . . . . . 300.00
30 CB(c). . . . . . . . . . . . . . . . . 300.00
31 thru 39. . . . . . . . . . . . . . @200.00
40 . . . . . . . . . . . . . . . . . . . . 175.00
41 . . . . . . . . . . . . . . . . . . . . 175.00
42 . . . . . . . . . . . . . . . . . . . . 175.00
43 . . . . . . . . . . . . . . . . . . . . 175.00
44. . . . . . . . . . . . . . . . . . . . 175.00
45 CB. . . . . . . . . . . . . . . . . . 350.00
46 CB; "Secret of Hondorica" . . . 500.00
47 thru 51 . . . . . . . . . . . . . . @200.00
52 CB; "Lost Peg-Leg Mine" . . . . 350.00
53 . . . . . . . . . . . . . . . . . . . . 200.00
54 CB; "Forbidden Valley" . . . . . . 500.00
55 thru 59 . . . . . . . . . . . . . . @175.00
60 CB; "Donald Duck & the
    Titanic Ants". . . . . . . . . . 350.00
61 thru 67 . . . . . . . . . . . . . . @150.00
68 CB . . . . . . . . . . . . . . . . . . 300.00
69 thru 78 . . . . . . . . . . . . . . @150.00
79 CB (1 page) . . . . . . . . . . . . 200.00
80 . . . . . . . . . . . . . . . . . . . . 125.00
81 CB (1 page) . . . . . . . . . . . . 150.00
82 . . . . . . . . . . . . . . . . . . . . 125.00
83 . . . . . . . . . . . . . . . . . . . . 125.00
84 . . . . . . . . . . . . . . . . . . . . 125.00

## DON FORTUNE
## MAGAZINE
**Don Fortune Publ. Co.,**
**Aug., 1946**
1 CCB . . . . . . . . . . . . . 400.00
2 CCB . . . . . . . . . . . . . 250.00
3 CCB,Bondage(c) . . . . . . . 225.00
4 CCB . . . . . . . . . . . . . 200.00
5 CCB . . . . . . . . . . . . . 200.00
6 CCB, Jan., 1947 . . . . . . . 200.00

## DON NEWCOMBE
**Fawcett Publications, 1950**
1 Baseball Star . . . . . . . . . . . . 650.00

## DON WINSLOW
## OF THE NAVY
**Fawcett Publ./**
**Charlton Comics, Feb., 1943**
1 Captain Marvel (c) . . . . . . . 2,000.00
2 Nips the Nipponese in
    the Solomons . . . . . . . . . . . 850.00
3 Single-Handed invasion of
    the Philippines . . . . . . . . . . 600.00
4 Undermines the Nazis! . . . . . . 500.00
5 Stolen Battleship Mystery . . . . 500.00
6 War Stamps for Victory (c) . . . 500.00
7 Coast Guard . . . . . . . . . . . . 400.00
8 U.S. Marines . . . . . . . . . . . . 400.00
9 Fighting Marines . . . . . . . . . . 400.00
10 Fighting Seabees . . . . . . . . . 400.00
11 . . . . . . . . . . . . . . . . . . . . 350.00
12 Tuned for Death . . . . . . . . . . 350.00
13 Hirohito's Hospitality . . . . . . . 350.00
14 Catapults against the Axis . . . . 350.00
15 Fighting Merchant Marine. . . . 300.00
16 V:The Most Diabolical Villain
    of all Time . . . . . . . . . . . . . 300.00
17 Buy War Stamps (c) . . . . . . . 300.00
18 The First Underwater Convoy. 300.00
19 Bonape Excersion. . . . . . . . . 300.00
20 The Nazi Prison Ship . . . . . . 300.00
21 Prisoner of the Nazis . . . . . . 225.00
22 Suicide Football . . . . . . . . . . 225.00
23 Peril on the High Seas . . . . . . 225.00
24 Adventures on the High Seas. 225.00
25 Shanghaied Red Cross Ship . 225.00
26 V:The Scorpion . . . . . . . . . . 225.00
27 Buy War Stamps . . . . . . . . . 225.00
28 . . . . . . . . . . . . . . . . . . . . 225.00
29 Invitation to Trouble . . . . . . . 225.00
30 . . . . . . . . . . . . . . . . . . . . 225.00
31 Man or Myth? . . . . . . . . . . . 150.00
32 Return of the Renegade . . . . . 150.00
33 Service Ribbons . . . . . . . . . . 150.00
34 Log Book. . . . . . . . . . . . . . . 150.00
35 . . . . . . . . . . . . . . . . . . . . 150.00
36 V:Octopus . . . . . . . . . . . . . . 150.00
37 V: Sea Serpent . . . . . . . . . . 150.00
38 Climbs Mt. Everest . . . . . . . . 150.00
39 Scorpion's Death Ledger . . . . 150.00
40 Kick Off! . . . . . . . . . . . . . . . 150.00
41 Rides the Skis! . . . . . . . . . . 125.00
42 Amazon Island . . . . . . . . . . 125.00
43 Ghastly Doll Murder Case . . . 125.00
44 The Scorpions Web . . . . . . . 125.00
45 V:Highwaymen of the Seas . . 125.00
46 Renegades Jailbreak . . . . . . . 125.00
47 The Artic Expedition . . . . . . . 125.00

48 Maelstrom of the Deep . . . . . . 125.00
49 The Vanishing Ship! . . . . . . . . 125.00
50 V:The Snake . . . . . . . . . . . . . 125.00
51 A:Singapore Sal . . . . . . . . . . . 125.00
52 Ghost of the Fishing Ships . . . 125.00
53 . . . . . . . . . . . . . . . . . . . . . . 125.00
54 . . . . . . . . . . . . . . . . . . . . . . 125.00
55 . . . . . . . . . . . . . . . . . . . . . . 125.00
56 Far East . . . . . . . . . . . . . . . . 125.00
57 A:Singapore Sal . . . . . . . . . . . 125.00
58 . . . . . . . . . . . . . . . . . . . . . . 125.00
59 . . . . . . . . . . . . . . . . . . . . . . 125.00
60 thru 63. . . . . . . . . . . . . . @125.00
64 MB. . . . . . . . . . . . . . . . . . . . 125.00
65 Ph(c) . . . . . . . . . . . . . . . . . . 200.00
66 Ph(c) . . . . . . . . . . . . . . . . . . 200.00
67 Ph(c) . . . . . . . . . . . . . . . . . . 200.00
68 Ph(c) . . . . . . . . . . . . . . . . . . 200.00
69 Ph(c), Jaws of Destruction . . . 200.00
70 . . . . . . . . . . . . . . . . . . . . . . 125.00
71 . . . . . . . . . . . . . . . . . . . . . . 125.00
72 . . . . . . . . . . . . . . . . . . . . . . 125.00
73 Sept., 1955 . . . . . . . . . . . . . 125.00

## DOPEY DUCK COMICS
**Marvel Timely, Fall, 1945**
1 A:Casper Cat,Krazy Krow . . . . 250.00
2 A:Casper Cat,Krazy Krow . . . . 225.00
**Becomes:**

## WACKY DUCK
**Marvel, 1946**
3 Paperchase(c) . . . . . . . . . . . 225.00
4 Wacky Duck(c) . . . . . . . . . . . 200.00
5 Duck & Devil(c) . . . . . . . . . . . 175.00
6 Cliffhanger(c) . . . . . . . . . . . . 175.00
1 Baketball(c) . . . . . . . . . . . . . 125.00
2 Traffic Light(c) . . . . . . . . . . . . 125.00
**Becomes:**

## JUSTICE COMICS

## DOROTHY LAMOUR
### See: JUNGLE LIL

## DOTTY
### See: FOUR TEENERS

## DOTTY DRIPPLE
**Magazine Enterprises/**
**Harvey Publications, 1946**
1 . . . . . . . . . . . . . . . . . . . . . . 150.00
2 . . . . . . . . . . . . . . . . . . . . . . 125.00

*Double Comics 1942 (#3)*
© Elliot Publications

*Dudley #2*
© Prize Publications

*Durango Kid #17*
© Magazine Enterprises

3 thru 10 . . . . . . . . . . . . . . . . @100.00
11 thru 20 . . . . . . . . . . . . . . . @100.00
21 thru 23 . . . . . . . . . . . . . . . @75.00
24 June, 1952 . . . . . . . . . . . . . . 75.00
**Becomes:**

## HORACE &
## DOTTY DRIPPLE
**Aug., 1952**

25 thru 42 . . . . . . . . . . . . . . . @75.00
43 Oct., 1955 . . . . . . . . . . . . . . 75.00

## DOUBLE ACTION
## COMICS
**DC Comics, Jan., 1940**
2 Pre-Hero DC . . . . . . . . . . 27,000.00

## DOUBLE COMICS
**Elliot Publications**
1 ('40),Masked Marvel . . . . . . 4,000.00
2 ('41),Tornado Tim . . . . . . . . 3,000.00
3 ('42) . . . . . . . . . . . . . . . . 2,500.00
4 ('43) . . . . . . . . . . . . . . . . 2,000.00
5 ('44) . . . . . . . . . . . . . . . . 2,000.00

## DOUBLE LIFE OF
## PRIVATE STRONG
**Archie Publications, 1959**
1 JSm/JK,I:Lancelot Strong/
   Shield, The Fly . . . . . . . . . . 850.00
2 JSm/JK,GT A:Fly . . . . . . . . . . 550.00

## DOUBLE TALK
**Feature Publications**
1 Anti-communist . . . . . . . . . . . 150.00

## DOUBLE TROUBLE
**St. John Publishing Co., 1957**
1 Funny kids . . . . . . . . . . . . . . 125.00

## DOUBLE UP
**Elliot Publications, 1941**
1 . . . . . . . . . . . . . . . . . . . 2,000.00

## DOVER THE BIRD
**Famous Funnies Publ. 1955**
1 Funny animal . . . . . . . . . . . . 100.00

## DOWN WITH CRIME
**Fawcett Publications,
Nov., 1951**
1 A:Desarro . . . . . . . . . . . . . . 650.00
2 BP, A:Scanlon Gang . . . . . . . 400.00
3 H-is for Heroin . . . . . . . . . . . 375.00
4 BP, A:Desarro . . . . . . . . . . . 350.00
5 No Jail Can Hold Me . . . . . . . 400.00
6 The Puncture-Proof Assassin . 400.00
7 The Payoff, Nov., 1952 . . . . . 400.00

## DO YOU BELIEVE
## IN NIGHTMARES
**St. John Publ. Co., 1957**
1 SD . . . . . . . . . . . . . . . . . . 900.00
2 DAy . . . . . . . . . . . . . . . . . 500.00

## DREAM BOOK OF LOVE,
## and DREAM BOOK
## OF ROMANCE
**See: A-1 COMICS**

## DUDLEY
**Prize Publications,
Nov.–Dec., 1952**
1 . . . . . . . . . . . . . . . . . . . . 175.00
2 . . . . . . . . . . . . . . . . . . . . 125.00
3 March–April, 1950 . . . . . . . . 100.00

## DUMBO WEEKLY
**The Walt Disney Co., 1942**
1 Gas giveaways . . . . . . . . . 2,100.00
2 . . . . . . . . . . . . . . . . . . . 1,500.00
3 . . . . . . . . . . . . . . . . . . . 1,500.00
4 thru 16 . . . . . . . . . . . @1,500.00

## DO YOU BELIEVE
## IN NIGHTMARES?
**St. John Publishing Co.,
1957–58**
1 SD . . . . . . . . . . . . . . . . . . 650.00
2 DAy . . . . . . . . . . . . . . . . . 400.00

## DURANGO KID
**Magazine Enterprises,
Oct.–Nov., 1949**
1 FF, Charles Starrett photo (c)
   B:Durango Kid & Raider . . 1,200.00

2 FF, Charles Starrett Ph(c) . . . . 700.00
3 FF, Charles Starrett Ph(c) . . . . 600.00
4 FF, Charles Starrett Ph(c),
   Two-Timing Guns . . . . . . . . 500.00
5 FF, Charles Starrett Ph(c),
   Tracks Across the Trail . . . . . 500.00
6 FF . . . . . . . . . . . . . . . . . . 300.00
7 FF,Atomic(c) . . . . . . . . . . . . 350.00
8 FF . . . . . . . . . . . . . . . . . . 300.00
9 FF . . . . . . . . . . . . . . . . . . 300.00
10 FF . . . . . . . . . . . . . . . . . 300.00
11 FF . . . . . . . . . . . . . . . . . 250.00
12 FF . . . . . . . . . . . . . . . . . 250.00
13 FF . . . . . . . . . . . . . . . . . 250.00
14 thru 16 FF . . . . . . . . . . . @250.00
17 O:Durango Kid . . . . . . . . . . 300.00
18 FMe,DAy(c) . . . . . . . . . . . . 200.00
19 FMe,FGu . . . . . . . . . . . . . . 175.00
20 FMe,FGu . . . . . . . . . . . . . . 175.00
21 FMe,FGu . . . . . . . . . . . . . . 175.00
22 FMe,FGu . . . . . . . . . . . . . . 200.00
23 FMe,FGu,I:Red Scorpion . . . 200.00
24 thru 30 FMe,FGu . . . . . . . @200.00
31 FMe,FGu . . . . . . . . . . . . . . 200.00
32 thru 40 FGu . . . . . . . . . . @200.00
41 FGu,Oct., 1941 . . . . . . . . . 200.00

## DYNAMIC COMICS
**Dynamic Publications
(Harry 'A' Chesler),
Oct., 1941**
1 EK,O:Major Victory, Dynamic Man,
   Hale the Magician, A:Black
   Cobra . . . . . . . . . . . . . . 3,500.00
2 O:Dynamic Boy & Lady
   Satan,I:Green Knight,
   Lance Cooper. . . . . . . . . . 2,500.00
3 GT . . . . . . . . . . . . . . . . . 2,200.00
8 Horror (c) . . . . . . . . . . . . . 2,500.00
9 MRa,GT,B:Mr.E . . . . . . . . . 2,500.00
10 . . . . . . . . . . . . . . . . . . 1,500.00
11 GT . . . . . . . . . . . . . . . . 1,350.00
12 GT . . . . . . . . . . . . . . . . 1,200.00
13 GT . . . . . . . . . . . . . . . . 1,300.00
14 . . . . . . . . . . . . . . . . . . 1,200.00
15 Sky Chief . . . . . . . . . . . . 1,200.00
16 GT,Bondage(c),Marijuana . . 1,500.00
17 . . . . . . . . . . . . . . . . . . 1,700.00
18 Ric . . . . . . . . . . . . . . . . 1,000.00
19 A:Dynamic Man . . . . . . . . . 1,000.00
20 same,Nude Woman . . . . . . 2,000.00
21 same,Dinosaur(c). . . . . . . . 1,000.00
22 same . . . . . . . . . . . . . . . 1,000.00
23 A:Yankee Girl,1.0948 . . . . . 1,000.00

---

Dynamite #1
© Comic Media

Eerie #4
© Avon Periodicals

Ellery Queen #1
© Superior Comics

## DYNAMITE
**Comic Media/Allen Hardy Publ.,**
**May, 1953**
1 DH(c),A:Danger#6 . . . . . . . . 400.00
2 . . . . . . . . . . . . . . . . . . . . . . . 200.00
3 PMo(a&c),B:Johnny
  Dynamite,Drug. . . . . . . . . . 300.00
4 PMo(a&c),Prostitution . . . . . . 350.00
5 PMo(a&c) . . . . . . . . . . . . . . . 200.00
6 PMo(a&c) . . . . . . . . . . . . . . . 200.00
7 PMo(a&c) . . . . . . . . . . . . . . . 200.00
8 PMo(a&c) . . . . . . . . . . . . . . . 200.00
9 PMo(a&c) . . . . . . . . . . . . . . . 200.00
Becomes:

## JOHNNY DYNAMITE
**Charlton Comics, June, 1955**
10 PMo(c) . . . . . . . . . . . . . . . . 150.00
11 . . . . . . . . . . . . . . . . . . . . . . 125.00
12 . . . . . . . . . . . . . . . . . . . . . . 125.00
Becomes:

## FOREIGN INTRIGUES
**1956**
13 A:Johnny Dynamite. . . . . . . . 150.00
14 same. . . . . . . . . . . . . . . . . . 125.00
15 same. . . . . . . . . . . . . . . . . . 125.00
Becomes:

## BATTLEFIELD ACTION
**Nov., 1957**
16 . . . . . . . . . . . . . . . . . . . . . . 150.00
17 . . . . . . . . . . . . . . . . . . . . . . 100.00
18 . . . . . . . . . . . . . . . . . . . . . . 100.00
19 . . . . . . . . . . . . . . . . . . . . . . 100.00
20 . . . . . . . . . . . . . . . . . . . . . . 100.00
21 thru 30. . . . . . . . . . . . . . . . @100.00

## EAGLE, THE
**Fox Features Syndicate,**
**July, 1941**
1 B:The Eagle,A:Rex Dexter
  of Mars . . . . . . . . . . . . . . 4,000.00
2 B:Spider Queen . . . . . . . . . . 2,000.00
3 B:Joe Spook . . . . . . . . . . . 1,800.00
4 Jan., 1942 . . . . . . . . . . . . . 1,800.00

## EAGLE
**Rural Home Publ.,**
**Feb.–March, 1945**
1 LbC . . . . . . . . . . . . . . . . . . . 800.00
2 LbC,April–May, 1945 . . . . . . 500.00

## EAT RIGHT
## TO WORK AND WIN
**Swift Co., 1942**
N# Flash Gordon,Popeye . . . . . 750.00

## EDDIE STANKY
**Fawcett Publications, 1951**
N# New York Giants . . . . . . . . 450.00

## EERIE
**Avon Periodicals,**
**May–June, 1951–**
**Aug.–Sept., 1954**
1 JKa,Horror from the Pit,
  Bondage(c) . . . . . . . . . . . 5,500.00
2,WW(a&c), Chamber of Death 1,000.00
3 WW(a&c),JKa,JO
  Monster of the Storm . . . . . 1,100.00
4 WW(c),Phantom of Reality . 1,000.00
5 WW(c), Operation Horror . . . 900.00
6 Devil Keeps a Date . . . . . . . . 450.00
7 WW(c),JKa,JO,Blood for
  the Vampire . . . . . . . . . . . . 700.00
8 EK, Song of the Undead . . . . 400.00
9 JKa, Hands of Death . . . . . . 400.00
10 Castle of Terror . . . . . . . . . . 400.00
11 Anatomical Monster . . . . . . 400.00
12 Dracula . . . . . . . . . . . . . . . 500.00
13 . . . . . . . . . . . . . . . . . . . . . . 400.00
14 Master of the Dead. . . . . . . 400.00
15 Reprint #1 . . . . . . . . . . . . . 300.00
16 WW, Chamber of Death . . . . 300.00
17 WW(c),JO,JKa, . . . . . . . . . 350.00

## EERIE ADVENTURES
**Approved Comics**
**(Ziff-Davis), Winter, 1951**
1 BP,JKa,Bondage . . . . . . . . . . 500.00

## EGBERT
**Arnold Publications/**
**Comic Magazine,**
**Spring, 1946**
1 I:Egbert & The Count . . . . . . 400.00
2 . . . . . . . . . . . . . . . . . . . . . . . 250.00
3 . . . . . . . . . . . . . . . . . . . . . . . 200.00
4 . . . . . . . . . . . . . . . . . . . . . . . 200.00
5 . . . . . . . . . . . . . . . . . . . . . . . 200.00
6 . . . . . . . . . . . . . . . . . . . . . . . 250.00
7 thru 10 . . . . . . . . . . . . . . . . @200.00
11 thru 17 . . . . . . . . . . . . . . . @150.00
18 1950 . . . . . . . . . . . . . . . . . . 150.00

## EH!
**Charlton Comics,**
**Dec., 1953–Nov., 1954**
1 DAy(c),DG,Atomic Mouse . . . . 400.00
2 DAy(c) . . . . . . . . . . . . . . . . . 250.00
3 DAy(c) . . . . . . . . . . . . . . . . . 225.00
4 DAy(c),Sexual . . . . . . . . . . . 250.00
5 DAy(c) . . . . . . . . . . . . . . . . . 225.00
6 DAy(c),Sexual . . . . . . . . . . . 250.00
7 DAy(c) . . . . . . . . . . . . . . . . . 225.00

## EL BOMBO COMICS
**Frances M. McQueeny, 1945**
1 . . . . . . . . . . . . . . . . . . . . . . . 175.00

## ELLA CINDERS
**St. John Publishing Co. 1948**
1 . . . . . . . . . . . . . . . . . . . . . . . 250.00
2 . . . . . . . . . . . . . . . . . . . . . . . 150.00
3 . . . . . . . . . . . . . . . . . . . . . . . 100.00
4 . . . . . . . . . . . . . . . . . . . . . . . 100.00
5 . . . . . . . . . . . . . . . . . . . . . . . 100.00

## ELLERY QUEEN
**Superior Comics,**
**May–Nov., 1949**
1 LbC(c),JKa,Horror . . . . . . . . . 700.00
2 . . . . . . . . . . . . . . . . . . . . . . . 500.00
3 Drug issue . . . . . . . . . . . . . . 600.00
4 The Crooked Mile . . . . . . . . . 500.00

## ELLERY QUEEN
**Approved Comics**
**(Ziff-Davis),**
**Jan.–March, 1952**
1 NS(c),The Corpse the Killed . . 600.00
2 NS,Killer's Revenge,
  Summer, 1952 . . . . . . . . . . 500.00

## ELMO COMICS
**St. John Publishing Co., 1948**
1 . . . . . . . . . . . . . . . . . . . . . . . 200.00

## ELSIE THE COW
**D.S. Publishing Co.,**
**Oct.–Nov., 1949**
1 P(c) . . . . . . . . . . . . . . . . . . . 450.00
2 Bondage(c) . . . . . . . . . . . . . 300.00
3 July–Aug., 1950 . . . . . . . . . . 200.00

*Exciting Comics #1*
© *Standard Comics*

*Exciting Comics #33*
© *Standard Comics*

*Exciting Comics #59*
© *Standard Comics*

Ex

## ENCHANTING LOVE
### Kirby Publishing Co.
### Oct., 1949
1 Branded Guilty, Ph(c) . . . . . . . 150.00
2 Ph(c),BP . . . . . . . . . . . . . . . 100.00
3 Ph(c),Utter Defeat was Our
  Victory; Jimmy Stewart . . . . . 150.00
4 thru 6 . . . . . . . . . . . . . . . . . @100.00

## ERNIE COMICS
### See: SCREAM COMICS

## ESCAPE FROM FEAR
### Planned Parenthood
### of America, 1956
1 . . . . . . . . . . . . . . . . . . . . . . . 150.00
2 (1962) . . . . . . . . . . . . . . . . . 100.00

## ETTA KETT
### Best Books, Inc.
### (Standard Comics),
### Dec., 1948
11 . . . . . . . . . . . . . . . . . . . . . . 150.00
12 . . . . . . . . . . . . . . . . . . . . . . 100.00
13 . . . . . . . . . . . . . . . . . . . . . . 100.00
14 Sept., 1949 . . . . . . . . . . . . . 100.00

## EVA THE IMP
### Red Top Comic/Decker, 1957
1 . . . . . . . . . . . . . . . . . . . . . . . 100.00
2 . . . . . . . . . . . . . . . . . . . . . . . 100.00

## EVERYTHING HAPPENS
## TO HARVEY
### DC Comics, 1953–54
1 Teen-age humor. . . . . . . . . . . 300.00
2 . . . . . . . . . . . . . . . . . . . . . . . 175.00
3 . . . . . . . . . . . . . . . . . . . . . . . 125.00
4 . . . . . . . . . . . . . . . . . . . . . . . 125.00
5 . . . . . . . . . . . . . . . . . . . . . . . 125.00
6 . . . . . . . . . . . . . . . . . . . . . . . 125.00
7 . . . . . . . . . . . . . . . . . . . . . . . 125.00

## EXCITING COMICS
### Better Publ./Visual Editions
### (Standard Comics),
### April, 1940
1 O:Mask, Jim Hatfield,
  Dan Williams . . . . . . . . . . 7,000.00
2 B:Sphinx . . . . . . . . . . . . . . 4,000.00

3 V;Robot . . . . . . . . . . . . . . . 3,000.00
4 V:Sea Monster . . . . . . . . . . 2,500.00
5 V:Gargoyle . . . . . . . . . . . . . 2,500.00
6 . . . . . . . . . . . . . . . . . . . . . . 2,500.00
7 AS(c) . . . . . . . . . . . . . . . . . 2,000.00
8 . . . . . . . . . . . . . . . . . . . . . . 2,000.00
9 O:Black Terror & Tim,
  Bondage(c) . . . . . . . . . . 17,000.00
10 A:Black Terror . . . . . . . . . . 5,000.00
11 same . . . . . . . . . . . . . . . . 3,000.00
12 Bondage(c) . . . . . . . . . . . . 2,800.00
13 Bondage(c) . . . . . . . . . . . . 2,800.00
14 O:Sphinx . . . . . . . . . . . . . . 2,500.00
15 O:Liberator. . . . . . . . . . . . . 2,600.00
16 Black Terror . . . . . . . . . . . . 2,400.00
17 same . . . . . . . . . . . . . . . . 2,400.00
18 same . . . . . . . . . . . . . . . . 2,400.00
19 same . . . . . . . . . . . . . . . . 2,400.00
20 E:Mask,Bondage(c) . . . . . . 2,200.00
21 A:Liberator . . . . . . . . . . . . . 2,200.00
22 O:The Eaglet,B:American
  Eagle . . . . . . . . . . . . . . . 2,200.00
23 Black Terror . . . . . . . . . . . . 1,800.00
24 Black Terror . . . . . . . . . . . . 1,800.00
25 Bondage(c) . . . . . . . . . . . . 1,800.00
26 ASh(c) . . . . . . . . . . . . . . . 1,800.00
27 ASh(c) . . . . . . . . . . . . . . . 1,800.00
28 ASh(c),B:Crime Crusader . . 2,000.00
29 ASh(c) . . . . . . . . . . . . . . . 1,800.00
30 ASh(c),Bondage(c). . . . . . . 2,000.00
31 ASh(c) . . . . . . . . . . . . . . . 1,500.00
32 ASh(c) . . . . . . . . . . . . . . . 1,500.00
33 ASh(c) . . . . . . . . . . . . . . . 1,500.00
34 ASh(c) . . . . . . . . . . . . . . . 1,500.00
35 ASh(c),E:Liberator . . . . . . . 1,500.00
36 ASh(c) . . . . . . . . . . . . . . . 1,500.00
37 ASh(c) . . . . . . . . . . . . . . . 1,500.00
38 ASh(c) . . . . . . . . . . . . . . . 1,500.00
39 ASh(c)O:Kara, Jungle
  Princess . . . . . . . . . . . . . 3,400.00
40 ASh(c) . . . . . . . . . . . . . . . 3,000.00
41 ASh(c) . . . . . . . . . . . . . . . 3,000.00
42 ASh(c),B:Scarab . . . . . . . . 3,000.00
43 ASh(c) . . . . . . . . . . . . . . . 1,200.00
44 ASh(c) . . . . . . . . . . . . . . . 1,200.00
45 ASh(c),V:Robot . . . . . . . . . 1,200.00
46 ASh(c) . . . . . . . . . . . . . . . 1,200.00
47 ASh(c) . . . . . . . . . . . . . . . 1,200.00
48 ASh(c) . . . . . . . . . . . . . . . 1,200.00
49 ASh(c),E:Kara &
  American Eagle . . . . . . . . 1,200.00
50 ASh(c),E:American Eagle . . 1,200.00
51 ASh(c),B:Miss Masque . . . . 1,500.00
52 ASh(c),Miss Masque . . . . . 1,000.00
53 ASh(c),Miss Masque . . . . . 1,000.00
54 ASh(c),E:Miss Masque . . . . 1,000.00

55 ASh(c),O&B:Judy o/t Jungle 1,000.00
56 ASh(c) . . . . . . . . . . . . . . . 1,000.00
57 ASh(c) . . . . . . . . . . . . . . . 1,000.00
58 ASh(c) . . . . . . . . . . . . . . . 1,000.00
59 ASh(c),FF,Bondage(c) . . . . 1,200.00
60 ASh(c),The Mystery Rider . 1,000.00
61 ASh(c) . . . . . . . . . . . . . . . 1,000.00
62 ASh(c),CQ . . . . . . . . . . . . 1,000.00
63 ASh(c) . . . . . . . . . . . . . . . 1,000.00
64 ASh(c) . . . . . . . . . . . . . . . 1,000.00
65 ASh(c),CQ . . . . . . . . . . . . 1,000.00
66 . . . . . . . . . . . . . . . . . . . . 1,000.00
67 GT . . . . . . . . . . . . . . . . . . 1,000.00
68 . . . . . . . . . . . . . . . . . . . . 1,000.00
69 Sept., 1949 . . . . . . . . . . . . 1,000.00

## EXCITING ROMANCES
### Fawcett Publications, 1949
1 Ph(c) . . . . . . . . . . . . . . . . . . 200.00
2 . . . . . . . . . . . . . . . . . . . . . . . 150.00
3 . . . . . . . . . . . . . . . . . . . . . . . 150.00
4 Ph(c) . . . . . . . . . . . . . . . . . . 150.00
5 thru 14 . . . . . . . . . . . . . . . @100.00

## EXCITING WAR
### Visual Editions
### (Standard Comics), 1952
5 Korean war . . . . . . . . . . . . . . 150.00
6 . . . . . . . . . . . . . . . . . . . . . . . 100.00
7 . . . . . . . . . . . . . . . . . . . . . . . 100.00
8 ATh. . . . . . . . . . . . . . . . . . . . 125.00

## EXOTIC ROMANCE
### See: TRUE WAR
## ROMANCES

## EXPLOITS OF
## DANIEL BOONE
### Comic Magazines
### (Quality Comics Group), 1955
1 Frontier hero . . . . . . . . . . . . . 350.00
2 . . . . . . . . . . . . . . . . . . . . . . . 200.00
3 . . . . . . . . . . . . . . . . . . . . . . . 175.00
4 thru 6 . . . . . . . . . . . . . . . . @175.00

## EXPLORER JOE
### Approved Comics
### (Ziff-Davis), Winter, 1951
1 NS,The Fire Opal
  of Madagscar . . . . . . . . . . . 150.00
2 BK, Oct.–Nov., 1952 . . . . . . . 165.00

---

All comics prices listed are for *Near Mint* condition.          **Page 111**

*Exposed #6*
© D.S. Publishing

*Fairy Tales #10*
© Ziff-Davis Publications

*Famous Crimes #3*
© Fox Features Syndicate

## EXPOSED
**D.S. Publishing Co.,**
**March–April, 1948**
1 Corpses Cash and Carry .... 275.00
2 Giggling Killer ............. 350.00
3 One Bloody Night .......... 150.00
4 JO,Deadly Dummy .......... 150.00
5 Body on the Beach ........ 150.00
6 Fatal Masquerade ......... 450.00
7 The Midnight Guest........ 450.00
8 Grl,The Secret in the Snow .. 450.00
9 The Gypsy Baron,
  July–Aug., 1949 ......... 450.00

## EXTRA COMICS
**Magazine Enterprises, 1947**
1 ........................ 750.00

## EXTRA!
**E.C. Comics,**
**March–April, 1955**
1 JCr,RC,JSe ............. 400.00
2 JCr,RC,JSe ............. 300.00
3 JCr,RC,JSe ............. 300.00
4 JCr,RC,JSe ............. 300.00
5 Nov.–Dec., 1955 .......... 300.00

## FACE, THE
**Publication Enterprises**
**(Columbia Comics), 1942**
1 MBi(c),The Face......... 2,000.00
2 MBi(c) ............... 1,500.00
Becomes:

## TONY TRENT
**1948**
3 MBi,A:The Face........... 350.00
4 1949 ................. 300.00

## FAIRY TALE PARADE
**Dell Publishing Co., 1942**
1 WK,Giant .............. 2,500.00
2 WK,Flying Horse........ 1,500.00
3 WK............... 1,000.00
4 WK.................. 900.00
5 WK.................. 900.00
6 WK.................. 600.00
7 WK.................. 600.00
8 WK.................. 600.00
9 WK,Reluctant Dragon ...... 600.00

## FAIRY TALES
**Approved Comics**
**(Ziff-Davis), 1951**
10 ..................... 350.00
11 ..................... 300.00

## FAITHFUL
**Marvel, Nov., 1949**
1 Ph(c),I Take This Man ...... 200.00
2 Ph(c),Love Thief,Feb.,1950 ... 200.00

## FALLING IN LOVE
**Arleigh Publ./**
**National Periodical Publ., 1955**
1 ..................... 475.00
2 ..................... 250.00
3 ..................... 150.00
4 ..................... 150.00
5 ..................... 150.00
6 ..................... 150.00
7 ..................... 150.00
8 ..................... 150.00
9 ..................... 150.00
10 .................... 150.00
11 thru 20 ............ @125.00
21 thru 47 ........... @100.00

## FAMILY FUNNIES
**Harvey Publications, 1950**
1 Mandrake.............. 200.00
2 Flash Gordon............ 150.00
3 ..................... 125.00
4 Flash Gordon............ 125.00
5 Flash Gordon............ 125.00
6 ..................... 125.00
7 Flash Gordon............ 125.00
8 ..................... 125.00
Becomes:

## TINY TOT FUNNIES
**Harvey Publications, 1951**
9 Dagwood (c),Flash Gordon ... 150.00
Becomes:

## JUNIOR FUNNIES
**Harvey Publications, 1951–52**
10 Blondie, Popeye .......... 100.00
11 ..................... 100.00
12 ..................... 100.00
13 ..................... 100.00

## FAMOUS COMICS
**Whitman Publ. Co., 1934**
1 3"x8", three per box ...... 1,200.00
2 .................... 1,000.00
3 .................... 1,000.00

## FAMOUS COMICS
**Zain-Eppy Publ.**
N# Joe Palooka ............. 600.00

## FAMOUS CRIMES
**Fox Features Syndicate,**
**June, 1948**
1 Cold Blooded Killer ........ 700.00
2 Near Nudity (c) ........... 550.00
3 Crime Never Pays ........ 650.00
4 ..................... 300.00
5 ..................... 300.00
6 ..................... 300.00
7 Drug issue ............. 550.00
8 thru 19 ............. @300.00
20 Aug., 1951 ............ 250.00
51 1952 ............... 200.00

## FAMOUS FAIRY TALES
**K.K. Publication Co., 1942**
N# WK, Giveaway........... 500.00
N# WK, Giveaway ........... 400.00
N# WK, Giveaway ........... 400.00

## FAMOUS FEATURE
## STORIES
**Dell Publishing Co., 1938**
1A:Tarzan, Terry and the Pirates
  Dick Tracy,Smilin' Jack.... 2,500.00

## FAMOUS FUNNIES
**Eastern Color Printing Co.,**
**1933**
N# A Carnival of Comics .... 30,000.00
N# Feb., 1934,
  1st 10-cent comic....... 50,000.00
1 July, 1934 ............ 35,000.00
2 .................... 15,000.00
3 B:Buck Rogers .......... 12,000.00
4 Football (c) ........... 5,000.00
5 Christmas ............. 4,500.00
6 ..................... 3,000.00
7 ..................... 3,000.00
8 ..................... 3,000.00
9 ..................... 3,000.00

All comics prices listed are for *Near Mint* condition.

*Famous Funnies #17*
© *Eastern Color Printing*

*Famous Funnies #209*
© *Eastern Color Printing*

*Famous Stars #5*
© *Ziff-Davis Publications*

**Fa**

| | |
|---|---|
| 10 | 3,000.00 |
| 11 Four pages of Buck Rogers | 1,500.00 |
| 12 Four pages of Buck Rogers | 1,500.00 |
| 13 | 1,200.00 |
| 14 | 1,200.00 |
| 15 Football (c) | 1,200.00 |
| 16 | 1,200.00 |
| 17 Christmas (c) | 1,200.00 |
| 18 Four pages of Buck Rogers | 1,500.00 |
| 19 | 1,200.00 |
| 20 | 1,200.00 |
| 21 Baseball | 1,100.00 |
| 22 Buck Rogers | 1,300.00 |
| 23 | 1,100.00 |
| 24 B: War on Crime | 1,100.00 |
| 25 | 1,100.00 |
| 26 | 1,100.00 |
| 27 G-Men (c) | 1,100.00 |
| 28 | 1,100.00 |
| 29 Christmas | 1,100.00 |
| 30 | 1,100.00 |
| 31 | 800.00 |
| 32 Phantom Magician | 1,000.00 |
| 33 A:Baby Face Nelson & John Dillinger | 800.00 |
| 34 | 800.00 |
| 35 Buck Rogers | 900.00 |
| 36 | 800.00 |
| 37 | 800.00 |
| 38 Portrait,Buck Rogers | 900.00 |
| 39 | 800.00 |
| 40 | 800.00 |
| 41 thru 50 | @700.00 |
| 51 thru 57 | @600.00 |
| 58 Baseball (c) | 600.00 |
| 59 | 600.00 |
| 60 | 600.00 |
| 61 | 500.00 |
| 62 | 500.00 |
| 63 | 500.00 |
| 64 | 500.00 |
| 65 JK | 500.00 |
| 66 | 500.00 |
| 67 | 500.00 |
| 68 JK | 500.00 |
| 69 | 500.00 |
| 70 | 500.00 |
| 71 BEv | 400.00 |
| 72 BEv,B:Speed Spaulding | 400.00 |
| 73 BEv | 400.00 |
| 74 BEv | 400.00 |
| 75 BEv | 400.00 |
| 76 BEv | 400.00 |
| 77 BEv,Merry Christmas (c) | 400.00 |
| 78 BEv | 400.00 |
| 79 BEv | 400.00 |

| | |
|---|---|
| 80 BEv,Buck Rogers | 400.00 |
| 81 O:Invisible Scarlet O'Neil | 300.00 |
| 82 Buck Rogers (c) | 400.00 |
| 83 Dickie Dare | 250.00 |
| 84 Scotty Smith | 250.00 |
| 85 Eagle Scout,Roy Rogers | 250.00 |
| 86 Moon Monsters | 250.00 |
| 87 Scarlet O'Neil | 250.00 |
| 88 Dickie Dare | 250.00 |
| 89 O:Fearless Flint | 250.00 |
| 90 Bondage (c) | 350.00 |
| 91 | 250.00 |
| 92 | 250.00 |
| 93 | 250.00 |
| 94 War Bonds | 300.00 |
| 95 Invisible Scarlet O'Neil | 200.00 |
| 96 | 200.00 |
| 97 War Bonds Promo | 200.00 |
| 98 | 200.00 |
| 99 | 200.00 |
| 100 Anniversary issue | 200.00 |
| 101 thru 110 | @200.00 |
| 111 thru 130 | @125.00 |
| 131 thru 150 | @100.00 |
| 151 thru 162 | @100.00 |
| 163 Valentine's Day (c) | 100.00 |
| 164 | 100.00 |
| 165 | 100.00 |
| 166 | 100.00 |
| 167 | 100.00 |
| 168 | 100.00 |
| 169 AW | 125.00 |
| 170 AW | 125.00 |
| 171 thru 190 | @150.00 |
| 191 thru 203 | @125.00 |
| 204 War (c) | 100.00 |
| 205 thru 208 | @100.00 |
| 209 FF(c),Buck Rogers | 3,000.00 |
| 210 FF(c),Buck Rogers | 3,000.00 |
| 211 FF(c),Buck Rogers | 3,000.00 |
| 212 FF(c),Buck Rogers | 3,000.00 |
| 213 FF(c),Buck Rogers | 3,000.00 |
| 214 FF(c),Buck Rogers | 3,000.00 |
| 215 FF(c),Buck Rogers | 3,000.00 |
| 216 FF(c),Buck Rogers | 3,000.00 |
| 217 | 100.00 |
| 218 July, 1955 | 100.00 |

## FAMOUS GANG, BOOK OF COMICS
## See: DONALD AND MICKEY MERRY CHRISTMAS

## FAMOUS GANGSTERS
### Avon Periodicals, 1951
| | |
|---|---|
| 1 Al Capone, Dillinger, Luciano & Shultz | 500.00 |
| 2 WW(c),Dillinger Machine-Gun Killer | 450.00 |
| 3 Lucky Luciano & Murder Inc... | 450.00 |

**Becomes:**

## CRIME ON THE WATERFRONT
### May, 1952
| | |
|---|---|
| 4 Underworld Gangsters who Control the Shipment of Drugs! | 400.00 |

## FAMOUS STARS
### Ziff-Davis Publ. Co., 1950
| | |
|---|---|
| 1 OW,Shelley Winter,Susan Peters & Shirley Temple | 1,000.00 |
| 2 BEv,Betty Hutton, Bing Crosby | 750.00 |
| 3 OW,Judy Garland, Alan Ladd | 800.00 |
| 4 RC,Jolson, Bob Mitchum | 750.00 |
| 5 BK,Elizabeth Taylor, Esther Williams | 900.00 |
| 6 Gene Kelly, Spring, 1952 | 700.00 |

## FAMOUS STORIES
### Dell Publishing Co., 1942
| | |
|---|---|
| 1 Treasure Island | 375.00 |
| 2 Tom Sawyer | 350.00 |

## FAMOUS WESTERN BADMEN
## See: REDSKIN

## FANTASTIC
## See: CAPTAIN SCIENCE

## FANTASTIC COMICS
### Fox Features Syndicate, 1939
| | |
|---|---|
| 1 LF(c),I&O:Samson,B:Star Dust, Super Wizard, Space Smith & Capt. Kid | 9,000.00 |
| 2 BP,LF(c),Samson Destroyed the Battery & Routed the Foe | 4,500.00 |
| 3 BP,LF(c),Slays the Iron Monster | 12,000.00 |
| 4 GT,LF(c),Demolishes the Closing Torture Walls | 3,000.00 |

---

All comics prices listed are for *Near Mint* condition.

Fantastic Comics #23
© Fox Features Syndicate

Fast Fiction #4
© Seaboard Publications

Gunfighter #8
© E.C. Comics

**Fa**

5 GT,LF(c),Crumbles the
   Mighty War Machine...... 2,700.00
6 JSm(c),Bondage(c) ....... 2,500.00
7 JSm(c) ................. 2,500.00
8 GT,Destroys the Mask of
   Fire,Bondage(c) ......... 2,000.00
9 Mighty Muscles saved the
   Drowning Girl ........... 2,000.00
10 I&O:David.............. 2,000.00
11 Wrecks the Torture Machine
   to save his fellow American 1,800.00
12 Heaved the Huge Ship high
   into the Air ............. 1,800.00
13 Samson(c).............. 1,800.00
14 Samson(c).............. 1,800.00
15 Samson(c)............. 1,800.00
16 E:Stardust ............. 1,800.00
17 Samson(c)............. 1,800.00
18 I:Black Fury & Chuck..... 1,800.00
19 Samson(c).............. 1,700.00
20 Samson(c)............. 1,700.00
21 B&I: The Banshee,Hitler(c) . 2,000.00
22 Hittler & Samson(c)....... 1,800.00
23 O:The Gladiator, Hitler (c)
   Nov., 1941 ............. 2,000.00

## FANTASTIC FEARS
**Farrell Publications
(Ajax), 1953
(Formerly: CAPTAIN JET)**
1 (7) Tales of Stalking Terror.... 650.00
2 (8) ...................... 400.00
3 ......................... 325.00
4 ......................... 325.00
5 SD,1st art .............. 1,100.00
6 Decapitation............... 700.00
7 ......................... 300.00
8 Decapitation............... 500.00
9 ......................... 300.00
Becomes:

## FANTASTIC COMICS
**Ajax, 1954**
10 Tales of Enchantment....... 250.00
11 Amazing Adventures........ 275.00

## FANTASTIC WORLDS
**Visual Editions
(Standard Comics), 1952–53**
5 ATh,Triumph Over Terror, Sci-fi 400.00
6 ATh,The Cosmic Terror ...... 350.00
7 The Asteroid God.......... 250.00

## FANTOMAN
## See: AMAZING
## ADVENTURE FUNNIES

## FARGO KID
## See: JUSTICE TRAPS OF
## THE GUILTY

## THE FARMER'S
## DAUGHTER
**Trojan Magazines/
Stanhall Publ., 1954**
1 Sexy humor, nudity ........ 350.00
2 ......................... 200.00
3 ......................... 200.00
4 ......................... 200.00

## FAST FICTION
**Seaboard Publ.,
Oct., 1949**
1 Scarlet Pimpernel ......... 500.00
2 HcK,Captain Blood ........ 400.00
3 She ..................... 500.00
4 The 39 Steps ............. 350.00
5 HcK,Beau Geste ........... 350.00
Becomes:

## STORIES BY FAMOUS
## AUTHORS ILLUSTRATED
**Famous Author Illustrated,
Aug., 1950**
1a Scarlet Pimpernel ......... 400.00
2a Captain Blood ............ 400.00
3a She ................... 500.00
4a The 39 Steps ............ 325.00
5a Beau Geste ............. 300.00
6 HcK,MacBeth.............. 325.00
7 HcK,Window .............. 275.00
8 HcK,Hamlet .............. 300.00
9 Nicholas Nickleby ......... 275.00
10 HcK,Romeo & Juliet ....... 275.00
11 GS,Ben Hur.............. 290.00
12 GS,La Svengali........... 275.00
13 HcK,Scaramouche ........ 275.00

## FAT AND SLAT
## JOKE BOOK
**William H. Wise, 1944**
N# ...................... 500.00

## FAT AND SLAT
**Fables Publ., Inc.
(E.C. Comics), 1947**
1 I&O:Voltage, Man of Lightning. 400.00
2 ......................... 275.00
3 ......................... 275.00
4 ......................... 275.00
Becomes:

## GUNFIGHTER
**Fables Publ., Inc.
(E.C. Comics), 1948–50**
5 JCr(c),Wild West .......... 700.00
6 Grl,JCr(c),Moon Girl ....... 500.00
7 AF,Grl................... 500.00
8 AF,Grl................... 500.00
9 AF,Grl................... 500.00
10 JCr,AF,Grl .............. 500.00
11 AF,Grl ................. 500.00
12 Grl.................... 500.00
13 JCr,WW,Grl............. 550.00
14 JCr,WW,Grl,Bondage ...... 550.00
Becomes:

## HAUNT OF FEAR

## FAUNTLEROY COMICS
**Close-Up Publ.
(Archie Publ.) 1950–52**
1 F:Super Duck............. 150.00
2 ......................... 100.00
3 ......................... 100.00

## FAVORITE COMICS
**1934**
1 Giveaways,Nebbs,Joe
   Palooka................ 1,500.00
2 same................... 1,000.00
3 same.................. 1,000.00

## FAWCETT
## FUNNY ANIMALS
**Fawcett Publications,
Dec., 1942**
1 I:Hoppy the Marvel Bunny,
   Captain Marvel (c) ...... 1,200.00
2 X-Mas Issue ............. 600.00
3 Spirit of '43 ............. 500.00
4 and 5 .................. @500.00
6 Buy War Bonds and Stamps . 400.00
7 ......................... 400.00
8 Flag (c).................. 400.00

*Fawcett Funny Animals #31*
© *Fawcett Publications*

*Feature Books #6*
© *David McKay Publications*

*Feature Funnies #10*
© *Harry A. Chesler Publications*

**Fe**

9 and 10 . . . . . . . . . . . . . . . . . @400.00
11 thru 20 . . . . . . . . . . . . . . . @250.00
21 thru 30 . . . . . . . . . . . . . . . @200.00
31 thru 40 . . . . . . . . . . . . . . . @200.00
41 thru 83 . . . . . . . . . . . . . . . @150.00

**Charlton Comics**
84 . . . . . . . . . . . . . . . . . . . . . . . 150.00
85 thru 91 Feb., 1956. . . . . . . @100.00

## FAWCETT MINIATURES
**Fawcett Publ.**
**(Wheaties Giveaways), 1946**
1 Capt. Marvel . . . . . . . . . . . . . . 250.00
2 Capt. Marvel . . . . . . . . . . . . . . 250.00
3 Capt. Marvel Jr. . . . . . . . . . . . . 250.00
4 Delecta of the Planets . . . . . . . 400.00

## FAWCETT MOVIE COMICS
**Fawcett Publications, 1949**
N# Dakota Lil . . . . . . . . . . . . . . . 375.00
N#a Copper Canyon . . . . . . . . 300.00
N# Destination the Moon . . . . 1,100.00
N# Montana . . . . . . . . . . . . . . . 300.00
N# Pioneer Marshal . . . . . . . . . 300.00
N# Powder River Rustlers . . . . . 450.00
N# Singing Guns . . . . . . . . . . . 275.00
7 Gunmen of Abilene . . . . . . . . 325.00
8 King of the Bull Whip . . . . . . 425.00
9 BP,The Old Frontier . . . . . . . . 300.00
10 The Missourians . . . . . . . . . . 300.00
11 The Thundering Trail. . . . . . . 400.00
12 Rustlers on Horseback . . . . . 325.00
13 Warpath. . . . . . . . . . . . . . . . . 250.00
14 Last Outpost,RonaldReagan . . . . 3,000.00
15 The Man from Planet-X . . . . 3,000.00
16 10 Tall Men . . . . . . . . . . . . . . 200.00
17 Rose Cimarron . . . . . . . . . . . 150.00
18 The Brigand . . . . . . . . . . . . . 175.00
19 Carbine Williams. . . . . . . . . . 175.00
20 Ivanhoe, Dec., 1952 . . . . . . . 300.00

## FEATURE BOOKS
**David McKay Publications,**
**May, 1937**
N# Dick Tracy . . . . . . . . . . . . 10,000.00
N# Popeye. . . . . . . . . . . . . . . . 9,000.00
1 Zane Grey's King of the
    Royal Mounted . . . . . . . . . . 800.00
2 Popeye . . . . . . . . . . . . . . . . 1,200.00
3 Popeye and the "Jeep" . . . . 1,000.00
4 Dick Tracy . . . . . . . . . . . . . 2,000.00
5 Popeye and his Poppa . . . . 1,000.00

6 Dick Tracy . . . . . . . . . . . . . 1,200.00
7 Little Orphan Annie . . . . . . 1,400.00
8 Secret Agent X-9 . . . . . . . . . 750.00
9 Tracy & the Famon Boys . . . 1,200.00
10 Popeye & Susan . . . . . . . . 1,000.00
11 Annie Rooney . . . . . . . . . . . 350.00
12 Blondie. . . . . . . . . . . . . . . . 1,100.00
13 Inspector Wade. . . . . . . . . . . 325.00
14 Popeye in Wild Oats . . . . . 1,200.00
15 Barney Baxter in the Air . . . . 500.00
16 Red Eagle . . . . . . . . . . . . . . . 400.00
17 Gang Busters . . . . . . . . . . . . 900.00
18 Mandrake the Magician . . . . 850.00
19 Mandrake . . . . . . . . . . . . . . . 850.00
20 The Phantom . . . . . . . . . . . 1,200.00
21 Lone Ranger . . . . . . . . . . . . 1,100.00
22 The Phantom . . . . . . . . . . . . 900.00
23 Mandrake in Teibe Castle. . . . 850.00
24 Lone Ranger . . . . . . . . . . . . 1,100.00
25 Flash Gordon on the
    Planet Mongo . . . . . . . . . . 1,500.00
26 Prince Valiant. . . . . . . . . . . 1,300.00
27 Blondie . . . . . . . . . . . . . . . . . 250.00
28 Blondie and Dagwood. . . . . . 250.00
29 Blondie at the Home
    Sweet Home . . . . . . . . . . . . 250.00
30 Katzenjammer Kids . . . . . . . 250.00
31 Blondie Keeps the Home
    Fires Burning. . . . . . . . . . . . 250.00
32 Katzenjammer Kids. . . . . . . . 200.00
33 Romance of Flying . . . . . . . . 200.00
34 Blondie Home is Our Castle . . 250.00
35 Katzenjammer Kids. . . . . . . . 200.00
36 Blondie on the Home Front. . . 225.00
37 Katzenjammer Kids. . . . . . . . 250.00
38 Blondie the ModelHomemaker 225.00
39 The Phantom . . . . . . . . . . . . 700.00
40 Blondie . . . . . . . . . . . . . . . . . 225.00
41 Katzenjammer Kids. . . . . . . . 250.00
42 Blondie in Home-Spun Yarns . 225.00
43 Blondie Home-Cooked Scraps 225.00
44 Katzenjammer Kids in
    Monkey Business . . . . . . . . . 250.00
45 Blondie in Home of the Free
    and the Brave . . . . . . . . . . . 225.00
46 Mandrake in Fire World . . . . . 500.00
47 Blondie in Eaten Out of
    House and Home . . . . . . . . . 225.00
48 The Maltese Falcon . . . . . . . 1,200.00
49 Perry Mason - The Case of
    the Lucky Legs . . . . . . . . . . . 350.00
50 The Shoplifters Shoe,
    P. Mason . . . . . . . . . . . . . . . 350.00
51 Rip Kirby - Mystery of
    the Mangler . . . . . . . . . . . . . 350.00
52 Mandrake in the Land of X . . . 450.00

53 Phantom in Safari Suspense . 500.00
54 Rip Kirby - Case of the
    Master Menace . . . . . . . . . . 425.00
55 Mandrake in 5-Numbers
    Treasue Hunt. . . . . . . . . . . . 450.00
56 Phantom Destroys the
    Sky Band . . . . . . . . . . . . . . . 500.00
57 Phantom in the Blue Gang,
    1948. . . . . . . . . . . . . . . . . . . 500.00

## FEATURE FILMS
**DC Comics, 1950**
1 Captain China . . . . . . . . . . . 1,200.00
2 Riding High, Bing Crosby . . 1,200.00
3 The Eagle and the Hawk . . . 1,100.00
4 Fancy Pants, Bob Hope . . . . 1,400.00

## FEATURE FUNNIES
**Harry A. Chesler Publ./**
**Comic Favorites, Oct., 1937**
1 RuG(a&c),A:Joe Palooka,
    Mickey Finn, Bungles, Dixie
    Dugan, Big Top, Strange as
    It Seems, Off the Record . . 3,500.00
2 A: The Hawk . . . . . . . . . . . 1,600.00
3 WE,Joe Palooka,The Clock . 1,200.00
4 RuG,WE,RuG(c),JoePalooka 1,200.00
5 WE, Joe Palooka drawing . . 1,200.00
6 WE, Joe Palooka (c) . . . . . . 1,200.00
7 WE,LLe, Gallant Knight story
    by Vernon Henkel . . . . . . . 1,000.00
8 WE . . . . . . . . . . . . . . . . . . . 1,000.00
9 WE, Joe Palooka story . . . . 1,200.00
10 WE,Micky Finn(c). . . . . . . . 1,000.00
11 WE,LLe,The Bungles(c). . . . 1,000.00
12 WE, Joe Palooka(c). . . . . . . 1,000.00
13 WE,LLe, World Series(c) . . . 1,100.00
14 WE,Ned Brant(c). . . . . . . . . . 800.00
15 WE,Joe Palooka(c). . . . . . . . 900.00
16 Mickey Finn(c) . . . . . . . . . . . 800.00
17 WE . . . . . . . . . . . . . . . . . . . . 800.00
18 Joe Palooka (c). . . . . . . . . . . 900.00
19 WE,LLe,Mickey Finn(c). . . . . 800.00
20 WE,LLe . . . . . . . . . . . . . . . . 800.00
**Becomes:**

## FEATURE COMICS
**Quality Comics Group,**
**June. 1939–May, 1950**
21 Joe Palooka(c). . . . . . . . . . 1,200.00
22 LLe(c),Mickey Finn(c) . . . . . . 700.00
23 B:Charlie Chan . . . . . . . . . . . 700.00
24 AIA,Joe Palooka(c) . . . . . . . . 700.00
25 AIA,The Clock(c). . . . . . . . . . 700.00

# STANDARD GUIDE TO GOLDEN AGE COMICS

*Feature Comics #36*
*© Quality Comics Group*

*Feature Presentation #2 (#6)*
*© Fox Features Syndicate*

*Felix the Cat #11*
*© Dell Publishing Co.*

Fe

26 AIA,The Bundles(c). . . . . . . . 700.00
27 WE,AIA,I:Doll Man . . . . . . . 6,500.00
28 LF,AIA,The Clock(c). . . . . . . 2,500.00
29 LF,AIA,The Clock(c). . . . . . . 1,400.00
30 LF,AIA,Doll Man(c) . . . . . . 1,400.00
31 LF,AIA,Mickey Finn(c) . . . . . 1,700.00
32 PGv,LF,GFx,Doll Man(c). . . . . 900.00
33 PGv,LF,GFx,Bundles(c) . . . . . 750.00
34 PGv,LF,GFx,Doll Man(c). . . . . 900.00
35 PGv,LF,GFx,Bundles(c) . . . . . 750.00
36 PGv,LF,GFx,Doll Man(c). . . . . 900.00
37 PGv,LF,GFx,Bundles(c) . . . . . 750.00
38 PGv,GFx,Doll Man(c) . . . . . . 650.00
39 PGv,GFx,Bundles(c). . . . . . . 650.00
40 PGv,GFx,WE(c),Doll Man(c) . 650.00
41 PGv,GFx,WE(c),Bundles(c) . . 500.00
42 GFx,Doll Man(c) . . . . . . . . . . 500.00
43 RC,GFx,Bundles(c). . . . . . . . 425.00
44 RC,GFx,Doll Man(c) . . . . . . . 500.00
45 RC,GFx,Bundles(c). . . . . . . . 400.00
46 RC,PGv,GFx,Doll Man(c) . . . . 600.00
47 RC,GFx,Bundles(c). . . . . . . . 400.00
48 RC,GFx,Doll Man(c) . . . . . . . 600.00
49 RC,GFx,Bundles(c). . . . . . . . 400.00
50 RC,GFx,Doll Man(c) . . . . . . . 600.00
51 RC,GFx,Bundles(c). . . . . . . . 400.00
52 RC,GFx,Doll Man(c) . . . . . . . 500.00
53 RC,GFx,Bundles(c). . . . . . . . 325.00
54 RC,GFx,Doll Man(c) . . . . . . . 500.00
55 RC,GFx,Bundles(c). . . . . . . . 325.00
56 RC,GFx,Doll Man(c) . . . . . . . 500.00
57 RC,GFx,Bundles(c). . . . . . . . 325.00
58 RC,GFx,Doll Man (c) . . . . . . . 500.00
59 RC,GFx,Mickey Finn(c) . . . . . 325.00
60 RC,GFx,Doll Man(c) . . . . . . . 500.00
61 RC,GFx,Bundles(c). . . . . . . . 350.00
62 RC,GFx,Doll Man(c) . . . . . . . 500.00
63 RC,GFx,Bundles(c). . . . . . . . 350.00
64 BP,GFx,Doll Man(c) . . . . . . . 600.00
65 BP,GFx(c),Bundles(c) . . . . . . 300.00
66 BP,GFx,Doll Man(c) . . . . . . . 400.00
67 BP. . . . . . . . . . . . . . . . . . . . . 300.00
68 BP,Doll Man vs.Bearded
Lady. . . . . . . . . . . . . . . . . . 700.00
69 BP,GFx(c),Devil (c) . . . . . . . . 300.00
70 BP,Doll Man(c) . . . . . . . . . . . 700.00
71 BP,GFx(c) . . . . . . . . . . . . . . . 300.00
72 BP,Doll Man(c) . . . . . . . . . . . 500.00
73 BP,GFx(c),Bundles(c) . . . . . . 250.00
74 Doll Man(c) . . . . . . . . . . . . . . 500.00
75 GFx(c). . . . . . . . . . . . . . . . . . 300.00
76 GFx(c). . . . . . . . . . . . . . . . . . 300.00
77 Doll Man (c) until #140 . . . . . . 400.00
78 Knows no Fear but the
Knife Does. . . . . . . . . . . . . . 300.00

79 Little Luck God . . . . . . . . . . . 300.00
80 . . . . . . . . . . . . . . . . . . . . . . . 300.00
81 Wanted for Murder . . . . . . . . 250.00
82 V:Shawunkas the Shaman . . . 250.00
83 V:Mechanical Man . . . . . . . . 250.00
84 V:Masked Rider, Death
Goes to the Rodeo . . . . . . . 250.00
85 V:King of Beasts . . . . . . . . . . 250.00
86 Is He A Killer?. . . . . . . . . . . . 250.00
87 The Maze of Murder . . . . . . . 250.00
88 V:The Phantom Killer . . . . . . . 250.00
89 Crook's Goose . . . . . . . . . . . 250.00
90 V:Whispering Corpse . . . . . . 250.00
91 V:The Undertaker . . . . . . . . . 250.00
92 V:The Image . . . . . . . . . . . . . 250.00
93 . . . . . . . . . . . . . . . . . . . . . . . 250.00
94 V:The Undertaker . . . . . . . . . 250.00
95 Flatten's the Peacock's Pride . 250.00
96 Doll Man Proves
Justice is Blind. . . . . . . . . . 250.00
97 V:Peacock. . . . . . . . . . . . . . . 250.00
98 V:Master Diablo . . . . . . . . . . 250.00
99 On the Warpath Again! . . . . . 250.00
100 Crushes the City of Crime . . 300.00
101 Land of the Midget Men!. . . . 200.00
102 The Angle . . . . . . . . . . . . . . 200.00
103 V:The Queen of Ants . . . . . . 200.00
104 V:The Botanist . . . . . . . . . . . 200.00
105 Dream of Death . . . . . . . . . . 200.00
106 V:The Sword Fish . . . . . . . . . 200.00
107 Hand of Horror!. . . . . . . . . . . 200.00
108 V:Cateye . . . . . . . . . . . . . . . 200.00
109 V:The Brain. . . . . . . . . . . . . . 200.00
110 V:Fat Cat . . . . . . . . . . . . . . . 200.00
111 V:The Undertaker . . . . . . . . . 200.00
112 I:Mr. Curio & His Miniatures . 200.00
113 V:Highwayman . . . . . . . . . . . 200.00
114 V:Tom Thumb . . . . . . . . . . . . 200.00
115 V:The Sphinx. . . . . . . . . . . . . 200.00
116 V:Elbows . . . . . . . . . . . . . . . . 200.00
117 Polka Dot on the Spot . . . . . . 200.00
118 thru 144 . . . . . . . . . . . . . . @ 200.00

## A FEATURE PRESENTATION
### Fox Features Syndicate, 1950
1 (5) The Black Tarantula . . . . . 700.00
2 (6) WW,Moby Dick. . . . . . . . . 600.00
3 Jungle Thrills, bondage . . . . . 500.00

## FEDERAL MEN COMICS
### Gerard Publ. Co., 1942
2 S&S,Spanking . . . . . . . . . . . . 800.00

## FELIX THE CAT
### Dell Publishing Co., Feb.–March, 1948
1 . . . . . . . . . . . . . . . . . . . . . . . . 450.00
2 . . . . . . . . . . . . . . . . . . . . . . . . 300.00
3 . . . . . . . . . . . . . . . . . . . . . . . . 200.00
4 . . . . . . . . . . . . . . . . . . . . . . . . 200.00
5 . . . . . . . . . . . . . . . . . . . . . . . . 200.00
6 . . . . . . . . . . . . . . . . . . . . . . . . 175.00
7 . . . . . . . . . . . . . . . . . . . . . . . . 175.00
8 . . . . . . . . . . . . . . . . . . . . . . . . 175.00
9 . . . . . . . . . . . . . . . . . . . . . . . . 175.00
10 . . . . . . . . . . . . . . . . . . . . . . . 175.00
11 thru 19 . . . . . . . . . . . . . . . @150.00
### Toby Press
20 thru 30. . . . . . . . . . . . . . . @350.00
31 . . . . . . . . . . . . . . . . . . . . . . . 150.00
32 . . . . . . . . . . . . . . . . . . . . . . . 350.00
33 . . . . . . . . . . . . . . . . . . . . . . . 350.00
34 & 35 . . . . . . . . . . . . . . . . . . . 150.00
36 . . . . . . . . . . . . . . . . . . . . . . . 300.00
37 Giant, Christmas(c). . . . . . . . 750.00
38 thru 60 . . . . . . . . . . . . . . . @300.00
61 . . . . . . . . . . . . . . . . . . . . . . . 275.00
### Harvey
62 thru 80. . . . . . . . . . . . . . . @125.00
81 thru 99. . . . . . . . . . . . . . . @100.00
100 . . . . . . . . . . . . . . . . . . . . . . 125.00
101 thru 118. . . . . . . . . . . . . . @100.00
Spec., 100 pgs, 1952. . . . . . . . 350.00
Summer Ann., 100 pgs. 1953 . . 500.00
Winter Ann.,#2 100 pgs, 1954. . 500.00

## FELIX AND HIS FRIENDS
### Toby, 1953
1 F:Felix the Cat . . . . . . . . . . . . 350.00
2 . . . . . . . . . . . . . . . . . . . . . . . . 400.00
3 . . . . . . . . . . . . . . . . . . . . . . . . 400.00

## FELIX'S NEPHEWS INKY & DINKY
### Harvey Publications, 1957
1 . . . . . . . . . . . . . . . . . . . . . . . . 150.00
2 . . . . . . . . . . . . . . . . . . . . . . . . 100.00
3 . . . . . . . . . . . . . . . . . . . . . . . . 100.00
4 thru 7 . . . . . . . . . . . . . . . . @100.00

## FERDINAND THE BULL
### Dell Publishing Co., 1938
1 . . . . . . . . . . . . . . . . . . . . . . . . 500.00

All comics prices listed are for *Near Mint* condition.

*Fight Against Crime #10*
© Story Comics

*Fight Comics #24*
© Fiction House Magazines

*Fight Comics #49*
© Fiction House Magazines

Fi

## FIGHT AGAINST CRIME
### Story Comics, May, 1951
1 Scorpion of Crime Inspector
  "Brains" Carroway . . . . . . . 700.00
2 Ganglands Double Cross . . . . 400.00
3 Killer Dolan's Double Cross . . 300.00
4 Hopped Up Killers - The
  Con's Slaughter,Drug issue . 400.00
5 FF,Horror o/t Avenging Corpse 400.00
6 Terror of the Crazy Killer . . . . 250.00
7 . . . . . . . . . . . . . . . . . . . . . . . 250.00
8 Killer with the Two-Bladed
  Knife . . . . . . . . . . . . . . . . . 250.00
9 Rats Die by Gas,Horror . . . . . 600.00
10 Horror of the Con's Revenge . 600.00
11 Case of the Crazy Killer . . . . 600.00
12 Horror,Drug issue . . . . . . . . 700.00
13 The Bloodless Killer . . . . . . . 600.00
14 Electric Chair (c) . . . . . . . . . 700.00
15 . . . . . . . . . . . . . . . . . . . . . . 600.00
16 RA,Bondage(c) . . . . . . . . . . 700.00
17 Knife in Neck(c) . . . . . . . . . . 700.00
18 Attempted Hanging (c) . . . . . 700.00
19 Bondage(c) . . . . . . . . . . . . . 700.00
20 Severed Head (c) . . . . . . . 1,000.00
21 . . . . . . . . . . . . . . . . . . . . . . 500.00
Becomes:

## FIGHT AGAINST
## THE GUILTY
### Dec., 1954
22 RA,Electric Chair . . . . . . . . . 500.00
23 March, 1955 . . . . . . . . . . . . . 350.00

## FIGHT COMICS
### (Fiction House Magazines),
### Jan., 1940
1 LF,GT,WE(c),O:Spy Fighter . 7,000.00
2 GT,WE(c),Joe Lewis . . . . . . 3,000.00
3 WE(c),GT,B:Rip Regan,
  The Powerman . . . . . . . . . 2,600.00
4 GT,LF(c) . . . . . . . . . . . . . . . 2,500.00
5 WE(c) . . . . . . . . . . . . . . . . . 2,500.00
6 GT,BP(c) . . . . . . . . . . . . . . 1,500.00
7 GT,BP(c),Powerman-Blood
  Money . . . . . . . . . . . . . . . 1,500.00
8 GT,Chip Collins-Lair of
  the Vulture . . . . . . . . . . . . 1,500.00
9 GT,Chip Collins-Prey of the
  War Eagle . . . . . . . . . . . . 1,500.00
10 GT,Wolves of the Yukon . . . 1,500.00
11 . . . . . . . . . . . . . . . . . . . . . 1,200.00
12 RA,Powerman-Monster of
  Madness. . . . . . . . . . . . . . 1,600.00

13 Shark Broodie-Legion
  of Satan . . . . . . . . . . . . . . 1,200.00
14 Shark Broodie-Lagoon
  of Death . . . . . . . . . . . . . . 1,200.00
15 Super-American-Hordes of
  the Secret Dicator. . . . . . . 1,500.00
16 B:Capt. Fight, Swastika
  Plague . . . . . . . . . . . . . . . 1,500.00
17 Super-American-Blaster of
  the Pig-Boat Pirates . . . . . . 1,500.00
18 Shark Broodie-Plague of
  the Yellow Devils . . . . . . . . 1,500.00
19 E:Capt. Fight . . . . . . . . . . . 1,500.00
20 . . . . . . . . . . . . . . . . . . . . . 1,100.00
21 Rip Carson-Hell's Sky-Riders . 900.00
22 Rip Carson-Sky Devil's
  Mission . . . . . . . . . . . . . . . 900.00
23 Rip Carson-Angels of
  Vengeance. . . . . . . . . . . . . 900.00
24 Baynonets for the Banzai
  Breed! Bondage(c) . . . . . . 1,500.00
25 Rip Carson-Samurai
  Showdown . . . . . . . . . . . . 1,000.00
26 Rip Carson-Fury of
  the Sky-Brigade . . . . . . . . 1,000.00
27 War-Loot for the Mikado
  Bondage(c). . . . . . . . . . . . 2,000.00
28 Rip Carson. . . . . . . . . . . . . 1,000.00
29 Rip Carson-Charge of the
  Lost Region . . . . . . . . . . . 1,000.00
30 Rip Carson-Jeep-Raiders of
  the Torture Jungle . . . . . . . 1,000.00
31 Gangway for the Gyrenes,
  Decapitation (c) . . . . . . . . 1,500.00
32 Vengeance of the Hun-
  Hunters,Bondage(c) . . . . . . 1,500.00
33 B:Tiger Girl . . . . . . . . . . . . . 750.00
34 Bondage(c) . . . . . . . . . . . . 1,000.00
35 MB. . . . . . . . . . . . . . . . . . . . 750.00
36 MB. . . . . . . . . . . . . . . . . . . . 750.00
37 MB. . . . . . . . . . . . . . . . . . . . 750.00
38 MB,Bondage(c) . . . . . . . . . 1,000.00
39 MB,Senorita Rio-Slave Brand
  of the Spider Cult. . . . . . . . 750.00
40 MB,Bondage (c) . . . . . . . . 1,000.00
41 MB,Bondage (c). . . . . . . . . 1,000.00
42 MB. . . . . . . . . . . . . . . . . . . . 600.00
43 MB,Senorita Rio-The Fire-Brides
  of the Lost Atlantis,
  Bondage(c) . . . . . . . . . . . . 500.00
44 MB,R:Capt. Fight . . . . . . . . . 600.00
45 MB,Tonight Don Diablo Rides. 600.00
46 MB. . . . . . . . . . . . . . . . . . . . 600.00
47 MB,SenoritaRio-Horror's
  Hacienda . . . . . . . . . . . . . . 600.00

48 MB. . . . . . . . . . . . . . . . . . . . 600.00
49 MB,JKa,B:Tiger Girl(c) . . . . . 600.00
50 MB. . . . . . . . . . . . . . . . . . . . 600.00
51 MB,O:Tiger Girl . . . . . . . . . . 800.00
52 MB,Winged Demons of Doom 375.00
53 MB,Shadowland Shrine . . . . . 375.00
54 MB,Flee the Cobra Fury . . . . 375.00
55 MB,Jungle Juggernaut . . . . . 375.00
56 MB. . . . . . . . . . . . . . . . . . . . 375.00
57 MB,Jewels of Jeopardy. . . . . 375.00
58 MB. . . . . . . . . . . . . . . . . . . . 375.00
59 MB,Vampires ofCrystalCavern 375.00
60 MB,Kraal of DeadlyDiamonds 375.00
61 MB,Seekers of the Sphinx,
  O:Tiger Girl . . . . . . . . . . . . 750.00
62 MB,Graveyard of the
  Tree Tribe . . . . . . . . . . . . . 500.00
63 MB. . . . . . . . . . . . . . . . . . . . 500.00
64 MB,DawnBeast from
  Karama-Zan! . . . . . . . . . . . 500.00
65 Beware the Congo Girl . . . . . 350.00
66 Man or Ape! . . . . . . . . . . . . 350.00
67 Head-Hunters of Taboo Trek . 350.00
68 Fangs of Dr. Voodoo. . . . . . . 350.00
69 Cage of the Congo Fury . . . . 350.00
70 Kraal of Traitor Tusks . . . . . . 350.00
71 Captives for the Golden
  Crocodile . . . . . . . . . . . . . . 350.00
72 Land of the Lost Safaris . . . . 350.00
73 War-Gods of the Jungle . . . . 350.00
74 Advengers of the Jungle. . . . 350.00
75 Perils of Momba-Kzar . . . . . 350.00
76 Kraal of Zombi-Zaro . . . . . . . 350.00
77 Slave-Queen of the Ape Man . 350.00
78 Great Congo Diamond
  Robbery. . . . . . . . . . . . . . . 500.00
79 A:Space Rangers . . . . . . . . . 600.00
80 . . . . . . . . . . . . . . . . . . . . . . 300.00
81 E:Tiger Girl(c) . . . . . . . . . . . 300.00
82 RipCarson-CommandoStrike . 300.00
83 NobodyLoves a Minesweeper 300.00
84 Rip Carson-Suicide Patrol . . . 300.00
85 . . . . . . . . . . . . . . . . . . . . . . 300.00
86 GE,Tigerman,Summer,1954 . . 350.00

## FIGHT FOR LOVE
### United Features
### Syndicate, 1952
N# Romance. . . . . . . . . . . . . . . 125.00

## FIGHTIN' AIR FORCE
### Charlton Comics, 1956–60
3 . . . . . . . . . . . . . . . . . . . . . . 150.00
4 . . . . . . . . . . . . . . . . . . . . . . 100.00

Fighting American #2
© Prize Publications

Fighting Undersea Commandos #1
© Avon Periodicals

Firehair Comics #1
© Fiction House

**Fi**

| | |
|---|---|
| 5 | 100.00 |
| 6 | 100.00 |
| 7 | 100.00 |
| 8 | 100.00 |
| 9 | 100.00 |
| 10 | 100.00 |
| 11 giant | 125.00 |
| 12 US,Russia Nuclear attack | 200.00 |
| 13 thru 20 | @100.00 |
| 21 thru 30 | @100.00 |

## FIGHTING AMERICAN
### Headline Publications
### (Prize), April–May, 1954
| | |
|---|---|
| 1 S&K,O:Fighting American & Speedboy | 2,500.00 |
| 2 S&K(a&c) | 1,200.00 |
| 3 S&K(a&c) | 850.00 |
| 4 S&K(a&c) | 850.00 |
| 5 S&K(a&c) | 850.00 |
| 6 S&K(a&c),O:Fighting American | 800.00 |
| 7 S&K(a&c), April–May, 1955 | 700.00 |

## FIGHTING FRONTS!
### Harvey Publications, 1952–53
| | |
|---|---|
| 1 War | 200.00 |
| 2 BP,violence | 250.00 |
| 3 BP | 150.00 |
| 4 | 125.00 |
| 5 | 125.00 |

## FIGHTING DAVY CROCKETT
## See: KIT CARSON

## FIGHTING INDIANS OF THE WILD WEST
### Avon Periodicals, March, 1952
| | |
|---|---|
| 1 EK,EL,Geronimo, Crazy Horse, Chief Victorio | 200.00 |
| 2 EK,Same, Nov., 1952 | 150.00 |

## FIGHTING LEATHERNECKS
### Toby Press, Feb., 1952
| | |
|---|---|
| 1 JkS,Duke's Diary | 150.00 |
| 2 | 125.00 |
| 3 | 100.00 |

| | |
|---|---|
| 4 | 100.00 |
| 5 | 100.00 |
| 6 Dec., 1952 | 100.00 |

## THE FIGHTING MAN
### Excellent Publications
### (Ajax/Farrell), 1952–53
| | |
|---|---|
| 1 War | 150.00 |
| 2 | 125.00 |
| 3 | 100.00 |
| 4 | 100.00 |
| 5 | 100.00 |
| 6 | 100.00 |
| 7 | 100.00 |
| 8 | 100.00 |
| Ann.#1 (1952) | 300.00 |

## FIGHTIN' TEXAN
## See: TEXAN, THE

## FIGHTING UNDERSEA COMMANDOS
### Avon Periodicals, 1952–53
| | |
|---|---|
| 1 Navy Frogmen | 175.00 |
| 2 | 125.00 |
| 3 | 100.00 |
| 4 BK | 110.00 |
| 5 | 100.00 |

## FIGHTING WAR STORIES
### Men's Publications, 1952
| | |
|---|---|
| 1 | 150.00 |
| 2 | 100.00 |
| 3 | 100.00 |
| 4 | 100.00 |
| 5 | 100.00 |

## FIGHTING YANK
### Nedor Publ./Better Publ.
### (Standard Comics) Sept., 1942
| | |
|---|---|
| 1 JaB,B:Fighting Yank, A:Wonder Man, Mystico, bondage (c) | 6,000.00 |
| 2 JaB | 3,200.00 |
| 3 Shark, bondage (c) | 3,000.00 |
| 4 ASh(c), bondage (c) | 3,000.00 |
| 5 ASh(c) | 1,600.00 |
| 6 ASh(c) | 1,600.00 |
| 7 ASh(c),Bomb(c) | 1,500.00 |
| 8 ASh(c), bondage(c) | 1,600.00 |
| 9 ASh(c) | 1,500.00 |
| 10 ASh(c),bondage-torture(c) | 1,600.00 |

| | |
|---|---|
| 11 ASh(c), A:Grim Reaper, bondage (c) | 1,500.00 |
| 12 ASh(c), Hirohito bondage (c) | 1,500.00 |
| 13 ASh(c),kid bondage,snake(c) | 1,500.00 |
| 14 ASh(c) | 1,000.00 |
| 15 ASh(c),bondage-torture(c) | 1,500.00 |
| 16 ASh(c) | 1,000.00 |
| 17 ASh(c),bondage(c) | 1,500.00 |
| 18 ASh(c), A:American Eagle | 1,200.00 |
| 19 ASh(c) | 1,000.00 |
| 20 ASh(c) Shark | 1,000.00 |
| 21 ASh(c) A:Kara,Jungle Princess | 1,000.00 |
| 22 ASh(c) A:Miss Masque-(c) story | 1,400.00 |
| 23 ASh(c) Klu Klux Klan parody (c) | 1,900.00 |
| 24 ASh(c),A:Miss Masque | 800.00 |
| 25 ASh(c),JRo,MMe,A:Cavalier | 1,500.00 |
| 26 ASh(c),JRo,MMe,A:Cavalier | 800.00 |
| 27 ASh(c),JRo,MMe,A:Cavalier | 800.00 |
| 28 ASh(c),JRo,MMe,AW A:Cavalier | 1,000.00 |
| 29 ASh(c),JRo,MMe,Aug., 1949 | 1,000.00 |

## FILM FUNNIES
### Marvel Chipiden Publ., 1949–50
| | |
|---|---|
| 1 Funny animal | 200.00 |
| 2 | 150.00 |

## FILM STAR ROMANCES
### Star Publications, 1950
| | |
|---|---|
| 1 LbC(c), Rudy Valentino story | 650.00 |
| 2 Liz Taylor & Robert Taylor, photo (c) | 700.00 |
| 3 May–June, 1950, photo(c) | 350.00 |

## FIREHAIR COMICS
### Flying Stories, Inc.
### (Fiction House Magazine),
### Winter, 1948–Spring, 1952
| | |
|---|---|
| 1 I:Firehair, Riders on the Pony Express | 750.00 |
| 2 Bride of the Outlaw Guns | 400.00 |
| 3 Kiss of the Six-Gun Siren! | 350.00 |
| 4 | 350.00 |
| 5 | 350.00 |
| 6 | 325.00 |
| 7 War Drums at Buffalo Bend | 250.00 |
| 8 Raid on the Red Arrows | 250.00 |
| 9 French Flags and Tomahawks | 250.00 |
| 10 Slave Maiden of the Crees | 250.00 |
| 11 Wolves of the Overland Trail | 250.00 |

*First Love Illustrated #67*
© Harvey Publications

*The Flame #1 (#5)*
© Ajax/Farrell

*Flash Comics #17*
© DC Comics

FI

## FIRST KISS
### Charlton Comics, 1957
| | |
|---|---|
| 1 | 125.00 |
| 2 thru 5 | @100.00 |
| 6 thru 10 | @100.00 |
| 11 thru 40 | @50.00 |

## FIRST LOVE ILLUSTRATED
### Harvey Publications, 1949–58
| | |
|---|---|
| 1 | 250.00 |
| 2 | 175.00 |
| 3 | 150.00 |
| 4 | 150.00 |
| 5 thru 10 | @150.00 |
| 11 thru 30 | @100.00 |
| 31 thru 34 | @100.00 |
| 35 | 250.00 |
| 36 "Love Slaves" Communism | 200.00 |
| 37 thru 49 | @75.00 |
| 50 thru 66 | @75.00 |
| 67 thru 70 JK(c) | @100.00 |
| 71 thru 88 | @50.00 |

## FIRST ROMANCE MAGAZINE
### (Home Comics (Harvey Publications), 1949
| | |
|---|---|
| 1 BP,True love stories | 250.00 |
| 2 BP | 150.00 |
| 3 BP | 125.00 |
| 4 BP | 125.00 |
| 5 BP | 125.00 |
| 6 | 100.00 |
| 7 | 100.00 |
| 8 BP | 100.00 |
| 9 BP | 100.00 |
| 10 BP | 100.00 |
| 11 thru 20 BP (in many) | @100.00 |
| 21 thru 40 | @75.00 |
| 41 thru 43 JK(c) | @ 100.00 |
| 44 thru 52 BP(in many) | @ 100.00 |

## 5 CENT COMICS
### Fawcett Publications, 1940
| | |
|---|---|
| 1 B&W, I:Dan Dare, very rare | 10,000.00 |

## FLAME, THE
### Fox Feature Syndicate, Summer, 1940
| | |
|---|---|
| 1 LF,O:The Flame | 7,000.00 |

| | |
|---|---|
| 2 GT,LF,Wing Turner | 3,000.00 |
| 3 BP,Wonderworld | 2,500.00 |
| 4 | 2,500.00 |
| 5 GT | 2,500.00 |
| 6 GT | 2,500.00 |
| 7 A:The Yank | 2,500.00 |
| 8 The Finger of the Frozen Death!, Jan., 1942 | 2,500.00 |

## FLAME, THE
### Ajax/Farrell, 1954–55
| | |
|---|---|
| 1 (#5) superhero,O:Flame | 600.00 |
| 2 | 350.00 |
| 3 | 350.00 |

## FLAMING LOVE
### Comic Magazines (Quality Comics Group), Dec., 1949
| | |
|---|---|
| 1 BWa,BWa(c),The Temptress I Feared in His Arms | 500.00 |
| 2 Torrid Tales of Turbulent Passion | 250.00 |
| 3 BWa,RC,My Heart's at Sea | 300.00 |
| 4 One Women Who Made a Mockery of Love, Ph(c) | 250.00 |
| 5 Bridge of Longing, Ph(c) | 250.00 |
| 6 Men Both Loved & Feared Me, Oct., 1950 | 250.00 |

## FLAMING WESTERN ROMANCES
### Star Publ., 1950
| | |
|---|---|
| 3 LbC,Robert Taylor Photo(c) | 500.00 |

## FLASH COMICS
### DC Comics, Jan., 1940
| | |
|---|---|
| 1 SMo,SMo(c),O:Flash,Hawkman,The Whip & Johnny Thunder,B:Cliff Cornwall,Minute Movies | 150,000.00 |
| 2 B:Rod Rain | 25,000.00 |
| 3 SMo,SMo(c),B:The King | 15,000.00 |
| 4 SMo,SMo(c),F:The Whip | 12,000.00 |
| 5 SMo,SMo(c),F:The King | 10,000.00 |
| 6 F:Flash | 15,000.00 |
| 7 Hawkman(c) | 12,000.00 |
| 8 Male bondage(c) | 6,500.00 |
| 9 Hawkman(c) | 7,000.00 |
| 10 SMo,SMo(c),Flash(c) | 7,000.00 |
| 11 SMo,SMo(c) | 5,500.00 |
| 12 SMo,SMo(c),B:Les Watts | 5,500.00 |
| 13 SMo,SMo(c) | 5,500.00 |

| | |
|---|---|
| 14 SMo,SMo(c) | 6,000.00 |
| 15 SMo,SMo(c) | 6,000.00 |
| 16 SMo,SMo(c) | 6,000.00 |
| 17 SMo,SMo(c),E:CliffCornwall | 6,000.00 |
| 18 SMo,SMo(c) | 6,000.00 |
| 19 SMo,SMo(c) | 6,000.00 |
| 20 SMo,SMo(c) | 6,000.00 |
| 21 SMo(c) | 7,000.00 |
| 22 SMo,SMo(c) | 6,000.00 |
| 23 SMo,SMo(c) | 6,000.00 |
| 24 SMo,SMo(c),Flash V:Spider-Men of Mars,A:Hawkgirl | 7,000.00 |
| 25 SMo,SMo(c) | 4,000.00 |
| 26 SMo,SMo(c) | 4,000.00 |
| 27 SMo,SMo(c),Flash goes to Hollywood | 4,000.00 |
| 28 SMo,SMo(c) | |
| 29 SMo,SMo(c) | 4,000.00 |
| 30 SMo,SMo(c),Flash inAdventure of the Curiosity Ray! | 4,000.00 |
| 31 SMo,SMo(c),Hawkman(c) | 4,000.00 |
| 32 SMo,SM(c),Flash inAdventure of the Fictious Villians | 4,000.00 |
| 33 SMo,SMo(c) | 4,000.00 |
| 34 SMo,SMo(c),Flash in The Robbers of the Round Table | 4,000.00 |
| 35 SMo,SMo(c) | 4,000.00 |
| 36 SMo,SMo(c),F:Flash,Mystery of Doll Who Walks Like a Man | 4,000.00 |
| 37 SMo,SMo(c) | 3,500.00 |
| 38 SMo,SMo(c) | 3,200.00 |
| 39 SMo,SMo(c) | 3,200.00 |
| 40 SMo,SMo(c),F:Flash, Man Who Could Read Man's Souls! | 4,000.00 |
| 41 SMo,SMo(c) | 4,000.00 |
| 42 SMo,SMo(c),Flash V:The Gangsters Baby! | 4,000.00 |
| 43 SMo,SMo(c) | 4,000.00 |
| 44 SMo,SMo(c),Flash V:The Liars Club | 4,000.00 |
| 45 SMo,SMo(c),F:Hawkman,Big Butch Makes Hall of Fame | 4,000.00 |
| 46 SMo,SMo(c) | 4,000.00 |
| 47 SMo,SMo(c),Hawkman in Crime Canned for the Duration | 2,500.00 |
| 48 SMo,SMo(c) | 2,500.00 |
| 49 SMo,SMo(c) | 2,500.00 |
| 50 SMo,SMo(c),Hawkman, Tale of the 1,000 Dollar Bill | 2,500.00 |
| 51 SMo,SMo(c) | 2,500.00 |
| 52 SMo,SMo(c),Flash, Machine that Thinks Like a Man | 2,500.00 |
| 53 SMo,SMo(c),Hawkman, Simple Simon Met the Hawkman | 2,500.00 |
| 54 SMo,SMo(c),Flash, Mysterious Bottle from the Sea | 2,500.00 |

Flash Comics #83
© DC Comics

The Flash #113
© DC Comics

Flash Gordon #2
© Dell Publishing Co.

55 SMo,SMo(c),Hawkman, Riddle of
  the Stolen Statuette!......2,500.00
56 SMo,SMo(c)............2,500.00
57 SMo,SMo(c),Hawkman,
  Adventure of the Gangster
  & the Ghost ...........2,500.00
58 SMo,SMo(c),Merman meets
  the Flash............2,500.00
59 SMo,SMo(c),Hawkman
  V:Pied Piper.........2,500.00
60 SMo,SMo(c),Flash
  V:The Wind Master.......2,500.00
61 SMo,SMo(c),Hawkman
  V:The Beanstalk........2,500.00
62 JKu,Flash in High Jinks
  on the Rinks.........3,000.00
63 JKu(c),Hawkman in The
  Tale of the Mystic Urn.....2,400.00
64 ...................2,400.00
65 JKu(c),Hawkman in Return
  of the Simple Simon......2,400.00
66 ...................2,400.00
67 JKu(c)...............2,400.00
68 Flash in The Radio that
  Ran Wild............2,400.00
69 ...................2,400.00
70 JKu(c)...............2,400.00
71 JKu(c),Hawkman in Battle
  of the Birdmen.........2,400.00
72 JKu.................2,400.00
73 JKu(c)...............2,400.00
74 JKu(c)...............2,400.00
75 JKu(c),Hawkman in Magic
  at the Mardi Gras.......2,400.00
76 A:Worry Wart..........2,400.00
77 Hawkman in The Case of
  the Curious Casket......2,400.00
78 ...................2,400.00
79 Hawkman in The Battle
  of the Birds...........2,400.00
80 Flash in The Story of
  the Boy Genius.........2,400.00
81 JKu(c),Hawkman's Voyage
  to Venus.............2,400.00
82 A:Walter Jordan........2,400.00
83 JKu,JKu(c),Hawkman in
  Destined for Disaster.....2,500.00
84 Flash V:The Changeling...2,500.00
85 JKu,JKu(c),Hawkman in
  Hollywood............2,500.00
86 JKu,1st Black Canary,Flash
  V:Stone Age Menace....8,000.00
87 Hawkman meets the Foil..3,200.00
88 JKu,Flash in The Case
  of the Vanished Year!.....3,200.00

89 I:The Thorn.............4,500.00
90 Flash in Nine Empty
  Uniforms..............3,200.00
91 Hawkman V:The Phantom
  Menace................4,000.00
92 1st full-length Black
  Canary story...........10,000.00
93 Flash V:Violin of Villainy...4,000.00
94 JKu(c)................4,000.00
95 ....................4,000.00
96 ....................4,000.00
97 Flash in The Dream
  that Didn't Vanish........4,000.00
98 JKu(c),Hawkman in
  Crime Costume!.........4,000.00
99 Flash in The Star Prize
  of the Year.............4,000.00
100 Hawkman in The Human
  -Fly Bandits!...........6,500.00
101 ...................5,500.00
102 Hawkman in The Flying
  Darkness.............5,500.00
103 ...................6,500.00
104 JKu,Hawkman in Flaming
  Darkness' Feb., 1949....20,000.00
**Revived as:**

## FLASH, THE
**DC Comics, Feb.–March, 1959**

105 CI,O:Flash,I:Mirror
  Master..............17,000.00
106 CI,I&O:Gorilla Grodd,
  O:Pied Piper...........5,000.00
107 CI,A:Grodd............3,000.00
108 CI,A:Grodd............2,200.00
109 CI,A:Mirror Master......2,000.00
110 CI,MA,I:Kid Flash,
  Weather Wizard.........4,000.00
111 CI,A:Kid Flash,The Invasion
  Of the Cloud Creatures...1,300.00
112 CI,I&O:Elongated Man,
  A:Kid Flash............1,500.00
113 CI,I&O:Trickster.........1,300.00
114 CI,A:Captain Cold........900.00
115 CI,A:Grodd.............800.00
116 CI,A:Kid Flash,The Man
  Who Stole Central City.....800.00
117 CI,MA,I:Capt.Boomerang..1,000.00
118 CI,MA ................700.00
119 CI,W:Elongated Man......700.00
120 CI,A:Kid Flash,Land of
  Golden Giants...........700.00
121 CI,A:Trickster...........600.00
122 CI,I&O:The Top..........600.00
123 I:Earth 2,R:G.A.Flash....3,500.00
124 CI,A:Capt.Boomerang.....450.00

125 CI,A:Kid Flash,The
  Conquerors of Time........450.00
126 CI,A:Mirror Master ........450.00
127 CI,A:Grodd..............450.00
128 CI,O:Abra Kadabra........450.00
129 CI,A:Capt.Cold,Trickster,A:Gold.
  Age Flash,C:JLA (flashback).700.00
130 CI,A:Mirror Master,
  Weather Wizard...........400.00
Ann.#1 O:ElongatedMan,
  G.Grodd.................800.00

## FLASH GORDON
**Harvey Publications,**
**Oct., 1950**

1 AR,Bondage(c)...........600.00
2 AR....................300.00
3 AR Bondage(c)...........400.00
4 AR, April, 1951...........275.00

## FLASH GORDON
**Dell Publishing Co., 1953**

2 .......................200.00
*See also FOUR COLOR*

## FLAT TOP
**Magazine Publ., 1953–55**

1 Teen-age...............125.00
2 .....................100.00
3 .....................100.00
4 .....................100.00
5 .....................100.00
6 .....................100.00
7 .....................100.00

## FLIP
**Harvey Publications,**
**April, 1954**

1 HN....................275.00
2 HN,BP,June, 1954 ........275.00

## FLIPPITY & FLOP
**DC Comics, 1952**

1 Funny animal............325.00
2 .....................175.00
3 .....................150.00
4 .....................150.00
5 .....................150.00
6 .....................100.00
7 .....................100.00
8 .....................100.00
9 .....................100.00

    All comics prices listed are for *Near Mint* condition.

Fo

*The Flying A's Range Rider #11*
© Dell Publishing Co.

*Forbidden Love #1*
© Quality Comics Group

*Forbidden Worlds #1*
© American Comics Group

10 . . . . . . . . . . . . . . . . . . . . . . . 100.00
11 thru 20 . . . . . . . . . . . . . . @125.00
21 thru 47 . . . . . . . . . . . . . . @100.00

### FLY BOY
**Approved Comics**
**(Ziff-Davis) Spring, 1952**
1 NS(c),Angels without Wings . . 300.00
2 NS(c),Flyboy's Flame-Out,
  Oct.–Nov., 1952 . . . . . . . . . 200.00

### FLYING ACES
**Key Publications, 1955–56**
1 War . . . . . . . . . . . . . . . . . . . . 125.00
2 . . . . . . . . . . . . . . . . . . . . . . . . 100.00
3 . . . . . . . . . . . . . . . . . . . . . . . . 100.00
4 . . . . . . . . . . . . . . . . . . . . . . . . 100.00
5 . . . . . . . . . . . . . . . . . . . . . . . . 100.00

### FLYING A'S RANGE RIDER, THE
**Dell Publishing Co.,**
**June–Aug., 1953**
(1) = *Dell Four Color #404*
2 Ph(c) all . . . . . . . . . . . . . . . 200.00
3 . . . . . . . . . . . . . . . . . . . . . . . . 150.00
4 . . . . . . . . . . . . . . . . . . . . . . . . 125.00
5 . . . . . . . . . . . . . . . . . . . . . . . . 125.00
6 . . . . . . . . . . . . . . . . . . . . . . . . 125.00
7 . . . . . . . . . . . . . . . . . . . . . . . . 125.00
8 . . . . . . . . . . . . . . . . . . . . . . . . 125.00
9 . . . . . . . . . . . . . . . . . . . . . . . . 125.00
10 . . . . . . . . . . . . . . . . . . . . . . . 125.00
11 . . . . . . . . . . . . . . . . . . . . . . . 100.00
12 . . . . . . . . . . . . . . . . . . . . . . . 100.00
13 . . . . . . . . . . . . . . . . . . . . . . . 100.00
14 . . . . . . . . . . . . . . . . . . . . . . . 100.00
15 . . . . . . . . . . . . . . . . . . . . . . . 100.00
16 . . . . . . . . . . . . . . . . . . . . . . . 100.00
17 ATh . . . . . . . . . . . . . . . . . . . 150.00
19 . . . . . . . . . . . . . . . . . . . . . . . 100.00
20 . . . . . . . . . . . . . . . . . . . . . . . 100.00
21 . . . . . . . . . . . . . . . . . . . . . . . 100.00
22 . . . . . . . . . . . . . . . . . . . . . . . 100.00
23 . . . . . . . . . . . . . . . . . . . . . . . 100.00
24 . . . . . . . . . . . . . . . . . . . . . . . 100.00

### FLYING CADET
**Flying Cadet Publ. Co., 1943**
1 Aviation for student Airmen . . . 200.00
2 . . . . . . . . . . . . . . . . . . . . . . . . 150.00
3 Photo(c) . . . . . . . . . . . . . . . . 125.00

4 Photo(c) . . . . . . . . . . . . . . . . 125.00
5 Photo(c) . . . . . . . . . . . . . . . . 125.00
6a Photo(c) . . . . . . . . . . . . . . . 125.00
6b Photo(c) . . . . . . . . . . . . . . . 125.00
7 Photo(c) . . . . . . . . . . . . . . . . 125.00
8 Photo(c) . . . . . . . . . . . . . . . . 125.00
9 Photo(c) . . . . . . . . . . . . . . . . 125.00
10 . . . . . . . . . . . . . . . . . . . . . . . 100.00
11 . . . . . . . . . . . . . . . . . . . . . . . 100.00
12 . . . . . . . . . . . . . . . . . . . . . . . 100.00
13 . . . . . . . . . . . . . . . . . . . . . . . 100.00
14 . . . . . . . . . . . . . . . . . . . . . . . 100.00
15 . . . . . . . . . . . . . . . . . . . . . . . 100.00
16 . . . . . . . . . . . . . . . . . . . . . . . 100.00
17 nudity-woman . . . . . . . . . . . 300.00

### FLYIN' JENNY
**Pentagon Publ. Co, 1946**
N# . . . . . . . . . . . . . . . . . . . . . . 300.00
2 . . . . . . . . . . . . . . . . . . . . . . . . 350.00

### FLYING MODELS
**Health-Knowledge**
**Publications, 1954**
1 . . . . . . . . . . . . . . . . . . . . . . . . 200.00

### FOODINI
**Continental Publications,**
**March, 1950**
1 TV Puppet . . . . . . . . . . . . . . . 275.00
2 Jingle Dingle . . . . . . . . . . . . . 150.00
3 . . . . . . . . . . . . . . . . . . . . . . . . 100.00
4 Aug., 1950 . . . . . . . . . . . . . . 100.00

### FOOTBALL THRILLS
**Approved Comics**
**(Ziff-Davis),**
**Fall-Winter, 1952**
1 BP,NS(c),Red Grange story . . 350.00
2 NS(c),Bronko Nagurski,
  Spring,1952 . . . . . . . . . . . . 250.00

### FORBIDDEN LOVE
**Comic Magazine**
**(Quality Comics Group),**
**March, 1950**
1 RC,Ph(c),Heartbreak Road . 1,000.00
2 Ph(c),I Loved a Gigolo . . . . . 800.00
3 Kissless Bride . . . . . . . . . . . . 500.00
4 BWa,Brimstone Kisses,
  Sept., 1950 . . . . . . . . . . . . . 500.00

### FORBIDDEN WORLDS
**American Comics Group,**
**July–Aug., 1951**
1 AW,FF . . . . . . . . . . . . . . . 2,500.00
2 . . . . . . . . . . . . . . . . . . . . . 1,200.00
3 AW,WW,JD . . . . . . . . . . . . 1,400.00
4 Werewolf (c) . . . . . . . . . . . . . 750.00
5 AW . . . . . . . . . . . . . . . . . . . . 850.00
6 AW,King Kong (c) . . . . . . . . . 750.00
7 . . . . . . . . . . . . . . . . . . . . . . . . 500.00
8 . . . . . . . . . . . . . . . . . . . . . . . . 500.00
9 Atomic Bomb . . . . . . . . . . . . 600.00
10 JyD . . . . . . . . . . . . . . . . . . . 375.00
11 The Mummy's Treasure . . . . 275.00
12 Chest of Death . . . . . . . . . . 275.00
13 Invasion from Hades. . . . . . . 275.00
14 Million-Year Monster . . . . . . 275.00
15 The Vampire Cat. . . . . . . . . . 275.00
16 The Doll . . . . . . . . . . . . . . . . 275.00
17 . . . . . . . . . . . . . . . . . . . . . . . 275.00
18 The Mummy . . . . . . . . . . . . 275.00
19 Pirate and the Voodoo Queen 275.00
20 Terror Island . . . . . . . . . . . . 275.00
21 The Ant Master . . . . . . . . . . 250.00
22 The Cursed Casket. . . . . . . . 250.00
23 Nightmare for Two . . . . . . . . 250.00
24 . . . . . . . . . . . . . . . . . . . . . . . 250.00
25 Hallahan's Head . . . . . . . . . . 250.00
26 The Champ. . . . . . . . . . . . . . 250.00
27 SMo,The Thing with the
   Golden Hair . . . . . . . . . . . . 250.00
28 Portrait of Carlotta. . . . . . . . . 250.00
29 The Frogman . . . . . . . . . . . . 250.00
30 The Things on the Beach . . . 250.00
31 SMo,The Circle of the
   Doomed. . . . . . . . . . . . . . . 225.00
32 The Invasion of the
   Dead Things . . . . . . . . . . . 225.00
33 . . . . . . . . . . . . . . . . . . . . . . . 225.00
34 Atomic Bomb. . . . . . . . . . . . 300.00
35 Comics Code . . . . . . . . . . . . 250.00
36 thru 62. . . . . . . . . . . . . . @150.00
63 AW . . . . . . . . . . . . . . . . . . . 150.00
64 . . . . . . . . . . . . . . . . . . . . . . . 100.00
65 . . . . . . . . . . . . . . . . . . . . . . . 100.00
66 . . . . . . . . . . . . . . . . . . . . . . . 100.00
67 . . . . . . . . . . . . . . . . . . . . . . . 100.00
68 OW(c) . . . . . . . . . . . . . . . . . 100.00
69 AW . . . . . . . . . . . . . . . . . . . 150.00
70 . . . . . . . . . . . . . . . . . . . . . . . 100.00
71 . . . . . . . . . . . . . . . . . . . . . . . 100.00
72 . . . . . . . . . . . . . . . . . . . . . . . 100.00
73 OW,I:Herbie . . . . . . . . . . . . 475.00
74 . . . . . . . . . . . . . . . . . . . . . . . 100.00
75 JB . . . . . . . . . . . . . . . . . . . . 100.00

All comics prices listed are for *Near Mint* condition. **Page 121**

*Forbidden Worlds #103*
*© American Comics Group*

*Four Color, 1st Series #4*
*© Walt Disney Co.*

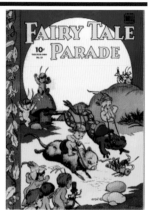

*Four Color, 2nd Series #69*
*© Oskar Lebeck*

**Fo**

| | |
|---|---|
| 76 AW | 150.00 |
| 77 | 100.00 |
| 78 AW,OW(c) | 125.00 |
| 79 thru 85 JB | @100.00 |
| 86 Flying Saucer | 110.00 |
| 87 | 100.00 |
| 88 | 100.00 |
| 89 | 100.00 |
| 90 | 100.00 |
| 91 | 100.00 |
| 92 | 100.00 |
| 93 | 100.00 |
| 94 OW(c),A:Herbie | 150.00 |
| 95 | 100.00 |
| 96 AW | 125.00 |
| 97 thru 115 | @100.00 |
| 116 OW(c)A:Herbie | 110.00 |
| 117 | 100.00 |
| 118 | 100.00 |
| 119 | 100.00 |
| 120 thru 124 | @100.00 |
| 125 I:O:Magic Man | 100.00 |
| 126 A:Magic Man | 100.00 |
| 127 same | 100.00 |
| 128 same | 100.00 |
| 129 same | 100.00 |
| 130 same | 100.00 |
| 131 same | 100.00 |
| 132 same | 100.00 |
| 133 I:O:Dragona | 100.00 |
| 134 A:Magic Man | 100.00 |
| 135 A:Magic Man | 100.00 |
| 136 A:Nemesis | 100.00 |
| 137 A:Magic Man | 100.00 |
| 138 A:Magic Man | 100.00 |
| 139 A:Magic Man | 100.00 |
| 140 SD,A:Mark Midnight | 125.00 |
| 141 thru 145 | @100.00 |

## FOREIGN INTRIGUES
### See: DYNAMITE

## FOUR COLOR
**Dell Publishing Co., 1939**

| | |
|---|---|
| N# Dick Tracy | 10,000.00 |
| N# Don Winslow of the Navy | 2,500.00 |
| N# Myra North | 1,300.00 |
| 4 Disney's Donald Duck (1940) | 25,000.00 |
| 5 Smilin' Jack | 1,000.00 |
| 6 Dick Tracy | 2,300.00 |
| 7 Gang Busters | 600.00 |
| 8 Dick Tracy | 1,200.00 |
| 9 Terry and the Pirates | 1,000.00 |

| | |
|---|---|
| 10 Smilin' Jack | 900.00 |
| 11 Smitty | 600.00 |
| 12 Little Orphan Annie | 750.00 |
| 13 Walt Disney's Reluctant Dragon (1941) | 3,000.00 |
| 14 Moon Mullins | 600.00 |
| 15 Tillie the Toiler | 600.00 |
| 16 W.Disney's Mickey Mouse Outwits the Phantom Blob (1941) | 25,000.00 |
| 17 W.Disney's Dumbo the Flying Elephant (1941) | 5,000.00 |
| 18 Jiggs and Maggie | 600.00 |
| 19 Barney Google and Snuffy Smith | 600.00 |
| 20 Tiny Tim | 500.00 |
| 21 Dick Tracy | 1,000.00 |
| 22 Don Winslow | 550.00 |
| 23 Gang Busters | 500.00 |
| 24 Captain Easy | 700.00 |
| 25 Popeye | 1,200.00 |

### [Second Series, 1942]

| | |
|---|---|
| 1 Little Joe | 1,000.00 |
| 2 Harold Teen | 500.00 |
| 3 Alley Oop | 900.00 |
| 4 Smilin' Jack | 700.00 |
| 5 Raggedy Ann and Andy | 900.00 |
| 6 Smitty | 350.00 |
| 7 Smokey Stover | 500.00 |
| 8 Tillie the Toiler | 400.00 |
| 9 Donald Duck finds Pirate Gold! | 20,000.00 |
| 10 Flash Gordon | 1,600.00 |
| 11 Wash Tubs | 500.00 |
| 12 Bambi | 1,200.00 |
| 13 Mr. District Attorney | 500.00 |
| 14 Smilin' Jack | 600.00 |
| 15 Felix the Cat | 1,200.00 |
| 16 Porky Pig | 1,500.00 |
| 17 Popeye | 800.00 |
| 18 Little Orphan Annie's Junior Commandos | 650.00 |
| 19 W.Disney's Thumper meets the Seven Dwarfs | 1,200.00 |
| 20 Barney Baxter | 500.00 |
| 21 Oswald the Rabbit | 800.00 |
| 22 Tillie the Toiler | 300.00 |
| 23 Raggedy Ann and Andy | 600.00 |
| 24 Gang Busters | 500.00 |
| 25 Andy Panda | 900.00 |
| 26 Popeye | 800.00 |
| 27 Mickey Mouse and the Seven Colored Terror | 2,500.00 |
| 28 Wash Tubbs | 375.00 |
| 29 CB,Donald Duck and the Mummy's Ring | 12,000.00 |

| | |
|---|---|
| 30 Bambi's Children | 900.00 |
| 31 Moon Mullins | 300.00 |
| 32 Smitty | 250.00 |
| 33 Bugs Bunny | 1,800.00 |
| 34 Dick Tracy | 700.00 |
| 35 Smokey Stover | 275.00 |
| 36 Smilin' Jack | 400.00 |
| 37 Bringing Up Father | 350.00 |
| 38 Roy Rogers | 4,000.00 |
| 39 Oswald the Rabbit | 650.00 |
| 40 Barney Google and Snuffy Smith | 375.00 |
| 41 WK,Mother Goose | 375.00 |
| 42 Tiny Tim | 300.00 |
| 43 Popeye | 550.00 |
| 44 Terry and the Pirates | 600.00 |
| 45 Raggedy Ann | 550.00 |
| 46 Felix the Cat and the Haunted House | 700.00 |
| 47 Gene Autry | 750.00 |
| 48 CB,Porky Pig of the Mounties | 2,000.00 |
| 49 W.Disney's Snow White and the Seven Dwarfs | 1,400.00 |
| 50 WK,Fairy Tale Parade | 450.00 |
| 51 Bugs Bunny Finds the Lost Treasure | 600.00 |
| 52 Little Orphan Annie | 500.00 |
| 53 Wash Tubbs | 250.00 |
| 54 Andy Panda | 500.00 |
| 55 Tillie the Toiler | 250.00 |
| 56 Dick Tracy | 600.00 |
| 57 Gene Autry | 700.00 |
| 58 Smilin' Jack | 400.00 |
| 59 WK,Mother Goose | 350.00 |
| 60 Tiny Folks Funnies | 275.00 |
| 61 Santa Claus Funnies | 400.00 |
| 62 CB,Donald Duck in Frozen Gold | 3,000.00 |
| 63 Roy Rogers-photo (c) | 900.00 |
| 64 Smokey Stover | 225.00 |
| 65 Smitty | 225.00 |
| 66 Gene Autry | 700.00 |
| 67 Oswald the Rabbit | 300.00 |
| 68 WK,Mother Goose | 300.00 |
| 69 WK,Fairy Tale Parade | 400.00 |
| 70 Popeye and Wimpy | 450.00 |
| 71 WK,Walt Disney's Three Caballeros | 1,300.00 |
| 72 Raggedy Ann | 450.00 |
| 73 The Grumps | 250.00 |
| 74 Marge's Little Lulu | 1,800.00 |
| 75 Gene Autry and the Wildcat | 500.00 |
| 76 Little Orphan Annie | 400.00 |
| 77 Felix the Cat | 600.00 |
| 78 Porky Pig & the Bandit Twins | 700.00 |

All comics prices listed are for *Near Mint* condition.

Fo

*Four Color, 2nd Series #118*
*© Lone Ranger, Inc.*

*Four Color, 2nd Series #155*
*© King Features*

*Four Color, 2nd Series #182*
*© Warner Bros.*

79 Mickey Mouse in the Riddle
of the Red Hat . . . . . . . . . . 2,000.00
80 Smilin' Jack . . . . . . . . . . . . 300.00
81 Moon Mullins. . . . . . . . . . . . 200.00
82 Lone Ranger. . . . . . . . . . . . . 750.00
83 Gene Autry in Outlaw Trail . . . 500.00
84 Flash Gordon . . . . . . . . . . . . 750.00
85 Andy Panda and the
Mad Dog Mystery . . . . . . . . 300.00
86 Roy Rogers-photo (c) . . . . . . 600.00
87 WK,DNo(c),Fairy Tale Parade 400.00
88 Bugs Bunny . . . . . . . . . . . . . 375.00
89 Tillie the Toiler. . . . . . . . . . . . 250.00
90 WK,Christmas with
Mother Goose . . . . . . . . . . . 300.00
91 WK,Santa Claus Funnies . . . . 300.00
92 WK,W.Disney's Pinocchio . . 1,000.00
93 Gene Autry . . . . . . . . . . . . . 500.00
94 Winnie Winkle. . . . . . . . . . . . 200.00
95 Roy Rogers,Ph(c). . . . . . . . . 600.00
96 Dick Tracy. . . . . . . . . . . . . . 500.00
97 Marge's Little Lulu. . . . . . . . . 900.00
98 Lone Ranger. . . . . . . . . . . . . 600.00
99 Smitty . . . . . . . . . . . . . . . . . 200.00
100 Gene Autry Comics-photo(c) 500.00
101 Terry and the Pirates . . . . . . 500.00
102 WK,Oswald the Rabbit . . . . . 250.00
103 WK,Easter with
Mother Goose . . . . . . . . . . . 300.00
104 WK,Fairy Tale Parade. . . . . . 325.00
105 WK,Albert the Alligator. . . . 1,200.00
106 Tillie the Toiler. . . . . . . . . . . 200.00
107 Little Orphan Annie. . . . . . . . 350.00
108 Donald Duck in the
Terror of the River . . . . . . . 2,600.00
109 Roy Rogers Comics . . . . . . . 500.00
110 Marge's Little Lulu . . . . . . . . 600.00
111 Captain Easy. . . . . . . . . . . . 250.00
112 Porky Pig's Adventure in
Gopher Gulch . . . . . . . . . . . 600.00
113 Popeye . . . . . . . . . . . . . . . . 250.00
114 WK,Fairy Tale Parade. . . . . . 325.00
115 Marge's Little Lulu. . . . . . . . . 550.00
116 Mickey Mouse and the
House of Many Mysteries . . . 600.00
117 Roy Rogers Comics, Ph(c) . . 350.00
118 Lone Ranger. . . . . . . . . . . . . 500.00
119 Felix the Cat . . . . . . . . . . . . 550.00
120 Marge's Little Lulu . . . . . . . . 500.00
121 Fairy Tale Parade . . . . . . . . . 225.00
122 Henry . . . . . . . . . . . . . . . . . 250.00
123 Bugs Bunny's Dangerous
Venture . . . . . . . . . . . . . . . . 275.00
124 Roy Rogers Comics,Ph(c) . . 350.00
125 Lone Ranger. . . . . . . . . . . . . 350.00
126 WK,Christmas with

Mother Goose . . . . . . . . . . . 250.00
127 Popeye . . . . . . . . . . . . . . . . 250.00
128 WK,Santa Claus Funnies . . . 250.00
129 W.Disney's Uncle Remus
& His Tales of Brer Rabbit. . 500.00
130 Andy Panda . . . . . . . . . . . . 200.00
131 Marge's Little Lulu. . . . . . . . . 500.00
132 Tillie the Toiler. . . . . . . . . . . 200.00
133 Dick Tracy. . . . . . . . . . . . . . 350.00
134 Tarzan and the Devil Ogre. 1,100.00
135 Felix the Cat . . . . . . . . . . . . 400.00
136 Lone Ranger. . . . . . . . . . . . . 375.00
137 Roy Rogers Comics . . . . . . . 375.00
138 Smitty . . . . . . . . . . . . . . . . . 175.00
139 Marge's Little Lulu. . . . . . . . . 500.00
140 WK,Easter with
Mother Goose . . . . . . . . . . . 250.00
141 Mickey Mouse and the
Submarine Pirates. . . . . . . . 500.00
142 Bugs Bunny and the
Haunted Mountain . . . . . . . . 250.00
143 Oswald the Rabbit & the
Prehistoric Egg . . . . . . . . . 175.00
144 Poy Rogers Comics,Ph(c) . . 350.00
145 Popeye . . . . . . . . . . . . . . . . 250.00
146 Marge's Little Lulu. . . . . . . . . 475.00
147 W.Disney's Donald Duck
in Volcano Valley . . . . . . . 1,800.00
148 WK,Albert the Alligator
and Pogo Possum. . . . . . . . 950.00
149 Smilin' Jack. . . . . . . . . . . . . 175.00
150 Tillie the Toiler . . . . . . . . . . . 150.00
151 Lone Ranger. . . . . . . . . . . . . 325.00
152 Little Orphan Annie. . . . . . . . 250.00
153 Roy Rogers Comics . . . . . . . 325.00
154 Andy Panda . . . . . . . . . . . . 200.00
155 Henry . . . . . . . . . . . . . . . . . 200.00
156 Porky Pig and the Phantom . 600.00
157 W.Disney's Mickey Mouse
and the Beanstalk . . . . . . . . 500.00
158 Marge's Little Lulu. . . . . . . . . 500.00
159 CB,W.Disney's Donald Duck
in the Ghost of the Grotto . 3,000.00
160 Roy Rogers Comics,Ph(c) . . 350.00
161 Tarzan & the Fires of Tohr . . 900.00
162 Felix the Cat . . . . . . . . . . . . 300.00
163 Dick Tracy. . . . . . . . . . . . . . 300.00
164 Bugs Bunny Finds the
Frozen Kingdom . . . . . . . . . 275.00
165 Marge's Little Lulu. . . . . . . . . 500.00
166 Roy Rogers Comics,Ph(c) . . 325.00
167 Lone Ranger. . . . . . . . . . . . . 325.00
168 Popeye . . . . . . . . . . . . . . . . 250.00
169 Woody Woodpecker,Drug. . . 400.00
170 W.Disney's Mickey Mouse
on Spook's Island . . . . . . . . 350.00

171 Charlie McCarthy . . . . . . . . 450.00
172 WK,Christmas with
Mother Goose . . . . . . . . . . . 250.00
173 Flash Gordon . . . . . . . . . . . 300.00
174 Winnie Winkle . . . . . . . . . . . 150.00
175 WK,Santa Claus Funnies . . . 250.00
176 Tillie the Toiler. . . . . . . . . . . 150.00
177 Roy Rogers Comics,Ph(c) . . 325.00
178 CB,W.Disney's Donald
Duck Christmas on Bear
Mountain. . . . . . . . . . . . . 2,400.00
179 WK,Uncle Wiggily. . . . . . . . . 275.00
180 Ozark the Ike . . . . . . . . . . . 200.00
181 W.Disney's Mickey Mouse
in Jungle Magic. . . . . . . . . . 500.00
182 Porky Pig in Never-
Never Land . . . . . . . . . . . . . 600.00
183 Oswald the Rabbit . . . . . . . . 175.00
184 Tillie the Toiler. . . . . . . . . . . 175.00
185 WK,Easter with
Mother Goose . . . . . . . . . . . 250.00
186 W.Disney's Bambi. . . . . . . . . 300.00
187 Bugs Bunny and the
Dreadful Bunny . . . . . . . . . . 200.00
188 Woody Woodpecker . . . . . . . 200.00
189 W.Disney's Donald Duck in
The Old Castle's Secret . . . 1,500.00
190 Flash Gordon . . . . . . . . . . . 350.00
191 Porky Pig to the Rescue. . . . 500.00
192 WK,The Brownies. . . . . . . . . 250.00
193 Tom and Jerry. . . . . . . . . . . 350.00
194 W.Disney's Mickey Mouse
in the World Under the Sea. . 500.00
195 Tillie the Toiler. . . . . . . . . . . 125.00
196 Charlie McCarthy in The
Haunted Hide-Out . . . . . . . . 300.00
197 Spirit of the Border . . . . . . . 200.00
198 Andy Panda . . . . . . . . . . . . 200.00
199 W.Disney's Donald Duck in
Sheriff of Bullet Valley . . . . 1,600.00
200 Bugs Bunny, Super Sleuth . . 225.00
201 WK,Christmas with
Mother Goose . . . . . . . . . . . 200.00
202 Woody Woodpecker . . . . . . . 150.00
203 CB,W.Disney's Donald Duck in
The Golden Christmas Tree 1,400.00
204 Flash Gordon . . . . . . . . . . . 250.00
205 WK,Santa Claus Funnies . . . 275.00
206 Little Orphan Funnies . . . . . . 200.00
207 King of the Royal Mounted . . 250.00
208 W.Disney's Brer Rabbit
Does It Again. . . . . . . . . . . . 200.00
209 Harold Teen . . . . . . . . . . . . 100.00
210 Tippe and Cap Stubbs . . . . . 100.00
211 Little Beaver . . . . . . . . . . . . 150.00
212 Dr. Bobbs . . . . . . . . . . . . . . . 75.00

All comics prices listed are for *Near Mint* condition. **Page 123**

Four Color, 2nd Series #239
© Western Printing

Four Color, 2nd Series #287
© Gene Autry

Four Color, 2nd Series #300
© Walt Disney Co.

213 Tillie the Toiler . . . . . . . . . . . 125.00
214 W.Disney's Mickey Mouse
and his Sky Adventure . . . . . 400.00
215 Sparkle Plenty . . . . . . . . . . . 200.00
216 Andy Panda and the
Police Pup . . . . . . . . . . . . . . 150.00
217 Bugs Bunny in Court Jester . 200.00
218 W.Disney's 3 Little Pigs . . . . 225.00
219 Swee'pea . . . . . . . . . . . . . . 150.00
220 WK,Easter with
Mother Goose . . . . . . . . . . . 200.00
221 WK,Uncle Wiggly . . . . . . . . . 175.00
222 West of the Pecos . . . . . . . . 125.00
223 CB,W.Disney's Donald Duck in
Lost in the Andes . . . . . . . . 1,600.00
224 Little Iodine . . . . . . . . . . . . . 200.00
225 Oswald the Rabbit . . . . . . . . 125.00
226 Porky Pig and Spoofy . . . . . 400.00
227 W.Disney's Seven Dwarfs. . . 225.00
228 The Mark of Zorro . . . . . . . . 400.00
229 Smokey Stover . . . . . . . . . . 125.00
230 Sunset Press . . . . . . . . . . . 125.00
231 W.Disney's Mickey Mouse
and the Rajah's Treasure . . . 400.00
232 Woody Woodpecker . . . . . . . 125.00
233 Bugs Bunny . . . . . . . . . . . . 200.00
234 W.Disney's Dumbo in Sky
Voyage. . . . . . . . . . . . . . . . . 250.00
235 Tiny Tim . . . . . . . . . . . . . . . . 75.00
236 Heritage of the Desert . . . . . 125.00
237 Tillie the Toiler. . . . . . . . . . . 125.00
238 CB,W.Disney's Donald Duck
in Voodoo Hoodoo . . . . . . . 1,300.00
239 Adventure Bound . . . . . . . . . 90.00
240 Andy Panda . . . . . . . . . . . . . 125.00
241 Porky Pig . . . . . . . . . . . . . . 300.00
242 Tippie and Cap Stubbs . . . . . 90.00
243 W.Disney's Thumper
Follows his Nose. . . . . . . . . 200.00
244 WK,The Brownies. . . . . . . . . 175.00
245 Dick's Adventures in
Dreamland. . . . . . . . . . . . . . 100.00
246 Thunder Mountain. . . . . . . . . 75.00
247 Flash Gordon . . . . . . . . . . . 500.00
248 W.Disney's Mickey Mouse
and the Black Sorcerer . . . . 275.00
249 Woody Woodpecker . . . . . . . 150.00
250 Bugs Bunny in
Diamond Daze . . . . . . . . . . 200.00
251 Hubert at Camp Moonbeam . 100.00
252 W.Disney's Pinocchio . . . . . 225.00
253 WK,Christmas with
Mother Goose . . . . . . . . . . . 225.00
254 WK,Santa Claus Funnies,
A:Pogo. . . . . . . . . . . . . . . . . 250.00
255 The Ranger. . . . . . . . . . . . . 100.00

256 CB,W.Disney's Donald Duck in
Luck of the North . . . . . . . . 1,000.00
257 Little Iodine . . . . . . . . . . . . . 150.00
258 Andy Panda and the
Ballon Race . . . . . . . . . . . . 150.00
259 Santa and the Angel . . . . . . 100.00
260 Porky Pig, Hero of the
Wild West . . . . . . . . . . . . . . 250.00
261 W.Disney's Mickey Mouse
and the Missing Key . . . . . . 300.00
262 Raggedy Ann and Andy . . . . 150.00
263 CB,W.Disney's Donald Duck in
Land of the Totem Poles . . 1,000.00
264 Woody Woodpecker in
the Magic Lantern . . . . . . . . 150.00
265 King of the Royal Mountain . 150.00
266 Bugs Bunny on the Isle of
Hercules . . . . . . . . . . . . . . . 175.00
267 Little Beaver . . . . . . . . . . . . 300.00
268 W.Disney's Mickey Mouse's
Surprise Visitor . . . . . . . . . . 300.00
269 Johnny Mack Brown,Ph(c) . . 400.00
270 Drift Fence . . . . . . . . . . . . . 100.00
271 Porky Pig . . . . . . . . . . . . . . 250.00
272 W.Disney's Cinderella . . . . . 200.00
273 Oswald the Rabbit . . . . . . . . 100.00
274 Bugs Bunny . . . . . . . . . . . . 150.00
275 CB,W.Disney's Donald Duck
in Ancient Persia . . . . . . . . . 900.00
276 Uncle Wiggly . . . . . . . . . . . . 150.00
277 PorkyPig in DesertAdventure 250.00
278 Bill Elliot Comics,Ph(c) . . . . 250.00
279 W.Disney's Mickey Mouse &
Pluto Battle the Giant Ants . . 300.00
280 Andy Panda in the Isle
of the Mechanical Men . . . . 150.00
281 Bugs Bunny in The Great
Circus Mystery. . . . . . . . . . . 175.00
282 CB,W.Disney's Donald Duck in
The Pixilated Parrot. . . . . . . 900.00
283 King of the Royal Mounted . . 150.00
284 Porky Pig in the Kingdom
of Nowhere . . . . . . . . . . . . . 250.00
285 Bozo the Clown. . . . . . . . . . 350.00
286 W.Disney's Mickey Mouse
and the Uninvited Guest . . . . 300.00
287 Gene Autry's Champion in the
Ghost of BlackMountain,Ph(c)200.00
288 Woody Woodpecker . . . . . . . 150.00
289 BugsBunny in IndianTrouble. 175.00
290 The Chief . . . . . . . . . . . . . . 125.00
291 CB,W.Disney's Donald Duck in
The Magic Hourglass . . . . . 900.00
292 The Cisco Kid Comics . . . . . 450.00
293 WK,The Brownies. . . . . . . . . 175.00
294 Little Beaver . . . . . . . . . . . . . 75.00

295 Porky Pig in President Pig . . 250.00
296 W.Disney's Mickey Mouse
Private Eye for Hire . . . . . . . 200.00
297 Andy Panda in The
Haunted Inn. . . . . . . . . . . . . 150.00
298 Bugs Bunny in Sheik
for a Day . . . . . . . . . . . . . . . 175.00
299 Buck Jones & the Iron Trail . 250.00
300 CB,W.Disney's Donald Duck in
Big-Top Bedlam. . . . . . . . . . 900.00
301 The Mysterious Rider . . . . . 100.00
302 Santa Claus Funnies . . . . . . 100.00
303 Porky Pig in The Land of
the Monstrous Flies. . . . . . . 200.00
304 W.Disney's Mickey Mouse
in Tom-Tom Island . . . . . . . . 250.00
305 Woody Woodpecker . . . . . . . 100.00
306 Raggedy Ann . . . . . . . . . . . 100.00
307 Bugs Bunny in Lumber
Jack Rabbit . . . . . . . . . . . . . 150.00
308 CB,W.Disney's Donald Duck in
Dangerous Disguise . . . . . . 800.00
309 Dollface and Her Gang. . . . . 100.00
310 King of the Royal Mounted . 125.00
311 Porky Pig in Midget Horses
of Hidden Valley . . . . . . . . . 200.00
312 Tonto . . . . . . . . . . . . . . . . . 200.00
313 W.Disney's Mickey Mouse in
the Mystery of the Double-
Cross Ranch . . . . . . . . . . . . 250.00
314 Ambush. . . . . . . . . . . . . . . . . 75.00
315 Oswald Rabbit . . . . . . . . . . 100.00
316 Rex Allen,Ph(c). . . . . . . . . . 250.00
317 Bugs Bunny in Hare Today
Gone Tomorrow . . . . . . . . . 150.00
318 CB,W.Disney's Donald Duck in
No Such Varmint . . . . . . . . . 800.00
319 Gene Autry's Champion . . . . 100.00
320 Uncle Wiggly . . . . . . . . . . . . 150.00
321 Little Scouts . . . . . . . . . . . . . 75.00
322 Porky Pig in Roaring Rockies 150.00
323 Susie Q. Smith . . . . . . . . . . . 75.00
324 I Met a Handsome Cowboy . 150.00
325 W.Disney's Mickey Mouse
in the Haunted Castle . . . . . 250.00
326 Andy Panda . . . . . . . . . . . . . 75.00
327 Bugs Bunny and the
Rajah's Treasure . . . . . . . . . 150.00
328 CB,W.Disney's Donald Duck
in Old California. . . . . . . . . . 850.00
329 Roy Roger's Trigger,Ph(c) . . 275.00
330 Porky Pig meets the
Bristled Bruiser . . . . . . . . . . 150.00
331 Disney's Alice in
Wonderland . . . . . . . . . . . . . 275.00
332 Little Beaver . . . . . . . . . . . . . 75.00

# STANDARD GUIDE TO GOLDEN AGE COMICS

Four Color, 2nd Series #375
© Edgar Rice Burroughs, Inc.

Four Color, 2nd Series #387
© Walt Disney Co.

Four Color, 2nd Series #421
© Videofeatures

**Fo**

333 Wilderness Trek . . . . . . . . . . 75.00
334 W.Disney's Mickey Mouse
 and Yukon Gold . . . . . . . . . . 250.00
335 Francis the Famous
 Talking Mule . . . . . . . . . . . . 200.00
336 Woody Woodpecker . . . . . . . 100.00
337 The Brownies . . . . . . . . . . . . 100.00
338 Bugs Bunny and the
 Rocking Horse Thieves . . . . . 200.00
339 W.Disney's Donald Duck
 and the Magic Fountain . . . . . 400.00
340 King of the Royal Mountain . 150.00
341 W.Disney's Unbirthday Party
 with Alice in Wonderland . . . . 275.00
342 Porky Pig the Lucky
 Peppermint Mine . . . . . . . . . 150.00
343 W.Disney's Mickey Mouse in
 Ruby Eye of Homar-Guy-Am 150.00
344 Sergeant Preston from
 Challenge of the Yukon . . . . . 250.00
345 Andy Panda in Scotland Yard 100.00
346 Hideout . . . . . . . . . . . . . . . . 100.00
347 Bugs Bunny the Frigid Hare . 150.00
348 CB,W.Disney's Donald Duck
 The Crocodile Collector . . . . . 600.00
349 Uncle Wiggly . . . . . . . . . . . . 125.00
350 Woody Woodpecker . . . . . . 100.00
351 Porky Pig and the Grand
 Canyon Giant . . . . . . . . . . . . 150.00
352 W.Disney's Mickey Mouse
 Mystery of Painted Valley . . . 200.00
353 CB(c),W.Disney'sDuckAlbum 300.00
354 Raggedy Ann & Andy . . . . . . 100.00
355 Bugs Bunny Hot-Rod Hair . . 150.00
356 CB(c),W.Disney's Donald
 Duck in Rags to Riches . . . . . 500.00
357 Comeback . . . . . . . . . . . . . . . 75.00
358 Andy Panada . . . . . . . . . . . . 100.00
359 Frosty the Snowman . . . . . . . 150.00
360 Porky Pig in Tree Fortune . . 100.00
361 Santa Claus Funnies . . . . . . 100.00
362 W.Disney's Mickey Mouse &
 the Smuggled Diamonds . . . . 250.00
363 King of the Royal Mounted . . 125.00
364 Woody Woodpecker . . . . . . . . 90.00
365 The Brownies . . . . . . . . . . . . . 90.00
366 Bugs Bunny Uncle
 Buckskin Comes to Town . . . 150.00
367 CB,W.Disney's Donald Duck in
 A Christmas for Shacktown . . 900.00
368 Bob Clampett's
 Beany and Cecil . . . . . . . . . 500.00
369 Lone Ranger's Famous
 Horse Hi-Yo Silver . . . . . . . . 175.00
370 Porky Pig in Trouble
 in the Big Trees . . . . . . . . . . 150.00

371 W.Disney's Mickey Mouse
 the Inca Idol Case . . . . . . . . 200.00
372 Riders of the Purple Sage . . . 75.00
373 Sergeant Preston . . . . . . . . . 150.00
374 Woody Woodpecker . . . . . . . . 75.00
375 John Carter of Mars . . . . . . . 600.00
376 Bugs Bunny . . . . . . . . . . . . . 200.00
377 Susie Q. Smith . . . . . . . . . . . . 75.00
378 Tom Corbett, Space Cadet . . 325.00
379 W.Disney's Donald Duck in
 Southern Hospitality . . . . . . . 300.00
380 Raggedy Ann & Andy . . . . . . 100.00
381 Marge's Tubby . . . . . . . . . . . 350.00
382 W.Disney's Show White and
 the Seven Dwarfs . . . . . . . . . 200.00
383 Andy Panda . . . . . . . . . . . . . . 75.00
384 King of the Royal Mounted . . 100.00
385 Porky Pig . . . . . . . . . . . . . . . 100.00
386 CB,W.Disney's Uncle Scrooge
 in Only A Poor Old Man . . . 2,700.00
387 W.Disney's Mickey Mouse
 in High Tibet . . . . . . . . . . . . 200.00
388 Oswald the Rabbit . . . . . . . . 100.00
389 Andy Hardy Comics . . . . . . . . 75.00
390 Woody Woodpecker . . . . . . . . 75.00
391 Uncle Wiggly . . . . . . . . . . . . 125.00
392 Hi-Yo Silver . . . . . . . . . . . . . 100.00
393 Bugs Bunny . . . . . . . . . . . . . 150.00
394 CB(c),W.Disney's Donald Duck
 in Malayalaya . . . . . . . . . . . . 500.00
395 Forlorn River . . . . . . . . . . . . . 75.00
396 Tales of the Texas Rangers,
 Ph(c) . . . . . . . . . . . . . . . . . . 200.00
397 Sergeant Preston o/t Yukon . 150.00
398 The Brownies . . . . . . . . . . . . . 75.00
399 Porky Pig in the Lost
 Gold Mine . . . . . . . . . . . . . . 100.00
400 AMc,Tom Corbett . . . . . . . . . 200.00
401 W.Disney's Mickey Mouse &
 Goofy's Mechanical Wizard . . 150.00
402 Mary Jane and Sniffles . . . . . 100.00
403 W.Disney's Li'l Bad Wolf . . . . 150.00
404 The Ranger Rider,Ph(c) . . . . 200.00
405 Woody Woodpecker . . . . . . . . 75.00
406 Tweety and Sylvester . . . . . . 125.00
407 Bugs Bunny, Foreign-
 Legion Hare . . . . . . . . . . . . . 125.00
408 CB,W.Disney's Donald Duck
 and the Golden Helmet . . . . 750.00
409 Andy Panda . . . . . . . . . . . . . . 75.00
410 Porky Pig in the
 Water Wizard . . . . . . . . . . . . 100.00
411 W.Disney's Mickey Mouse
 and the Old Sea Dog . . . . . . 150.00
412 Nevada . . . . . . . . . . . . . . . . . . 75.00
413 Disney's Robin Hood(movie),

Ph(c) . . . . . . . . . . . . . . . . . . 200.00
414 Bob Clampett's Beany
 and Cecil . . . . . . . . . . . . . . . 250.00
415 Rootie Kazootie . . . . . . . . . . 175.00
416 Woody Woodpecker . . . . . . . . 75.00
417 Double Trouble with Goober . . 75.00
418 Rusty Riley . . . . . . . . . . . . . . . 75.00
419 Sergeant Preston . . . . . . . . . 150.00
420 Bugs Bunny . . . . . . . . . . . . . 125.00
421 AMc,Tom Corbett . . . . . . . . . 175.00
422 CB,W.Disney's Donald Duck
 and the Gilded Man . . . . . . . 750.00
423 Rhubarb . . . . . . . . . . . . . . . . 100.00
424 Flash Gordon . . . . . . . . . . . . 175.00
425 Zorro . . . . . . . . . . . . . . . . . . . 200.00
426 Porky Pig . . . . . . . . . . . . . . . 100.00
427 W.Disney's Mickey Mouse &
 the Wonderful Whizzix . . . . . . 150.00
428 Uncle Wiggily . . . . . . . . . . . . 100.00
429 W.Disney's Pluto in
 Why Dogs Leave Home . . . . 200.00
430 Marge's Tubby . . . . . . . . . . . 200.00
431 Woody Woodpecker . . . . . . . 100.00
432 Bugs Bunny and the
 Rabbit Olympics . . . . . . . . . . 125.00
433 Wildfire . . . . . . . . . . . . . . . . . . 75.00
434 Rin Tin Tin,Ph(c) . . . . . . . . . . 250.00
435 Frosty the Snowman . . . . . . . 100.00
436 The Brownies . . . . . . . . . . . . . 75.00
437 John Carter of Mars . . . . . . . 400.00
438 W.Disney's Annie
 Oakley (TV) . . . . . . . . . . . . . 275.00
439 Little Hiawatha . . . . . . . . . . . 100.00
440 Black Beauty . . . . . . . . . . . . . 75.00
441 Fearless Fagan . . . . . . . . . . . . 75.00
442 W.Disney's Peter Pan . . . . . . 175.00
443 Ben Bowie and His
 Mountain Men . . . . . . . . . . . 125.00
444 Marge's Tubby . . . . . . . . . . . 200.00
445 Charlie McCarthy . . . . . . . . . 100.00
446 Captain Hook and Peter Pan 150.00
447 Andy Hardy Comics . . . . . . . . 75.00
448 Beany and Cecil . . . . . . . . . . 275.00
449 Tappan's Burro . . . . . . . . . . . . 75.00
450 CB(c),W.Disney's Duck
 Album . . . . . . . . . . . . . . . . . 200.00
451 Rusty Riley . . . . . . . . . . . . . . . 65.00
452 Raggedy Ann and Andy . . . . 100.00
453 Susie Q. Smith . . . . . . . . . . . . 65.00
454 Krazy Kat Comics . . . . . . . . . . 65.00
455 Johnny Mack Brown Comics,
 Ph(c) . . . . . . . . . . . . . . . . . . 125.00
456 W.Disney's Uncle Scrooge
 Back to the Klondike . . . . . 1,500.00
457 Daffy . . . . . . . . . . . . . . . . . . . 150.00
458 Oswald the Rabbit . . . . . . . . . 75.00

All comics prices listed are for *Near Mint* condition.          **Page 125**

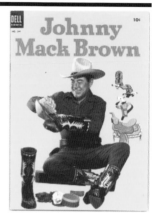

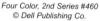

Four Color, 2nd Series #460
© Dell Publishing Co.

Four Color, 2nd Series #520
© S. Slesinger

Four Color, 2nd Series #541
© Johnny Mack Brown

459 Rootie Kazootie . . . . . . . . . 150.00
460 Buck Jones . . . . . . . . . . . . 175.00
461 Marge's Tubby . . . . . . . . . . 175.00
462 Little Scouts . . . . . . . . . . . . 50.00
463 Petunia . . . . . . . . . . . . . . . . 75.00
464 Bozo . . . . . . . . . . . . . . . . . 150.00
465 Francis the Talking Mule . . . . 100.00
466 Rhubarb, the Millionaire Cat . . 75.00
467 Desert Gold . . . . . . . . . . . . . 75.00
468 W.Disney's Goofy . . . . . . . . 300.00
469 Beetle Bailey . . . . . . . . . . . 175.00
470 Elmer Fudd . . . . . . . . . . . . 100.00
471 Double Trouble with Goober . . 40.00
472 Wild Bill Elliot,Ph(c). . . . . . . . 150.00
473 W.Disney's Li'l Bad Wolf . . . . . 75.00
474 Mary Jane and Sniffles . . . . . 125.00
475 M.G.M.'s the Two
      Mouseketeers . . . . . . . . . . 125.00
476 Rin Tin Tin,Ph(c). . . . . . . . . 150.00
477 Bob Clampett's Beany and
      Cecil. . . . . . . . . . . . . . . . . 275.00
478 Charlie McCarthy . . . . . . . . 100.00
479 Queen o/t West Dale Evans . 400.00
480 Andy Hardy Comics . . . . . . . 50.00
481 Annie Oakley and Tagg. . . . . 150.00
482 Brownies . . . . . . . . . . . . . . . 75.00
483 Little Beaver . . . . . . . . . . . . 75.00
484 River Feud . . . . . . . . . . . . . . 75.00
485 The Little People. . . . . . . . . 125.00
486 Rusty Riley . . . . . . . . . . . . . . 75.00
487 Mowgli, the Jungle Book. . . . 100.00
488 John Carter of Mars . . . . . . 350.00
489 Tweety and Sylvester . . . . . . 100.00
490 Jungle Jim . . . . . . . . . . . . . 125.00
491 EK,Silvertip . . . . . . . . . . . . 150.00
492 W.Disney's Duck Album . . . . 150.00
493 Johnny Mack Brown,Ph(c) . . 125.00
494 The Little King. . . . . . . . . . . 175.00
495 CB, W.Disney's Uncle
      Scrooge . . . . . . . . . . . . . 1,000.00
496 The Green Hornet. . . . . . . . 900.00
497 Zorro, (Sword of). . . . . . . . . 225.00
498 Bugs Bunny's Album . . . . . . 100.00
499 M.G.M.'s Spike and Tyke . . . . 90.00
500 Buck Jones . . . . . . . . . . . . 100.00
501 Francis the Famous
      Talking Mule . . . . . . . . . . . . 90.00
502 Rootie Kazootie . . . . . . . . . 135.00
503 Uncle Wiggily . . . . . . . . . . . . 90.00
504 Krazy Kat . . . . . . . . . . . . . . . 75.00
505 W.Disney's the Sword and
      the Rose (TV),Ph(c) . . . . . . 150.00
506 The Little Scouts . . . . . . . . . . 40.00
507 Oswald the Rabbit . . . . . . . . . 75.00
508 Bozo . . . . . . . . . . . . . . . . . 150.00
509 W.Disney's Pluto. . . . . . . . . 100.00

510 Son of Black Beauty . . . . . . . 60.00
511 EK,Outlaw Trail . . . . . . . . . . . 75.00
512 Flash Gordon . . . . . . . . . . . 125.00
513 Ben Bowie and His
      Mountain Men . . . . . . . . . . . 60.00
514 Frosty the Snowman. . . . . . . 100.00
515 Andy Hardy . . . . . . . . . . . . . 50.00
516 Double Trouble With Goober . 40.00
517 Walt Disney's Chip 'N' Dale . 200.00
518 Rivets . . . . . . . . . . . . . . . . . 50.00
519 Steve Canyon . . . . . . . . . . . 150.00
520 Wild Bill Elliot,Ph(c). . . . . . . . 125.00
521 Beetle Bailey. . . . . . . . . . . . 100.00
522 The Brownies . . . . . . . . . . . . 75.00
523 Rin Tin Tin,Ph(c). . . . . . . . . 150.00
524 Tweety and Sylvester . . . . . . . 90.00
525 Santa Claus Funnies . . . . . . 100.00
526 Napoleon. . . . . . . . . . . . . . . 50.00
527 Charlie McCarthy . . . . . . . . 100.00
528 Queen o/t West Dale Evans,
      Ph(c) . . . . . . . . . . . . . . . . 200.00
529 Little Beaver . . . . . . . . . . . . . 75.00
530 Bob Clampett's Beany
      and Cecil . . . . . . . . . . . . . 275.00
531 W.Disney's Duck Album . . . . 150.00
532 The Rustlers . . . . . . . . . . . . . 60.00
533 Raggedy Ann and Andy . . . . 100.00
534 EK,Western Marshal. . . . . . . 125.00
535 I Love Lucy,Ph(c). . . . . . . . 1,000.00
536 Daffy . . . . . . . . . . . . . . . . . 100.00
537 Stormy, the Thoroughbred . . . 75.00
538 EK,The Mask of Zorro . . . . . 250.00
539 Ben and Me . . . . . . . . . . . . . 75.00
540 Knights of the Round Table,
      Ph(c) . . . . . . . . . . . . . . . . 150.00
541 Johnny Mack Brown,Ph(c) . . 125.00
542 Super Circus Featuring
      Mary Hartline . . . . . . . . . . . 125.00
543 Uncle Wiggly. . . . . . . . . . . . 100.00
544 W.Disney's Rob Roy(Movie),
      Ph(c) . . . . . . . . . . . . . . . . 150.00
545 The Wonderful Adventures
      of Pinocchio. . . . . . . . . . . . 150.00
546 Buck Jones . . . . . . . . . . . . . 100.00
547 Francis the Famous
      Talking Mule . . . . . . . . . . . . 90.00
548 Krazy Kat . . . . . . . . . . . . . . . 75.00
549 Oswald the Rabbit . . . . . . . . . 75.00
550 The Little Scouts . . . . . . . . . . 40.00
551 Bozo . . . . . . . . . . . . . . . . . 150.00
552 Beetle Bailey. . . . . . . . . . . . 100.00
553 Susie Q. Smith . . . . . . . . . . . 50.00
554 Rusty Riley . . . . . . . . . . . . . . 60.00
555 Range War . . . . . . . . . . . . . . 60.00
556 Double Trouble with Goober . . 40.00

557 Ben Bowie and His
      Mountain Men . . . . . . . . . . . 60.00
558 Elmer Fudd . . . . . . . . . . . . . 75.00
559 I Love Lucy,Ph(c) . . . . . . . . 600.00
560 W.Disney's Duck Album . . . . 150.00
561 Mr. Magoo. . . . . . . . . . . . . . 200.00
562 W.Disney's Goofy . . . . . . . . 150.00
563 Rhubarb, the Millionaire Cat . 100.00
564 W.Disney's Li'l Bad Wolf . . . . 100.00
565 Jungle Jim . . . . . . . . . . . . . . 75.00
566 Son of Black Beauty . . . . . . . 60.00
567 BF,Prince Valiant,Ph(c). . . . . 250.00
568 Gypsy Cat . . . . . . . . . . . . . . 90.00
569 Priscilla's Pop . . . . . . . . . . . . 75.00
570 Bob Clampett's Beany
      and Cecil . . . . . . . . . . . . . 275.00
571 Charlie McCarthy . . . . . . . . 100.00
572 EK,Silvertip . . . . . . . . . . . . . 90.00
573 The Little People. . . . . . . . . 100.00
574 The Hand of Zorro . . . . . . . 225.00
575 Annie and Oakley and Tagg,
      Ph(c) . . . . . . . . . . . . . . . . 175.00
576 Angel. . . . . . . . . . . . . . . . . . 40.00
577 M.G.M.'s Spike and Tyke . . . . 60.00
578 Steve Canyon . . . . . . . . . . . . 90.00
579 Francis the Talking Mule. . . . . 75.00
580 Six Gun Ranch . . . . . . . . . . . 75.00
581 Chip 'N' Dale. . . . . . . . . . . . 100.00
582 Mowgli, the Jungle Book. . . . 100.00
583 The Lost Wagon Train . . . . . . 75.00
584 Johnny Mack Brown,Ph(c) . . 125.00
585 Bugs Bunny's Album. . . . . . . 100.00
586 W.Disney's Duck Album . . . . 160.00
587 The Little Scouts . . . . . . . . . . 50.00
588 MB,King Richard and the
      Crusaders,Ph(c) . . . . . . . . . 175.00
589 Buck Jones . . . . . . . . . . . . . 100.00
590 Hansel and Gretel. . . . . . . . 125.00
591 EK,Western Marshal. . . . . . . 100.00
592 Super Circus. . . . . . . . . . . . 125.00
593 Oswald the Rabbit . . . . . . . . . 60.00
594 Bozo . . . . . . . . . . . . . . . . . 160.00
595 Pluto . . . . . . . . . . . . . . . . . . 75.00
596 Turok, Son of Stone . . . . . . 1,000.00
597 The Little King. . . . . . . . . . . 100.00
598 Captain Davy Jones . . . . . . . 90.00
599 Ben Bowie and His
      Mountain Men . . . . . . . . . . . 75.00
600 Daisy Duck's Diary . . . . . . . 150.00
601 Frosty the Snowman. . . . . . . 100.00
602 Mr. Magoo and the Gerald
      McBoing-Boing . . . . . . . . . . 225.00
603 M.G.M.'s The Two
      Mouseketeers . . . . . . . . . . . 90.00
604 Shadow on the Trail . . . . . . . 75.00
605 The Brownies . . . . . . . . . . . . 75.00

Fo

*Four Color, 2nd Series #610*
© Dell Publishing Co.

*Four Color, 2nd Series #671*
© Walt Disney Co.

*Four Color, 2nd Series #716*
© Walt Disney Co.

606 Sir Lancelot . . . . . . . . . . . . . 150.00
607 Santa Claus Funnies . . . . . . 100.00
608 EK,Silver Tip . . . . . . . . . . . . 75.00
609 The Littlest Outlaw,Ph(c). . . . 125.00
610 Drum Beat,Ph(c) . . . . . . . . 175.00
611 W.Disney's Duck Album . . . . 150.00
612 Little Beaver . . . . . . . . . . . . . 65.00
613 EK,Western Marshal . . . . . . . 100.00
614 W.Disney's 20,000 Leagues
    Under the Sea (Movie) . . . . . 200.00
615 Daffy . . . . . . . . . . . . . . . . . 100.00
616 To The Last Man . . . . . . . . . . 75.00
617 The Quest of Zorro . . . . . . . . 225.00
618 Johnny Mack Brown,Ph(c) . . 125.00
619 Krazy Kat . . . . . . . . . . . . . . . 65.00
620 Mowgli, Jungle Book . . . . . . . 90.00
621 Francis the Famous
    Talking Mule . . . . . . . . . . . . . 65.00
622 Beetle Bailey . . . . . . . . . . . . 100.00
623 Oswald the Rabbit . . . . . . . . . 65.00
624 Treasure Island,Ph(c) . . . . . . 150.00
625 Beaver Valley . . . . . . . . . . . . 125.00
626 Ben Bowie and His
    Mountain Men . . . . . . . . . . . . 65.00
627 Goofy . . . . . . . . . . . . . . . . . 150.00
628 Elmer Fudd . . . . . . . . . . . . . . 65.00
629 Lady & The Tramp with Jock 150.00
630 Priscilla's Pop . . . . . . . . . . . 65.00
631 W.Disney's Davy Crockett
    Indian Fighter (TV),Ph(c). . . . 350.00
632 Fighting Caravans. . . . . . . . . . 65.00
633 The Little People. . . . . . . . . . . 65.00
634 Lady and the Tramp Album. . 100.00
635 Bob Clampett's Beany
    and Cecil . . . . . . . . . . . . . . . 300.00
636 Chip 'N' Dale. . . . . . . . . . . . . 100.00
637 EK,Silvertip . . . . . . . . . . . . . . 75.00
638 M.G.M.'s Spike and Tyke . . . . 50.00
639 W.Disney's Davy Crockett
    at the Alamo (TV),Ph(c). . . . . 275.00
640 EK,Western Marshal . . . . . . 100.00
641 Steve Canyon . . . . . . . . . . . . 110.00
642 M.G.M.'s The Two
    Mouseketeers . . . . . . . . . . . . 75.00
643 Wild Bill Elliott,Ph(c) . . . . . . . 65.00
644 Sir Walter Raleigh,Ph(c) . . . . 125.00
645 Johnny Mack Brown,Ph(c) . . 125.00
646 Dotty Dripple and Taffy . . . . . 60.00
647 Bugs Bunny's Album . . . . . . 100.00
648 Jace Pearson of the
    Texas Rangers,Ph(c) . . . . . . 100.00
649 Duck Album. . . . . . . . . . . . . 100.00
650 BF,Prince Valiant . . . . . . . . . 125.00
651 EK,King Colt . . . . . . . . . . . . . 60.00
652 Buck Jones . . . . . . . . . . . . . . 60.00
653 Smokey Bear . . . . . . . . 200.00

654 Pluto . . . . . . . . . . . . . . . . . . . 75.00
655 Francis the Famous
    Talking Mule . . . . . . . . . . . . . 75.00
656 Turok, Son of Stone . . . . . . . 550.00
657 Ben Bowie and His
    Mountain Men . . . . . . . . . . . . 60.00
658 Goofy . . . . . . . . . . . . . . . . . 150.00
659 Daisy Duck's Diary . . . . . . . . 125.00
660 Little Beaver . . . . . . . . . . . . . 65.00
661 Frosty the Snowman. . . . . . . 100.00
662 Zoo Parade. . . . . . . . . . . . . 100.00
663 Winky Dink . . . . . . . . . . . . . 150.00
664 W.Disney's Davy Crockett in
    the Great Keelboat
    Race (TV),Ph(c) . . . . . . . . . 300.00
665 The African Lion . . . . . . . . . . 100.00
666 Santa Claus Funnies . . . . . . 100.00
667 EK,Silvertip and the Stolen
    Stallion . . . . . . . . . . . . . . . . 100.00
668 W.Disney's Dumbo . . . . . . . 325.00
668a W.Disney's Dumbo . . . . . . 300.00
669 W.Disney's Robin Hood
    (Movie),Ph(c) . . . . . . . . . . . 100.00
670 M.G.M.'s Mouse Musketeers . 75.00
671 W.Disney's Davey Crockett &
    the River Pirates(TV),Ph(c). . 275.00
672 Quentin Durward,Ph(c) . . . . . 125.00
673 Buffalo Bill Jr.,Ph(c) . . . . . . . 125.00
674 The Little Rascals . . . . . . . . . 125.00
675 EK,Steve Donovan,Ph(c) . . . 150.00
676 Will-Yum!. . . . . . . . . . . . . . . . 50.00
677 Little King . . . . . . . . . . . . . . 100.00
678 The Last Hunt,Ph(c) . . . . . . . 150.00
679 Gunsmoke. . . . . . . . . . . . . . 350.00
680 Out Our Way with the
    Worry Wart . . . . . . . . . . . . . . 50.00
681 Forever, Darling,Lucile
    Ball Ph(c). . . . . . . . . . . . . . . 225.00
682 When Knighthood Was
    in Flower,Ph(c) . . . . . . . . . . 150.00
683 Hi and Lois . . . . . . . . . . . . . . 60.00
684 SB,Helen of Troy,Ph(c) . . . . . 200.00
685 Johnny Mack Brown,Ph(c) . . 150.00
686 Duck Album. . . . . . . . . . . . . 150.00
687 The Indian Fighter,Ph(c) . . . . 150.00
688 SB,Alexander the Great,
    Ph(c) . . . . . . . . . . . . . . . . . 150.00
689 Elmer Fudd . . . . . . . . . . . . . . 60.00
690 The Conqueror,
    John Wayne Ph(c). . . . . . . . 300.00
691 Dotty Dripple and Taffy . . . . . 50.00
692 The Little People. . . . . . . . . . . 60.00
693 W.Disney's Brer Rabbit
    Song of the South . . . . . . . . 175.00
694 Super Circus,Ph(c) . . . . . . . . 125.00
695 Little Beaver . . . . . . . . . . . . . 60.00

696 Krazy Kat . . . . . . . . . . . . . . . 60.00
697 Oswald the Rabbit . . . . . . . . . 60.00
698 Francis the Famous
    Talking Mule . . . . . . . . . . . . . 60.00
699 BA,Prince Valiant . . . . . . . . . 150.00
700 Water Birds and the
    Olympic Elk . . . . . . . . . . . . 100.00
701 Jimmy Cricket . . . . . . . . . . . 150.00
702 The Goofy Success Story . . . 135.00
703 Scamp. . . . . . . . . . . . . . . . . 175.00
704 Priscilla's Pop . . . . . . . . . . . . 60.00
705 Brave Eagle,Ph(c). . . . . . . . . 125.00
706 Bongo and Lumpjaw. . . . . . . 100.00
707 Corky and White Shadow,
    Ph(c) . . . . . . . . . . . . . . . . . 135.00
708 Smokey the Bear . . . . . . . . . 100.00
709 The Searchers,John
    Wayne Ph(c) . . . . . . . . . . . . 450.00
710 Francis the Famous
    Talking Mule . . . . . . . . . . . . . 60.00
711 M.G.M.'s Mouse Musketeers. . 50.00
712 The Great Locomotive
    Chase, Ph(c) . . . . . . . . . . . . 135.00
713 The Animal World . . . . . . . . . 60.00
714 W.Disney's Spin
    & Marty (TV) . . . . . . . . . . . . 250.00
715 Timmy . . . . . . . . . . . . . . . . . . 60.00
716 Man in Space . . . . . . . . . . . . 150.00
717 Moby Dick,Ph(c) . . . . . . . . . 150.00
718 Dotty Dripple and Taffy . . . . . 50.00
719 BF,Prince Valiant . . . . . . . . . 125.00
720 Gunsmoke,Ph(c). . . . . . . . . . 175.00
721 Captain Kangaroo,Ph(c) . . . . 300.00
722 Johnny Mack Brown,Ph(c) . . 125.00
723 EK,Santiago . . . . . . . . . . . . . 175.00
724 Bugs Bunny's Album. . . . . . . . 75.00
725 Elmer Fudd . . . . . . . . . . . . . . 50.00
726 Duck Album. . . . . . . . . . . . . 100.00
727 The Nature of Things . . . . . . 110.00
728 M.G.M.'s Mouse Musketeers . 50.00
729 Bob Son of Battle . . . . . . . . . 60.00
730 Smokey Stover . . . . . . . . . . . 75.00
731 EK,Silvertip and The
    Fighting Four . . . . . . . . . . . . . 75.00
732 Zorro, (the Challenge of) . . . 250.00
733 Buck Rogers . . . . . . . . . . . . . 65.00
734 Cheyenne,C.Walker Ph(c) . . . 300.00
735 Crusader Rabbit . . . . . . . . . . 550.00
736 Pluto . . . . . . . . . . . . . . . . . . . 75.00
737 Steve Canyon . . . . . . . . . . . 100.00
738 Westward Ho, the Wagons,
    Ph(c) . . . . . . . . . . . . . . . . . 200.00
739 MD,Bounty Guns . . . . . . . . . . 75.00
740 Chilly Willy . . . . . . . . . . . . . . 100.00
741 The Fastest Gun Alive,Ph(c). 150.00
742 Buffalo Bill Jr.,Ph(c) . . . . . . . 100.00

All comics prices listed are for *Near Mint* condition. **Page 127**

Fo

*Four Color, 2nd Series #760*
© Walt Disney Co.

*Four Color, 2nd Series #811*
© Dell Publishing Co.

*Four Color, 2nd Series #866*
© Walt Disney Co.

743 Daisy Duck's Diary . . . . . . . 110.00
744 Little Beaver . . . . . . . . . . . . . 65.00
745 Francis the Famous
    Talking Mule . . . . . . . . . . . . 65.00
746 Dotty Dripple and Taffy . . . . . 50.00
747 Goofy . . . . . . . . . . . . . . . . 135.00
748 Frosty the Snowman. . . . . . 100.00
749 Secrets of Life,Ph(c). . . . . . 100.00
750 The Great Cat . . . . . . . . . . 125.00
751 Our Miss Brooks,Ph(c) . . . . 150.00
752 Mandrake, the Magician . . . 175.00
753 Walt Scott's Little People . . . 75.00
754 Smokey the Bear . . . . . . . . 100.00
755 The Littlest Snowman . . . . . . 75.00
756 Santa Claus Funnies . . . . . 100.00
757 The True Story of
    Jesse James,Ph(c) . . . . . . . 175.00
758 Bear Country. . . . . . . . . . . 100.00
759 Circus Boy,Ph(c). . . . . . . . 250.00
760 W.Disney's Hardy Boys(TV) . 250.00
761 Howdy Doody . . . . . . . . . . 250.00
762 SB,The Sharkfighters,Ph(c) . 150.00
763 GrandmaDuck'sFarmFriends 150.00
764 M.G.M.'s Mouse Musketeers . 50.00
765 Will-Yum!. . . . . . . . . . . . . . . 50.00
766 Buffalo Bill,Ph(c). . . . . . . . 100.00
767 Spin and Marty . . . . . . . . . 175.00
768 EK,Steve Donovan, Western
    Marshal,Ph(c) . . . . . . . . . . 125.00
769 Gunsmoke. . . . . . . . . . . . . 200.00
770 Brave Eagle,Ph(c) . . . . . . . . 65.00
771 MD,Brand of Empire . . . . . . . 65.00
772 Cheyenne,C.Walker Ph(c) . . 150.00
773 The Brave One,Ph(c) . . . . . 100.00
774 Hi and Lois . . . . . . . . . . . . . 50.00
775 SB,Sir Lancelot and
    Brian,Ph(c). . . . . . . . . . . . 175.00
776 Johnny Mack Brown,Ph(c) . . 125.00
777 Scamp. . . . . . . . . . . . . . . . 135.00
778 The Little Rascals . . . . . . . . 100.00
779 Lee Hunter, Indian Fighter . . 100.00
780 Captain Kangaroo,Ph(c) . . . 250.00
781 Fury,Ph(c). . . . . . . . . . . . . 150.00
782 Duck Album. . . . . . . . . . . . 100.00
783 Elmer Fudd . . . . . . . . . . . . . 50.00
784 Around the World in 80
    Days,Ph(c). . . . . . . . . . . . 125.00
785 Circus Boys,Ph(c). . . . . . . . 250.00
786 Cinderella . . . . . . . . . . . . . 125.00
787 Little Hiawatha . . . . . . . . . . 100.00
788 BF,Prince Valiant. . . . . . . . 125.00
789 EK,Silvertip-Valley Thieves. . 100.00
790 ATh,The Wings of Eagles,
    J.Wayne Ph(c) . . . . . . . . . 300.00
791 The 77th Bengal Lancers,
    Ph(c) . . . . . . . . . . . . . . . . 150.00

792 Oswald the Rabbit . . . . . . . . 65.00
793 Morty Meekle . . . . . . . . . . . 50.00
794 SB,The Count of Monte
    Cristo. . . . . . . . . . . . . . . . 150.00
795 Jiminy Cricket . . . . . . . . . . 125.00
796 Ludwig Bemelman's
    Madeleine and Genevieve. . . 60.00
797 Gunsmoke,Ph(c). . . . . . . . 175.00
798 Buffalo Bill,Ph(c) . . . . . . . . 100.00
799 Priscilla's Pop . . . . . . . . . . . 60.00
800 The Buccaneers,Ph(c) . . . . 150.00
801 Dotty Dripple and Taffy . . . . 50.00
802 Goofy . . . . . . . . . . . . . . . . 150.00
803 Cheyenne,C.Walker Ph(c) . . 150.00
804 Steve Canyon . . . . . . . . . . 100.00
805 Crusader Rabbit . . . . . . . . . 450.00
806 Scamp. . . . . . . . . . . . . . . . 125.00
807 MB,Savage Range . . . . . . . . 65.00
808 Spin and Marty,Ph(c) . . . . . 175.00
809 The Little People. . . . . . . . . 75.00
810 Francis the Famous
    Talking Mule . . . . . . . . . . . . 65.00
811 Howdy Doody . . . . . . . . . . 200.00
812 The Big Land,A.Ladd Ph(c) . 200.00
813 Circus Boy,Ph(c) . . . . . . . . 225.00
814 Covered Wagon,A:Mickey
    Mouse . . . . . . . . . . . . . . . 125.00
815 Dragoon Wells Massacre . . 150.00
816 Brave Eagle,Ph(c). . . . . . . . 65.00
817 Little Beaver . . . . . . . . . . . . 65.00
818 Smokey the Bear . . . . . . . . 100.00
819 Mickey Mouse in Magicland . 100.00
820 The Oklahoman,Ph(c). . . . . 175.00
821 Wringle Wrangle,Ph(c) . . . . 150.00
822 ATh,W.Disney's Paul Revere's
    Ride (TV). . . . . . . . . . . . . . 175.00
823 Timmy . . . . . . . . . . . . . . . . 50.00
824 The Pride and the Passion,
    Ph(c) . . . . . . . . . . . . . . . . 150.00
825 The Little Rascals . . . . . . . . 100.00
826 Spin and Marty and Annette,
    Ph(c) . . . . . . . . . . . . . . . . 400.00
827 Smokey Stover . . . . . . . . . . 90.00
828 Buffalo Bill, Jr,Ph(c). . . . . . . 90.00
829 Tales of the Pony Express,
    Ph(c) . . . . . . . . . . . . . . . . . 90.00
830 The Hardy Boys,Ph(c) . . . . 175.00
831 No Sleep 'Til Dawn,Ph(c) . . 125.00
832 Lolly and Pepper. . . . . . . . . 65.00
833 Scamp. . . . . . . . . . . . . . . . 125.00
834 Johnny Mack Brown,Ph(c) . . 125.00
835 Silvertip- The Fake Rider . . . 90.00
836 Man in Fight . . . . . . . . . . . 135.00
837 All-American Athlete
    Cotton Woods . . . . . . . . . . . 55.00

838 Bugs Bunny's Life
    Story Album. . . . . . . . . . . . . 75.00
839 The Vigilantes . . . . . . . . . . 125.00
840 Duck Album . . . . . . . . . . . . 100.00
841 Elmer Fudd . . . . . . . . . . . . . 50.00
842 The Nature of Things . . . . . . 100.00
843 The First Americans . . . . . . 150.00
844 Gunsmoke,Ph(c). . . . . . . . 150.00
845 ATh,The Land Unknown . . . . 225.00
846 ATh,Gun Glory . . . . . . . . . . 175.00
847 Perri . . . . . . . . . . . . . . . . . . 90.00
848 Marauder's Moon . . . . . . . . . 55.00
849 BF,Prince Valiant. . . . . . . . 125.00
850 Buck Jones . . . . . . . . . . . . . 60.00
851 The Story of Mankind,
    V.Price Ph(c) . . . . . . . . . . . 135.00
852 Chilly Willy . . . . . . . . . . . . . 65.00
853 Pluto . . . . . . . . . . . . . . . . . . 75.00
854 Hunchback of Notre Dame,
    Ph(c) . . . . . . . . . . . . . . . . 225.00
855 Broken Arrow,Ph(c). . . . . . . 100.00
856 Buffalo Bill, Jr.,Ph(c) . . . . . . 100.00
857 The Goofy Adventure Story . 150.00
858 Daisy Duck's Diary . . . . . . . . 90.00
859 Topper and Neil. . . . . . . . . . 80.00
860 Wyatt Earp,Ph(c) . . . . . . . . 175.00
861 Frosty the Snowman. . . . . . . 75.00
862 Truth About Mother Goose . . 135.00
863 Francis the Famous
    Talking Mule . . . . . . . . . . . . 60.00
864 The Littlest Snowman . . . . . . 75.00
865 Andy Burnett,Ph(c) . . . . . . . 175.00
866 Mars and Beyond . . . . . . . . 150.00
867 Santa Claus Funnies . . . . . 100.00
868 The Little People. . . . . . . . . 90.00
869 Old Yeller,Ph(c). . . . . . . . . 110.00
870 Little Beaver . . . . . . . . . . . . 65.00
871 Curly Kayoe . . . . . . . . . . . . 50.00
872 Captain Kangaroo,Ph(c) . . . 235.00
873 Grandma Duck's
    Farm Friends . . . . . . . . . . . . 90.00
874 Old Ironsides. . . . . . . . . . . 125.00
875 Trumpets West . . . . . . . . . . 60.00
876 Tales of Wells Fargo,Ph(c) . . 175.00
877 ATh,Frontier Doctor,Ph(c) . . . 175.00
878 Peanuts. . . . . . . . . . . . . . . 275.00
879 Brave Eagle,Ph(c). . . . . . . . 60.00
880 MD,Steve Donovan,Ph(c) . . . 75.00
881 The Captain and the Kids . . . 60.00
882 ATh,W.DisneyPresentsZorro. 275.00
883 The Little Rascals . . . . . . . . 100.00
884 Hawkeye and the Last
    of the Mohicans,Ph(c) . . . . . 135.00
885 Fury,Ph(c) . . . . . . . . . . . . . 125.00
886 Bongo and Lumpjaw. . . . . . . 90.00
887 The Hardy Boys,Ph(c) . . . . 175.00

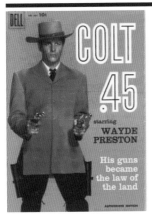

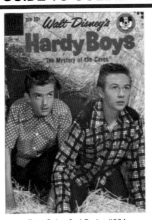

Fo

*Four Color, 2nd Series #924*
© Dell Publishing Co.

*Four Color, 2nd Series #964*
© Walt Disney Co.

*Four Color, 2nd Series #1010*
© Walt Disney Co.

888 Elmer Fudd . . . . . . . . . . . . . . 50.00
889 ATh,W.Disney's Clint
   & Mac(TV),Ph(c) . . . . . . . . . 225.00
890 Wyatt Earp,Ph(c) . . . . . . . . 135.00
891 Light in the Forest,
   C.Parker,Ph(c). . . . . . . . . . . 135.00
892 Maverick,J.Garner Ph(c). . . . 450.00
893 Jim Bowie,Ph(c) . . . . . . . . . 100.00
894 Oswald the Rabbit . . . . . . . . 60.00
895 Wagon Train,Ph(c) . . . . . . . 200.00
896 Adventures of Tinker Bell . . 150.00
897 Jiminy Cricket . . . . . . . . . . 125.00
898 EK,Silvertip . . . . . . . . . . . . . 90.00
899 Goofy . . . . . . . . . . . . . . . . . 100.00
900 BF,Prince Valiant . . . . . . . . 125.00
901 Little Hiawatha . . . . . . . . . . . 90.00
902 Will-Yum! . . . . . . . . . . . . . . . 60.00
903 Dotty Dripple and Taffy . . . . . 50.00
904 Lee Hunter, Indian Fighter . . . 60.00
905 W.Disney's Annette (TV),
   Ph(c) . . . . . . . . . . . . . . . . . 500.00
906 Francis the Famous
   Talking Mule . . . . . . . . . . . . . 60.00
907 Ath,Sugarfoot,Ph(c). . . . . . . 235.00
908 The Little People
   and the Giant. . . . . . . . . . . . . 75.00
909 Smitty . . . . . . . . . . . . . . . . . . 60.00
910 ATh,The Vikings,
   K.Douglas Ph(c) . . . . . . . . . 150.00
911 The Gray Ghost,Ph(c). . . . . . 150.00
912 Leave it to Beaver,Ph(c) . . . . 300.00
913 The Left-Handed Gun,
   Paul Newman Ph(c) . . . . . . . 175.00
914 ATh,No Time for Sergeants,
   Ph(c) . . . . . . . . . . . . . . . . . 175.00
915 Casey Jones,Ph(c) . . . . . . . . 100.00
916 Red Ryder Ranch Comics . . . 90.00
917 The Life of Riley,Ph(c) . . . . . 225.00
918 Beep Beep, the Roadrunner. 200.00
919 Boots and Saddles,Ph(c) . . . 135.00
920 Ath,Zorro,Ph(c) . . . . . . . . . 225.00
921 Wyatt Earp,Ph(c) . . . . . . . . . 135.00
922 Johnny Mack Brown,Ph(c) . . 135.00
923 Timmy . . . . . . . . . . . . . . . . . 50.00
924 Colt .45,Ph(c) . . . . . . . . . . . 175.00
925 Last of the Fast Guns,Ph(c) . 135.00
926 Peter Pan . . . . . . . . . . . . . . . 75.00
927 SB,Top Gun . . . . . . . . . . . . . 60.00
928 Sea Hunt,L.Bridges Ph(c) . . 225.00
929 Brave Eagle,Ph(c) . . . . . . . . . 60.00
930 Maverick,J. Garner Ph(c) . . . 200.00
931 Have Gun, Will Travel,Ph(c) . 250.00
932 Smokey the Bear . . . . . . . . . 100.00
933 ATh,W.Disney's Zorro . . . . . 225.00
934 Restless Gun . . . . . . . . . . . 225.00
935 King of the Royal Mounted . . . 65.00

936 The Little Rascals . . . . . . . . 100.00
937 Ruff and Ready. . . . . . . . . . . 225.00
938 Elmer Fudd . . . . . . . . . . . . . 60.00
939 Steve Canyon . . . . . . . . . . . . 90.00
940 Lolly and Pepper . . . . . . . . . 50.00
941 Pluto . . . . . . . . . . . . . . . . . . 60.00
942 Pony Express . . . . . . . . . . . . 90.00
943 White Wilderness . . . . . . . . . 125.00
944 SB,7th Voyage of Sinbad . . . 250.00
945 Maverick,J.Garner Ph(c). . . . 250.00
946 The Big Country,Ph(c) . . . . . 150.00
947 Broken Arrow,Ph(c). . . . . . . . 90.00
948 Daisy Duck's Diary . . . . . . . . 90.00
949 High Adventure,Ph(c) . . . . . . 90.00
950 Frosty the Snowman . . . . . . . 75.00
951 ATh,Lennon Sisters
   Life Story,Ph(c) . . . . . . . . . . 250.00
952 Goofy . . . . . . . . . . . . . . . . . . 90.00
953 Francis the Famous
   Talking Mule . . . . . . . . . . . . . 60.00
954 Man in Space . . . . . . . . . . . 135.00
955 Hi and Lois . . . . . . . . . . . . . . 50.00
956 Ricky Nelson,Ph(c). . . . . . . . 350.00
957 Buffalo Bee . . . . . . . . . . . . . 175.00
958 Santa Claus Funnies . . . . . . . 90.00
959 Christmas Stories . . . . . . . . . 75.00
960 ATh,W.Disney's Zorro . . . . . 225.00
961 Jace Pearson's Tales of
   Texas Rangers,Ph(c). . . . . . . 90.00
962 Maverick,J.Garner Ph(c) . . . 200.00
963 Johnny Mack Brown,Ph(c) . . 125.00
964 The Hardy Boys,Ph(c) . . . . . 175.00
965 GrandmaDuck'sFarmFriends . 90.00
966 Tonka,Ph(c). . . . . . . . . . . . . 150.00
967 Chilly Willy . . . . . . . . . . . . . . 60.00
968 Tales of Wells Fargo,Ph(c) . . 150.00
969 Peanuts. . . . . . . . . . . . . . . . 200.00
970 Lawman,Ph(c). . . . . . . . . . . 225.00
971 Wagon Train,Ph(c) . . . . . . . 125.00
972 Tom Thumb. . . . . . . . . . . . . 175.00
973 SleepingBeauty & the Prince 200.00
974 The Little Rascals . . . . . . . . 125.00
975 Fury,Ph(c) . . . . . . . . . . . . . . 125.00
976 ATh,W.Disney's Zorro,Ph(c) . 200.00
977 Elmer Fudd . . . . . . . . . . . . . 50.00
978 Lolly and Pepper. . . . . . . . . . 50.00
979 Oswald the Rabbit . . . . . . . . 60.00
980 Maverick,J.Garner Ph(c). . . . 200.00
981 Ruff and Ready. . . . . . . . . . . 150.00
982 The New Adventures of
   Tinker Bell . . . . . . . . . . . . . . 150.00
983 Have Gun, Will Travel,Ph(c) . 175.00
984 Sleeping Beauty's Fairy
   Godmothers, . . . . . . . . . . . . 165.00
985 Shaggy Dog,Ph(c) . . . . . . . . 150.00
986 Restless Gun,Ph(c). . . . . . . . 150.00

987 Goofy . . . . . . . . . . . . . . . . . . 90.00
988 Little Hiawatha . . . . . . . . . . . 90.00
989 Jimmy Cricket . . . . . . . . . . . 125.00
990 Huckleberry Hound . . . . . . . 235.00
991 Francis the Famous
   Talking Mule . . . . . . . . . . . . . 60.00
992 ATh,Sugarfoot,Ph(c) . . . . . . 200.00
993 Jim Bowie,Ph(c) . . . . . . . . . . 90.00
994 Sea HuntL.Bridges Ph(c) . . . 150.00
995 Donald Duck Album . . . . . . . 125.00
996 Nevada . . . . . . . . . . . . . . . . . 60.00
997 Walt Disney Presents,Ph(c) . 150.00
998 Ricky Nelson,Ph(c) . . . . . . . . 350.00
999 Leave It To Beaver,Ph(c) . . . 300.00
1000 The Gray Ghost,Ph(c). . . . . 150.00
1001 Lowell Thomas' High
   Adventure,Ph(c). . . . . . . . . . . 90.00
1002 Buffalo Bee . . . . . . . . . . . . 125.00
1003 ATh,W.Disney's Zorro,Ph(c) 200.00
1004 Colt .45,Ph(c) . . . . . . . . . . 150.00
1005 Maverick,J.Garner Ph(c). . . 200.00
1006 SB,Hercules . . . . . . . . . . . 175.00
1007 John Paul Jones,Ph(c) . . . . 90.00
1008 Beep, Beep, the
   Road Runner. . . . . . . . . . . . . 90.00
1009 CB,The Rifleman,Ph(c) . . . 450.00
1010 Grandma Duck's Farm
   Friends. . . . . . . . . . . . . . . . 225.00
1011 Buckskin,Ph(c) . . . . . . . . . 150.00
1012 Last Train from Gun
   Hill,Ph(c) . . . . . . . . . . . . . . 155.00
1013 Bat Masterson,Ph(c). . . . . . 225.00
1014 ATh,The Lennon Sisters,
   Ph(c) . . . . . . . . . . . . . . . . . 250.00
1015 Peanuts. . . . . . . . . . . . . . . 200.00
1016 Smokey the Bear . . . . . . . . 75.00
1017 Chilly Willy . . . . . . . . . . . . . 60.00
1018 Rio Bravo,J.Wayne Ph(c) . . 400.00
1019 Wagon Train,Ph(c) . . . . . . 125.00
1020 Jungle . . . . . . . . . . . . . . . . 60.00
1021 Jace Pearson's Tales of
   the Texas Rangers,Ph(c). . . . 90.00
1022 Timmy . . . . . . . . . . . . . . . . 50.00
1023 Tales of Wells Fargo,Ph(c) . 150.00
1024 ATh,Darby O'Gill and
   the Little People,Ph(c). . . . . 175.00
1025 CB,W.Disney's Vacation in
   Disneyland. . . . . . . . . . . . . 350.00
1026 Spin and Marty,Ph(c) . . . . . 135.00
1027 The Texan,Ph(c) . . . . . . . . 150.00
1028 Rawhide,
   Clint Eastwood Ph(c). . . . . . 425.00
1029 Boots and Saddles,Ph(c) . . 100.00
1030 Spanky and Alfalfa, the
   Little Rascals . . . . . . . . . . 100.00
1031 Fury,Ph(c) . . . . . . . . . . . . . 125.00

All comics prices listed are for *Near Mint* condition.

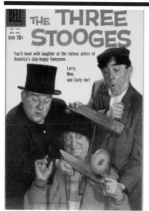

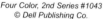

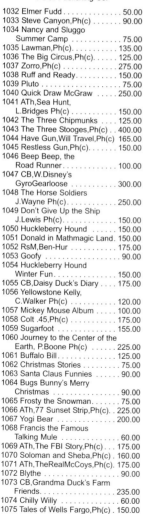

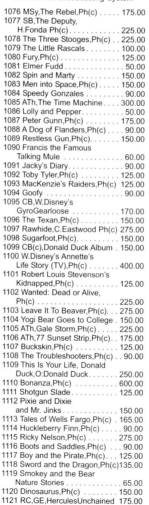

*Four Color, 2nd Series #1043*
© Dell Publishing Co.

*Four Color, 2nd Series #1097*
© Columbia Broadcasting System

*Four Color, 2nd Series #1166*
© P. A. T. Ward

1032 Elmer Fudd . . . . . . . . . . . . . 50.00
1033 Steve Canyon,Ph(c) . . . . . . . 90.00
1034 Nancy and Sluggo
      Summer Camp . . . . . . . . . . 75.00
1035 Lawman,Ph(c). . . . . . . . . . . 135.00
1036 The Big Circus,Ph(c). . . . . 125.00
1037 Zorro,Ph(c) . . . . . . . . . . . . . 275.00
1038 Ruff and Ready . . . . . . . . . 150.00
1039 Pluto . . . . . . . . . . . . . . . . . . 75.00
1040 Quick Draw McGraw . . . . . 250.00
1041 ATh,Sea Hunt,
      L.Bridges Ph(c) . . . . . . . . . 150.00
1042 The Three Chipmunks . . . . 125.00
1043 The Three Stooges,Ph(c) . . 400.00
1044 Have Gun,Will Travel,Ph(c) 165.00
1045 Restless Gun,Ph(c). . . . . . . 150.00
1046 Beep Beep, the
      Road Runner. . . . . . . . . . . . 100.00
1047 CB,W.Disney's
      GyroGearloose . . . . . . . . . . 300.00
1048 The Horse Soldiers
      J.Wayne Ph(c) . . . . . . . . . . 250.00
1049 Don't Give Up the Ship
      J.Lewis Ph(c). . . . . . . . . . . . 150.00
1050 Huckleberry Hound . . . . . . 100.00
1051 Donald in Mathmagic Land . 150.00
1052 RsM,Ben-Hur . . . . . . . . . . 175.00
1053 Goofy . . . . . . . . . . . . . . . . . . 90.00
1054 Huckleberry Hound
      Winter Fun. . . . . . . . . . . . . . 150.00
1055 CB,Daisy Duck's Diary . . . . 175.00
1056 Yellowstone Kelly,
      C.Walker Ph(c) . . . . . . . . . . 120.00
1057 Mickey Mouse Album . . . . . 100.00
1058 Colt .45,Ph(c) . . . . . . . . . . . 175.00
1059 Sugarfoot . . . . . . . . . . . . . . 155.00
1060 Journey to the Center of the
      Earth, P.Boone Ph(c) . . . . . 225.00
1061 Buffalo Bill. . . . . . . . . . . . . . 125.00
1062 Christmas Stories . . . . . . . . 75.00
1063 Santa Claus Funnies . . . . . 90.00
1064 Bugs Bunny's Merry
      Christmas . . . . . . . . . . . . . . 90.00
1065 Frosty the Snowman. . . . . . 75.00
1066 ATh,77 Sunset Strip,Ph(c). . 225.00
1067 Yogi Bear . . . . . . . . . . . . . . 200.00
1068 Francis the Famous
      Talking Mule . . . . . . . . . . . . 60.00
1069 ATh,The FBI Story,Ph(c) . . . 175.00
1070 Soloman and Sheba,Ph(c) . 160.00
1071 ATh,TheRealMcCoys,Ph(c). 175.00
1072 Blythe . . . . . . . . . . . . . . . . . . 90.00
1073 CB,Grandma Duck's Farm
      Friends. . . . . . . . . . . . . . . . . 235.00
1074 Chilly Willy . . . . . . . . . . . . . 60.00
1075 Tales of Wells Fargo,Ph(c) . 150.00

1076 MSy,The Rebel,Ph(c) . . . . . 175.00
1077 SB,The Deputy,
      H.Fonda Ph(c). . . . . . . . . . . 225.00
1078 The Three Stooges,Ph(c) . . 225.00
1079 The Little Rascals . . . . . . . 100.00
1080 Fury,Ph(c) . . . . . . . . . . . . . . 125.00
1081 Elmer Fudd . . . . . . . . . . . . . 50.00
1082 Spin and Marty . . . . . . . . . . 150.00
1083 Men into Space,Ph(c) . . . . . 150.00
1084 Speedy Gonzales . . . . . . . . 90.00
1085 ATh,The Time Machine. . . . 300.00
1086 Lolly and Pepper. . . . . . . . . 50.00
1087 Peter Gunn,Ph(c) . . . . . . . . 175.00
1088 A Dog of Flanders,Ph(c) . . . 90.00
1089 Restless Gun,Ph(c). . . . . . . 150.00
1090 Francis the Famous
      Talking Mule . . . . . . . . . . . . 60.00
1091 Jacky's Diary. . . . . . . . . . . . 90.00
1092 Toby Tyler . . . . . . . . . . . . . . 125.00
1093 MacKenzie's Raiders,Ph(c) 125.00
1094 Goofy . . . . . . . . . . . . . . . . . . 90.00
1095 CB,W.Disney's
      GyroGearloose . . . . . . . . . . 170.00
1096 The Texan,Ph(c) . . . . . . . . . 150.00
1097 Rawhide,C.Eastwood Ph(c) 275.00
1098 Sugarfoot,Ph(c). . . . . . . . . . 150.00
1099 CB(c),Donald Duck Album . 150.00
1100 W.Disney's Annette's
      Life Story (TV),Ph(c) . . . . . . 400.00
1101 Robert Louis Stevenson's
      Kidnapped,Ph(c) . . . . . . . . . 125.00
1102 Wanted: Dead or Alive,
      Ph(c) . . . . . . . . . . . . . . . . . . 225.00
1103 Leave It To Beaver,Ph(c). . . 275.00
1104 Yogi Bear Goes to College . 150.00
1105 ATh,Gale Storm,Ph(c) . . . . 225.00
1106 ATh,77 Sunset Strip,Ph(c). . 175.00
1107 Buckskin,Ph(c) . . . . . . . . . . 125.00
1108 The Troubleshooters,Ph(c) . . 90.00
1109 This Is Your Life, Donald
      Duck,O:Donald Duck. . . . . . 250.00
1110 Bonanza,Ph(c) . . . . . . . . . . 600.00
1111 Shotgun Slade . . . . . . . . . . 125.00
1112 Pixie and Dixie
      and Mr. Jinks . . . . . . . . . . . 150.00
1113 Tales of Wells Fargo,Ph(c) . 165.00
1114 Huckleberry Finn,Ph(c) . . . . 90.00
1115 Ricky Nelson,Ph(c) . . . . . . . 275.00
1116 Boots and Saddles,Ph(c) . . . 90.00
1117 Boy and the Pirate,Ph(c). . . 125.00
1118 Sword and the Dragon,Ph(c)135.00
1119 Smokey and the Bear
      Nature Stories . . . . . . . . . . . 65.00
1120 Dinosaurus,Ph(c) . . . . . . . . 150.00
1121 RC,GE,HerculesUnchained 175.00
1122 Chilly Willy. . . . . . . . . . . . . . 60.00

1123 Tombstone Territory,Ph(c) . . 175.00
1124 Whirlybirds,Ph(c). . . . . . . . . 165.00
1125 GK,RH,Laramie,Ph(c) . . . . 175.00
1126 Sundance,Ph(c) . . . . . . . . . 125.00
1127 The Three Stooges,Ph(c) . . 225.00
1128 Rocky and His Friends . . . . 600.00
1129 Pollyanna,H.Mills Ph(c). . . . 135.00
1130 SB,The Deputy,
      H.Fonda Ph(c) . . . . . . . . . . 175.00
1131 Elmer Fudd . . . . . . . . . . . . . 50.00
1132 Space Mouse . . . . . . . . . . . . 75.00
1133 Fury,Ph(c) . . . . . . . . . . . . . . 125.00
1134 ATh,Real McCoys,Ph(c) . . . 175.00
1135 M.G.M.'s Mouse Musketeers. 90.00
1136 Jungle Cat,Ph(c) . . . . . . . . . 120.00
1137 The Little Rascals . . . . . . . . 90.00
1138 The Rebel,Ph(c) . . . . . . . . . 165.00
1139 SB,Spartacus,Ph(c). . . . . . . 225.00
1140 Donald Duck Album . . . . . . 150.00
1141 Huckleberry Hound for
      President . . . . . . . . . . . . . . . 150.00
1142 Johnny Ringo,Ph(c) . . . . . . 135.00
1143 Pluto . . . . . . . . . . . . . . . . . . . 60.00
1144 The Story of Ruth,Ph(c) . . . 150.00
1145 GK,The Lost World,Ph(c) . . 175.00
1146 Restless Gun,Ph(c). . . . . . . 135.00
1147 Sugarfoot,Ph(c). . . . . . . . . . 150.00
1148 I aim at the Stars,Ph(c) . . . . 135.00
1149 Goofy . . . . . . . . . . . . . . . . . . 90.00
1150 CB,Daisy Duck's Diary . . . . 200.00
1151 Mickey Mouse Album . . . . . 60.00
1152 Rocky and His Friends . . . . 400.00
1153 Frosty the Snowman. . . . . . . 90.00
1154 Santa Claus Funnies. . . . . . 175.00
1155 North to Alaska . . . . . . . . . . 275.00
1156 Walt Disney Swiss
      Family Robinson . . . . . . . . . 135.00
1157 Master of the World. . . . . . . . 90.00
1158 Three Worlds of Gulliver . . . 125.00
1159 ATh,77 Sunset Strip . . . . . . 170.00
1160 Rawhide . . . . . . . . . . . . . . . 250.00
1161 CB,Grandma Duck's
      Farm Friends. . . . . . . . . . . . 225.00
1162 Yogi Bera joins the Marines 135.00
1163 Daniel Boone . . . . . . . . . . . . 90.00
1164 Wanted: Dead or Alive . . . . 175.00
1165 Ellery Queen . . . . . . . . . . . . 200.00
1166 Rocky and His Friends . . . . 375.00
1167 Tales of Wells Fargo,Ph(c) . 135.00
1168 The Detectives,
      R.Taylor Ph(c) . . . . . . . . . . . 175.00
1169 New Adventures of
      Sherlock Holmes . . . . . . . . . 275.00
1170 The Three Stooges,Ph(c) . . 225.00
1171 Elmer Fudd . . . . . . . . . . . . . 50.00
1172 Fury,Ph(c) . . . . . . . . . . . . . . 125.00

All comics prices listed are for *Near Mint* condition.

Fo

*Four Color, 2nd Series #1191*
© Gomalco Productions

*Four Color, 2nd Series #1237*
© Dell Publishing Co.

*Four Color, 2nd Series #1275*
© P. A. T. Ward

1173 The Twilight Zone . . . . . . . 400.00
1174 The Little Rascals . . . . . . . . 75.00
1175 M.G.M.'s Mouse Musketeers . 45.00
1176 Dondi,Ph(c) . . . . . . . . . . . . 75.00
1177 Chilly Willy . . . . . . . . . . . . . 60.00
1178 Ten Who Dared . . . . . . . . . 135.00
1179 The Swamp Fox,
 L.Nielson Ph(c) . . . . . . . . . . 150.00
1180 The Danny Thomas Show . 275.00
1181 Texas John Slaughter,Ph(c) 135.00
1182 Donald Duck Album . . . . . . 100.00
1183 101 Dalmatians . . . . . . . . . 175.00
1184 CB,W.Disney's
 Gyro Gearloose . . . . . . . . . . 165.00
1185 Sweetie Pie . . . . . . . . . . . . 75.00
1186 JDa,Yak Yak . . . . . . . . . . . 145.00
1187 The Three Stooges,Ph(c) . . 200.00
1188 Atlantis the Lost
 Continent,Ph(c) . . . . . . . . . 200.00
1189 Greyfriars Bobby,Ph(c) . . . 135.00
1190 CB(c),Donald and
 the Wheel . . . . . . . . . . . . . . 135.00
1191 Leave It to Beaver,Ph(c) . . . 250.00
1192 Rocky Nelson,Ph(c) . . . . . . 265.00
1193 The Real McCoys,Ph(c) . . . 150.00
1194 Pepe,Ph(c) . . . . . . . . . . . . . 50.00
1195 National Velvet,Ph(c) . . . . . 125.00
1196 Pixie and Dixie
 and Mr. Jinks . . . . . . . . . . . . 90.00
1197 The Aquanauts,Ph(c) . . . . . 135.00
1198 Donald in Mathmagic Land . 125.00
1199 Absent-Minded Professor,
 Ph(c) . . . . . . . . . . . . . . . . . . 150.00
1200 Hennessey,Ph(c) . . . . . . . . 125.00
1201 Goofy . . . . . . . . . . . . . . . . . 90.00
1202 Rawhide,C.Eastwood Ph(c) 275.00
1203 Pinocchio . . . . . . . . . . . . . 100.00
1204 Scamp . . . . . . . . . . . . . . . . 65.00
1205 David & Goliath,Ph(c) . . . . . 125.00
1206 Lolly and Pepper . . . . . . . . . 40.00
1207 MSy,The Rebel,Ph(c) . . . . . 150.00
1208 Rocky and His Friends . . . . 375.00
1209 Sugarfoot,Ph(c) . . . . . . . . . 150.00
1210 The Parent Trap,
 H.Mills Ph(c) . . . . . . . . . . . . 175.00
1211 RsM,77 Sunset Strip,Ph(c) . 150.00
1212 Chilly Willy . . . . . . . . . . . . . 60.00
1213 Mysterious Island,Ph(c) . . . 150.00
1214 Smokey the Bear . . . . . . . . . 65.00
1215 Tales of Wells Fargo,Ph(c) . 135.00
1216 Whirlybirds,Ph(c) . . . . . . . . 135.00
1218 Fury,Ph(c) . . . . . . . . . . . . . 125.00
1219 The Detectives,
 Robert Taylor Ph(c) . . . . . . . 150.00
1220 Gunslinger,Ph(c) . . . . . . . . 150.00
1221 Bonanza,Ph(c) . . . . . . . . . . 300.00

1222 Elmer Fudd . . . . . . . . . . . . . 50.00
1223 GK,Laramie,Ph(c) . . . . . . . 125.00
1224 The Little Rascals . . . . . . . . 75.00
1225 The Deputy,H.Fonda Ph(c) . 175.00
1226 Nikki, Wild Dog of the North . 90.00
1227 Morgan the Pirate,Ph(c) . . . 135.00
1229 Thief of Bagdad,Ph(c) . . . . . 125.00
1230 Voyage to the Bottom
 of the Sea,Ph(c) . . . . . . . . . 200.00
1231 Danger Man,Ph(c) . . . . . . . 200.00
1232 On the Double . . . . . . . . . . . 75.00
1233 Tammy Tell Me True . . . . . . 125.00
1234 The Phantom Planet . . . . . . 135.00
1235 Mister Magoo . . . . . . . . . . . 150.00
1236 King of Kings,Ph(c) . . . . . . . 135.00
1237 ATh,The Untouchables,
 Ph(c) . . . . . . . . . . . . . . . . . . 375.00
1238 Deputy Dawg . . . . . . . . . . . 200.00
1239 CB(c),Donald Duck Album . 150.00
1240 The Detectives,
 R.Taylor Ph(c) . . . . . . . . . . . 150.00
1241 Sweetie Pies . . . . . . . . . . . . 50.00
1242 King Leonardo and
 His Short Subjects . . . . . . . . 225.00
1243 Ellery Queen . . . . . . . . . . . . 150.00
1244 Space Mouse . . . . . . . . . . . . 75.00
1245 New Adventures of
 Sherlock Holmes . . . . . . . . . 250.00
1246 Mickey Mouse Album . . . . 100.00
1247 Daisy Duck's Diary . . . . . . . 125.00
1248 Pluto . . . . . . . . . . . . . . . . . . 60.00
1249 The Danny Thomas Show,
 Ph(c) . . . . . . . . . . . . . . . . . . 275.00
1250 Four Horseman of the
 Apocalypse,Ph(c) . . . . . . . . 125.00
1251 Everything's Ducky . . . . . . . . 85.00
1252 The Andy Griffith Show,
 Ph(c) . . . . . . . . . . . . . . . . . . 600.00
1253 Spaceman . . . . . . . . . . . . . 135.00
1254 'Diver Dan' . . . . . . . . . . . . . . 90.00
1255 The Wonders of Aladdin . . . 125.00
1256 Kona, Monarch of
 Monster Isle . . . . . . . . . . . . . 135.00
1257 Car 54, Where Are You?,
 Ph(c) . . . . . . . . . . . . . . . . . . 150.00
1258 GE,The Frogmen . . . . . . . . 135.00
1259 El Cid,Ph(c) . . . . . . . . . . . . 135.00
1260 The Horsemasters,Ph(c) . . 225.00
1261 Rawhide,C.Eastwood Ph(c) 250.00
1262 The Rebel,Ph(c) . . . . . . . . . 150.00
1263 RsM,77 Sunset Strip,Ph(c) . 150.00
1264 Pixie & Dixie & Mr.Jinks . . . 100.00
1265 The Real McCoys,Ph(c) . . . 150.00
1266 M.G.M.'s Spike and Tyke . . . 50.00
1267 CB,GyroGearloose . . . . . . . 125.00
1268 Oswald the Rabbit . . . . . . . . 60.00

1269 Rawhide,C.Eastwood Ph(c) 250.00
1270 Bullwinkle and Rocky . . . . . 350.00
1271 Yogi Bear Birthday Party . . . . 90.00
1272 Frosty the Snowman . . . . . . . 90.00
1273 Hans Brinker,Ph(c) . . . . . . . 100.00
1274 Santa Claus Funnies . . . . . . 75.00
1275 Rocky and His Friends . . . . 375.00
1276 Dondi . . . . . . . . . . . . . . . . . . 45.00
1278 King Leonardo and
 His Short Subjects . . . . . . . . 225.00
1279 Grandma Duck's Farm
 Friends . . . . . . . . . . . . . . . . . 75.00
1280 Hennessey,Ph(c) . . . . . . . . 110.00
1281 Chilly Willy . . . . . . . . . . . . . 60.00
1282 Babes in Toyland,Ph(c) . . . . 225.00
1283 Bonanza,Ph(c) . . . . . . . . . . 300.00
1284 RH,Laramie,Ph(c) . . . . . . . . 125.00
1285 Leave It to Beaver,Ph(c) . . . 275.00
1286 The Untouchables,Ph(c) . . . 275.00
1287 Man from Wells Fargo,Ph(c) 100.00
1288 RC,GE,The Twilight Zone . . 225.00
1289 Ellery Queen . . . . . . . . . . . . 150.00
1290 M.G.M.'s Mouse
 Musketeers . . . . . . . . . . . . . . 45.00
1291 RsM,77 Sunset Strip,Ph(c) . 150.00
1293 Elmer Fudd . . . . . . . . . . . . . 50.00
1294 Ripcord . . . . . . . . . . . . . . . 125.00
1295 Mr. Ed, the Talking Horse,
 Ph(c) . . . . . . . . . . . . . . . . . . 225.00
1296 Fury,Ph(c) . . . . . . . . . . . . . 125.00
1297 Spanky, Alfalfa and the
 Little Rascals . . . . . . . . . . . . 75.00
1298 The Hathaways,Ph(c) . . . . . . 75.00
1299 Deputy Dawg . . . . . . . . . . . 200.00
1300 The Comancheros . . . . . . . 275.00
1301 Adventures in Paradise . . . . 100.00
1302 JohnnyJason,TeenReporter . 50.00
1303 Lad: A Dog,Ph(c) . . . . . . . . . 65.00
1304 Nellie the Nurse . . . . . . . . . 125.00
1305 Mister Magoo . . . . . . . . . . . 150.00
1306 Target: The Corruptors,
 Ph(c) . . . . . . . . . . . . . . . . . . 100.00
1307 Margie . . . . . . . . . . . . . . . . . 90.00
1308 Tales of the Wizard of Oz . . 200.00
1309 BK,87th Precinct,Ph(c) . . . . 175.00
1310 Huck and Yogi Winter
 Sports . . . . . . . . . . . . . . . . . 150.00
1311 Rocky and His Friends . . . . 375.00
1312 National Velvet,Ph(c) . . . . . . 60.00
1313 Moon Pilot,Ph(c) . . . . . . . . . 135.00
1328 GE,The Underwater
 City,Ph(c) . . . . . . . . . . . . . . 125.00
1330 GK,Brain Boy . . . . . . . . . . . 225.00
1332 Bachelor Father . . . . . . . . . 135.00
1333 Short Ribs . . . . . . . . . . . . . . 90.00
1335 Aggie Mack . . . . . . . . . . . . . 60.00

Four Favorites #18
© Ace Magazines

Foremost Boys #39
© Star Publications

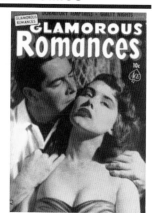

Glamorous Romances #67
© Ace Magazines

**Fo**

| | |
|---|---|
| 1336 On Stage | 75.00 |
| 1337 Dr. Kildare,Ph(c) | 150.00 |
| 1341 The Andy Griffith Show, Ph(c) | 575.00 |
| 1348 JDa,Yak Yak | 150.00 |
| 1349 Yogi Berra Visits the U.N. | 175.00 |
| 1350 Commanche,Ph(c) | 90.00 |
| 1354 Calvin and the Colonel | 150.00 |

### FOUR FAVORITES
**Ace Magazines, Sept., 1941**

| | |
|---|---|
| 1 B:Vulcan, Lash Lighting, Magno the Magnetic Man, Raven, Flag (c),Hitler | 3,000.00 |
| 2 A: Black Ace | 1,400.00 |
| 3 E:Vulcan | 1,200.00 |
| 4 E:Raven,B:Unknown Soldiers | 1,000.00 |
| 5 B:Captain Courageous | 1,000.00 |
| 6 A: The Flag, B: Mr. Risk | 900.00 |
| 7 JM | 900.00 |
| 8 | 900.00 |
| 9 RP,HK | 1,000.00 |
| 10 HK | 1,200.00 |
| 11 HK,LbC,UnKnown Soldier | 1,500.00 |
| 12 LbC | 800.00 |
| 13 LbC | 700.00 |
| 14 Fer | 700.00 |
| 15 Fer | 700.00 |
| 16 Bondage(c) | 800.00 |
| 17 Magno Lighting | 700.00 |
| 18 Magno Lighting | 700.00 |
| 19 RP(a&c) | 400.00 |
| 20 RP(a&c) | 400.00 |
| 21 RP(a&c) | 400.00 |
| 22 RP(c) | 350.00 |
| 23 RP(c) | 350.00 |
| 24 RP(c) | 350.00 |
| 25 RP(c) | 350.00 |
| 26 RP(c) | 350.00 |
| 27 RP(c) | 300.00 |
| 28 | 300.00 |
| 29 | 300.00 |
| 30 thru 32 | @250.00 |

### 4MOST
**Novelty Publ./Star Publ., Winter 1941**

| | |
|---|---|
| 1 The Target, The Cadet | 2,500.00 |
| 2 The Target | 1,500.00 |
| 3 Dan'l Flannel, Flag(c) | 700.00 |
| 4 Dr. Seuss (1pg.) | 700.00 |
| 2-1 | 400.00 |

| | |
|---|---|
| 2-2 | 400.00 |
| 2-3 | 400.00 |
| 2-4 Hitler,Tojo,Mussolini (c) | 600.00 |
| 3-1 | 300.00 |
| 3-2 | 300.00 |
| 3-3 | 300.00 |
| 3-4 | 300.00 |
| 4-1 | 250.00 |
| 4-2 Walter Johnson(c) | 250.00 |
| 4-3 | 250.00 |
| 4-4 | 250.00 |
| 5-1 The Target, Football(c) | 200.00 |
| 5-2 | 200.00 |
| 5-3 | 200.00 |
| 5-4 Football(c) | 200.00 |
| 6-1 Skiing(c) | 200.00 |
| 6-2 LbC(c) | 500.00 |
| 6-3 Tennis(c) | 200.00 |
| 6-4 Football(c) | 200.00 |
| 6-5 | 300.00 |
| 7-1 Basketball(c) | 200.00 |
| 7-2 LbC(c) | 500.00 |
| 7-3 | 250.00 |
| 7-4 LbC(c) | 500.00 |
| 7-5 | 250.00 |
| 7-6 LbC(c) | 500.00 |

**Becomes:**

### FOREMOST BOYS
**Jan., 1949**

| | |
|---|---|
| 8-1 | 250.00 |
| 8-2 LbC(c),Surfing(c) | 500.00 |
| 8-3 LbC(c) | 500.00 |
| 8-4 LbC | 500.00 |
| 8-5 LbC(c) | 500.00 |
| 8-6 LbC | 500.00 |
| 38 LbC(c), Johnny Weismuller | 500.00 |
| 39 LbC(c), Johnny Weismuller | 500.00 |
| 40 LbC(c), White Rider | 500.00 |

**Becomes:**

### THRILLING CRIME CASES

### FOUR TEENERS
A.A. Wyn, Inc. (Ace Magazines), 1948

| | |
|---|---|
| 34 | 125.00 |

**Becomes:**

### DOTTY
**A.A. Wyn, Inc (Ace Magazines), 1948**

| | |
|---|---|
| 35 Teen-age | 150.00 |
| 36 | 100.00 |
| 37 Transvestism | 250.00 |
| 38 thru 40 | @100.00 |

**Becomes:**

### GLAMOROUS ROMANCES
**A.A. Wyn, Inc.
(Ace Magazines), 1949–56**

| | |
|---|---|
| 41 Dotty | 150.00 |
| 42 thru 68 | @100.00 |
| 69 thru 72 Photo(c) | @100.00 |
| 73 JbC | 150.00 |
| 74 thru 90 Photo(c) | @100.00 |

### FOX AND THE CROW
**DC Comics, Dec.–Jan., 1951**

| | |
|---|---|
| 1 | 1,450.00 |
| 2 | 675.00 |
| 3 | 400.00 |
| 4 | 400.00 |
| 5 | 400.00 |
| 6 thru 10 | @300.00 |
| 11 thru 20 | @225.00 |
| 21 thru 40 | @150.00 |
| 41 thru 60 | @125.00 |
| 61 thru 80 | @100.00 |
| 81 thru 94 | @100.00 |
| 95 | 125.00 |
| 96 thru 99 | @75.00 |
| 100 | 75.00 |
| 101 thru 108 | @75.00 |

### FOX GIANTS
**Fox Features Syndicate 1944–50**

Over 40 different "titles" consisting of four remainder comics, rebound Romance or western titles 400 to 500.00. Crime or jungle titles.... 500 to 750.00

### FOXHOLE
**Mainline Publ., 1954**

| | |
|---|---|
| 1 JK | 575.00 |
| 2 JK | 400.00 |
| 3 JK(c) | 225.00 |
| 4 JK(c) | 225.00 |

**Charlton Comics, 1955–56**

| | |
|---|---|
| 5 JK(c) | 350.00 |
| 6 JK | 350.00 |
| 7 | 150.00 |

### FOXY FAGAN
**Dearfield Publ. Co., 1946–48**

| | |
|---|---|
| 1 | 200.00 |
| 2 | 150.00 |
| 3 | 125.00 |
| 4 | 125.00 |

All comics prices listed are for *Near Mint* condition.

*Frankenstein Comics #26*
© *Prize Publications*

*Freedom Train N#*
© *Street & Smith Publications*

*Frisky Fables #40*
© *Star Publications*

Fr

```
5 . . . . . . . . . . . . . . . . . . . . . . . 125.00
6 Rocket . . . . . . . . . . . . . . . . . . 125.00
7 . . . . . . . . . . . . . . . . . . . . . . . 125.00
```

## FRANK BUCK
**Fox Features Syndicate, 1950**
```
1 (70) WW. . . . . . . . . . . . . . . . . 400.00
2 (71) WW. . . . . . . . . . . . . . . . . 225.00
3 . . . . . . . . . . . . . . . . . . . . . . . 150.00
```

## FRANKENSTEIN COMICS
**Crestwood Publications
(Prize Publ.), Summer, 1945**
```
1 B:Frankenstein,DBr(a&c) . . . 2,000.00
2 DBr(a&c) . . . . . . . . . . . . . . . 1,000.00
3 DBr(a&c). . . . . . . . . . . . . . . . 750.00
4 DBr(a&c). . . . . . . . . . . . . . . . 750.00
5 DBr(a&c). . . . . . . . . . . . . . . . 750.00
6 DBr(a&c),S&K . . . . . . . . . . . 600.00
7 DBr(a&c),S&K . . . . . . . . . . . 600.00
8 DBr(a&c),S&K . . . . . . . . . . . 600.00
9 DBr(a&c),S&K . . . . . . . . . . . 600.00
10 DBr(a&c),S&K. . . . . . . . . . 600.00
11 DBr(a&c)A:Boris Karloff . . . . 500.00
12 DBr(a&c). . . . . . . . . . . . . . . 500.00
13 DBr(a&c). . . . . . . . . . . . . . . 500.00
14 DBr(a&c). . . . . . . . . . . . . . . 500.00
15 DBr(a&c). . . . . . . . . . . . . . . 500.00
16 DBr(a&c). . . . . . . . . . . . . . . 500.00
17 DBr(a&c). . . . . . . . . . . . . . . 500.00
18 DBr,B:Horror . . . . . . . . . . . 750.00
19 DBr . . . . . . . . . . . . . . . . . . . 400.00
3-4 DBr. . . . . . . . . . . . . . . . . . . 350.00
3-5 DBr. . . . . . . . . . . . . . . . . . . 350.00
3-6 DBr. . . . . . . . . . . . . . . . . . . 350.00
4-1 thru 4-6 DBr . . . . . . . . . . @350.00
5-1 thru 5-4 DBr . . . . . . . . . . @350.00
5-5 DBr, Oct.–Nov., 1954 . . . . 350.00
```

## FRANKIE
**See: ANIMATED MOVIE-
TUNES**

## FRANKIE & LANA
**See: ANIMATED MOVIE-
TUNES**

## FRANKIE FUDDLE
**See: ANIMATED
MOVIE TUNES**

## FRANK LUTHER'S
## SILLY PILLY COMICS
**Children's Comics, 1949**
```
1 Radio characters . . . . . . . . . . 150.00
```

## FRANK MERRIWELL
## AT YALE
**Charlton Comics, 1955–56**
```
1 . . . . . . . . . . . . . . . . . . . . . . . 125.00
2 thru 4 . . . . . . . . . . . . . . . . @100.00
```

## FRECKLES
## AND HIS FRIENDS
**Visual Editions
(Standard Comics), 1947–49**
```
5 . . . . . . . . . . . . . . . . . . . . . . . 150.00
6 . . . . . . . . . . . . . . . . . . . . . . . 100.00
7 . . . . . . . . . . . . . . . . . . . . . . . 100.00
8 . . . . . . . . . . . . . . . . . . . . . . . 100.00
9 . . . . . . . . . . . . . . . . . . . . . . . 100.00
10 . . . . . . . . . . . . . . . . . . . . . . 100.00
11 Lingerie . . . . . . . . . . . . . . . . 250.00
12. . . . . . . . . . . . . . . . . . . . . . . 100.00
```

## FRECKLES AND
## HIS FRIENDS
**Argo Publ., 1955**
```
1 . . . . . . . . . . . . . . . . . . . . . . . 125.00
2 . . . . . . . . . . . . . . . . . . . . . . . 100.00
3 . . . . . . . . . . . . . . . . . . . . . . . 100.00
4 . . . . . . . . . . . . . . . . . . . . . . . 100.00
```

## FREEDOM TRAIN
**Street & Smith Publications**
```
1 BP . . . . . . . . . . . . . . . . . . . . . 250.00
```

## FRIENDLY GHOST
## CASPER, THE
**Harvey Publications, 1958**
```
1 . . . . . . . . . . . . . . . . . . . . . . . 500.00
2 . . . . . . . . . . . . . . . . . . . . . . . 200.00
3 thru 10 . . . . . . . . . . . . . . . @150.00
11 thru 20 . . . . . . . . . . . . . . @125.00
21 thru 30. . . . . . . . . . . . . . . @100.00
31 thru 50. . . . . . . . . . . . . . . @100.00
51 thru 100. . . . . . . . . . . . . . . @75.00
101 thru 159. . . . . . . . . . . . . . @50.00
160 thru 163 52 pgs. . . . . . . . . @30.00
164 thru 253 . . . . . . . . . . . . . . @30.00
```

## FRISKY ANIMALS
## ON PARADE
**Ajax-Farrell Publ., 1957**
```
1 LbC(c) . . . . . . . . . . . . . . . . . . 250.00
2 . . . . . . . . . . . . . . . . . . . . . . . 125.00
3 LbC(c) . . . . . . . . . . . . . . . . . . 250.00
```

## FRISKY FABLES
**Novelty Press/Premium Group/
Star Publ., Spring, 1945**
```
1 AFa . . . . . . . . . . . . . . . . . . . . 250.00
2 AFa . . . . . . . . . . . . . . . . . . . . 150.00
3 AFa . . . . . . . . . . . . . . . . . . . . 150.00
4 AFa . . . . . . . . . . . . . . . . . . . . 125.00
5 AFa . . . . . . . . . . . . . . . . . . . . 125.00
6 AFa . . . . . . . . . . . . . . . . . . . . 125.00
7 AFa,Flag (c) . . . . . . . . . . . . . . 150.00
2-1 AFa,Rainbow(c). . . . . . . . . 150.00
2-2 AFa . . . . . . . . . . . . . . . . . . 135.00
2-3 AFa . . . . . . . . . . . . . . . . . . 135.00
2-4 AFa . . . . . . . . . . . . . . . . . . 135.00
2-5 AFa . . . . . . . . . . . . . . . . . . 135.00
2-6 AFa . . . . . . . . . . . . . . . . . . 135.00
2-7 AFa . . . . . . . . . . . . . . . . . . 135.00
2-8 AFa,Halloween (c) . . . . . . . 135.00
2-9 AFa,Thanksgiving(c) . . . . . . 125.00
2-10 AFa,Christmas (c) . . . . . . 135.00
2-11 AFa. . . . . . . . . . . . . . . . . 135.00
2-12 AFa,Valentine's Day (c) . . . . 125.00
3-1 AFa . . . . . . . . . . . . . . . . . . 125.00
3-2 AFa . . . . . . . . . . . . . . . . . . 125.00
3-3 AFa . . . . . . . . . . . . . . . . . . 135.00
3-4 AFa . . . . . . . . . . . . . . . . . . 125.00
3-5 AFa . . . . . . . . . . . . . . . . . . 125.00
3-6 AFa . . . . . . . . . . . . . . . . . . 125.00
3-7 AFa . . . . . . . . . . . . . . . . . . 125.00
3-8 AFa,Turkey (c) . . . . . . . . . . 125.00
3-9 AFa . . . . . . . . . . . . . . . . . . 125.00
3-10 AFa . . . . . . . . . . . . . . . . . 125.00
3-11 AFa,1948(c). . . . . . . . . . . 125.00
3-12 AFa . . . . . . . . . . . . . . . . . 125.00
4-1 thru 4-7 AFa . . . . . . . . . . @125.00
5-1 AFa . . . . . . . . . . . . . . . . . . 125.00
5-2 AFa . . . . . . . . . . . . . . . . . . 125.00
5-3 . . . . . . . . . . . . . . . . . . . . . 125.00
5-4 Star Publications . . . . . . . . 125.00
39 LbC(c) . . . . . . . . . . . . . . . . . 250.00
40 LbC(c), Christmas . . . . . . . . 250.00
41 LbC(c) . . . . . . . . . . . . . . . . . 250.00
42 LbC(c) . . . . . . . . . . . . . . . . . 250.00
43 LbC(c) . . . . . . . . . . . . . . . . . 100.00
```
**Becomes:**

*Frisky Animals #52*
© Star Publications

*From Here to Insanity #11*
© Charlton Comics

*Frontline Combat #13*
© E.C. Comics

## FRISKY ANIMALS
**Star Publications Jan., 1951**
44 LbC, Super Cat. . . . . . . . . . . 250.00
45 LbC . . . . . . . . . . . . . . . . . . . 350.00
46 LbC,Baseball. . . . . . . . . . . . . 250.00
47 LbC . . . . . . . . . . . . . . . . . . . 250.00
48 LbC . . . . . . . . . . . . . . . . . . . 250.00
49 LbC . . . . . . . . . . . . . . . . . . . 250.00
50 LbC . . . . . . . . . . . . . . . . . . . 250.00
51 LbC(c). . . . . . . . . . . . . . . . . 250.00
52 LbC(c), Christmas. . . . . . . . . 275.00
53 LbC(c). . . . . . . . . . . . . . . . . 250.00
54 LbC(c),Supercat(c) . . . . . . . 250.00
55 LbC(c),same . . . . . . . . . . . . 250.00
56 LbC(c),same . . . . . . . . . . . . 250.00
57 LbC(c),same . . . . . . . . . . . . 250.00
58 LbC(c),same,July, 1954 . . . . 250.00

## FRITZI RITZ
**United Features Syndicate/
St. John Publications,
Fall, 1948**
N# Special issue . . . . . . . . . . . . 250.00
2 . . . . . . . . . . . . . . . . . . . . . . . 150.00
3 . . . . . . . . . . . . . . . . . . . . . . . 125.00
4 and 5 . . . . . . . . . . . . . . . @125.00
6 A:Abbie & Slats . . . . . . . . . . . 150.00
7 . . . . . . . . . . . . . . . . . . . . . . . 125.00
Becomes:

## UNITED COMICS
**United Features, 1950**
8 thru 26 Bushmiller(c) . . . . . @125.00
Becomes:

## FRITZI RITZ
**United Features, 1953**
27 thru 59 . . . . . . . . . . . . . . @125.00

## FROGMAN COMICS
**Hillman Periodicals,
Jan.–Feb., 1952–May, 1953**
1 . . . . . . . . . . . . . . . . . . . . . . . 200.00
2 . . . . . . . . . . . . . . . . . . . . . . . 150.00
3 . . . . . . . . . . . . . . . . . . . . . . . 150.00
4 MMe. . . . . . . . . . . . . . . . . . . 150.00
5 BK,AT. . . . . . . . . . . . . . . . . . 150.00
6 thru 11 . . . . . . . . . . . . . . @100.00

## FROM HERE TO INSANITY
**Charlton Comics, 1955**
8 . . . . . . . . . . . . . . . . . . . . . . . 200.00
9 . . . . . . . . . . . . . . . . . . . . . . . 150.00

10 SD(c). . . . . . . . . . . . . . . . . . 250.00
11 JK . . . . . . . . . . . . . . . . . . . . 250.00
12 JK . . . . . . . . . . . . . . . . . . . . 250.00
3-1 . . . . . . . . . . . . . . . . . . . . . . 350.00

## FRONTIER FIGHTER
## See: DAVY CROCKETT

## FRONTIER FIGHTERS
**DC Comics, 1955–56**
1 JKu,Davy Crocket, Buffalo Bill. 750.00
2 JKu. . . . . . . . . . . . . . . . . . . . 500.00
3 thru 8 JKu. . . . . . . . . . . . . . @475.00

## FRONTIER ROMANCES
**Avon Periodicals,
Nov.–Dec., 1949**
1 She Learned to Ride and Shoot,
  and Kissing Came Natural . . 600.00
2 Bronc-Busters Sweetheart,
  Jan.–Feb., 1950 . . . . . . . . . 450.00

## FRONTIER SCOUT
## DANIEL BOONE
## See: DEATH VALLEY

## FRONTIER TRAIL
## See: RIDER, THE

## FRONTIER WESTERN
**Marvel, Feb., 1956**
1 RH,. . . . . . . . . . . . . . . . . . . . 300.00
2 AW,GT,GC,JMn . . . . . . . . . . . 200.00
3 MD . . . . . . . . . . . . . . . . . . . . 200.00
4 MD,Ringo Kid. . . . . . . . . . . . . 150.00
5 RC,DW,JDa . . . . . . . . . . . . . . 200.00
6 AW,GC . . . . . . . . . . . . . . . . . 175.00
7 JR,JMn. . . . . . . . . . . . . . . . . 150.00
8 RC,DW. . . . . . . . . . . . . . . . . 150.00
9 JMn . . . . . . . . . . . . . . . . . . . 150.00
10 SC,Aug., 1957 . . . . . . . . . . . 150.00

## FRONTLINE COMBAT
**Tiny Tot Publications
(E.C. Comics), ,
July–Aug., 1951**
1 HK(c),WW, JSe,JDa,Hanhung
  Changjn (c) . . . . . . . . . . . 1,500.00
2 HK(c),WW,Tank Battle (c) . . . . 600.00

3 HK(c),WW,Naval Battleship
  fire (c) . . . . . . . . . . . . . . . . . 900.00
4 HK(c),WW, Bazooka (c) . . . . . 700.00
5 HK(c),JSe . . . . . . . . . . . . . . . 900.00
6 HK(c),WW,JSe. . . . . . . . . . . . 500.00
7 HK(c),WW,JSe,Document of the
  Action at Iwo Jima . . . . . . . . 500.00
8 HK(c),WW,ATh . . . . . . . . . . . 500.00
9 HK(c),WW,JSe,Civil War iss. . 500.00
10 GE,HK(c),WW,
  Crying Child (c) . . . . . . . . . . 400.00
11 GE . . . . . . . . . . . . . . . . . . . 300.00
12 GE,Air Force issue . . . . . . . . 300.00
13 JSe,GE,WW(c),
  Bi-Planes (c) . . . . . . . . . . . . 300.00
14 JKu,GE,WW(c) . . . . . . . . . . 300.00
15 JSe,GE,WW(c), Jan., 1954 . 300.00

## FRONT PAGE
## COMIC BOOK
**Front Page Comics, 1945**
1 JKu,BP,BF(c),I:Man in Black . . 500.00

## FUGITIVES FROM
## JUSTICE
**St. John Publishing Co.,
Feb., 1952**
1 . . . . . . . . . . . . . . . . . . . . . . . 250.00
2 MB, Killer Boomerang . . . . . . . 300.00
3 GT . . . . . . . . . . . . . . . . . . . . 250.00
4 . . . . . . . . . . . . . . . . . . . . . . . 200.00
5 Bondage (c), Oct., 1952 . . . . . 275.00

## FULL OF FUN
**Decker Publications
(Red Top), 1957**
1 . . . . . . . . . . . . . . . . . . . . . . . 125.00
2 . . . . . . . . . . . . . . . . . . . . . . . 100.00

## FUN COMICS
## See: HOLIDAY COMICS

## FUNLAND
**Approved Comics
(Ziff-Davis), 1949**
N# . . . . . . . . . . . . . . . . . . . . . . 225.00

## FUNLAND COMICS
**Croyden Publ., 1945**
1 Funny Animal. . . . . . . . . . . . . 600.00

Fu

*The Funnies 2nd Series #1*
© Dell Publishing Co.

*New Funnies #84*
© Dell Publishing Co.

*Funny Films #11*
© American Comics Group

## FUNNIES, THE
## (1ST SERIES)
**Dell Publishing Co.,
1929-30**
1 B:Foxy Grandpa, Sniffy..... 3,000.00
2 thru 21................ @1,000.00
N#(22) .................... 800.00
N#(23) thru (36) .......... @800.00

## FUNNIES, THE
## (2ND SERIES)
**Dell Publishing Co.,
Oct., 1936**
1 Tailspin Tommy,Mutt & Jeff,
   Capt. Easy,D.Dixon ...... 6,000.00
2 Scribbly................ 3,000.00
3 ....................... 2,500.00
4 Christmas issue ......... 2,000.00
5 ....................... 2,000.00
6 thru 10............... @1,500.00
11 thru 22 .............. 1,200.00
23 thru 29 ............. @1,000.00
30 B:John Carter of Mars .... 3,500.00
31 inc. Dick Tracy .......... 1,500.00
32 ...................... 1,500.00
33 ...................... 1,500.00
34 ...................... 1,500.00
35 John Carter (c).......... 1,500.00
36 John Carter (c).......... 1,500.00
37 John Carter (c).......... 1,500.00
38 Rex King of the Deep (c)... 1,500.00
39 Rex King (c)............. 1,500.00
40 John Carter (c).......... 1,500.00
41 Sky Ranger (c)........... 1,500.00
42 Rex King (c)............. 1,500.00
43 Rex King (c)............. 1,500.00
44 Rex King (c)............. 1,500.00
45 I&O:Phantasmo:Master of
   the World ............. 1,600.00
46 Phantasmo (c) ........... 900.00
47 Phantasmo (c) ........... 800.00
48 Phantasmo (c) ........... 800.00
49 Phantasmo (c) ........... 800.00
50 Phantasmo (c) ........... 800.00
51 Phantasmo (c) ........... 800.00
52 Phantasmo (c) ........... 750.00
53 Phantasmo (c) ........... 750.00
54 Phantasmo (c) ........... 750.00
55 Phantasmo (c) ........... 750.00
56 Phantasmo (c) E:John Carter  750.00
57 I&O:Captain Midnight...... 6,000.00
58 Captain Midnight (c)....... 1,800.00
59 Captain Midnight (c)....... 1,800.00

60 Captain Midnight (c)...... 1,800.00
61 Captain Midnight (c)...... 1,500.00
62 Captain Midnight (c)...... 1,200.00
63 Captain Midnight (c)...... 1,200.00
64 B: Woody Woodpecker .... 1,650.00
**Becomes:**

## NEW FUNNIES
**Dell Publishing Co. July, 1942**
65 Andy Panda, Raggedy Ann &
   Andy, Peter Rabbit ....... 1,600.00
66 same.................. 750.00
67 Felix the Cat ............. 750.00
68 ....................... 750.00
69 WK, The Brownies ........ 750.00
70 ....................... 750.00
71 ....................... 500.00
72 WK .................... 500.00
73 ....................... 500.00
74 ....................... 500.00
75 WK,Brownies ............ 500.00
76 CB,Andy Panda, Woody
   Woodpecker ........... 2,000.00
77 same.................. 500.00
78 Andy Panda ............. 500.00
79 ....................... 350.00
80 ....................... 350.00
81 ....................... 350.00
82 WK,Brownies ............ 400.00
83 WK,Brownies ............ 400.00
84 WK,Brownies ............ 400.00
85 WK,Brownies ............ 400.00
86 ....................... 300.00
87 Woody Woodpecker ........ 250.00
88 same.................. 250.00
89 same.................. 250.00
90 same.................. 250.00
91 thru 99 ............... @200.00
100 ..................... 175.00
101 thru 110 ............. @150.00
111 thru 118 ............. @150.00
119 Christmas ............. 150.00
120 thru 142.............. @150.00
143 Christmas (c) .......... 150.00
144 thru 149............ @150.00
150 thru 154............. @100.00
155 Christmas (c) .......... 150.00
156 thru 167............. @100.00
168 Christmas (c) .......... 150.00
169 thru 181............. @100.00
182 I&O:Knothead & Splinter.... 100.00
183 thru 200............. @100.00
201 thru 240............. @100.00
241 thru 288............. @75.00

## THE FUNNIES ANNUAL
**Avon Periodicals, 1959**
1 Best newspaper strips ....... 600.00

## FUNNIES ON PARADE
**Eastern Color Printing Co.,
1933**
N# Mutt & Jeff, Joe Palooka.. 18,000.00

## FUNNY BONE
**LaSalle Publishing Co., 1944**
N# ....................... 350.00

## FUNNY BOOK
**Funny Book Publ. Corp.,
(Parents Magazine) Dec., 1952**
1 Alec, the Funny Bunny,
   Alice in Wonderland ....... 200.00
2 Gulliver in Giant-Land ....... 150.00
3 ....................... 125.00
4 Adventures of Robin Hood ... 100.00
5 ....................... 100.00
6 ....................... 100.00
7 ....................... 100.00
8 ....................... 100.00
9 ....................... 100.00

## FUNNY FABLES
**Decker Publ.
(Red Top Comics), 1957**
1 ....................... 125.00
2 ....................... 100.00

## FUNNY FILMS
**Best Syndicated Features
(American Comics Group),
Sept.–Oct., 1949**
1 B:Puss An' Boots,
   Blunderbunny ........... 225.00
2 ....................... 100.00
3 ....................... 125.00
4 ....................... 100.00
5 ....................... 100.00
6 ....................... 100.00
7 ....................... 100.00
8 ....................... 100.00
9 ....................... 100.00
10 ...................... 100.00
11 thru 20............... @100.00
21 thru 28............... @100.00
29 May–June, 1954 .......... 100.00

Fu

*Funny Folks #10*
© DC Comics

*Funny Pages #36*
© Comics Magazine

*Funny Stuff #7*
© DC Comics

## FUNNY FOLKS
**DC Comics, 1946–1950**

| | |
|---|---|
| 1 Nutsy Squirrel | 500.00 |
| 2 | 250.00 |
| 3 | 175.00 |
| 4 1st Nutsy Squirrel(c) | 175.00 |
| 5 HK | 175.00 |
| 6 | 125.00 |
| 7 | 125.00 |
| 8 | 125.00 |
| 9 | 125.00 |
| 10 | 125.00 |
| 11 thru 20 | @125.00 |
| 21 thru 26 | @125.00 |

**Becomes:**

## HOLLYWOOD FUNNY FOLKES
**DC Comics, 1950–54**

| | |
|---|---|
| 27 | 150.00 |
| 28 thru 40 | @125.00 |
| 41 thru 60 | @100.00 |

## FUNNY FROLICS
**Marvel, Summer, 1945**

| | |
|---|---|
| 1 Shardy Fox,KrazyKroid,(fa) | 250.00 |
| 2 | 150.00 |
| 3 | 100.00 |
| 4 | 100.00 |
| 5 HK | 125.00 |

## FUNNY FUNNIES
**Nedor Publ. Co., April, 1943**

| | |
|---|---|
| 1 Funny Animals | 225.00 |

## COMICS MAGAZINE
**Comics Magazine/Centaur, May, 1936**

| | |
|---|---|
| 1 S&S, Dr. Mystic. | 17,000.00 |
| 2 S&S, Federal Agent | 4,000.00 |
| 3 | 3,000.00 |
| 4 | 3,000.00 |
| 5 | 3,000.00 |

**Becomes:**

## FUNNY PAGES
**Nov., 1936**

| | |
|---|---|
| 6 I:The Clock,1st masked hero | 3,500.00 |
| 7 WE | 1,500.00 |
| 8 WE | 1,500.00 |
| 9 | 1,500.00 |
| 10 WE | 1,500.00 |

| | |
|---|---|
| 11 | 1,500.00 |
| 12 | 1,000.00 |
| 13 FGu,BoW | 1,000.00 |
| 14 JCo,FGu,BoW | 1,000.00 |
| 15 JCo. | 1,000.00 |
| 16 JCo,FGu. | 1,000.00 |
| 17 Centaur | 1,500.00 |
| 18 | 1,000.00 |
| 19 | 1,000.00 |
| 20 | 1,000.00 |
| 21 B:The Arrow | 5,000.00 |
| 22 BEv,GFx. | 2,500.00 |
| 23 | 2,500.00 |
| 24 BKa,B.Wayne prototype. | 2,800.00 |
| 25 JCo. | 2,000.00 |
| 26 | 2,000.00 |
| 27 | 2,000.00 |
| 28 | 2,000.00 |
| 29 JCo,BoW | 2,000.00 |
| 30 BoW,The Arrow(c) | 4,000.00 |
| 31 | 4,000.00 |
| 32 JCo,BoW | 2,000.00 |
| 33 JCo,BoW,The Arrow(c) | 3,000.00 |
| 34 JCo,The Arrow(c). | 4,000.00 |
| 35 BoW,The Arrow(c) | 4,000.00 |
| 36 Mad Ming (c) | 2,000.00 |
| 37 JCo,Mad Ming (c) | 2,000.00 |
| 38 Mad Ming(c). | 2,000.00 |
| 39 The Arrow(c) | 3,000.00 |
| 40 BoW,The Arrow(c) | 3,000.00 |
| 41 BoW,The Arrow(c) | 3,000.00 |
| 42 BoW,The Arrow(c) | 3,000.00 |

## FUNNY PICTURE STORIES
**Comics Magazine/Centaur Publ., Nov., 1936**

| | |
|---|---|
| 1 B:The Clock | 4,500.00 |
| 2 The Spinner Talks | 1,600.00 |
| 3 Tyrant Gold | 1,000.00 |
| 4 WE,The Brothers Three | 1,000.00 |
| 5 Timber Terror | 1,000.00 |
| 6 War in Asia (c) | 1,000.00 |
| 7 Racist Humor (c). | 1,000.00 |

**Vol 2**

| | |
|---|---|
| #1(10) | 700.00 |
| #2 (11) BoW | 700.00 |
| #3 (12)BoW | 600.00 |
| #4 (13) Christmas (c). | 700.00 |
| #5 (14) BoW. | 600.00 |
| #6 (15) Centaur. | 1,000.00 |
| #7 (16) | 550.00 |
| #8 (17) | 550.00 |
| #9 (18) | 550.00 |
| #10 (19) | 550.00 |
| #11 (20) | 550.00 |

**Vol 3**

| | |
|---|---|
| #1 | 550.00 |
| #2 | 550.00 |
| #3 | 550.00 |

**Becomes:**

## COMIC PAGES
**July, 1939**

| | |
|---|---|
| 4 BoW | 800.00 |
| 5 | 600.00 |
| 6 | 600.00 |

## FUNNYMAN
**Magazine Enterprises of Canada, Dec., 1947**

| | |
|---|---|
| 1 S&K(a&c) | 600.00 |
| 2 S&K(a&c) | 325.00 |
| 3 S&K(a&c) | 250.00 |
| 4 S&K(a&c) | 250.00 |
| 5 S&K(a&c) | 250.00 |
| 6 S&K(a&c), Aug., 1948 | 250.00 |

## FUNNY STUFF
**DC Comics, Summer, 1944**

| | |
|---|---|
| 1 B:3 Mouseketeers Terrific Whatzit | 1,800.00 |
| 2 | 800.00 |
| 3 | 500.00 |
| 4 | 500.00 |
| 5 | 500.00 |
| 6 thru 10 | @300.00 |
| 11 thru 20 | @250.00 |
| 21 | 175.00 |
| 22 C:Superman | 600.00 |
| 23 thru 30. | @200.00 |
| 31 thru 78. | @150.00 |
| 79 July-Aug., 1954. | 150.00 |

**Becomes:**

## DODO AND THE FROG
**DC Comics, 1954**

| | |
|---|---|
| 80 F:Doodles Duck | 250.00 |
| 81 | 150.00 |
| 82 | 150.00 |
| 83 thru 91 | @150.00 |
| 92 scarce | 200.00 |

## FUNNY TUNES
**Marvel Timely, 1944–46 (KRAZY KOMICS spinoff)**

| | |
|---|---|
| 16 Animated Funny Comic-Tunes | 250.00 |
| 17 | 200.00 |
| 18 | 200.00 |
| 19 | 200.00 |

*Funny Tunes #22*
© Marvel Comics Group

*Gang Busters #1*
© DC Comics

Gabby Hayes Western #18
© Fawcett Publications

**Ga**

| | |
|---|---|
| 20 | 200.00 |
| 21 | 200.00 |
| 22 | 200.00 |
| 23 HK | 200.00 |
| Becomes: | |

## OSCAR

## FUNNY TUNES
**Avon Periodicals, July, 1953**

1 (fa),Space Mouse, Peter Rabbit
   Merry Mouse,Cicero the Cat . 150.00
2 same . . . . . . . . . . . . . . . . . 100.00
3 same . . . . . . . . . . . . . . . . . 100.00
Becomes:

## SPACE COMICS
**Avon Periodicals, March–April, 1954**

4 (fa),F:Space Mouse . . . . . . . 125.00
5 (fa),F:Space Mouse . . . . . . . 100.00

## FUNNY WORLD
**Marbak Press, 1947–48**

1 . . . . . . . . . . . . . . . . . . . . . . 150.00
2 . . . . . . . . . . . . . . . . . . . . . . 125.00
3 . . . . . . . . . . . . . . . . . . . . . . 125.00

## FUN TIME
**Ace Periodicals, 1953**

N# Funny animal . . . . . . . . . . . . 200.00
2 . . . . . . . . . . . . . . . . . . . . . . 160.00
3 . . . . . . . . . . . . . . . . . . . . . . 160.00
4 . . . . . . . . . . . . . . . . . . . . . . 160.00

## FUTURE COMICS
**David McKay Publications, June, 1940**

1 Lone Ranger,Phantom . . . . . 4,000.00
2 Lone Ranger. . . . . . . . . . . . 2,000.00
3 Lone Ranger. . . . . . . . . . . . 1,600.00
4 Lone Ranger,Sept., 1940 . . . 1,500.00

## FUTURE WORLD COMICS
**George W. Dougherty, Summer, 1946**

1 . . . . . . . . . . . . . . . . . . . . . . 600.00
2 Fall, 1946 . . . . . . . . . . . . . . 500.00

## GABBY
**Comic Favorites (Quality Comics Group), 1953 (KEN SHANNON spinoff)**

1 (11) teen-age . . . . . . . . . . . . 150.00
2 . . . . . . . . . . . . . . . . . . . . . . 100.00
3 . . . . . . . . . . . . . . . . . . . . . . 100.00
4 . . . . . . . . . . . . . . . . . . . . . . 100.00
5 . . . . . . . . . . . . . . . . . . . . . . 100.00
6 . . . . . . . . . . . . . . . . . . . . . . 100.00
7 . . . . . . . . . . . . . . . . . . . . . . 100.00
8 . . . . . . . . . . . . . . . . . . . . . . 100.00
9 . . . . . . . . . . . . . . . . . . . . . . 100.00

## GABBY HAYES WESTERN
**Fawcett Publ., Nov., 1948**

1 Ph(c) . . . . . . . . . . . . . . . . . 650.00
2 Ph(c) . . . . . . . . . . . . . . . . . 300.00
3 The Rage of the Purple Sage,
   Ph(c) . . . . . . . . . . . . . . . . . 200.00
4 Ph(c) . . . . . . . . . . . . . . . . . 200.00
5 Ph(c) . . . . . . . . . . . . . . . . . 175.00
6 Ph(c) . . . . . . . . . . . . . . . . . 175.00
7 Ph(c) . . . . . . . . . . . . . . . . . 150.00
8 Ph(c) . . . . . . . . . . . . . . . . . 150.00
9 Ph(c),V:The Kangaroo Crook . 150.00
10 Ph(c) . . . . . . . . . . . . . . . . 150.00
11 Ph(c), Chariot Race . . . . . . 150.00
12 V:Beaver Ben, The Biting
   Bandit,Ph(c). . . . . . . . . . . . 125.00
13 thru 15 . . . . . . . . . . . . . . @125.00
16 . . . . . . . . . . . . . . . . . . . . 125.00
17 . . . . . . . . . . . . . . . . . . . . 125.00
18 thru 20 . . . . . . . . . . . . . . @125.00
21 thru 50 . . . . . . . . . . . . . . @125.00

### Charlton Comics
51 . . . . . . . . . . . . . . . . . . . . 125.00
52 thru 59 Dec., 1954 . . . . . . . @75.00

## GAGS
**United Features Syndicate, 1937**

1 Jokes and Cartoons. . . . . . . . 300.00

## GANDY GOOSE
**St. John Publ. Co., 1953**

1 Funny animal. . . . . . . . . . . . 150.00
2 . . . . . . . . . . . . . . . . . . . . . . 125.00
3 . . . . . . . . . . . . . . . . . . . . . . 125.00
4 . . . . . . . . . . . . . . . . . . . . . . 125.00

### Pines, 1956–58
5 . . . . . . . . . . . . . . . . . . . . . . 100.00
6 . . . . . . . . . . . . . . . . . . . . . . 100.00

## GANG BUSTERS
**DC Comics, 1947–58**

1 . . . . . . . . . . . . . . . . . . . . 1,200.00
2 . . . . . . . . . . . . . . . . . . . . . 500.00
3 . . . . . . . . . . . . . . . . . . . . . 400.00
4 . . . . . . . . . . . . . . . . . . . . . 400.00
5 . . . . . . . . . . . . . . . . . . . . . 400.00
6 . . . . . . . . . . . . . . . . . . . . . 400.00
7 . . . . . . . . . . . . . . . . . . . . . 400.00
8 . . . . . . . . . . . . . . . . . . . . . 400.00
9 Ph(c) . . . . . . . . . . . . . . . . . 275.00
10 Ph(c) . . . . . . . . . . . . . . . . 275.00
11 Ph(c) . . . . . . . . . . . . . . . . 225.00
12 Ph(c) . . . . . . . . . . . . . . . . 225.00
13 Ph(c) . . . . . . . . . . . . . . . . 225.00
14 Ph(c),FF . . . . . . . . . . . . . . 500.00
15 . . . . . . . . . . . . . . . . . . . . 200.00
16 . . . . . . . . . . . . . . . . . . . . 200.00
17 . . . . . . . . . . . . . . . . . . . . 500.00
18 . . . . . . . . . . . . . . . . . . . . 175.00
19 . . . . . . . . . . . . . . . . . . . . 175.00
20 . . . . . . . . . . . . . . . . . . . . 175.00
21 thru 25 . . . . . . . . . . . . . . @150.00
26 JK . . . . . . . . . . . . . . . . . . 150.00
27 thru 40 . . . . . . . . . . . . . . @150.00
41 thru 44 . . . . . . . . . . . . . . @125.00
45 Comics Code . . . . . . . . . . . 125.00
46 thru 50 . . . . . . . . . . . . . . @125.00
51 MD . . . . . . . . . . . . . . . . . . 125.00
52 thru 67 . . . . . . . . . . . . . . @125.00

## GANGSTERS AND GUN MOLLS
**Realistic Comics (Avon), Sept., 1951**

1 WW,A:Big Jim Colosimo,
   Evelyn Ellis . . . . . . . . . . . . 600.00
2 JKa, A:Bonnie Parker, The
   Kissing Bandit . . . . . . . . . . 500.00
3 EK, A:Juanita Perez, Crimes
   Homicide Squad . . . . . . . . . 400.00
4 A:Mara Hite, Elkins Boys,
   June, 1952 . . . . . . . . . . . . . 350.00

## GANGSTERS CAN'T WIN
**D.S. Publishing Co., Feb.–March, 1948**

1 Shot Cop (c) . . . . . . . . . . . . 400.00
2 A:Eddie Bentz . . . . . . . . . . . 200.00

---

All comics prices listed are for *Near Mint* condition.     ****

# STANDARD GUIDE TO GOLDEN AGE COMICS

**Ga**

Gay Comics #20
© Marvel Comics Group

Gene Autry Comics #62
© Dell Publishing Co.

Georgie Comics #3
© Marvel Comics Group

3 Twin Trouble Trigger Man . . . . 175.00
4 Suicide on SoundStageSeven  225.00
5 Trail of Terror . . . . . . . . . . . . . 175.00
6 Mystery at the Circus . . . . . . . 175.00
7 Talisman Trail . . . . . . . . . . . . . 150.00
8 . . . . . . . . . . . . . . . . . . . . . . . . 150.00
9 Suprise at Buoy 13,
    June–July, 1949 . . . . . . . . . 150.00

## GANG WORLD
**Literary Enterprises
(Standard Comics),
Oct., 1952**
5 Bondage (c) . . . . . . . . . . . . . 350.00
6 Mob Payoff, Jan., 1953 . . . . . 150.00

## GASOLINE ALLEY
**Star Publications,
Oct., 1950**
1 . . . . . . . . . . . . . . . . . . . . . . . . 250.00
2 LBc . . . . . . . . . . . . . . . . . . . . . 275.00
3 LBc(c), April, 1950 . . . . . . . . . 250.00

## GAY COMICS
**Marvel Timely, 1944**
1 BW,Guys and gals humor . . . . 600.00
18 BW . . . . . . . . . . . . . . . . . . . . 375.00
19 BW . . . . . . . . . . . . . . . . . . . . 300.00
20 BW . . . . . . . . . . . . . . . . . . . . 300.00
21 BW . . . . . . . . . . . . . . . . . . . . 300.00
22 BW . . . . . . . . . . . . . . . . . . . . 300.00
23 BW . . . . . . . . . . . . . . . . . . . . 300.00
24 BW,HK,Hey Look . . . . . . . . . . 300.00
25 BW . . . . . . . . . . . . . . . . . . . . 300.00
26 BW . . . . . . . . . . . . . . . . . . . . 300.00
27 BW . . . . . . . . . . . . . . . . . . . . 300.00
28 BW . . . . . . . . . . . . . . . . . . . . 300.00
29 BW,HK,Hey Look . . . . . . . . . . 300.00
30 HK,Hey Look. . . . . . . . . . . . . 200.00
31 HK,Hey Look. . . . . . . . . . . . . 200.00
32 . . . . . . . . . . . . . . . . . . . . . . . 100.00
33 HK,Hey Look. . . . . . . . . . . . . 200.00
34 HK,Hey Look. . . . . . . . . . . . . 200.00
35 thru 40 . . . . . . . . . . . . . . . @100.00
**Becomes:**

## HONEYMOON
**Marvel Comics, 1950**
41 Photo(c) . . . . . . . . . . . . . . . . 125.00

## GEM COMICS
**Spotlight Publ. April, 1945**
1 A:Steve Strong,Bondage(c) . . 600.00

## GENE AUTRY COMICS
**Fawcett Publications,
Jan., 1942**
1 The Mark of Cloven Hoof . . 12,000.00
2 . . . . . . . . . . . . . . . . . . . . . . 2,200.00
3 Secret o/t Aztec Treasure . . 1,600.00
4 . . . . . . . . . . . . . . . . . . . . . . 1,400.00
5 Mystery of Paint Rock
    Canyon . . . . . . . . . . . . . . 1,400.00
6 Outlaw Round-up . . . . . . . . 1,300.00
7 Border Bullets . . . . . . . . . . . 1,300.00
8 Blazing Guns . . . . . . . . . . . . 1,300.00
9 Range Robbers . . . . . . . . . . 1,300.00
10 Fightin' Buckaroo, Danger's
    Trail, Sept., 1943 . . . . . . . 1,300.00
11 . . . . . . . . . . . . . . . . . . . . . 1,200.00
12 . . . . . . . . . . . . . . . . . . . . . 1,200.00

## GENE AUTRY COMICS
**Dell Publishing Co.,
May/June, 1946**
1 . . . . . . . . . . . . . . . . . . . . . . 1,000.00
2 Ph(c) . . . . . . . . . . . . . . . . . . . 600.00
3 Ph(c) . . . . . . . . . . . . . . . . . . . 400.00
4 Ph(c),I:Flap Jack . . . . . . . . . . 400.00
5 Ph(c), all. . . . . . . . . . . . . . . . . 400.00
6 thru 10 . . . . . . . . . . . . . . . @300.00
11 thru 19 . . . . . . . . . . . . . . . @300.00
20 . . . . . . . . . . . . . . . . . . . . . . . 275.00
21 thru 29 . . . . . . . . . . . . . . . @200.00
30 thru 40, B:Giants . . . . . . . . @175.00
41 thru 56 E:Giants . . . . . . . . @150.00
57 . . . . . . . . . . . . . . . . . . . . . . . 150.00
58 Christmas (c) . . . . . . . . . . . . 125.00
59 thru 66. . . . . . . . . . . . . . . @125.00
67 thru 80, B:Giant. . . . . . . . . @125.00
81 thru 90, E:Giant. . . . . . . . . @100.00
91 thru 93. . . . . . . . . . . . . . . @100.00
94 Christmas (c) . . . . . . . . . . . . 100.00
95 thru 99 . . . . . . . . . . . . . . . @100.00
100 . . . . . . . . . . . . . . . . . . . . . . 150.00
101 thru 111 . . . . . . . . . . . . . @125.00
112 thru 121 . . . . . . . . . . . . . @125.00

## GENE AUTRY'S CHAMPION
**Dell Publishing Co.,
Aug., 1950**
(1) *see Dell Four Color #287*
(2) *see Dell Four Color #319*
3 . . . . . . . . . . . . . . . . . . . . . . . . 150.00
4 thru 19 . . . . . . . . . . . . . . . . @125.00

## GEORGE PAL'S PUPPETOON'S
**Fawcett Publications,
Dec., 1945**
1 Captain Marvel (c) . . . . . . . . . 700.00
2 . . . . . . . . . . . . . . . . . . . . . . . . 400.00
3 . . . . . . . . . . . . . . . . . . . . . . . . 300.00
4 thru 17 . . . . . . . . . . . . . . . @250.00
18 Dec., 1947 . . . . . . . . . . . . . 200.00

## GEORGIE COMICS
**Marvel, Spring, 1945**
1 Georgie stories begin . . . . . . . 275.00
2 Pet Shop (c) . . . . . . . . . . . . . 150.00
3 Georgie/Judy(c) . . . . . . . . . . . 125.00
4 Wedding Dress(c) . . . . . . . . . 125.00
5 Monty/Policeman(c) . . . . . . . . 125.00
6 Classroom(c) . . . . . . . . . . . . 125.00
7 Fishing(c) . . . . . . . . . . . . . . . 135.00
8 Soda Jerk(c) . . . . . . . . . . . . . 135.00
9 Georgie/Judy(c),HK,Hey Look  135.00
10 Georgie/Girls(c),HK,Hey Look  135.00
11 Table Tennis(c),A:Margie,Millie 100.00
12 Camping(c) . . . . . . . . . . . . . 100.00
13 Life Guard(c),HK,Hey Look. . . 150.00
14 Classroom(c),HK,Hey Look . . 150.00
15 Winter Sports(c) . . . . . . . . . . 100.00
16 . . . . . . . . . . . . . . . . . . . . . . 100.00
17 HK,Hey Look. . . . . . . . . . . . . 150.00
18 . . . . . . . . . . . . . . . . . . . . . . 100.00
19 Baseball(c) . . . . . . . . . . . . . 100.00
**Becomes:**

## GEORGIE & JUDY COMICS
20 . . . . . . . . . . . . . . . . . . . . . . 125.00
21 . . . . . . . . . . . . . . . . . . . . . . 100.00
**Becomes:**

## GEORGIE COMICS
22 Georgie comics . . . . . . . . . . 100.00
23 . . . . . . . . . . . . . . . . . . . . . . 100.00
24 . . . . . . . . . . . . . . . . . . . . . . 100.00
25 Driben painted (c). . . . . . . . . 125.00
26 thru 28. . . . . . . . . . . . . . . @100.00
29 . . . . . . . . . . . . . . . . . . . . . . 125.00
30 thru 38. . . . . . . . . . . . . . . @100.00
39 Oct., 1952. . . . . . . . . . . . . . 100.00

## GENERAL DOUGLAS MACARTHUR
**Fox Features Syndicate, 1950**
N# True life story . . . . . . . . . . . 250.00

Geronimo #1
© Avon Periodicals

Giant Comics Editions #4
© St. John Publications

G. I. Combat #15
© Quality Comics Group

**Gi**

## GERALD McBOING-BOING AND THE NEARSIGHTED MR. MAGOO
**Dell Publishing Co., Aug.–Oct., 1952**
1 . . . . . . . . . . . . . . . . . . . . . . . 225.00
2 thru 5 . . . . . . . . . . . . . . . . . @175.00

## GERONIMO
**Avon Periodicals, 1950**
1 Massacre at San Pedro Pass . 200.00
2 EK(c), Murderous Battle
   at Kiskayah . . . . . . . . . . . . . 150.00
3 EK(c) . . . . . . . . . . . . . . . . . . . 150.00
4 EK(c),Apache Death Trap,
   Feb., 1952 . . . . . . . . . . . . . 125.00

## GET LOST
**Mikeross Publications, Feb.–March, 1954**
1 . . . . . . . . . . . . . . . . . . . . . . . 350.00
2 . . . . . . . . . . . . . . . . . . . . . . . 225.00
3 June–July, 1954 . . . . . . . . . . 200.00

## GHOST
**Fiction House Magazine, Winter, 1951–Summer, 1954**
1 The Banshee Bells . . . . . . . 1,500.00
2 I Woke In Terror . . . . . . . . . . 900.00
3 The Haunted Hand of X . . . . 800.00
4 Flee the Mad Furies . . . . . . . . 350.00
5 The Hex of Ruby Eye . . . . . . 800.00
6 The Sleepers in the Crypt . . . . 800.00
7 When Dead Rogues Ride . . . . 800.00
8 Curse of the Mist-Thing . . . . . 800.00
9 It Crawls by Night,
   Bondage(c). . . . . . . . . . . . . 1,000.00
10 Halfway to Hades . . . . . . . . . 800.00
11 GE, The Witch's Doll. . . . . . . . 800.00

## GHOST BREAKERS
**Street & Smith Publ., 1948**
1 BP(a&c), A:Dr. Neff . . . . . . . 1,000.00
2 BP(a&c), Breaks the Voodoo
   Hoodoo,Dec., 1948 . . . . . . . . 800.00

## GHOSTLY WEIRD STORIES
**See: BLUE BOLT**

## GHOST RIDER
**See: A-1 COMICS**

## GIANT BOY BOOK OF COMICS
**Newsbook Publ. (Lev Gleason), 1945**
1 A:Crime Buster & Young
   Robin Hood . . . . . . . . . . . 1,200.00

## GIANT COMICS
**Charlton Comics Summer, 1957**
1 A:Atomic Mouse,Hoppy . . . . . 250.00
2 A:Atomic Mouse. . . . . . . . . . . 200.00
3 . . . . . . . . . . . . . . . . . . . . . . . 200.00

## GIANT COMICS EDITION
**St. John Publ., 1948**
1 Mighty Mouse . . . . . . . . . . . . . 650.00
2 Abbie and Slats . . . . . . . . . . . 325.00
3 Terry Toons . . . . . . . . . . . . . . . 500.00
4 Crime Comics . . . . . . . . . . . . . 750.00
5 MB, Police Case Book . . . . . . 750.00
6 MB(a&c), Western
   Picture Story . . . . . . . . . . . . . 650.00
7 Mopsy . . . . . . . . . . . . . . . . . . . 400.00
8 Adventures of Mighty Mouse . . 450.00
9 JKu,MB,Romance & Confession
   Stories,Ph(c) . . . . . . . . . . . . . 750.00
10 Terry Toons . . . . . . . . . . . . . . . 450.00
11 MB(a&c),JKu,Western
   Picture Stories . . . . . . . . . . . . 650.00
12 MB(a&c),Diary Secrets,
   Prostitute . . . . . . . . . . . . . . 1,500.00
13 MB,JKu, Romances . . . . . . . . 650.00
14 Mighty Mouse Album . . . . . . . 450.00
15 MB(c),Romance . . . . . . . . . . . 750.00
16 Little Audrey . . . . . . . . . . . . . . 450.00
N#, Mighty Mouse Album . . . . . . 450.00

## GIANT COMICS EDITION
**United Features Syndicate, 1945**
1 A:Abbie & Slats, Jim Hardy,
   Ella Cinders,Iron Vic . . . . . . . 500.00
2 Elmo, Jim Hardy, Abbie &
   Slats, 1945 . . . . . . . . . . . . . 350.00

## G.I. COMBAT
**Quality Comics Group, 1952**
1 RC(c), Beyond the Call
   of Duty . . . . . . . . . . . . . . . 900.00
2 RC(c), Operation Massacre . . 400.00
3 An Indestructible Marine . . . . . 375.00
4 Bridge to Blood Hill . . . . . . . . . 375.00
5 Hell Breaks loose on
   Suicide Hill. . . . . . . . . . . . . . 375.00
6 Beachhead Inferno . . . . . . . . . 300.00
7 Fire Power Assault . . . . . . . . . 250.00
8 RC(c),Death-trap Hill . . . . . . . 250.00
9 Devil Riders . . . . . . . . . . . . . . . 250.00
10 RC(c), Two-Ton Booby Trap . . 350.00
11 Hell's Heroes. . . . . . . . . . . . . . 225.00
12 Hand Grenade Hero . . . . . . . . 225.00
13 Commando Assault. . . . . . . . . 225.00
14 Spear Head Assault . . . . . . . . 225.00
15 Vengeance Assault. . . . . . . . . 225.00
16 Trapped Under Fire. . . . . . . . . 200.00
17 Attack on Death Mountain. . . . 200.00
18 Red Battle Ground . . . . . . . . . 200.00
19 Death on Helicopter Hill . . . . . 200.00
20 Doomed Legion-Death Trap . . 200.00
21 Red Sneak Attack . . . . . . . . . . 175.00
22 Vengeance Raid . . . . . . . . . . . 175.00
23 No Grandstand in Hell . . . . . . 175.00
24 Operation Steel
   Trap,Comics Code. . . . . . . . 175.00
25 Charge of the Commie
   Brigade . . . . . . . . . . . . . . . . 175.00
26 Red Guerrilla Trap . . . . . . . . . 175.00
27 Trapped Behind Commie
   Lines . . . . . . . . . . . . . . . . . . 175.00
28 Atomic Battleground . . . . . . . . 175.00
29 Patrol Ambush . . . . . . . . . . . . 175.00
30 Operation Booby Trap . . . . . . 175.00
31 Human Fly on Heartbreak
   Hill . . . . . . . . . . . . . . . . . . . . 175.00
32 Atomic Rocket Assault . . . . . . 200.00
33 Bridge to Oblivion . . . . . . . . . . 175.00
34 RC,Desperate Mission . . . . . . 200.00
35 Doom Patrol . . . . . . . . . . . . . . 175.00
36 Fire Power Assault . . . . . . . . . 175.00
37 Attack at Dawn . . . . . . . . . . . . 175.00
38 Get That Tank . . . . . . . . . . . . . 175.00
39 Mystery of No Man's Land . . . 175.00
40 Maneuver Battleground . . . . . 175.00
41 Trumpet of Doom . . . . . . . . . . 175.00
42 March of Doom . . . . . . . . . . . . 175.00
43 Operation Showdown . . . . . . . 175.00

**DC Comics, Jan., 1957**
44 RH,JKu,The Eagle and
   the Wolves. . . . . . . . . . . . . . 900.00
45 RH,JKu,Fireworks Hill. . . . . . . 400.00

---

Gi

*G.I. Combat #56*
© DC Comics

*Giggle Comics #49*
© American Comics Group

*G.I. Joe #11*
© Ziff-Davis Publication Co.

46 JKu,The Long Walk
   To Wansan. . . . . . . . . . . . . . . 350.00
47 RH, The Walking Weapon . . . 350.00
48 No Fence For A Jet. . . . . . . . 350.00
49 Frying Pan Seat . . . . . . . . . . 350.00
50 Foxhole Pilot . . . . . . . . . . . . 350.00
51 RH,The Walking Grenade. . . . 350.00
52 JKu,JKu(c),Call For A Tank. . . 250.00
53 JKu,The Paper Trap . . . . . . . 250.00
54 RH,JKu,Sky Tank . . . . . . . . . 250.00
55 Call For A Gunner. . . . . . . . . 250.00
56 JKu,JKu(c),The D.I.-And the
   Sand Fleas . . . . . . . . . . . . . 350.00
57 RH,Live Wire For Easy . . . . . . 300.00
58 JKu(c),Flying Saddle. . . . . . . . 300.00
59 JKu,Hot Corner. . . . . . . . . . . 250.00
60 RH,Bazooka Crossroads . . . . 250.00
61 JKu(c),The Big Run . . . . . . . . 225.00
62 RH,JKu,Drop An Inch . . . . . . 225.00
63 MD,JKu(c),Last Stand . . . . . . 225.00
64 MD,RH,JKu,JKu(c),The
   Silent Jet . . . . . . . . . . . . . . 225.00
65 JKu,Battle Parade. . . . . . . . . 225.00
66 MD,The Eagle of Easy
   Company . . . . . . . . . . . . . . . 300.00
67 JKu(c),I:Tank Killer . . . . . . . . 300.00
68 JKu,RH,The Rock . . . . . . . 1,000.00
69 JKu,RH,The Steel Ribbon. . . . 200.00
70 JKu,Bull's-Eye Bridge . . . . . . 200.00
71 MD,JKu(c),Last Stand . . . . . . 200.00
72 MD,JKu(c),Ground Fire. . . . . . 200.00
73 RH,JKu(c),Window War . . . . . 200.00
74 RH,A Flag For Joey . . . . . . . . 200.00
75 RH,Dogtag Hill . . . . . . . . . . . 250.00
76 MD,RH,JKu,Bazooka For
   A Mouse . . . . . . . . . . . . . . . 250.00
77 RH,JKu,H-Hour For A Gunner 250.00
78 MD,RH,JKu(c),Who Cares
   About The Infantry. . . . . . . . 250.00
79 JKu,RH,Big Gun-Little Gun. . . 250.00
80 JKu,RH(c),Flying Horsemen. . 250.00
81 Jump For Glory. . . . . . . . . . . 200.00
82 IN,Get Off My Back. . . . . . . . 200.00
83 Too Tired To Fight . . . . . . . . . 200.00
84 JKu(c),Dog Company
   Is Holding . . . . . . . . . . . . . 180.00
85 IN,JKu(c),The T.N.T. Trio . . . . 180.00
86 JKu,RH(c),Not Return. . . . . . . 180.00
87 RH(c),I:Haunted Tank . . . . . . 900.00
88 RH,JKu(c),Haunted Tank Vs.
   Ghost Tank . . . . . . . . . . . . . 325.00
89 JA,RH,IN,Tank With Wings. . . 200.00
90 JA,IN,RH,Tank Raiders. . . . . . 200.00
91 IN,RH,Tank and the Turtle . . . 200.00
92 JA,IN,The Tank of Doom . . . . 200.00
93 RH(c),JA,No-Return Mission . 200.00

94 IN,RH(c),Haunted Tank Vs.
   The Killer Tank. . . . . . . . . . . 200.00
95 JA,RH(c),The Ghost of
   the Haunted Tank . . . . . . . . 200.00
96 JA,RH(c),The Lonesome Tank 200.00
97 IN,RH(c),The Decoy Tank. . . . 200.00
98 JA,RH(c),Trap of Dragon's
   Teeth . . . . . . . . . . . . . . . . . 200.00
99 JA,JKu,RH(c),Battle of the
   Thirsty Tanks . . . . . . . . . . . 200.00
100 JA,JKu,Return of the
   Ghost Tank . . . . . . . . . . . . 200.00

## GIFT COMICS
**Fawcett Publications,
March, 1942**
1 A:Captain Marvel, Bulletman,
   Golden Arrow,Ibis, the
   Invincible, Spy Smasher. . . 4,000.00
2 . . . . . . . . . . . . . . . . . . . . . 2,500.00
3 . . . . . . . . . . . . . . . . . . . . . 1,800.00
4 A:Marvel Family, 1949 . . . . . 1,500.00

## GIGGLE COMICS
**Creston Publ./
American Comics Group,
Oct., 1943**
1 (fa)same. . . . . . . . . . . . . . . . 400.00
2 KHu . . . . . . . . . . . . . . . . . . . 250.00
3 KHu . . . . . . . . . . . . . . . . . . . 225.00
4 KHu . . . . . . . . . . . . . . . . . . . 200.00
5 KHu . . . . . . . . . . . . . . . . . . . 200.00
6 KHu . . . . . . . . . . . . . . . . . . . 150.00
7 KHu . . . . . . . . . . . . . . . . . . . 150.00
8 KHu . . . . . . . . . . . . . . . . . . . 150.00
9 I:Super Katt . . . . . . . . . . . . . 175.00
10 KHu. . . . . . . . . . . . . . . . . . . 125.00
11 thru 20 KHu. . . . . . . . . . . @125.00
21 thru 30 KHu. . . . . . . . . . . @125.00
31 thru 40 KHu. . . . . . . . . . . @100.00
41 thru 94 KHu. . . . . . . . . . . @100.00
95 A:Spencer Spook . . . . . . . . 100.00
96 KHu . . . . . . . . . . . . . . . . . . 100.00
97 KHu . . . . . . . . . . . . . . . . . . 100.00
98 KHu . . . . . . . . . . . . . . . . . . 100.00
99 KHu. . . . . . . . . . . . . . . . . . . 100.00
100 and 101 March–April,1955 @100.00

## G.I. IN BATTLE
**Ajax/Farrell, 1952**
1 War stories. . . . . . . . . . . . . . 150.00
2 . . . . . . . . . . . . . . . . . . . . . . . 100.00
3 . . . . . . . . . . . . . . . . . . . . . . . 100.00

4 . . . . . . . . . . . . . . . . . . . . . . . 100.00
5 . . . . . . . . . . . . . . . . . . . . . . . 100.00
6 . . . . . . . . . . . . . . . . . . . . . . . 100.00
7 . . . . . . . . . . . . . . . . . . . . . . . 100.00
8 . . . . . . . . . . . . . . . . . . . . . . . 100.00
9 . . . . . . . . . . . . . . . . . . . . . . . 100.00
Ann #1 100 pgs. (1952) . . . . . . 300.00
**Ajax, 1957**
1 . . . . . . . . . . . . . . . . . . . . . . . 125.00
2 . . . . . . . . . . . . . . . . . . . . . . . 100.00
3 thru 6 . . . . . . . . . . . . . . . . @100.00

## G.I. JANE
**Stanhall Publ.,
May, 1953**
1 . . . . . . . . . . . . . . . . . . . . . . . 150.00
2 thru 6 . . . . . . . . . . . . . . . . @125.00
7 thru 9 . . . . . . . . . . . . . . . . @100.00
10 Dec., 1954 . . . . . . . . . . . . . . 100.00

## G.I. JOE
**Ziff-Davis Publication Co.,
1950**
10 NS(c),Red Devils of Korea,
   V:Seoul City Lou . . . . . . . . . 175.00
11 NS(c),The Guerrilla's Lair . . . . 125.00
12 NS(c). . . . . . . . . . . . . . . . . . 125.00
13 NS(c),Attack at Dawn . . . . . . 125.00
14 NS(c),Temple of Terror,
   A:Peanuts the Great . . . . . . 135.00
2-6 It's a Foot Soldiers Job,
   I:Frankie of the Pump . . . . . 125.00
2-7 BP,NS(c),The Rout at
   Sugar Creek . . . . . . . . . . . 125.00
8 BP,NS(c),Waldo'sSqueezeBox 125.00
9 NS(c),Dear John . . . . . . . . . . 125.00
10 NS(c),Joe Flies the Payroll . . 125.00
11 NS(c),For the Love of Benny . 125.00
12 NS(c),Patch work Quilt. . . . . . 125.00
13 NS(c). . . . . . . . . . . . . . . . . . 125.00
14 NS(c),The Wedding Ring . . . . 125.00
15 The Lacrosse Whoopee . . . . . 125.00
16 Mamie's Mortar. . . . . . . . . . . 125.00
17 A Time for Waiting. . . . . . . . . 125.00
18 Giant . . . . . . . . . . . . . . . . . . 275.00
19 Old Army Game..Buck Passer 125.00
20 General Confusion . . . . . . . . . 125.00
21 Save 'Im for Brooklyn . . . . . . 125.00
22 Portrait of a Lady . . . . . . . . . 125.00
23 Take Care of My Little Wagon 125.00
24 Operation 'Operation' . . . . . . . 125.00
25 The Two-Leaf Clover . . . . . . . 125.00
26 NS(c),Nobody Flies Alone
   Mud & Wings. . . . . . . . . . . . 125.00

All comics prices listed are for *Near Mint* condition.

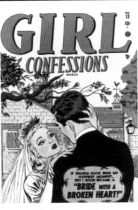

*Girl Confessions #13*
© Marvel Comics Group

*Girls' Love Stories #17*
© DC Comics

*Golden Arrow #1*
© Fawcett Publications

**Go**

27 'Dear Son...Come Home' .... 125.00
28 They Alway's Come Back
  Bondage (c). . . . . . . . . . . . . . 125.00
29 What a Picnic . . . . . . . . . . . . . 100.00
30 NS(c),The One-Sleeved
  Kimono . . . . . . . . . . . . . . . . 125.00
31 NS(c),Get a Horse . . . . . . . . 100.00
32 thru 47. . . . . . . . . . . . . . . . @100.00
48 Atom Bomb . . . . . . . . . . . . . . 125.00
49 thru 51 June, 1957 . . . . . . . @100.00

## GINGER
**Close-Up Publ.
(Archie Publications),
Jan., 1951**
1 GFs . . . . . . . . . . . . . . . . . . . . 200.00
2 . . . . . . . . . . . . . . . . . . . . . . . 150.00
3 . . . . . . . . . . . . . . . . . . . . . . . 125.00
4 . . . . . . . . . . . . . . . . . . . . . . . 125.00
5 . . . . . . . . . . . . . . . . . . . . . . . 100.00
6 . . . . . . . . . . . . . . . . . . . . . . . 100.00
7 thru 9 . . . . . . . . . . . . . . . . @125.00
10 A:Katy Keene,Summer,1954. . 150.00

## GIRL COMICS
**Marvel Atlas, Nov., 1949**
1 Ph(c),True love stories,I Could
  Escape From Love . . . . . . . 250.00
2 Ph(c),JKu,Blind Date . . . . . . 135.00
3 BEv,Ph(c),Liz Taylor . . . . . . . 300.00
4 PH(c),Borrowed Love . . . . . . 100.00
5 Love stories . . . . . . . . . . . . . 100.00
6 same . . . . . . . . . . . . . . . . . . 100.00
7 same . . . . . . . . . . . . . . . . . . 100.00
8 same . . . . . . . . . . . . . . . . . . 100.00
9 same . . . . . . . . . . . . . . . . . . 100.00
10 The Deadly Double-Cross . . . 100.00
11 Love stories. . . . . . . . . . . . . 100.00
12 BK,The Dark Hallway . . . . . . 125.00
**Becomes:**

## GIRL CONFESSIONS
**Marvel, 1952**
13 . . . . . . . . . . . . . . . . . . . . . . 150.00
14 . . . . . . . . . . . . . . . . . . . . . . 125.00
15 . . . . . . . . . . . . . . . . . . . . . . 125.00
16 BEv. . . . . . . . . . . . . . . . . . . 150.00
17 BEv. . . . . . . . . . . . . . . . . . . 150.00
18 BEv. . . . . . . . . . . . . . . . . . . 150.00
19 . . . . . . . . . . . . . . . . . . . . . . 110.00
20 . . . . . . . . . . . . . . . . . . . . . . 110.00
21 thru 34 . . . . . . . . . . . . . . . @100.00
35 Aug., 1954. . . . . . . . . . . . . . 100.00

## GIRLS IN LOVE
**Fawcett Publications,
May, 1950**
1 . . . . . . . . . . . . . . . . . . . . . . . 125.00
2 Ph(c),July, 1950 . . . . . . . . . . 100.00

## GIRLS IN LOVE
**See: DIARY LOVES**

## GIRLS' LIFE
**Marvel Atlas, Jan., 1954**
1 . . . . . . . . . . . . . . . . . . . . . . . 150.00
2 . . . . . . . . . . . . . . . . . . . . . . . 125.00
3 . . . . . . . . . . . . . . . . . . . . . . . 100.00
4 . . . . . . . . . . . . . . . . . . . . . . . 100.00
5 . . . . . . . . . . . . . . . . . . . . . . . 100.00
6 November, 1954 . . . . . . . . . . 100.00

## GIRLS' LOVE STORIES
**DC Comics, 1949**
1 ATh,EK,Romance . . . . . . . . . 700.00
2 EK . . . . . . . . . . . . . . . . . . . . 375.00
3 . . . . . . . . . . . . . . . . . . . . . . . 250.00
4 . . . . . . . . . . . . . . . . . . . . . . . 250.00
5 . . . . . . . . . . . . . . . . . . . . . . . 250.00
6 . . . . . . . . . . . . . . . . . . . . . . . 250.00
7 CI . . . . . . . . . . . . . . . . . . . . . 250.00
8 . . . . . . . . . . . . . . . . . . . . . . . 250.00
9 . . . . . . . . . . . . . . . . . . . . . . . 250.00
10 . . . . . . . . . . . . . . . . . . . . . . 250.00
11 thru 20 . . . . . . . . . . . . . . . @200.00
21 EK . . . . . . . . . . . . . . . . . . . 150.00
22 thru 83 . . . . . . . . . . . . . . . @100.00

## GIRLS' ROMANCES
**DC Comics, 1950**
1 Ph(c) . . . . . . . . . . . . . . . . . . 700.00
2 ATh,Ph(c). . . . . . . . . . . . . . . 375.00
3 Ph(c) . . . . . . . . . . . . . . . . . . 275.00
4 Ph(c) . . . . . . . . . . . . . . . . . . 250.00
5 Ph(c) . . . . . . . . . . . . . . . . . . 250.00
6 Ph(c) . . . . . . . . . . . . . . . . . . 250.00
7 . . . . . . . . . . . . . . . . . . . . . . . 250.00
8 . . . . . . . . . . . . . . . . . . . . . . . 250.00
9 . . . . . . . . . . . . . . . . . . . . . . . 250.00
10 . . . . . . . . . . . . . . . . . . . . . . 250.00
11 . . . . . . . . . . . . . . . . . . . . . . 175.00
12 . . . . . . . . . . . . . . . . . . . . . . 175.00
13 ATh(c) . . . . . . . . . . . . . . . . 200.00
14 thru 20 . . . . . . . . . . . . . . . @175.00
21 thru 31 . . . . . . . . . . . . . . . @150.00

32 thru 50 . . . . . . . . . . . . . . . @125.00
51 thru 80 . . . . . . . . . . . . . . . @100.00

## G.I. SWEETHEARTS
**See: DIARY LOVES**

## G.I. TALES
**See: SERGEANT
BARNEY BARKER**

## G.I. WAR BRIDES
**Superior Publ. Ltd.,
April, 1954**
1 . . . . . . . . . . . . . . . . . . . . . . . 150.00
2 . . . . . . . . . . . . . . . . . . . . . . . 125.00
3 thru 7 . . . . . . . . . . . . . . . . @100.00
8 June, 1955 . . . . . . . . . . . . . . 100.00

## GLAMOROUS ROMANCES
**See: FOUR TEENERS**

## GOING STEADY
**See: TEEN-AGE
TEMPTATIONS**

## GOLDEN ARROW
**Fawcett Publications,
Spring, 1942**
1 B:Golden Arrow . . . . . . . . . 1,100.00
2 . . . . . . . . . . . . . . . . . . . . . . . 550.00
3 . . . . . . . . . . . . . . . . . . . . . . . 400.00
4 . . . . . . . . . . . . . . . . . . . . . . . 375.00
5 Spring, 1947 . . . . . . . . . . . . . 375.00
6 BK . . . . . . . . . . . . . . . . . . . . 400.00
6a 1944 Well Known Comics
  (Giveaway) . . . . . . . . . . . . . 450.00

## GOLDEN LAD
**Spark Publications,
July, 1945–June, 1946**
1 MMe(a&c),A:Kid Wizards,
  Swift Arrow,B:Golden Ladd. 1,200.00
2 MMe(a&c) . . . . . . . . . . . . . . 600.00
3 MMe(a&c) . . . . . . . . . . . . . . 600.00
4 MMe(a&c), The Menace of
  the Minstrel . . . . . . . . . . . . 600.00
5 MMe(a&c),O:Golden Girl . . . . . 600.00

---

All comics prices listed are for *Near Mint* condition.     **Page 141**

*Goofy Comics #7*
© Standard Comics

*Green Giant Comics #1*
© Pelican Publications

*Green Lama #4*
© Prize Publications

## GOLDEN WEST LOVE
**Kirby Publishing Co.,**
**Sept.–Oct., 1949**
1 BP,I Rode Heartbreak Hill,
  Ph(c) . . . . . . . . . . . . . . . . . . 250.00
2 BP . . . . . . . . . . . . . . . . . . . . . 175.00
3 BP,Ph(c) . . . . . . . . . . . . . . . . 175.00
4 BP,April, 1950 . . . . . . . . . . . . 175.00

## GOLD MEDAL COMICS
**Cambridge House, 1945**
N# Captain Truth . . . . . . . . . . . . 600.00

## GOOFY COMICS
**Nedor Publ. Co./**
**Animated Cartoons**
**(Standard Comics),**
**June, 1943**
1 (fa) . . . . . . . . . . . . . . . . . . . . . 500.00
2 . . . . . . . . . . . . . . . . . . . . . . . . 300.00
3 VP . . . . . . . . . . . . . . . . . . . . . 250.00
4 VP . . . . . . . . . . . . . . . . . . . . . 225.00
5 VP . . . . . . . . . . . . . . . . . . . . . 225.00
6 thru 10 VP . . . . . . . . . . . . . @225.00
11 thru 15 . . . . . . . . . . . . . . . @200.00
15 thru 19 . . . . . . . . . . . . . . . @200.00
20 thru 35 FF . . . . . . . . . . . . @150.00
36 thru 48 . . . . . . . . . . . . . . . @125.00

## GREAT AMERICAN
## COMICS PRESENTS–
## THE SECRET VOICE
**4 Star Publ., 1944**
1 Hitler,Secret Weapon . . . . . . . 700.00

## GREAT COMICS
**Novak Publ. Co., 1945**
1 LbC(c) . . . . . . . . . . . . . . . . . . 650.00

## GREAT COMICS
**Great Comics Publications,**
**Nov., 1941**
1 I:The Great Zorro . . . . . . . . 2,000.00
2 Buck Johnson . . . . . . . . . . . 1,000.00
3 The Lost City, Jan., 1942 . . . 4,000.00

## GREAT EXPLOITS
**Decker Publ./Red Top, 1957**
91 BK, Rep. Daring Adventure . . 125.00

## GREAT LOVER
## ROMANCES
**Toby Press, March, 1951**
1 Jon Juan,A:Dr. King . . . . . . . . 200.00
2 Hollywood Girl . . . . . . . . . . . 100.00
3 Love in a Taxi . . . . . . . . . . . . 125.00
4 The Experimental Kiss . . . . . . 125.00
5 After the Honeymoon . . . . . . 125.00
6 HK,The Kid Sister Falls
  in Love . . . . . . . . . . . . . . . . 150.00
7 Man Crazy . . . . . . . . . . . . . . . 125.00
8 Stand-in Boyfriend . . . . . . . . 125.00
9 The Cheat . . . . . . . . . . . . . . . 125.00
10 Heart Breaker . . . . . . . . . . . 125.00
11 . . . . . . . . . . . . . . . . . . . . . . 125.00
12 . . . . . . . . . . . . . . . . . . . . . . 125.00
13 Powerhouse of Deceit . . . . . . 125.00
14 . . . . . . . . . . . . . . . . . . . . . . 125.00
15 Ph(c),Still Undecided,
  Liz Taylor . . . . . . . . . . . . . . 200.00
16 thru 21 . . . . . . . . . . . . . . @100.00
22 May, 1955 . . . . . . . . . . . . . 100.00

## GREAT WESTERN
## See: A-1 COMICS

## GREEN GIANT COMICS
**Pelican Publications, 1941**
1 Black Arrow, Dr. Nerod
  O:Colossus . . . . . . . . . . . 17,000.00

## GREEN HORNET
## COMICS
**Helnit Publ. Co./**
**Family Comics**
**(Harvey Publ.), Dec., 1940**
1 B:Green Hornet,P(c) . . . . . 10,000.00
2 . . . . . . . . . . . . . . . . . . . . . 3,500.00
3 BWh(c) . . . . . . . . . . . . . . . 2,500.00
4 BWh(c) . . . . . . . . . . . . . . . 2,000.00
5 BWh(c) . . . . . . . . . . . . . . . 2,000.00
6 . . . . . . . . . . . . . . . . . . . . . 2,000.00
7 BP, O:Zebra, B:Robin
  Hood & Spirit of 76 . . . . . . 1,800.00
8 BP,Bondage (c). . . . . . . . . . 2,200.00
9 BP,JK(c),Behind the (c) . . . . 1,800.00
10 BP . . . . . . . . . . . . . . . . . . 2,000.00
11 Who is Mr. Q? . . . . . . . . . . 1,500.00
12 BP,A:Mr.Q . . . . . . . . . . . . . 1,800.00
13 Hitler (c) . . . . . . . . . . . . . . 2,200.00
14 BP,Spirit of 76-Twinkle
  Twins, Bondage(c) . . . . . . 1,500.00

15 ASh(c),Nazi Ghost Ship . . . . 1,500.00
16 BP,Prisoner of War . . . . . . . . 1,500.00
17 BP,ASh(c),Nazis' Last Stand 1,500.00
18 BP,ASh(c),Jap's Treacherous
  Plot,Bondage (c). . . . . . . . 1,500.00
19 BP,ASh(c),Clash with the
  Rampaging Japs. . . . . . . . 1,500.00
20 BP,ASh(c),Tojo's
  Propaganda Hoax . . . . . . . 2,200.00
21 BP,ASh(c),Unwelcome
  Cargo . . . . . . . . . . . . . . . . 1,200.00
22 ASh(c),Rendezvous with
  Jap Saboteurs . . . . . . . . . . . 600.00
23 BF,ASh(c),Jap's Diabolical
  Plot #B2978 . . . . . . . . . . . 1,200.00
24 BF,Science Fiction (c) . . . . . 1,500.00
25 thru 29 . . . . . . . . . . . . . @1,200.00
30 BP,JKu,AAv . . . . . . . . . . . 1,200.00
31 BP,JKu . . . . . . . . . . . . . . . 1,200.00
32 BP,JKu . . . . . . . . . . . . . . . 1,000.00
33 BP,JKu,AAv . . . . . . . . . . . 1,000.00
34 BP,JKu . . . . . . . . . . . . . . . 1,000.00
35 BP,JKu . . . . . . . . . . . . . . . 1,000.00
36 BP,JKu,Bondage (c). . . . . . 1,500.00
37 BP,JKu,AAv,S&K . . . . . . . . 1,000.00
38 BP,JKu . . . . . . . . . . . . . . . 1,000.00
39 S&K,AAv . . . . . . . . . . . . . 1,400.00
40 thru 45 . . . . . . . . . . . . . . @900.00
46 Drug . . . . . . . . . . . . . . . . . 1,100.00
47 AAv,Sept., 1949 . . . . . . . . . . 800.00

## GREEN LAMA
**Spark Publications/Prize Publ.,**
**Dec., 1944**
1 I:Green Lama, Lt. Hercules
  & Boy Champions . . . . . . 2,500.00
2 MRa,Forward to Victory
  in 1945 . . . . . . . . . . . . . . 2,000.00
3 MRa,The Riddles of Toys . 1,500.00
4 MRa,Dive Bombs Japan . . . 1,400.00
5 MRa(a&c),Fights for
  the Four Freedoms . . . . . . 1,400.00
6 MRa,Smashes a Plot
  against America . . . . . . . . 1,400.00
7 MRa,Merry X-Mas . . . . . . . . 1,000.00
8 MRa,Smashes Toy Master
  of Crime, March, 1946 . . . . 1,000.00

## GREEN LANTERN
**DC Comics, Autumn, 1941**
1 O:Green Lantern, V:Master of
  Light, Arson in the Slums . 55,000.00
2 V:Baldy,Tycoon's Legacy . . 10,000.00
3 War cover . . . . . . . . . . . . . . 7,500.00

# STANDARD GUIDE TO GOLDEN AGE COMICS

Green Lantern #13
© DC Comics

The Green Mask Volume 2, #4
© Fox Features Syndicate

Gunsmoke #2
© Western Comics

**Gu**

4 Doiby and Green Lantern
 join the Army . . . . . . . . . . . 6,000.00
5 V:Nazis and Black
 Prophet,A:General Prophet 4,000.00
6 V:Nordo & Hordes of War Hungry
 Henchmen,Exhile of Exiles,
 A:Shiloh . . . . . . . . . . . . . . 3,000.00
7 The Wizard of Odds . . . . . . . 3,100.00
8 The Lady and Her Jewels,
 A:Hop Harrigan . . . . . . . . . 3,000.00
9 V:The Whistler, The School
 for Vandals . . . . . . . . . . . . . 2,500.00
10 V:Vandal Savage,The Man Who
 Wanted the World,O:Vandal
 Savage . . . . . . . . . . . . . . . 2,500.00
11 The Distardly Designs of
 Doiby Dickles' Pals . . . . . . . 1,900.00
12 O:The Gambler . . . . . . . . . 1,900.00
13 A:Angela Van Enters . . . . . . 1,900.00
14 Case of the Crooked Cook . 1,900.00
15 V:Albert Zero, One...Two...
 Three...Stop Thinking . . . . . 1,900.00
16 V:The Lizard . . . . . . . . . . . . 1,900.00
17 V:Kid Triangle, Reward for
 Green Lantern . . . . . . . . . . . 1,900.00
18 V:The Dandy,The Connoisseur
 of Crime, X-mas(c) . . . . . . . 2,200.00
19 V:Harpies, Sing a Song of
 Disaster A:Fate . . . . . . . . . . 1,800.00
20 A:Gambler . . . . . . . . . . . . . . 1,800.00
21 V:The Woodman,The Good
 Humor Man . . . . . . . . . . . . . 1,500.00
22 A:Dapper Dan Crocker . . . . . 1,500.00
23 Doiby Dickles Movie
 Ajax Pictures . . . . . . . . . . . 1,500.00
24 A:Mike Mattson,OnceA Cop. 1,500.00
25 The Diamond Magnet . . . . . 1,500.00
26 The Scourge of the Sea . . . . 1,500.00
27 V:Sky Pirate . . . . . . . . . . . . . 1,500.00
28 The Tricks of the
 Sports Master . . . . . . . . . . . 1,500.00
29 Meets the Challenge of
 the Harlequin . . . . . . . . . . . 1,500.00
30 I:Streak the Wonder Dog . . . 1,500.00
31 The Terror of the Talismans . 1,300.00
32 The Case of the
 Astonishing Juggler . . . . . . 1,300.00
33 Crime Goes West . . . . . . . . 1,300.00
34 Streak meets the Princess . . 1,300.00
35 V:Three-in-One Criminal . . . 1,300.00
36 The Mystery of the
 Missing Messenger . . . . . . 1,700.00
37 A:Sargon . . . . . . . . . . . . . . . 1,700.00
38 DoublePlay,May-June,1949 . 1,700.00

## GREEN MASK, THE
**Fox Features Syndicate,**
**Summer, 1940**
1 LF(c),O:Green Mask &
 Domino . . . . . . . . . . . . . . 6,500.00
2 A:Zanzibar . . . . . . . . . . . . . 2,200.00
3 BP . . . . . . . . . . . . . . . . . . . 1,500.00
4 B:Navy Jones . . . . . . . . . . . 1,200.00
5 . . . . . . . . . . . . . . . . . . . . . . 1,000.00
6 B:Nightbird,E:Navy Jones,
 Bondage (c) . . . . . . . . . . . . 900.00
7 B:Timothy Smith &
 The Tumbler . . . . . . . . . . . . 800.00
8 JSs . . . . . . . . . . . . . . . . . . . . 750.00
9 E:Nightbird, Death Wields
 a Scalpel! . . . . . . . . . . . . . . 750.00
10 . . . . . . . . . . . . . . . . . . . . . . . 500.00
11 The Banshee of Dead
 Man's Hill . . . . . . . . . . . . . . 500.00
2-1 Election of Skulls . . . . . . . . 400.00
2-2 Pigeons of Death . . . . . . . . 400.00
2-3 Wandering Gold Brick . . . . . 350.00
2-4 Time on His Hands . . . . . . . 350.00
2-5 JFe,SFd . . . . . . . . . . . . . . . 450.00
2-6 Adventure of the Disappearing
 Trains, Oct.–Nov., 1946 . . . . 450.00

## GUMPS, THE
**Dell Publishing Co., 1945**
1 . . . . . . . . . . . . . . . . . . . . . . . . 300.00
2 . . . . . . . . . . . . . . . . . . . . . . . . 250.00
3 thru 5 . . . . . . . . . . . . . . . . @200.00

## GUNHAWK, THE
## See: BLAZE CARSON

## GUNFIGHTER
## See: FAT AND SLAT

## GUNSLINGER
## See: TEX DAWSON,
## GUNSLINGER

## GUNS AGAINST
## GANGSTERS
**Curtis Publ./Novelty Press,**
**Sept.–Oct., 1948**
1 LbC(a&c),B:Toni Gayle . . . . . . 500.00
2 LbC(a&c) . . . . . . . . . . . . . . . . 350.00

3 LbC(a&c) . . . . . . . . . . . . . . . . 300.00
4 LbC(a&c) . . . . . . . . . . . . . . . . 300.00
5 LbC(a&c) . . . . . . . . . . . . . . . . 300.00
6 LbC(a&c),Shark . . . . . . . . . . . 300.00
2-1 LbC(a&c),Sept.–Oct., 1949 . 300.00

## GUNSMOKE
**Western Comics, Inc.,**
**April–May, 1949**
1 Grl(a&c),Gunsmoke & Masked
 Marvel,Bondage (c) . . . . . . 500.00
2 Grl(a&c) . . . . . . . . . . . . . . . . 350.00
3 Grl(a&c) . . . . . . . . . . . . . . . . 275.00
4 Grl(c),Bondage(c) . . . . . . . . . 250.00
5 Grl(c) . . . . . . . . . . . . . . . . . . 250.00
6 . . . . . . . . . . . . . . . . . . . . . . . 225.00
7 . . . . . . . . . . . . . . . . . . . . . . . 150.00
8 . . . . . . . . . . . . . . . . . . . . . . . 150.00
9 . . . . . . . . . . . . . . . . . . . . . . . 150.00
10 . . . . . . . . . . . . . . . . . . . . . . . 150.00
11 thru 15 . . . . . . . . . . . . . . . . @125.00
16 Jan., 1952 . . . . . . . . . . . . . . 125.00

## GUNSMOKE
**Dell Publishing Co., 1956**
1 J.Arness Ph(c) all . . . . . . . . . 300.00
2 . . . . . . . . . . . . . . . . . . . . . . . 175.00
3 . . . . . . . . . . . . . . . . . . . . . . . 175.00
4 . . . . . . . . . . . . . . . . . . . . . . . 175.00
5 . . . . . . . . . . . . . . . . . . . . . . . 175.00
6 . . . . . . . . . . . . . . . . . . . . . . . 150.00
7 . . . . . . . . . . . . . . . . . . . . . . . 150.00
8 . . . . . . . . . . . . . . . . . . . . . . . 155.00
9 . . . . . . . . . . . . . . . . . . . . . . . 155.00
10 AW,RC . . . . . . . . . . . . . . . . . 165.00
11 . . . . . . . . . . . . . . . . . . . . . . . 155.00
12 AW . . . . . . . . . . . . . . . . . . . . 165.00
13 thru 27 . . . . . . . . . . . . . . . . @125.00

## GUNSMOKE TRAIL
**Four Star Comic. Corp**
**(Ajax/Farrell), 1957**
1 Western action . . . . . . . . . . . . 125.00
2 . . . . . . . . . . . . . . . . . . . . . . . 100.00
3 . . . . . . . . . . . . . . . . . . . . . . . 100.00
4 . . . . . . . . . . . . . . . . . . . . . . . 100.00

## GUNSMOKE WESTERN
## See: ALL WINNERS
## COMICS

---

All comics prices listed are for *Near Mint* condition.

**Page 143**

Ha Ha Comics #53
© American Comics Group

Hans Christian Andersen N#
© Ziff-Davis Publications

Harvey Comic Hits #51
© Harvey Publications

## HA HA COMICS
**Creston Publ.**
**(American Comics Group),**
**Oct., 1943**
1 Funny Animal, all . . . . . . . . . 350.00
2 . . . . . . . . . . . . . . . . . . . . . . . . 200.00
3 . . . . . . . . . . . . . . . . . . . . . . . . 150.00
4 . . . . . . . . . . . . . . . . . . . . . . . . 150.00
5 . . . . . . . . . . . . . . . . . . . . . . . . 150.00
6 thru 10 . . . . . . . . . . . . . . . @125.00
11 . . . . . . . . . . . . . . . . . . . . . . . 100.00
12 thru 15 KHu . . . . . . . . . . . @100.00
16 thru 20 KHu . . . . . . . . . . . @100.00
21 thru 30 KHu . . . . . . . . . . . @100.00
31 thru 101 . . . . . . . . . . . . . . @100.00
102 Feb.–March, 1955 . . . . . . . 100.00

## MISTER RISK
**Humor Publ.,**
**Oct., 1950**
1 (7) B:Mr. Risk . . . . . . . . . . . 200.00
2 . . . . . . . . . . . . . . . . . . . . . . . . 200.00
Becomes:

## MEN AGAINST CRIME
**Ace Magazines, Feb., 1951**
3 A:Mr. Risk, Case of the Carnival
Killer . . . . . . . . . . . . . . . . . 200.00
4 Murder-And the Crowd Roars 150.00
5 . . . . . . . . . . . . . . . . . . . . . . . . 150.00
6 . . . . . . . . . . . . . . . . . . . . . . . . 150.00
7 Get Them! . . . . . . . . . . . . . . 150.00
Becomes:

## HAND OF FATE
**Ace Magazines, Dec., 1951**
8 . . . . . . . . . . . . . . . . . . . . . . . . 600.00
9 LC . . . . . . . . . . . . . . . . . . . . . 400.00
10 LC . . . . . . . . . . . . . . . . . . . . 400.00
11 Genie(c) . . . . . . . . . . . . . . . 300.00
12 . . . . . . . . . . . . . . . . . . . . . . . 275.00
13 Hanging(c) . . . . . . . . . . . . . 500.00
14 . . . . . . . . . . . . . . . . . . . . . . . 275.00
15 . . . . . . . . . . . . . . . . . . . . . . . 275.00
16 . . . . . . . . . . . . . . . . . . . . . . . 275.00
17 . . . . . . . . . . . . . . . . . . . . . . . 275.00
18 . . . . . . . . . . . . . . . . . . . . . . . 275.00
19 Drug issue,Quicksand(c) . . . . 400.00
20 . . . . . . . . . . . . . . . . . . . . . . . 300.00
21 Drug issue. . . . . . . . . . . . . . 400.00
22 . . . . . . . . . . . . . . . . . . . . . . . 300.00
23 Graveyard(c) . . . . . . . . . . . . 400.00
24 LC,Electric Chair. . . . . . . . . . 500.00
25 Nov., 1954. . . . . . . . . . . . . . 250.00
25a Dec., 1954 . . . . . . . . . . . . . 275.00

## HANGMAN COMICS
## See: LAUGH COMICS

## HANK
**Pentagon Publications, 1946**
N# War stories . . . . . . . . . . . . . . 200.00

## HANS CHRISTIAN ANDERSEN
**Ziff-Davis Publications, 1953**
N# Movie comic . . . . . . . . . . . . . 200.00

## HAP HAZARD COMICS
**A.A. Wyn/Red Seal Publ./**
**Readers Research,**
**Summer, 1944**
1 Funny Teen . . . . . . . . . . . . . 300.00
2 Dog Show . . . . . . . . . . . . . . 250.00
3 Sgr, . . . . . . . . . . . . . . . . . . . . 200.00
4 Sgr, . . . . . . . . . . . . . . . . . . . . 200.00
5 thru 10 Sgr, . . . . . . . . . . . . @200.00
11 thru 13 Sgr, . . . . . . . . . . . @150.00
14 AF(c) . . . . . . . . . . . . . . . . . . 175.00
15 . . . . . . . . . . . . . . . . . . . . . . . 150.00
16 thru 24 . . . . . . . . . . . . . . . @150.00
Becomes:

## REAL LOVE
**April, 1949**
25 Dangerous Dates . . . . . . . . . 250.00
26 . . . . . . . . . . . . . . . . . . . . . . . 200.00
27 LbC(c), Revenge Conquest . . 275.00
28 thru 40 . . . . . . . . . . . . . . . @150.00
41 thru 66 . . . . . . . . . . . . . . . @125.00
67 Comics code . . . . . . . . . . . . 100.00
68 thru 76, Nov., 1956 . . . . . . @100.00

## HAPPY COMICS
**Nedor Publications/**
**Animated Cartoons,**
**Aug., 1943**
1 Funny Animal in all . . . . . . . . 400.00
2 . . . . . . . . . . . . . . . . . . . . . . . . 300.00
3 . . . . . . . . . . . . . . . . . . . . . . . . 200.00
4 . . . . . . . . . . . . . . . . . . . . . . . . 200.00
5 thru 10 . . . . . . . . . . . . . . . @200.00
11 thru 20 . . . . . . . . . . . . . . . @150.00
21 thru 31 . . . . . . . . . . . . . . . @150.00
32 FF . . . . . . . . . . . . . . . . . . . . 350.00
33 FF . . . . . . . . . . . . . . . . . . . . 500.00
34 thru 37 FF . . . . . . . . . . . . @200.00

38 thru 40 . . . . . . . . . . . . . . . @100.00
Becomes:

## HAPPY RABBIT
**Standard Comics, Feb., 1951**
41 Funny Animal in all . . . . . . . . 125.00
42 thru 50 . . . . . . . . . . . . . . . @100.00

## HAPPY HOULIHANS
## See: SADDLE JUSTICE

## HAPPY JACK
**Decker Publ. (Red Top), 1957**
1 . . . . . . . . . . . . . . . . . . . . . . . . 100.00
2 . . . . . . . . . . . . . . . . . . . . . . . . 100.00

## HARVEY COMIC HITS
**Harvey Publications, Oct., 1951**
**(Formerly: JOE PALOOKA)**
51 Phantom . . . . . . . . . . . . . . . 400.00
52 Steve Canyon's Air Power . . . 200.00
53 Mandrake . . . . . . . . . . . . . . 300.00
54 Tim Tyler's Tales of Jungle
Terror . . . . . . . . . . . . . . . . . 175.00
55 Love Stories of Mary Worth . . 125.00
56 Phantom, Bondage (c) . . . . . 400.00
57 AR,Kidnap Racket . . . . . . . . 250.00
58 Girls in White . . . . . . . . . . . 150.00
59 Tales of the Invisible . . . . . . 200.00
60 Paramount Animated Comics 600.00
61 Casper the Friendly Ghost . . . 750.00
62 Paramount Animated Comics,
April, 1953 . . . . . . . . . . . . . 225.00

## HARVEY COMICS LIBRARY
**Harvey Publications, 1952**
1 Teen-age dope slaves . . . . . 1,500.00
2 Sparkle Plenty . . . . . . . . . . . . 275.00

## HARVEY HITS
**Harvey Publications, 1957**
1 The Phantom . . . . . . . . . . . . 400.00
2 Rags Rabbit . . . . . . . . . . . . . . 60.00
3 Richie Rich . . . . . . . . . . . . . 2,000.00
4 Little Dot's Uncles . . . . . . . . . 250.00
5 Stevie Mazie's Boy Friend . . . . 50.00
6 JK(c),BP,The Phantom . . . . . . 300.00
7 Wendy the Witch . . . . . . . . . . 500.00
8 Sad Sack's Army Life . . . . . . 100.00
9 Richie Rich's Golden Deeds . . 700.00

Ha

*Harvey Hits #48*
© Harvey Publications

*Haunt of Fear #6*
© E.C. Comics

*Headline Comics #23*
© Prize Publications

**Ha**

10 Little Lotta . . . . . . . . . . . . . . . 175.00
11 Little Audrey Summer Fun . . . 150.00
12 The Phantom . . . . . . . . . . . . . 300.00
13 Little Dot's Uncles . . . . . . . . . 100.00
14 Herman & Katnip . . . . . . . . . . 50.00
15 The Phantom . . . . . . . . . . . . . 300.00
16 Wendy the Witch . . . . . . . . . . 300.00
17 Sad Sack's Army Life . . . . . . . 75.00
18 Buzzy & the Crow . . . . . . . . . . 50.00
19 Little Audrey . . . . . . . . . . . . . . 75.00
20 Casper & Spooky . . . . . . . . . . 100.00
21 Wendy the Witch . . . . . . . . . . 250.00
22 Sad Sack's Army Life . . . . . . . 75.00
23 Wendy the Witch . . . . . . . . . . 250.00
24 Little Dot's Uncles . . . . . . . . . 150.00
25 Herman & Katnip . . . . . . . . . . 50.00
26 The Phantom . . . . . . . . . . . . . 250.00
27 Wendy the Good Little Witch . 300.00
28 Sad Sack's Army Life . . . . . . . 50.00
29 Harvey-Toon . . . . . . . . . . . . . . 75.00
30 Wendy the Witch . . . . . . . . . . 200.00
31 Herman & Katnip . . . . . . . . . . 40.00
32 Sad Sack's Army Life . . . . . . . 50.00
33 Wendy the Witch . . . . . . . . . . 200.00
34 Harvey-Toon . . . . . . . . . . . . . . 50.00
35 Funday Funnies . . . . . . . . . . . 40.00
36 The Phantom . . . . . . . . . . . . . 200.00
37 Casper & Nightmare . . . . . . . . 75.00
38 Harvey-Toon . . . . . . . . . . . . . . 50.00
39 Sad Sack's Army Life . . . . . . . 50.00
40 Funday Funnies . . . . . . . . . . . 35.00
41 Herman & Katnip . . . . . . . . . . 35.00
42 Harvey-Toon . . . . . . . . . . . . . . 40.00
43 Sad Sack's Army Life . . . . . . . 40.00
44 The Phantom . . . . . . . . . . . . . 200.00
45 Casper & Nightmare . . . . . . . . 75.00
46 Harvey-Toon . . . . . . . . . . . . . . 40.00
47 Sad Sack's Army Life . . . . . . . 40.00
48 The Phantom . . . . . . . . . . . . . 200.00
49 Stumbo the Giant . . . . . . . . . . 150.00
50 Harvey-Toon . . . . . . . . . . . . . . 30.00

## HAUNTED THRILLS
**Four Star Publ.**
**(Ajax/Farrell), June, 1952**
1 Ellery Queen . . . . . . . . . . . . . . 600.00
2 LbC,Ellery Queen . . . . . . . . . . 450.00
3 Drug Story . . . . . . . . . . . . . . . 600.00
4 Ghouls Castle . . . . . . . . . . . . . 350.00
5 Fatal Scapel . . . . . . . . . . . . . . 350.00
6 Pit of Horror . . . . . . . . . . . . . . 400.00
7 Trail to a Tomb . . . . . . . . . . . . 300.00
8 Vanishing Skull . . . . . . . . . . . . 300.00
9 Madness of Terror . . . . . . . . . 300.00
10 . . . . . . . . . . . . . . . . . . . . . . . 300.00

11 Nazi Concentration Camp . . . . 400.00
12 RWb . . . . . . . . . . . . . . . . . . . 225.00
13 . . . . . . . . . . . . . . . . . . . . . . . 225.00
14 RWb . . . . . . . . . . . . . . . . . . . 250.00
15 The Devil Collects . . . . . . . . . . 225.00
16 . . . . . . . . . . . . . . . . . . . . . . . 225.00
17 Mirror of Madness . . . . . . . . . 225.00
18 No Place to Go,
   Nov.–Dec., 1954 . . . . . . . . . 250.00

## HAUNT OF FEAR
**Fables Publ. (E.C. Comics) ,**
**May–June, 1950**
15 JCr(a&c),AF,WW . . . . . . . . 5,000.00
16 JCr(a&c),AF,WW . . . . . . . . 2,500.00
17 JCr(a&c),AF,WW,O:Crypt
   of Terror,Vault of Horror
   & Haunt of Fear . . . . . . . . 2,400.00
4 AF(c),WW,JDa . . . . . . . . . . . 1,800.00
5 JCr(a&c),WW,JDa,Eye Injury 1,500.00
6 JCr(a&c),WW,JDa . . . . . . . . . 1,200.00
7 JCr(a&c),WW,JDa . . . . . . . . . 1,200.00
8 AF(c),JKa,JDa,
   Shrunken Head . . . . . . . . . 1,200.00
9 AF(c),JCr,JDa . . . . . . . . . . . . 1,200.00
10 AF(c),Grl,JDa . . . . . . . . . . . . . 900.00
11 JKa,Grl,JDa . . . . . . . . . . . . . 1,200.00
12 JCr,Grl,JDa . . . . . . . . . . . . . . . 900.00
13 Grl,JDa . . . . . . . . . . . . . . . . . . 900.00
14 Grl(a&c),JDa,O:Old Witch . . 1,200.00
15 JDa . . . . . . . . . . . . . . . . . . . . 700.00
16 Grl(c),JDa,Ray Bradbury
   adaptation . . . . . . . . . . . . . . 700.00
17 JDa,Grl(c),Classic
   Ghastly (c) . . . . . . . . . . . . . . 700.00
18 JDa,Grl(c),JKa,Ray Bradbury
   adaptation . . . . . . . . . . . . . . 700.00
19 JDa,Guillotine (c),
   Bondage (c) . . . . . . . . . . . . . . 900.00
20 RC,JDa,Grl(a&c) . . . . . . . . . 1,000.00
21 JDa,Grl(a&c) . . . . . . . . . . . . . . 900.00
22 JDa,Grl(a&c) . . . . . . . . . . . . . . 900.00
23 JDa,Grl(a&c) . . . . . . . . . . . . . . 900.00
22 JDa,Grl(a&c) . . . . . . . . . . . . . . 900.00
23 JDa,Grl(a&c) . . . . . . . . . . . . . . 900.00
24 JDa,Grl(a&c) . . . . . . . . . . . . . . 900.00
25 JDa,Grl(a&c) . . . . . . . . . . . . . . 900.00
26 RC,JDa,Grl (a&c) . . . . . . . . 1,000.00
27 JDa,Grl(a&c), Cannibalism . 1,000.00
28 Dec., 1954 . . . . . . . . . . . . . . . 900.00

## HAVE GUN, WILL TRAVEL
**Dell Publishing Co., 1958**
1 Richard Boone Ph(c) all . . . . . 250.00

2 . . . . . . . . . . . . . . . . . . . . . . . . 200.00
3 . . . . . . . . . . . . . . . . . . . . . . . . 200.00
5 . . . . . . . . . . . . . . . . . . . . . . . . 150.00
6 . . . . . . . . . . . . . . . . . . . . . . . . 150.00
7 . . . . . . . . . . . . . . . . . . . . . . . . 150.00
8 thru 14 . . . . . . . . . . . . . . . . @150.00

## HAWK, THE
**Approved Comics**
**(Ziff-Davis), Winter, 1951**
1 MA,The Law of the Colt,P(c) . 250.00
2 JKu,Iron Caravan of the
   Mojave, P(c) . . . . . . . . . . . . 125.00
3 Leverett's Last Stand,P(c) . . . . 110.00
4 Killer's Town,P(c) . . . . . . . . . . 100.00
5 . . . . . . . . . . . . . . . . . . . . . . . . 100.00
6 . . . . . . . . . . . . . . . . . . . . . . . . 100.00
7 . . . . . . . . . . . . . . . . . . . . . . . . 100.00
8 MB(c),Dry River Rampage . . . 135.00
9 MB(a&c),JKu . . . . . . . . . . . . . 135.00
10 MB(c) . . . . . . . . . . . . . . . . . . . 135.00
11 MB(c) . . . . . . . . . . . . . . . . . . . 135.00
12 MB(a&c), May, 1955 . . . . . . . . 135.00

## HEADLINE COMICS
**American Boys Comics/**
**Headline Publ. (Prize Publ.),**
**Feb., 1943**
1 B:Jr. Rangers . . . . . . . . . . . . 1,000.00
2 JaB(a&c) . . . . . . . . . . . . . . . . . 500.00
3 JaB(a&c) . . . . . . . . . . . . . . . . . 450.00
4 . . . . . . . . . . . . . . . . . . . . . . . . 350.00
5 HcK . . . . . . . . . . . . . . . . . . . . 350.00
6 HcK . . . . . . . . . . . . . . . . . . . . 350.00
7 HcK,Jr. Rangers . . . . . . . . . . . 350.00
8 HcK,Hitler (c) . . . . . . . . . . . . . 900.00
9 HcK . . . . . . . . . . . . . . . . . . . . 350.00
10 HcK,Hitler story,Wizard(c) . . . . 400.00
11 . . . . . . . . . . . . . . . . . . . . . . . . 325.00
12 HcK,Heroes of Yesterday . . . . 325.00
13 HcK,A:Blue Streak . . . . . . . . . 325.00
14 HcK,A:Blue Streak . . . . . . . . . 325.00
15 HcK,A:Blue Streak . . . . . . . . . 325.00
16 HcK,O:Atomic Man . . . . . . . . . 450.00
17 Atomic Man(c) . . . . . . . . . . . . 250.00
18 Atomic Man(c) . . . . . . . . . . . . 250.00
19 S&K,Atomic Man(c) . . . . . . . 500.00
20 Atomic Man(c) . . . . . . . . . . . . 250.00
21 E:Atomic Man . . . . . . . . . . . . 250.00
22 HcK . . . . . . . . . . . . . . . . . . . . 200.00
23 S&K(a&c),Valentines Day
   Massacre . . . . . . . . . . . . . . . 400.00
24 S&K(a&c),You Can't Forget
   a Killer . . . . . . . . . . . . . . . . . 400.00

*Headline Comics #60*
*© Prize Publications*

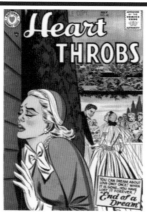

*Heart Throbs #48*
*© DC Comics*

*Hedy Hollywood #40*
*© Marvel Comics Group*

He

25 S&K(a&c),Crime Never Pays . 400.00
26 S&K(a&c),Crime Never Pays . 400.00
27 S&K(a&c),Crime Never Pays . 400.00
28 S&K(a&c),Crime Never Pays . 400.00
29 S&K(a&c),Crime Never Pays . 400.00
30 S&K(a&c),Crime Never Pays . 400.00
31 S&K(a&c),Crime Never Pays . 400.00
32 S&K(a&c),Crime Never Pays . 400.00
33 S&K(a&c),Police and FBI
     Heroes . . . . . . . . . . . . . . . . 400.00
34 S&K(a&c),same . . . . . . . . . . 400.00
35 S&K(a&c),same . . . . . . . . . . 400.00
36 S&K,same,Ph(c) . . . . . . . . . . 350.00
37 S&K,MvS,same,Ph(c) . . . . . . 400.00
38 S&K,same,Ph(c) . . . . . . . . . . 200.00
39 S&K,same,Ph(c) . . . . . . . . . . 200.00
40 S&K,Ph(c)Violent Crime . . . . 200.00
41 Ph(c),J.Edgar Hoover(c) . . . . . 200.00
42 Ph(c) . . . . . . . . . . . . . . . . . . 150.00
43 Ph(c) . . . . . . . . . . . . . . . . . . 150.00
44 MMe,MvS,WE,S&K . . . . . . . . 300.00
45 JK . . . . . . . . . . . . . . . . . . . . 250.00
46 . . . . . . . . . . . . . . . . . . . . . . 200.00
47 . . . . . . . . . . . . . . . . . . . . . . 200.00
48 . . . . . . . . . . . . . . . . . . . . . . 200.00
49 MMe . . . . . . . . . . . . . . . . . . 200.00
50 . . . . . . . . . . . . . . . . . . . . . . 200.00
51 JK . . . . . . . . . . . . . . . . . . . . 200.00
52 . . . . . . . . . . . . . . . . . . . . . . 200.00
53 . . . . . . . . . . . . . . . . . . . . . . 200.00
54 . . . . . . . . . . . . . . . . . . . . . . 200.00
55 . . . . . . . . . . . . . . . . . . . . . . 200.00
56 S&K . . . . . . . . . . . . . . . . . . 275.00
57 . . . . . . . . . . . . . . . . . . . . . . 150.00
58 . . . . . . . . . . . . . . . . . . . . . . 150.00
59 . . . . . . . . . . . . . . . . . . . . . . 150.00
60 MvS(c) . . . . . . . . . . . . . . . . 150.00
61 MMe,MvS(c) . . . . . . . . . . . . 150.00
62 MMe(a&c) . . . . . . . . . . . . . . 150.00
63 MMe(a&c) . . . . . . . . . . . . . . 150.00
64 MMe(a&c) . . . . . . . . . . . . . . 150.00
65 MMe(a&c) . . . . . . . . . . . . . . 150.00
66 MMe(a&c) . . . . . . . . . . . . . . 150.00
67 MMe(a&c) . . . . . . . . . . . . . . 150.00
68 MMe(a&c) . . . . . . . . . . . . . . 150.00
69 MMe(a&c) . . . . . . . . . . . . . . 150.00
70 MMe(a&c) . . . . . . . . . . . . . . 150.00
71 MMe(a&c) . . . . . . . . . . . . . . 150.00
72 MMe(a&c) . . . . . . . . . . . . . . 150.00
73 MMe(a&c) . . . . . . . . . . . . . . 150.00
74 MMe(a&c) . . . . . . . . . . . . . . 150.00
75 MMe(a&c) . . . . . . . . . . . . . . 150.00
76 MMe(a&c) . . . . . . . . . . . . . . 150.00
77 MMe(a&c),Oct., 1956 . . . . . . 150.00

## HEART THROBS
### Comics Magazines
### (Quality), Aug., 1949
1 BWa(c),PG,Spoiled Brat . . . . . 500.00
2 BWa(c),PG,Siren of
     the Tropics . . . . . . . . . . . . . 300.00
3 PG . . . . . . . . . . . . . . . . . . . . 150.00
4 BWa(c),Greed Turned Me into
     a Scheming Vixen,Ph(c) . . . . 200.00
5 Ph(c) . . . . . . . . . . . . . . . . . . 150.00
6 BWa . . . . . . . . . . . . . . . . . . 200.00
7 . . . . . . . . . . . . . . . . . . . . . . 150.00
8 BWa . . . . . . . . . . . . . . . . . . 250.00
9 I Hated Men,Ph(c) . . . . . . . . 200.00
10 BWa,My Secret Fears. . . . . . 275.00
11 . . . . . . . . . . . . . . . . . . . . . 150.00
12 . . . . . . . . . . . . . . . . . . . . . 150.00
13 . . . . . . . . . . . . . . . . . . . . . 150.00
14 BWa . . . . . . . . . . . . . . . . . 150.00
15 My Right to Happiness,Ph(c) . 200.00
16 . . . . . . . . . . . . . . . . . . . . . 125.00
17 . . . . . . . . . . . . . . . . . . . . . 125.00
18 . . . . . . . . . . . . . . . . . . . . . 125.00
19 . . . . . . . . . . . . . . . . . . . . . 125.00
20 . . . . . . . . . . . . . . . . . . . . . 125.00
21 BWa . . . . . . . . . . . . . . . . . 200.00
22 BWa . . . . . . . . . . . . . . . . . 200.00
23 BWa . . . . . . . . . . . . . . . . . 200.00
24 thru 30 . . . . . . . . . . . . . . @125.00
31 thru 33 . . . . . . . . . . . . . . @125.00
34 thru 39 . . . . . . . . . . . . . . @125.00
40 BWa . . . . . . . . . . . . . . . . . 200.00
41 . . . . . . . . . . . . . . . . . . . . . 125.00
42 . . . . . . . . . . . . . . . . . . . . . 100.00
43 thru 46 . . . . . . . . . . . . . . @125.00
### DC Comics, 1957
47 . . . . . . . . . . . . . . . . . . . . . 350.00
48 . . . . . . . . . . . . . . . . . . . . . 150.00
49 . . . . . . . . . . . . . . . . . . . . . 125.00
50 thru 60 . . . . . . . . . . . . . . @100.00
61 thru 74 . . . . . . . . . . . . . . @100.00

## HECKLE AND JECKLE
### St. John Publ./Pines,
### Nov., 1951
1 Blue Ribbon Comics . . . . . . . . 300.00
2 Blue Ribbon Comics . . . . . . . . 150.00
3 . . . . . . . . . . . . . . . . . . . . . . 125.00
4 . . . . . . . . . . . . . . . . . . . . . . 125.00
5 . . . . . . . . . . . . . . . . . . . . . . 125.00
6 . . . . . . . . . . . . . . . . . . . . . . 125.00
7 . . . . . . . . . . . . . . . . . . . . . . 125.00
8 . . . . . . . . . . . . . . . . . . . . . . 100.00
9 . . . . . . . . . . . . . . . . . . . . . . 100.00

10 . . . . . . . . . . . . . . . . . . . . . 100.00
11 . . . . . . . . . . . . . . . . . . . . . 100.00
12 . . . . . . . . . . . . . . . . . . . . . 100.00
13 . . . . . . . . . . . . . . . . . . . . . 100.00
14 . . . . . . . . . . . . . . . . . . . . . 100.00
15 . . . . . . . . . . . . . . . . . . . . . 125.00
16 thru 20 . . . . . . . . . . . . . . @100.00
21 thru 33 . . . . . . . . . . . . . . @100.00
34 June, 1959 . . . . . . . . . . . . . 100.00

## HECTOR COMICS
### Key Publications, 1953
1 Teen-age humor . . . . . . . . . . 125.00
2 . . . . . . . . . . . . . . . . . . . . . . 100.00
3 . . . . . . . . . . . . . . . . . . . . . . 100.00

## HEDY DEVINE COMICS
### Marvel, Aug., 1947—Sept., 1952
22 I:Hedy Devine . . . . . . . . . . . 275.00
23 BW,Beauty and the Beach,
     HK,Hey Look . . . . . . . . . . . 200.00
24 High Jinx in Hollywood,
     HK, Hey Look . . . . . . . . . . . 200.00
25 Hedy/Bull(c),HK,Hey Look . . . 200.00
26 Skating(c),HK,Giggles&Grins . 225.00
27 Hedy at Show(c),HK,HeyLook 200.00
28 Hedy/Charlie(c),HK,HeyLook . 200.00
29 Tennis(c),HK,Hey Look . . . . . 200.00
30 . . . . . . . . . . . . . . . . . . . . . 150.00
31 thru 35 . . . . . . . . . . . . . . @150.00
**Becomes:**

## HEDY HOLLYWOOD
36 thru 50 . . . . . . . . . . . . . . @150.00

## HEDY WOLFE
### Marvel Atlas, Aug., 1957
1 Patsy Walker's Rival . . . . . . . . 125.00

## HELLO PAL COMICS
### Harvey Publications,
### Jan., 1943
1 B:Rocketman & Rocket Girl,
     Mickey Rooney, Ph(c) . . . . 2,000.00
2 Charlie McCarthy, Ph(c) . . . . 1,500.00
3 Bob Hope, Ph(c), May, 1943 1,700.00

## HE-MAN
### Approved Comics
### (Ziff-Davis)/Toby Press, 1952
1 "Real-Life Adventure" . . . . . . . 175.00
1a . . . . . . . . . . . . . . . . . . . . . 165.00
2a . . . . . . . . . . . . . . . . . . . . . 165.00

*Henry #14*
© Dell Publishing Co.

*Heroic Comics #9*
© Eastern Color Printing Co.

*Heroic Comics #81*
© Eastern Color Printing Co.

**Hi**

## HENRY

**Dell Publishing Co.,
Oct., 1946**

1 . . . . . . . . . . . . . . . . . . . . . . . 250.00
2 . . . . . . . . . . . . . . . . . . . . . . . 150.00
3 thru 10 . . . . . . . . . . . . . @150.00
11 thru 20 . . . . . . . . . . . . . @125.00
21 thru 30 . . . . . . . . . . . . @125.00
31 thru 40 . . . . . . . . . . . . @100.00
41 thru 50 . . . . . . . . . . . @75.00
51 thru 65 . . . . . . . . . . . @75.00

## HENRY ALDRICH COMICS

**Dell Publishing Co.,
Aug.–Sept., 1950**

1 . . . . . . . . . . . . . . . . . . . . . . 200.00
2 . . . . . . . . . . . . . . . . . . . . . . 150.00
3 . . . . . . . . . . . . . . . . . . . . . . 125.00
4 . . . . . . . . . . . . . . . . . . . . . . 125.00
5 . . . . . . . . . . . . . . . . . . . . . . 125.00
6 . . . . . . . . . . . . . . . . . . . . . . 100.00
7 . . . . . . . . . . . . . . . . . . . . . . 100.00
8 . . . . . . . . . . . . . . . . . . . . . . 100.00
9 . . . . . . . . . . . . . . . . . . . . . . 100.00
10 . . . . . . . . . . . . . . . . . . . . . 100.00
11 thru 22 . . . . . . . . . . . . @100.00

## HERE'S HOWIE COMICS

**DC Comics, 1952–54**

1 Teen-age humor. . . . . . . . . . . 300.00
2 . . . . . . . . . . . . . . . . . . . . . . 200.00
3 . . . . . . . . . . . . . . . . . . . . . . 150.00
4 . . . . . . . . . . . . . . . . . . . . . . 150.00
5 Military humor . . . . . . . . . . . 150.00
6 . . . . . . . . . . . . . . . . . . . . . . 125.00
7 . . . . . . . . . . . . . . . . . . . . . . 125.00
8 . . . . . . . . . . . . . . . . . . . . . . 125.00
9 . . . . . . . . . . . . . . . . . . . . . . 125.00
10 . . . . . . . . . . . . . . . . . . . . . 125.00
11 . . . . . . . . . . . . . . . . . . . . . 100.00
12 . . . . . . . . . . . . . . . . . . . . . 100.00
13 . . . . . . . . . . . . . . . . . . . . . 100.00
14 . . . . . . . . . . . . . . . . . . . . . 100.00
15 . . . . . . . . . . . . . . . . . . . . . 100.00
16 . . . . . . . . . . . . . . . . . . . . . 100.00
17 . . . . . . . . . . . . . . . . . . . . . 100.00
18 . . . . . . . . . . . . . . . . . . . . . 100.00

## HEROES OF
## THE WILD FRONTIER
See: BAFFLING
MYSTERIES

## HEROIC COMICS

**Eastern Color Printing Co./
Famous Funnies Aug., 1940**

1 BEv(a&c),O:Hydroman,Purple
  Zombie, B:Man of India . . . 3,000.00
2 BEv(a&c),B:Hydroman (c)s. . 1,500.00
3 BEv(a&c) . . . . . . . . . . . . . . . . . 750.00
4 BEv(a&c) . . . . . . . . . . . . . . . . . 750.00
5 BEv(a&c) . . . . . . . . . . . . . . . . . 700.00
6 BEv(a&c) . . . . . . . . . . . . . . . . . 650.00
7 BEv(a&c),O:Man O'Metal . . . . 750.00
8 BEv(a&c) . . . . . . . . . . . . . . . . . 500.00
9 BEv . . . . . . . . . . . . . . . . . . . . . 500.00
10 BEv . . . . . . . . . . . . . . . . . . . . 500.00
11 BEv,E:Hydroman (c)s . . . . . . 500.00
12 BEv,B&0:Music Master . . . . . 550.00
13 BEv,RC,LF . . . . . . . . . . . . . . . 500.00
14 BEv . . . . . . . . . . . . . . . . . . . . 550.00
15 BEv,I:Downbeat . . . . . . . . . . 550.00
16 BEv,BTh,CCB(c),A:Lieut
  Nininger, Major Heidger,Lieut
  Welch,B:P(c) . . . . . . . . . . . . 300.00
17 BEv,A:JohnJames Powers,Hewitt
  T.Wheless, Irving Strobing. . . 300.00
18 HcK,BEv,Pass the
  Ammunition . . . . . . . . . . . . 300.00
19 HcK,BEv,A:Barney Ross. . . . 300.00
20 HcK,BEv . . . . . . . . . . . . . . . . 300.00
21 HcK,BEv . . . . . . . . . . . . . . . . 200.00
22 HcK,BEv,Howard Gilmore. . . 200.00
23 HcK,BEv . . . . . . . . . . . . . . . . 200.00
24 HcK,BEv . . . . . . . . . . . . . . . . 200.00
25 HcK,BEv . . . . . . . . . . . . . . . . 200.00
26 HcK,BEv . . . . . . . . . . . . . . . . 200.00
27 HcK,BEv . . . . . . . . . . . . . . . . 200.00
28 HcK,BEv,E:Man O'Metal. . . . 200.00
29 HcK,BEv,E:Hydroman. . . . . . 200.00
30 BEv . . . . . . . . . . . . . . . . . . . . 200.00
31 BEv,CCB,Capt. Tootsie. . . . . 125.00
32 ATh,CCB,WWII(c),
  Capt. Tootsie . . . . . . . . . . . 150.00
33 ATh, . . . . . . . . . . . . . . . . . . . 175.00
34 WWII(c) . . . . . . . . . . . . . . . . 125.00
35 Ath,B:Rescue(c) . . . . . . . . . . 175.00
36 HcK,ATh . . . . . . . . . . . . . . . . 150.00
37 same . . . . . . . . . . . . . . . . . . . 75.00
38 ATh . . . . . . . . . . . . . . . . . . . . 150.00
39 HcK,ATh . . . . . . . . . . . . . . . . 125.00
40 ATh,Boxing . . . . . . . . . . . . . . 125.00
41 Grl(c),ATh . . . . . . . . . . . . . . . 125.00
42 ATh . . . . . . . . . . . . . . . . . . . . 125.00
43 ATh . . . . . . . . . . . . . . . . . . . . 100.00
44 HcK,ATh . . . . . . . . . . . . . . . . 100.00
45 HcK . . . . . . . . . . . . . . . . . . . . 100.00
46 HcK . . . . . . . . . . . . . . . . . . . . 100.00

47 HcK . . . . . . . . . . . . . . . . . . . . 100.00
48 HcK . . . . . . . . . . . . . . . . . . . . 125.00
49 HcK . . . . . . . . . . . . . . . . . . . . 100.00
50 HcK . . . . . . . . . . . . . . . . . . . . 100.00
51 HcK,ATh,AW . . . . . . . . . . . . . 150.00
52 HcK,AW . . . . . . . . . . . . . . . . . 125.00
53 HcK . . . . . . . . . . . . . . . . . . . . 125.00
54 . . . . . . . . . . . . . . . . . . . . . . . 125.00
55 ATh . . . . . . . . . . . . . . . . . . . . 125.00
56 ATh(c) . . . . . . . . . . . . . . . . . . 100.00
57 ATh(c) . . . . . . . . . . . . . . . . . . 100.00
58 ATh(c) . . . . . . . . . . . . . . . . . . 100.00
59 ATh(c) . . . . . . . . . . . . . . . . . . 100.00
60 ATh(c) . . . . . . . . . . . . . . . . . . 100.00
61 BEv(c) . . . . . . . . . . . . . . . . . . 100.00
62 BEv(c) . . . . . . . . . . . . . . . . . . 100.00
63 BEv(c) . . . . . . . . . . . . . . . . . . 100.00
64 GE,BEv(c). . . . . . . . . . . . . . . 100.00
65 HcK(c),FF,ATh,AW,GE . . . . . 150.00
66 HcK(c),FF . . . . . . . . . . . . . . . 125.00
67 HcK(c),FF,Korean War(c) . . . . 125.00
68 HcK(c),Korean War(c). . . . . . 100.00
69 HcK(c),FF . . . . . . . . . . . . . . . 150.00
70 HcK(c),FF,B:Korean War(c) . . 100.00
71 HcK(c),FF . . . . . . . . . . . . . . . 100.00
72 HcK(c),FF . . . . . . . . . . . . . . . 150.00
73 HcK(c),FF . . . . . . . . . . . . . . . 100.00
74 HcK(c). . . . . . . . . . . . . . . . . . 100.00
75 HcK(c),FF . . . . . . . . . . . . . . . 100.00
76 thru 80 HcK,HcK(c). . . . . . . @100.00
81 FF,HcK(c) . . . . . . . . . . . . . . . 100.00
82 FF,HcK(c) . . . . . . . . . . . . . . . 100.00
83 FF,HcK(c) . . . . . . . . . . . . . . . 100.00
84 HcK(c). . . . . . . . . . . . . . . . . . 100.00
85 HcK(c). . . . . . . . . . . . . . . . . . 100.00
86 HcK(c) . . . . . . . . . . . . . . . . . 120.00
87 FF,HcK(c) . . . . . . . . . . . . . . . 120.00
88 HcK(c),E:Korean War (c)s . . . 100.00
89 HcK(c) . . . . . . . . . . . . . . . . . 100.00
90 HcK(c). . . . . . . . . . . . . . . . . . 100.00
91 HcK(c) . . . . . . . . . . . . . . . . . 100.00
92 HcK(c) . . . . . . . . . . . . . . . . . 100.00
93 HcK(c) . . . . . . . . . . . . . . . . . 100.00
94 HcK(c) . . . . . . . . . . . . . . . . . 120.00
95 HcK(c) . . . . . . . . . . . . . . . . . 100.00
96 HcK(c) . . . . . . . . . . . . . . . . . 100.00
97 HcK(c),E:P(c),June, 1955. . . . 100.00

## HICKORY

**Comic Magazine
(Quality Comics Group),
Oct., 1949**

1 HSa, . . . . . . . . . . . . . . . . . . . 200.00
2 HSa, . . . . . . . . . . . . . . . . . . . 125.00
3 HSa, . . . . . . . . . . . . . . . . . . . 100.00

*Hi-School Romance #57*
© Harvey Publications

*Hit Comics #5*
© Quality Comics Group

*Hit Comics #58*
© Quality Comics Group

4 HSa, . . . . . . . . . . . . . . . . . . . . 100.00
5 HSa, . . . . . . . . . . . . . . . . . . . . 100.00
6 HSa,Aug., 1950 . . . . . . . . . . 100.00

## HIGH ADVENTURE
**Decker Publ. (Red Top), 1957**
1 BK . . . . . . . . . . . . . . . . . . . 100.00

## HI-HO COMICS
**Four Star Publications, 1946**
1 LbC(c) . . . . . . . . . . . . . . . . . . 600.00
2 LbC(c) . . . . . . . . . . . . . . . . . . 300.00
3 1946 . . . . . . . . . . . . . . . . . . 250.00

## HI-JINX
**B & I Publ. Co. (American Comics Group), July–Aug., 1947**
1 (fa) all . . . . . . . . . . . . . . . . . 250.00
2 . . . . . . . . . . . . . . . . . . . . . . . 175.00
3 . . . . . . . . . . . . . . . . . . . . . . . 125.00
4 thru 7 . . . . . . . . . . . . . . . @100.00
N# . . . . . . . . . . . . . . . . . . . . . 150.00

## HI-LITE COMICS
**E.R. Ross Publ. Fall, 1945**
1 . . . . . . . . . . . . . . . . . . . . . . 350.00

## HILLBILLY COMICS
**Charlton Comics, 1955**
1 . . . . . . . . . . . . . . . . . . . . . . 125.00
2 thru 4 July 1956 . . . . . . . . . @100.00

## HI-SCHOOL ROMANCE
**Harvey Publications, 1949–58**
1 BP,Ph(c). . . . . . . . . . . . . . . . 175.00
2 BP,Ph(c). . . . . . . . . . . . . . . . 150.00
3 BP,Ph(c). . . . . . . . . . . . . . . . 125.00
4 Ph(c) . . . . . . . . . . . . . . . . . . 125.00
5 BPPh(c) . . . . . . . . . . . . . . . . 125.00
6 . . . . . . . . . . . . . . . . . . . . . . . 125.00
7 . . . . . . . . . . . . . . . . . . . . . . . 125.00
8 BP . . . . . . . . . . . . . . . . . . . . 125.00
9 . . . . . . . . . . . . . . . . . . . . . . . 125.00
10 Rare . . . . . . . . . . . . . . . . . 150.00
11 thru 20 BP(in many) . . . . . @100.00
21 thru 50 . . . . . . . . . . . . . . @100.00
51 thru 75 . . . . . . . . . . . . . . @75.00

## HI-SPOT COMICS
**See: RED RYDER COMICS**

## HIT COMICS
**Comics Magazine (Quality Comics Group), July, 1940**
1 LF(c),O:Neon,Hercules,I:The Red Bee, B:Bob & Swab, Blaze Barton Strange Twins,X-5 Super Agent Casey Jones,Jack & Jill . . . 9,500.00
2 GT,LF(c),B:Old Witch . . . . . 3,500.00
3 GT,LF(c),E:Casey Jones. . . . 3,200.00
4 GT,LF(c),B:Super Agent & Betty Bates,E:X-5. . . . . . . 2,900.00
5 GT,LF(c),B:Red Bee (c) . . . . 8,000.00
6 GT,LF(c) . . . . . . . . . . . . . . 2,500.00
7 GT,LF(c),E:Red Bee (c) . . . . 2,500.00
8 GT,LF(c),B:Neon (c) . . . . . . 2,500.00
9 JCo,LF(c),E:Neon (c) . . . . . . 2,500.00
10 JCo,RC,LF(c),B:Hercules(c) 2,500.00
11 JCo,RC,LF(c),A:Hercules. . 2,200.00
12 JCo,RC,LF(c),A:Hercules . . 2,200.00
13 JCo,RC,LF(c),A:Hercules . . 2,200.00
14 JCo,RC,LF(c),A:Hercules . . 2,200.00
15 JCo,RC,A:Hercules . . . . . . . 1,500.00
16 JCo,RC,LF(c),A:Hercules . . 1,500.00
17 JCo,RC,LF(c),E:Hercules(c) 1,500.00
18 JCo,RC(a&c),O:Stormy Foster,B:Ghost of Flanders 1,600.00
19 JCo,RC(c),B:Stormy Foster(c) . . . . . . . . . . . . . . 1,300.00
20 JCo,RC(c),A:Stormy Foster . 1,400.00
21 JCo,RC(c) . . . . . . . . . . . . . 1,350.00
22 JCo. . . . . . . . . . . . . . . . . . 1,350.00
23 JCo,RC(a&c) . . . . . . . . . . . 1,300.00
24 JCo,E:Stormy Foster (c) . . . 1,300.00
25 JCo,RP,O:Kid Eternity . . . . . 2,500.00
26 JCo,RP,A:Black Hawk . . . . . 1,400.00
27 JCo,RP,B:Kid Eternity (c)s . . . 700.00
28 JCo,RP,A:Her Highness . . . . . 700.00
29 JCo,RP . . . . . . . . . . . . . . . . . 700.00
30 JCo,RP,HK,V:Julius Caesar and his Legion of Warriors . . 600.00
31 JCo,RP . . . . . . . . . . . . . . . . . 600.00
32 JCo,RP,V:Merlin the Wizard . . 350.00
33 JCo,RP . . . . . . . . . . . . . . . . . 300.00
34 JCo,RP,E:Stormy Foster . . . . 300.00
35 JCo,Kid Eternity Accused of Murder. . . . . . . . . . . . . . . 300.00
36 JCo,The Witch's Curse. . . . . 300.00
37 JCo,V:Mr. Silence . . . . . . . . . 300.00
38 JCo . . . . . . . . . . . . . . . . . . . 300.00
39 JCo,Runaway River Boat . . . 300.00
40 PG,V:Monster from the Past . 300.00
41 PG,Did Kid Eternity Lose His Power? . . . . . . . . . . . . 250.00

42 PG,Kid Eternity Loses Killer Cronson. . . . . . . . . . . . . . . 250.00
43 JCo,PG,V:Modern Bluebeard . . . . . . . . . . . . . 250.00
44 JCo,PG,Trips up the Shoe . . . 250.00
45 JCo,PG,Pancho Villa against Don Pablo . . . . . . . . . . . . . 250.00
46 JCo,V:Mr. Hardeel. . . . . . . . . 250.00
47 A Polished Diamond Can Be Rough on Rats . . . . . . . . . . 250.00
48 EhH,A Treasure Chest of Trouble . . . . . . . . . . . . . . 250.00
49 EhH,V:Monsters from the Mirror . . . . . . . . . . . . . . 250.00
50 EhH,Heads for Trouble . . . . 250.00
51 EhH,Enters the Forgotten World . . . . . . . . . . . . . . . . 225.00
52 EhH,Heroes out of the Past . . 225.00
53 EhH,V:Mr. Puny . . . . . . . . . . 225.00
54 V:Ghost Town Killer. . . . . . . . 225.00
55 V:The Brute. . . . . . . . . . . . . . 225.00
56 V:Big Odds . . . . . . . . . . . . . . 225.00
57 Solves the Picture in a Frame. . . . . . . . . . . . . . . 225.00
58 Destroys Oppression! . . . . . . 225.00
59 Battles Tomorrow's Crimes Today! . . . . . . . . . . . . . . . . 225.00
60 E:Kid Eternity (c)s, V:The Mummy . . . . . . . . . . 225.00
61 RC(a&c),I:Jeb Rivers . . . . . . . 250.00
62 RC(c). . . . . . . . . . . . . . . . . . . 225.00
63 RC(c),A:Jeb Rivers. . . . . . . . . 250.00
64 RC,A:Jeb Rivers . . . . . . . . . . . 250.00
65 Bondage (c),RC,July, 1950. . . 275.00

## HOLIDAY COMICS
**Fawcett Publ., Nov., 1942**
1 Captain Marvel (c) . . . . . . . . 2,100.00

## HOLIDAY COMICS
**Marvel Star, Jan., 1951**
1 LbC(c),Christmas(c). . . . . . . . 450.00
2 LbC(c),Easter Parade(c) . . . . . 450.00
3 LbC(c),4th of July(c) . . . . . . . 300.00
4 LbC(c),Summer Vacation. . . . 275.00
5 LbC(c),Christmas(c). . . . . . . . 275.00
6 LbC(c),Birthday(c) . . . . . . . . . 275.00
7 LbC(c),Rodeo (c) . . . . . . . . . . 275.00
8 LbC(c),Xmas(c) Oct., 1952 . . 275.00
**Becomes:**

## FUN COMICS
**Marvel Star, 1953**
9 LbC . . . . . . . . . . . . . . . . . . . . 275.00

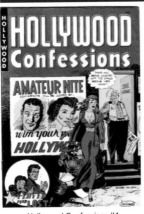

*Hollywood Confessions #1*
*© St. John Publ. Co.*

*Holyoke One-Shot #3*
*© Holyoke Publ. Co.*

*Hoot Gibson Western #6*
*© Fox Features Syndicate*

**Ho**

10 LbC . . . . . . . . . . . . . . . . . . . 250.00
11 LbC . . . . . . . . . . . . . . . . . . . 250.00
12 LbC . . . . . . . . . . . . . . . . . . . 250.00
Becomes:

## MIGHTY BEAR
**Marvel Star, 1954**
13 LbC . . . . . . . . . . . . . . . . . . . 100.00
14 LbC . . . . . . . . . . . . . . . . . . . 100.00
Becomes:

## UNSANE
**Marvel Star, 1954**
15 . . . . . . . . . . . . . . . . . . . . . . 475.00

## HOLLYWOOD COMICS
**New Age Publishers,**
**Winter, 1944**
1 (fa) . . . . . . . . . . . . . . . . . . . . 200.00

## HOLLYWOOD CONFESSIONS
**St. John Publ. Co.,**
**Oct., 1949**
1 JKu(a&c) . . . . . . . . . . . . . . . 350.00
2 JKu(a&c), Dec., 1949 . . . . . . 400.00

## HOLLYWOOD DIARY
**Comics Magazine**
**(Quality Comics), Dec., 1949**
1 . . . . . . . . . . . . . . . . . . . . . . . 250.00
2 Photo (c) . . . . . . . . . . . . . . . 200.00
3 Photo (c) . . . . . . . . . . . . . . . 150.00
4 . . . . . . . . . . . . . . . . . . . . . . . 150.00
5 Photo (c), Aug., 1950 . . . . . . 150.00

## HOLLYWOOD FILM STORIES
**Feature Publications,**
**(Prize) April, 1950**
1 June Allison,Ph(c) . . . . . . . . . 250.00
2 Lizabeth Scott,Ph(c) . . . . . . . 150.00
3 Barbara Stanwick,Ph(c) . . . . . 150.00
4 Beth Hutton, Aug., 1950 . . . . 150.00

## HOLLYWOOD FUNNY FOLKES
**See: FUNNY FOLKES**

## HOLLYWOOD SECRETS
**Comics Magazine**
**(Quality Comics Group),**
**Nov., 1949**
1 BWa,BWa(c) . . . . . . . . . . . . 400.00
2 BWa,BWa(c),RC . . . . . . . . . 300.00
3 Ph(c) . . . . . . . . . . . . . . . . . 200.00
4 Ph(c),May, 1950 . . . . . . . . . 200.00
5 Ph(c) . . . . . . . . . . . . . . . . . 200.00
6 Ph(c) . . . . . . . . . . . . . . . . . 200.00

## HOLYOKE ONE-SHOT
**Tem Publ.**
**(Holyoke Publ. Co.), 1944**
1 Grit Grady . . . . . . . . . . . . . . 300.00
2 Rusty Dugan . . . . . . . . . . . . 300.00
3 JK,Miss Victory,O:Cat Woman. 400.00
4 Mr. Miracle . . . . . . . . . . . . . 250.00
5 U.S. Border Patrol . . . . . . . . 250.00
6 Capt. Fearless . . . . . . . . . . . 250.00
7 Strong Man . . . . . . . . . . . . . 300.00
8 Blue Streak . . . . . . . . . . . . . 200.00
9 S&K, Citizen Smith . . . . . . . . 300.00
10 S&K, Capt. Stone . . . . . . . . . 300.00

## HOMER, THE HAPPY GHOST
**Marvel, March, 1955**
1 . . . . . . . . . . . . . . . . . . . . . . . 250.00
2 . . . . . . . . . . . . . . . . . . . . . . . 150.00
3 . . . . . . . . . . . . . . . . . . . . . . . 125.00
4 thru 15 . . . . . . . . . . . . . . @125.00
16 thru 22 . . . . . . . . . . . . . . @100.00

## HOMER HOOPER
**Marvel Atlas, 1953**
1 Teen-age romance humor . . . . 150.00
2 . . . . . . . . . . . . . . . . . . . . . . . 100.00
3 . . . . . . . . . . . . . . . . . . . . . . . 100.00
4 . . . . . . . . . . . . . . . . . . . . . . . 100.00

## HONEYMOON
**See: GAY COMICS**

## HONEYMOON ROMANCE
**Artful Publications**
**(Digest Size), April, 1950**
1 . . . . . . . . . . . . . . . . . . . . . . . 450.00
2 July, 1950 . . . . . . . . . . . . . . 425.00

## THE HOODED HORSEMAN
**See: BLAZING WEST**
**Also: OUT OF THE NIGHT**

## HOORAY COMICS
**Tendon Publishing Co., 1946**
1 Funny animal . . . . . . . . . . . . . 250.00

## HOOT GIBSON WESTERN
**Fox Features Syndicate, 1950**
**(Formerly: MY LOVE STORY)**
1 (5) Ph(c) . . . . . . . . . . . . . . . . 350.00
2 (6) . . . . . . . . . . . . . . . . . . . . 325.00
3 WW . . . . . . . . . . . . . . . . . . . 350.00

## HOPALONG CASSIDY
**Fawcett Publications,**
**Feb., 1943**
1 B:Hopalong Cassidy & Topper,
    Captain Marvel (c) . . . . . . 7,000.00
2 . . . . . . . . . . . . . . . . . . . . . . 1,000.00
3 Blazing Trails . . . . . . . . . . . . 600.00
4 5-full length story . . . . . . . . . 500.00
5 Death in the Saddle, Ph(c) . . . 450.00
6 . . . . . . . . . . . . . . . . . . . . . . . 450.00
7 . . . . . . . . . . . . . . . . . . . . . . . 450.00
8 Phantom Stage Coach . . . . . . 450.00
9 The Last Stockade . . . . . . . . 450.00
10 4-spine tingling adventures. . . 450.00
11 Desperate Jetters! Ph(c) . . . . 300.00
12 The Mysterious Message . . . . 300.00
13 The Human Target, Ph(c) . . . . 300.00
14 Land of the Lawless, Ph(c). . . 300.00
15 Death holds the Reins, Ph(c) . 300.00
16 Webfoot's Revenge, Ph(c) . . . 300.00
17 The Hangman's Noose, Ph(c) 300.00
18 The Ghost of Dude Ranch,
    Ph(c) . . . . . . . . . . . . . . . . 300.00
19 A:William Boyd,Ph(c) . . . . . . 300.00
20 The Notorious Nellie Blaine!,
    B:P(c) . . . . . . . . . . . . . . . . 225.00
21 V:Arizona Kid . . . . . . . . . . . . 225.00
22 V:Arizona Kid . . . . . . . . . . . . 225.00
23 Hayride Horror . . . . . . . . . . . 225.00
24 Twin River Giant . . . . . . . . . . 225.00
25 On the Trails of the Wild
    and Wooly West . . . . . . . . . 225.00
26 thru 30 . . . . . . . . . . . . . . . @200.00
31 52 pages . . . . . . . . . . . . . . . 150.00
32 36 pages . . . . . . . . . . . . . . . 150.00
33 52 pages . . . . . . . . . . . . . . . 150.00

---

All comics prices listed are for *Near Mint* condition.          **Page 149**

Hopalong Cassidy #25
© Fawcett Publications

Hopalong Cassidy #86
© DC Comics

Hoppy the Marvel Bunny #1
© Fawcett Publications

34 52 pages . . . . . . . . . . . . . . . 150.00
35 52 pages . . . . . . . . . . . . . . . 150.00
36 36 pages . . . . . . . . . . . . . . . 125.00
37 thru 40, 52 pages . . . . . . . @150.00
40 36 pages . . . . . . . . . . . . . . . 150.00
41 E:P(c) . . . . . . . . . . . . . . . . 150.00
42 B:Ph(c) . . . . . . . . . . . . . . . 150.00
43 . . . . . . . . . . . . . . . . . . . . . 150.00
44 . . . . . . . . . . . . . . . . . . . . . 125.00
45 . . . . . . . . . . . . . . . . . . . . . 135.00
46 thru 51 . . . . . . . . . . . . . . . @125.00
52 . . . . . . . . . . . . . . . . . . . . . 100.00
53 . . . . . . . . . . . . . . . . . . . . . 125.00
54 . . . . . . . . . . . . . . . . . . . . . 125.00
55 . . . . . . . . . . . . . . . . . . . . . 100.00
56 . . . . . . . . . . . . . . . . . . . . . 125.00
57 thru 70 . . . . . . . . . . . . . . . @125.00
71 thru 84 . . . . . . . . . . . . . . . @100.00
85 E:Ph(c),Jan., 1954 . . . . . . . . 125.00

## HOPALONG CASSIDY
### DC Comics, Feb., 1954
86 GC,Ph(c):William Boyd & Topper,
    Secret o/t Tattooed Burro . . . 500.00
87 GC,Ph(c),Tenderfoot Outlaw. . 250.00
88 Ph(c),GC,15 Robbers of Rimfire
    Ridge . . . . . . . . . . . . . . . . . . 175.00
89 GC,Ph(c),One-Day Boom
    Town . . . . . . . . . . . . . . . . . . 175.00
90 GC,Ph(c),Cowboy Clown
    Robberies . . . . . . . . . . . . . . 175.00
91 GC,Ph(c),The Riddle of
    the Roaring R Ranch . . . . . . 175.00
92 GC,Ph(c),Sky-RidingOutlaws . 150.00
93 GC,Ph(c),Silver Badge
    of Courage. . . . . . . . . . . . . . 150.00
94 GC,Ph(c),Mystery of the
    Masquerading Lion . . . . . . . . 150.00
95 GC,Ph(c),Showdown at the
    Post-Hole Bank . . . . . . . . . . 150.00
96 GC,Ph(c),Knights of
    the Range . . . . . . . . . . . . . . 150.00
97 GC,Ph(c),The Mystery of
    the Three-Eyed Cowboy . . . . 150.00
98 GC,Ph(c),Hopalong's
    Unlucky Day . . . . . . . . . . . . . 150.00
99 GC,Ph(c),Partners in Peril . . . 150.00
100 GC,Ph(c),The Secrets
    of a Sheriff. . . . . . . . . . . . . . 175.00
101 GC,Ph(c),Way Out West
    Where The East Begins . . . . 125.00
102 GC,Ph(c),Secret of the
    Buffalo Hat. . . . . . . . . . . . . . 125.00
103 GC,Ph(c),The Train-Rustlers
    of Avalanche Valley . . . . . . . . 125.00

104 GC,Ph(c),Secret of the
    Surrendering Outlaws . . . . . 125.00
105 GC,Ph(c),Three Signs
    to Danger. . . . . . . . . . . . . . . 125.00
106 GC,Ph(c),The Secret of
    the Stolen Signature . . . . . . . 125.00
107 GC,Ph(c),The Mystery Trail
    to Stagecoach Town . . . . . . . 125.00
108 GC,Ph(c),The Mystery
    Stage From Burro Bend . . . . 125.00
109 GC,The Big Gun on Saddletop
    Mountain . . . . . . . . . . . . . . . 125.00
110 GC,The Dangerous Stunts
    of Hopalong Cassidy . . . . . . . 100.00
111 GC,Sheriff Cassidy's
    Mystery Clue . . . . . . . . . . . . 100.00
112 GC,Treasure Trail to
    Thunderbolt Ridge. . . . . . . . . 100.00
113 GC,The Shadow of the
    Toy Soldier. . . . . . . . . . . . . . 100.00
114 GC,Ambush at Natural
    Bridge . . . . . . . . . . . . . . . . . 100.00
115 GC,The Empty-Handed
    Robberies . . . . . . . . . . . . . . 100.00
116 GC,Mystery of the
    Vanishing Cabin. . . . . . . . . . . 100.00
117 GC,School for Sheriffs . . . . . 100.00
118 GC,The Hero of
    Comanche Ridge. . . . . . . . . . 100.00
119 GC,The Dream Sheriff of
    Twin Rivers . . . . . . . . . . . . . 100.00
120 GC,Salute to a Star-Wearer . 100.00
121 GC,The Secret of the
    Golden Caravan . . . . . . . . . . 100.00
122 GC,The Rocking
    Horse Bandits . . . . . . . . . . . 100.00
123 GK,Mystery of the
    One-Dollar Bank Robbery . . . 100.00
124 GK,Mystery of the
    Double-X Brand. . . . . . . . . . . 100.00
125 GK,Hopalong Cassidy's
    Secret Brother . . . . . . . . . . . 100.00
126 GK,Trail of the
    Telltale Clues. . . . . . . . . . . . . 100.00
127 GK,Hopalong Cassidy's
    Golden Riddle . . . . . . . . . . . . 100.00
128 GK,The House That
    Hated Outlaws. . . . . . . . . . . . 100.00
129 GK,Hopalong Cassidy's
    Indian Sign . . . . . . . . . . . . . . 100.00
130 GK,The Return of the
    Canine Sheriff . . . . . . . . . . . . 100.00
131 GK&GK(c),The Amazing
    Sheriff of Double Creek. . . . . 100.00
132 GK,Track of the
    Invisible Indians. . . . . . . . . . . 100.00

133 GK,Golden Trail to Danger . . 100.00
134 GK,Case of the
    Three Crack-Shots . . . . . . . . 100.00
135 GK,May-June, 1959 . . . . . . . 100.00

## HOPPY THE
## MARVEL BUNNY
### Fawcett Publications,
### Dec., 1945
1 A:Marvel Bunny . . . . . . . . . . 650.00
2 . . . . . . . . . . . . . . . . . . . . . . 300.00
3 . . . . . . . . . . . . . . . . . . . . . . 250.00
4 . . . . . . . . . . . . . . . . . . . . . . 250.00
5 . . . . . . . . . . . . . . . . . . . . . . 250.00
6 thru 14 . . . . . . . . . . . . . . . . @200.00
15 Sept., 1947 . . . . . . . . . . . . . 200.00

## HORACE &
## DOTTY DRIPPLE
## See: DOTTY DRIPPLE

## HORRIFIC
### Artful/Comic Media/
### Harwell Publ./Mystery,
### Sept., 1952
1 Conductor in Flames(c) . . . . . . 700.00
2 Human Puppets(c). . . . . . . . . . 400.00
3 DH(c),Bullet hole in
    head(c) . . . . . . . . . . . . . . . . 800.00
4 DH(c),head on a stick (c) . . . . 350.00
5 DH(c) . . . . . . . . . . . . . . . . . . 350.00
6 DH(c),Jack the Ripper . . . . . . 350.00
7 DH(c),Shrunken Skulls . . . . . . 350.00
8 DH(c),I:The Teller . . . . . . . . . . 400.00
9 DH(c),Claws of Horror, Wolves
    of Midnight . . . . . . . . . . . . . . 350.00
10 DH(c),The Teller-Four
    Eerie Tales of Horror . . . . . . . 350.00
11 DH(c),A:Gary Ghoul,Freddie,
    Demon,Victor Vampire
    Walter Werewolf . . . . . . . . . . 300.00
12 DH(c),A:Gary Ghoul,Freddie
    Demon,Victor Vampire,
    Walter Werewolf . . . . . . . . . . 300.00
13 DH(c),A:Gary Ghoul,Freddie
    Demom,Victor Vampire,
    Walter Werewolf . . . . . . . . . . 300.00
**Becomes:**

## TERRIFIC COMICS
### Dec., 1954
14 Eye Injury . . . . . . . . . . . . . . . 800.00

*Horrors #15*
*© Marvel Comics Group*

*Hot Rods and Racing Cars #9*
*© Charlton Comics*

*House of Mystery #8*
*© DC Comics*

Ho

15 . . . . . . . . . . . . . . . . . . . . . . . 400.00
16 B:Wonderboy . . . . . . . . . . . . 400.00
**Becomes:**

## WONDERBOY

**Ajax/Farrell Publ., May, 1955**
17 The Enemy's Enemy. . . . . . . 600.00
18 Success Is No Accident,
  July, 1955 . . . . . . . . . . . . . . 500.00

## HORROR FROM
## THE TOMB
### See: MYSTERIOUS
### STORIES

## HORRORS, THE

**Marvel Star Publications,**
**Jan., 1953–April, 1954**
11 LbC(c),JyD,Horrors of War . . . 350.00
12 LbC(c),Horrors of War . . . . . . 350.00
13 LbC(c),Horrors of Mystery . . . 300.00
14 LbC(c),Horrors of the
  Underworld . . . . . . . . . . . . . 350.00
15 LbC(c),Horrors of the
  Underworld . . . . . . . . . . . . . 350.00

## HORSE FEATHER
## COMICS

**Lev Gleason Publications,**
**Nov., 1947**
1 BW . . . . . . . . . . . . . . . . . . . . 350.00
2 . . . . . . . . . . . . . . . . . . . . . . . 250.00
3 . . . . . . . . . . . . . . . . . . . . . . . 200.00
4 Summer, 1948 . . . . . . . . . . . 200.00

## HOT DOG
### See: A-1 COMICS

## HOT ROD AND
## SPEEDWAY COMICS

**Hillman Periodicals**
**Feb.–March, 1952**
1 . . . . . . . . . . . . . . . . . . . . . . . 350.00
2 BK . . . . . . . . . . . . . . . . . . . . . 250.00
3 . . . . . . . . . . . . . . . . . . . . . . . 200.00
4 . . . . . . . . . . . . . . . . . . . . . . . 200.00
5 April–May, 1953 . . . . . . . . . . 200.00

## HOT ROD COMICS

**Fawcett Publications,**
**Feb., 1952–53**
N# BP,BP(c),F:Clint Curtis . . . . 600.00
2 BP,BP(c),Safety comes First . . 375.00
3 BP,BP(c),The Racing Game . . 200.00
4 BP,BP(c),Bonneville National
  Championships . . . . . . . . . . 200.00
5 BP,BP(c), . . . . . . . . . . . . . . . 200.00
6 BP,BP(c),Race to Death . . . . . 200.00

## HOT ROD KING

**Approved Comics**
**(Ziff-Davis), Fall, 1952**
1 P(c) . . . . . . . . . . . . . . . . . . . . 300.00

## HOT RODS
## AND RACING CARS

**Motor Mag./**
**Charlton Comics, 1951**
1 Speedy Davis. . . . . . . . . . . . . 350.00
2 . . . . . . . . . . . . . . . . . . . . . . . 200.00
3 . . . . . . . . . . . . . . . . . . . . . . . 150.00
4 . . . . . . . . . . . . . . . . . . . . . . . 150.00
5 . . . . . . . . . . . . . . . . . . . . . . . 150.00
6 . . . . . . . . . . . . . . . . . . . . . . . 150.00
7 . . . . . . . . . . . . . . . . . . . . . . . 150.00
8 . . . . . . . . . . . . . . . . . . . . . . . 150.00
9 . . . . . . . . . . . . . . . . . . . . . . . 150.00
10 . . . . . . . . . . . . . . . . . . . . . . 150.00
11 thru 20 . . . . . . . . . . . . . . . @125.00
21 thru 70 . . . . . . . . . . . . . . . @100.00

## HOT STUFF,
## THE LITTLE DEVIL

**Harvey Publications, 1957**
1 . . . . . . . . . . . . . . . . . . . . . . . 650.00
2 1st Stumbo the Giant . . . . . . . 300.00
3 thru 5 . . . . . . . . . . . . . . . . . @225.00
6 thru 10 . . . . . . . . . . . . . . . . @200.00
11 thru 20 . . . . . . . . . . . . . . . @150.00
21 thru 40. . . . . . . . . . . . . . . . @125.00
41 thru 60 . . . . . . . . . . . . . . . @100.00

## HOT STUFF SIZZLERS

**Harvey Publications, 1960**
1 F:Hot Stuff . . . . . . . . . . . . . . 225.00
2 . . . . . . . . . . . . . . . . . . . . . . . 150.00
3 . . . . . . . . . . . . . . . . . . . . . . . 125.00
4 . . . . . . . . . . . . . . . . . . . . . . . 125.00
5 . . . . . . . . . . . . . . . . . . . . . . . 125.00

6 . . . . . . . . . . . . . . . . . . . . . . . 100.00
7 . . . . . . . . . . . . . . . . . . . . . . . 100.00
8 . . . . . . . . . . . . . . . . . . . . . . . 100.00
9 . . . . . . . . . . . . . . . . . . . . . . . 100.00
10 . . . . . . . . . . . . . . . . . . . . . . 100.00
11 thru 15 . . . . . . . . . . . . . . . . @75.00

## HOUSE OF MYSTERY

**DC Comics, Dec.–Jan., 1952**
1 I Fell In Love With
  a Monster . . . . . . . . . . . . . 3,500.00
2 The Mark of X . . . . . . . . . . . 1,500.00
3 The Dummy of Death . . . . . . 1,100.00
4 The Man With the Evil Eye . . . 750.00
5 The Man With the Strangler
  Hands! . . . . . . . . . . . . . . . . 750.00
6 The Monster in Clay! . . . . . . . 650.00
7 Nine Lives of Alger Denham!. . 650.00
8 Tattoos of Doom . . . . . . . . . . 650.00
9 Secret of the Little Black Bag . 650.00
10 The Wishes of Doom . . . . . . 650.00
11 Deadly Game of G-H-O-S-T . . 550.00
12 The Devil's Chessboard . . . . . 550.00
13 The Theater Of A
  Thousand Thrills! . . . . . . . . . 550.00
14 The Deadly Dolls . . . . . . . . . 550.00
15 The Man Who Could Change
  the World . . . . . . . . . . . . . . . 550.00
16 Dead Men Tell No Tales!. . . . . 450.00
17 Man With the X-Ray Eyes . . . 325.00
18 Dance of Doom. . . . . . . . . . . 325.00
19 The Strange Faces of Death. . 325.00
20 The Beast Of Bristol . . . . . . . 325.00
21 Man Who Could See Death . . 325.00
22 The Phantom's Return . . . . . . 325.00
23 Stamps of Doom . . . . . . . . . . 325.00
24 Kill The Black Cat . . . . . . . . . 325.00
25 The Man With Three Eyes!. . . 325.00
26 The Man with Magic Ears. . . . 300.00
27 Fate Held Four Aces! . . . . . . . 300.00
28 The Wings Of Mr. Milo!. . . . . . 300.00
29 . . . . . . . . . . . . . . . . . . . . . . 300.00
30 . . . . . . . . . . . . . . . . . . . . . . 300.00
31 The Incredible Illusions! . . . . 300.00
32 Pied Piper of the Sea . . . . . . . 300.00
33 Mr. Misfortune! . . . . . . . . . . . 300.00
34 The Hundred Year Duel . . . . . 300.00
35 . . . . . . . . . . . . . . . . . . . . . . 300.00
36 The Treasure of Montezuma! . 250.00
37 MD,The Statue That
  Came to Life . . . . . . . . . . . . 250.00
38 The Voyage Of No Return . . . 250.00
39 . . . . . . . . . . . . . . . . . . . . . . 250.00
40 The Coins That Came To Life. 250.00
41 The Impossible Tricks! . . . . . . 250.00

---

*House of Mystery #53*
*© DC Comics*

*House of Mystery #113*
*© DC Comics*

*House of Secrets #17*
*© DC Comics*

42 The Stranger From Out There 250.00
43 . . . . . . . . . . . . . . . . . . . . . . 250.00
44 The Secret Of Hill 14 . . . . . . . 250.00
45 . . . . . . . . . . . . . . . . . . . . . . 250.00
46 The Bird of Fate . . . . . . . . . . . 250.00
47 The Robot Named Think. . . . . 250.00
48 The Man Marooned On Earth. 250.00
49 The Mysterious Mr. Omen . . . 250.00
50 . . . . . . . . . . . . . . . . . . . . . . 275.00
51 Man Who Stole Teardrops . . . 225.00
52 The Man With The Golden
    Shoes . . . . . . . . . . . . . . . . . 225.00
53 The Man Who Hated Mirrors . 225.00
54 The Woman Who Lived Twice 225.00
55 I Turned Back Time. . . . . . . . 225.00
56 The Thing In The Black Box . . 225.00
57 The Untamed . . . . . . . . . . . . 225.00
58 . . . . . . . . . . . . . . . . . . . . . . 225.00
59 The Tomb Of Ramfis. . . . . . . 225.00
60 The Prisoner On Canvas . . . . 225.00
61 JK,Superstition Day . . . . . . . . 225.00
62 The Haunting Scarecrow . . . . 200.00
63 JK,The Lady & The Creature . 225.00
64 The Golden Doom . . . . . . . . . 200.00
65 JK,The Magic Lantern. . . . . . . 275.00
66 JK,Sinister Shadow. . . . . . . . . 275.00
67 The Wizard of Water. . . . . . . . 200.00
68 The Book That Bewitched. . . . 200.00
69 The Miniature Disasters . . . . . 200.00
70 JK,The Man With Nine Lives . 200.00
71 Menace of the Mole Man . . . . 200.00
72 JK,Dark Journey . . . . . . . . . . . 200.00
73 Museum That Came to Life . . 200.00
74 Museum That Came To Life . . 200.00
75 Assignment Unknown! . . . . . . 200.00
76 JK,Prisoners Of The Tiny
    Universe . . . . . . . . . . . . . . . . 200.00
77 The Eyes That Went Berserk . 175.00
78 JK(c),The 13th Hour . . . . . . . . 200.00
79 JK(c),The Fantastic Sky
    Puzzle . . . . . . . . . . . . . . . . . 200.00
80 Man With Countless Faces! . . 175.00
81 The Man Who Made Utopia . . 175.00
82 The Riddle of the Earth's
    Second Moon . . . . . . . . . . . 175.00
83 The Mystery of the
    Martian Eye . . . . . . . . . . . . . 175.00
84 JK,BK,100-Century Doom . . . 250.00
85 JK(c),Earth's Strangest
    Salesman. . . . . . . . . . . . . . . 225.00
86 The Baffling Bargains . . . . . . . 200.00
87 The Human Diamond . . . . . . . 200.00
88 Return of the Animal Man. . . . 200.00
89 The Cosmic Plant! . . . . . . . . . 200.00
90 The Invasion Of the Energy
    Creatures! . . . . . . . . . . . . . . . 200.00

91 DD&SMo(c),The Riddle of the
    Alien Satellite. . . . . . . . . . . . 200.00
92 DD(c),Menace of the
    Golden Globule . . . . . . . . . . 200.00
93 NC(c),I Fought The
    Molten Monster . . . . . . . . . . 200.00
94 DD&SMo(c),The Creature
    In Echo Lake . . . . . . . . . . . . 200.00
95 The Wizard's Gift . . . . . . . . . . 200.00
96 The Amazing 70-Ton Man. . . . 200.00
97 The Alien Who Change
    History . . . . . . . . . . . . . . . . . 200.00
98 DD&SMo(c),The Midnight
    Creature. . . . . . . . . . . . . . . . 200.00
99 The Secret of the
    Leopard God . . . . . . . . . . . . 200.00
100 The Beast Beneath Earth . . . 225.00
101 The Magnificent Monster . . . 175.00
102 Cellmate to a Monster . . . . . 175.00
103 Hail the Conquering Aliens . . 175.00
104 I was the Seeing-Eye Man . . 175.00
105 Case of the Creature X-14 . . 175.00
106 Invaders from the Doomed
    Dimension . . . . . . . . . . . . . . 175.00
107 Captives o/t Alien
    Fisherman . . . . . . . . . . . . . . 175.00
108 RMo,Four Faces of Frank
    Forbes . . . . . . . . . . . . . . . . . 175.00
109 ATh,JKu,Secret of the Hybrid
    Creatures. . . . . . . . . . . . . . . 175.00
110 Beast Who Stalked Through
    Time. . . . . . . . . . . . . . . . . . . 175.00
111 Operation Beast Slayer . . . . . 175.00
112 Menace of Craven's
    Creatures. . . . . . . . . . . . . . . 175.00
113 RMo,Prisoners of Beast
    Asteroid . . . . . . . . . . . . . . . . 175.00
114 The Movies from Nowhere . . 175.00
115 Prisoner o/t Golden Mask . . . 175.00
116 RMo,Return of the
    Barsfo Beast . . . . . . . . . . . . 175.00

## HOUSE OF SECRETS
### DC Comics, Nov.–Dec., 1956
1 MD,JM,The Hand of Doom. . 2,100.00
2 MMe,RMo,NC,Mask of Fear . . 700.00
3 JM,JK,MMe,The Three
    Prophecies. . . . . . . . . . . . . . 600.00
4 JM,JK,MMe,Master of
    Unknown . . . . . . . . . . . . . . . 500.00
5 MMe,The Man Who
    Hated Fear . . . . . . . . . . . . . 325.00
6 NC,MMe,Experiment 1000 . . . 325.00
7 RMo,Island o/t Enchantress . . 325.00
8 JK,RMo,The Electrified Man . . 350.00

9 JM,JSt,The Jigsaw Creatures . 275.00
10 JSt,NC,I was a Prisoner
    of the Sea . . . . . . . . . . . . . . 275.00
11 KJ(c),NC,The Man who
    Couldn't Stop Growing. . . . . 275.00
12 JK,The Hole in the Sky. . . . . . 300.00
13 The Face in the Mist. . . . . . . . 200.00
14 MMe,The Man who Stole Air . 200.00
15 The Creature in the Camera. . 200.00
16 NC,We Matched Wits with a
    Gorilla Genius . . . . . . . . . . . 175.00
17 DW,Lady in the Moon . . . . . . . 175.00
18 MMe,The Fantastic
    Typewriter . . . . . . . . . . . . . . 175.00
19 MMe,NC,Lair of the
    Dragonfly . . . . . . . . . . . . . . . 175.00
20 Incredible Fireball Creatures. . 175.00
21 Girl from 50,000 Fathoms. . . . 175.00
22 MMe,Thing from Beyond . . . . 175.00
23 MMe,I&O:Mark Merlin. . . . . . . 200.00
24 NC,Mark Merlin story . . . . . . . 175.00
25 MMe,Mark Merlin story . . . . . 150.00
26 NC,MMe, Mark Merlin story . . 150.00
27 MMe,Mark Merlin . . . . . . . . . . 150.00
28 MMe,Mark Merlin . . . . . . . . . . 150.00
29 NC,MMe,Mark Merlin . . . . . . . 150.00
30 JKu,MMe,Mark Merlin. . . . . . . 150.00
31 DD,MMe,RH,Mark Merlin . . . . 140.00
32 MMe,Mark Merlin . . . . . . . . . . 140.00
33 MMe,Mark Merlin . . . . . . . . . . 140.00
34 MMe,Mark Merlin . . . . . . . . . . 140.00
35 MMe,Mark Merlin . . . . . . . . . . 140.00
36 MMe,Mark Merlin . . . . . . . . . . 140.00
37 MMe,Mark Merlin . . . . . . . . . . 140.00
38 MMe,Mark Merlin . . . . . . . . . . 140.00
39 JKu,MMe,Mark Merlin. . . . . . . 140.00
40 NC,MMe,Mark Merlin. . . . . . . 140.00
41 MMe,Mark Merlin . . . . . . . . . . 140.00
42 MMe,Mark Merlin . . . . . . . . . . 140.00
43 RMo,MMe,CI,Mark Merlin. . . . 140.00
44 MMe,Mark Merlin . . . . . . . . . . 140.00
45 MMe,Mark Merlin . . . . . . . . . . 140.00
46 MMe,Mark Merlin . . . . . . . . . . 140.00
47 MMe,Mark Merlin . . . . . . . . . . 140.00
48 ATh,MMe,Mark Merlin. . . . . . . 140.00
49 MMe,Mark Merlin . . . . . . . . . . 140.00
50 MMe,Mark Merlin . . . . . . . . . . 140.00
51 MMe,Mark Merlin . . . . . . . . . . 140.00
52 MMe,Mark Merlin . . . . . . . . . . 140.00
53 CI,Mark Merlin . . . . . . . . . . . . 140.00
54 RMo,MMe,Mark Merlin . . . . . . 140.00
55 MMe,Mark Merlin . . . . . . . . . . 140.00
56 MMe,Mark Merlin . . . . . . . . . . 140.00
57 MMe,Mark Merlin . . . . . . . . . . 140.00
58 MMe,O:Mark Merlin . . . . . . . . 140.00
59 MMe,Mark Merlin . . . . . . . . . . 140.00

*Howdy Doody #1*
© Dell Publishing Co.

*Human Torch #12*
© Marvel Comics Group

*Humbug #2*
© Harvey Kurtzman

**Hu**

60 MMe,Mark Merlin . . . . . . . . . 140.00
61 I:Eclipso,A:Mark Merlin . . . . . 250.00
62 MMe,Eclipso,Mark Merlin . . . . 140.00

## HOWDY DOODY
**Dell Publishing Co.,
Jan., 1950**

1 Ph(c) . . . . . . . . . . . . . . . . 1,600.00
2 Ph(c) . . . . . . . . . . . . . . . . . 750.00
3 Ph(c) . . . . . . . . . . . . . . . . . 350.00
4 Ph(c) . . . . . . . . . . . . . . . . . 350.00
5 Ph(c) . . . . . . . . . . . . . . . . . 350.00
6 P(c) . . . . . . . . . . . . . . . . . . 400.00
7 thru 10 . . . . . . . . . . . . . . . @250.00
11 & 12. . . . . . . . . . . . . . . . @225.00
13 Christmas (c) . . . . . . . . . . 225.00
14 thru 20. . . . . . . . . . . . . . @225.00
21 thru 38. . . . . . . . . . . . . . @175.00

## HOW STALIN
## HOPES WE WILL
## DESTROY AMERICA
**Pictorial News, 1951**
N# (Giveaway) . . . . . . . . . . . . . 600.00

## HOW TO SHOOT
**Remington, 1952**
N# (promotional) . . . . . . . . . . . 100.00

## HUCKLEBERRY HOUND
**Dell Publishing Co.,
May-July, 1959**

1 . . . . . . . . . . . . . . . . . . . . . 200.00
2 . . . . . . . . . . . . . . . . . . . . . 150.00
3 thru 7 . . . . . . . . . . . . . . . . @125.00
8 thru 10 . . . . . . . . . . . . . . . @100.00
11 thru 17. . . . . . . . . . . . . . . @75.00

## RED RAVEN COMICS
**Marvel Timely Comics Aug.,
1940**
1 JK,O:Red Raven,I:Magar,A:Comet
Pierce & Mercury,Human Top,
Eternal Brain . . . . . . . . . 25,000.00
**Becomes:**

## HUMAN TORCH
**Marvel Comcis, 1940–49**
2 (#1)ASh(c),BEv,B:Sub-Mariner
A:Fiery Mask,Falcon,Mantor,
Microman . . . . . . . . . . . 55,000.00

3 (#2)Ash(c),BEv,V:Sub-
Mariner,Bondage(c) . . . . 10,000.00
4 (#3)ASh(c),BEv,O:Patriot . . . 7,500.00
5 (#4)V:Nazis,A:Patriot,Angel
crossover . . . . . . . . . . . . 6,000.00
5a(#5)ASh(c),V:Sub-Mariner . . 9,000.00
6 ASh(c),Doom Dungeon. . . . . 4,500.00
7 ASh(c),V:Japanese. . . . . . . 4,700.00
8 ASh(c),BW,V:Sub-Mariner . . 6,000.00
9 ASh(c),V:General Rommel . . 5,000.00
10 ASh(c),BW,V:Sub-Mariner . . 5,000.00
11 ASh(c),Nazi Oil Refinery . . . 3,000.00
12 ASh(c),V:Japanese,
Bondage(c). . . . . . . . . . . 5,000.00
13 ASh(c),V:Japanese,
Bondage(c). . . . . . . . . . . 3,000.00
14 ASh(c),V:Nazis. . . . . . . . . 3,000.00
15 ASh(c),Toro Trapped . . . . . 3,000.00
16 ASh(c),V:Japanese . . . . . . 2,500.00
17 ASh(c),V:Japanese . . . . . . 2,500.00
18 ASh(c),V:Japanese,
MacArthurs HQ. . . . . . . . 2,500.00
19 ASh(c),Bondage(c). . . . . . . 2,700.00
20 ASh(c),Last War Issue . . . 2,500.00
21 ASh(c),V:Organized Crime. . 2,500.00
22 ASh(c),V:Smugglers. . . . . . 2,500.00
23 ASh(c),V:Giant Robot. . . . 2,800.00
24 SSh(c),V:Mobsters . . . . . . . 4,000.00
25 The Masked Monster. . . . . 3,500.00
26 SSh(c),Her Diary of Terror . . 3,500.00
27 SSh(c),BEv,V:The Asbestos
Lady. . . . . . . . . . . . . . . . 3,500.00
28 BEv,The Twins Who Weren't 3,500.00
29 SSh(c),You'll Die Laughing . 3,500.00
30 SSh(c),BEv,The Stranger,
A:Namora . . . . . . . . . . . 2,500.00
31 A:Namora. . . . . . . . . . . . . 2,200.00
32 SSh(c),A:Sungirl,Namora. . . 1,300.00
33 Capt.America crossover . . . 2,500.00
34 The Flat of the Land . . . . . 2,200.00
35 A;Captain America,Sungirl . . 2,500.00
**Becomes:**

## LOVE TALES
**Revived As:**

## HUMAN TORCH
**Marvel Comics, 1954**

36 A:Submariner . . . . . . . . . 2,000.00
37 BEv,A:Submariner . . . . . . . 1,800.00
38 BEv,A:Submariner . . . . . . . 1,800.00

## HUMBUG
**Harvey Kurtzman, 1957**
1 JDa,WW,WE,End of the World 400.00

2 JDa,WE,Radiator . . . . . . . . . . 200.00
3 JDa,WE . . . . . . . . . . . . . . . . 150.00
4 JDa,WE,Queen Victoria(c). . . . 150.00
5 JDa,WE . . . . . . . . . . . . . . . . 150.00
6 JDa,WE . . . . . . . . . . . . . . . . 150.00
7 JDa,WE,Sputnik(c). . . . . . . . . 175.00
8 JDa,WE,Elvis/George
Washington(c) . . . . . . . . . . . 150.00
9 JDa,WE . . . . . . . . . . . . . . . . 150.00
10 JDa,Magazine. . . . . . . . . . . . 250.00
11 JDa,WE,HK,Magazine . . . . . . 200.00

## HUMDINGER
**Novelty Press/Premium
Service, May–June, 1946**
1 B:Jerkwater Line,Dink,
Mickey Starlight . . . . . . . . . 500.00
2 . . . . . . . . . . . . . . . . . . . . . 300.00
3 . . . . . . . . . . . . . . . . . . . . . 250.00
4 . . . . . . . . . . . . . . . . . . . . . 250.00
5 . . . . . . . . . . . . . . . . . . . . . 250.00
6 . . . . . . . . . . . . . . . . . . . . . 250.00
2-1 . . . . . . . . . . . . . . . . . . . . 225.00
2-2 July–Aug., 1947 . . . . . . . . . 225.00

## HUMPHREY COMICS
**Harvey Publications,
Oct., 1948**

1 BP,Joe Palooka . . . . . . . . . . . 250.00
2 BP . . . . . . . . . . . . . . . . . . . 150.00
3 BP . . . . . . . . . . . . . . . . . . . 135.00
4 BP,A:Boy Heroes . . . . . . . . . 150.00
5 BP . . . . . . . . . . . . . . . . . . . 125.00
6 BP . . . . . . . . . . . . . . . . . . . 125.00
7 BP,A:Little Dot . . . . . . . . . . . 125.00
8 BP,O:Humphrey . . . . . . . . . . 125.00
9 BP . . . . . . . . . . . . . . . . . . . 100.00
10 BP . . . . . . . . . . . . . . . . . . . 100.00
11 thru 21 . . . . . . . . . . . . . . . @100.00
22 April, 1952. . . . . . . . . . . . . . 100.00

## HUNTED
**Fox Features Syndicate, 1950
(Formerly: MY LOVE
MEMOIRS)**
1 (13) Famous Crime Cases . . . 400.00
2 . . . . . . . . . . . . . . . . . . . . . 200.00

## HURRICANE COMICS
**Cambridge House, 1945**
1 F:Hurry Kane . . . . . . . . . . . . 350.00

---

*Hyper Mystery Comics #1*
© Hyper Publications

*Ideal Comics #2*
© Marvel Comics Group

*I Love Lucy #4*
© Dell Publishing Co.

## HYPER MYSTERY COMICS
**Hyper Publications, May, 1940**
1 B:Hyper . . . . . . . . . . . . . . . 3,000.00
2 June, 1940 . . . . . . . . . . . . 2,000.00

## IBIS, THE INVINCIBLE
**Fawcett Publications, Jan., 1942–Spring, 1948**
1 MRa(c),O:Ibis . . . . . . . . . . . 3,500.00
2 Bondage (c) . . . . . . . . . . . . 2,000.00
3 BW . . . . . . . . . . . . . . . . . . . 1,500.00
4 BW,A:Mystic Snake People . . 900.00
5 BW,Bondage (c),The
  Devil's Ibistick . . . . . . . . . 1,000.00
6 BW, The Book of Evil . . . . . . 1,000.00

## IDEAL
**Marvel Timely, July, 1948**
1 Antony and Cleopatra . . . . . . 400.00
2 The Corpses of Dr.Sacotti . . . 350.00
3 Joan of Arc . . . . . . . . . . . . . 325.00
4 Richard the Lionhearted
  A:The Witness . . . . . . . . . . . 500.00
5 Phc,Love and Romance . . . . 250.00
**Becomes:**

## LOVE ROMANCES
6 Ph(c),I Loved a Scoundrel . . . 250.00
7 Ph(c) . . . . . . . . . . . . . . . . . . 175.00
8 Ph(c) . . . . . . . . . . . . . . . . . . 200.00
9 thru 12 Ph(c) . . . . . . . . . . @150.00
13 thru 20 . . . . . . . . . . . . . . @150.00
21 BK . . . . . . . . . . . . . . . . . . . 125.00
22 . . . . . . . . . . . . . . . . . . . . . . 125.00
23 . . . . . . . . . . . . . . . . . . . . . . 125.00
24 BK . . . . . . . . . . . . . . . . . . . 125.00
25 . . . . . . . . . . . . . . . . . . . . . . 125.00
26 thru 35 . . . . . . . . . . . . . . @125.00
36 BK . . . . . . . . . . . . . . . . . . . 125.00
37 . . . . . . . . . . . . . . . . . . . . . . 125.00
38 BK . . . . . . . . . . . . . . . . . . . 150.00
39 thru 44 . . . . . . . . . . . . . . @125.00
45 MB . . . . . . . . . . . . . . . . . . . 150.00
46 . . . . . . . . . . . . . . . . . . . . . . 150.00
47 . . . . . . . . . . . . . . . . . . . . . . 150.00
48 . . . . . . . . . . . . . . . . . . . . . . 125.00
49 ATh . . . . . . . . . . . . . . . . . . 150.00
50 . . . . . . . . . . . . . . . . . . . . . . 125.00
51 . . . . . . . . . . . . . . . . . . . . . . 125.00
52 . . . . . . . . . . . . . . . . . . . . . . 125.00
53 ATh . . . . . . . . . . . . . . . . . . 140.00
54 . . . . . . . . . . . . . . . . . . . . . . 125.00
55 . . . . . . . . . . . . . . . . . . . . . . 125.00

56 . . . . . . . . . . . . . . . . . . . . . . 125.00
57 MB . . . . . . . . . . . . . . . . . . . 135.00
58 thru 74 . . . . . . . . . . . . . . @135.00
75 MB . . . . . . . . . . . . . . . . . . . 135.00
76 . . . . . . . . . . . . . . . . . . . . . . 125.00
77 MB . . . . . . . . . . . . . . . . . . . 135.00
78 . . . . . . . . . . . . . . . . . . . . . . 125.00
79 . . . . . . . . . . . . . . . . . . . . . . 125.00
80 RH(c) . . . . . . . . . . . . . . . . . 125.00
81 . . . . . . . . . . . . . . . . . . . . . . 125.00
82 MB,JK(c) . . . . . . . . . . . . . . 150.00
83 JSe,JK(c) . . . . . . . . . . . . . . 150.00
84 JK . . . . . . . . . . . . . . . . . . . . 150.00
85 JK . . . . . . . . . . . . . . . . . . . . 150.00
86 thru 95 . . . . . . . . . . . . . . @100.00
96 JK . . . . . . . . . . . . . . . . . . . . 150.00
97 . . . . . . . . . . . . . . . . . . . . . . 150.00
98 JK . . . . . . . . . . . . . . . . . . . . 160.00
99 JK . . . . . . . . . . . . . . . . . . . . 160.00
100 thru 104 . . . . . . . . . . . . . @160.00
105 JK . . . . . . . . . . . . . . . . . . . 160.00
106 JK,July, 1963 . . . . . . . . . . 160.00

## IDEAL COMICS
**Marvel Timely, Fall, 1944**
1 B:Super Rabbit,Giant Super
  Rabbit V:Axis(c) . . . . . . . . . 275.00
2 Super Rabbit at Fair(c) . . . . . 200.00
3 Beach Party(c) . . . . . . . . . . . 200.00
4 How to Catch Robbers . . . . . 200.00
**Becomes:**

## WILLIE COMICS
**Marvel, 1946**
5 B:Willie,George,Margie,Nellie
  Football(c) . . . . . . . . . . . . . 250.00
6 Record Player(c) . . . . . . . . . 175.00
7 Soda Fountain(c),HK . . . . . . 175.00
8 Fancy Dress(c) . . . . . . . . . . 150.00
9 . . . . . . . . . . . . . . . . . . . . . . 150.00
10 HK,Hey Look . . . . . . . . . . . 175.00
11 HK,Hey Look . . . . . . . . . . . 175.00
12 . . . . . . . . . . . . . . . . . . . . . . 150.00
13 . . . . . . . . . . . . . . . . . . . . . . 150.00
14 . . . . . . . . . . . . . . . . . . . . . . 150.00
15 . . . . . . . . . . . . . . . . . . . . . . 175.00
16 thru 18 . . . . . . . . . . . . . . @150.00
19 . . . . . . . . . . . . . . . . . . . . . . 175.00
20 Li'L Willie Comics . . . . . . . . 150.00
21 Li'L Willie Comics . . . . . . . . 150.00
22 . . . . . . . . . . . . . . . . . . . . . . 150.00
23 May, 1950 . . . . . . . . . . . . . 150.00
**Becomes:**

### CRIME CASES

## IDEAL ROMANCE
**See: TENDER ROMANCE**

## IF THE DEVIL WOULD TALK
**Catechetical Guild, 1950**
N# Rare . . . . . . . . . . . . . . . . 1,000.00
N#, 1958 Very Rare . . . . . . . . . 850.00

## ILLUSTRATED STORIES OF THE OPERAS
**B. Bailey Publ. Co., 1943**
N# Faust . . . . . . . . . . . . . . . . . 800.00
N# Aida . . . . . . . . . . . . . . . . . 750.00
N# Carman . . . . . . . . . . . . . . . 750.00
N# Rigoletto . . . . . . . . . . . . . . 750.00

## I LOVED
**See: ZOOT COMICS**

## I LOVE LUCY COMICS
**Dell Publishing Co., 1954**
(1) see Dell Four Color #535
(2) see Dell Four Color #559
3 Lucile Ball Ph(c) all . . . . . . . . 400.00
4 . . . . . . . . . . . . . . . . . . . . . . 350.00
5 . . . . . . . . . . . . . . . . . . . . . . 350.00
6 thru 10 . . . . . . . . . . . . . . . @300.00
11 thru 20 . . . . . . . . . . . . . . @200.00
21 thru 35 . . . . . . . . . . . . . . @175.00

## I LOVE YOU
**Fawcett Publications, 1950**
1 Photo(c) . . . . . . . . . . . . . . . . 175.00

## I'M A COP
**See: A-1 COMICS**

## IMPACT
**E.C. Comics, March–April, 1955**
1 RC,GE,BK,Grl . . . . . . . . . . . 400.00
2 RC,JDu,Grl,BK,JO . . . . . . . . 300.00
3 JO,RC,JDU,Grl,JKa,BK . . . . . 275.00
4 RC,JO,JDa,GE,Grl,BK . . . . . . 275.00
5 Nov.–Dec., 1955 . . . . . . . . . 275.00

All comics prices listed are for *Near Mint* condition.

*Indian Fighter #5*
*© Youthful Magazines*

*Indians #2*
*© Fiction House*

*Inside Crime #3*
*© Fox Features Syndicate*

## INCREDIBLE
## SCIENCE FANTASY
### See: WEIRD SCIENCE

## INCREDIBLE
## SCIENCE FICTION
### E.C. Comics, July–Aug., 1955

```
30 JDa,BK,JO,WW . . . . . . . . . . 800.00
31 AW,WW,BK . . . . . . . . . . . . . 750.00
32 AW,JDa,BK,JO . . . . . . . . . . . 750.00
33 JDa,BK,JO,WW . . . . . . . . . . . 750.00
```

## INDIAN BRAVES
### See: BAFFLING
### MYSTERIES

## INDIAN CHIEF
### Dell Publishing Co.,
### July–Sept., 1951

```
3 P(c) all . . . . . . . . . . . . . . . . . . 150.00
4 . . . . . . . . . . . . . . . . . . . . . . . . . 125.00
5 . . . . . . . . . . . . . . . . . . . . . . . . . 125.00
6 A:White Eagle . . . . . . . . . . . . 125.00
7 . . . . . . . . . . . . . . . . . . . . . . . . . 125.00
8 . . . . . . . . . . . . . . . . . . . . . . . . . 125.00
9 . . . . . . . . . . . . . . . . . . . . . . . . . 125.00
10 . . . . . . . . . . . . . . . . . . . . . . . . 125.00
11 . . . . . . . . . . . . . . . . . . . . . . . . 125.00
12 I:White Eagle . . . . . . . . . . . . 135.00
13 thru 29 . . . . . . . . . . . . . . . @100.00
30 SB . . . . . . . . . . . . . . . . . . . . . 100.00
31 thru 33 SB . . . . . . . . . . . . . @100.00
```

## INDIAN FIGHTER
### Youthful Magazines,
### May, 1950

```
1 Revenge of Chief Crazy
   Horse . . . . . . . . . . . . . . . . . . 250.00
2 Bondage (c) . . . . . . . . . . . . . 250.00
3 . . . . . . . . . . . . . . . . . . . . . . . . . 125.00
4 Cheyenne Warpath . . . . . . . . 125.00
5 . . . . . . . . . . . . . . . . . . . . . . . . . 125.00
6 Davy Crockett in Death Stalks
   the Alamo . . . . . . . . . . . . . . 125.00
7 Tom Horn-Bloodshed at
   Massacre Valley . . . . . . . . . 125.00
8 Tales of Wild Bill Hickory,
   Jan., 1952 . . . . . . . . . . . . . . 125.00
```

## INDIANS
### Wings Publ. Co.
### (Fiction House), Spring, 1950

```
1 B:Long Bow, Manzar, White
   Indian & Orphan . . . . . . . . . 350.00
2 B:Starlight . . . . . . . . . . . . . . . 175.00
3 Longbow(c) . . . . . . . . . . . . . . 150.00
4 Longbow(c) . . . . . . . . . . . . . . 125.00
5 Manzar(c) . . . . . . . . . . . . . . . . 150.00
6 Captive of the Semecas . . . . 125.00
7 Longbow(c) . . . . . . . . . . . . . . 125.00
8 A:Long Bow . . . . . . . . . . . . . . 125.00
9 A:Long Bow . . . . . . . . . . . . . . 125.00
10 Manzar(c) . . . . . . . . . . . . . . . 125.00
11 thru 16 . . . . . . . . . . . . . . . @100.00
17 Spring, 1953,Longbow(c) . . . . 100.00
```

## INDIANS ON
## THE WARPATH
### St. John Publ. Co., 1950

```
N# MB(c). . . . . . . . . . . . . . . . . . 400.00
```

## INDIAN WARRIORS
### See: OUTLAWS, THE

## INFORMER, THE
### Feature Television
### Productions, April, 1954

```
1 MSy,The Greatest Social
   Menace of our Time! . . . . . . 200.00
2 MSy . . . . . . . . . . . . . . . . . . . . 150.00
3 MSy . . . . . . . . . . . . . . . . . . . . 100.00
4 MSy . . . . . . . . . . . . . . . . . . . . 100.00
5 Dec., 1954 . . . . . . . . . . . . . . 100.00
```

## IN LOVE
### Mainline, Aug., 1954

```
1 S&K,Bride of the Star . . . . . . 450.00
2 S&K,Marilyn's Men . . . . . . . . 250.00
3 S&K . . . . . . . . . . . . . . . . . . . . 250.00
4 S&K,Comics Code . . . . . . . . . 275.00
5 S&K(c) . . . . . . . . . . . . . . . . . . 125.00
6 . . . . . . . . . . . . . . . . . . . . . . . . . 100.00
```
**Becomes:**

## I LOVE YOU
### Charlton Comics, Sept., 1955

```
7 JK(c),BP . . . . . . . . . . . . . . . . 150.00
8 . . . . . . . . . . . . . . . . . . . . . . . . . 125.00
9 . . . . . . . . . . . . . . . . . . . . . . . . . 125.00
10 . . . . . . . . . . . . . . . . . . . . . . . . 125.00
```

```
11 thru 16 . . . . . . . . . . . . . . . . @100.00
17 Giant . . . . . . . . . . . . . . . . . . . 150.00
18 . . . . . . . . . . . . . . . . . . . . . . . . 100.00
19 . . . . . . . . . . . . . . . . . . . . . . . . 100.00
20 . . . . . . . . . . . . . . . . . . . . . . . . 100.00
21 thru 50 . . . . . . . . . . . . . . . . @75.00
51 thru 59 . . . . . . . . . . . . . . . . @75.00
60 Elvis . . . . . . . . . . . . . . . . . . . 225.00
61 thru 100 . . . . . . . . . . . . . . . @75.00
101 thru 130 . . . . . . . . . . . . . . @25.00
```

## INSIDE CRIME
### Hero Books/
### Fox Feature Syndicate, 1950

```
1 . . . . . . . . . . . . . . . . . . . . . . . . . 325.00
2 . . . . . . . . . . . . . . . . . . . . . . . . . 275.00
N# . . . . . . . . . . . . . . . . . . . . . . . 700.00
```

## INTERNATIONAL COMICS
### See: CRIME PATROL

## INTERNATIONAL
## CRIME PATROL
### See: CRIME PATROL

## INTIMATE
### Charlton Comics, 1957

```
1 thru 3 . . . . . . . . . . . . . . . . . @100.00
```
**Becomes:**

## TEEN-AGE LOVE

```
4 . . . . . . . . . . . . . . . . . . . . . . . . . . 75.00
5 thru 9 . . . . . . . . . . . . . . . . . . @50.00
10 thru 35 . . . . . . . . . . . . . . . . @50.00
36 thru 96 . . . . . . . . . . . . . . . . @50.00
```

## INTIMATE
## CONFESSIONS
### Fawcett Publ./
### Realistic Comics, 1951

```
1a P(c) all, Unmarried Bride . . 1,000.00
1 EK,EK(c),Days of Temptation...
   Nights of Desire . . . . . . . . . 250.00
2 Doomed to Silence . . . . . . . . 250.00
3 EK(c), The Only Man For Me . 175.00
3a Robert Briffault . . . . . . . . . . 275.00
4 EK(c),Tormented Love . . . . . . 250.00
5 Her Secret Sin . . . . . . . . . . . . 250.00
6 Reckless Pick-up . . . . . . . . . . 250.00
7 A Love Like Ours,Spanking . . 275.00
8 Fatal Woman, March, 1953 . . 250.00
```

**In**

Intrigue #1
© Quality Comics Group

Is This Tomorrow #1
© Catechetical Guild

Jace Pearson of the Texas Rangers #8
© Dell Publishing Co.

**In**

## INTIMATE LOVE
**Standard Magazines,
Jan., 1950**
5 Wings on My Heart,Ph(c) .... 150.00
6 WE,JSe,Ph(c) ............. 175.00
7 WE,JSe,Ph(c),I Toyed
   with Love .............. 175.00
8 WE,JSe,Ph(c) ............. 175.00
9 Ph(c) .................... 100.00
10 Ph(c),My Hopeless Heart .... 175.00
11 ........................ 100.00
12 ........................ 100.00
13 thru 18................. @100.00
19 ATh .................... 125.00
20 ........................ 100.00
21 ATh .................... 125.00
22 ATh .................... 125.00
23 ATh .................... 100.00
24 ATh .................... 125.00
25 ATh .................... 100.00
26 ATh .................... 125.00
27 ATh .................... 100.00
28 ATh,Aug., 1954 .......... 100.00

## INTIMATE SECRETS OF ROMANCE
**Star Publications,
Sept., 1953**
1 LbC(c) ................... 275.00
2 LbC(c) ................... 250.00

## INTRIGUE
**Comics Magazine (Quality
Comics Group), 1955**
1 LbC,Ghost Ship ........... 400.00

## INVISIBLE SCARLET O'NEIL
**Harvey Publications,
Dec., 1950**
1 ......................... 200.00
2 ......................... 150.00
3 April, 1951 .............. 150.00

## IRON VIC
**United Features Syndicate/
St. John Publ. Co., 1940**
1-shot .................... 600.00

## IS THIS TOMORROW?
**Catechetical Guild, 1950**
1 Communist threat ......... 200.00
2 (1) Canada............... 150.00
3 (1) America ............. 200.00
4 (1) Turkey.............. 100.00
5 (1) Australia ........... 150.00

## IT REALLY HAPPENED
**William H. Wise/
Visual Editions, 1945**
1 Benjamin Franklin, Kit Carson 300.00
2 The Terrible Tiddlers ....... 200.00
3 Maid of the Margiris ........ 150.00
4 Chaplain Albert J. Hoffman ... 150.00
5 AS(c),Monarchs of the Sea,Lou
   Gehrig, Amelia Earhart ..... 275.00
6 AS(c),Ernie Pyle .......... 150.00
7 FGu,Teddy Roosevelt,Jefferson
   Davis,Story of the Helicopter. 150.00
8 FGu,Man O' War,Roy Rogers . 250.00
9 AS(c),The Story of
   Old Ironsides .......... 150.00
10 AS(c),Honus Wagner, The
   Story of Mark Twain....... 200.00
11 AS(c),MB,Queen of the Spanish
   Main, Oct., 1947 ......... 175.00

## IT'S A DUCK'S LIFE
**Marvel, Feb., 1950**
1 F;Buck Duck,Super Rabbit ... 150.00
2 ......................... 100.00
3 thru 11 ................. @100.00

## IT'S FUN TO STAY ALIVE
**Nat.'l Auto Dealers Assoc.,
1947**
1 Bugs Bunny .............. 250.00

## IT'S GAMETIME
**DC Comics, Sept.–Oct., 1955**
1 ........................ 1,000.00
2 Dodo and the Frog......... 700.00
3 ......................... 700.00
4 March-April, 1956 ......... 700.00

## IT'S LOVE, LOVE, LOVE
**St. John Publishing Co., 1957**
1 ......................... 100.00
2 ......................... 100.00

## JACE PEARSON OF THE TEXAS RANGERS
**Dell Publishing Co.,
May, 1952**
(1) see Dell Four Color #396
2 Ph(c),Joel McRae .......... 150.00
3 Ph(c),Joel McRae .......... 150.00
4 Ph(c),Joel McRae .......... 150.00
5 Ph(c),Joel McRae .......... 150.00
6 Ph(c),Joel McRae .......... 150.00
7 Ph(c),Joel McRae .......... 150.00
8 Ph(c),Joel McRae .......... 150.00
9 Ph(c),Joel McRae .......... 150.00
(10) see Dell Four Color #648
Becomes:

## TALES OF JACE PEARSON OF THE TEXAS RANGERS
**Feb., 1955**
11 ........................ 125.00
12 ........................ 125.00
13 ........................ 125.00
14 ........................ 125.00
15 ATh .................... 150.00
16 ATh .................... 150.00
17 thru 20................. @100.00

## JACK ARMSTRONG
**Parents' Institute,
Nov., 1947**
1 Artic Mystery ............. 600.00
2 Den of the Golden Dragon ... 250.00
3 Lost Valley of Ice ......... 200.00
4 Land of the Leopard Men .... 200.00
5 Fight against Racketeers of
   the Ring ............... 200.00
6 ......................... 175.00
7 Baffling Mystery on the
   Diamond ............... 175.00
8 ......................... 175.00
9 Mystery of the Midgets ..... 175.00
10 Secret Cargo............ 175.00
11 ........................ 175.00
12 Madman's Island, rare ..... 200.00
13 Sept., 1949 ............. 175.00

## JACKIE GLEASON
**St. John Publishing Co.,
Sept., 1955**
1 Ph(c) ................... 900.00
2 ......................... 550.00

Jackie Gleason and the Honeymooners
#11 © DC Comics

Jamboree #1
© Round Publishing

Jesse James #7
© Avon Periodicals

3 . . . . . . . . . . . . . . . . . . . 500.00
4 Dec., 1955 . . . . . . . . . . . . . . 500.00

## JACKIE GLEASON AND THE HONEYMOONERS
DC Comics, June-July, 1956
1 Based on TV show . . . . . . . 1,300.00
2 . . . . . . . . . . . . . . . . . . . . . 700.00
3 . . . . . . . . . . . . . . . . . . . . . 500.00
4 . . . . . . . . . . . . . . . . . . . . . 500.00
5 . . . . . . . . . . . . . . . . . . . . . 500.00
6 . . . . . . . . . . . . . . . . . . . . . 500.00
7 . . . . . . . . . . . . . . . . . . . . . 500.00
8 . . . . . . . . . . . . . . . . . . . . . 500.00
9 . . . . . . . . . . . . . . . . . . . . . 500.00
10 . . . . . . . . . . . . . . . . . . . . 500.00
11 . . . . . . . . . . . . . . . . . . . . 500.00
12 April-May, 1958 . . . . . . . . . . . 850.00

## JACKIE ROBINSON
Fawcett Publications, May, 1950
N# Ph(c) all issues. . . . . . . . . 1,800.00
2 . . . . . . . . . . . . . . . . . . . . 1,000.00
3 . . . . . . . . . . . . . . . . . . . . . 900.00
4 . . . . . . . . . . . . . . . . . . . . . 900.00
5 . . . . . . . . . . . . . . . . . . . . . 900.00
6 May, 1952 . . . . . . . . . . . . . . 900.00

## JACK IN THE BOX
See: YELLOW JACKET COMICS

## JACKPOT COMICS
MLJ Magazines, Spring, 1941
1 CBi(c),B:Black Hood,Mr.Justice, Steel Sterling,Sgt.Boyle . . . 4,500.00
2 SCp(c), . . . . . . . . . . . . . . . 2,000.00
3 Bondage (c) . . . . . . . . . . . 1,800.00
4 First Archie . . . . . . . . . . . . 5,500.00
5 Hitler(c) . . . . . . . . . . . . . . . 2,000.00
6 Son of the Skull v:Black Hood, Bondage(c) . . . . . . 1,800.00
7 Bondage (c) . . . . . . . . . . . 1,800.00
8 Sal(c), . . . . . . . . . . . . . . . 1,500.00
9 Sal(c), . . . . . . . . . . . . . . . 1,500.00
Becomes:
## JOLLY JINGLES
Summer, 1943
10 Super Duck,(fa). . . . . . . . . . 450.00

11 Super Duck . . . . . . . . . . . . . 225.00
12 Hitler parody (c),A:Woody Woodpecker . . . . . . . . . . . 250.00
13 thru 15 Super Duck . . . . . . @150.00
16 Dec., 1944 . . . . . . . . . . . . . 150.00

## JACK THE GIANT KILLER
Bimfort & Co., Aug.–Sept., 1953
1 HcK,HcK(c) . . . . . . . . . . . . . 250.00

## JAMBOREE
Round Publishing Co., Feb., 1946
1 . . . . . . . . . . . . . . . . . . . . . 250.00
2 March, 1946 . . . . . . . . . . . . . 150.00

## JANE ARDEN
St. John Publ. Co., March, 1948
1 . . . . . . . . . . . . . . . . . . . . . 200.00
2 June, 1948 . . . . . . . . . . . . . . 150.00

## JANN OF THE JUNGLE
See: JUNGLE TALES

## JEANIE COMICS
See: DARING MYSTERY

## JEEP COMICS
R.B. Leffingwell & Co., Winter, 1944
1 B;Captain Power . . . . . . . . . . 700.00
2 . . . . . . . . . . . . . . . . . . . . . 400.00
3 LbC(c),March–April, 1948 . . . . 600.00

## JEFF JORDAN, U.S. AGENT
D.S. Publ. Co., Dec., 1947
1 . . . . . . . . . . . . . . . . . . . . . 250.00

## JERRY DRUMMER
Charlton Comics, 1957
1 Revolutionary War . . . . . . . . . 100.00
2 . . . . . . . . . . . . . . . . . . . . . 100.00

## JESSE JAMES
Avon Periodicals/ Realistic Publ., Aug., 1950
1 JKu,The San Antonio Stage Robbery . . . . . . . . . . . . . . 250.00
2 JKu,The Daring Liberty Bank Robbery . . . . . . . . . . . . . . 175.00
3 JKu,The California Stagecoach Robberies . . . . . . . . . . . . 175.00
4 EK(c),Deadliest Deed! . . . . . . 100.00
5 JKu,WW,Great Prison Break . 175.00
6 JKu,Wanted Dead or Alive . . . 175.00
7 JKu,Six-Gun Slaughter at San Romano! . . . . . . . . . . 150.00
8 EK,Daring Train Robbery! . . . . 125.00
9 EK . . . . . . . . . . . . . . . . . . . 100.00
10 thru 14 {Do not exist}
15 EK . . . . . . . . . . . . . . . . . . 125.00
16 EK, Butch Cassidy . . . . . . . . 100.00
17 EK, Jessie James . . . . . . . . . 100.00
18 JKu . . . . . . . . . . . . . . . . . . 100.00
19 JKu . . . . . . . . . . . . . . . . . . 100.00
20 AW,FF,A:Chief Vic,Kit West . . 200.00
21 EK, Two Jessie James . . . . . . 100.00
22 EK,Chuck Wagon . . . . . . . . . 100.00
23 EK . . . . . . . . . . . . . . . . . . . 100.00
24 EK,B:New McCarty . . . . . . . . 100.00
25 EK . . . . . . . . . . . . . . . . . . . 100.00
26 EK . . . . . . . . . . . . . . . . . . . 100.00
27 EK,E:New McCarty . . . . . . . . 100.00
28 Quantrells Raiders . . . . . . . . 100.00
29 Aug., 1956 . . . . . . . . . . . . . 100.00

## JEST
Harry 'A' Chesler, 1944
10 J. Rebel,Yankee Boy . . . . . . 350.00
11 1944,Little Nemo . . . . . . . . . 400.00

## JET ACES
Real Adventure Publ. Co. (Fiction House), 1952
1 Set 'em up in MIG Alley . . . . . 250.00
2 Kiss-Off for Moscow Molly . . . 150.00
3 Red Task Force Sighted . . . . . 150.00
4 Death-Date at 40,000, 1953 . . 150.00

## JET FIGHTERS
Standard Magazines, Nov., 1953
5 ATh,Korean War Stories . . . . . 150.00
6 Circus Pilot . . . . . . . . . . . . . 125.00
7 ATh, Iron Curtains for Ivan, March, 1953 . . . . . . . . . . . 150.00

Je

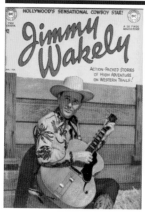

Jimmy Wakely #3
© DC Comics

Jingle Jangle Comics #6
© Eastern Color Printing

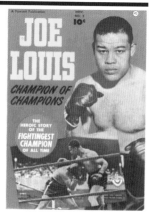

Joe Louis #2
© Fawcett Periodicals

## JET POWERS
### See: A-1 COMICS

## JETTA OF THE
## 21st CENTURY
**Standard Comics, Dec., 1952**
5 Teen Stories . . . . . . . . . . . . . 250.00
6 Robot (c) . . . . . . . . . . . . . . . 250.00
7 April, 1953 . . . . . . . . . . . . . . 150.00

## JIGGS AND MAGGIE
**Best Books (Standard)/
Harvey Publ., June, 1949**
11 . . . . . . . . . . . . . . . . . . . . . . . 125.00
12 thru 21 . . . . . . . . . . . . . . @100.00
22 thru 25 . . . . . . . . . . . . . . @100.00
26 Part 3-D . . . . . . . . . . . . . . 250.00
27 Feb.–March, 1954 . . . . . . . . 100.00

## JIM BOWIE
### See: DANGER

## JIM DANDY
**Dandy Magazine
(Lev Gleason), 1956**
1 Teen-age humor . . . . . . . . . . . 125.00
2 . . . . . . . . . . . . . . . . . . . . . . . 100.00
3 . . . . . . . . . . . . . . . . . . . . . . . 100.00

## JIM HARDY
**Spotlight Publ., 1944**
N# Dynamite Jim,Mirror Man . . . 700.00

## JIMMY OLSEN
### See: SUPERMAN'S PAL
### JIMMY OLSEN

## JIMMY WAKELY
**DC Comics, Sept.–Oct., 1949**
1 Ph(c),ATh,The Cowboy
  Swordsman . . . . . . . . . . 1,800.00
2 Ph(c),ATh,The Prize Pony . . . . 750.00
3 Ph(c),ATh,The Return of
  Tulsa Tom . . . . . . . . . . . . . 650.00
4 Ph(c),ATh,FF,HK,Where There's
  Smoke There's Gunfire . . . . . 625.00
5 ATh,The Return of the
  Conquistadores . . . . . . . . . 500.00

6 ATh,Two Lives of
  Jimmy Wakely . . . . . . . . . . . 500.00
7 The Secret of Hairpin Canyon . 500.00
8 ATh,The Lost City of
  Blue Valley . . . . . . . . . . . . . . 500.00
9 ATh,The Return of the
  Western Firebrands . . . . . . . 350.00
10 ATh,Secret of Lantikin'sLight . 350.00
11 ATh,Trail o/a Thousand Hoofs. 350.00
12 ATh,JKU,The King of Sierra
  Valley . . . . . . . . . . . . . . . . . . 350.00
13 ATh,The Raiders of Treasure
  Mountain . . . . . . . . . . . . . . . 350.00
14 ATh(c),JKu,The Badmen
  of Roaring Flame Valley . . . . 350.00
15 GK(c),Tommyguns on the
  Range . . . . . . . . . . . . . . . . . 350.00
16 GK(c),The Bad Luck Boots . . . 300.00
17 GK(c),Terror atThunderBasin . 300.00
18 July-Aug., 1952 . . . . . . . . . . . 350.00

## JIM RAY'S AVIATION
## SKETCH BOOK
**Vital Publishers, Feb., 1946**
1 Radar, the Invisible eye . . . . 550.00
2 Gen.Hap Arnold, May, 1946 . . 350.00

## JINGLE JANGLE
## COMICS
**Eastern Color Printing Co.,
Feb., 1942**
1 B:Benny Bear,Pie Face Prince,
  Jingle Jangle Tales,Hortense 700.00
2 GCn . . . . . . . . . . . . . . . . . . . 350.00
3 GCn . . . . . . . . . . . . . . . . . . . 300.00
4 GCn,Pie Face (c) . . . . . . . . . . 300.00
5 GCn,B:Pie Face . . . . . . . . . . . 300.00
6 GCn, . . . . . . . . . . . . . . . . . . . 250.00
7 . . . . . . . . . . . . . . . . . . . . . . . 250.00
8 . . . . . . . . . . . . . . . . . . . . . . . 250.00
9 . . . . . . . . . . . . . . . . . . . . . . . 250.00
10 . . . . . . . . . . . . . . . . . . . . . . . 250.00
11 . . . . . . . . . . . . . . . . . . . . . . . 200.00
12 . . . . . . . . . . . . . . . . . . . . . . . 200.00
13 . . . . . . . . . . . . . . . . . . . . . . . 200.00
14 . . . . . . . . . . . . . . . . . . . . . . . 200.00
15 E:Pie Face . . . . . . . . . . . . . @200.00
16 thru 20 . . . . . . . . . . . . . . . . @175.00
21 thru 25 . . . . . . . . . . . . . . . . @150.00
26 thru 30 . . . . . . . . . . . . . . . . @150.00
31 thru 41 . . . . . . . . . . . . . . . . @100.00
42 Dec., 1949 . . . . . . . . . . . . . . 100.00

## JING PALS
**Victory Publ. Corp.,
Feb., 1946**
1 Johnny Rabbit . . . . . . . . . . . . 250.00
2 . . . . . . . . . . . . . . . . . . . . . . . 200.00
3 . . . . . . . . . . . . . . . . . . . . . . . 200.00
4 Aug., 1948 . . . . . . . . . . . . . . 200.00

## JOE COLLEGE
**Hillman Periodicals,
Fall, 1949**
1 BP,DPr . . . . . . . . . . . . . . . . . 150.00
2 BP, Winter, 1949 . . . . . . . . . . 125.00

## JOE LOUIS
**Fawcett Periodicals,
Sept., 1950**
1 Ph(c),Life Story . . . . . . . . . . . 750.00
2 Ph(c),Nov., 1950 . . . . . . . . . . 500.00

## JOE PALOOKA
**Publication Enterprises
(Columbia Comics Group) 1943**
1 Lost in the Desert . . . . . . . 1,200.00
2 Hitler (c) . . . . . . . . . . . . . . . . 850.00
3 KO's the Nazis! . . . . . . . . . . . 700.00
4 Eiffel tower (c), 1944 . . . . . . . 375.00

## JOE PALOOKA
**Harvey Publications,
Nov., 1945–March, 1961**
1 Joe Tells How He Became
  World Champ . . . . . . . . . . . 600.00
2 Skiing (c) . . . . . . . . . . . . . . . . 300.00
3 . . . . . . . . . . . . . . . . . . . . . . . 175.00
4 Welcome Home Pals! . . . . . . . 175.00
5 S&K,The Great Carnival
  Murder Mystery . . . . . . . . . 250.00
6 Classic Joe Palooka (c) . . . . . 175.00
7 BP,V:Grumpopski . . . . . . . . . 150.00
8 BP,Mystery of the Ghost Ship . 150.00
9 Drooten Island Mystery . . . . . 150.00
10 BP . . . . . . . . . . . . . . . . . . . . 150.00
11 . . . . . . . . . . . . . . . . . . . . . . . 100.00
12 BP,Boxing Course . . . . . . . . . 100.00
13 . . . . . . . . . . . . . . . . . . . . . . . 110.00
14 BP,Palooka's Toughest Fight . . 110.00
15 BP,O:Humphrey . . . . . . . . . . 175.00
16 BP,A:Humphrey . . . . . . . . . . . 110.00
17 BP,I:Little Max,A:Humphrey . . 175.00
18 A:Little Max . . . . . . . . . . . . . . 110.00
19 BP,Freedom Train(c) . . . . . . . 125.00

Je

*Joe Palooka #25*
© Harvey Publications

*Joe Yank #13*
© Standard Comics

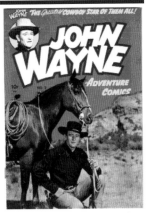

*John Wayne Adventure Comics #2*
© Toby Press

**Jo**

20 Punch Out(c). . . . . . . . . . . . . 110.00
21 . . . . . . . . . . . . . . . . . . . . . . . 100.00
22 V:Assassin . . . . . . . . . . . . . . 100.00
23 Big Bathing Beauty Issue . . . . 100.00
24 . . . . . . . . . . . . . . . . . . . . . . . 100.00
25 . . . . . . . . . . . . . . . . . . . . . . . 100.00
26 BP,Big Prize Fight Robberies . 100.00
27 BP,Mystery of Bal
 Eagle Cabin,A:Little Max. . . . 100.00
28 BP,Fights Out West, Babe
 Ruth. . . . . . . . . . . . . . . . . . . 100.00
29 BP,Joe Busts Crime
 Wide Open . . . . . . . . . . . . . . 100.00
30 BP,V:Hoodlums, Nude
 Painting . . . . . . . . . . . . . . . . 125.00
31 BP, Dizzy Dean. . . . . . . . . . . . 125.00
32 BP,Fight Palooka Was Sure
 to Lose. . . . . . . . . . . . . . . . . 100.00
33 BP,Joe finds Ann. . . . . . . . . . 100.00
34 BP,How to Box like a Champ . 100.00
35 BP,More Adventures of Little
 Max, Joe Louis . . . . . . . . . . . 125.00
36 BP . . . . . . . . . . . . . . . . . . . . . 100.00
37 BP,Joe as a Boy . . . . . . . . . . 100.00
38 BP . . . . . . . . . . . . . . . . . . . . . 100.00
39 BP,Original Hillbillies with
 Big Leviticus . . . . . . . . . . . . . 100.00
40 BP,Joe's Toughest Fight . . . . 100.00
41 BP,Humphrey's Grudge Fight . 100.00
42 BP . . . . . . . . . . . . . . . . . . . . . 100.00
43 BP . . . . . . . . . . . . . . . . . . . . . 100.00
44 BP,M:Ann Howe, Markies . . . . 125.00
45 BP . . . . . . . . . . . . . . . . . . . . . . 90.00
46 Champ of Champs . . . . . . . . . . 90.00
47 BreathtakingUnderwaterBattle . 90.00
48 BP,Exciting Indian Adventure . . 90.00
49 BP . . . . . . . . . . . . . . . . . . . . . . 90.00
50 BP,Bondage(c) . . . . . . . . . . . . . 90.00
51 BP, Babe Ruth . . . . . . . . . . . . . 90.00
52 BP,V:Balonki . . . . . . . . . . . . . . 90.00
53 BP . . . . . . . . . . . . . . . . . . . . . . 90.00
54 V:Bad Man Trigger McGehee . . 90.00
55 . . . . . . . . . . . . . . . . . . . . . . . . 90.00
56 Foul Play on the High Seas . . . 90.00
57 Curtains for the Champ . . . . . . 90.00
58 V:The Man-Eating Swamp
 Terror. . . . . . . . . . . . . . . . . . . 90.00
59 The Enemy Attacks. . . . . . . . . . 90.00
60 Joe Fights Escaped Convict . . 90.00
61 . . . . . . . . . . . . . . . . . . . . . . . . 90.00
62 S&K, Boy Explorers . . . . . . . . 125.00
63 . . . . . . . . . . . . . . . . . . . . . . . . 90.00
64 . . . . . . . . . . . . . . . . . . . . . . . . 90.00
65 . . . . . . . . . . . . . . . . . . . . . . . . 90.00
66 Drug . . . . . . . . . . . . . . . . . . . 125.00
67 Drug . . . . . . . . . . . . . . . . . . . 150.00

68 . . . . . . . . . . . . . . . . . . . . . . . . 90.00
69 Torture. . . . . . . . . . . . . . . . . . 150.00
70 BP, Vs. "Gooks" . . . . . . . . . . . . 90.00
71 Bloody Bayonets. . . . . . . . . . . . 90.00
72 Tank . . . . . . . . . . . . . . . . . . . . . 90.00
73 BP . . . . . . . . . . . . . . . . . . . . . . 90.00
74 thru 115 . . . . . . . . . . . . . . . @90.00
116 thru 117 giants . . . . . . . . . @150.00
118 Giant, Jack Dempsey . . . . @150.00
Giant 1 Body Building . . . . . . . . 150.00
Giant 2 Fights His Way Back. . . . 200.00
Giant 3 Visits Lost City. . . . . . . . 125.00
Giant 4 All in Family. . . . . . . . . . 150.00

## JOE YANK
### Visual Editions
### (Standard Comics),
### March, 1952

5 ATh,WE,Korean Jackpot! . . . . 150.00
6 Bacon and Bullets,
 G.I.Renegade . . . . . . . . . . . . 150.00
7 Two-Man War,A:Sgt. Glamour 100.00
8 ATh(c),Miss Foxhole of 1952, . 125.00
9 G.I.'s and Dolls,Colonel Blood 100.00
10 A Good Way to Die,
 A:General Joe . . . . . . . . . . . 100.00
11 . . . . . . . . . . . . . . . . . . . . . . . 100.00
12 RA. . . . . . . . . . . . . . . . . . . . . 100.00
13 . . . . . . . . . . . . . . . . . . . . . . . 100.00
14 . . . . . . . . . . . . . . . . . . . . . . . 100.00
15 . . . . . . . . . . . . . . . . . . . . . . . 100.00
16 July, 1954 . . . . . . . . . . . . . . . 100.00

## JOHN HIX SCRAPBOOK
### Eastern Color Printing Co.,
### 1937

1 Strange as It Seems . . . . . . . . 650.00
2 Strange as It Seems . . . . . . . . 500.00

## JOHNNY DANGER
### Toby Press, Aug., 1954

1 Ph(c),Private Detective . . . . . . 200.00

## JOHNNY DYNAMITE
### See: DYNAMITE

## JOHNNY HAZARD
### Best Books
### (Standard Comics),
### Aug., 1948

5 FR . . . . . . . . . . . . . . . . . . . . . 250.00
6 FR,FR(c) . . . . . . . . . . . . . . . . 225.00

7 FR(c) . . . . . . . . . . . . . . . . . . . 200.00
8 FR,FR(c), May, 1949 . . . . . . . 200.00

## JOHNNY LAW,
## SKY RANGER
### Good Comics (Lev Gleason),
### April, 1955

1 . . . . . . . . . . . . . . . . . . . . . . . 125.00
2 . . . . . . . . . . . . . . . . . . . . . . . 100.00
3 . . . . . . . . . . . . . . . . . . . . . . . 100.00
4 Nov., 1955 . . . . . . . . . . . . . . . 100.00

## JOHNNY MACK BROWN
### Dell Publishing Co., 1950–52

1 See: FOUR COLOR
2 Western hero . . . . . . . . . . . . . 200.00
3 . . . . . . . . . . . . . . . . . . . . . . . 150.00
4 . . . . . . . . . . . . . . . . . . . . . . . 125.00
5 . . . . . . . . . . . . . . . . . . . . . . . 125.00
6 . . . . . . . . . . . . . . . . . . . . . . . 125.00
7 . . . . . . . . . . . . . . . . . . . . . . . 125.00
8 . . . . . . . . . . . . . . . . . . . . . . . 125.00
9 . . . . . . . . . . . . . . . . . . . . . . . 125.00
10 . . . . . . . . . . . . . . . . . . . . . . . 125.00

## JOHN WAYNE
## ADVENTURE COMICS
### Toby Press, Winter, 1949

1 Ph(c),The Mysterious Valley
 of Violence . . . . . . . . . . . . . 2,200.00
2 AW,FF,Ph(c) . . . . . . . . . . . . . 1,000.00
3 AW,FF,Flying Sheriff . . . . . . 1,000.00
4 AW,FF,Double-Danger,Ph(c) 1,000.00
5 Volcano of Death,Ph(c) . . . . . 650.00
6 AW,FF,Caravan of Doom,
 Ph(c) . . . . . . . . . . . . . . . . . . 800.00
7 AW,FF,Ph(c) . . . . . . . . . . . . . 700.00
8 AW,FF,Duel of Death,Ph(c) . . 900.00
9 Ghost Guns,Ph(c) . . . . . . . . . 500.00
10 Dangerous Journey,Ph(c). . . . 450.00
11 Manhunt!,Ph(c) . . . . . . . . . . . 450.00
12 HK,Joins the Marines,Ph(c) . . 450.00
13 V:Frank Stacy . . . . . . . . . . . . 400.00
14 Operation Peeping John. . . . . 400.00
15 Bridge Head . . . . . . . . . . . . . 400.00
16 AW,FF,Golden Double-Cross . 400.00
17 Murderer's Music . . . . . . . . . . 400.00
18 AW,FF,Larson's Folly . . . . . . 475.00
19 . . . . . . . . . . . . . . . . . . . . . . . 350.00
20 Whale (c) . . . . . . . . . . . . . . . 350.00
21 . . . . . . . . . . . . . . . . . . . . . . . 350.00
22 Flash Flood! . . . . . . . . . . . . . 350.00

*Jo-Jo Comics #18*
© Fox Features Syndicate

*Joker Comics #4*
© Marvel Comics Group

*Adventures Into Terror #20*
© Marvel Comics Group

**Jo**

23 Death on Two Wheels . . . . . . 350.00
24 Desert . . . . . . . . . . . . . . . . . . 350.00
25 AW,FF,Hondo!,Ph(c) . . . . . . . 475.00
26 Ph(c) . . . . . . . . . . . . . . . . . . 400.00
27 Ph(c) . . . . . . . . . . . . . . . . . . 400.00
28 Dead Man's Boots! . . . . . . . . 400.00
29 AW,FF,Ph(c),Crash in
   California Desert . . . . . . . . . . 450.00
30 The Wild One, Ph(c) . . . . . . 400.00
31 AW,FF,May, 1955 . . . . . . . . . 450.00

### JO-JO COMICS
**Fox Features Syndicate,
Spring, 1946**
N# (fa) JoJo . . . . . . . . . . . . . . . 250.00
2 (fa) Electro . . . . . . . . . . . . . . . 150.00
3 (fa) . . . . . . . . . . . . . . . . . . . . 150.00
4 (fa) . . . . . . . . . . . . . . . . . . . . 150.00
5 (fa) . . . . . . . . . . . . . . . . . . . . 150.00
6 (fa) . . . . . . . . . . . . . . . . . . . . 150.00
7 B:Jo-Jo Congo King . . . . . . 1,200.00
8 (7)B:Tanee,V:The
   Giant Queen . . . . . . . . . . . 900.00
9 (8)The Mountain of Skulls . . . . 750.00
10 (9)Death of the Fanged Lady . 750.00
11 (10) . . . . . . . . . . . . . . . . . . . 750.00
12 (11)Bondage(c),
   Water Warriors. . . . . . . . . . . 625.00
13 (12) Jade Juggernaut . . . . . . 600.00
14 The Leopards of Learda . . . . 600.00
15 The Flaming Fiend . . . . . . . . 600.00
16 Golden Gorilla,bondage(c) . . . 600.00
17 Stark-Mad Thespian,
   bondage(c) . . . . . . . . . . . . . 675.00
18 The Death Traveler. . . . . . . . 600.00
19 Gladiator of Gore . . . . . . . . . 600.00
20 . . . . . . . . . . . . . . . . . . . . . . 600.00
21 . . . . . . . . . . . . . . . . . . . . . . 600.00
22 . . . . . . . . . . . . . . . . . . . . . . 600.00
23 . . . . . . . . . . . . . . . . . . . . . . 600.00
24 . . . . . . . . . . . . . . . . . . . . . . 600.00
25 Bondage(c) . . . . . . . . . . . . . 675.00
26 . . . . . . . . . . . . . . . . . . . . . . 600.00
27 . . . . . . . . . . . . . . . . . . . . . . 600.00
28 . . . . . . . . . . . . . . . . . . . . . . 600.00
29 July, 1949 . . . . . . . . . . . . . . 650.00

### JOKER COMICS
**Marvel Timely, April, 1942**
1 BW,I&B:Powerhouse Pepper,
   A:Stuporman . . . . . . . . . 5,000.00
2 BW,I:Tessie the Typist . . . . 2,000.00
3 BW,A:Tessie the Typist,
   Squat Car Squad . . . . . . 1,500.00

4 BW,Squat Car (c) . . . . . . . . 1,400.00
5 BW,same . . . . . . . . . . . . . 1,400.00
6 BW, . . . . . . . . . . . . . . . . . 1,000.00
7 BW . . . . . . . . . . . . . . . . . . 1,000.00
8 BW . . . . . . . . . . . . . . . . . . 1,000.00
9 BW . . . . . . . . . . . . . . . . . . 1,000.00
10 BW,Shooting Gallery (c) . . . 1,000.00
11 BW . . . . . . . . . . . . . . . . . 1,000.00
12 BW . . . . . . . . . . . . . . . . . 1,000.00
13 BW . . . . . . . . . . . . . . . . . 1,000.00
14 BW . . . . . . . . . . . . . . . . . 1,000.00
15 BW . . . . . . . . . . . . . . . . . 1,000.00
16 BW . . . . . . . . . . . . . . . . . 1,000.00
17 BW . . . . . . . . . . . . . . . . . 1,000.00
18 BW . . . . . . . . . . . . . . . . . 1,000.00
19 BW . . . . . . . . . . . . . . . . . 1,000.00
20 BW . . . . . . . . . . . . . . . . . 1,000.00
21 BW . . . . . . . . . . . . . . . . . 1,000.00
22 BW . . . . . . . . . . . . . . . . . 1,000.00
23 BW,HK,Hey Look . . . . . . . 1,000.00
24 BW,HK,Laff Favorites . . . . . . 800.00
25 BW,HK,same . . . . . . . . . . 1,100.00
26 BW,HK,same . . . . . . . . . . 1,100.00
27 BW . . . . . . . . . . . . . . . . . 1,100.00
28 . . . . . . . . . . . . . . . . . . . . . 250.00
29 BW . . . . . . . . . . . . . . . . . 1,100.00
30 BW . . . . . . . . . . . . . . . . . 1,100.00
31 BW . . . . . . . . . . . . . . . . . 1,100.00
32 B:Millie,Hedy . . . . . . . . . . . 250.00
33 HK . . . . . . . . . . . . . . . . . . . 275.00
34 . . . . . . . . . . . . . . . . . . . . . 250.00
35 HK . . . . . . . . . . . . . . . . . . . 275.00
36 HK . . . . . . . . . . . . . . . . . . . 250.00
37 . . . . . . . . . . . . . . . . . . . . . 250.00
38 . . . . . . . . . . . . . . . . . . . . . 250.00
39 . . . . . . . . . . . . . . . . . . . . . 250.00
40 . . . . . . . . . . . . . . . . . . . . . 250.00
41 A:Nellie the Nurse. . . . . . . . 250.00
42 I:Patty Pin-up . . . . . . . . . . . 275.00
Becomes:

### ADVENTURES INTO TERROR
**Marvel, 1950**
43(1)AH,B:Horror Stories . . . . . . 900.00
44(2)AH,Won't You Step Into
   My Palor . . . . . . . . . . . . . . . 600.00
3 GC,I Stalk By Night . . . . . . . . 400.00
4 DR,The Torture Room . . . . . . 400.00
5 GC,DR,The Hitchhiker . . . . . . 375.00
6 RH,The Dark Room . . . . . . . . 325.00
7 GT(c),BW,JMn,Where Monsters
   Dwell . . . . . . . . . . . . . . . . . 750.00
8 JSt,Enter... the Lizard . . . . . . 400.00

9 RH(c),JSt,The Dark
   Dungeon . . . . . . . . . . . . . . . 375.00
10 JMn,When the Vampire Calls . 375.00
11 JMn,JSt,Dead Man's Escape . 325.00
12 BK,Man Who Cried Ghost . . . 350.00
13 BEv(c),The Hands of Death . . 350.00
14 GC,GT,The Hands . . . . . . . . 300.00
15 Trapped by the Tarantula . . . . 300.00
16 RH(c),Her Name Is Death . . . 300.00
17 I Die Too Often,Bondage(c) . . 350.00
18 He's Trying to Kill Me . . . . . . 300.00
19 The Girl Who Couldn't Die . . . 275.00
20 . . . . . . . . . . . . . . . . . . . . . 275.00
21 GC,JMn. . . . . . . . . . . . . . . . 250.00
22 JMn . . . . . . . . . . . . . . . . . . 250.00
23 . . . . . . . . . . . . . . . . . . . . . 250.00
24 MF,GC. . . . . . . . . . . . . . . . . 250.00
25 MF. . . . . . . . . . . . . . . . . . . . 300.00
26 GC . . . . . . . . . . . . . . . . . . . 250.00
27 . . . . . . . . . . . . . . . . . . . . . 250.00
28 GC. . . . . . . . . . . . . . . . . . . . 250.00
29 GC,JMn. . . . . . . . . . . . . . . . 250.00
30 . . . . . . . . . . . . . . . . . . . . . 250.00
31 May, 1954 . . . . . . . . . . . . . . 250.00

### JOLLY JINGLES
### See: JACKPOT

### JONESY
**Comic Favorites (Quality
Comics Group), 1953—54**
1 teen-age. . . . . . . . . . . . . . . . 125.00
2 . . . . . . . . . . . . . . . . . . . . . . 100.00
3 . . . . . . . . . . . . . . . . . . . . . . 100.00
4 . . . . . . . . . . . . . . . . . . . . . . 100.00
5 . . . . . . . . . . . . . . . . . . . . . . 100.00
6 . . . . . . . . . . . . . . . . . . . . . . 100.00
7 . . . . . . . . . . . . . . . . . . . . . . 100.00
8 . . . . . . . . . . . . . . . . . . . . . . 100.00

### JON JUAN
**Toby Press, 1950**
1 ASh(c),Superlover . . . . . . . . . 800.00

### JOURNEY INTO FEAR
**Superior Publications,
May, 1951—Sept., 1954**
1 MB,Preview of Chaos . . . . . 1,000.00
2 Debt to the Devil . . . . . . . . . . 600.00
3 Midnight Prowler . . . . . . . . . . 500.00
4 Invisible Terror . . . . . . . . . . . 500.00
5 Devil Cat . . . . . . . . . . . . . . . 350.00

*Journey Into Fear #6*
*© Superior Publications*

*Journey Into Mystery #72*
*© Marvel Comics Group*

*Jughead's Fantasy #3*
*© Archie Publications*

6 Partners in Blood . . . . . . . . . 350.00
7 The Werewolf Lurks . . . . . . . . 350.00
8 Bells of the Damned . . . . . . . 350.00
9 Masked Death . . . . . . . . . . . 350.00
10 Gallery of the Dead. . . . . . . . 350.00
11 Beast of Bedlam . . . . . . . . . 300.00
12 No Rest for the Dead . . . . . . 300.00
13 Cult of the Dead . . . . . . . . . . 300.00
14 Jury of the Undead . . . . . . . . 300.00
15 Corpse in Make-up . . . . . . . . 350.00
16 Death by Invitation . . . . . . . . 300.00
17 Deadline for Death . . . . . . . . 300.00
18 Here's to Horror . . . . . . . . . . 300.00
19 This Body is Mine! . . . . . . . . 300.00
20 Masters of the Dead . . . . . . . 300.00
21 Horror in the Clock . . . . . . . . 300.00

## JOURNEY INTO MYSTERY
### Marvel, June, 1952
1 RH(c),B:Mystery/Horror
   stories . . . . . . . . . . . . . . 4,500.00
2 Don't Look . . . . . . . . . . . . . 1,500.00
3 I Didn't See Anything . . . . . . 1,200.00
4 RH,BEv(c),I'm Drowning,
   Severed Hand (c) . . . . . . . 1,200.00
5 RH,BEv(c),Fright . . . . . . . . . . 750.00
6 BEv(c),Till Death Do
   Us Part . . . . . . . . . . . . . . . 750.00
7 BEv(c),Ghost Guard . . . . . . . 750.00
8 He Who Hesitates . . . . . . . . . 750.00
9 BEv(c),I Made A Monster . . . . 750.00
10 The Assassin of Paris . . . . . . 750.00
11 RH,GT,Meet the Dead. . . . . . 700.00
12 A Night At Dragmoor Castle . . 600.00
13 The Living and the Dead . . . . 600.00
14 DAy,RH,The Man Who
   Owned A World . . . . . . . . . 600.00
15 RH(c),Till Death Do Us Part . . 600.00
16 DW,Vampire Tale . . . . . . . . . 600.00
17 SC,Midnight On Black
   Mountain . . . . . . . . . . . . . 600.00
18 He Wouldn't Stay Dead. . . . . 600.00
19 JF,The Little Things. . . . . . . . 600.00
20 BEv,BP,After Man, What. . . . . 600.00
21 JKu,The Man With No Past . . 600.00
22 Haunted House . . . . . . . . . . 600.00
23 GC,Gone, But Not Forgotten . 450.00
24 The Locked Drawer . . . . . . . 450.00
25 The Man Who Lost Himself . . 450.00
26 The Man From Out There. . . . 450.00
27 BP,JSe,Masterpiece . . . . . . . 450.00
28 The Survivor . . . . . . . . . . . . 450.00
29 Three Frightened People . . . . 450.00
30 JO,The Lady Who Vanished . . 450.00
31 The Man Who Had No Fear . . 450.00

32 Elevator In The Sky . . . . . . . . 450.00
33 SD,AW,There'll Be Some
   Changes Made . . . . . . . . . . 500.00
34 BP,BK,The Of The
   Mystic Ring . . . . . . . . . . . . 450.00
35 LC,JF,Turn Back The Clock . . 450.00
36 I, The Pharaoh . . . . . . . . . . . 450.00
37 BEv(c),The Volcano . . . . . . . 450.00
38 SD,Those Who Vanish . . . . . . 450.00
39 BEv(c),DAy,WW,The
   Forbidden Room . . . . . . . . . 450.00
40 BEv(c),JF,The Strange
   Secret Of Henry Hill . . . . . . . 450.00
41 BEv(c),GM,RC,I Switched
   Bodies . . . . . . . . . . . . . . . . 400.00
42 BEv(c),GM,What Was
   Farley's Other Face. . . . . . . . 400.00
43 AW,Ghost Ship . . . . . . . . . . . 400.00
44 SD,JK,BEv . . . . . . . . . . . . . . 400.00
45 BEv,JO . . . . . . . . . . . . . . . . 375.00
46 . . . . . . . . . . . . . . . . . . . . . . 375.00
47 BEv . . . . . . . . . . . . . . . . . . . 375.00
48 . . . . . . . . . . . . . . . . . . . . . . 375.00
49 . . . . . . . . . . . . . . . . . . . . . . 375.00
50 SD . . . . . . . . . . . . . . . . . . . 375.00
51 SD,JK . . . . . . . . . . . . . . . . . 400.00
52 JK . . . . . . . . . . . . . . . . . . . . 375.00
53 DH . . . . . . . . . . . . . . . . . . . 375.00
54 AW . . . . . . . . . . . . . . . . . . . 400.00
55 . . . . . . . . . . . . . . . . . . . . . . 400.00
56 thru 61 SD,JK . . . . . . . . . . @350.00
62 SD,JK,I:Xemnu. . . . . . . . . . . 600.00
63 SD,JK . . . . . . . . . . . . . . . . . 500.00
64 SD,JK . . . . . . . . . . . . . . . . . 500.00
65 SD,JK . . . . . . . . . . . . . . . . . 500.00
66 Hulk Type . . . . . . . . . . . . . . 600.00
67 SD,JK . . . . . . . . . . . . . . . . . 500.00
68 SD,JK . . . . . . . . . . . . . . . . . 500.00
69 SD,JK . . . . . . . . . . . . . . . . . 500.00
70 Sandman Type . . . . . . . . . . 550.00
71 JK,SD . . . . . . . . . . . . . . . . . 500.00
72 JK,SD . . . . . . . . . . . . . . . . . 500.00
73 JK,DH,Spider-Man type . . . . . 700.00
74 . . . . . . . . . . . . . . . . . . . . . . 400.00
75 JK,DH . . . . . . . . . . . . . . . . . 400.00
76 JK,DH . . . . . . . . . . . . . . . . . 350.00
77 DH,SD,JK . . . . . . . . . . . . . . 350.00
78 DH,Dr.Strange Type . . . . . . . 450.00
79 JK,DH,SD . . . . . . . . . . . . . . 400.00
80 JK,DH,SD . . . . . . . . . . . . . . 300.00
81 JK,DH,SD . . . . . . . . . . . . . . 300.00
82 JK,DH,SD . . . . . . . . . . . . . . 300.00
83 JK,SD,I&O:Thor. . . . . . . . . . 9,500.00
84 JK,SD,DH,I:Executioner. . . . 2,500.00
85 JK,SD,I:Loki,Heimdall,Balder,
   Tyr,Odin,Asgard . . . . . . . . 1,500.00

86 JK,SD,DH,V:Tomorrow Man 1,000.00
87 JK,SD,V:Communists . . . . . . 650.00
88 JK,SD,V:Loki. . . . . . . . . . . . 650.00
89 JK,SD,O:Thor(rep) . . . . . . . . 650.00
90 SD,I:Carbon Copy. . . . . . . . . 500.00
91 JSt,SD,I:Sandu . . . . . . . . . . 450.00
92 JSt,SD,V:Loki,I:Frigga. . . . . . 450.00
93 DAy,JK,SD,I:Radioactive Man 500.00
94 JSt,SD,V:Loki . . . . . . . . . . . 450.00
95 JSt,SD,I:Duplicator . . . . . . . 450.00
96 JSt,SD,I:Merlin II . . . . . . . . . 450.00
97 JK,I:Lava Man,O:Odin . . . . . 500.00
98 DH,JK,I&O:Cobra . . . . . . . . 350.00
99 DH,JK,I:Mr.Hyde,Surtur . . . . 350.00
100 DH,JK,V:Mr.Hyde . . . . . . . . 350.00

## JOURNEY INTO
## UNKNOWN WORLDS
## See: ALL WINNERS
## COMICS

## JUDE,
## THE FORGOTTEN SAINT
### Catechetical Guild, 1953
N# . . . . . . . . . . . . . . . . . . . . . . 100.00

## JUDGE PARKER
### Argo, Feb., 1956
1 . . . . . . . . . . . . . . . . . . . . . . . 100.00
2 . . . . . . . . . . . . . . . . . . . . . . . 100.00

## JUDO JOE
### Jay-Jay Corp.,
### Aug., 1952
1 Drug. . . . . . . . . . . . . . . . . . . . 250.00
2 . . . . . . . . . . . . . . . . . . . . . . . 150.00
3 Drug, Dec., 1953 . . . . . . . . . 200.00

## JUDY CANOVA
## See: ALL TOP COMICS

## JUGHEAD'S FANTASY
### Archie Publications, 1960
1 Sir Jugalot . . . . . . . . . . . . . . . 275.00
2 Peter Goon . . . . . . . . . . . . . . 200.00
3 Superjughead . . . . . . . . . . . . .15000

Ju

*Jughead's Folly #1*
© Archie Publications

*Jumbo Comics #26*
© Fiction House

*Jumbo Comics #80*
© Fiction House

## JUGHEAD'S FOLLY
**Archie Publications, 1957**
1 Jughead like Elvis . . . . . . . . . 650.00

## JUKE BOX
**Famous Funnies,
March, 1948**
1 ATh(c),Spike Jones . . . . . . . . 500.00
2 Dinah Shore,Transvestitism. . . 500.00
3 Vic Damone, Peggie Lee. . . . . 250.00
4 Jimmy Durante. . . . . . . . . . . . 250.00
5 . . . . . . . . . . . . . . . . . . . . . . . . 250.00
6 Jan., 1949,Desi Arnaz  . . . . . . 300.00

## JUMBO COMICS
**Real Adventure Publ. Co.
(Fiction House),
Sept., 1938**
1 LF,BKa,JK,WE(a&c),B:Sheena
   Queen of the Jungle,The Hawk
   The Hunchback . . . . . . . . 30,000.00
2 LF,JK,WE,BKa,BP,
   O:Sheena . . . . . . . . . . . . 10,000.00
3 JK,WE(a&c),BP,LF,BKa . . . . 6,000.00
4 WE(a&c),MMe,LF,BKa,
   O:The Hawk . . . . . . . . . . . 5,800.00
5 WE(a&c),BP,BKa . . . . . . . . . 5,000.00
6 WE(a&c),BP,BKa . . . . . . . . . 4,500.00
7 WE,BKa,BP . . . . . . . . . . . . . 4,400.00
8 LF(c),BP,BKa,World of
   Tommorow . . . . . . . . . . . . . 4,400.00
9 LF(c),BP . . . . . . . . . . . . . . . 3,500.00
10 WE,LF(c),BKa,Regular size
   issues begin . . . . . . . . . . . 2,500.00
11 LF(c),WE&BP,War of the
   Emerald Gas . . . . . . . . . . . 2,000.00
12 WE(c),WE&BP,Hawk in Buccaneer
   Vengeance,Bondage(c) . . . 2,500.00
13 WE(c),BP,Sheena in The
   Thundering Herds. . . . . . . . 2,000.00
14 WE(c),LF,BP,Hawk in Siege
   of Thunder Isle,B:Lightning  2,100.00
15 BP(a&c),Sheena(c) . . . . . . . 1,100.00
16 BP(a&c),The Lightning
   Strikes Twice . . . . . . . . . . . 1,500.00
17 BP(c), B:Sheena covers
   and lead stories . . . . . . . . 1,100.00
18 BP . . . . . . . . . . . . . . . . . . . 1,100.00
19 BP(c),BKa,Warriors of
   the Bush. . . . . . . . . . . . . . . 1,100.00
20 BP,BKa,Spoilers of the
   Wild. . . . . . . . . . . . . . . . . . . 1,100.00
21 BP,BKa,Prey of the
   Giant Killers. . . . . . . . . . . . . . 800.00

22 BP,BKa,Victims of the
   Super-Ape,O:Hawk . . . . . . . . 900.00
23 BP,BKa,Swamp of the
   Green Terror . . . . . . . . . . . . 900.00
24 BP,BKa,Curse of the Black
   Venom . . . . . . . . . . . . . . . . . 900.00
25 BP,BKa,Bait for the Beast. . . . 800.00
26 BP,BKa,Tiger-Man Terror . . . . 800.00
27 BP,BKa,Sabre-Tooth Terror. . . 800.00
28 BKa,RWd,The Devil of
   the Congo . . . . . . . . . . . . . . 800.00
29 BKa,RWd,Elephant-Scourge . 800.00
30 BKa,RWd,Slashing Fangs . . . 800.00
31 BKa,RWd,Voodoo Treasure
   of Black Slave Lake. . . . . . . 750.00
32 BKa,RWd,AB,Captives of
   the Gorilla-Men . . . . . . . . . . 750.00
33 BKa,RWd,AB,Stampede
   Tusks . . . . . . . . . . . . . . . . . 750.00
34 BKa,RWd,AB,Claws of the
   Devil-Cat . . . . . . . . . . . . . . . 750.00
35 BKa,RWd,AB,Hostage of the
   Devil Apes . . . . . . . . . . . . . . 750.00
36 BKa,RWd,AB,Voodoo Flames 750.00
37 BKa,RWd,AB,Congo Terror . . 750.00
38 BKa,RWd,AB,Death-Trap of
   the River Demons . . . . . . . . 750.00
39 BKa,RWd,AB,Cannibal Bait . . 750.00
40 BKa,RWd,AB,
   Assagai Poison . . . . . . . . . 750.00
41 BKa,RWd,AB,Killer's Kraal,
   Bondage(c) . . . . . . . . . . . . . 600.00
42 BKa,RWd,AB,Plague of
   Spotted Killers . . . . . . . . . . 600.00
43 BKa,RWd,AB,Beasts of the
   Devil Queen. . . . . . . . . . . . . 600.00
44 BKa,RWd,AB,Blood-Cult of
   K'Douma . . . . . . . . . . . . . . . 600.00
45 BKa,RWd,AB,Fanged
   Keeper of the Fire-Gem . . . . 600.00
46 BKa,RWd,AB,Lair of the
   Armored Monsters. . . . . . . . 600.00
47 BKa,RWd,AB,The Bantu
   Blood-Monster . . . . . . . . . . . 600.00
48 BKa,RWd,AB,Red Meat for
   the Cat-Pack . . . . . . . . . . . . 600.00
49 BKa,RWd,AB,Empire of the
   Hairy Ones . . . . . . . . . . . . . 600.00
50 BKa,RWd,AB,Eyrie of the
   Leopard Birds . . . . . . . . . . . 600.00
51 BKa,RWd.AB,Monsters with
   Wings. . . . . . . . . . . . . . . . . 500.00
52 BKa,RWd,AB,Man-Eaters
   Paradise . . . . . . . . . . . . . . . 500.00
53 RWd,AB,Slaves of the
   Blood Moon . . . . . . . . . . . . . 500.00

54 RWd,AB,Congo Kill. . . . . . . . 500.00
55 RWd,AB,Bait for the Silver
   King Cat. . . . . . . . . . . . . . . . 500.00
56 RWd,AB,Sabre Monsters of
   the Aba-Zanzi,Bondage(c). . . 700.00
57 RWd,AB,Arena of Beasts . . . . 500.00
58 RWd,AB,Sky-Atlas of the
   Thunder-Birds . . . . . . . . . . . 500.00
59 RWd,AB,Kraal of Shrunken
   Heads . . . . . . . . . . . . . . . . . 500.00
60 RWd,AB,Land of the
   Stalking Death . . . . . . . . . . . 400.00
61 RWd,AB,King-Beast of
   the Masai. . . . . . . . . . . . . . . 400.00
62 RWd,AB,Valley of Golden
   Death. . . . . . . . . . . . . . . . . . 400.00
63 RWd,AB,The Dwarf Makers . . 400.00
64 RWd,The Slave-Brand of Ibn
   Ben Satan,Male Bondage . . . 600.00
65 RWd,The Man-Eaters of
   Linpopo . . . . . . . . . . . . . . . . 400.00
66 RWd,Valley of Monsters . . . . 400.00
67 RWd,Land of Feathered Evil . 400.00
68 RWd,Spear of Blood Ju-Ju . . . 400.00
69 RWd,AB,Slaves for the
   White Sheik . . . . . . . . . . . . . 400.00
70 RWd,AB,MB,The Rogue
   Beast's Prey . . . . . . . . . . . . 400.00
71 RWd,AB,MB,The Serpent-
   God Speaks. . . . . . . . . . . . . 350.00
72 RWd,AB,MB,Curse of the
   Half-Dead . . . . . . . . . . . . . . 350.00
73 RWd,AB,MB,War Apes of
   the T'Kanis. . . . . . . . . . . . . . 350.00
74 RWd,AB,MB,Drums of the
   Voodoo God . . . . . . . . . . . . . 350.00
75 RWd,AB,MB,Terror Trail of
   the Devil's Horn. . . . . . . . . . 350.00
76 RWd,AB,MB,Fire Gems of
   Skull Valley . . . . . . . . . . . . . 350.00
77 RWd,AB,MB,Blood Dragons
   from Fire Valley . . . . . . . . . . 350.00
78 RWd,AB,MB,Veldt of the
   Vampire Apes . . . . . . . . . . . 350.00
79 RWd,AB,MB,Dancing
   Skeletons. . . . . . . . . . . . . . . 350.00
80 RWd,AB,MB,Banshee
   Cats . . . . . . . . . . . . . . . . . . 350.00
81 RWd,MB,AB,JKa,Heads for
   King' Hondo's Harem. . . . . . . 300.00
82 RWd,MB,AB,JKa,Ghost Riders
   of the Golden Tuskers. . . . . . 300.00
83 RWd,AB,MB,JKa,Charge of
   the Condo Juggernauts. . . . . 300.00
84 RWd,MB,AB,JKa,Valley of
   the Whispering Fangs . . . . . . 300.00

All comics prices listed are for *Near Mint* condition.

**Ju**

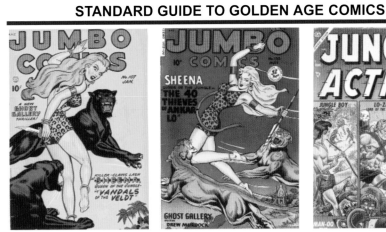

*Jumbo Comics #107*
© Fiction House

*Jumbo Comics #135*
© Fiction House

*Jungle Action #2*
© Marvel Comics Group

85 RWd,MB,AB,JKa,Red Tusks
of Zulu-Za'an . . . . . . . . . . . . 300.00
86 RWd,MB,AB,JKa,Witch-Maiden
of the Burning Blade . . . . . . . 300.00
87 RWd,AB,MB,JKa,Sargasso of
Lost Safaris . . . . . . . . . . . . . 300.00
88 RWd,AB,MB,JKa,Kill-Quest
of the Ju-Ju Tusks . . . . . . . . . 300.00
89 RWd,AB,MB,JKa,Ghost Slaves
of Bwana Rojo . . . . . . . . . . . 300.00
90 RWd,AB,MB,JKa,Death Kraal
of the Mastadons . . . . . . . . . 300.00
91 RWd,AB,MB,JKa,Spoor of
the Sabre-Horn Tiger . . . . . . 275.00
92 RWd,MB,JKa,Pied Piper
of the Congo . . . . . . . . . . . . 275.00
93 RWd,MB,JKa,The Beasts
that Dawn Begot . . . . . . . . . 275.00
94 RWd,MB,JKa,Wheel of a
Thousand Deaths . . . . . . . . 350.00
95 RWd,MB,JKa,Flame Dance
of the Ju-Ju Witch . . . . . . . . 275.00
96 RWd,MB,JKa,Ghost
Safari . . . . . . . . . . . . . . . . . . 275.00
97 RWd,MB,JKa,Banshee Wail
of the Undead,Bondage(c) . . 400.00
98 RWd,MB,JKa,Seekers of
the Terror Fangs . . . . . . . . . 300.00
99 RWd,MB,JKa,Shrine of
the Seven Souls . . . . . . . . . 300.00
100 RWd,MB,Slave Brand
of Hassan Bey . . . . . . . . . . . 350.00
101 RWd,MB,Quest of the
Two-Face Ju Ju . . . . . . . . . . 300.00
102 RWd,MB,Viper Gods of
Vengeance Veldt . . . . . . . . . 300.00
103 RWd,MB,Blood for the
Idol of Blades . . . . . . . . . . . . 300.00
104 RWd,MB,Valley of Eternal
Sleep . . . . . . . . . . . . . . . . . . 300.00
105 RWd,MB,Man Cubs from
Momba-Zu . . . . . . . . . . . . . . 350.00
106 RWd,MB,The River of
No-Return . . . . . . . . . . . . . . 350.00
107 RWd,MB,Vandals of
the Veldt . . . . . . . . . . . . . . . 300.00
108 RWd,MB,The Orphan of
Vengeance Vale . . . . . . . . . . 300.00
109 RWd,MB,The Pygmy's Hiss
is Poison . . . . . . . . . . . . . . . 300.00
110 RWd,MB,Death Guards the
Congo Keep . . . . . . . . . . . . . 300.00
111 RWd,MB,Beware of the
Witch-Man's Brew . . . . . . . . 300.00
112 RWd,MB,The Blood-Mask
from G'Shinis Grave . . . . . . . 275.00

113 RWd,MB,The Mask's of
Zombi-Zan . . . . . . . . . . . . . . 275.00
114 RWd,MB . . . . . . . . . . . . . . . 275.00
115 RWd,MB,Svengali of
the Apes . . . . . . . . . . . . . . . 275.00
116 RWd,MB,The Vessel of
Marbel Monsters . . . . . . . . . 275.00
117 RWd,MB,Lair of the Half-
Man King . . . . . . . . . . . . . . . 275.00
118 RWd,MB,Quest of the
Congo Dwarflings . . . . . . . . . 275.00
119 RWd,MB,King Crocodile's
Domain . . . . . . . . . . . . . . . . 275.00
120 RWd,MB,The Beast-Pack
Howls the Moon . . . . . . . . . 275.00
121 RWd,MB,The Kraal of
Evil Ivory . . . . . . . . . . . . . . . 275.00
122 RWd,MB,Castaways of
the Congo . . . . . . . . . . . . . . 250.00
123 RWd,MB, . . . . . . . . . . . . . . 250.00
124 RWd,MB,The Voodoo Beasts
of Changra-Lo . . . . . . . . . . . 250.00
125 RWd,MB,JKa(c),The Beast-
Pack Strikes at Dawn . . . . . . 250.00
126 RWd,MB,JKa(c),Lair of the
Swamp Beast . . . . . . . . . . . 250.00
127 RWd,MB,JKa(c),The Phantom
of Lost Lagoon . . . . . . . . . . . 250.00
128 RWd,MB,JKa(c),Mad Mistress
of the Congo-Tuskers . . . . . . 250.00
129 RWd,MB,JKa(c),Slaves of
King Simbas Kraal . . . . . . . . 250.00
130 RWd,MB,JKa(c),Quest of
the Pharaoh's Idol . . . . . . . . 250.00
131 RWd,JKa(c),Congo Giants
at Bay . . . . . . . . . . . . . . . . . 250.00
132 RWd,JKa(c),The Doom of
the Devil's Gorge . . . . . . . . . 250.00
133 RWd,JKa(c),Blaze the
Pitfall Trail . . . . . . . . . . . . . . 250.00
134 RWd,JKa(c),Catacombs of
the Jackal-Men . . . . . . . . . . 250.00
135 RWd,JKa(c),The 40 Thieves
of Ankar-Lo . . . . . . . . . . . . . 250.00
136 RWd,JKa(c),The Perils of
Paradise Lost . . . . . . . . . . . . 250.00
137 RWd,JKa(c),The Kraal of
Missing Men . . . . . . . . . . . . 250.00
138 RWd,JKa(c),The Panthers
of Kajo-Kazar . . . . . . . . . . . . 250.00
139 RWd,JKa(c),Stampede of
the Congo Lancers . . . . . . . . 250.00
140 RWd,JKa(c),The Moon
Beasts from Vulture Valley . . 250.00
141 RWd,JKa(c),B:Long
Bow . . . . . . . . . . . . . . . . . . . 275.00

142 RWd,JKa(c),Man-Eaters
of N'Gamba . . . . . . . . . . . . . 250.00
143 RWd,JKa(c),The Curse of
the Cannibal Drum . . . . . . . . 250.00
144 RWd,JKa(c),The Secrets of
Killers Cave . . . . . . . . . . . . . 250.00
145 RWd,JKa(c),Killers of
the Crypt . . . . . . . . . . . . . . . 250.00
146 RWd,JKa(c),Sinbad of the
Lost Lagoon . . . . . . . . . . . . . 250.00
147 RWd,JKa(c),The Wizard of
Gorilla Glade . . . . . . . . . . . . 250.00
148 RWd,JKa(c),Derelict of
the Slave King . . . . . . . . . . . 250.00
149 RWd,JKa(c),Lash Lord of
the Elephants . . . . . . . . . . . . 250.00
150 RWd,JKa(c),Queen of
the Pharaoh's Idol . . . . . . . . 250.00
151 RWd,The Voodoo Claws
of Doomsday Trek . . . . . . . . 250.00
152 RWd,Red Blades of Africa . . 250.00
153 RWd,Lost Legions of the
Nile . . . . . . . . . . . . . . . . . . . 250.00
154 RWd,The Track of the
Black Devil . . . . . . . . . . . . . . 250.00
155 RWd,The Ghosts of
Blow- Gun Trail . . . . . . . . . . . 250.00
156 RWd,The Slave-Runners
of Bambaru . . . . . . . . . . . . . 250.00
157 RWd,Cave of the
Golden Skull . . . . . . . . . . . . 250.00
158 RWd,Gun Trek to
Panther Valley . . . . . . . . . . . 250.00
159 RWd,A:Space Scout . . . . . . 225.00
160 RWd,Savage Cargo,
E:Sheena covers . . . . . . . . . 225.00
161 RWd,Dawns of the Pit . . . . . 225.00
162 RWd,Hangman's Haunt . . . . 225.00
163 RWd,Cagliostro Cursed
Thee . . . . . . . . . . . . . . . . . . 225.00
164 RWd,Death Bars the Door . . 225.00
165 RWd,Day off from a Corpse . 225.00
166 RWd,The Gallows Bird . . . . . 225.00
167 RWd,Cult of the Clawmen,
March, 1953 . . . . . . . . . . . . 225.00

## JUNGLE ACTION
**Marvel Atlas, Oct., 1954**
1 JMn,JMn(c),B:Leopard Girl . . . 450.00
2 JMn,JMn(c) . . . . . . . . . . . . . . 475.00
3 JMn,JMn(c) . . . . . . . . . . . . . . 300.00
4 JMn,JMn(c) . . . . . . . . . . . . . . 300.00
5 JMn,JMn(c) . . . . . . . . . . . . . . 300.00
6 JMn,JMn(c),Aug., 1955 . . . . . 300.00

**Ju**

Jungle Comics #
© Fiction House

Jungle Comics #34
© Fiction House

Jungle Comics #68
© Fiction House

## JUNGLE COMICS

### Glen Kel Publ./Fiction House, Jan., 1940

1 HcK,DBr,LF(c),O:The White Panther,Kaanga,Tabu, B:The Jungle Boy,Camilla, all Kaanga covers & stories . . 7,000.00
2 HcK,DBr,WE(c),B:Fantomah 2,300.00
3 HcK,DBr,GT,The Crocodiles of Death River . . . . . . . . . 1,900.00
4 HcK,DBr,Wambi in Thundering Herds. . . . . . . 1,700.00
5 WE(c),GT,HcK,DBr,Empire of the Ape Men. . . . . . . . . 1,900.00
6 WE(c),GT,DBr,HcK,Tigress of the Deep Jungle Swamp 1,200.00
7 BP(c),DBr,GT,HcK,Live Sacrifice,Bondage(c) . . . . . 1,100.00
8 BP(c),GT,HcK,Safari into Shadowland . . . . . . . . . . . 1,100.00
9 GT,HcK,Captive of the Voodoo Master . . . . . . . . . . 1,100.00
10 GT,HcK,BP,Lair of the Renegade Killer . . . . . . . . . 1,100.00
11 GT,HcK,V:Beasts of Africa's Ancient Primeival Swamp Land . . . . . 750.00
12 GT,HcK,The Devil's Death-Trap . . . . . . . . . . . . . 750.00
13 GT(c),GT,HcK,Stalker of the Beasts . . . . . . . . . . . . . . 800.00
14 HcK,Vengeance of the Gorilla Hordes . . . . . . . . . . . 750.00
15 HcK,Terror of the Voodoo Cauldron . . . . . . . . . . . . . 750.00
16 HcK,Caveman Killers . . . . . . . 750.00
17 HcK,Valley of the Killer-Birds . 750.00
18 HcK,Trap of the Tawny Killer, Bondage(c) . . . . . . . . 800.00
19 HcK,Revolt of the Man-Apes . 750.00
20 HcK,One-offering to Ju-Ju Demon . . . . . . . . . . . 750.00
21 HcK,Monster of the Dismal Swamp, Bondage(c) . . . . . . 600.00
22 HcK,Lair o/t Winged Fiend . . . 550.00
23 HcK,Man-Eater Jaws . . . . . . . 550.00
24 HcK,Battle of the Beasts. . . . . 550.00
25 HcK,Kaghis the Blood God, Bondage(c) . . . . . . . . . . . . . 700.00
26 HcK,Gorillas of the Witch-Queen . . . . . . . . . . . . 550.00
27 HcK,Spore o/t Gold-Raiders . . 550.00
28 HcK,Vengeance of the Flame God, Bondage(c) . . . . . . . . . 700.00
29 HcK,Juggernaut of Doom . . . . 550.00
30 HcK,Claws o/t Black Terror . . 550.00

31 HcK,Land of Shrunken Skulls. . . . . . . . . . . . . . . . . 500.00
32 HcK,Curse of the King-Beast . 500.00
33 HcK,Scaly Guardians of Massacre Pool,Bondage(c) . . 600.00
34 HcK,Bait of the Spotted Fury,Bondage(c) . . . . . . . . . 600.00
35 HcK,Stampede of the Slave-Masters . . . . . . . . . . . 500.00
36 HcK,GT,The Flame-Death of Ju Ju Mountain . . . . . . . . . . 500.00
37 HcK,GT,Scaly Sentinel of Taboo Swamp . . . . . . . . . . . 500.00
38 HcK,GT,Duel of the Congo Destroyers . . . . . . . . . . . . . 500.00
39 HcK,Land of Laughing Bones. 500.00
40 HcK,Killer Plague . . . . . . . . . 500.00
41 Hck,The King Ape Feeds at Dawn . . . . . . . . . . . 400.00
42 Hck,RC,Master of the Moon-Beasts . . . . . . . . . . . . 425.00
43 Hck,The White Shiek . . . . . . . 400.00
44 HcK,Monster of the Boiling Pool . . . . . . . . . . . . . 400.00
45 HcK,The Bone-Grinders of B'Zambi, Bondage(c). . . . . . 500.00
46 HcK,Blood Raiders of Tree Trail . . . . . . . . . . . . . . 400.00
47 HcK,GT,Monsters of the Man Pool, Bondage(c). . . . . . . . . 500.00
48 HcK,GT,Strangest Congo Adventure . . . . . . . . . . . . . 350.00
49 HcK,GT,Lair of the King -Serpent. . . . . . . . . . . . . . . 350.00
50 HcK,GT,Juggernaut of the Bush . . . . . . . . . . . . . . 350.00
51 HcK,GT,The Golden Lion of Genghis Kahn . . . . . . . . . . . 350.00
52 HcK,Feast for the River Devils, Bondage(c) . . . . . . . 500.00
53 HcK,GT,Slaves for Horrors Harem . . . . . . . . . . . . . . . 375.00
54 HcK,GT,Blood Bride of the Crocodile . . . . . . . . . . . . 350.00
55 HcK,GT,The Tree Devil. . . . . 350.00
56 HcK,Bride for the Rainmaker Raj. . . . . . . . . . . . 350.00
57 HcK,Fire Gems of T'ulaki . . . . 350.00
58 HcK,Land of the Cannibal God . . . . . . . . . . . 350.00
59 HcK,Dwellers of the Mist Bondage(c) . . . . . . . . . . . . . 450.00
60 HcK,Bush Devil's Spoor . . . . . 400.00
61 HcK,Curse of the Blood Madness . . . . . . . . . . . . . . 400.00
62 Bondage(c) . . . . . . . . . . . . . . 450.00

63 HcK,Fire-Birds for the Cliff Dwellers . . . . . . . . . . . 350.00
64 Valley of the Ju-Ju Idols . . . . . 350.00
65 Shrine of the Seven Ju Jus, Bondage(c) . . . . . . . . . . . . . 400.00
66 Spoor of the Purple Skulls . . . 350.00
67 Devil Beasts of the Golden Temple. . . . . . . . . . . . . . . . . 350.00
68 Satan's Safari . . . . . . . . . . . . 350.00
69 Brides for the Serpent King . . 350.00
70 Brides for the King Beast, Bondage(c) . . . . . . . . . . . . . 400.00
71 Congo Prey,Bondage(c) . . . . . 400.00
72 Blood-Brand o/t Veldt Cats . . . 350.00
73 The Killer of M'omba Raj, Bondage(c) . . . . . . . . . . . . . 400.00
74 AgF,GoldenJaws, Bondage(c) . . . . . . . . . . . . . 400.00
75 AgF,Congo Kill . . . . . . . . . . . 350.00
76 AgF,Blood Thirst of the Golden Tusk . . . . . . . . . . . . . 350.00
77 AgF,The Golden Gourds Shriek Blood,Bondage(c) . . . 400.00
78 AgF,Bondage(c) . . . . . . . . . . . 400.00
79 AgF,Death has a Thousand Fangs . . . . . . . . . . 375.00
80 AgF,Salome of the Devil-Cats Bondage(c) . . . . . 400.00
81 AgF,Colossus of the Congo . . 375.00
82 AgF,Blood Jewels of the Fire-Bird. . . . . . . . . . . . . . . 375.00
83 AgF,Vampire Veldt, Bondage(c) . . . . . . . . . . . . . 400.00
84 AgF,Blood Spoor of the Faceless Monster . . . . . . . . . 375.00
85 AgF,Brides for the Man-Apes Bondage(c) . . . . . . . . . . . . . 400.00
86 AgF,Firegems of L'hama Lost, Bondage(c). . . . . . . . . 400.00
87 AgF,Horror Kraal of the Legless One,Bondage(c). . . . 400.00
88 AgF,Beyond the Ju-Ju Mists . . 375.00
89 AgF,Blood-Moon over the Whispering Veldt . . . . . . . . . 350.00
90 AgF,The Skulls for the Altar of Doom,Bondage(c) . . 425.00
91 AgF,Monsters from the Mist Lands, Bondage(c) . . . . . . . 425.00
92 AgF,Vendetta of the Tree Tribes . . . . . . . . . . . . . 400.00
93 AgF,Witch Queen of the Hairy Ones . . . . . . . . . . . . . 400.00
94 AgF,Terror Raid of the Congo Caesar . . . . . . . . . 400.00
95 Agf,Flame-Tongues of the Sky Gods. . . . . . . . . . . . . . . 400.00

*Jungle Comics #115*
© *Fiction House*

*Jungle Comics #146*
© *Fiction House*

*Jungle Jim #10*
© *Dell Publishing Co.*

96 Agf,Phantom Guardians of the
Enchanted Lake,Bondage(c). 400.00
97 AgF,Wizard of the Whirling
Doom,Bondage(c) . . . . . . . . 375.00
98 AgF,Ten Tusks of Zulu Ivory . . 450.00
99 AgF,Cannibal Caravan,
Bondage(c) . . . . . . . . . . . . . 375.00
100 AgF,Hate has a
Thousand Claws . . . . . . . . . 375.00
101 AgF,The Blade of
Buddha, Bondage(c) . . . . . . 375.00
102 AgF,Queen of the
Amazon Lancers . . . . . . . . . 350.00
103 AgF,The Phantoms of
Lost Lagoon. . . . . . . . . . . . . 350.00
104 AgF . . . . . . . . . . . . . . . . . . . 350.00
105 AgF,The Red Witch
of Ubangi-Shan . . . . . . . . . . 350.00
106 AgF,Bondage(c) . . . . . . . . . 375.00
107 Banshee Valley . . . . . . . . . . 375.00
108 HcK,Merchants of Murder. . . 375.00
109 HcK,Caravan of the
Golden Bones . . . . . . . . . . . 350.00
110 HcK,Raid of the Fire-Fangs . 350.00
111 HcK,The Trek of the
Terror-Paws. . . . . . . . . . . . . 350.00
112 HcK,Morass of the
Mammoths. . . . . . . . . . . . . . 350.00
113 HcK,Two-Tusked Terror . . . . 350.00
114 HcK,Mad Jackals Hunt
by Night . . . . . . . . . . . . . . . . 350.00
115 HcK,Treasure Trove in
Vulture Sky . . . . . . . . . . . . . 350.00
116 HcK,The Banshees of
Voodoo Veldt . . . . . . . . . . . . 350.00
117 HcK,The Fangs of the
Hooded Scorpion. . . . . . . . . 350.00
118 HcK,The Muffled Drums
of Doom. . . . . . . . . . . . . . . . 350.00
119 HcK,Fury of the Golden
Doom. . . . . . . . . . . . . . . . . . 350.00
120 HcK,Killer King Domain . . . . 350.00
121 HcK,Wolves of the
Desert Night . . . . . . . . . . . . 350.00
122 HcK,The Veldt of
Phantom Fangs. . . . . . . . . . 350.00
123 HcK,The Ark of the
Mist-Maids . . . . . . . . . . . . . 350.00
124 HcK,The Trail of the
Pharaoh's Eye . . . . . . . . . . . 350.00
125 HcK,Skulls for Sale on
Dismal River . . . . . . . . . . . . 350.00
126 HcK,Safari Sinister . . . . . . . . 300.00
127 HcK,Bondage(c) . . . . . . . . . 300.00
128 HcK,Dawn-Men of the
Congo . . . . . . . . . . . . . . . . . 300.00

129 HcK,The Captives of
Crocodile Swamp . . . . . . . . 300.00
130 HcK,Phantoms of the Congo 300.00
131 HcK,Treasure-Tomb of the
Ape-King . . . . . . . . . . . . . . . 300.00
132 HcK,Bondage(c) . . . . . . . . . 350.00
133 HcK,Scourge of the Sudan
Bondage(c) . . . . . . . . . . . . . 350.00
134 HcK,The Black Avengers of
Kaffir Pass. . . . . . . . . . . . . . 300.00
135 HcK . . . . . . . . . . . . . . . . . . . 300.00
136 HcK,The Death Kraals
of Kongola . . . . . . . . . . . . . . 300.00
137 BWg(c),HcK,The Safari of
Golden Ghosts . . . . . . . . . . 300.00
138 BWg(c),HcK,Track of the
Black Terror Bondage(c) . . . . 350.00
139 BWg(c),HcK,Captain Kidd
of the Congo . . . . . . . . . . . . 300.00
140 BWg(c),HcK, The Monsters
of Kilimanjaro . . . . . . . . . . . 300.00
141 BWg(c)HcK,The Death Hunt
of the Man Cubs . . . . . . . . . 300.00
142 BWg(c),Hck,Sheba of the
Terror Claws,Bondage(c). . . . 350.00
143 BWg(c)Hck,The Moon of
Devil Drums. . . . . . . . . . . . . 300.00
144 BWg(c)Hck,Quest of the
Dragon's Claw . . . . . . . . . . . 300.00
145 BWg(c)Hck,Spawn of the
Devil's Moon . . . . . . . . . . . . 300.00
146 BWg(c),HcK,Orphans of
the Congo . . . . . . . . . . . . . . 300.00
147 BWG(c),HcK,The Treasure
of Tembo Wanculu. . . . . . . . 300.00
148 BWg(c),HcK,Caged Beasts
of Plunder-Men,Bondage(c) . 350.00
149 BWg(c),HcK . . . . . . . . . . . . . 275.00
150 BWg(c),HcK,Rhino Rampage,
Bondage(c). . . . . . . . . . . . . 350.00
151 BWg(c),HcK . . . . . . . . . . . . . 275.00
152 BWg(c),HcK,The Rogue of
Kopje Kull . . . . . . . . . . . . . . 275.00
153 BWg(c),HcK,The Wild Men
of N'Gara . . . . . . . . . . . . . . . 275.00
154 BWg(c),HcK,The Fire Wizard 275.00
155 BWg(c),HcK,Swamp of
the Shrieking Dead . . . . . . . 275.00
156 BWg(c),HcK . . . . . . . . . . . . . 275.00
157 BWg(c),HcK . . . . . . . . . . . . . 275.00
158 BWg(c),HcK,A:Sheena . . . . . 275.00
159 BWg(c),HcK,The Blow-Gun
Kill . . . . . . . . . . . . . . . . . . . . 275.00
160 BWg,HcK,King Fang. . . . . . . 275.00
161 BWg(c),HcK,The Barbarizi
Man-Eaters . . . . . . . . . . . . . 275.00

162 BWg(c) . . . . . . . . . . . . . . . . . 275.00
163 BWg(c),Jackals at the
Kill, Summer,1954 . . . . . . . . 275.00

## JUNGLE JIM
### Best Books
### (Standard Comics), Jan., 1949
11 . . . . . . . . . . . . . . . . . . . . . . . 125.00
12 Mystery Island. . . . . . . . . . . . 100.00
13 Flowers of Peril. . . . . . . . . . . . 100.00
14 . . . . . . . . . . . . . . . . . . . . . . . 100.00
15 . . . . . . . . . . . . . . . . . . . . . . . 100.00
16 . . . . . . . . . . . . . . . . . . . . . . . 100.00
17 . . . . . . . . . . . . . . . . . . . . . . . 100.00
18 . . . . . . . . . . . . . . . . . . . . . . . 100.00
19 . . . . . . . . . . . . . . . . . . . . . . . 100.00
20 1951 . . . . . . . . . . . . . . . . . . . 100.00

## JUNGLE JIM
### Dell Publishing Co., Aug., 1953
(1) *see Dell Four Color #490*
(1) *see Dell Four Color #565*
3 P(c) all . . . . . . . . . . . . . . . . . . 125.00
4 . . . . . . . . . . . . . . . . . . . . . . . . 125.00
5 . . . . . . . . . . . . . . . . . . . . . . . . 125.00
6 . . . . . . . . . . . . . . . . . . . . . . . . 100.00
7 . . . . . . . . . . . . . . . . . . . . . . . . 100.00
8 thru 12 . . . . . . . . . . . . . . . @100.00
13 'Mystery Island'. . . . . . . . . . . 100.00
14 'Flowers of Peril' . . . . . . . . . . 100.00
15 thru 20. . . . . . . . . . . . . . . @100.00

## JUNGLE JO
### Hero Books
### (Fox Features Syndicate),
### March, 1950
N# Congo King . . . . . . . . . . . . . . 550.00
1 WW,Mystery of Doc Jungle . . 600.00
2 Tangl . . . . . . . . . . . . . . . . . . . 450.00
3 The Secret of Youth,
Sept., 1950 . . . . . . . . . . . . . 450.00

## JUNGLE LIL
### Hero Books, April, 1950
1 Betrayer of the Kombe Dead. . 500.00
**Becomes:**

## DOROTHY LAMOUR
### Fox Features Syndicate,
### June 1950
2 WW,Ph(c)The Lost Safari . . . . 500.00
3 WW,Ph(c), Aug., 1950 . . . . . . 300.00

**Ju**

Jungle Tales #2
© Marvel Comics Group

Junior Miss #27
© Marvel Comics Group

Justice Traps the Guilty #45
© Prize Publications

**Ju**

## JUNGLE TALES
**Marvel Atlas, Sept., 1954**
1 B:Jann of the Jungle,Cliff
　Mason,Waku . . . . . . . . . . . 450.00
2 GT,Jann Stories cont. . . . . . . 300.00
3 Cliff Mason,White Hunter,
　Waku Unknown Jungle . . . . . 300.00
4 Cliff Mason,Waku,Unknown
　Jungle . . . . . . . . . . . . . . . . 300.00
5 RH(c),SSh,Cliff Mason,Waku,
　Unknown Jungle . . . . . . . . . 300.00
6 DH,SSh,Cliff Mason,Waku,
　Unknown Jungle . . . . . . . . . 300.00
7 DH,SSh,Cliff Mason,Waku,
　Unknown Jungle . . . . . . . . . 300.00
Becomes:

## JANN OF THE JUNGLE
**Marvel, 1955**
8 SH,SSh,The Jungle Outlaw . . . 400.00
9 With Fang and Talons . . . . . . . 250.00
10 AW,The Jackal's Lair. . . . . . . 250.00
11 Bottomless Pit . . . . . . . . . . . . 250.00
12 The Lost Safari . . . . . . . . . . . 250.00
13 When the Trap Closed . . . . . 250.00
14 V:Hunters . . . . . . . . . . . . . . 250.00
15 BEv(c),DH,V:Hunters . . . . . . 250.00
16 BEv(c),AW,JungleVengeance. 275.00
17 BEv(c),DH,AW,June, 1957 . . . 275.00

## JUNGLE THRILLS
**See: TERRORS OF
THE JUNGLE**

## JUNIE PROM
**Dearfield Publishing Co.
Winter, 1947**
1 Teenage Stories . . . . . . . . . . . 150.00
2 . . . . . . . . . . . . . . . . . . . . . . . . 125.00
3 thru 5 . . . . . . . . . . . . . . . . @100.00
6 June, 1949 . . . . . . . . . . . . . . 100.00

## JUNIOR COMICS
**Fox Features Syndicate,
Sept., 1947**
9 AF(a&c),Teenage Stories. . . 1,200.00
10 AF(a&c) . . . . . . . . . . . . . . 1,000.00
11 AF(a&c) . . . . . . . . . . . . . . 1,000.00
12 AF(a&c) . . . . . . . . . . . . . . 1,000.00
13 AF(a&c) . . . . . . . . . . . . . . 1,000.00
14 AF(a&c) . . . . . . . . . . . . . . 1,000.00

15 AF(a&c) . . . . . . . . . . . . . . . 1,000.00
16 AF(a&c),July,1948 . . . . . . . 1,000.00

## JUNIOR FUNNIES
**See: FAMILY FUNNIES**

## JUNIOR HOOP COMICS
**Stanmor Publications,
Jan., 1952**
1 . . . . . . . . . . . . . . . . . . . . . . . . 125.00
2 . . . . . . . . . . . . . . . . . . . . . . . . 100.00
3 July, 1952 . . . . . . . . . . . . . . . 100.00

## JUNIOR MISS
**Marvel Timely, 1944, 1947–50**
1 F:Frank Sinatra &June Allyson 350.00
24 . . . . . . . . . . . . . . . . . . . . . . . 150.00
25 thru 38 Cindy . . . . . . . . . @125.00
39 HK. . . . . . . . . . . . . . . . . . . . . 150.00

## JUSTICE COMICS
**Marvel Atlas, Fall, 1947**
7(1) B:FBI in Action,Mystery of
　White Death. . . . . . . . . . . . . 350.00
8(2),HK,Crime is For Suckers . . . 250.00
9(3),FBI Raid . . . . . . . . . . . . . . 200.00
4 Bank Robbery . . . . . . . . . . . . 200.00
5 Subway(c) . . . . . . . . . . . . . . . 175.00
6 E:FBI In Action . . . . . . . . . . . . 175.00
7 Symbolic(c) . . . . . . . . . . . . . . 175.00
8 Funeral(c) . . . . . . . . . . . . . . . 175.00
9 B:True Cases Proving Crime
　Can't Win. . . . . . . . . . . . . . . 175.00
10 Ph(c),Bank Hold Up . . . . . . . 175.00
11 Ph(c),Behind Bars. . . . . . . . . 175.00
12 Ph(c),The Crime of
　Martin Blaine . . . . . . . . . . . . 135.00
13 Ph(c),The Cautious Crook . . . 135.00
14 Ph(c) . . . . . . . . . . . . . . . . . . 135.00
15 Ph(c) . . . . . . . . . . . . . . . . . . 135.00
16 F:"Ears"Karpik-Mobster. . . . . 125.00
17 The Ragged Stranger . . . . . . . 125.00
18 Criss-Cross . . . . . . . . . . . . . . 125.00
19 Death Of A Spy . . . . . . . . . . . 125.00
20 Miami Mob . . . . . . . . . . . . . . 125.00
21 Trap. . . . . . . . . . . . . . . . . . . . 125.00
22 The Big Break. . . . . . . . . . . . . 125.00
23 thru 40 . . . . . . . . . . . . . . @100.00
41 Electrocution cover . . . . . . . . 200.00
42 thru 51 . . . . . . . . . . . . . . @100.00
52 Flare Up . . . . . . . . . . . . . . . . 100.00
Becomes:

## TALES OF JUSTICE
**Marvel, May, 1955—Aug., 1957**
53 BEv,Keeper Of The Keys . . . . 200.00
54 thru 57. . . . . . . . . . . . . . . @175.00
58 BK. . . . . . . . . . . . . . . . . . . . . 150.00
59 BK. . . . . . . . . . . . . . . . . . . . . 150.00
60 thru 63. . . . . . . . . . . . . . . @100.00
64 RC,DW,JSe. . . . . . . . . . . . . . 125.00
65 RC. . . . . . . . . . . . . . . . . . . . . 125.00
66 JO,AT . . . . . . . . . . . . . . . . . . 125.00
67 DW . . . . . . . . . . . . . . . . . . . . 125.00

## JUSTICE TRAPS THE GUILTY
**Headline Publications,
(Prize) Oct.–Nov., 1947**
2-1 S&K(a&c),Electric chair (c) . 800.00
2 S&K(a&c) . . . . . . . . . . . . . . . 450.00
3 S&K(a&c) . . . . . . . . . . . . . . . 400.00
4 S&K(a&c),True Confession
　of a Girl Gangleader . . . . . . . 400.00
5 S&K(a&c) . . . . . . . . . . . . . . . 400.00
6 S&K(a&c) . . . . . . . . . . . . . . . 400.00
7 S&K(a&c) . . . . . . . . . . . . . . . 400.00
8 S&K(a&c) . . . . . . . . . . . . . . . 400.00
9 S&K(a&c) . . . . . . . . . . . . . . . 400.00
10 S&K(a&c) . . . . . . . . . . . . . . 400.00
11 S&K(a&c) . . . . . . . . . . . . . . 175.00
12 . . . . . . . . . . . . . . . . . . . . . . 125.00
13 . . . . . . . . . . . . . . . . . . . . . . 150.00
14 . . . . . . . . . . . . . . . . . . . . . . 125.00
15 . . . . . . . . . . . . . . . . . . . . . . 125.00
16 . . . . . . . . . . . . . . . . . . . . . . 125.00
17 . . . . . . . . . . . . . . . . . . . . . . 125.00
18 S&K(a&c) . . . . . . . . . . . . . . 150.00
19 S&K(a&c) . . . . . . . . . . . . . . 150.00
20 . . . . . . . . . . . . . . . . . . . . . . 150.00
21 S&K. . . . . . . . . . . . . . . . . . . 175.00
22 S&K(c). . . . . . . . . . . . . . . . . 175.00
23 S&K(c). . . . . . . . . . . . . . . . . 175.00
24 . . . . . . . . . . . . . . . . . . . . . . 100.00
25 . . . . . . . . . . . . . . . . . . . . . . 100.00
26 . . . . . . . . . . . . . . . . . . . . . . 100.00
27 S&K(c). . . . . . . . . . . . . . . . . 175.00
28 . . . . . . . . . . . . . . . . . . . . . . 100.00
29 . . . . . . . . . . . . . . . . . . . . . . 100.00
30 S&K. . . . . . . . . . . . . . . . . . . 150.00
31 thru 50 . . . . . . . . . . . . . . @100.00
51 thru 54 . . . . . . . . . . . . . . @100.00
55 . . . . . . . . . . . . . . . . . . . . . . 100.00
56 . . . . . . . . . . . . . . . . . . . . . . 100.00
57 . . . . . . . . . . . . . . . . . . . . . . 100.00
58 Drug . . . . . . . . . . . . . . . . . . 300.00
59 thru 92. . . . . . . . . . . . . . . @100.00

*Ka'a'nga Comics #12*
© Fiction House

*Katy Keene #44*
© Archie Publications

*Katzenjammer Kids #20*
© Standard Comics

**Becomes:**

## FARGO KID
**Headline Publications
(Prize),  June–July. 1958**
93 AW,JSe,O:Kid Fargo . . . . . . . 175.00
94 JSe . . . . . . . . . . . . . . . . . . 125.00
95 June–July, 1958,JSe . . . . . . . 125.00

## JUST MARRIED
**Charlton Comics, 1958**
1 . . . . . . . . . . . . . . . . . . . . . . . 125.00
2 . . . . . . . . . . . . . . . . . . . . . . . 125.00
3 . . . . . . . . . . . . . . . . . . . . . . . 100.00
4 . . . . . . . . . . . . . . . . . . . . . . . 100.00
5 . . . . . . . . . . . . . . . . . . . . . . . 100.00
6 . . . . . . . . . . . . . . . . . . . . . . . 100.00
7 . . . . . . . . . . . . . . . . . . . . . . . 100.00
8 . . . . . . . . . . . . . . . . . . . . . . . 100.00
9 . . . . . . . . . . . . . . . . . . . . . . . 100.00
10 . . . . . . . . . . . . . . . . . . . . . . 100.00

## KA'A'NGA COMICS
**Glen-Kel Publ.
(Fiction House),
Spring, 1949–Summer, 1954**
1 Phantoms of the Congo . . . . . 700.00
2 V:The Jungle Octopus . . . . . . 350.00
3 . . . . . . . . . . . . . . . . . . . . . . . 250.00
4 The Wizard Apes of
   Inkosi-Khan . . . . . . . . . . . . . 235.00
5 A:Camilla . . . . . . . . . . . . . . . 225.00
6 Captive of the Devil Apes . . . . 175.00
7 GT,Beast-Men of Mombassa . 200.00
8 The Congo Kill-Cry . . . . . . . . . 175.00
9 Tabu-Wizard . . . . . . . . . . . . . 175.00
10 Stampede for Congo Gold . . . 175.00
11 Claws of the Roaring Congo. . 125.00
12 Bondage(c) . . . . . . . . . . . . . 250.00
13 Death Web of the Amazons . . 125.00
14 Slave Galley of the Lost
   Nile Bondage(c) . . . . . . . . . . 250.00
15 Crocodile Moon,Bondage(c). . 250.00
16 Valley of Devil-Dwarfs,Sheena 150.00
17 Tembu the Elephants . . . . . . 125.00
18 The Red Claw of Vengeance . 125.00
19 The Devil-Devil Trail . . . . . . . 125.00
20 The Cult of the Killer Claws . . 125.00

## KASCO COMICS
**Kasco Grainfeed
(Giveaway), 1945**
1 BWo . . . . . . . . . . . . . . . . . . 300.00
2 1949,BWo . . . . . . . . . . . . . . 250.00

## KATHY
**Standard Comics,
Sept., 1949**
1 Teen-Age Stories . . . . . . . . . . 150.00
2 ASh . . . . . . . . . . . . . . . . . . . 125.00
3 thru 6 . . . . . . . . . . . . . . . . @100.00
7 thru 17 . . . . . . . . . . . . . . . . @100.00

## KATHY
**Marvel Atlas, Oct., 1959—Feb.,
1964**
1 Teenage Tornado . . . . . . . . . . 125.00
2 . . . . . . . . . . . . . . . . . . . . . . . 100.00
3 thru 15 . . . . . . . . . . . . . . . . . @75.00
16 thru 27 . . . . . . . . . . . . . . . . @60.00

## KATY KEENE
**Archie Publications/Close-Up
Radio Comics, 1949**
1 BWo . . . . . . . . . . . . . . . . 1,700.00
2 BWo . . . . . . . . . . . . . . . . 1,200.00
3 BWo . . . . . . . . . . . . . . . . 1,000.00
4 BWo . . . . . . . . . . . . . . . . 1,000.00
5 BWo . . . . . . . . . . . . . . . . . 900.00
6 BWo . . . . . . . . . . . . . . . . . 800.00
7 BWo . . . . . . . . . . . . . . . . . 600.00
8 thru 12 BWo . . . . . . . . . . . @500.00
13 thru 20 BWo . . . . . . . . . . @400.00
21 thru 29 BWo . . . . . . . . . . @300.00
30 thru 38 BWo . . . . . . . . . . @300.00
39 thru 62 BWo . . . . . . . . . . @300.00
Ann.#1 . . . . . . . . . . . . . . . . . 1,200.00
Ann.#2 thru #6 . . . . . . . . . . . @700.00

## KATY KEENE FASHION BOOK MAGAZINE
**Archie Publications, 1955**
1 Woggon(a&c). . . . . . . . . . . . . 800.00
2 . . . . . . . . . . . . . . . . . . . . . . . 500.00
3 thru 10 not published
11 thru 18 . . . . . . . . . . . . . . . @300.00
19 . . . . . . . . . . . . . . . . . . . . . . 250.00
20 . . . . . . . . . . . . . . . . . . . . . . 250.00
21 . . . . . . . . . . . . . . . . . . . . . . 250.00
22 . . . . . . . . . . . . . . . . . . . . . . 250.00
23 Winter 1958-59 . . . . . . . . . . 250.00

## KATY KEENE PINUP PARADE
**Archie Publications, 1955**
1 . . . . . . . . . . . . . . . . . . . . . . . 750.00

2 . . . . . . . . . . . . . . . . . . . . . . . 400.00
3 . . . . . . . . . . . . . . . . . . . . . . . 350.00
4 . . . . . . . . . . . . . . . . . . . . . . . 350.00
5 . . . . . . . . . . . . . . . . . . . . . . . 350.00
6 . . . . . . . . . . . . . . . . . . . . . . . 275.00
7 . . . . . . . . . . . . . . . . . . . . . . . 275.00
8 . . . . . . . . . . . . . . . . . . . . . . . 275.00
9 . . . . . . . . . . . . . . . . . . . . . . . 275.00
10 Woggon art . . . . . . . . . . . . . 275.00
11 Story on comics. . . . . . . . . . 350.00
12 . . . . . . . . . . . . . . . . . . . . . . 275.00
13 . . . . . . . . . . . . . . . . . . . . . . 275.00
14 . . . . . . . . . . . . . . . . . . . . . . 275.00
15 Sept., 1961 . . . . . . . . . . . . . 500.00

## KATZENJAMMER KIDS
**David McKay Publ., 1947–50**
1 . . . . . . . . . . . . . . . . . . . . . . . 250.00
2 . . . . . . . . . . . . . . . . . . . . . . . 125.00
3 . . . . . . . . . . . . . . . . . . . . . . . 100.00
4 . . . . . . . . . . . . . . . . . . . . . . . 100.00
5 . . . . . . . . . . . . . . . . . . . . . . . 100.00
6 . . . . . . . . . . . . . . . . . . . . . . . 100.00
7 . . . . . . . . . . . . . . . . . . . . . . . 100.00
8 . . . . . . . . . . . . . . . . . . . . . . . 100.00
9 . . . . . . . . . . . . . . . . . . . . . . . 100.00
10 . . . . . . . . . . . . . . . . . . . . . . 100.00
11 . . . . . . . . . . . . . . . . . . . . . . 100.00
**Standard Comics, 1950–53**
12 thru 22 . . . . . . . . . . . . . . . @100.00
**Harvey Publ., 1953–54**
22 thru 25 . . . . . . . . . . . . . . . @100.00

## KAYO
**See: SCOOP COMICS**

## KEEN DETECTIVE FUNNIES
**Centaur Publications,
July, 1938**
1-8 B:The Clock, . . . . . . . . . . 3,000.00
1-9 WE . . . . . . . . . . . . . . . . 1,200.00
1-10 . . . . . . . . . . . . . . . . . . 1,100.00
1-11 Dean Denton . . . . . . . . 1,100.00
2-1 The Eye Sees. . . . . . . . . . . 900.00
2-2 JCo . . . . . . . . . . . . . . . . . 900.00
2-3 TNT. . . . . . . . . . . . . . . . . . 900.00
2-4 Gabby Flynn . . . . . . . . . . . 900.00
5 . . . . . . . . . . . . . . . . . . . . . 1,000.00
6 . . . . . . . . . . . . . . . . . . . . . . . 900.00
7 Masked Marvel . . . . . . . . . . 3,300.00

**Ke**

---

All comics prices listed are for *Near Mint* condition.　　　　　**Page 167**

*Keen Detective Funnies #8*
© *Centaur Publications*

*Kerry Drake Detective Cases #12*
© *Harvey Publications*

*Key Comics #4*
© *Consolidated Magazines*

8 PGv,Gabby Flynn,Nudity
Expanded 16 pages . . . . . . 1,400.00
9 Dean Denton . . . . . . . . . . . 1,000.00
10 . . . . . . . . . . . . . . . . . . . . . . 1,000.00
11 BEv,Sidekick . . . . . . . . . . . 1,000.00
12 Masked Marvel(c) . . . . . . . 1,200.00
3-1 Masked Marvel(c) . . . . . . . 1,000.00
3-2 Masked Marvel(c) . . . . . . . 1,000.00
3-3 BEv . . . . . . . . . . . . . . . . . 1,000.00
16 BEv . . . . . . . . . . . . . . . . . . 1,000.00
17 JSm . . . . . . . . . . . . . . . . . . 1,000.00
18 The Eye Sees,Bondage(c). . 1,200.00
19 LFe . . . . . . . . . . . . . . . . . . . 950.00
20 BEv,The Eye Sees. . . . . . . 1,400.00
21 Masked Marvel(c) . . . . . . . . 950.00
22 Masked Marvel(c) . . . . . . . . 950.00
23 B:Airman . . . . . . . . . . . . . . 1,300.00
24 Airman . . . . . . . . . . . . . . . . 1,400.00

## KEEN KOMICS
### Centaur Publications, May, 1939
1 Teenage Stories . . . . . . . . . 1,300.00
2 PGv,JaB,CBu,Cut Carson . . . . 800.00
3 JCo,Saddle Sniffl . . . . . . . . . . 800.00

## KEEN TEENS
### Life's Romances Publ./Leader/ Magazine Enterprises, 1945
N# P(c),Claire Voyant . . . . . . . 450.00
N# Ph(c),Van Johnson . . . . . . . 350.00
3 Ph(c), . . . . . . . . . . . . . . . . . 125.00
4 Ph(c),Glenn Ford . . . . . . . . . 150.00
5 Ph(c),Perry Como . . . . . . . . 150.00
6 . . . . . . . . . . . . . . . . . . . . . . 125.00

## KELLYS, THE
### See: KID KOMICS

## KEN MAYNARD WESTERN
### Fawcett Publications, Sept., 1950–Feb., 1952
1 B:Ken Maynard & Tarzan (horse)
The Outlaw Treasure Trail . . 800.00
2 Invasion of the Badmen . . . . 500.00
3 Pied Piper of the West . . . . . 350.00
4 Outlaw Hoax . . . . . . . . . . . . 350.00
5 Mystery of Badman City . . . . 350.00
6 Redwood Robbery . . . . . . . . 350.00
7 Seven Wonders of the West . . 350.00
8 Mighty Mountain Menace . . . 350.00

## KEN SHANNON
### Quality Comics Group, Oct., 1951–April, 1953
1 RC, Evil Eye of Count Ducrie . 500.00
2 RC, Cut Rate Corpses . . . . . . 350.00
3 RC, Corpse that Wouldn't
Sleep . . . . . . . . . . . . . . . . 275.00
4 RC, Stone Hatchet Murder . . . 275.00
5 RC, Case of the Carney Killer 275.00
6 Weird Vampire Mob . . . . . . . . 275.00
7 RC,Ugliest Man in the World . 225.00
8 Chinatown Murders,Drug . . . . 350.00
9 RC, Necklace of Blood . . . . . 200.00
10 RC, Shadow of the Chair . . . . 200.00

## KEN STUART
### Publication Enterprises, 1949
1 . . . . . . . . . . . . . . . . . . . . . . 150.00

## KENT BLAKE OF THE SECRET SERVICE
### Marvel, May, 1951—July, 1953
1 U.S. Govt. Secret Agent
stories,Bondage cover . . . . . 400.00
2 JSt,Drug issue,Man without
A Face . . . . . . . . . . . . . . . . 350.00
3 JMn,Trapped By The Chinese
Reds . . . . . . . . . . . . . . . . . 125.00
4 Secret Service Stories . . . . . . 125.00
5 RH(c),Condemned To Death . . 125.00
6 Cases from Kent Blake files . . 125.00
7 RH(c),Behind Enemy Lines . . 125.00
8 GT,V:Communists . . . . . . . . . 125.00
9 thru 14 . . . . . . . . . . . . . . . . @125.00

## KERRY DRAKE DETECTIVE CASES
### Life's Romances/M.E., 1944
(1) see N# A-1 Comics
2 A:The Faceless Horror . . . . . . 200.00
3 . . . . . . . . . . . . . . . . . . . . . . 150.00
4 A:Squirrel, Dr. Zero, Caresse . 150.00
5 Bondage (c) . . . . . . . . . . . . . 500.00
### Harvey Publ., Jan., 1952
6 A:Stitches . . . . . . . . . . . . . . 250.00
7 A:Shuteye . . . . . . . . . . . . . . 275.00
8 Bondage (c) . . . . . . . . . . . . . 350.00
9 Drug . . . . . . . . . . . . . . . . . . 350.00
10 BP,A:Meatball,Drug . . . . . . . . 350.00
11 BP,I:Kid Gloves . . . . . . . . . . . 150.00
12 BP . . . . . . . . . . . . . . . . . . . . 150.00
13 BP,A:Torso . . . . . . . . . . . . . . 125.00

14 BP,Bullseye Murder Syndicate 125.00
15 BP,Fake Mystic Racket . . . . . . 125.00
16 BP,A:Vixen . . . . . . . . . . . . . . 100.00
17 BP,Case of the $50,000
Robbery . . . . . . . . . . . . . . . 100.00
18 BP,A:Vixen . . . . . . . . . . . . . . 100.00
19 BP,Case of the Dope
Smugglers . . . . . . . . . . . . . 250.00
20 BP,Secret Treasury Agent . . . . 100.00
21 BP,Murder on Record . . . . . . . 100.00
22 BP,Death Rides the Air Waves 100.00
23 BP,Blackmailer's Secret
Weapon . . . . . . . . . . . . . . . 100.00
24 Blackmailer's Trap . . . . . . . . . 100.00
25 Pretty Boy Killer . . . . . . . . . . 100.00
26 . . . . . . . . . . . . . . . . . . . . . . 100.00
27 . . . . . . . . . . . . . . . . . . . . . . 100.00
28 BP . . . . . . . . . . . . . . . . . . . . 100.00
29 BP . . . . . . . . . . . . . . . . . . . . 100.00
30 Mystery Mine,Bondage(c) . . . 250.00
31 . . . . . . . . . . . . . . . . . . . . . . 100.00
32 . . . . . . . . . . . . . . . . . . . . . . 100.00
33 Aug., 1952. . . . . . . . . . . . . . . 100.00

## KEWPIES
### Will Eisner Publications, Spring, 1949
1 . . . . . . . . . . . . . . . . . . . . . . 600.00

## KEY COMICS
### Consolidated Magazines Jan., 1944
1 B:The Key, Will-O-The-Wisp . . 550.00
2 . . . . . . . . . . . . . . . . . . . . . . 300.00
3 . . . . . . . . . . . . . . . . . . . . . . 250.00
4 WJo(c) O:John Quincy,
B:The Atom . . . . . . . . . . . . . 275.00
5 HoK,Aug., 1946 . . . . . . . . . . . 300.00

## KEY RING COMICS
### Dell Publishing Co., 1941
1 . . . . . . . . . . . . . . . . . . . . . . 250.00
(1) Radior. . . . . . . . . . . . . . . . . 300.00

## KID CARROTS
### St. John Publishing Co., 1953
1 Funny animal . . . . . . . . . . . . . 100.00

## KID COLT OUTLAW
### Marvel Atlas, Aug., 1948
1 B:Kid Colt,A:Two-Gun Kid . . 1,400.00
2 Gun-Fighter and the Girl . . . . 700.00

# STANDARD GUIDE TO GOLDEN AGE COMICS

*Kid Colt Outlaw #10*
© *Marvel Comics Group*

*Kid Eternity #1*
© *Comics Magazine*

*Kid Komics #8*
© *Marvel Comics Group*

3 SSh,Colt-Quick Killers
For Hire . . . . . . . . . . . . . . . 550.00
4 Wanted,A:Tex Taylor . . . . . . . 550.00
5 Mystery of the Misssing
Mine,A:Blaze Carson. . . . . . 550.00
6 A:Tex Taylor,Valley of
the Werewolf . . . . . . . . . . . 350.00
7 B:Nimo the Lion . . . . . . . . . . 350.00
8 . . . . . . . . . . . . . . . . . . . . . . . 350.00
9 . . . . . . . . . . . . . . . . . . . . . . . 350.00
10 The Whip Strikes,E:Nimo
the Lion . . . . . . . . . . . . . . 350.00
11 O:Kid Colt . . . . . . . . . . . . . . 400.00
12 . . . . . . . . . . . . . . . . . . . . . . 225.00
13 DRi . . . . . . . . . . . . . . . . . . . 225.00
14 . . . . . . . . . . . . . . . . . . . . . . 225.00
15 Gun Whipped in ShotgunCity . 225.00
16 . . . . . . . . . . . . . . . . . . . . . . 225.00
17 . . . . . . . . . . . . . . . . . . . . . . 225.00
18 DRi . . . . . . . . . . . . . . . . . . . 225.00
19 . . . . . . . . . . . . . . . . . . . . . . 200.00
20 The Outlaw . . . . . . . . . . . . . 200.00
21 thru 30 . . . . . . . . . . . . . . . @200.00
31 . . . . . . . . . . . . . . . . . . . . . . 200.00
32 . . . . . . . . . . . . . . . . . . . . . . 200.00
33 thru 45 A:Black Rider . . . . . @150.00
46 RH(c). . . . . . . . . . . . . . . . . . 150.00
47 DW . . . . . . . . . . . . . . . . . . . 150.00
48 RH(c),JKu . . . . . . . . . . . . . . 150.00
49 . . . . . . . . . . . . . . . . . . . . . . 150.00
50 . . . . . . . . . . . . . . . . . . . . . . 150.00
51 thru 56 . . . . . . . . . . . . . . . @125.00
57 AW . . . . . . . . . . . . . . . . . . . 125.00
58 AW . . . . . . . . . . . . . . . . . . . 125.00
59 AW . . . . . . . . . . . . . . . . . . . 125.00
60 AW . . . . . . . . . . . . . . . . . . . 125.00
61 . . . . . . . . . . . . . . . . . . . . . . 100.00
62 . . . . . . . . . . . . . . . . . . . . . . 100.00
63 . . . . . . . . . . . . . . . . . . . . . . 100.00
64 RC . . . . . . . . . . . . . . . . . . . . 110.00
65 RC . . . . . . . . . . . . . . . . . . . . 110.00
66 AW . . . . . . . . . . . . . . . . . . . 150.00
67 thru 78 . . . . . . . . . . . . . . . @100.00
79 Origin Retold . . . . . . . . . . . . 110.00
80 thru 86 . . . . . . . . . . . . . . . @100.00
87 JDa(reprint) . . . . . . . . . . . . . 110.00
88 AW . . . . . . . . . . . . . . . . . . . 120.00
89 AW,Matt Slade . . . . . . . . . . . 120.00
90 thru 99 . . . . . . . . . . . . . . . @100.00
100 JK . . . . . . . . . . . . . . . . . . . 120.00

## KID COWBOY
### Approved Comics/
### St. John Publ. Co., 1950
1 B:Lucy Belle & Red Feather . . 200.00

2 Six-Gun Justice . . . . . . . . . . 150.00
3 Shadow on Hangman's Bridge 125.00
4 Red Feather V:Eagle of Doom 100.00
5 Killers on the Rampage . . . . . 100.00
6 The Stovepipe Hat . . . . . . . . 100.00
7 Ghost Town of Twin Buttes . . . 100.00
8 Thundering Hoofs . . . . . . . . . 100.00
9 Terror on the Salt Flats . . . . . 100.00
10 Valley of Death . . . . . . . . . . 100.00
11 Vanished Herds,Bondage(c) . . 200.00
12 . . . . . . . . . . . . . . . . . . . . . . 100.00
13 . . . . . . . . . . . . . . . . . . . . . . 100.00
14 1954 . . . . . . . . . . . . . . . . . . 100.00

## KIDDIE KARNIVAL
### Approved Comics, 1952
N# . . . . . . . . . . . . . . . . . . . . . 450.00

## KIDDY KAPERS
### Farrell Publ./Red Top/
### Decker Publ., 1946
1 Funny animal, Little Bit . . . . . . 125.00
1a (1957) . . . . . . . . . . . . . . . . . 100.00

## KID ETERNITY
### Comics Magazine,
### Spring, 1946
1 . . . . . . . . . . . . . . . . . . . . . 1,300.00
2 . . . . . . . . . . . . . . . . . . . . . . 500.00
3 Follow Him Out of This World . 550.00
4 Great Heroes of the Past . . . . 350.00
5 Don't Kid with Crime . . . . . . . 300.00
6 Busy Battling Crime . . . . . . . . 300.00
7 Protects the World . . . . . . . . . 300.00
8 Fly to the Rescue . . . . . . . . . . 300.00
9 Swoop Down on Crime . . . . . 300.00
10 Golden Touch from Mr. Midas. 300.00
11 Aid the Living by Calling
the Dead . . . . . . . . . . . . . . 250.00
12 Finds Death . . . . . . . . . . . . . 250.00
13 Invades General Poschka. . . . 250.00
14 Battles Double . . . . . . . . . . . 250.00
15 A: Master Man. . . . . . . . . . . . 250.00
16 Balance Scales of Justice. . . . 225.00
17 A:Baron Roxx . . . . . . . . . . . . 225.00
18 A:Man with Two Faces . . . . . . 225.00
**Becomes:**

## BUCCANEERS
### Quality Comics Group,
### Jan., 1950
19 RC,Sword Fight(c) . . . . . . . . 700.00
20 RC,Treasure Chest . . . . . . . 450.00
21 RC,Death Trap . . . . . . . . . . . 500.00

22 A:Lady Dolores,Snuff,
Bondage(c) . . . . . . . . . . . . 400.00
23 RC,V:Treasure Hungry
Plunderers of the Sea . . . . . 375.00
24 A:Adam Peril,Black Roger,
Eric Falcon . . . . . . . . . . . . . 300.00
25 V:Clews . . . . . . . . . . . . . . . 300.00
26 V:Admiral Blood . . . . . . . . . . 300.00
27 RC(a&c)May, 1951 . . . . . . . . 450.00

## KID FROM DODGE CITY
### Marvel Atlas, July, 1957—Sept.,
### 1957
1 . . . . . . . . . . . . . . . . . . . . . . 150.00
2 . . . . . . . . . . . . . . . . . . . . . . 100.00

## KID FROM TEXAS
### Marvel Atlas, June, 1957—Aug.,
### 1957
1 . . . . . . . . . . . . . . . . . . . . . . 125.00
2 . . . . . . . . . . . . . . . . . . . . . . 100.00

## KID KOMICS
### Marvel Timely, Feb., 1943
1 SSh(c),BW,O:Captain Wonder
& Tim Mulrooney I:Whitewash,
Knuckles,Trixie Trouble,
Pinto Pete Subbie. . . . . . . 7,500.00
2 AsH(c),F:Captain Wonder
Subbie, B:Young Allies,
B:Red Hawk,Tommy Tyme 3,500.00
3 ASh(c),AAv,SSh,A:The Vision
& Daredevils . . . . . . . . . . 3,000.00
4 ASh(c),B:Destroyer,A:Sub-Mariner,
E:Red Hawk,Tommy Tyme 2,200.00
5 ASh(c),V:Nazis . . . . . . . . . . 1,800.00
6 ASh(c),V:Japanese . . . . . . . 1,800.00
7 ASh(c),B;Whizzer . . . . . . . . 1,600.00
8 ASh(c),V:Train Robbers . . . . 1,600.00
9 ASh(c),V:Elves . . . . . . . . . . 1,600.00
10 ASh(c),E:Young Allies,
The Destoyer,The Whizzer 1,600.00
**Becomes:**

## KID MOVIE KOMICS
### Marvel, 1946
11 F:Silly Seal,Ziggy Pig
HK,Hey Look . . . . . . . . . . . 300.00
**Becomes:**

## RUSTY COMICS
### Marvel, 1947
12 F:Rusty,A:Mitzi . . . . . . . . . . . 225.00
13 Do not Disturb(c). . . . . . . . . . 125.00

---

All comics prices listed are for *Near Mint* condition.                    **Page 169**

# STANDARD GUIDE TO GOLDEN AGE COMICS

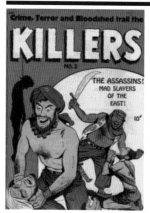

The Killers #2
© Magazine Enterprises

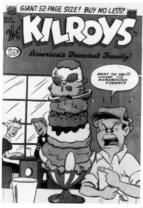

The Kilroys #33
© American Comics

King Comics #19
© David McKay Publications

14 Beach(c),BW,HK,Hey Look... 250.00
15 Picnic(c),HK,Hey Look ..... 175.00
16 Juniors Grades,HK,HeyLook . 175.00
17 John in Trouble,HK,HeyLook . 175.00
18 John Fired............... 125.00
19 Fridge raid(c),HK .......... 125.00
20 And Her Family,HK ........ 200.00
21 And Her Family,HK ........ 250.00
22 HK..................... 250.00
**Becomes:**

## KELLYS, THE
**Marvel, 1950**
23 F:The Kelly Family(Pop,
Mom,Mike,Pat & Goliath) ... 125.00
24 Mike's Date,A;Margie ........ 75.00
25 Wrestling(c)............... 75.00
**Becomes:**

## SPY CASES
**Marvel, 1950**
26(#1) Spy stories ........... 350.00
27(#2) BEv,Bondage(c) ........ 300.00
28(#3) Sabotage,A:Douglas
Grant Secret Agent....... 175.00
4 The Secret Invasion ........ 150.00
5 The Vengeance of Comrade
de Casto ............... 150.00
6 A:Secret Agent Doug Grant . 150.00
7 GT,A:Doug Grant .......... 150.00
8 Atom Bomb(c),Frozen
Horror ................. 250.00
9 Undeclared War .......... 125.00
10 Battlefield Adventures...... 125.00
11 Battlefield Adventures...... 125.00
12 Battlefield Adventures...... 125.00
13 Battlefield Adventures...... 125.00
14 Battlefield Adventures...... 125.00
15 Doug Grant.............. 125.00
16 Doug Grant.............. 125.00
17 Doug Grant.............. 125.00
18 Contact in Ankara......... 125.00
19 Final Issue,Oct., 1953...... 125.00

## KID MONTANA
**See: DAVY CROCKETT**

## KID SLADE GUNFIGHTER
**See: MATT SLADE**

## KID ZOO COMICS
**Street & Smith Publ., 1948**
1 (fa) .................... 325.00

## KILLERS, THE
**Magazine Enterprises, 1947**
1 LbC(c),Thou Shall Not Kill .. 1,500.00
2 Grl,OW,Assassins Mad Slayers
of the East,Hanging(c),Drug 1,300.00

## KILROYS, THE
**B&L Publishing Co./
American Comics,
June–July, 1947**
1 Three Girls in Love(c) ....... 300.00
2 Flat Tire(c) .............. 150.00
3 Right to Swear(c) .......... 125.00
4 Kissing Booth(c) .......... 125.00
5 Skiing(c) ................ 125.00
6 Prom(c) ................. 100.00
7 To School ............... 100.00
8 ...................... 100.00
9 ...................... 100.00
10 B:Solid Jackson solo........ 100.00
11 ..................... 100.00
12 Life Guard(c)............. 100.00
13 thru 21................ @100.00
22 thru 30................ @100.00
31 thru 40................ @100.00
41 thru 47................ @100.00
48 3-D effect ............. 200.00
49 3-D effect ............. 200.00
50 thru 54, July, 1954....... @100.00

## KING COMICS
**David McKay Publications,
April, 1936
(all have Popeye covers)**
1 AR,EC,B:Popeye,Flash Gordon,B:
Henry,Mandrake ...... 15,000.00
2 AR,EC,Flash Gordon ..... 3,500.00
3 AR,EC,Flash Gordon ..... 2,500.00
4 AR,EC,Flash Gordon ..... 2,000.00
5 AR,EC,Flash Gordon ..... 1,500.00
6 AR,EC,Flash Gordon ..... 1,100.00
7 AR,EC,King Royal Mounties 1,050.00
8 AR,EC,Thanksgiving(c) .... 1,000.00
9 AR,EC,Christmas(c) ....... 1,000.00
10 AR,EC,Flash Gordon ..... 1,000.00
11 AR,EC,Flash Gordon ....... 750.00
12 AR,EC,Flash Gordon ....... 750.00
13 AR,EC,Flash Gordon ....... 750.00
14 AR,EC,Flash Gordon ....... 750.00
15 AR,EC,Flash Gordon ....... 750.00
16 AR,EC,Flash Gordon ....... 750.00
17 AR,EC,Flash Gordon ....... 700.00
18 AR,EC,Flash Gordon ...... 700.00

**Covers say: "Starring Popeye"**
19 AR,EC,Flash Gordon ....... 700.00
20 AR,EC,Football(c).......... 700.00
21 AR,EC,Flash Gordon ....... 600.00
22 AR,EC,Flash Gordon ....... 600.00
23 AR,EC,Flash Gordon ....... 600.00
24 AR,EC,Flash Gordon ....... 600.00
25 AR,EC,Flash Gordon ....... 600.00
26 AR,EC,Flash Gordon ....... 550.00
27 AR,EC,Flash Gordon ....... 550.00
28 AR,EC,Flash Gordon ....... 550.00
29 AR,EC,Flash Gordon ....... 550.00
30 AR,EC,Flash Gordon ....... 550.00
31 AR,EC,Flash Gordon ....... 550.00
32 AR,EC,Flash Gordon ....... 550.00
33 AR,EC,Skiing(c) .......... 550.00
34 AR,Ping Pong(c)........... 450.00
35 AR,Flash Gordon ......... 450.00
36 AR,Flash Gordon ......... 450.00
37 AR,Flash Gordon ......... 450.00
38 AR,Flash Gordon ......... 450.00
39 AR,Baseball(c) ........... 450.00
40 AR,Flash Gordon ......... 450.00
41 AR,Flash Gordon ......... 400.00
42 AR,Flash Gordon ......... 400.00
43 AR,Flash Gordon ......... 400.00
44 AR,Popeye golf(c)......... 400.00
45 AR,Flash Gordon ......... 400.00
46 AR,B:Little Lulu .......... 400.00
47 AR,Flash Gordon ......... 400.00
48 AR,Flash Gordon ......... 400.00
49 AR,Weather Vane ......... 400.00
50 AR,B:Love Ranger ........ 400.00
51 AR,Flash Gordon ......... 300.00
52 AR,Flash Gordon ......... 300.00
53 AR,Flash Gordon ......... 300.00
54 AR,Flash Gordon ......... 300.00
55 AR,Magic Carpet.......... 300.00
56 AR,Flash Gordon ......... 300.00
57 AR,Cows Over Moon(c) .... 300.00
58 AR,Flash Gordon ......... 300.00
59 AR,Flash Gordon ......... 300.00
60 AR,Flash Gordon ......... 300.00
61 AR,B:Phantom,Baseball(c) ... 300.00
62 AR,Flash Gordon ......... 300.00
63 AR,Flash Gordon ......... 200.00
64 AR,Flash Gordon ......... 200.00
65 AR,Flash Gordon ......... 200.00
66 AR,Flash Gordon ......... 200.00
67 AR,Sweet Pea............ 200.00
68 AR,Flash Gordon ......... 200.00
69 AR,Flash Gordon ......... 200.00
70 AR,Flash Gordon ......... 200.00
71 AR,Flash Gordon ......... 200.00
72 AR,Flash Gordon ......... 200.00
73 AR,Flash Gordon ......... 200.00

All comics prices listed are for *Near Mint* condition.

King Comics #127
© David McKay

Kit Carson #5
© Avon Periodicals

Krazy Komics #2
© Marvel Comics Group

74 AR,Flash Gordon . . . . . . . . . 200.00
75 AR,Flash Godron . . . . . . . . . 200.00
76 AR,Flag(c). . . . . . . . . . . . . . 200.00
77 AR,Flash Gordon . . . . . . . . . 200.00
78 AR,Popeye,Olive Oil(c). . . . . 200.00
79 AR,Sweet Pea. . . . . . . . . . . . 200.00
80 AR,Wimpy(c). . . . . . . . . . . . 200.00
81 AR,B:Blondie(c). . . . . . . . . . 200.00
82 thru 91 AR . . . . . . . . . . @150.00
92 thru 98 AR . . . . . . . . . . . @150.00
99 AR,Olive Oil(c) . . . . . . . . . . 150.00
100 . . . . . . . . . . . . . . . . . . . . 200.00
101 thru 116 AR . . . . . . . . . @175.00
117 O:Phantom . . . . . . . . . . . . 200.00
118 Flash Gordon . . . . . . . . . . 175.00
119 Flash Gordon . . . . . . . . . . 150.00
120 Wimpy(c). . . . . . . . . . . . . 150.00
121 thru 140. . . . . . . . . . . . @125.00
141 Flash Gordon . . . . . . . . . . 125.00
142 Flash Gordon . . . . . . . . . . 125.00
143 Flash Gordon . . . . . . . . . . 125.00
144 Flash Gordon . . . . . . . . . . 125.00
145 Prince Valiant . . . . . . . . . . 100.00
146 Prince Valiant . . . . . . . . . . 100.00
147 Prince Valiant . . . . . . . . . . 100.00
148 thru 154. . . . . . . . . . . . . @75.00
155 E:Flash Gordon. . . . . . . . . . 75.00
156 Baseball(c) . . . . . . . . . . . . . 75.00
157 thru 159 . . . . . . . . . . . . @75.00

## KING OF THE
## ROYAL MOUNTED
### Dell Publishing Co.,
### Dec., 1948–1958
(1) see Dell Four Color #207
(2) see Dell Four Color #265
(3) see Dell Four Color #283
(4) see Dell Four Color #310
(5) see Dell Four Color #340
(6) see Dell Four Color #363
(7) see Dell Four Color #384
8 Zane Grey adapt. . . . . . . . . . 150.00
9 . . . . . . . . . . . . . . . . . . . . . 125.00
10 . . . . . . . . . . . . . . . . . . . . 125.00
11 thru 28 . . . . . . . . . . . . . . @100.00

## KIT CARSON
### Avon Periodicals, 1950
N# EK(c) Indian Scout . . . . . . . 200.00
2 EK(c),Kit Carson's Revenge,
Doom Trail . . . . . . . . . . . . 150.00
3 EK(c),V:Comanche Raiders . . 100.00
4 . . . . . . . . . . . . . . . . . . . . . 100.00
5 EK(c),Trail of Doom . . . . . . . 100.00

6 EK(c) . . . . . . . . . . . . . . . . . 100.00
7 EK(c) . . . . . . . . . . . . . . . . . 100.00
8 EK(c) . . . . . . . . . . . . . . . . . 100.00
Becomes:

## FIGHTING DAVY
## CROCKETT
### Oct.–Nov, 1955
9 EK(c) . . . . . . . . . . . . . . . . . 100.00

## KITTY
### St. John Publishing Co., 1948
1 . . . . . . . . . . . . . . . . . . . . . 150.00

## KNOCK KNOCK
### Whitman Publications, 1936
1 . . . . . . . . . . . . . . . . . . . . . 200.00

## KNOCKOUT ADVENTURES
### Fiction House, 1953
1 Rep. Fight Comics #53 . . . . . 150.00

## KOKEY KOALA
### Toby Press, 1952
1 . . . . . . . . . . . . . . . . . . . . . 125.00

## KOKO AND KOLA
### Compix/Magazine Enterprises,
### Fall, 1946
1 (fa) . . . . . . . . . . . . . . . . . . 175.00
2 X-Mas Issue . . . . . . . . . . . . 150.00
3 . . . . . . . . . . . . . . . . . . . . . 100.00
4 . . . . . . . . . . . . . . . . . . . . . 100.00
5 . . . . . . . . . . . . . . . . . . . . . 100.00
6 May, 1947 . . . . . . . . . . . . . 100.00

## KO KOMICS
### Gerona Publications,
### Oct., 1945
1 . . . . . . . . . . . . . . . . . . . . . 900.00

## KOKONUT KOMICS
### Gerona Publications, 1945
1 . . . . . . . . . . . . . . . . . . . . . 150.00

## KOMIC KARTOONS
### Marvel Timely, 1945
1 Funny Animal. . . . . . . . . . . . 225.00
2 . . . . . . . . . . . . . . . . . . . . . 225.00

## KOMIK PAGES
## See: SCOOP COMICS

## KRAZY KAT COMICS
### Dell Publishing Co.,
### May–June, 1951
1 . . . . . . . . . . . . . . . . . . . . . 125.00
2 . . . . . . . . . . . . . . . . . . . . . 100.00
3 . . . . . . . . . . . . . . . . . . . . . 100.00
4 . . . . . . . . . . . . . . . . . . . . . 100.00
5 . . . . . . . . . . . . . . . . . . . . . 100.00

## KRAZY KOMICS
### Marvel Timely, July, 1942
1 B:Ziggy Pig,Silly Seal . . . . . . 750.00
2 Toughy Tomcat(c) . . . . . . . . 325.00
3 Toughy Tomcat/Bunny(c) . . . 250.00
4 Toughy Tomcat/Ziggy(c) . . . . 250.00
5 Ziggy/Buzz Saw(c) . . . . . . . 250.00
6 Toughy/Cannon(c) . . . . . . . . 250.00
7 Cigar Store Indian(c) . . . . . . 250.00
8 Toughy/Hammock(c) . . . . . . 250.00
9 Hitler(c) . . . . . . . . . . . . . . . 275.00
10 Newspaper(c) . . . . . . . . . . 225.00
11 Canoe(c) . . . . . . . . . . . . . . 225.00
12 Circus(c) . . . . . . . . . . . . . . 300.00
13 Pirate Treasure(c). . . . . . . . 200.00
14 Fishing(c) . . . . . . . . . . . . . 200.00
15 Ski-Jump(c). . . . . . . . . . . . 175.00
16 Airplane(c). . . . . . . . . . . . . 125.00
17 Street corner(c) . . . . . . . . . 125.00
18 Mallet/Bell(c) . . . . . . . . . . . 125.00
19 Bicycle(c) . . . . . . . . . . . . . 125.00
20 Ziggy(c) . . . . . . . . . . . . . . 125.00
21 Toughy's date(c) . . . . . . . . 125.00
22 Crystal Ball(c) . . . . . . . . . . 125.00
23 Sharks in bathtub(c) . . . . . . 150.00
24 Baseball(c) . . . . . . . . . . . . 125.00
25 HK,Krazy Krow(c). . . . . . . . 150.00
26 Super Rabbit(c). . . . . . . . . . 125.00
Becomes:

## CINDY COMICS
### Marvel, 1947
27 HK,B:Margie,Oscar. . . . . . . 250.00
28 HK,Snow sled(c) . . . . . . . . 150.00
29 . . . . . . . . . . . . . . . . . . . . 150.00
30 . . . . . . . . . . . . . . . . . . . . 150.00
31 HK. . . . . . . . . . . . . . . . . . 150.00
32 . . . . . . . . . . . . . . . . . . . . 100.00
33 A;Georgie . . . . . . . . . . . . . 100.00
34 thru 40. . . . . . . . . . . . . . @100.00
Becomes:

*Krazy Krow #1*
*© Marvel Comics Group*

*Land of the Lost #3*
*© E.C. Comics*

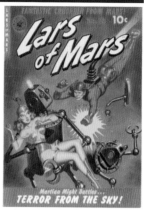

*Lars of Mars #10*
*© Ziff-Davis Publishing Co.*

## CRIME CAN'T WIN
**Marvel, 1950**
41 Crime stories. . . . . . . . . . . . . 300.00
42 . . . . . . . . . . . . . . . . . . . . . . 175.00
43 GT,Horror story . . . . . . . . . . . 250.00
4 thru 11 . . . . . . . . . . . . . . . . @150.00
12 Sept., 1953 . . . . . . . . . . . . . 125.00

## KRAZY KOMICS
**Marvel Timely**
**[2nd Series], 1948**
1 BW,HK,B:Eustice Hayseed . . . 600.00
2 BW,O:Powerhouse Pepper . . . 400.00

## KRAZY KROW
**Marvel, Summer, 1945**
1 B:Krazy Krow . . . . . . . . . . . . 250.00
2 . . . . . . . . . . . . . . . . . . . . . . 150.00
3 Winter, 1945-46 . . . . . . . . . . 150.00

## KRAZY LIFE
## See: PHANTOM LADY

## LABOR IS A PARTNER
**Catechetical Guild**
**Educational Society, 1949**
1 . . . . . . . . . . . . . . . . . . . . . . 250.00

## LADY LUCK
## See: SMASH

## LAFFY-DAFFY COMICS
**Rural Home Publ. Co.,**
**Feb., 1945**
1 (fa) . . . . . . . . . . . . . . . . . . . 150.00
2 . . . . . . . . . . . . . . . . . . . . . . 150.00

## LANA
**Marvel, Aug., 1948**
1 F:Lana Lane The Show Girl,
  A:Rusty,B:Millie . . . . . . . . . . 225.00
2 HK,Hey Look,A:Rusty . . . . . . 200.00
3 Show(c),B:Nellie . . . . . . . . . . 100.00
4 Ship(c) . . . . . . . . . . . . . . . . . 100.00
5 Audition(c) . . . . . . . . . . . . . . 100.00
6 Stop sign(c) . . . . . . . . . . . . . 100.00
7 Beach(c) . . . . . . . . . . . . . . . . 100.00
**Becomes:**

## LITTLE LANA
**Marvel, 1949**
8 Little Lana(c) . . . . . . . . . . . . 100.00
9 Final Issue,March, 1950 . . . . . 100.00

## LANCE O'CASEY
**Fawcett, 1946–47**
1 High Seas Adventure
  from Whiz comics . . . . . . . . 400.00
2 thru 4 . . . . . . . . . . . . . . . . @250.00

## LAND OF THE LOST
**E.C. Comics,**
**July–Aug., 1946–Spring 1948**
1 Radio show adapt. . . . . . . . . . 400.00
2 . . . . . . . . . . . . . . . . . . . . . . 275.00
3 thru 9 . . . . . . . . . . . . . . . . @225.00

## LARGE FEATURE
## COMICS
**Dell Publishing Co., 1939**
1 Dick Tracy vs. the Blank . . . . 2,100.00
2 Terry and the Pirates . . . . . . 1,100.00
3 Heigh-Yo Silver!
  the Lone Ranger. . . . . . . . 1,700.00
4 Dick Tracy gets his man . . . . 1,200.00
5 Tarzan of the Apes . . . . . . . 2,000.00
6 Terry and the Pirates . . . . . . 1,200.00
7 Lone Ranger to the rescue. . 1,600.00
8 Dick Tracy, Racket Buster . . 1,200.00
9 King of the Royal Mounted . . . 700.00
10 Gang Busters . . . . . . . . . . . . 800.00
11 Dick Tracy, Mad Doc Hump . 1,200.00
12 Smilin' Jack . . . . . . . . . . . . . 750.00
13 Dick Tracy and Scottie
  of Scotland Yard . . . . . . . . 1,200.00
14 Smilin' Jack helps G-Men . . . . 750.00
15 Dick Tracy and
  the Kidnapped Princes . . . . 1,200.00
16 Donald Duck, 1st Daisy. . . . 9,000.00
17 Gang Busters . . . . . . . . . . . . 600.00
18 Phantasmo The Master
  of the World . . . . . . . . . . . . 500.00
19 Walt Disney's Dumbo. . . . . 4,000.00
20 Donald Duck . . . . . . . . . . . 10,000.00
21 Private Buck . . . . . . . . . . . . . 150.00
22 Nuts and Jolts . . . . . . . . . . . . 150.00
23 The Nebbs . . . . . . . . . . . . . . 200.00
24 Popeye in 'Thimble Theatre'. . 900.00
25 Smilin'Jack . . . . . . . . . . . . . . 700.00
26 Smitty . . . . . . . . . . . . . . . . . . 300.00
27 Terry and the Pirates . . . . . . 750.00

28 Grin and Bear It . . . . . . . . . . 100.00
29 Moon Mullins. . . . . . . . . . . . 300.00
30 Tillie the Toiler . . . . . . . . . . . 275.00
**[Series 2]**
1 Peter Rabbit. . . . . . . . . . . . . 500.00
2 Winnie Winkle . . . . . . . . . . . 250.00
3 Dick Tracy . . . . . . . . . . . . . 1,000.00
4 Tiny Tim . . . . . . . . . . . . . . . . 300.00
5 Toots and Casper. . . . . . . . . 150.00
6 Terry and the Pirates . . . . . . 750.00
7 Pluto saves the Ship. . . . . . 2,000.00
8 Bugs Bunny . . . . . . . . . . . 2,000.00
9 Bringing Up Father . . . . . . . . 250.00
10 Popeye . . . . . . . . . . . . . . . . 650.00
11 Barney Google&SnuffySmith . 300.00
12 Private Buck . . . . . . . . . . . . . 150.00
13 1001 Hours of Fun . . . . . . . . 200.00

## LARRY DOBY,
## BASEBALL HERO
**Fawcett Publications, 1950**
1 Ph(c),BW . . . . . . . . . . . . . 1,100.00

## LARS OF MARS
**Ziff-Davis Publishing Co.,**
**April–May, 1951**
10 MA,'Terror from the Sky' . . . 1,100.00
11 GC, The Terror Weapon . . . . 900.00

## LASH LARUE WESTERN
**Fawcett Publications,**
**Summer, 1949**
1 Ph(c),The Fatal Roundups . . 1,500.00
2 Ph(c),Perfect Hide Out . . . . . 750.00
3 Ph(c),The Suspect. . . . . . . . . 600.00
4 Ph(c),Death on Stage . . . . . . 600.00
5 Ph(c),Rustler's Haven . . . . . . 600.00
6 Ph(c) . . . . . . . . . . . . . . . . . . 500.00
7 Ph(c),Shadow of the Noose. . 425.00
8 Ph(c),Double Deadline. . . . . . 425.00
9 Ph(c),Generals Last Stand . . 425.00
10 Ph(c) . . . . . . . . . . . . . . . . . . 425.00
11 Ph(c) . . . . . . . . . . . . . . . . . . 350.00
12 thru 20 Ph(c) . . . . . . . . . . @300.00
21 thru 29 Ph(c) . . . . . . . . . . @250.00
30 thru 46 Ph(c). . . . . . . . . . . @225.00
46 Ph(c),Lost Chance . . . . . . . . 225.00

## LASSIE
**Dell Publishing Co.,**
**Oct.–Dec., 1950**
1 Ph(c) all . . . . . . . . . . . . . . . . 250.00

Kr

*Lassie*
© Dell Publishing Co.

*Laugh Comics #47*
© Archie Publications

*Laurel and Hardy #3*
© St. John Publishing Co.

La

| | |
|---|---|
| 2 | 150.00 |
| 3 | 125.00 |
| 4 | 125.00 |
| 5 | 125.00 |
| 6 | 125.00 |
| 7 | 125.00 |
| 8 | 125.00 |
| 9 | 125.00 |
| 10 | 125.00 |
| 11 | 100.00 |
| 12 Rocky Langford | 100.00 |
| 13 | 100.00 |
| 14 | 100.00 |
| 15 I:Timbu | 100.00 |
| 16 | 100.00 |
| 17 | 100.00 |
| 18 | 100.00 |
| 19 | 100.00 |
| 20 MB | 125.00 |
| 21 MB | 125.00 |
| 22 MB | 125.00 |
| 23 thru 38 | @100.00 |
| 39 I:Timmy | 100.00 |
| 40 thru 62 | @100.00 |
| 63 E:Timmy | 100.00 |
| 64 thru 70 | @100.00 |

## LATEST COMICS
**Spotlight Publ./
Palace Promotions,
March, 1945**

| | |
|---|---|
| 1 Funny Animal-Super Duper | 250.00 |
| 2 | 200.00 |

## SPECIAL COMICS
**MLJ Magazines,
Winter, 1941**

| | |
|---|---|
| 1 O:Boy Buddies & Hangman, D:The Comet | 4,000.00 |

Becomes:

## HANGMAN COMICS
**Spring, 1942**

| | |
|---|---|
| 2 B:Hangman & Boy Buddies | 2,700.00 |
| 3 V:Nazis (c),Bondage(c) | 1,800.00 |
| 4 V:Nazis (c) | 1,500.00 |
| 5 Bondage (c) | 1,500.00 |
| 6 | 1,500.00 |
| 7 BF,Graveyard (c) | 1,500.00 |
| 8 BF | 1,500.00 |

Becomes:

## BLACK HOOD
**Winter, 1943–44**

| | |
|---|---|
| 9 BF, Hang Man | 1,500.00 |

| | |
|---|---|
| 10 BF,A:Dusty, the Boy Detective | 800.00 |
| 11 Here lies the Black Hood | 600.00 |
| 12 | 500.00 |
| 13 EK(c) | 500.00 |
| 14 EK(c) | 500.00 |
| 15 EK | 500.00 |
| 16 EK(c) | 500.00 |
| 17 Bondage (c) | 650.00 |
| 18 | 500.00 |
| 19 I.D. Revealed | 700.00 |

Becomes:

## LAUGH COMICS
**Archie Comics, Fall, 1946**

| | |
|---|---|
| 20 BWo,B:Archie,Katy Keene | 850.00 |
| 21 BWo | 400.00 |
| 22 BWo | 400.00 |
| 23 Bwo | 400.00 |
| 24 BWo,JK,Pipsy | 425.00 |
| 25 BWo | 400.00 |
| 26 BWo | 225.00 |
| 27 BWo | 225.00 |
| 28 BWo | 225.00 |
| 29 BWo | 225.00 |
| 30 BWo | 225.00 |
| 31 thru 40 BWo | @200.00 |
| 41 thru 50 BWo | @175.00 |
| 51 thru 60 BWo | @150.00 |
| 61 thru 80 BWo | @150.00 |
| 81 thru 99 BWo | @150.00 |
| 100 BWo | 150.00 |
| 101 thru 126 BWo | @125.00 |
| 127 A:Jaguar | 150.00 |
| 128 A:The Fly | 150.00 |
| 129 A:The Fly | 150.00 |
| 130 A:Jaguar | 150.00 |
| 131 A:Jaguar | 150.00 |
| 132 A:The Fly | 150.00 |
| 133 A:Jaguar | 150.00 |
| 134 A:The Fly | 150.00 |
| 135 A:Jaguar | 150.00 |
| 136 A:Fly Girl | 150.00 |
| 137 A:Fly Girl | 150.00 |
| 138 A:The Fly | 150.00 |
| 139 A:The Fly | 150.00 |
| 140 A:Jaguar | 150.00 |
| 141 A:Jaguar | 150.00 |
| 142 | 150.00 |
| 143 | 150.00 |
| 144 | 150.00 |

## LAUGH COMIX
See: TOP-NOTCH COMICS

## LAUREL AND HARDY
**St. John Publishing Co.,
March, 1949**

| | |
|---|---|
| 1 | 900.00 |
| 2 | 500.00 |
| 3 | 350.00 |
| 26 Rep #1 | 200.00 |
| 27 Rep #2 | 200.00 |
| 28 Rep #3 | 200.00 |

## LAWBREAKERS
**Law & Order Magazines
(Charlton), March, 1951**

| | |
|---|---|
| 1 | 500.00 |
| 2 | 250.00 |
| 3 | 200.00 |
| 4 Drug | 300.00 |
| 5 | 200.00 |
| 6 LM(c) | 225.00 |
| 7 Drug | 300.00 |
| 8 | 200.00 |
| 9 StC(c) | 200.00 |

Becomes:

## LAWBREAKERS
## SUSPENSE STORIES
**Jan., 1953**

| | |
|---|---|
| 10 StC(c) | 500.00 |
| 11 LM(c),Negligee(c) | 1,300.00 |
| 12 LM(c) | 275.00 |
| 13 DG(c) | 275.00 |
| 14 DG(c),Sharks | 275.00 |
| 15 DG(c),Acid in Face(c) | 750.00 |

Becomes:

## STRANGE SUSPENSE
## STORIES
**Jan., 1954**

| | |
|---|---|
| 16 DG(c) | 400.00 |
| 17 DG(c) | 300.00 |
| 18 SD,SD(c) | 450.00 |
| 19 SD,SD(c),Electric Chair | 600.00 |
| 20 SD,SD(c) | 500.00 |
| 21 SD,SD(c) | 300.00 |
| 22 SD,SD(c) | 450.00 |

Becomes:

## THIS IS SUSPENSE
**Feb., 1955**

| | |
|---|---|
| 23 WW; Comics Code | 325.00 |
| 24 GE,DG(c) | 175.00 |
| 25 DG(c) | 150.00 |
| 26 DG(c) | 50.00 |

Becomes:

---

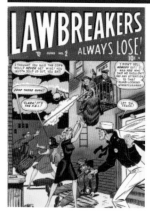

Lawbreakers Always Lose #2
© Marvel Comics Group

Leading Comics #9
© DC Comics

Leave It To Binky #1
© DC Comics

## STRANGE SUSPENSE STORIES

### Oct., 1955

| | |
|---|---|
| 27 | 150.00 |
| 28 | 125.00 |
| 29 | 125.00 |
| 30 | 125.00 |
| 31 SD | 250.00 |
| 32 SD | 250.00 |
| 33 SD | 250.00 |
| 34 SD | 600.00 |
| 35 SD | 250.00 |
| 36 SD | 250.00 |
| 37 SD | 250.00 |
| 38 | 125.00 |
| 39 SD | 200.00 |
| 40 SD | 225.00 |
| 41 SD | 200.00 |
| 42 | 100.00 |
| 43 | 100.00 |
| 44 | 100.00 |
| 45 | 100.00 |
| 46 | 100.00 |
| 47 SD | 225.00 |
| 48 SD | 225.00 |
| 49 | 100.00 |
| 50 SD | 225.00 |
| 51 SD | 225.00 |
| 52 SD | 225.00 |
| 53 SD | 225.00 |
| 54 thru 60 | @100.00 |
| 61 thru 74 | @100.00 |
| 75 SD,SD(c), Captain Atom | 200.00 |
| 77 Oct 1965 | 125.00 |

## LAWBREAKERS ALWAYS LOSE

### Marvel Crime Bureau Stories, 1948–49

| | |
|---|---|
| 1 HK; FBI Reward Poster Photo Adam and Eve, HK,Giggles and Grins | 500.00 |
| 2 FBI V:Fur Theives | 250.00 |
| 3 | 200.00 |
| 4 AyB(c),Vampire | 200.00 |
| 5 AyB(c) | 200.00 |
| 6 Anti Wertham Edition | 225.00 |
| 7 Crime at Midnight | 350.00 |
| 8 Prison Break | 150.00 |
| 9 Ph(c),He Prowled at Night | 150.00 |
| 10 Phc(c),I Met My Murderer | 150.00 |

## LAW-CRIME

### Essenkay Publications, April, 1948

| | |
|---|---|
| 1 LbC,LbC-(c);Raymond Hamilton Dies In The Chair | 1,000.00 |
| 2 LbC,LbC-(c);Strangled Beauty Puzzles Police | 750.00 |
| 3 LbC,LbC-(c);Lipstick Slayer Sought; Aug., 1943 | 900.00 |

## LAWMAN

### Dell Publishing Co., 1959

| | |
|---|---|
| 1 Ph(c) all | 200.00 |
| 2 | 100.00 |
| 3 ATh | 125.00 |
| 4 | 100.00 |
| 5 | 100.00 |
| 6 | 100.00 |
| 7 | 100.00 |
| 8 thru 11 | @100.00 |

## LEADING COMICS

### DC Comics, Winter, 1941–42

| | |
|---|---|
| 1 O:Seven Soldiers of Victory, B:Crimson Avenger,Green Arrow & Speedy,Shining Knight, A:The Dummy | 9,000.00 |
| 2 MMe,V:Black Star | 4,000.00 |
| 3 V:Dr. Doome | 3,000.00 |
| 4 Seven Steps to Conquest, V:The Sixth Sense | 2,500.00 |
| 5 The Miracles that Money Couldn't Buy | 2,500.00 |
| 6 Treasure that Time Forgot | 2,000.00 |
| 7 The Wizard of Wisstark | 2,000.00 |
| 8 Seven Soldiers Go back through the Centuries | 2,000.00 |
| 9 V:Mr. X,Chameleon of Crime | 2,000.00 |
| 10 King of the Hundred Isles | 2,000.00 |
| 11 The Hard Luck Hat! | 1,400.00 |
| 12 The Million Dollar Challenge! | 1,400.00 |
| 13 The Trophies of Crime | 1,400.00 |
| 14 Bandits from the Book | 1,400.00 |
| 15 (fa) | 300.00 |
| 16 thru 22 (fa) | @125.00 |
| 23 (fa),I:Peter Porkchops | 250.00 |
| 24 thru 30 (fa) | @125.00 |
| 31 (fa) | 100.00 |
| 32 (fa) | 100.00 |
| 33 (fa) | 100.00 |
| 34 thru 40 (fa) | @100.00 |
| 41 (fa),Feb.–March, 1950 | 100.00 |

Becomes:

## LEADING SCREEN COMICS

### DC Comics, 1950

| | |
|---|---|
| 42 thru 50 Funny Animal | @125.00 |
| 51 thru 60 | @100.00 |
| 61 thru 70 | @100.00 |
| 71 thru 77 | @100.00 |

## LEAVE IT TO BINKY

### DC Comics, 1948

| | |
|---|---|
| 1ShM, teen-age | 400.00 |
| 2 ShM | 200.00 |
| 3 | 135.00 |
| 4 | 135.00 |
| 5 A:Superman | 200.00 |
| 6 | 125.00 |
| 7 | 125.00 |
| 8 | 125.00 |
| 9 | 125.00 |
| 10 | 125.00 |
| 11 thru 13 | @100.00 |
| 14 ShM | 125.00 |
| 15 thru 20 | @90.00 |
| 21 thru 27 | @100.00 |
| 28 MD | 125.00 |
| 29 | 100.00 |
| 30 | 100.00 |
| 31 thru 60 | @100.00 |

## LEGENDS OF DANIEL BOONE, THE

### DC Comics, Oct., 1955–Jan., 1957

| | |
|---|---|
| 1 | 750.00 |
| 2 | 550.00 |
| 3 thru 8 | 450.00 |

## LEROY

### Visual Editions (Standard Comics), Nov., 1949

| | |
|---|---|
| 1 FunniestTeenager of them All | 150.00 |
| 2 | 125.00 |
| 3 thru 6 | @100.00 |

## LET'S PRETEND

### D.S. Publishing Company, May–June, 1950

| | |
|---|---|
| 1 From Radio Nursery Tales | 200.00 |
| 2 | 150.00 |
| 3 Nov., 1950 | 150.00 |

All comics prices listed are for *Near Mint* condition.

La

*Liberty Scouts #3*
*© Comic Corp. of America*

*Life With Archie #1*
*© Archie Publications*

*Li'l Abner #68*
*© Harvey Publications*

## LET'S TAKE A TRIP
**Pines Publ., 1958**
1 . . . . . . . . . . . . . . . . . . . . . . . 40.00

## MISS LIBERTY
**Burten Publishing, circa 1944**
1 Reprints-Shield,Wizard . . . . . 550.00
Becomes:

## LIBERTY COMICS
**Green Publishing, May, 1946**
10 Reprints,Hangman . . . . . . . . 250.00
11 Wilbur in women's clothes . . . 225.00
12 Black Hood, Skull(c) . . . . . . . 500.00
14 Patty of Airliner . . . . . . . . . . . 150.00
15 Patty of Airliner . . . . . . . . . . . 150.00

## LIBERTY GUARDS
**Chicago Mail Order
(Comic Corp of America),
Circa 1942**
1 PG(c),Liberty Scouts . . . . . . . 500.00
Becomes:

## LIBERTY SCOUTS
**June, 1941–Aug., 1941**
PG(a&c)O:Fireman,Liberty
   Scouts . . . . . . . . . . . . . . 1,800.00
3 PG,PG(c),O:Sentinel . . . . . . . 1,200.00

## LIFE STORY
**Fawcett Publications,
April, 1949**
1 Ph(c) . . . . . . . . . . . . . . . . . . 200.00
2 Ph(c) . . . . . . . . . . . . . . . . . . 150.00
3 Ph(c) . . . . . . . . . . . . . . . . . . 125.00
4 Ph(c) . . . . . . . . . . . . . . . . . . 125.00
5 Ph(c) . . . . . . . . . . . . . . . . . . 125.00
6 Ph(c) . . . . . . . . . . . . . . . . . . 125.00
7 Ph(c) . . . . . . . . . . . . . . . . . . 100.00
8 Ph(c) . . . . . . . . . . . . . . . . . . 100.00
9 Ph(c) . . . . . . . . . . . . . . . . . . 100.00
10 Ph(c) . . . . . . . . . . . . . . . . . . 100.00
11 . . . . . . . . . . . . . . . . . . . . . . 100.00
12 . . . . . . . . . . . . . . . . . . . . . . 100.00
13 WW, Drug . . . . . . . . . . . . . . 250.00
14 . . . . . . . . . . . . . . . . . . . . . . 100.00
15 . . . . . . . . . . . . . . . . . . . . . . 100.00
16 thru 21 . . . . . . . . . . . . . . . @100.00
22 Drug . . . . . . . . . . . . . . . . . . 200.00
23 . . . . . . . . . . . . . . . . . . . . . . 100.00
24 . . . . . . . . . . . . . . . . . . . . . . 100.00
25 thru 35 . . . . . . . . . . . . . . . @100.00

36 Drug . . . . . . . . . . . . . . . . . . 200.00
37 . . . . . . . . . . . . . . . . . . . . . . 100.00
38 . . . . . . . . . . . . . . . . . . . . . . 100.00
39 . . . . . . . . . . . . . . . . . . . . . . 100.00
40 . . . . . . . . . . . . . . . . . . . . . . 100.00
41 . . . . . . . . . . . . . . . . . . . . . . 100.00
42 . . . . . . . . . . . . . . . . . . . . . . 100.00
43 GE . . . . . . . . . . . . . . . . . . . 125.00
44 . . . . . . . . . . . . . . . . . . . . . . 100.00
45 1952 . . . . . . . . . . . . . . . . . . 100.00

## LIFE WITH ARCHIE
**Archie Publications, 1958**
1 . . . . . . . . . . . . . . . . . . . . . . 400.00
2 . . . . . . . . . . . . . . . . . . . . . . 200.00
3 . . . . . . . . . . . . . . . . . . . . . . 150.00
4 . . . . . . . . . . . . . . . . . . . . . . 150.00
5 . . . . . . . . . . . . . . . . . . . . . . 150.00
6 . . . . . . . . . . . . . . . . . . . . . . 125.00
7 . . . . . . . . . . . . . . . . . . . . . . 125.00
8 . . . . . . . . . . . . . . . . . . . . . . 125.00
9 . . . . . . . . . . . . . . . . . . . . . . 125.00
10 . . . . . . . . . . . . . . . . . . . . . . 125.00
11 thru 20 . . . . . . . . . . . . . . . @100.00

## LIFE WITH SNARKY PARKER
**Fox Feature Syndicate,
Aug., 1950**
1 . . . . . . . . . . . . . . . . . . . . . . 300.00

## SURE-FIRE
**Ace Magazines, 1940**
1 O:Flash Lightning . . . . . . . . 2,200.00
2 Whiz Wilson . . . . . . . . . . . . 1,100.00
3 The Raven,Sept., 1940 . . . . . . 800.00
3a Ace McCoy,Oct., 1940 . . . . . 800.00
Becomes:

## LIGHTNING COMICS
**Dec., 1940**
4 Sure-Fire Stories . . . . . . . . . 1,700.00
5 JM . . . . . . . . . . . . . . . . . . 1,000.00
6 JM,Dr. Nemesis . . . . . . . . . 1,000.00
**Vol. 2**
1 JM . . . . . . . . . . . . . . . . . . . 750.00
2 JM,Flash Lightning . . . . . . . . . 750.00
3 JM . . . . . . . . . . . . . . . . . . . 750.00
4 JM . . . . . . . . . . . . . . . . . . . 750.00
5 JM . . . . . . . . . . . . . . . . . . . 750.00
6 JM, bondage(c) . . . . . . . . . . 900.00
**Vol. 3**
1 I:Lightning Girl . . . . . . . . . . . 750.00

## LINDA
**Ajax/Farrell Publications, 1954**
1 . . . . . . . . . . . . . . . . . . . . . . 200.00
2 Lingerie . . . . . . . . . . . . . . . . 150.00
3 . . . . . . . . . . . . . . . . . . . . . . 125.00
4 . . . . . . . . . . . . . . . . . . . . . . 125.00

## LINDA
**See: PHANTOM LADY**

## LI'L ABNER
**Harvey Publications,
Dec., 1947**
61 BP,BW,Sadie Hawkins Day . . . 400.00
62 . . . . . . . . . . . . . . . . . . . . . . 250.00
63 . . . . . . . . . . . . . . . . . . . . . . 250.00
64 . . . . . . . . . . . . . . . . . . . . . . 250.00
65 BP . . . . . . . . . . . . . . . . . . . 250.00
66 . . . . . . . . . . . . . . . . . . . . . . 200.00
67 . . . . . . . . . . . . . . . . . . . . . . 200.00
68 FearlessFosdick V:Any Face . 275.00
69 . . . . . . . . . . . . . . . . . . . . . . 275.00
70 . . . . . . . . . . . . . . . . . . . . . . 200.00

**Toby Press**
71 . . . . . . . . . . . . . . . . . . . . . . 175.00
72 . . . . . . . . . . . . . . . . . . . . . . 175.00
73 . . . . . . . . . . . . . . . . . . . . . . 175.00
74 . . . . . . . . . . . . . . . . . . . . . . 175.00
75 HK . . . . . . . . . . . . . . . . . . . 200.00
76 . . . . . . . . . . . . . . . . . . . . . . 175.00
77 HK . . . . . . . . . . . . . . . . . . . 200.00
78 HK . . . . . . . . . . . . . . . . . . . 200.00
79 HK . . . . . . . . . . . . . . . . . . . 200.00
80 . . . . . . . . . . . . . . . . . . . . . . 175.00
81 . . . . . . . . . . . . . . . . . . . . . . 150.00
82 . . . . . . . . . . . . . . . . . . . . . . 150.00
83 Baseball . . . . . . . . . . . . . . . 175.00
84 . . . . . . . . . . . . . . . . . . . . . . 150.00
85 . . . . . . . . . . . . . . . . . . . . . . 150.00
86 HK . . . . . . . . . . . . . . . . . . . 250.00
87 . . . . . . . . . . . . . . . . . . . . . . 150.00
88 . . . . . . . . . . . . . . . . . . . . . . 150.00
89 . . . . . . . . . . . . . . . . . . . . . . 150.00
90 . . . . . . . . . . . . . . . . . . . . . . 150.00
91 Rep. #77 . . . . . . . . . . . . . . . 165.00
92 . . . . . . . . . . . . . . . . . . . . . . 150.00
93 Rep. #71 . . . . . . . . . . . . . . . 165.00
94 . . . . . . . . . . . . . . . . . . . . . . 150.00
95 Fearless Fosdick . . . . . . . . . . 175.00
96 . . . . . . . . . . . . . . . . . . . . . . 150.00
97 Jan., 1955 . . . . . . . . . . . . . . 150.00

**Li**

---

All comics prices listed are for *Near Mint* condition.

*Little Al of the Secret Service #10*
© Ziff Davis

*Little Audrey #17*
© St. John Publ. Co.

*Little Dot #17*
© Harvey Publications

## LITTLE AL OF THE F.B.I.

**Approved Comics (Ziff Davis), 1950**

| | |
|---|---|
| 10 | 200.00 |
| 11 | 150.00 |

## LITTLE AL OF THE SECRET SERVICE

**Approved Comics (Ziff Davis), 1951**

| | |
|---|---|
| 1 | 200.00 |
| 2 | 150.00 |
| 3 | 150.00 |

## LITTLE AMBROSE

**Archie Publications, 1958**

| | |
|---|---|
| 1 | 150.00 |

## LITTLE ANGEL

**Standard Comics, 1954–59**

| | |
|---|---|
| 5 | 125.00 |
| 6 | 100.00 |
| 7 | 100.00 |
| 8 | 100.00 |
| 9 | 100.00 |
| 10 | 100.00 |
| 11 | 100.00 |
| 12 | 100.00 |
| 13 | 100.00 |
| 14 | 100.00 |
| 15 | 100.00 |
| 16 | 100.00 |

## LITTLE ARCHIE

**Archie Publications, 1956**

| | |
|---|---|
| 1 | 1,000.00 |
| 2 | 400.00 |
| 3 | 250.00 |
| 4 | 250.00 |
| 5 | 250.00 |
| 6 thru 10 | @200.00 |
| 11 thru 20 | @150.00 |
| 21 thru 30 | @100.00 |

## LITTLE ANNIE ROONEY

**St. John Publishing Co./Standard, 1948**

| | |
|---|---|
| 1 | 175.00 |
| 2 | 100.00 |
| 3 | 100.00 |

## LITTLE ASPIRIN

**Marvel Comics, 1949**

| | |
|---|---|
| 1 HK | 200.00 |
| 2 HK | 125.00 |
| 3 | 100.00 |

## LITTLE AUDREY

**St. John Publ. Co./ Harvey Comics, April, 1948**

| | |
|---|---|
| 1 | 550.00 |
| 2 | 300.00 |
| 3 thru 6 | @175.00 |
| 7 thru 10 | @150.00 |
| 11 thru 20 | @125.00 |
| 21 thru 24 | @100.00 |
| 25 B:Harvey Comics | 200.00 |
| 26 A: Casper | 150.00 |
| 27 A: Casper | 150.00 |
| 28 A: Casper | 150.00 |
| 29 thru 31 | @125.00 |
| 32 A: Casper | 125.00 |
| 33 A: Casper | 125.00 |
| 34 A: Casper | 125.00 |
| 35 A: Casper | 125.00 |
| 36 thru 53 | @100.00 |

## LITTLE BEAVER

**Dell Publishing Co., 1951**

| | |
|---|---|
| 3 | 100.00 |
| 4 | 100.00 |
| 5 | 100.00 |
| 6 | 100.00 |
| 7 | 100.00 |
| 8 | 100.00 |

## LITTLE BIT

**Jubilee Publishing Company, March, 1949**

| | |
|---|---|
| 1 | 150.00 |
| 2 June, 1949 | 125.00 |

## LITTLE DOT

**Harvey Publications, Sept., 1953**

| | |
|---|---|
| 1 I: Richie Rich & Little Lotta | 2,200.00 |
| 2 | 900.00 |
| 3 | 550.00 |
| 4 | 450.00 |
| 5 O:Dots on Little Dot's Dress | 550.00 |
| 6 1st Richie Rich(c) | 450.00 |
| 7 | 300.00 |
| 8 | 275.00 |
| 9 | 275.00 |
| 10 | 275.00 |
| 11 thru 20 | @175.00 |
| 21 thru 30 | @150.00 |
| 31 thru 39 | @125.00 |
| 40 thru 50 | @100.00 |
| 51 thru 60 | @100.00 |
| 61 thru 70 | @100.00 |
| 71 thru 80 | @100.00 |
| 81 thru 100 | @100.00 |
| 101 thru 130 | @75.00 |
| 131 thru 140 | @75.00 |
| 141 thru 145, 52 pages | @75.00 |
| 146 thru 163 | @50.00 |

## LITTLE EVA

**St. John Publishing Co., May, 1952**

| | |
|---|---|
| 1 | 200.00 |
| 2 | 150.00 |
| 3 | 125.00 |
| 4 | 125.00 |
| 5 thru 10 | @100.00 |
| 11 thru 30 | @100.00 |
| 31 Nov., 1956 | 100.00 |

## LI'L GENIUS

**Charlton Comics, 1955**

| | |
|---|---|
| 1 | 125.00 |
| 2 | 100.00 |
| 3 thru 15 | @100.00 |
| 16 Giants | 125.00 |
| 17 Giants | 125.00 |
| 18 Giants,100 pages | 150.00 |
| 19 thru 40 | @75.00 |
| 41 thru 54 | @75.00 |
| 55 1965 | 75.00 |

## LI'L GHOST

**St. John Publishing/ Fago Magazine Co.**

| | |
|---|---|
| 1 | 150.00 |
| 2a | 100.00 |
| 3 | 100.00 |

## LITTLE GIANT COMICS

**Centaur Publications, July, 1938**

| | |
|---|---|
| 1 PG, B&W with Color(c) | 900.00 |
| 2 B&W with Color(c) | 750.00 |
| 3 B&W with Color(c) | 750.00 |
| 4 B&W with Color(c) | 750.00 |

All comics prices listed are for *Near Mint* condition.

*Little Iodine #13*
© Dell Publishing Co.

*Little Lotta #1*
© Harvey Publications

*Little Orphan Annie #1*
© Dell Publishing Co.

## LITTLE GIANT DETECTIVE FUNNIES
**Centaur Publications, Oct., 1938–Jan., 1939**
1 B&W . . . . . . . . . . . . . . . . . . 1,000.00
2 B&W . . . . . . . . . . . . . . . . . 750.00
3 B&W . . . . . . . . . . . . . . . . . 750.00
4 WE . . . . . . . . . . . . . . . . . . 750.00

## LITTLE GIANT MOVIE FUNNIES
**Centaur Publications, Aug., 1938**
1 Ed Wheelan-a . . . . . . . . . . 1,000.00
2 Ed Wheelan-a, Oct., 1938 . . . 750.00

## LITTLE GROUCHO
**Reston Publ., Co. 1955**
1 . . . . . . . . . . . . . . . . . . . . . . 125.00
2 . . . . . . . . . . . . . . . . . . . . . . 100.00

## LITTLE IKE
**St. John Publishing Co., April, 1953**
1 . . . . . . . . . . . . . . . . . . . . . . 125.00
2 . . . . . . . . . . . . . . . . . . . . . . 100.00
3 . . . . . . . . . . . . . . . . . . . . . . 100.00
4 Oct., 1953 . . . . . . . . . . . . . 100.00

## LITTLE IODINE
**Dell Publishing Co., April, 1949**
1 . . . . . . . . . . . . . . . . . . . . . . 175.00
2 . . . . . . . . . . . . . . . . . . . . . . 125.00
3 . . . . . . . . . . . . . . . . . . . . . . 125.00
4 . . . . . . . . . . . . . . . . . . . . . . 125.00
5 . . . . . . . . . . . . . . . . . . . . . . 125.00
6 thru 10 . . . . . . . . . . . . . . . @100.00
11 thru 30 . . . . . . . . . . . . . . . @100.00
31 thru 50 . . . . . . . . . . . . . . . @100.00
51 thru 56 . . . . . . . . . . . . . . . @100.00

## LITTLE JACK FROST
**Avon Periodicals, 1951**
1 . . . . . . . . . . . . . . . . . . . . . . 100.00

## LI'L JINX
**Archie Publications, 1956**
11 . . . . . . . . . . . . . . . . . . . . . 150.00
12 . . . . . . . . . . . . . . . . . . . . . 125.00

13 . . . . . . . . . . . . . . . . . . . . . 125.00
14 . . . . . . . . . . . . . . . . . . . . . 125.00
15 . . . . . . . . . . . . . . . . . . . . . 125.00
16 . . . . . . . . . . . . . . . . . . . . . 125.00

## LITTLE JOE
**St. John Publishing Co., 1953**
1 . . . . . . . . . . . . . . . . . . . . . . 100.00

## LITTLE LANA
**See: LANA**

## LITTLE LENNY
**Marvel Classic Detective, 1949**
1 . . . . . . . . . . . . . . . . . . . . . . 125.00
2 . . . . . . . . . . . . . . . . . . . . . . 100.00
3 . . . . . . . . . . . . . . . . . . . . . . 100.00

## LITTLE LIZZIE
**Marvel, June, 1949**
1 Roller Skating(c) . . . . . . . . . . 150.00
2 Soda(c) . . . . . . . . . . . . . . . . 100.00
3 Movies(c) . . . . . . . . . . . . . . 100.00
4 Lizzie(c) . . . . . . . . . . . . . . . 100.00
5 Lizzie/Swing(c) April,1950 . . . 100.00
**Marvel, [2nd Series] Sept., 1953**
1 . . . . . . . . . . . . . . . . . . . . . . 100.00
2 . . . . . . . . . . . . . . . . . . . . . . 75.00
3 Jan., 1954 . . . . . . . . . . . . . . 75.00

## LITTLE LOTTA
**Harvey Publications, 1955**
1 B:Richie Rich and Little Lotta . 550.00
2 . . . . . . . . . . . . . . . . . . . . . . 250.00
3 . . . . . . . . . . . . . . . . . . . . . . 200.00
4 . . . . . . . . . . . . . . . . . . . . . . 150.00
5 . . . . . . . . . . . . . . . . . . . . . . 150.00
6 . . . . . . . . . . . . . . . . . . . . . . 125.00
7 . . . . . . . . . . . . . . . . . . . . . . 125.00
8 . . . . . . . . . . . . . . . . . . . . . . 125.00
9 . . . . . . . . . . . . . . . . . . . . . . 125.00
10 . . . . . . . . . . . . . . . . . . . . . 125.00
11 thru 20 . . . . . . . . . . . . . . . @100.00
21 thru 40 . . . . . . . . . . . . . . . @100.00
41 thru 60 . . . . . . . . . . . . . . . @100.00
61 thru 80 . . . . . . . . . . . . . . . @75.00
81 thru 99 . . . . . . . . . . . . . . . @75.00
100 thru 103 52 pgs . . . . . . . . . @75.00

## LITTLE LULU
**See: MARGE'S LITTLE LULU**

## LI'L MENACE
**Fago Magazine Co., 1958**
1 . . . . . . . . . . . . . . . . . . . . . . 125.00
2 . . . . . . . . . . . . . . . . . . . . . . 100.00

## LITTLE MAX COMICS
**Harvey Publications, Oct., 1949**
1 I: Little Dot,Joe Palooka(c) . . . 300.00
2 A: Little Dot,Joe Palooka(c) . . . 250.00
3 A: Little Dot,Joe Palooka(c) . . 200.00
4 . . . . . . . . . . . . . . . . . . . . . . 150.00
5 C: Little Dot . . . . . . . . . . . . . 150.00
6 thru 10 . . . . . . . . . . . . . . . @100.00
11 thru 22 . . . . . . . . . . . . . . . @100.00
23 A: Little Dot . . . . . . . . . . . . . 100.00
24 thru 37 . . . . . . . . . . . . . . . @100.00
38 Rep. #20 . . . . . . . . . . . . . . . 100.00
39 thru 72 . . . . . . . . . . . . . . . @100.00
73 A: Richie Rich; Nov.'61 . . . . . . 100.00

## LITTLE MISS MUFFET
**Best Books (Standard Comics), Dec., 1948**
11 Strip Reprints . . . . . . . . . . . 150.00
12 Strip Reprints . . . . . . . . . . . 125.00
13 Strip Reprints; Mar.'49 . . . . . 125.00

## LITTLE MISS SUNBEAM COMICS
**Magazine Enterprises, June–July, 1950**
1 . . . . . . . . . . . . . . . . . . . . . . 175.00
2 . . . . . . . . . . . . . . . . . . . . . . 100.00
3 . . . . . . . . . . . . . . . . . . . . . . 100.00
4 Dec.–Jan., 1951 . . . . . . . . . . 100.00

## LITTLE ORPHAN ANNIE
**Dell Publishing Co., 1948**
1 . . . . . . . . . . . . . . . . . . . . . . 250.00
2 Orphan Annie and the Rescue 150.00
3 . . . . . . . . . . . . . . . . . . . . . . 150.00
See also: *Four Color*

*The Living Bible #3*
*© Living Bible Corp.*

*Lone Ranger #28*
*© Dell Publishing Co.*

*The Lone Ranger's Companion Tonto*
*#7 © Dell Publishing Co.*

**Li**

## LI'L PAN

**Fox Features Syndicate,
Dec.–Jan., 1946-47**

| | |
|---|---|
| 6 | 150.00 |
| 7 | 125.00 |
| 8 April–May, 1947 | 125.00 |

## LITTLE ROQUEFORT

**St. John Publishing Co.,
June,1952**

| | |
|---|---|
| 1 | 125.00 |
| 2 | 100.00 |
| 3 thru 9 | @100.00 |

### Pines

| | |
|---|---|
| 10 Summer 1958 | 100.00 |

## LITTLE SCOUTS

**Dell Publishing Co.,
March, 1951**

(1) *see Dell Four Color #321*

| | |
|---|---|
| 2 | 125.00 |
| 3 | 100.00 |
| 4 | 100.00 |
| 5 | 100.00 |
| 6 | 100.00 |

## LITTLEST SNOWMAN

**Dell Publishing Co.,
Dec., 1956**

| | |
|---|---|
| 1 | 100.00 |

## LIVING BIBLE, THE

**Living Bible Corp.
Autumn, 1945**

| | |
|---|---|
| 1 LbC-(c) Life of Paul | 500.00 |
| 2 LbC-(c) Joseph &His Brethern. | 400.00 |
| 3 LbC-(c) Chaplains At War | 475.00 |

## LOIS LANE

See: SUPERMAN'S GIRL
FRIEND LOIS LANE

## LONE EAGLE

**Ajax/Farrell,
April–May, 1954**

| | |
|---|---|
| 1 | 200.00 |
| 2 | 150.00 |
| 3 Bondage(c) | 250.00 |
| 4 Oct.–Nov., 1954 | 150.00 |

## LONELY HEART

**Excellent Publications
(Ajax/Farrell), 1955**

| | |
|---|---|
| 9 | 150.00 |
| 10 | 100.00 |
| 11 | 100.00 |
| 12 | 100.00 |
| 13 | 100.00 |
| 14 | 100.00 |

Becomes:

## DEAR HEART

**Ajax/Farrell Publ., 1956**

| | |
|---|---|
| 15 | 100.00 |
| 16 | 100.00 |

## LONE RANGER

**Dell Publishing Co.,
Jan.–Feb., 1948**

| | |
|---|---|
| 1 B:Lone Ranger & Tonto B:Strip Reprint | 1,400.00 |
| 2 | 600.00 |
| 3 | 400.00 |
| 4 | 400.00 |
| 5 | 400.00 |
| 6 | 350.00 |
| 7 | 350.00 |
| 8 O:Retold. | 400.00 |
| 9 | 350.00 |
| 10 | 350.00 |
| 11 B:Young Hawk. | 250.00 |
| 12 thru 20 | @250.00 |
| 21 | 200.00 |
| 22 | 200.00 |
| 23 O:Retold | 275.00 |
| 24 thru 30 | @200.00 |
| 31 (1st Mask Logo) | 250.00 |
| 32 thru 36 | @175.00 |
| 37 (E:Strip reprints) | 150.00 |
| 38 thru 50 | @150.00 |
| 51 thru 75 | @150.00 |
| 76 thru 99 | @125.00 |
| 100 | 150.00 |
| 101 thru 111 | @150.00 |
| 112 B:Clayton Moore Ph(c) | 350.00 |
| 113 thru 117 | @200.00 |
| 118 O:Lone Ranger & Tonto retold, Anniv. issue | 400.00 |
| 119 thru 144 | @200.00 |
| 145 final issue,May/July, 1962 | 200.00 |

## THE LONE RANGER'S COMPANION TONTO

**Dell Publishing Co., Jan., 1951**

(1) *see Dell Four Color #312*

| | |
|---|---|
| 2 P(c) all | 200.00 |
| 3 | 150.00 |
| 4 | 125.00 |
| 5 | 125.00 |
| 6 thru 10 | @125.00 |
| 11 thru 20 | @100.00 |
| 21 thru 25 | @100.00 |
| 26 thru 33 | @100.00 |

## THE LONE RANGER'S FAMOUS HORSE HI-YO SILVER

**Dell Publishing Co., Jan., 1952**

(1) *see Dell Four Color #369*
(1) *see Dell Four Color #392*

| | |
|---|---|
| 3 P(c) all | 125.00 |
| 4 | 125.00 |
| 5 | 125.00 |
| 6 thru 10 | @125.00 |
| 11 thru 36 | @100.00 |

## LONE RIDER

**Farrell (Superior Comics), April, 1951**

| | |
|---|---|
| 1 | 350.00 |
| 2 I&O: Golden Arrow; 52 pgs. | 200.00 |
| 3 | 175.00 |
| 4 | 175.00 |
| 5 | 175.00 |
| 6 E: Golden Arrow | 175.00 |
| 7 G.Arrow Becomes Swift Arrow | 175.00 |
| 8 O: Swift Arrow | 200.00 |
| 9 thru 14 | @100.00 |
| 15 O: Golden Arrow Rep. #2 | 125.00 |
| 16 thru 19 | @100.00 |
| 20 | 100.00 |
| 21 3-D (c). | 250.00 |
| 22 | 100.00 |
| 23 A: Apache Kid | 100.00 |
| 24 | 100.00 |
| 25 | 100.00 |
| 26 July, 1955 | 100.00 |

## LONG BOW

**Real Adventures Publ.
(Fiction House), Winter, 1950**

| | |
|---|---|
| 1 | 200.00 |

*Looney Tunes and Merrie Melodies #24 © Warner Bros.*

*Looney Tunes #169 © Warner Bros.*

*Lost Worlds #5 © Standard Comics*

2 . . . . . . . . . . . . . . . . . . . . . . 125.00
3 'Red Arrows Means War' . . . . . 125.00
4 'Trial of Tomahawk' . . . . . . . . 125.00
5 . . . . . . . . . . . . . . . . . . . . . . 125.00
6 'Rattlesnake Raiders' . . . . . . . 100.00
7 . . . . . . . . . . . . . . . . . . . . . . 100.00
8 . . . . . . . . . . . . . . . . . . . . . . 100.00
9 Spring, 1953 . . . . . . . . . . . . . 100.00

## LONG JOHN SILVER
## AND THE PIRATES
### See: TERRY
## AND THE PIRATES

## LOONEY TUNES AND
## MERRIE MELODIES
**Dell Publishing Co., 1941**
1 B:&1st Comic App. Bugs Bunny
Daffy Duck,Elmer Fudd . . 20,000.00
2 Bugs/Porky(c) . . . . . . . . . 4,000.00
3 Bugs/Porky(c) B:WK,
Kandi the Cave . . . . . . . . . 3,000.00
4 Bugs/Porky(c),WK . . . . . . . 3,000.00
5 Bugs/Porky(c),WK,
A:Super Rabbit . . . . . . . . 2,500.00
6 Bugs/Porky/Elmer(c),E:WK,
Kandi the Cave . . . . . . . . . 2,200.00
7 Bugs/Porky(c) . . . . . . . . . 1,500.00
8 Bugs/Porky swimming(c),F:WK,
Kandi the Cave . . . . . . . . . 2,000.00
9 Porky/Elmer car painted(c) . 1,500.00
10 Porky/Bugs/Elmer Parade(c) 1,500.00
11 Bugs/Porky(c),F:WK,
Kandi the Cave . . . . . . . . . 1,500.00
12 Bugs/Porky rollerskating(c) . 1,100.00
13 Bugs/Porky(c) . . . . . . . . . . 1,100.00
14 Bugs/Porky(c) . . . . . . . . . . 1,100.00
15 Bugs/Porky X-Mas(c),F:WK
Kandi the Cave . . . . . . . . . 1,000.00
16 Bugs/Porky ice-skating(c) . . 1,000.00
17 Bugs/Petunia Valentines(c) . 1,000.00
18 Sgt.Bugs Marine(c) . . . . . . 1,000.00
19 Bugs/Painting(c) . . . . . . . . . 1,000.00
20 Bugs/Porky/ElmerWarBonds(c),
B:WK,Pat,Patsy&Pete . . . 1,000.00
21 Bugs/Porky 4th July(c) . . . . 1,000.00
22 Porky(c) . . . . . . . . . . . . . . . 1,000.00
23 Bugs/Porky Fishing(c) . . . . . 1,000.00
24 Bugs/Porky Football(c) . . . . 1,000.00
25 Bugs/Porky/Petunia Halloween
(c),E:WK,Pat, Patsy & Pete 1,000.00
26 Bugs Thanksgiving(c) . . . . . . 750.00

27 Bugs/Porky New Years(c) . . . . 750.00
28 Bugs/Porky Ice-Skating(c) . . . 750.00
29 Bugs Valentine(c) . . . . . . . . . 750.00
30 Bugs(c) . . . . . . . . . . . . . . . . 750.00
31 Bugs(c) . . . . . . . . . . . . . . . . 600.00
32 Bugs/Porky Hot Dogs(c) . . . . 600.00
33 Bugs/Porky War Bonds(c) . . . 750.00
34 Bugs/Porky Fishing(c) . . . . . . 500.00
35 Bugs/Porky Swimming(c) . . . . 500.00
36 Bugs/Porky(c) . . . . . . . . . . . . 500.00
37 Bugs Halloween(c) . . . . . . . . 500.00
38 Bugs Thanksgiving(c) . . . . . . 500.00
39 Bugs X-Mas(c) . . . . . . . . . . . 500.00
40 Bugs(c) . . . . . . . . . . . . . . . . 500.00
41 Bugs Washington's
Birthday(c) . . . . . . . . . . . . . 400.00
42 Bugs Magician(c) . . . . . . . . . 400.00
43 Bugs Dream(c) . . . . . . . . . . . 400.00
44 Bugs/Porky(c) . . . . . . . . . . . . 400.00
45 Bugs War Bonds(c) . . . . . . . . 400.00
46 Bugs/Porky(c) . . . . . . . . . . . . 400.00
47 Bugs Beach(c) . . . . . . . . . . . 350.00
48 Bugs/Porky Picnic(c) . . . . . . . 350.00
49 Bugs(c) . . . . . . . . . . . . . . . . 350.00
50 Bugs(c) . . . . . . . . . . . . . . . . 350.00
51 thru 60 . . . . . . . . . . . . . . . . @300.00
61 thru 80 . . . . . . . . . . . . . . . . @250.00
81 thru 86 . . . . . . . . . . . . . . . . @150.00
87 Bugs X-Mas(c) . . . . . . . . . . . 175.00
88 thru 99 . . . . . . . . . . . . . . . . @150.00
100 . . . . . . . . . . . . . . . . . . . . . . 150.00
101 thru 110 . . . . . . . . . . . . . . . @150.00
111 thru 125 . . . . . . . . . . . . . . . @150.00
126 thru 150 . . . . . . . . . . . . . . . @150.00
151 thru 165 . . . . . . . . . . . . . . . @100.00
**Becomes:**

## LOONEY TUNES
**Aug., 1955**
166 thru 200 . . . . . . . . . . . . . . @100.00
201 thru 245 . . . . . . . . . . . . . . @100.00
246 final issue,Sept.1962 . . . . . . 100.00

## LORNA, THE
## JUNGLE GIRL
**Marvel Atlas, 1953–57**
1 Terrors of the Jungle,O:Lorna . 450.00
2 Headhunter's Strike
I:Greg Knight . . . . . . . . . . . 225.00
3 . . . . . . . . . . . . . . . . . . . . . . 200.00
4 . . . . . . . . . . . . . . . . . . . . . . 200.00
5 . . . . . . . . . . . . . . . . . . . . . . 200.00
6 RH(c),GT . . . . . . . . . . . . . . 150.00
7 RH(c) . . . . . . . . . . . . . . . . . 150.00
8 Jungle Queen Strikes Again . . 150.00

9 . . . . . . . . . . . . . . . . . . . . . . 150.00
10 White Fang . . . . . . . . . . . . . 150.00
11 Death From the Skies . . . . . . 150.00
12 Day of Doom . . . . . . . . . . . . 125.00
13 thru 17 . . . . . . . . . . . . . . . . @125.00
18 AW(c) . . . . . . . . . . . . . . . . . 150.00
19 thru 26 . . . . . . . . . . . . . . . @100.00

## LOST WORLDS
**Literary Enterprises
(Standard Comics),
Oct., 1952**
5 ATh, Alice in Terrorland . . . . . . 600.00
6 ATh . . . . . . . . . . . . . . . . . . . . 450.00

## LOVE ADVENTURES
**Marvel Atlas, Oct., 1949**
1 Ph(c) . . . . . . . . . . . . . . . . . . . 250.00
2 BP,Ph(c),Tyrone Power/
Gene Tierney . . . . . . . . . . . . 225.00
3 thru 12 . . . . . . . . . . . . . . . @150.00
**Becomes:**

## ACTUAL CONFESSIONS
**Marvel, 1952**
13 . . . . . . . . . . . . . . . . . . . . . . 100.00
14 Dec., 1952 . . . . . . . . . . . . . . 100.00

## LOVE AND MARRIAGE
**Superior Comics Ltd.,
March, 1952**
1 . . . . . . . . . . . . . . . . . . . . . . 150.00
2 . . . . . . . . . . . . . . . . . . . . . . 125.00
3 . . . . . . . . . . . . . . . . . . . . . . 100.00
4 . . . . . . . . . . . . . . . . . . . . . . 100.00
5 . . . . . . . . . . . . . . . . . . . . . . 100.00
6 . . . . . . . . . . . . . . . . . . . . . . 100.00
7 thru 15 . . . . . . . . . . . . . . . @100.00
16 Sept., 1954 . . . . . . . . . . . . . 100.00

## LOVE AT FIRST SIGHT
**Periodical House
(Ace Magazines),
Oct., 1949**
1 P(c) . . . . . . . . . . . . . . . . . . . 200.00
2 P(c) . . . . . . . . . . . . . . . . . . . 150.00
3 . . . . . . . . . . . . . . . . . . . . . . 125.00
4 P(c) . . . . . . . . . . . . . . . . . . . 125.00
5 thru 10 . . . . . . . . . . . . . . . @125.00
11 thru 33 . . . . . . . . . . . . . . . @125.00
34 1st Edition Under Code . . . . 100.00
35 thru 41 . . . . . . . . . . . . . . . @100.00
42 1956 . . . . . . . . . . . . . . . . . . 100.00

**Lo**

Love Confessions #8
© Quality Comics Group

Love Lessons #1
© Harvey Publications

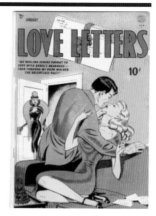

Love Letters #1
© Quality Comics Group

**Lo**

## LOVE CLASSICS
**Marvel Classic Detective, 1949**
| | |
|---|---|
| 1 | 160.00 |
| 2 | 150.00 |

## LOVE CONFESSIONS
**Comics Magazine (Quality Comics Group), Oct., 1949**
| | |
|---|---|
| 1 PG,BWa(c)& Some-a | 400.00 |
| 2 PG,BWa(c) | 300.00 |
| 3 | 150.00 |
| 4 RC | 175.00 |
| 5 BWa | 200.00 |
| 6 Ph(c) | 125.00 |
| 7 Ph(c) Van Johnson | 125.00 |
| 8 BWa,Robert Mitchum | 125.00 |
| 9 Ph(c)Jane Russell/Robert Mitchum | 125.00 |
| 10 BWa | 200.00 |
| 11 thru 18 Ph(c) | @150.00 |
| 19 | 150.00 |
| 20 BWa | 175.00 |
| 21 | 100.00 |
| 22 BWa | 150.00 |
| 23 thru 28 | @100.00 |
| 29 BWa | 150.00 |
| 30 thru 38 | @100.00 |
| 39 MB. | 150.00 |
| 40 thru 42 | @100.00 |
| 43 1st Edition Under Code | 100.00 |
| 44 | 100.00 |
| 45 BWa(a) | 150.00 |
| 46 | 100.00 |
| 47 BWa(c) | 150.00 |
| 48 | 100.00 |
| 49 MB. | 150.00 |
| 50 thru 54 Dec., 1956 | @100.00 |

## LOVE DIARY
**Our Publishing Co./Toytown, July, 1949–Oct., 1955**
| | |
|---|---|
| 1 BK,Ph(c) | 250.00 |
| 2 BK,Ph(c) | 200.00 |
| 3 BK,Ph(c) | 200.00 |
| 4 thru 9 Ph(c) | @150.00 |
| 10 BEv, Ph(c). | 150.00 |
| 11 thru 24 Ph(c) | @125.00 |
| 25 | 100.00 |
| 26 | 100.00 |
| 27 Ph(c) | 125.00 |
| 28 | 100.00 |
| 29 Ph(c) | 100.00 |
| 30 | 100.00 |

| | |
|---|---|
| 31 JB(c) | 100.00 |
| 32 thru 41 | @100.00 |
| 42 MB(c) | 100.00 |
| 43 thru 47 | @100.00 |
| 48 1st Edition Under Code | 100.00 |

## LOVE DIARY
**Quality Comics Group, Sept., 1949**
| | |
|---|---|
| 1 BWa(c) | 400.00 |

## LOVE DIARY
**Charlton Comics, 1958**
| | |
|---|---|
| 1 | 150.00 |
| 2 | 125.00 |
| 3 | 100.00 |
| 4 | 100.00 |
| 5 | 100.00 |
| 6 | 100.00 |
| 7 | 100.00 |
| 8 | 100.00 |
| 9 | 100.00 |
| 10 | 100.00 |
| 11 thru 15 | @100.00 |
| 16 thru 20 | @100.00 |
| 21 thru 40 | @75.00 |

## LOVE DRAMAS
**Marvel, Oct., 1949**
| | |
|---|---|
| 1 Ph(c),JKa | 200.00 |
| 2 Jan., 1950 | 150.00 |

## LOVE JOURNAL
**Our Publishing Co., 1951–54**
| | |
|---|---|
| 10 | 150.00 |
| 11 | 125.00 |
| 12 | 125.00 |
| 13 | 125.00 |
| 14 | 125.00 |
| 15 | 125.00 |
| 16 | 125.00 |
| 17 | 125.00 |
| 18 | 125.00 |
| 19 | 125.00 |
| 20 | 125.00 |
| 21 thru 25 | @125.00 |

## LOVELAND
**Marvel, 1949**
| | |
|---|---|
| 1 Ph(c) | 150.00 |
| 2 Ph(c) | 150.00 |

## LOVE LESSONS
**Harvey Publications, Oct., 1949**
| | |
|---|---|
| 1 Silver(c) | 350.00 |
| 2 BP | 250.00 |
| 3 Ph(c) | 200.00 |
| 4 | 200.00 |
| 5 June, 1950 | 200.00 |

## LOVE LETTERS
**Comic Magazines (Quality Comics Group), Nov., 1949**
| | |
|---|---|
| 1 PG,BWa(c) | 350.00 |
| 2 PG,BWa(c) | 300.00 |
| 3 PG,Ph(c) | 250.00 |
| 4 BWa,Ph(c) | 300.00 |
| 5 Ph(c) | 150.00 |
| 6 Ph(c) | 150.00 |
| 7 Ph(c) | 150.00 |
| 8 Ph(c) | 150.00 |
| 9 Ph(c) of Robert Mitchum | 175.00 |
| 10 Ph(c) | 150.00 |
| 11 BWa,Ph(c) Broadway Romances | 200.00 |
| 12 Ph(c) | 125.00 |
| 13 Ph(c) | 125.00 |
| 14 Ph(c) | 125.00 |
| 15 Ph(c) | 125.00 |
| 16 Ph(c) of Anthony Quinn | 200.00 |
| 17 BWa, Ph(c) of Jane Russell | 200.00 |
| 18 thru 28 Ph(c) | @125.00 |
| 29 | 125.00 |
| 30 & 31 BWa | @200.00 |
**Becomes:**

## LOVE SECRETS
**Aug., 1953**
| | |
|---|---|
| 32 | 200.00 |
| 33 | 125.00 |
| 34 BWa | 200.00 |
| 35 thru 39 | @150.00 |
| 40 MB(c)1st Edition Under Code | 125.00 |
| 41 thru 48 | @100.00 |
| 49 MB | 150.00 |
| 50 MB | 150.00 |
| 51 MB(c) | 150.00 |
| 52 thru 56 | @100.00 |

## LOVELORN
**Best Syndicated/Michel Publ. (American Comics Group), Aug.–Sept., 1949**
| | |
|---|---|
| 1 | 200.00 |

*Love Secrets #35*
© Quality Comics Group

*Love Mystery #2*
© Fawcett Publications

*Lovers' Lane #2*
© Lev Gleason Publications

| | |
|---|---|
| 2 | 150.00 |
| 3 thru 10 | @135.00 |
| 11 thru 17 | @125.00 |
| 18 2pgs. MD-a | 125.00 |
| 19 | 125.00 |
| 20 | 125.00 |
| 21 Prostitution Story | 200.00 |
| 22 thru 50 | @125.00 |
| 51 July, 1954, 3-D | 250.00 |

Becomes:

### CONFESSIONS OF THE LOVELORN
**Aug., 1954**

| | |
|---|---|
| 52 3-D | 350.00 |
| 53 | 100.00 |
| 54 3-D | 350.00 |
| 55 | 150.00 |
| 56 Communist Story | 150.00 |
| 57 Comics Code | 125.00 |
| 58 thru 90 | @125.00 |
| 91 AW | 150.00 |
| 92 thru 105 | @100.00 |
| 106 P(c) | 100.00 |
| 107 P(c) | 100.00 |
| 108 thru 114 | @100.00 |

### LOVE MEMORIES
**Fawcett Publications, Autumn, 1949**

| | |
|---|---|
| 1 Ph(c) | 175.00 |
| 2 Ph(c) | 125.00 |
| 3 Ph(c) | 125.00 |
| 4 Ph(c) | 125.00 |

### LOVE MYSTERY
**Fawcett Publications, June, 1950**

| | |
|---|---|
| 1 GE, Ph(c) | 250.00 |
| 2 GE, Ph(c) | 200.00 |
| 3 GE & BP, Ph(c); Oct., 1950 | 200.00 |

### LOVE PROBLEMS AND ADVICE ILLUSTRATED
**McCombs/Harvey Publications Home Comics, June, 1949**

| | |
|---|---|
| 1 BP | 250.00 |
| 2 BP | 200.00 |
| 3 | 150.00 |
| 4 | 150.00 |
| 5 LEI(c) | 125.00 |
| 6 | 125.00 |
| 7 BP | 125.00 |

| | |
|---|---|
| 8 BP | 125.00 |
| 9 BP | 125.00 |
| 10 BP | 125.00 |
| 11 BP | 100.00 |
| 12 BP | 100.00 |
| 13 BP | 100.00 |
| 14 BP | 100.00 |
| 15 | 100.00 |
| 16 | 100.00 |
| 17 thru 23 BP | @100.00 |
| 24 BP, Rape Scene | 150.00 |
| 25 BP | 100.00 |
| 26 | 100.00 |
| 27 | 100.00 |
| 28 BP | 100.00 |
| 29 BP | 100.00 |
| 30 | 100.00 |
| 31 | 100.00 |
| 32 Comics Code | 100.00 |
| 33 BP | 100.00 |
| 34 | 100.00 |
| 35 | 100.00 |
| 36 | 100.00 |
| 37 | 100.00 |
| 38 S&K (c) | 100.00 |
| 39 | 100.00 |
| 40 BP | 100.00 |
| 41 BP | 100.00 |
| 42 | 100.00 |
| 43 | 100.00 |
| 44 March, 1957 | 100.00 |

### LOVE ROMANCES
**See: IDEAL**

### LOVERS
**See: ALL-SELECT COMICS**

### LOVE SCANDALS
**Comic Magazines (Quality Comics Group), Feb., 1950**

| | |
|---|---|
| 1 BW(a&c) | 300.00 |
| 2 PG-a, Ph(c) | 125.00 |
| 3 PG-a, Ph(c) | 125.00 |
| 4 BWa(a&c) 18Pgs.; GFx-a | 250.00 |
| 5 Ph(c), Oct., 1950 | 125.00 |

### LOVE SECRETS
**Marvel, Oct., 1949**

| | |
|---|---|
| 1 | 175.00 |
| 2 Jan., 1950 | 125.00 |

### LOVE SECRETS
**See: LOVE LETTERS**

### LOVERS LANE
**Lev Gleason Publications, Oct., 1949**

| | |
|---|---|
| 1 CBi (c),FGu-a | 250.00 |
| 2 P(c) | 150.00 |
| 3 P(c) | 125.00 |
| 4 P(c) | 125.00 |
| 5 P(c) | 125.00 |
| 6 GT,P(c) | 125.00 |
| 7 P(c), | 125.00 |
| 8 P(c), | 125.00 |
| 9 P(c), | 125.00 |
| 10 P(c) | 125.00 |
| 11 thru 19 P(c) | @100.00 |
| 20 Ph(c); FF 1 page Ad, | 125.00 |
| 21 Ph(c) | 100.00 |
| 22 Ph(c) | 100.00 |
| 23 | 100.00 |
| 24 | 100.00 |
| 25 | 100.00 |
| 26 Ph(c) | 100.00 |
| 27 Ph(c) | 100.00 |
| 28 Ph(c) | 100.00 |
| 29 thru 38 | @100.00 |
| 39 Story Narrated by Frank Sinatra | 150.00 |
| 40 | 100.00 |
| 41 June, 1954 | 100.00 |

### LOVE STORIES OF MARY WORTH
**Harvey Publications, Sept., 1949**

| | |
|---|---|
| 1 Newspaper Reprints | 150.00 |
| 2 Newspaper Reprints | 125.00 |
| 3 Newspaper Reprints | 100.00 |
| 4 Newspaper Reprints, | 100.00 |
| 5 May, 1950 | 100.00 |

### LOVE TALES
**Marvel Atlas, 1949–56**
**(Formerly: The Human Torch)**

| | |
|---|---|
| 36 Ph(c) | 250.00 |
| 37 | 175.00 |
| 38 | 150.00 |
| 39 thru 41 | @150.00 |
| 42 thru 44 | @125.00 |
| 45 BP | 150.00 |

**Lo**

Lucky Comics #5
© Consolidated Magazines

Meet Miss Pepper #6
© St. John Publishing Co.

Mad Magazine #45
© E.C. Comics

46 thru 51 . . . . . . . . . . . . . . . @125.00
52 BK . . . . . . . . . . . . . . . . . . . 150.00
53 thru 68 . . . . . . . . . . . . . . . @125.00
69 BEv . . . . . . . . . . . . . . . . . . 150.00
70 thru 75 . . . . . . . . . . . . . . . @100.00

### LOVE TRAILS
**Marvel Current Detective, 1949**
1 western romance . . . . . . . . . . 175.00
2 . . . . . . . . . . . . . . . . . . . . . . . 175.00

**Lo**

### LUCKY COMICS
**Consolidated Magazines,
Jan., 1944–Summer 1946**
1 Lucky Star . . . . . . . . . . . . . . . 300.00
2 HcK(c) . . . . . . . . . . . . . . . . . . 200.00
3 . . . . . . . . . . . . . . . . . . . . . . . 200.00
4 . . . . . . . . . . . . . . . . . . . . . . . 200.00
5 Devil(c) . . . . . . . . . . . . . . . . . 200.00

### LUCKY DUCK
**Standard Comics
(Literary Enterprises),
Jan.–Sept., 1953**
5 IS(a&c) . . . . . . . . . . . . . . . . . 125.00
6 IS(a&c) . . . . . . . . . . . . . . . . . 100.00
7 IS(a&c) . . . . . . . . . . . . . . . . . 100.00
8 IS(a&c) . . . . . . . . . . . . . . . . . 100.00

### LUCKY FIGHTS
### IT THROUGH
**Educational Comics, 1949**
N# HK-a, V.D. Prevention . . . . 1,500.00

### LUCKY "7" COMICS
**Howard Publications, 1944**
1 Bondage(c) Pioneer . . . . . . . . 700.00

### LUCKY STAR
**Nationwide Publications,
1950**
1 JDa,B:52 pages western . . . . 225.00
2 JDa . . . . . . . . . . . . . . . . . . . . 150.00
3 JDa . . . . . . . . . . . . . . . . . . . . 150.00
4 JDa . . . . . . . . . . . . . . . . . . . . 125.00
5 JDa . . . . . . . . . . . . . . . . . . . . 125.00
6 JDa . . . . . . . . . . . . . . . . . . . . 125.00
7 JDa . . . . . . . . . . . . . . . . . . . . 125.00
8 thru 13 . . . . . . . . . . . . . . . . @100.00
14 1955,E:52 pages western . . . . 100.00

### LUCY, THE REAL
### GONE GAL
**St. John Publishing Co.,
June, 1953**
1 Negligee Panels,Teenage . . . . 300.00
2 . . . . . . . . . . . . . . . . . . . . . . . 150.00
3 MD-a . . . . . . . . . . . . . . . . . . . 125.00
4 Feb., 1954 . . . . . . . . . . . . . . . 100.00
**Becomes:**

### MEET MISS PEPPER
**April, 1954**
5 JKu-a . . . . . . . . . . . . . . . . . . . 225.00
6 JKu (a&c), June,1954 . . . . . . 175.00

### MAD
**E.C. Comics,
Oct.–Nov., 1952**
1 JSe,HK(c),JDa,WW . . . . . 15,000.00
2 JSe,JDa(c),JDa,WW. . . . . . 4,500.00
3 JSe,HK(c),JDa,WW . . . . . . 2,700.00
4 JSe,HK(c),JDa-Flob Was
  A Slob,JDa,WW . . . . . . . . 2,500.00
5 JSe,BE(c).JDa,WW . . . . . . 3,000.00
6 JSe,HK(c),Jda,WW. . . . . . . 1,500.00
7 HK(c),JDa,WW . . . . . . . . . 1,500.00
8 HK(c),JDa,WW . . . . . . . . . 1,500.00
9 JSe,HK(c),JDa,WW . . . . . . 1,500.00
10 JSe,HK(c),JDa,WW . . . . . . 1,600.00
11 BW,BW(c),JDa,WW,Life(c). . 1,500.00
12 BK,JDa,WW. . . . . . . . . . . . 1,400.00
13 HK(c),JDa,WW,Red(c). . . . . 1,400.00
14 RH,HK(c),JDa,WW,
  Mona Lisa(c). . . . . . . . . . . 1,400.00
15 JDa,WW,Alice in
  Wonderland(c) . . . . . . . . . . 1,400.00
16 HK(c),JDa,WW,
  Newspaper(c). . . . . . . . . . . 1,400.00
17 BK,BW,JDa,WW . . . . . . . . 1,400.00
18 HK(c),JDa,WW. . . . . . . . . . 1,400.00
19 JDa,WW,Racing Form(c). . . 1,000.00
20 JDa,WW,Composition(c) . . . 1,200.00
21 JDa,WW,1st A.E.Neuman(c) 1,500.00
22 BE,JDa,WW,Picasso(c) . . . . 1,500.00
23 Last Comic Format Edition,
  JDa,WW Think(c) . . . . . . 1,000.00
24 BK,WW, HK Logo & Border;
  1st Magazine Format . . . . . 1,800.00
25 WW,AlJaffee Becomes Reg. 1,000.00
26 BK,WW,WW(c) . . . . . . . . . . 500.00
27 WWa,RH,JDa(c) . . . . . . . . . 400.00
28 WW,BE(c),RH Back(c) . . . . . 400.00
29 JKa,BW,WW,WW(c);
  1st Don Martin Artwork . . . . . 400.00
30 BE,WW,RC; 1st A.E.
  Neuman(c) By Mingo . . . . . 600.00
31 JDa,WW,BW,Mingo(c) . . . . . 350.00
32 MD,JO 1st as reg.;Mingo(c);
  WW-Back(c) . . . . . . . . . . . 350.00
33 WWa,Mingo(c);JO-Back(c) . . 350.00
34 WWa,Mingo(c);1st Berg
  as Reg. . . . . . . . . . . . . . . . 250.00
35 WW,RC,Mingo
  Wraparound(c). . . . . . . . . . 225.00
36 WW,BW,Mingo(c),JO,MD . . 200.00
37 WW,Mingo(c)JO,MD . . . . . . 200.00
38 WW,JO,MD . . . . . . . . . . . . 200.00
39 WW,JO,MD . . . . . . . . . . . . 200.00
40 WW,BW,JO,MD . . . . . . . . . 200.00
41 WW,JO,MD . . . . . . . . . . . . 150.00
42 WW,JO,MD . . . . . . . . . . . . 150.00
43 WW,JO,MD . . . . . . . . . . . . 150.00
44 WW,JO,MD . . . . . . . . . . . . 150.00
45 WW,JO,MD . . . . . . . . . . . . 150.00
46 JO,MD . . . . . . . . . . . . . . . . 150.00
47 JO,MD. . . . . . . . . . . . . . . . . 150.00
48 JO,MD . . . . . . . . . . . . . . . . 150.00
49 JO,MD . . . . . . . . . . . . . . . . 150.00
50 JO,MD . . . . . . . . . . . . . . . . 150.00
51 JO,MD . . . . . . . . . . . . . . . . 125.00
52 JO,MD . . . . . . . . . . . . . . . . 125.00
53 JO,MD. . . . . . . . . . . . . . . . . 125.00
54 JO,MD . . . . . . . . . . . . . . . . 125.00
55 JO,MD. . . . . . . . . . . . . . . . . 125.00
56 JO,MD . . . . . . . . . . . . . . . . 125.00
57 JO,MD . . . . . . . . . . . . . . . . 125.00
58 JO,MD. . . . . . . . . . . . . . . . . 125.00
59 WW,JO,MD . . . . . . . . . . . . 150.00
60 JO,MD. . . . . . . . . . . . . . . . . 150.00

### MAD HATTER, THE
**O.W. Comics, 1946**
1 Freddy the Firefly . . . . . . . . 1,200.00
2 V:Humpty Dumpty . . . . . . . . . 600.00

### MADHOUSE
**Ajax/Farrell Publ., 1954**
1 . . . . . . . . . . . . . . . . . . . . . . . 375.00
2 . . . . . . . . . . . . . . . . . . . . . . . 200.00
3 . . . . . . . . . . . . . . . . . . . . . . . 200.00
4 . . . . . . . . . . . . . . . . . . . . . . . 300.00

**Second Series, 1957**
1 . . . . . . . . . . . . . . . . . . . . . . . 150.00
2 . . . . . . . . . . . . . . . . . . . . . . . 125.00
3 . . . . . . . . . . . . . . . . . . . . . . . 125.00

All comics prices listed are for *Near Mint* condition.

# STANDARD GUIDE TO GOLDEN AGE COMICS

Magic Comics #1
© David McKay Publications

Magic Comics #54
© David McKay Publications

Man Comics #12
© Marvel Comics Group

## MAGIC COMICS

**David McKay Publications,
Aug.,1939–Nov.-Dec., 1949**
1 Mandrake the Magician, Henry,
Popeye,Blondie, Barney Baxter,
Secret Agent X-9, Bunky,
Henry on(c) . . . . . . . . . . . 3,800.00
2 Henry on(c) . . . . . . . . . . . . 1,400.00
3 Henry on(c) . . . . . . . . . . . . 1,000.00
4 Henry on(c),Mandrake-Logo . . 850.00
5 Henry on(c),Mandrake-Logo . . 750.00
6 Henry on(c),Mandrake-Logo . . 525.00
7 Henry on(c),Mandrake-Logo . . 525.00
8 B:Inspector Wade,Tippie . . . . 500.00
9 Henry-Mandrake Interact(c) . . 500.00
10 Henry-Mandrake Interact(c) . . 500.00
11 Henry-Mandrake Interact(c) . . 425.00
12 Mandrake on(c). . . . . . . . . . 425.00
13 Mandrake on(c). . . . . . . . . . 425.00
14 Mandrake on(c). . . . . . . . . . 425.00
15 Mandrake on(c). . . . . . . . . . 425.00
16 Mandrake on(c). . . . . . . . . . 425.00
17 B:Lone Ranger . . . . . . . . . . 500.00
18 Mandrake/Robot on(c) . . . . . 400.00
19 Mandrake on(c). . . . . . . . . . 500.00
20 Mandrake on(c) . . . . . . . . . . 400.00
21 Mandrake on(c). . . . . . . . . . 300.00
22 Mandrake on(c). . . . . . . . . . 300.00
23 Mandrake on(c). . . . . . . . . . 300.00
24 Mandrake on(c). . . . . . . . . . 300.00
25 B:Blondie; Mandrake in
Logo for Duration. . . . . . . . 300.00
26 Blondie (c). . . . . . . . . . . . . 275.00
27 Blondie(c); HighSchoolHeroes 275.00
28 Blondie(c); HighSchoolHeroes 275.00
29 Blondie(c); HighSchoolHeroes 275.00
30 Blondie (c) . . . . . . . . . . . . . 275.00
31 Blondie(c);High School
Sports Page. . . . . . . . . . . . 225.00
32 Blondie (c);Secret Agent X-9 . 225.00
33 C.Knight's-Romance of Flying 225.00
34 ClaytonKnight's-War in the Air 225.00
35 Blondie (c). . . . . . . . . . . . . 225.00
36 July'42; Patriotic-(c) . . . . . . . 225.00
37 Blondie (c). . . . . . . . . . . . . 225.00
38 ClaytonKnight's-Flying Tigers . 225.00
39 Blondie (c). . . . . . . . . . . . . 225.00
40 Jimmie Doolittle bombs Tokyo 225.00
41 How German Refuse
British Censor . . . . . . . . . . . 200.00
42 Joe Musial's-Dollar-a-Dither . . 200.00
43 Clay Knight's-War in the Air . . 200.00
44 Flying Fortress in Action . . . . 200.00
45 Clayton Knight's-Gremlins . . . 200.00
46 Adventures of Aladdin Jr. . . . . 200.00

47 Secret Agent X-9. . . . . . . . . . 200.00
48 General Arnold U.S.A.F. . . . . . 200.00
49 Joe Musial's-Dollar-a-Dither . . 200.00
50 The Lone Ranger . . . . . . . . . 200.00
51 Joe Musial's-Dollar-a-Dither . . 150.00
52 C. Knights-Heroes on Wings . 150.00
53 C. Knights-Heroes on Wings . 150.00
54 High School Heroes . . . . . . . . 150.00
55 Blondie (c). . . . . . . . . . . . . . 175.00
56 High School Heroes . . . . . . . . 150.00
57 Joe Musial's-Dollar-a-Dither . . 150.00
58 Private Breger Abroad . . . . . . 150.00
59 . . . . . . . . . . . . . . . . . . . . . . 150.00
60 . . . . . . . . . . . . . . . . . . . . . . 150.00
61 Joe Musial's-Dollar-a-Dither . . 125.00
62 . . . . . . . . . . . . . . . . . . . . . . 125.00
63 B:Buz Sawyer, Naval Pilot . . . 125.00
64 thru 70. . . . . . . . . . . . . . @125.00
71 thru 80 . . . . . . . . . . . . . @125.00
81 thru 90 . . . . . . . . . . . . . @100.00
91 thru 99 . . . . . . . . . . . . . @100.00
100 . . . . . . . . . . . . . . . . . . . . 125.00
101 thru 108. . . . . . . . . . . . @100.00
108 Flash Gordon . . . . . . . . . . . 125.00
109 Flash Gordon . . . . . . . . . . . 125.00
110 thru 113 . . . . . . . . . . . . @125.00
114 The Lone Ranger . . . . . . . . 125.00
115 thru 119 . . . . . . . . . . . . @125.00
120 Secret Agent X-9 . . . . . . . . 150.00
121 Secret Agent X-9. . . . . . . . . 150.00
122 Secret Agent X-9. . . . . . . . . 150.00
123 Sec. Agent X-9 . . . . . . . . . . 150.00

## MAJOR HOOPLE COMICS

**Nedor Publications, 1942**
1 Mary Worth,Phantom Soldier;
Buy War Bonds On(c) . . . . . 500.00

## MAJOR INAPAK THE SPACE ACE

**Magazine Enterprises, 1951**
1 BP,Sci-Fi . . . . . . . . . . . . . . . 200.00

## MAJOR VICTORY COMICS

**H. Clay Glover Svcs./
Harry A. Chestler, 1944**
1 O:Major Victory,I:Spider
Woman . . . . . . . . . . . . . . . 850.00
2 A: Dynamic Boy . . . . . . . . . . 500.00
3 A: Rocket Boy . . . . . . . . . . . . 450.00

## MAMMOTH COMICS

**K.K. Publications, 1938**
1 Alley Oop, Dick Tracy, etc. . . 3,000.00

## MAN COMICS

**Marvel Atlas, 1949–53**
1 GT . . . . . . . . . . . . . . . . . . . . 350.00
2 GT . . . . . . . . . . . . . . . . . . . . 250.00
3 . . . . . . . . . . . . . . . . . . . . . . 200.00
4 . . . . . . . . . . . . . . . . . . . . . . 200.00
5 . . . . . . . . . . . . . . . . . . . . . . 200.00
6 . . . . . . . . . . . . . . . . . . . . . . 200.00
7 JeR . . . . . . . . . . . . . . . . . . . 200.00
8 BEv . . . . . . . . . . . . . . . . . . . 200.00
9 EC,TSe,War format begins . . . 150.00
10 JeR,MMe(c) . . . . . . . . . . . . 150.00
11 RH,TSe,MMe . . . . . . . . . . . 150.00
12 . . . . . . . . . . . . . . . . . . . . . 150.00
13 . . . . . . . . . . . . . . . . . . . . . 150.00
14 GT,JeR . . . . . . . . . . . . . . . . 175.00
15 . . . . . . . . . . . . . . . . . . . . . 150.00
16 . . . . . . . . . . . . . . . . . . . . . 150.00
17 RH . . . . . . . . . . . . . . . . . . . 175.00
18 . . . . . . . . . . . . . . . . . . . . . 150.00
19 . . . . . . . . . . . . . . . . . . . . . 150.00
20 . . . . . . . . . . . . . . . . . . . . . 150.00
21 EC-RH. . . . . . . . . . . . . . . . . 175.00
22 BEv(c),BK . . . . . . . . . . . . . . 175.00
23 GT,JSt . . . . . . . . . . . . . . . . . 175.00
24 . . . . . . . . . . . . . . . . . . . . . 150.00
25 BEv(c). . . . . . . . . . . . . . . . . 175.00
26 . . . . . . . . . . . . . . . . . . . . . 150.00
27 . . . . . . . . . . . . . . . . . . . . . 150.00
28 Where Mummies Prowl. . . . . . 150.00

## MANHUNT!

**Magazine Enterprises, 1953**
1 LbC,FGu,OW(c);B:Red Fox,
Undercover Girl, Space Ace . 650.00
2 LbC,FGu,OW(c);
Electrocution(c) . . . . . . . . . 500.00
3 LbC,FGu,OW,OW(c) . . . . . . . 400.00
4 LbC,FGu,OW,OW(c) . . . . . . . 400.00
5 LbC,FGu,OW,OW(c) . . . . . . . 400.00
6 LbC,OW,OW(c) . . . . . . . . . . 375.00
7 LbC,OW; E:Space Ace . . . . . . 350.00
8 LbC,OW,FGu(c);B:Trail Colt . . 350.00
9 LbC,OW . . . . . . . . . . . . . . . 350.00
10 LbC,OW,OW(c),Gwl . . . . . . . 350.00
11 LbC,FF,OW;B:The Duke,
Scotland Yard . . . . . . . . . . 500.00
12 LbC,OW . . . . . . . . . . . . . . . 300.00
13 See: A-1 Comics #63
14 See: A-1 Comics #77

**Ma**

*Man in Black #1*
*© Harvey Publications*

*March of Comics #25*
*© K. K. Publications*

*March of Comics #66*
*© K. K. Publications*

## MAN IN BLACK

### Harvey Publications, 1957

1 BP . . . . . . . . . . . . . . . . . . . . . 200.00
2 BP . . . . . . . . . . . . . . . . . . . . . 150.00
3 BP . . . . . . . . . . . . . . . . . . . . . 150.00
4 BP, March, 1958 . . . . . . . . . . 150.00

## MAN OF WAR

### Comic Corp. of America
### (Centaur Publ.), Nov., 1941

1 PG,PG(c);Flag(c);B:The Fire-
  Man,Man of War,The Sentinel,
  Liberty Guards,Vapoman . . 3,000.00
2 PG,PG(c);I: The Ferret . . . . 2,500.00

## MAN O'MARS

### Fiction House/
### I.W. Enterprises, 1953

1 MA, Space Rangers . . . . . . . 550.00
1 MA, Rep. Space Rangers . . . . 100.00

## MARCH OF COMICS

### K.K. Publications/
### Western Publ., 1946
### (All were Giveaways)

N# WK back(c),Goldilocks . . . . . 325.00
N# WK,How Santa got His
  Red Suit . . . . . . . . . . . . . . . 325.00
N# WK,Our Gang . . . . . . . . . . 450.00
N# CB,Donald Duck;
  'Maharajah Donald' . . . . . . 8,500.00
5 Andy Panda . . . . . . . . . . . . 200.00
6 WK,Fairy Tales . . . . . . . . . . 250.00
7 Oswald the Lucky Rabbit . . . . 200.00
8 Mickey Mouse . . . . . . . . . . . 600.00
9 Gloomey Bunny . . . . . . . . . . 125.00
10 Santa Claus . . . . . . . . . . . . 125.00
11 Santa Claus. . . . . . . . . . . . . 100.00
12 Santa's Toys . . . . . . . . . . . . 100.00
13 Santa's Suprise. . . . . . . . . . . 100.00
14 Santa's Kitchen. . . . . . . . . . . 100.00
15 Hip-It-Ty Hop. . . . . . . . . . . . 100.00
16 Woody Woodpecker . . . . . . . 150.00
17 Roy Rogers. . . . . . . . . . . . . . 275.00
18 Fairy Tales . . . . . . . . . . . . . 125.00
19 Uncle Wiggily . . . . . . . . . . . 100.00
20 CB,Donald Duck . . . . . . . . 5,000.00
21 Tom and Jerry. . . . . . . . . . . . 125.00
22 Andy Panda . . . . . . . . . . . . 100.00
23 Raggedy Ann and Andy . . . . 150.00
24 Felix the Cat; By
  Otto Messmer . . . . . . . . . . 250.00
25 Gene Autrey . . . . . . . . . . . . 250.00

26 Our Gang . . . . . . . . . . . . . . . 275.00
27 Mickey Mouse. . . . . . . . . . . . 450.00
28 Gene Autry . . . . . . . . . . . . . . 250.00
29 Easter . . . . . . . . . . . . . . . . . . 60.00
30 Santa . . . . . . . . . . . . . . . . . . 50.00
31 Santa. . . . . . . . . . . . . . . . . . . 50.00
32 Does Not Exist
33 A Christmas Carol. . . . . . . . . . 50.00
34 Woody Woodpecker . . . . . . . 125.00
35 Roy Rogers. . . . . . . . . . . . . . 275.00
36 Felix the Cat . . . . . . . . . . . . . 225.00
37 Popeye . . . . . . . . . . . . . . . . 150.00
38 Oswald the Lucky Rabbit . . . . 90.00
39 Gene Autry . . . . . . . . . . . . . . 250.00
40 Andy and Woody . . . . . . . . . . 90.00
41 CB,DonaldDuck,SouthSeas. 4,500.00
42 Porky Pig . . . . . . . . . . . . . . . 100.00
43 Henry . . . . . . . . . . . . . . . . . . 100.00
44 Bugs Bunny . . . . . . . . . . . . . 100.00
45 Mickey Mouse. . . . . . . . . . . . 350.00
46 Tom and Jerry. . . . . . . . . . . . 100.00
47 Roy Rogers. . . . . . . . . . . . . . 250.00
48 Santa. . . . . . . . . . . . . . . . . . 100.00
49 Santa. . . . . . . . . . . . . . . . . . 100.00
50 Santa . . . . . . . . . . . . . . . . . . 100.00
51 Felix the Cat . . . . . . . . . . . . . 175.00
52 Popeye . . . . . . . . . . . . . . . . 150.00
53 Oswald the Lucky Rabbit . . . . 100.00
54 Gene Autrey . . . . . . . . . . . . . 250.00
55 Andy and Woody. . . . . . . . . . 100.00
56 CB back(c),Donald Duck . . . . 350.00
57 Porky Pig . . . . . . . . . . . . . . . 100.00
58 Henry . . . . . . . . . . . . . . . . . . 100.00
59 Bugs Bunny . . . . . . . . . . . . . 125.00
60 Mickey Mouse . . . . . . . . . . . 300.00
61 Tom and Jerry. . . . . . . . . . . . 100.00
62 Roy Rogers. . . . . . . . . . . . . . 250.00
63 Santa. . . . . . . . . . . . . . . . . . 100.00
64 Santa. . . . . . . . . . . . . . . . . . 100.00
65 Jingle Bells . . . . . . . . . . . . . 100.00
66 Popeye . . . . . . . . . . . . . . . . 125.00
67 Oswald the Lucky Rabbit . . . . 100.00
68 Roy Rogers. . . . . . . . . . . . . . 225.00
69 Donald Duck . . . . . . . . . . . . 300.00
70 Tom and Jerry . . . . . . . . . . . 100.00
71 Porky Pig . . . . . . . . . . . . . . . 100.00
72 Krazy Kat . . . . . . . . . . . . . . . 100.00
73 Roy Rogers. . . . . . . . . . . . . . 200.00
74 Mickey Mouse. . . . . . . . . . . . 300.00
75 Bugs Bunny . . . . . . . . . . . . . 100.00
76 Andy and Woody. . . . . . . . . . 100.00
77 Roy Rogers. . . . . . . . . . . . . . 175.00
78 Gene Autrey; last regular
  sized issue . . . . . . . . . . . . 175.00
79 Andy Panda,5"x7" format . . . . 100.00
80 Popeye . . . . . . . . . . . . . . . . 100.00

81 Oswald the Lucky Rabbit . . . . . 75.00
82 Tarzan. . . . . . . . . . . . . . . . . . 200.00
83 Bugs Bunny . . . . . . . . . . . . . 100.00
84 Henry . . . . . . . . . . . . . . . . . . 100.00
85 Woody Woodpecker . . . . . . . . 100.00
86 Roy Rogers. . . . . . . . . . . . . . 150.00
87 Krazy Kat . . . . . . . . . . . . . . . 100.00
88 Tom and Jerry. . . . . . . . . . . . 100.00
89 Porky Pig . . . . . . . . . . . . . . . 100.00
90 Gene Autrey . . . . . . . . . . . . . 125.00
91 Roy Rogers and Santa . . . . . . 150.00
92 Christmas w/Santa . . . . . . . . . 75.00
93 Woody Woodpecker . . . . . . . . 75.00
94 Indian Chief. . . . . . . . . . . . . . 100.00
95 Oswald the Lucky Rabbit . . . . . 75.00
96 Popeye . . . . . . . . . . . . . . . . 125.00
97 Bugs Bunny . . . . . . . . . . . . . 100.00
98 Tarzan,Lex Barker Ph(c). . . . . 200.00
99 Porky Pig . . . . . . . . . . . . . . . . 75.00
100 Roy Rogers. . . . . . . . . . . . . . 125.00
101 Henry . . . . . . . . . . . . . . . . . . 75.00
102 Tom Corbet,P(c) . . . . . . . . . . 150.00
103 Tom and Jerry. . . . . . . . . . . . 75.00
104 Gene Autrey . . . . . . . . . . . . . 100.00
105 Roy Rogers. . . . . . . . . . . . . . 125.00
106 Santa's Helpers. . . . . . . . . . . . 75.00
107 *Not Published*
108 Fun with Santa . . . . . . . . . . . 75.00
109 Woody Woodpecker . . . . . . . . 75.00
110 Indian Chief . . . . . . . . . . . . . 75.00
111 Oswald the Lucky Rabbit . . . . . 75.00
112 Henry. . . . . . . . . . . . . . . . . . . 75.00
113 Porky Pig . . . . . . . . . . . . . . . . 75.00
114 Tarzan,RsM . . . . . . . . . . . . . 175.00
115 Bugs Bunny . . . . . . . . . . . . . . 75.00
116 Roy Rogers . . . . . . . . . . . . . 125.00
117 Popeye . . . . . . . . . . . . . . . . 100.00
118 Flash Gordon, P(c) . . . . . . . . 150.00
119 Tom and Jerry . . . . . . . . . . . . 75.00
120 Gene Autrey . . . . . . . . . . . . . 100.00
121 Roy Rogers. . . . . . . . . . . . . . 125.00
122 Santa's Suprise. . . . . . . . . . . . 75.00
123 Santa's Christmas Book . . . . . 75.00
124 Woody Woodpecker . . . . . . . . 75.00
125 Tarzan, Lex Barker Ph(c) . . . . 175.00
126 Oswald the Lucky Rabbit . . . . . 75.00
127 Indian Chief. . . . . . . . . . . . . . 100.00
128 Tom and Jerry . . . . . . . . . . . . 75.00
129 Henry . . . . . . . . . . . . . . . . . . . 75.00
130 Porky Pig . . . . . . . . . . . . . . . . 75.00
131 Roy Rogers . . . . . . . . . . . . . 125.00
132 Bugs Bunny . . . . . . . . . . . . . . 75.00
133 Flash Gordon,Ph(c) . . . . . . . 125.00
134 Popeye . . . . . . . . . . . . . . . . 100.00
135 Gene Autrey . . . . . . . . . . . . . 100.00
136 Roy Rogers. . . . . . . . . . . . . . 100.00

Ma

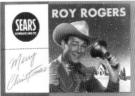

*March of Comics #98 & #151*
© Edgar Rice Burroughs. & Roy Rogers

*March of Comics #205*
© K. K. Publications

*Marge's Little Lulu #28*
© Dell Publishing Co.

137 Gifts from Santa . . . . . . . . . . . 50.00
138 Fun at Christmas . . . . . . . . . . 50.00
139 Woody Woodpecker . . . . . . . . 50.00
140 Indian Chief . . . . . . . . . . . . . . 75.00
141 Oswald the Lucky Rabbit . . . . 50.00
142 Flash Gordon . . . . . . . . . . . . . 100.00
143 Porky Pig . . . . . . . . . . . . . . . . 50.00
144 RsM,Ph(c),Tarzan . . . . . . . . . 150.00
145 Tom and Jerry . . . . . . . . . . . . 50.00
146 Roy Rogers,Ph(c) . . . . . . . . . 125.00
147 Henry . . . . . . . . . . . . . . . . . . 50.00
148 Popeye . . . . . . . . . . . . . . . . . 100.00
149 Bugs Bunny . . . . . . . . . . . . . 50.00
150 Gene Autrey . . . . . . . . . . . . . 100.00
151 Roy Rogers. . . . . . . . . . . . . . 100.00
152 The Night Before Christmas . . 50.00
153 Merry Christmas . . . . . . . . . . 50.00
154 Tom and Jerry . . . . . . . . . . . . 50.00
155 Tarzan,Ph(c) . . . . . . . . . . . . . 150.00
156 Oswald the Lucky Rabbit . . . . 50.00
157 Popeye . . . . . . . . . . . . . . . . . 100.00
158 Woody Woodpecker . . . . . . . . 50.00
159 Indian Chief. . . . . . . . . . . . . . 100.00
160 Bugs Bunny . . . . . . . . . . . . . 50.00
161 Roy Rogers. . . . . . . . . . . . . . 100.00
162 Henry . . . . . . . . . . . . . . . . . . 50.00
163 Rin Tin Tin. . . . . . . . . . . . . . . 125.00
164 Porky Pig . . . . . . . . . . . . . . . . 50.00
165 The Lone Ranger . . . . . . . . . 100.00
166 Santa & His Reindeer. . . . . . . 50.00
167 Roy Rogers and Santa . . . . . 100.00
168 Santa Claus' Workshop . . . . 50.00
169 Popeye . . . . . . . . . . . . . . . . . 100.00
170 Indian Chief . . . . . . . . . . . . . 100.00
171 Oswald the Lucky Rabbit . . . . 50.00
172 Tarzan. . . . . . . . . . . . . . . . . . 175.00
173 Tom and Jerry . . . . . . . . . . . . 50.00
174 The Lone Ranger . . . . . . . . . 125.00
175 Porky Pig . . . . . . . . . . . . . . . . 50.00
176 Roy Rogers . . . . . . . . . . . . . 125.00
177 Woody Woodpecker . . . . . . . . 50.00
178 Henry . . . . . . . . . . . . . . . . . . 50.00
179 Bugs Bunny . . . . . . . . . . . . . 50.00
180 Rin Tin Tin . . . . . . . . . . . . . . 100.00
181 Happy Holiday . . . . . . . . . . . . 50.00
182 Happi Tim . . . . . . . . . . . . . . . 50.00
183 Welcome Santa. . . . . . . . . . . 50.00
184 Woody Woodpecker . . . . . . . . 50.00
185 Tarzan, Ph(c) . . . . . . . . . . . . 150.00
186 Oswald the Lucky Rabbit . . . . 50.00
187 Indian Chief. . . . . . . . . . . . . . 100.00
188 Bugs Bunny . . . . . . . . . . . . . 50.00
189 Henry . . . . . . . . . . . . . . . . . . 50.00
190 Tom and Jerry . . . . . . . . . . . . 50.00
191 Roy Rogers. . . . . . . . . . . . . . 100.00
192 Porky Pig . . . . . . . . . . . . . . . . 50.00

193 The Lone Ranger . . . . . . . . 125.00
194 Popeye . . . . . . . . . . . . . . . . . 100.00
195 Rin Tin Tin. . . . . . . . . . . . . . . 150.00
196 *Not Published*
197 Santa is Coming . . . . . . . . . . 50.00
198 Santa's Helper . . . . . . . . . . . 50.00
199 Huckleberry Hound. . . . . . . . 150.00
200 Fury . . . . . . . . . . . . . . . . . . . 100.00
201 Bugs Bunny . . . . . . . . . . . . . 75.00
202 Space Explorer . . . . . . . . . . . 100.00
203 Woody Woodpecker . . . . . . . . 50.00
204 Tarzan . . . . . . . . . . . . . . . . . 125.00
205 Mighty Mouse . . . . . . . . . . . . 100.00
206 Roy Rogers,Ph(c) . . . . . . . . . 100.00
207 Tom and Jerry . . . . . . . . . . . . 50.00
208 The Lone Ranger,Ph(c) . . . . 150.00
209 Porky Pig . . . . . . . . . . . . . . . . 50.00
210 Lassie . . . . . . . . . . . . . . . . . 100.00
211 *Not Published*
212 Christmas Eve . . . . . . . . . . . 50.00
213 Here Comes Santa . . . . . . . . 50.00
214 Huckleberry Hound . . . . . . . . 125.00
215 Hi Yo Silver . . . . . . . . . . . . . 125.00
216 Rocky & His Friends . . . . . . . 125.00
217 Lassie . . . . . . . . . . . . . . . . . 100.00
218 Porky Pig . . . . . . . . . . . . . . . . 50.00
219 Journey to the Sun . . . . . . . . 100.00
220 Bugs Bunny . . . . . . . . . . . . . 50.00
221 Roy and Dale,Ph(c) . . . . . . . 150.00
222 Woody Woodpecker . . . . . . . . 50.00
223 Tarzan . . . . . . . . . . . . . . . . . 125.00
224 Tom and Jerry . . . . . . . . . . . . 50.00
225 The Lone Ranger . . . . . . . . . 100.00
226 Christmas Treasury. . . . . . . . 50.00
227 *Not Published*
228 Letters to Santa . . . . . . . . . . 50.00
229 The Flintstones . . . . . . . . . . . 150.00
230 Lassie . . . . . . . . . . . . . . . . . 100.00
231 Bugs Bunny . . . . . . . . . . . . . 50.00
232 The Three Stooges . . . . . . . . 275.00
233 Bullwinkle . . . . . . . . . . . . . . . 150.00
234 Smokey the Bear . . . . . . . . . 50.00
235 Huckleberry Hound . . . . . . . . 100.00
236 Roy and Dale . . . . . . . . . . . . 125.00
237 Mighty Mouse . . . . . . . . . . . . 50.00
238 The Lone Ranger . . . . . . . . . 100.00
239 Woody Woodpecker . . . . . . . . 50.00
240 Tarzan . . . . . . . . . . . . . . . . . 125.00
241 Santa Around the World . . . . 50.00
242 Santa Toyland . . . . . . . . . . . . 50.00
243 The Flintstones . . . . . . . . . . . 150.00
244 Mr.Ed,Ph(c). . . . . . . . . . . . . . 75.00
245 Bugs Bunny . . . . . . . . . . . . . 50.00
246 Popeye . . . . . . . . . . . . . . . . . 75.00
247 Mighty Mouse . . . . . . . . . . . . 75.00
248 The Three Stooges . . . . . . . . 250.00

249 Woody Woodpecker . . . . . . . . 50.00
250 Roy and Dale . . . . . . . . . . . . 125.00

## MARCH OF CRIME
### See: MY LOVE AFFAIR

## MARGE'S LITTLE LULU
### Dell Publishing Co., 1948
1 B:Lulu's Diary . . . . . . . . . . . 1,000.00
2 I:Gloria,Miss Feeny . . . . . . . . 500.00
3 . . . . . . . . . . . . . . . . . . . . . . . . 450.00
4 . . . . . . . . . . . . . . . . . . . . . . . . 450.00
5 . . . . . . . . . . . . . . . . . . . . . . . . 450.00
6 . . . . . . . . . . . . . . . . . . . . . . . . 350.00
7 I:Annie,X-Mas (c). . . . . . . . . . 350.00
8 . . . . . . . . . . . . . . . . . . . . . . . . 350.00
9 . . . . . . . . . . . . . . . . . . . . . . . . 350.00
10 . . . . . . . . . . . . . . . . . . . . . . . 350.00
11 thru 18 . . . . . . . . . . . . . . . . @300.00
19 I:Wilbur . . . . . . . . . . . . . . . . . 300.00
20 I:Mr.McNabbem. . . . . . . . . . . 300.00
21 thru 25 . . . . . . . . . . . . . . . . @250.00
26 rep.Four Color#110. . . . . . . . 250.00
27 thru 29 . . . . . . . . . . . . . . . . @250.00
30 Christmas (c) . . . . . . . . . . . . 250.00
31 thru 34 . . . . . . . . . . . . . . . . @225.00
35 B:Mumday Story . . . . . . . . . . 225.00
36 thru 38 . . . . . . . . . . . . . . . . @225.00
39 I:Witch Hazel. . . . . . . . . . . . . 250.00
40 Halloween (c) . . . . . . . . . . . . 175.00
41 . . . . . . . . . . . . . . . . . . . . . . . 175.00
42 Christmas (c) . . . . . . . . . . . . 175.00
43 Skiing (c). . . . . . . . . . . . . . . . 175.00
44 Valentines Day (c). . . . . . . . . 175.00
45 2nd A:Witch Hazel . . . . . . . . 175.00
46 thru 60 . . . . . . . . . . . . . . . . @175.00
61 . . . . . . . . . . . . . . . . . . . . . . . 150.00
62 . . . . . . . . . . . . . . . . . . . . . . . 150.00
63 I:Chubby . . . . . . . . . . . . . . . . 150.00
64 thru 67 . . . . . . . . . . . . . . . . @150.00
68 I:Professor Cleff . . . . . . . . . . 150.00
69 thru 77 . . . . . . . . . . . . . . . . @150.00
78 Christmas (c) . . . . . . . . . . . . 150.00
79 . . . . . . . . . . . . . . . . . . . . . . . 150.00
80 . . . . . . . . . . . . . . . . . . . . . . . 150.00
81 thru 89 . . . . . . . . . . . . . . . . @125.00
90 Christmas (c) . . . . . . . . . . . . 125.00
91 thru 99 . . . . . . . . . . . . . . . . @125.00
100 . . . . . . . . . . . . . . . . . . . . . . 150.00
101 thru 122. . . . . . . . . . . . . . . @125.00
123 I:Fifi . . . . . . . . . . . . . . . . . . . 110.00
124 thru 164 . . . . . . . . . . . . . . . @100.00
165 giant sized. . . . . . . . . . . . . . 200.00
166 giant sized. . . . . . . . . . . . . . 200.00

**Ma**

Marmaduke Mouse #1
© Quality Comics Group

Marvel Mystery Comics #2
© Marvel Comics Group

Marvel Mystery Comics #33
© Marvel Comics Group

## MARGE'S TUBBY
**Dell Publishing Co., 1953**
1 . . . . . . . . . . . . . . . . . . . . . . . 350.00
2 . . . . . . . . . . . . . . . . . . . . . . . 200.00
3 & 4 . . . . . . . . . . . . . . . . . @175.00
5 thru 10 . . . . . . . . . . . . . . . @135.00
11 thru 20 . . . . . . . . . . . . . . @125.00
21 thru 49 . . . . . . . . . . . . . . @100.00

## MARGIE COMICS
### See: COMEDY COMICS

## MARINES AT WAR
### See: DEVIL-DOG DUGAN

## MARINES IN ACTION
**Marvel Atlas, June, 1955**
1 B:Rock Murdock,Boot Camp
Brady . . . . . . . . . . . . . . . . 125.00
2 thru 13 . . . . . . . . . . . . . . @100.00
14 Sept., 1957 . . . . . . . . . . . . . 100.00

## MARINES IN BATTLE
**Marvel Atlas, Aug., 1954**
1 RH,B:Iron Mike McGraw . . . . . 250.00
2 . . . . . . . . . . . . . . . . . . . . . . 150.00
3 thru 6 . . . . . . . . . . . . . . . . @125.00
7 thru 17 . . . . . . . . . . . . . . . @125.00
18 thru 22 . . . . . . . . . . . . . . @100.00
23 . . . . . . . . . . . . . . . . . . . . . 125.00
24 . . . . . . . . . . . . . . . . . . . . . 100.00
25 Sept., 1958 . . . . . . . . . . . . . 125.00

## MARK TRAIL
**Standard Magazines/
Fawcett/Pines, 1955**
1 . . . . . . . . . . . . . . . . . . . . . . 125.00
5 . . . . . . . . . . . . . . . . . . . . . . 100.00
A1 . . . . . . . . . . . . . . . . . . . . . 150.00

## MARMADUKE MOUSE
**Quality Comics Group
(Arnold Publications), 1946**
1 Funny Animal . . . . . . . . . . . . . 250.00
2 Funny Animal . . . . . . . . . . . . 200.00
3 thru 8 Funny Animal . . . . . . @150.00
9 Funny Animal . . . . . . . . . . . . 100.00
10 Funny Animal . . . . . . . . . . . 100.00
11 thru 20 Funny Animal . . . . . @100.00
21 thru 30 Funny Animal . . . . . . @75.00

31 thru 40 Funny Animal . . . . . . @75.00
41 thru 50 Funny Animal . . . . . . @75.00
51 thru 65 Funny Animal . . . . . . @75.00

## MARTIN KANE
**Hero Books (Fox Features
Syndicate), June, 1950**
1 WW,WW-(c) . . . . . . . . . . . . . 350.00
2 WW,JO, Auguat, 1950 . . . . . . 250.00

## MARVEL BOY
### See: ASTONISHING

## MARVEL COMICS
**Marvel, Oct.-Nov., 1939**
1 FP(c),BEv,CBu,O:Sub-Mariner
I&B:The Angel,A:Human Torch,
Ka-Zar,Jungle Terror,
B:The Masked Raider . . 400,000.00
**Becomes:**

## MARVEL MYSTERY
## COMICS
2 CSM(c),BEv,CBu,PGv,
B:American, Ace,Human
Torch,Sub-Mariner,Ka-Zar 50,000.00
3 ASh(c),BEv,CBu,PGv,
E:American Ace . . . . . . . . 27,000.00
4 ASh(c),BEv,CBu,PGv,
I&B:Electro,The Ferret,
Mystery Detective . . . . . . 25,000.00
5 ASh(c),BEv,CBu,PGv,
Human Torch(c) . . . . . . . 45,000.00
6 ASh(c),BEv,CBu,PGv,
Angel(c) . . . . . . . . . . . 15,000.00
7 ASh(c),BEv,CBu,PGv,
Bondage(c) . . . . . . . . . . 15,000.00
8 ASh(c),BEv,CBu,PGv,Human
TorchV:Sub-Mariner . . . . . 18,000.00
9 ASh(c),BEv,CBu,PGv,Human
Torch V:Sub-Mariner(c) . . 45,000.00
10 ASh(c),BEv,CBu,PGv,B:Terry
Vance Boy Detective . . . . 16,000.00
11 ASh(c),BEv,CBu,PGv,
Human Torch V:Nazis(c). . . 6,500.00
12 ASh(c),BEv,CBu,
PGv,Angel(c) . . . . . . . . . . 7,000.00
13 ASh(c),BEv,CBu,PGv,S&K,
I&B:The Vision . . . . . . . . . 9,000.00
14 ASh(c),BEv,CBu,PGv,S&K,
Sub-Mariner V:Nazis . . . . . 4,800.00
15 ASh(c),BEv,CBu,PGv,S&K,
Sub-Mariner(c) . . . . . . . . . 4,800.00

16 ASh(c),BEv,CBu,PGv,S&K,
HumanTorch/NaziAirbase. . 4,800.00
17 ASh(c),BEv,CBu,PGv,S&K
Human Torch/Sub-Mariner 5,000.00
18 ASh(c),BEv,CBu,PGv,S&K,
Human Torch & Toro(c) . . . 4,500.00
19 ASh(c),BEv,CBu,PGv,S&K,
O:Toro,E:Electro . . . . . . . . 4,500.00
20 ASh(c),BEv,CBu,PGv,S&K,
O:The Angel . . . . . . . . . . . 4,500.00
21 ASh(c),BEv,CBu,PGv,S&K,
I&B:The Patriot . . . . . . . . . 4,500.00
22 ASh(c),BEv,CBu,PGv,S&K,
AAv,Toro/Bomb(c). . . . . . . 4,000.00
23 ASh(c),BEv,CBu,PGv,S&K,
O:Vision,E:The Angel . . . . . 4,000.00
24 ASh(c),BEv,CBu,S&K,
AAv,Human Torch(c). . . . . . 4,000.00
25 BEv,CBu,S&K,ASh Nazi(c) . 4,000.00
26 ASh(c),BEv,CBu,S&K,
Sub-Mariner(c) . . . . . . . . . 3,500.00
27 ASh(c),BEv,CBu,
S&K,E:Ka-Zar. . . . . . . . . . 3,500.00
28 ASh(c),BEv,CBu,S&K,Bondage
(c),B:Jimmy Jupiter . . . . . . 3,500.00
29 ASh(c),BEv,CBu,SSh,
Bondage(c). . . . . . . . . . . . 3,500.00
30 BEv,CBu,SSh,Pearl
Harbor(c) . . . . . . . . . . . . . 3,500.00
31 BEv,CBu,Human Torch(c) . . 4,200.00
32 CBu,I:The Boboes . . . . . . . 3,500.00
33 ASh(c),CBu,SSh,Jap(c) . . . . 3,000.00
34 ASh(c),CBu,SSh,V:Hitler . . . 3,500.00
35 ASh(c),SSh,BeachAssault(c) 3,000.00
36 ASh(c),Nazi Invasion of NY . 3,000.00
37 SSh(c),Nazi(c) . . . . . . . . . . 3,000.00
38 SSh(c),Battlefield(c). . . . . . . 3,000.00
39 ASh(c),Nazis/U.S(c). . . . . . . 3,000.00
40 ASh(c),SSh,Zeppelin(c) . . . 3,000.00
41 ASh(c),Jap. Command(c) . . . 2,700.00
42 ASh(c),Japanese Sub(c) . . . 2,700.00
43 ASh(c),SSh,Destroyed
Bridge(c). . . . . . . . . . . . . . 2,700.00
44 ASh(c),Nazi Super Plane(c). 2,700.00
45 ASh(c),SSh,Nazi(c) . . . . . . . 2,700.00
46 ASh(c),Hitler Bondage(c). . . 2,700.00
47 ASh(c),Ruhr Valley Dam(c) . 2,700.00
48 ASh(c),E:Jimmy Jupiter,
Vision,Allied Invasion(c) . . . 2,700.00
49 SSh(c),O:Miss America,
Bondage(c) . . . . . . . . . . . 3,000.00
50 ASh(c),Bondage(c),Miss
Patriot . . . . . . . . . . . . . . . 2,700.00
51 ASh(c),Nazi Torture(c) . . . . . 2,500.00
52 ASh(c),Bondage(c). . . . . . . 2,500.00
53 ASh(c),Bondage(c). . . . . . . 2,500.00

All comics prices listed are for *Near Mint* condition.

*Marvel Mystery Comics #67*
© *Marvel Comics Group*

*Marvel Tales #97*
© *Marvel Comics Group*

*The Marvel Family #1*
© *Fawcett Publications*

54 ASh(c),Bondage(c) . . . . . . . 2,500.00
55 ASh(c),Bondage(c) . . . . . . . 2,500.00
56 ASh(c),Bondage(c) . . . . . . . 2,500.00
57 ASh(c),Torture/Bondage(c) . 2,500.00
58 ASh(c),Torture(c) . . . . . . . . . 2,500.00
59 ASh(c),Testing Room(c) . . . . 2,500.00
60 ASh(c),Japanese Gun(c) . . 2,500.00
61 ASh(c),Torturer Chamber(c) . 2,500.00
62 ASh(c),Violent(c) . . . . . . . . . 2,500.00
63 ASh(c),Nazi High
  Command(c) . . . . . . . . . . . . 2,500.00
64 ASh(c),Last Nazi(c) . . . . . . . 2,500.00
65 ASh(c),Bondage(c) . . . . . . . 2,500.00
66 ASh(c),Last Japanese(c) . . . 2,500.00
67 ASh(c),Treasury raid(c) . . . . 2,500.00
68 ASh(c),Torture Chamber(c) . 3,600.00
69 ASh(c),Torture Chamber(c) . 2,500.00
70 Cops & Robbers(c) . . . . . . . 2,500.00
71 ASh(c),Egyptian(c) . . . . . . . 2,500.00
72 Police(c) . . . . . . . . . . . . . . . 2,500.00
73 Werewolf Headlines(c) . . . . . 2,500.00
74 ASh(c),Robbery(c),E:The
  Patriot . . . . . . . . . . . . . . . . . 2,500.00
75 SSh,Tavern(c),B:YoungAllies 2,500.00
76 ASh(c),Shoot-out(c),B:Miss
  America . . . . . . . . . . . . . . . . 2,500.00
77 SSh,Human Torch/Sub-
  Mariner(c) . . . . . . . . . . . . . . 2,500.00
78 SSh,Safe Robbery(c) . . . . . . 2,500.00
79 SSh,Super Villians(c),E:The
  Angel . . . . . . . . . . . . . . . . . . 2,500.00
80 SSh,I:Capt.America
  (in Marvel) . . . . . . . . . . . . . 3,000.00
81 SSh,Mystery o/t Crimson
  Terror . . . . . . . . . . . . . . . . . . 2,200.00
82 SSh,I:Sub-Mariner/Namora
  Team-up, O:Namora,A:Capt.
  America . . . . . . . . . . . . . . . . 4,500.00
83 SSh,The Photo Phantom,
  E;Young Allies . . . . . . . . . . . 1,800.00
84 SSh,BEv,B:Blonde Phantom 3,000.00
85 SSh,BEv,A:Blonde Phantom,
  E;Miss America . . . . . . . . . 2,000.00
86 BEv,Blonde Phantom ID
  Revealed,E:Bucky . . . . . . . . 1,800.00
87 SSh,BEv,I:Capt.America/Golden
  Girl Team-up . . . . . . . . . . . 3,200.00
88 SSh,BEv,E:Toro . . . . . . . . . 1,800.00
89 SSh,BEv,AAv,I:Human Torch/
  Sun Girl Team-up . . . . . . . . 1,800.00
90 BEv,Giant of the Mountains 1,800.00
91 BEv,I:Venus,E:Blonde
  Phantom,Sub-Mariner . . . . 1,800.00
92 BEv,How the Human Torch was
  Born,D:Professor Horton,I:The
  Witness,A:Capt.America. . . 5,500.00

92a Marvel #33(c)rare,reps. . . 40,000.00
**Becomes:**

## MARVEL TALES
### Marvel, Aug., 1949
93 The Ghoul Strikes . . . . . . . . 2,000.00
94 BEv,The Haunted Love . . . . 1,300.00
95 The Living Death. . . . . . . . . . 900.00
96 MSy,SSh(c),Monster Returns . 900.00
97 DRi,MSy,The Wooden
  Horror . . . . . . . . . . . . . . . . 1,100.00
98 BEv,BK,MSy,The Curse of
  the Black Cat. . . . . . . . . . . . . 900.00
99 DRi,The Secret of the Wax
  Museum. . . . . . . . . . . . . . . . . 900.00
100 The Eyes of Doom . . . . . . . 900.00
101 The Man Who Died Twice . . 900.00
102 BW,A Witch Among Us . . . 1,300.00
103 RA,A Touch of Death . . . . . 1,000.00
104 RH(c),BW,BEv,The Thing
  in the Mirror . . . . . . . . . . . . 1,300.00
105 RH(c),GC,JSt,The Spider. . 1,000.00
106 RH(c),BK,BEv,In The Dead of
  the Night . . . . . . . . . . . . . . . . 750.00
107 GC,OW,BK,The Thing in the
  Sewer . . . . . . . . . . . . . . . . . . 750.00
108 RH(c),BEv,JR,Horror in the
  Moonlight . . . . . . . . . . . . . . . 500.00
109 BEv(c),Sight for Sore Eyes . . 500.00
110 RH,SSh,A Coffin for Carlos . 500.00
111 BEv,Horror Under the Earth . 500.00
112 The House That Death Built . 500.00
113 RH,Terror Tale. . . . . . . . . . . 500.00
114 BEv(c),GT,JM,2 for Zombie . 500.00
115 The Man With No Face. . . . . 500.00
116 JSt . . . . . . . . . . . . . . . . . . . . 500.00
117 BEv(c),GK,Terror in the
  North. . . . . . . . . . . . . . . . . . . 500.00
118 RH,DBr,GC,A World
  Goes Mad . . . . . . . . . . . . . . . 500.00
119 RH,They Gave Him A Grave . 500.00
120 GC,Graveyard(c) . . . . . . . . . 500.00
121 GC,Graveyard(c). . . . . . . . . . 400.00
122 JKu,Missing One Body . . . . . 400.00
123 No Way Out . . . . . . . . . . . . . 400.00
124 He Waits at the Tombstone. . 400.00
125 JF,Horror House . . . . . . . . . . 400.00
126 DW,It Came From Nowhere . 375.00
127 BEv(c),GC,MD,Gone is the
  Gargoyle. . . . . . . . . . . . . . . . 375.00
128 Emily,Flying Saucer(c) . . . . . 375.00
129 You Can't Touch Bottom . . . 375.00
130 RH(c),JF,The Giant Killer . . . 375.00
131 GC,BEv,Five Fingers . . . . . . 375.00
132 . . . . . . . . . . . . . . . . . . . . . . . 250.00
133 . . . . . . . . . . . . . . . . . . . . . . . 250.00

134 BK,JKu,Flying Saucer(c). . . . 250.00
135 thru 143. . . . . . . . . . . . . . @250.00
144 . . . . . . . . . . . . . . . . . . . . . . . 265.00
145 . . . . . . . . . . . . . . . . . . . . . . . 250.00
146 . . . . . . . . . . . . . . . . . . . . . . . 200.00
147 . . . . . . . . . . . . . . . . . . . . . . . 225.00
148 thru 151. . . . . . . . . . . . . . @200.00
152 . . . . . . . . . . . . . . . . . . . . . . . 225.00
153 . . . . . . . . . . . . . . . . . . . . . . . 250.00
154 thru 158. . . . . . . . . . . . . . @200.00
159 Aug., 1957. . . . . . . . . . . . . . 225.00

## MARVEL FAMILY, THE
### Fawcett Publications,
### Dec., 1945–Jan., 1954
1 O:Captain Marvel,Captain Marvel Jr.,
  Mary Marvel,Uncle Marvel;
  V:Black Adam . . . . . . . . . . 2,700.00
2 Uncle Marvel. . . . . . . . . . . . 1,300.00
3 . . . . . . . . . . . . . . . . . . . . . . . . 900.00
4 The Witch's Tale . . . . . . . . . . 700.00
5 Civilization of a
  Prehistoric Race . . . . . . . . . 600.00
6 . . . . . . . . . . . . . . . . . . . . . . . . 550.00
7 The Rock of Eternity . . . . . . . 500.00
8 The Marvel Family
  Round Table . . . . . . . . . . . . . 500.00
9 V: The Last Vikings . . . . . . . . 500.00
10 CCB(c),JaB,BTh,V:Sivana
  Family . . . . . . . . . . . . . . . . . . 500.00
11 V: The Well of Evil. . . . . . . . . 450.00
12 V: The Iron Horseman . . . . . 450.00
13 BTh,CCB,PrC(c) . . . . . . . . . . 450.00
14 Captain Marvel Invalid . . . . . 450.00
15 V: Mr. Triangle. . . . . . . . . . . . 425.00
16 World's Mightiest Quarrell. . . 425.00
17 . . . . . . . . . . . . . . . . . . . . . . . . 425.00
18 . . . . . . . . . . . . . . . . . . . . . . . . 425.00
19 V: The Monster Menace . . . . 425.00
20 The Marvel Family Feud. . . . 425.00
21 V: The Trio of Terror . . . . . . . 400.00
22 V: The Triple Threat . . . . . . . 400.00
23 March of Independence (c). . . 425.00
24 V: The Fighting Xergos . . . . . 400.00
25 Trial of the Marvel Family . . . 400.00
26 V: Mr. Power . . . . . . . . . . . . . 400.00
27 V: The Amoeba Men. . . . . . . 400.00
28 . . . . . . . . . . . . . . . . . . . . . . . . 400.00
29 V: The Monarch of Money . . . 400.00
30 A:World's Greatest Magician . 400.00
31 V:Sivana & The Great Hunger 350.00
32 The Marvel Family Goes
  Into Buisness. . . . . . . . . . . . . 350.00
33 I: The Hermit Family . . . . . . . 350.00
34 V: Sivana's Miniature Menace 350.00

**Ma**

*The Marvel Family #71*
© Fawcett Publications

*Mary Marvel Comics #25*
© Fawcett Publications

*Monte Hale Western #46*
© Fawcett Publications

35 V: The Berzerk Machines . . . . 350.00
36 V: The Invaders From Infinity . 350.00
37 V: The Earth Changer. . . . . . . 350.00
38 V: Sivana's Instinct
   Exterminator Gun . . . . . . . . 350.00
39 The Legend of Atlantis . . . . . . 350.00
40 Seven Wonders of the
   Modern World . . . . . . . . . . . 350.00
41 The Great Oxygen Theft. . . . . 350.00
42 V: The Endless Menace . . . . . 300.00
43 . . . . . . . . . . . . . . . . . . . . . . . 300.00
44 V: The Rust That Menaced
   the World . . . . . . . . . . . . . . . 300.00
45 The Hoax City . . . . . . . . . . . . 300.00
46 The Day Civilization Vanished 300.00
47 V: The Interplanetary Thieves. 350.00
48 V: The Four Horsemen . . . . . . 300.00
49 ...Proves Human Hardness. . . 300.00
50 The Speech Scrambler
   Machine . . . . . . . . . . . . . . . . 300.00
51 The Living Statues . . . . . . . . 325.00
52 The School of Witches . . . . . . 300.00
53 V:Man Who Changed World . . 300.00
54 . . . . . . . . . . . . . . . . . . . . . . . 300.00
55 . . . . . . . . . . . . . . . . . . . . . . . 300.00
56 The World's Mightiest Project . 300.00
57 . . . . . . . . . . . . . . . . . . . . . . . 300.00
58 The Triple Time Plot . . . . . . . . 300.00
59 . . . . . . . . . . . . . . . . . . . . . . . 300.00
60 . . . . . . . . . . . . . . . . . . . . . . . 300.00
61 . . . . . . . . . . . . . . . . . . . . . . . 300.00
62 . . . . . . . . . . . . . . . . . . . . . . . 300.00
63 V: The Pirate Planet . . . . . . . . 300.00
64 . . . . . . . . . . . . . . . . . . . . . . . 300.00
65 . . . . . . . . . . . . . . . . . . . . . . . 300.00
66 The Miracle Stone. . . . . . . . . . 300.00
67 . . . . . . . . . . . . . . . . . . . . . . . 300.00
68 . . . . . . . . . . . . . . . . . . . . . . . 300.00
69 V: The Menace of Old Age . . . 300.00
70 V: The Crusade of Evil . . . . . 300.00
71 . . . . . . . . . . . . . . . . . . . . . . . 300.00
72 . . . . . . . . . . . . . . . . . . . . . . . 300.00
73 . . . . . . . . . . . . . . . . . . . . . . . 300.00
74 . . . . . . . . . . . . . . . . . . . . . . . 300.00
75 The Great Space Struggle . . . 300.00
76 . . . . . . . . . . . . . . . . . . . . . . . 325.00
77 Anti-Communist. . . . . . . . . . . 400.00
78 V: The Red Vulture . . . . . . . . 300.00
79 Horror . . . . . . . . . . . . . . . . . . 250.00
80 . . . . . . . . . . . . . . . . . . . . . . . 250.00
81 . . . . . . . . . . . . . . . . . . . . . . . 250.00
82 . . . . . . . . . . . . . . . . . . . . . . . 250.00
83 V: The Flying Skull . . . . . . . . 250.00
84 thru 87 . . . . . . . . . . . . . @250.00
88 Jokes of Jeopardy. . . . . . . . . 250.00
89 And Then There Were None. . 250.00

## MARVEL MYSTERY COMICS
### See: MARVEL COMICS

## MARVELS OF SCIENCE
### Charlton Comics, 1946
1 1st Charlton Book; Atomic
   Bomb Story . . . . . . . . . . . . . 400.00
2 . . . . . . . . . . . . . . . . . . . . . . . 350.00
3 . . . . . . . . . . . . . . . . . . . . . . . 350.00
4 President Truman(c); Jun.'6 . . 350.00

## MARVEL TALES
### See: MARVEL COMICS

## MARVIN MOUSE
### Marvel Atlas, Sept., 1957
1 BEv,F:Marvin Mouse . . . . . . 125.00

## MARY MARVEL COMICS
### Fawcett Publications, Dec., 1945
1 Intro: Mary Marvel. . . . . . . . 2,700.00
2 . . . . . . . . . . . . . . . . . . . . . . 1,000.00
3 . . . . . . . . . . . . . . . . . . . . . . . 750.00
4 On a Leave of Absence . . . . 700.00
5 Butterfly (c) Bullet Girl . . . . . . 500.00
6 A:Freckles,Teenager of
   Mischief . . . . . . . . . . . . . . . 500.00
7 The Kingdom Undersea . . . . 500.00
8 Holiday Special Issue . . . . . . 500.00
9 Air Race (c) . . . . . . . . . . . . . 450.00
10 A: Freckles . . . . . . . . . . . . . . 450.00
11 A: The Sad Dryads . . . . . . . . 300.00
12 Red Cross Appeal on(c) . . . . 300.00
13 Keep the Homefires Burning . 300.00
14 Meets Ghosts (c) . . . . . . . . . 300.00
15 A: Freckles . . . . . . . . . . . . . . 300.00
16 The Jukebox Menace . . . . . . 275.00
17 Aunt Agatha's Adventures. . . 275.00
18 . . . . . . . . . . . . . . . . . . . . . . . 275.00
19 Witch (c) . . . . . . . . . . . . . . . . 275.00
20 . . . . . . . . . . . . . . . . . . . . . . . 275.00
21 V: Dice Head. . . . . . . . . . . . . 225.00
22 The Silver Slippers . . . . . . . . 225.00
23 The Pendulum Strikes. . . . . . 225.00
24 V: The Nightowl. . . . . . . . . . . 225.00
25 A: Freckles . . . . . . . . . . . . . . 225.00
26 A:Freckles dressed as Clown 225.00
27 The Floating Oceanliner . . . . 225.00
28 Western, Sept., 1948 . . . . . . 225.00

Becomes:
## MONTE HALE WESTERN
### Fawcett Publications, Oct., 1948
29 Ph(c),B:Monte Hale & His
   Horse Pardner . . . . . . . . . . . 650.00
30 Ph(c),B:Big Bow-Little
   Arrow; CCB,Captain Tootsie . 300.00
31 Ph(c),Giant . . . . . . . . . . . . . . 250.00
32 Ph(c),Giant . . . . . . . . . . . . . . 250.00
33 Ph(c),Giant . . . . . . . . . . . . . . 250.00
34 Ph(c),E:Big Bow-Little
   Arrow;B:Gabby Hayes,Giant . 250.00
35 Ph(c),Gabby Hayes, Giant . . . 250.00
36 Ph(c),Gabby Hayes, Giant . . . 250.00
37 Ph(c),Gabby Hayes . . . . . . . . 150.00
38 Ph(c),Gabby Hayes, Giant . . . 200.00
39 Ph(c);CCB, Captain Tootsie;
   Gabby Hayes, Giant . . . . . . . 200.00
40 Ph(c),Gabby Hayes, Giant . . . 200.00
41 Ph(c),Gabby Hayes . . . . . . . . 150.00
42 Ph(c),Gabby Hayes, Giant . . . 175.00
43 Ph(c),Gabby Hayes, Giant . . . 175.00
44 Ph(c),Gabby Hayes, Giant . . . 175.00
45 Ph(c),Gabby Hayes . . . . . . . . 150.00
46 Ph(c),Gabby Hayes, Giant . . . 150.00
47 Ph(c),A:Big Bow-Little Arrow;
   Gabby Hayes, Giant . . . . . . . 150.00
48 Ph(c),Gabby Hayes, Giant . . . 150.00
49 Ph(c),Gabby Hayes . . . . . . . . 150.00
50 Ph(c),Gabby Hayes, Giant . . . 150.00
51 Ph(c),Gabby Hayes, Giant . . . 135.00
52 Ph(c),Gabby Hayes, Giant . . . 135.00
53 Ph(c),A:Slim Pickens;
   Gabby Hayes. . . . . . . . . . . . . 125.00
54 Ph(c),Gabby Hayes, Giant . . . 135.00
55 Ph(c),Gabby Hayes, Giant . . . 135.00
56 Ph(c),Gabby Hayes, Giant . . . 125.00
57 Ph(c),Gabby Hayes . . . . . . . . 100.00
58 Ph(c),Gabby Hayes, Giant . . . 125.00
59 Ph(c),Gabby Hayes, Giant . . . 125.00
60 thru 79 Ph(c),Gabby Hayes @100.00
80 Ph(c),E: Gabby Hayes . . . . . . 100.00
81 Ph(c) . . . . . . . . . . . . . . . . . . . 100.00
82 Final Ph(c) . . . . . . . . . . . . . . 125.00

### Charlton Comics, Feb., 1955
83 R:G. Hayes Back B&W Ph(c) . 150.00
84 . . . . . . . . . . . . . . . . . . . . . . . 100.00
85 . . . . . . . . . . . . . . . . . . . . . . . 100.00
86 E: Gabby Hayes . . . . . . . . . . 100.00
87 . . . . . . . . . . . . . . . . . . . . . . . 100.00
88 Jan., 1956. . . . . . . . . . . . . . . 100.00

**Ma**

Mask Comics #1
© Rural Home Publications

Master Comics #23
© Fawcett Publications

Master Comics #46
© Fawcett Publications

## MARY WORTH
### ARGO, 1956
1 . . . . . . . . . . . . . . . . . . . . . . . 100.00

## MASK COMICS
### Rural Home Publications, Feb.–March, 1945
1 LbC,LbC-(c), Evil . . . . . . 4,000.00
2 LbC-(c),A:Black Rider,The
  Collector The Boy Magician;
  Apr-May'45, Devil (c) . . . . . 2,500.00

## MASKED MARVEL
### Centaur Publications, Sept., 1940
1 I: The Masked Marvel . . . . . 2,400.00
2 PG, . . . . . . . . . . . . . . . . . . . 1,500.00
3 Dec., 1940 . . . . . . . . . . . . . 1,400.00

## THE MASKED RAIDER
### Charlton Comics, 1955
1 . . . . . . . . . . . . . . . . . . . . . . . 150.00
2 . . . . . . . . . . . . . . . . . . . . . . . 125.00
3 . . . . . . . . . . . . . . . . . . . . . . . 100.00
4 . . . . . . . . . . . . . . . . . . . . . . . 100.00
5 . . . . . . . . . . . . . . . . . . . . . . . 100.00
6 . . . . . . . . . . . . . . . . . . . . . . . 100.00
7 . . . . . . . . . . . . . . . . . . . . . . . 100.00
8 Billy the Kid . . . . . . . . . . . . . . 100.00
9 . . . . . . . . . . . . . . . . . . . . . . . 100.00
10 . . . . . . . . . . . . . . . . . . . . . . 100.00
11 thru 14 . . . . . . . . . . . . . . . . @100.00
15 AW . . . . . . . . . . . . . . . . . . . 125.00
16 thru 30 . . . . . . . . . . . . . . . @100.00

## MASKED RANGER
### Premier Magazines, April, 1954
1 FF,O&B:The Masked Ranger,
  Streak the Horse,The
  Crimson Avenger . . . . . . . . . 500.00
2 . . . . . . . . . . . . . . . . . . . . . . . 175.00
3 . . . . . . . . . . . . . . . . . . . . . . . 175.00
4 B: Jessie James,Billy the Kid,
  Wild Bill Hickok,
  Jim Bowie's Life Story . . . . . 200.00
5 . . . . . . . . . . . . . . . . . . . . . . . 200.00
6 . . . . . . . . . . . . . . . . . . . . . . . 200.00
7 . . . . . . . . . . . . . . . . . . . . . . . 200.00
8 . . . . . . . . . . . . . . . . . . . . . . . 200.00
9 AT,E:All Features; A:Wyatt
  Earp Aug., 1955. . . . . . . . . 225.00

## MASTER COMICS
### Fawcett Publications, March, 1940
**1-6 Oversized,7-Normal Format**
1 O:Master Man; B:The Devil's
  Dagger, El Carin-Master of
  Magic, Rick O'Say, Morton
  Murch, White Rajah, Shipwreck
  Roberts, Frontier Marshall,
  Mr. Clue, Streak Sloan . . . 16,000.00
2 Master Man (c) . . . . . . . . . . 5,000.00
3 Master Man (c) Bondage . . 4,600.00
4 Master Man (c) . . . . . . . . . . 4,500.00
5 Master Man (c) . . . . . . . . . . 4,500.00
6 E: All Above Features . . . . . 4,600.00
7 B:Bulletman,Zorro,The Mystery
  Man, Lee Granger, Jungle
  King,Buck Jones . . . . . . . . 6,000.00
8 B:The Red Gaucho,Captain
  Venture, Planet Princess . . 3,600.00
9 Bulletman & Steam Roller . . 3,500.00
10 E: Lee Granger . . . . . . . . . 5,500.00
11 O: Minute Man . . . . . . . . . 5,500.00
12 Minute Man (c). . . . . . . . . 3,500.00
13 O:Bulletgirl; E:Red Gaucho . 4,000.00
14 B: The Companions Three . . 3,200.00
15 MRa, Bulletman & Girl (c) . . 3,200.00
16 MRa, Minute Man (c) . . . . . 3,200.00
17 B:MRa on Bulletman . . . . . . 3,000.00
18 MRa, . . . . . . . . . . . . . . . . . 3,000.00
19 MRa, Bulletman & Girl (c) . . 3,000.00
20 MRa,C:Cap.Marvel-
  Bulletman . . . . . . . . . . . . . 3,000.00
21 MRa-(c),Capt. Marvel in
  Bulletman,I&O:Captain
  Nazi . . . . . . . . . . . . . . . . . . 9,000.00
22 MRa-(c),E:Mystery Man,Captain
  Venture; Bondage(c);Capt.
  Marvel Jr. X-Over In
  Bulletman; A:Capt. Nazi . . . 8,000.00
23 MRa(a&c),B:Capt. Marvel Jr.
  V:Capt. Nazi . . . . . . . . . . . 5,000.00
24 MRa(a&c),Death By Radio . 3,000.00
25 MRa(a&c),The Jap Invasion 3,000.00
26 MRa(a&c),Capt. Marvel Jr.
  Avenges Pearl Harbor . . . 3,000.00
27 MRa(a&c),V For Victory(c). . 3,000.00
28 MRa(a&c)Liberty Bell(c). . . . 3,000.00
29 MRa(a&c),Hitler &
  Hirohito(c). . . . . . . . . . . . . 3,200.00
30 MRa(a&c),Flag (c);Capt.
  Marvel Jr, V: Capt. Nazi . . 3,000.00
31 MRa(a&c),E:Companions
  Three,Capt.Marvel Jr,
  V:Mad Dr. Macabre . . . . . . 2,000.00
32 MRa(a&c),E: Buck Jones;
  CMJr Strikes Terror Castle . 2,000.00
33 MRa(a&c),B:Balbo the Boy
  Magician,Hopalong Cassidy 2,000.00
34 MRa(a&c),Capt.Marvel Jr
  V: Capt.Nazi . . . . . . . . . . . 2,500.00
35 MRa(a&c),CMJr Defies
  the Flame . . . . . . . . . . . . . 2,000.00
36 MRa(a&c),Statue Of
  Liberty(c). . . . . . . . . . . . . . 2,000.00
37 MRa(a&c),CMJr Blasts
  the Nazi Raiders. . . . . . . . . 1,800.00
38 MRa(a&c),CMJr V:the Japs . 1,800.00
39 MRa(a&c),CMJr Blasts
  Nazi Slave Ship . . . . . . . . . 1,800.00
40 MRa(a&c),Flag (c) . . . . . . . 1,800.00
41 MRa(a&c),Bulletman,Bulletgirl,
  CMJr X-over In Minuteman 1,800.00
42 MRa(a&c),CMJr V: Hitler's
  Dream Soldier . . . . . . . . . . 1,000.00
43 MRa(c),CMJr Battles For
  Stalingrad . . . . . . . . . . . . . 1,000.00
44 MRa(c),CMJr In Crystal City
  of the Peculiar Penguins . . 1,000.00
45 MRa(c), . . . . . . . . . . . . . . . 1,000.00
46 MRa(c) . . . . . . . . . . . . . . . . 1,000.00
47 MRa(c),A:Hitler; E: Balbo. . . 1,100.00
48 MRa(c),I:Bulletboy;Capt.
  Marvel A: in Minuteman . . . 1,200.00
49 MRa(c),E: Hopalong Cassidy,
  Minuteman . . . . . . . . . . . . 1,000.00
50 I&O: Radar,A:Capt. Marvel,
  B:Nyoka the Jungle Girl . . 1,000.00
51 MRa(c),CMJr V: Japanese . . 750.00
52 MRa(c),CMJr & Radar Pitch
  War Stamps on (c). . . . . . . . 750.00
53 CMJR V: Dr. Sivana . . . . . . . 750.00
54 MRa(c),Capt.Marvel Jr
  Your Pin-Up Buddy . . . . . . . 750.00
55 . . . . . . . . . . . . . . . . . . . . . . . 750.00
56 MRa(c) . . . . . . . . . . . . . . . . . 700.00
57 CMJr V: Dr. Sivana . . . . . . . . 700.00
58 MRa(a&c), . . . . . . . . . . . . . . 700.00
59 MRa(c),A:The Upside
  Downies. . . . . . . . . . . . . . . . 750.00
60 MRa(c) . . . . . . . . . . . . . . . . . 750.00
61 CMJr Meets Uncle Marvel . . . 750.00
62 Uncle Sam on (c) . . . . . . . . . 750.00
63 W/ Radar (c) . . . . . . . . . . . . . 700.00
64 W/ Radar (c) . . . . . . . . . . . . . 700.00
65 BTh(c),JkS . . . . . . . . . . . . . . 700.00
66 CMJr & Secret Of the Sphinx . 700.00
67 Knight (c) . . . . . . . . . . . . . . . . 700.00
68 CMJr in the Range of
  the Beasts . . . . . . . . . . . . . . 700.00
69 . . . . . . . . . . . . . . . . . . . . . . . 700.00

**Ma**

*Master Comics #77*
© *Fawcett Publications*

*Maverick #11*
© *Dell Publishing Co.*

*Meet Corliss Archer #3*
© *Fox Features Syndicate*

**Ma**

70 . . . . . . . . . . . . . . . . . . . . . . 700.00
71 CMJr,V:Man in Metal Mask. . . 650.00
72 CMJr V: Sivana & The Whistle
That Wouldn't Stop . . . . . . . 650.00
73 CMJr V: The Ghost of Evil . . . 650.00
74 CMJr & The Fountain of Age . 650.00
75 CMJr V: The Zombie Master. . 650.00
76 . . . . . . . . . . . . . . . . . . . . . . 650.00
77 BTh(c),BK,Pirate Treasure . . . 650.00
78 CMJr in Death on the Scenic
Railway . . . . . . . . . . . . . . . . 650.00
79 CMJr V: The Black Shroud . . . 650.00
80 CMJr-The Land of Backwards 650.00
81 CMJr & The Voyage 'Round
the Horn. . . . . . . . . . . . . . . . 450.00
82 CMJr,IN,Death at the
Launching . . . . . . . . . . . . . . 450.00
83 . . . . . . . . . . . . . . . . . . . . . . 450.00
84 BTh(c&a) CMJr V: The Human
Magnet. . . . . . . . . . . . . . . . . 450.00
85 CMJr-Crime on the Campus . 300.00
86 CMJr V: The City of Machines. 300.00
87 CMJr & The Root of Evil. . . . . 300.00
88 CMJr V: The Wreckers;
B: Hopalong Cassidy. . . . . . . 300.00
89 . . . . . . . . . . . . . . . . . . . . . . 300.00
90 CMJr V: The Caveman . . . . . 300.00
91 CMJr V: The Blockmen. . . . . . 300.00
92 CMJr V: The Space Slavers . . 300.00
93 BK,CMJr,V:TheGrowingGiant . 300.00
94 E: Hopalong Cassidy. . . . . . . 300.00
95 B: Tom Mix; CMJr Meets
the Skyhawk . . . . . . . . . . . . 300.00
96 CMJr Meets the World's
Mightiest Horse . . . . . . . . . . 300.00
97 CMJr Faces the Doubting
Thomas . . . . . . . . . . . . . . . . 300.00
98 KKK Type . . . . . . . . . . . . . . . 300.00
99 Witch (c) . . . . . . . . . . . . . . . . 300.00
100 CMJr V: The Ghost Ship. . . . 350.00
101 thru 105 . . . . . . . . . . . . . . @250.00
106 E: Bulletman. . . . . . . . . . . . . 250.00
107 CMJr Faces the Disappearance
of the Statue of Liberty . . . . . 300.00
108 . . . . . . . . . . . . . . . . . . . . . . 300.00
109 . . . . . . . . . . . . . . . . . . . . . . 300.00
110 CMJr & The Hidden Death . . 300.00
111 thru 122 . . . . . . . . . . . . . . @300.00
123 CMJr V: The Flying
Desperado. . . . . . . . . . . . . . . 300.00
124 . . . . . . . . . . . . . . . . . . . . . . 300.00
125 CMJr & The Bed of Mystery . 300.00
126 thru 131. . . . . . . . . . . . . . @300.00
132 V: Migs . . . . . . . . . . . . . . . . 300.00
133 E: Tom Mix; April, 1953. . . . . 350.00

## MATT SLADE, GUNFIGHTER
### Marvel Atlas, May, 1956
1 AW,AT,F:Matt Slade,Crimson
Avenger . . . . . . . . . . . . . . . . 225.00
2 AW,A:Crimson Avenger . . . . . 175.00
3 A:Crimson Avenger . . . . . . . . . 150.00
4 A:Crimson Avenger . . . . . . . . . 125.00
**Becomes:**

## KID SLADE GUNFIGHTER
5 F:Kid Slade . . . . . . . . . . . . . . 125.00
6 . . . . . . . . . . . . . . . . . . . . . . . 100.00
7 AW,Duel in the Night . . . . . . . 110.00
8 July, 1957 . . . . . . . . . . . . . . . 100.00

## MAVERICK
### Dell Publishing Co., 1958
1 Ph(c) Garner photos . . . . . . . 400.00
2 Ph(c) . . . . . . . . . . . . . . . . . . . 200.00
3 Ph(c) . . . . . . . . . . . . . . . . . . . 200.00
4 Ph(c) . . . . . . . . . . . . . . . . . . . 200.00
5 Ph(c) . . . . . . . . . . . . . . . . . . . 200.00
6 thru 14 Ph(c) last Garner . . . @150.00
15 thru 19 Ph(c) R. Moore . . . . @125.00

## MAVERICK MARSHALL
### Charlton Comics, 1958
1 . . . . . . . . . . . . . . . . . . . . . . . 125.00
2 . . . . . . . . . . . . . . . . . . . . . . . 100.00
3 . . . . . . . . . . . . . . . . . . . . . . . 100.00
4 . . . . . . . . . . . . . . . . . . . . . . . 100.00
5 . . . . . . . . . . . . . . . . . . . . . . . 100.00
6 . . . . . . . . . . . . . . . . . . . . . . . 100.00
7 May, 1960 . . . . . . . . . . . . . . . 100.00

## MAZIE
### Nationwide Publ./ Magazine Publ./ Harvey Publ., 1951–58
1 . . . . . . . . . . . . . . . . . . . . . . . 150.00
2 . . . . . . . . . . . . . . . . . . . . . . . 100.00
3 . . . . . . . . . . . . . . . . . . . . . . . 100.00
4 . . . . . . . . . . . . . . . . . . . . . . . 100.00
5 . . . . . . . . . . . . . . . . . . . . . . . 100.00
6 . . . . . . . . . . . . . . . . . . . . . . . 100.00
7 . . . . . . . . . . . . . . . . . . . . . . . 100.00
8 . . . . . . . . . . . . . . . . . . . . . . . 100.00
9 . . . . . . . . . . . . . . . . . . . . . . . 100.00
10 . . . . . . . . . . . . . . . . . . . . . . 100.00
11 thru 20. . . . . . . . . . . . . . . . @100.00
21 thru 28 . . . . . . . . . . . . . . . @75.00

## MD
### E.C. Comics, April, 1955–Jan., 1956
1 RC,GE,Grl,JO,JCr(c). . . . . . . . 600.00
2 thru 5 RC,GE,Grl,JO,JCr(c). @500.00

## MEDAL OF HONOR COMICS
### Stafford Publication, Spring, 1947
1 True Stories of Medal of Honor
Recipients . . . . . . . . . . . . . . 250.00

## MEET CORLISS ARCHER
### Fox Features Syndicate, March, 1948
1 AF,AF(c), Teenage . . . . . . . . 1,300.00
2 AF(c) . . . . . . . . . . . . . . . . . . . 750.00
3 . . . . . . . . . . . . . . . . . . . . . . . 600.00
**Becomes:**

## MY LIFE
### Sept., 1948
4 JKa,AF, . . . . . . . . . . . . . . . . . 500.00
5 JKa, . . . . . . . . . . . . . . . . . . . . 250.00
6 JKa,AF, . . . . . . . . . . . . . . . . . 275.00
7 WW,Watercolor & Ink Drawing
on(c) . . . . . . . . . . . . . . . . . . 300.00
8 . . . . . . . . . . . . . . . . . . . . . . . 150.00
9 . . . . . . . . . . . . . . . . . . . . . . . 150.00
10 WW, July, 1950. . . . . . . . . . . 300.00

## MEET MERTON
### Toby Press, Dec., 1953
1 DBe,Teen Stories. . . . . . . . . . 125.00
2 DBe . . . . . . . . . . . . . . . . . . . . 100.00
3 DBe . . . . . . . . . . . . . . . . . . . . 100.00
4 DBe; June, 1954 . . . . . . . . . . 100.00

## MEET MISS BLISS
### Marvel Atlas, 1955
1 . . . . . . . . . . . . . . . . . . . . . . . 150.00
2 . . . . . . . . . . . . . . . . . . . . . . . 100.00
3 . . . . . . . . . . . . . . . . . . . . . . . 100.00
4 . . . . . . . . . . . . . . . . . . . . . . . 100.00

## MEET MISS PEPPER
### See: LUCY THE REAL GONE GAL

Menace #2
© Marvel Comics Group

Mickey Finn #1
© Eastern Color Printing

Mickey Mouse #40
© Walt Disney

## MEET THE NEW POST GAZETTE SUNDAY FUNNIES

**Pittsburg Post Gazette, 1949**
N# One Shot Insert F: Several
Syndicated Characters in Stories
Exclusive to This Edition . . 7,000.00

## MEL ALLEN SPORTS COMICS

**Visual Editions, 1949**
1 GT . . . . . . . . . . . . . . . . . . . . 250.00
2 Lou Gehrig . . . . . . . . . . . . . . 200.00

## MELVIN THE MONSTER

**Marvel Atlas, July, 1956**
1 JMn . . . . . . . . . . . . . . . . . . . . 150.00
2 thru 6 . . . . . . . . . . . . . . . . @125.00
Becomes:

## DEXTER THE DEMON

**Marvel, Sept., 1957**
7 . . . . . . . . . . . . . . . . . . . . . . . 100.00

## MENACE

**Marvel Atlas, May, 1953**
1 RH,BEv,GT,One Head Too
Many . . . . . . . . . . . . . . . . . . . 900.00
2 RH,BEv,GT,JSt,Burton'sBlood . 650.00
3 BEv,RH,JR,The Werewolf . . . . 450.00
4 BEv,RH,The Four Armed Man . 450.00
5 BEv,RH,GC,GT,I&O:Zombie . . 750.00
6 BEv,RH,JR,The Graymoor
Ghost . . . . . . . . . . . . . . . . . 450.00
7 JSt,RH,Fresh out of Flesh . . . 350.00
8 RH,The Lizard Man . . . . . . . . 350.00
9 BEv,The Walking Dead . . . . . 400.00
10 RH(c),Half Man,Half . . . . . . . 350.00
11 JKz,JR,Locked In,May, 1954 . 350.00

## MEN AGAINST CRIME
## See: HAND OF FATE

## MEN IN ACTION

**Marvel Atlas, April, 1952**
1 Sweating it Out . . . . . . . . . . . 200.00
2 US Infantry stories . . . . . . . . 150.00
3 RH . . . . . . . . . . . . . . . . . . . . 100.00
4 War stories . . . . . . . . . . . . . . 100.00
5 JMn,Squad Charge . . . . . . . . 100.00

6 War stories . . . . . . . . . . . . . 100.00
7 RH(c),BK,No Risk Too Great . 150.00
8 JRo(c),They Strike By Night . . 100.00
9 SSh(c),Rangers Strike Back . . 100.00
Becomes:

## BATTLE BRADY

10 SSh(c),F:Battle Brady . . . . . . 150.00
11 SSh(c) . . . . . . . . . . . . . . . . . 100.00
12 SSh(c),Death to the Reds . . . 100.00
13 . . . . . . . . . . . . . . . . . . . . . . 100.00
14 Final Issue,June, 1953 . . . . . 100.00

## MEN IN ACTION

**Ajax/Farrell Publ., 1957**
1 . . . . . . . . . . . . . . . . . . . . . . 125.00
2 . . . . . . . . . . . . . . . . . . . . . . 100.00
3 . . . . . . . . . . . . . . . . . . . . . . 100.00
4 . . . . . . . . . . . . . . . . . . . . . . 100.00
5 . . . . . . . . . . . . . . . . . . . . . . 100.00
6 . . . . . . . . . . . . . . . . . . . . . . 100.00

## MEN OF COURAGE

**Catechetical Guild**
N# . . . . . . . . . . . . . . . . . . . . . 100.00

## MEN'S ADVENTURES
## See: TRUE WESTERN

## MERRY COMICS

**Carlton Comics, 1945**
N# A:Boogeyman . . . . . . . . . . . 300.00

## MERRY-GO-ROUND COMICS

**LaSalle/Croyden/ Rotary Litho., 1944**
1 LaSalle Publications Edition . . 200.00
1a 1946, Croyden Edition . . . . . 100.00
1b Sept-Oct.'47,Rotary Litho Ed. 125.00
2 . . . . . . . . . . . . . . . . . . . . . . 125.00

## MERRY MOUSE

**Avon Periodicals, June, 1953**
1 (fa),F. Carin (a&c) . . . . . . . . . 150.00
2 (fa),F. Carin (a&c) . . . . . . . . . 100.00
3 (fa),F. Carin (a&c) . . . . . . . . . 100.00
4 (fa),F. Carin (a&c);Jan.'54 . . . 100.00

## METEOR COMICS

**Croyden Publications, Nov., 1945**
1 Captain Wizard & Baldy Bean . 500.00

## MICKEY FINN

**Eastern Color/ Columbia Comics Group, 1942**
1 . . . . . . . . . . . . . . . . . . . . . . 400.00
2 . . . . . . . . . . . . . . . . . . . . . . 300.00
3 A: Charlie Chan . . . . . . . . . . . 250.00
4 . . . . . . . . . . . . . . . . . . . . . . 200.00
5 thru 9 . . . . . . . . . . . . . . . @150.00
10 thru 15 . . . . . . . . . . . . . . @125.00

## (WALT DISNEY'S) MICKEY MOUSE

**Dell Publishing Co., Dec., 1952**
#1-#27 Dell Four Color
28 . . . . . . . . . . . . . . . . . . . . . 150.00
29 . . . . . . . . . . . . . . . . . . . . . 125.00
30 . . . . . . . . . . . . . . . . . . . . . 125.00
31 . . . . . . . . . . . . . . . . . . . . . 125.00
32 thru 34 . . . . . . . . . . . . . . @125.00
35 thru 50 . . . . . . . . . . . . . . @125.00
51 thru 73 . . . . . . . . . . . . . . @100.00
74 . . . . . . . . . . . . . . . . . . . . . 125.00
75 thru 99 . . . . . . . . . . . . . . @100.00
100 thru 105 rep. . . . . . . . . . @125.00
106 thru 120 . . . . . . . . . . . . @150.00
121 thru 130 . . . . . . . . . . . . @100.00
131 thru 146 . . . . . . . . . . . . . @30.00
147 rep,Phantom Fires . . . . . . . 30.00
148 rep. . . . . . . . . . . . . . . . . . 100.00
149 thru 158 . . . . . . . . . . . . . @60.00
159 rep. . . . . . . . . . . . . . . . . . . 60.00
160 thru 170 . . . . . . . . . . . . . @60.00
171 thru 199 . . . . . . . . . . . . . @25.00
200 rep. . . . . . . . . . . . . . . . . . . 25.00
201 thru 218 . . . . . . . . . . . . . @25.00

## MICKEY MOUSE MAGAZINE

**Kay Kamen, 1933**
1 scarce . . . . . . . . . . . . . . . . 20,000.00
2 . . . . . . . . . . . . . . . . . . . . . 5,000.00
3 thru 8 . . . . . . . . . . . . . . . @4,000.00
9 . . . . . . . . . . . . . . . . . . . . . 3,500.00

Mickey Mouse Magazine Vol. 1 #1
© Walt Disney (1935)

Mickey Mouse Magazine Vol 4 #7
© Walt Disney

Midget Comics #1
© St. John Publishing Co.

## MICKEY MOUSE MAGAZINE
### Kay Kamen, 1933–34
1 digest size (1933) . . . . . . . . 4,000.00
2 dairy give-away promo . . . . 2,000.00
3 dairy give-away promo . . . . 1,500.00
4 dairy give-away promo . . . . 1,500.00
5 dairy give-away promo . . . . 1,500.00
6 dairy give-away promo . . . . 1,500.00
7 dairy give-away promo . . . . 1,500.00
8 dairy give-away promo . . . . 1,500.00
9 dairy give-away promo . . . . 1,500.00
10 dairy give-away promo . . . . 1,500.00
11 dairy give-away promo . . . . 1,500.00
12 dairy give-away promo . . . . 1,500.00

### Volume II, 1934–35
1 dairy give-away promo . . . . 1,500.00
2 Christmas issue . . . . . . . . . 1,500.00
3 dairy give-away promo . . . . 1,500.00
4 dairy give-away promo . . . . 1,500.00
5 1st Donald Duck as Sailor . 5,000.00
6 dairy give-away promo . . . . 1,500.00
7 dairy give-away promo . . . . 1,500.00
8 dairy give-away promo . . . . 1,500.00
9 dairy give-away promo . . . . 1,500.00
10 dairy give-awaypromo . . . . 1,500.00
11 dairy give-awaypromo . . . . 1,500.00
12 dairy give-awaypromo . . . . 1,500.00

## MICKEY MOUSE MAGAZINE
### K.K. Pub./Westen Pub., 1935
1 (1935) 13¼"x10¼" . . . . . . . 35,000.00
2 OM, new size 11½"x8½". . . . 6,000.00
3 OM . . . . . . . . . . . . . . . . . . . 3,000.00
4 OM . . . . . . . . . . . . . . . . . . . 3,000.00
5 (1936) Donald Duck solo . . . 5,000.00
6 Donald Duck editor . . . . . . . 4,500.00
7 . . . . . . . . . . . . . . . . . . . . . . 3,000.00
8 Donald Duck solo . . . . . . . . 4,500.00
9 1st Minnie & Minnie . . . . . . . 4,500.00
10 . . . . . . . . . . . . . . . . . . . . . 3,000.00
11 Mickey & Pluto . . . . . . . . . 3,500.00
12 . . . . . . . . . . . . . . . . . . . . . 3,000.00

### Volume II
1 OM . . . . . . . . . . . . . . . . . . . 2,500.00
2 OM . . . . . . . . . . . . . . . . . . . 2,500.00
3 OM,Christmas issue, 100pg . 7,500.00
4 OM (1937) Roy Ranger
 adv.strip . . . . . . . . . . . . . . 2,000.00
5 Ted True strip . . . . . . . . . . . 1,500.00
6 Mickey Mouse cut-outs . . . . 1,500.00
7 Mickey Mouse cut-outs . . . . 1,500.00

8 Mickey Mouse cut-outs . . . . 1,500.00
9 Mickey Mouse cut-outs . . . . 1,500.00
10 Full color . . . . . . . . . . . . . 2,200.00
11 . . . . . . . . . . . . . . . . . . . . . 1,500.00
12 Hiawatha . . . . . . . . . . . . . . 1,500.00
13 . . . . . . . . . . . . . . . . . . . . . 1,500.00

### Volume III
2 Big Bad Wolf (c) . . . . . . . . . 1,700.00
3 CB,First Snow White . . . . . 5,000.00
4 CB,(1938) Snow White . . . . 3,000.00
5 Snow White (c) . . . . . . . . . . 3,000.00
6 Snow White ends . . . . . . . . 1,600.00
7 CB,7 Dwarfs Easter (c) . . . . 1,500.00
8 . . . . . . . . . . . . . . . . . . . . . . 1,400.00
9 CB,Dopey(c) . . . . . . . . . . . . 1,400.00
10 Goofy(c) . . . . . . . . . . . . . . 1,400.00
11 Mickey Mouse Sheriff . . . . . 1,400.00
12 CB,A:Snow White . . . . . . . 1,400.00

### Volume IV
1 OM,Practile Pig & Brave
 Little Tailor . . . . . . . . . . . . 1,500.00
2 I:Huey,Louis & Dewey(c) . . . 2,000.00
3 Ferdinand the Bull . . . . . . . . 1,500.00
4 (1939),B:Spotty . . . . . . . . . . 1,400.00
5 Pluto solo . . . . . . . . . . . . . . 1,500.00
7 Ugly Duckling . . . . . . . . . . . 1,500.00
7a Goofy & Wilber . . . . . . . . . 1,500.00
8 Big Bad Wolf(c) . . . . . . . . . . 1,500.00
9 CB,The Pointer . . . . . . . . . . 1,500.00
10 CB,July 4th . . . . . . . . . . . . 1,700.00
11 Slick, oversize . . . . . . . . . . 1,500.00
12 CB,Donald's Penguin. . . . . 1,600.00

### Volume V
1 Black Pete. . . . . . . . . . . . . . 1,600.00
2 Goofy(c),I:Pinocchio . . . . . . 2,000.00
3 Pinocchio . . . . . . . . . . . . . . 2,200.00
4 (1940) . . . . . . . . . . . . . . . . . 1,500.00
5 Jiminy Cricket(c) . . . . . . . . . 1,500.00
6 Tugboat Mickey. . . . . . . . . . 1,500.00
7 Huey, Louis & Dewey(c) . . . . 1,500.00
8 Figaro & Cleo . . . . . . . . . . . 1,500.00
9 Donald(c),J.Cricket . . . . . . . 1,700.00
10 July 4th . . . . . . . . . . . . . . . 1,700.00
11 Mickey's Tailor . . . . . . . . . . 1,700.00
12 Change of comic format . . . 8,000.00
becomes:

## WALT DISNEY COMICS & STORIES

## MICKEY MOUSE
### Whitman
904 W.Disney's Mickey Mouse
 and His Friends (1934). . . . 3,000.00

948 Disney'sMickeyMouse('34) 3,000.00

## MIDGET COMICS
### St. John Publishing Co., Feb., 1950
1 MB(c),Fighting Indian Stories . 200.00
2 April, 1950;Tex West-Cowboy
 Marshall . . . . . . . . . . . . . . . 150.00

## MIDNIGHT
### Ajax/Farrell, 1957
1 Voodoo & Strange Fantasy . . . 175.00
2 . . . . . . . . . . . . . . . . . . . . . . . 125.00

## MIGHTY ATOM, THE
### See: PIXIES

## MIGHTY BEAR
### See: HOLIDAY COMICS

## MIGHTY MIDGET COMICS
### 4"x5" Format
### Samuel E. Lowe & Co./ Fawcett, 1942-43
1 Bulletman . . . . . . . . . . . . . . . 500.00
2 Captain Marvel . . . . . . . . . . . 500.00
3 Captain Marvel Jr. . . . . . . . . . 500.00
4 Golden Arrow . . . . . . . . . . . . 400.00
5 Ibis the Invincible . . . . . . . . . 500.00
6 Spy Smasher . . . . . . . . . . . . 450.00
7 Balbo, The Boy Magician . . . 250.00
8 Bulletman . . . . . . . . . . . . . . . 300.00
9 Commando Yank . . . . . . . . . . 200.00
10 Dr. Voltz, The Human
 Generator . . . . . . . . . . . . . . 250.00
11 Lance O'Casey . . . . . . . . . . 250.00
12 Leatherneck the Marine . . . . 250.00
13 Minute Man . . . . . . . . . . . . . 250.00
14 Mister Q . . . . . . . . . . . . . . . 275.00
15 Mr. Scarlet & Pinky . . . . . . . 250.00
16 Pat Wilson & His
 Flying Fortress . . . . . . . . . . 225.00
17 Phantom Eagle . . . . . . . . . . 250.00
18 State Trooper Stops Crime . . . 250.00
19 Tornado Tom . . . . . . . . . . . . 250.00

## MIGHTY MOUSE
### Marvel [1st Series], Fall, 1946
1 Terrytoons Presents . . . . . . . 1,700.00

All comics prices listed are for *Near Mint* condition.

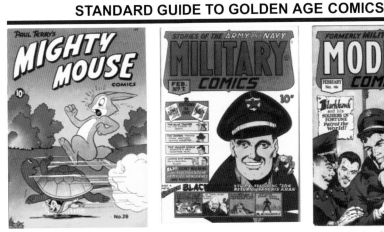

Mighty Mouse #28
© St. John Publishing Co.

Military Comics #7
© Quality Comics Group

Modern Comics #46
© Quality Comics Group

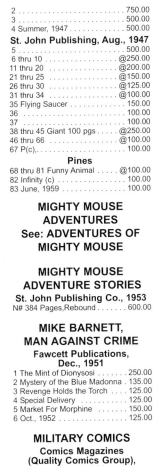

2 . . . . . . . . . . . . . . . . . . . . . . . 750.00
3 . . . . . . . . . . . . . . . . . . . . . . . 500.00
4 Summer, 1947 . . . . . . . . . . . . . 500.00

**St. John Publishing, Aug., 1947**
5 . . . . . . . . . . . . . . . . . . . . . . . 500.00
6 thru 10 . . . . . . . . . . . . . . . . @250.00
11 thru 20 . . . . . . . . . . . . . . . @200.00
21 thru 25 . . . . . . . . . . . . . . . @150.00
26 thru 30 . . . . . . . . . . . . . . . @125.00
31 thru 34 . . . . . . . . . . . . . . . @100.00
35 Flying Saucer . . . . . . . . . . . . 150.00
36 . . . . . . . . . . . . . . . . . . . . . . 100.00
37 . . . . . . . . . . . . . . . . . . . . . . 100.00
38 thru 45 Giant 100 pgs . . . . . @250.00
46 thru 66 . . . . . . . . . . . . . . . @100.00
67 P(c), . . . . . . . . . . . . . . . . . . 100.00

**Pines**
68 thru 81 Funny Animal . . . . . @100.00
82 Infinity (c) . . . . . . . . . . . . . . 100.00
83 June, 1959 . . . . . . . . . . . . . . 100.00

## MIGHTY MOUSE
## ADVENTURES
## See: ADVENTURES OF
## MIGHTY MOUSE

## MIGHTY MOUSE
## ADVENTURE STORIES
**St. John Publishing Co., 1953**
N# 384 Pages,Rebound . . . . . . . 600.00

## MIKE BARNETT,
## MAN AGAINST CRIME
**Fawcett Publications,
Dec., 1951**
1 The Mint of Dionysosi . . . . . . 250.00
2 Mystery of the Blue Madonna . 135.00
3 Revenge Holds the Torch . . . . 125.00
4 Special Delivery . . . . . . . . . . 125.00
5 Market For Morphine . . . . . . . 150.00
6 Oct., 1952 . . . . . . . . . . . . . . 125.00

## MILITARY COMICS
**Comics Magazines
(Quality Comics Group),
Aug., 1941**
1 JCo,CCu,FGu,BP,WE(c),O:Black-
hawk, Miss America, Death Patrol,
Blue Tracer; B:X of the Under-
ground, Yankee Eagle,Q-Boat,

Shot & Shell, Archie Atkins,
Loops & Banks . . . . . . . . 20,000.00
2 JCo,FGu,BP,CCu,CCu(c),B:
Secret War News . . . . . . 5,000.00
3 JCo,FGu,BP,AMc,CCu,CCu(c),
I&O:Chop Chop . . . . . . . 4,000.00
4 FGu,BP,AMc,CCu,CCu(c) . . 3,500.00
5 FGu,BP,AMc,CCu,CCu(c)
B: The Sniper . . . . . . . . . 3,000.00
6 FGu,BP,AMc,CCu,CCu(c) . . 2,600.00
7 FGu,BP,AMc,CCu,CCu(c)
E:Death Patrol . . . . . . . . 2,600.00
8 FGu,BP,AMc,RC(a&c) . . . . 2,600.00
9 FGu,BP,AMc,CCu,CCu(c)
B: The Phantom Clipper . . 2,600.00
10 FGu,BP,CCu,AMc,WE(c) . . 2,700.00
11 FGu,BP,CCu,AMc,
WE(c),Flag(c) . . . . . . . . . 2,500.00
12 FGu,BP,AMc,RC(a&c) . . . . 2,600.00
13 FGu,BP,AMc,RC(a&c),E:X of
the Underground . . . . . . . 2,500.00
14 FGu,AMc,RC(a&c),B:Private
Dogtag . . . . . . . . . . . . . 2,500.00
15 FGu,AMc,RC(a&c), . . . . . . 2,500.00
16 FGu,AMc,RC(a&c),E:The Phantom
Clipper,Blue Tracer . . . . . . 2,000.00
17 FGu,AMc,RC(a&c),
B:P.T. Boat . . . . . . . . . . . 2,000.00
18 FGu,AMc,RC(a&c), V:
The Thunderer . . . . . . . . 2,000.00
19 FGu,RC(a&c), V:King Cobra 2,000.00
20 GFx,RC(a&c), Death Patrol 2,000.00
21 FGu,GFx . . . . . . . . . . . . . 1,800.00
22 FGu,GFx . . . . . . . . . . . . . 1,800.00
23 FGu,GFx . . . . . . . . . . . . . 1,800.00
24 FGu,GFx,V: Man-Heavy
Glasses . . . . . . . . . . . . . 1,800.00
25 FGu,GFx,V: Wang The Tiger 1,800.00
26 FGu,GFx,V: Skull . . . . . . . . 1,500.00
27 FGu,JCo,R:The Death Patrol 1,500.00
28 FGu,JCo, Dungeon of Doom 1,500.00
29 FGu,JCo,V: Xanukhara . . 1,500.00
30 FGu,JCo,BWa(a&c),Blackhawk
V: Dr. Koro . . . . . . . . . . . 1,500.00
31 FGu,JCo,BWa,E:Death
Patrol; I: Captain Hitsu . . . . 1,500.00
32 JCo,A: Captain Hitsu . . . . . 1,400.00
33 W/ Civil War Veteran . . . . . 1,400.00
34 A: Eve Rice . . . . . . . . . . . 1,400.00
35 Shipwreck Island . . . . . . . . 1,400.00
36 Cult of the Wailing Tiger . . 1,400.00
37 Pass of Bloody Peace . . . . 1,400.00
38 B.Hawk Faces Bloody Death 1,400.00
39 A: Kwan Yin . . . . . . . . . . . 1,400.00
40 V: Ratru . . . . . . . . . . . . . . 1,300.00
41 W/ Chop Chop (c) . . . . . . . 1,300.00

42 V: Jap Mata Hari . . . . . . . . 1,300.00
43 . . . . . . . . . . . . . . . . . . . . 1,300.00
**Becomes:**

## MODERN COMICS
**Nov., 1945**
44 Duel of Honor. . . . . . . . . . . 1,200.00
45 V: Sakyo the Madman . . . . . 750.00
46 RC, Soldiers of Fortune . . . . 750.00
47 RC,PG,V:Count Hokoy . . . . . 750.00
48 RC,PG,V:Pirates of Perool . . . 750.00
49 RC,PG,I:Fear,Lady
Adventuress. . . . . . . . . . . . 750.00
50 RC,PG . . . . . . . . . . . . . . . 750.00
51 RC,PG, Ancient City of Evil. . . 500.00
52 PG,BWa,V: The Vulture. . . . . 500.00
53 PG,BWa,B: Torchy . . . . . . . 850.00
54 PG,RC,RC/CCu,BWa . . . . . . 500.00
55 PG,RC,RC/CCu,BWa . . . . . . 500.00
56 PG,RC/CCu,BWa . . . . . . . . 500.00
57 PG,RC/CCu,BWa . . . . . . . . 500.00
58 PG,RC,RC/CCu,BWa,
V:The Grabber. . . . . . . . . . 500.00
59 PG,RC,RC/CCu,BWa . . . . . . 500.00
60 PG,RC/CCu,BWa,RC(c),
V:Green Plague. . . . . . . . . . 500.00
61 PG,RC/CCu,BWa,RC(c) . . . . 475.00
62 PG,RC/CCu,BWa,RC(c) . . . . 475.00
63 PG,RC/CCu,BWa,RC(c) . . . . 450.00
64 PG,RC/CCu,BWa,RC(c) . . . . 450.00
65 PG,RC/CCu,BWa,RC(c) . . . . 450.00
66 PG,RC/CCu,BWa . . . . . . . . 450.00
67 PG,RC/CCu,BWa,RC(c) . . . . 450.00
68 PG,RC/CCu,BWa,RC(c);
I:Madame Butterfly . . . . . . . 450.00
69 PG,RC/CCu,BWa,RC(c) . . . . 450.00
70 PG,RC/CCu,BWa,RC(c) . . . . 450.00
71 PG,RC/CCu,BWa,RC(c) . . . . 450.00
72 PG,RC/CCu,BWa,RC(c) . . . . 450.00
73 PG,RC/CCu,BWa,RC(c) . . . . 450.00
74 PG,RC/CCu,BWa,RC(c) . . . . 450.00
75 PG,RC/CCu,BWa,RC(c) . . . . 450.00
76 PG,RC/CCu,BWa,RC(c) . . . . 450.00
77 PG,RC/CCu,BWa,RC(c) . . . . 450.00
78 PG,RC/CCu,BWa,JCo,RC(c) . 500.00
79 PG,RC/CCu,BWa,JCo,RC(c) . 450.00
80 PG,RC/CCu,BWa,JCo,RC(c) . 475.00
81 PG,RC/CCu,BWa,JCo,RC(c) . 475.00
82 PG,RC/CCu,BWa,JCo,RC(c) . 450.00
83 PG,RC/CCu,BWa,JCo,RC(c);
E: Private Dogtag . . . . . . . . 450.00
84 PG,RC/CCu,BWa,RC(c) . . . . 450.00
85 PG,RC/CCu,BWa,RC(c) . . . . 450.00
86 PG,RC/CCu,BWa,RC(c) . . . . 450.00
87 PG,RC/CCu,BWa,RC(c) . . . . 450.00
88 PG,RC/CCu,BWa,RC(c) . . . . 450.00

**All comics prices listed are for *Near Mint* condition.**

*Millie The Model #6*
*© Marvel Comics Group*

*Miss America Magazine #2*
*© Marvel Comics Group*

*Miss Fury Comics #6*
*© Marvel Comics Group*

89 PG,RC/CCu,BWa,RC(c) . . . . . 450.00
90 PG,RC/CCu,GFx,RC(c) . . . . . 450.00
91 RC/CCu,GFx,RC(c) . . . . . . . 450.00
92 RC/CCu,GFx,RC(c) . . . . . . . 450.00
93 RC/CCu,GFx,RC(c) . . . . . . . 450.00
94 RC/CCu,GFx,RC(c) . . . . . . . 450.00
95 RC/CCu,GFx,RC(c) . . . . . . . 450.00
96 RC/CCu,GFx,RC/CCu(c) . . . . 450.00
97 RC/CCu,GFx,RC/CCu(c) . . . . 450.00
98 RC/CCu,GFx,RC/CCu(c) . . . . 450.00
99 RC/CCu,GFx,JCo,RC/CCu(c). 450.00
100 GFx,JCo,RC/CCu(c) . . . . . . 475.00
101 GFx,JCo,RC/CCu(c) . . . . . . 450.00
102 GFx,JCo,WE,BWa,
   RC/CCu(c). . . . . . . . . . . . 600.00

## MILLIE THE MODEL
### Marvel, Winter, 1945
1 O:Millie the Model,
   Bowling(c) . . . . . . . . . . . . 1,500.00
2 Totem Pole(c) . . . . . . . . . . . 750.00
3 Anti-Noise(c) . . . . . . . . . . . . 500.00
4 Bathing Suit(c) . . . . . . . . . . 500.00
5 Blame it on Fame . . . . . . . . . 500.00
6 Beauty and the Beast . . . . . . 500.00
7 Bathing Suit(c) . . . . . . . . . . 500.00
8 Fancy Dress(c),HK,Hey Look . 500.00
9 Paris(c),BW . . . . . . . . . . . . . 600.00
10 Jewelry(c),HK,Hey Look . . . . 500.00
11 HK,Giggles and Grins . . . . . 350.00
12 A;Rusty,Hedy Devine . . . . . . 250.00
13 A;Hedy Devine,HK,Hey Look . 275.00
14 HK,Hey Look. . . . . . . . . . . . 275.00
15 HK,Hey Look. . . . . . . . . . . . 250.00
16 HK,Hey Look. . . . . . . . . . . . 250.00
17 thru 20. . . . . . . . . . . . . . . @275.00
21 thru 30. . . . . . . . . . . . . . . @225.00
31 thru 75. . . . . . . . . . . . . . . @225.00
76 thru 99. . . . . . . . . . . . . . . @150.00
100 . . . . . . . . . . . . . . . . . . . . 200.00
101 thru 126. . . . . . . . . . . . . @150.00
127 Millie/Clicker . . . . . . . . . . . 165.00
128 A:Scarlet Mayfair. . . . . . . . . 125.00
129 The Truth about Agnes . . . . . 125.00
130 thru 153. . . . . . . . . . . . . . @125.00
154 B:New Millie . . . . . . . . . . . . 125.00
155 thru 206. . . . . . . . . . . . . . @125.00
207 Dec., 1973 . . . . . . . . . . . . . 125.00
Ann.#1 How Millie Became
   a Model . . . . . . . . . . . . . . . . 450.00
Ann.#2 Millies Guide to
   the World of Modeling . . . . . 300.00
Ann.#3 Many Lives of Millie. . . . 200.00
Ann.#4 Many Lives of Millie. . . . 150.00

## MILT GROSS FUNNIES
### Milt Gross, Inc.,
### Aug., 1947
1 Gag Oriented Caricature . . . . 225.00
2 Gag Oriented Caricature . . . . 150.00

## MINUTE MAN
### Fawcett Publications,
### Summer, 1941
1 V: The Nazis . . . . . . . . . . . 3,000.00
2 V: The Mongol Horde . . . . . 2,000.00
3 V: The Black Poet;Spr'42 . . 2,000.00

## MIRACLE COMICS
### E.C. Comics,
### Feb.,1940
1 B:Sky Wizard,Master of Space,
   Dash Dixon,Man of Might,Dusty
   Doyle,Pinkie Parker, The Kid
   Cop,K-7 Secret Agent,Scorpion
   & Blandu,Jungle Queen . . 2,500.00
2 . . . . . . . . . . . . . . . . . . . . . 1,400.00
3 B:Bill Colt,The Ghost Rider . 1,400.00
4 A:The Veiled Prophet,
   Bullet Bob; Mar'41 . . . . . . 1,100.00

## MISS AMERICA COMICS
### Marvel, 1944
1 Miss America(c),pin-ups . . 2,200.00

## MISS AMERICA MAGAZINE
### Marvel, Nov., 1944—Nov., 1958
2 Ph(c),Miss America costume
   I;Patsy Walker,Buzz Baxter,
   Hedy Wolfe . . . . . . . . . . . 1,700.00
3 Ph(c),A:Patsy Walker,Miss
   America . . . . . . . . . . . . . . . 650.00
4 Ph(c),Betty Page,A:Patsy
   Walker,Miss America . . . . . 650.00
5 Ph(c),A:Patsy Walker,Miss
   America . . . . . . . . . . . . . . . 650.00
6 Ph(c),A:Patsy Walker. . . . . . . 175.00
7 Patsy Walker stories . . . . . . . 150.00
8 same . . . . . . . . . . . . . . . . . . 150.00
9 same . . . . . . . . . . . . . . . . . . 150.00
10 same . . . . . . . . . . . . . . . . . 150.00
11 same . . . . . . . . . . . . . . . . . 150.00
12 same . . . . . . . . . . . . . . . . . 150.00
13 thru 18. . . . . . . . . . . . . . . @150.00
21 . . . . . . . . . . . . . . . . . . . . . 175.00
22 thru 93. . . . . . . . . . . . . . . @100.00

## MISS BEVERLY HILLS OF HOLLYWOOD
### DC Comics, 1949–50
1 Alan Ladd. . . . . . . . . . . . . . . 800.00
2 William Holden. . . . . . . . . . . 600.00
3 . . . . . . . . . . . . . . . . . . . . . . 500.00
4 . . . . . . . . . . . . . . . . . . . . . . 500.00
5 Bob Hope. . . . . . . . . . . . . . . 500.00
6 Lucile Ball . . . . . . . . . . . . . . 425.00
7 . . . . . . . . . . . . . . . . . . . . . . 425.00
8 Ronald Reagan . . . . . . . . . . . 500.00
9 . . . . . . . . . . . . . . . . . . . . . . 425.00

## MISS CAIRO JONES
### Croyden Publishers, 1944
1 BO,Rep. Newspaper Strip . . . 250.00

## MISS FURY COMICS
### Marvel Timely, Winter, 1942-43
1 Newspaper strip reprints,
   ASh(c) O:Miss Fury . . . . . . 5,500.00
2 V:Nazis(c) . . . . . . . . . . . . . 2,500.00
3 Hitler/Nazi Flag(c) . . . . . . . 2,000.00
4 ASh(c),Japanese(c) . . . . . . 1,500.00
5 ASh(c),Gangster(c) . . . . . . 1,300.00
6 ASh(c),Gangster(c). . . . . . . 1,200.00
7 Gangster(c) . . . . . . . . . . . . 1,100.00
8 Atom-Bomb Secrets(c)
   Winter, 1946 . . . . . . . . . . . 1,100.00

## MISS LIBERTY
### See: LIBERTY COMICS

## MISS MELODY LANE OF BROADWAY
### DC Comics, 1950
1 . . . . . . . . . . . . . . . . . . . . . . 800.00
2 . . . . . . . . . . . . . . . . . . . . . . 500.00
3 Ed Sullivan. . . . . . . . . . . . . . 500.00

## MR. ANTHONY'S LOVE CLINIC
### Hillman Periodicals, 1945
1 Ph(c) . . . . . . . . . . . . . . . . . . 250.00
2 . . . . . . . . . . . . . . . . . . . . . . 150.00
3 . . . . . . . . . . . . . . . . . . . . . . 100.00
4 . . . . . . . . . . . . . . . . . . . . . . 100.00
5 Ph(c),Apr/May'50 . . . . . . . . . 100.00

Mi

Mr. District Attorney #13
© DC Comics

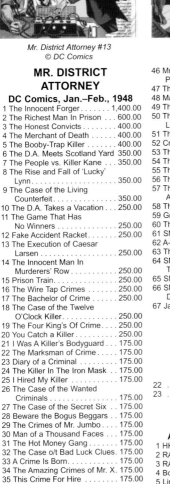

Mister Mystery #14
© Aragon Publishing

Modern Love #3
© E. C. Comics

## MR. DISTRICT ATTORNEY
### DC Comics, Jan.–Feb., 1948
1 The Innocent Forger . . . . . . . 1,400.00
2 The Richest Man In Prison . . . 600.00
3 The Honest Convicts . . . . . . . 400.00
4 The Merchant of Death . . . . . . 400.00
5 The Booby-Trap Killer . . . . . . . 400.00
6 The D.A. Meets Scotland Yard 350.00
7 The People vs. Killer Kane . . . 350.00
8 The Rise and Fall of 'Lucky'
    Lynn. . . . . . . . . . . . . . . . . . . 350.00
9 The Case of the Living
    Counterfeit. . . . . . . . . . . . . . . 350.00
10 The D.A. Takes a Vacation . . . 250.00
11 The Game That Has
    No Winners . . . . . . . . . . . . . 250.00
12 Fake Accident Racket. . . . . . . 250.00
13 The Execution of Caesar
    Larsen . . . . . . . . . . . . . . . . . 250.00
14 The Innocent Man In
    Murderers' Row . . . . . . . . . . . 250.00
15 Prison Train. . . . . . . . . . . . . . 250.00
16 The Wire Tap Crimes . . . . . . . 250.00
17 The Bachelor of Crime . . . . . . 250.00
18 The Case of the Twelve
    O'Clock Killer. . . . . . . . . . . . . 250.00
19 The Four King's Of Crime. . . . 250.00
20 You Catch a Killer . . . . . . . . . . 250.00
21 I Was A Killer's Bodyguard . . . 175.00
22 The Marksman of Crime . . . . . 175.00
23 Diary of a Criminal . . . . . . . . . 175.00
24 The Killer In The Iron Mask . . 175.00
25 I Hired My Killer . . . . . . . . . . . 175.00
26 The Case of the Wanted
    Criminals . . . . . . . . . . . . . . . . 175.00
27 The Case of the Secret Six . . 175.00
28 Beware the Bogus Beggars . . 175.00
29 The Crimes of Mr. Jumbo . . . . 175.00
30 Man of a Thousand Faces . . . 175.00
31 The Hot Money Gang . . . . . . . 175.00
32 The Case o/t Bad Luck Clues. 175.00
33 A Crime Is Born. . . . . . . . . . . . 175.00
34 The Amazing Crimes of Mr. X. 175.00
35 This Crime For Hire . . . . . . . . 175.00
36 The Chameleon of Crime . . . . 175.00
37 Miss Miller's Big Case . . . . . . 175.00
38 The Puzzle Shop For Crime . . 175.00
39 Man Who Killed Daredevils . . 175.00
40 The Human Vultures. . . . . . . . 175.00
41 The Great Token Take . . . . . . 175.00
42 Super-Market Sleuth. . . . . . . . 175.00
43 Hotel Detective . . . . . . . . . . . . 175.00
44 S.S. Justice,B:Comics Code. . 150.00
45 Miss Miller, Widow . . . . . . . . 150.00
46 Mr. District Attorney,
    Public Defender. . . . . . . . . . 150.00
47 The Missing Persons Racket . 150.00
48 Manhunt With the Mounties . . 150.00
49 The TV Dragnet . . . . . . . . . . . 150.00
50 The Case of Frank Bragan,
    Little Shot . . . . . . . . . . . . . . . 150.00
51 The Big Heist . . . . . . . . . . . . . 150.00
52 Crooked Wheels of Fortune . . 150.00
53 The Courtroom Patrol . . . . . . . 150.00
54 The Underworld Spy Squad . . 150.00
55 The Flying Saucer Mystery . . . 150.00
56 The Underworld Oracle. . . . . . 150.00
57 The Underworld Employment
    Agency. . . . . . . . . . . . . . . . . . 150.00
58 The Great Bomb Scare. . . . . . 150.00
59 Great Underworld Spy Plot . . . 150.00
60 The D.A.'s TV Rival . . . . . . . . . 150.00
61 SMo(c),Architect of Crime. . . . 150.00
62 A-Bombs For Sale. . . . . . . . . . 150.00
63 The Flying Prison . . . . . . . . . . 150.00
64 SMo(c),The Underworld
    Treasure Hunt . . . . . . . . . . . 150.00
65 SMo(c),World Wide Dragnet. . 150.00
66 SMo(c),The Secret of the
    D.A.'s Diary . . . . . . . . . . . . . 150.00
67 Jan.–Feb., 1959 . . . . . . . . . . . 150.00

## MR. MUSCLES
### See: THING, THE

## MR. MUSCLES
### Charlton Comics, 1956
22 . . . . . . . . . . . . . . . . . . . . . . . . 100.00
23 . . . . . . . . . . . . . . . . . . . . . . . . . 75.00

## MISTER MYSTERY
### Media Publ./SPM Publ./
### Aragon Publ., Sept., 1951
1 HK,RA,Horror . . . . . . . . . . . . 1,400.00
2 RA,RA(c) . . . . . . . . . . . . . . . . . 800.00
3 RA(c) . . . . . . . . . . . . . . . . . . . . 800.00
4 Bondage(c) . . . . . . . . . . . . . . . 900.00
5 Lingerie(c) . . . . . . . . . . . . . . . 800.00
6 Bondage(c) . . . . . . . . . . . . . . . 800.00
7 BW,Bondage(c);The Brain
    Bats of Venus . . . . . . . . . 1,700.00
8 Lingerie(c) . . . . . . . . . . . . . . . 750.00
9 HN . . . . . . . . . . . . . . . . . . . . . . 750.00
10 . . . . . . . . . . . . . . . . . . . . . . . . . 750.00
11 BW,Robot Woman . . . . . . . . 1,100.00
12 Flaming Object to Eye (c) . . 1,600.00
13 . . . . . . . . . . . . . . . . . . . . . . . . 525.00
14 . . . . . . . . . . . . . . . . . . . . . . . . 525.00
15 The Coffin & Medusa's Head . 500.00
16 Bondage(c) . . . . . . . . . . . . . . 500.00
17 Severed Heads . . . . . . . . . . . 500.00
18 BW,Bondage(c). . . . . . . . . . . . 850.00
19 Reprints . . . . . . . . . . . . . . . . . 500.00

## MISTER RISK
### See: HAND OF FATE

## MISTER UNIVERSE
### Mr. Publ./Media Publ./
### Stanmore, July, 1951
1 . . . . . . . . . . . . . . . . . . . . . . . . 250.00
2 RA(c);Jungle That time Forgot 150.00
3 Marijuana Story . . . . . . . . . . . 150.00
4 Mr. Universe Goes to War . . . . 125.00
5 Mr. Universe Goes to War;
    April, 1952 . . . . . . . . . . . . . 125.00

## MITZI COMICS
### Marvel Timely, Spring, 1948
1 HK:Hey Look,Giggles
    and Grins . . . . . . . . . . . . . . 300.00
Becomes:

## MITZI'S BOYFRIEND
2 F:Chip,Mitzi/Chip(c) . . . . . . . . 150.00
3 Chips adventures . . . . . . . . . . 125.00
4 thru 7 same . . . . . . . . . . . . . . @125.00
Becomes:

## MITZI'S ROMANCES
8 Mitzi/Chip(c) . . . . . . . . . . . . . . 125.00
9 . . . . . . . . . . . . . . . . . . . . . . . . 100.00
10 Dec., 1949 . . . . . . . . . . . . . . . 100.00

## MODEL FUN
### Harle Publications, 1954
2 . . . . . . . . . . . . . . . . . . . . . . . . 100.00
3 . . . . . . . . . . . . . . . . . . . . . . . . . 75.00
4 . . . . . . . . . . . . . . . . . . . . . . . . . 75.00
5 . . . . . . . . . . . . . . . . . . . . . . . . . 75.00

## MODERN COMICS
### See: MILITARY COMICS

## MODERN LOVE
### Tiny Tot Comics
### (E.C. Comics),
### June–July, 1949
1 Grl,AF,Stolen Romance . . . . . 900.00

### Mo

*Molly Manton's Romances #1*
© *Marvel Comics Group*

*Monster Crime #1*
© *Hillman Periodicals*

*Moon Girl #6*
© *E.C. Comics*

2 Grl,JcR,AF(c),I Craved
    Excitement . . . . . . . . . . . . . 600.00
3 AF(c);Our Families Clashed . . 500.00
4 AF(c);I Was a B Girl, panties . 700.00
5 RP,AF(c);Saved From Shame 700.00
6 AF(c);The Love That
    Might Have Been . . . . . . . . 700.00
7 Grl,WW,AF(c);They Won't Let
    Me Love Him . . . . . . . . . . . 500.00
8 Grl,AF(c);Aug-Sept'50 . . . . . . 550.00

## MOE & SHMOE COMICS
### O.S. Publishing Co.,
### Spring, 1948
1 Gag Oriented Caricature . . . . 100.00
2 Gag Oriented Caricature . . . . . 60.00

## MOLLY MANTON'S
## ROMANCES
### Marvel, Sept., 1949
1 Ph(c),Dare Not Marry . . . . . . . 175.00
2 Ph(c),Romances of . . . . . . . . 150.00
Becomes:
### ROMANTIC AFFAIRS
3 Ph(c) . . . . . . . . . . . . . . . . . . . 125.00

## MOLLY O'DAY
### Avon Periodicals,
### Feb., 1945
1 GT;The Enchanted Dagger . . . 700.00

## THE MONKEY
## AND THE BEAR
### Marvel Atlas, 1953
1 . . . . . . . . . . . . . . . . . . . . . . . 100.00
2 . . . . . . . . . . . . . . . . . . . . . . . 125.00

## MONKEYSHINES COMICS
### Publ. Specialists/Ace/
### Summer, 1944
1 (fa),Several Short Features . . 150.00
2 (fa),Same Format Throughout
    Entire Run . . . . . . . . . . . . . 125.00
3 thru 16 Funny Animal . . . . . @100.00
### Ace
17 Funny Animal . . . . . . . . . . . . 125.00
18 thru 21 . . . . . . . . . . . . . . . @100.00
### Unity Publ.
22 (fa). . . . . . . . . . . . . . . . . . . 100.00
23 (fa). . . . . . . . . . . . . . . . . . . 100.00

24 (fa),AFa,AFa(c) . . . . . . . . . . . 100.00
25 (fa). . . . . . . . . . . . . . . . . . . . 100.00
26 (fa). . . . . . . . . . . . . . . . . . . . 100.00
27 (fa),July, 1949 . . . . . . . . . . . 100.00

## MONSTER
### Fiction House Magazines, 1953
1 Dr. Drew. . . . . . . . . . . . . . . . 750.00
2 . . . . . . . . . . . . . . . . . . . . . . . 500.00

## MONSTER CRIME
## COMICS
### Hillman Periodicals,
### Oct., 1952
1 52 Pgs,15 Cent (c) Price . . . 1,400.00

## MONSTERS ON
## THE PROWL
## See: CHAMBER OF
## DARKNESS

## MONTE HALL
## WESTERN
## See: MARY MARVEL
## COMICS

## MONTY HALL OF
## THE U.S. MARINES
### Toby Press, Aug., 1951
1 JkS,:Monty Hall,Pin-Up Pete;
    (All Issues) . . . . . . . . . . . . . 150.00
2 JkS. . . . . . . . . . . . . . . . . . . . 125.00
3 thru 5 JkS. . . . . . . . . . . . . . @100.00
6 JkS. . . . . . . . . . . . . . . . . . . . 100.00
7 JkS,The Fireball Express . . . . 100.00
8 JkS. . . . . . . . . . . . . . . . . . . . 100.00
9 JkS. . . . . . . . . . . . . . . . . . . . 100.00
10 The Vial of Death . . . . . . . . . 100.00
11 Monju Island Prison Break . . . 100.00

## MOON GIRL AND
## THE PRINCE
### E.C. Comics, Autumn, 1947
1 JCr(c),O:Moon Girl . . . . . . 1,400.00
Becomes:

## MOON GIRL
### E.C. Comics, 1947
2 JCr(c),Battle of the Congo . . . 800.00
3 . . . . . . . . . . . . . . . . . . . . . . . 750.00
4 V: A Vampire . . . . . . . . . . . . . 750.00
5 1st E.C. Horror-Zombie
    Terror . . . . . . . . . . . . . . . 1,500.00
6 . . . . . . . . . . . . . . . . . . . . . . . 700.00
Becomes:

## MOON GIRL
## FIGHTS CRIME
### E.C. Comics, 1949
7 O:Star;The Fiend Who
    Fights With Fire . . . . . . . . . 700.00
8 True Crime Feature . . . . . . . . 700.00
Becomes:

## A MOON, A GIRL
## ...ROMANCE
### Sept.–Oct., 1949
9 AF,Grl,AF(c),C:Moon Girl;
    Spanking Panels . . . . . . . . 1,000.00
10 AF,Grl,WW,AF(c),Suspicious
    of His Intentions. . . . . . . . . . 800.00
11 AF,Grl,WW,AF(c),Hearts
    Along the Ski Trail . . . . . . . . 800.00
12 AF,Grl,AF(c),
    March–April, 1950 . . . . . . . 1,100.00
Becomes:
### WEIRD FANTASY

## MOON MULLINS
### Michael Publ. (American
### Comics Group), 1948
1 . . . . . . . . . . . . . . . . . . . . . . . 275.00
2 . . . . . . . . . . . . . . . . . . . . . . . 150.00
3 . . . . . . . . . . . . . . . . . . . . . . . 150.00
4 . . . . . . . . . . . . . . . . . . . . . . . 150.00
5 . . . . . . . . . . . . . . . . . . . . . . . 150.00
6 . . . . . . . . . . . . . . . . . . . . . . . 150.00
7 . . . . . . . . . . . . . . . . . . . . . . . 150.00
8 . . . . . . . . . . . . . . . . . . . . . . . 150.00

## MOPSY
### St. John Publishing Co.,
### Feb., 1948
1 Paper Dolls Enclosed . . . . . . 800.00
2 . . . . . . . . . . . . . . . . . . . . . . . 550.00
3 . . . . . . . . . . . . . . . . . . . . . . . 550.00
4 Paper Dolls Enclosed . . . . . . 550.00
5 Paper Dolls Enclosed . . . . . . 550.00

**Mo**

*Motion Picture Comics #113*
© *Fawcett Publications*

*Movie Love #14*
© *Famous Funnies Publ.*

*Murder Incorporated #9*
© *Fox Features Syndicate*

6 Paper Dolls Enclosed . . . . . . . 550.00
7 . . . . . . . . . . . . . . . . . . . . . . . . . 525.00
8 Paper Dolls Enclosed;
   Lingerie Panels . . . . . . . . . . 550.00
9 . . . . . . . . . . . . . . . . . . . . . . . . . 500.00
10 . . . . . . . . . . . . . . . . . . . . . . . . 500.00
11 . . . . . . . . . . . . . . . . . . . . . . . . 500.00
12 . . . . . . . . . . . . . . . . . . . . . . . . 500.00
13 Paper Dolls Enclosed . . . . . . . 500.00
14 thru 18 . . . . . . . . . . . . . . @500.00
19 Lingerie(c);Paper
   Dolls Enclosed . . . . . . . . . . 500.00

## MORE FUN COMICS
### See: NEW FUN COMICS

## MORTIE
**Magazine Publishers,**
**Dec., 1952**
1 ...Mazie's Friend . . . . . . . . . . 125.00
2 . . . . . . . . . . . . . . . . . . . . . . . . . 100.00
3 . . . . . . . . . . . . . . . . . . . . . . . . . 100.00

## MOTION PICTURE
## COMICS
**Fawcett Publications,**
**Nov., 1950**
101 Ph(c),Monte Hale's-
   Vanishing Westerner . . . . . . . 450.00
102 Ph(c),Rocky Lane's-Code
   of the Silver Sage . . . . . . . . 400.00
103 Ph(c),Rocky Lane's-Covered
   Wagon Raid . . . . . . . . . . . . . 400.00
104 BP,Ph(c),Rocky Lane's-
   Vigilante Hideout . . . . . . . . . 400.00
105 BP,Ph(c),Audie Murphy's-
   Red Badge of Courage . . . . 500.00
106 Ph(c),George Montgomery's-
   The Texas Rangers . . . . . . . . 450.00
107 Ph(c),Rocky Lane's-Frisco
   Tornado . . . . . . . . . . . . . . . . 400.00
108 Ph(c),John Derek's-Mask
   of the Avenger . . . . . . . . . . . 350.00
109 Ph(c),Rocky Lane's-Rough
   Rider of Durango . . . . . . . . . 375.00
110 GE,Ph(c), When Worlds
   Collide . . . . . . . . . . . . . . . 2,000.00
111 Ph(c),Lash LaRue's-The
   Vanishing Outpost . . . . . . . . 500.00
112 Ph(c),Jay Silverheels'-
   Brave Warrior . . . . . . . . . . . 300.00
113 KS,Ph(c),George Murphy's-
   Walk East on Beacon . . . . . . 250.00

114 Ph(c),George Montgomery's-
   Cripple Creek;Jan, 1953 . . . . 250.00

## MOTION PICTURES
## FUNNIES WEEKLY
**1st Funnies Incorporated, 1939**
1 BEv,1st Sub-Mariner . . . . . 35,000.00
2 Cover Only . . . . . . . . . . . . . 1,500.00
3 Cover Only . . . . . . . . . . . . . 1,500.00
4 Cover Only . . . . . . . . . . . . . 1,500.00

## MOVIE COMICS
**DC Comics, 1939**
1 Gunga Din . . . . . . . . . . . . . 4,500.00
2 Stagecoach . . . . . . . . . . . . . 3,000.00
3 East Side of Heaven . . . . . . . 2,500.00
4 Captain Fury,B:Oregon Trail . 1,800.00
5 Man in the Iron Mask . . . . . . 1,800.00
6 Phantom Creeps . . . . . . . . . 2,500.00

## MOVIE COMICS
**Fiction House Magazines,**
**Dec., 1946**
1 Big Town on(c) . . . . . . . . . . . 700.00
2 MB,White Tie & Tails . . . . . . . 500.00
3 MB,Andy Hardy Laugh Hit . . . 500.00
4 MB,Slave Girl . . . . . . . . . . . . 650.00

## MOVIE LOVE
**Famous Funnies Publ.,**
**Feb., 1950**
1 Ph(c),Dick Powell(c) . . . . . . . 200.00
2 Ph(c),Myrna Loy(c) . . . . . . . . 150.00
3 Ph(c),Cornell Wilde(c) . . . . . 125.00
4 Ph(c),Paulette Goddard(c) . . 125.00
5 Ph(c),Joan Fontaine(c) . . . . . 125.00
6 Ph(c),Ricardo Montalban(c) . . 125.00
7 Ph(c),Fred Astaire(c) . . . . . . 150.00
8 AW,FF,Ph(c),Corinne
   Calvert(c) . . . . . . . . . . . . . . . 600.00
9 Ph(c),John Lund(c) . . . . . . . . 125.00
10 Ph(c),Mona Freeman(c) . . . . 600.00
11 Ph(c),James Mason(c) . . . . . 150.00
12 Ph(c),Jerry Lewis &
   Dean Martin(c) . . . . . . . . . . 200.00
13 Ph(c),Ronald Reagan(c) . . . . 200.00
14 Ph(c),Janet Leigh,Gene Kelly . 125.00
15 Ph(c),John Payne . . . . . . . . 125.00
16 Ph(c),Angela Lansbury . . . . . 150.00
17 FF,Ph(c),Leslie Caron . . . . . . 150.00
18 Ph(c),Cornel Wilde . . . . . . . . 125.00
19 Ph(c),John Derek . . . . . . . . . 125.00

20 Ph(c),Debbie Reynolds . . . . . 150.00
21 Ph(c),Patricia Medina . . . . . . 125.00
22 Ph(c),John Payne . . . . . . . . . 125.00

## MOVIE THRILLERS
**Magazine Enterprises 1949**
1 Ph(c),Burt Lancaster's-
   Rope of Sand . . . . . . . . . . . 375.00

## MOVIE TUNES
### See: ANIMATED
### MOVIE-TUNES

## MUGGSY MOUSE
### See: A-1 COMICS

## MUGGY-DOO, BOY CAT
**Stanhall Publications,**
**July, 1953**
1 . . . . . . . . . . . . . . . . . . . . . . . . . 125.00
2 and 3 . . . . . . . . . . . . . . . . @100.00
4 Jan., 1954 . . . . . . . . . . . . . . . 100.00

## MURDER,
## INCORPORATED
**Fox Features Incorporated,**
**Jan., 1948–Aug., 1951**
1 For Adults Only-on(c) . . . . . . 750.00
2 For Adults Only-on(c);Male
   Bondage(c),Electrocution sty 500.00
3 Dutch Schultz-Beast of Evil . . 275.00
4 The Ray Hamilton Case,
   Lingerie(c) . . . . . . . . . . . . . 275.00
5 . . . . . . . . . . . . . . . . . . . . . . . . . 275.00
6 . . . . . . . . . . . . . . . . . . . . . . . . . 275.00
7 . . . . . . . . . . . . . . . . . . . . . . . . . 275.00
8 . . . . . . . . . . . . . . . . . . . . . . . . . 275.00
9 Bathrobe (c) . . . . . . . . . . . . . 350.00
9a Lingerie (c) . . . . . . . . . . . . . 350.00
10 . . . . . . . . . . . . . . . . . . . . . . . . 250.00
11 . . . . . . . . . . . . . . . . . . . . . . . . 250.00
12 . . . . . . . . . . . . . . . . . . . . . . . . 250.00
13 . . . . . . . . . . . . . . . . . . . . . . . . 275.00
14 Bill Hale-King o/t Murderers . 250.00
15 . . . . . . . . . . . . . . . . . . . . . . . . 250.00
16(5),Second Series . . . . . . . . 200.00
17(2) . . . . . . . . . . . . . . . . . . . . . . 200.00
18(3), Bondage(c) w/Lingerie . . 300.00

*Murderous Gangsters #2*
*© Avon Periodicals*

*My Desire #4*
*© Fox Features Syndicate*

*My Greatest Adventure #10*
*© DC Comics*

## MURDEROUS GANGSTERS

**Avon Periodicals/Realistic, July, 1951**

1 WW,Pretty Boy Floyd,
   Leggs Diamond . . . . . . . . . 550.00
2 WW,Baby Face Nelson,Mad
   Dog Esposito . . . . . . . . . . . 350.00
3 P(c),Tony & Bud Fenner,
   Jed Hawkins . . . . . . . . . . . 300.00
4 EK(c),Murder By Needle-
   Drug Story, June, 1952 . . . . . 400.00

## MUTINY

**Aragon Magazines, Oct., 1954**

1 AH(c),Stormy Tales of the
   Seven Seas . . . . . . . . . . . . 200.00
2 AH(c) . . . . . . . . . . . . . . . . . 150.00
3 Bondage(c),Feb., '55 . . . . . . 300.00

## MUTT AND JEFF

**DC Comics, 1939**

1 . . . . . . . . . . . . . . . . . . . . . 2,000.00
2 . . . . . . . . . . . . . . . . . . . . . . 900.00
3 Bucking Broncos . . . . . . . . . . 700.00
4 and 5 . . . . . . . . . . . . . . . . @600.00
6 thru 10 . . . . . . . . . . . . . . @350.00
11 thru 20 . . . . . . . . . . . . . @250.00
21 thru 30 . . . . . . . . . . . . . @225.00
31 thru 50 . . . . . . . . . . . . . @200.00
51 thru 70 . . . . . . . . . . . . . @150.00
71 thru 80 . . . . . . . . . . . . . @125.00
81 thru 99 . . . . . . . . . . . . . @100.00
100 . . . . . . . . . . . . . . . . . . . . 125.00
101 thru 103 . . . . . . . . . . . @100.00
104 thru 148 . . . . . . . . . . . @100.00

## MY CONFESSIONS
### See: WESTERN TRUE CRIME

## MY DATE COMICS

**Hillman Periodicals, July, 1944**

1 S&K,S&K (c), Teenage . . . . . 400.00
2 S&K,DB,S&K(c) . . . . . . . . . . 300.00
3 S&K,DB,S&K(c) . . . . . . . . . . 300.00
4 S&K,DB,S&K(c) . . . . . . . . . . 300.00

## MY DESIRE

**Fox Features Syndicate, Oct., 1949**

1 Intimate Confessions . . . . . . . 200.00
2 WW,They Called Me Wayward 200.00
3 I Hid My Lover . . . . . . . . . . . 125.00
4 WW, April, 1950 . . . . . . . . . 250.00

## MY DIARY

**Marvel, Dec., 1949–March, 1950**

1 Ph(c),The Man I Love . . . . . . 175.00
2 Ph(c),I Was Anybody's Girl . . . 150.00

## MY EXPERIENCE
### See: ALL TOP

## WESTERN LIFE ROMANCES

**Marvel Comics, 1949**

1 . . . . . . . . . . . . . . . . . . . . . . 225.00
2 . . . . . . . . . . . . . . . . . . . . . . 200.00
Becomes:

## MY FRIEND IRMA

**Marvel Atlas, 1950**

3 . . . . . . . . . . . . . . . . . . . . . . 200.00
4 HK . . . . . . . . . . . . . . . . . . . 225.00
5 HK . . . . . . . . . . . . . . . . . . . 175.00
6 . . . . . . . . . . . . . . . . . . . . . . 125.00
7 HK . . . . . . . . . . . . . . . . . . . 125.00
8 . . . . . . . . . . . . . . . . . . . . . . 125.00
9 Paper dolls. . . . . . . . . . . . . . 150.00
10 . . . . . . . . . . . . . . . . . . . . . 125.00
11 . . . . . . . . . . . . . . . . . . . . . 100.00
12 thru 22 . . . . . . . . . . . . . @100.00
23 FF(one page) . . . . . . . . . . . 125.00
24 thru 48 . . . . . . . . . . . . . @100.00

## MY GIRL PEARL

**Marvel Atlas, 1955–61**

1 . . . . . . . . . . . . . . . . . . . . . . 175.00
2 . . . . . . . . . . . . . . . . . . . . . . 150.00
3 . . . . . . . . . . . . . . . . . . . . . . 125.00
4 . . . . . . . . . . . . . . . . . . . . . . 125.00
5 . . . . . . . . . . . . . . . . . . . . . . 125.00
6 . . . . . . . . . . . . . . . . . . . . . . 125.00
7 . . . . . . . . . . . . . . . . . . . . . . 100.00
8 . . . . . . . . . . . . . . . . . . . . . . 100.00
9 . . . . . . . . . . . . . . . . . . . . . . 100.00
10 . . . . . . . . . . . . . . . . . . . . . 100.00
11 . . . . . . . . . . . . . . . . . . . . . 100.00

## MY GREATEST ADVENTURE

**DC Comics, Jan.–Feb., 1955**

1 LSt,I Was King Of
   Danger Island . . . . . . . . . . 2,200.00
2 My Million Dollar Dive . . . . . . 900.00
3 I Found Captain
   Kidd's Treasure . . . . . . . . . . 600.00
4 I Had A Date With Doom . . . . 600.00
5 I Escaped From Castle Morte . 500.00
6 I Had To Spend A Million . . . . 500.00
7 I Was A Prisoner On Island X . 475.00
8 The Day They Stole My Face . 475.00
9 I Walked Through The Doors
   of Destiny . . . . . . . . . . . . . . 475.00
10 We Found A World Of
   Tiny Cavemen . . . . . . . . . . . 475.00
11 LSt(c),My Friend, Madcap
   Manning. . . . . . . . . . . . . . . . 350.00
12 MMe(c),I Hunted Big Game
   in Outer Space. . . . . . . . . . . 350.00
13 LSt(c),I Hunted Goliath
   The Robot . . . . . . . . . . . . . . 350.00
14 LSt,I Had the Midas
   Touch of Gold . . . . . . . . . . . 350.00
15 JK, I Hunted the Worlds
   Wildest Animals . . . . . . . . . . 350.00
16 JK,I Died a Thousand Times . 350.00
17 JK,I Doomed the World . . . . 350.00
18 JK(c),We Discovered The
   Edge of the World . . . . . . . . 450.00
19 I Caught Earth's
   Strangest Criminal. . . . . . . . . 350.00
20 JK,I Was Big-Game
   on Neptune . . . . . . . . . . . . . 350.00
21 JK,We Were Doomed By
   The Metal-Eating Monster . . . 350.00
22 I Was Trapped In The
   Magic Mountains . . . . . . . . . 325.00
23 I Was A Captive In
   Space Prison . . . . . . . . . . . . 325.00
24 NC(c),I Was The Robinson
   Crusoe of Space . . . . . . . . . 325.00
25 I Led Earth's Strangest
   Safari! . . . . . . . . . . . . . . . . . 325.00
26 NC(c),We Battled The
   Sand Creature. . . . . . . . . . . . 325.00
27 I Was the Earth's First Exile . . 325.00
28 I Stalked the Camouflage
   Creatures. . . . . . . . . . . . . . . 325.00
29 I Tracked the
   Forbidden Powers . . . . . . . . . 200.00
30 We Cruised Into the
   Supernatural!. . . . . . . . . . . . . 200.00
31 I Was a Modern Hercules . . . . 175.00

**Mu**

All comics prices listed are for *Near Mint* condition.

*My Greatest Adventure #57*
© DC Comics

*My Greatest Adventure #81*
© DC Comics

*My Love Affair #2*
© Fox Features Syndicate

32 We Were Trapped In A Freak
  Valley! . . . . . . . . . . . . . . . . . . 175.00
33 I Was Pursued by
  the Elements . . . . . . . . . . . . . 175.00
34 DD,We Unleashed The Cloud
  Creatures. . . . . . . . . . . . . . . . 175.00
35 I Solved the Mystery of
  Volcano Valley . . . . . . . . . . . . 175.00
36 I Was Bewitched
  By Lady Doom. . . . . . . . . . . . 175.00
37 DD&SMo(c),I Hunted the
  Legendary Creatures! . . . . . . 175.00
38 DD&SMo(c),I Was the Slave
  of the Dream-Master . . . . . . . 175.00
39 DD&SMo(c),We were Trapped
  in the Valley of no Return . . . 175.00
40 We Battled the StormCreature 175.00
41 DD&SMo(c),I Was Tried
  by a Robot Court. . . . . . . . . . 150.00
42 DD&SMo(c),My Brother
  Was a Robot . . . . . . . . . . . . . 150.00
43 DD&SMo(c),I Fought the
  Sonar Creatures . . . . . . . . . . 150.00
44 DD&SMo(c),We Fought the
  Beasts of Petrified Island . . . 150.00
45 DD&SMo(c),We Battled the
  Black Narwahl . . . . . . . . . . . . 150.00
46 DD&SMo(c),We Were Prisoners
  of the Sundial of Doom . . . . . 150.00
47 We Became Partners of the
  Beast Brigade . . . . . . . . . . . . 150.00
48 DD&SMo(c),I Was Marooned
  On Earth . . . . . . . . . . . . . . . . 150.00
49 DD&SMo(c),I Was An Ally
  Of A Criminal Creature . . . . . 150.00
50 DD&SMo(c),I Fought the
  Idol King . . . . . . . . . . . . . . . . 150.00
51 DD&SMo(c),We Unleashed
  the Demon of the Dungeon . . 135.00
52 DD&SMo(c),I Was A
  Stand-In For an Alien. . . . . . . 135.00
53 DD&SMo(c),I, Creature Slayer 135.00
54 I Was Cursed With
  an Alien Pal . . . . . . . . . . . . . . 135.00
55 DD&SMo(c),I Became The
  Wonder-Man of Space. . . . . . 135.00
56 DD&SMo(c),My Brother-The
  Alien. . . . . . . . . . . . . . . . . . . . 135.00
57 DD&SMo(c),Don't Touch Me
  Or You'll Die. . . . . . . . . . . . . . 135.00
58 DD&SMo(c),ATh,I was Trapped
  in the Land of L'Oz . . . . . . . . 150.00
59 DD&SMo(c),Listen Earth-I
  Am Still Alive . . . . . . . . . . . . . 150.00
60 DD&SMo(c),ATh,I Lived in
  Two Worlds . . . . . . . . . . . . . . 150.00

61 DD&SMo(c),ATh,I Battled For
  the Doom-Stone . . . . . . . . . . 150.00
62 DD&SMo(c),I Fought For
  An Alien Enemy. . . . . . . . . . . 100.00
63 DD&SMo(c),We Braved the
  Trail of the Ancient Warrior . . 100.00
64 DD&SMo(c),They Crowned My
  Fiance Their King! . . . . . . . . . 100.00
65 DD&SMo(c),I Lost the Life
  or Death Secret . . . . . . . . . . . 100.00
66 DD&SMo(c),I Dueled with
  the Super Spirits . . . . . . . . . . 100.00
67 I Protected the Idols
  of Idoro! . . . . . . . . . . . . . . . . . 100.00
68 DD&SMo(c),My Deadly Island
  of Space . . . . . . . . . . . . . . . . 100.00
69 DD&SMo(c),I Was A Courier
  From the Past . . . . . . . . . . . . 100.00
70 DD&SMo(c),We Tracked the
  Fabled Fish-Man! . . . . . . . . . 100.00
71 We Dared to open the Door
  of Danger Dungeon . . . . . . . . 100.00
72 The Haunted Beach . . . . . . . . 100.00
73 I Defeiller Mountain. . . . . . . . . 100.00
74 GC(c),We Were Challenged
  By The River Spirit . . . . . . . . 100.00
75 GC(c),Castaway Cave-Men
  of 1950 . . . . . . . . . . . . . . . . . 100.00
76 MMe(c),We Battled the
  Micro-Monster . . . . . . . . . . . . 100.00
77 ATh,We Found the Super-
  Tribes of Tomorrow . . . . . . . . 125.00
78 Destination-'Dead Man's Alley' 100.00
79 Countdown in Dinosaur Valley 100.00
80 BP,I:Doom Patrol . . . . . . . . . . 750.00
81 BP,ATh,I:Dr. Janus . . . . . . . . 250.00
82 BP,F:Doom Patrol . . . . . . . . . 225.00
83 BP,F:Doom Patrol . . . . . . . . . 225.00
84 BP,V:General Immortus . . . . . 225.00
85 BP,ATh,F:Doom Patrol . . . . . . 225.00

## MY GREAT LOVE
### Fox Features Syndicate,
### Oct., 1949–Apr., 1950
1 Reunion In a Shack . . . . . . . . 175.00
2 My Crazy Dreams . . . . . . . . . 100.00
3 He Was Ashamed of Me . . . . . 100.00
4 My Two Wedding Rings . . . . . 100.00

## MY INTIMATE AFFAIR
### Fox Features Syndicate,
### March, 1950
1 I Sold My Love . . . . . . . . . . . 175.00
2 I Married a Jailbird;May'50 . . . 100.00

## MY LIFE
## See: MEET CORLISS
## ARCHER

## MY LITTLE MARGIE
### Charlton Comics, 1954–65
1 Ph(c) . . . . . . . . . . . . . . . . . . . 400.00
2 Ph(c) . . . . . . . . . . . . . . . . . . . 175.00
3 thru 8 . . . . . . . . . . . . . . . . . @125.00
9 . . . . . . . . . . . . . . . . . . . . . . . 110.00
10 . . . . . . . . . . . . . . . . . . . . . . . 125.00
11 . . . . . . . . . . . . . . . . . . . . . . . 100.00
12 . . . . . . . . . . . . . . . . . . . . . . . 100.00
13 . . . . . . . . . . . . . . . . . . . . . . . 100.00
14 thru 19 . . . . . . . . . . . . . . . . @100.00
20 Giant Size . . . . . . . . . . . . . . . 125.00
21 thru 35 . . . . . . . . . . . . . . . . @100.00
36 thru 53 . . . . . . . . . . . . . . . . @100.00
54 Beatles (c). . . . . . . . . . . . . . . 225.00

## MY LITTLE MARGIE'S
## BOY FRIEND
### Charlton Comics, 1955–58
1 . . . . . . . . . . . . . . . . . . . . . . . . 200.00
2 . . . . . . . . . . . . . . . . . . . . . . . . 150.00
3 . . . . . . . . . . . . . . . . . . . . . . . . 100.00
4 . . . . . . . . . . . . . . . . . . . . . . . . 100.00
5 . . . . . . . . . . . . . . . . . . . . . . . . 100.00
6 . . . . . . . . . . . . . . . . . . . . . . . . 100.00
7 . . . . . . . . . . . . . . . . . . . . . . . . 100.00
8 . . . . . . . . . . . . . . . . . . . . . . . . 100.00
9 . . . . . . . . . . . . . . . . . . . . . . . . 100.00
10 . . . . . . . . . . . . . . . . . . . . . . . 100.00
11 . . . . . . . . . . . . . . . . . . . . . . . 100.00

## MY LOVE
### Marvel, July, 1949
1 Ph(c),One Heart to Give . . . . . 175.00
2 Ph(c),Hate in My Heart . . . . . . 125.00
3 Ph(c), . . . . . . . . . . . . . . . . . . . 100.00
4 Ph(c),Betty Page, April,1950 . . 400.00

## MY LOVE AFFAIR
### Fox Features Syndicate,
### July, 1949
1 Truck Driver's Sweetheart . . . 175.00
2 My Dreadful Secret . . . . . . . . 100.00
3 WW,I'll Make Him Marry Me . . 250.00
4 WW,They Called Me Wild . . . . 250.00
5 WW,Beauty Was My Bait . . . . 250.00
6 WW,The Man Downstairs . . . . 250.00

*My Love Story #1*
© Fox Features Syndicate

*My Secret Life #24*
© Fox Features Syndicate

*My Secret Romance #2*
© Fox Features Syndicate

Becomes:

## MARCH OF CRIME
**Fox Features Syndicate, 1950**
1 (7) WW . . . . . . . . . . . . . . . 475.00
2 WW . . . . . . . . . . . . . . . . . . 450.00
3 . . . . . . . . . . . . . . . . . . . . . . 225.00

## MY LOVE MEMORIES
### See: WOMEN OUTLAWS

## MY LOVE LIFE
### See: ZEGRA, JUNGLE EMPRESS

## MY LOVE STORY
**Fox Features Syndicate, Sept., 1949**
1 Men Gave Me Jewels . . . . . . . 175.00
2 He Dared Me . . . . . . . . . . . . 100.00
3 WW,I Made Love a Plaything . 250.00
4 WW,I Tried to Be Good . . . . . 250.00

## MY PAST CONFESSIONS
### See: WESTERN THRILLERS

## MY PERSONAL PROBLEM
**Ajax/Farrell Publ., 1955**
1 . . . . . . . . . . . . . . . . . . . . . . 125.00
2 thru 4 . . . . . . . . . . . . . . . . @100.00

## MY PRIVATE LIFE
**Fox Features Syndicate, Feb., 1950**
16 My Friendship Club Affair . . . . 150.00
17 My Guilty Kisses;April'50 . . . . 135.00

## MY ROMANCE
**Marvel, Sept., 1948**
1 Romance Stories . . . . . . . . . . 175.00
2 . . . . . . . . . . . . . . . . . . . . . . 125.00
3 . . . . . . . . . . . . . . . . . . . . . . 125.00
Becomes:
## MY OWN ROMANCE
4 Romance Stories Continue . . . 250.00
5 thru 10 . . . . . . . . . . . . . . . . @150.00

11 thru 20 . . . . . . . . . . . . . . . @150.00
21 thru 50 . . . . . . . . . . . . . . . @125.00
51 thru 54 . . . . . . . . . . . . . . . @100.00
55 ATh . . . . . . . . . . . . . . . . . . 125.00
56 thru 60 . . . . . . . . . . . . . . . @100.00
61 thru 70 . . . . . . . . . . . . . . . @100.00
71 AW . . . . . . . . . . . . . . . . . . 125.00
72 thru 76 . . . . . . . . . . . . . . . @100.00
Becomes:

## TEENAGE ROMANCE
77 Romance Stories Continue . . . 100.00
78 thru 85 . . . . . . . . . . . . . . . @100.00
86 March, 1962 . . . . . . . . . . . . 100.00

## MY SECRET
**Superior Comics, Aug., 1949**
1 True Love Stories . . . . . . . . . 150.00
2 I Was Guilty of Being a
   Cheating Wife . . . . . . . . . . . 125.00
3 Was I His Second Love?; . . . . 125.00
Becomes:
## OUR SECRET
**Nov., 1949–June, 1950**
4 JKa,She Loves Me,She Loves
   Me Not . . . . . . . . . . . . . . . . . 200.00
5 . . . . . . . . . . . . . . . . . . . . . . 125.00
6 . . . . . . . . . . . . . . . . . . . . . . 125.00
7 How Do You Fall In Love? . . . . 135.00
8 His Kiss Tore At My Heart . . . . 125.00

## MY SECRET AFFAIR
**Hero Books
(Fox Features Syndicate),
Dec., 1949**
1 WW,SHn,My Stormy
   Love Affair . . . . . . . . . . . . . 250.00
2 WW,I Loved a Weakling . . . . . 250.00
3 WW, April, 1950 . . . . . . . . . . 250.00

## MY SECRET CONFESSION
**Sterling Comics, 1955**
1 MSy . . . . . . . . . . . . . . . . . . . 100.00

## MY SECRET LIFE
**Fox Features Syndicate, July, 1949**
22 I Loved More Than Once . . . . 150.00
23 WW . . . . . . . . . . . . . . . . . . 250.00
24 Love Was a Habit . . . . . . . . . 100.00
25 . . . . . . . . . . . . . . . . . . . . . 100.00
Becomes:

## ROMEO TUBBS
**Dec., 1952**
26 WW,That Lovable Teen-ager . 250.00

## MY LOVE SECRET
### See: PHANTOM LADY

## MY SECRET MARRIAGE
**Superior Comics, May, 1953**
1 I Was a Cheat . . . . . . . . . . . 150.00
2 . . . . . . . . . . . . . . . . . . . . . . 125.00
3 We Couldn't Wait . . . . . . . . . 100.00
4 . . . . . . . . . . . . . . . . . . . . . . 100.00
5 . . . . . . . . . . . . . . . . . . . . . . 100.00
6 . . . . . . . . . . . . . . . . . . . . . . 100.00
7 thru 23 . . . . . . . . . . . . . . . @100.00
24 1956 . . . . . . . . . . . . . . . . . 100.00

## MY SECRET ROMANCE
**Hero Books
(Fox Features Syndicate),
Jan., 1950**
1 WW,They Called Me 'That'
   Woman . . . . . . . . . . . . . . . . 250.00
2 WW,They Called Me Cheap . . 250.00

## MY SECRET STORY
### See: DAGAR, DESERT HAWK

## MYSTERIES OF UNEXPLORED WORLDS/ SON OF VULCAN
**Charlton Comics, 1956**
1 . . . . . . . . . . . . . . . . . . . . . . 400.00
2 . . . . . . . . . . . . . . . . . . . . . . 175.00
3 SD,SD(c) . . . . . . . . . . . . . . . 300.00
4 SD,Forbidden Room . . . . . . . . 350.00
5 SD,SD(c) . . . . . . . . . . . . . . . 350.00
6 SD . . . . . . . . . . . . . . . . . . . . 350.00
7 SD, giant . . . . . . . . . . . . . . . 375.00
8 SD . . . . . . . . . . . . . . . . . . . . 325.00
9 SD . . . . . . . . . . . . . . . . . . . . 325.00
10 SD,SD(c). . . . . . . . . . . . . . . 325.00
11 SD,SD(c). . . . . . . . . . . . . . . 325.00
12 SD,Charm Bracelet. . . . . . . . 250.00
13 thru 18 . . . . . . . . . . . . . . . @100.00
19 SD(c). . . . . . . . . . . . . . . . . . 250.00

All comics prices listed are for *Near Mint* condition.

*Mysteries of Unexplored Worlds #20*
© Charlton Comics

*Mysterious Adventures #22*
© Story Comics

*Mystery in Space #11*
© DC Comics

20 . . . . . . . . . . . . . . . . . . . . . . 100.00
21 thru 24 SD . . . . . . . . . . . . . @250.00
25 . . . . . . . . . . . . . . . . . . . . . . 100.00
26 SD . . . . . . . . . . . . . . . . . . . . 250.00
27 thru 30 . . . . . . . . . . . . . . . @100.00

## MYSTERIES WEIRD AND STRANGE
### Superior Comics/ Dynamic Publ., May, 1953
1 The Stolen Brain . . . . . . . . . . 500.00
2 The Screaming Room,
  Atomic Bomb . . . . . . . . . . . . 350.00
3 SD,The Avenging Corpse . . . . 300.00
4 SD,Ghost on the Gallows . . . . 300.00
5 SD,Horror a la Mode . . . . . . . . 300.00
6 SD,Howling Horror . . . . . . . . 300.00
7 SD,Demon in Disguise . . . . . . 200.00
8 SD,The Devil's Birthmark . . . . 200.00
9 SD . . . . . . . . . . . . . . . . . . . . . 200.00
10 SD . . . . . . . . . . . . . . . . . . . . 300.00
11 SD . . . . . . . . . . . . . . . . . . . . 300.00

## MYSTERIOUS ADVENTURES
### Story Comics, March, 1951
1 WJo(c),Wild Terror of the
  Vampire Flag . . . . . . . . . . . 900.00
2 Terror of the Ghoul's Corpse . 450.00
3 Terror of the Witche's Curse . . 400.00
4 The Little Coffin That Grew . . . 400.00
5 LC,Curse of the Jungle,
  Bondage(c) . . . . . . . . . . . . . 450.00
6 LC,Ghostly Terror in the
  Cave . . . . . . . . . . . . . . . . . . 400.00
7 LC,Terror of the Ghostly
  Castle . . . . . . . . . . . . . . . . . 500.00
8 Terror of the Flowers of Death. 650.00
9 The Ghostly Ghouls-
  Extreme Violence . . . . . . . . . 450.00
10 Extreme Violence . . . . . . . . . 400.00
11 The Trap of Terror . . . . . . . . . 450.00
12 SHn,Vultures of Death-
  Extreme Violence . . . . . . . . . 450.00
13 Extreme Violence . . . . . . . . . 450.00
14 Horror of the Flame Thrower
  Extreme Violence . . . . . . . . . 450.00
15 DW,Ghoul Crazy . . . . . . . . . . 500.00
16 Chilling Tales of Horror . . . . . 500.00
17 DW,Bride of the Dead . . . . . . 500.00
18 Extreme Violence . . . . . . . . . 500.00
19 The Coffin . . . . . . . . . . . . . . . 500.00

20 Horror o/t Avenging Corpse . . 500.00
21 Mother Ghoul's Nursery
  Tales, Bondage (c) . . . . . . . . 500.00
22 RA,Insane . . . . . . . . . . . . . . . 400.00
23 RA,Extreme Violence . . . . . . . 400.00
24 KS, . . . . . . . . . . . . . . . . . . . . 350.00
25 KS,Aug., 1955 . . . . . . . . . . . . 350.00

## HORROR FROM THE TOMB
### Premier Magazines, Sept., 1954
1 AT,GWb,The Corpse Returns . 500.00
Becomes:

## MYSTERIOUS STORIES
### Dec., 1954–Jan., 1955
2 GWb(c),Eternal Life . . . . . . . 600.00
3 GWb,The Witch Doctor . . . . . . 350.00
4 That's the Spirit . . . . . . . . . . . 325.00
5 King Barbarossa . . . . . . . . . . 325.00
6 GWb,Strangers in the Night. . . 350.00
7 KS,The Pipes of Pan;Dec'55 . . 325.00

## MYSTERIOUS TRAVELER COMICS
### Trans-World Publications, Nov., 1948
1 BP,BP(c),Five Miles Down . . . . 700.00

## MYSTERY COMICS
### William H. Wise & Co., 1944
1 ASh(c),B:Brad Spencer-Wonderman,
  King of Futeria,The Magnet, Zudo-
  Jungle Boy,Silver Knight. . . 1,500.00
2 ASh(c),Bondage (c) . . . . . . . . 900.00
3 ASh(c),Robot(c),LanceLewis,B 800.00
4 ASh(c),E:All Features,
  KKK Type(c) . . . . . . . . . . . . 800.00

## MYSTERY IN SPACE
### DC Comics, April-May, 1951
1 CI&FrG(c),FF,B:Knights of the
  Galaxy,Nine Worlds to
  Conquer . . . . . . . . . . . . . . 5,500.00
2 CI(c),MA,A:Knights of the
  Galaxy, Jesse James-
  Highwayman of Space . . . . 2,500.00
3 CI(c),A:Knights of the
  Galaxy, Duel of the Planets 1,500.00
4 CI(c),S&K,MA,A:Knights of the
  Galaxy, Master of Doom. . . 1,400.00

5 CI(c),A:Knights of the Galaxy,
  Outcast of the Lost World. . 1,400.00
6 CI(c),A:Knights of the Galaxy,
  The Day the World Melted . 1,000.00
7 GK(c),ATh,A:Knights of the
  Galaxy, Challenge o/t Robot Knight 1,000.00
8 MA,It's a Women's World . . . 1,000.00
9 MA(c),The Seven Wonders
  of Space . . . . . . . . . . . . . . . 900.00
10 MA(c),The Last Time I
  Saw Earth . . . . . . . . . . . . . . 900.00
11 GK(c),Unknown Spaceman. . . 750.00
12 MA,The Sword in the Sky . . . . 750.00
13 MA(c),MD,Signboard
  in Space. . . . . . . . . . . . . . . . 750.00
14 MA,GK(c),Hollywood
  in Space. . . . . . . . . . . . . . . . 750.00
15 MA(c),Doom from Station X . . 750.00
16 MA(c),Honeymoon in Space . 750.00
17 MA(c),The Last Mile of
  Space. . . . . . . . . . . . . . . . . . 750.00
18 MA(c),GK,Chain Gang
  of Space . . . . . . . . . . . . . . . 750.00
19 MA(c),The Great
  Space-Train Robbery . . . . . . 750.00
20 MA(c),The Man in the
  Martian Mask. . . . . . . . . . . . 600.00
21 MA(c),Interplanetary
  Merry- Go-Round . . . . . . . . . 600.00
22 MA(c),The Square Earth. . . . . 600.00
23 MA(c),Monkey-Rocket
  to Mars . . . . . . . . . . . . . . . . 600.00
24 MA(c),A:Space Cabby,
  Hitchhiker of Space . . . . . . . 600.00
25 MA(c),Station Mars on the Air. 500.00
26 GK(c),Earth is the Target . . . . 500.00
27 The Human Fishbowl . . . . . . 500.00
28 The Radio Planet . . . . . . . . . . 500.00
29 GK(c),Space-Enemy
  Number One . . . . . . . . . . . . . 500.00
30 GK(c),The Impossible
  World Named Earth. . . . . . . . 500.00
31 GK(c),The Day the Earth
  Split in Two . . . . . . . . . . . . . 475.00
32 GK(c),Riddle of the
  Vanishing Earthmen . . . . . . 475.00
33 The Wooden World War . . . . . 475.00
34 GK(c),The Man Who
  Moved the World . . . . . . . . . 475.00
35 The Counterfeit Earth . . . . . . 475.00
36 GK(c),Secret of the
  Moon Sphinx . . . . . . . . . . . 475.00
37 GK(c),Secret of the
  Masked Martians . . . . . . . . . 475.00
38 GK(c),The Canals of Earth . . . 475.00
39 GK(c),Sorcerers of Space. . . . 475.00

**My**

Mystery in Space #48
© DC Comics

Mystery in Space #76
© DC Comics

Mystery Men Comics #3
© Fox Features Syndicate

40 GK(c),Riddle of the
  Runaway Earth . . . . . . . . . . 475.00
41 GK(c),The Miser of Space . . . 375.00
42 GK(c),The Secret of the
  Skyscraper Spaceship . . . . . . 375.00
43 GK(c),Invaders From the
  Space Satellites . . . . . . . . . . 375.00
44 GK(c),Amazing Space Flight
  of North America . . . . . . . . . 375.00
45 GK(c),MA,Flying Saucers
  Over Mars . . . . . . . . . . . . . . 375.00
46 GK(c),MA,Mystery of the
  Moon Sniper . . . . . . . . . . . . 375.00
47 GK(c),MA,Interplanetary Tug
  of War . . . . . . . . . . . . . . . . . 375.00
48 GK(c),MA,Secret of the
  Scarecrow World . . . . . . . . . 375.00
49 GK(c),The Sky-High Man . . . . 375.00
50 GK(c),The Runaway
  Space-Train . . . . . . . . . . . . . 375.00
51 GK(c),MA,Battle of the
  Moon Monsters . . . . . . . . . . 375.00
52 GK(c),MSy,Mirror Menace
  of Mars . . . . . . . . . . . . . . . . 375.00
53 GK(c),B:Adam Strange stories,
  Menace o/t Robot Raiders . 3,500.00
54 GK(c),Invaders of the
  Underground World . . . . . . . 850.00
55 GK(c),The Beast From
  the Runaway World . . . . . . . 700.00
56 GK(c),The Menace of
  the Super-Atom . . . . . . . . . . 375.00
57 GK(c),Mystery of the
  Giant Footsteps . . . . . . . . . . 375.00
58 GK(c),Chariot in in the Sky . . . 375.00
59 GK(c),The Duel of the
  Two Adam Stranges . . . . . . . 375.00
60 GK(c),The Attack of the
  Tentacle World . . . . . . . . . . . 375.00
61 CI&MA(c),Threat of the
  Tornado Tyrant . . . . . . . . . . . 300.00
62 CI&MA(c),The Beast with
  the Sizzling Blue Eyes . . . . . 300.00
63 The Weapon that
  Swallowed Men . . . . . . . . . . 300.00
64 The Radioactive Menace . . . . 300.00
65 Mechanical Masters of
  Rann . . . . . . . . . . . . . . . . . . 300.00
66 Space-Island of Peril . . . . . . . 300.00
67 Challenge of the
  Giant Fireflies . . . . . . . . . . . 300.00
68 CI&MA(c),Fadeaway Doom . . 300.00
69 CI&MA(c),Menace of the
  Aqua-Ray Weapon . . . . . . . . 300.00
70 CI&MA(c),Vengeance of
  the Dust Devil . . . . . . . . . . . 300.00

71 CI&MA(c),The Challenge of
  the Crystal Conquerors . . . . 300.00
72 The Multiple Menace Weapon 250.00
73 CI&MA(c),The Invisible
  Invaders of Rann . . . . . . . . . 250.00
74 CI&MA(c),The Spaceman
  Who Fought Himself . . . . . . . 250.00
75 CI&MA(c),The Planet That
  Came to a Standstill . . . . . . 500.00
76 CI&MA(c),Challenge of
  the Rival Starman . . . . . . . . 250.00
77 CI&MA(c),Ray-Gun in the Sky 250.00
78 CI&MA(c),Shadow People
  of the Eclipse . . . . . . . . . . . . 250.00
79 CI&MA(c),The Metal
  Conqueror of Rann . . . . . . . 250.00
80 CI&MA(c),The Deadly
  Shadows of Adam Strange . . 250.00
81 CI&MA(c),The Cloud-Creature
  That Menaced Two Worlds . . 200.00
82 CI&MA(c),World War on
  Earth and Rann . . . . . . . . . . 200.00
83 CI&MA(c),The Emotion-Master
  of Space . . . . . . . . . . . . . . . 200.00
84 CI&MA(c),The Powerless
  Weapons of Adam Strange . . 200.00
85 CI&MA(c),Riddle of the
  Runaway Rockets . . . . . . . . . 200.00
86 CI&MA(c),Attack of the
  Underworld Giants . . . . . . . . 200.00
87 MA(c),The Super-Brain of
  Adam Strange,B:Hawkman . . 400.00
88 CI&MA(c),The Robot Wraith
  of Rann . . . . . . . . . . . . . . . . 300.00
89 MA(c),Siren o/t Space Ark . . . 275.00
90 CI&MA(c),Planets and
  Peril, E:Hawkman . . . . . . . . 275.00
91 CI&MA(c),Puzzle of
  the Perilous Prisons . . . . . . . 150.00
92 DD&SMo(c),The Alien Invasion
  From Earth,B:Space Ranger . 150.00
93 DD&SMo(c),The Convict
  Twins of Space . . . . . . . . . . 150.00
94 DD&SMo(c),The Adam
  Strange Story . . . . . . . . . . . . 150.00
95 The Hydra-Head From
  Outer Space . . . . . . . . . . . . 150.00
96 The Coins That Doomed
  Two Planets . . . . . . . . . . . . . 150.00
97 The Day Adam Strange
  Vanished . . . . . . . . . . . . . . . 150.00
98 The Wizard of the Cosmos . . . 150.00
99 DD&SMo(c),The World-
  Destroyer From Space . . . . . 150.00
100 DD&SMo(c),GK,The Death
  of Alanna . . . . . . . . . . . . . . 150.00

101 GK(c),The Valley of
  1,000 Dooms . . . . . . . . . . . . 150.00
102 GK,The Robot World of Rann150.00
103 The Billion-Dollar Time-
  Capsule(Space Ranger),I:Ultra
  the Multi-Agent . . . . . . . . . . 150.00
104 thru 109 . . . . . . . . . . . . . @125.00
110 Series ends, Sept., 1966 . . . 125.00

## MYSTERY MEN COMICS
### Fox Features Syndicate,
### Aug., 1939
1 GT,DBr,LF(c),Bondage(c),I:Blue
  Beetle,Green Mask,Rex Dexter
  of Mars,Zanzibar,Lt.Drake,D-13
  Secret Agent,Chen Chang,
  Wing Turner,Capt. Denny  15,000.00
2 GT,BP,DBr,LF(c),
  Rex Dexter (c) . . . . . . . . . . 5,000.00
3 LF(c) . . . . . . . . . . . . . . . . . 6,000.00
4 LF(c),B:Captain Savage . . . . 3,500.00
5 GT,BP,LF(c),Green Mask (c) 3,500.00
6 GT,BP . . . . . . . . . . . . . . . . 3,000.00
7 GT,BP,Bondage(c),
  Blue Beetle(c) . . . . . . . . . . 3,500.00
8 GT,BP,LF(c),Bondage(c),
  Blue Beetle . . . . . . . . . . . . . 3,200.00
9 GT,BP,DBr(c),B:The Moth . . . 1,500.00
10 GT,BP,JSm(c),A:Wing
  Turner; Bondage(c) . . . . . . . 1,400.00
11 GT,BP,JSm(c),I:The Domino 1,400.00
12 GT,BP,JSm(c),BlueBeetle(c) 1,400.00
13 GT,I:The Lynx & Blackie . . . 1,000.00
14 GT,Male Bondage (c) . . . . . . . 950.00
15 GT,Blue Beetle (c) . . . . . . . . . 900.00
16 GT,Hypo(c),MaleBondage(c) . 950.00
17 GT,BP,Blue Beetle (c) . . . . . . 900.00
18 GT,Blue Beetle (c) . . . . . . . . . 900.00
19 GT,I&B:Miss X . . . . . . . . . . 1,000.00
20 GT,DBr,Blue Beetle (c) . . . . . 900.00
21 GT,E:Miss X . . . . . . . . . . . . . 900.00
22 GT,CCu(c),Blue Beetle (c) . . . 900.00
23 GT,Blue Beetle (c) . . . . . . . . . 900.00
24 GT,BP,DBr, Blue Beetle (c) . . 900.00
25 GT,Bondage(c);
  A:Private O'Hara . . . . . . . . . 950.00
26 GT,Bondage(c);B:The Wraith . 950.00
27 GT,Bondage(c),BlueBeetle(c). 950.00
28 GT,Bondage(c);Satan's
  Private Needlewoman . . . . . . 950.00
29 GT,Bondage(c),Blue
  Beetle (c) . . . . . . . . . . . . . . . 950.00
30 Holiday of Death . . . . . . . . . . 900.00
31 Bondage(c);Feb'42 . . . . . . . . 950.00

*Mystery Tales #6*
© Marvel Comics Group

*Mystic Comics #2*
© Marvel Comics Group

*Mystic #11*
© Marvel Comics Group

## MYSTERY TALES

### Marvel Atlas, March, 1952

1 GC,Horror Strikes at
   Midnight . . . . . . . . . . . . . . 1,400.00
2 BK,BEv,OW,The Corpse
   is Mine . . . . . . . . . . . . . . . 700.00
3 RH,GC,JM, Vampire Strikes . . 550.00
4 Funeral of Horror . . . . . . . . . 550.00
5 Blackout at Midnight . . . . . . . 550.00
6 A-Bomb Picture . . . . . . . . . . . 550.00
7 JRo,The Ghost Hunter . . . . . . 550.00
8 BEv . . . . . . . . . . . . . . . . . . . 550.00
9 BEv(c),the Man in the Morgue  550.00
10 BEV(c),GT,What Happened
   to Harry . . . . . . . . . . . . . . . 550.00
11 BEv(c) . . . . . . . . . . . . . . . . 450.00
12 GT,MF . . . . . . . . . . . . . . . . 475.00
13 . . . . . . . . . . . . . . . . . . . . . 450.00
14 BEv(c),GT . . . . . . . . . . . . . 450.00
15 RH(c),EK. . . . . . . . . . . . . . 450.00
16 . . . . . . . . . . . . . . . . . . . . . 450.00
17 RH(c). . . . . . . . . . . . . . . . . 450.00
18 AW,DAy,GC . . . . . . . . . . . . 475.00
19 . . . . . . . . . . . . . . . . . . . . . 450.00
20 Electric Chair . . . . . . . . . . . 450.00
21 JF,MF,BP,Decapitation . . . . . 450.00
22 JF,MF . . . . . . . . . . . . . . . . 450.00
23 thru 27. . . . . . . . . . . . . . @400.00
28 . . . . . . . . . . . . . . . . . . . . . 350.00
29 thru 32. . . . . . . . . . . . . . @375.00
33 BEv . . . . . . . . . . . . . . . . . . 350.00
34 . . . . . . . . . . . . . . . . . . . . . 350.00
35 BEv,GC . . . . . . . . . . . . . . . 350.00
36 . . . . . . . . . . . . . . . . . . . . . 375.00
37 DW,BP,JR . . . . . . . . . . . . . 350.00
38 BP . . . . . . . . . . . . . . . . . . . 350.00
39 BK . . . . . . . . . . . . . . . . . . . 350.00
40 JM . . . . . . . . . . . . . . . . . . . 375.00
41 MD,BEv. . . . . . . . . . . . . . . 350.00
42 JeR . . . . . . . . . . . . . . . . . . 350.00
41 GC. . . . . . . . . . . . . . . . . . . 350.00
44 AW . . . . . . . . . . . . . . . . . . 350.00
45 SD . . . . . . . . . . . . . . . . . . . 325.00
46 RC,SD,JP . . . . . . . . . . . . . 325.00
47 DAy,BP . . . . . . . . . . . . . . . 325.00
48 BEv . . . . . . . . . . . . . . . . . . 350.00
49 GM,AT,DAy . . . . . . . . . . . . 350.00
50 JO,AW,GM . . . . . . . . . . . . 325.00
51 DAy,JO . . . . . . . . . . . . . . . 325.00
52 DAy . . . . . . . . . . . . . . . . . . 325.00
53 BEv . . . . . . . . . . . . . . . . . . 325.00
54 RC,Aug., 1957 . . . . . . . . . . 350.00

## MYSTICAL TALES

### Marvel Atlas, June, 1956

1 BEv,BP,JO,Say the Magical
   Words . . . . . . . . . . . . . . . . 600.00
2 BEv(c),JO,Black Blob . . . . . . 300.00
3 BEv(c),RC,Four Doors To . . . 325.00
4 BEv(c).The Condemned . . . . 325.00
5 AW,Meeting at Midnight . . . . . 350.00
6 BK,AT,He Hides in the Tower . 275.00
7 BEv,JF,JO,AT,FBe,The
   Haunted Tower . . . . . . . . . . 275.00
8 BK,SC, Stone Walls Can't
   Stop Him,Aug., 1957 . . . . . . 275.00

## MYSTIC COMICS

### Marvel Timely, March, 1940
### [1st Series]

1 ASh(c),SSh,O:Blue Blaze,Dynamic,
   Man,Flexo,B:Dakor the Magician,
   A:Zephyr Jones,3X's, Deep Sea,
   Demon,bondage(c). . . . . 22,000.00
2 ASh(c),B:The Invisible Man
   Mastermind,Blue Blaze . . . 6,500.00
3 ASh(c),O:Hercules . . . . . . . . 4,500.00
4 ASh(c),O:Thin Man,Black Widow
   E:Hercules,Blue Blazes,Dynamic
   Man,Flexo,Invisible Man. . . 4,800.00
5 ASh(c)O:The Black Marvel,
   Blazing Skull,Super Slave
   Terror,Sub-Earth Man . . . . 4,500.00
6 ASh(c),O:The Challenger,
   B:The Destroyer . . . . . . . . 5,500.00
7 S&K(c),B:The Witness,O:Davey
   and the Demon,E:The Black
   Widow,Hitler(c) . . . . . . . . 5,500.00
8 Bondage(c) . . . . . . . . . . . . 3,000.00
9 MSy,DRi,Hitler/Bondage(c) . 3,000.00
10 E:Challenger,Terror . . . . . . . 3,000.00

### Marvel, [2nd Series] Oct., 1944

1 SSh,B:The Angel,Human Torch,
   Destroyer,Terry Vance,
   Tommy Tyme,Bondage(c) . 3,200.00
2 E:Human Torch,Terry
   Vance,Bondage(c) . . . . . . . 1,600.00
3 E:The Angel,Tommy Tyme
   Bondage(c) . . . . . . . . . . . . 1,500.00
4 ASh(c),A:Young Allies
   Winter, 1944-45 . . . . . . . . . 1,500.00

## MYSTIC

### Marvel, [3rd Series], March, 1951

1 MSy,Strange Tree . . . . . . . . 1,700.00

2 MSy,Dark Dungeon . . . . . . . . 900.00
3 GC,Jaws of Creeping Death . . 850.00
4 BW,MSy,The Den of the
   Devil Bird . . . . . . . . . . . . . 1,500.00
5 MSy,Face . . . . . . . . . . . . . . 650.00
6 BW,She Wouldn't Stay Dead 1,500.00
7 GC,Untold Horror waits
   in the Tomb . . . . . . . . . . . . 650.00
8 DAy(c),BEv,GK,A Monster
   Among Us . . . . . . . . . . . . . 650.00
9 BEv . . . . . . . . . . . . . . . . . . 650.00
10 GC. . . . . . . . . . . . . . . . . . . 650.00
11 JR,The Black Gloves . . . . . . 600.00
12 GC. . . . . . . . . . . . . . . . . . . 600.00
13 In the Dark . . . . . . . . . . . . . 600.00
14 The Corpse and I . . . . . . . . . 600.00
15 GT,JR,House of Horror . . . . . 500.00
16 A Scream in the Dark . . . . . . 500.00
17 BEv,Behold the Vampire . . . . 500.00
18 BEv(c),The Russian Devil . . . 500.00
19 Swamp Girl . . . . . . . . . . . . . 500.00
20 RH(c). . . . . . . . . . . . . . . . . 500.00
21 BEv(c),GC. . . . . . . . . . . . . . 450.00
22 RH(c). . . . . . . . . . . . . . . . . 450.00
23 RH(c),RA,RMn,Chilling Tales . 450.00
24 GK,RMn,How Many Times Can
   You Die . . . . . . . . . . . . . . . 450.00
25 RH(c),RA,E.C.Swipe. . . . . . . 450.00
26 Severed Head(c). . . . . . . . . . 450.00
27 Who Walks with a Zombie . . . 350.00
28 DW,RMn(c),Not Enough Dead 350.00
29 SMo,RMn(c),The Unseen . . . . 350.00
30 RH(c),DW . . . . . . . . . . . . . . 350.00
31 SC,JKz,RMn(c). . . . . . . . . . . 350.00
32 The Survivor . . . . . . . . . . . . 350.00
33 thru 36. . . . . . . . . . . . . . @350.00
37 thru 51. . . . . . . . . . . . . . @325.00
52 WW,RC . . . . . . . . . . . . . . . 350.00
53 thru 57. . . . . . . . . . . . . . @325.00
58 thru 60. . . . . . . . . . . . . . @350.00
61 . . . . . . . . . . . . . . . . . . . . . 325.00

## MY STORY

### See: ZAGO, JUNGLE PRINCE

## MY TRUE LOVE

### Fox Features Syndicate, 1949

65 . . . . . . . . . . . . . . . . . . . . . . 175.00
66 . . . . . . . . . . . . . . . . . . . . . . 125.00
67 WW . . . . . . . . . . . . . . . . . . . 250.00
68 . . . . . . . . . . . . . . . . . . . . . . 125.00
69 PMo. . . . . . . . . . . . . . . . . . . 150.00

*Namora #1*
© Marvel Comics Group

*National Comics #33*
© Quality Comics Group

*Navy Combat #1*
© Marvel Comics Group

## NAMORA
**Marvel, Fall, 1948–Dec., 1948**
1 BEv,DR . . . . . . . . . . . . . . . . 3,500.00
2 BEv,A:Sub-Mariner,Blonde
  Phantom . . . . . . . . . . . . . 1,700.00
3 BEv,A:Sub-Mariner . . . . . . . 1,900.00

## NANCY AND SLUGGO
## See: SPARKLER COMICS

## NAPOLEON
## AND UNCLE ELBY
**Eastern Color Printing, 1942**
1 . . . . . . . . . . . . . . . . . . . . . . . 600.00

## NATIONAL COMICS
**Comics Magazines
(Quality Comics Group),
July, 1940**
1 GT,HcK,LF(c),B:Uncle Sam,
  Wonder Boy,Merlin the Magician,
  Cyclone, Kid Patrol,Sally O'Neil-
  Police-woman, Pen Miller,
  Prop Powers,PaulBunyan 10,000.00
2 WE,GT,HcK,LF&RC(c) . . . . . 4,500.00
3 GT,HcK,LF,WE&RC(c) . . . . . 3,000.00
4 GT,HcK,LF&RC(c),E:Cyclone;
  Torpedo Islands of Death . . 3,400.00
5 GT,LF&RC(c),B:Quicksilver;
  O:Uncle Sam . . . . . . . . . . 3,000.00
6 GT,LF&RC(c) . . . . . . . . . . . 2,500.00
7 GT,LF&RC(c) . . . . . . . . . . . 3,500.00
8 GT,LF&RC(c) . . . . . . . . . . . 2,500.00
9 JCo,LF&RC(c) . . . . . . . . . . 2,500.00
10 RC,JCo,LF&RC(c) . . . . . . . 2,500.00
11 RC,JCo,LF&RC(c) . . . . . . . 2,500.00
12 RC,JCo,LF&RC(c) . . . . . . . 1,800.00
13 RC,JCo,LF,LF&RC(c). . . . . 1,600.00
14 RC,JCo,LF,PG,LF&RC(c). . . 1,800.00
15 RC,JCo,LF,PG,LF&RC(c). . . 1,800.00
16 RC,JCo,LF,PG,LF&RC(c). . . 1,800.00
17 RC,JCo,LF,PG,LF&RC(c). . . 2,000.00
18 JCo,LF,PG,LF&RC(c),
  Pearl Harbor. . . . . . . . . . . 2,700.00
19 JCo,LF,PG,RC(c),The Black
  Fog Mystery . . . . . . . . . . 2,000.00
20 JCo,LF,PG,LF&RC(c) . . . . . 2,000.00
21 LF,JCo,PG,LF(c). . . . . . . . . 2,000.00
22 JCo,LF,PG,FGu,GFx,LF(c),
  E:Jack & Jill,Pen Miller,
  Paul Bunyan. . . . . . . . . . . 2,000.00

23 JCo,PG,FGu,GFx,AMc,LF
  & GFx(c),B:The Unknown,
  Destroyer 171. . . . . . . . . . 2,200.00
24 JCo,PG,RC,AMc,FGu,
  GFx,RC(c) . . . . . . . . . . . . 2,200.00
25 AMc,RC,JCo,PG,FGu,
  GFx,RC(c) . . . . . . . . . . . . 1,500.00
26 AMc,Jco,RC,PG,RC(c),
  E:Prop Powers,WonderBoy 1,500.00
27 JCo,AMc . . . . . . . . . . . . . . 1,500.00
28 JCo,AMc . . . . . . . . . . . . . . 1,500.00
29 JCo,O:The Unknown;U.Sam
  V:Dr. Dirge . . . . . . . . . . . . 1,600.00
30 JCo,RC(c) . . . . . . . . . . . . . 1,200.00
31 JCo,RC(c) . . . . . . . . . . . . . 1,400.00
32 JCo,RC(c) . . . . . . . . . . . . . 1,400.00
33 JCo,GFx,RC(c),B:Chic Carter;
  U.Sam V:Boss Spring. . . . . 1,400.00
34 JCo,GFx,U.Sam V:Big John
  Fales. . . . . . . . . . . . . . . . . 1,400.00
35 JCo,GFx,E:Kid Patrol. . . . . . 1,200.00
36 JCo. . . . . . . . . . . . . . . . . . . 1,200.00
37 JCo,FGu,A:The Vagabond. . 1,200.00
38 JCo,FGu,Boat of the Dead . 1,200.00
39 JCo,FGu,Hitler(c);U.Sam
  V:The Black Market . . . . . 1,700.00
40 JCo,FGu,U.Sam V:The
  Syndicate of Crime . . . . . . . 750.00
41 JCo,FGu . . . . . . . . . . . . . . . 750.00
42 JCo,FGu,JCo(c),B:The Barker 600.00
43 JCo,FGu,JCo(c) . . . . . . . . . . 600.00
44 JCo,FGu . . . . . . . . . . . . . . . 600.00
45 JCo,FGu,E:Merlin Magician . 600.00
46 JCo,JCo(c),Murder is no Joke 600.00
47 JCo,JCo(c),E:Chic Carter . . . 600.00
48 JCo,O:The Whistler . . . . . . . 600.00
49 JCo,JCo(c),A Corpse
  for a Cannonball . . . . . . . . . 600.00
50 JCo,JCo(c),V:Rocks Myzer . . 600.00
51 JCo,BWa,JCo(c),
  A:Sally O'Neil . . . . . . . . . . . 700.00
52 JCo,A Carnival of Laughs. . . 500.00
53 PG,V:Scramolo . . . . . . . . . . 500.00
54 PG,V:Raz-Ma-Taz . . . . . . . . 500.00
55 JCo,AMc,V:The Hawk. . . . . . 500.00
56 GFx,JCo,AMc,V:The Grifter . . 500.00
57 GFx,JCo,AMc,V:Witch Doctor. 500.00
58 GFz,JCo,AMc,Talking Animals 500.00
59 GFx,JCo,AMc,V:The Birdman. 500.00
60 GFx,JCo,AMc,V:Big Ed Grew  500.00
61 GFx,AMc,Trouble Comes in
  Small Packages. . . . . . . . . . 400.00
62 GFx,AMc,V:Crocodile Man . . 400.00
63 GFx,AMc,V:Bearded Lady . . . 400.00
64 GFx,V:The Human Fly . . . . . 400.00
65 GFx,GFx(c)V:The King . . . . . 400.00

66 GFx,GFx(c)V:The Man Who
  Hates the Circus . . . . . . . . . 400.00
67 GFx,Gfx(c),A:Quicksilver;
  V:Ali Ben Riff Raff . . . . . . . . 400.00
68 GFx,GFx(c),V:Leo theLionMan 400.00
69 GFx,Gfx(c),A:Percy the
  Powerful. . . . . . . . . . . . . . . . 400.00
70 GFx,GFx(c),Barker Tires
  of the Big Top . . . . . . . . . . . 400.00
71 PG,GFx(c),V:SpellbinderSmith 400.00
72 PG,GFx(c),The Oldest Man
  in the World . . . . . . . . . . . . . 400.00
73 PG,GFx(c),V:A CountrySlicker 400.00
74 PG,GFx(c),V:Snake Oil Sam. . 400.00
75 PG,GFx(c),Barker Breaks the
  Bank at Monte Marlo;Nov'49. 400.00

## NATURE BOY
## See: DANNY BLAZE

## NAVY ACTION
**Marvel, Aug., 1954**
1 BP,US Navy War Stories . . . . 225.00
2 TLn,Navy(c) . . . . . . . . . . . . . 125.00
3 BEv . . . . . . . . . . . . . . . . . . . 100.00
4 and 5 . . . . . . . . . . . . . . . . . @100.00
6 JH(c) . . . . . . . . . . . . . . . . . . 100.00
7 MD,JMn . . . . . . . . . . . . . . . . 100.00
8 JMn,GC. . . . . . . . . . . . . . . . . 100.00
9 thru 15 . . . . . . . . . . . . . . . . @100.00
16 BEv(c) . . . . . . . . . . . . . . . . . 100.00
17 MD,BEv(c). . . . . . . . . . . . . . 100.00
18 Aug., 1957. . . . . . . . . . . . . . 100.00

## NAVY COMBAT
**Marvel Atlas, June, 1955**
1 DH,JMn(c),B:Torpedo Taylor . . 225.00
2 DH . . . . . . . . . . . . . . . . . . . . 125.00
3 DH,BEv . . . . . . . . . . . . . . . . 100.00
4 DH . . . . . . . . . . . . . . . . . . . . 100.00
5 DH . . . . . . . . . . . . . . . . . . . . 100.00
6 JMn,A:Battleship Burke . . . . . 100.00
7 thru 10 . . . . . . . . . . . . . . . . @100.00
11 MD,GC,JMn . . . . . . . . . . . . 100.00
12 RC. . . . . . . . . . . . . . . . . . . . 125.00
13 GT . . . . . . . . . . . . . . . . . . . . 100.00
14 AT,GT . . . . . . . . . . . . . . . . . 100.00
15 GT . . . . . . . . . . . . . . . . . . . . 100.00
16 . . . . . . . . . . . . . . . . . . . . . . 100.00
17 AW,AT,JMn . . . . . . . . . . . . . 110.00
18 . . . . . . . . . . . . . . . . . . . . . . 100.00
19 . . . . . . . . . . . . . . . . . . . . . . 100.00
20 BEv,BP,AW,Oct., 1958 . . . . . 110.00

**Na**

*Negro Heroes #2*
© *National Urban League*

*Nellie the Nurse #1*
© *Marvel Comics Group*

*New Fun Comics #2*
© *DC Comics*

## NAVY HEROES
**Almanac Publ. Co., 1945**
1 Propaganda . . . . . . . . . . . . . 135.00

## NAVY PATROL
**Key Publications, 1955**
1 . . . . . . . . . . . . . . . . . . . . . . 125.00
2 . . . . . . . . . . . . . . . . . . . . . . 100.00
3 . . . . . . . . . . . . . . . . . . . . . . 100.00
4 . . . . . . . . . . . . . . . . . . . . . . 100.00

## NAVY TALES
**Marvel Atlas, Jan., 1957**
1 BEv(c),BP,Torpedoes . . . . . . 175.00
2 AW,RC,JMn(c),One Hour
  to Live . . . . . . . . . . . . . . . . 175.00
3 JSe(c) . . . . . . . . . . . . . . . . . 150.00
4 JSe(c),GC,JSt,RC,July, 1957 . 150.00

## NAVY TASK FORCE
**Stanmor Publ./
Aragon Publ., 1953**
1 . . . . . . . . . . . . . . . . . . . . . . 150.00
2 . . . . . . . . . . . . . . . . . . . . . . 100.00
3 . . . . . . . . . . . . . . . . . . . . . . 100.00
4 . . . . . . . . . . . . . . . . . . . . . . 100.00
5 . . . . . . . . . . . . . . . . . . . . . . 100.00
6 . . . . . . . . . . . . . . . . . . . . . . 100.00
7 . . . . . . . . . . . . . . . . . . . . . . 100.00
8 . . . . . . . . . . . . . . . . . . . . . . 100.00

## NEBBS, THE
**Dell Publishing Co., 1941**
1 rep. . . . . . . . . . . . . . . . . . . . 250.00

## NEGRO HEROES
**National Urban League, 1947**
1 . . . . . . . . . . . . . . . . . . . . . 1,500.00
2 Jackie Robinson . . . . . . . . . 2,000.00

## NEGRO ROMANCE
**Fawcett Publications,
June, 1950**
1 GE,Ph(c), Love's Decoy . . . . 1,600.00
2 GE,Ph(c), A Tragic Vow . . . . 1,200.00
3 GE,Ph(c), My Love
  Betrayed Me . . . . . . . . . . 1,200.00
**Charlton Comics**
4 Rep.FawcettEd.#2;May,1955 1,000.00

## NELLIE THE NURSE
**Marvel Atlas, 1945**
1 Beach(c) . . . . . . . . . . . . . . . 500.00
2 Nellie's Date(c) . . . . . . . . . . 250.00
3 Swimming Pool(c) . . . . . . . . 175.00
4 Roller Coaster(c) . . . . . . . . . 175.00
5 Hospital(c),HK,Hey Look . . . . 175.00
6 Bedside Manner(c) . . . . . . . . 175.00
7 Comic book(c)A:Georgie . . . . 175.00
8 Hospital(c),A:Georgie . . . . . . 175.00
9 BW,Nellie/Swing(c)A:Millie . . 175.00
10 Bathing Suit(c),A:Millie . . . . . 175.00
11 HK,Hey Look . . . . . . . . . . . . 200.00
12 HK,Giggles 'n' Grins . . . . . . . 175.00
13 HK. . . . . . . . . . . . . . . . . . . . 125.00
14 HK . . . . . . . . . . . . . . . . . . . . 150.00
15 HK. . . . . . . . . . . . . . . . . . . . 150.00
16 HK. . . . . . . . . . . . . . . . . . . . 150.00
17 HK.A:Annie Oakley . . . . . . . . 150.00
18 HK. . . . . . . . . . . . . . . . . . . . 150.00
19 . . . . . . . . . . . . . . . . . . . . . . 125.00
20 . . . . . . . . . . . . . . . . . . . . . . 125.00
21 . . . . . . . . . . . . . . . . . . . . . . 100.00
22 . . . . . . . . . . . . . . . . . . . . . . 100.00
23 . . . . . . . . . . . . . . . . . . . . . . 100.00
24 . . . . . . . . . . . . . . . . . . . . . . 100.00
25 . . . . . . . . . . . . . . . . . . . . . . 100.00
26 . . . . . . . . . . . . . . . . . . . . . . 100.00
27 . . . . . . . . . . . . . . . . . . . . . . 100.00
28 HK,Rusty Reprint . . . . . . . . . 100.00
29 thru 35. . . . . . . . . . . . . . . . @100.00
36 Oct., 1952 . . . . . . . . . . . . . . 100.00

## NEW ADVENTURES
## OF CHARLIE CHAN
**DC Comics, 1958**
1 GK,SGe . . . . . . . . . . . . . . . . 900.00
2 . . . . . . . . . . . . . . . . . . . . . . 600.00
3 SGe . . . . . . . . . . . . . . . . . . . 500.00
4 SGe . . . . . . . . . . . . . . . . . . . 500.00
5 SGe . . . . . . . . . . . . . . . . . . . 500.00
6 SGe . . . . . . . . . . . . . . . . . . . 500.00

## NEW BOOK OF COMICS
**DC Comics, 1937**
1 Dr.Occult. . . . . . . . . . . . . . 20,000.00
2 Dr.Occult. . . . . . . . . . . . . . 10,000.00

## NEW COMICS
**DC Comics, 1935**
1 . . . . . . . . . . . . . . . . . . . . 30,000.00
2 . . . . . . . . . . . . . . . . . . . . 14,000.00

3 thru 6 . . . . . . . . . . . . . . @9,000.00
7 thru 11 . . . . . . . . . . . . . @8,000.00
**Becomes:**

## NEW ADVENTURE
## COMICS
**DC Comics, Jan., 1937**
12 S&S . . . . . . . . . . . . . . . . . 7,500.00
13 thru 20 . . . . . . . . . . . . . @6,000.00
21 . . . . . . . . . . . . . . . . . . . . . 5,000.00
22 thru 31 . . . . . . . . . . . . . @4,000.00
**Becomes:**

## ADVENTURE COMICS

## NEW FUN COMICS
**DC Comics, Feb., 1935**
1 B:Oswald the Rabbit,
  Jack Woods . . . . . . . . . . . 60,000.00
2 . . . . . . . . . . . . . . . . . . . . 30,000.00
3 . . . . . . . . . . . . . . . . . . . . 15,000.00
4 . . . . . . . . . . . . . . . . . . . . 15,000.00
5 . . . . . . . . . . . . . . . . . . . . 15,000.00
6 S&S,B:Dr.Occult,
  Henri Duval. . . . . . . . . . . 30,000.00
**Becomes:**

## MORE FUN COMICS
**DC Comics, Jan., 1936**
7 S&S,WK . . . . . . . . . . . . . . 17,000.00
8 S&S,WK . . . . . . . . . . . . . . 15,000.00
9 S&S,E:Henri Duval . . . . . . . 18,000.00
10 S&S . . . . . . . . . . . . . . . . . 10,000.00
11 S&S,B:Calling all Girls . . . . 10,000.00
12 S&S . . . . . . . . . . . . . . . . . 10,000.00
13 S&S . . . . . . . . . . . . . . . . . 10,000.00
14 S&S,Color,Dr.Occult. . . . . . 19,000.00
15 S&S . . . . . . . . . . . . . . . . . 10,000.00
16 S&S,Christmas(c) . . . . . . . 10,000.00
17 S&S . . . . . . . . . . . . . . . . . . 9,000.00
18 S&S . . . . . . . . . . . . . . . . . . 3,500.00
19 S&S . . . . . . . . . . . . . . . . . . 3,500.00
20 HcK,S&S . . . . . . . . . . . . . . 3,500.00
21 S&S . . . . . . . . . . . . . . . . . . 3,800.00
22 S&S . . . . . . . . . . . . . . . . . . 3,800.00
23 S&S . . . . . . . . . . . . . . . . . . 3,800.00
24 S&S . . . . . . . . . . . . . . . . . . 3,800.00
25 S&S . . . . . . . . . . . . . . . . . . 3,500.00
26 S&S . . . . . . . . . . . . . . . . . . 3,200.00
27 S&S . . . . . . . . . . . . . . . . . . 3,200.00
28 S&S . . . . . . . . . . . . . . . . . . 3,000.00
29 S&S . . . . . . . . . . . . . . . . . . 3,000.00
30 S&S . . . . . . . . . . . . . . . . . . 3,000.00
31 S&S . . . . . . . . . . . . . . . . . . 3,200.00
32 S&S,E:Dr. Occult . . . . . . . . 3,000.00

**Ne**

---

All comics prices listed are for *Near Mint* condition.                **Page 205**

*More Fun #41*
© DC Comics

*More Fun #101*
© DC Comics

*Nickel Comics #6*
© Fawcett Publications

33 . . . . . . . . . . . . . . . . . . . . . . . 3,000.00
34 . . . . . . . . . . . . . . . . . . . . . . . 3,000.00
35 . . . . . . . . . . . . . . . . . . . . . . . 3,000.00
36 B:Masked Ranger . . . . . . . 3,000.00
37 thru 40 . . . . . . . . . . . . . . @4,500.00
41 E:Masked Ranger . . . . . . . . 6,200.00
42 thru 50 . . . . . . . . . . . . . . @3,500.00
51 I:The Spectre . . . . . . . . . . . 9,000.00
52 O:The Spectre,pt.1,
  E:Wing Brady . . . . . . . . 135,000.00
53 O:The Spectre,pt.2,
  B:Capt.Desmo . . . . . . . . 80,000.00
54 E:King Carter,Spectre(c) . . 25,000.00
55 I:Dr.Fate,E:Bulldog Martin,
  Spectre(c) . . . . . . . . . . . 30,000.00
56 B:Congo Bill,Dr.Fate(c) . . 12,000.00
57 Spectre(c) . . . . . . . . . . . . 10,000.00
58 Spectre(c) . . . . . . . . . . . . 10,000.00
59 A:Spectre . . . . . . . . . . . . 10,000.00
60 Spectre(c) . . . . . . . . . . . . 10,000.00
61 Spectre(c) . . . . . . . . . . . . 10,000.00
62 Spectre(c) . . . . . . . . . . . . . 7,000.00
63 Spectre(c),E:St.Bob Neal . . 7,000.00
64 Spectre(c),B:Lance Larkin . . 7,000.00
65 Spectre(c) . . . . . . . . . . . . . 7,000.00
66 Spectre(c) . . . . . . . . . . . . . 7,000.00
67 Spectre(c),O:Dr. Fate,
  E:Congo Bill,Biff Bronson . 12,000.00
68 Dr.Fate(c),B:Clip Carson . . . 7,000.00
69 Dr.Fate(c) . . . . . . . . . . . . . 7,000.00
70 Dr.Fate(c),E:Lance Larkin . . 7,000.00
71 Dr.Fate(c),I:Johnny Quick . 10,000.00
72 Dr. Fate has Smaller Helmet,
  E:Sgt. Carey,Sgt.O'Malley . 7,000.00
73 Dr.Fate(c),I:Aquaman,Green
  Arrow,Speedy . . . . . . . . . 27,000.00
74 Dr.Fate(c),A:Aquaman . . . . . 7,500.00
75 Dr.Fate(c) . . . . . . . . . . . . . 7,000.00
76 Dr.Fate(c),MMe,E:Clip Carson,
  B:Johnny Quick . . . . . . . . . 7,000.00
77 MMe,Green Arrow(c) . . . . . . 7,000.00
78 MMe,Green Arrow(c) . . . . . . 7,000.00
79 MMe,Green Arrow(c) . . . . . . 7,000.00
80 MMe,Green Arrow(c) . . . . . . 4,500.00
81 MMe,Green Arrow(c) . . . . . . 5,000.00
82 MMe,Green Arrow(c) . . . . . . 5,000.00
83 MMe,Green Arrow(c) . . . . . . 5,000.00
84 MMe,Green Arrow(c) . . . . . . 6,000.00
85 MMe,Green Arrow(c) . . . . . . 3,500.00
86 MMe . . . . . . . . . . . . . . . . 3,500.00
87 MMe,E:Radio Squad . . . . . . 3,500.00
88 MMe,Green Arrow(c) . . . . . . 3,500.00
89 MMe,O:Gr.Arrow&Speedy . . 3,600.00
90 MMe,Green Arrow(c) . . . . . . 5,000.00
91 MMe,Green Arrow(c) . . . . . . 3,000.00
92 MMe,Green Arrow(c) . . . . . . 3,000.00

93 MMe,B:Dover & Clover . . . . 4,000.00
94 MMe,Green Arrow(c) . . . . . . 2,500.00
95 MMe,Green Arrow(c) . . . . . . 2,500.00
96 MMe,Green Arrow(c) . . . . . . 2,500.00
97 MMe,JKu,E:Johnny Quick . . 3,200.00
98 E:Dr. Fate . . . . . . . . . . . . . 3,700.00
99 Green Arrow(c) . . . . . . . . . 3,500.00
100 Anniversary Issue . . . . . . . 3,500.00
101 O&I:Superboy,
  E:The Spectre . . . . . . . . 17,000.00
102 A:Superboy . . . . . . . . . . . 4,000.00
103 A:Superboy . . . . . . . . . . . 3,500.00
104 Superboy(c) . . . . . . . . . . . 3,000.00
105 Superboy(c) . . . . . . . . . . . 3,000.00
106 . . . . . . . . . . . . . . . . . . . 3,000.00
107 E:Superboy . . . . . . . . . . . 3,000.00
108 A:Genius Jones,Genius
  Meets Genius . . . . . . . . . . . 800.00
109 A:Genius Jones, The
  Disappearing Deposits . . . . 800.00
110 A:Genius Jones, Birds,
  Brains and Burglary . . . . . . . 800.00
111 A:Genius Jones, Jeepers
  Creepers . . . . . . . . . . . . . . . 800.00
112 A:Genius Jones, The
  Tell-Tale Tornado . . . . . . . . . 800.00
113 A:Genius Jones, Clocks
  and Shocks . . . . . . . . . . . . . 800.00
114 A:Genius Jones, The
  Milky Way . . . . . . . . . . . . . . 800.00
115 A:Genius Jones,Foolish
  Questions . . . . . . . . . . . . . . 800.00
116 A:Genius Jones,Palette
  For Plunder . . . . . . . . . . . . . 800.00
117 A:Genius Jones,Battle of
  the Pretzel Benders . . . . . . . 800.00
118 A:Genius Jones, The
  Sinister Siren . . . . . . . . . . . . 800.00
119 A:Genius Jones,A
  Perpetual Jackpot . . . . . . . . 800.00
120 A:Genius Jones,The Man
  in the Moon . . . . . . . . . . . . . 800.00
121 A:Genius Jones,The
  Mayor Goes Haywire . . . . . . 800.00
122 A:Genius Jones,When Thug-
  Hood Was In Floor . . . . . . . . 800.00
123 A:Genius Jones,Hi Diddle Diddle,
  the Cat and the Fiddle . . . . . . 800.00
124 A:Genius Jones,
  The Zany Zoo . . . . . . . . . . . 800.00
125 Genius Jones,
  Impossible But True . . . . . . 1,500.00
126 A:Genius Jones,The Case
  of the Gravy Spots . . . . . . . . 500.00
127 Nov.–Dec., 1947 . . . . . . . 1,000.00

## NEW FUNNIES
## See: FUNNIES

## NEW ROMANCES
**Standard Comics,**
**May, 1951**
5 Ph(c), The Blame I Bore . . . . . 175.00
6 Ph(c), No Wife Was I . . . . . . . 150.00
7 Ph(c), My Runaway Heart,
  Ray Miland . . . . . . . . . . . . . 125.00
8 Ph(c) . . . . . . . . . . . . . . . . . 125.00
9 Ph(c) . . . . . . . . . . . . . . . . . 125.00
10 ATh,Ph(c) . . . . . . . . . . . . . 150.00
11 ATh,Ph(c) of Elizabeth Taylor . 250.00
12 Ph(c) . . . . . . . . . . . . . . . . 125.00
13 Ph(c) . . . . . . . . . . . . . . . . 125.00
14 ATh,Ph(c) . . . . . . . . . . . . . 150.00
15 Ph(c) . . . . . . . . . . . . . . . . 125.00
16 ATh,Ph(c) . . . . . . . . . . . . . 150.00
17 Ath, . . . . . . . . . . . . . . . . . 150.00
18 and 19 . . . . . . . . . . . . . . @125.00
20 GT, . . . . . . . . . . . . . . . . . 125.00
21 April, 1954 . . . . . . . . . . . . . 125.00

## NEW YORK
## WORLD'S FAIR
**DC Comics, 1939–40**
1 1939 . . . . . . . . . . . . . . . . 30,000.00
2 1940 . . . . . . . . . . . . . . . . 17,000.00

## NICKEL COMICS
**Dell Publishing Co., 1938**
1 Bobby & Chip . . . . . . . . . . . 1,000.00

## NICKEL COMICS
**Fawcett Publications,**
**May, 1940**
1 JaB(c),O&I: Bulletman . . . . . 6,000.00
2 JaB(c), . . . . . . . . . . . . . . . 1,800.00
3 JaB(c), . . . . . . . . . . . . . . . 1,400.00
4 JaB(c), B: Red Gaucho . . . . 1,300.00
5 CCB(c),Bondage(c) . . . . . . . 1,300.00
6 and 7 CCB(c) . . . . . . . . . @1,200.00
8 CCB(c),Aug. 23, 1940,
  World's Fair . . . . . . . . . . . 1,300.00

## NICK HALIDAY
**Argo, 1956**
1 Strip reprints . . . . . . . . . . . . . 150.00

Nightmare #2
© Ziff-Davis Publishing Co.

Nutty Comics #6
© Harvey Publications

Nyoka The Jungle Girl #2
© Fawcett Publications

## NIGHTMARE

### See: WEIRD HORRORS

## NIGHTMARE

**Ziff-Davis Publishing Co., 1952**
1 EK,GT,P(c),The Corpse That
  Wouldn't Stay Dead ....... 750.00
2 EK,P(c),Vampire Mermaid ... 500.00
**St. John Publishing Co.**
3 EK,P(c),The Quivering Brain . 400.00
4 P(c),1953 ............... 350.00

## NORTHWEST MOUNTIES

**Jubilee Publications/
St. John Publ. Co.,
Oct., 1948**
1 MB,BLb(c),Rose of the Yukon 600.00
2 MB,BLb(c),A:Ventrilo ....... 500.00
3 MB, Bondage(c) ........... 550.00
4 MB(c),A:Blue Monk,July'49 . 450.00

## NO TIME
## FOR SERGEANTS

**Dell Publishing Co., 1958**
1 Ph(c) .................... 175.00
2 Ph(c) .................... 100.00
3 Ph(c) .................... 100.00

## NURSERY RHYMES

**Ziff-Davis Publishing Co., 1950**
1 How John Came Clean ..... 175.00
2 The Old Woman Who
  Lived in a Shoe ......... 175.00

## NUTS!

**Premere Comics Group,
March, 1954**
1 ......................... 350.00
2 ......................... 250.00
3 Mention of "Reefers" ....... 275.00
4 ......................... 250.00
5 Captain Marvel Spoof;Nov.'54 250.00

## NUTSY SQUIRREL

**DC Comics, Sept.–Oct., 1954**
61 SM...................... 125.00
62 thru 71................. @100.00
72 Nov., 1957............... 100.00

## NUTTY COMICS

**Harvey Publications, 1945**
1 BW,Funny animal.......... 125.00
2 ......................... 125.00
3 ......................... 110.00
4 ......................... 100.00
5 ......................... 100.00
6 ......................... 100.00
7 ......................... 100.00
8 ......................... 100.00

## NUTTY COMICS

**Fawcett Publications,
Winter, 1946**
1 (fa),F:Capt. Kid,Richard Richard,
  Joe Miller...Among others ... 250.00

## NUTTY LIFE
### See: PHANTOM LADY

## NYOKA THE
## JUNGLE GIRL

**Fawcett Publications,
Winter, 1945**
1 Bondage(c);Partial Ph(c) of
  Kay Aldridge as Nyoka ..... 750.00
2 ......................... 400.00
3 ......................... 400.00
4 Bondage(c) .............. 500.00
5 Barbacosi Madness;
  Bondage(c) .............. 500.00
6 ......................... 275.00
7 North Pole Jungle;
  Bondage(c) .............. 400.00
8 Bondage(c) .............. 400.00
9 ......................... 225.00
10 ......................... 225.00
11 Danger! Death! in an
  Unexplored Jungle ....... 225.00
12 ......................... 200.00
13 The Human Leopards....... 225.00
14 The Mad Witch Doctor;
  Bondage(c) .............. 400.00
15 Sacred Goat of Kristan..... 200.00
16 BK,The Vultures of Kalahari . . 225.00
17 BK ...................... 225.00
18 BK,The Art of Murder ...... 225.00
19 The Elephant Battle ....... 225.00
20 Explosive Volcano Action ... 225.00
21 ......................... 150.00
22 The Weird Monsters ....... 150.00
23 Danger in Duplicate ....... 150.00

24 The Human Jaguar;
  Bondage(c) .............. 400.00
25 Hand Colored Ph(c) ....... 135.00
26 A Jungle Stampede........ 135.00
27 Adventure Laden......... 135.00
28 The Human Statues of
  the Jungle .............. 135.00
29 Ph(c) .................... 135.00
30 Ph(c) .................... 135.00
31 thru 40 Ph(c) ........... @125.00
41 thru 50 Ph(c) ........... @135.00
51 thru 59 Ph(c)............ @100.00
60 Ph(c) ................... 100.00
61 Ph(c),The Sacred Sword of
  the Jungle .............. 100.00
62 & 63 Ph(c)............. @100.00
64 Ph(c), The Jungle Idol .... 100.00
65 Ph(c).................... 100.00
66 Ph(c).................... 100.00
67 Ph(c), The Sky Man ....... 100.00
68 thru 74 Ph(c).......... @100.00
75 Ph(c), The Jungle Myth
  of Terror................ 100.00
76 Ph(c) ................... 100.00
77 Ph(c),The Phantoms of the
  Elephant Graveyard;Jun'53. . 100.00

## NYOKA, JUNGLE GIRL

**Charlton Comics, 1955–57**
14 ......................... 125.00
15 ......................... 100.00
16 ......................... 100.00
17 ......................... 100.00
18 ......................... 100.00
19 ......................... 100.00
20 ......................... 100.00
21 ......................... 100.00
22 ......................... 100.00

## OAKY DOAKS

**Eastern Color Printing Co.,
July, 1942**
1 Humor Oriented .......... 450.00

## OBIE

**Food Store Comics, 1953**
1 ......................... 100.00

## OFFICIAL TRUE
## CRIME CASES

**Marvel, Fall, 1947**
24 (1)SSh(c),The Grinning Killer . 275.00

---

# STANDARD GUIDE TO GOLDEN AGE COMICS

*Okay Comics #1*
*© United Features Syndicate*

*Operation Peril #4*
*© American Comics Group*

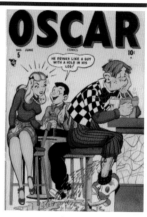

*Oscar #5*
*© Marvel Comics Group*

25 (2)She Made Me a Killer,HK . . 225.00
Becomes:

## ALL-TRUE CRIME
### Marvel, 1948
26 SSh(c),The True Story of Wilbur
  Underhill . . . . . . . . . . . . . . 400.00
27 Electric Chair(c),Robert Mais . 300.00
28 Cops V:Gangsters(c) . . . . . . . 125.00
29 Cops V:Gangsters(c) . . . . . . . 125.00
30 He Picked a Murderous Mind . 125.00
31 Hitchiking Thugs(c) . . . . . . . . 125.00
32 Jewel Thieves(c). . . . . . . . . . . 125.00
33 The True Story of Dinton
  Phillips . . . . . . . . . . . . . . . . 125.00
34 Case of the Killers Revenge . . 125.00
35 Ph(c),Date with Danger . . . . . 125.00
36 Ph(c) . . . . . . . . . . . . . . . . . . . 125.00
37 Ph(c),Story of Robert Marone . 125.00
38 Murder Weapon,Nick Maxim . 125.00
39 Story of Vince Vanderee . . . . . 125.00
40 . . . . . . . . . . . . . . . . . . . . . . . 125.00
41 Lou 'Lucky' Raven . . . . . . . . . 125.00
42 BK,Baby Face Nelson. . . . . . . 150.00
43 Doc Channing Paulson. . . . . . 125.00
44 Murder in the Big House. . . . . 125.00
45 While the City Sleeps . . . . . . . 125.00
46 . . . . . . . . . . . . . . . . . . . . . . . 125.00
47 Gangster Terry Craig . . . . . . . 125.00
48 GT,They Vanish By Night . . . . 125.00
49 BK,Squeeze Play . . . . . . . . . . 150.00
50 Shoot to Kill. . . . . . . . . . . . . . 125.00
51 Panic in the Big House. . . . . . . 125.00
52 Prison Break, Sept., 1952. . . . 125.00

## OH, BROTHER!
### Stanhall Publications, Jan., 1953
1 Bill Williams-a . . . . . . . . . . . 125.00
2 thru 5 . . . . . . . . . . . . . . . . . @100.00

## OKAY COMICS
### United Features Syndicate, 1940
1 . . . . . . . . . . . . . . . . . . . . . . . 600.00

## OK COMICS
### United Features Syndicate, July, 1940
1 B:Pal Peyton,Little Giant, Phantom
  Knight,Sunset Smith,Teller Twins,
  Don Ramon, Jerrry Sly,Kip Jaxon,
  Leatherneck,Ulysses . . . . . 1,000.00
2 Oct., 1940 . . . . . . . . . . . . . 1,100.00

## OKLAHOMA KID
### Ajax/Farrell Publ., 1957
1 . . . . . . . . . . . . . . . . . . . . . . . 150.00
2 . . . . . . . . . . . . . . . . . . . . . . . 125.00
3 . . . . . . . . . . . . . . . . . . . . . . . 125.00
4 . . . . . . . . . . . . . . . . . . . . . . . 125.00

## 100 PAGES OF COMICS
### Dell Publishing Co., 1937
101 Alley Oop,OG,Wash Tubbs,
  Tom Mix,Dan Dunn. . . . . . 2,000.00

## ON THE AIR
### NBC Network Comics, 1947
1 Giveaway, no cover . . . . . . . . 275.00

## ON THE SPOT
### Fawcett Publications, Autumn, 1948
N# Bondage(c),PrettyBoyFloyd . . 450.00

## OPERATION PERIL
### American Comics Group (Michel Publ.), Oct.–Nov., 1950
1 LSt,OW,OW(c),B:TyphoonTyler,
  DannyDanger,TimeTravellers 450.00
2 OW,OW(c),War (c). . . . . . . . . 275.00
3 OW,OW(c),Horror . . . . . . . . . 250.00
4 OW,OW(c), Flying Saucers . . . 250.00
5 OW,OW(c), Science Fiction. . . 250.00
6 OW, Tyr. Rex . . . . . . . . . . . . . 250.00
7 OW,OW(c),Sabretooth. . . . . . . 250.00
8 OW,OW(c) . . . . . . . . . . . . . . . 225.00
9 OW,OW(c) . . . . . . . . . . . . . . . 225.00
10 OW,OW(c),science fiction. . . 225.00
11 OW,OW(c), War . . . . . . . . . . 225.00
12 OW,OW(c),E:Time Travellers . 225.00
13 OW,OW(c),War Stories . . . . . 150.00
14 OW,OW(c),War Stories . . . . . 150.00
15 OW,OW(c),War Stories . . . . . 150.00
16 OW,OW(c),April–May,1953,
  War Stories . . . . . . . . . . . . . 150.00

## OSCAR COMICS
### Marvel USA Comics, 1947–49 (FUNNY TUNES spin-off)
1 (24) . . . . . . . . . . . . . . . . . . . . 200.00
2 (25) BW,HK,Hey Look . . . . . . 250.00
3 . . . . . . . . . . . . . . . . . . . . . . . 135.00
4 . . . . . . . . . . . . . . . . . . . . . . . 135.00

5 . . . . . . . . . . . . . . . . . . . . . . . 135.00
6 . . . . . . . . . . . . . . . . . . . . . . . 135.00
7 . . . . . . . . . . . . . . . . . . . . . . . 135.00
8 . . . . . . . . . . . . . . . . . . . . . . . 135.00
9 . . . . . . . . . . . . . . . . . . . . . . . 135.00
10 HK . . . . . . . . . . . . . . . . . . . . 175.00
Becomes:

## AWFUL OSCAR
### Marvel USA Comics, 1949
11 . . . . . . . . . . . . . . . . . . . . . . 125.00
12 . . . . . . . . . . . . . . . . . . . . . . 125.00
Becomes:

## OSCAR
13 . . . . . . . . . . . . . . . . . . . . . . 135.00

## OUR ARMY AT WAR
### DC Comics, Aug., 1952
1 CI(c),Dig Your FoxholeDeep . 2,800.00
2 CI(c),Champ . . . . . . . . . . . . 1,200.00
3 GK(c),No Exit. . . . . . . . . . . . . 850.00
4 IN(c),Last Man. . . . . . . . . . . . 700.00
5 IN(c),T.N.T. Bouquet . . . . . . . 650.00
6 IN(c),Battle Flag. . . . . . . . . . . 650.00
7 IN(c),Dive Bomber . . . . . . . . 650.00
8 IN(c),One Man Army . . . . . . . 650.00
9 GC(c),Undersea Raider. . . . . . 650.00
10 IN(c),Soldiers on the
  High Wire. . . . . . . . . . . . . . . 650.00
11 IN(c),Scratch One Meatball. . . 650.00
12 IN(c),The Big Drop . . . . . . . . 500.00
13 BK(c),Ghost Ace . . . . . . . . . . 650.00
14 IN(c),Drummer of Waterloo . . 650.00
15 IN(c),Thunder in the Skies . . . 500.00
16 IN(c),A Million To One Shot . 500.00
17 IN(c),The White Death . . . . . 500.00
18 IN(c),Frontier Fighter . . . . . . 500.00
19 IN(c),The Big Ditch . . . . . . . . 500.00
20 IN(c),Abandon Ship . . . . . . . 500.00
21 IN(c),Dairy of a Flattop . . . . . 350.00
22 JGr(c),Ranger Raid. . . . . . . . . 350.00
23 IN(c),Jungle Navy . . . . . . . . . 350.00
24 IN(c),Suprise Landing. . . . . . . 350.00
25 JGr(c),Take 'Er Down . . . . . . . 350.00
26 JGr(c),Sky Duel . . . . . . . . . . . 350.00
27 IN(c),MD,Diary of a Frogman . 350.00
28 JGr(c),Detour-War . . . . . . . . . 350.00
29 IN(c),Grounded Fighter. . . . . . 350.00
30 JGr(c),Torpedo Raft . . . . . . . . 350.00
31 IN(c),Howitzer Hill. . . . . . . . . 350.00
32 JGr(c),Battle Mirror. . . . . . . . . 350.00
33 JGr(c),Fighting Gunner. . . . . . 350.00
34 JGr(c),Point-Blank War. . . . . . 350.00
35 JGr(c),Frontline Tackle . . . . . 350.00
36 JGr(c),Foxhole Mascot . . . . . 350.00

**Of**

     All comics prices listed are for *Near Mint* condition.

*Our Army at War #29*
© DC Comics

*Our Fighting Forces #2*
© DC Comics

*Our Fighting Forces #29*
© DC Comics

37 JGr(c),Walking Battle Pin .... 350.00
38 JGr(c),Floating Pillbox ....... 350.00
39 JGr(c),Trench Trap ........... 350.00
40 RH(c),Tank Hunter .......... 350.00
41 JGr(c),Jungle Target ........ 350.00
42 IN(c),Shadow Targets ....... 250.00
43 JGr(c),A Bridge For Billy ..... 250.00
44 JGr(c),Thunder In The Desert  250.00
45 JGr(c),Diary of a Fighter Pilot. 250.00
46 JGr(c),Prize Package ....... 250.00
47 JGr(c),Flying Jeep ......... 250.00
48 JGr(c),Front Seat .......... 250.00
49 JKu(c),Landing Postponed ... 250.00
50 JGr(c),RH,Mop-Up Squad ... 250.00
51 JGr(c),Battle Tag.......... 250.00
52 JGr(c),Pony Express Pilot. ... 250.00
53 JGr(c),One Ringside-For War. 250.00
54 JKu(c),No-Man Secret ...... 250.00
55 JGr(c),No Rest For A Raider . 250.00
56 JKu(c),You're Next ......... 250.00
57 JGr(c),Ten-Minute Break..... 250.00
58 JKu(c),The Fighting SnowBird 250.00
59 JGr(c),The Mustang Had
  My Number ............. 250.00
60 JGr(c),Ranger Raid. ....... 250.00
61 JGr(c),A Pigeon For Easy Co. 225.00
62 JKu(c),Trigger Man ........ 225.00
63 JGr(c),The Big Toss ....... 225.00
64 JKu(c),Tank Rider.......... 225.00
65 JGr(c),Scramble-War Upstairs 225.00
66 RH(c),Gunner Wanted ..... 225.00
67 JKu(c),MD,Boiling Point ..... 225.00
68 JKu(c),MD,End of the Line ... 225.00
69 JGr(c),Combat Cage....... 225.00
70 JGr(c),Torpedo Tank ....... 225.00
71 JGr(c),Flying Mosquitoes .... 225.00
72 JGr(c),No. 1 Pigeon ....... 225.00
73 JKu(c),Shooting Gallery ..... 225.00
74 JGr(c),Ace Without Guns .... 225.00
75 JGr(c),Blind Night Fighter.... 225.00
76 JKu(c),Clipped Hellcat ...... 225.00
77 JGr(c),Jets Don't Dream..... 225.00
78 IN(c),Battle Nurse.......... 225.00
79 JGr(c),MD,What's the Price
  of a B-17? ............. 225.00
80 JGr(c),The Sparrow And
  The...Hawk ............ 225.00
81 JGr(c),Sgt. Rock in The
  Rock of Easy Co......... 4,000.00
82 JGr(c),MD,Gun Jockey...... 900.00
83 JGr(c),MD,B:Sgt.Rock Stories,
  The Rock and the Wall.... 3,000.00
84 JKu(c),Laughter On
  Snakehead Hill .......... 450.00
85 JGr(c),Ice Cream Soldier .... 600.00
86 RH(c),Tank 711............ 400.00

87 RH(c),Calling Easy Co....... 400.00
88 JKu(c),The Hard Way....... 400.00
89 RH(c),No Shoot From Easy .. 400.00
90 JKu(c),3 Stripes Hill ........ 400.00
91 JGr(c),No Answer from
  Sarge ............... 1,200.00
92 JGr(c),Luck of Easy ........ 250.00
93 JGr(c),Deliver One Airfield ... 250.00
94 JKu(c),Target-Easy Company. 250.00
95 JKu(c),Battle of the Stripes... 250.00
96 JGr(c),MD,Last Stand
  For Easy ............... 250.00
97 JKu(c),What Makes A
  Sergeant Run? .......... 250.00
98 JKu(c),Soldiers Never Die ... 250.00
99 JKu(c),Easy's Hardest Battle . 250.00
100 JKu(c),No Exit For Easy .... 250.00

## OUR FIGHTING FORCES
### DC Comics, Oct.–Nov., 1954
1 IN,JGr(c),Human Booby Trap 1,800.00
2 RH,IN,IN(c),Mile-Long Step... 700.00
3 RA,JKu(c),Winter Ambush.... 550.00
4 RA,JGr(c),The Hot Seat ..... 450.00
5 IN,RA,JGr(c),The Iron Punch . 450.00
6 IN,RA,JGr(c),The Sitting Tank . 375.00
7 RA,JKu,JGr(c),Battle Fist..... 375.00
8 IN,RA,JGr(c),No War
  For A Gunner............ 375.00
9 JKu,RH,JGr(c),Crash-
  Landing At Dawn.......... 375.00
10 WW,RA,JGr(c),Grenade
  Pitcher................. 375.00
11 JKu,JGr(c),Diary of a Sub.... 300.00
12 IN,JKu,JGr(c),Jump Seat .... 300.00
13 RA,JGr(c),Beach Party ..... 300.00
14 JA,RA,IN,JGr(c),Unseen War . 300.00
15 RH,JKu,JGr(c),Target For
  A Lame Duck............ 300.00
16 RH,JGr(c),Night Fighter ..... 300.00
17 RA,JGr(c),Anchored Frogman 300.00
18 RH,JKu,JGr(c),Cockpit Seat . 300.00
19 RA,JKu(c),StraightenThatLine 300.00
20 RA,MD,JGr(c),The
  Floating Pilot ............ 350.00
21 RA,JKu(c),The Bouncing
  Baby of Company B ...... 200.00
22 JKu,RA,JGr(c),3 Doorways
  To War ................ 200.00
23 RA,IN,JA,JGr(c),Tin Fish Pilot 200.00
24 RA,RH,JGr(c),Frogman Duel . 200.00
25 RA,JKu(c),Dead End ...... 200.00
26 IN,RH,JKu(c),Tag Day ...... 200.00
27 MD,RA,JKu(c),TNT Escort ... 200.00
28 RH,MD,JKu(c),AllQuiet atC.P. 200.00

29 JKu,JKu(c),Listen To A Jet ... 200.00
30 IN,RA,JKu(c),Fort
  For A Gunner............ 200.00
31 MD,RA,JKu(c),Silent Sub .... 200.00
32 RH,MD,RH(c),PaperWorkWar 200.00
33 RH,JKu,JKu(c),Frogman
  In A Net ............... 200.00
34 JA,JGr,JKu(c),Calling U-217.. 200.00
35 JA,JGr,JKu(c),Mask of
  a Frogman ............. 200.00
36 MD,JA,JKu(c),Steel Soldier .. 200.00
37 JA,JGr,JGr(c),Frogman
  In A Bottle ............. 200.00
38 RH,RA,JA,JGr(c),Sub Sinker . 200.00
39 JA,RH,RH(c),Last Torpedo ... 200.00
40 JGr,JA,JKu,JKu(c),The
  Silent Ones ............ 200.00
41 JGr,RH,JA,JKu(c),Battle
  Mustang ............... 250.00
42 RH,MD,JGr(c),Sorry-
  Wrong Hill ............. 175.00
43 MD,JKu,JGr(c),Inside Battle .. 175.00
44 MD,RH,RA,JGr(c),Big Job
  For Baker............... 175.00
45 RH,RA,JGr(c),B:Gunner and
  Sarge, Mop-Up Squad...... 600.00
46 RH,RA,JGr(c),Gunner's
  Squad ................ 250.00
47 RH,JKu(c),TNT Birthday..... 175.00
48 JA,RH,JGr(c),A Statue
  For Sarge .............. 175.00
49 MD,RH,JGr(c),Blind Gunner.. 225.00
50 JA,RH,JGr(c),I:Pooch,My
  Pal, The Pooch ......... 175.00
51 RA,JA,RH(c),Underwater
  Gunner................ 150.00
52 MD,JKu,JKu(c),The Gunner
  and the Nurse ........... 125.00
53 JA,RA,JGr(c),An Egg
  For Sarge .............. 125.00
54 .................... 125.00
55 MD,RH,JGr(c),The Last Patrol 125.00
56 RH,RA,JGr(c),Bridge of
  Bullets ................ 125.00
57 JA,IN,JGr(c),A Tank For Sarge 125.00
58 JA,JGr(c),Return of the Pooch 125.00
59 RH,JA,JGr(c),Pooch-Patrol
  Leader ................ 125.00
60 RH,JA,JGr(c),Tank Target.... 125.00
61 JA,JGr(c),Pass to Peril ...... 125.00
62 JA,JGr(c),The Flying Pooch . 125.00
63 JA,RH,JGr(c),Pooch-Tank
  Hunter ................ 125.00
64 JK,RH,JGr(c),A Lifeline
  For Sarge .............. 125.00
65 IN,JA,JGr(c),Dogtag Patrol... 125.00

**Ou**

All comics prices listed are for *Near Mint* condition.                    **Page 209**

Our Flag #2
© Ace Magazines

Tom and Jerry #72
© Dell Publishing Co.

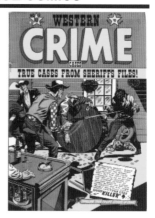

Western Crime Cases #9
© Star Publications

66 JKu,JA,JGr(c),Trail of the
  Ghost Bomber . . . . . . . . . . . 125.00
67 IN,JA,JGr(c),Purple Heart
  For Pooch . . . . . . . . . . . . . . 125.00
68 JA,JGr(c),Col. Hakawa's
  Birthday Party . . . . . . . . . . . 125.00
69 JA,JKu,JGr(c),
  Destination Doom . . . . . . . . 125.00
70 JA,JKu(c),The Last Holdout . . 125.00

## OUR FIGHTING MEN
## IN ACTION
### Ajax/Farrell, 1957
1 . . . . . . . . . . . . . . . . . . . . . . . 125.00
2 . . . . . . . . . . . . . . . . . . . . . . . 100.00
3 . . . . . . . . . . . . . . . . . . . . . . . 100.00
4 . . . . . . . . . . . . . . . . . . . . . . . 100.00
5 . . . . . . . . . . . . . . . . . . . . . . . 100.00
6 . . . . . . . . . . . . . . . . . . . . . . . 100.00

## OUR FLAG COMICS
### Ace Magazines,
### Aug., 1941–April, 1942
1 MA,JM,B:Capt.Victory,Unknown
  Soldier,The Three Cheers . 3,700.00
2 JM,JM(c),O:The Flag . . . . . . 1,500.00
3 Tank Battle (c). . . . . . . . . . . 1,200.00
4 MA . . . . . . . . . . . . . . . . . . . 1,200.00
5 I:Mr. Risk, Male Bondage . . . 1,400.00

## OUR GANG COMICS
### Dell Publishing Co.,
### Sept.–Oct., 1942
1 WK,Barney Bear, Tom &
  Jerry . . . . . . . . . . . . . . . . . 1,500.00
2 WK . . . . . . . . . . . . . . . . . . . . 750.00
3 WK,Benny Burro . . . . . . . . . . 500.00
4 WK . . . . . . . . . . . . . . . . . . . . 500.00
5 WK . . . . . . . . . . . . . . . . . . . . 500.00
6 WK . . . . . . . . . . . . . . . . . . . . 750.00
7 WK . . . . . . . . . . . . . . . . . . . . 350.00
8 WK,CB,Benny Burro . . . . . . . 900.00
9 WK,CB,Benny Burro . . . . . . . 850.00
10 WK,CB,Benny Burro . . . . . . 600.00
11 WK,I:Benny Bear . . . . . . . . . 850.00
12 thru 20 WK . . . . . . . . . . @400.00
21 thru 29 WK . . . . . . . . . . @300.00
30 WK,Christmas(c). . . . . . . . . 250.00
31 thru 34 WK . . . . . . . . . . @250.00
35 WK,CB . . . . . . . . . . . . . . . . 200.00
36 WK,CB . . . . . . . . . . . . . . . . 200.00
37 thru 40 WK . . . . . . . . . . @125.00
41 thru 50 WK . . . . . . . . . . @125.00

51 thru 56 WK . . . . . . . . . . . . @125.00
57 . . . . . . . . . . . . . . . . . . . . . . 100.00
58 Our Gang . . . . . . . . . . . . . . 100.00
59 Our Gang . . . . . . . . . . . . . . 100.00
Becomes:

## TOM AND JERRY
### July, 1949
60 . . . . . . . . . . . . . . . . . . . . . . 175.00
61 . . . . . . . . . . . . . . . . . . . . . . 125.00
62 . . . . . . . . . . . . . . . . . . . . . . 100.00
63 . . . . . . . . . . . . . . . . . . . . . . 100.00
64 . . . . . . . . . . . . . . . . . . . . . . 100.00
65 . . . . . . . . . . . . . . . . . . . . . . 100.00
66 Christmas (c) . . . . . . . . . . . 120.00
67 thru 70 . . . . . . . . . . . . . @125.00
71 thru 76 . . . . . . . . . . . . . @125.00
77 Christmas (c) . . . . . . . . . . . 125.00
78 thru 80 . . . . . . . . . . . . . @125.00
81 thru 89 . . . . . . . . . . . . . @100.00
90 Christmas (c) . . . . . . . . . . . 125.00
91 thru 99 . . . . . . . . . . . . . @100.00
100 . . . . . . . . . . . . . . . . . . . . . 125.00
101 thru 120 . . . . . . . . . . . . @100.00
121 thru 150 . . . . . . . . . . . . @100.00
151 thru 212 . . . . . . . . . . . . @100.00

## OUR LOVE
### Marvel, Sept., 1949
1 Ph(c),Guilt of Nancy Crane . . 175.00
2 Ph(c),My Kisses Were Cheap . 125.00

## OUR SECRET
### See: MY SECRET

## OUTER SPACE
### See: CHARLIE CHAN

## OUTLAW FIGHTERS
### Marvel Atlas, Aug., 1954
1 GT,Western Tales . . . . . . . . . 150.00
2 GT ,JMn(c). . . . . . . . . . . . . . 100.00
3 . . . . . . . . . . . . . . . . . . . . . . . 100.00
4 A;Patch Hawk . . . . . . . . . . . . 100.00
5 RH, Final Issue,April, 1955 . . 100.00

## OUTLAW KID
### Marvel Atlas, Sept., 1954
1 SSh,DW,JMn(c),B&O:Outlaw Kid,
  A;Black Rider . . . . . . . . . . . 350.00
2 DW,JMn(c),A:Black Rider . . . 175.00
3 DW,AW,GWb,JMN(c) . . . . . . . 175.00

4 DW(c),Death Rattle . . . . . . . . 150.00
5 JMn . . . . . . . . . . . . . . . . . . . 150.00
6 JMn . . . . . . . . . . . . . . . . . . . 150.00
7 JMn . . . . . . . . . . . . . . . . . . . 150.00
8 AW,DW,JMn . . . . . . . . . . . . . 150.00
9 . . . . . . . . . . . . . . . . . . . . . . . 125.00
10 JSe . . . . . . . . . . . . . . . . . . . 125.00
11 thru 17 . . . . . . . . . . . . . . @100.00
18 AW,JMn. . . . . . . . . . . . . . . . 100.00
19 JSe,Sept., 1957 . . . . . . . . . . 100.00

## OUTLAWS
### D.S. Publishing Co.,
### Feb.–March, 1948
1 HcK,Western Crime Stories . . 400.00
2 Grl,Doc Dawson's Dilema . . . 400.00
3 Cougar City Cleanup . . . . . . 175.00
4 JO,Death Stakes A Claim . . . . 200.00
5 RJ,RJ(c),Man Who Wanted
  Mexico . . . . . . . . . . . . . . . . 175.00
6 AMc,RJ,RJ(c),The Ghosts of
  Crackerbox Hill . . . . . . . . . . 175.00
7 Grl,Dynamite For Boss Cavitt . 300.00
8 Grl,The Gun & the Boss . . . . 300.00
9 FF,Shoot to Kill;June–
  July, 1949 . . . . . . . . . . . . . 600.00

## WHITE RIDER AND
## SUPER HORSE
### Star Publications,
### Sept., 1950
1 LbC(c) . . . . . . . . . . . . . . . . . 250.00
2 LbC(c) . . . . . . . . . . . . . . . . . 200.00
3 LbC(c) . . . . . . . . . . . . . . . . . 200.00
4 LbC(c) . . . . . . . . . . . . . . . . . 200.00
5 LbC(c),Stampede of Hard
  Riding Thrills . . . . . . . . . . . 225.00
6 LbC(c),Drums of the Sioux . . . 225.00
Becomes:

## INDIAN WARRIORS
### June, 1951
7 LbC(c),Winter on the Great
  Plains . . . . . . . . . . . . . . . . . 250.00
8 LbC(c) . . . . . . . . . . . . . . . . . 225.00
Becomes:

## WESTERN CRIME
## CASES
### Dec., 1951
9 LbC(c),The Card Sharp Killer . 250.00
Becomes:

All comics prices listed are for *Near Mint* condition.

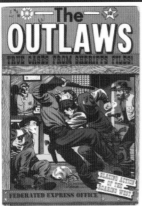

Outlaws #10
© Star Publications

Out of the Shadows #7
© Standard Comics

Oxydol-Dreft giveaways #3, #4 & #6
© Oxydol Dreft

## OUTLAWS, THE

### May, 1952

10 LbC(c),Federated Express . . . 250.00
11 LbC(c),Frontier Terror!!!. . . . . 225.00
12 LbC(c),Ruthless Killer!!! . . . . . 225.00
13 LbC(c),The Grim Avengers. . . 225.00
14 AF,JKa,LbC(c),Trouble in
   Dark Canyon,April, 1954 . . . . 225.00

## OUTLAWS OF THE WEST
### See: BULLS-EYE

## OUT OF THE NIGHT

### American Comics Group/
### Best Synd. Feature,
### Feb.–March, 1952

1 AW . . . . . . . . . . . . . . . . . . . . . 900.00
2 AW . . . . . . . . . . . . . . . . . . . . 600.00
3 . . . . . . . . . . . . . . . . . . . . . . . . 350.00
4 AW . . . . . . . . . . . . . . . . . . . . 500.00
5 . . . . . . . . . . . . . . . . . . . . . . . . 350.00
6 The Ghoul's Revenge . . . . . . . 350.00
7 . . . . . . . . . . . . . . . . . . . . . . . . 350.00
8 The Frozen Ghost . . . . . . . . . . 350.00
9 Death Has Wings,
   Science Fiction . . . . . . . . . . . 350.00
10 Ship of Death . . . . . . . . . . . . . 350.00
11 . . . . . . . . . . . . . . . . . . . . . . . . 275.00
12 Music for the Dead . . . . . . . . 275.00
13 HN,From the Bottom of
   the Well . . . . . . . . . . . . . . . . . 275.00
14 Out of the Screen . . . . . . . . . . 275.00
15 The Little Furry Thing . . . . . . . 250.00
16 Nightmare From the Past . . . . 250.00
17 The Terror of the Labyrinth . . . 250.00
Becomes:

## HOODED HORSEMAN

### Dec., 1954–Jan., 1955

18 B: The Hooded Horseman . . . 125.00
19 The Horseman's Strangest
   Adventure . . . . . . . . . . . . . . . 175.00
20 OW,O:Johnny Injun. . . . . . . . 125.00
21 OW,OW(c). . . . . . . . . . . . . . . 175.00
22 OW . . . . . . . . . . . . . . . . . . . . 125.00
23 . . . . . . . . . . . . . . . . . . . . . . . . 125.00
24 . . . . . . . . . . . . . . . . . . . . . . . . 125.00
25 . . . . . . . . . . . . . . . . . . . . . . . . 100.00
26 O&I:Cowboy Sahib . . . . . . . . 125.00
27 Jan.–Feb., 1953 . . . . . . . . . . 110.00

## OUT OF THE SHADOWS

### Visual Editions
### (Standard Comics),
### July, 1952–Aug., 1954

5 ATh,GT,The Shoremould
   Horror . . . . . . . . . . . . . . . . . . 750.00
6 ATh,JKz,Salesman of Death . . 500.00
7 JK,Plant of Death . . . . . . . . . . 350.00
8 Mask of Death . . . . . . . . . . . . 625.00
9 RC,Till Death Do Us Part . . . . 350.00
10 MSy,We Vowed,Till Death
   Do Us Part. . . . . . . . . . . . . . . 350.00
11 ATh,Fountain of Fear. . . . . . . . 350.00
12 ATh,Hand of Death . . . . . . . . 500.00
13 MSy,The Cannibal . . . . . . . . . 350.00
14 ATh,The Werewolf. . . . . . . . . . 350.00

## OUT OF THIS WORLD

### Charlton Comics, 1956–59

1 . . . . . . . . . . . . . . . . . . . . . . . . 300.00
2 . . . . . . . . . . . . . . . . . . . . . . . . 150.00
3 SD . . . . . . . . . . . . . . . . . . . . . 350.00
4 SD . . . . . . . . . . . . . . . . . . . . . 350.00
5 SD . . . . . . . . . . . . . . . . . . . . . 350.00
6 SD . . . . . . . . . . . . . . . . . . . . . 350.00
7 SD,SD(c) . . . . . . . . . . . . . . . . 375.00
8 SD . . . . . . . . . . . . . . . . . . . . . 300.00
9 SD . . . . . . . . . . . . . . . . . . . . . 250.00
10 SD,Perfect Forcaster . . . . . . . 250.00
11 SD . . . . . . . . . . . . . . . . . . . . . 300.00
12 SD . . . . . . . . . . . . . . . . . . . . . 250.00
13 thru 15. . . . . . . . . . . . . . . @125.00
16 . . . . . . . . . . . . . . . . . . . . . . . . 325.00

## OXYDOL-DREFT

### Giveaways, 1950
### The Set is More Valuable if the
### Original Envelope is Present

1 L'il Abner . . . . . . . . . . . . . . . . 150.00
2 Daisy Mae . . . . . . . . . . . . . . . 150.00
3 Shmoo . . . . . . . . . . . . . . . . . . 175.00
4 AW&FF(c),John Wayne . . . . . 150.00
5 Archie . . . . . . . . . . . . . . . . . . . 175.00
6 Terry Toons Comics . . . . . . . . 150.00

## OZARK IKE

### Visual Editions
### (Standard Comics), 1948

11 . . . . . . . . . . . . . . . . . . . . . . . . 175.00
12 . . . . . . . . . . . . . . . . . . . . . . . . 100.00
13 . . . . . . . . . . . . . . . . . . . . . . . . 100.00
14 . . . . . . . . . . . . . . . . . . . . . . . . 100.00
15 . . . . . . . . . . . . . . . . . . . . . . . . 100.00

16 . . . . . . . . . . . . . . . . . . . . . . . . 100.00
17 . . . . . . . . . . . . . . . . . . . . . . . . 100.00
18 . . . . . . . . . . . . . . . . . . . . . . . . 100.00
19 . . . . . . . . . . . . . . . . . . . . . . . . 100.00
20 . . . . . . . . . . . . . . . . . . . . . . . . 100.00
21 thru 25 . . . . . . . . . . . . . . . @100.00

## OZZIE AND BABS

### Fawcett Publications,
### Winter, 1946

1 Humor Oriented, Teenage . . . . 150.00
2 Humor Oriented . . . . . . . . . . . 100.00
3 Humor Oriented . . . . . . . . . . . 100.00
4 Humor Oriented . . . . . . . . . . . 100.00
5 Humor Oriented . . . . . . . . . . . 100.00
6 Humor Oriented . . . . . . . . . . . 100.00
7 Humor Oriented . . . . . . . . . . . 100.00
8 Humor Oriented . . . . . . . . . . . 100.00
9 Humor Oriented . . . . . . . . . . . 100.00
10 Humor Oriented . . . . . . . . . . . 100.00
11 Humor Oriented . . . . . . . . . . . 100.00
12 Humor Oriented . . . . . . . . . . . 100.00
13 Humor Oriented;1949 . . . . . . 100.00

## PAGEANT OF COMICS

### St. John Publishing Co.,
### Sept., 1947

1 Rep. Mopsy . . . . . . . . . . . . . . 250.00
2 Rep. Jane Arden,Crime
   Reporter. . . . . . . . . . . . . . . . 250.00

## PANHANDLE PETE
## AND JENNIFER

### J. Charles Lave
### Publishing Co., July, 1951

1 (fa) . . . . . . . . . . . . . . . . . . . . 125.00
2 (fa) . . . . . . . . . . . . . . . . . . . . 100.00
3 (fa),Nov.'51 . . . . . . . . . . . . . . 100.00

## PANIC

### Tiny Tot Publications
### (E.C. Comics), March, 1954
### "Humor in a Jugular Vein"

1 BE,JKa,JO,JDa,AF(c) . . . . . . . 750.00
2 BE,JO,WW,JDa,A:Bomb . . . . 500.00
3 BE,JO,BW,WW,JDa,AF(c) . . . 400.00
4 BE,JO,WW,JDa,BW(c),
   Infinity(c) . . . . . . . . . . . . . . . 400.00
5 BE,JO,WW,JDa,AF(c) . . . . . . 350.00
6 BE,JO,WW,JDa,Blank (c) . . . . 350.00
7 BE,JO,WW,JDa . . . . . . . . . . . 350.00
8 BE,JO,WW,JDa,Eye Chart (c) . 275.00

**Pa**

*Paramount Animated Comics #8*
© *Harvey Publications*

*Parole Breakers #3*
© *Avon Periodicals*

*Patsy Walker #21*
© *Marvel Comics Group*

9 BE,JO,WW,JDa,Ph(c),
　Confidential(c) . . . . . . . . . 1,000.00
10 BE,JDa, Postal Package(c) . . 500.00
11 BE,WW,JDa,Wheaties parody
　as Weedies (c) . . . . . . . . . . 400.00
12 BE,WW,JDa,JDa(c);
　Dec.–Jan., 1955–56 . . . . . . 375.00

## PARAMOUNT ANIMATED COMICS
### Family Publications (Harvey Publ.), June, 1953
1 (fa),B:Baby Herman & Katnip,
　Baby Huey,Buzzy the Crow . 275.00
2 (fa) . . . . . . . . . . . . . . . . . . 125.00
3 (fa) . . . . . . . . . . . . . . . . . . 100.00
4 (fa) . . . . . . . . . . . . . . . . . . 100.00
5 (fa) . . . . . . . . . . . . . . . . . . 100.00
6 (fa) . . . . . . . . . . . . . . . . . . 100.00
7 (fa), Baby Huey (c) . . . . . . . 250.00
8 (fa), Baby Huey (c) . . . . . . . 100.00
9 (fa), Infinity(c),Baby Huey (c). . 100.00
10 thru 21 (fa),Baby Huey(c) . . @100.00
22 (fa), July, 1956, Baby Huey (c) 100.00

## PAROLE BREAKERS
### Avon Periodicals/Realistic, Dec., 1951–July, 1952
1 P(c),Hellen Willis,Gun
　Crazed Gun Moll . . . . . . . . 550.00
2 JKu,P(c),Vinnie Sherwood,
　The Racket King . . . . . . . . . 400.00
3 EK(c),John "Slicer" Berry,
　Hatchetman of Crime . . . . . . 350.00

## PAT BOONE
### DC Comics, 1959
1 . . . . . . . . . . . . . . . . . . . . . 600.00
2 Fabian, Paul Anka . . . . . . . . . 450.00
3 . . . . . . . . . . . . . . . . . . . . . 450.00
4 Bobby Darin, Johnny Mathis . . 450.00
5 Dick Clark, Frankie Avalon . . . 450.00

## PATCHES
### Rural Home Publ./ Patches Publ., March–April, 1945
1 LbC(c),Imagination In Bed(c). . 500.00
2 Dance (c). . . . . . . . . . . . . . . 200.00
3 Rocking Horse (c) . . . . . . . . . 150.00
4 Music Band (c). . . . . . . . . . . 150.00
5 LbC(c),A:Danny Kaye,Football 250.00

6 A: Jackie Kelk . . . . . . . . . . . 150.00
7 A: Hopalong Cassidy . . . . . . . 225.00
8 A: Smiley Burnettte . . . . . . . . 150.00
9 BK,A: Senator Claghorn . . . . . 150.00
10 A: Jack Carson . . . . . . . . . . . 150.00
11 A: Red Skeleton; Dec'47. . . . 200.00

## PATSY & HEDY
### Marvel Atlas, Feb., 1952
1 AJ(c),B:Patsy Walker &
　Hedy Wolfe . . . . . . . . . . . . 250.00
2 Skating(c) . . . . . . . . . . . . . . 175.00
3 Boyfriend Trouble . . . . . . . . . 150.00
4 Swimsuit(c) . . . . . . . . . . . . . 150.00
5 Patsy's Date(c) . . . . . . . . . . . 150.00
6 Swimsuit/Picnic(c) . . . . . . . . 150.00
7 Double-Date(c) . . . . . . . . . . 150.00
8 AJ(c),The Dance . . . . . . . . . . 150.00
9 . . . . . . . . . . . . . . . . . . . . . 150.00
10 . . . . . . . . . . . . . . . . . . . . . 150.00
11 thru 25 . . . . . . . . . . . . . . . @125.00
26 thru 50. . . . . . . . . . . . . . . @100.00
51 thru 60 . . . . . . . . . . . . . . . @100.00
61 thru 109. . . . . . . . . . . . . . @100.00
110 Feb., 1967 . . . . . . . . . . . . . 100.00

## PATSY & HER PALS
### Marvel, May, 1953
1 MWs(c),F:Patsy Walker . . . . . 225.00
2 MWs(c),Swimsuit(c) . . . . . . . 125.00
3 MWs(c),Classroom(c) . . . . . . 100.00
4 MWs(c),Golfcourse(c) . . . . . . 100.00
5 MWs(c).Patsy/Buzz(c) . . . . . 100.00
6 thru 10 . . . . . . . . . . . . . . . @100.00
11 thru 28. . . . . . . . . . . . . . . @100.00
29 Aug., 1957. . . . . . . . . . . . . . 100.00

## PATSY WALKER
### Marvel, 1945
1 F:Patsy Walker Adventures . . 650.00
2 Patsy/Car(c) . . . . . . . . . . . . 300.00
3 Skating(c) . . . . . . . . . . . . . . 225.00
4 Perfume(c) . . . . . . . . . . . . . 225.00
5 Archery Lesson, Eye Injury(c) 225.00
6 Bus(c) . . . . . . . . . . . . . . . . 225.00
7 Charity Drive(c) . . . . . . . . . . 225.00
8 Organ Driver Monkey(c) . . . . 225.00
9 Date(c) . . . . . . . . . . . . . . . . 225.00
10 Skating(c),Wedding Bells,
　A:Millie. . . . . . . . . . . . . . . 225.00
11 Date with a Dream,A:Mitzi . . . 175.00
12 Love in Bloom,Artist(c),
　A:Rusty . . . . . . . . . . . . . . 175.00

13 Swimsuit(c),There Goes My
　Heart;HK,Hey Look . . . . . . . 175.00
14 An Affair of the Heart,
　HK,Hey Look . . . . . . . . . . . 175.00
15 Dance(c) . . . . . . . . . . . . . . . 135.00
16 Skating(c) . . . . . . . . . . . . . . 150.00
17 Patsy's Diary(c),HK,Hey Look 225.00
18 Autograph(c) . . . . . . . . . . . . 200.00
19 HK,Hey Look. . . . . . . . . . . . 200.00
20 HK,Hey Look. . . . . . . . . . . . 200.00
21 HK,Hey Look. . . . . . . . . . . . 200.00
22 HK,Hey Look. . . . . . . . . . . . 200.00
23 . . . . . . . . . . . . . . . . . . . . . 150.00
24 . . . . . . . . . . . . . . . . . . . . . 150.00
25 HK,Rusty. . . . . . . . . . . . . . . 200.00
26 . . . . . . . . . . . . . . . . . . . . . 150.00
27 . . . . . . . . . . . . . . . . . . . . . 150.00
28 . . . . . . . . . . . . . . . . . . . . . 150.00
29 . . . . . . . . . . . . . . . . . . . . . 150.00
30 HK,Egghead Double . . . . . . . 150.00
31 . . . . . . . . . . . . . . . . . . . . . 125.00
32 thru 56. . . . . . . . . . . . . . . @100.00
57 thru 58 AJ(c) . . . . . . . . . . . @125.00
59 thru 99. . . . . . . . . . . . . . . @100.00
100 . . . . . . . . . . . . . . . . . . . . . 100.00
Fashion Parade #1 . . . . . . . . . . 150.00

## PAT THE BRAT
### Radio Comics (Archie Publications), 1955–59
1 . . . . . . . . . . . . . . . . . . . . . 175.00
2 . . . . . . . . . . . . . . . . . . . . . 150.00
3 . . . . . . . . . . . . . . . . . . . . . 125.00
4 . . . . . . . . . . . . . . . . . . . . . 125.00
15 thru 20. . . . . . . . . . . . . . . @100.00
21 thru 33 . . . . . . . . . . . . . . . @100.00

## PATTY POWERS
### See: DELLA VISION

## PAUL TERRY'S COMICS
### See: TERRY-TOONS COMICS

## PAWNEE BILL
### Story Comics, Feb.–July, 1951
1 A:Bat Masterson,Wyatt Earp,
　Indian Massacre
　at Devil's Gulch . . . . . . . . . 125.00
2 Blood in Coffin Canyon . . . . . 100.00

**Pa**

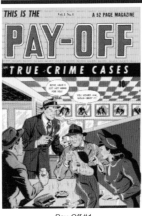

Pay-Off #1
© D.S. Publishing Co.

Pep Comics #17
© Archie Publications

The Perfect Crime #24
© Cross Publications

3 LC,O:Golden Warrior,Fiery
Arrows at Apache Pass..... 100.00

## PAY-OFF
### D.S. Publishing Co.,
### July–Aug., 1948–
### March–April, 1949
1 True Crime 1 & 2.......... 300.00
2 The Pennsylvania Blue-Beard . 175.00
3 The Forgetful Forger ........ 150.00
4 RJ(c),Lady and the Jewels ... 150.00
5 The Beautiful Embezzeler .... 150.00

## PEANUTS
### Dell Publishing Co., 1958
1 ........................ 250.00
2 ........................ 200.00
3 ........................ 150.00
4 ........................ 125.00
5 thru 13 ............... @100.00

## PEDRO
### Fox Features Syndicate,
### Jan., 1950
1 WW,WW(c),Humor Oriented . 250.00
2 Aug., 1950 ............. 175.00

## PENNY
### Avon Publications, 1947
1 The Slickest Chick of 'em All . 125.00
2 ........................ 100.00
3 America's Teen-age
Sweetheart .............. 100.00
4 ........................ 100.00
5 ........................ 100.00
6 Perry Como Ph(c),Sept.–
Oct., 1949 ............. 125.00

## PEP COMICS
### MJL Magazines/
### Archie Publications,
### Jan., 1940
1 IN,JCo,MMe,IN(c),I:Shield,
O:Comet,Queen of Diamonds,
B:The Rocket,Press Guardian,
Sergeant Boyle Chang,Bently
of Scotland Yard........ 17,000.00
2 CBi,JCo,IN,IN(c),O:Rocket.. 4,500.00
3 JCo,IN,IN(c),Shield (c) ..... 3,000.00
4 Cbi,JCo,MMe,IN,IN(c),
C:Wizard(not Gareb) ..... 2,400.00

5 Cbi,JCo,MMe,IN,IN(c),
C:Wizard............... 2,400.00
6 IN,IN(c), Shield (c) ........ 1,800.00
7 IN,IN(c),Bondage(c),Shield(c)1,800.00
8 JCo,IN, Shield (c) ......... 1,800.00
9 IN, Shield (c)............. 1,800.00
10 IN,IN(c), Shield (c)........ 1,800.00
11 MMe,IN,IN(c),I:Dusty,
Boy Detective ........... 2,000.00
12 IN,IN(c),O:Fireball
Bondage(c), E:Rocket,
Queen of Diamonds ..... 2,200.00
13 IN,IN(c),Bondage(c)....... 1,500.00
14 IN,IN(c)................. 1,500.00
15 IN,Bondage(c) ........... 1,500.00
16 IN,O:Madam Satan ...... 2,400.00
17 IN,IN(c),O:Hangman,
D:Comet.............. 6,000.00
18 IN,IN(c),Bondage(c) ..... 1,500.00
19 IN ................... 1,500.00
20 IN,IN(c),E:Fireball ....... 1,500.00
21 IN,IN(c),Bondage(c),
E: Madam Satan........ 1,500.00
22 IN,IN(c)I:Archie,
Jughead, Betty ........ 25,000.00
23 IN,IN(c)................. 2,200.00
24 IN,IN(c)................. 1,500.00
25 IN,IN(c)................. 1,500.00
26 IN,IN(c),I:Veronica ....... 2,200.00
27 IN,IN(c),Bill of Rights (c) ... 1,500.00
28 IN,IN(c), V:Capt. Swastika.. 1,500.00
29 ASh (c)................. 1,500.00
30 B:Capt.Commando ...... 1,500.00
31 Bondage(c) ............. 1,500.00
32 Bondage(c) ............. 1,100.00
33 ...................... 1,100.00
34 Bondage(c) ............. 1,100.00
35 ...................... 1,100.00
36 1st Archie(c)............. 2,500.00
37 Bondage(c).............. 750.00
38 ASh(c).................. 700.00
39 ASh(c), Human Shield ..... 700.00
40 ...................... 700.00
41 2nd Archie; I:Jughead....... 500.00
42 F:Archie & Jughead ........ 500.00
43 F:Archie & Jughead ........ 500.00
44 ........................ 500.00
45 ........................ 500.00
46 ........................ 500.00
47 E:Hangman,Infinity(c)....... 500.00
48 B:Black Hood ............ 500.00
49 ........................ 500.00
50 ........................ 500.00
51 ........................ 350.00
52 B:Suzie ................. 350.00
53 ........................ 350.00

54 E:Captain Commando ...... 350.00
55 ........................ 350.00
56 thru 58................. @300.00
59 E:Suzie ................. 300.00
60 B:Katy Keene ............ 300.00
61 ........................ 275.00
62 I L'il Jinx ............... 275.00
63 ........................ 275.00
64 ........................ 275.00
65 E:Shield................. 275.00
66 thru 71................. @150.00
72 thru 80................. @125.00
81 thru 90................. @100.00
91 thru 99................. @100.00
100 ...................... 150.00
101 thru 110............... @125.00
111 thru 120............... @100.00
121 thru 130............... @125.00
131 thru 140............... @100.00
141 thru 150............... @100.00
151 thru 160,A:Super Heroes . @100.00

## PERFECT CRIME, THE
### Cross Publications,
### Oct., 1949

**Pe**

1 BP,DW ................. 400.00
2 BP .................... 200.00
3 ...................... 175.00
4 BP .................... 175.00
5 DW ................... 175.00
6 ...................... 175.00
7 B:Steve Duncan ......... 175.00
8 Drug Story ............. 300.00
9 ...................... 175.00
10 ...................... 175.00
11 Bondage (c) ............ 300.00
12 ...................... 175.00
13 ...................... 175.00
14 Poisoning (c)............ 350.00
15 'The Most Terrible Menace,'
Drug................. 300.00
16 ...................... 150.00
17 ...................... 150.00
18 Drug (c)................ 400.00
19 ...................... 150.00
20 thru 25................ @125.00
26 Drug w/ Hypodermic (c) ... 400.00
27 ...................... 150.00
28 ...................... 150.00
29 ...................... 150.00
30 E:Steve Duncan, Rope
Strangulation (c) ......... 400.00
31 ...................... 125.00
32 ...................... 125.00
33 ...................... 125.00

*Perfect Love #3*
© St. John Publ. Co.

*Personal Love #32*
© Famous Funnies

*Phantom Lady #14*
© Fox Features Syndicate

### PERFECT LOVE

**Approved Comics (Ziff-Davis)/
St. John Publ. Co.,
Aug.–Sept., 1951**

1 (10),P(c),Our Kiss was a
  Prelude to Love Adrift . . . . . 250.00
2 . . . . . . . . . . . . . . . . . . . . . . . 150.00
3 P(c) . . . . . . . . . . . . . . . . . . . 125.00
4 . . . . . . . . . . . . . . . . . . . . . . . 100.00
5 . . . . . . . . . . . . . . . . . . . . . . . 100.00
6 . . . . . . . . . . . . . . . . . . . . . . . 100.00
7 . . . . . . . . . . . . . . . . . . . . . . . 100.00
8 EK . . . . . . . . . . . . . . . . . . . . 125.00
9 EK,P(c) . . . . . . . . . . . . . . . . 100.00
10 Ph(c), Dec '53 . . . . . . . . . . . . 100.00

### PERSONAL LOVE

**Famous Funnies, Jan., 1950**

1 Ph(c) Are You in Love . . . . . . . 225.00
2 Ph(c) Serenade for Suzette
  Mario Lanzo . . . . . . . . . . . . . 125.00
3 Ph(c) . . . . . . . . . . . . . . . . . . . 100.00
4 Ph(c) . . . . . . . . . . . . . . . . . . . 100.00
5 Ph(c) . . . . . . . . . . . . . . . . . . . 100.00
6 Ph(c) Be Mine Forever . . . . . . 110.00
7 Ph(c) You'll Always Be
  Mine, Robert Walker . . . . . . . 110.00
8 EK,Ph(c),Esther Williams &
  Howard Keel . . . . . . . . . . . . 125.00
9 EK,Ph(c),Debra Paget & Louis
  Jordan . . . . . . . . . . . . . . . . . 125.00
10 Ph(c),Loretta Young
  Joseph Cotton . . . . . . . . . . . 100.00
11 ATh, Ph(c),Gene Tierney &
  Glenn Ford . . . . . . . . . . . . . 150.00
12 Ph(c) Jane Greer &
  William Lundigan . . . . . . . . . 100.00
13 Ph(c) Debra Paget &
  Louis Jordan . . . . . . . . . . . . 100.00
14 Ph(c) Kirk Douglas &
  Patrice Wymore . . . . . . . . . . 110.00
15 Ph(c) Dale Robertson &
  Joanne Dru . . . . . . . . . . . . . 100.00
16 Ph(c) Take Back Your Love . . 100.00
17 Ph(c) My Cruel Deception . . . 100.00
18 Ph(c) Gregory Peck &
  Susan Hayward . . . . . . . . . . 125.00
19 Ph(c) Anthony Quinn . . . . . . . 125.00
20 Ph(c) The Couple in the
  Next Apartment, Bob Wagner 125.00
21 Ph(c) I'll Make You Care . . . . . 125.00
22 Ph(c) Doorway To Heartbreak 125.00
23 Ph(c) SaveMe from that Man . 125.00

24 FF, Ph(c) Tyrone Power . . . . 500.00
25 FF, Ph(c) The Dark Light . . . 500.00
26 Ph(c) Love Needs A Break . . . 100.00
27 FF, Ph(c) Champ or Chump? . 500.00
28 FF, Ph(c) A Past to Forget . . . 500.00
29 Ph(c) Charlton Heston . . . . . 125.00
30 Ph(c) The Lady is Lost . . . . . 100.00
31 Ph(c) Marlon Brando . . . . . . . 125.00
32 FF, Ph(c) The Torment,
  Kirk Douglas . . . . . . . . . . . . 700.00
33 Ph(c) June, 1955 . . . . . . . . . 100.00

### PETER COTTONTAIL

**Key Publications,
Jan., 1954**

1 No 3-D (fa) . . . . . . . . . . . . . . . 100.00
1 Feb '54 3-D (fa) . . . . . . . . . . . 250.00
2 Rep of 3-D #1,not in 3-D . . . . . 100.00

### PETER PANDA

**DC Comics, Aug.–Sept., 1953**

1 . . . . . . . . . . . . . . . . . . . . . . . 500.00
2 . . . . . . . . . . . . . . . . . . . . . . . 250.00
3 thru 9 . . . . . . . . . . . . . . . . . @200.00
10 Aug.–Sept., 1958 . . . . . . . . . 200.00

### PETER PAUL'S 4 IN 1 JUMBO COMIC BOOK

**Capitol Stories, 1953**

1 F: Racket Squad in Action,
  Space Adventures,Crime &
  Justice,Space Western . . . . . 500.00

### PETER PENNY AND HIS MAGIC DOLLAR

**American Bakers Assn., 1947**

1 History from Colonial
  America to the 1950's . . . . . . 200.00
2 . . . . . . . . . . . . . . . . . . . . . . . 125.00

### PETER PIG

**Literary Enterprises
(Standard Comics), 1953**

5 . . . . . . . . . . . . . . . . . . . . . . . 100.00
6 . . . . . . . . . . . . . . . . . . . . . . . 100.00

### PETER PORKCHOPS

**DC Comics, Nov.–Dec., 1949**

1 . . . . . . . . . . . . . . . . . . . . . . . 350.00
2 . . . . . . . . . . . . . . . . . . . . . . . 175.00

3 thru 10 . . . . . . . . . . . . . . . . @125.00
11 thru 30 . . . . . . . . . . . . . . . . @100.00
31 thru 61 . . . . . . . . . . . . . . . . @100.00
62 Oct.–Dec., 1960 . . . . . . . . . . 100.00

### PETER RABBIT

**Avon Periodicals, 1947**

1 HCa . . . . . . . . . . . . . . . . . . . 450.00
2 HCa . . . . . . . . . . . . . . . . . . . 275.00
3 HCa . . . . . . . . . . . . . . . . . . . 250.00
4 HCa . . . . . . . . . . . . . . . . . . . 250.00
5 HC . . . . . . . . . . . . . . . . . . . . 250.00
6 HCa . . . . . . . . . . . . . . . . . . . 250.00
7 thru 10 . . . . . . . . . . . . . . . . @100.00
11 . . . . . . . . . . . . . . . . . . . . . . 100.00

### PETE THE PANIC

**Stanmor Publications, 1955**

N# . . . . . . . . . . . . . . . . . . . . . . 100.00

### KRAZY LIFE

**Fox Features Syndicate, 1945**

1 (fa) . . . . . . . . . . . . . . . . . . . . 100.00
Becomes:

### NUTTY LIFE

**Summer, 1946**

2 (fa) . . . . . . . . . . . . . . . . . . . . 100.00
Becomes:

### WOTALIFE

**Fox Features Synd./
Green Publ., Aug.–Sept., 1946**

3 (fa)B:L'il Pan,Cosmo Cat . . . . 150.00
4 . . . . . . . . . . . . . . . . . . . . . . . 100.00
5 thru 11 . . . . . . . . . . . . . . . . @100.00
12 July, 1947 . . . . . . . . . . . . . . 100.00
9a rep (1959) . . . . . . . . . . . . . . 100.00
Becomes:

### PHANTOM LADY

**Fox Features Syndicate,
Aug., 1947**

13(#1) MB,MB(c) Knights of
  the Crooked Cross . . . . . . . 6,000.00
14(#2) MB,MB(c) Scoundrels
  and Scandals . . . . . . . . . . . 3,300.00
15 MB,MB(c) The Meanest
  Crook In the World . . . . . . . 3,200.00
16 MB,MB(c) Claa Peete The
  Beautiful Beast, Negligee . . 3,200.00
17 MB.MB(c) The Soda Mint
  Killer, Bondage (c) . . . . . . . 8,000.00

**Pe**

*My Love Secret #26*
© Fox Features Syndicate

*Pictorial Romances #8*
© St. John Publishing Co.

*Picture News #1*
© 299 Lafayette Street Corp.

18 MB,MB(c) The Case of
　Irene Shroeder . . . . . . . . . . 2,500.00
19 MB,MB(c) The Case of
　the Murderous Model . . . . 2,500.00
20 MB,MB(c) Ace of Spades . . . 2,000.00
21 MB,MB(c) . . . . . . . . . . . . . 1,800.00
22 MB,JKa . . . . . . . . . . . . . . 1,800.00
23 MB,JKa Bondage (c) . . . . . . 2,000.00
**Becomes:**

## MY LOVE SECRET
### June, 1949
24 JKa, My Love Was For Sale . . 200.00
25 Second Hand Love . . . . . . . . 125.00
26 WW I Wanted Both Men . . . . . 250.00
27 I Was a Love Cheat . . . . . . . 100.00
28 WW, I Gave Him Love . . . . . . 250.00
29 . . . . . . . . . . . . . . . . . . . . . 100.00
30 Ph(c) . . . . . . . . . . . . . . . . . 100.00

## LINDA
### Ajax/Farrell, April–May, 1954
1 . . . . . . . . . . . . . . . . . . . . . . 175.00
2 Lingerie section . . . . . . . . . . . 150.00
3 . . . . . . . . . . . . . . . . . . . . . . 100.00
4 Oct.–Nov.,1954 . . . . . . . . . . . 100.00
**Becomes:**

## PHANTOM LADY
### Dec., 1954–Jan., 1955
5(1) MB . . . . . . . . . . . . . . . . 1,500.00
2 Last Pre-Code Edition . . . . . 1,250.00
3 Comics Code . . . . . . . . . . . 1,000.00
4 Red Rocket,June, 1955 . . . . 1,000.00

## PHANTOM STRANGER
### DC Comics, Aug.–Sept., 1952
1 . . . . . . . . . . . . . . . . . . . . . 2,500.00
2 . . . . . . . . . . . . . . . . . . . . . 1,500.00
3 thru 5 . . . . . . . . . . . . . . . . @1,200.00
6, June-July, 1953 . . . . . . . . . 1,200.00

## PHIL RIZZUTO
### Fawcett Publications, 1951
Ph(c) The Sensational Story of
　The American Leagues MVP 950.00

## PICTORIAL
## CONFESSIONS
### St. John Publishing Co., Sept., 1949
1 MB,MB(c),I Threw Away My Repu-
　tation on a Worthless Love . . 350.00

2 MB,Ph(c) I Tried to be a
　Hollywood Glamour Girl . . . . 250.00
3 JKY,MB,MB(c),They Caught
　Me Cheating . . . . . . . . . . . . 300.00
**Becomes:**

## PICTORIAL ROMANCES
### Jan., 1950
4 Ph(c) MB, Trapped By Kisses
　I Couldn't Resist . . . . . . . . . 350.00
5 MB,MB(c). . . . . . . . . . . . . . . 300.00
6 MB,MB(c) I Was Too Free
　With Boys . . . . . . . . . . . . . . 250.00
7 MB,MB(c) . . . . . . . . . . . . . . 250.00
8 MB,MB(c) I Made a
　Sinful Bargain . . . . . . . . . . . 250.00
9 MB,MB(c) Dishonest Love . . . . 250.00
10 MB,MB(c) I Was The
　Other Woman . . . . . . . . . . . . 200.00
11 MB,MB(c) The Worst
　Mistake A Wife Can Make . . . 225.00
12 MB,MB(c) Love Urchin . . . . . 200.00
13 MB,MB(c) Temptations of a
　Hatcheck Girl . . . . . . . . . . . . 200.00
14 MB,MB(c) I Was A
　Gamblers Wife . . . . . . . . . . . 200.00
15 MB,MB(c) Wife Without
　Pride or Principles . . . . . . . . 200.00
16 MB,MB(c) The Truth of My
　Affair With a Farm Boy . . . . . 200.00
17 MB,MB(c) True Confessions
　of a Girl in Love . . . . . . . . . . 300.00
18 MB,MB(c) . . . . . . . . . . . . . . 300.00
20 MB,MB(c) . . . . . . . . . . . . . . 300.00
21 thru 23 MB,MB(c) . . . . . . . . @175.00
24 MB,MB(c) March,1954 . . . . . 175.00

## PICTORIAL
## LOVE STORIES
## See: ZOO FUNNIES

## PICTORIAL LOVE
## STORIES
### St. John Publishing Co., Oct., 1952
1 MB,MB(c) I Lost My Head, My
　Heart and My Resistance . . . 350.00

## PICTURE CRIMES
### 1937
1 . . . . . . . . . . . . . . . . . . . . . 1,500.00

## PICTURE NEWS
### 299 Lafayette Street Corp., Jan., 1946–Jan.-Feb., 1947
1 Will The Atom Blow The
　World Apart . . . . . . . . . . . . 1,000.00
2 Meet America's 1st Girl Boxing
　Expert,Atomic Bomb . . . . . . 500.00
3 Hollywood's June Allison Shows
　You How to be Beautiful,
　Atomic Bomb . . . . . . . . . . . . 400.00
4 Amazing Marine Who Became
　King of 10,000 Voodoos,
　Atomic Bomb . . . . . . . . . . . . 450.00
5 G.I.Babies,Hank Greenberg . . . 400.00
6 Joe Louis(c) . . . . . . . . . . . . . 450.00
7 Lovely Lady, Englands
　Future Queen . . . . . . . . . . . . 350.00
8 Champion of them All . . . . . . . 350.00
9 Bikini Atom Bomb,
　Joe DiMaggio . . . . . . . . . . . . 400.00
10 Dick Quick, Ace Reporter,
　Atomic Bomb . . . . . . . . . . . . 400.00

## PICTURE PARADE
### Gilberton Co., 1953
1 A-Bomb . . . . . . . . . . . . . . . . 300.00
2 . . . . . . . . . . . . . . . . . . . . . . 150.00
3 . . . . . . . . . . . . . . . . . . . . . . 150.00
4 Christmas issue . . . . . . . . . . . 150.00
**Becomes:**

## PICTURE PROGRESS
### Gilberton Co., 1954
5 1953 News . . . . . . . . . . . . . . 100.00
6 Birth of America . . . . . . . . . . . 100.00
7 . . . . . . . . . . . . . . . . . . . . . . 100.00
8 Paul Revere . . . . . . . . . . . . . . 100.00
9 Hawaian Islands . . . . . . . . . . . 100.00
10 Flight . . . . . . . . . . . . . . . . . . 100.00
11 thru 20 . . . . . . . . . . . . . . @100.00

## PICTURE SCOPE
## JUNGLE ADVENTURES
### Star Publications, 1954
7 LbC(c) . . . . . . . . . . . . . . . . . 650.00

## PICTURE STORIES FROM
## AMERICAN HISTORY
### E.C. Comics, 1946–47
1 . . . . . . . . . . . . . . . . . . . . . . 750.00
2 thru 4 . . . . . . . . . . . . . . . . @550.00

**Pi**

*Picture Stories From Science #1*
© Educational Comics

*Piracy #6*
© E.C. Comics

*Planet Comics #39*
© Fiction House Magazines

## PICTURE STORIES FROM SCIENCE

**Educational Comics, Spring, 1947**
1 Understanding Air and Water . 500.00
2 Fall '47 Amazing Discoveries
  About Food & Health. . . . . . . 400.00

## PICTURE STORIES FROM THE BIBLE

**DC Comics, Autumn, 1942–43**
1 thru 4 Old Testament . . . . . . @700.00
1 thru 3 New Testament . . . . . . . 900.00

## PICTURE STORIES FROM WORLD HISTORY

**E.C. Comics, Spring, 1947**
1 Ancient World to the
  Fall of Rome . . . . . . . . . . . . 350.00
2 Europes Struggle for
  Civilization . . . . . . . . . . . . . . 300.00

## PINHEAD AND FOODINI

**Fawcett Publications, July, 1951–Jan., 1952**
1 Ph(c) . . . . . . . . . . . . . . . . . . . 350.00
2 Ph(c) . . . . . . . . . . . . . . . . . . . 200.00
3 Ph(c) Too Many Pinheads . . . . 150.00
4 Foodini's Talking Camel. . . . . . 150.00

## PIN-UP PETE

**Toby Publishers, 1952**
1 Loves of a GI Casanova . . . . . 250.00

## PIONEER PICTURE STORIES

**Street & Smith Publ., Dec., 1941**
1 Red Warriors in Blackface. . . . 500.00
2 Life Story Of Errol Flynn . . . . . 400.00
3 Success Stories of Brain
  Muscle in Action . . . . . . . . . 300.00
4 Legless Ace & Boy Commando
  Raid Occupied France . . . . . 300.00
5 How to Tell Uniform and
  Rank of Any Navy Man . . . . . 300.00
6 General Jimmy Doolittle . . . . . 350.00
7 Life Story of Admiral Halsey . . 350.00

8 Life Story of Timoshenko . . . . . 300.00
9 Dec., '43,Man Who Conquered
  The Wild Frozen North . . . . . 300.00

## PIRACY

**E.C. Comics, Oct.–Nov., 1954**
1 WW,JDa,AW,WW(c),RC,AT . . 750.00
2 RC,JDa(c),WW,AW,AT. . . . . . 600.00
3 RC,GE, RC(c),Grl . . . . . . . . . 500.00
4 RC,GE,RC(c),Grl . . . . . . . . . 450.00
5 RC,GE,BK(c),Grl . . . . . . . . . 450.00
6 JDa,RC,GE,BK(c),Grl . . . . . . 450.00
7 Oct Nov GE(c),RC,GE,Grl . . . 450.00

## PIRATES COMICS

**Hillman Periodicals, Feb., 1950**
1 . . . . . . . . . . . . . . . . . . . . . . . . 300.00
2 . . . . . . . . . . . . . . . . . . . . . . . . 200.00
3 . . . . . . . . . . . . . . . . . . . . . . . . 175.00
4 Aug–Sept., 1950 . . . . . . . . . . 175.00

## PIXIES, THE

**Magazine Enterprises, Winter, 1946**
1 Mighty Atom. . . . . . . . . . . . . . 200.00
2 . . . . . . . . . . . . . . . . . . . . . . . . 150.00
3 . . . . . . . . . . . . . . . . . . . . . . . . 150.00
4 . . . . . . . . . . . . . . . . . . . . . . . . 150.00
5 . . . . . . . . . . . . . . . . . . . . . . . . 150.00
**Becomes:**

## MIGHTY ATOM, THE
### 1949
6 . . . . . . . . . . . . . . . . . . . . . . . . 150.00

## PLANET COMICS

**Love Romance Publ.
(Fiction House Magazines),
Jan., 1940–Winter, 1953**
1 AB,DBr,HcK, Planet Comics,
  WE&LF,O:Aura,B:Flint Baker,
  Red Comet,Spurt Hammond,
  Capt. Nelson Cole . . . . . . 17,000.00
2 HcK,LF(c) . . . . . . . . . . . . . . 6,500.00
3 WE(c),HcK . . . . . . . . . . . . . . 4,000.00
4 HcK,B:Gale Allan and
  the Girl Squad . . . . . . . . . 3,500.00
5 BP,HcK . . . . . . . . . . . . . . . . 3,200.00
6 BP,HcK,BP(c),The Ray
  Pirates of Venus. . . . . . . . 3,400.00
7 BP,AB,HcK,BP(c) B:Buzz
  Crandall Planet Payson . . . 3,000.00
8 BP,AB HcK . . . . . . . . . . . . . 3,000.00

9 BP,AB,GT,HcK,B:Don
  Granville Cosmo Corrigan . 3,000.00
10 BP,AB,GT HcK . . . . . . . . . . 3,000.00
11 HcK, B:Crash Parker . . . . . . 3,000.00
12 Dri,B:Star Fighter . . . . . . . . . 3,000.00
13 Dri,B:Reef Ryan. . . . . . . . . . 2,000.00
14 Dri B:Norge Benson . . . . . . 2,000.00
15 B: Mars,God of War . . . . . . 3,900.00
16 Invasion From The Void. . . . 1,800.00
17 Warrior Maid of Mercury . . . 1,800.00
18 Bondage(c) . . . . . . . . . . . . . 2,000.00
19 Monsters of the Inner
  World . . . . . . . . . . . . . . . . 1,800.00
20 RP, Winged Man Eaters
  of the Exile Star . . . . . . . . 1,800.00
21 RP,B:Lost World
  Hunt Bowman. . . . . . . . . . 2,000.00
22 Inferno on the Fifth Moon . . 1,800.00
23 GT,Lizard Tyrant of
  the Twilight World . . . . . . . 1,700.00
24 GT,Grl Raiders From
  The Red Moon . . . . . . . . . 1,700.00
25 Grl,B:Norge Benson . . . . . . 1,700.00
26 Grl,B:The Space Rangers
  Bondage(c). . . . . . . . . . . . 1,800.00
27 Grl, The Fire Eaters of
  Asteroid Z. . . . . . . . . . . . . 1,500.00
28 Grl, Bondage (c) . . . . . . . . . 2,200.00
29 Grl,Dragon Raiders of Aztla. 2,600.00
30 GT,Grl City of Lost Souls . . . 2,000.00
31 Grl,Fire Priests of Orbit6X . . 1,600.00
32 Slaver's Planetoid . . . . . . . . 1,700.00
33 MA . . . . . . . . . . . . . . . . . . . 1,600.00
34 MA,Bondage . . . . . . . . . . . . 1,800.00
35 MA B:Mysta of The Moon . . 1,600.00
36 MA Collosus of the
  Blood Moon . . . . . . . . . . . 1,600.00
37 MA, Behemoths of the
  Purple Void. . . . . . . . . . . . 1,600.00
38 MA . . . . . . . . . . . . . . . . . . . 1,500.00
39 MA.Death Webs Of Zenith 3 1,500.00
40 Chameleon Men from
  Galaxy 9 . . . . . . . . . . . . . . 1,500.00
41 MA,AgF,New O: Auro
  Bondage (c) . . . . . . . . . . . 1,500.00
42 MA,AgF,E:Gale Allan . . . . . 1,500.00
43 MA,AgF Death Rays
  From the Sun. . . . . . . . . . . 1,500.00
44 MA,Bbl,B:Futura . . . . . . . . . 1,500.00
45 Ma,Bbl,Her Evilness
  from Xanado . . . . . . . . . . . 1,500.00
46 MA,Bbl,GE The Mecho-Men
  From Mars . . . . . . . . . . . . 1,500.00
47 MA,Bbl,GE,The Great
  Green Spawn . . . . . . . . . . 1,200.00
48 MA,GE . . . . . . . . . . . . . . . . 1,200.00

     All comics prices listed are for *Near Mint* condition.

*Planet Comics #60*
© Fiction House Magazines

*Plastic Man #17*
© Quality Comics Group

*Playful Little Audrey #7*
© Harvey Publications

49 MA,GE, Werewolves From
   Hydra Hell. . . . . . . . . . . . . 1,200.00
50 MA,GE,The Things of Xeves 1,200.00
51 MA,GE, Mad Mute X-Adapts 1,000.00
52 GE,Mystery of the Time
   Chamber. . . . . . . . . . . . . . 1,000.00
53 MB,GE,Bondage(c)
   Dwarflings From Oceania. . 1,000.00
54 MB,GE,Robots From Inferno 1,000.00
55 MB,GE,Giants of the
   Golden Atom. . . . . . . . . . . 1,000.00
56 MB,GE,Grl . . . . . . . . . . . . . . 900.00
57 MB,GE,Grl . . . . . . . . . . . . . . 900.00
58 MB,GE,Grl . . . . . . . . . . . . . . 900.00
59 MB,GE,Grl,LSe . . . . . . . . . . . 900.00
60 GE,Grl,Vassals of Volta . . . . . 900.00
61 GE,Grl, The Brute in the
   Bubble . . . . . . . . . . . . . . . . . 800.00
62 GE,Musta,Moon Goddess . . 800.00
63 GE,Paradise or Inferno. . . . . 800.00
64 GE,Monkeys From the Blue . . 800.00
65 The Lost World . . . . . . . . . . . 800.00
66 The Plague of the
   Locust Men . . . . . . . . . . . . . 800.00
67 The Nymphs of Neptune. . . . 800.00
68 Synthoids of the 9th Moon . . 800.00
69 The Mentalists of Mars . . . . . 800.00
70 Cargo For Amazonia . . . . . . 800.00
71 Sandhogs of Mars. . . . . . . . 700.00
72 Last Ship to Paradise . . . . . . 700.00
73 The Martian Plague . . . . . . . 700.00

## PLASTIC MAN
### Comics Magazines
### (Quality Comics Group),
### Summer, 1943–Nov., 1956
1 JCo(a&c)Game of Death . . . 6,000.00
2 JCo(a&c)The Gay Nineties
   Nightmare . . . . . . . . . . . . . 2,500.00
3 JCo(a&c). . . . . . . . . . . . . . . 1,600.00
4 JCo(a&c). . . . . . . . . . . . . . . 1,500.00
5 JCo(a&c). . . . . . . . . . . . . . . 1,400.00
6 JCo(a&c). . . . . . . . . . . . . . . 1,500.00
7 JCo(a&c). . . . . . . . . . . . . . . 1,500.00
8 JCo(a&c). . . . . . . . . . . . . . . 1,500.00
9 JCo(a&c). . . . . . . . . . . . . . . 1,500.00
10 JCo(a&c) . . . . . . . . . . . . . . 1,500.00
11 JCo(a&c) . . . . . . . . . . . . . . 1,500.00
12 JCo(a&c),V:Spadehead . . . . 1,500.00
13 JCo(a&c),V:Mr.Hazard . . . . . 1,500.00
14 JCo(a&c),Words,Symbol
   of Crime . . . . . . . . . . . . . . 1,500.00
15 JCo(a&c),V:BeauBrummel . . 1,500.00
16 JCo(a&c),Money
   Means Trouble . . . . . . . . . 1,500.00

17 JCo(a&c),A:The Last
   Man on Earth . . . . . . . . . . 1,200.00
18 JCo(a&c),Goes Back
   to the Farm. . . . . . . . . . . . 1,200.00
19 JCo(a&c),V;Prehistoric
   Plunder. . . . . . . . . . . . . . . 1,200.00
20 JCo(a&c),A:Sadly,Sadly. . . 1,200.00
21 JCo(a&c),V:Crime Minded
   Mind Reader . . . . . . . . . . . 800.00
22 JCo(a&c), Which Twin
   is the Phony. . . . . . . . . . . . 800.00
23 JCo(a&c),The Fountain
   of Age . . . . . . . . . . . . . . . . 800.00
24 JCo(a&c),The Black Box
   of Terror . . . . . . . . . . . . . . . 800.00
25 JCo(a&c),A:Angus
   MacWhangus . . . . . . . . . . 800.00
26 JCo(a&c),On the Wrong
   Side of the Law? . . . . . . . . 800.00
27 JCo(a&c),V:The Leader . . . . 800.00
28 JCo(a&c),V:Shasta . . . . . . . 800.00
29 JCo(a&c),V:Tricky Toledo . . . 800.00
30 JCo(a&c),V:Weightless
   Wiggins . . . . . . . . . . . . . . . 800.00
31 JCo(a&c),V:Raka the
   Witch Doctor . . . . . . . . . . . 600.00
32 JCo(a&c),V:Mr.Fission . . . . . 600.00
33 JCo(a&c),V:The Mad
   Professor . . . . . . . . . . . . . . 600.00
34 JCo(a&c),V:Smuggler'sHaven . . 600.00
35 JCo(a&c),V:The Hypnotist . . . 600.00
36 JCo(a&c),The Uranium
   Underground . . . . . . . . . . . 600.00
37 JCo(a&c),V:Gigantic Ants . . . . 600.00
38 JCo(a&c),The Curse of
   Monk Mauley . . . . . . . . . . 600.00
39 JCo(a&c),The Stairway
   to Madness . . . . . . . . . . . . 600.00
40 JCo(a&c),The Ghoul of
   Ghost Swamp . . . . . . . . . . 600.00
41 JCo(a&c),The Beast with
   the Bloody Claws. . . . . . . . 500.00
42 JCo(a&c),The King of
   Thunderbolts . . . . . . . . . . . 500.00
43 JCo(a&c),The Evil Terror . . . . 500.00
44 JCo(a&c),The Magic Cup . . . 500.00
45 The Invisible Raiders . . . . . . . 500.00
46 V:The Spider . . . . . . . . . . . . 500.00
47 The Fiend of a
   Thousand Faces . . . . . . . . 500.00
48 Killer Crossbones . . . . . . . . . 500.00
49 JCo,The Weapon for Evil . . . . 500.00
50 V:Iron Fist . . . . . . . . . . . . . . 500.00
51 Incredible Sleep Weapon . . . 500.00
52 V:Indestructible Wizard. . . . . . 500.00

53 V:Dazzia,Daughter of
   Darkness . . . . . . . . . . . . . . 500.00
54 V:Dr.Quomquat. . . . . . . . . . 500.00
55 The Man Below Zero . . . . . . 500.00
56 JCo, The Man Who Broke
   the Law of Gravity . . . . . . . . 500.00
57 The Chemist's Cauldron . . . . 500.00
58 JCo,The Amazing
   Duplicating Machine . . . . . . 500.00
59 JCo,V:The Super Spy . . . . . . 500.00
60 The Man in the Fiery
   Disguise. . . . . . . . . . . . . . . 450.00
61 V:King of the Thunderbolts . . . 450.00
62 V:The Smokeweapon . . . . . . 450.00
63 V:Reflecto . . . . . . . . . . . . . . 450.00
64 The Invisible Raiders . . . . . . . 450.00

## PLAYFUL LITTLE AUDREY
### Harvey Publications, 1957
1 . . . . . . . . . . . . . . . . . . . . . . . 350.00
2 . . . . . . . . . . . . . . . . . . . . . . . 200.00
3 . . . . . . . . . . . . . . . . . . . . . . . 135.00
4 . . . . . . . . . . . . . . . . . . . . . . . 135.00
5 . . . . . . . . . . . . . . . . . . . . . . . 135.00
6 . . . . . . . . . . . . . . . . . . . . . . . 100.00
7 . . . . . . . . . . . . . . . . . . . . . . . 100.00
8 . . . . . . . . . . . . . . . . . . . . . . . 100.00
9 . . . . . . . . . . . . . . . . . . . . . . . 100.00
10 thru 30 . . . . . . . . . . . . . . @100.00

## POCAHONTAS
### Pocahontas Fuel Co.,
### Oct., 1941
N# . . . . . . . . . . . . . . . . . . . . . 350.00
2 . . . . . . . . . . . . . . . . . . . . . . . 325.00

## POCKET COMICS
### Harvey Publications,
### Aug., 1941
1 100 pages,O:Black Cat,Spirit
   of '76,Red Blazer Phantom
   Sphinx & Zebra,B:Phantom
   Ranger,British Agent #99,
   Spin Hawkins,Satan . . . . . . 1,400.00
2 . . . . . . . . . . . . . . . . . . . . . . . 900.00
3 . . . . . . . . . . . . . . . . . . . . . . . 650.00
4 Jan.'42,All Features End . . . . . 650.00

## POGO POSSUM
### Dell Publishing Co., 1941
1 WK,A:Swamp Land Band . . . 1,700.00
2 WK . . . . . . . . . . . . . . . . . . . 1,000.00
3 WK. . . . . . . . . . . . . . . . . . . . . 600.00

**Po**

*Police Against Crime #1*
*© Premier Magazines*

*Police Comics #29*
*© Quality Comics Group*

*Police Comics #76*
*© Quality Comics Group*

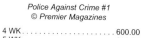

4 WK . . . . . . . . . . . . . . . . . . 600.00
5 WK . . . . . . . . . . . . . . . . . . 600.00
6 thru 10 WK . . . . . . . . . . . . . @450.00
11 WK, Christmas (c) . . . . . . . @400.00
12 thru 16 WK . . . . . . . . . . . . @500.00

## POLICE ACTION
### Marvel, Jan., 1954
1 JF,GC,JMn(c),Riot Squad . . . . 225.00
2 JF,Over the Wall . . . . . . . . . . 150.00
3 JMn . . . . . . . . . . . . . . . . . . . 125.00
4 DAy . . . . . . . . . . . . . . . . . . . 125.00
5 DAy,JMn. . . . . . . . . . . . . . . 125.00
6 . . . . . . . . . . . . . . . . . . . . . . . 125.00
7 BPNov., 1954 . . . . . . . . . . . . 125.00

## POLICE AGAINST CRIME
### Premier Magazines, 1954
1 Knife in Face . . . . . . . . . . . . . 300.00
2 . . . . . . . . . . . . . . . . . . . . . . . 165.00
3 . . . . . . . . . . . . . . . . . . . . . . . 125.00
4 thru 9 . . . . . . . . . . . . . . . . . @125.00

## POLICE BADGE
### See: SPY THRILLERS

## POLICE BADGE #479
### Marvel Atlas, 1955
5 . . . . . . . . . . . . . . . . . . . . . . . 125.00

## POLICE COMICS
### Comic Magazines
### (Quality Comics Group),
### Aug., 1941
1 JCo,WE,PGv,RC,FGu,AB,
GFx(a&c),B&O:Plastic Man
The Human Bomb,#711,I&B,
Chic Canter,The Firebrand
Mouthpiece,Phantom Lady
The Sword . . . . . . . . . . . 11,000.00
2 JCo,PGv,WE,RC,FGu,
GFx(a&c) . . . . . . . . . . . . . 5,000.00
3 JCo,PGv,WE,RC,FGu,
GFx(a&c) . . . . . . . . . . . . . 3,000.00
4 JCo,GFx,PGv,WE,RC,FGu,
GFx&WEC(c) . . . . . . . . . . 2,600.00
5 JCo,PGv,WE,RC,FGu,
GFx(a&c) . . . . . . . . . . . . . 2,500.00
6 JCo,PGv,WE,RC,FGu,
GFx(a&c) . . . . . . . . . . . . . 2,200.00
7 JCo,PGv,WE,RC,FGu,
GFx(a&c) . . . . . . . . . . . . . 2,200.00

8 JCo,PGv,WE,RC,FGu,
GFx(a&c),B&O:Manhunter  2,500.00
9 JCo,PGv,WE,RC,FGu,
GFx(a&c) . . . . . . . . . . . . . 1,800.00
10 JCo,PGv,WE,RC,FGu,
GFx(a&c) . . . . . . . . . . . . . 1,700.00
11 JCo,PGv,WE,RC,FGu,GFx(a&c),
B:Rep:Rep.Spirit Strips. . . . 3,000.00
12 JCo,GFx,PGv,WE,FGu,AB,
RC(c) I:Ebony . . . . . . . . . . 1,700.00
13 JCo,GFx,PGv,WE,FGu,AB,RC(c)
E:Firebrand,I:Woozy Winks 1,700.00
14 JCo,PGv,WE,Jku,GFx(a&c). 1,500.00
15 JCo,PGv,WE,Jku,GFx(a&c)
E#711,B:Destiny . . . . . . . . 1,500.00
16 JCo,PGv,WE,JKu. . . . . . . . . 1,500.00
17 PGv,WE,JKu,JCo(a&c) . . . . 1,500.00
18 PGv,WE,JCo(a&c) . . . . . . . 1,500.00
19 PGv,WE,JCo(a&c) . . . . . . . 1,500.00
20 PGv,WE,JCo(a&c),A:Jack
Cole in Phantom Lady . . . . 1,500.00
21 PGv,WE,JCo(a&c) . . . . . . . 1,400.00
22 PGv,WE,RP,JCo(a&c)
The Eyes Have it . . . . . . . 1,400.00
23 WE,RP,JCo(a&c),E:Phantom
Lady . . . . . . . . . . . . . . . . . 1,200.00
24 WE,HK,JCo(a&c),B:Flatfoot
Burns . . . . . . . . . . . . . . . . 1,200.00
25 WE,HK,RP,JCo(a&c),The
Bookstore Mysrery . . . . . . 1,200.00
26 WE,Hk,JCo(a&c)E:Flatfoot
Burns . . . . . . . . . . . . . . . . 1,200.00
27 WE,JCo(a&c). . . . . . . . . . . 1,200.00
28 WE,JCo(a&c) . . . . . . . . . . . 1,200.00
29 WE,JCo(a&c) . . . . . . . . . . . 1,200.00
30 WE,JCo(a&c),A Slippery
Racket . . . . . . . . . . . . . . . 1,200.00
31 WE,JCo(a&c),Is Plastic
Man Washed Up?. . . . . . . 1,100.00
32 WE,JCo(a&c),Fiesta Turns
Into a Fracas . . . . . . . . . . 1,100.00
33 JCo,WE . . . . . . . . . . . . . . . 1,100.00
34 WE,JCo(a&c). . . . . . . . . . . 1,100.00
35 WE,JCo(a&c) . . . . . . . . . . . 1,100.00
36 WE,JCo(a&c),Rest In Peace 1,100.00
37 WE,PGv,JCo(a&c),Love
Comes to Woozy . . . . . . . 1,100.00
38 WE,PGv,JCo(a&c) . . . . . . . 1,100.00
39 WE,PGv,JCo(a&c) . . . . . . . 1,100.00
40 WE,PGv,JCo(a&c) . . . . . . . 1,100.00
41 WE,PGv,JCo(a&c),E:Reps.
of Spirit Strip . . . . . . . . . . 1,100.00
42 LF&WE,PGv,JCo(a&c),
Woozy Cooks with Gas . . . 1,100.00
43 LF&WE,PGv,JCo(a&c). . . . 1,100.00
44 PGv,LF,JCo(a&c) . . . . . . . . 1,100.00

45 PGv,LF,JCo(a&c) . . . . . . . . 1,100.00
46 PGv,LF,JCo(a&c) . . . . . . . . 1,100.00
47 PGv,LF,JCo(a&c),V:Dr.Slicer 1,100.00
48 PGv,LF,JCo(a&c),V:Big
Beaver . . . . . . . . . . . . . . . 1,100.00
49 PGv,LF,JCo(a&c),V:Thelma
Twittle . . . . . . . . . . . . . . . 1,100.00
50 PGv,LF,JCo(a&c) . . . . . . . . 1,100.00
51 PGv,LF,JCo(a&c),V:The
Granite Lady. . . . . . . . . . . 1,000.00
52 PGv,LF,JCo(a&c) . . . . . . . . 1,000.00
53 PGv,LF,JCo(a&c),V:Dr.
Erudite . . . . . . . . . . . . . . . 1,000.00
54 PGv,LF,JCo(a&c) . . . . . . . . 1,000.00
55 PGv,LF,JCo(a&c),V:The
Sleepy Eyes . . . . . . . . . . . 1,000.00
56 PGv,LF,JCo(a&c),V:The
Yes Man . . . . . . . . . . . . . . 1,000.00
57 PGv,LF,JCo(a&c),V:Mr.Misfit 1,000.00
58 PGv,LF,JCo(a&c),E:The
Human Bomb . . . . . . . . . . 1,000.00
59 PGv,LF,JCo(a&c),A:Mr.
Happiness. . . . . . . . . . . . . 1,000.00
60 PGv,LF,JCo(a&c) . . . . . . . . . 500.00
61 PGv,LF,JCo(a&c) . . . . . . . . 1,000.00
62 PGv,LF,JCo(a&c) . . . . . . . . 1,000.00
63 PGv,LF,JCo(a&c),V:The
Crab . . . . . . . . . . . . . . . . . 1,000.00
64 PGv,LF,HK,JCo(a&c) . . . . . 1,000.00
65 PGv,LF,JCo(a&c) . . . . . . . . 1,000.00
66 PGv,LF,JCo(a&c) Love
Can Mean Trouble . . . . . . 1,000.00
67 LF,JCo(a&c),
V:The Gag Man . . . . . . . . 1,000.00
68 LF,JCo(a&c). . . . . . . . . . . . 1,000.00
69 LF,JCo(a&c),V:Strecho. . . . 1,000.00
70 LF,JCo(a&c),V:Strecho. . . . 1,000.00
71 LF,JCo(a&c) . . . . . . . . . . . . . 600.00
72 LF,JCo(a&c),V:Mr.Cat . . . . . 600.00
73 LF,JCo(a&c) . . . . . . . . . . . . . 600.00
74 LF,JCo(a&c),V:Prof.Dimwit . 600.00
75 LF,JCo(a&c) . . . . . . . . . . . . . 600.00
76 LF,JCo(a&c),V:Mr.Morbid . . 600.00
77 LF,JCo(a&c),V:Skull Face
& Eloc . . . . . . . . . . . . . . . . . 600.00
78 LF,JCo(a&c),A Hot Time In
Dreamland. . . . . . . . . . . . . . 600.00
79 LF,JCo(a&c),V:Eaglebeak . . . 600.00
80 LF,JCo(a&c),V:Penetro . . . . . 600.00
81 LF,JCo(a&c),V:A Gorilla . . . . 600.00
82 LF,JCo(a&c) . . . . . . . . . . . . . 600.00
83 LF,JCo(a&c) . . . . . . . . . . . . . 600.00
84 LF,JCo(a&c) . . . . . . . . . . . . . 600.00
85 LF,JCo(a&c),V:Lucky 7 . . . . . 600.00
86 LF,JCo(a&c),V:The Baker . . . 600.00
87 LF,JCo(a&c) . . . . . . . . . . . . . 600.00

All comics prices listed are for *Near Mint* condition.

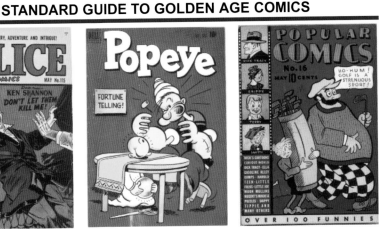

*Police Comics #115*
© Quality Comics Group

*Popeye #14*
© Dell Publishing Co.

*Popular Comics #16*
© Dell Publishing Co.

88 LF,JCo(a&c),V:The Seen . . . . 600.00
89 JCo(a&c),V:The Vanishers . . . 550.00
90 LF,JCo(a&c),V:Capt.Rivers . . . 550.00
91 JCo(a&c),The Forest Primeval 600.00
92 LF,JCo(a&c),V:Closets
　　Kennedy . . . . . . . . . . . . . . . . 600.00
93 JCo(a&c),V:The Twinning
　　Terror . . . . . . . . . . . . . . . . 500.00
94 JCo(a&c),WE . . . . . . . . . . . 800.00
95 JCo(a&c),WE,V:Scowls . . . . . 800.00
96 JCo(a&c),WE,V:Black Widow . 800.00
97 JCo(a&c),WE,V:The Mime . . . 800.00
98 JCo(a&c),WE . . . . . . . . . . . 800.00
99 JCo(a&c),WE . . . . . . . . . . . 800.00
100 JCo(a&c) . . . . . . . . . . . . . 1,000.00
101 JCo(a&c) . . . . . . . . . . . . . 1,000.00
102 JCo(a&c),E:Plastic Man . . . 1,000.00
103 JCo,LF,B&I:Ken Shannon;
　　Bondage(c) . . . . . . . . . . . . 550.00
104 The Handsome of Homocide 400.00
105 Invisible Hands of Murder . . . 400.00
106 Museum of Murder . . . . . . . . 400.00
107 Man with the Shrunken
　　Head . . . . . . . . . . . . . . . . . 400.00
108 The Headless Horse Player . 400.00
109 LF,Bondage(c),Blood on the
　　Chinese Fan . . . . . . . . . . . . 400.00
110 Murder with a Bang . . . . . . . 400.00
111 Diana, Homocidal Huntress . 400.00
112 RC,The Corpse on the
　　Sidewalk . . . . . . . . . . . . . . 450.00
113 RC(a&c), The Dead Man
　　with the Size 13 Shoe . . . . . 450.00
114 The Terrifying Secret of
　　the Black Bear. . . . . . . . . . . 400.00
115 Don't Let Them Kill Me . . . . 400.00
116 Stage Was Set For Murder . . 400.00
117 Bullet Riddled Bookkeeper . . 400.00
118 Case of the Absent Corpse. . 400.00
119 A Fast & Bloody Buck . . . . . 400.00
120 Death & The Derelict . . . . . . 400.00
121 Curse of the Clawed Killer . . 400.00
122 The Lonely Hearts Killer . . . . 400.00
123 Death Came Screaming . . . . 400.00
124 Masin Murder . . . . . . . . . . . 400.00
125 Bondage(c),The Killer of
　　King Arthur's Court . . . . . . . . 450.00
126 Hit & Run Murders . . . . . . . . 400.00
127 Oct'53,Death Drivers . . . . . . 400.00

## POLICE LINE-UP
### Avon Periodicals/
### Realistic Comics, Aug., 1951
1 WW,P(c). . . . . . . . . . . . . . . . 500.00
2 P(c),Drugs . . . . . . . . . . . . . . 400.00

3 JKu,EK,P(c) . . . . . . . . . . . . . . 250.00
4 July, '52;EK . . . . . . . . . . . . . . 250.00

## POLICE TRAP
### Mainline, Sept., 1954
1 S&K(c) . . . . . . . . . . . . . . . . . 350.00
2 S&K(c) . . . . . . . . . . . . . . . . . 200.00
3 S&K(c) . . . . . . . . . . . . . . . . . 200.00
4 S&K(c) . . . . . . . . . . . . . . . . . 200.00

### Charlton Comics, July, 1955
5 S&K,S&K(c) . . . . . . . . . . . . . . 300.00
6 S&K,S&K(c) . . . . . . . . . . . . . . 300.00
Becomes:

## PUBLIC DEFENDER
## IN ACTION
### Charlton Comics, March, 1956
7 . . . . . . . . . . . . . . . . . . . . . . . 125.00
8 and 9 . . . . . . . . . . . . . . . . @100.00
10 thru 12, . . . . . . . . . . . . . . @100.00

## POLLY PIGTAILS
### Parents' Magazine Institute,
### Jan., 1946
1 Ph(c) . . . . . . . . . . . . . . . . . . 150.00
2 Ph(c) . . . . . . . . . . . . . . . . . . 125.00
3 Ph(c) . . . . . . . . . . . . . . . . . . 100.00
4 Ph(c) . . . . . . . . . . . . . . . . . . 100.00
5 Ph(c) . . . . . . . . . . . . . . . . . . 100.00
6 Ph(c) . . . . . . . . . . . . . . . . . . 100.00
7 Ph(c) . . . . . . . . . . . . . . . . . . 100.00
8 . . . . . . . . . . . . . . . . . . . . . . 100.00
9 . . . . . . . . . . . . . . . . . . . . . . 100.00
10 . . . . . . . . . . . . . . . . . . . . . 100.00
11 thru 22 . . . . . . . . . . . . . . . @100.00
22 Ph(c) . . . . . . . . . . . . . . . . . 100.00
23 Ph(c) . . . . . . . . . . . . . . . . . 100.00
34 thru 43 . . . . . . . . . . . . . . . @100.00

## POPEYE
### Dell Publishing Co., 1948
1 . . . . . . . . . . . . . . . . . . . . . . 450.00
2 . . . . . . . . . . . . . . . . . . . . . . 250.00
3 'Welcome to Ghost Island' . . . 225.00
4 . . . . . . . . . . . . . . . . . . . . . . 225.00
5 . . . . . . . . . . . . . . . . . . . . . . 225.00
6 . . . . . . . . . . . . . . . . . . . . . . 225.00
7 . . . . . . . . . . . . . . . . . . . . . . 225.00
8 . . . . . . . . . . . . . . . . . . . . . . 225.00
9 . . . . . . . . . . . . . . . . . . . . . . 225.00
10 . . . . . . . . . . . . . . . . . . . . . 225.00
11 . . . . . . . . . . . . . . . . . . . . . 200.00
12 . . . . . . . . . . . . . . . . . . . . . 200.00

13 . . . . . . . . . . . . . . . . . . . . . . 200.00
14 thru 20 . . . . . . . . . . . . . . . @200.00
21 thru 30 . . . . . . . . . . . . . . . @150.00
31 thru 40 . . . . . . . . . . . . . . . @135.00
41 thru 45 . . . . . . . . . . . . . . . @125.00
46 O:Swee' Pea . . . . . . . . . . . . 150.00
47 thru 50 . . . . . . . . . . . . . . . @125.00
51 thru 60 . . . . . . . . . . . . . . . @100.00
61 thru 65 . . . . . . . . . . . . . . . @100.00

## POP-POP COMICS
### R.B. Leffingwell Co., 1946
2 . . . . . . . . . . . . . . . . . . . . . . 150.00

## POPSICLE PETE
## FUN BOOK
### Joe Lowe Corp., 1947
N# . . . . . . . . . . . . . . . . . . . . . . 125.00

## POPULAR COMICS
### Dell Publishing Co.,
### Feb., 1936
1 Dick Tracy, Little Orphan
　　Annie . . . . . . . . . . . . . . . . 9,000.00
2 Terry Pirates . . . . . . . . . . . 4,000.00
3 Terry,Annie,Dick Tracy . . . . 3,000.00
4 . . . . . . . . . . . . . . . . . . . . . 2,000.00
5 B:Tom Mix . . . . . . . . . . . . . 2,000.00
6 I:Scribbu . . . . . . . . . . . . . . 1,800.00
7 . . . . . . . . . . . . . . . . . . . . . 1,500.00
8 Scribbu & Reg Fellers. . . . . 1,500.00
9 . . . . . . . . . . . . . . . . . . . . . 1,500.00
10 Terry,Annie,Tracy . . . . . . . 1,500.00
11 Terry,Annie,Tracy . . . . . . . 1,000.00
12 Christmas(c). . . . . . . . . . . 1,000.00
13 Terry,Annie,Tracy . . . . . . . 1,000.00
14 Terry,Annie,Tracy . . . . . . . 1,000.00
15 Terry,Annie,Tracy . . . . . . . 1,000.00
16 Terry,Annie,Tracy . . . . . . . 1,000.00
17 Terry,Annie,Tracy . . . . . . . 1,000.00
18 Terry,Annie,Tracy . . . . . . . 1,000.00
19 Terry,Annie,Tracy . . . . . . . 1,000.00
20 Terry,Annie,Tracy . . . . . . . 1,000.00
21 Terry,Annie,Tracy . . . . . . . . 750.00
22 Terry,Annie,Tracy . . . . . . . . 750.00
23 Terry,Annie,Tracy . . . . . . . . 750.00
24 Terry,Annie,Tracy . . . . . . . . 750.00
25 Terry,Annie,Tracy . . . . . . . . 750.00
26 Terry,Annie,Tracy . . . . . . . . 750.00
27 E:Terry,Annie,Tracy. . . . . . . 750.00
28 A:Gene Autry. . . . . . . . . . . . 550.00
29 . . . . . . . . . . . . . . . . . . . . . 550.00
30 . . . . . . . . . . . . . . . . . . . . . 550.00

**Po**

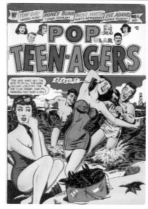

Popular Comics #61
© Dell Publishing Co.

Popular Teen-Agers #8
© Star Publications

Powerhouse Pepper Comics #1
© Marvel Comics Group

31 A:Jim McCoy . . . . . . . . . . . . . 550.00
32 A:Jim McCoy . . . . . . . . . . . . . 550.00
33 . . . . . . . . . . . . . . . . . . . . . . . . 550.00
34 . . . . . . . . . . . . . . . . . . . . . . . . 550.00
35 Christmas(c),Tex Ritter . . . . . 550.00
36 . . . . . . . . . . . . . . . . . . . . . . . . 550.00
37 . . . . . . . . . . . . . . . . . . . . . . . . 550.00
38 B:Gang Busters . . . . . . . . . . . 600.00
39 . . . . . . . . . . . . . . . . . . . . . . . . 550.00
40 . . . . . . . . . . . . . . . . . . . . . . . . 550.00
41 . . . . . . . . . . . . . . . . . . . . . . . . 550.00
42 . . . . . . . . . . . . . . . . . . . . . . . . 550.00
43 F:Gang Busters . . . . . . . . . . . 550.00
44 . . . . . . . . . . . . . . . . . . . . . . . . 400.00
45 Tarzan(c) . . . . . . . . . . . . . . . . 400.00
46 O:Martan the Marvel Man . . . . 500.00
47 F:Martan the Marvel Man . . . . 350.00
48 F:Martan the Marvel Man . . . . 350.00
49 F:Martan the Marvel Man . . . . 350.00
50 . . . . . . . . . . . . . . . . . . . . . . . . 350.00
51 B&O:Voice . . . . . . . . . . . . . . . 350.00
52 A:Voice . . . . . . . . . . . . . . . . . . 350.00
53 F:The Voice . . . . . . . . . . . . . . 325.00
54 F:Gang Busters,A:Voice . . . . . 325.00
55 F:Gang Busters . . . . . . . . . . . 350.00
56 F:Gang Busters . . . . . . . . . . . 325.00
57 F:The Marvel Man . . . . . . . . . 325.00
58 F:The Marvel Man . . . . . . . . . 325.00
59 F:The Marvel Man . . . . . . . . . 325.00
60 O:Prof. Supermind . . . . . . . . 350.00
61 Prof. Supermind & Son . . . . . 275.00
62 Supermind & Son . . . . . . . . . 275.00
63 B:Smilin' Jack . . . . . . . . . . . . 275.00
64 Smilin'Jack,Supermind . . . . . 275.00
65 Professor Supermind . . . . . . . 275.00
66 . . . . . . . . . . . . . . . . . . . . . . . . 275.00
67 Gasoline Alley . . . . . . . . . . . . 275.00
68 F:Smilin' Jack . . . . . . . . . . . . 275.00
69 F:Smilin' Jack . . . . . . . . . . . . 275.00
70 F:Smilin' Jack . . . . . . . . . . . . 275.00
71 F:Smilin' Jack . . . . . . . . . . . . 275.00
72 B:Owl,Terry & the Pirates . . . . 500.00
73 F:Terry and the Pirates . . . . . . 300.00
74 F:Smilin' Jack . . . . . . . . . . . . 300.00
75 F:Smilin'Jack,A:Owl . . . . . . . . 300.00
76 Captain Midnight . . . . . . . . . . 425.00
77 Captain Midnight . . . . . . . . . . 425.00
78 Captain Midnight . . . . . . . . . . 425.00
79 A:Owl . . . . . . . . . . . . . . . . . . . 300.00
80 F:Smilin' Jack,A:Owl . . . . . . . . 300.00
81 F: Terry&thePirates,A:Owl . . . 300.00
82 F:Smilin' Jack,A:Owl . . . . . . . . 300.00
83 F:Smilin' Jack,A:Owl . . . . . . . . 300.00
84 F:Smilin' Jack,A:Owl . . . . . . . . 300.00
85 F:ThreeLittleGremlins,A:Owl . . 300.00
86 F:Three Little Gremlins . . . . . . 200.00

87 F:Smilin' Jack . . . . . . . . . . . . 200.00
88 F:Smilin' Jack . . . . . . . . . . . . 200.00
89 F:Smokey Stover . . . . . . . . . . 200.00
90 F:Terry and the Pirates . . . . . . 200.00
91 F:Smokey Stover . . . . . . . . . . 200.00
92 F:Terry and the Pirates . . . . . . 200.00
93 F:Smilin' Jack . . . . . . . . . . . . 200.00
94 F:Terry and the Pirates . . . . . . 200.00
95 F:Smilin' Jack . . . . . . . . . . . . 200.00
96 F:Gang Busters . . . . . . . . . . . 200.00
97 F:Smilin' Jack . . . . . . . . . . . . 200.00
98 B:Felix Cat . . . . . . . . . . . . . . 225.00
99 F:Bang Busters . . . . . . . . . . . 200.00
100 . . . . . . . . . . . . . . . . . . . . . . 250.00
101 thru 141 . . . . . . . . . . . . . @175.00
142 E:Terry & the Pirates . . . . . . 125.00
143 . . . . . . . . . . . . . . . . . . . . . . 125.00
144 . . . . . . . . . . . . . . . . . . . . . . 125.00
145 F:Harold Teen . . . . . . . . . . . 125.00

## POPULAR ROMANCES
### Better Publications
### (Standard Comics), Dec., 1949
5 B:Ph(c) . . . . . . . . . . . . . . . . . . 150.00
6 Ph(c) . . . . . . . . . . . . . . . . . . . . 100.00
7 RP . . . . . . . . . . . . . . . . . . . . . . 100.00
8 Ph(c) . . . . . . . . . . . . . . . . . . . . 100.00
9 Ph(c) . . . . . . . . . . . . . . . . . . . . 100.00
10 WW . . . . . . . . . . . . . . . . . . . . 150.00
11 thru 16 . . . . . . . . . . . . . . . @100.00
17 WE . . . . . . . . . . . . . . . . . . . . 100.00
18 thru 21 . . . . . . . . . . . . . . . @100.00
22 thru 27 ATh,Ph(c) . . . . . . . @125.00

## SCHOOL DAY ROMANCES
### Star Publications,
### Nov.–Dec., 1949
1 LbC(c),Teen-Age . . . . . . . . . . 375.00
2 LbC(c) . . . . . . . . . . . . . . . . . . 350.00
3 LbC(c),Ph(c) . . . . . . . . . . . . . 350.00
4 LbC(c),JyD,RonaldReagan . . . 400.00
**Becomes:**

## POPULAR TEEN-AGERS
### Sept., 1950
5 LbC(c),Toni Gay, Eve Adams . 400.00
6 LbC(c),Ginger Bunny,
Midge Martin . . . . . . . . . . . . 350.00
7 LbC(c) . . . . . . . . . . . . . . . . . . 350.00
8 LbC(c) . . . . . . . . . . . . . . . . . . 350.00
9 LbC(c) Romances . . . . . . . . . . 250.00
10 LbC(c) Secrets of Love . . . . . 225.00
11 LbC(c) Secrets of Love . . . . . 225.00
12 LbC(c) Secrets of Love . . . . . 225.00

13 LbC(c),JyD Secrets of Love . . 225.00
14 LbC,WW, Secrets of Love
Spanking . . . . . . . . . . . . . . 300.00
15 LbC(c),JyD Secrets of Love . . 225.00
16 Secrets of Love . . . . . . . . . . . 200.00
17 LbC(c),JyD Secrets of Love . . 200.00
18 LbC(c) Secrets of Love . . . . . 200.00
19 LbC(c) Secrets of Love . . . . . 200.00
20 LbC(c),JyD Secrets of Love . . 225.00
21 LbC(c),JyD Secrets of Love . . 225.00
22 LbC(c) Secrets of Love . . . . . 200.00
23 LbC(c) Secrets of Love . . . . . 200.00

## POWER COMICS
### Holyoke/Narrative Publ., 1944
1 LbC(c) . . . . . . . . . . . . . . . . . 2,000.00
2 B:Dr.Mephisto,Hitler(c) . . . . . 2,100.00
3 LbC(c) . . . . . . . . . . . . . . . . . 2,400.00
4 LbC(c) . . . . . . . . . . . . . . . . . 2,000.00

## POWERHOUSE PEPPER COMICS
### Marvel, 1943—Nov., 1948
1 BW,Movie Auditions(c) . . . . . 2,500.00
2 BW,Dinner(c) . . . . . . . . . . . . 1,200.00
3 BW,Boxing Ring(c) . . . . . . . 1,100.00
4 BW,Subway(c) . . . . . . . . . . . 1,100.00
5 BW,Bankrobbers(c) . . . . . . . 1,300.00

## PRIDE OF THE YANKEES
### Magazine Enterprises, 1949
1 N#,OW,Ph(c),The Life
of Lou Gehrig . . . . . . . . . . 1,100.00

## PRISON BREAK
### Avon Periodicals/Realistic, Sept., 1951
1 WW(c),WW . . . . . . . . . . . . . . 550.00
2 WW(c),WW,JKu . . . . . . . . . . . 400.00
3 JD,JO . . . . . . . . . . . . . . . . . . 300.00
4 EK . . . . . . . . . . . . . . . . . . . . . 250.00
5 EK,CI . . . . . . . . . . . . . . . . . . . 250.00

## PRIVATE EYE
### Marvel Atlas, Jan., 1951
1 . . . . . . . . . . . . . . . . . . . . . . . 250.00
2 . . . . . . . . . . . . . . . . . . . . . . . 175.00
3 GT . . . . . . . . . . . . . . . . . . . . . 175.00
4 . . . . . . . . . . . . . . . . . . . . . . . 125.00
5 . . . . . . . . . . . . . . . . . . . . . . . 125.00

All comics prices listed are for *Near Mint* condition.

Prize Comics #8
© Prize Publications

Prize Comics #51
© Prize Publications

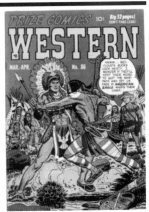

Prize Comics Western #86
© Prize Comics

6 JSt . . . . . . . . . . . . . . . . . . . . 125.00
7 . . . . . . . . . . . . . . . . . . . . . . . 125.00
8 March, 1952 . . . . . . . . . . . . . . 125.00

## PRIZE COMICS
### Feature Publications
### (Prize Publ.), March, 1940
1 O&B:Power Nelson,Jupiter.
  B:Ted O'Neil,Jaxon of
  the Jungle,Bucky Brady,
  Storm Curtis, Rocket(c) . . . 6,000.00
2 B:The Owl . . . . . . . . . . . . . 3,000.00
3 Power Nelson(c) . . . . . . . . . 2,700.00
4 Power Nelson(c) . . . . . . . . . 2,700.00
5 A:Dr.Dekkar. . . . . . . . . . . . 2,400.00
6 A:Dr.Dekkar. . . . . . . . . . . . 2,400.00
7 S&K,DBr,JK(c),O&B DR Frost,
  Frankenstein,B:GreenLama,
  Capt Gallant,Voodini
  Twist Turner . . . . . . . . . . . . 4,500.00
8 S&K,DBr . . . . . . . . . . . . . . 2,600.00
9 S&K,DBr,Black Owl(c) . . . . . 2,500.00
10 DBr,Black Owl(c) . . . . . . . 2,000.00
11 DBr,O:Bulldog Denny . . . . . 1,800.00
12 DBr. . . . . . . . . . . . . . . . . 1,800.00
13 DBr,O&B:Yank and
  Doodle,Bondage(c). . . . . . 2,000.00
14 DBr,Black Owl(c) . . . . . . . . 1,800.00
15 DBr,Black Owl(c) . . . . . . . . 1,800.00
16 DBr,JaB,B:Spike Mason. . . . 1,800.00
17 DBr,Black Owl(c) . . . . . . . . 1,800.00
18 DBr,Black Owl(c) . . . . . . . . 1,800.00
19 DBr,Yank&Doodle(c) . . . . . . 1,800.00
20 DBr,Yank&Doodle(c) . . . . . . 1,800.00
21 DBr,JaB(c),Yank&Doodle(c). 1,500.00
22 DBr,Yank&Doodle(c) . . . . . . 1,500.00
23 DBr,Uncle Sam(c) . . . . . . . . 1,500.00
24 DBr,Abe Lincoln(c) . . . . . . . 1,500.00
25 DBr,JaB,Yank&Doodle(c). . . 1,500.00
26 DBr,JaB,JaB(c),Liberty
  Bell(c) . . . . . . . . . . . . . . . 1,500.00
27 DBr,Yank&Doodle(c) . . . . . . 1,000.00
28 DBr,Yank&Doodle(c) . . . . . . . 900.00
29 DBr,JaB(c)Yank&Doodle(c). . 900.00
30 DBr,Yank&Doodle(c) . . . . . . 1,000.00
31 DBr,Yank&Doodle(c) . . . . . . . 900.00
32 DBr,Yank&Doodle(c) . . . . . . . 900.00
33 DBr,Bondage(c),Yank
  & Doodle. . . . . . . . . . . . . 1,000.00
34 DBr,O:Airmale;New
  Black Owl . . . . . . . . . . . . . 1,000.00
35 DBr,B:Flying Fist & Bingo . . . . 750.00
36 DBr,Yank&Doodle(c). . . . . . . 750.00
37 DBr,I:Stampy,Hitler(c) . . . . . . 800.00
38 DBr,B.Owl,Yank&Doodle(c) . . 750.00

39 DBr,B.Owl,Yank&Doodle(c) . . 750.00
40 DBr,B.Owl,Yank&Doodle(c) . . 750.00
41 DBr,B.Owl,Yank&Doodle(c) . . 750.00
42 DBr,B.Owl,Yank&Doodle(c) . . 500.00
43 DBr,B.Owl,Yank&Doodle(c) . . 500.00
44 DBr, B&I:Boom Boom
  Brannigan . . . . . . . . . . . . . . 500.00
45 DBr . . . . . . . . . . . . . . . . . . . 500.00
46 DBr . . . . . . . . . . . . . . . . . . . 500.00
47 DBr . . . . . . . . . . . . . . . . . . . 500.00
48 DBr,B:Prince Ra;Bondage(c) . 600.00
49 DBr,Boom Boom(c). . . . . . . . 500.00
50 DBr,Frankenstein(c) . . . . . . . 500.00
51 DBr . . . . . . . . . . . . . . . . . . . 500.00
52 DBr, B:Sir Prize. . . . . . . . . . . 500.00
53 DBr, The Man Who Could
  Read Features. . . . . . . . . . . 500.00
54 DBr . . . . . . . . . . . . . . . . . . . 500.00
55 DBr,Yank&Doodle(c). . . . . . . 500.00
56 DBr,Boom Boom (c) . . . . . . . 500.00
57 DBr,Santa Claus(c). . . . . . . . 500.00
58 DBr,The Poisoned Punch . . . . 500.00
59 DBr,Boom Boom(c) . . . . . . . . 500.00
60 DBr,Sir Prise(c) . . . . . . . . . . 500.00
61 DBr,The Man wih the
  Fighting Feet . . . . . . . . . . . . 500.00
62 DBr,Hck(c),Yank&Doodle(c) . . 500.00
63 DBr,S&K,S&K(c),Boom
  Boom(c). . . . . . . . . . . . . . . 550.00
64 DBr,Blackowl Retires . . . . . . . 400.00
65 DBr,DBr(c),Frankenstein. . . . . 400.00
66 DBr,DBr(c),Frankenstein. . . . . 400.00
67 DBr,B:Brothers in Crime . . . . . 400.00
68 DBr,RP(c) . . . . . . . . . . . . . . 400.00
**Becomes:**

## PRIZE COMICS
## WESTERN
### Feature Publ., April–May, 1948
69 ACa(c),B:Dusty Ballew . . . . . 150.00
70 ACa(c). . . . . . . . . . . . . . . . . 125.00
71 ACa(c). . . . . . . . . . . . . . . . . 125.00
72 ACa(c),JSe . . . . . . . . . . . . . 125.00
73 ACa(c). . . . . . . . . . . . . . . . . 125.00
74 ACa(c). . . . . . . . . . . . . . . . . 125.00
75 JSe,S&K(c),6-Gun Showdown
  at Rattlesnake Gulch . . . . . . . 135.00
76 Ph(c),Randolph Scott . . . . . . 150.00
77 Ph(c),JSe,Streets of
  Laredo,movie. . . . . . . . . . . . 135.00
78 Ph(c),JSe,HK,Bullet
  Code, movie . . . . . . . . . . . . 200.00
79 Ph(c),JSe,Stage to
  China, movie . . . . . . . . . . . . 200.00
80 Ph(c),Gunsmoke Justice. . . . . 150.00

81 Ph(c),The Man Who Shot
  Billy The Kid . . . . . . . . . . . . 150.00
82 Ph(c),MBi,JSe&BE,Death
  Draws a Circle. . . . . . . . . . . 150.00
83 JSe,S&K(c) . . . . . . . . . . . . . 125.00
84 JSe . . . . . . . . . . . . . . . . . . . 100.00
85 JSe,B:American Eagle . . . . . . 300.00
86 JSe . . . . . . . . . . . . . . . . . . . 150.00
87 JSe&BE. . . . . . . . . . . . . . . . 150.00
88 JSe&BE. . . . . . . . . . . . . . . . 150.00
89 JSe&BE. . . . . . . . . . . . . . . . 150.00
90 JSe&Be. . . . . . . . . . . . . . . . 150.00
91 JSe&BE,JSe&BE(c) . . . . . . . 150.00
92 JSe,JSe&BE(c) . . . . . . . . . . 150.00
93 JSe,JSe&BE(c), . . . . . . . . . . 150.00
94 JSe,JSe&BE(c) . . . . . . . . . . 150.00
95 JSe,JSe&BE(c) . . . . . . . . . . 150.00
96 JSe,JSe&BE,JSe&BE(c). . . . 150.00
97 JSe,JSe&BE,JSeBE(c). . . . . 150.00
98 JSe&BE,JSe&BE(c) . . . . . . . 150.00
99 JSe&BE,JSe&BE(c) . . . . . . . 150.00
100 JSe,JSe(c) . . . . . . . . . . . . . 175.00
101 JSe . . . . . . . . . . . . . . . . . . 150.00
102 JSe . . . . . . . . . . . . . . . . . . 150.00
103 JSe . . . . . . . . . . . . . . . . . . 150.00
104 JSe . . . . . . . . . . . . . . . . . . 150.00
105 JSe . . . . . . . . . . . . . . . . . . 150.00
106 JSe . . . . . . . . . . . . . . . . . . 100.00
107 JSe . . . . . . . . . . . . . . . . . . 100.00
108 JSe . . . . . . . . . . . . . . . . . . 110.00
109 JSe&AW . . . . . . . . . . . . . . 125.00
110 JSe&BE . . . . . . . . . . . . . . . 125.00
111 JSe&BE . . . . . . . . . . . . . . . 125.00
112 . . . . . . . . . . . . . . . . . . . . . 100.00
113 AW&JSe . . . . . . . . . . . . . . 125.00
114 MMe,B:The Drifter. . . . . . . . 100.00
115 MMe . . . . . . . . . . . . . . . . . 100.00
116 MMe . . . . . . . . . . . . . . . . . 100.00
117 MMe . . . . . . . . . . . . . . . . . 100.00
118 MMe,E:The Drifter. . . . . . . . 100.00
119 Nov/Dec'56 . . . . . . . . . . . . 100.00

## PRIZE MYSTERY
### Key Publications, 1955
1 . . . . . . . . . . . . . . . . . . . . . . 125.00
2 and 3 . . . . . . . . . . . . . . . . . @100.00

## PSYCHOANALYSIS
### E.C. Comics,
### March–April, 1955
1 JKa,JKa(c) . . . . . . . . . . . . . . 250.00
2 JKa,JKa(c) . . . . . . . . . . . . . . 200.00
3 JKa,JKa(c) . . . . . . . . . . . . . . 200.00
4 JKa,JKa(c) Sept.–Oct., 1955 . . 200.00

*Punch and Judy Comics #4*
*© Hillman Periodicals*

*Punch Comics #14*
*© Harry A Chesler*

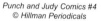

*Race For the Moon #1*
*© Harvey Publications*

## PUBLIC DEFENDER IN ACTION

See: POLICE TRAP

## PUBLIC ENEMIES

**D.S. Publishing Co., 1948**

| | |
|---|---|
| 1 AMc | 300.00 |
| 2 AMc | 250.00 |
| 3 AMc | 200.00 |
| 4 AMc | 200.00 |
| 5 AMc | 200.00 |
| 6 AMc | 150.00 |
| 7 AMc,Eye Injury | 200.00 |
| 8 | 150.00 |
| 9 | 150.00 |

## PUDGY PIG

**Charlton Comics, 1958**

| | |
|---|---|
| 1 | 125.00 |
| 2 | 100.00 |

## PUNCH AND JUDY COMICS

**Hillman Periodicals, 1944**

| | |
|---|---|
| 1 (fa) | 300.00 |
| 2 | 250.00 |
| 3 | 200.00 |
| 4 thru 12 | @175.00 |
| 2-1 | 150.00 |
| 2-2 JK | 250.00 |
| 2-3 | 150.00 |
| 2-4 | 150.00 |
| 2-5 | 150.00 |
| 2-6 | 150.00 |
| 2-7 | 150.00 |
| 2-8 | 150.00 |
| 2-9 | 150.00 |
| 2-10 JK | 250.00 |
| 2-11 JK | 250.00 |
| 2-12 JK | 250.00 |
| 3-1 JK | 250.00 |
| 3-2 | 200.00 |
| 3-3 | 100.00 |
| 3-4 | 100.00 |
| 3-5 | 100.00 |
| 3-6 | 100.00 |
| 3-7 | 100.00 |
| 3-8 | 100.00 |
| 3-9 | 100.00 |

## PUNCH COMICS

**Harry 'A' Chesler, Dec., 1941**

| | |
|---|---|
| 1 B:Mr.E,The Sky Chief,Hale the Magician,Kitty Kelly | 3,000.00 |
| 2 A:Capt.Glory | 2,400.00 |
| 3-8 Do Not Exist | |
| 9 B:Rocket Man & Rocket girl,Master Ken | 2,400.00 |
| 10 JCo,A:Sky Chief | 1,700.00 |
| 11 JCo,O:Master Key,A:Little Nemo | 1,700.00 |
| 12 A:Rocket Boy,Capt.Glory | 4,000.00 |
| 13 Ric(c) | 1,700.00 |
| 14 GT | 1,200.00 |
| 15 FSm(c) | 1,200.00 |
| 16 | 1,200.00 |
| 17 | 1,200.00 |
| 18 FSm(c),Bondage(c),Drug | 1,500.00 |
| 19 FSm(c) | 1,200.00 |
| 20 Women semi-nude(c) | 1,800.00 |
| 21 Drug | 1,200.00 |
| 22 I:Baxter,Little Nemo | 700.00 |
| 23 A:Little Nemo | 700.00 |

## PUPPET COMICS

**Dougherty, Co., Spring, 1946**

| | |
|---|---|
| 1 Funny Animal | 125.00 |
| 2 | 125.00 |

## PURPLE CLAW, THE

**Minoan Publishing Co./ Toby Press, Jan., 1953**

| | |
|---|---|
| 1 O:Purple Claw | 400.00 |
| 2 and 3 | @250.00 |

## PUZZLE FUN COMICS

**George W. Dougherty Co., Spring, 1946**

| | |
|---|---|
| 1 PGv | 275.00 |
| 2 | 200.00 |

## QUEEN OF THE WEST, DALE EVANS

**Dell Publishing Co., July, 1953**

| | |
|---|---|
| (1) see Dell Four Color #479 | |
| (1) see Dell Four Color #528 | |
| 3 ATh, Ph(c) all | 125.00 |
| 4 ATh,RsM | 110.00 |
| 5 RsM | 100.00 |
| 6 RsM | 100.00 |

| | |
|---|---|
| 7 RsM | 100.00 |
| 8 RsM | 100.00 |
| 9 RsM | 100.00 |
| 10 RsM | 100.00 |
| 11 | 75.00 |
| 12 RsM | 85.00 |
| 13 RsM | 85.00 |
| 14 RsM | 85.00 |
| 15 RsM | 85.00 |
| 16 RsM | 85.00 |
| 17 RsM | 85.00 |
| 18 RsM | 85.00 |
| 19 | 75.00 |
| 20 RsM | 85.00 |
| 21 | 75.00 |
| 22 RsM | 85.00 |

## QUICK-TRIGGER WESTERN

See: WESTERN THRILLERS

## RACE FOR THE MOON

**Harvey Publications, 1958**

| | |
|---|---|
| 1 BP | 175.00 |
| 2 JK,AW,JK/AW(c) | 300.00 |
| 3 JK,AW,JK/AW(c) | 350.00 |

## RACKET SQUAD IN ACTION

**Capitol Stories/ Charlton Comics, May–June, 1952**

| | |
|---|---|
| 1 Carnival(c) | 350.00 |
| 2 | 175.00 |
| 3 Roulette | 175.00 |
| 4 FFr(c) | 250.00 |
| 5 Just off the Boat | 250.00 |
| 6 The Kidnap Racket | 200.00 |
| 7 | 150.00 |
| 8 | 150.00 |
| 9 2 Fisted fix | 150.00 |
| 10 Explosion Blast (c) | 250.00 |
| 11 SD(a&c),Racing(c) | 350.00 |
| 12 JoS,SD(c),Explosion(c) | 900.00 |
| 13 JoS(c),The Notorious Modelling Agency Racket,Acid | 150.00 |
| 14 DG(c),Drug | 200.00 |
| 15 Photo Extortion Racket | 150.00 |
| 16 thru 28 | @150.00 |
| 29 March, 1958 | 150.00 |

**Pu**

All comics prices listed are for *Near Mint* condition.

Raggedy Ann and Andy #36
© Dell Publishing Co.

Range Romances #1
© Quality Comics

Rangers Comics #33
© Fiction House

## RADIANT LOVE
### See: DARING LOVE

## RAGGEDY ANN AND ANDY
**Dell Publishing Co., 1942**
1 Billy & Bonnie Bee . . . . . . . . . 600.00
2 . . . . . . . . . . . . . . . . . . . . . . . . 350.00
3 DNo,B:Egbert Elephant . . . . . 350.00
4 DNo,WK . . . . . . . . . . . . . . . . 400.00
5 DNo . . . . . . . . . . . . . . . . . . . . 300.00
6 DNo . . . . . . . . . . . . . . . . . . . . 300.00
7 Little Black Sambo . . . . . . . . . 300.00
8 . . . . . . . . . . . . . . . . . . . . . . . . 300.00
9 . . . . . . . . . . . . . . . . . . . . . . . . 300.00
10 . . . . . . . . . . . . . . . . . . . . . . . 300.00
11 . . . . . . . . . . . . . . . . . . . . . . . 250.00
12 . . . . . . . . . . . . . . . . . . . . . . . 250.00
13 . . . . . . . . . . . . . . . . . . . . . . . 250.00
14 . . . . . . . . . . . . . . . . . . . . . . . 250.00
15 . . . . . . . . . . . . . . . . . . . . . . . 250.00
16 thru 20 . . . . . . . . . . . . . . . @250.00
21 Alice in Wonderland . . . . . . . 300.00
22 thru 27 . . . . . . . . . . . . . . . . @200.00
28 WK . . . . . . . . . . . . . . . . . . . . 225.00
29 thru 39 . . . . . . . . . . . . . . . @200.00

## RAGS RABBIT
**Harvey Publications, 1957**
11 . . . . . . . . . . . . . . . . . . . . . . . 120.00
12 . . . . . . . . . . . . . . . . . . . . . . . 100.00
13 . . . . . . . . . . . . . . . . . . . . . . . 100.00
14 . . . . . . . . . . . . . . . . . . . . . . . 100.00
15 . . . . . . . . . . . . . . . . . . . . . . . 100.00
16 . . . . . . . . . . . . . . . . . . . . . . . 100.00
17 . . . . . . . . . . . . . . . . . . . . . . . 100.00
18 . . . . . . . . . . . . . . . . . . . . . . . 100.00

## RALPH KINER HOME RUN KING
**Fawcett Publications, 1950**
1 N#, Life Story of the
    Famous Pittsburgh Slugger. . 800.00

## RAMAR OF THE JUNGLE
**Toby Press/ Charlton Comics, 1954**
1 Ph(c),TV Show . . . . . . . . . . . . 250.00
2 Ph(c) . . . . . . . . . . . . . . . . . . . 200.00

3 . . . . . . . . . . . . . . . . . . . . . . . . 200.00
4 . . . . . . . . . . . . . . . . . . . . . . . . 200.00
5 Sept '56 . . . . . . . . . . . . . . . . . 200.00

## RANGE BUSTERS
**Charlton Comics, 1955**
8 . . . . . . . . . . . . . . . . . . . . . . . . 150.00
9 & 10 . . . . . . . . . . . . . . . . . . @100.00

## RANGELAND LOVE
**Marvel Comics, 1949**
1 Robert Taylor . . . . . . . . . . . . . 200.00
2 . . . . . . . . . . . . . . . . . . . . . . . . 150.00

## RANGE ROMANCES
**Comics Magazines (Quality Comics), Dec., 1949**
1 PGv(a&c) . . . . . . . . . . . . . . . . 300.00
2 RC(a&c) . . . . . . . . . . . . . . . . . 350.00
3 RC,Ph(c) . . . . . . . . . . . . . . . . . 275.00
4 RC,Ph(c) . . . . . . . . . . . . . . . . . 250.00
5 RC,PGv,Ph(c) . . . . . . . . . . . . . 250.00

## RANGERS OF FREEDOM
**Flying Stories, Inc. (Fiction House), Oct., 1941**
1 I:Ranger Girl & Rangers
    of Freedom;V:Super-Brain . 5,000.00
2 V:Super -Brain . . . . . . . . . . . 1,800.00
3 Bondage(c) The Headsman
    of Hate . . . . . . . . . . . . . . . . 1,500.00
4 Hawaiian Inferno . . . . . . . . . . 1,200.00
5 RP,V:Super-Brain . . . . . . . . . 1,200.00
6 RP,Bondage(c);Bugles
    of the Damned . . . . . . . . . . 1,200.00
7 RP,Death to Tojo's Butchers . 1,000.00
**Becomes:**

## RANGERS COMICS
**Dec., 1942**
8 RP,B:US Rangers . . . . . . . . . 1,000.00
9 GT,BLb,Commando Steel
    for Slant Eyes . . . . . . . . . . 1,000.00
10 BLb,Bondage (c) . . . . . . . . . 1,100.00
11 Raiders of the
    Purple Death . . . . . . . . . . . . 900.00
12 A:Commando Rangers . . . . . . 900.00
13 Grl,B:Commando Ranger . . 1,000.00
14 Grl,Bondage(c) . . . . . . . . . . 1,100.00
15 GT,Grl,Bondage(c) . . . . . . . 1,100.00
16 Grl,GT;Burma Raid . . . . . . . . 650.00
17 GT,GT,Bondage(c),Raiders
    of the Red Dawn . . . . . . . . 1,000.00

18 GT . . . . . . . . . . . . . . . . . . . . . 650.00
19 GE,BLb,GT,Bondage(c) . . . 1,100.00
20 GT . . . . . . . . . . . . . . . . . . . . . 500.00
21 GT,Bondage(c) . . . . . . . . . . . 650.00
22 GT,B&O:Firehair . . . . . . . . . . 500.00
23 GT,BLb,B:Kazana . . . . . . . . . 450.00
24 Bondage(c) . . . . . . . . . . . . . . 450.00
25 Bondage(c) . . . . . . . . . . . . . . 450.00
26 Angels From Hell . . . . . . . . . . 400.00
27 Bondage(c) . . . . . . . . . . . . . . 500.00
28 BLb,E:Kazana;B&O Tiger
    Man . . . . . . . . . . . . . . . . . . . 450.00
29 Bondage(c) . . . . . . . . . . . . . . 500.00
30 BLb,B:Crusoe Island . . . . . . . 450.00
31 BLb,Bondage(c) . . . . . . . . . . 400.00
32 BLb . . . . . . . . . . . . . . . . . . . . 400.00
33 BLb,Drug . . . . . . . . . . . . . . . . 550.00
34 BLb . . . . . . . . . . . . . . . . . . . . 300.00
35 Bl b,Bondage(c) . . . . . . . . . . 400.00
36 BLb,MB . . . . . . . . . . . . . . . . . 300.00
37 BLb,Mb . . . . . . . . . . . . . . . . . 350.00
38 BLb,MB,GE,Bondage(c) . . . . 400.00
39 BLb,GE . . . . . . . . . . . . . . . . . 500.00
40 BLb,GE,BLb(c) . . . . . . . . . . . 300.00
41 BLb,GE, L:Werewolf Hunter . . 300.00
42 BLb,GE . . . . . . . . . . . . . . . . . 300.00
43 BLb,GE . . . . . . . . . . . . . . . . . 300.00
44 BLb,GE . . . . . . . . . . . . . . . . . 300.00
45 BLb,GEl . . . . . . . . . . . . . . . . . 300.00
46 BLb,GE . . . . . . . . . . . . . . . . . 300.00
47 BLb,JGr, Dr. Drew . . . . . . . . . 300.00
48 BLb,JGr, L:Glory Forces . . . . . 300.00
49 BLb,JGr . . . . . . . . . . . . . . . . . 300.00
50 BLb,JGr,Bondage(c) . . . . . . . 350.00
51 BLb,JGr . . . . . . . . . . . . . . . . . 300.00
52 BLb,JGr,Bondage(c) . . . . . . . 350.00
53 BLb,JGr,Prisoners of
    Devil Pass . . . . . . . . . . . . . . 250.00
54 JGr,When The Wild
    Commanches Ride . . . . . . . 250.00
55 JGr,Massacre Guns at
    Pawnee Pass . . . . . . . . . . . 250.00
56 JGr, Gun Smuggler of
    Apache Mesa . . . . . . . . . . . 250.00
57 JGr,Redskins to the
    Rescue . . . . . . . . . . . . . . . . 225.00
58 JGr,Brides of the
    Buffalo Men . . . . . . . . . . . . . 225.00
59 JGr,Plunder Portage . . . . . . . 225.00
60 JGr, Buzzards of
    Bushwack Trail . . . . . . . . . . 225.00
61 BWh(c)Devil Smoke at
    Apache Basin . . . . . . . . . . . 150.00
62 BWh(c)B:Cowboy Bob . . . . . 150.00
63 BWh(c) . . . . . . . . . . . . . . . . . 150.00
64 BWh(c)B:Suicide Smith . . . . 150.00

**Ra**

*Rawhide Kid #1*
© Marvel Comics Group

*Real Heroes #1*
© Parents' Magazine Institute

*Real Life Comics #18*
© Standard Publications

65 BWh(c):Wolves of the
  Overland Trail,Bondage(c) . . 165.00
66 BWh(c) . . . . . . . . . . . . . . . . 150.00
67 BWh(c)B:Space Rangers . . . . 150.00
68 BWh(c);Cargo for Coje . . . . . . 150.00
69 BWh(c);Great Red Death Ray 150.00

## RAWHIDE KID
### Marvel Atlas, March, 1955
1 JMn,B:Rawhide Kid & Randy,
  A:Wyatt Earp . . . . . . . . . . 1,200.00
2 JMn,Shoot-out(c) . . . . . . . . . 500.00
3 V:Hustler . . . . . . . . . . . . . . . 350.00
4 Rh(c) . . . . . . . . . . . . . . . . . . 350.00
5 GC,JMn . . . . . . . . . . . . . . . . 350.00
6 JMn,Six-Gun Lesson . . . . . . . 250.00
7 AW . . . . . . . . . . . . . . . . . . . 250.00
8 . . . . . . . . . . . . . . . . . . . . . . 250.00
9 . . . . . . . . . . . . . . . . . . . . . . 250.00
10 thru 16 Sept. 1957 . . . . . . . @225.00
17 JK,O:Rawhide Kid; Aug. 1960 225.00
18 thru 20 . . . . . . . . . . . . . . . @225.00
21 . . . . . . . . . . . . . . . . . . . . . 225.00
22 . . . . . . . . . . . . . . . . . . . . . 225.00
23 JK,O:Rawhide Kid Retold . . . . 300.00
24 thru 30 . . . . . . . . . . . . . . . @200.00
31 JK,DAy,No Law in Mesa . . . . . 200.00
32 JK,DAy,Beware of the
  Parker Brothers . . . . . . . . . . 200.00
33 JK(c),JDa,V:Jesse James. . . . 200.00
34 JDa,JK,V:Mister Lightning. . . . 200.00
35 JK(c),GC,JDa,
  I&D:The Raven . . . . . . . . . . 200.00

## REAL ADVENTURE
## COMICS
## See: ACTION ADVENTURE

## REAL CLUE
## CRIME STORIES
## See: CLUE COMICS

## REAL EXPERIENCES
## See: TESSIE THE TYPIST

## REAL FACT COMICS
### DC Comics, March-April, 1946
1 S&K,Harry Houdini story. . . . 1,000.00
2 S&K,Rin-Tin-Tin story. . . . . . . 750.00
3 H.G. Wells story . . . . . . . . . . 600.00

4 Jimmy Stewart story,B:Just
  Imagine . . . . . . . . . . . . . . . 650.00
5 Batman & Robin(c) . . . . . . . 3,000.00
6 O:Tommy Tomorrow . . . . . . 2,400.00
7 The Flying White House . . . . 300.00
8 VF,A:Tommy Tomorrow. . . . 1,200.00
9 S&K,Glen Miller story . . . . . . 500.00
10 MMe(s),The Vigilante . . . . . . 500.00
11 EK,How the G-Men Capture
  Public Enemies!. . . . . . . . . . 300.00
12 How G-Men are Trained . . . . 300.00
13 Dale Evans story. . . . . . . . . . 650.00
14 Will Rogers Story,Diary of
  Death . . . . . . . . . . . . . . . . 400.00
15 A:The Master Magician-
  Thurston,A-Bomb . . . . . . . . 400.00
16 A:Four Reno Brothers,
  T.Tommorrow. . . . . . . . . . . . 900.00
17 I Guard an Armored Car . . . . 400.00
18 The Mystery Man of
  Tombstone. . . . . . . . . . . . . 400.00
19 Weapon that Won the West . . 400.00
20 JKu,Daniel Boone. . . . . . . . . 450.00
21 JKu,KitCarson,July-Aug.,1949 400.00

## REAL FUNNIES
### Nedor Publishing Co.,
### Jan., 1943
1 (fa) . . . . . . . . . . . . . . . . . . . 350.00
2 and 3 (fa) . . . . . . . . . . . . . . @200.00

## REAL HEROES COMICS
### Parents' Magazine Institiute,
### Sept., 1941
1 HcK,Franklin Roosevelt . . . . . . 500.00
2 J, Edgar Hoover. . . . . . . . . . . 300.00
3 General Wavell . . . . . . . . . . . 250.00
4 Chiang Kai Shek, Churchill . . . 275.00
5 Stonewall Jackson . . . . . . . . . 300.00
6 Lou Gehrig. . . . . . . . . . . . . . 400.00
7 Chennault and his
  Flying Tigers . . . . . . . . . . . . 300.00
8 Admiral Nimitz . . . . . . . . . . . 300.00
9 The Panda Man . . . . . . . . . . . 250.00
10 Carl Akeley-Jungle
  Adventurer. . . . . . . . . . . . . . 250.00
11 Wild Jack Howard . . . . . . . . . 200.00
12 General Robert L
  Eichelberger . . . . . . . . . . . . 200.00
13 HcK,Victory at Climback . . . . . 200.00
14 Pete Gray . . . . . . . . . . . . . . 200.00
15 Alexander Mackenzie . . . . . . 200.00
16 Balto of Nome Oct '46 . . . . . 200.00

## REAL LIFE STORY
## OF FESS PARKER
### Dell Publishing Co., 1955
1 . . . . . . . . . . . . . . . . . . . . . . 125.00

## REALISTIC ROMANCES
### Avon Periodicals/
### Realistic Comics,
### July–Aug., 1951
1 EK,Ph(c) . . . . . . . . . . . . . . . 250.00
2 Ph(c) . . . . . . . . . . . . . . . . . 150.00
3 P(c) . . . . . . . . . . . . . . . . . . 125.00
4 P(c) . . . . . . . . . . . . . . . . . . 125.00
5 . . . . . . . . . . . . . . . . . . . . . . 125.00
6 EK . . . . . . . . . . . . . . . . . . . 150.00
7 GE, Avon (c) . . . . . . . . . . . . 150.00
8 EK . . . . . . . . . . . . . . . . . . . 110.00
9 thru 14 . . . . . . . . . . . . . . . @100.00
15 . . . . . . . . . . . . . . . . . . . . . 100.00
16 EK,Drug . . . . . . . . . . . . . . . 125.00
17 EK . . . . . . . . . . . . . . . . . . . 100.00

## REAL LIFE COMICS
### Visual Editions/Better/
### Standard/Nedor, Sept., 1941
1 ASh(c),Lawrence of
  Arabia,Uncle Sam(c) . . . . . 1,500.00
2 ASh(c),Liberty(c) . . . . . . . . . 600.00
3 Adolph Hitler(c). . . . . . . . . . 2,500.00
4 ASh(c)Robert Fulton,
  Charles DeGaulle, Old Glory. 400.00
5 ASh(c)Alexander the Great . . . 400.00
6 ASh(c)John Paul Jones,CDR . 350.00
7 ASh(c)Thomas Jefferson . . . . 350.00
8 Leonardo Da Vinci . . . . . . . . . 350.00
9 US Coast Guard Issue. . . . . . 350.00
10 Sir Hubert Wilkens . . . . . . . . 350.00
11 ASh(c),Odyssey on a Raft. . . . 300.00
12 ASh(c),ImpossibleLeatherneck 300.00
13 ASh(c)The Eternal Yank . . . . 300.00
14 ASh(c),Sir Isaac Newton. . . . . 300.00
15 ASh(c),William Tell . . . . . . . . 300.00
16 ASh(c),Marco Polo . . . . . . . . 300.00
17 ASh(c),Albert Einstein. . . . . . 350.00
18 ASh(c),Ponce De Leon . . . . . 300.00
19 ASh(c),The Fighting Seabees. 300.00
20 ASh(c),Joseph Pulitzer . . . . . 300.00
21 ASh(c),Admiral Farragut . . . . 250.00
22 ASh(c),Thomas Paine. . . . . . 250.00
23 ASh(c),Pedro Menendez . . . 250.00
24 ASh(c),Babe Ruth . . . . . . . . . 450.00
25 ASh(c),CQ,Marcus Whitman . 250.00
26 ASh(c),CQ,Benvenuto Cellini . 250.00

Ra

*Real Life Comics #57*
© Standard Publications

*Real West Romances #2*
© Prize Publications

*Red Dragon Comics #7*
© Street & Smith

27 ASh(c),CQ,A-Bomb Story . . . . 350.00
28 ASh(c),CQ,Robert Blake. . . . . 250.00
29 ASh(c),CQ,Daniel DeFoe,
A-Bomb . . . . . . . . . . . . . . . 300.00
30 ASh(c),CQ,Baron Robert Clive 250.00
31 ASh(c),CQ,Anthony Wayne . . 250.00
32 ASh(c),CQ,Frank Sinatra . . . . 275.00
33 ASh(c),CQ,Frederick Douglas 200.00
34 ASh(c),CQ,P Revere,J.Stewart 225.00
35 ASh(c),CQ,Rudyard Kipling . . 200.00
36 ASh(c),CQ,Story of the
Automobile. . . . . . . . . . . . . 200.00
37 ASh(c),CQ,Francis Manion,
Motion Picture, Bing Crosby . 200.00
38 ASh(c),CQ,Richard Henry
Dana . . . . . . . . . . . . . . . . . 150.00
39 ASh(c),CQ,Samuel FB Morse. 150.00
40 FGu,CQ,ASh(c),Hans Christian
Anderson, Bob Feller. . . . . . . 250.00
41 CQ,Abe Lincoln,Jimmy Foxx . 200.00
42 Joseph Conrad,Fred Allen . . . 150.00
43 Louis Braille,O.W.Holmes . . . . 100.00
44 Citizens of Tomorrow . . . . . . 100.00
45 ASh(c),FrancoisVillon,
Olympics, Burl Ives . . . . . . . . 200.00
46 ASh(c),The Pony Express. . . . 200.00
47 ASh(c),Montezuma, Gershwin 200.00
48 ASh(c). . . . . . . . . . . . . . . . . . 200.00
49 ASh(c),Gene Bearden,
Baseball. . . . . . . . . . . . . . . . 200.00
50 FF,ASh(c),Lewis & Clark. . . . . 600.00
51 GE,ASh(c),Sam Houston . . . . 450.00
52 GE,FF,ASh(c),JSe&BE
Leif Erickson . . . . . . . . . . . . 650.00
53 GT,JSe&BE,Henry Wells &
William Fargo . . . . . . . . . . . . 300.00
54 GT,Alexander Graham Bell . . . 300.00
55 ASh(c),JSe&BE,The James
Brothers . . . . . . . . . . . . . . . . 300.00
56 JSe&BE. . . . . . . . . . . . . . . . . 300.00
57 JSe&BE. . . . . . . . . . . . . . . . . 300.00
58 JSe&BE,Jim Reaves. . . . . . . . 350.00
59 FF,JSe&BE,Battle Orphan
Sept '52 . . . . . . . . . . . . . . . . 300.00

## REAL LOVE
### See: HAP HAZARD
### COMICS

## REAL SCREEN COMICS
### DC Comics, Spring, 1945
1 B:Fox & the Crow,Flippity
& Flop. . . . . . . . . . . . . . . 1,400.00

2 (fa) . . . . . . . . . . . . . . . . . . . 650.00
3 (fa) . . . . . . . . . . . . . . . . . . . 400.00
4 thru 7 (fa) . . . . . . . . . . . . . . @250.00
8 thru 11 (fa) . . . . . . . . . . . . . @200.00
12 thru 20 (fa) . . . . . . . . . . . . @175.00
21 thru 30 (fa) . . . . . . . . . . . . @150.00
31 thru 40 (fa) . . . . . . . . . . . . @125.00
41 thru 128 (fa) . . . . . . . . . . . @100.00
**Becomes:**

## TV SCREEN CARTOONS
129 thru 137 . . . . . . . . . . . . . @100.00
138 Jan.–Feb., 1961 . . . . . . . . . 100.00

## REAL LIFE SECRETS
### Ace Books, 1949
1 . . . . . . . . . . . . . . . . . . . . . . 150.00
**Becomes:**

## REAL SECRETS
### Ace Periodicals, 1949
2 . . . . . . . . . . . . . . . . . . . . . . 125.00
3 thru 5 . . . . . . . . . . . . . . . . @100.00

## REAL SPORTS COMICS
## See: ALL SPORTS
## COMICS

## REAL WESTERN HERO
## See: WOW COMICS

## REAL WEST ROMANCES
### Crestwoood Publishing Co./
### Prize Publ., April–May, 1949
1 S&K,Ph(c) . . . . . . . . . . . . . . 275.00
2 Ph(c),Spanking . . . . . . . . . . 150.00
3 JSe,BE,Ph(c) . . . . . . . . . . . . 150.00
4 S&K,JSe,BE,Ph(c) . . . . . . . . 250.00
5 S&K,MMe,JSe,Audie
Murphy Ph(c) . . . . . . . . . . 225.00
6 S&K,JSe,BE,Ph(c) . . . . . . . . 150.00

## RECORD BOOK OF
## FAMOUS POLICE CASES
### St. John Publishing Co., 1949
1 N#,JKu,MB(c) . . . . . . . . . . . 450.00

## RED ARROW
### P.L. Publishing Co.,
### May, 1951
1 Bondage(c) . . . . . . . . . . . . . 550.00

2 . . . . . . . . . . . . . . . . . . . . . . 250.00
3 P(c) . . . . . . . . . . . . . . . . . . . 250.00

## RED BAND COMICS
### Enwil Associates,
### Nov., 1944
1 The Bogeyman . . . . . . . . . . . 500.00
2 O:Bogeyman,same(c)as#1 . . . 350.00
3 A:Captain Wizard. . . . . . . . . . 300.00
4 May, '45,Repof#3,Same(c) . . . 300.00

## RED CIRCLE COMICS
### Enwil Associates
### (Rural Home Public),
### Jan., 1945
1 B:Red Riot,The Prankster . . . . 500.00
2 LSt,A:The Judge . . . . . . . . . . 400.00
3 LSt(A&c). . . . . . . . . . . . . . . . 250.00
4 LSt(a&c) covers of #4
stapled over other comics . . . 250.00

## TRAIL BLAZERS
### Street & Smith Publ., Jan., 1942
1 Wright Brothers . . . . . . . . . . . 400.00
2 Benjamin Franklin,Dodgers . . . 400.00
3 Red Barber,Yankees . . . . . . . . 500.00
4 Famous War song . . . . . . . . . 250.00
**Becomes:**

## RED DRAGON COMICS
### Jan., 1943
5 JaB(c),B&O:Red Rover:
B:Capt.Jack Commando
Rex King&Jet,Minute Man . 1,500.00
6 O:Red Dragon. . . . . . . . . . . 3,000.00
7 The Curse of the
Boneless Men. . . . . . . . . . 2,400.00
8 China V:Japan . . . . . . . . . . 1,000.00
9 The Reducing Ray,Jan '44 . 1,000.00
### (2nd Series) Nov., 1947
1 B:Red Dragon. . . . . . . . . . . 1,250.00
2 BP . . . . . . . . . . . . . . . . . . . 900.00
3 BP,BP(c),I:Dr Neff . . . . . . . . . 750.00
4 BP,BP(c) . . . . . . . . . . . . . . 1,000.00
5 MMe,BP,BP(c) . . . . . . . . . . . 550.00
6 BP,BP(c) . . . . . . . . . . . . . . . 550.00
7 MMe,BP,BP(c),May, 49 . . . . . 550.00

## REDDY KILOWATT
### Educational Comics, 1958
N# . . . . . . . . . . . . . . . . . . . . . 100.00
2 . . . . . . . . . . . . . . . . . . . . . . 150.00
3 . . . . . . . . . . . . . . . . . . . . . . 100.00

**Re**

Red Rabbit #7
© J. Charles Lave Publ. Co.

Red Ryder Comics #89
© Dell Publishing Co.

Rex Dexter of Mars #1
© Fox Features Syndicate

## RED MASK
### See: TIM HOLT

## RED RAVEN
### See: HUMAN TORCH

## RED RABBIT
**Dearfield/**
**J. Charles Lave Publ. Co.,**
**Jan., 1941**
1 (fa) . . . . . . . . . . . . . . . . . . . . 250.00
2 . . . . . . . . . . . . . . . . . . . . . . . 150.00
3 . . . . . . . . . . . . . . . . . . . . . . . 125.00
4 . . . . . . . . . . . . . . . . . . . . . . . 125.00
5 . . . . . . . . . . . . . . . . . . . . . . . 125.00
6 thru 10 . . . . . . . . . . . . . . . @125.00
11 thru 22 . . . . . . . . . . . . . . @100.00

## RED RYDER COMICS
**Hawley Publ./**
**Dell Publ. Co. 1940**
1 . . . . . . . . . . . . . . . . . . . . . 4,000.00
Becomes:

## HI-SPOT COMICS
**Hawley Publications, 1940**
2 Alley Oop, Capt. Easy. . . . . 1,700.00
Becomes:

## RED RYDER COMICS
**Hawley Publ./Dell**
**Publ. Co., 1941**
3 Alley Oop, Capt. Easy. . . . . 2,000.00
4 . . . . . . . . . . . . . . . . . . . . . . . 900.00
5 . . . . . . . . . . . . . . . . . . . . . . . 900.00
6 . . . . . . . . . . . . . . . . . . . . . . . 900.00
7 . . . . . . . . . . . . . . . . . . . . . . . 700.00
8 . . . . . . . . . . . . . . . . . . . . . . . 700.00
9 . . . . . . . . . . . . . . . . . . . . . . . 700.00
10 . . . . . . . . . . . . . . . . . . . . . . 700.00
11 thru 20 . . . . . . . . . . . . . . @500.00
21 thru 30 . . . . . . . . . . . . . . @500.00
31 thru 40 . . . . . . . . . . . . . . @500.00
41 thru 50 . . . . . . . . . . . . . . @250.00
51 thru 60 . . . . . . . . . . . . . . @200.00
61 thru 70 . . . . . . . . . . . . . . @200.00
71 thru 80 . . . . . . . . . . . . . . @200.00
80 thru 99 . . . . . . . . . . . . . . @100.00
100 . . . . . . . . . . . . . . . . . . . . . 150.00
101 thru 151 . . . . . . . . . . . . @100.00
Giant #1 . . . . . . . . . . . . . . . . . 100.00
Giant #2 . . . . . . . . . . . . . . . . . 100.00

## REDSKIN
**Youthful Magazines,**
**Sept., 1950**
1 Redskin,Bondage(c) . . . . . . . 400.00
2 Apache Dance of Death. . . . . 125.00
3 Daniel Boone . . . . . . . . . . . . 100.00
4 Sitting Bull- Red Devil
   of the Black Hills . . . . . . . . . 100.00
5 . . . . . . . . . . . . . . . . . . . . . . . 100.00
6 Geronimo- Terror of the
   Desert,Bondage. . . . . . . . . 350.00
7 Firebrand of the Sioux . . . . . . 100.00
8 . . . . . . . . . . . . . . . . . . . . . . . 100.00
9 . . . . . . . . . . . . . . . . . . . . . . . 100.00
10 Dead Man's Magic . . . . . . . . 100.00
11 . . . . . . . . . . . . . . . . . . . . . . 100.00
12 Quanah Parker,Bondage(c) . . 300.00
Becomes:

## FAMOUS WESTERN
## BADMEN
**Dec., 1952**
13 Redskin- Last of the
   Comanches . . . . . . . . . . . . 150.00
14 . . . . . . . . . . . . . . . . . . . . . . 100.00
15 The Dalton Boys Apr '52. . . . 100.00

## RED WARRIOR
**Marvel Atlas, Jan.–Dec., 1951**
1 GT,Indian Tales . . . . . . . . . . . 200.00
2 GT(c),The Trail of the Outcast 125.00
3 The Great Spirit Speaks . . . . . 100.00
4 O:White Wing . . . . . . . . . . . . 100.00
5 . . . . . . . . . . . . . . . . . . . . . . . 100.00
6 JMn(c) final issue. . . . . . . . . . 100.00

## REG'LAR FELLERS
**Visual Editions (Standard),**
**1947**
5 . . . . . . . . . . . . . . . . . . . . . . . 100.00
6 . . . . . . . . . . . . . . . . . . . . . . . 100.00

## REMEMBER
## PEARL HARBOR
**Street & Smith Publ., 1942**
1 N# JaB,Battle of the
   Pacific,Uncle Sam(c) . . . . . . 600.00

## RENO BROWNE
### See: COMEDY COMICS

## RETURN OF THE
## OUTLAW
**Minoan Publishing Co.,**
**Feb., 1953**
1 Billy The Kid . . . . . . . . . . . . . 150.00
2 . . . . . . . . . . . . . . . . . . . . . . . 125.00
3 thru 11 . . . . . . . . . . . . . . . . @100.00

## REVEALING ROMANCES
**A.A. Wyn**
**(Ace Magazines), Sept., 1949**
1 . . . . . . . . . . . . . . . . . . . . . . . 135.00
2 . . . . . . . . . . . . . . . . . . . . . . . 125.00
3 thru 6 . . . . . . . . . . . . . . . . . @100.00

## REX ALLEN COMICS
**Dell Publishing Co.,**
**Feb., 1951**
(1) *see Dell Four Color #316*
2 Western, Ph(c) all . . . . . . . . . 175.00
3 thru 10 . . . . . . . . . . . . . . . . @125.00
11 thru 23 . . . . . . . . . . . . . . . @100.00
24 ATh . . . . . . . . . . . . . . . . . . . 110.00
25 thru 31 . . . . . . . . . . . . . . . @100.00

## REX DEXTER OF MARS
**Fox Features Syndicate,**
**Autumn, 1940**
1 DBr,DBr(c) Battle ofKooba . . 2,800.00

## REX HART
### See: BLAZE CARSON

## REX MORGAN, M.D.
**Argo Publications, 1950**
1 . . . . . . . . . . . . . . . . . . . . . . . 150.00
2 . . . . . . . . . . . . . . . . . . . . . . . 100.00

## RIBTICKLER
**Fox Features Syndicate, 1945**
1 . . . . . . . . . . . . . . . . . . . . . . . 200.00
2 . . . . . . . . . . . . . . . . . . . . . . . 150.00
3 Cosmo Cat. . . . . . . . . . . . . . . 125.00
4 thru 6 . . . . . . . . . . . . . . . . . @100.00
7 Cosmo Cat. . . . . . . . . . . . . . . 100.00
8 thru 9 . . . . . . . . . . . . . . . . . @100.00

**Re**

*The Rifleman #2*
© Dell Publishing Co

*Rin Tin Tin #7*
© Dell Publishing Co.

*Rocket Ship X #1*
© Fox Features Syndicate

## RICKY
**Visual Editions (Standard Comics), 1953**
1 . . . . . . . . . . . . . . . . . . . . . 100.00

## THE RIDER
**Four Star Comics (Ajax-Farrell Publ.), 1957**
1 Swift Arrow. . . . . . . . . . . . . 150.00
2 thru 5 . . . . . . . . . . . . . . . . @100.00
Becomes:

## FRONTIER TRAIL
**Ajax-Farrell Publ., 1958**
6 . . . . . . . . . . . . . . . . . . . . . . 100.00

## RIFLEMAN, THE
**Dell Publishing Co., 1959**
1 Chuck Connors Ph(c) all . . . . 350.00
2 Ph(c) . . . . . . . . . . . . . . . . . . 200.00
3 ATh,Ph(c). . . . . . . . . . . . . . . 175.00
4 Ph(c) . . . . . . . . . . . . . . . . . . 165.00
5 Ph(c) . . . . . . . . . . . . . . . . . . 165.00
6 ATh . . . . . . . . . . . . . . . . . . . 175.00
7 thru 10 Ph(c) . . . . . . . . . . . @150.00
11 thru 20 . . . . . . . . . . . . . . . @125.00

## RINGO KID WESTERN
**Marvel Atlas, Aug., 1954**
1 JMn,JSt,O:Ringo Kid,
 B:Ringo Kid . . . . . . . . . . . . 350.00
2 JMn,I&O:Arab,A:Black Rider . 200.00
3 JMn . . . . . . . . . . . . . . . . . . . 125.00
4 JMn . . . . . . . . . . . . . . . . . . . 125.00
5 JMn . . . . . . . . . . . . . . . . . . . 125.00
6 . . . . . . . . . . . . . . . . . . . . . . 125.00
7 . . . . . . . . . . . . . . . . . . . . . . 125.00
8 JSe. . . . . . . . . . . . . . . . . . . . 125.00
9 . . . . . . . . . . . . . . . . . . . . . . 100.00
10 JSe(c),AW. . . . . . . . . . . . . . 125.00
11 JSe(c) . . . . . . . . . . . . . . . . 100.00
12 JO . . . . . . . . . . . . . . . . . . . 100.00
13 AW . . . . . . . . . . . . . . . . . . 125.00
14 thru 20. . . . . . . . . . . . . . . @100.00
21 Sept., 1957 . . . . . . . . . . . . 100.00

## RIN TIN TIN
**Dell Publishing Co., Nov., 1952**
(1) *see Dell Four Color #434*
(1) *see Dell Four Color #476*
(1) *see Dell Four Color #523*

4 thru 10 Ph(c) all . . . . . . . . @100.00
11 thru 20 . . . . . . . . . . . . . . @125.00

## RIOT
**Marvel Atlas, 1954–56**
1 RH,MMe,GC,BEv. . . . . . . . . . 350.00
2 MMe,Li'l Abner. . . . . . . . . . . 275.00
3 MMe(c). . . . . . . . . . . . . . . . . 250.00
4 JSe,MMe,BEv,Marilyn Monroe 300.00
5 JSe,MMe,BEv,Marilyn Monroe 325.00
6 MMe,JSe . . . . . . . . . . . . . . . 250.00

## RIPLEY's BELIEVE IT OR NOT!
**Harvey Publications, 1953–54**
1 BP . . . . . . . . . . . . . . . . . . . . 150.00
2 Li'l Abner . . . . . . . . . . . . . . . 125.00
3 . . . . . . . . . . . . . . . . . . . . . . 125.00
4 . . . . . . . . . . . . . . . . . . . . . . 125.00

## RIVETS
**Argo Publications, 1956**
1 . . . . . . . . . . . . . . . . . . . . . . 125.00
2 . . . . . . . . . . . . . . . . . . . . . . 100.00
3 . . . . . . . . . . . . . . . . . . . . . . 100.00

## ROBIN HOOD
**Sussex Publ. Co (Magazine Enterprises), 1955**
1 FBe . . . . . . . . . . . . . . . . . . . 200.00
2 FBe . . . . . . . . . . . . . . . . . . . 150.00
3 FBe . . . . . . . . . . . . . . . . . . . 150.00
4 FBe . . . . . . . . . . . . . . . . . . . 150.00
5 FBe . . . . . . . . . . . . . . . . . . . 150.00
6 FBe,BP . . . . . . . . . . . . . . . . . 150.00
Becomes:

## ADVENTURES OF ROBIN HOOD
**Magazine Enterprises, 1957**
7 BP, Richard Green Ph(c) . . . . 200.00
8 Richard Green Ph(c) . . . . . . . 200.00

## ROBIN HOOD AND HIS MERRY MEN
**See: THIS MAGAZINE IS HAUNTED**

## ROBIN HOOD TALES
**Quality Comics Group, 1956**
1 MB . . . . . . . . . . . . . . . . . . . . 400.00
2 MB . . . . . . . . . . . . . . . . . . . . 375.00
3 MB . . . . . . . . . . . . . . . . . . . . 375.00
4 MB . . . . . . . . . . . . . . . . . . . . 375.00
5 MB . . . . . . . . . . . . . . . . . . . . 375.00
6 MB . . . . . . . . . . . . . . . . . . . . 375.00

**DC Comics, 1957–58**
7 . . . . . . . . . . . . . . . . . . . . . . 450.00
8 thru 14 . . . . . . . . . . . . . . . @400.00

## ROCKET COMICS
**Hillman Periodicals, March, 1940**
1 O:Red Roberts;B:Rocket
 Riley,Phantom Ranger,Steel
 Shank,Buzzard Baynes,Lefty
 Larson,The Defender,Man
 with 1,000 Faces . . . . . . . . 4,500.00
2 . . . . . . . . . . . . . . . . . . . . . 2,000.00
3 May, '40 E:All Features . . . . 2,500.00

## ROCKET KELLY
**Fox Features Syndicate, Autumn, 1945–Oct., Nov., 1946**
N# . . . . . . . . . . . . . . . . . . . . . 400.00
1 . . . . . . . . . . . . . . . . . . . . . . 300.00
2 A:The Puppeteer . . . . . . . . . . 275.00
3 thru 6 . . . . . . . . . . . . . . . . @250.00

## ROCKETMAN
**Ajax/Farrell Publications, June, 1952**
1 Space Stories of the Future . . . 500.00

## ROCKET SHIP X
**Fox Features Syndicate, Sept., 1951**
1 . . . . . . . . . . . . . . . . . . . . . . 900.00
2 N# Variant of Original . . . . . . 500.00

## ROCKY LANE WESTERN
**Fawcett/Charlton Comics, May, 1949**
1 Ph(c)B:Rocky Lane,Slim
 Pickins . . . . . . . . . . . . . . . 1,400.00
2 Ph(c) . . . . . . . . . . . . . . . . . . 600.00
3 Ph(c) . . . . . . . . . . . . . . . . . . 500.00
4 Ph(c)CCB,Rail Riders
 Rampage,F Capt Tootsie. . . . 500.00

**Ro**

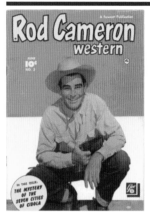

Rod Cameron Western #3
© Fawcett Publications

Romance Trail #1
© DC Comics

Romantic Adventures #2
© American Comics Group

5 Ph(c)The Missing
 Stagecoaches . . . . . . . . . . . 450.00
6 Ph(c)Ghost Town Showdown . 300.00
7 Ph(c)The Border Revolt . . . . . . 350.00
8 Ph(c)The Sunset Feud . . . . . . 350.00
9 Ph(c)Hermit of the Hills . . . . . . 350.00
10 Ph(c)Badman's Reward . . . . . 300.00
11 Ph(c)Fool's Gold Fiasco . . . . . 250.00
12 Ph(c),CCB,Coyote Breed
 F:Capt Tootsie,Giant . . . . . . . 250.00
13 Ph(c),Giant . . . . . . . . . . . . . . 250.00
14 Ph(c) . . . . . . . . . . . . . . . . . . 200.00
15 Ph(c)B:Black Jacks
 Hitching Post,Giant . . . . . . . . 225.00
16 Ph(c),Giant . . . . . . . . . . . . . 200.00
17 Ph(c),Giant . . . . . . . . . . . . . 200.00
18 Ph(c) . . . . . . . . . . . . . . . . . . 225.00
19 Ph(c),Giant . . . . . . . . . . . . . 235.00
20 Ph(c)The Rodeo Rustler
 E:Slim Pickens . . . . . . . . . . . 235.00
21 Ph(c)B: Dee Dickens . . . . . . 200.00
22 Ph(c) . . . . . . . . . . . . . . . . . . 175.00
23 thru 30 . . . . . . . . . . . . . . . @200.00
31 thru 40 . . . . . . . . . . . . . . . @175.00
41 thru 55 . . . . . . . . . . . . . . . @175.00
56 thru 87 . . . . . . . . . . . . . . . @150.00

## ROD CAMERON WESTERN
**Fawcett Publications, Feb., 1950**

1 Ph(c) . . . . . . . . . . . . . . . . . . . 750.00
2 Ph(c) . . . . . . . . . . . . . . . . . . . 350.00
3 Ph(c),Seven Cities of Cipiola . 300.00
4 Ph(c),Rip-Roaring Wild West . 250.00
5 Ph(c),Six Gun Sabotage . . . . 250.00
6 Ph(c),Medicine Bead Murders 250.00
7 Ph(c),Wagon Train Of Death . 250.00
8 Ph(c),Bayou Badman . . . . . . 250.00
9 Ph(c),Rustlers Ruse . . . . . . . 250.00
10 Ph(c),White Buffalo Trail . . . . 250.00
11 Ph(c),Lead Poison . . . . . . . . 225.00
12 Ph(c) . . . . . . . . . . . . . . . . . . 225.00
13 Ph(c) . . . . . . . . . . . . . . . . . . 225.00
14 Ph(c) . . . . . . . . . . . . . . . . . . 225.00
15 Ph(c) . . . . . . . . . . . . . . . . . . 225.00
16 thru 19 Ph(c) . . . . . . . . . . . @225.00
20 Phc(c),Great Army Hoax . . . . 225.00

## ROGER DODGER
**Standard Comics, 1952**

5 . . . . . . . . . . . . . . . . . . . . . . . 100.00

## ROLY-POLY COMICS
**Green Publishing Co., 1945**

1 B:Red Rube&Steel Sterling . 400.00
6 A:Blue Cycle . . . . . . . . . . . . . 250.00
10 A:Red Rube . . . . . . . . . . . . . 300.00
11 . . . . . . . . . . . . . . . . . . . . . . 250.00
12 Black Hood . . . . . . . . . . . . . 250.00
13 . . . . . . . . . . . . . . . . . . . . . . 250.00
14 A:Black Hood, Decapitation . . 450.00
15 A:Steel Fist;1946 . . . . . . . . . 400.00

## ROMANCE AND CONFESSION STORIES
**St. John Publishing Co., 1949**

1 MB(c),MB . . . . . . . . . . . . . . . 500.00

## ROMANCE DIARY
**Marvel, Dec., 1949**

1 . . . . . . . . . . . . . . . . . . . . . . . 150.00
2 March, 1950 . . . . . . . . . . . . . 125.00

## THE ROMANCES OF NURSE HELEN GRANT
**Marvel Atlas, 1957**

1 . . . . . . . . . . . . . . . . . . . . . . . 100.00

## ROMANCES OF THE WEST
**Marvel, Nov., 1949**

1 Ph(c),Calamity Jane,
 Sam Bass . . . . . . . . . . . . . . 300.00
2 March, 1950 . . . . . . . . . . . . . 175.00

## ROMANCE STORIES OF TRUE LOVE
**See: TRUE LOVE PROBLEMS AND ADVICE ILLUSTRATED**

## ROMANCE TALES
**Marvel, Oct., 1949**
**(no #1 thru 6)**

7 . . . . . . . . . . . . . . . . . . . . . . . 150.00
8 . . . . . . . . . . . . . . . . . . . . . . . 100.00
9 March, 1950 . . . . . . . . . . . . . 100.00

## ROMANCE TRAIL
**DC Comics, 1949–50**

1 EK,ATh . . . . . . . . . . . . . . . . . 800.00
2 EK . . . . . . . . . . . . . . . . . . . . 400.00
3 EK,ATh . . . . . . . . . . . . . . . . . 425.00
4 ATh . . . . . . . . . . . . . . . . . . . . 300.00
5 . . . . . . . . . . . . . . . . . . . . . . . 275.00
6 EK . . . . . . . . . . . . . . . . . . . . 275.00

## ROMANTIC ADVENTURES
**B & I Publishing Co.
(American Comics Group),
1949**

1 . . . . . . . . . . . . . . . . . . . . . . . 200.00
2 . . . . . . . . . . . . . . . . . . . . . . . 150.00
3 thru 10 . . . . . . . . . . . . . . . . @125.00
11 thru 20 . . . . . . . . . . . . . . . @125.00
20 thru 45 . . . . . . . . . . . . . . . @100.00
46 thru 50 3-D type . . . . . . . . . @75.00
51 thru 100 . . . . . . . . . . . . . . @100.00

## ROMANTIC AFFAIRS
**See: MOLLY MANTON'S ROMANCES**

## ROMANTIC CONFESSIONS
**Hillman Periodicals, 1949–53**

1 . . . . . . . . . . . . . . . . . . . . . . . 175.00
2 . . . . . . . . . . . . . . . . . . . . . . . 125.00
3 . . . . . . . . . . . . . . . . . . . . . . . 150.00
4 . . . . . . . . . . . . . . . . . . . . . . . 125.00
5 . . . . . . . . . . . . . . . . . . . . . . . 125.00
6 . . . . . . . . . . . . . . . . . . . . . . . 125.00
7 . . . . . . . . . . . . . . . . . . . . . . . 125.00
8 . . . . . . . . . . . . . . . . . . . . . . . 125.00
9 . . . . . . . . . . . . . . . . . . . . . . . 125.00
10 . . . . . . . . . . . . . . . . . . . . . . 125.00
11 . . . . . . . . . . . . . . . . . . . . . . 125.00
12 . . . . . . . . . . . . . . . . . . . . . . 125.00
**Vol 2**
1 . . . . . . . . . . . . . . . . . . . . . . . 150.00
2 . . . . . . . . . . . . . . . . . . . . . . . 150.00
3 BK . . . . . . . . . . . . . . . . . . . . 150.00
4 thru 8 . . . . . . . . . . . . . . . . @125.00
9 FF,AD . . . . . . . . . . . . . . . . . 125.00
10 thru 13 . . . . . . . . . . . . . . . @100.00

## ROMANTIC HEARTS
**Story Comics/Master Publ./Merrit Publ., 1951**

1 . . . . . . . . . . . . . . . . . . . . . . . 200.00

Ro

*Romantic Love #1*
*© Avon Periodicals*

*Romantic Picture Novelettes #1*
*© Magazine Enterprises*

*Roundup #4*
*© D.S. Publishing Co.*

2 . . . . . . . . . . . . . . . . . . . . . . . 150.00
3 LC . . . . . . . . . . . . . . . . . . . . 125.00
4 LC . . . . . . . . . . . . . . . . . . . . 125.00
5 LC . . . . . . . . . . . . . . . . . . . . 125.00
6 LC . . . . . . . . . . . . . . . . . . . . 125.00
7 LC . . . . . . . . . . . . . . . . . . . . 125.00
8 LC . . . . . . . . . . . . . . . . . . . . 125.00
9 LC . . . . . . . . . . . . . . . . . . . . 125.00
10 LC . . . . . . . . . . . . . . . . . . . 125.00
11 . . . . . . . . . . . . . . . . . . . . . 150.00

**Second Series, 1953**
1 . . . . . . . . . . . . . . . . . . . . . . 125.00
2 thru 12 . . . . . . . . . . . . . . . @125.00

## ROMANTIC LOVE
**Avon Periodicals/Realistic,**
**Sept.–Oct., 1949**
1 P(c) . . . . . . . . . . . . . . . . . . . 275.00
2 P(c) . . . . . . . . . . . . . . . . . . . 200.00
3 P(c) . . . . . . . . . . . . . . . . . . . 200.00
4 Ph(c) . . . . . . . . . . . . . . . . . . 200.00
5 P(c) . . . . . . . . . . . . . . . . . . . 200.00
6 Ph(c),Drug,Thrill Crazy . . . . . . 250.00
7 P(c) . . . . . . . . . . . . . . . . . . . 200.00
8 P(c) . . . . . . . . . . . . . . . . . . . 200.00
9 EK,P(c) . . . . . . . . . . . . . . . . . 225.00
10 thru 11 P(c) . . . . . . . . . . . @225.00
12 EK . . . . . . . . . . . . . . . . . . . 225.00
20 . . . . . . . . . . . . . . . . . . . . . . 200.00
21 . . . . . . . . . . . . . . . . . . . . . . 200.00
22 EK . . . . . . . . . . . . . . . . . . . 200.00
23 EK . . . . . . . . . . . . . . . . . . . 200.00

## ROMANTIC MARRIAGE
**Ziff-Davis/**
**St. John Publishing Co.,**
**Nov.–Dec., 1950**
1 Ph(c),Selfish Wife . . . . . . . . . 250.00
2 P(c),Mother's Boy . . . . . . . . . 150.00
3 P(c),Hen Peck House . . . . . . . 135.00
4 P(c) . . . . . . . . . . . . . . . . . . . 135.00
5 Ph(c) . . . . . . . . . . . . . . . . . . 135.00
6 Ph(c) . . . . . . . . . . . . . . . . . . 125.00
7 Ph(c) . . . . . . . . . . . . . . . . . . 125.00
8 P(c) . . . . . . . . . . . . . . . . . . . 125.00
9 P(c) . . . . . . . . . . . . . . . . . . . 125.00
10 P/PH(c) . . . . . . . . . . . . . . . 250.00
11 . . . . . . . . . . . . . . . . . . . . . 125.00
12 . . . . . . . . . . . . . . . . . . . . . 125.00
13 Ph(c) . . . . . . . . . . . . . . . . . 125.00
14 thru 20 . . . . . . . . . . . . . . @125.00
20 Ph(c) . . . . . . . . . . . . . . . . . 125.00
21 . . . . . . . . . . . . . . . . . . . . . 125.00
22 . . . . . . . . . . . . . . . . . . . . . 125.00

23 MB. . . . . . . . . . . . . . . . . . . 135.00
24 . . . . . . . . . . . . . . . . . . . . . 125.00

## ROMANTIC PICTURE NOVELETTES
**Magazine Enterprises, 1946**
1 Mary Worth Adventure . . . . . . . 200.00

## ROMANTIC SECRETS
**Fawcett Publ./Charlton Comics,**
**Sept., 1949**
1 Ph(c) . . . . . . . . . . . . . . . . . . 250.00
2 MSy(c) . . . . . . . . . . . . . . . . . 175.00
3 MSy(c) . . . . . . . . . . . . . . . . . 175.00
4 GE . . . . . . . . . . . . . . . . . . . 175.00
5 BP . . . . . . . . . . . . . . . . . . . 150.00
6 . . . . . . . . . . . . . . . . . . . . . . 150.00
7 BP . . . . . . . . . . . . . . . . . . . 150.00
8 . . . . . . . . . . . . . . . . . . . . . . 150.00
9 GE . . . . . . . . . . . . . . . . . . . 150.00
10 BP . . . . . . . . . . . . . . . . . . . 150.00
11 . . . . . . . . . . . . . . . . . . . . . 125.00
12 BP . . . . . . . . . . . . . . . . . . . 150.00
13 . . . . . . . . . . . . . . . . . . . . . 125.00
14 . . . . . . . . . . . . . . . . . . . . . 125.00
15 . . . . . . . . . . . . . . . . . . . . . 125.00
16 BP,MSy . . . . . . . . . . . . . . . 150.00
17 BP . . . . . . . . . . . . . . . . . . . 150.00
18 . . . . . . . . . . . . . . . . . . . . . 125.00
19 . . . . . . . . . . . . . . . . . . . . . 125.00
20 BP,MBi . . . . . . . . . . . . . . . . 150.00
21 . . . . . . . . . . . . . . . . . . . . . 125.00
22 . . . . . . . . . . . . . . . . . . . . . 125.00
23 . . . . . . . . . . . . . . . . . . . . . 125.00
24 GE . . . . . . . . . . . . . . . . . . . 150.00
25 MSy . . . . . . . . . . . . . . . . . . 125.00
26 BP,MSy . . . . . . . . . . . . . . . 125.00
27 MSy . . . . . . . . . . . . . . . . . . 125.00
28 . . . . . . . . . . . . . . . . . . . . . 125.00
29 BP . . . . . . . . . . . . . . . . . . . 125.00
30 thru 32 . . . . . . . . . . . . . . @125.00
33 MSy . . . . . . . . . . . . . . . . . . 125.00
34 BP . . . . . . . . . . . . . . . . . . . 125.00
35 . . . . . . . . . . . . . . . . . . . . . 125.00
36 BP . . . . . . . . . . . . . . . . . . . 125.00
37 BP . . . . . . . . . . . . . . . . . . . 125.00
38 thru 52 . . . . . . . . . . . . . . @100.00

## ROMANTIC STORY
**Fawcett Publ./Charlton Comics,**
**Nov., 1949**
1 Ph(c) . . . . . . . . . . . . . . . . . . 250.00
2 Ph(c) . . . . . . . . . . . . . . . . . . 200.00

3 Ph(c) . . . . . . . . . . . . . . . . . . 175.00
4 Ph(c) . . . . . . . . . . . . . . . . . . 175.00
5 Ph(c) . . . . . . . . . . . . . . . . . . 175.00
6 Ph(c) . . . . . . . . . . . . . . . . . . 175.00
7 BP,Ph(c). . . . . . . . . . . . . . . . 150.00
8 BP,Ph(c). . . . . . . . . . . . . . . . 150.00
9 Ph(c) . . . . . . . . . . . . . . . . . . 150.00
10 Ph(c) . . . . . . . . . . . . . . . . . 150.00
11 Ph(c) . . . . . . . . . . . . . . . . . 150.00
12 Ph(c) . . . . . . . . . . . . . . . . . 150.00
13 Ph(c) . . . . . . . . . . . . . . . . . 150.00
14 Ph(c) . . . . . . . . . . . . . . . . . 150.00
15 GE,Ph(c). . . . . . . . . . . . . . . 200.00
16 BP,Ph(c). . . . . . . . . . . . . . . 125.00
17 Ph(c) . . . . . . . . . . . . . . . . . 125.00
18 Ph(c) . . . . . . . . . . . . . . . . . 125.00
19 Ph(c) . . . . . . . . . . . . . . . . . 125.00
20 BP,Ph(c). . . . . . . . . . . . . . . 125.00
22 ATh,Ph(c). . . . . . . . . . . . . . 125.00

**Charlton Comics**
23 . . . . . . . . . . . . . . . . . . . . . 125.00
24 Ph(c) . . . . . . . . . . . . . . . . . 100.00
25 thru 29 . . . . . . . . . . . . . . @100.00
30 BP . . . . . . . . . . . . . . . . . . . 125.00
31 thru 39 . . . . . . . . . . . . . . @100.00

## ROMANTIC WESTERN
**Fawcett Publications,**
**Winter, 1949**
1 Ph(c) . . . . . . . . . . . . . . . . . . 300.00
2 Ph(c),AW,AMc . . . . . . . . . . . . 325.00
3 Ph(c) . . . . . . . . . . . . . . . . . . 250.00

## ROMEO TUBBS
See: MY SECRET LIFE

## ROOKIE COP
**Charlton, 1955**
27 . . . . . . . . . . . . . . . . . . . . . 150.00
28 . . . . . . . . . . . . . . . . . . . . . 100.00
29 . . . . . . . . . . . . . . . . . . . . . 100.00
30 . . . . . . . . . . . . . . . . . . . . . 100.00
31 thru 33 . . . . . . . . . . . . . . @100.00

## ROUNDUP
**D.S. Publishing Co.,**
**July–Aug., 1948**
1 HcK . . . . . . . . . . . . . . . . . . . 200.00
2 Drug. . . . . . . . . . . . . . . . . . . 150.00
3 . . . . . . . . . . . . . . . . . . . . . . 125.00
4 . . . . . . . . . . . . . . . . . . . . . . 125.00
5 Male Bondage . . . . . . . . . . . . 135.00

**Ro**

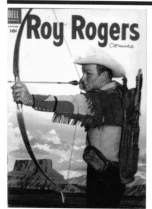

*Roy Rogers #83*
*© Dell Publishing Co.*

*Rugged Action #1*
*© Marvel Comics Group*

*Saddle Romances #10*
*© E.C. Comics*

## ROY CAMPANELLA, BASEBALL HERO

**Fawcett Publications, 1950**
N# Ph(c),Life Story of the
   Battling Dodgers Catcher . . 1,000.00

## ROY ROGERS COMICS

**Dell Publishing Co., 1948**
1 photo (c) . . . . . . . . . . . . . . 1,500.00
2 . . . . . . . . . . . . . . . . . . . . . . 500.00
3 . . . . . . . . . . . . . . . . . . . . . . 350.00
4 . . . . . . . . . . . . . . . . . . . . . . 350.00
5 . . . . . . . . . . . . . . . . . . . . . . 350.00
6 thru 10 . . . . . . . . . . . . . . . @250.00
11 thru 18 . . . . . . . . . . . . . . @225.00
19 Chuck Wagon Charlie . . . . . . 200.00
20 Trigger . . . . . . . . . . . . . . . . . 200.00
21 thru 30 . . . . . . . . . . . . . . . @200.00
31 thru 46 . . . . . . . . . . . . . . . @150.00
47 thru 50 . . . . . . . . . . . . . . . @125.00
51 thru 56 . . . . . . . . . . . . . . . @110.00
57 Drug . . . . . . . . . . . . . . . . . . 125.00
58 Drug . . . . . . . . . . . . . . . . . . 135.00
59 thru 80 . . . . . . . . . . . . . . . @125.00
81 thru 91 . . . . . . . . . . . . . . . @100.00
**Becomes:**

## ROY ROGERS AND TRIGGER

**Aug., 1955**
92 . . . . . . . . . . . . . . . . . . . . . . 100.00
93 . . . . . . . . . . . . . . . . . . . . . . 100.00
94 . . . . . . . . . . . . . . . . . . . . . . 100.00
95 . . . . . . . . . . . . . . . . . . . . . . 100.00
96 thru 99 . . . . . . . . . . . . . . . @100.00
100 Trigger Returns . . . . . . . . . . 125.00
101 thru 118 . . . . . . . . . . . . . . @100.00
119 thru 125 ATn . . . . . . . . . . @150.00
126 thru 131 . . . . . . . . . . . . . . @120.00
132 Dale Evans . . . . . . . . . . . . . 150.00
133 thru 144 RsM . . . . . . . . . . @110.00
145 . . . . . . . . . . . . . . . . . . . . . 150.00

## ROY ROGER'S TRIGGER

**Dell Publishing Co., May, 1951**
(1) see Dell Four Color #329
2 Ph(c) . . . . . . . . . . . . . . . . . . 250.00
3 P(c) . . . . . . . . . . . . . . . . . . . 100.00
4 P(c) . . . . . . . . . . . . . . . . . . . 100.00
5 P(c) . . . . . . . . . . . . . . . . . . . 100.00
6 thru 17 P(c) . . . . . . . . . . . . @100.00

## RUDOLPH THE RED–NOSED REINDEER

**DC Comics, Dec., 1950**
1950 . . . . . . . . . . . . . . . . . . . . 250.00
1951 thru 1954 . . . . . . . . . . . @125.00
1955 thru 1962 Winter . . . . . . @100.00

## RUFF AND READY

**Dell Publishing Co., 1958**
1 . . . . . . . . . . . . . . . . . . . . . . 200.00
2 . . . . . . . . . . . . . . . . . . . . . . 150.00
3 . . . . . . . . . . . . . . . . . . . . . . 150.00
4 thru 12 . . . . . . . . . . . . . . . @100.00

## RUGGED ACTION

**Marvel Atlas, Dec., 1954**
1 AyB,Man-Eater . . . . . . . . . . . 150.00
2 JSe,DAy,JMn(c),Manta-Ray . . 100.00
3 DAy,JMn(c) . . . . . . . . . . . . . 100.00
4 . . . . . . . . . . . . . . . . . . . . . . 100.00
**Becomes:**

## STRANGE STORIES OF SUSPENSE

5 RH,JMn(c),Little Black Box . . . 500.00
6 BEv,The Illusion . . . . . . . . . . 300.00
7 JSe(c),BEv,Old John's House . 325.00
8 AW,BP,Thumbs Down . . . . . . 325.00
9 BEv(c),Nightmare . . . . . . . . . 350.00
10 RC,MME,AT . . . . . . . . . . . 350.00
11 BEv(c) . . . . . . . . . . . . . . . . 225.00
12 AT . . . . . . . . . . . . . . . . . . . 225.00
13 BEv,GM . . . . . . . . . . . . . . . 225.00
14 AW . . . . . . . . . . . . . . . . . . 250.00
15 BK . . . . . . . . . . . . . . . . . . . 250.00
16 MF,BP, Aug., 1957 . . . . . . . . 250.00

## RULAH, JUNGLE GODDESS

**See: ZOOT COMICS**

## RUSTY, BOY DETECTIVE

**Good Comics/Lev Gleason Publ., 1955**
1 . . . . . . . . . . . . . . . . . . . . . . 125.00
2 . . . . . . . . . . . . . . . . . . . . . . 100.00
3 . . . . . . . . . . . . . . . . . . . . . . 100.00
4 . . . . . . . . . . . . . . . . . . . . . . 100.00
5 . . . . . . . . . . . . . . . . . . . . . . 100.00

## RUSTY COMICS

**See: KID KOMICS**

## SAARI, THE JUNGLE GODDESS

**P.L. Publishing Co., Nov., 1951**
1 The Bantu Blood Curse . . . . 600.00

## SABU, ELEPHANT BOY

**Fox Features Syndicate, June, 1950**
1(30) WW,Ph(c) . . . . . . . . . . . 300.00
2 JKa,Ph(c),Aug.'50 . . . . . . . . . 250.00

## HAPPY HOULIHANS

**Fables Publications (E.C. Comics), Autumn, 1947**
1 O:Moon Girl . . . . . . . . . . . . . 650.00
2 . . . . . . . . . . . . . . . . . . . . . . 350.00
**Becomes:**

## SADDLE JUSTICE

**Spring, 1948**
3 HcK,JCr,AF . . . . . . . . . . . . . . 700.00
4 AF,JCr, Grl . . . . . . . . . . . . . . 600.00
5 AF,Grl . . . . . . . . . . . . . . . . . 500.00
6 AF,Grl . . . . . . . . . . . . . . . . . 450.00
7 AF,Grl . . . . . . . . . . . . . . . . . 450.00
8 AF,Grl, . . . . . . . . . . . . . . . . . 500.00
**Becomes:**

## SADDLE ROMANCES

**Nov., 1949**
9 Grl(c),Grl . . . . . . . . . . . . . . . 600.00
10 AF(c),WW,Grl . . . . . . . . . . . 550.00
11 AF(c),Grl . . . . . . . . . . . . . . 600.00

## SAD SACK AND THE SARGE

**Harvey Publications, 1957**
1 . . . . . . . . . . . . . . . . . . . . . . 200.00
2 . . . . . . . . . . . . . . . . . . . . . . 150.00
3 . . . . . . . . . . . . . . . . . . . . . . 125.00
4 . . . . . . . . . . . . . . . . . . . . . . 125.00
5 . . . . . . . . . . . . . . . . . . . . . . 125.00
thru 10 . . . . . . . . . . . . . . . . . @125.00
11 thru 20 . . . . . . . . . . . . . . . @125.00
21 thru 40 . . . . . . . . . . . . . . . @50.00
41 thru 50 . . . . . . . . . . . . . . . @50.00

**Ro**

Sad Sack Comics #10
© Harvey Publications

The Saint #9
© Avon Periodicals

Science Comics #1
© Fox Features Syndicate

## SAD SACK COMICS
### Harvey Publications, Sept., 1949
1 I:Little Dot. . . . . . . . . . . . . . 900.00
2 Flying Fool . . . . . . . . . . . . . . 500.00
3 . . . . . . . . . . . . . . . . . . . . . . . 400.00
4 . . . . . . . . . . . . . . . . . . . . . . . 300.00
5 . . . . . . . . . . . . . . . . . . . . . . . 300.00
6 thru 10 . . . . . . . . . . . . . . . @300.00
11 thru 21 . . . . . . . . . . . . . . @200.00
22 Back in the Army Again,
  The Specialist . . . . . . . . . . . 250.00
23 thru 50 . . . . . . . . . . . . . @150.00
51 thru 100 . . . . . . . . . . . . . @100.00

## SAD SACK'S FUNNY FRIENDS
### Harvey Publications, 1955
1 . . . . . . . . . . . . . . . . . . . . . . . 150.00
2 . . . . . . . . . . . . . . . . . . . . . . . 100.00
3 . . . . . . . . . . . . . . . . . . . . . . . 100.00
4 . . . . . . . . . . . . . . . . . . . . . . . 100.00
5 . . . . . . . . . . . . . . . . . . . . . . . 100.00
6 thru 10 . . . . . . . . . . . . . . . @100.00
11 thru 20 . . . . . . . . . . . . . . @75.00

## SAD SACK LAUGH SPECIAL
### Harvey Publications, 1958
1 . . . . . . . . . . . . . . . . . . . . . . . 160.00
2 . . . . . . . . . . . . . . . . . . . . . . . 120.00
3 . . . . . . . . . . . . . . . . . . . . . . . 100.00
4 . . . . . . . . . . . . . . . . . . . . . . . 100.00
5 . . . . . . . . . . . . . . . . . . . . . . . 100.00
6 . . . . . . . . . . . . . . . . . . . . . . . 100.00
7 . . . . . . . . . . . . . . . . . . . . . . . 100.00
8 . . . . . . . . . . . . . . . . . . . . . . . 100.00
9 . . . . . . . . . . . . . . . . . . . . . . . 100.00
10 . . . . . . . . . . . . . . . . . . . . . . 100.00
11 thru 20 . . . . . . . . . . . . . . @100.00

## SAINT, THE
### Avon Periodicals, Aug., 1947
1 JKa,JKa(c),Bondage(c) . . . . 1,500.00
2 . . . . . . . . . . . . . . . . . . . . . . 1,000.00
3 Rolled Stocking Leg(c). . . . . . 800.00
4 MB(c) Longerie . . . . . . . . . . . 800.00
5 Spanking Panel . . . . . . . . . . . 900.00
6 B:Miss Fury . . . . . . . . . . . . . 900.00
7 WJo(c),Detective Cases(c) . . . 700.00
8 P(c),Detective Cases(c) . . . . . 750.00

9 EK(c),The Notorious
  Murder Mob . . . . . . . . . . . . 750.00
10 WW,P(c),V:The Communist
  Menace . . . . . . . . . . . . . . . 700.00
11 P(c),Wanted For Robbery . . . . 500.00
12 P(c),The Blowpipe Murders
  March, 1952 . . . . . . . . . . . . 500.00

## SAM HILL PRIVATE EYE
### Close-Up Publications, 1950
1 The Double Trouble Caper . . . 200.00
2 . . . . . . . . . . . . . . . . . . . . . . . 150.00
3 . . . . . . . . . . . . . . . . . . . . . . . 125.00
4 Negligee panels . . . . . . . . . . . 200.00
5 . . . . . . . . . . . . . . . . . . . . . . . 100.00
6 . . . . . . . . . . . . . . . . . . . . . . . 100.00
7 . . . . . . . . . . . . . . . . . . . . . . . 100.00

## SAMSON
### Fox Features Syndicate, Autumn, 1940
1 BP,GT,A:Wing Turner . . . . . . 3,500.00
2 BP,A:Dr. Fung . . . . . . . . . . 1,400.00
3 JSh(c),A:Navy Jones . . . . . . . 900.00
4 WE,B:Yarko . . . . . . . . . . . . . 800.00
5 WE . . . . . . . . . . . . . . . . . . . 750.00
6 WE,O:The Topper;Sept'41 . . . 750.00

## SAMSON
### Ajax Farrell Publ (Four Star), April, 1955
12 The Electric Curtain . . . . . . . 350.00
13 Assignment Danger . . . . . . . . 300.00
14 The Red Raider;Aug'55 . . . . . 300.00

## SANDS OF THE SOUTH PACIFIC
### Toby Press, Jan., 1953
1 2-Fisted Romantic Adventure . 250.00

## SANTA CLAUS FUNNIES
### Dell Publishing Co., 1942
N# WK . . . . . . . . . . . . . . . . . . 600.00
2 WK . . . . . . . . . . . . . . . . . . . 400.00

## SANTA CLAUS PARADE
### Approved Comics (Ziff-Davis)/ St. John Publ., 1951
N# . . . . . . . . . . . . . . . . . . . . . 350.00
2 . . . . . . . . . . . . . . . . . . . . . . . 250.00
3 . . . . . . . . . . . . . . . . . . . . . . . 225.00

## SANTA'S CHRISTMAS COMICS
### Best Books (Standard Comics), 1952
N# Dizzy Duck . . . . . . . . . . . . . 225.00

## SANTA'S FUN BOOK
### Promotional Publ., 1951
N# . . . . . . . . . . . . . . . . . . . . . 100.00

## SANTA'S SECRET
### Sam B. Anson, 1951
N# . . . . . . . . . . . . . . . . . . . . . 100.00

## SANTA'S TOYTOWN FUN BOOK
### Promotional Publications, 1952
N# . . . . . . . . . . . . . . . . . . . . . 100.00

## SCHOOL DAY ROMANCES
### See: POPULAR TEEN-AGERS

## SCIENCE COMICS
### Fox Features Syndicate, Feb., 1940
1 GT,LF(c),O&B:Electro,Perisphere
  Payne,The Eagle,Navy Jones;
  B:Marga,Cosmic Carson,
  Dr. Doom; Bondage(c) . . 10,000.00
2 GT,LF(c) . . . . . . . . . . . . . . . 6,000.00
3 GT,LF(c),Dynamo . . . . . . . . 5,000.00
4 JK,Cosmic Carson . . . . . . . . 5,000.00
5 Giant Comiscope Offer
  Eagle(c) . . . . . . . . . . . . . . 2,500.00
6 Dynamop(c) . . . . . . . . . . . . 2,500.00
7 Bondage(c),Dynamo . . . . . . 2,700.00
8 Sept., 1940 Eagle(c). . . . . . . 2,500.00

## SCIENCE COMICS
### Humor Publications, Jan., 1946
1 RP(c),Story of the A-Bomb . . . 250.00
2 RP(c),How Museum Pieces
  Are Assembled . . . . . . . . . . 100.00
3 AF,RP(c),How Underwater
  Tunnels Are Made . . . . . . . 175.00

Sc

Scoop Comics #8
© Harry A Chesler Jr.

Red Seal Comics #21
© Harry A Chesler, Jr.

Scribbly #4
© DC Comics

4 RP(c),Behind the Scenes at
 A TV Broadcast . . . . . . . . . 100.00
5 The Story of the World's
 Bridges; Sept., 1946 . . . . . . 100.00

## SCIENCE COMICS
**Ziff-Davis Publ. Co.,
May, 1946**
N# Used For A Mail Order
 Test Market . . . . . . . . . . . 500.00

## SCIENCE COMICS
**Export Publication Enterprises,
March, 1951**
1 How to resurrect a dead rat. . . 125.00

## SCOOP COMICS
**Harry 'A' Chesler Jr.,
Nov., 1941**
1 I&B:Rocketman&Rocketgirl;B:Dan
 Hastings;O&B:Master Key . 1,800.00
2 A:Rocketboy,Eye Injury. . . . . 2,000.00
3 Partial rep. of #2 . . . . . . . . . . 900.00
4 thru 7 do not exist
8 1945 . . . . . . . . . . . . . . . . 600.00
Becomes:

## SNAP
**Harry 'A' Chesler Jr.,
1944**
N# Humorous . . . . . . . . . . . . . 150.00
Becomes:

## KOMIK PAGES
**Harry 'A' Chesler Jr.,
1944**
1(10) JK,Duke of Darkness . . . . 350.00
Becomes:

## BULLS-EYE
**Harry 'A' Chesler Jr.,
1944**
11 Green Knight, Skull (c) . . . . . . 550.00
Becomes:

## KAYO
**Harry 'A' Chesler Jr.,
1945**
12 Green Knight. . . . . . . . . . . . . 200.00
Becomes:

## CARNIVAL
**Harry 'A' Chesler Jr., 1945**
(13) Guardineer. . . . . . . . . . . . . 225.00
Becomes:

## RED SEAL COMICS
**Harry 'A' Chesler, Jr./Superior,
Oct., 1945**
14 GT,Bondage(c),Black Dwarf 1,000.00
15 GT,Torture . . . . . . . . . . . . . . 650.00
16 GT. . . . . . . . . . . . . . . . . . . . 800.00
17 GT,Lady Satan,Sky Chief . . . 700.00
18 Lady Satan,Sky Chief. . . . . . 700.00
19 Lady Satan,Sky Chief. . . . . . 600.00
20 Lady Satan,Sky Chief. . . . . . 600.00
21 Lady Satan,Sky Chief. . . . . . 550.00
22 Rocketman . . . . . . . . . . . . . . 450.00

## SCOOTER COMICS
**Rucker Publications, 1946**
1 . . . . . . . . . . . . . . . . . . . . . . 200.00

## SCOTLAND YARD
**Charlton Comics, 1955**
1 . . . . . . . . . . . . . . . . . . . . . . 165.00
2 . . . . . . . . . . . . . . . . . . . . . . 125.00
3 . . . . . . . . . . . . . . . . . . . . . . 125.00
4 . . . . . . . . . . . . . . . . . . . . . . 125.00

## SCREAM COMICS
**Humor Publ./Current Books
(Ace Magazines),
Autumn, 1944**
1 . . . . . . . . . . . . . . . . . . . . . . 350.00
2 . . . . . . . . . . . . . . . . . . . . . . 250.00
3 thru 15 . . . . . . . . . . . . . . . @200.00
16 I:Lily Belle . . . . . . . . . . . . . . 225.00
17 . . . . . . . . . . . . . . . . . . . . . 200.00
18 Drug . . . . . . . . . . . . . . . . . 400.00
19 . . . . . . . . . . . . . . . . . . . . . 200.00
Becomes:

## ANDY COMICS
**June, 1948**
20 Teenage . . . . . . . . . . . . . . . 150.00
21 . . . . . . . . . . . . . . . . . . . . . 150.00
Becomes:

## ERNIE COMICS
**Sept., 1948**
22 Teenage . . . . . . . . . . . . . . . 150.00
23 thru 25. . . . . . . . . . . . . . . @100.00
Becomes:

## ALL LOVE ROMANCES
**May, 1949**
26 Ernie . . . . . . . . . . . . . . . . . 125.00
27 LbC. . . . . . . . . . . . . . . . . . 250.00
28 thru 32. . . . . . . . . . . . . . . @100.00

## SCRIBBLY
**DC Comics, Aug.,
1948–Dec.–Jan., 1951–52**
1 SM . . . . . . . . . . . . . . . . . 1,000.00
2 . . . . . . . . . . . . . . . . . . . . . . 650.00
3 . . . . . . . . . . . . . . . . . . . . . . 500.00
4 . . . . . . . . . . . . . . . . . . . . . . 500.00
5 . . . . . . . . . . . . . . . . . . . . . . 500.00
6 thru 10 . . . . . . . . . . . . . . . @350.00
11 thru 15 . . . . . . . . . . . . . . @300.00

## (Capt. Silvers Log of...)
## SEA HOUND, THE
**Avon Periodicals, 1945**
N# The Esmerelda's Treasure . . 250.00
2 Adventures in Brazil . . . . . . . . 200.00
3 Louie the Llama . . . . . . . . . . 150.00
4 In Greed & Vengence;
 Jan-Feb, 1946 . . . . . . . . . . . 150.00

## SEA HUNT
**Dell Publishing Co., 1958**
1 L.BridgesPh(c) all . . . . . . . . . 200.00
2 . . . . . . . . . . . . . . . . . . . . . . 150.00
3 ATh. . . . . . . . . . . . . . . . . . . 165.00
4 RsM . . . . . . . . . . . . . . . . . . 150.00
5 RsM . . . . . . . . . . . . . . . . . . 150.00
6 RsM . . . . . . . . . . . . . . . . . . 150.00
7 . . . . . . . . . . . . . . . . . . . . . . 125.00
8 RsM . . . . . . . . . . . . . . . . . . 150.00
9 RsM . . . . . . . . . . . . . . . . . . 150.00
10 RsM. . . . . . . . . . . . . . . . . . 150.00
11 RsM . . . . . . . . . . . . . . . . . . 150.00
12 . . . . . . . . . . . . . . . . . . . . . 150.00
13 RsM. . . . . . . . . . . . . . . . . . 150.00

## SEARCH FOR LOVE
**Best Syndicated Features
(American Comics), 1950**
1 . . . . . . . . . . . . . . . . . . . . . . 125.00
2 . . . . . . . . . . . . . . . . . . . . . . 100.00

## SECRET HEARTS
**DC Comics, Sept.–Oct.,
1949–July, 1971**
1 Make Believe Sweetheart . . . . 700.00
2 ATh,Love Is Not A Dream . . . . 350.00
3 Sing Me A Love Song . . . . . . 275.00
4 ATh. . . . . . . . . . . . . . . . . . . 275.00
5 ATh. . . . . . . . . . . . . . . . . . . 275.00
6 . . . . . . . . . . . . . . . . . . . . . . 275.00
7 . . . . . . . . . . . . . . . . . . . . . . 500.00

All comics prices listed are for *Near Mint* condition.

*Secret Missions #1*
© St. John Publishing Co.

*Select Detective #1*
© D.S. Publishing Co.

*Sensation Comics #19*
© DC Comics

```
8 thru 20 . . . . . . . . . . . . . . . @175.00
21 thru 26 . . . . . . . . . . . . . . @150.00
27 B:Comics Code . . . . . . . . . . . 125.00
28 thru 30 . . . . . . . . . . . . . . @125.00
31 thru 70 . . . . . . . . . . . . . . @100.00
71 thru 75 . . . . . . . . . . . . . . @100.00
```

## SECRET LOVE

### Ajax/Farrell (Four Star Comic Corp.), 1955–57

```
1 . . . . . . . . . . . . . . . . . . . . 150.00
2 . . . . . . . . . . . . . . . . . . . . 125.00
3 . . . . . . . . . . . . . . . . . . . . 125.00
```

**Second Series, Ajax, 1957**

```
1 . . . . . . . . . . . . . . . . . . . . 150.00
2 . . . . . . . . . . . . . . . . . . . . 100.00
3 . . . . . . . . . . . . . . . . . . . . 100.00
4 . . . . . . . . . . . . . . . . . . . . 100.00
5 . . . . . . . . . . . . . . . . . . . . 100.00
6 . . . . . . . . . . . . . . . . . . . . 100.00
```

## SECRET LOVES

### Comics Magazines (Quality Comics), Nov., 1949

```
1 BWa(c) . . . . . . . . . . . . . . . . 300.00
2 BWa(c),Lingerie(c) . . . . . . . . . . 250.00
3 RC . . . . . . . . . . . . . . . . . . 200.00
4 . . . . . . . . . . . . . . . . . . . . 150.00
5 Boom Town Babe . . . . . . . . . 200.00
6 . . . . . . . . . . . . . . . . . . . . 150.00
```

## SECRET MISSIONS

### St. John Publishing Co., 1950

```
1 JKu . . . . . . . . . . . . . . . . . . 225.00
```

## SECRET MYSTERIES
## See: CRIME MYSTERIES

## SECRET ROMANCES

### Superior Publications, 1951

```
1 . . . . . . . . . . . . . . . . . . . . 175.00
2 . . . . . . . . . . . . . . . . . . . . 125.00
3 . . . . . . . . . . . . . . . . . . . . 125.00
4 . . . . . . . . . . . . . . . . . . . . 125.00
5 . . . . . . . . . . . . . . . . . . . . 125.00
6 . . . . . . . . . . . . . . . . . . . . 125.00
7 . . . . . . . . . . . . . . . . . . . . 125.00
8 . . . . . . . . . . . . . . . . . . . . 125.00
9 . . . . . . . . . . . . . . . . . . . . 125.00
10 . . . . . . . . . . . . . . . . . . . 125.00
11 thru 18 . . . . . . . . . . . . . . @100.00
```

```
19 Lingerie . . . . . . . . . . . . . . . 200.00
20 . . . . . . . . . . . . . . . . . . . 100.00
21 thru 27 . . . . . . . . . . . . . . @100.00
```

## SECRET STORY ROMANCES

### Marvel Atlas, 1953

```
1 BEv . . . . . . . . . . . . . . . . . . 175.00
2 . . . . . . . . . . . . . . . . . . . . 125.00
3 . . . . . . . . . . . . . . . . . . . . 100.00
4 . . . . . . . . . . . . . . . . . . . . 100.00
5 . . . . . . . . . . . . . . . . . . . . 100.00
6 . . . . . . . . . . . . . . . . . . . . 100.00
7 . . . . . . . . . . . . . . . . . . . . 100.00
8 . . . . . . . . . . . . . . . . . . . . 100.00
9 . . . . . . . . . . . . . . . . . . . . 100.00
10 ViC . . . . . . . . . . . . . . . . . 100.00
11 thru 21 ViC (in many) . . . . . @100.00
```

## SELECT DETECTIVE

### D.S. Publishing Co., Aug.–Sept., 1948

```
1 MB,Exciting New Mystery
   Cases . . . . . . . . . . . . . . . . 350.00
2 MB,AMc,Dead Men . . . . . . . . . 200.00
3 Face in theFrame;Dec-Jan'48 . 175.00
```

## SENSATIONAL POLICE CASES

### Avon Periodicals, 1952

```
N# JKu,EK(c) . . . . . . . . . . . . . 475.00
2 . . . . . . . . . . . . . . . . . . . . 200.00
3 . . . . . . . . . . . . . . . . . . . . 200.00
4 . . . . . . . . . . . . . . . . . . . . 200.00
```

## SENSATION COMICS

### DC Comics, 1942–52

```
1 I:Wonder Woman,Wildcat . . 60,000.00
2 I:Etta Candy & the Holiday
   Girls, Dr. Poison . . . . . . . . 10,000.00
3 Diana Price joins Military
   Intelligence . . . . . . . . . . . 5,000.00
4 I:Baroness PaulaVonGunther 4,000.00
5 V:Axis Spies . . . . . . . . . . . . 3,500.00
6 Wonder Woman receives magic
   lasso,V:Baroness Gunther . 3,500.00
7 V:Baroness Gunther . . . . . . 2,500.00
8 Meets Gloria Bullfinch . . . . . 2,500.00
9 A:The Real Diana Prince . . . 2,500.00
10 V:Ishti . . . . . . . . . . . . . . . 2,500.00
11 I:Queen Desira . . . . . . . . . 2,500.00
12 V:Baroness Gunther . . . . . 2,000.00
```

```
13 V:Olga,Hitler(c) . . . . . . . . . 2,500.00
14 . . . . . . . . . . . . . . . . . . . 2,000.00
15 V:Simon Slikery . . . . . . . . . 2,000.00
16 V:Karl Schultz . . . . . . . . . . 2,000.00
17 V:Princess Yasmini . . . . . . 2,000.00
18 V:Quito . . . . . . . . . . . . . . 2,000.00
19 Wonder Woman Goes
   Berserk . . . . . . . . . . . . . . 2,000.00
20 V:Stoffer . . . . . . . . . . . . . . 2,000.00
21 V:American Adolf . . . . . . . . 1,800.00
22 V:Cheetah . . . . . . . . . . . . 1,800.00
23 'War Laugh Mania' . . . . . . . 1,800.00
24 I:Wonder Woman's
   Mental Radio . . . . . . . . . . 1,800.00
25 . . . . . . . . . . . . . . . . . . . 1,800.00
26 A:Queen Hippolyte . . . . . . . 1,800.00
27 V:Ely Close . . . . . . . . . . . . 1,800.00
28 V:Mayor Prude . . . . . . . . . . 1,800.00
29 V:Mimi Mendez . . . . . . . . . 1,800.00
30 V:Anton Unreal . . . . . . . . . 1,800.00
31 Grow Down Land . . . . . . . . 1,400.00
32 V:Crime Chief . . . . . . . . . . 1,400.00
33 Meets Percy Pringle . . . . . . 1,400.00
34 I:Sargon . . . . . . . . . . . . . . 1,500.00
35 V:Sontag Henya in Atlantis . 1,200.00
36 V:Bedwin Footh . . . . . . . . . 1,200.00
37 A:Mala((1st app. All-Star #8) 1,200.00
38 V:The Gyp . . . . . . . . . . . . 1,200.00
39 V:Nero . . . . . . . . . . . . . . . 1,200.00
40 I:Countess Draska Nishki . . 1,200.00
41 V:Creeper Jackson . . . . . . . 1,100.00
42 V:Countess Nishki . . . . . . . 1,100.00
43 Meets Joel Heyday . . . . . . . 1,100.00
44 V:Lt. Sturm . . . . . . . . . . . . 1,100.00
45 V:Jose Perez . . . . . . . . . . . 1,100.00
46 V:Lawbreakers Protective
   League . . . . . . . . . . . . . . 1,100.00
47 V:Unknown . . . . . . . . . . . . 1,100.00
48 V:Topso and Teena . . . . . . . 1,100.00
49 V:Zavia . . . . . . . . . . . . . . . 1,100.00
50 V:'Ears' Fellock . . . . . . . . . 1,100.00
51 V:Boss Brekel . . . . . . . . . . 1,000.00
52 Meets Prof. Toxino . . . . . . . 1,000.00
53 V:Wanta Wynn . . . . . . . . . . 1,000.00
54 V:Dr. Fiendo . . . . . . . . . . . 1,000.00
55 V:Bughumans . . . . . . . . . . 1,000.00
56 V:Dr. Novel . . . . . . . . . . . . 1,000.00
57 V:Syonide . . . . . . . . . . . . . 1,000.00
58 Meets Olive Norton . . . . . . 1,000.00
59 V:Snow Man . . . . . . . . . . . . 750.00
60 V:Bifton Jones . . . . . . . . . . . 750.00
61 V:Bluff Robust . . . . . . . . . . . 750.00
62 V:Black Robert of Dogwood . . 750.00
63 V:Prof. Vibrate . . . . . . . . . . . 750.00
64 V:Cloudmen . . . . . . . . . . . . 750.00
65 V:Lim Slait . . . . . . . . . . . . . 800.00
```

**Se**

Sensation Comics #88
© DC Comics

Sensation Mystery #115
© DC Comics

Seven Seas Comics #4
© Universal Phoenix Features

66 V:Slick Skeener. . . . . . . . . . . 800.00
67 V:Daredevil Dix . . . . . . . . . . . 800.00
68 Secret of the Menacing
Octopus. . . . . . . . . . . . . . . . 800.00
69 V:Darcy Wells . . . . . . . . . . . . 900.00
70 Unconquerable Woman of
Cocha Bamba . . . . . . . . . . . 900.00
71 V:Queen Flaming . . . . . . . . . 900.00
72 V:Blue Seal Gang . . . . . . . . . 900.00
73 Wonder Woman time
travel story. . . . . . . . . . . . . . 900.00
74 V:Spug Spangle . . . . . . . . . . 900.00
75 V:Shark. . . . . . . . . . . . . . . . . 900.00
76 V:King Diamond . . . . . . . . . . 900.00
77 V:Boss Brekel . . . . . . . . . . . . 900.00
78 V:Furiosa. . . . . . . . . . . . . . . . 900.00
79 Meets Leila and Solala . . . . . 900.00
80 V:Don Enrago . . . . . . . . . . . . 900.00
81 V:Dr. Frenzi. . . . . . . . . . . . . . 750.00
82 V:King Lunar. . . . . . . . . . . . . 600.00
83 V:Prowd . . . . . . . . . . . . . . . . 600.00
84 V:Duke Daxo. . . . . . . . . . . . . 600.00
85 Meets Leslie M. Gresham. . . . 600.00
86 Secret of the Amazing
Bracelets . . . . . . . . . . . . . . . 600.00
87 In Twin Peaks(in Old West) . . 600.00
88 Wonder Woman in Holywood. . 600.00
89 V:Abacus Rackeett Gang . . . . 600.00
90 The Secret of the Modern
Sphinx . . . . . . . . . . . . . . . . . 600.00
91 . . . . . . . . . . . . . . . . . . . . . . . 600.00
92 V:Duke of Deceptions . . . . . . . 600.00
93 V:Talbot. . . . . . . . . . . . . . . . . 600.00
94 Girl Issue. . . . . . . . . . . . . . . . 650.00
95 . . . . . . . . . . . . . . . . . . . . . . . 750.00
96 . . . . . . . . . . . . . . . . . . . . . . . 750.00
97 . . . . . . . . . . . . . . . . . . . . . . . 750.00
98 Strange Mission . . . . . . . . . . 750.00
99 I:Astra . . . . . . . . . . . . . . . . . 750.00
100 . . . . . . . . . . . . . . . . . . . . . . 800.00
101 Battle for the Atom World . . . 750.00
102 Queen of the South Seas. . . 750.00
103 V:Robot Archers . . . . . . . . . 750.00
104 The End of Paradise
Island. . . . . . . . . . . . . . . . . 750.00
105 Secret of the Giant Forest . . 750.00
106 E:Wonder Woman. . . . . . . . . 750.00
107 ATh,Mystery issue . . . . . . . 1,200.00
108 ATh,GK,I:Johnny Peril . . . . 1,000.00
109 Ath,GK,A:Johnny Peril . . . . 1,500.00
Becomes:

## SENSATION MYSTERY
### DC Comics, 1952–53
110 MA(c),B:Johnny Peril . . . . . 800.00
111 GK,Spectre in the Flame. . . . 750.00

112 GK,Death Has 5 Guesses . . 750.00
113 GK, . . . . . . . . . . . . . . . . . . 750.00
114 GK,GC,The Haunted
Diamond . . . . . . . . . . . . . . 750.00
115 GK,The Phantom Castle. . . . 750.00
116 The Toy Assassins . . . . . . . 750.00

## SERGEANT
## BARNEY BARKER
### Marvel, Aug., 1956
1 JSe,Comedy . . . . . . . . . . . . . 250.00
2 JSe,Army Inspection(c) . . . . . 150.00
3 JSe,Tank(c) . . . . . . . . . . . . . 150.00
Becomes:

## G.I. TALES
4 JSe,At Grips with the Enemy . 125.00
5 . . . . . . . . . . . . . . . . . . . . . . . 100.00
6 JO,BP,GWb, July, 1957 . . . . . 100.00

## SERGEANT BILKO
### DC Comics, May-June, 1957
1 Based on TV show . . . . . . . . 1,000.00
2 . . . . . . . . . . . . . . . . . . . . . . . 500.00
3 . . . . . . . . . . . . . . . . . . . . . . . 400.00
4 . . . . . . . . . . . . . . . . . . . . . . . 350.00
5 . . . . . . . . . . . . . . . . . . . . . . . 350.00
6 thru 17 . . . . . . . . . . . . . . . . @300.00
18 March-April, 1960 . . . . . . . . 300.00

## SERGEANT BILKO'S
## PVT. DOBERMAN
### DC Comics, June-July, 1958
1 . . . . . . . . . . . . . . . . . . . . . . . 550.00
2 . . . . . . . . . . . . . . . . . . . . . . . 300.00
3 . . . . . . . . . . . . . . . . . . . . . . . 225.00
4 . . . . . . . . . . . . . . . . . . . . . . . 225.00
5 photo (c). . . . . . . . . . . . . . . . 225.00
6 thru 10 . . . . . . . . . . . . . . . . @150.00
11 Feb.–March, 1960. . . . . . . . . 150.00

## SERGEANT PRESTON
## OF THE YUKON
### Dell Publishing Co., Aug., 1951
(1 thru 4) see Dell Four Color #344;
#373, 397, 419
5 P(c) . . . . . . . . . . . . . . . . . . . 150.00
6 Bondage, P(c) . . . . . . . . . . . . 200.00
7 thru 11 P(c) . . . . . . . . . . . . . 150.00
12 P(c) . . . . . . . . . . . . . . . . . . . 150.00
13 P(c),O:Sergeant Preston . . . . 200.00
14 thru 17 P(c) . . . . . . . . . . . . @150.00

18 Yukon King,P(c) . . . . . . . . . . 200.00
19 thru 29 Ph(c). . . . . . . . . . . . @250.00

## SEVEN SEAS COMICS
### Universal Phoenix Features/
### Leader Publ., April, 1946
1 MB,RWb(c),B:South Sea
Girl, Captain Cutlass . . . . . 1,400.00
2 MB,RWb(c) . . . . . . . . . . . . 1,200.00
3 MB,AF,MB(c) . . . . . . . . . . . 1,100.00
4 MB,MB(c) . . . . . . . . . . . . . 1,200.00
5 MB,MB(c),Hangman's
Noose . . . . . . . . . . . . . . . 1,100.00
6 MB,MB(c);1947 . . . . . . . . . 1,000.00

## SHADOW COMICS
### Street & Smith Publ.,
### March, 1940
1-1 P(c),B:Shadow,Doc Savage,
Bill Barnes,Nick Carter,
Frank Merriwell,Iron Munro 7,000.00
1-2 P(c),B: The Avenger . . . . . 2,500.00
1-3 P(c),A: Norgill the
Magician . . . . . . . . . . . . . 2,000.00
1-4 P(c),B:The Three
Musketeers. . . . . . . . . . . . 1,500.00
1-5 P(c),E: Doc Savage . . . . . 1,500.00
1-6 A: Captain Fury . . . . . . . . 1,200.00
1-7 O&B: The Wasp . . . . . . . . 1,300.00
1-8 A:Doc Savage . . . . . . . . . 1,200.00
1-9 A:Norgill the Magician . . . 1,200.00
1-10 O:Iron Ghost;B:The Dead
End Kids . . . . . . . . . . . . . 1,200.00
1-11 O:Hooded Wasp . . . . . . 1,200.00
1-12 Crime Does Not pay . . . . 1,100.00
2-1 . . . . . . . . . . . . . . . . . . . . 1,200.00
2-2 Shadow Becomes Invisible 1,700.00
2-3 O&B:Supersnipe;
F:Little Nemo . . . . . . . . . . 1,500.00
2-4 F:Little Nemo . . . . . . . . . 1,200.00
2-5 V:The Ghost Faker . . . . . 1,200.00
2-6 A:Blackstone the Magician 1,000.00
2-7 V:The White Dragon . . . . 1,000.00
2-8 A:Little Nemo . . . . . . . . . 1,000.00
2-9 The Hand of Death . . . . . 1,000.00
2-10 A:Beebo the WonderHorse 1,000.00
2-11 V:Devil Kyoti . . . . . . . . . 1,000.00
2-12 V:Devil Kyoti . . . . . . . . . . 900.00
3-1 JaB(c),V:Devil Kyoti . . . . . . 900.00
3-2 Red Skeleton Life Story . . . . 900.00
3-3 V:Monstrodamus . . . . . . . . . 900.00
3-4 V:Monstrodamus . . . . . . . . . 900.00
3-5 V:Monstrodamus . . . . . . . . . 900.00
3-6 V:Devil's of the Deep . . . . . . 900.00

Se

*Shadow Comics Vol. 4 #9*
© Street & Smith Publications

*Sheena, Queen of the Jungle #8*
© Fiction House

*Shield-Wizard Comics #11*
© MLJ Magazines

3-7 V: Monstrodamus . . . . . . . . 900.00
3-8 E: The Wasp . . . . . . . . . . . . . 900.00
3-9 The Stolen Lighthouse . . . . . 900.00
3-10 A:Doc Savage . . . . . . . . . . 900.00
3-11 P(c),V: Thade . . . . . . . . . . . 900.00
3-12 V: Thade . . . . . . . . . . . . . . 900.00
4-1 Red Cross Appeal on (c) . . . . 800.00
4-2 V:The Brain of Nippon . . . . . 800.00
4-3 Little Men in Space . . . . . . . . 800.00
4-4 ...Mystifies Berlin . . . . . . . . . 800.00
4-5 ...Brings Terror to Tokio . . . . 800.00
4-6 V:The Tarantula . . . . . . . . . . 800.00
4-7 Crypt of the Seven Skulls . . . 800.00
4-8 V:the Indigo Mob . . . . . . . . . 800.00
4-9 Ghost Guarded Treasure
 of the Haunted Glen . . . . . . . 800.00
4-10 V:The Hydra . . . . . . . . . . . . 800.00
4-11 V:The Seven Sinners . . . . . . 800.00
4-12 Club Curio . . . . . . . . . . . . . 1,000.00
5-1 A:Flatty Foote . . . . . . . . . . 1,000.00
5-2 Bells of Doom . . . . . . . . . . 1,000.00
5-3 The Circle of Death . . . . . . 1,000.00
5-4 The Empty Safe Riddle . . . 1,000.00
5-5 The Mighty Master Nomad . 1,200.00
5-6 ...Fights Piracy Among
 the Golden Isles . . . . . . . . . . 750.00
5-7 V:The Talon . . . . . . . . . . . . . 750.00
5-8 V:The Talon . . . . . . . . . . . . . 750.00
5-9 V:The Talon . . . . . . . . . . . . . 750.00
5-10 V:The Crime Master . . . . . . 750.00
5-11 The Clutch of the Talon . . . . 750.00
5-12 Most Dangerous Criminal . . 750.00
6-1 Double Z . . . . . . . . . . . . . . . 600.00
6-2 Riddle of Prof.Mentalo . . . . . 600.00
6-3 V:Judge Lawless . . . . . . . . . 600.00
6-4 V:Dr. Zenith . . . . . . . . . . . . . 600.00
6-5 . . . . . . . . . . . . . . . . . . . . . . 600.00
6-6 ...Invades the
 Crucible of Death . . . . . . . . . 600.00
6-7 Four Panel (c) . . . . . . . . . . . 600.00
6-8 Crime Among the Aztecs . . . 600.00
6-9 I:Shadow Jr. . . . . . . . . . . . . . 650.00
6-10 Devil's Passage . . . . . . . . . 600.00
6-11 The Black Pagoda . . . . . . . . 600.00
6-12 BP,BP(c),Atomic Bomb
 Secrets Stolen . . . . . . . . . . . . 650.00
7-1 The Yellow Band . . . . . . . . . 650.00
7-2 A:Shadow Jr. . . . . . . . . . . . . 650.00
7-3 BP,BP(c),Crime Under
 the Border . . . . . . . . . . . . . . 800.00
7-4 BP,BP(c),One Tree Island,
 Atomic Bomb . . . . . . . . . . . . 900.00
7-5 A:Shadow Jr. . . . . . . . . . . . . 650.00
7-6 BP,BP(c),The Sacred Sword
 of Sanjorojo . . . . . . . . . . . . . 800.00
7-7 Crime K.O. . . . . . . . . . . . . . . 650.00

7-8 ...Raids Crime Harbor . . . . . . 650.00
7-9 BP.BP(c),Kilroy Was Here . . 800.00
7-10 BP,BP(c),The Riddle of
 the Flying Saucer . . . . . . . . 1,000.00
7-11 BP,BP(c),Crime
 Doesn't Pay . . . . . . . . . . . . . 800.00
7-12 BP,BP(c)Back From
 the Grave. . . . . . . . . . . . . . . 800.00
8-1 BP,BP(c),Curse of the Cat . . 800.00
8-2 BP,BP(c),Decay,Vermin &
 Murder in the Bayou . . . . . . . 800.00
8-3 BP,BP(c),The Spider Boy . . . 800.00
8-4 BP,BP(c),Death Rises
 Out of the Sea . . . . . . . . . . . 800.00
8-5 BP,BP(c),Jekyll-
 Hyde Murders . . . . . . . . . . . 800.00
8-6 Secret of Valhalla Hall . . . . . 800.00
8-7 BP,BP(c),Shadow in Danger 800.00
8-8 BP,BP(c),...Solves a
 Twenty Year Old Crime . . . . 800.00
8-9 BP,BP(c),3-D Effect(c) . . . . . 800.00
8-10 BP,BP(c),Up&Down(c). . . . . 800.00
8-11 BP,BP(c). . . . . . . . . . . . . . . 800.00
8-12 BP,BP(c),Arabs,Boat(c) . . . . 800.00
9-1 Airport(c) . . . . . . . . . . . . . . . 800.00
9-2 BP,BP(c),Flying Cannon(c) . . 800.00
9-3 BP,BP(c),Shadow's Shadow . 800.00
9-4 BP,BP(c) . . . . . . . . . . . . . . . 800.00
9-5 Death in the Stars;Aug'49 . . . 800.00

## SHARP COMICS
### H.C. Blackerby,
### Winter, 1945
1 O:Planetarian(c) . . . . . . . . . . . 550.00
2 O:The Pioneer . . . . . . . . . . . . 400.00

## SHEENA, QUEEN OF
## THE JUNGLE
### Real Adventures
### (Fiction House)
### Spring, 1942–Winter, 1952
1 Blood Hunger . . . . . . . . . . . . 3,500.00
2 Black Orchid of Death . . . . . . 1,500.00
3 Harem Shackles . . . . . . . . . 1,100.00
4 The Zebra Raiders . . . . . . . . . 700.00
5 War of the Golden Apes . . . . . 650.00
6 . . . . . . . . . . . . . . . . . . . . . . . 625.00
7 They Claw By Night . . . . . . . . 600.00
8 The Congo Colossus . . . . . . . 600.00
9 and 10 . . . . . . . . . . . . . . . . . @550.00
11 Red Fangs of the Tree Tribe. . 550.00
12 . . . . . . . . . . . . . . . . . . . . . . . 450.00
13 Veldt o/t Voo Doo Lions . . . . . 450.00

14 The Hoo Doo Beasts of
 Mozambique . . . . . . . . . . . . . 450.00
15 . . . . . . . . . . . . . . . . . . . . . . . 450.00
16 Black Ivory . . . . . . . . . . . . . . 450.00
17 Great Congo Treasure Trek . . 450.00
18 Doom of the Elephant Drum. . 450.00

## SHERIFF OF
## TOMBSTONE
### Charlton Comics, 1958–61
1 AW,JSe . . . . . . . . . . . . . . . . . 150.00
2 thru 10 . . . . . . . . . . . . . . . . @100.00
11 thru 17 . . . . . . . . . . . . . . . . . @75.00

## SHERLOCK HOLMES
### Charlton Comics, 1955
1 . . . . . . . . . . . . . . . . . . . . . . . 500.00
2 . . . . . . . . . . . . . . . . . . . . . . . 450.00

## SHERRY THE SHOWGIRL
### Marvel Atlas, 1956
1 . . . . . . . . . . . . . . . . . . . . . . . 200.00
2 . . . . . . . . . . . . . . . . . . . . . . . 135.00
3 . . . . . . . . . . . . . . . . . . . . . . . 125.00
4 . . . . . . . . . . . . . . . . . . . . . . . 125.00
5 thru 7 . . . . . . . . . . . . . . . . . @125.00

## SHIELD-WIZARD
## COMICS
### MLJ Magazines,
### Summer, 1940
1 IN,EA,O:Shield . . . . . . . . . . . 7,000.00
2 O:Shield;I:Roy . . . . . . . . . . . 3,000.00
3 Roy,Child Bondage(c). . . . . . 2,000.00
4 Shield,Roy,Wizard . . . . . . . . 1,800.00
5 B:Dusty-Boy Dectective,Child
 Bondage . . . . . . . . . . . . . . . 1,700.00
6 B:Roy the Super Boy,Child
 Bondage . . . . . . . . . . . . . . . 1,500.00
7 Shield(c),Roy Bondage(c) . . 1,600.00
8 Bondage(c) . . . . . . . . . . . . . 1,500.00
9 Shield/Roy(c) . . . . . . . . . . . 1,200.00
10 Shield/Roy(c) . . . . . . . . . . . 1,200.00
11 Shield/Roy(c) . . . . . . . . . . . 1,200.00
12 Shield/Roy(c) . . . . . . . . . . . 1,200.00
13 Bondage (c);Spring'44 . . . . . 1,500.00

## SHIP AHOY
### Spotlight Publishers,
### Nov., 1944
1 LbC(c) . . . . . . . . . . . . . . . . . 250.00

All comics prices listed are for *Near Mint* condition.     **Page 235**

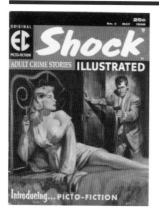

*Shock Illustrated #3*
© E.C. Comics

*Showcase #17*
© DC Comics

*Silver Streak Comics #20*
© Lev Gleason

## SHOCK DETECTIVE CASE(S)
### See: CRIMINALS ON THE RUN

## SHOCK ILLUSTRATED
### E.C. Comics, 1955

| | |
|---|---|
| 1 Drugs | 300.00 |
| 2 AW,GI,RC | 200.00 |
| 3 RC | 4,000.00 |

## SHOCK SUSPENSTORIES
### Tiny Tot Comics (E.C. Comics), Feb.–March, 1952

| | |
|---|---|
| 1 JDa,JKa,AF(c),ElectricChair | 2,500.00 |
| 2 WW,JDa,Grl,JKa,WW(c) | 1,800.00 |
| 3 WW,JDa,JKa,WW(c) | 1,200.00 |
| 4 WW,JDa,JKa,WW(c) | 1,200.00 |
| 5 WW,JDa,JKa,WW(c), Hanging | 1,400.00 |
| 6 WW,AF,JKa,WW(c), Bondage(c) | 1,500.00 |
| 7 JKa,WW,GE,AF(c),Face Melting | 1,500.00 |
| 8 JKa,AF,AW,GE,WW,AF(c) | 1,100.00 |
| 9 JKa,AF,RC,WW,AF(c) | 1,000.00 |
| 10 JKa,WW,RC,JKa(c),Drug | 1,000.00 |
| 11 JCr,JKa,WW,RC,JCr(c) | 900.00 |
| 12 AF,JKa,WW,RC,AF(c) Drug(c) | 1,000.00 |
| 13 JKa,WW,FF,JKa(c) | 1,200.00 |
| 14 JKa,WW,BK,WW(c) | 900.00 |
| 15 JKa,WW,RC,JDa(c) Strangulation | 750.00 |
| 16 GE,RC,JKa,GE(c),Rape | 750.00 |
| 17 GE,RC,JKa,GE(c) | 600.00 |
| 18 GE,RC,JKa,GE(c);Jan'55 | 600.00 |

## SHOCKING MYSTERY CASES
### See: THRILLING CRIME CASES

## SHORTY SHINER
### Dandy Comics, 1956

| | |
|---|---|
| 1 | 125.00 |
| 2 | 100.00 |
| 3 | 100.00 |

## SHOWCASE
### DC Comics, 1956–70

| | |
|---|---|
| 1 F:Fire Fighters | 5,500.00 |
| 2 JKu,F:Kings of Wild | 1,600.00 |
| 3 F:Frogmen | 1,500.00 |
| 4 CI,JKu,I&O:S.A. Flash (Barry Allen) | 42,000.00 |
| 5 F:Manhunters | 1,400.00 |
| 6 JK,I&O:Challengers of the Unknown | 6,000.00 |
| 7 JK,F:Challengers | 2,800.00 |
| 8 CI,F:Flash,I:Capt.Cold | 17,500.00 |
| 9 F:Lois Lane | 12,000.00 |
| 10 F:Lois Lane | 4,600.00 |
| 11 JK(c),F:Challengers | 2,500.00 |
| 12 JK(c),F:Challengers | 2,500.00 |
| 13 CI,F:Flash,Mr.Element | 6,500.00 |
| 14 CI,F:Flash,Mr.Element | 6,800.00 |
| 15 I:Space Ranger | 3,000.00 |
| 16 F:Space Ranger | 1,400.00 |
| 17 GK(c),I:Adam Strange | 3,700.00 |
| 18 GK(c),F:Adam Strange | 1,800.00 |
| 19 GK(c),F:Adam Strange | 2,000.00 |
| 20 I:Rip Hunter | 1,500.00 |
| 21 F:Rip Hunter | 750.00 |
| 22 GK,I&O:S.A. Green Lantern (Hal Jordan) | 7,200.00 |
| 23 GK,F:Green Lantern | 2,400.00 |
| 24 GK,F:Green Lantern | 2,400.00 |
| 25 JKu,F:Rip Hunter | 500.00 |
| 26 JKu,F:Rip Hunter | 500.00 |
| 27 RH,I:Sea Devils | 1,300.00 |
| 28 RH,F:Sea Devils | 600.00 |
| 29 RH,F:Sea Devils | 600.00 |
| 30 O:Aquaman | 1,200.00 |
| 31 GK(c),F:Aquaman | 600.00 |
| 32 F:Aquaman | 600.00 |
| 33 F:Aquaman | 650.00 |
| 34 GK,MA,I&O:S.A. Atom | 2,400.00 |
| 35 GK,MA,F:Atom | 1,200.00 |
| 36 GK,MA,F:Atom | 900.00 |
| 37 RA,I:Metal Man | 1,000.00 |
| 38 RA,F:Metal Man | 650.00 |
| 39 RA,F:Metal Man | 500.00 |
| 40 RA,F:Metal Man | 425.00 |
| 41 & 42 F:Tommy Tomorrow | @275.00 |
| 43 F:Dr.No(James Bond 007) | 675.00 |
| 44 F:Tommy Tomorrow | 200.00 |
| 45 JKu,O:Sgt.Rock | 450.00 |

## SHOWGIRLS
### Marvel Atlas, 1957

| | |
|---|---|
| 1 | 150.00 |
| 2 | 125.00 |

## SILLY TUNES
### Marvel Timely, 1945–47

| | |
|---|---|
| 1 Ziggy Pig | 125.00 |
| 2 | 125.00 |
| 3 | 110.00 |
| 4 | 110.00 |
| 5 | 110.00 |
| 6 | 110.00 |
| 7 | 110.00 |

## SILVER KID WESTERN
### Key Publ./Stanmor Publ., 1954

| | |
|---|---|
| 1 | 125.00 |
| 2 | 100.00 |
| 3 | 100.00 |
| 4 | 100.00 |

## SILVER STREAK COMICS
### Your Guide/New Friday/ Comic House/Newsbrook Publications/Lev Gleason, Dec., 1939

| | |
|---|---|
| 1 JCo(a&c),I&B:The Claw,Red Reeves Capt.Fearless;B:Mr.Midnight,Wasp;A:Spiritman | 16,500.00 |
| 2 JSm,JCo,JSm(c) | 6,000.00 |
| 3 JaB(c),I&O:Silver Streak; B:Dickie Dean,Lance Hale, Ace Powers,Bill Wayne, Planet Patrol | 5,000.00 |
| 4 JCo,JaB(c)B:Sky Wolf; N:Silver Streak,I:Lance Hale's Sidekick-Jackie | 2,500.00 |
| 5 JCo(a&c),Dickie Dean V:The Raging Flood | 3,000.00 |
| 6 JCo,JaB,JCo(a&c),O&I:Daredevil [Blue & Yellow Costume]; R:The Claw | 21,000.00 |
| 7 JCo,N: Daredevil | 15,000.00 |
| 8 JCo(a&c) | 5,000.00 |
| 9 JCo,BoW(c) | 3,000.00 |
| 10 BoW,BoW(c) | 2,500.00 |
| 11 DRi(c) I:Mercury | 2,000.00 |
| 12 DRi(c) | 1,500.00 |
| 13 JaB,JaB(c),O:Thun-Dohr | 1,500.00 |
| 14 JaB,JaB(c),A:Nazi Skull Men | 1,500.00 |
| 15 JaB,DBr,JaB(c), B:Bingham Boys | 1,200.00 |
| 16 DBr,BoW(c),Hitler(c) | 1,600.00 |
| 17 DBr,JaB(c),E:Daredevil | 1,200.00 |
| 18 DBr,JaB(c),B:The Saint | 1,100.00 |

**Sh**

*Crime Does Not Pay #35*
© Lev Gleason

*Crime Does Not Pay #117*
© Lev Gleason

*Single Series #20*
© United Features Syndicate

19 DBr,EA . . . . . . . . . . . . . . . 900.00
20 BW,BEv,EA . . . . . . . . . . . . . 900.00
21 BW,BEv. . . . . . . . . . . . . . . . 900.00
**Becomes:**

## CRIME DOES NOT PAY
### June, 1942
22(23) CBi(c),The Mad Musician
   & Tunes of Doom . . . . . . . 3,500.00
23 CBi(c),John Dillinger-One
   Man Underworld . . . . . . . . . . 1,900.00
24 CBi(c),The Mystery of the
   Indian Dick . . . . . . . . . . . . 1,500.00
25 CBi(c),Dutch Shultz-King
   of the Underworld . . . . . . . . 800.00
26 CBi(c),Lucky Luciano-The
   Deadliest of Crime Rats . . . . 800.00
27 CBi(c),Pretty Boy Floyd . . . . . 800.00
28 CBi(c), . . . . . . . . . . . . . . . . . 800.00
29 CBi(c),Two-Gun Crowley-The
   Bad Kid with the Itchy
   Trigger Finger . . . . . . . . . . 750.00
30 CBi(c),"Monk"Eastman
   V:Thompson's Mob . . . . . . . . 750.00
31 CBi(c) The Million Dollar
   Bank Robbery . . . . . . . . . . . 500.00
32 CBi(c),Seniorita of Sin . . . . . . 500.00
33 CBi(c),Meat Cleaver Murder . . 550.00
34 CBi(c),Elevator Shaft . . . . . . 500.00
35 CBi(c),Case o/t MissingToe . . 500.00
36 CBi(c) . . . . . . . . . . . . . . . . . 450.00
37 CBi(c) . . . . . . . . . . . . . . . . . 400.00
38 CBi(c) . . . . . . . . . . . . . . . . . 400.00
39 FGu,CBi(c) . . . . . . . . . . . . . 400.00
40 CBi(c),CBi(c) . . . . . . . . . . . . 450.00
41 FGu,RP,CBi(c),The Cocksure
   Counterfeiter . . . . . . . . . . . 350.00
42 FGu,RP,CBi(c) . . . . . . . . . . 350.00
43 FGu,RP,CBi(c)Electrocution . . 500.00
44 FGu,CBi(c),The Most Shot
   At Gangster . . . . . . . . . . . . 250.00
45 CBi(c) . . . . . . . . . . . . . . . . . 250.00
46 FGu,CBi(c),ChildKidnapping(c)300.00
47 FGu,CBi(c),ElectricChair. . . . . 400.00
48 FGu,CBi(c) . . . . . . . . . . . . . 250.00
49 FGu,CBi(c) . . . . . . . . . . . . . 250.00
50 FGu,CBi(c) . . . . . . . . . . . . . 250.00
51 FGu,GT,CBi(c),1st Monthly. . . 225.00
52 FGu,GT,CBi(c) . . . . . . . . . . . 225.00
53 FGu,CBi(c) . . . . . . . . . . . . . 225.00
54 FGu,CBi(c) . . . . . . . . . . . . . 225.00
55 FGu,CBi(c) . . . . . . . . . . . . . 225.00
56 FGu,GT,CBi(c) . . . . . . . . . . . 225.00
57 FGu,CBi(c) . . . . . . . . . . . . . 225.00
58 FGu,CBi(c) . . . . . . . . . . . . . 225.00
59 FGu,Cbi(c) . . . . . . . . . . . . . 225.00

60 FGu,CBi(c) . . . . . . . . . . . . . 225.00
61 FGu,GT,CBi(c) . . . . . . . . . . . 225.00
62 FGu,CBi(c),Bondage(c) . . . . . 225.00
63 FGu,GT,CBi(c) . . . . . . . . . . . 200.00
64 FGu,GT,CBi(c) . . . . . . . . . . . 200.00
65 FGu,CBi(c) . . . . . . . . . . . . . 200.00
66 FGu,GT,CBi(c) . . . . . . . . . . . 200.00
67 FGu,GT,CBi(c) . . . . . . . . . . . 200.00
68 FGu,CBi(c) . . . . . . . . . . . . . 200.00
69 FGu,CBi(c) . . . . . . . . . . . . . 200.00
70 FGu,CBi(c) . . . . . . . . . . . . . 200.00
71 FGu,CBi(c) . . . . . . . . . . . . . 150.00
72 FGu,CBi(c) . . . . . . . . . . . . . 150.00
73 FGu,CBi(c) . . . . . . . . . . . . . 150.00
74 FGu,CBi(c) . . . . . . . . . . . . . 150.00
75 FGu,CBi(c) . . . . . . . . . . . . . 150.00
76 FGu,CBi(c) . . . . . . . . . . . . . 150.00
77 FGu,CBi(c),Electrified Safe. . . 175.00
78 FGu,CBi(c) . . . . . . . . . . . . . 150.00
79 FGu . . . . . . . . . . . . . . . . . . 150.00
80 FGu . . . . . . . . . . . . . . . . . . 150.00
81 FGu . . . . . . . . . . . . . . . . . . 150.00
82 FGu . . . . . . . . . . . . . . . . . . 150.00
83 FGu . . . . . . . . . . . . . . . . . . 150.00
84 FGu . . . . . . . . . . . . . . . . . . 150.00
85 FGu . . . . . . . . . . . . . . . . . . 150.00
86 FGu . . . . . . . . . . . . . . . . . . 150.00
87 FGu,P(c),The Rock-A-Bye
   Baby Murder . . . . . . . . . . . . 150.00
88 FGu,P(c),Death Carries Torch 150.00
89 FGu,BF,BF P(c),The Escort
   Murder Case . . . . . . . . . . . . 150.00
90 FGu,BF P(c),The Alhambra
   Club Murders . . . . . . . . . . . 150.00
91 FGu,AMc,BF P(c),Death
   Watches The Clock . . . . . . . 150.00
92 BF,FGu,BF P(c) . . . . . . . . . . 150.00
93 BF,FGu,AMc,BF P(c) . . . . . . 150.00
94 BF,FGu,BF P(c) . . . . . . . . . . 150.00
95 FGu,AMc,BF P(c) . . . . . . . . . 150.00
96 BF,FGu,BF P(c),The Case of
   the Movie Star's Double . . . . 150.00
97 FGu,BF P(c) . . . . . . . . . . . . 150.00
98 BF,FGu,BF P(c),Bondage(c). . 150.00
99 BF,FGu,BF P(c) . . . . . . . . . . 150.00
100 FGu,BF,AMc,P(c),The Case
   of the Jittery Patient . . . . . . . 150.00
101 FGu,BF,AMc,P(c) . . . . . . . . 125.00
102 FGu,BF,AMc,BF P(c) . . . . . . 125.00
103 FGu,BF,AMc,BF P(c) . . . . . . 125.00
104 thru 110 FGu . . . . . . . . . . @125.00
111 thru 120 . . . . . . . . . . . . . @125.00
121 thru 140 . . . . . . . . . . . . . @100.00
141 JKu . . . . . . . . . . . . . . . . . 100.00
142 JKu,CBi(c). . . . . . . . . . . . . 100.00
143 JKu,Comic Code. . . . . . . . . 100.00

144 I Helped Capture "Fat Face"
   George Klinerz . . . . . . . . . . . 75.00
145 RP,Double Barrelled Menace . 75.00
146 BP,The Con & The Canary . . . 75.00
147 JKu,BP,A Long Shoe On the
   Highway;July, 1955 . . . . . . . 125.00

## SINGLE SERIES
### United Features Syndicate, 1938
1 Captain & The Kids . . . . . . . 1,200.00
2 Bronco Bill . . . . . . . . . . . . . . 650.00
3 Ella Cinders . . . . . . . . . . . . . 500.00
4 Li'l Abner . . . . . . . . . . . . . . 1,000.00
5 Fritzi Ritz . . . . . . . . . . . . . . . 300.00
6 Jim Hardy . . . . . . . . . . . . . . . 500.00
7 Frankie Doodle . . . . . . . . . . . 400.00
8 Peter Pat . . . . . . . . . . . . . . . 400.00
9 Strange As it Seems . . . . . . . 400.00
10 Little Mary Mixup. . . . . . . . . . 400.00
11 Mr. & Mrs. Beans . . . . . . . . . 400.00
12 Joe Jinx. . . . . . . . . . . . . . . . 350.00
13 Looy Dot Dope . . . . . . . . . . . 350.00
14 Billy Make Believe. . . . . . . . . 350.00
15 How It Began . . . . . . . . . . . . 400.00
16 Illustrated Gags. . . . . . . . . . . 250.00
17 Danny Dingle . . . . . . . . . . . . 300.00
18 Li'l Abner. . . . . . . . . . . . . . . 800.00
19 Broncho Bill. . . . . . . . . . . . . 550.00
20 Tarzan . . . . . . . . . . . . . . . 1,500.00
21 Ella Cinders . . . . . . . . . . . . . 400.00
22 Iron Vic . . . . . . . . . . . . . . . . 400.00
23 Tailspin Tommy . . . . . . . . . . . 500.00
24 Alice In Wonderland . . . . . . . 550.00
25 Abbie an' Slats . . . . . . . . . . . 450.00
26 Little Mary Mixup. . . . . . . . . . 400.00
27 Jim Hardy . . . . . . . . . . . . . . 400.00
28 Ella Cinders & Abbie AN'
   Slats 1942 . . . . . . . . . . . . . 400.00

## SIX GUN HEROES
### Fawcett Publications, 1950
1 Rocky Lane,Hopalong Cassidy 600.00
2 . . . . . . . . . . . . . . . . . . . . . . 350.00
3 . . . . . . . . . . . . . . . . . . . . . . 250.00
4 . . . . . . . . . . . . . . . . . . . . . . 250.00
5 Lash Larue. . . . . . . . . . . . . . 250.00
6 . . . . . . . . . . . . . . . . . . . . . . 175.00
7 . . . . . . . . . . . . . . . . . . . . . . 175.00
8 . . . . . . . . . . . . . . . . . . . . . . 175.00
9 . . . . . . . . . . . . . . . . . . . . . . 175.00
10 . . . . . . . . . . . . . . . . . . . . . 175.00
11 thru 23 . . . . . . . . . . . . . . @125.00

**Si**

*Skeleton Hand #2*
© American Comics Group

*Slave Girl Comics #1*
© Avon Periodicals

*Smash Comics #17*
© Comics Magazine, Inc.

**Charlton Comics, 1954**
24 . . . . . . . . . . . . . . . . . . . . . . . 225.00
25 . . . . . . . . . . . . . . . . . . . . . . . 125.00
26 thru 50 . . . . . . . . . . . . . @100.00
51 thru 70 . . . . . . . . . . . . . @100.00

### SIX-GUN WESTERN
**Marvel Atlas, Jan., 1957**
1 JSe(c),RC,JR,Kid Yukon
  Gunslinger . . . . . . . . . . . . . 225.00
2 SSh,AW,DAy,JO,His Guns
  Hang Low . . . . . . . . . . . . . . 150.00
3 AW,BP,DAy . . . . . . . . . . . . . 150.00
4 JSe(c),JR,GWb . . . . . . . . . . . 125.00

### SKELETON HAND
**American Comics Group,
Sept.–Oct., 1952**
1 . . . . . . . . . . . . . . . . . . . . . . . 600.00
2 The Were-Serpent of Karnak. . 400.00
3 Waters of Doom . . . . . . . . . . . 300.00
4 Black Dust . . . . . . . . . . . . . . 300.00
5 The Rise & Fall of the
  Bogey Man . . . . . . . . . . . . . . 300.00
6 July–Aug., 1953 . . . . . . . . . . . 300.00

### SKIPPY'S OWN
### BOOK OF COMICS
**M.C. Gaines, 1934**
N# . . . . . . . . . . . . . . . . . . . . . 6,000.00

### SKY BLAZERS
**Hawley Publications,
Sept., 1940**
1 Flying Aces,Sky Pirates . . . . . 800.00
2 Nov., 1940 . . . . . . . . . . . . . . 600.00

### SKYMAN
**Columbia Comics Group, 1941**
1 OW,OW(c),O:Skyman,Face . 1,600.00
2 OW,OW(c),Yankee Doodle . . 800.00
3 OW,OW(c) . . . . . . . . . . . . . 500.00
4 OW,OW(c),Statue of
  Liberty(c) 1948 . . . . . . . . . 500.00

### SKY PILOT
**Ziff-Davis Publishing Co.,
1950**
10 NS, P(c),Lumber Pirates. . . . 175.00
11 NS, P(c),The 2,00 Foot Drop;
  April–May, 1951. . . . . . . . . 150.00

### SKY ROCKET
**Home Guide Publ.
(Harry 'A' Chesler), 1944**
1 Alias the Dragon,Skyrocket . . . 400.00

### SKY SHERIFF
**D.S. Publishing,
Summer, 1948**
1 I:Breeze Lawson & the Prowl
  Plane Patrol . . . . . . . . . . . . . 150.00

### SLAM BANG COMICS
**Fawcett Publications,
Jan., 1940**
1 B:Diamond Jack,Mark Swift,
  Lee Granger,Jungle King . . 5,000.00
2 F:Jim Dolan Two-Fisted
  Crime Buster . . . . . . . . . . . 2,000.00
3 A: Eric the Talking Lion . . . . 3,500.00
4 F: Hurricane Hansen-Sea
  Adventurer . . . . . . . . . . . . 2,000.00
5 . . . . . . . . . . . . . . . . . . . . . 2,000.00
6 I: Zoro the Mystery Man;
  Bondage(c) . . . . . . . . . . . 2,000.00
7 Bondage(c);Sept., 1940 . . . . 2,000.00

### SLAPSTICK COMICS
**Comic Magazine
Distrib., Inc., 1945**
N# Humorous Parody . . . . . . . . 300.00

### SLASH-D DOUBLECROSS
**St. John Publishing Co., 1950**
N# . . . . . . . . . . . . . . . . . . . . . . 250.00

### SLAVE GIRL COMICS
**Avon Periodicals, Feb., 1949**
1 EL . . . . . . . . . . . . . . . . . . . 1,250.00
2 EL . . . . . . . . . . . . . . . . . . . . 900.00

### SLICK CHICK COMICS
**Leader Enterprises, Inc., 1947**
1 Teen-Aged Humor . . . . . . . . . 125.00
2 Teen-Aged Humor . . . . . . . . 100.00
3 1947. . . . . . . . . . . . . . . . . . . 100.00

### SLUGGER
**Lev Gleason Publications, 1956**
1 CBi(c). . . . . . . . . . . . . . . . . . 100.00

### SMASH COMICS
**Comics Magazine, Inc.
(Quality Comics Group),
Aug., 1939**
1 WE,O&B:Hugh Hazard, Bozo
  the Robot,Black X, Invisible
  Justice: B:Wings Wendall,
  Chic Carter . . . . . . . . . . . 6,000.00
2 WE,A:Lone Star Rider . . . . . 1,800.00
3 WE,B:Captain Cook, John
  Law . . . . . . . . . . . . . . . . . 1,100.00
4 WE,PGv,B:Flash Fulton . . . . 1,000.00
5 WE,PGv,Bozo Robot . . . . . . 1,000.00
6 WE,PGv,GFx,Black X(c). . . . 1,000.00
7 WE,PGv,GFx,Wings
  Wendell(c) . . . . . . . . . . . . . 900.00
8 WE,PGv,GFx,Bozo Robot . . . . 900.00
9 WE,PGv,GFx,Black X(c) . . . . . 900.00
10 WE,PGv,GFx,Bozo Robot(c) . 900.00
11 WE,PGv,GFx,BP,Black X(c) . . 900.00
12 WE,PGv,GFx,BP,Bozo(c) . . . . 900.00
13 WE,PGv,GFx,AB,BP,B:Mango,
  Purple Trio,BlackX(c). . . . . . 900.00
14 BP,LF,AB,PGv,I:The Ray . . 4,500.00
15 BP,LF,AB,PGv,The Ram(c) . 2,000.00
16 BP,LF,AB,PGv,Bozo(c). . . . . 1,900.00
17 BP,LF,AB,PGv,JCo,
  The Ram(c) . . . . . . . . . . . 1,900.00
18 BP,LF,AB,JCo,PGv,
  B&O:Midnight . . . . . . . . . 2,500.00
19 BP,LF,AB,JCo,PGv,Bozo(c) . 1,400.00
20 BP,LF,AB,JCo,PGv,
  The Ram(c) . . . . . . . . . . . 1,400.00
21 BP,LF,AB,JCo,PGv. . . . . . . 1,400.00
22 BP,LF,AB,JCo,PGv,
  B:The Jester. . . . . . . . . . . 1,400.00
23 BP,AB,JCo,RC,PGv,
  The Ram(c) . . . . . . . . . . . 1,300.00
24 BP,AB,JCo,RC,PGv,A:Sword,
  E:ChicCarter,
  N:WingsWendall. . . . . . . . 1,300.00
25 AB,JCo,RC,PGv,O:Wildfire . 1,300.00
26 AB,JCo,RC,PGv,Bozo(c) . . . 1,200.00
27 AB,JCo,RC,PGv,
  The Ram(c) . . . . . . . . . . . 1,200.00
28 AB,JCo,RC,PGv,
  1st Midnight (c) . . . . . . . . 1,200.00
29 AB,JCo,Rc,PGv,B;
  Midnight(c) . . . . . . . . . . . 1,200.00
30 AB,JCo,PGv. . . . . . . . . . . . 1,200.00
31 AB,JCo,PGv . . . . . . . . . . . 1,000.00
32 AB,JCo,PGv . . . . . . . . . . . 1,000.00
33 AB,JCo,PGv,O:Marksman . . 1,100.00
34 AB,JCo,PGv. . . . . . . . . . . . 1,000.00
35 AB,JCo,RC,PGv. . . . . . . . . 1,000.00

Si

*Smash Comics #60*
© Comics Magazine, Inc.

*Snappy Comics #1*
© Cima Publications

*Soldier Comics #4*
© Fawcett Publications

36 AB,JCo,RC,PGv,
   E:Midnight(c) . . . . . . . . . . . 1,000.00
37 AB,JCo,RC,PGv,Doc Wacky
   Becomes Fastest Human
   on Earth . . . . . . . . . . . . . . . 1,000.00
38 JCo,RC,PGv,B:YankeeEagle 1,500.00
39 PGv,B:Midnight(c) . . . . . . . 1,000.00
40 PGv,E:Ray . . . . . . . . . . . . . 1,000.00
41 PGv . . . . . . . . . . . . . . . . . . . 800.00
42 PGv,B:Lady Luck . . . . . . . . 2,200.00
43 PGv,A:Lady Luck . . . . . . . . . . 900.00
44 PGv . . . . . . . . . . . . . . . . . . . 800.00
45 PGv,E:Midnight(c) . . . . . . . . . 800.00
46 RC,Twelve Hours to Live . . . . 800.00
47 Wanted Midnight,
   Dead or Alive . . . . . . . . . . . . 800.00
48 Midnight Meets the
   Menace from Mars . . . . . . . . 800.00
49 PGv,FGu,Mass of Muscle . . . . 800.00
50 I:Hyram the Hermit . . . . . . . . 800.00
51 A:Wild Bill Hiccup . . . . . . . . . 500.00
52 PGv,FGu,Did Ancient Rome Fall,
   or was it Pushed? . . . . . . . . . 500.00
53 Is ThereHonorAmongThieves. 400.00
54 A:Smear-Faced Schmaltz . . . . 450.00
55 Never Trouble Trouble until
   Trouble Troubles You . . . . . . 450.00
56 The Laughing Killer. . . . . . . . . 450.00
57 A Dummy that Turns Into
   A Curse . . . . . . . . . . . . . . . . 450.00
58 . . . . . . . . . . . . . . . . . . . . . . . 450.00
59 A Corpse that Comes Alive. . . 450.00
60 The Swooner & the Trush. . . . 450.00
61 . . . . . . . . . . . . . . . . . . . . . . . 400.00
62 V:The Lorelet . . . . . . . . . . . . 400.00
63 PGv . . . . . . . . . . . . . . . . . . . 400.00
64 PGv,In Search of King Zoris . . 450.00
65 PGv,V:Cyanide Cindy . . . . . . . 450.00
66 Under Circle's Spell . . . . . . . . 450.00
67 A Living Clue. . . . . . . . . . . . . 450.00
68 JCo,Atomic Dice . . . . . . . . . . 450.00
69 JCo,V:Sir Nuts . . . . . . . . . . . 450.00
70 . . . . . . . . . . . . . . . . . . . . . . . 450.00
71 . . . . . . . . . . . . . . . . . . . . . . . 350.00
72 JCo,Angela,the Beautiful
   Bovine . . . . . . . . . . . . . . . . . 350.00
73 . . . . . . . . . . . . . . . . . . . . . . . 350.00
74 . . . . . . . . . . . . . . . . . . . . . . . 350.00
75 The Revolution . . . . . . . . . . . 350.00
76 Bowl Over Crime. . . . . . . . . . . 350.00
77 Who is Lilli Dilli? . . . . . . . . . . 350.00
78 JCo,Win Over Crime. . . . . . . . 350.00
79 V:The Men From Mars . . . . . . 350.00
80 JCo,V:Big Hearted Bosco . . . . 350.00
81 V:Willie the Kid . . . . . . . . . . . 350.00
82 V:Woodland Boy . . . . . . . . . . 350.00

83 JCo,Quizmaster . . . . . . . . . . . 350.00
84 A Date With Father Time. . . . 350.00
85 JCo,A Singing Swindle . . . . . 350.00
Becomes:

## LADY LUCK
### Comics Magazine
### (Quality Comics), 1949
86 (1) . . . . . . . . . . . . . . . . . . 1,200.00
87 thru 90 . . . . . . . . . . . . . . . @900.00

## SMASH HITS
## SPORTS COMICS
### Essankay Publications,
### Jan., 1949
1 LbC,LbC(c) . . . . . . . . . . . . . . . 350.00

## SMILEY BURNETTE
## WESTERN
### Fawcett Publications,
### March, 1950
1 Ph(c),B:Red Eagle. . . . . . . . . . 650.00
2 Ph(c) . . . . . . . . . . . . . . . . . . . 500.00
3 Ph(c) . . . . . . . . . . . . . . . . . . . 500.00
4 Ph(c) . . . . . . . . . . . . . . . . . . . 500.00

## SMILIN' JACK
### Dell Publishing Co., 1948
1 . . . . . . . . . . . . . . . . . . . . . . . 150.00
2 thru 8 . . . . . . . . . . . . . . . . . @100.00

## SMITTY
### Dell Publishing Co., 1948
1 . . . . . . . . . . . . . . . . . . . . . . . 150.00
2 . . . . . . . . . . . . . . . . . . . . . . . 125.00
3 thru 7 . . . . . . . . . . . . . . . . . @100.00

## SNAP
## See: SCOOP COMICS

## SNAPPY COMICS
### Cima Publications,
### (Prize), 1945
1 A:Animale . . . . . . . . . . . . . . . 400.00

## SNIFFY THE PUP
### Animated Cartoons
### (Standard Comics), Nov., 1949
5 FF,Funny Animal . . . . . . . . . . 125.00

6 thru 9 Funny Animal . . . . . @100.00
10 thru 17 Funny Animal . . . . . @100.00
18 Sept., 1953 . . . . . . . . . . . . . . 100.00

## SOLDIER AND MARINE
## COMICS
### Charlton Comics, 1954
11 . . . . . . . . . . . . . . . . . . . . . . 125.00
12 thru 15. . . . . . . . . . . . . . . . @100.00
Vol 2 #9 . . . . . . . . . . . . . . . . . . 100.00

## SOLDIER COMICS
### Fawcett Publications,
### Jan., 1952
1 Fighting Yanks on Flaming
   Battlefronts . . . . . . . . . . . . . 250.00
2 Blazing Battles Exploding
   with Combat . . . . . . . . . . . . 200.00
3 . . . . . . . . . . . . . . . . . . . . . . . 150.00
4 A Blow for Freedom . . . . . . . . 150.00
5 Only The Dead Are Free . . . . 150.00
6 Blood & Guts . . . . . . . . . . . . . 150.00
7 The Phantom Sub . . . . . . . . . . 150.00
8 More Plasma! . . . . . . . . . . . . . 170.00
9 Red Artillery . . . . . . . . . . . . . . 150.00
10 . . . . . . . . . . . . . . . . . . . . . . 150.00
11 Sept., 1953 . . . . . . . . . . . . . . 150.00

## SOLDIERS OF FORTUNE
### Creston Publications
### (American Comics Group),
### Feb.–March, 1952

1 OW(c),B:Ace Carter,
   Crossbones, Lance Larson . 300.00
2 OW(c) . . . . . . . . . . . . . . . . . . 175.00
3 OW(c) . . . . . . . . . . . . . . . . . . 125.00
4 . . . . . . . . . . . . . . . . . . . . . . . 125.00
5 OW(c) . . . . . . . . . . . . . . . . . . 125.00
6 OW(c),OW,Bondage(c) . . . . . . 250.00
7 . . . . . . . . . . . . . . . . . . . . . . . 125.00
8 OW thru 10. . . . . . . . . . . . . . @125.00
11 OW,Format Change to War . . 100.00
12 . . . . . . . . . . . . . . . . . . . . . . 100.00
13 OW,Feb.–March, 1953 . . . . . . 100.00

## SON OF SINBAD
### St. John Publishing Co.,
### Feb., 1950
1 JKu,JKu(c),The Curse of the
   Caliph's Dancer . . . . . . . . . 500.00

**So**

Space Action #2
© Ace Magazines

Space Detective #3
© Avon Periodicals

Space Worlds #6
© Marvel Comics Group

## SORORITY SECRETS
### Toby Press, 1954
1 . . . . . . . . . . . . . . . . . . . . . . 100.00

## SPACE ACTION
### Junior Books
### (Ace Magazines),
### June, 1952–Oct., 1952
1 Invaders from a Lost Galaxy  1,500.00
2 The Silicon Monster from
   Galaxy X . . . . . . . . . . . . . 1,000.00
3 Attack on Ishtar . . . . . . . . . . 1,000.00

## SPACE ADVENTURES
### Capitol Stories/
### Charlton Comics,
### July, 1952
1 AFa&LM(c) . . . . . . . . . . . . . . 700.00
2 . . . . . . . . . . . . . . . . . . . . . . 325.00
3 DG(c) . . . . . . . . . . . . . . . . . 250.00
4 DG(c) . . . . . . . . . . . . . . . . . 250.00
5 StC(c) . . . . . . . . . . . . . . . . . 250.00
6 StC(c),Two Worlds . . . . . . . . 225.00
7 DG(c),Transformation . . . . . . 250.00
8 DG(c),All For Love . . . . . . . . 225.00
9 DG(c) . . . . . . . . . . . . . . . . . 225.00
10 SD,SD(c) . . . . . . . . . . . . . . 650.00
11 SD,JoS . . . . . . . . . . . . . . . 750.00
12 SD(c) . . . . . . . . . . . . . . . . . 800.00
13 A:Blue Beetle . . . . . . . . . . . 250.00
14 A:Blue Beetle . . . . . . . . . . . 250.00
15 Ph(c) of Rocky Jones . . . . . . 250.00
16 BKa,A:Rocky Jones . . . . . . . 250.00
17 A:Rocky Jones . . . . . . . . . . 225.00
18 A:Rocky Jones . . . . . . . . . . 225.00
19 . . . . . . . . . . . . . . . . . . . . . 200.00
20 First Trip to the Moon . . . . . . 350.00
21 War at Sea . . . . . . . . . . . . . 200.00
22 Does Not Exist
23 SD,Space Trip to the Moon . . . 300.00
24 . . . . . . . . . . . . . . . . . . . . . 225.00
25 Brontosaurus . . . . . . . . . . . 225.00
26 SD,Flying Saucers . . . . . . . . 300.00
27 SD,Flying Saucers . . . . . . . . 300.00
28 Moon Trap . . . . . . . . . . . . . 100.00
29 Captive From Space . . . . . . . 100.00
30 Peril in the Sky . . . . . . . . . . 100.00
31 SD,SD(c),Enchanted Planet . . 250.00
32 SD,SD(c),Last Ship
   from Earth . . . . . . . . . . . . . 250.00
33 Galactic Scourge,
   I&O:Captain Atom . . . . . . . . 650.00
34 SD,SD(c),A:Captain Atom . . . . 275.00

35 thru 40 SD,SD(c),
   A:Captain Atom . . . . . . . . . @275.00

## SPACE BUSTERS
### Ziff-Davis Publishing Co.,
### Spring, 1952
1 BK,NS(c),Ph(c),Charge of
   the Battle Women . . . . . . . 1,200.00
2 EK,BK,MA,NS(c),
   Bondage(c),Ph(c) . . . . . . . . 800.00
3 Autumn, 1952 . . . . . . . . . . . . 750.00

## SPACE COMICS
## See: FUNNY TUNES

## SPACE DETECTIVE
### Avon Periodicals,
### July, 1951
1 WW,WW(c),Opium Smugglers
   of Venus . . . . . . . . . . . . . 1,500.00
2 WW,WW(c),Batwomen of
   Mercury . . . . . . . . . . . . . . 1,200.00
3 EK(c),SeaNymphs ofNeptune  600.00
4 EK,Flame Women of Vulcan,
   Bondage(c) . . . . . . . . . . . . 650.00

## SPACEMAN
### Marvel Atlas, Sept., 1953
1 BEv(c),F:Speed Carter and
   the Space Sentinels . . . . . . . 900.00
2 JMn,Trapped in Space . . . . . . 600.00
3 BEv(c),JMn,V:Ice Monster . . . . 450.00
4 JMn, A-Bomb . . . . . . . . . . . . 500.00
5 GT . . . . . . . . . . . . . . . . . . . 450.00
6 JMn,Thing From Outer Space  450.00

## SPACE MOUSE
### Avon Periodicals,
### April, 1953
1 Funny Animal . . . . . . . . . . . . 150.00
2 Funny Animal . . . . . . . . . . . . 125.00
3 thru 5 Funny Animal . . . . . . @100.00

## SPACE PATROL
### Approved Comics
### (Ziff-Davis),
### Summer, 1952
1 BK,NS,Ph(c), The Lady of
   Diamonds . . . . . . . . . . . . 1,400.00
2 BK,NS,Ph(c),Slave King of
   Pluto,Oct.–Nov., 1952 . . . . . 850.00

## SPACE SQUADRON
### Marvel Atlas, June, 1951
1 AyB,F:Capt. Jet Dixon,Blast,
   Dawn,Revere,Rusty Blake . . 900.00
2 GT(c), . . . . . . . . . . . . . . . . . 750.00
3 Planet of Madness,GT . . . . . . 600.00
4 . . . . . . . . . . . . . . . . . . . . . 600.00
5 AyB . . . . . . . . . . . . . . . . . . 600.00
Becomes:

## SPACE WORLDS
### Marvel, April, 1952
6 Midnight Horror . . . . . . . . . . . 550.00

## SPACE THRILLERS
### Avon Periodicals, 1954
N# Contents May Vary . . . . . . . 1,500.00

## SPACE WAR
### Charlton Comics, 1959
1 . . . . . . . . . . . . . . . . . . . . . 200.00
2 . . . . . . . . . . . . . . . . . . . . . 100.00
3 . . . . . . . . . . . . . . . . . . . . . 100.00
4 SD,SD(c) . . . . . . . . . . . . . . . 200.00
5 SD,SD(c) . . . . . . . . . . . . . . . 200.00
6 SD . . . . . . . . . . . . . . . . . . . 200.00
7 . . . . . . . . . . . . . . . . . . . . . 100.00
8 SD,SD(c) . . . . . . . . . . . . . . . 200.00
9 . . . . . . . . . . . . . . . . . . . . . 100.00
10 SD,SD(c) . . . . . . . . . . . . . . 200.00
11 . . . . . . . . . . . . . . . . . . . . . 100.00
12 thru 15 . . . . . . . . . . . . . . @100.00
16 thru 27 . . . . . . . . . . . . . . @100.00

## SPACE WESTERN
## COMICS
## See: YELLOWJACKET
## COMICS

## SPARKIE, RADIO PIXIE
### Approved Publ.
### (Ziff-Davis), 1951
1 Radio Narration . . . . . . . . . . . 350.00
2 . . . . . . . . . . . . . . . . . . . . . 250.00
Becomes:

## BIG JON AND SPARKIE
### Approved Publ.
### (Ziff-Davis), 1952
3 . . . . . . . . . . . . . . . . . . . . . 250.00
4 . . . . . . . . . . . . . . . . . . . . . 250.00

So

Sparkle Comics #2
© United Features Syndicate

Sparkler Comics #14
© United Features Syndicate

Sparkler Comics #120
© United Features Syndicate

## SPARKLE COMICS
### United Features
### Syndicate, 1948
1 Nancy, Li'l Abner . . . . . . . . . . 250.00
2 . . . . . . . . . . . . . . . . . . . . 150.00
3 . . . . . . . . . . . . . . . . . . . . 125.00
4 . . . . . . . . . . . . . . . . . . . . 125.00
5 . . . . . . . . . . . . . . . . . . . . 125.00
6 . . . . . . . . . . . . . . . . . . . . 125.00
7 . . . . . . . . . . . . . . . . . . . . 125.00
8 thru 10 . . . . . . . . . . . . . . @125.00
11 thru 20 . . . . . . . . . . . . . @100.00
21 thru 32 . . . . . . . . . . . . . @100.00
33 Peanuts. . . . . . . . . . . . . . . 125.00

## SPARKLER COMICS
### United Features Syndicate, July, 1940
1 Jim Handy . . . . . . . . . . . . . . 500.00
2 Frankie Doodle,Aug., 1940 . . . 400.00

## SPARKLER COMICS
### United Features Syndicate, July, 1941
1 BHg,O:Sparkman;B:Tarzan,Captain
  & the Kids,Ella Cinders,Danny
  Dingle,Dynamite Dunn, Nancy,
  Abbie an' Slats, Frankie
  Doodle,Broncho Bill . . . . . . 4,000.00
2 BHg, The Case of Poisoned
  Fruit . . . . . . . . . . . . . . . . . 1,800.00
3 BHg . . . . . . . . . . . . . . . . . . 1,500.00
4 BHg,Case of Sparkman &
  the Firefly . . . . . . . . . . . . . 1,500.00
5 BHg,Sparkman,Natch . . . . . . 1,200.00
6 BHg,Case of the Bronze
  Bees . . . . . . . . . . . . . . . . 1,200.00
7 BHg,Case of the Green
  Raiders . . . . . . . . . . . . . . 1,200.00
8 BHg,V:River Fiddler . . . . . . . 1,200.00
9 BHg,N:Sparkman . . . . . . . . . 1,200.00
10 BHg,B:Hap Hopper,
  Sparkman's ID revealed . . . 1,200.00
11 BHg,V:Japanese . . . . . . . . . . 900.00
12 BHg,Another N:Sparkman . . . 900.00
13 BHg,Hap Hopper Rides
  For Freedom . . . . . . . . . . . . 900.00
14 BHg,BHg(c),Tarzan
  V:Yellow Killer. . . . . . . . . . 1,000.00
15 BHg. . . . . . . . . . . . . . . . . . . 700.00
16 BHg,Sparkman V:Japanese . . 700.00
17 BHg,Nancy(c) . . . . . . . . . . . . 700.00
18 BHg,Sparkman in Crete . . . . . 700.00

19 BHg,I&B:Race Riley,
  Commandos . . . . . . . . . . . . 700.00
20 BHg,Nancy(c) . . . . . . . . . . . . 700.00
21 BHg,Tarzan(c). . . . . . . . . . . . 750.00
22 BHg,Nancy(c) . . . . . . . . . . . . 600.00
23 BHg,Capt&Kids(c). . . . . . . . . 600.00
24 BHg,Nancy(c) . . . . . . . . . . . . 600.00
25 BHg,BHg(c),Tarzan(c). . . . . . 750.00
26 BHg,Capt&Kids(c). . . . . . . . . 600.00
27 BHg,Nancy(c) . . . . . . . . . . . . 600.00
28 BHg,BHg(c),Tarzan(c). . . . . . 750.00
29 BHg,Capt&Kids(c). . . . . . . . . 600.00
30 BHg,Nancy(c) . . . . . . . . . . . . 600.00
31 BHg,BHg(c),Tarzan(c). . . . . . 750.00
32 BHg,Capt&Kids(c). . . . . . . . . 400.00
33 BHg,Nancy(c) . . . . . . . . . . . . 400.00
34 BHg,BHg(c),Tarzan(c). . . . . . 750.00
35 BHg,Capt&Kids(c). . . . . . . . . 400.00
36 BHg,Nancy(c) . . . . . . . . . . . . 400.00
37 BHg,BHg(c),Tarzan(c). . . . . . 750.00
38 BHg,Capt&Kids(c). . . . . . . . . 350.00
39 BHg,BHg(c),Tarzan(c). . . . . . 800.00
40 BHg,Nancy(c) . . . . . . . . . . . . 350.00
41 BHg,Capt&Kids(c). . . . . . . . . 300.00
42 BHg,BHg,Tarzan(c) . . . . . . . . 500.00
43 BHg,Nancy(c) . . . . . . . . . . . . 300.00
44 BHg,Tarzan(c). . . . . . . . . . . . 500.00
45 BHg,Capt&Kids(c). . . . . . . . . 300.00
46 BHg,Nancy(c) . . . . . . . . . . . . 300.00
47 BHg,Tarzan(c). . . . . . . . . . . . 500.00
48 BHg,Nancy(c) . . . . . . . . . . . . 300.00
49 BHg,Capt&Kids(c). . . . . . . . . 300.00
50 BHg,BHg(c),Tarzan(c). . . . . . 500.00
51 BHg,Capt&Kids(c). . . . . . . . . 300.00
52 BHg,Nancy(c) . . . . . . . . . . . . 300.00
53 BHg,BHg(c),Tarzan(c). . . . . . 500.00
54 BHg,Capt&Kids(c). . . . . . . . . 250.00
55 BHg,Nancy(c) . . . . . . . . . . . . 250.00
56 BHg,Capt&Kids(c). . . . . . . . . 250.00
57 BHg,F:Li'l Abner . . . . . . . . . . 250.00
58 BHg,A:Fearless Fosdick . . . . 350.00
59 BHg,B:Li'l Abner . . . . . . . . . . 350.00
60 BHg,Nancy(c) . . . . . . . . . . . . 250.00
61 BHg,Capt&Kids(c). . . . . . . . . 250.00
62 BHg,Li'L Abner(c) . . . . . . . . . 250.00
63 BHg,Capt&Kids(c). . . . . . . . . 250.00
64 BHg,Valentines (c) . . . . . . . . 250.00
65 BHg,Nancy(c) . . . . . . . . . . . . 250.00
66 BHg,Capt&Kids(c). . . . . . . . . 250.00
67 BHg,Nancy(c) . . . . . . . . . . . . 250.00
68 BHg, . . . . . . . . . . . . . . . . . . 250.00
69 BHg,B:Nancy (c). . . . . . . . . . 250.00
70 BHg. . . . . . . . . . . . . . . . . . . 250.00
71 thru 80 BHg. . . . . . . . . . . . @200.00
81 BHg,E:Nancy(c) . . . . . . . . . . 200.00
82 BHg. . . . . . . . . . . . . . . . . . . 200.00

83 BHg,Tarzan(c) . . . . . . . . . . . . 350.00
84 BHg. . . . . . . . . . . . . . . . . . . 175.00
85 BHg,E:Li'l Abner . . . . . . . . . . 175.00
86 BHg. . . . . . . . . . . . . . . . . . . 175.00
87 BHg,Nancy(c) . . . . . . . . . . . . 175.00
88 thru 96 BHg. . . . . . . . . . . . @175.00
97 BHg,O:Lady Ruggles . . . . . . 350.00
98 BHg . . . . . . . . . . . . . . . . . . . 150.00
99 BHg,Nancy(c) . . . . . . . . . . . . 150.00
100 BHg,Nancy(c) . . . . . . . . . . . 175.00
101 thru 107 BHg. . . . . . . . . . . @125.00
108 & 109 BHg,ATh. . . . . . . . . 200.00
110 BHg . . . . . . . . . . . . . . . . . . 125.00
111 BHg . . . . . . . . . . . . . . . . . . 125.00
112 BHg . . . . . . . . . . . . . . . . . . 125.00
113 BHg,ATh. . . . . . . . . . . . . . . 200.00
114 thru 120 BHg. . . . . . . . . . . @150.00
**Becomes:**

## NANCY AND SLUGGO
### St. John/Dell Publ. 1955
121 . . . . . . . . . . . . . . . . . . . . 150.00
122 thru 130. . . . . . . . . . . . . @125.00
131 thru 145. . . . . . . . . . . . . @100.00

### Dell Publishing Co., 1957
146 B:Peanuts . . . . . . . . . . . . . 150.00
147 Peanuts . . . . . . . . . . . . . . 125.00
148 Peanuts . . . . . . . . . . . . . . 125.00
149 Peanuts . . . . . . . . . . . . . . 125.00
150 thru 161. . . . . . . . . . . . . @125.00
162 thru 165. . . . . . . . . . . . . @200.00
166 thru 176 A:OONA . . . . . . . @200.00
177 thru 180. . . . . . . . . . . . . @125.00
181 thru 187. . . . . . . . . . . . . @125.00

## SPARKLING STARS
### Holyoke Publishing Co., June, 1944
1 B:Hell's Angels,Ali Baba,FBI,
  Boxie Weaver,Petey & Pop . 350.00
2 Speed Spaulding . . . . . . . . . . 300.00
3 FBI. . . . . . . . . . . . . . . . . . . . 200.00
4 thru 12 . . . . . . . . . . . . . . @200.00
13 O&I:Jungo, The Man-Beast . . 225.00
14 thru 19. . . . . . . . . . . . . . @200.00
20 I:Fangs the Wolfboy . . . . . . . 200.00
21 thru 28. . . . . . . . . . . . . . @200.00
29 Bondage(c). . . . . . . . . . . . . 350.00
30 thru 32. . . . . . . . . . . . . . @150.00
33 March, 1948 . . . . . . . . . . . . 150.00

## SPARKMAN
### Frances M. McQueeny, 1944
1 O:Sparkman. . . . . . . . . . . . . 375.00

**Sp**

*Special Edition Comics #1*
© Fawcett Publications

*A Spectacular Feature Magazine #11*
© Fox Features Syndicate

*Spellbound #11*
© Marvel Comics Group

## SPARKY WATTS

**Columbia Comics Group, 1942**
1 A:Skyman,Hitler(c) . . . . . . . 1,500.00
2 . . . . . . . . . . . . . . . . . . . . . . . . 500.00
3 . . . . . . . . . . . . . . . . . . . . . . . . 400.00
4 O:Skyman . . . . . . . . . . . . . . . 400.00
5 A:Skyman . . . . . . . . . . . . . . . 350.00
6 . . . . . . . . . . . . . . . . . . . . . . . . 200.00
7 . . . . . . . . . . . . . . . . . . . . . . . . 200.00
8 . . . . . . . . . . . . . . . . . . . . . . . . 250.00
9 . . . . . . . . . . . . . . . . . . . . . . . . 200.00
10 1949 . . . . . . . . . . . . . . . . . . . 200.00

## [STEVE SAUNDERS]
## SPECIAL AGENT

**Parents Magazine/
Commended Comics,
Dec., 1947**
1 J. Edgar Hoover, Ph(c) . . . . . 250.00
2 . . . . . . . . . . . . . . . . . . . . . . . . 150.00
3 thru 7 . . . . . . . . . . . . . . . . . . @125.00
8 Sept., 1949 . . . . . . . . . . . . . 125.00

## SPECIAL COMICS
## See: LAUGH COMICS

## SPECIAL EDITION

**DC Comics, 1944–45
(Reprint giveaways
for U.S. Navy)**
1 Action Comics #80,WB . . . . . . 750.00
2 Action Comics#81,WB . . . . . . . 750.00
3 Superman #33 . . . . . . . . . . . . 750.00
4 Detective Comics#97 . . . . . . . 750.00
5 Superman #34 . . . . . . . . . . . . 750.00
6 Action Comics #84,WB . . . . . . 750.00

## SPECIAL EDITION
## COMICS

**Fawcett Publications,
Aug., 1940**
1 CCB,CCB(c),F:Captain
Marvel . . . . . . . . . . . . . . 20,000.00

## A SPECTACULAR
## FEATURE MAGAZINE

**Fox Features Syndicate, 1950**
1 (11) Samson and Delilah . . . . . 350.00
**Becomes:**

## SPECTACULAR
## FEATURES MAGAZINE

**Fox Features Syndicate, 1950**
2 (12) Iwo Jima . . . . . . . . . . . . . 360.00
3 True Crime Cases . . . . . . . . . 275.00

## SPECTACULAR STORIES
## MAGAZINE

**Hero Books (Fox Features
Syndicate), 1950**
3 Actual Crime Cases . . . . . . . . 500.00
4 Sherlock Holmes . . . . . . . . . . 325.00

## SPEED COMICS

**Brookwood/Speed Publ.
Harvey Publications,
Oct., 1939**
1 BP,B&O:Shock Gibson,B:Spike
Marlin,Biff Bannon . . . . . . . 5,000.00
2 BP,B:Shock Gibson(c) . . . . . 1,500.00
3 BP,GT . . . . . . . . . . . . . . . . . 1,200.00
4 BP . . . . . . . . . . . . . . . . . . . . 1,000.00
5 BP,DBr . . . . . . . . . . . . . . . . . 1,000.00
6 BP,GT . . . . . . . . . . . . . . . . . . 900.00
7 GT,JKu,Bondage, B:Mars
Mason . . . . . . . . . . . . . . . . 900.00
8 JKu . . . . . . . . . . . . . . . . . . . . 850.00
9 JKu . . . . . . . . . . . . . . . . . . . . 850.00
10 JKu,E:Shock Gibson(c) . . . . . 850.00
11 JKu,E:Mars Mason . . . . . . . . 850.00
12 B:The Wasp . . . . . . . . . . . . 1,000.00
13 I:Captain Freedom;B:Girls
Commandos,Pat Parker . . 1,100.00
14 AAv,Pocket sized-100pgs. . . 1,200.00
15 AAv,Pocket size . . . . . . . . . 1,200.00
16 JKu,AAv,Pocket size . . . . . . 1,200.00
17 O:Black Cat . . . . . . . . . . . . 1,500.00
18 B:Capt.Freedom,Bondage(c) 1,200.00
19 S&K . . . . . . . . . . . . . . . . . . 1,000.00
20 S&K . . . . . . . . . . . . . . . . . . 1,000.00
21 JKu(c),Hitler & Tojo . . . . . . . 1,400.00
22 JKu(c) . . . . . . . . . . . . . . . . . 1,000.00
23 JKu(c),O:Girl Commandos . . 1,000.00
24 Hitler,Tojo & Mussilini(c) . . . 1,200.00
25 . . . . . . . . . . . . . . . . . . . . . . 1,200.00
26 GT,Flag (c),Black Cat . . . . . 1,000.00
27 GT,Black Cat . . . . . . . . . . . . 1,000.00
28 E:Capt Freedom . . . . . . . . . 1,000.00
29 Case o/t Black Marketeers . 1,000.00
30 POW Death Chambers . . . . 1,000.00
31 ASh(c),Nazi Thrashing(c) . . . 1,200.00
32 ASh(c) . . . . . . . . . . . . . . . . . 1,100.00
33 ASh(c) . . . . . . . . . . . . . . . . . 1,100.00

34 ASh(c) . . . . . . . . . . . . . . . . . 1,100.00
35 ASh(c),BlackCat'sDeathTrap 1,150.00
36 ASh(c) . . . . . . . . . . . . . . . . . 1,100.00
37 RP(c) . . . . . . . . . . . . . . . . . . 1,100.00
38 RP(c),War Bond Plea with Iwo
Jima flag allusion(c) . . . . . 1,100.00
39 RP(c),B:Capt Freedom(c) . . 1,200.00
40 RP(c) . . . . . . . . . . . . . . . . . . 1,200.00
41 RP(c) . . . . . . . . . . . . . . . . . . 1,200.00
42 JKu,RP(c) . . . . . . . . . . . . . . 1,200.00
43 JKu,AAv,E:Capt Freedom(c) 1,250.00
44 BP,JKu,Four Kids on a raft,
Jan.–Feb., 1947 . . . . . . . . 1,300.00

## SPEED SMITH
## THE HOT ROD KING

**Ziff-Davis Publishing Co.,
Spring, 1952**
1 INS,Ph(c),A:Roscoe
the Rascal . . . . . . . . . . . . . 250.00

## SPELLBOUND

**Marvel Atlas, March, 1952**
1 AyB(c),Step into my Coffin . . 1,200.00
2 BEv,RH,Horror Story,
A:Edgar A. Poe . . . . . . . . . . 700.00
3 RH(c),OW . . . . . . . . . . . . . . . 600.00
4 RH,Decapitation story . . . . . . 600.00
5 AyB,BEv,JM,Its in the Bag . . . 600.00
6 AyB,BK,The Man Who Couldn't
be Killed. . . . . . . . . . . . . . . . 600.00
7 AyB,BEv,JMn,Don't Close
the Door. . . . . . . . . . . . . . . . 500.00
8 BEv(c),RH,JSt,DAy,
The Operation . . . . . . . . . . . 500.00
9 BEv(c),RH,The Death of
Agatha Slurl. . . . . . . . . . . . . 500.00
10 AyB,BEv,RH,JMn(c),The Living
Mummy . . . . . . . . . . . . . . . . 500.00
11 The Empty Coffin . . . . . . . . . 400.00
12 RH,My Friend the Ghost. . . . 400.00
13 JM,AyB,The Dead Men. . . . . 400.00
14 BEv(c),RH,JMn,Close Shave . 400.00
15 AyB,Cl,Get Out of my
Graveyard . . . . . . . . . . . . . . 400.00
16 RH,BEv,JF,JSt,Behind
the Door. . . . . . . . . . . . . . . . 400.00
17 BEv(c),GC,BK,Goodbye
Forever . . . . . . . . . . . . . . . . 400.00
18 BEv(c),JM . . . . . . . . . . . . . . 350.00
19 BEv(c),BP,Witch Doctor . . . . 350.00
20 RH(c),BP . . . . . . . . . . . . . . . 350.00
21 RH(c). . . . . . . . . . . . . . . . . . 325.00
22 . . . . . . . . . . . . . . . . . . . . . . 325.00

All comics prices listed are for *Near Mint* condition.

Sp

*The Spirt 8/8/43*
© Will Eisner

*The Spirit #3*
© Quality Comics Group

*Spitfire Comics #2*
© Harvey Publications

23 .......................... 325.00
24 JMn(c),JR ............... 300.00
25 JO,AyB,Look Into My Eyes . . . 300.00
26 JR,AyB,Things in the Box . . . . 300.00
27 JMn,JR,AyB,Trap in the
   Mirage .................... 300.00
28 BEv ...................... 300.00
29 JSe(c),SD ............... 325.00
30 BEv(c) ................... 300.00
31 ......................... 300.00
32 BP,AyB,Almost Human ...... 300.00
33 AT ...................... 300.00
34 June, 1957 .............. 300.00

## SPIRIT, THE
### Will Eisner
### (Weekly Coverless
### Comic Book), June, 1940
WE,O:SPirit .............. 1,000.00
  6/9/40 WE ................. 600.00
  6/16/40 WE,Black Queen ... 300.00
  6/23/40 WE,Mr Mystic ..... 250.00
  6/30/40 WE ............... 250.00
  7/7/40 WE,Black Queen ... 250.00
  7/14/40 WE .............. 200.00
  7/21/40 WE .............. 200.00
  7/28/40 WE .............. 200.00
  8/4/40 WE ............... 200.00
  7/7/40-11/24/40,WE ...... 165.00
  11/10/40 WE,Black Queen . . 150.00
  12/1/40 WE,Ellen
    Spanking(c) .............. 225.00
  12/8/40-12/29/40 ......... 125.00
1941 WE Each ............... 125.00
  3/16 WE I:Silk Satin ....... 200.00
  6/15 WE I Twilight ........ 125.00
  6/22 WE Hitler ........... 125.00
1942 WE Each ............... 100.00
  2-1 Duchess ............. 125.00
  2-15 .................... 100.00
  2-23 .................... 150.00
1943 WE Each,LF,WE scripts . . . 100.00
1944 JCo,LF ................ 100.00
1945 LF Each, ............. 100.00
1946 WE Each ............... 100.00
  1/13 WE,O:The Spirit ....... 125.00
  1/20 WE,Satin ........... 125.00
  3/17 WE,I:Nylon .......... 125.00
  4/21 WE,I:Mr.Carrion ...... 150.00
  7/7 WE,I:Dulcet Tone&Skinny 125.00
  10/6 WE,I:F:Gell ......... 100.00
1947 WE Each ............... 100.00
  7/13.,WE,Hansel &Gretel ... 125.00
  7/20,WE,A:Bomb ......... 125.00
  9/28,WE,Flying Saucers .... 100.00

10/5,WE, Cinderella ....... 125.00
12/7,WE,I:Power Puff ...... 125.00
1948 WE Each .............. 125.00
  1/11,WE,Sparrow Fallon .... 125.00
  1/25,WE,I:Last A Net ...... 125.00
  3/14,WE,A:Kretuama ....... 125.00
  4/4,WE,A:Wildrice ........ 125.00
  7/25,The Thing .......... 100.00
  8/22,Poe Tale,Horror ...... 125.00
  9/18, A:Lorelei .......... 100.00
  11/7,WE,A:Plaster of Paris . . 100.00
1949 WE Each .............. 100.00
  1/23 WE,I:Thorne ......... 100.00
  8/21 WE,I:Monica Veto ..... 100.00
  9/25 WE,A:Ice ........... 100.00
  12/4 WE,I:Flaxen ......... 100.00
1950 WE Each .............. 100.00
  1/8 WE,I:Sand Saref ...... 150.00
  2/10, Horror Issue ....... 100.00
1951 WE(Last WE 8/12/51) . . @100.00
  Non-Eisners ........... @25.00
1952 Non-Eisners .......... @25.00
  7/27 WW,Denny Colt ...... 500.00
  8/3 WW,Moon ........... 500.00
  8/10 WW.Moon .......... 500.00
  8/17 WW,WE,Heart ....... 400.00
  8/24 WW,Rescue ......... 400.00
  8/31 WW,Last Man ....... 400.00
  9/7 WW,Man Moon ....... 550.00
  9/14 WE................. 150.00
  9/21 WE Space .......... 350.00
  9/28 WE Moon. .......... 400.00
  10/5 WE Last Story ....... 250.00

## SPIRIT, THE
### Quality Comics Group/
### Vital Publ., 1944
N# Wanted Dead or Alive! . . . 1,000.00
N# ...in Crime Doesn't Pay,LF(c) 600.00
N# ...In Murder Runs Wild ..... 500.00
4 ...Flirts with Death .......... 400.00
5 ...Wanted Dead or Alive..... 350.00
6 ...Gives You Triple Value ..... 300.00
7 ...Rocks the Underworld ..... 300.00
8 ...Cracks Down on Crime,LF(c) 300.00
9 ...Throws Fear Into the
   Heart of Crime .......... 300.00
10 ...Stalks Crime,RC(c) ....... 300.00
11 ...America's Greatest
   Crime Buster ............ 250.00
12 WE(c),....The Famous Outlaw
   Who Smashes Crime .... 400.00
13 WE(c),...and Ebony Cleans Out
   the Underworld;Bondage(c) . 400.00
14 WE(c) .................... 400.00

15 WE(c),Bank Robber at Large . 400.00
16 WE(c),The Case of the
   Uncanny Cat ............. 400.00
17 WE(c),The Organ Grinding
   Bank Robber ............. 400.00
18 WE,WE(c),'The Bucket
   of Blood ................. 450.00
19 WE,WE(c),'The Man Who
   Murdered the Spirit' ........ 450.00
20 WE,WE(c),'The Vortex' ...... 450.00
21 WE,WE(c),'P'Gell of Paris' . . 450.00
22 WE(c),TheOctopus,Aug.1950. 800.00

## SPIRIT, THE
### Fiction House Magazines,
### 1952
1 Curse of Claymore Castle . . . 500.00
2 WE,WE(c),Who Says Crime
   Doesn't Pay ............. 450.00
3 WE/JGr(c),League of Lions . . 400.00
4 WE,WE&JGr(c),Last Prowl of
   Mr. Mephisto;Bondage (c) . . 450.00
5 WE,WE(c),Ph(c)1954 ....... 450.00

## SPIRITMAN
### Will Eisner, 1944
1 3 Spirit Sections from
   1944 Bound Together ..... 250.00
2 LF, 2 Spirit Sections
   from 1944 Bound Together . . 200.00

## SPITFIRE COMICS
### Harvey Publ., Aug., 1941
1 MKd(c),100-pgs.,Pocket-size 1,000.00
2 100-pgs.,Pocket-size,
   Oct., 1941 .............. 950.00

## SPITFIRE
### Malverne Herald/
### Elliot Publ. Co., 1944
132 & 133................. @300.00

## SPOOK COMICS
### Baily Publications, 1946
1 A:Mr. Lucifer ............. 400.00

## SPOOK
## DETECTIVE CASES
## See: CRIMINALS
## ON THE RUN

*Spooky #1*
*© Harvey Publications*

*Spotlight Comics #2*
*© Harry A Chesler*

*Spy Fighters #1*
*© Marvel Comics Group*

## SPOOK

## SUSPENSE MYSTERY

### See: CRIMINALS ON THE RUN

## SPOOKY

**Harvey Publications, Nov., 1955**

| | |
|---|---|
| 1 Funny Apparition | 600.00 |
| 2 same | 300.00 |
| 3 | 200.00 |
| 4 | 200.00 |
| 5 | 200.00 |
| 6 thru 10 same | @200.00 |
| 11 thru 20 same | @150.00 |
| 21 thru 30 same | @125.00 |
| 31 thru 40 same | @125.00 |
| 41 thru 70 same | @125.00 |
| 71 thru 90 same | @100.00 |

## SPOOKY MYSTERIES

**Your Guide Publishing Co., 1946**

| | |
|---|---|
| 1 Rib-Tickling Horror | 250.00 |

## SPORT COMICS

### See: TRUE SPORT PICTURE STORIES

## SPORTS STARS

**Sport Stars, Inc. (Parents' Magazine), 1946**

| | |
|---|---|
| 1 Johnny Weissmuller | 500.00 |
| 2 Baseball Greats | 350.00 |
| 3 | 275.00 |
| 4 | 275.00 |

## SPORT STARS

**Marvel, Nov., 1949**

| | |
|---|---|
| 1 The Life of Knute Rockne | 600.00 |

**Becomes:**

## SPORTS ACTION

| | |
|---|---|
| 2 BP(c),Life of George Gipp | 550.00 |
| 3 BEv,Hack Wilson | 300.00 |
| 4 Art Houtteman | 250.00 |
| 5 Nile Kinnick | 250.00 |
| 6 Warren Gun | 250.00 |
| 7 Jim Konstanty | 250.00 |
| 8 Ralph Kiner | 275.00 |

| | |
|---|---|
| 9 Ed 'Strangler' Lewis | 250.00 |
| 10 JMn,The Yella-Belly | 250.00 |
| 11 The Killers | 250.00 |
| 12 BEv,Man Behind the Mask | 250.00 |
| 13 BEv,Lew Andrews | 260.00 |
| 14 MWs,Ken Roper,Sept.,1952 | 260.00 |

## SPORTS THRILLS

### See: DICK COLE

## SPOTLIGHT COMICS

**Harry 'A' Chesler Jr. Publications, Nov., 1944**

| | |
|---|---|
| 1 GT,GT(c),B:Veiled Avenger, Black Dwarf,Barry Kuda | 900.00 |
| 2 | 750.00 |
| 3 1945,Eye Injury | 800.00 |

## SPOTTY THE PUP

**Avon Periodicals, 1953**

| | |
|---|---|
| N# | 125.00 |
| 3 | 100.00 |

## SPUNKY

**Standard Comics, April, 1949**

| | |
|---|---|
| 1 FF,Adventures of a Junior Cowboy | 125.00 |
| 2 FF | 100.00 |
| 3 | 100.00 |
| 4 | 100.00 |
| 5 | 100.00 |
| 6 | 100.00 |
| 7 Nov., 1951 | 100.00 |

## SPUNKY
## THE SMILING SPOOK

**Four Star Comic (Ajax/Farrell Publ.), 1957**

| | |
|---|---|
| 1 rep. Frisky Fables | 125.00 |
| 2 thru 4 | @100.00 |

## SPY AND COUNTERSPY

**Best Syndicated Features (American Comics Group), Aug.–Sept., 1949**

| | |
|---|---|
| 1 I&O:Jonathan Kent | 350.00 |
| 2 | 200.00 |

**Becomes:**

## SPY-HUNTERS

**Dec., 1949–Jan., 1950**

| | |
|---|---|
| 3 Jonathan Kent | 300.00 |
| 4 J.Kent | 150.00 |
| 5 J.Kent | 150.00 |
| 6 J.Kent | 150.00 |
| 7 OW(c),J.Kent | 150.00 |
| 8 OW(c),J.Kent | 150.00 |
| 9 OW(c),J.Kent | 150.00 |
| 10 OW(c),J.Kent | 150.00 |
| 11 | 125.00 |
| 12 OW(c),MD | 125.00 |
| 13 and 14 | @125.00 |
| 15 OW(c) | 125.00 |
| 16 AW | 175.00 |
| 17 | 100.00 |
| 18 War (c) | 100.00 |
| 19 and 20 | @100.00 |
| 21 B:War Content | 100.00 |
| 22 | 100.00 |
| 23 Torture | 250.00 |
| 24 'BlackmailBrigade',July,1953 | 100.00 |

## SPY CASES

### See: KID KOMICS

## SPY FIGHTERS

**Marvel, March, 1951**

| | |
|---|---|
| 1 GT | 300.00 |
| 2 GT | 150.00 |
| 3 | 125.00 |
| 4 thru 13 | @125.00 |
| 14 thru 15 July, 1953 | @135.00 |

## SPY SMASHER

**Fawcett Publications, Autumn, 1941**

| | |
|---|---|
| 1 B;Spy Smasher | 6,000.00 |
| 2 MRa(c) | 2,800.00 |
| 3 Bondage (c) | 2,000.00 |
| 4 | 1,800.00 |
| 5 MRa,Mt. Rushmore(c) | 1,800.00 |
| 6 MRa(a&c),V:The Sharks of Steel | 1,500.00 |
| 7 MRa | 1,500.00 |
| 8 AB | 1,300.00 |
| 9 AB,Hitler,Tojo, Mussolini(c) | 1,600.00 |
| 10 AB,Did Spy Smasher Kill Hitler? | 1,500.00 |
| 11 AB,Feb., 1943 | 1,300.00 |

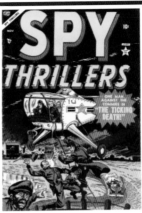

*Spy Thrillers #1*
© Marvel Comics Group

*Starlet O'Hara in Hollywood #2*
© Standard Comics

*Stars and Stripes Comics #3*
© Centaur Publications

## SPY THRILLERS
**Marvel Atlas, Nov., 1954**
1 AyB(c),The Tickling Death . . . . 250.00
2 V:Communists . . . . . . . . . . . . 150.00
3 . . . . . . . . . . . . . . . . . . . . . . . . 100.00
4 . . . . . . . . . . . . . . . . . . . . . . . . 100.00
Becomes:

## POLICE BADGE
5 Sept., 1955 . . . . . . . . . . . . . . 125.00

## SQUEEKS
**Lev Gleason Publications,
Oct., 1953**
1 CBi(c),(fa) . . . . . . . . . . . . . . . 150.00
2 CBi(c),(fa) . . . . . . . . . . . . . . . 100.00
3 CBi(c),(fa) . . . . . . . . . . . . . . . 100.00
4 (fa) . . . . . . . . . . . . . . . . . . . . 100.00
5 (fa),Jan., 1954 . . . . . . . . . . . 100.00

## STAMPS COMICS
**Youthful Magazines/Stamp
Comics, Inc.,
Oct., 1951**
1 HcK,Birth of Liberty . . . . . . . . 350.00
2 HcK,RP,Battle of White Plains 200.00
3 HcK,DW,RP,Iwo Jima . . . . . . . 150.00
4 HcK,DW,RP . . . . . . . . . . . . . . 150.00
5 HcK,Von Hindenberg disaster . 175.00
6 HcK,The Immortal Chaplains. . 150.00
7 HcK,RKr,RP,B&O:Railroad . . . 250.00
Becomes:

## THRILLING ADVENTURES
## IN STAMPS
**Jan., 1953**
8 HcK, 100 Pgs. . . . . . . . . . . . 1,000.00

## STANLEY & HIS
## MONSTER
**See: FOX AND
THE CROW**

## STAR COMICS
**Comic Magazines/Ultem
Publ./Chesler
Centaur Publications,
Feb., 1937**
1 B:Dan Hastings. . . . . . . . . . 2,500.00
2 . . . . . . . . . . . . . . . . . . . . . 1,100.00
3 . . . . . . . . . . . . . . . . . . . . . . 900.00

4 WMc(c) . . . . . . . . . . . . . . . . . 900.00
5 WMc(c),A:Little Nemo . . . . . . 900.00
6 CBi(c),FGu . . . . . . . . . . . . . . . 850.00
7 FGu . . . . . . . . . . . . . . . . . . . . 800.00
8 BoW,BoW(c),FGu,A:Little
Nemo,Horror . . . . . . . . . . . . 850.00
9 FGu,CBi(c) . . . . . . . . . . . . . . . 800.00
10 FGu,CBi(c),BoW,A:Impyk . . 1,100.00
11 FGu,BoW,JCo . . . . . . . . . . . 850.00
12 FGu,BoW,B:Riders of the
Golden West . . . . . . . . . . . . 750.00
13 FGu,BoW . . . . . . . . . . . . . . . 750.00
14 FGu,GFx(c). . . . . . . . . . . . . . 750.00
15 CBu,B:The Last Pirate . . . . . 750.00
16 CBu,B:Phantom Rider . . . . . 750.00
2-1 CBu,B:Phantom Rider(c) . . 800.00
2-2 CBu,A:Diana Deane . . . . . . 750.00
2-3 GFx(c),CBu . . . . . . . . . . . . . 700.00
2-4 CBu . . . . . . . . . . . . . . . . . . . 700.00
2-5 CBu . . . . . . . . . . . . . . . . . . . 700.00
2-6 CBu,E:Phantom Rider . . . . 700.00
2-7 CBu,Aug., 1939 . . . . . . . . . 700.00

## STARLET O'HARA IN
## HOLLYWOOD
**Standard Comics,
Dec., 1948**
1 The Terrific Tee-Age Comic . . . 275.00
2 Her Romantic Adventures in
Movie land . . . . . . . . . . . . . . 150.00
3 and 4, Sept., 1949 . . . . . . @125.00

## STAR RANGER
**Comics Magazines/Ultem/
Centaur Publ.,
Feb., 1937**
1 FGu,I:Western Comic . . . . . 2,500.00
2 . . . . . . . . . . . . . . . . . . . . . 1,300.00
3 FGu . . . . . . . . . . . . . . . . . . 1,100.00
4 . . . . . . . . . . . . . . . . . . . . . 1,100.00
5 . . . . . . . . . . . . . . . . . . . . . 1,100.00
6 FGu . . . . . . . . . . . . . . . . . . 1,000.00
7 FGu . . . . . . . . . . . . . . . . . . . 900.00
8 GFx,FGu,PGv,BoW . . . . . . . 900.00
9 GFx,FGu,PGv,BoW . . . . . . . 900.00
10 JCo,GFx,FGu,PGv,BoW . . 1,300.00
11 . . . . . . . . . . . . . . . . . . . . . . 850.00
12 JCo(a&c),FGu,PGv. . . . . . . 850.00
Becomes:

## COWBOY COMICS
**July, 1938**
13 FGu,PGv . . . . . . . . . . . . . . 1,000.00
14 FGu,PGv . . . . . . . . . . . . . . . 900.00

Becomes:
## STAR RANGER
## FUNNIES
**Oct., 1938**
15 WE,PGv . . . . . . . . . . . . . . 1,300.00
2-1(16) JCo(a&c) . . . . . . . . . . 1,000.00
2-2(17) PGv,JCo,A:Night Hawk . . 900.00
2-3(18) JCo,FGu . . . . . . . . . . . . 750.00
2-4(19) A:Kit Carson . . . . . . . . . 750.00
2-5(20) Oct., 1939 . . . . . . . . . . . 750.00

## STARS AND STRIPES
## COMICS
**Comic Corp of America
(Centaur Publications),
May, 1941**
2 PGv,PGv(c),'Called to Colors',
The Shark,The Voice . . . . . 3,000.00
3 PGv,PGv(c),O:Dr.Synthe . . . 1,700.00
4 PGv,PGv(c),I:The Stars
& Stripes . . . . . . . . . . . . . 1,500.00
5 . . . . . . . . . . . . . . . . . . . . . 1,000.00
6(5), Dec., 1941 . . . . . . . . . . 1,000.00

## STAR SPANGLED
## COMICS
**DC Comics, Oct., 1941**
1 O:Tarantula,B:Captain X of the
R.A.F.,Star Spangled Kid,
Armstrong of the Army . . . . 7,500.00
2 V:Dr. Weerd . . . . . . . . . . . . 3,000.00
3 . . . . . . . . . . . . . . . . . . . . . 2,500.00
4 V:The Needle . . . . . . . . . . . 2,500.00
5 V:Dr. Weerd . . . . . . . . . . . . 2,500.00
6 E:Armstrong . . . . . . . . . . . . 1,700.00
7 S&K,O&1st app:The Guardian,
B:Robotman,The Newsboy
Legion, TNT . . . . . . . . . . 11,000.00
8 O:TNT & Dan the Dyna-Mite 3,500.00
9 . . . . . . . . . . . . . . . . . . . . . 3,000.00
10 . . . . . . . . . . . . . . . . . . . . . 3,000.00
11 . . . . . . . . . . . . . . . . . . . . . 2,700.00
12 Newsboy Legion stories,
Prevue of Peril!. . . . . . . . . 2,700.00
13 Kill Dat Story!. . . . . . . . . . . 2,700.00
14 Meanest Man on Earth . . . . 2,700.00
15 Playmates of Peril . . . . . . . 2,700.00
16 Playboy of Suicide Slum!. . . 2,700.00
17 V:Rafferty Mob . . . . . . . . . . 2,700.00
18 O:Star Spangled Kid . . . . . . 3,000.00
19 E:Tarantula . . . . . . . . . . . . . 2,700.00
20 B:Liberty Belle . . . . . . . . . . 2,700.00

**St**

*Star Spangled Comics #25*
© DC Comics

*Star Spangled Comics #91*
© DC Comics

*Star Spangled War Stories #14*
© DC Comics

21 . . . . . . . . . . . . . . . . . . 2,500.00
22 Brains for Sale . . . . . . . . 2,500.00
23 Art for Scrapper's Sake . . . . 2,500.00
24 . . . . . . . . . . . . . . . . . . 2,500.00
25 Victuals for Victory . . . . . . 2,500.00
26 Louie the Lug goes Literary . 2,500.00
27 Turn on the Heat! . . . . . . . . 2,500.00
28 Poor Man's Rich Man . . . . . . 2,500.00
29 Cabbages and Comics . . . . 2,500.00
30 . . . . . . . . . . . . . . . . . . 1,500.00
31 Questions Please! . . . . . . . 1,500.00
32 . . . . . . . . . . . . . . . . . . 1,500.00
33 . . . . . . . . . . . . . . . . . . 1,500.00
34 From Rags to Run! . . . . . . . 1,500.00
35 The Proud Poppas . . . . . . . 1,500.00
36 Cowboy of Suicide Slum . . . 1,500.00
37 . . . . . . . . . . . . . . . . . . 1,500.00
38 . . . . . . . . . . . . . . . . . . 1,500.00
39 Two Guardians are a Crowd 1,500.00
40 . . . . . . . . . . . . . . . . . . 1,400.00
41 Back the 6th War Loan(c) . . 1,200.00
42 . . . . . . . . . . . . . . . . . . 1,200.00
43 American Red Cross(c) . . . . 1,200.00
44 . . . . . . . . . . . . . . . . . . 1,200.00
45 7th War Loan (c) . . . . . . . . 1,200.00
46 . . . . . . . . . . . . . . . . . . 1,200.00
47 . . . . . . . . . . . . . . . . . . 1,200.00
48 . . . . . . . . . . . . . . . . . . 1,200.00
49 . . . . . . . . . . . . . . . . . . 1,200.00
50 . . . . . . . . . . . . . . . . . . 1,200.00
51 A:Robot Robber . . . . . . . . . 1,200.00
52 Rehearsal for Crime . . . . . . 1,200.00
53 The Poet of Suicide Slum . . 1,200.00
54 Dead-Shot Dade's Revenge 1,200.00
55 Gabby Strikes a Gusher . . . 1,200.00
56 The Treasurer of Araby . . . . 1,200.00
57 Recruit for the Legion . . . . . 1,200.00
58 Matadors of Suicide Slum . . 1,200.00
59 . . . . . . . . . . . . . . . . . . 1,200.00
60 . . . . . . . . . . . . . . . . . . 1,200.00
61 . . . . . . . . . . . . . . . . . . 1,200.00
62 Prevue of Tomorrow . . . . . . 1,200.00
63 . . . . . . . . . . . . . . . . . . 1,200.00
64 Criminal Cruise . . . . . . . . . 1,200.00
65 B:Robin,(c) & stories . . . . . 2,700.00
66 V:No Face . . . . . . . . . . . . 1,600.00
67 The Castle of Doom . . . . . . 1,500.00
68 . . . . . . . . . . . . . . . . . . 1,500.00
69 The Stolen Atom Bomb . . . . 2,000.00
70 V:The Clock . . . . . . . . . . . 1,500.00
71 Perils of the Stone Age . . . . 1,500.00
72 Robin Crusoe . . . . . . . . . . 1,500.00
73 V:The Black Magician . . . . . 1,500.00
74 V:The Clock . . . . . . . . . . . 1,500.00
75 The State vs. Robin . . . . . . 1,500.00
76 V:The Fence . . . . . . . . . . . 1,500.00

77 The Boy who Wanted Robin
 for Christmas . . . . . . . . . . 1,500.00
78 Rajah Robin . . . . . . . . . . . 1,500.00
79 V:The Clock,The Tick-Tock
 Crimes . . . . . . . . . . . . . . 1,500.00
80 The Boy Disc Jockey . . . . . 1,400.00
81 The Seeing-Eye Dog Crimes 1,300.00
82 The Boy who Hated Robin . . 1,200.00
83 Who is Mr. Mystery,B:Captain
 Compass backup story . . . . 1,200.00
84 How can we Fight Juvenile
 Delinquency? . . . . . . . . . . 1,400.00
85 Peril at the Pole . . . . . . . . . 1,200.00
86 . . . . . . . . . . . . . . . . . . 1,200.00
87 V:Sinister Knight . . . . . . . . 1,500.00
88 Robin Declares War on
 Batman, B:Batman app. . . 1,400.00
89 Batman's Utility Belt? . . . . . 1,400.00
90 Rancho Fear! . . . . . . . . . . 1,400.00
91 Cops 'n' Robbers? . . . . . . . 1,400.00
92 Movie Hero No. 1? . . . . . . . 1,400.00
93 . . . . . . . . . . . . . . . . . . 1,400.00
94 Underworld Playhouse . . . . 1,500.00
95 The Man with the Midas Touch,
 E:Robin(c),Batman story . . 1,500.00
96 B:Tomahawk(c) & stories . . 1,000.00
97 The 4 Bold Warriors . . . . . . 800.00
98 . . . . . . . . . . . . . . . . . . 800.00
99 The Second Pocahontas . . . 800.00
100 The Frontier Phantom . . . . 1,000.00
101 Peril on the High Seas . . . . 800.00
102 . . . . . . . . . . . . . . . . . . 800.00
103 Tomahawk's Death Duel! . . . 800.00
104 Race with Death! . . . . . . . . 800.00
105 The Unhappy Hunting
 Grounds . . . . . . . . . . . . . . 800.00
106 Traitor in the War Paint . . . . 800.00
107 The Brave who Hunted
 Tomahawk . . . . . . . . . . . . 800.00
108 'The Ghost called Moccasin
 Foot!' . . . . . . . . . . . . . . . 800.00
109 The Land Pirates of
 Jolly Roger Hill! . . . . . . . . 800.00
110 Sally Raines Frontier Girl . . . 800.00
111 The Death Map of Thunder
 Hill . . . . . . . . . . . . . . . . . 800.00
112 . . . . . . . . . . . . . . . . . . 800.00
113 FF,V:The Black Cougar . . . 1,100.00
114 Return of the Black Cougar 1,100.00
115 Journey of a Thousand
 Deaths . . . . . . . . . . . . . . 800.00
116 The Battle of Junction Fort . . 800.00
117 Siege? . . . . . . . . . . . . . . 800.00
118 V:Outlaw Indians . . . . . . . . 750.00
119 The Doomed Stockade? . . . . 750.00
120 Revenge of Raven Heart! . . . 800.00

121 Adventure in New York! . . . . 750.00
122 I:Ghost Breaker,(c)& stories 1,000.00
123 The Dolls of Doom . . . . . . . 700.00
124 Suicide Tower . . . . . . . . . . 700.00
125 The Hermit's Ghost Dog! . . . 700.00
126 The Phantom of Paris! . . . . . 700.00
127 The Supernatural Alibi! . . . . 700.00
128 C:Batman,The Girl who
 lived 5,000 Years! . . . . . . . 700.00
129 The Human Orchids . . . . . . 750.00
130 The Haunted Town,
 July, 1952 . . . . . . . . . . . . 800.00
**Becomes:**

## STAR SPANGLED
## WAR STORIES
### DC Comics, Aug., 1952

131 CS&StK(c),I Was A Jap
 Prisoner of War . . . . . . . . 2,000.00
132 CS&StK(c),I.E. With
 The Million-Dollar Arm . . . . 1,600.00
133 CS&StK(c),Mission-San
 Marino . . . . . . . . . . . . . . 1,400.00
3 CS&StK(c),Hundred-Mission
 Mitchell . . . . . . . . . . . . . . 900.00
4 CS&StK(c),The Hot Rod Tank . 900.00
5 LSt(c),Jet Pilot . . . . . . . . . . 900.00
6 CS(c),Operation Davy Jones . . 900.00
7 CS(c),Rookie Ranger,The . . . . 800.00
8 CS(c),I Was A
 Hollywood Soldier . . . . . . . 800.00
9 CS&StK(c),Sad Sack Squad . . 800.00
10 CS,The G.I. & The Gambler . . 800.00
11 LSt(c),The Lucky Squad . . . . 800.00
12 CS(c),The Four Horseman of
 Barricade Hill . . . . . . . . . . 800.00
13 No Escape . . . . . . . . . . . . 800.00
14 LSt(c),Pitchfork Army . . . . . 800.00
15 The Big Fish . . . . . . . . . . . 800.00
16 The Yellow Ribbon . . . . . . . 800.00
17 IN(c),Prize Target . . . . . . . . 800.00
18 IN(c),The Gladiator . . . . . . . 800.00
19 IN(c),The Big Lift . . . . . . . . 800.00
20 JGr(c),The Battle of
 the Frogmen . . . . . . . . . . . 800.00
21 JGr(c),Dead Man's Bridge . . . 600.00
22 JGr(c),Death Hurdle . . . . . . 600.00
23 JGr(c),The Silent Frogman . . 600.00
24 JGr(c),Death Slide . . . . . . . 600.00
25 JGr(c),S.S. Liferaft . . . . . . . 600.00
26 JGr(c),Bazooka Man . . . . . . 600.00
27 JGr(c),Taps for a Tail Gunner . 600.00
28 JGr(c),Tank Duel . . . . . . . . 700.00
29 JGr(c),A Gun Called Slugger . 600.00
30 JGr(c),The Thunderbolt Tank . 600.00

*Star Spangled War Stories #44*
© DC Comics

*Startling Comics #11*
© Nedor Publications

*Startling Terror Tales #6*
© Star Publications

31 IN(c),Tank Block . . . . . . . . . . 400.00
32 JGr(c),Bridge to Battle . . . . . . 400.00
33 JGr(c),Pocket War . . . . . . . . 400.00
34 JGr(c),Fighting...Snowbirds . 400.00
35 JGr(c),Zero Hour. . . . . . . . . . 400.00
36 JGr(c),A G.I. Passed Here . . . 400.00
37 JGr(c),A Handful of T.N.T. . . . . 400.00
38 RH(c),One-Man Army . . . . . . 400.00
39 JGr(c),Flying Cowboy . . . . . . . 400.00
40 JGr(c),Desert Duel . . . . . . . . . 400.00
41 IN(c),A Gunner's Hands . . . . . 350.00
42 JGr(c),Sniper Alley . . . . . . . . . 350.00
43 JGr(c),Top Kick Brother . . . . . 350.00
44 JGr(c),Tank 711
    Doesn't Answer . . . . . . . . . . 350.00
45 JGr(c),Flying Heels . . . . . . . . . 350.00
46 JGr(c),Gunner's Seat . . . . . . . 350.00
47 JGr(c),Sidekick . . . . . . . . . . . 350.00
48 JGr(c),Battle Hills . . . . . . . . . . 350.00
49 JGr(c),Payload . . . . . . . . . . . . 350.00
50 JGr(c),Combat Dust . . . . . . . . 350.00
51 JGr(c),Battle Pigeon . . . . . . . . 250.00
52 JGr(c),Cannon-Man . . . . . . . . 250.00
53 JGr(c),Combat Close-Ups . . . 250.00
54 JGr(c),Flying Exit . . . . . . . . . . 250.00
55 JKu(c),The Burning Desert . . . 250.00
56 JKu(c),The Walking Sub . . . . . 250.00
57 JGr(c),Call For a Frogman . . . 250.00
58 JGr(c),MD,Waist Punch . . . . . 250.00
59 JGr(c),Kick In The Door . . . . . 250.00
60 JGr(c),Hotbox . . . . . . . . . . . . 250.00
61 JGr(c),MD,Tow Pilot . . . . . . . . 250.00
62 JGr(c),The Three GIs . . . . . . . 250.00
63 JGr(c),Flying Range Rider . . . . 250.00
64 JGr(c),MD,Frogman Ambush . 250.00
65 JGr(c),JSe,Frogman Block . . . 250.00
66 JGr(c),Flattop Pigeon . . . . . . . 250.00
67 RH(c),MD,Ashcan Alley . . . . . 250.00
68 JGr(c),The Long Step . . . . . . . 250.00
69 JKu(c),Floating Tank, The . . . . 250.00
70 JKu(c),No Medal For
    Frogman . . . . . . . . . . . . . . 250.00
71 JKu(c),Shooting Star . . . . . . . . 250.00
72 JGr(c),Silent Fish . . . . . . . . . . 250.00
73 JGr(c),MD,The Mouse &
    the Tiger . . . . . . . . . . . . . . . 250.00
74 JGr(c),MD,Frogman Bait . . . . . 250.00
75 JGr(c),MD,Paratroop
    Mousketeers . . . . . . . . . . . . 250.00
76 JKu(c),Odd Man . . . . . . . . 250.00
77 MD,JKu(c),Room to Fight . . . . 250.00
78 MD,JGr(c),Fighting Wingman . 250.00
79 MD,JKu(c),Zero Box . . . . . . . . 250.00
80 MD,JGr(c),Top Gunner . . . . . . 250.00
81 MD,RH(c),Khaki Mosquito . . . 250.00

82 MD,JKu(c),Ground Flier . . . . . 250.00
83 MD,JGr(c),Jet On
    My Shoulder . . . . . . . . . . . . 250.00
84 MD,IN(c),O:Mademoiselle
    Marie . . . . . . . . . . . . . . . . . 500.00
85 IN(c),A Medal For Marie . . . . 300.00
86 JGr(c),A Medal For Marie . . . 300.00
87 JGr(c),T.N.T. Spotlight . . . . . . 300.00
88 JGr(c),The Steel Trap . . . . . . 300.00
89 IN(c),Trail of the Terror . . . . . 300.00
90 RA(c),Island of
    Armored Giants . . . . . . . . . 1,000.00
91 JGr(c),The Train of Terror . . . . 250.00
92 Last Battle of the
    Dinosaur Age . . . . . . . . . . . . 400.00
93 Goliath of the Western Front . 250.00
94 JKu(c),The Frogman and
    the Dinosaur . . . . . . . . . . . . 550.00
95 Guinea Pig Patrol,Dinosaurs . 400.00
96 Mission X,Dinosaur . . . . . . . . 400.00
97 The Sub-Crusher, Dinosaur . . 400.00
98 Island of Thunder, Dinosaur . . 400.00
99 The Circus of Monsters,
    Dinosaur . . . . . . . . . . . . . . . 400.00
100 The Volcano of Monsters,
    Dinosaur . . . . . . . . . . . . . . . 450.00

## STAR STUDDED
### Cambridge House, 1945
N# 25 cents (c) price;128 pgs.;
    32 F:stories . . . . . . . . . . . . . 400.00
N# The Cadet,Hoot Gibson,
    Blue Beetle . . . . . . . . . . . . . 350.00

## STARTLING COMICS
### Better Publ./Nedor Publ.,
### June, 1940
1 WE,LF,B&O:Captain Future,
    Mystico, Wonder Man;
    B:Masked Rider . . . . . . . . . 7,000.00
2 Captain Future(c) . . . . . . . . . 2,500.00
3 same . . . . . . . . . . . . . . . . . . 2,100.00
4 same . . . . . . . . . . . . . . . . . . 1,900.00
5 same . . . . . . . . . . . . . . . . . . 1,800.00
6 same . . . . . . . . . . . . . . . . . . 1,800.00
7 same . . . . . . . . . . . . . . . . . . 1,800.00
8 ASh(c),Captain Future . . . . . 1,800.00
9 Bondage(c) . . . . . . . . . . . . . 1,800.00
10 O:Fighting Yank . . . . . . . . . 7,000.00
11 Fighting Yank(c) . . . . . . . . . 2,500.00
12 Hitler,Mussolini,Tojo (c) . . . . 2,200.00
13 JBi . . . . . . . . . . . . . . . . . . . 1,900.00
14 JBi . . . . . . . . . . . . . . . . . . . 1,900.00
15 Fighting Yank (c) . . . . . . . . . 1,900.00

16 Bondage(c),O:Four
    Comrades . . . . . . . . . . . . . 1,900.00
17 Fighting Yank (c),
    E:Masked Rider . . . . . . . . . 1,700.00
18 JBi,B&O:Pyroman . . . . . . . . 2,500.00
19 Pyroman(c) . . . . . . . . . . . . . 1,500.00
20 Pyroman(c),B:Oracle . . . . . . 1,500.00
21 HcK,ASh(c)Bondage(c)
    O:Ape . . . . . . . . . . . . . . . . 1,800.00
22 HcK,ASh(c),Fighting Yank(c) 1,500.00
23 HcK,BEv,ASh(c),Pyroman(c) 1,500.00
24 HcK,BEv,ASh(c),Fighting
    Yank(c) . . . . . . . . . . . . . . . 1,500.00
25 HcK,BEv,ASh(c),Pyroman(c) 1,500.00
26 BEv,ASh(c),Fighting Yank(c) 1,500.00
27 BEv,ASh(c),Pyroman(c) . . . . 1,500.00
28 BEv,ASh(c),Fighting Yank(c) 1,500.00
29 BEv,ASh(c),Pyroman(c) . . . . 1,500.00
30 ASh(c),Fighting Yank(c) . . . . 1,500.00
31 ASh(c),Pyroman(c) . . . . . . . 1,500.00
32 ASh(c),Fighting Yank(c) . . . . 1,500.00
33 ASh(c),Pyroman(c) . . . . . . . 1,500.00
34 ASh(c),Fighting Yank(c),
    O:Scarab . . . . . . . . . . . . . . 1,800.00
35 ASh(c),Pyroman(c) . . . . . . . 1,500.00
36 ASh(c),Fighting Yank(c) . . . . 1,200.00
37 ASh(c),Bondage (c) . . . . . . . 1,200.00
38 ASh(c),Bondage(c) . . . . . . . 1,500.00
39 ASh(c),Pyroman(c) . . . . . . . 1,500.00
40 ASh(c),E:Captain Future . . . 1,500.00
41 ASh(c),Pyroman(c) . . . . . . . 1,500.00
42 ASh(c),Fighting Yank(c) . . . . 1,500.00
43 ASh(c),Pyroman(c),
    E:Pyroman . . . . . . . . . . . . . 1,500.00
44 Grl(c),Lance Lewis(c) . . . . . 1,700.00
45 Grl(c),I:Tygra . . . . . . . . . . . . 1,700.00
46 Grl,Grl(c),Bondage(c) . . . . . 1,700.00
47 ASh(c),Bondage(c) . . . . . . . . 3,000.00
48 ASh(c),Lance Lewis(c) . . . . 1,500.00
49 ASh(c),Bondage(c),
    E:Fighting Yank . . . . . . . . . 7,500.00
50 ASh(c),Lance Lewis(c),
    Sea Eagle . . . . . . . . . . . . . 1,100.00
51 ASh(c),Sea Eagle . . . . . . . . 1,100.00
52 ASh(c) . . . . . . . . . . . . . . . . 1,100.00
53 ASh(c),Sept., 1948 . . . . . . . 1,100.00

## STARTLING TERROR
## TALES
### Star Publications,
### May, 1952
10 WW,LbC(c),The Story Starts 1,000.00
11 LbC(c),The Ghost Spider
    of Death . . . . . . . . . . . . . . 1,700.00

**St**

---

*Steve Roper #4*
*© Famous Funnies*

*Straight Arrow #15*
*© Magazine Enterprises*

*Strange Adventures #14*
*© DC Comics*

12 LbC(c),White Hand Horror . . . 350.00
13 JyD,LbC(c),Love From
   a Gorgor . . . . . . . . . . . . . . . 375.00
14 LbC(c),Trapped by the
   Color of Blood . . . . . . . . . . 350.00
4 LbC(c),Crime at the Carnival . 300.00
5 LbC(c),The Gruesome
   Demon of Terror . . . . . . . . . 300.00
6 LbC(c),Footprints of Death . . . 300.00
7 LbC(c),The Case of the
   Strange Murder . . . . . . . . . . 300.00
8 RP,LbC(c),Phantom Brigade . . 300.00
9 LbC(c),The Forbidden Tomb . . 275.00
10 LbC(c),The Horrible Entity . . . 325.00
11 RP,LbC(c),The Law Will
   Win, July, 1954 . . . . . . . . . . 300.00

## STEVE CANYON COMICS
**Harvey Publications, Feb., 1948–Dec., 1948**
1 MC,BP,O:Steve Canyon. . . . . 275.00
2 MC,BP . . . . . . . . . . . . . . . . . 175.00
3 MC,BP,Canyon's Crew . . . . . 150.00
4 MC,BP,Chase of Death . . . . . 150.00
5 MC,BP,A:Happy Easter . . . . . 150.00
6 MC,BP,A:Madame Lynx. . . . . . 165.00

## STEVE ROPER
**Famous Funnies, April, 1948**
1 Reprints newspaper strips . . . 150.00
2 . . . . . . . . . . . . . . . . . . . . . . . 75.00
3 . . . . . . . . . . . . . . . . . . . . . . . 60.00
4 . . . . . . . . . . . . . . . . . . . . . . . 60.00
5 Dec., 1948 . . . . . . . . . . . . . . . 60.00

## STEVIE
**Magazine Publications (Mazie), 1952**
1 teenage . . . . . . . . . . . . . . . . . . 80.00
2 . . . . . . . . . . . . . . . . . . . . . . . 50.00

## STONY CRAIG
**Pentagon Publishing, 1945**
N# . . . . . . . . . . . . . . . . . . . . . . . 75.00

## STORIES BY FAMOUS AUTHORS ILLUSTRATED
**See: FAST FICTION**

## STORIES OF ROMANCE
**Marvel Atlas, 1956**
5 MB,ViC(c) . . . . . . . . . . . . . . . 150.00
6 . . . . . . . . . . . . . . . . . . . . . . . 100.00
7 . . . . . . . . . . . . . . . . . . . . . . . 100.00
8 . . . . . . . . . . . . . . . . . . . . . . . 100.00
9 ViC . . . . . . . . . . . . . . . . . . . . 125.00
10 . . . . . . . . . . . . . . . . . . . . . . . 100.00
11 MB,ViC,JR. . . . . . . . . . . . . . . 150.00
12 . . . . . . . . . . . . . . . . . . . . . . . 120.00
13 ABr . . . . . . . . . . . . . . . . . . . . 150.00

## STORY OF HARRY S. TRUMAN, THE
**Democratic National Committee, 1948**
N# Giveaway-The Life of Our
   33rd President . . . . . . . . . . 200.00

## THE STORY OF MARTHA WAYNE
**Argo Publications, 1956**
1 . . . . . . . . . . . . . . . . . . . . . . . 100.00

## STRAIGHT ARROW
**Magazine Enterprises, Feb.–March, 1950**
1 OW,B:Straight Arrow & his
   Horse Fury . . . . . . . . . . . . 1,200.00
2 BP,B&O:Red Hawk . . . . . . . . . 550.00
3 BP,FF(c) . . . . . . . . . . . . . . . . 700.00
4 BP,Cave(c). . . . . . . . . . . . . . . 500.00
5 BP,StraightArrow'sGreatLeap . 500.00
6 BP . . . . . . . . . . . . . . . . . . . . . 450.00
7 BP,The Railroad Invades
   Comanche Country . . . . . . . 450.00
8 BP . . . . . . . . . . . . . . . . . . . . . 450.00
9 BP . . . . . . . . . . . . . . . . . . . . . 450.00
10 BP . . . . . . . . . . . . . . . . . . . . . 450.00
11 BP,The Valley of Time. . . . . . . 500.00
12 thru 19 BP . . . . . . . . . . . . . . @500.00
20 BP,Straight Arrow's
   Great War Shield. . . . . . . . . 450.00
21 BP,O:Fury . . . . . . . . . . . . . . . 500.00
22 BP,FF(c) . . . . . . . . . . . . . . . . 550.00
23 BP . . . . . . . . . . . . . . . . . . . . . 300.00
24 BP,The Dragons of Doom. . . . 400.00
25 BP, Secret Cave . . . . . . . . . . 300.00
26 BP,Red Hawk vs. Vikings . . . . 300.00
27 BP . . . . . . . . . . . . . . . . . . . . . 250.00
28 BP,Red Hawk . . . . . . . . . . . . 250.00
29 thru 35 BP . . . . . . . . . . . . . @250.00

36 BP Red Hawk, Drug . . . . . . . . 225.00
37 BP . . . . . . . . . . . . . . . . . . . . . 225.00
38 BP . . . . . . . . . . . . . . . . . . . . . 225.00
39 BP,The Canyon Beasts. . . . . . 250.00
40 BP,Secret of the
   Spanish Specters. . . . . . . . . 250.00
41 BP . . . . . . . . . . . . . . . . . . . . . 200.00
42 BP . . . . . . . . . . . . . . . . . . . . . 200.00
43 BP,I:Blaze . . . . . . . . . . . . . . . 250.00
44 BP . . . . . . . . . . . . . . . . . . . . . 200.00
45 thru 53 BP . . . . . . . . . . . . . @200.00
54 BP,March, 1956 . . . . . . . . . . 200.00

## STRANGE ADVENTURES
**DC Comics, 1950–74**
1 The Menace of the Green
   Nebula . . . . . . . . . . . . . . . 6,000.00
2 S&K,JM(c),Doom From
   Planet X . . . . . . . . . . . . . . 3,000.00
3 The Metal World . . . . . . . . . 1,800.00
4 BP,The Invaders From the
   Nth Dimension . . . . . . . . . . 1,800.00
5 The World Inside the Atom . . 1,800.00
6 Confessions of a Martian . . . 1,800.00
7 The World of Giant Ants . . . . 1,800.00
8 MA,ATh,Evolution Plus . . . . . 1,800.00
9 MA,B:Captain Comet,The
   Origin of Captain Comet. . . 3,500.00
10 MA,CI,The Air Bandits
   From Space . . . . . . . . . . . . 1,800.00
11 MA,CI,Day the Past
   Came Back. . . . . . . . . . . . . 1,000.00
12 MA,CI,GK(c),The Girl From
   the Diamond Planet . . . . . . 1,000.00
13 MA,CI,GK(c),When the Earth
   was Kidnapped. . . . . . . . . . 1,000.00
14 MA,CI,GK(c),Destination
   Doom . . . . . . . . . . . . . . . . 1,000.00
15 MA,CI,GK(c),Captain Comet-
   Enemy of Earth. . . . . . . . . . 1,000.00
16 MA,CI,GK(c),The Ghost of
   Captain Comet . . . . . . . . . . 1,000.00
17 MA,CI,GK(c),Beware the
   Synthetic Men. . . . . . . . . . . 1,000.00
18 CI,MA(c),World of Flying
   Men. . . . . . . . . . . . . . . . . . 1,000.00
19 CI,MA(c),Secret of the
   Twelve Eternals . . . . . . . . . 1,500.00
20 CI,Slaves of the Sea Master 1,500.00
21 CI,MA(c),Eyes of the
   Other Worlds . . . . . . . . . . . . 800.00
22 CI,The Guardians of the
   Clockwork Universe. . . . . . . 800.00
23 CI,MA(c),The Brain Pirates
   of Planet X. . . . . . . . . . . . . . 800.00

**St**

    All comics prices listed are for *Near Mint* condition.

# STANDARD GUIDE TO GOLDEN AGE COMICS

Strange Adventures #51
© DC Comics

Strange Adventures #75
© DC Comics

Strange Adventures #123
© DC Comics

24 CI,MA(c),Doomsday on Earth. 800.00
25 CI,GK(c),The Day
  That Vanished . . . . . . . . . . . 800.00
26 CI,Captain Vs. Miss Universe. 800.00
27 CI,MA(c),The Counterfeit
  Captain Comet . . . . . . . . . . 800.00
28 CI,Devil's Island in Space . . . . 800.00
29 CI,The Time Capsule From
  1,000,000 B.C. . . . . . . . . . . 800.00
30 CI,MA(c),Menace From the
  World of Make-Believe . . . . . 750.00
31 CI,Lights Camera Action . . . . . 750.00
32 CI,MA(c),The Challenge of
  Man-Ape the Mighty . . . . . . 750.00
33 CI,MA(c),The Human Beehive 750.00
34 CI,MA(c) . . . . . . . . . . . . . . . . 750.00
35 CI,MA(c),Cosmic Chessboard 750.00
36 CI,MA(c),The Grab-Bag
  Planet . . . . . . . . . . . . . . . . . 750.00
37 CI,MA(c),The Invaders From
  the Golden Atom . . . . . . . . . 750.00
38 CI,MA(c),Seeing-Eye Humans 750.00
39 CI,MA(c),The Guilty Gorilla . . . 750.00
40 CI,MA(c),The Mind Monster . . 750.00
41 CI,MA(c),The Beast From Out
  of Time. . . . . . . . . . . . . . . . . 750.00
42 CI,MD,MA(c),The Planet of
  Ancient Children . . . . . . . . . 750.00
43 CI,MD,MA(c),The Phantom
  Prize Fighter . . . . . . . . . . . . 750.00
44 CI,MA(c),The Planet That
  Plotted Murder. . . . . . . . . . . 750.00
45 CI,MD,MA(c),Gorilla World . . . 750.00
46 CI,MA(c),E:Captain Comet
  Interplanetary War Base . . . . 750.00
47 CI,MA(c),The Man Who Sold
  the Earth . . . . . . . . . . . . . . . 750.00
48 CI,MA(c),Human Phantom . . . 750.00
49 CI,MA(c),The Invasion
  from Indiana . . . . . . . . . . . . 750.00
50 CI,MA(c),The World Wrecker . 600.00
51 CI,MA(c),The Man Who
  Stole Air . . . . . . . . . . . . . . . 600.00
52 CI,MA(c),Prisoner of the
  Parakeets . . . . . . . . . . . . . . 600.00
53 CI,MA(c),The Human Icicle. . . 600.00
54 CI,MA(c),The Electric Man . . . 500.00
55 CI,MA(c),The Gorilla Who
  Challanged the World,pt.I . . . 500.00
56 CI,The Jungle Emperor,pt.II . . 500.00
57 CI,The Spy from Saturn . . . . . 500.00
58 CI,I Hunted the Radium Man . 500.00
59 CI,The Ark From Planet X. . . . 500.00
60 CI,Across the Ages . . . . . . . . 500.00
61 CI,The Mirages From Space. . 500.00
62 CI,The Fireproof Man . . . . . . . 500.00

63 CI,I Was the Man in the Moon 500.00
64 CI,GK(c),Gorillas In Space . . . 500.00
65 CI,GK(c),Prisoner From Pluto. 500.00
66 CI,GK(c),The Human Battery . 500.00
67 CI,GK(c),Martian Masquerader 500.00
68 CI,The Man Who Couldn't
  Drown . . . . . . . . . . . . . . . . . 500.00
69 CI,Gorilla Conquest of Earth. . 500.00
70 CI,Triple Life of Dr. Pluto . . . . 500.00
71 CI,MSy,Zero Hour For Earth . . 400.00
72 CI,The Skyscraper That Came
  to Life. . . . . . . . . . . . . . . . . . 400.00
73 CI,Amazing Rain of Gems . . . 400.00
74 CI,The Invisible Invader
  From Dimension X. . . . . . . . . 400.00
75 CI,Secret of the Man-Ape . . . . 400.00
76 CI,B:Darwin Jones,The Robot
  From Atlantis . . . . . . . . . . . . 400.00
77 CI,A:Darwin Jones,The World
  That Slipped Out of Space . . 400.00
78 CI,The Secret of the Tom
  Thumb Spaceman . . . . . . . . 400.00
79 CI,A:Darwin Jones,Invaders
  from the Ice World . . . . . . . . 400.00
80 CI,Mind Robbers of Venus . . . 400.00
81 CI,The Secret of the
  Shrinking Twins . . . . . . . . . . 400.00
82 CI,Giants of the Cosmic Ray . 300.00
83 CI,Assignment in Eternity . . . . 300.00
84 CI,Prisoners of the Atom
  Universe . . . . . . . . . . . . . . . 300.00
85 CI,The Amazing Human Race 300.00
86 CI,The Dog That Saved the
  Earth . . . . . . . . . . . . . . . . . . 300.00
87 CI,New Faces For Old . . . . . . 300.00
88 CI,A:Darwin Jones,The Gorilla
  War Against Earth . . . . . . . . 300.00
89 CI,Earth For Sale . . . . . . . . . . 300.00
90 CI,The Day I Became a
  Martian . . . . . . . . . . . . . . . . 300.00
91 CI,Midget Earthmen of Jupiter 300.00
92 CI,GK(c),The Amazing Ray
  of Knowledge. . . . . . . . . . . . 300.00
93 CI,GK(c),A:Darwin Jones,
  Space-Rescue By Proxy . . . . 300.00
94 MA,CI,GK(c),Fisherman of
  Space. . . . . . . . . . . . . . . . . . 300.00
95 CI,The World at my Doorstep. 300.00
96 CI,MA(c),The Menace of
  Saturn's Rings . . . . . . . . . . . 300.00
97 CI,MA(c),MSy,Secret of the
  Space-Giant. . . . . . . . . . . . . 300.00
98 CI,GK(c),MSy,Attack on Fort
  Satellite . . . . . . . . . . . . . . . . 300.00
99 CI,MSy,GK(c),Big Jump Into
  Space. . . . . . . . . . . . . . . . . . 300.00

100 CI,MSy,The Amazing Trial
  of John (Gorilla) Doe . . . . . . 400.00
101 CI,MSy,GK(c),Giant From
  Beyond . . . . . . . . . . . . . . . . 250.00
102 MSy,GK(c),The Three Faces
  of Barry Morrell . . . . . . . . . . 250.00
103 GK(c),The Man Who
  Harpooned Worlds. . . . . . . . 250.00
104 MSy,GK(c),World of Doomed
  Spacemen . . . . . . . . . . . . . . 250.00
105 MSy,GK(c),Fisherman From
  the Sea . . . . . . . . . . . . . . . . 250.00
106 MSy,CI,GK(c),Genie in the
  Flying Saucer . . . . . . . . . . . 250.00
107 MSy,CI,GK(c),War of the
  Jovian Bubble-Men . . . . . . . 250.00
108 MSy,CI,GK(c),The Human
  Pet of Gorilla Land . . . . . . . . 250.00
109 MSy,CI,GK(c),The Man Who
  Weighed 100 Tons. . . . . . . . 250.00
110 MSy,CI,GK(c),Hand From
  Beyond . . . . . . . . . . . . . . . . 250.00
111 MSy,CI,GK(c),Secret of
  the Last Earth-Man . . . . . . . 250.00
112 MSy,CI,GK(c),Menace of
  the Size-Changing Spaceman 250.00
113 MSy,CI,GK(c),Deluge From
  Space. . . . . . . . . . . . . . . . . . 250.00
114 MSy,CI,GK(c),Secret of the
  Flying Buzz Saw . . . . . . . . . 250.00
115 MSy,CI,GK(c),The Great
  Space-Tiger Hunt. . . . . . . . . 250.00
116 MSy,CI,RH,GK(c),Invasion
  of the Water Warriors . . . . . . 250.00
117 MSy,CI,GK(c),I:Atomic
  Knights . . . . . . . . . . . . . . . 1,000.00
118 MSy,CI,The Turtle-Men of
  Space. . . . . . . . . . . . . . . . . . 275.00
119 MSy,CI,MA(c),Raiders
  From the Giant World . . . . . . 250.00
120 MSy,CI,MA,Attack of the Oil
  Demons . . . . . . . . . . . . . . . . 500.00
121 MSy,CI,MA(c),Invasion of the
  Flying Reptiles . . . . . . . . . . . 225.00
122 MSy,CI,MA(c),David and the
  Space-Goliath . . . . . . . . . . . 225.00
123 MSy,CI,MA(c),Secret of the
  Rocket-Destroyer. . . . . . . . . 300.00
124 MSy,CI,MA(c),The Face-Hunter
  From Saturn . . . . . . . . . . . . 250.00
125 MSy,CI,The Flying Gorilla
  Menace . . . . . . . . . . . . . . . . 225.00
126 MSy,CI,MA(c),Return of the
  Neanderthal Man. . . . . . . . . 400.00
127 MSy,CI,MA(c),Menace
  From the Earth-Globe . . . . . . 225.00

**St**

All comics prices listed are for *Near Mint* condition.          **Page 249**

*Strange Fantasy #6*
© Farrell Publications

*Strange Mysteries #19*
© Superior Publications

*Strange Suspense Stories #22*
© Charlton Comics

128 MSy,CI,MA(c),The Man
With the Electronic Brain.... 225.00
129 MSy,CI,MA(c),The Giant
Who Stole Mountains ...... 250.00
130 MSy,CI,MA.War With the
Giant Frogs ............. 225.00
131 MSy,CI,MA(c),Emperor
of the Earth ............. 225.00
132 MSy,CI,MA(c),The Dreams
of Doom ............... 250.00
133 MSy,CI,MA(c),The Invisible
Dinosaur .............. 225.00
134 MSy,CI,MA(c), The Aliens
Who Raided New York ..... 250.00

## STRANGE CONFESSIONS
**Approved Publications
(Ziff-Davis),
Spring, 1952**
1 EK,Ph(c) ................ 650.00
2 Ph(c) .................. 400.00
3 EK,Ph(c),Girls Reformatory ... 400.00
4 Ph(c),Girls Reformatory ...... 400.00

## STRANGE FANTASY
**Farrell Publications/
Ajax Comics,
Aug., 1952**
(2)1 Jungle Princess......... 600.00
2 Drug & Horror ............ 500.00
3 The Dancing Ghost ........ 500.00
4 Demon in the Dungeon,
A:Rocketman............ 500.00
5 Visiting Corpse .......... 300.00
6 ..................... 300.00
7 A:Madam Satan .......... 450.00
8 A:Black Cat ............. 300.00
9 S&K,SD, Black Cat ....... 400.00
10 .................... 300.00
11 Fearful Things Can Happen
in a Lonely Place......... 400.00
12 The Undying Fiend ........ 300.00
13 Terror in the Attic,
Bondage(c) ............ 400.00
14 Monster in the Building,
Oct.–Nov., 1954.......... 300.00

## STRANGE JOURNEY
**America's Best, 1957**
1 ..................... 250.00
2 Flying Saucer............ 175.00
3 ..................... 150.00
4 ..................... 150.00

## STRANGE MYSTERIES
**Superior Publ./Dynamic Publ.,
1951**
1 LKa,Horror .............. 800.00
2 ..................... 425.00
3 thru 5 ............... @400.00
6 ..................... 350.00
7 ..................... 350.00
8 ..................... 350.00
9 Bondage,3-D type ........ 400.00
10 .................... 300.00
11 thru 18 ............. @250.00
19 MB ................. 275.00
20 reprint #1, new (c). ....... 200.00
21 reprint ............... 200.00

## UNKNOWN WORLD
**Fawcett Publications,
June, 1952**
1 NS(c),Ph(c),Will You Venture
to Meet the Unknown ...... 600.00
Becomes:

## STRANGE STORIES FROM ANOTHER WORLD
**Aug., 1952**
2 NS(c),Ph(c),Will You?
Dare You .............. 750.00
3 NS(c),Ph(c),The Dark Mirror .. 500.00
4 NS(c),Ph(c),Monsters of
the Mind .............. 500.00
5 NS(c),Ph(c),Dance of the
Doomed, Feb., 1953 ...... 500.00

## STRANGE STORIES OF SUSPENSE
**See: RUGGED ACTION**

## STRANGE SUSPENSE STORIES
**Fawcett Publications,
June, 1952**
1 BP,MSy,MBi ............. 1,500.00
2 MBi,GE ............... 1,000.00
3 MBi,GE(c) .............. 800.00
4 BP .................. 800.00
5 MBi(c),Voodoo(c). ......... 800.00
6 BEv .................. 400.00
7 BEv .................. 400.00
8 AW .................. 400.00

9 ..................... 400.00
10 .................... 500.00
11 thru 13 ............. @300.00
14 .................... 350.00
15 AW,BEv(c). ............ 350.00

## Charlton Comics
16 .................... 350.00
17 .................... 300.00
18 SD,SD(c). ............. 500.00
19 SD,SD(c). ............. 700.00
20 SD,SD(c). ............. 500.00
21 .................... 250.00
22 SD(c). ............... 450.00
Becomes:

## THIS IS SUSPENSE!
**Feb., 1955**
23 WW .................. 400.00
24 .................... 150.00
25 .................... 100.00
26 .................... 100.00
Becomes:

## STRANGE SUSPENSE STORIES
**Oct., 1955**
27 .................... 200.00
28 thru 30 ............. @150.00
31 SD(c). ............... 300.00
32 SD ................. 300.00
33 SD ................. 300.00
34 SD,SD(c). ............. 600.00
35 SD ................. 300.00
36 SD,SD(c). ............. 300.00
37 SD ................. 375.00
38 .................... 300.00
39 SD ................. 350.00
40 SD ................. 300.00
41 SD ................. 300.00
42 thru 44 ............. @125.00
45 SD ................. 250.00
46 .................... 125.00
47 SD ................. 250.00
48 SD ................. 250.00
49 .................... 125.00
50 SD ................. 250.00
51 SD ................. 150.00
52 SD ................. 150.00
53 SD ................. 150.00
54 thru 60 ............. @125.00
61 thru 74 ............. @100.00
75 Capt. Atom ........... 250.00
76 Capt. Atom ........... 100.00
77 Capt. Atom ........... 100.00

All comics prices listed are for *Near Mint* condition.

*Strange Tales #13*
© Marvel Comics Group

*Strange Tales #67*
© Marvel Comics Group

*Strange Tales of the Unusual #8*
©Marvel Comics Group

## STRANGE SUSPENSE
### STORIES
### See: LAWBREAKERS

## STRANGE TALES
**Marvel, June, 1951**
1 The Room . . . . . . . . . . . . . 4,000.00
2 Trapped In A Tomb . . . . . . . 1,300.00
3 JMn,Man Who Never Was . . 1,000.00
4 BEv,Terror in the Morgue . . . 1,100.00
5 A Room Without A Door . . . . 1,000.00
6 RH(c),The Ugly Man . . . . . . . . 700.00
7 Who Stands Alone . . . . . . . . . 700.00
8 BEv(c),Something in the Fog. . 700.00
9 Drink Deep Vampire . . . . . . . . 700.00
10 BK,Hidden Head. . . . . . . . . . . 800.00
11 BEv(c),GC,'O'Malley's Friend . 500.00
12 Graveyard At Midnight . . . . . . 500.00
13 BEv(c),Death Makes A Deal . . 500.00
14 GT,Horrible Herman . . . . . . . 500.00
15 BK,Don't Look Down. . . . . . . . 550.00
16 Decapitation cover . . . . . . . . 500.00
17 DBr,JRo,Death Feud. . . . . . . . 500.00
18 Witch Hunt . . . . . . . . . . . . . . 500.00
19 RH(c),The Rag Doll . . . . . . . . 500.00
20 RH(c),GC,SMo,Lost World . . . 500.00
21 BEv . . . . . . . . . . . . . . . . . . . 400.00
22 BK,JF . . . . . . . . . . . . . . . . . . 400.00
23 Strangest Tale in the World. . . 400.00
24 The Thing in the Coffin . . . . . 400.00
25 . . . . . . . . . . . . . . . . . . . . . . . 400.00
26 . . . . . . . . . . . . . . . . . . . . . . . 400.00
27 JF,The Garden of Death . . . . . 400.00
28 Come into my Coffin . . . . . . . 400.00
29 Witch-Craft . . . . . . . . . . . . . . 400.00
30 The Thing in the Box . . . . . . . 400.00
31 Man Who Played with Blocks . 400.00
32 . . . . . . . . . . . . . . . . . . . . . . . 400.00
33 JMn(c),Step Lively Please . . . 400.00
34 Flesh and Blood . . . . . . . . . . 375.00
35 The Man in the Bottle . . . . . . 300.00
36 . . . . . . . . . . . . . . . . . . . . . . . 300.00
37 Out of the Storm . . . . . . . . . . 300.00
38 . . . . . . . . . . . . . . . . . . . . . . . 300.00
39 Karnoff's Plan . . . . . . . . . . . . 300.00
40 BEv,Man Who Caught
a Mermaid . . . . . . . . . . . . . . 300.00
41 BEv,Riddle of the Skull . . . . . 325.00
42 DW,BEv,JMn,Faceless One . . 325.00
43 JF,The Mysterious Machine . . 300.00
44 . . . . . . . . . . . . . . . . . . . . . . . 300.00
45 JKa,Land of Vanishing Men . . 325.00
46 thru 57 . . . . . . . . . . . . . . . @300.00

58 AW . . . . . . . . . . . . . . . . . . . . 300.00
59 BK. . . . . . . . . . . . . . . . . . . . . 300.00
60 The Abyss. . . . . . . . . . . . . . . 275.00
61 BK. . . . . . . . . . . . . . . . . . . . . 300.00
62 . . . . . . . . . . . . . . . . . . . . . . . 275.00
63 The Melting Pot. . . . . . . . . . . 300.00
64 AW . . . . . . . . . . . . . . . . . . . . 300.00
65 Afraid to Open the Door . . . . 275.00
66 . . . . . . . . . . . . . . . . . . . . . . . 275.00
67 Trapped Between Two Worlds 350.00
68 Evacuate Earth . . . . . . . . . . . 350.00
69 . . . . . . . . . . . . . . . . . . . . . . . 350.00
70 When Wakes the Sphinx. . . . . 350.00
71 I Defied the Black Magic. . . . . 350.00
72 . . . . . . . . . . . . . . . . . . . . . . . 350.00
73 . . . . . . . . . . . . . . . . . . . . . . . 350.00
74 . . . . . . . . . . . . . . . . . . . . . . . 350.00
75 I Am Taboo . . . . . . . . . . . . . . 350.00
76 I Am Dragoom. . . . . . . . . . . . 350.00
77 Taboo Returns . . . . . . . . . . . 350.00
78 A Martian Prowls Among Us . . 350.00
79 SD,JK,Dr.Strange Prototype . . 350.00
80 thru 83 SD,JK . . . . . . . . . . @250.00
84 SD,JK,Magneto Prototype . . . 250.00
85 SD,JK . . . . . . . . . . . . . . . . . . 250.00
86 SD,JK,I Created Mechano . . . 250.00
87 SD,JK,Return of Grogg. . . . . . 250.00
88 SD,JK,Zzutak . . . . . . . . . . . . . 250.00
89 SD,JK,Fin Fang Foom . . . . . . 700.00
90 SD,JK,Orrgo Unconquerable . 250.00
91 SD,JK,The Sacrifice . . . . . . . . 250.00
92 SD,JK,Thing That Waits . . . . . 250.00
93 SD,JK,The Wax People . . . . . 250.00
94 SD,JK,Pildorr the Plunderer . . 250.00
95 SD,JK,Two-Headed Thing . . . 250.00
96 SD,JK,I Dream of Doom. . . . . 250.00
97 SD,JK,When A Planet Dies. . . 600.00
98 SD,JK,No Human Can
Beat Me . . . . . . . . . . . . . . . . 250.00
99 SD,JK,Mister Morgan's
Monster . . . . . . . . . . . . . . . . 250.00
100 SD,JK,I Was Trapped
in the Crazy Maze . . . . . . . . 250.00
101 B:StL(s),SD,JK,
B:Human Torch. . . . . . . . . 1,600.00
102 SD,JK,I:Wizard . . . . . . . . . . 500.00
103 SD,JK,I:Zemu . . . . . . . . . . . 450.00
104 SD,JK,I:The Trapster . . . . . . 450.00
105 SD,JK,V:Wizard . . . . . . . . . 450.00
106 SD,A:Fantastic Four . . . . . . 300.00
107 SD,V:Sub-Mariner. . . . . . . . 375.00
108 SD,JK,A:FF,I:The Painter . . . 300.00
109 SD,JK,I:Sorcerer. . . . . . . . . 300.00
110 SD,I&B:Dr.Strange,
Nightmare. . . . . . . . . . . . 2,000.00

## STRANGE TALES
## OF THE UNUSUAL
**Marvel, Dec., 1955—Aug., 1957**
1 JMn(c),BP,DH,JR,Man Lost. . . 600.00
2 BEv,Man Afraid . . . . . . . . . . . 300.00
3 AW,The Invaders . . . . . . . . . . 325.00
4 The Long Wait . . . . . . . . . . . . 225.00
5 RC,SD,The Threat. . . . . . . . . . 275.00
6 BEv . . . . . . . . . . . . . . . . . . . . 225.00
7 JK,JO . . . . . . . . . . . . . . . . . . 225.00
8 . . . . . . . . . . . . . . . . . . . . . . . . 225.00
9 BEv(c),BK . . . . . . . . . . . . . . . 250.00
10 GM,AT. . . . . . . . . . . . . . . . . . 225.00
11 BEv(c),Aug., 1957. . . . . . . . . 225.00

## STRANGE TERRORS
**St. John Publishing Co.,**
**June, 1952**
1 The Ghost of Castle
Karloff, Bondage(c) . . . . . . . 900.00
2 Unshackled Flight into Nowhere 700.00
3 JKu,Ph(c),The Ghost Who
Ruled Crazy Heights . . . . . . 750.00
4 JKu,Ph(c),Terror from
the Tombs . . . . . . . . . . . . . . 900.00
5 JKu,Ph(c),No Escaping
the Pool of Death . . . . . . . . 750.00
6 LC,PMo,Bondage(c),Giant. . . 900.00
7 JKu,JKu(c),Cat's Death,Giant 1,000.00

## STRANGE WORLD OF
## YOUR DREAMS
**Prize Group,**
**Aug., 1952**
1 S&K(c),What Do They Mean–
Messages Rec'd in Sleep . 1,200.00
2 MMe,S&K(c),Why did I Dream
That I Was Being Married
to a Man without a Face? . . . 700.00
3 S&K(c) . . . . . . . . . . . . . . . . . 500.00
4 MMe,S&K(c),The Story of
a Man Who Dreamed a Murder
that Happened . . . . . . . . . . . 450.00

## STRANGE WORLDS
**Avon Periodicals,**
**Nov., 1950**
1 JKu,Spider God of Akka . . . 2,200.00
2 WW,Dara of the Vikings . . . 2,000.00
3 AW&FF,EK(c),WW,JO. . . . . . 3,200.00
4 JO,WW,WW(c),The
Enchanted Dagger . . . . . . 2,300.00

**St**

Strange Worlds #8
© Avon Periodicals

Sub-Mariner Comics #39
© Marvel Comics Group

Sun Girl #1
© Marvel Comics Group

5 WW,WW(c),JO,Bondage(c);
Sirens of Space . . . . . . . . 2,400.00
6 EK,WW(c),JO,SC,
Maid o/t Mist . . . . . . . . . . 1,000.00
7 EK, Sabotage on
Space Station 1 . . . . . . . . . 900.00
8 JKu,EK,The Metal Murderer . . 900.00
9 The Radium Monsters . . . . . . 900.00
18 JKu . . . . . . . . . . . . . . . . . . . . 800.00
19 Astounding Super
Science Fantasies . . . . . . . . 800.00
20 WW(c),Fighting War Stories . . 250.00
21 EK(c) . . . . . . . . . . . . . . . . . . . 200.00
22 EK(c),Sept.–Oct., 1955 . . . . . . 200.00

## STRANGE WORLDS
### Marvel, Dec., 1958
1 JK,SD,Flying Saucer . . . . . . . 1,200.00
2 SD . . . . . . . . . . . . . . . . . . . . . 650.00
3 JK . . . . . . . . . . . . . . . . . . . . . 500.00
4 AW . . . . . . . . . . . . . . . . . . . . . 450.00
5 SD . . . . . . . . . . . . . . . . . . . . . 400.00

## STRICTLY PRIVATE
### Eastern Color Printing,
### July, 1942
1 You're in theArmyNow-Humor . 275.00
2 F:Peter Plink, 1942 . . . . . . . . . 250.00

## STUNTMAN COMICS
### Harvey Publications,
### April–May, 1946
1 S&K,O:Stuntman . . . . . . . . 2,000.00
2 S&K,New Champ of Split-
Second Action . . . . . . . . . . 1,200.00
3 S&K,Digest sized,Mail Order
Only, B&W interior,
Oct.–Nov., 1946 . . . . . . . . 1,500.00

## SUB-MARINER COMICS
### Marvel Timely, Spring, 1941
1 ASh(c),BEv,PGv,B:Sub-
Mariner, The Angel . . . . . 65,000.00
2 ASh(c),BEv,Nazi
Submarine (c) . . . . . . . . 10,000.00
3 ASh(c),BEv,Churchill . . . . . . 9,500.00
4 ASh(c),BEv,BW . . . . . . . . . 6,000.00
5 V:Axis Powers . . . . . . . . . . 5,000.00
6 ASh(c),Panama Canal . . . . 4,500.00
7 ASm&FrG(c) . . . . . . . . . . . 4,500.00
8 ASh(c),PGv . . . . . . . . . . . . 4,500.00
9 ASh(c),BW,Flag(c) . . . . . . . 4,500.00
10 ASh(c),GS . . . . . . . . . . . . 4,500.00

11 ASh(c),Dragon(c) . . . . . . . . 4,500.00
12 ASh(c) . . . . . . . . . . . . . . . . 3,500.00
13 ASh(c),Bondage(c) . . . . . . . 3,500.00
14 ASh(c) . . . . . . . . . . . . . . . . 3,500.00
15 ASh(c),V:Japs . . . . . . . . . . 3,500.00
16 ASh(c),CI,ASm,GS . . . . . . . 2,500.00
17 ASh(c),V:Japs . . . . . . . . . . 2,500.00
18 ASh(c),ASm . . . . . . . . . . . 2,500.00
19 . . . . . . . . . . . . . . . . . . . . . 2,500.00
20 ASh(c),V:Crooks . . . . . . . . 2,500.00
21 SSh(c),BEv,Last Angel . . . . 2,200.00
22 SSh(c),BEv,A:Young Allies . . 2,200.00
23 SSh(c),BEv,Human Torch . . 2,200.00
24 MSy(c),BEv,A:Namora,
bondage cover . . . . . . . . . 2,200.00
25 MSy(c),HK,B:The Blonde
Phantom, A:Namora,
bondage(c) . . . . . . . . . . . . 2,400.00
26 BEv,SSh,A:Namora . . . . . . 2,000.00
27 DRi(c),BEv,A:Namora . . . . 2,000.00
28 DRi(c),BEv,A:Namora . . . . 2,000.00
29 BEv,SSh,A:Namora,Human
Torch . . . . . . . . . . . . . . . . 2,000.00
30 DRi(c),BEv,Slaves Under
the Sea . . . . . . . . . . . . . . 2,000.00
31 BEv,The Man Who Grew,
A:Capt. America,E:Blonde
Phantom . . . . . . . . . . . . . 2,000.00
32 BEv,O:Sub-Mariner . . . . . . 2,500.00
33 BEv,O:Sub-Mariner,A:Human
Torch,B:Namora . . . . . . . . 2,200.00
34 BEv,A:Human Torch,bondage
cover . . . . . . . . . . . . . . . . 2,000.00
35 BEv,A:Human Torch . . . . . . 2,000.00
36 BEv,Hidden World . . . . . . . 2,000.00
37 JMn(c),BEv . . . . . . . . . . . . 2,000.00
38 SSh(c),BEv,JMn,
O:Sub-Mariner . . . . . . . . . 2,300.00
39 JMn(c),BEv,Commie
Frogman . . . . . . . . . . . . . 2,000.00
40 JMn(c),BEv,Secret Tunnel . . 2,000.00
41 JMn(c),BEv,A:Namora . . . . 2,000.00
42 BEv,Oct., 1955 . . . . . . . . . . 2,400.00

## SUGAR AND SPIKE
### DC Comics, April-May, 1956
1 SM . . . . . . . . . . . . . . . . . . 3,000.00
2 SM . . . . . . . . . . . . . . . . . . 1,000.00
3 SM . . . . . . . . . . . . . . . . . . . 750.00
4 SM . . . . . . . . . . . . . . . . . . . 750.00
5 SM . . . . . . . . . . . . . . . . . . . 750.00
6 thru 10 SM . . . . . . . . . . . . @450.00
11 thru 20 SM . . . . . . . . . . . . @350.00
21 thru 29 SM . . . . . . . . . . . @250.00
30 SM,A:Scribbly . . . . . . . . . . . 250.00

## SUGAR BOWL COMICS
### Famous Funnies,
### May, 1948
1 ATh,ATh(c),The Newest in
Teen Age! . . . . . . . . . . . . . . 175.00
2 . . . . . . . . . . . . . . . . . . . . . . 100.00
3 ATh . . . . . . . . . . . . . . . . . . . 125.00
4 . . . . . . . . . . . . . . . . . . . . . . . 75.00
5 Jan., 1949 . . . . . . . . . . . . . . . 75.00

## SUN FUN KOMIKS
### Sun Publications, 1939
1 F:Spineless Sam the
Sweetheart . . . . . . . . . . . . . 600.00

## SUN GIRL
### Marvel Comics, 1948
1 Miss America . . . . . . . . . . . 2,100.00
2 Blonde Phantom . . . . . . . . . 1,450.00
3 . . . . . . . . . . . . . . . . . . . . . 1,450.00

## SUNNY, AMERICA'S SWEETHEART
### Fox Features Syndicate,
### Dec., 1947
11 AF,AF(c) . . . . . . . . . . . . . . 2,000.00
12 AF,AF(c) . . . . . . . . . . . . . . 1,500.00
13 AF,AF(c) . . . . . . . . . . . . . . 1,500.00
14 AF,AF(c) . . . . . . . . . . . . . . 1,500.00

## SUNSET CARSON
### Charlton Comics,
### Feb., 1951–Aug., 1951
1 Painted, Ph(c);Wyoming
Mail . . . . . . . . . . . . . . . . . 1,200.00
2 Kit Carson-Pioneer . . . . . . . . 800.00
3 . . . . . . . . . . . . . . . . . . . . . . 700.00
4 Panhandle Trouble . . . . . . . . . 700.00

## SUPER BOOK OF COMICS
### Western Publishing Co., 1943
N# Dick Tracy . . . . . . . . . . . . . 700.00
1 Dick Tracy, Smuggling . . . . . . 700.00
1a Smilin' Jack . . . . . . . . . . . . . 400.00
2 Smitty,Magic Morro . . . . . . . . 400.00
3 Capt. Midnight . . . . . . . . . . . 700.00
3a Moon Mullins . . . . . . . . . . . 300.00
4 Red Ryder,Magic Morro . . . . . 400.00
4a Smitty . . . . . . . . . . . . . . . . . 300.00

St

Super-Book of Comics 2nd Series #13
© Western Publishing

Superboy #20
© DC Comics

Superboy #42
© DC Comics

5 Don Winslow,Magic Morro . . . . 400.00
5a DonWinslow,StratosphereJim 400.00
5a Terry & the Pirates . . . . . . . . 500.00
6 Don Winslow . . . . . . . . . . . . . . 500.00
6a King of the Royal Mounties . . 500.00
7 Little Orphan Annie . . . . . . . . . 300.00
7a Dick Tracy . . . . . . . . . . . . . . . 600.00
8 Dick Tracy . . . . . . . . . . . . . . . . 500.00
8a Dan Dunn. . . . . . . . . . . . . . . . 300.00
9 Terry & the Pirates . . . . . . . . . . 500.00
10 Red Ryder, Magic Morro . . . . . 300.00

## SUPER-BOOK OF COMICS

**Western Publishing Co., 1944**

1 Dick Tracy (Omar) . . . . . . . . . . 350.00
1 Dick Tracy (Hancock) . . . . . . . 250.00
2 Bugs Bunny (Omar) . . . . . . . . . 250.00
2 Bugs Bunny (Hancock) . . . . . . 250.00
3 Terry & the Pirates (Omar) . 300.00
3 Terry & the Pirates (Hancock) . 300.00
4 Andy Panda (Omar). . . . . . . . . 200.00
4 Andy Panda (Hancock) . . . . . . 200.00
5 Smokey Stover (Omar) . . . . . . 200.00
5 Smokey Stover (Hancock) . . . 200.00
6 Porky Pig (Omar). . . . . . . . . . . 250.00
6 Porky Pig (Hancock) . . . . . . . . 225.00
7 Smilin' Jack (Omar) . . . . . . . . . 200.00
7 Smilin' Jack (Hancock) . . . . . . 200.00
8 Oswald the Rabbit (Omar). . . . 200.00
8 Oswald the Rabbit (Hancock) . 175.00
9 Alley Oop (Omar) . . . . . . . . . . 300.00
9 Alley Oop (Hancock) . . . . . . . . 275.00
10 Elmer Fudd (Omar). . . . . . . . . 200.00
10 Elmer Fudd (Hancock) . . . . . . 175.00
11 Little Orphan Annie (Omar). . . 200.00
11 Little Orphan Amnie (Hancock)200.00
12 Woody Woodpecker (Omar). . 225.00
12 WoodyWoodpecker(Hancock) 200.00
13 Dick Tracy (Omar). . . . . . . . . 300.00
13 Dick Tracy (Hancock) . . . . . . 275.00
14 Bugs Bunny (Omar) . . . . . . . . 300.00
14 Bugs Bunny (Hanock). . . . . . . 250.00
15 Andy Panda (Omar) . . . . . . . . 200.00
15 Andy Panda (Hancock) . . . . . . 175.00
16 Terry & the Pirates (Omar) . . . 300.00
16 Terry & the Pirates (Hancock) . 275.00
17 Smokey Stover (Omar) . . . . . . 200.00
17 Smokey Stover (Hancock) . . . 175.00
18 Porky Pig (Omar) . . . . . . . . . . 250.00
18 Smokey Stover (Hancock) . . . 175.00
19 Smilin' Jack (Omar) . . . . . . . . 175.00
N# Smilin' Jack (Hancock). . . . . . 150.00
20 Oswald the Rabbit (Omar) . . . 150.00

N# Oswald the Rabbit (Hancock) 125.00
21 Gasoline Alley (Omar). . . . . . . 150.00
N# Gasoline Alley (Hancock). . . . 125.00
22 Elmer Fudd (Omar). . . . . . . . . 150.00
N# Elmer Fudd (Hancock) . . . . . . 135.00
23 Little Orphan Annie (Omar). . 150.00
N# Little Orphan Annie (Hancock) 135.00
24 Woody Woodpecker (Omar) . . 125.00
N# WoodyWoodpecker(Hancock) 100.00
25 Dick Tracy (Omar). . . . . . . . . . 175.00
N# Dick Tracy (Hancock) . . . . . . 150.00
26 Bugs Bunny (Omar) . . . . . . . . 150.00
N# Bugs Bunny (Hancock) . . . . . 125.00
27 Andy Panda (Omar) . . . . . . . . 125.00
27 Andy Panda (Hancock) . . . . . . 100.00
28 Terry & the Pirates (Omar) . . . 250.00
28 Terry & the Pirates (Hancock). 225.00
29 Smokey Stover (Omar) . . . . . . 100.00
29 Smokey Stover (Hancock) . . . 100.00
30 Porky Pig (Omar) . . . . . . . . . . 150.00
30 Porky Pig (Hancock). . . . . . . . 125.00
N# Bugs Bunny (Hancock) . . . . . 125.00

## SUPERBOY

**DC Comics, 1949**

1 Superman (c) . . . . . . . . . . . 20,000.00
2 Superboy Day. . . . . . . . . . . 5,000.00
3 . . . . . . . . . . . . . . . . . . . . . . 3,700.00
4 The Oracle of Smallville . . 3,200.00
5 Superboy meets Supergirl,
  Pre-Adventure #252 . . . . . . 3,200.00
6 I:Humpty Dumpty,the Hobby
  Robber . . . . . . . . . . . . . . . 2,700.00
7 WB,V:Humpty Dumpty . . . . . 2,700.00
8 CS,I:Superbaby,V:Humpty
  Dumpty . . . . . . . . . . . . . . . 2,500.00
9 V:Humpty Dumpty. . . . . . . . 2,500.00
10 CS,I:Lana Lang . . . . . . . . . 2,500.00
11 CS,2nd Lang,V:Humpty
  Dumpty . . . . . . . . . . . . . . . 2,200.00
12 CS,The Heroes Club . . . . . 2,000.00
13 CS,Scout of Smallville . . . . 2,000.00
14 CS,I:Marsboy . . . . . . . . . . . 2,000.00
15 CS,A:Superman . . . . . . . . 2,200.00
16 CS,A:Marsboy . . . . . . . . . . 2,000.00
17 CS,Superboy's Double . . . . 2,000.00
18 CS,Lana Lang-Hollywood
  Star . . . . . . . . . . . . . . . . . . 2,000.00
19 CS,The Death of Young
  Clark Kent. . . . . . . . . . . . . 2,000.00
20 CS,The Ghost that Haunted
  Smallville . . . . . . . . . . . . . . 2,000.00
21 CS,Lana Lang-Magician . . . 1,000.00
22 CS,The New Clark Kent . . . 1,000.00
23 CS,The Super Superboy . . . 1,000.00

24 CS,The Super Fat Boy of
  Steel . . . . . . . . . . . . . . . . . 1,000.00
25 CS,Cinderella of Smallville . 1,000.00
26 CS,A:Superbaby . . . . . . . . 1,000.00
27 CS,Clark Kent-Runaway. . . . 1,000.00
28 CS,The Man Who Defeated
  Superboy . . . . . . . . . . . . . . 1,000.00
29 CS,The Puppet Superboy . . 1,000.00
30 CS,I:Tommy Tuttle . . . . . . . . 800.00
31 CS,The Amazing Elephant
  Boy From Smallville. . . . . . . 800.00
32 CS,His Majesty King
  Superboy . . . . . . . . . . . . . . . 800.00
33 CS,The Crazy Costumes of
  the Boy of Steel . . . . . . . . . . 800.00
34 CS,Hep Cats o/Smallville . . . . 800.00
35 CS,The Five Superboys . . . . . 800.00
36 . . . . . . . . . . . . . . . . . . . . . . . 800.00
37 CS,I:Thaddeus Lang. . . . . . . . 800.00
38 CS,Public Chimp #1 . . . . . . . . 800.00
39 CS,Boy w/Superboy Powers. . 800.00
40 CS,The Magic Necklace . . . . . 700.00
41 CS,Superboy Meets
  Superbrave . . . . . . . . . . . . . . 700.00
42 CS,Gaucho of Smallville. . . . . 700.00
43 CS,Super-Farmer of
  Smallville . . . . . . . . . . . . . . . . 700.00
44 The Amazing Adventure of
  Superboy's Costume. . . . . . . 700.00
45 A Trap For Superboy. . . . . . . . 700.00
46 The Battle of Fort Smallville . . 700.00
47 CS,A:Superman . . . . . . . . . . . 700.00
48 CS,Boy Without Super-Suit . . 700.00
49 I:Metallo (Jor-El's Robot) . . . 700.00
50 The Super-Giant of
  Smallville . . . . . . . . . . . . . . . . 700.00
51 I:Krypto . . . . . . . . . . . . . . . . . 500.00
52 CS,The Powerboy from
  Earth . . . . . . . . . . . . . . . . . . . 500.00
53 CS,A:Superman . . . . . . . . . . . 500.00
54 CS,The Silent Superboy . . . . . 500.00
55 CS,A:Jimmy Olson . . . . . . . . . 500.00
56 CS,A:Krypto . . . . . . . . . . . . . . 500.00
57 CS,One-Man Baseball Team . 500.00
58 CS,The Great Kryptonite
  Mystery . . . . . . . . . . . . . . . . . 500.00
59 CS,A:Superbaby . . . . . . . . . . . 500.00
60 The 100,000 Cowboy . . . . . . . 500.00
61 The School For Superboys. . . 400.00
62 I:Gloria Kent . . . . . . . . . . . . . . 400.00
63 CS,The Two Boys of Steel . . . 400.00
64 CS,A:Krypto . . . . . . . . . . . . . . 400.00
65 Superboy's Moonlight Spell . . 400.00
66 The Family with X-Ray Eyes . 400.00
67 I:Klax-Ar . . . . . . . . . . . . . . . . . 400.00
68 O&I:Bizarro . . . . . . . . . . . . . 1,400.00

**Su**

Superboy #77
© DC Comics

Super Comics #10
© Dell Publishing Co.

Super Comics #54
© Dell Publishing Co.

69 How Superboy Learned
  To Fly . . . . . . . . . . . . . . . . 300.00
70 O:Superboy's Glasses . . . . . . 300.00
71 A:Superbaby . . . . . . . . . . . . . 300.00
72 The Flying Girl of Smallville . . 300.00
73 CS,A:Superbaby . . . . . . . . . . 300.00
74 A:Jor-El & Lara . . . . . . . . . . . 300.00
75 A:Superbaby . . . . . . . . . . . . . 300.00
76 I:Super Monkey. . . . . . . . . . . 300.00
77 Superboy's Best Friend . . . . . 300.00
78 O:Mr.Mzyzptlk . . . . . . . . . . . 500.00
79 A:Jar-El & Lara . . . . . . . . . . . 300.00
80 Superboy meets Supergirl . . . 400.00
81 The Weakling From Earth. . . . 275.00
82 A:Bizarro Krypto . . . . . . . . . . 275.00
83 I:Kryptonite Kid . . . . . . . . . . . 275.00
84 A:William Tell. . . . . . . . . . . . . 275.00
85 Secret of Mighty Boy . . . . . . 275.00
86 I:PeteRoss,A:Legion . . . . . . . 500.00
87 I:Scarlet Jungle of Krypton . . 275.00
88 The Invader from Earth. . . . . . 275.00
89 I:Mon-El. . . . . . . . . . . . . . . . . 275.00
90 A:Pete Ross . . . . . . . . . . . . . 150.00
91 CS,Superboy in Civil War . . . . 150.00
92 CS,I:Destructo,A:Lex Luthor . . 150.00
93 A:Legion . . . . . . . . . . . . . . . . 150.00
94 I:Superboy Revenge Squad,
  A:Pete Ross . . . . . . . . . . . . 150.00
95 Imaginary Story,The Super
  Family From Krypton . . . . . . . 150.00
96 A:Pete Ross,Lex Luther . . . . . 150.00
97 Krypto Story . . . . . . . . . . . . . 150.00
98 Legion,I&O:Ultraboy . . . . . . . 150.00
99 O: The Kryptonite Kid . . . . . . 100.00
100 I:Phantom Zone . . . . . . . . . . 275.00
101 The Handsome Hound
  of Steel . . . . . . . . . . . . . . . 125.00
102 O:Scarlet Jungle of Krypton . 125.00
103 CS,A:King Arthur,Jesse James
  Red Kryptonite. . . . . . . . . . . 125.00
104 O:Phantom Zone . . . . . . . . . 125.00
105 CS,The Simpleton of Steel . . 125.00
106 CS,A:Brainiac . . . . . . . . . . . . 125.00
107 CS,I:Superboy Club of
  Smallville . . . . . . . . . . . . . . 150.00
108 The Kent's First Super Son . . 125.00
109 The Super Youth of Bronze . 125.00
110 A:Jor-El . . . . . . . . . . . . . . . . 125.00

## SUPER BRAT
### Toby Press, 1954
1 . . . . . . . . . . . . . . . . . . . . . . . . 125.00
2 . . . . . . . . . . . . . . . . . . . . . . . . 100.00
3 . . . . . . . . . . . . . . . . . . . . . . . . 100.00
4 Li'l Teevy . . . . . . . . . . . . . . . . 100.00

## SUPER CAT
### Four Star Comic Corp.
### (Ajax Comics/Farrell
### Publ.), 1957
1 . . . . . . . . . . . . . . . . . . . . . . . . 125.00
2 thru 4 . . . . . . . . . . . . . . . . @100.00

## SUPER CIRCUS
### Cross Publishing Co.,
### Jan., 1951
1 Partial Ph(c) . . . . . . . . . . . . . 150.00
2 . . . . . . . . . . . . . . . . . . . . . . . . 125.00
3 . . . . . . . . . . . . . . . . . . . . . . . . 100.00
4 . . . . . . . . . . . . . . . . . . . . . . . . 100.00
5 1951 . . . . . . . . . . . . . . . . . . . . 100.00

## SUPER COMICS
### Dell Publishing Co.,
### May, 1938
1 Dick Tracy and the
  Pirates,Smilin'Jack,Smokey
  Stover,Orphan Annie,etc. . . 3,200.00
2 . . . . . . . . . . . . . . . . . . . . . 1,400.00
3 . . . . . . . . . . . . . . . . . . . . . 1,200.00
4 . . . . . . . . . . . . . . . . . . . . . 1,100.00
5 Gumps(c) . . . . . . . . . . . . . 1,000.00
6 . . . . . . . . . . . . . . . . . . . . . . 750.00
7 Smokey Stover(c) . . . . . . . . . 750.00
8 Dick Tracy(c) . . . . . . . . . . . . . 750.00
9 . . . . . . . . . . . . . . . . . . . . . . 750.00
10 Dick Tracy(c). . . . . . . . . . . . . 750.00
11 . . . . . . . . . . . . . . . . . . . . . . 550.00
12 . . . . . . . . . . . . . . . . . . . . . . 550.00
13 . . . . . . . . . . . . . . . . . . . . . . 550.00
14 . . . . . . . . . . . . . . . . . . . . . . 550.00
15 . . . . . . . . . . . . . . . . . . . . . . 550.00
16 Terry & the Pirates . . . . . . . . 500.00
17 Dick Tracy(c) . . . . . . . . . . . . 500.00
18 . . . . . . . . . . . . . . . . . . . . . . 500.00
19 . . . . . . . . . . . . . . . . . . . . . . 500.00
20 Smilin'Jack(c) . . . . . . . . . . . 525.00
21 B:Magic Morro . . . . . . . . . . . 400.00
22 Magic Morro(c) . . . . . . . . . . 450.00
23 all star(c) . . . . . . . . . . . . . . . 400.00
24 Dick Tracy(c) . . . . . . . . . . . . 450.00
25 Magic Morro(c) . . . . . . . . . . 400.00
26 . . . . . . . . . . . . . . . . . . . . . . 400.00
27 Magic Morro(c) . . . . . . . . . . 400.00
28 Jim Ellis(c) . . . . . . . . . . . . . . 450.00
29 Smilin'Jack(c) . . . . . . . . . . . 400.00
30 inc.The Sea Hawk. . . . . . . . . 450.00
31 Dick Tracy(c) . . . . . . . . . . . . 350.00
32 Smilin' Jack(c). . . . . . . . . . . . 365.00

33 Jim Ellis(c) . . . . . . . . . . . . . . 350.00
34 Magic Morro(c) . . . . . . . . . . 350.00
35 thru 40 Dick Tracy(c). . . . . @350.00
41 B:Lightning Jim . . . . . . . . . . . 300.00
42 thru 50 Dick Tracy(c). . . . . @300.00
51 thru 54 Dick Tracy(c). . . . . @250.00
55 . . . . . . . . . . . . . . . . . . . . . . 250.00
56 . . . . . . . . . . . . . . . . . . . . . . 250.00
57 Dick Tracy(c). . . . . . . . . . . . . 250.00
58 Smitty(c) . . . . . . . . . . . . . . . 250.00
59 . . . . . . . . . . . . . . . . . . . . . . 250.00
60 Dick Tracy(c). . . . . . . . . . . . . 275.00
61 . . . . . . . . . . . . . . . . . . . . . . 235.00
62 Flag(c). . . . . . . . . . . . . . . . . 235.00
63 Dick Tracy(c) . . . . . . . . . . . . 235.00
64 Smitty(c) . . . . . . . . . . . . . . . 225.00
65 Dick Tracy(c) . . . . . . . . . . . . 235.00
66 Dick Tracy(c) . . . . . . . . . . . . 235.00
67 Christmas(c) . . . . . . . . . . . . . 235.00
68 Dick Tracy(c) . . . . . . . . . . . . 235.00
69 Dick Tracy(c) . . . . . . . . . . . . 235.00
70 Dick Tracy(c) . . . . . . . . . . . . 235.00
71 Dick Tracy(c) . . . . . . . . . . . . 200.00
72 Dick Tracy(c) . . . . . . . . . . . . 200.00
73 Smitty(c) . . . . . . . . . . . . . . . 200.00
74 War Bond(c) . . . . . . . . . . . . . 200.00
75 Dick Tracy(c) . . . . . . . . . . . . 200.00
76 Dick Tracy(c) . . . . . . . . . . . . 200.00
77 Dick Tracy(c) . . . . . . . . . . . . 200.00
78 Smitty(c) . . . . . . . . . . . . . . . 150.00
79 Dick Tracy(c) . . . . . . . . . . . . 150.00
80 Smitty(c) . . . . . . . . . . . . . . . 150.00
81 Dick Tracy(c) . . . . . . . . . . . . 150.00
82 Dick Tracy(c) . . . . . . . . . . . . 150.00
83 Smitty(c) . . . . . . . . . . . . . . . 135.00
84 Dick Tracy(c) . . . . . . . . . . . . 150.00
85 Smitty(c) . . . . . . . . . . . . . . . 135.00
86 All on cover . . . . . . . . . . . . . 150.00
87 All on cover . . . . . . . . . . . . . 150.00
88 Dick Tracy(c) . . . . . . . . . . . . 150.00
89 Smitty(c) . . . . . . . . . . . . . . . 135.00
90 Dick Tracy(c) . . . . . . . . . . . . 150.00
91 Smitty(c) . . . . . . . . . . . . . . . 135.00
92 Dick Tracy(c) . . . . . . . . . . . . 150.00
93 Dick Tracy(c) . . . . . . . . . . . . 150.00
94 Dick Tracy(c) . . . . . . . . . . . . 150.00
95 thru 99 . . . . . . . . . . . . . . . @135.00
100 . . . . . . . . . . . . . . . . . . . . . . 150.00
101 thru 115 . . . . . . . . . . . . . @150.00
116 Smokey Stover(c) . . . . . . . . 100.00
117 Gasoline Alley(c) . . . . . . . . . 100.00
118 Smokey Stover(c) . . . . . . . . 100.00
119 Terry and the Pirates(c). . . . 110.00
120 . . . . . . . . . . . . . . . . . . . . . . 100.00
121 . . . . . . . . . . . . . . . . . . . . . . 100.00

*Super Duck Comics #22*
*© Archie Publications*

*Super Magician Comics Vol. 3 #12*
*© Street & Smith Publications*

*Superman #14*
*© DC Comics*

## SUPER-DOOPER COMICS

**Able Manufacturing Co., 1946**
1 A:Gangbuster . . . . . . . . . . . . . 250.00
2 . . . . . . . . . . . . . . . . . . . . . . . . . 200.00
3 & 4 . . . . . . . . . . . . . . . . . . . . @150.00
5 A:Captain Freedom,Shock
    Gibson . . . . . . . . . . . . . . . . . 150.00
6 & 7 same . . . . . . . . . . . . . . . @150.00
8 A:Shock Gibson, 1946 . . . . . . 150.00

## SUPER DUCK COMICS

**MLJ Magazines/Close-Up (Archie Publ.), Autumn, 1944**
1 O:Super Duck, Hitler . . . . . . . . 750.00
2 . . . . . . . . . . . . . . . . . . . . . . . . . 300.00
3 I:Mr. Monster . . . . . . . . . . . . . 250.00
4 & 5 . . . . . . . . . . . . . . . . . . . . @225.00
6 thru 10 . . . . . . . . . . . . . . . . . @200.00
11 thru 20 . . . . . . . . . . . . . . . . @150.00
21 thru 40 . . . . . . . . . . . . . . . . @125.00
41 thru 60 . . . . . . . . . . . . . . . . @100.00
61 thru 94 . . . . . . . . . . . . . . . . @100.00

## SUPER DUPER COMICS

**F.E. Howard Publications, 1947**
3 Mr Monster 1st. . . . . . . . . . . . 175.00

## SUPER FUN

**Gilmor Magazines, 1956**
1 Puzzles & comics . . . . . . . . . 100.00

## SUPER FUNNIES

**Superior Comics Publishers, March, 1954**
1 Dopey Duck . . . . . . . . . . . . . . 500.00
2 Out of the Booby-Hatch . . . . . 200.00
**Becomes:**

## SUPER WESTERN FUNNIES

**1954**
3 F:Phantom Ranger . . . . . . . . . 100.00
4 F:Phantom Ranger,Sept., 1954 100.00

## SUPERIOR STORIES

**Nesbit Publishing Co., 1955**
1 Wells-The Invisible Man . . . . . 275.00
2 Ingrahams-Pirate of the Gulf . . 125.00
3 Clark-Wreck of Grosvenor . . . . 125.00
4 O'Henry-Texas Rangers . . . . . 125.00

## SUPER MAGICIAN COMICS

**Street & Smith Publ., May, 1941**
1 B:The Mysterious Blackstone . 800.00
2 V:Wild Tribes of Africa . . . . . . 500.00
3 V:Oriental Wizard . . . . . . . . . . 500.00
4 V:Quetzal Wizard,O:Transo . . . 475.00
5 A:The Moylan Sisters . . . . . . . 475.00
6 JaB,JaB(c),The Eddie
    Cantor story . . . . . . . . . . . . . 475.00
7 In the House of Skulls . . . . . . 500.00
8 A:Abbott & Costello . . . . . . . . 500.00
9 V:Duneen the Man-Ape . . . . . 500.00
10 V:Pirates o/t Sargasso Sea . . 500.00
11 JaB(c),V:Fire Wizards . . . . . . 500.00
12 V:Baal . . . . . . . . . . . . . . . . . . 500.00
2-1 A:The Shadow . . . . . . . . . . 500.00
2-2 Temple of the 10,000 Idols . 250.00
2-3 Optical Illusion on (c)-
    turn Jap into Monkey . . . . . . 250.00
2-4 V:Cannibal Killers . . . . . . . . 250.00
2-5 V:The Pygmies of Lemuriai . 250.00
2-6 V:Pirates & Indians . . . . . . . 250.00
2-7 Can Blackstone Catch the
    Cannonball? . . . . . . . . . . . . . 250.00
2-8 V:Marabout,B:Red Dragon . 250.00
2-9 . . . . . . . . . . . . . . . . . . . . . . . 250.00
2-10 Pearl Dives Swallowed By
    Sea Demons . . . . . . . . . . . . . 250.00
2-11 Blackstone Invades
    Pelican Islands . . . . . . . . . . . 250.00
2-12 V:Bubbles of Death . . . . . . 250.00
3-1 . . . . . . . . . . . . . . . . . . . . . . . 275.00
3-2 Bondage(c),Midsummers
    Eve . . . . . . . . . . . . . . . . . . . . 250.00
3-3 The Enchanted Garden . . . . 250.00
3-4 Fabulous Aztec Treasure . . . 250.00
3-5 A:Buffalo Bill . . . . . . . . . . . . 250.00
3-6 Magic Tricks to Mystify . . . . 250.00
3-7 V:Guy Fawkes . . . . . . . . . . . 250.00
3-8 V:Hindu Spook Maker . . . . . 250.00
3-9 . . . . . . . . . . . . . . . . . . . . . . . 250.00
3-10 V:The Water Wizards . . . . . 250.00
3-11 V:The Green Goliath . . . . . . 250.00
3-12 Lady in White . . . . . . . . . . . 250.00
4-1 Cannibal of Crime . . . . . . . . 225.00
4-2 The Devil's Castle . . . . . . . . 225.00
4-3 V:Demons of Golden River . . 225.00
4-4 V:Dr. Zero . . . . . . . . . . . . . . . 225.00
4-5 Bondage(c) . . . . . . . . . . . . . 225.00
4-6 V:A Terror Gang . . . . . . . . . . 225.00
4-7 . . . . . . . . . . . . . . . . . . . . . . . 225.00
4-8 Mystery of the
    Disappearing Horse . . . . . . . 225.00
4-9 A Floating Light? . . . . . . . . . 225.00

4-10 Levitation . . . . . . . . . . . . . . 225.00
4-11 Lost, Strange Land
    of Shangri . . . . . . . . . . . . . . . 225.00
4-12 I:Nigel Elliman . . . . . . . . . . 225.00
5-1 V:Voodoo Wizards of the
    Everglades,Bondage (c) . . . . 225.00
5-2 Treasure of the Florida
    Keys; Bondage (c) . . . . . . . . . 225.00
5-3 Elliman Battles Triple Crime . 225.00
5-4 Can A Human Being Really
    Become Invisible . . . . . . . . . . 225.00
5-5 Mystery of the Twin Pools . . 225.00
5-6 A:Houdini . . . . . . . . . . . . . . . 225.00
5-7 F:Red Dragon . . . . . . . . . . . . 500.00
5-8 F:Red Dragon,
    Feb.–March, 1947 . . . . . . . . . 500.00

## SUPERMAN

**DC Comics, 1939**
1 JoS,O:Superman,reprints Action
    Comics #1–#4 . . . . . . . . 280,000.00
2 JoS,I:George Taylor . . . . . . 18,000.00
3 JoS,V:Superintendent
    Lyman . . . . . . . . . . . . . . . 11,000.00
4 JoS,V:Lex Luthor . . . . . . . . 11,000.00
5 JoS,V:Lex Luthor . . . . . . . . . 8,000.00
6 JoS,V:Brute' Bashby . . . . . . . 4,500.00
7 JoS,I:Perry White . . . . . . . . . 3,800.00
8 JoS,V:Jackal . . . . . . . . . . . . . 3,600.00
9 JoS,V:Joe Gatson . . . . . . . . . 3,600.00
10 JoS,V:Lex Luthor . . . . . . . . . 3,500.00
11 JoS,V:Rolf Zimba . . . . . . . . . 2,800.00
12 JoS,V:Lex Luthor . . . . . . . . . 2,800.00
13 JoS,I:Jimmy Olsen,V:Lex
    Luthor,The Archer . . . . . . . . 2,800.00
14 JoS,I:Lightning Master . . . . . 4,500.00
15 JoS,V:The Evolution King . . 2,800.00
16 JoS,V:Mr. Sinus . . . . . . . . . . 2,300.00
17 JoS,V:Lex Luthor,Lois Lane
    first suspects Clark
    is Superman . . . . . . . . . . . . 2,300.00
18 JoS,V:Lex Luthor . . . . . . . . . 2,200.00
19 JoS,V:Funnyface,
    1st Imaginary story . . . . . . . 2,200.00
20 JoS,V:Puzzler,Leopard . . . . 2,200.00
21 JoS,V:Sir Gauntlet . . . . . . . . 1,800.00
22 JoS,V:Prankster . . . . . . . . . . 1,800.00
23 JoS,Propaganda story . . . . . 1,800.00
24 V:Cobra King . . . . . . . . . . . . 2,500.00
25 Propaganda story . . . . . . . . 1,700.00
26 I:J.Wilbur Wolfingham,
    A:Mercury . . . . . . . . . . . . . . 1,700.00
27 V:Toyman . . . . . . . . . . . . . . . 1,700.00
28 V:J.Wilbur Wolfingham,
    A:Hercules . . . . . . . . . . . . . . 1,700.00

# STANDARD GUIDE TO GOLDEN AGE COMICS

*Superman #36*
© DC Comics

*Superman #95*
© DC Comics

*Superman #130*
© DC Comics

29 V:Prankster . . . . . . . . . . . . . 1,700.00
30 I&O:Mr. Mxyztplk . . . . . . . . 3,000.00
31 V:Lex Luthor . . . . . . . . . . . . 1,400.00
32 V:Toyman . . . . . . . . . . . . . . 1,400.00
33 V:Mr. Mxyztplk . . . . . . . . . . 1,400.00
34 V:Lex Luthor . . . . . . . . . . . . 1,400.00
35 V:J.Wilbur Wolfingham . . . . 1,400.00
36 V:Mr. Mxyztplk . . . . . . . . . . 1,400.00
37 V:Prankster,A:Sinbad . . . . . 1,400.00
38 V:Lex Luthor . . . . . . . . . . . . 1,400.00
39 V:J.Wilbur Wolfingham . . . . 1,400.00
40 V:Mr. Mxyztplk,A:Susie
   Thompkins . . . . . . . . . . . . . 1,400.00
41 V:Prankster . . . . . . . . . . . . . 1,100.00
42 V:J.Wilbur Wolfingham . . . . 1,100.00
43 V:Lex Luthor . . . . . . . . . . . . 1,100.00
44 V:Toyman,A:Shakespeare . . 1,100.00
45 A:Hocus & Pocus,Lois Lane
   as Superwoman . . . . . . . . . 1,100.00
46 V:Mr. Mxyztplk,Lex Luthor,
   Superboy flashback . . . . . . 1,100.00
47 V:Toyman . . . . . . . . . . . . . . 1,100.00
48 V:Lex Luthor . . . . . . . . . . . . 1,100.00
49 V:Toyman . . . . . . . . . . . . . . 1,100.00
50 V:Prankster . . . . . . . . . . . . . 1,100.00
51 V:Mr. Mxyztplk . . . . . . . . . . . 900.00
52 V:Prankster . . . . . . . . . . . . . . 900.00
53 WB,O:Superman . . . . . . . . . 3,800.00
54 V:Wrecker . . . . . . . . . . . . . . . 900.00
55 V:Prankster . . . . . . . . . . . . . . 900.00
56 V:Prankster . . . . . . . . . . . . . . 900.00
57 V:Lex Luthor . . . . . . . . . . . . . 900.00
58 V:Tiny Trix . . . . . . . . . . . . . . . 900.00
59 V:Mr.Mxyzptlk . . . . . . . . . . . . 900.00
60 V:Toyman . . . . . . . . . . . . . . . 900.00
61 I:Kryptonite,V:Prankster . . . 1,800.00
62 V:Mr.Mxyzptlk,A:Orson
   Welles . . . . . . . . . . . . . . . . . 900.00
63 V:Toyman . . . . . . . . . . . . . . . 900.00
64 V:Prankster . . . . . . . . . . . . . . 900.00
65 V:Mala,Kizo and U-Ban . . . . 900.00
66 V:Prankster . . . . . . . . . . . . . . 900.00
67 A:Perry Como,I:Brane
   Taylor . . . . . . . . . . . . . . . . . . 900.00
68 V:Lex Luthor . . . . . . . . . . . . . 900.00
69 V:Prankster,A:Inspector
   Erskine Hawkins . . . . . . . . . 900.00
70 V:Prankster . . . . . . . . . . . . . . 900.00
71 V:Lex Luthor . . . . . . . . . . . . . 800.00
72 V:Prankster . . . . . . . . . . . . . . 800.00
72a giveaway . . . . . . . . . . . . . 1,000.00
73 Flashback story . . . . . . . . . . . 800.00
74 V:Lex Luthor . . . . . . . . . . . . . 800.00
75 V:Prankster . . . . . . . . . . . . . . 800.00

76 A:Batman, Superman &
   Batman reveal each other's
   identities . . . . . . . . . . . . . . 2,200.00
77 A:Pocahontas . . . . . . . . . . . . 750.00
78 V:Kryptonian snagriff,
   A:Lana Lang . . . . . . . . . . . . . 750.00
79 V:Lex Luthor,A:Inspector
   Erskine Hawkins . . . . . . . . . 750.00
80 A:Halk Kar . . . . . . . . . . . . . . . 750.00
81 V:Lex Luthor . . . . . . . . . . . . . 750.00
82 V:Mr. Mxyzptlk . . . . . . . . . . . 650.00
83 V:The Brain . . . . . . . . . . . . . . 650.00
84 Time-travel story . . . . . . . . . . 650.00
85 V:Lex Luthor . . . . . . . . . . . . . 650.00
86 V:Mr.Mxyzptlk . . . . . . . . . . . . 650.00
87 WB,V:The Thing from
   40,000 AD . . . . . . . . . . . . . . 650.00
88 WB,V:Lex Luthor,Toyman,
   Prankster team . . . . . . . . . . . 750.00
89 V:Lex Luthor . . . . . . . . . . . . . 650.00
90 V:Lex Luthor . . . . . . . . . . . . . 700.00
91 The Superman Stamp . . . . . . 650.00
92 Goes back to 12th Century
   England . . . . . . . . . . . . . . . . 650.00
93 V:The Thinker . . . . . . . . . . . . 650.00
94 Clark Kent's Hillbilly Bride . . . 650.00
95 A:Susie Thompkins . . . . . . . . 650.00
96 V:Mr. Mxyzptlk . . . . . . . . . . . 475.00
97 Superboy's Last Day In
   Smallville . . . . . . . . . . . . . . . 475.00
98 Clark Kent, Outlaw! . . . . . . . . 475.00
99 V:Midnite gang . . . . . . . . . . . 475.00
100 F:Superman-Substitute
   Schoolteacher . . . . . . . . . . 2,800.00
101 A:Lex Luthor . . . . . . . . . . . . . 475.00
102 I:Superman Stock
   Company . . . . . . . . . . . . . . . 475.00
103 A:Mr.Mxyzptlk . . . . . . . . . . . . 475.00
104 F:Clark Kent,Jailbird . . . . . . . 475.00
105 A:Mr.Mxyzptlk . . . . . . . . . . . . 475.00
106 A:Lex Luthor . . . . . . . . . . . . . 500.00
107 F:Superman In 30th century
   (pre-Legion) . . . . . . . . . . . . . 475.00
108 I:Perry White Jr. . . . . . . . . . . 475.00
109 I:Abner Hokum . . . . . . . . . . . 475.00
110 A:Lex Luthor . . . . . . . . . . . . . 475.00
111 Becomes Mysto the Great . . 400.00
112 A:Lex Luthor . . . . . . . . . . . . . 400.00
113 A:Jor-El . . . . . . . . . . . . . . . . . 400.00
114 V:The Great Mento . . . . . . . . 400.00
115 V:The Organizer . . . . . . . . . . 400.00
116 Return to Smallville . . . . . . . . 400.00
117 A:Lex Luthor . . . . . . . . . . . . . 400.00
118 F:Jimmy Olsen . . . . . . . . . . . 400.00
119 A:Zoll Orr . . . . . . . . . . . . . . . 400.00
120 V:Gadget Grim . . . . . . . . . . . 400.00

121 I:XL-49 (Futureman) . . . . . . . 350.00
122 In the White House . . . . . . . . 350.00
123 CS,pre-Supergirl tryout
   A:Jor-El & Lara . . . . . . . . . . . 375.00
124 F:Lois Lane . . . . . . . . . . . . . . 350.00
125 F:Superman College Story . . 350.00
126 F:Lois Lane . . . . . . . . . . . . . . 350.00
127 WB,I&O:Titano . . . . . . . . . . . 375.00
128 V:Vard & Boka . . . . . . . . . . . 350.00
129 WB,I&O:Lori Lemaris . . . . . . 375.00
130 A:Krypto,the Superdog . . . . . 350.00
131 A:Mr. Mxyzptlk . . . . . . . . . . . 275.00
132 A:Batman & Robin . . . . . . . . 275.00
133 F:Superman Joins Army . . . . 275.00
134 A:Supergirl & Krypto . . . . . . . 275.00
135 A:Lori Lemaris,Mr.Mxyzptlk . . 275.00
136 O:Discovery Kryptonite . . . . . 275.00
137 CS,I:Super-Menace . . . . . . . 275.00
138 A:Titano,Lori Lemaris . . . . . . 275.00
139 CS,O:Red Kryptonite . . . . . . 275.00
140 WB,I:Bizarro Jr,Bizarro
   Supergirl,Blue Kryptonite . . . 275.00
141 I:Lyla Lerrol,A:Jor-EL
   & Lara . . . . . . . . . . . . . . . . . 225.00
142 WB,CS,A:Al Capone . . . . . . . 225.00
143 WB,F:Bizarro meets
   Frankenstein . . . . . . . . . . . . 225.00
144 O:Superboy's 1st Public
   Appearance . . . . . . . . . . . . . 225.00
145 F:April Fool's Issue . . . . . . . . 225.00
146 F:Superman's life story . . . . . 275.00
147 CS,I:Adult Legion . . . . . . . . . 275.00
148 CS,V:Mxyzptlk . . . . . . . . . . . 225.00
149 CS:A:Luthor,C:JLA . . . . . . . . 225.00
150 CS,KS,V:Mxyzptlk . . . . . . . . 150.00
Ann.#1 I:Supergirl Rep . . . . . . 1,700.00
Ann.#2 I&O:Titano . . . . . . . . . . 650.00
Ann.#3 I:Legion . . . . . . . . . . . . 450.00
Ann.#4 O:Legion . . . . . . . . . . . 350.00
Ann.#5 A:Krypton . . . . . . . . . . . 275.00
Ann.#6 A:Legion . . . . . . . . . . . . 275.00
Ann.#7 O:Superman,Silver Anniv. 200.00
Ann.#8 F:Secret origins . . . . . . 175.00

## SUPERMAN'S BUDDY
### DC Comics, 1954
1 w/costume, giveaway . . . . . . . 1,800.00
1 w/out costume, giveaway . . . . 800.00

## SUPERMAN'S
## CHRISTMAS ADVENTURE
### DC Comics, 1940–44
1 (1940) giveaway . . . . . . . . . 6,000.00
2 (1944) giveaway . . . . . . . . . 1,500.00

All comics prices listed are for *Near Mint* condition.

Superman-Tim Store Stamp Album 9-48
© DC Comics

Superman's Girl Friend, Lois Lane #37
© DC Comics

Superman's Pal Jimmy Olsen #39
© DC Comics

## SUPERMAN AND THE GREAT CLEVELAND FIRE
**DC Comics, 1948**
1 for Hospital Fund, giveaway . . 800.00

## SUPERMAN (miniature)
**DC Comics, 1942**
1 Py-Co-Pay Tooth Powder
Give- Away . . . . . . . . . . . . 900.00
2 CS,Superman Time Capsule . . 500.00
3 CS,Duel in Space . . . . . . . . . 450.00
4 CS,Super Show in Metropolis . 450.00

## SUPERMAN-TIM STORE PAMPHLETS
**DC Comics, 1942**
Superman-Tim store Monthly Member-
ship Pamphlets, stories, games
(1942), each . . . . . . . . . . . 1,500.00
(1943), each . . . . . . . . . . . . 500.00
(1944), each . . . . . . . . . . . . 475.00
(1945), each . . . . . . . . . . . . 450.00
(1946), color(c) each . . . . . . 550.00
(1947), color(c) each . . . . . . 350.00
(1948), color(c) each . . . . . . 300.00
(1949), color(c) each . . . . . . 300.00
(1950), color(c) each . . . . . . 350.00
Superman-Tim stamp albums,
(1946) . . . . . . . . . . . . . . . . 400.00
(1947) Superman story . . . . . 500.00
(1948) . . . . . . . . . . . . . . . . 400.00

## SUPERMAN WORKBOOK
**DC Comics, 1945**
1 rep. Superman #14 . . . . . . . . 1,300.00

## SUPERMAN'S GIRL FRIEND, LOIS LANE
**DC Comics, 1958**
1 CS,KS . . . . . . . . . . . . . . . . 6,000.00
2 CS,KS . . . . . . . . . . . . . . . . 1,500.00
3 CS,KS,spanking panel . . . . . 1,000.00
4 CS,KS . . . . . . . . . . . . . . . . . 750.00
5 CS,KS . . . . . . . . . . . . . . . . . 750.00
6 CS,KS . . . . . . . . . . . . . . . . . 550.00
7 CS,KS . . . . . . . . . . . . . . . . . 550.00
8 CS,KS . . . . . . . . . . . . . . . . . 450.00
9 CS,KS, A:Pat Boone . . . . . . . 450.00
10 CS,KS . . . . . . . . . . . . . . . . 450.00
11 CS,KS . . . . . . . . . . . . . . . . 300.00
12 CS,KS . . . . . . . . . . . . . . . . 300.00

13 CS,KS . . . . . . . . . . . . . . . . 300.00
14 KS,Three Nights in the
Fortress of Solitude . . . . . . . 300.00
15 KS,I:Van-Zee . . . . . . . . . . . 300.00
16 KS, Lois' Signal-Watch . . . . . 300.00
17 KS,CS,A:Brainiac . . . . . . . . . 300.00
18 KS,A:Astounding Man. . . . . . 300.00
19 KS,Superman of the Past . . . 300.00
20 KS,A:Superman . . . . . . . . . . . 325.00
21 KS,A:Van-Zee . . . . . . . . . . . 225.00
22 KS,A:Robin Hood . . . . . . . . . 225.00
23 KS,A:Elastic Lass, Supergirl. . 225.00
24 KS,A:Van-Zee, Bizarro . . . . . 225.00
25 KS,Lois' Darkest Secret . . . . 225.00
26 KS,A:Jor-El . . . . . . . . . . . . . 225.00
27 KS,CS,A:Bizarro . . . . . . . . . . 225.00
28 KS,A:Luthor . . . . . . . . . . . . . 225.00
29 CS,A:Aquaman,Batman,Green
Arrow . . . . . . . . . . . . . . . . 225.00
30 KS,A:Krypto,Aquaman . . . . . . 150.00
31 KS,A:Lori Lemaris . . . . . . . . . 150.00
32 KS,CS,A:Bizarro . . . . . . . . . . 150.00
33 KS,CS,A:Phantom Zone,Lori
Lemaris, Mon-El . . . . . . . . . 150.00
34 KS,A:Luthor,Supergirl . . . . . . 150.00
35 KS,CS,A:Supergirl . . . . . . . . 150.00
36 KS,CS,Red Kryptonite Story. . 150.00
37 KS,CS,The Forbidden Box . . . 150.00
38 KS,CS,A:Prof.Potter,
Supergirl . . . . . . . . . . . . . . 150.00
39 KS,CS,A:Supergirl,Jor-El,
Krypto, Lori Lemaris . . . . . . 150.00
40 KS,Lois Lane, Hag! . . . . . . . . 150.00
41 KS,CS,The Devil and
Lois Lane . . . . . . . . . . . . . . 150.00
42 KS,A:Lori Lemaris . . . . . . . . . 150.00
43 KS,A:Luthor . . . . . . . . . . . . . 150.00
44 KS,A:Lori Lemaris,Braniac,
Prof. Potter . . . . . . . . . . . . 150.00
45 KS,CS,The Superman-Lois
Hit Record . . . . . . . . . . . . . 150.00
46 KS,A:Luthor . . . . . . . . . . . . . 150.00
47 KS,The Incredible Delusion . . 150.00
48 KS,A:Mr. Mxyzptlk . . . . . . . . 150.00
49 KS,The Unknown Superman . 150.00
50 KS,A:Legion . . . . . . . . . . . . 160.00

## SUPERMAN'S PAL, JIMMY OLSEN
**DC Comics, 1954**
1 CS,The Boy of 100 Faces! . . 8,500.00
2 CS,The Flying Jimmy Olsen. 2,500.00
3 CS,The Man Who Collected
Excitement . . . . . . . . . . . . 1,300.00

4 CS,King For A Day! . . . . . . . . 900.00
5 CS,The Story of Superman's
Souvenirs. . . . . . . . . . . . . . 900.00
6 CS,Kryptonite story . . . . . . . . 650.00
7 CS,The King of Marbles . . . . . 650.00
8 CS,Jimmy Olsen, Crooner. . . . 600.00
9 CS,The Missile of Steel . . . . . 600.00
10 CS,Jungle Jimmy Olsen . . . . . 600.00
11 CS,TNT.Olsen,The Champ . . . 400.00
12 CS,Invisible Jimmy Olsen. . . . 400.00
13 CS,Jimmy Olsen's
Super Issue . . . . . . . . . . . . 400.00
14 CS,The Boy Superman. . . . . . 400.00
15 CS,Jimmy Olsen,Speed
Demon. . . . . . . . . . . . . . . . 400.00
16 CS,The Boy Superman. . . . . . 400.00
17 CS,J.Olsen as cartoonist . . . . 400.00
18 CS,A:Superboy . . . . . . . . . . . 400.00
19 CS,Supermam's Kid Brother. . 400.00
20 CS,Merman of Metropolis . . . . 400.00
21 CS,The Wedding of Jimmy
Olsen . . . . . . . . . . . . . . . . 250.00
22 CS,The Super Brain of
Jimmy Olsen . . . . . . . . . . . 250.00
23 CS,The Adventure of
Private Olsen. . . . . . . . . . . 250.00
24 CS,The Gorilla Reporter . . . . . 250.00
25 CS,The Day There Was
No Jimmy Olsen . . . . . . . . . 250.00
26 CS,Bird Boy of Metropolis . . . 250.00
27 CS,The Outlaw Jimmy Olsen . 250.00
28 CS,The Boy Who Killed
Superman . . . . . . . . . . . . . 250.00
29 CS,A:Krypto . . . . . . . . . . . . . 250.00
30 CS,The Son of Superman . . . 250.00
31 CS,I:Elastic Lad . . . . . . . . . . 225.00
32 CS,A:Prof.Potter . . . . . . . . . . 200.00
33 CS,Human Flame Thrower . . . 200.00
34 CS,Superman's Pal of Steel . . 200.00
35 CS,Superman's Enemy . . . . . 200.00
36 CS,I:Lois Lane,O:Jimmy Olsen
as Superman's Pal . . . . . . . . 200.00
37 CS,O:Jimmy Olsen's SignalWatch,
A:Elastic Lad(Jimmy Olsen) . 200.00
38 CS,Olsen's Super-Supper . . . 200.00
39 CS,The Super-Lad of Space. . 200.00
40 CS,A:Supergirl,Hank White
(Perry White's son) . . . . . . . 200.00
41 CS,The Human Octopus. . . . . 150.00
42 CS,Jimmy The Genie . . . . . . 150.00
43 WB,CS,Jimmy Olsen's Private
Monster . . . . . . . . . . . . . . 150.00
44 CS,Miss Jimmy Olsen. . . . . . 150.00
45 CS,A:Kandor. . . . . . . . . . . . . 150.00
46 CS,A:Supergirl,Elastic Lad . . . 150.00
47 CS,Monsters From Earth! . . . . 150.00

**Su**

*Supermouse #1*
*© Standard Comics*

*Super-Mystery Comics #13 (Vol. 3 #1)*
*© Ace Magazines*

*Supersnipe Comics Vol. 2 #1*
*© Street & Smith Publications*

48 CS,I:Superman Emergency
  Squad . . . . . . . . . . . . . . . . 150.00
49 CS,A:Congorilla & Congo Bill . 150.00
50 CS,A:Supergirl,Krypto,Bizarro 150.00
51 CS,A:Supergirl . . . . . . . . . . 125.00
52 CS,A:Mr. Mxyzptlk,
  Miss Gzptlsnz . . . . . . . . . . 125.00
53 CS,A:Kandor,Lori Lemaris,
  Mr.Mxyztlk . . . . . . . . . . . . 125.00
54 CS,A:Elastic Lad. . . . . . . . . 125.00
55 CS,A:Aquaman,Thor. . . . . . . 125.00
56 KS,Imaginary story . . . . . . . . 125.00

## SUPERMOUSE
### Standard Comics/Pines, Dec., 1948

1 FF,(fa) . . . . . . . . . . . . . . . . 350.00
2 FF,(fa) . . . . . . . . . . . . . . . . 150.00
3 FF,(fa) . . . . . . . . . . . . . . . . 135.00
4 FF,(fa) . . . . . . . . . . . . . . . . 135.00
5 FF,(fa) . . . . . . . . . . . . . . . . 135.00
6 FF,(fa) . . . . . . . . . . . . . . . . 135.00
7 thru 10 (fa) . . . . . . . . . . . @125.00
11 thru 20 (fa) . . . . . . . . . . @125.00
21 thru 44 (fa) . . . . . . . . . . @100.00
45 (fa),Autumn, 1958. . . . . . . . 100.00

## SUPER-MYSTERY COMICS
### Periodical House (Ace Magazines), July, 1940

1 B:Magno,Vulcan,Q-13,Flint
  of the Mountes . . . . . . . . 4,000.00
2 Bondage (c) . . . . . . . . . . . 1,300.00
3 JaB,B:Black Spider . . . . . . 1,000.00
4 O:Davy;A:Captain Gallant . . 750.00
5 JaB,JM(c),I&B:The Clown . . 750.00
6 JM,JM(c),V:The Clown . . . . . 650.00
2-1 JM,JM(c),O:Buckskin,
  Bondage(c) . . . . . . . . . . . 650.00
2-2 JM,JM(c),V:The Clown . . . . 600.00
2-3 JM,JM(c),V:The Clown . . . . 600.00
2-4 JM,JM(c),V:The Nazis . . . . 600.00
2-5 JM,JM(c),Bondage(c) . . . . 600.00
2-6 JM,JM(c),Bondage(c),
  'Foreign Correspondent' . . . 600.00
3-1 B:Black Ace . . . . . . . . . . . 600.00
3-2 A:Mr, Risk, Bondage(c) . . . 600.00
3-3 HK,HK(c),I:Lancer;B:Dr.
  Nemesis, The Sword . . . . . 650.00
3-4 HK . . . . . . . . . . . . . . . . . 600.00
3-5 HK,LbC,A:Mr. Risk . . . . . . 600.00
3-6 HK,LbC,A:Paul Revere Jr. . 600.00
4-1 HK, LbC,A:Twin Must Die . . . 550.00

4-2 A:Mr. Risk . . . . . . . . . . . . . 375.00
4-3 Mango out to Kill Davey! . . . 375.00
4-4 Danger Laughs at Mr. Risk . . 375.00
4-5 A:Mr. Risk . . . . . . . . . . . . . 375.00
4-6 RP,A:Mr. Risk . . . . . . . . . . 375.00
5-1 RP . . . . . . . . . . . . . . . . . 375.00
5-2 RP,RP(c),The Riddle of the
  Swamp-Land Spirit . . . . . . 375.00
5-3 RP,RP(c),The Case of the
  Whispering Death . . . . . . . 375.00
5-4 RP,RP(c) . . . . . . . . . . . . . 375.00
5-5 RP,Harry the Hack . . . . . . . 375.00
5-6 . . . . . . . . . . . . . . . . . . . . 375.00
6-1 . . . . . . . . . . . . . . . . . . . . 300.00
6-2 RP,A:Mr. Risk . . . . . . . . . . 300.00
6-3 Bondage (c) . . . . . . . . . . . 300.00
6-4 E:Mango;A:Mr. Risk . . . . . . 300.00
6-5 Bondage(c) . . . . . . . . . . . 300.00
6-6 A:Mr. Risk . . . . . . . . . . . . 300.00
7-1 . . . . . . . . . . . . . . . . . . . . 300.00
7-2 KBa(c) . . . . . . . . . . . . . . . 300.00
7-3 Bondage(c) . . . . . . . . . . . 300.00
7-4 . . . . . . . . . . . . . . . . . . . . 300.00
7-5 . . . . . . . . . . . . . . . . . . . . 300.00
7-6 . . . . . . . . . . . . . . . . . . . . 300.00
8-1 The Riddle of the Rowboat . . 275.00
8-2 Death Meets a Train . . . . . . 275.00
8-3 The Man Who Couldn't Die . 275.00
8-4 RP(c) . . . . . . . . . . . . . . . . 275.00
8-5 GT,MMe,Staged for Murder . 275.00
8-6 Unlucky Seven,July, 1949 . 275.00

## SUPER PUP
### Avon Periodicals, 1954

4 . . . . . . . . . . . . . . . . . . . . . 125.00
5 Robot(c). . . . . . . . . . . . . . . 150.00

## SUPER RABBIT
### Marvel Timely, 1943

1 Hitler . . . . . . . . . . . . . . . 1,200.00
2 . . . . . . . . . . . . . . . . . . . . . 500.00
3 . . . . . . . . . . . . . . . . . . . . . 350.00
4 . . . . . . . . . . . . . . . . . . . . . 350.00
5 . . . . . . . . . . . . . . . . . . . . . 350.00
6 Origin of Super Rabbit. . . . . . 325.00
7 . . . . . . . . . . . . . . . . . . . . . 225.00
8 . . . . . . . . . . . . . . . . . . . . . 225.00
9 . . . . . . . . . . . . . . . . . . . . . 225.00
10 . . . . . . . . . . . . . . . . . . . . 225.00
11 HK,Hey Look . . . . . . . . . . . 250.00
12 . . . . . . . . . . . . . . . . . . . . 250.00
13 . . . . . . . . . . . . . . . . . . . . 250.00
14 . . . . . . . . . . . . . . . . . . . . 250.00

## ARMY AND NAVY COMICS
### Street & Smith Publ., May, 1941

1 Hawaii is Calling You,Capt.
  Fury,Nick Carter. . . . . . . . . 750.00
2 Private Rock V;Hitler . . . . . . 600.00
3 The Fighting Fourth . . . . . . . 600.00
4 The Fighting Irish . . . . . . . . 600.00
5 I:Super Snipe . . . . . . . . . . . 700.00
Becomes:

## SUPERSNIPE COMICS
### Oct., 1942

6 A "Comic" With A Sense
  of Humor . . . . . . . . . . . . 1,300.00
7 A:Wacky, Rex King . . . . . . . 700.00
8 Axis Powers & Satan(c),
  Hitler(c) . . . . . . . . . . . . 1,000.00
9 Hitler Voodoo Doll (c) . . . . 1,100.00
10 Lighting (c) . . . . . . . . . . . 700.00
11 A:Little Nemo. . . . . . . . . . . 700.00
12 Football(c). . . . . . . . . . . . . 700.00
2-1 B:Huck Finn . . . . . . . . . 1,000.00
2-2 Battles Shark . . . . . . . . . . 550.00
2-3 Battles Dinosaur . . . . . . . . 500.00
2-4 Baseball(c). . . . . . . . . . . . 500.00
2-5 Battles Dinosaur . . . . . . . . 500.00
2-6 A:Pochontas. . . . . . . . . . . 500.00
2-7 A:Wing Woo Woo . . . . . . . 500.00
2-8 A:Huck Finn . . . . . . . . . . . 500.00
2-9 Dotty Loves Trouble. . . . . . 500.00
2-10 Assists Farm Labor
  Shortage . . . . . . . . . . . . . 500.00
2-11 Dotty & the Jelly Beans . . . . 500.00
2-12 Statue of Liberty. . . . . . . . 500.00
3-1 Ice Skating(c) . . . . . . . . . . 400.00
3-2 V:Pirates(c) . . . . . . . . . . . 400.00
3-3 Baseball(c). . . . . . . . . . . . 400.00
3-4 Jungle(c) . . . . . . . . . . . . . 400.00
3-5 Learn Piglatin. . . . . . . . . . 400.00
3-6 Football Hero . . . . . . . . . . 400.00
3-7 Saves Girl From Grisley . . . 400.00
3-8 Rides a Wild Horse . . . . . . 400.00
3-9 Powers Santa's Sleigh. . . . . 400.00
3-10 Plays Basketball . . . . . . . . 400.00
3-11 Is A Baseball Pitcher . . . . . 400.00
3-12 Flies with the Birds . . . . . . 400.00
4-1 Catches A Whale . . . . . . . . 300.00
4-2 Track & Field Athlete . . . . . 300.00
4-3 Think Machine(c) . . . . . . . . 300.00
4-4 Alpine Skiier. . . . . . . . . . . 300.00
4-5 Becomes a Boxer . . . . . . . 300.00
4-6 Race Car Driver. . . . . . . . . 300.00
4-7 Bomber(c). . . . . . . . . . . . . 300.00
4-8 Baseball Star . . . . . . . . . . 300.00

*Superworld Comics #3*
*© Hugo Gernsback*

*Suspense Comics #3*
*© Continental Magazines*

*Suspense Detective #5*
*© Fawcett Publications*

4-9 Football Hero . . . . . . . . . . . . . 300.00
4-10 Christmas(c) . . . . . . . . . . . . 300.00
4-11 Artic Adventure . . . . . . . . . . 300.00
4-12 The Ghost Remover . . . . . 300.00
5-1 Aug.–Sept., 1949 . . . . . . . . . 300.00

## SUPER SPY
### Centaur Publications, Oct.–Nov., 1940
1 O:Sparkler . . . . . . . . . . . . . 1,500.00
2 A:Night Hawk, Drew Ghost, Tim
 Blain, S.S. Swanson the Inner
 Circle, Duke Collins, Gentlemen
 of Misfortune . . . . . . . . . . . . 900.00

## SUPER WESTERN COMICS
### Youthful Magazines, Aug., 1950
1 BP,BP,(c),B:Buffalo Bill,Wyatt
 Earp,CalamityJane,SamSlade150.00
2 . . . . . . . . . . . . . . . . . . . . . . . 100.00
3 . . . . . . . . . . . . . . . . . . . . . . . 100.00
4 March, 1951 . . . . . . . . . . . . . 100.00

## SUPER WESTERN FUNNIES
### See: SUPER FUNNIES

## SUPERWORLD COMICS
### Komos Publications (Hugo Gernsback), April, 1940
1 FP,FP(c),B:MilitaryPowers,BuzzAllen
 Smarty Artie, Alibi Alige . . 10,000.00
2 FP,FP(c),A:Mario . . . . . . . . 6,000.00
3 FP,FP(c),V:Vest Wearing
 Giant Grasshoppers . . . . . 4,000.00

## SURE-FIRE COMICS
### See: LIGHTNING COMICS

## SURPRISE ADVENTURES
### See: TORMENTED

## SUSPENSE
### Marvel Atlas, Dec., 1949
1 BP,Ph(c),Sidney Greenstreet/
 Peter Lorne (Maltese Falcon) 800.00

2 Ph(c),Dennis O'Keefe/Gale
 Storm (Abandoned) . . . . . . . 400.00
3 B:Horror stories,The Black
 Pit . . . . . . . . . . . . . . . . . . . . 450.00
4 Thing In Black . . . . . . . . . . . 325.00
5 BEv,GT,RH,BK,DBr,
 Hangman's House . . . . . . . . 350.00
6 BEv,GT,PMo,RH,Madness
 of Scott Mannion . . . . . . . . . 350.00
7 DBr,GT,DR,Murder . . . . . . . 325.00
8 GC,DRi,RH,Don't Open
 the Door . . . . . . . . . . . . . . . 325.00
9 GC,DRi,Back From The Dead 325.00
10 JMn(c),WIP,RH,Trapped
 In Time . . . . . . . . . . . . . . . . 325.00
11 MSy,The Suitcase . . . . . . . . 275.00
12 GT,Dark Road . . . . . . . . . . . 275.00
13 JMn(c),Strange Man,
 bondage cover . . . . . . . . . . 275.00
14 RH,Death And Doctor Parker . 400.00
15 JMn(c),OW,The Machine . . . . 275.00
16 OW,Horror Backstage . . . . . . 275.00
17 Night Of Terror . . . . . . . . . . . 275.00
18 BK,The Cozy Coffin . . . . . . . 300.00
19 BEv,RH . . . . . . . . . . . . . . . . 275.00
20 . . . . . . . . . . . . . . . . . . . . . . 275.00
21 BEv(c) . . . . . . . . . . . . . . . . . 275.00
22 BEv(c),BK,OW . . . . . . . . . . . 275.00
23 BEv . . . . . . . . . . . . . . . . . . . 275.00
24 RH,GT . . . . . . . . . . . . . . . . . 300.00
25 I Died At Midnight . . . . . . . . . 350.00
26 BEv(c) . . . . . . . . . . . . . . . . . 225.00
27 DBr . . . . . . . . . . . . . . . . . . . 250.00
28 BEv . . . . . . . . . . . . . . . . . . . 250.00
29 JMn,BF,JRo,April, 1953 . . . . . 250.00

## SUSPENSE COMICS
### Et Es Go Mag. Inc. (Continental Magazines), Dec., 1945
1 LbC, Bondage(c),B:Grey
 Mask . . . . . . . . . . . . . . . . 6,500.00
2 DRi,I:The Mask . . . . . . . . . . 4,000.00
3 LbC,ASh(c),Bondage(c) . . . 20,000.00
4 LbC,LbC(c),Bondage(c) . . . . 3,000.00
5 LbC,LbC(c) . . . . . . . . . . . . 3,000.00
6 LbC,LbC(c),The End of
 the Road . . . . . . . . . . . . . . 3,000.00
7 LbC,LbC(c) . . . . . . . . . . . . 2,700.00
8 LbC,LbC(c) . . . . . . . . . . . . 6,500.00
9 LbC,LbC(c) . . . . . . . . . . . . 2,700.00
10 RP,LbC,LbC(c) . . . . . . . . . . 2,700.00
11 RP,LbC,EL,LbC(c),Satan(c) . 5,000.00
12 LbC,LbC(c),Dec., 1946 . . . . 2,500.00

## SUSPENSE DETECTIVE
### Fawcett Publications, June, 1952
1 GE,MBi,MBi(c),Death Poised
 to Strike . . . . . . . . . . . . . . . 650.00
2 GE,MSy . . . . . . . . . . . . . . . 400.00
3 A Furtive Footstep . . . . . . . . . 350.00
4 MBi,MSy,Bondage(c),A Blood
 Chilling Scream . . . . . . . . . . 350.00
5 MSy,MSy(c),MBi,A Hair-Trigger
 from Death, March, 1953 . . . 350.00

## SUZIE COMICS
## See: TOP-NOTCH COMICS

## SWAT MALONE
### Swat Malone Enterpriess, 1955
1 . . . . . . . . . . . . . . . . . . . . . . 125.00

## SWEENEY
### Standard Comics, June, 1949
4 Buzz Sawyer's Pal . . . . . . . . 150.00
5 Sept., 1949 . . . . . . . . . . . . . 125.00

## SWEETHEART DIARY
### Fawcett, Winter, 1949
1 . . . . . . . . . . . . . . . . . . . . . . 200.00
2 . . . . . . . . . . . . . . . . . . . . . . 125.00
3 WW . . . . . . . . . . . . . . . . . . . 250.00
4 WW . . . . . . . . . . . . . . . . . . . 250.00
5 thru 10 . . . . . . . . . . . . . . . . @150.00
11 thru 14 . . . . . . . . . . . . . . . . @100.00

## SWEETHEART DIARY
### Charlton Comics, Jan., 1953
32 . . . . . . . . . . . . . . . . . . . . . . 125.00
33 thru 40 . . . . . . . . . . . . . . . . @100.00
41 thru 65 . . . . . . . . . . . . . . . . @100.00

## SWEET HEART
## See: CAPTAIN MIDNIGHT

## SWEETHEARTS
### Charlton Comics, 1954
68 . . . . . . . . . . . . . . . . . . . . . . 200.00
69 . . . . . . . . . . . . . . . . . . . . . . 150.00

*Swift Arrow #1*
© Farrell Publications

*Taffy #1*
© Rural Home

*Tales of Horror #12*
© Tob Press

| | |
|---|---|
| 70 thru 80 | @125.00 |
| 81 thru 99 | @125.00 |
| 100 | 110.00 |
| 101 thru 106 | @110.00 |
| 107 BP | 110.00 |
| 108 thru 110 | @100.00 |
| 111 Ronald Reagan | 150.00 |
| 112 thru 116 | @100.00 |
| 117 GE | 125.00 |
| 118 | 100.00 |
| 119 Marilyn Monroe | 600.00 |
| 120 A-Bomb | 150.00 |
| 121 Liz Taylor | 200.00 |
| 122 Marijuana | 300.00 |

## SWEETIE PIE
**Farrell Publications/Pines, 1955**

| | |
|---|---|
| 1 | 150.00 |
| 2 | 100.00 |
| 3 thru 10 | @100.00 |
| 11 thru 15 | @100.00 |

## SWEET LOVE
**Harvey Publications (Home Comics), Sept., 1949**

| | |
|---|---|
| 1 Ph(c) | 150.00 |
| 2 Ph(c) | 125.00 |
| 3 BP | 125.00 |
| 4 Ph(c) | 100.00 |
| 5 BP,JKa,Ph(c) | 100.00 |

## SWEET SIXTEEN
**Parents' Magazine Group, Aug.–Sept., 1946**

| | |
|---|---|
| 1 Van Johnson story | 250.00 |
| 2 Alan Ladd story | 200.00 |
| 3 Rip Taylor | 150.00 |
| 4 Elizabeth Taylor ph(c) | 250.00 |
| 5 Gregory Peck story (c) | 150.00 |
| 6 Dick Haymes(c) | 150.00 |
| 7 Ronald Reagan(c) & story | 300.00 |
| 8 Shirley Jones(c) | 125.00 |
| 9 William Holden(c) | 125.00 |
| 10 James Stewart(c) | 150.00 |
| 11 | 125.00 |
| 12 Bob Cummings(c) | 125.00 |
| 13 Robert Mitchum(c) | 150.00 |

## SWIFT ARROW
**Farrell Publications (Ajax), Feb.–March, 1954**

| | |
|---|---|
| 1 Lone Rider's Redskin Brother | 200.00 |
| 2 | 125.00 |

| | |
|---|---|
| 3 | 100.00 |
| 4 | 100.00 |
| 5 Oct.–Nov., 1954 | 100.00 |

**(2nd Series) April, 1957**

| | |
|---|---|
| 1 | 100.00 |
| 2 B:Lone Rider | 100.00 |
| 3 Sept., 1957 | 100.00 |

## TAFFY
**Orbit Publications/Rural Home/ Taffy Publications, March–April, 1945**

| | |
|---|---|
| 1 LbC(c),(fa),Bondage(c) | 800.00 |
| 2 LbC(c),(fa) | 350.00 |
| 3 (fa) | 150.00 |
| 4 (fa) | 150.00 |
| 5 LbC(c),A:Van Johnson | 250.00 |
| 6 A:Perry Como | 150.00 |
| 7 A:Dave Clark | 150.00 |
| 8 A:Glen Ford | 150.00 |
| 9 A:Lon McCallister | 150.00 |
| 10 A:John Hodiak | 150.00 |
| 11 A:Mickey Rooney | 165.00 |
| 12 Feb., 1948 | 150.00 |

## TAILSPIN
**Spotlight Publications, Nov., 1944**

| | |
|---|---|
| N# LbC(c),A:Firebird | 350.00 |

## TALE OF THE MARINES
**See: DEVIL-DOG DUGAN**

## TALES FROM THE CRYPT
**See: CRIME PATROL**

## TALES FROM THE GREAT BOOK
**Famous Funnies, 1955**

| | |
|---|---|
| 1 Samson | 125.00 |
| 2 Joshua | 100.00 |
| 3 Joash the Boy King | 100.00 |
| 4 David | 100.00 |

## TALES OF HORROR
**Toby Press/Minoan Publ. Corp, June, 1952–Oct., 1954**

| | |
|---|---|
| 1 Demons of the Underworld | 500.00 |

| | |
|---|---|
| 2 What was the Thing in the Pool?,Torture | 400.00 |
| 3 The Big Snake | 300.00 |
| 4 The Curse of King Kala! | 300.00 |
| 5 Hand of Fate | 300.00 |
| 6 The Fiend of Flame | 300.00 |
| 7 Beast From The Deep | 300.00 |
| 8 The Snake that Held A City Captive | 300.00 |
| 9 It Came From the Bottom of the World | 350.00 |
| 10 The Serpent Strikes | 300.00 |
| 11 Death Flower? | 350.00 |
| 12 Guaranteed to Make Your Hair Stand on End,Torture | 350.00 |
| 13 Ghost with a Torch | 350.00 |

## TALES OF JACE PEARSON
**See: JACE PEARSON**

## TALES OF JUSTICE
**See: JUSTICE COMICS**

## TALES OF SUSPENSE
**Marvel Atlas, 1959**

| | |
|---|---|
| 1 AW,DH,JB,SD,JK | 2,600.00 |
| 2 SD,JK,RH,Robot | 900.00 |
| 3 SD,JK,JB(c),Flying Saucer | 900.00 |
| 4 AW,JK,BEv,SD | 750.00 |
| 5 JK,SD,JF | 600.00 |
| 6 SD,JK | 600.00 |
| 7 SD,JK, | 625.00 |
| 8 SD,BEv,JK,Lava Man | 550.00 |
| 9 SD,JK,TF,Iron man type | 600.00 |
| 10 SD,RH,JK | 550.00 |
| 11 SD,JK | 450.00 |
| 12 RC,SD,JK | 450.00 |
| 13 SK,JK,Elektro | 425.00 |
| 14 SD,JK,Colossus (1) | 550.00 |
| 15 SD,JK | 425.00 |
| 16 JK,Metallo (1) | 550.00 |
| 17 JK | 425.00 |
| 18 JK | 425.00 |
| 19 JK | 425.00 |
| 20 JK,Colossus (2) | 450.00 |

## TALES OF TERROR
**Toby Press, 1952**

| | |
|---|---|
| 1 Just A Bunch of Hokey Hogwash | 300.00 |

Tales of the Mysterious Traveler #8
© Charlton Comics

Tales of the Unexpected #35
© DC Comics

Tales to Astonish #20
© Marvel Comics Group

## TALES OF TERROR ANNUAL
### E.C. Comics, 1951
N# AF . . . . . . . . . . . . . . . . . . . . 6,000.00
2 AF . . . . . . . . . . . . . . . . . . . . 3,000.00
3 . . . . . . . . . . . . . . . . . . . . . . 2,700.00

## TALES OF THE MYSTERIOUS TRAVELER
### Charlton Comics, 1956
1 DG . . . . . . . . . . . . . . . . . . . . 600.00
2 SD . . . . . . . . . . . . . . . . . . . . 500.00
3 SD,SD(c) . . . . . . . . . . . . . . . 425.00
4 SD,SD(c) . . . . . . . . . . . . . . . 500.00
5 SD,SD(c) . . . . . . . . . . . . . . . 500.00
6 SD,SD(c) . . . . . . . . . . . . . . . 500.00
7 thru 9 SD . . . . . . . . . . . . . @450.00
10 SD,SD(c). . . . . . . . . . . . . . . 475.00
11 SD,SD(c). . . . . . . . . . . . . . . 475.00
12 . . . . . . . . . . . . . . . . . . . . . . 200.00
13 . . . . . . . . . . . . . . . . . . . . . . 225.00

## TALES OF THE UNEXPECTED
### DC Comics, 1956
1 The Out-Of-The-World Club . 1,700.00
2 . . . . . . . . . . . . . . . . . . . . . . 750.00
3 . . . . . . . . . . . . . . . . . . . . . . 500.00
4 Seven Steps to the Unknown . 500.00
5 . . . . . . . . . . . . . . . . . . . . . . 500.00
6 The Girl in the Bottle . . . . . . . 400.00
7 NC(c),Pen That Never Lied . . . 400.00
8 . . . . . . . . . . . . . . . . . . . . . . 400.00
9 LSt(c),The Amazing Cube . . . . 400.00
10 MMe(c),The Strangest Show On Earth . . . . . . . . . . . . . . . 400.00
11 LSt(c),Who Am I? . . . . . . . . . 250.00
12 JK,Four Threads of Doom . . . 350.00
13 JK(c),Weapons of Destiny . . . 350.00
14 SMo(c),The Forbidden Game . 250.00
15 JK,MMe,Three Wishes to Doom. . . . . . . . . . . . . . . 350.00
16 JK,The Magic Hammer. . . . . . 350.00
17 JK,Who Is Mr. Ashtar? . . . . . . 350.00
18 JK(c),MMe,A Man Without A World . . . . . . . . . . . . . . . . . 350.00
19 NC,Man From Two Worlds . . . 325.00
20 NC(c),The Earth Gladiator . . . 325.00
21 JK,The Living Phantoms. . . . . 325.00
22 JK(c),The Man From Robot Island. . . . . . . . . . . . . . . . . 325.00
23 JK,The Invitation From Mars! . 325.00

24 LC,The Secret Of Planetoid Zero! . . . . . . . . . . . . . . . . . 325.00
25 The Sorcerer's Asteroid! . . . . 225.00
26 MMe,The Frozem City . . . . . . 225.00
27 MMe,The Prison In Space . . . 225.00
28 The Melting Planet . . . . . . . . 225.00
29 The Phantom Raider. . . . . . . . 225.00
30 The Jinxed Planet. . . . . . . . . . 225.00
31 RH,Keep Off Our Planet . . . . 200.00
32 Great Space Cruise Mystery . 200.00
33 The Man Of 1,000 Planets . . . 200.00
34 Ambush In Outer Space . . . . . 200.00
35 MMe,I was a Space Refugee . 200.00
36 The Curse Of The Galactic Goodess . . . . . . . . 200.00
37 The Secret Prisoners Of Planet 13 . . . . . . . . . . . 200.00
38 The Stunt Man Of Space . . . . 200.00
39 The Creatures From The Space Globe . . . . . . . . . . . . 200.00
40 B:Space Ranger,The Last Days Of Planet Mars! . . . . . 1,600.00
41 SMo(c),The Destroyers From The Stars! . . . . . . . . . . . . . . 550.00
42 The Secret Of The Martian Helmet . . . . . . . . . . 550.00
43 The Riddle Of The Burning Treasures,I:Space Ranger . 1,200.00
44 DD&SMo(c),The Menace Of The Indian Aliens. . . . . . . . . 375.00
45 DD&SMo(c),The Sheriff From Jupiter . . . . . . . . . . . . 375.00
46 DD&SMo(c),The Duplicate Doom! . . . . . . . . . 375.00
47 DD(c),The Man Who Stole The Solar System . . . . . . . . 275.00
48 Bring 'Em Back Alive- From Space . . . . . . . . . . . . . 275.00
49 RH,The Fantastic Lunar-Land 275.00
50 MA,King Barney The Ape . . . . 275.00
51 Planet Earth For Sale. . . . . . . 275.00
52 Prisoner On Pluto . . . . . . . . . 275.00
53 InterplanetaryTroubleShooter . 275.00
54 The Ugly Sleeper Of Klanth, Dinosaur . . . . . . . . . . . . . . . 275.00
55 The Interplanetary Creature Trainer . . . . . . . . . . 275.00
56 B:Spaceman At Work,Invaders From Earth . . . . . . . . . . . . . 275.00
57 The Jungle Beasts Of Jupiter . 275.00
58 The Boss Of The Saturnian Legion . . . . . . . . . 275.00
59 The Man Who Won A World . . 275.00
60 School For Space Sleuths . . . 275.00
61 The Mystery Of The Mythical Monsters . . . . . . . . 225.00

62 The Menace Of The Red Snow Crystals . . . . . . . . . . . 225.00
63 Death To Planet Earth . . . . . . 225.00
64 Boy Usurper Of Planet Zonn . 225.00
65 The Creature That Couldn't Exist . . . . . . . . . . . 225.00
66 MMe,Trap Of The Space Convict. . . . . . . . . . . . . . . . . 225.00
67 The Giant That Devoured A Village . . . . . . . . 225.00

## TALES TO ASTONISH
### Marvel Atlas, Jan., 1959
1 JDa,Ninth Wonder of the World . . . . . . . . . . . . . . . . . 2,500.00
2 SD,Capture A Martian. . . . . . 1,000.00
3 SD,JK,The Giant From Outer Space . . . . . . . . . . . . 750.00
4 SD,JK,The Day The Martians Struck . . . . . . . . . . 750.00
5 SD,AW,The Things on Easter Island . . . . . . . . . . . . 800.00
6 SD,JK,Invasion of the Stone Men . . . . . . . . . . . . . . 600.00
7 SD,JK,The Thing on Bald Mountain . . . . . . . . . . . . . . . 600.00
8 DAy,SD,JK,Mmmex, King of the Mummies . . . . . . . . . . . 600.00
9 DAy,JK(c),SD,Droom, the Living Lizard . . . . . . . . . . . . 600.00
10 DAy,JK,SD,Titano . . . . . . . . . 600.00
11 DAy,JK,SD,Monstrom, the Dweller in the Black Swamp. . . . . . . 400.00
12 JK/DAy(c),SD,Gorgilla . . . . . . 400.00
13 JK,SD,Groot, the Monster From Planet X . . . . . . . . . . . . 400.00
14 JK,SD,Krang. . . . . . . . . . . . . . 400.00
15 JK/DAy,The Blip . . . . . . . . . . . 550.00
16 DAy,JK,SD,Thorr. . . . . . . . . . . 450.00
17 JK,SD,Vandoom . . . . . . . . . . . 400.00
18 DAy,JK,SD,Gorgilla Strikes Again . . . . . . . . . . . . . . . . . . 400.00
19 DAy,JK,SD,Rommbu. . . . . . . . 400.00
20 JK,SD,X, The Thing That Lived . . . . . . . . . . . . . . 400.00
21 JK,SD,Trull the Inhuman. . . . . 400.00
22 JK,SD,The Crawling Creature. . . . . . . . . . . . . . . . . 300.00
23 JK,SD,Moomba is Here!. . . . . 300.00
24 JK,SD,The Abominable Snowman. . . . . . . . . . . . . . . 300.00
25 JK,SD,The Creature From Krogarr. . . . . . . . . . . . . . . . . 300.00
26 JK,SD,Four-Armed Things . . . 300.00
27 StL(s),SD,JK,I:Ant-Man . . . . 7,000.00

**Ta**

*Tally-Ho Comics #N*
*© Baily Publishing Co.*

*Target Vol. 2 #11*
*© Novelty Publications*

*Target Vol. 9 #1*
*© Novelty Publications*

28 JK,SD,I Am the Gorilla Man . . 300.00
29 JK,SD,When the Space
   Beasts Attack. . . . . . . . . . . 300.00
30 JK,SD,Thing From the
   Hidden Swamp . . . . . . . . . 300.00
31 JK,SD,The Mummy's Secret. . 300.00
32 JK,SD,Quicksand . . . . . . . . . 300.00
33 JK,SD,Dead Storage. . . . . . . 300.00
34 JK,SD,Monster at Window . . . 300.00
35 StL(s),JK,SD, B:Ant-Man
   (2nd App.). . . . . . . . . . . . 3,000.00
36 JK,SD,V:Comrade X . . . . . . 1,000.00
37 JK,SD,V:The Protector . . . . . 700.00
38 JK,SD,Betrayed By the Ants. . 700.00
39 JK,DH,V:Scarlet Beetle. . . . . 700.00
40 JK,SD,DH,The Day Ant-Man
   Failed. . . . . . . . . . . . . . . . 700.00

## TALLY-HO COMICS
**Baily Publishing Co., 1944**
N# FF,A:Snowman . . . . . . . . . . 550.00

## TASTEE-FREEZ COMICS
**Harvey Comics, 1957**
1 Little Dot. . . . . . . . . . . . . . . 60.00
2 Rags Rabbit. . . . . . . . . . . . . 30.00
3 Casper. . . . . . . . . . . . . . . . . 40.00
4 Sad Sack . . . . . . . . . . . . . . 30.00
5 Mazie . . . . . . . . . . . . . . . . . 30.00
6 Dick Tracy . . . . . . . . . . . . . 50.00

## TARGET COMICS
**Funnnies Inc./Novelty Publ./
Premium Group/Curtis
Circulation Co./Star
Publications, Feb., 1940**
1 BEv,JCo,CBu,JSm;B,O&I:Manowar,
   White Streak,Bull's-Eye;B:City
   Editor,High Grass Twins,T-Men,
   Rip Rory,Fantastic Feature
   Films, Calling 2-R . . . . . . 10,000.00
2 BEv,JSm,JCo,CBu,White
   Streak(c). . . . . . . . . . . . . 6,000.00
3 BEv,JSm,JCo,CBu . . . . . . . 3,200.00
4 JSm,JCo . . . . . . . . . . . . . . 3,200.00
5 CBu,BW,O:White Streak . 9,000.00
6 CBu,BW,White Streak(c) . . 3,500.00
7 CBu,BW,BW(c),V:Planetoid
   Stories,Space Hawk(c) . . 10,000.00
8 CBu,BW,White Shark(c) . . . 3,000.00
9 CBu,BW,White Shark(c) . . . 3,000.00
10 CBu,BW,JK(c),The
   Target(c). . . . . . . . . . . . . 4,000.00

11 BW,The Target(c) . . . . . . . . 3,500.00
12 BW,same . . . . . . . . . . . . . . 3,200.00
2-1 BW,CBu . . . . . . . . . . . . . . 3,000.00
2-2 BW,BoW(c). . . . . . . . . . . . 2,700.00
2-3 BW,BoW(c),The Target(c). . 2,500.00
2-4 BW,B:Cadet . . . . . . . . . . . 2,500.00
2-5 BW,BoW(c),The Target(c). . 2,500.00
2-6 BW,The Target(c) . . . . . . . 2,000.00
2-7 BW,The Cadet(c) . . . . . . . 2,000.00
2-8 BW,same . . . . . . . . . . . . . 2,000.00
2-9 BW,The Target(c) . . . . . . . 2,000.00
2-10 BW,same . . . . . . . . . . . . 2,500.00
2-11 BW,The Cadet(c) . . . . . . 2,000.00
2-12 BW,same . . . . . . . . . . . . 2,000.00
3-1 BW,same . . . . . . . . . . . . . 2,000.00
3-2 BW . . . . . . . . . . . . . . . . . 2,000.00
3-3 BW,The Target(c) . . . . . . . 2,000.00
3-4 BW,The Cadet(c) . . . . . . . 2,000.00
3-5 BW . . . . . . . . . . . . . . . . . 2,000.00
3-6 BW,War Bonds(c). . . . . . . 2,500.00
3-7 BW . . . . . . . . . . . . . . . . . 2,000.00
3-8 BW,War Bonds(c). . . . . . . 2,500.00
3-9 BW . . . . . . . . . . . . . . . . . 2,000.00
3-10 BW . . . . . . . . . . . . . . . . 2,000.00
3-11 . . . . . . . . . . . . . . . . . . . 500.00
3-12 . . . . . . . . . . . . . . . . . . . 500.00
4-1 JJo(c) . . . . . . . . . . . . . . . 275.00
4-2 ERy(c) . . . . . . . . . . . . . . 275.00
4-3 AVi . . . . . . . . . . . . . . . . . 275.00
4-4 . . . . . . . . . . . . . . . . . . . . 275.00
4-5 API(c),Statue of Liberty(c) . . 275.00
4-6 BW . . . . . . . . . . . . . . . . . 275.00
4-7 AVi . . . . . . . . . . . . . . . . . 275.00
4-8,Christmas(c) . . . . . . . . . . 275.00
4-9 . . . . . . . . . . . . . . . . . . . . 275.00
4-10 . . . . . . . . . . . . . . . . . . . 275.00
4-11 . . . . . . . . . . . . . . . . . . . 275.00
4-12 . . . . . . . . . . . . . . . . . . . 275.00
5-1 . . . . . . . . . . . . . . . . . . . . 250.00
5-2 The Target . . . . . . . . . . . 125.00
5-3 Savings Checkers(c) . . . . 125.00
5-4 War Bonds Ph(c) . . . . . . . 125.00
5-5 thru 5-12 . . . . . . . . . . @125.00
6-1 The Target(c) . . . . . . . . . 125.00
6-2 . . . . . . . . . . . . . . . . . . . . 125.00
6-3 Red Cross(c) . . . . . . . . . 125.00
6-4 . . . . . . . . . . . . . . . . . . . . 125.00
6-5 Savings Bonds(c) . . . . . . 150.00
6-6 The Target(c) . . . . . . . . . 250.00
6-7 The Cadet(c) . . . . . . . . . 250.00
6-8 AFa . . . . . . . . . . . . . . . . 250.00
6-9 The Target(c) . . . . . . . . . 250.00
6-10 . . . . . . . . . . . . . . . . . . . 250.00
6-11 . . . . . . . . . . . . . . . . . . . 250.00
6-12 . . . . . . . . . . . . . . . . . . . 250.00
7-1 . . . . . . . . . . . . . . . . . . . . 250.00

7-2 Bondage(c) . . . . . . . . . . . 250.00
7-3 The Target(c) . . . . . . . . . 250.00
7-4 DRi,The Cadet(c) . . . . . . 250.00
7-5 . . . . . . . . . . . . . . . . . . . . 250.00
7-6 DRi(c). . . . . . . . . . . . . . . 250.00
7-7 The Cadet(c) . . . . . . . . . 250.00
7-8 DRi(c). . . . . . . . . . . . . . . 250.00
7-9 The Cadet(c) . . . . . . . . . 250.00
7-10 DRi,DRi(c) . . . . . . . . . . 250.00
7-11 . . . . . . . . . . . . . . . . . . . 250.00
7-12 JH(c) . . . . . . . . . . . . . . 250.00
8-1 . . . . . . . . . . . . . . . . . . . . 200.00
8-2 DRi,DRi(c),BK . . . . . . . . 200.00
8-3 DRi,The Cadet(c) . . . . . . 200.00
8-4 DRi,DRi(c) . . . . . . . . . . . 200.00
8-5 DRi,The Cadet(c) . . . . . . 200.00
8-6 DRi,DRi(c) . . . . . . . . . . . 200.00
8-7 BK,DRi,DRi(c) . . . . . . . . 200.00
8-8 DRi,The Cadet(c) . . . . . . 200.00
8-9 DRi,The Cadet(c) . . . . . . 200.00
8-10 DRi,KBa,LbC(c) . . . . . . 750.00
8-11 DRi,The Cadet. . . . . . . . 200.00
8-12 DRi,The Cadet. . . . . . . . 200.00
9-1 DRi,LbC(c). . . . . . . . . . . 750.00
9-2 DRi. . . . . . . . . . . . . . . . . 200.00
9-3 DRi,Bondage(c),The Cadet(c)275.00
9-4 DRi,LbC(c). . . . . . . . . . . 750.00
9-5 DRi,Baseball(c) . . . . . . . 250.00
9-6 DRi,LbC(c). . . . . . . . . . . 750.00
9-7 DRi. . . . . . . . . . . . . . . . . 250.00
9-8 DRi,LbC(c). . . . . . . . . . . 750.00
9-9 DRi,Football(c). . . . . . . . 250.00
9-10 DRi,LbC(c). . . . . . . . . . 750.00
9-11,The Cadet . . . . . . . . . . . 250.00
9-12 LbC(c),Gems(c). . . . . . . 750.00
10-1,The Cadet . . . . . . . . . . . 250.00
10-2 LbC(c) . . . . . . . . . . . . . 750.00
10-3 LbC(c) . . . . . . . . . . . . . 750.00
**Becomes:**

## TARGET WESTERN ROMANCES
**Star Publications,
Oct.–Nov., 1949**
106 LbC(c),The Beauty Scar . . . . 500.00
107 LbC(c),The Brand Upon His
   Heart . . . . . . . . . . . . . . . . 450.00

## TARZAN
**Dell Publishing Co.,
Jan.–Feb., 1948**
1 V:White Savages of Vari . . 2,500.00
2 Captives of Thunder Valley. . 1,000.00
3 Dwarfs of Didona . . . . . . . . . 700.00
4 The Lone Hunter . . . . . . . . . 700.00

*Tarzan #14*
© Edgar Rice Burroughs, Inc.

*Teen-Age Romances #7*
© St. John Publishing Co.

*Teen-Age Temptations #9*
© St. John Publishing Co.

5 The Men of Greed . . . . . . . . . 700.00
6 Outlaws of Pal-ul-Don . . . . . . 600.00
7 Valley of the Monsters . . . . . . 600.00
8 The White Pygmies . . . . . . . 600.00
9 The Men of A-Lur. . . . . . . . . 600.00
10 Treasure of the Bolgani . . . . 600.00
11 The Sable Lion . . . . . . . . . . 500.00
12 The Price of Peace . . . . . . . 500.00
13 B:Lex Barker photo(c). . . . . . 450.00
14 Lex Barker ph(c). . . . . . . . . 450.00
15 Lex Barker ph(c). . . . . . . . . 450.00
16 Lex Barker ph(c). . . . . . . . . 400.00
17 Lex Barker ph(c). . . . . . . . . 400.00
18 Lex Barker ph(c). . . . . . . . . 400.00
19 Lex Barker ph(c). . . . . . . . . 400.00
20 Lex Barker ph(c). . . . . . . . . 400.00
21 thru 24 Lex Barker ph(c). . . @350.00
25 Brothers of the Spear . . . . . . 375.00
26 thru 54 E:L.Barker ph(c) . . . @300.00
55 thru 70 . . . . . . . . . . . . . . . @250.00
71 thru 79 . . . . . . . . . . . . . . . @200.00
80 thru 90 B:ScottGordonPh(c) @150.00
91 thru 99 . . . . . . . . . . . . . . . @125.00
100 . . . . . . . . . . . . . . . . . . . . 150.00
101 thru 110 E:S.GordonPh(c). @150.00
111 thru 120 . . . . . . . . . . . . . @125.00
121 thru 131 . . . . . . . . . . . . . @100.00

## TEENA
### Standard Comics, 1949
20 . . . . . . . . . . . . . . . . . . . . . 100.00
21 . . . . . . . . . . . . . . . . . . . . . 100.00
22 . . . . . . . . . . . . . . . . . . . . . 100.00

## TEEN-AGE BRIDES
### Home Comics/
### Harvey Publications, 1953
1 BP . . . . . . . . . . . . . . . . . . . 150.00
2 BP . . . . . . . . . . . . . . . . . . . 125.00
3 BP . . . . . . . . . . . . . . . . . . . 125.00
4 . . . . . . . . . . . . . . . . . . . . . . 100.00
5 . . . . . . . . . . . . . . . . . . . . . . 100.00
6 BP . . . . . . . . . . . . . . . . . . . 150.00
7 . . . . . . . . . . . . . . . . . . . . . . 100.00
Becomes:

## TRUE BRIDES'
## EXPERIENCES
### Harvey Publications, 1954–56
8 . . . . . . . . . . . . . . . . . . . . . . 125.00
9 . . . . . . . . . . . . . . . . . . . . . . 100.00
10 . . . . . . . . . . . . . . . . . . . . . 100.00
11 thru 16 . . . . . . . . . . . . @ 100.00
Becomes:

## TRUE BRIDE-TO-BE
## ROMANCES
### Harvey Publications, 1956–58
17 S&K(c). . . . . . . . . . . . . . . . 150.00
18 thru 30 . . . . . . . . . . . . . . . 100.00

## TEEN-AGE DIARY
## SECRETS
### St. John Publishing Co.,
### Oct., 1949
6 MB,PH(c) . . . . . . . . . . . . . . 350.00
7 MB,PH(c) . . . . . . . . . . . . . . 300.00
8 MB,PH(c) . . . . . . . . . . . . . . 250.00
9 MB,PH(c) . . . . . . . . . . . . . . 300.00
Becomes:

## DIARY SECRETS
### Feb., 1952
10 MB. . . . . . . . . . . . . . . . . . . 250.00
11 MB. . . . . . . . . . . . . . . . . . . 200.00
12 thru 19 MB . . . . . . . . . . . @150.00
20 MB,JKu . . . . . . . . . . . . . . . 200.00
21 thru 28 MB . . . . . . . . . . . @100.00
29 MB,Comics Code . . . . . . . . . 100.00
30 MB. . . . . . . . . . . . . . . . . . . 100.00

## TEEN-AGE LOVE
## See: INTIMATE

## TEENAGE ROMANCE
## See: MY ROMANCE

## TEEN-AGE ROMANCES
### St. John Publishing Co.,
### Jan., 1949
1 MB(c),MB. . . . . . . . . . . . . . . 500.00
2 MB(c),MB. . . . . . . . . . . . . . . 300.00
3 MB(c),MB. . . . . . . . . . . . . . . 350.00
4 Ph(c) . . . . . . . . . . . . . . . . . 300.00
5 MB,Ph(c) . . . . . . . . . . . . . . 300.00
6 MB,Ph(c) . . . . . . . . . . . . . . 300.00
7 MB,Ph(c) . . . . . . . . . . . . . . 300.00
8 MB,Ph(c) . . . . . . . . . . . . . . 300.00
9 MB,MB(c),JKu . . . . . . . . . . . 325.00
10 thru 27 MB,MB(c),JKu . . . . @250.00
28 thru 30 . . . . . . . . . . . . . . @100.00
31 thru 34 MB(c) . . . . . . . . . . @125.00
35 thru 42 MB(c),MB . . . . . . . @125.00
43 MB(c),MB,Comics Code . . . . 150.00
44 MB(c),MB . . . . . . . . . . . . . 150.00
45 MB(c),MB . . . . . . . . . . . . . 150.00

## TEEN-AGE TEMPTATIONS
### St. John Publishing Co.,
### Oct., 1952
1 MB(c),MB. . . . . . . . . . . . . . . 600.00
2 MB(c),MB. . . . . . . . . . . . . . . 200.00
3 MB(c),MB. . . . . . . . . . . . . . . 275.00
4 MB(c),MB. . . . . . . . . . . . . . . 275.00
5 MB(c),MB. . . . . . . . . . . . . . . 275.00
6 MB(c),MB. . . . . . . . . . . . . . . 275.00
7 MB(c),MB. . . . . . . . . . . . . . . 275.00
8 MB(c),MB,Drug . . . . . . . . . . . 300.00
9 MB(c),MB. . . . . . . . . . . . . . . 275.00
Becomes:

## GOING STEADY
### Dec., 1954
10 MB(c),MB . . . . . . . . . . . . . 225.00
11 MB(c),MB . . . . . . . . . . . . . 125.00
12 MB(c),MB . . . . . . . . . . . . . 125.00
13 MB(c),MB . . . . . . . . . . . . . 175.00
14 MB(c),MB . . . . . . . . . . . . . 200.00

## TEEN COMICS
## See: ALL WINNERS
## COMICS

## TEEN CONFESSIONS
### Charlton Comics, 1959
1 . . . . . . . . . . . . . . . . . . . . . . 150.00
2 . . . . . . . . . . . . . . . . . . . . . . 125.00
3 thru 10 . . . . . . . . . . . . . . @100.00
11 thru 30 . . . . . . . . . . . . . @100.00

## TEENIE WEENIES, THE
### Ziff-Davis Publishing Co.,
### 1951
10 . . . . . . . . . . . . . . . . . . . . . 250.00
11 . . . . . . . . . . . . . . . . . . . . . 250.00

## TEEN LIFE
## See: YOUNG LIFE

## TEEN SECRET DIARY
### Charlton Comics, 1959–61
1 . . . . . . . . . . . . . . . . . . . . . . 125.00
2 . . . . . . . . . . . . . . . . . . . . . . 100.00
3 . . . . . . . . . . . . . . . . . . . . . . 100.00
4 . . . . . . . . . . . . . . . . . . . . . . 100.00
5 . . . . . . . . . . . . . . . . . . . . . . 100.00
6 thru 11 . . . . . . . . . . . . . . @100.00

**Te**

*Television Comics #5*
*© Standard Comics*

*Tense Suspense #2*
*© Fago Publications*

*Terrors of the Jungle #21*
*© Star Publications*

## TEGRA, JUNGLE EMPRESS
### See: ZEGRA, JUNGLE EMPRESS

## TELEVISION COMICS
**Animated Cartoons (Standard Comics), Feb., 1950**
5 Humorous Format,I:Willie Nilly 300.00
6 . . . . . . . . . . . . . . . . . . . . . . . 150.00
7 . . . . . . . . . . . . . . . . . . . . . . . 150.00
8 May, 1950 . . . . . . . . . . . . . . . 150.00

## TELEVISION PUPPET SHOW
**Avon Periodicals, 1950**
1 F:Sparky Smith,Spotty, Cheeta, Speedy . . . . . . . . . 250.00
2 Nov., 1950 . . . . . . . . . . . . . . 150.00

## TELL IT TO THE MARINES
**Toby Press, March, 1952**
1 I:Spike & Pat . . . . . . . . . . . . . 250.00
2 A:Madame Cobra . . . . . . . . . . 150.00
3 Spike & Bat on a Commando Raid! . . . . . . . . 125.00
4 Veil Dancing(c) . . . . . . . . . . . 125.00
5 . . . . . . . . . . . . . . . . . . . . . . . 125.00
6 To Paris . . . . . . . . . . . . . . . . 100.00
7 Ph(c),The Chinese Bugle . . . . 100.00
8 Ph(c),V:Communists in South Korea . . . . . . . . . . . 100.00
9 Ph(c) . . . . . . . . . . . . . . . . . . 100.00
10 . . . . . . . . . . . . . . . . . . . . . . 100.00
11 . . . . . . . . . . . . . . . . . . . . . . 100.00
12 . . . . . . . . . . . . . . . . . . . . . . 100.00
13 John Wayne Ph(c) . . . . . . . . 150.00
14 Ph(c). . . . . . . . . . . . . . . . . . 100.00
15 Ph(c),July, 1955 . . . . . . . . . . 100.00

## TENDER ROMANCE
**Key Publications, Dec., 1953**
1 . . . . . . . . . . . . . . . . . . . . . . . 200.00
2 . . . . . . . . . . . . . . . . . . . . . . . 125.00
Becomes:

## IDEAL ROMANCE
**April, 1954**
3 . . . . . . . . . . . . . . . . . . . . . . . 125.00
4 thru 8 . . . . . . . . . . . . . . . . @100.00
Becomes:

## DIARY CONFESSIONS
**May, 1955**
9 . . . . . . . . . . . . . . . . . . . . . . . 125.00
10 . . . . . . . . . . . . . . . . . . . . . . 100.00

## TENSE SUSPENSE
**Fago Publications, 1958–59**
1 . . . . . . . . . . . . . . . . . . . . . . . 125.00
2 . . . . . . . . . . . . . . . . . . . . . . . 100.00

## TERRIFIC COMICS
### See: HORRIFIC

## TERRIFIC COMICS
**Et Es Go Mag. Inc./ Continental Magazines, Jan., 1944**
1 LbC,DRi(c),F:Kid Terrific Drug . . . . . . . . . . . 5,000.00
2 LcC,ASh(c),B:Boomerang, 'Comics' McCormic . . . . . . 3,500.00
3 LbC,LbC(c) . . . . . . . . . . . . . 3,500.00
4 LbC,RP(c) . . . . . . . . . . . . . . 6,000.00

5 LbC,BF,ASh(c),Bondage(c) . 8,000.00
6 LbC,LbC(c),BF,Nov.,1944 . . 3,200.00

## TERRIFYING TALES
**Star Publications, Jan., 1953**
11 LbC,LbC(c),'TyrantsofTerror'. . 700.00
12 LbC,LbC(c),'Bondage(c), 'Jungle Mystery'. . . . . . . . . . 600.00
13 LbC(c),Bondage(c),'The Death-Fire,Devil Head(c). . . . 750.00
14 LbC(c),Bondage(c),'The Weird Idol' . . . . . . . . . . . . 550.00
15 LbC(c),'The Grim Secret', April, 1954 . . . . . . . . . . . . . . 550.00
Becomes:

## JUNGLE THRILLS
**Star Publications, Feb., 1952**
16 LbC(c),'Kingdom of Unseen Terror' . . . . . . . . . . . . . . . . 700.00
Becomes:

## TERRORS OF THE JUNGLE
**Star Publications, May, 1952**
17 LbC(c),Bondage(c) . . . . . . . . 700.00
18 LbC(c),Strange Monsters . . . . 450.00
19 JyD,LbC(c),Bondage(c),The Golden Ghost Gorilla. . . . . . 400.00
20 JyD,LbC(c),The Creeping Scourge . . . . . . . . . . . . . . . 400.00
21 LbC(c),Evil Eyes of Death! . . . 450.00
4 JyD,LbC(c),Morass of Death . 400.00
5 JyD,LbC(c),Bondage(c), Savage Train . . . . . . . . . . . 425.00
6 JyD,LbC(c),Revolt of the Jungle Monsters . . . . . . . . . . 425.00
7 JyD,LbC(c) . . . . . . . . . . . . . 450.00
8 JyD,LbC(c),Death's Grim Reflection . . . . . . . . . . . . . 450.00
9 JyD,LbC(c),Doom to Evil-Doers . . . . . . . . . . . . . 450.00
10 JyD,LbC(c),Black Magic, Sept., 1954 . . . . . . . . . . . . . 450.00

## TERROR ILLUSTRATED
**E.C. Comics, Nov.–Dec., 1955**
1 JCr,GE,Grl,JO,RC(c) . . . . . . . 250.00
2 Spring, 1956 . . . . . . . . . . . . . 150.00

## BOY EXPLORERS
**Harvey Comics, 1946**
1 S&K(c),S&K,The Cadet . . . . 1,500.00
2 S&K(c),S&K . . . . . . . . . . . . 2,000.00
Becomes:

## TERRY AND THE PIRATES
**Harvey Comics, April, 1947**
3 S&K,MC(c),MC,Terry and Dragon Lady . . . . . . . . . . . . 500.00
4 S&K,MC(c),MC . . . . . . . . . . 300.00
5 S&K,MC(c),MC,BP, Chop-Chop(c) . . . . . . . . . . 175.00
6 S&K..MC(c),MC . . . . . . . . . . 175.00
7 S&K,MC(c),MC,BP . . . . . . . . 175.00
8 S&K,MC(c),MC,BP . . . . . . . . 175.00
9 S&K,MC(c),MC,BP . . . . . . . . 175.00
10 S&K,MC(c),MC,BP . . . . . . . . 175.00
11 S&K,MC(c),MC,BP, A:Man in Black . . . . . . . . . . 150.00
12 S&K,MC(c),MC,BP . . . . . . . . 150.00
13 S&K,MC(c),MC,Belly Dancers 150.00
14 thru 20 S&K,MC(c),MC . . . @125.00
21 thru 26 S&K,MC(c),MC . . . . @110.00

**Te**

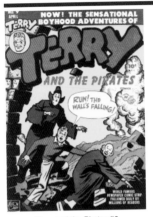

Terry and the Pirates #9
© Harvey Publications

Tessie the Typist #2
© Marvel Comics Group

Tex Farrell #1
© D.S. Publishing Co.

27 Charlton Comics . . . . . . . . . . 100.00
28 . . . . . . . . . . . . . . . . . . . . . . . 100.00
Becomes:

## LONG JOHN SILVER
## AND THE PIRATES
**Charlton Comics, 1956–57**
30 . . . . . . . . . . . . . . . . . . . . . . 125.00
31 . . . . . . . . . . . . . . . . . . . . . . 125.00
32 . . . . . . . . . . . . . . . . . . . . . . 125.00

## TERRY-BEARS COMICS
**St. John Publishing Co.,
June, 1952**
1 . . . . . . . . . . . . . . . . . . . . . . . 125.00
2 & 3 . . . . . . . . . . . . . . . . . . . @100.00

## TERRY-TOONS COMICS
**Select, Timely, Marvel,
St. Johns, 1942**
1 Paul Terry (fa) . . . . . . . . . . . 2,500.00
2 . . . . . . . . . . . . . . . . . . . . . . . 800.00
3 thru 6 . . . . . . . . . . . . . . . . . @500.00
7 Hitler,Hirohito,Mussolini(c) . . . . 700.00
8 thru 20 . . . . . . . . . . . . . . . . @400.00
21 thru 37 . . . . . . . . . . . . . . . . @300.00
38 I&(c):Mighty Mouse . . . . . . 1,600.00
39 Mighty Mouse . . . . . . . . . . . 500.00
40 thru 49 All Mighty Mouse . . @250.00
50 I:Heckle & Jeckle . . . . . . . . . 600.00
51 thru 60 . . . . . . . . . . . . . . . @150.00
61 thru 70 . . . . . . . . . . . . . . . @125.00
71 thru 86 . . . . . . . . . . . . . . . @125.00
Becomes:

## PAUL TERRY'S COMICS
**St. John Publishing Co.**
85a Mighty Mouse, etc. . . . . . . . 150.00
86a . . . . . . . . . . . . . . . . . . . . . 100.00
87 thru 100 . . . . . . . . . . . . . @100.00
101 thru 125 . . . . . . . . . . . . @100.00
Becomes:

## ADVENTURES OF
## MIGHTY MOUSE
**St. John Publ. Co., 1955**
126 thru 128 . . . . . . . . . . . . @150.00
**Pines, 1956**
129 thru 143 . . . . . . . . . . . . @150.00
**Dell Publ. Co., 1959**
144 thru 155 . . . . . . . . . . . . @125.00

## TESSIE THE TYPIST
**Marvel Timely, Summer, 1944**
1 BW,Doc Rockblock . . . . . . . . . 750.00
2 BW,Powerhouse Pepper . . . . . 400.00
3 Football cover . . . . . . . . . . . . 150.00
4 BW . . . . . . . . . . . . . . . . . . . . 300.00
5 BW . . . . . . . . . . . . . . . . . . . . 300.00
6 BW,HK,Hey Look . . . . . . . . . . 300.00
7 BW . . . . . . . . . . . . . . . . . . . . 300.00
8 BW . . . . . . . . . . . . . . . . . . . . 300.00
9 BW,HK,Powerhouse Pepper . . 325.00
10 BW,A:Rusty . . . . . . . . . . . . . 325.00
11 BW,A:Rusty . . . . . . . . . . . . . 325.00
12 BW,HK . . . . . . . . . . . . . . . . 325.00
13 BW,A:Millie The Model,Rusty . 275.00
14 BW . . . . . . . . . . . . . . . . . . . 275.00
15 HK,A:Millie,Rusty . . . . . . . . . 275.00
16 HK . . . . . . . . . . . . . . . . . . . 150.00
17 HK,A:Millie, Rusty . . . . . . . . . 150.00
18 HK . . . . . . . . . . . . . . . . . . . 150.00
19 Annie Oakley story . . . . . . . . 100.00
20 . . . . . . . . . . . . . . . . . . . . . . 100.00
21 A:Lana, Millie . . . . . . . . . . . . 100.00
22 . . . . . . . . . . . . . . . . . . . . . . 100.00
23 . . . . . . . . . . . . . . . . . . . . . . 100.00
Becomes:

## TINY TESSIE
24 . . . . . . . . . . . . . . . . . . . . . . 100.00
Becomes:

## REAL EXPERIENCES
25 Ph(c),Jan., 1950 . . . . . . . . . . 100.00

## TEXAN, THE
**St. John Publishing Co.,
Aug., 1948**
1 GT,F:Buckskin Belle,The Gay
Buckaroo,Mustang Jack . . . . 200.00
2 GT . . . . . . . . . . . . . . . . . . . . 125.00
3 BL(c) . . . . . . . . . . . . . . . . . . 100.00
4 MB,MB(c) . . . . . . . . . . . . . . . 200.00
5 MB,MB(c),Mystery Rustlers
of the Rio Grande . . . . . . . . 200.00
6 MB(c),Death Valley
Double-Cross . . . . . . . . . . . 125.00
7 MB,MB(c),Comanche Justice
Strikes at Midnight . . . . . . . 200.00
8 MB,MB(c),Scalp Hunters
Hide their Tracks . . . . . . . . 200.00
9 MB(c),Ghost Terror of
the Blackfeet . . . . . . . . . . . . 200.00
10 MB,MB(c),Treason Rides
the Warpath . . . . . . . . . . . . 125.00
11 MB,MB(c),Hawk Knife . . . . . . 200.00

12 MB . . . . . . . . . . . . . . . . . . . 250.00
13 MB,Doublecross at Devil'sDen 200.00
14 MB,Ambush at Buffalo Trail . . 200.00
15 MB,Twirling Blades Tame
Treachery . . . . . . . . . . . . . . 200.00
Becomes:

## FIGHTIN' TEXAN
**Sept., 1952**
16 GT,Wanted Dead or Alive . . . 125.00
17 LC,LC(c);Killers Trail,
Dec., 1952 . . . . . . . . . . . . . 100.00

## TEXAS KID
**Marvel Atlas, Jan., 1951**
1 GT,JMn,O:Texas Kid . . . . . . . 300.00
2 JMn . . . . . . . . . . . . . . . . . . . 200.00
3 JMn,Man Who Didn't Exist . . . 150.00
4 thru 9 JMn . . . . . . . . . . . . . @150.00
10 JMn,July, 1952 . . . . . . . . . . 150.00

## TEXAS RANGERS
## IN ACTION
**Charlton Comics, 1956**
5 . . . . . . . . . . . . . . . . . . . . . . . 150.00
6 and 7 . . . . . . . . . . . . . . . . . @100.00
8 SD . . . . . . . . . . . . . . . . . . . . 100.00
9 and 10 . . . . . . . . . . . . . . . . @100.00
11 AW . . . . . . . . . . . . . . . . . . . 100.00
12 . . . . . . . . . . . . . . . . . . . . . . 100.00
13 AW . . . . . . . . . . . . . . . . . . . 150.00
14 thru 20 . . . . . . . . . . . . . . . @100.00

## TEX FARRELL
**D.S. Publishing Co.,
March–April, 1948**
1 Pride of the Wild West . . . . . . 175.00

## TEX GRANGER
**See: CALLING ALL BOYS**

## TEX MORGAN
**Marvel, Aug., 1948**
1 Tex Morgan & Lobo . . . . . . . . 350.00
2 Boot Hill Welcome For A
Bad Man . . . . . . . . . . . . . . 225.00
3 A:Arizona Annie . . . . . . . . . . . 150.00
4 SSh,Trapped in the Outlaw's
Den, A:Arizona Annie . . . . . 125.00
5 Valley of Missing Cowboys . . . 125.00
6 Never Say Murder,
A:Tex Taylor . . . . . . . . . . . . 150.00

**Te**

Tex Ritter Western #13
© Fawcett Publications

The Thing #10
© Charlton Comics

This Magazine Is Haunted #8
© Fawcett Publications

7 CCB,Ph(c),Captain Tootsie,
  A:Tex Taylor . . . . . . . . . . . . 200.00
8 Ph(c),Terror Of Rimrock
  Valley, A:Diablo . . . . . . . . . 200.00
9 Ph(c),Death to Tex Taylor,
  Feb., 1950 . . . . . . . . . . . . . 200.00

## TEX RITTER WESTERN
### Fawcett Publications/ Charlton Comics, Oct., 1950–May, 1959
1 Ph(c),B:Tex Ritter, his Horse
  White Flash, his dog Fury, and
  his mom Nancy . . . . . . . . . . 900.00
2 Ph(c),Vanishing Varmints . . . 400.00
3 Ph(c),Blazing Six-Guns . . . . . 325.00
4 Ph(c),The Jaws of Terror . . . . 275.00
5 Ph(c),Bullet Trail . . . . . . . . . . 275.00
6 Ph(c),Killer Bait . . . . . . . . . . . 250.00
7 Ph(c),Gunsmoke Revenge . . . 225.00
8 Ph(c),Lawless Furnace Valley . 225.00
9 Ph(c),The Spider's Web . . . . . 225.00
10 Ph(c),The Ghost Town . . . . . 225.00
11 Ph(c),Saddle Conquest . . . . . 225.00
12 Ph(c),Prairie Inferno . . . . . . . 175.00
13 Ph(c) . . . . . . . . . . . . . . . . . . . 175.00
14 Ph(c) . . . . . . . . . . . . . . . . . . . 175.00
15 Ph(c) . . . . . . . . . . . . . . . . . . . 175.00
16 thru 19 Ph(c) . . . . . . . . . . @175.00
20 Ph(c),Stagecoach To Danger . 175.00
21 Ph(c), . . . . . . . . . . . . . . . . . . 200.00
22 Panic at Diamond B . . . . . . . 150.00
23 A:Young Falcon . . . . . . . . . . . 125.00
24 A:Young Falcon . . . . . . . . . . . 125.00
25 A:Young Falcon . . . . . . . . . . . 125.00
26 thru 38 . . . . . . . . . . . . . . @100.00
39 AW,AW(c) . . . . . . . . . . . . . . 100.00
40 thru 46 . . . . . . . . . . . . . . @100.00

## TEX TAYLOR
### Marvel, Sept., 1948
1 SSh,Boot Hill Showdown . . . . 325.00
2 When Two-Gun Terror Rides
  the Range . . . . . . . . . . . . . . 175.00
3 SSh,Thundering Hooves and
  Blazing Guns. . . . . . . . . . . . 150.00
4 Ph(c),Draw or Die Cowpoke . . 200.00
5 Ph(c),The Juggler of Yellow
  Valley,A:Blaze Carson . . . . . 200.00
6 Ph(c),Mystery of Howling Gap. 200.00
7 Ph(c),Trapped in Time's Lost
  Land,A:Diablo . . . . . . . . . . . 225.00
8 Ph(c),The Mystery of Devil-
  Tree Plateau,A:Diablo . . . . . 225.00

9 Ph(c),Guns Along the Border,
  A:Nimo,March, 1950 . . . . . . 225.00

## THING!, THE
### Song Hits/Capitol Stories/ Charlton Comics, Feb., 1952
1 Horror . . . . . . . . . . . . . . . . . 2,500.00
2 Crazy King(c) . . . . . . . . . . . 2,000.00
3 Green skinned creature . . . . 2,000.00
4 AFa(c),I Was A Zombie . . . . 1,500.00
5 LM(c),Severed Head(c) . . . . 1,500.00
6 . . . . . . . . . . . . . . . . . . . . . . . 1,500.00
7 Fingernail to Eye(c) . . . . . . . 1,600.00
8 . . . . . . . . . . . . . . . . . . . . . . . 1,500.00
9 Severe cruelty. . . . . . . . . . . . 2,000.00
10 Devil(c). . . . . . . . . . . . . . . . 1,250.00
11 SC,Cleaver, eye injury . . . . . 1,500.00
12 SD,SD(c),Neck Blood
   Sucking. . . . . . . . . . . . . . . 1,500.00
13 SD,SD(c) . . . . . . . . . . . . . . 1,500.00
14 SD,SD(c) torture . . . . . . . . . 1,500.00
15 SD,SD(c) . . . . . . . . . . . . . . 1,500.00
16 Eye Torture . . . . . . . . . . . . . . 750.00
17 BP,SD(c) . . . . . . . . . . . . . . 1,500.00
Becomes:

## BLUE BEETLE
### Feb., 1955
18 America's Fastest Moving
   Crusader Against Crime . . . . 250.00
19 JKa,Lightning Fast . . . . . . . . 275.00
20 JKa . . . . . . . . . . . . . . . . . . . 275.00
21 The Invincible . . . . . . . . . . . . 200.00
Becomes:

## MR. MUSCLES
### March, 1956
22 World's Most Perfect Man. . . . 150.00
23 Aug., 1956. . . . . . . . . . . . . . 100.00

## THIS IS SUSPENSE
See: LAWBREAKERS

## THIS IS SUSPENSE!
See: STRANGE SUSPENSE STORIES

## THIS IS WAR
### Standard Comics, July, 1952
5 ATh,Show Them How To Die . 150.00
6 ATh,Make Him A Soldier . . . . 125.00

7 One Man For Himself . . . . . . . 100.00
8 Miracle on Massacre Hill . . . . 100.00
9 ATh,May, 1953 . . . . . . . . . . . 125.00

## THIS MAGAZINE IS HAUNTED
### Fawcett Publications Oct., 1951
1 MBi,F:Doctor Death . . . . . . . . 850.00
2 GE . . . . . . . . . . . . . . . . . . . . 650.00
3 MBi,Quest of the Vampire . . . 400.00
4 BP,The Blind, The Doomed
  and the Dead . . . . . . . . . . . 400.00
5 BP,GE,The Slithering Horror
  of Skontong Swamp! . . . . . . 650.00
6 Secret of the Walking Dead. . . 300.00
7 The Man Who Saw Too Much . 300.00
8 The House in the Web. . . . . . . 300.00
9 The Witch of Tarlo . . . . . . . . . 300.00
10 I Am Dr Death,
   Severed Head(c) . . . . . . . . . 500.00
11 BP,Touch of Death . . . . . . . . 300.00
12 BP . . . . . . . . . . . . . . . . . . . . 300.00
13 BP,Severed Head(c) . . . . . . . 500.00
14 BP,Horrors of the Damned . . . 300.00
### Charlton Comics, 1954
15 DG(c) . . . . . . . . . . . . . . . . . . 250.00
16 SD(c). . . . . . . . . . . . . . . . . . 500.00
17 SD,SD(c). . . . . . . . . . . . . . . 600.00
18 SD,SD(c). . . . . . . . . . . . . . . 500.00
19 SD(c). . . . . . . . . . . . . . . . . . 450.00
20 SMz(c). . . . . . . . . . . . . . . . . 265.00
21 SD(c). . . . . . . . . . . . . . . . . . 400.00
Becomes:

## DANGER AND ADVENTURE
### Feb., 1955
22 The Viking King,F:Ibis the
   Invincible . . . . . . . . . . . . . . 150.00
23 F:Nyoka the Jungle Girl
   Comics Code. . . . . . . . . . . . 125.00
24 DG&AA(c) . . . . . . . . . . . . . . 100.00
25 thru 27. . . . . . . . . . . . . . @100.00
Becomes:

## ROBIN HOOD AND HIS MERRY MEN
### April, 1956
28 . . . . . . . . . . . . . . . . . . . . . . 150.00
29 thru 37. . . . . . . . . . . . . . @100.00
38 SD,Aug., 1958 . . . . . . . . . . . 150.00

*3-D Adventures of Superman*
© DC Comics

*3-D EC Classics #2*
© E.C. Comics

*3-D Sheena Jungle Queen #1*
© Fiction House

## THIS MAGAZINE
## IS HAUNTED
## See: CHARLIE CHAN

### 3-D ACTION
**Marvel Atlas 1954**
1 Battle Brady . . . . . . . . . . . . . . 450.00

### 3-D ADVENTURES OF
### SUPERMAN
**DC Comics, 1953**
N# O:Superman . . . . . . . . . . . 1,500.00

### 3-D ANIMAL FUN
**Premier Magazines, 1953**
1 Ziggy Pig, Silly Seal,etc. . . . . . 400.00

### 3-D BATMAN
### ADVENTURES
**DC Comics 1953**
1 with Bat-glasses . . . . . . . . . . 1,500.00

### CAPTAIN 3-D
**Harvey Publ, 1953**
1 . . . . . . . . . . . . . . . . . . . . . . . 125.00

### CHERRIOS 3D CLASSICS
**Walt Disney Productions, 1954**
1 . . . . . . . . . . . . . . . . . . . . . . . 150.00

### 3-D CIRCUS
**Fiction House, 1953**
1 . . . . . . . . . . . . . . . . . . . . . . . 500.00

### 3-D DARING
### ADVENTURES
**St. John Publ, 1953**
1 . . . . . . . . . . . . . . . . . . . . . . . 400.00

### 3-D-ELL
**Dell Publishing Co., 1953**
1 Rootie Kazootie . . . . . . . . . . . 500.00
3 Flunkey Louise. . . . . . . . . . . . 450.00

### 3-D DOLLY
**Harvey Publ, 1953**
1 Richie Rich. . . . . . . . . . . . . . 850.00

### 3-D EC CLASSICS
**E.C. Comics 1954**
1 . . . . . . . . . . . . . . . . . . . . . 1,200.00
2 Tales from the Crypt of Terror 1,200.00

### 3-D FELIX THE CAT
**Toby Press, 1953**
N# . . . . . . . . . . . . . . . . . . . . . 350.00

### 3-D FIRST CHRISTMAS
**Fiction House, 1953**
1 . . . . . . . . . . . . . . . . . . . . . . . 250.00

### 3-D FUNNY MOVIES
**Comic Media, 1953**
1 Bugsey Bear . . . . . . . . . . . . . 425.00

### FUNNY 3-D
**Harvey Publ., 1953**
1 . . . . . . . . . . . . . . . . . . . . . . . 350.00

### 3-D HAWK, THE
**St. John Publ, 1953**
1 Western . . . . . . . . . . . . . . . . 350.00

### 3-D HOUSE OF TERROR
**St. John Publ., 1953**
1 . . . . . . . . . . . . . . . . . . . . . . . 500.00

### 3-D I LOVE LUCY
1 Lucy, Desi, Ricky Jr. Ph(c). . . . 500.00

### 3-D INDIAN WARRIORS
**Star Publications, 1953**
1 . . . . . . . . . . . . . . . . . . . . . . . 250.00

### (3-D Features Presents)
### JET PUP
**Dimensions Publ., 1953**
1 . . . . . . . . . . . . . . . . . . . . . . . 500.00

### 3-D JUNGLE THRILLS
**Star Publications, 1953**
1 . . . . . . . . . . . . . . . . . . . . . . . 350.00

### 3-D KATY KEENE
**Archie Publications, 1953**
1 . . . . . . . . . . . . . . . . . . . . . . . 500.00

### 3-D LITTLE EVA
**St. John Publ, 1953**
1 . . . . . . . . . . . . . . . . . . . . . . . 350.00
2 . . . . . . . . . . . . . . . . . . . . . . . 350.00

### 3-D LOVE
**Steriographic Publ., 1953**
1 . . . . . . . . . . . . . . . . . . . . . . . 425.00

### (Three Dimension Comics)
### MIGHTY MOUSE
**St. John Publ, 1953**
1 . . . . . . . . . . . . . . . . . . . . . . . 350.00
2 . . . . . . . . . . . . . . . . . . . . . . . 350.00
3 . . . . . . . . . . . . . . . . . . . . . . . 350.00

### 3-D NOODNICK
**Comic Media, 1953**
1 . . . . . . . . . . . . . . . . . . . . . . . 350.00

### 3-D ROMANCE
**Steriographic Publ., 1954**
1 . . . . . . . . . . . . . . . . . . . . . . . 425.00

### (Harvey 3-D Hits)
### SAD SACK
**Harvey Publications, 1954**
1 . . . . . . . . . . . . . . . . . . . . . . . 350.00

### 3-D SHEENA,
### JUNGLE QUEEN
**Fiction House, 1953**
1 . . . . . . . . . . . . . . . . . . . . . . 1,000.00

### 3-D SPACE KAT-ETS
**Power Publishing, 1953**
1 . . . . . . . . . . . . . . . . . . . . . . . 350.00

**Th**

*True 3-D #1*
© *Harvey Publications*

*Three Stooges #9*
© *Dell Publishing Co.*

*Thrilling Comics #59*
© *Standard Comics*

### 3-D SUPER ANIMALS
**Star Publications, 1953**
1 Pidgy and the Magic Glasses . 350.00

### 3-D SUPER FUNNIES
**Superior Comics Publ., 1953**
1 Dopey Duck . . . . . . . . . . . . . 350.00

### 3-D TALES OF THE WEST
**Marvel Atlas, 1954**
1 . . . . . . . . . . . . . . . . . . . . . . 500.00

### 3-D THREE STOOGES
**St. John Publ., 1953**
1 . . . . . . . . . . . . . . . . . . . . . . 600.00
2 . . . . . . . . . . . . . . . . . . . . . . 600.00

### 3-D TRUE 3D
**Harvey Publ., 1953**
1 . . . . . . . . . . . . . . . . . . . . . . 400.00
2 . . . . . . . . . . . . . . . . . . . . . . 350.00

### 3-D WESTERN FIGHTERS
**Star Publications, 1953**
1 . . . . . . . . . . . . . . . . . . . . . . 350.00

### THE THREE MOUSEKETEERS
**DC Comics, 1956–60**
1 . . . . . . . . . . . . . . . . . . . . . . 275.00
2 . . . . . . . . . . . . . . . . . . . . . . 150.00
3 . . . . . . . . . . . . . . . . . . . . . . 125.00
4 . . . . . . . . . . . . . . . . . . . . . . 125.00
5 . . . . . . . . . . . . . . . . . . . . . . 125.00
6 thru 10 . . . . . . . . . . . . . . @125.00
11 thru 20 . . . . . . . . . . . . . @100.00
21 thru 26 . . . . . . . . . . . . . @100.00

### THREE RING COMICS
**Spotlight Publishers, March, 1945**
1 Funny Animal . . . . . . . . . . . 200.00

### THREE STOOGES
**Jubilee Publ., Feb., 1949**
1 JKu,Infinity(c) . . . . . . . . . 1,500.00
2 JKu,On the Set of the
  'The Gorilla Girl' . . . . . . . 1,200.00

### St. John Publishing Co.
1:JKu,'Hell Bent for
  Treasure,' Sept., 1953 . . . . 1,200.00
2 JKu. . . . . . . . . . . . . . . . . . 900.00
3 JKu,3D. . . . . . . . . . . . . . . . 900.00
4 JKu,Medical Mayhem . . . . . 800.00
5 JKu,Shempador-Matador
  Supreme . . . . . . . . . . . . . . 800.00
6 JKu,. . . . . . . . . . . . . . . . . . 800.00
7 JKu,Ocotber, 1954. . . . . . . . 800.00

### THREE STOOGES
**Dell Publishing Co., 1959**
6 Ph(c),B:Prof. Putter . . . . . . . 300.00
7 Ph(c) . . . . . . . . . . . . . . . . . 300.00
8 Ph(c) . . . . . . . . . . . . . . . . . 300.00
9 Ph(c) . . . . . . . . . . . . . . . . . 300.00

### THRILLING ADVENTURES IN STAMPS
**See: STAMPS COMICS**

### THRILLING COMICS
**Better Publ./Nedor/ Standard Comics, Feb., 1940**
1 B&O:Doc Strange,B:Nickie
  Norton . . . . . . . . . . . . . . 5,000.00
2 B:Rio Kid,Woman in Red
  Pinocchio . . . . . . . . . . . . 2,500.00
3 B:Lone Eagle,The Ghost . . 2,000.00
4 Dr Strange(c) . . . . . . . . . . 1,400.00
5 Bondage(c) . . . . . . . . . . . 1,600.00
6 Dr Strange(c) . . . . . . . . . . 1,400.00
7 Dr Strange(c) . . . . . . . . . . 1,500.00
8 V:Pirates . . . . . . . . . . . . . 1,500.00
9 ASh,Bondage(c) . . . . . . . . 1,500.00
10 V:Nazis. . . . . . . . . . . . . . 1,700.00
11 ASh(c),V:Nazis . . . . . . . . 1,400.00
12 ASh(c) . . . . . . . . . . . . . . 1,400.00
13 ASh(c),Bondage(c). . . . . . 1,600.00
14 ASh(c) . . . . . . . . . . . . . . 1,200.00
15 ASh(c),V:Nazis . . . . . . . . 1,200.00
16 Bondage(c) . . . . . . . . . . . 1,600.00
17 Dr Strange(c) . . . . . . . . . 1,200.00
18 Dr Strange(c) . . . . . . . . . 1,600.00
19 I&O:American Crusader. . . 1,500.00
20 Bondage(c) . . . . . . . . . . . 1,600.00
21 American Crusader(c) . . . . 1,200.00
22 Bondage(c) . . . . . . . . . . . 1,400.00
23 American Crusader . . . . . . 1,200.00
24 I:Mike in Doc Strange . . . . 1,200.00
25 DR Strange(c) . . . . . . . . . 1,200.00

26 Dr Strange(c) . . . . . . . . . . 1,200.00
27 Bondage(c) . . . . . . . . . . . 1,400.00
28 Bondage(c) . . . . . . . . . . . 1,400.00
29 E:Rio Kid;Bondage(c) . . . . 1,400.00
30 Bondage(c) . . . . . . . . . . . 1,400.00
31 Dr Strange(c) . . . . . . . . . . 1,100.00
32 Dr Strange(c) . . . . . . . . . . 1,100.00
33 Dr Strange(c) . . . . . . . . . . 1,100.00
34 Dr Strange(c) . . . . . . . . . . 1,100.00
35 Dr Strange . . . . . . . . . . . . 1,100.00
36 ASh(c),B:Commando . . . . . 1,200.00
37 BO,ASh(c) . . . . . . . . . . . . 1,100.00
38 ASh(c) . . . . . . . . . . . . . . . 1,100.00
39 ASh(c),E:American Crusader 1,100.00
40 ASh(c) . . . . . . . . . . . . . . . 1,100.00
41 ASh(c),F:American Crusader,
  Hitler. . . . . . . . . . . . . . . . 2,000.00
42 ASh(c). . . . . . . . . . . . . . . . 900.00
43 ASh(c). . . . . . . . . . . . . . . . 900.00
44 ASh(c),Hitler(c). . . . . . . . . 1,400.00
45 EK,ASh(c). . . . . . . . . . . . . . 800.00
46 ASh(c). . . . . . . . . . . . . . . . 800.00
47 ASh(c). . . . . . . . . . . . . . . . 800.00
48 EK,ASh(c). . . . . . . . . . . . . . 800.00
49 ASh(c). . . . . . . . . . . . . . . . 800.00
50 ASh(c). . . . . . . . . . . . . . . . 800.00
51 ASh(c). . . . . . . . . . . . . . . . 800.00
52 ASh(c),E:Th Ghost;
  Peto-Bondage(c) . . . . . . . . 900.00
53 ASh(c),B:Phantom Detective . 700.00
54 ASh(c),Bondage(c) . . . . . . . 900.00
55 ASh(c),E:Lone Eagle . . . . . . 700.00
56 ASh(c),B:Princess Pantha . . . 900.00
57 ASh(c). . . . . . . . . . . . . . . . 800.00
58 ASh(c). . . . . . . . . . . . . . . . 800.00
59 ASh(c). . . . . . . . . . . . . . . . 800.00
60 ASh(c). . . . . . . . . . . . . . . . 800.00
61 ASh(c),Grl,A:Lone Eagle . . . 800.00
62 ASh(c). . . . . . . . . . . . . . . . 800.00
63 ASh(c),GT. . . . . . . . . . . . . . 800.00
64 ASh(c). . . . . . . . . . . . . . . . 800.00
65 ASh(c),E:Commando Cubs,
  Phantom Detective . . . . . . . 800.00
66 ASh(c). . . . . . . . . . . . . . . . 800.00
67 FF,ASh(c) . . . . . . . . . . . . . . 900.00
68 FF,ASh(c) . . . . . . . . . . . . . . 900.00
69 FF,ASh(c) . . . . . . . . . . . . . . 900.00
70 FF,ASh(c) . . . . . . . . . . . . . . 900.00
71 FF,ASh(c) . . . . . . . . . . . . . . 900.00
72 FF,ASh(c),Sea Eagle . . . . . . 900.00
73 FF,ASh(c) . . . . . . . . . . . . . . 900.00
74 ASh(c),E:Princess Pantha;
  B:Buck Ranger . . . . . . . . . . 500.00
75 B:Western Front . . . . . . . . . 350.00
76 Western. . . . . . . . . . . . . . . 350.00
77 ASh(c). . . . . . . . . . . . . . . . . 350.00

All comics prices listed are for *Near Mint* condition.

**Th**

*Shocking Mystery Cases #54*
© Star Publications

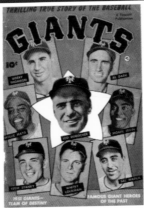

*Thrilling True Story of the Baseball Giants N# © Fawcett Publications*

*Tim Holt #38*
© Magazine Enterprises

78 Bondage(c) . . . . . . . . . . . . . . 400.00
79 BK . . . . . . . . . . . . . . . . . . . . 350.00
80 JSe,BE,April, 1951 . . . . . . . . 350.00

## THRILLING CRIME CASES
**Star Publications,**
**June–July, 1950**
41 LbC(c),The Unknowns . . . . . . 350.00
42 LbC(c),The Gunmaster . . . . . . 325.00
43 LbC,LbC(c),The Chameleon . . 350.00
44 LbC(c),Sugar Bowl Murder . . . 350.00
45 LbC(c),Maze of Murder . . . . . . 350.00
46 LbC,LbC(c),Modern
    Communications . . . . . . . . . 300.00
47 LbC(c),The Careless Killer . . . 300.00
48 LbC(c),Road Black . . . . . . . . . 300.00
49 LbC(c),The Poisoner . . . . . . . 550.00
**Becomes:**

## SHOCKING MYSTERY CASES
**Sept., 1952–Oct., 1954**
50 JyD,LbC(c),Dead Man's
    Revenge . . . . . . . . . . . . . . . 550.00
51 JyD,LbC(c),A Murderer's
    Reward . . . . . . . . . . . . . . . . 350.00
52 LbC(c),The Carnival Killer . . . 350.00
53 LbC(c),The Long Shot of Evil . 350.00
54 LbC(c),Double-Cross of Death 350.00
55 LbC(c),Return from Death . . . 350.00
56 LbC(c),The Chase . . . . . . . . . 375.00
57 LbC(c),Thrilling Cases . . . . . . 350.00
58 LbC(c),Killer at Large . . . . . . . 350.00
59 LbC(c),Relentless Huntdown . . 350.00
60 LbC(c),Lesson of the Law . . . . 350.00

## THRILLING ROMANCES
**Standard Comics,**
**Dec., 1949**
5 Ph(c) . . . . . . . . . . . . . . . . . . . 150.00
6 Ph(c) . . . . . . . . . . . . . . . . . . . 100.00
7 Ph(c),JSe,BE . . . . . . . . . . . . . 125.00
8 Ph(c) . . . . . . . . . . . . . . . . . . . 100.00
9 Ph(c),GT . . . . . . . . . . . . . . . . . 125.00
10 Ph(c),JSe,BE . . . . . . . . . . . . 125.00
11 Ph(c),JSe,BE . . . . . . . . . . . . 125.00
12 Ph(c),WW . . . . . . . . . . . . . . . 150.00
13 Ph(c),JSe . . . . . . . . . . . . . . . 100.00
14 Ph(c),Danny Kaye . . . . . . . . . 125.00
15 Ph(c),Tony Martin,Ph(c) . . . . . 100.00
16 Ph(c) . . . . . . . . . . . . . . . . . . 100.00
17 Ph(c) . . . . . . . . . . . . . . . . . . 100.00

18 thru 21 Ph(c) . . . . . . . . . . . @100.00
22 Ph(c),ATn . . . . . . . . . . . . . . . 125.00
23 Ph(c),ATn . . . . . . . . . . . . . . . 125.00
24 Ph(c),ATn3 . . . . . . . . . . . . . . 125.00
25 Ph(c),ATn . . . . . . . . . . . . . . . 125.00

## THRILLING TRUE STORY OF THE BASEBALL GIANTS
**Fawcett Publications, 1952**
N# Partial Ph(c),Famous Giants
    of the Past, Willie Mays . . . 1,200.00
2 Yankees Ph(c),Joe DiMaggio,
    Yogi Berra,Mickey Mantle,
    Casey Stengel . . . . . . . . . . . 900.00

## THRILLS OF TOMORROW
**See: TOMB OF TERROR**

## THUNDA
**See: A-1 COMICS**

## TICK TOCK TALES
**Magazine Enterprises,**
**Jan., 1946**
1 (fa) Koko & Kola . . . . . . . . . . . 250.00
2 (fa) Calender . . . . . . . . . . . . . 200.00
3 thru 10 (fa) . . . . . . . . . . . . . @150.00
11 thru 18 (fa) . . . . . . . . . . . . @125.00
19 (fa),Flag(c) . . . . . . . . . . . . . 125.00
20 thru 22 (fa) . . . . . . . . . . . . @125.00
23 (fa),Mugsy Mouse . . . . . . . . . 125.00
24 thru 33 (fa) . . . . . . . . . . . . @125.00
34 (fa), 1951 . . . . . . . . . . . . . . . 125.00

## TILLY AND TED TINKERTOTLAND
**W.T. Grant Co., 1945**
N# Christmas . . . . . . . . . . . . . . . 100.00

## TIM HOLT
**Magazine Enterprises,**
**Jan.–Feb., 1949**
1 thru 3 see: A-1 Comics #14, #17, #19
4 FBe,Ph(c) . . . . . . . . . . . . . 1,200.00
5 FBe,Ph(c) . . . . . . . . . . . . . . . 700.00
6 FBe,Ph(c),I:Calico Kid . . . . . . 600.00
7 FBe,Ph(c),Man-Killer Mustang 500.00
8 FBe,Ph(c) . . . . . . . . . . . . . . . 500.00

9 FBe,DAy(c),TerribleTenderfoot 500.00
10 FBe, DAy(c),The Devil Horse . 500.00
11 FBe,DAy(c),O&I:Ghost Rider . 750.00
12 FBe,DAy(c),Battle at
    Bullock Gap . . . . . . . . . . . . . 250.00
13 FBe,DAy(c),Ph(c) . . . . . . . . . 250.00
14 FBe,DAy(c),Ph(c),The
    Honest Bandits . . . . . . . . . . 250.00
15 FBe,DAy,Ph(c) . . . . . . . . . . . 250.00
16 FBe,DAy,Ph(c) . . . . . . . . . . . 250.00
17 FBe,DAy,Ph(c) . . . . . . . . . . . 750.00
18 FBe,DAy,Ph(c) . . . . . . . . . . . 300.00
19 FBe,DAy,They Dig By Night . . 175.00
20 FBe,DAy,O:Red Mask . . . . . . 300.00
21 FBe,DAy,FF(c) . . . . . . . . . . . 600.00
22 FBe,DAy . . . . . . . . . . . . . . . 175.00
23 FF,FBe,DAy . . . . . . . . . . . . . 500.00
24 FBe,DAy,FBe(c) . . . . . . . . . . 175.00
25 FBe,DAy,FBe(c) . . . . . . . . . . 350.00
26 FBe,DAy,FBe(c) . . . . . . . . . . 175.00
27 FBe,DAy,FBe(c),V:Straw Man. 175.00
28 FBe,DAy,FBe(c),Ph(c) . . . . . . 175.00
29 FBe,DAy,FBe,Ph(c), . . . . . . . 175.00
30 FBe,DAy,FBe(c),Lady Doom
    & The Death Wheel . . . . . . . 200.00
31 FBe,DAy,FBe(c) . . . . . . . . . . 200.00
32 FBe,DAy,FBe(c) . . . . . . . . . . 200.00
33 FBe,DAy,FBe(c) . . . . . . . . . . 200.00
34 FBe,DAy,FBe(c) . . . . . . . . . . 250.00
35 FBe,DAy,FBe(c) . . . . . . . . . . 250.00
36 FBe,DAy,FBe(c),Drugs . . . . . 350.00
37 FBe,DAy,FBe(c) . . . . . . . . . . 250.00
38 FBe,DAy,FBe(c) . . . . . . . . . . 250.00
39 FBe,DAy,FBe(c),3D Effect . . . 200.00
40 FBe,DAy,FBe(c) . . . . . . . . . . 200.00
41 FBe,DAy,FBe(c) . . . . . . . . . . 200.00
**Becomes:**

## RED MASK
**June–July, 1954**
42 FBe,DAy,FBe(c),3D . . . . . . . . 250.00
43 FBe,DAy,FBe(c),3D . . . . . . . . 225.00
44 FBe,DAy,FBe(c),Death at
    Split Mesa,3D . . . . . . . . . . . 225.00
45 FBe,DAy,FBe(c),V:False Red
    Mask . . . . . . . . . . . . . . . . . 225.00
46 FBe,DAy,FBe(c) . . . . . . . . . . 225.00
47 FBe,DAy,FBe(c) . . . . . . . . . . 225.00
48 FBe,DAy,FBe(c),Comics Code 200.00
49 FBe,DAy,FBe(c) . . . . . . . . . . 200.00
50 FBe,DAy . . . . . . . . . . . . . . . 200.00
51 FBe,DAy,The Magic of 'The
    Presto Kid' . . . . . . . . . . . . . 200.00
52 FBe,DAy,O:Presto Kid . . . . . 225.00
53 FBe,DAy . . . . . . . . . . . . . . . 150.00
54 FBe,DAy,Sept., 1957 . . . . . . . 225.00

**Ti**

All comics prices listed are for *Near Mint* condition.

Tim Tyler Cowboy #11
© Standard Comics

Tip Top Comics #34
© St. John Publishing Co.

T-Man #3
© Quality Comics Group

## TIM McCOY
### See: ZOO FUNNIES

## TIMMY THE TIMID GHOST
### See: WIN A PRIZE COMICS

## TIM TYLER COWBOY
### Standard Comics,
### Nov., 1948

| | |
|---|---:|
| 11 | 150.00 |
| 12 | 100.00 |
| 13 The Doll Told the Secret | 100.00 |
| 14 Danger at Devil's Acres | 100.00 |
| 15 Secret Treasure | 100.00 |
| 16 | 100.00 |
| 17 | 100.00 |
| 18 1950 | 100.00 |

## TINY TESSIE
### See: TESSIE THE TYPIST

## TINY TOT FUNNIES
### See: FAMILY FUNNIES

## TINY TOTS COMICS
### Dell Publishing Co., 1943

| | |
|---|---:|
| 1 WK,fairy tales | 500.00 |

## TINY TOTS COMICS
### E.C. Comics, March, 1946

| | |
|---|---:|
| N# Your First Comic Book | |
| B:Burton Geller(c) and art | 500.00 |
| 2 | 275.00 |
| 3 Celebrate the 4th | 225.00 |
| 4 Go Back to School | 250.00 |
| 5 Celebrate the Winter | 225.00 |
| 6 Do Their Spring Gardening | 225.00 |
| 7 On a Thrilling Ride | 225.00 |
| 8 On a Summer Vacation | 225.00 |
| 9 On a Plane Ride | 225.00 |
| 10 Merry X-Mas Tiny Tots | |
| E:Burton Geller(c)and art | 225.00 |

## TIP TOP COMICS
### United Features, St. John,
### Dell, 1936

| | |
|---|---:|
| 1 HF,Li'l Abner | 10,000.00 |
| 2 HF | 2,600.00 |
| 3 HF,Tarzan(c) | 2,400.00 |

| | |
|---|---:|
| 4 HF,Li'l Abner(c) | 1,500.00 |
| 5 HF,Capt&Kids(c) | 1,000.00 |
| 6 HF | 900.00 |
| 7 HF | 900.00 |
| 8 HF,Li'l Abner(c) | 900.00 |
| 9 HF,Tarzan(c) | 1,200.00 |
| 10 HF,Li'L Abner(c) | 900.00 |
| 11 HF,Tarzan(c) | 850.00 |
| 12 HF,Li'l Abner | 800.00 |
| 13 HF,Tarzan(c) | 850.00 |
| 14 HF,Li'L Abner(c) | 800.00 |
| 15 HF,Capt&kids(c) | 800.00 |
| 16 HF,Tarzan(c) | 850.00 |
| 17 HF,Li'l Abner(c) | 800.00 |
| 18 HF,Tarzan(c) | 850.00 |
| 19 HF,Football(c) | 750.00 |
| 20 HF,Capt&Kids(c) | 750.00 |
| 21 HF,Tarzan(c) | 750.00 |
| 22 HF,Li'l Abner(c) | 500.00 |
| 23 HF,Capt&Kids(c) | 500.00 |
| 24 HF,Tarzan(c) | 750.00 |
| 25 HF,Capt&Kids(c) | 500.00 |
| 26 HF,Li'L Abner(c) | 500.00 |
| 27 HF,Tarzan(c) | 750.00 |
| 28 HF,Li'l Abner(c) | 500.00 |
| 29 HF,Capt&Kids(c) | 500.00 |
| 30 HF,Tarzan(c) | 750.00 |
| 31 HF,Capt&Kids(c) | 500.00 |
| 32 HF,Tarzan(c) | 700.00 |
| 33 HF,Tarzan(c) | 750.00 |
| 34 HF,Capt&Kids(c) | 750.00 |
| 35 HF | 450.00 |
| 36 HF,HK,Tarzan(c) | 750.00 |
| 37 HF,Tarzan | 750.00 |
| 38 HF | 450.00 |
| 39 HF,Tarzan | 700.00 |
| 40 HF | 450.00 |
| 41 Tarzan(c) | 750.00 |
| 42 | 450.00 |
| 43 Tarzan(c) | 400.00 |
| 44 HF | 450.00 |
| 45 HF,Tarzan(c) | 400.00 |
| 46 HF | 450.00 |
| 47 HF,Tarzan(c) | 400.00 |
| 48 HF | 450.00 |
| 49 HF | 450.00 |
| 50 HF,Tarzan(c) | 400.00 |
| 51 | 375.00 |
| 52 Tarzan(c) | 450.00 |
| 53 | 375.00 |
| 54 | 475.00 |
| 55 | 350.00 |
| 56 | 350.00 |
| 57 BHg | 400.00 |
| 58 | 300.00 |
| 59 BHg | 400.00 |

| | |
|---|---:|
| 60 | 300.00 |
| 61 and 62 BHg | @400.00 |
| 63 thru 90 | @200.00 |
| 91 thru 99 | @150.00 |
| 100 | 175.00 |
| 101 thru 150 | @125.00 |
| 151 thru 188 | @100.00 |
| 189 thru 225 | @75.00 |

## TIP TOPPER COMICS
### United Features
### Syndicate, 1949

| | |
|---|---:|
| 1 Abbie & Slats, Li'l Abner, etc. | 200.00 |
| 2 | 150.00 |
| 3 | 125.00 |
| 4 | 125.00 |
| 5 Fearless Fosdick | 125.00 |
| 6 Fearless Fosdick | 125.00 |
| 7 | 100.00 |
| 8 | 100.00 |
| 9 | 100.00 |
| 10 | 100.00 |
| 11 thru 16 | @100.00 |
| 17 Peanuts (c) | 150.00 |
| 18 thru 24 | @100.00 |
| 25 Peanuts | 110.00 |
| 26 Peanuts | 110.00 |

## T-MAN
### Comics Magazines
### (Quality Comics Group),
### Sept., 1951

| | |
|---|---:|
| 1 JCo,Pete Trask-the | |
| Treasury Man | 500.00 |
| 2 RC(c),The Girl with Death | |
| in Her Hands | 250.00 |
| 3 RC(a&c),Death Trap in Iran | 250.00 |
| 4 RC(a&c),Panama Peril | 250.00 |
| 5 RC(a&c),Violence in Venice | 250.00 |
| 6 RC(c),The Man Who | |
| Could Be Hitler | 225.00 |
| 7 RC(c),Mr. Murder & The | |
| Black Hand | 225.00 |
| 8 RC(c),Red Ticket to Hell | 225.00 |
| 9 RC(c),Trial By Terror | 200.00 |
| 10 | 200.00 |
| 11 The Voice of Russia | 175.00 |
| 12 Terror in Tokyo | 175.00 |
| 13 Mind Assassins | 175.00 |
| 14 Trouble in Bavaria, Hitler | 200.00 |
| 15 The Traitor,Bondage(c) | 175.00 |
| 16 Hunt For a Hatchetman | 175.00 |
| 17 Red Triggerman | 175.00 |
| 18 Death Rides the Rails | 175.00 |

Ti

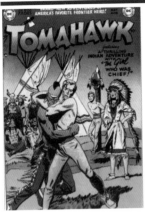

*Tomahawk #5*
© DC Comics

*Tomahawk #31*
© DC Comics

*Tom and Jerry Summer Fun #1*
© Dell Publishing Co.

19 Death Ambush . . . . . . . . . . . 175.00
20 The Fantastic H-Bomb Plot. . . 200.00
21 The Return of Mussolini . . . . . 150.00
22 Propaganda for Doom . . . . . . 165.00
23 Red Intrigue in Parid,H-Bomb. 150.00
24 Red Sabotage. . . . . . . . . . . . . 150.00
25 RC,The Ingenious Red Trap. . . 150.00
26 . . . . . . . . . . . . . . . . . . . . . . . . 125.00
27 . . . . . . . . . . . . . . . . . . . . . . . . 125.00
28 . . . . . . . . . . . . . . . . . . . . . . . . 125.00
29 . . . . . . . . . . . . . . . . . . . . . . . . 125.00
30 thru 37. . . . . . . . . . . . . . . @125.00
38 Dec., 1956 . . . . . . . . . . . . . . 125.00

## TNT COMICS

### Charles Publishing Co.,
### Feb., 1946

1 FBI story,YellowJacket. . . . . . 400.00

## TODAY'S BRIDES

### Ajax/Farrell Publishing Co.,
### Nov., 1955

1 . . . . . . . . . . . . . . . . . . . . . . . . . 125.00
2 thru 4 Nov., 1956 . . . . . . . . @100.00

## TODAY'S ROMANCE

### Standard Comics,
### March, 1952

5 Ph(c) . . . . . . . . . . . . . . . . . . . . 100.00
6 ATh, Ph(c) . . . . . . . . . . . . . . . 125.00
7 and 8 Ph(c) . . . . . . . . . . . . . @100.00

## TOMAHAWK

### DC Comics, 1950

1 Prisoner Called Tomahawk. . 2,500.00
2 FF(4pgs),Four Boys
　Against the Frontier . . . . . . 1,000.00
3 Warpath . . . . . . . . . . . . . . . . . . 800.00
4 Tomahawk Wanted: Dead
　or Alive. . . . . . . . . . . . . . . . . . . 800.00
5 The Girl Who Was Chief . . . . . 800.00
6 Tomahawk-King of the Aztecs . 700.00
7 Punishment of Tomahawk . . . . 700.00
8 The King's Messenger. . . . . . . 700.00
9 The Five Doomed Men . . . . . . 700.00
10 Frontied Sabotage . . . . . . . . . 700.00
11 Girl Who Hated Tomahawk. . . 500.00
12 Man From Magic Mountain. . . 500.00
13 Dan Hunter's Rival . . . . . . . . . 500.00
14 The Frontier Tinker . . . . . . . . . 500.00
15 The Wild Men of
　Wigwam Mountain. . . . . . . . . 500.00
16 Treasure of the Angelique. . . . 500.00

17 Short-Cut to Danger . . . . . . . 500.00
18 Bring In M'Sieur Pierre . . . . . . 500.00
19 The Lafayette Volunteers . . . . 500.00
20 NC(c),The Retreat of
　Tomahawk . . . . . . . . . . . . . . . 500.00
21 NC(c),The Terror of the
　Wrathful Spirit . . . . . . . . . . . . 350.00
22 CS(c),Admiral Tomahawk . . . . 350.00
23 CS(c),The Indian Chief
　from Oxford . . . . . . . . . . . . . . 350.00
24 NC(c),Adventure In the
　Everglades. . . . . . . . . . . . . . . 350.00
25 NC(c),The Star-Gazer of
　Freemont . . . . . . . . . . . . . . . . 350.00
26 NC(c),Ten Wagons For
　Tomahawk . . . . . . . . . . . . . . . 350.00
27 NC(c),Frontier Outcast . . . . . . 350.00
28 I:Lord Shilling . . . . . . . . . . . . . 375.00
29 Conspiracy of Wounded Bear. 400.00
30 The King of the Thieves . . . . 350.00
31 NC(c),The Buffalo Brave
　From Misty Mountain. . . . . . . 350.00
32 NC(c),The Clocks That
　Went to War. . . . . . . . . . . . . . 350.00
33 The Paleface Tribe . . . . . . . . . 350.00
34 The Capture of General
　Washington . . . . . . . . . . . . . . 350.00
35 Frontier Feud . . . . . . . . . . . . . 350.00
36 NC(c),A Cannon for Fort
　Reckless . . . . . . . . . . . . . . . . . 350.00
37 NC(c),Feathered Warriors. . . . 350.00
38 The Frontier Zoo. . . . . . . . . . . 350.00
39 The Redcoat Trickster. . . . . . . 350.00
40 Fearless Fettle-Daredevil . . . . 350.00
41 The Captured Chieftain. . . . . . 350.00
42 The Prisoner Tribe . . . . . . . . . 350.00
43 Tomahawk's Little Brother. . . . 350.00
44 The Brave Named Tomahawk 350.00
45 The Last Days of Chief Tory . . 350.00
46 The Chief With 1,000 Faces . . 200.00
47 The Frontier Rain-Maker. . . . . 200.00
48 Indian Twin Trouble. . . . . . . . . 200.00
49 The Unknown Warrior. . . . . . . 200.00
50 The Brave Who Was Jinxed. . 200.00
51 General Tomahawk. . . . . . . . . 200.00
52 Tom Thumb of the Frontier . . 200.00
53 The Four-Footed Renegade . . 200.00
54 Mystery of the 13th Arrows. . 200.00
55 Prisoners of the Choctaw . . . 200.00
56 The Riddle of the
　Five Little Indians . . . . . . . . . 200.00
57 The Strange Fight
　at Fort Bravo . . . . . . . . . . . . . 250.00
58 Track of the Mask. . . . . . . . . . 150.00
59 The Mystery Prisoner of
　Lost Island. . . . . . . . . . . . . . . 150.00

60 The Amazing Walking Fort . . . 150.00
61 Tomahawk's Secret Weapons. 100.00
62 Strongest Man in the World . . 100.00
63 The Frontier Super Men . . . . . 100.00
64 The Outcast Brave . . . . . . . . . 100.00
65 Boy Who Wouldn't Be Chief . . 100.00
66 DD&SMo(c),A Trap For
　Tomahawk . . . . . . . . . . . . . . . 100.00
67 DD&SMo(c),Frontier Sorcerer 100.00
68 DD&SMo(c),Tomahawk's
　Strange Ally . . . . . . . . . . . . . . 100.00
69 DD&SMo(c),Tracker-King
　of the Wolves. . . . . . . . . . . . . 100.00
70 DD&SMo(c),Three Tasks
　for Tomahawk . . . . . . . . . . . . 100.00
71 DD&SMo(c),The Boy Who
　Betrayed His Country . . . . . . 100.00
72 DD&SMo(c),The Frontier Pupil 100.00
73 DD&SMo(c),The Secret of
　the Indian Sorceress . . . . . . . 100.00
74 DD&SMo(c),The Great
　Paleface Masquerade . . . . . . 100.00
75 DD&SMo(c),The Ghost of
　Lord Shilling. . . . . . . . . . . . . . 100.00
76 DD&SMo(c),The Totem-Pole
　Trail . . . . . . . . . . . . . . . . . . . . 100.00
77 DD&SMo(c),The Raids of
　the One-Man Tribe . . . . . . . . 100.00

## TOM AND JERRY

### DELL GIANT EDITIONS
### Dell Publishing Co.,
### 1952–58

Back to School . . . . . . . . . . . . . . 300.00
Picnic Time. . . . . . . . . . . . . . . . . 250.00
Summer Fun 1 . . . . . . . . . . . . . . 350.00
Summer Fun 2 . . . . . . . . . . . . . . 200.00
Winter Carnival 1 . . . . . . . . . . . . 500.00
Winter Carnival 2 . . . . . . . . . . . . 350.00
Winter Fun 3 . . . . . . . . . . . . . . . 200.00
Winter Fun 4 . . . . . . . . . . . . . . . 175.00
Winter Fun 5 . . . . . . . . . . . . . . . 150.00
Winter Fun 6 . . . . . . . . . . . . . . . 150.00
Winter Fun 7 . . . . . . . . . . . . . . . 150.00

## TOM AND JERRY
### See: OUR GANG COMICS

## TOMB OF TERROR

### Harvey Publications,
### June, 1952

1 BP,The Thing From the
　Center of the Earth . . . . . . . . 750.00

**To**

---

All comics prices listed are for *Near Mint* condition.

Tom Corbett Space Cadet #4
© Dell Publishing Co.

Tom Mix Comics #8
© Ralston-Purina Co.

Tom Mix Western #56
© Fawcett Publications

2 RP,The Quagmire Beast . . . . . 600.00
3 BP,RP,Caravan of the
   Doomed, Bondage(c) . . . . . . 600.00
4 RP,I'm Going to Kill You,
   Torture . . . . . . . . . . . . . . . . 500.00
5 RP . . . . . . . . . . . . . . . . . . . . . 500.00
6 RP,Return From the Grave . . . 500.00
7 RP,Shadow of Death . . . . . . . 500.00
8 HN,The Hive . . . . . . . . . . . . . 500.00
9 BP,HN,The Tunnel . . . . . . . . 500.00
10 BP,HN,The Trial . . . . . . . . . . 500.00
11 BP,HN,The Closet . . . . . . . . . 500.00
12 BP,HN,Tale of Cain . . . . . . . . 550.00
13 BP,What Was Out There . . . . . 600.00
14 BP,SC,End Result . . . . . . . . . 600.00
15 BP,HN,Break-up, Exploding
   Head . . . . . . . . . . . . . . . . . 1,000.00
16 BP,Going,Going,Gone . . . . . . 600.00
Becomes:

## THRILLS OF
## TOMORROW
### Oct., 1954
17 RP,BP,The World of Mr. Chatt. 300.00
18 RP,BP,The Dead Awaken . . . . 200.00
19 S&K,S&K(c),A:Stuntman . . . . 600.00
20 S&K,S&K(c),A:Stuntman . . . . . 500.00

## TOM CAT
## See: BO

## TOM CORBETT
## SPACE CADET
### Dell Publishing Co.,
### Jan., 1952
See also Dell Four Color
4 based on TV show . . . . . . . . . 200.00
5 . . . . . . . . . . . . . . . . . . . . . . . 150.00
6 . . . . . . . . . . . . . . . . . . . . . . . 100.00
7 . . . . . . . . . . . . . . . . . . . . . . . 100.00
8 . . . . . . . . . . . . . . . . . . . . . . . 100.00
9 . . . . . . . . . . . . . . . . . . . . . . . 100.00
10 and 11 . . . . . . . . . . . . . . . . @100.00

## TOM CORBETT
## SPACE CADET
### Prize Publications,
### May–June, 1955
1 Robot(c) . . . . . . . . . . . . . . . . 400.00
2 . . . . . . . . . . . . . . . . . . . . . . . 300.00
3 Sept.–Oct., 1955 . . . . . . . . . . 300.00

## TOM MIX COMICS
### Ralston-Purina Co.,
### Sept., 1940
1 O:Tom Mix . . . . . . . . . . . . . 4,500.00
2 . . . . . . . . . . . . . . . . . . . . . . 1,500.00
3 . . . . . . . . . . . . . . . . . . . . . . . 800.00
4 thru 9 . . . . . . . . . . . . . . . . . @750.00
Becomes:

## TOM MIX
## COMMANDOS COMICS
### Nov., 1942
10 . . . . . . . . . . . . . . . . . . . . . . 700.00
11 Invisible Invaders . . . . . . . . . 700.00
12 Terrible Talons Of Tokyo . . . . 700.00

## TOM MIX WESTERN
### Fawcett Publications,
### Jan., 1948
1 Ph(c),Two-Fisted
   Adventures . . . . . . . . . . . . 1,500.00
2 Ph(c),Hair-Triggered Action . . 600.00
3 Ph(c),Double Barreled Action . 500.00
4 Ph(c),Cowpunching . . . . . . . . 500.00
5 Ph(c),Two Gun Action . . . . . . 500.00
6 CCB,Most Famous Cowboy . . 350.00
7 CCB,A Tattoo of Thrills . . . . . 250.00
8 EK,Ph(c),Gallant Guns . . . . . 325.00
9 CCB,Song o/t Deadly Spurs . . 325.00
10 CCB,Crack Shot Western . . . . 325.00
11 CCB,EK(C),Triple Revenge . . 325.00
12 King of the Cowboys . . . . . . . 250.00
13 Ph(c),Leather Burns . . . . . . . 250.00
14 Ph(c),Brand of Death . . . . . . 250.00
15 Ph(c),Masked Treachery . . . . 250.00
16 Ph(c),Death Spurting Guns . . . 250.00
17 Ph(c),Trail of Doom . . . . . . . 250.00
18 Ph(c),Reign of Terror . . . . . . 225.00
19 Hand Colored Ph(c) . . . . . . . 250.00
20 Ph(c),CCB,F:Capt Tootsie . . . 225.00
21 Ph(c) . . . . . . . . . . . . . . . . . . 225.00
22 Ph(c),The Human Beast . . . . . 225.00
23 Ph(c),Return of the Past . . . . . 225.00
24 Hand Colored Ph(c),
   The Lawless City . . . . . . . . . 225.00
25 Hand Colored Ph(c),
   The Signed Death Warrant . . 225.00
26 Hand Colored Ph(c),
   Dangerous Escape . . . . . . . 225.00
27 Hand Colored Ph(c),
   Hero Without Glory . . . . . . 225.00
28 Ph(c),The Storm Kings . . . . . 225.00
29 Hand Colored Ph(c),The
   Case of the Rustling Rose . . 225.00

30 Ph(c),Disappearance
   in the Hills . . . . . . . . . . . . . 225.00
31 Ph(c) . . . . . . . . . . . . . . . . . . 175.00
32 Hand Colored Ph(c),
   Mystery of Tremble Mountain 175.00
33 . . . . . . . . . . . . . . . . . . . . . . 175.00
34 . . . . . . . . . . . . . . . . . . . . . . 175.00
35 Partial Ph(c),The Hanging
   at Hollow Creek . . . . . . . . . . 175.00
36 Ph(c) . . . . . . . . . . . . . . . . . . 175.00
37 Ph(c) . . . . . . . . . . . . . . . . . . 175.00
38 Ph(c),36 pages . . . . . . . . . . . 150.00
39 Ph(c) . . . . . . . . . . . . . . . . . . 175.00
40 Ph(c) . . . . . . . . . . . . . . . . . . 175.00
41 Ph(c) . . . . . . . . . . . . . . . . . . 175.00
42 Ph(c) . . . . . . . . . . . . . . . . . . 175.00
43 Ph(c) . . . . . . . . . . . . . . . . . . 150.00
44 Ph(c) . . . . . . . . . . . . . . . . . . 150.00
45 Partial Ph(c),The Secret
   Letter . . . . . . . . . . . . . . . . . 150.00
46 Ph(c) . . . . . . . . . . . . . . . . . . 150.00
47 Ph(c) . . . . . . . . . . . . . . . . . . 150.00
48 Ph(c) . . . . . . . . . . . . . . . . . . 150.00
49 Partial Ph(c),Blind Date
   With Death . . . . . . . . . . . . . 150.00
50 Ph(c) . . . . . . . . . . . . . . . . . . 150.00
51 Ph(c) . . . . . . . . . . . . . . . . . . 150.00
52 Ph(c) . . . . . . . . . . . . . . . . . . 150.00
53 Ph(c) . . . . . . . . . . . . . . . . . . 150.00
54 Ph(c) . . . . . . . . . . . . . . . . . . 150.00
55 Ph(c) . . . . . . . . . . . . . . . . . . 150.00
56 Partial Ph(c),Deadly Spurs . . . 150.00
57 Ph(c)5 . . . . . . . . . . . . . . . . . 150.00
58 Ph(c) . . . . . . . . . . . . . . . . . . 150.00
59 Ph(c) . . . . . . . . . . . . . . . . . . 150.00
60 Ph(c) . . . . . . . . . . . . . . . . . . 150.00
61 Partial Ph(c),Lost in the
   Night,May, 1953 . . . . . . . . . . 175.00

## TOMMY OF THE
## BIG TOP
### King Features/
### Standard Comics, 1948
10 Thrilling Circus Adventures . . . 150.00
11 . . . . . . . . . . . . . . . . . . . . . . 100.00
12 March, 1949 . . . . . . . . . . . . . 100.00

## TOM TERRIFIC!
### Pines Comics
### Summer, 1957
1 . . . . . . . . . . . . . . . . . . . . . . . 250.00
2 thru 5 . . . . . . . . . . . . . . . . . @175.00
6 Fall, 1958 . . . . . . . . . . . . . . . 175.00

**To**

Topix Comics Vol. 8 #19
© Topix/Catechetical Guild

Top-Notch Comics #10
© MLJ Magazines

Suzie Comics #64
© MLJ Magazines

## TOM-TOM THE JUNGLE BOY
**Magazine Enterprises, 1946**
1 (fa) . . . . . . . . . . . . . . . . . . . . 200.00
2 (fa) . . . . . . . . . . . . . . . . . . . . 150.00
3 Winter 1947,(fa),X-mas issue . 125.00
1 . . . . . . . . . . . . . . . . . . . . . . . 100.00

## TONTO
### See: LONE RANGER'S COMPANION TONTO

## TONY TRENT
### See: FACE, THE

## TOODLES
**Approved Comics (Ziff-Davis Publ.), 1951**
10 . . . . . . . . . . . . . . . . . . . . . . 125.00

## THE TOODLES TWINS
**Argo Publ., 1956**
1 . . . . . . . . . . . . . . . . . . . . . . . 100.00

## TOP FLIGHT COMICS
**Four Star/St. John Publ. Co., July, 1949**
1 . . . . . . . . . . . . . . . . . . . . . . . 125.00
1 Hector the Inspector . . . . . . . . 100.00

## TOPIX COMICS
**Topix/Catechetical Guild, 1942**
1 Catholic . . . . . . . . . . . . . . . . 350.00
2 . . . . . . . . . . . . . . . . . . . . . . . 250.00
3 . . . . . . . . . . . . . . . . . . . . . . . 250.00
4 . . . . . . . . . . . . . . . . . . . . . . . 200.00
5 . . . . . . . . . . . . . . . . . . . . . . . 200.00
6 . . . . . . . . . . . . . . . . . . . . . . . 200.00
7 . . . . . . . . . . . . . . . . . . . . . . . 200.00
8 . . . . . . . . . . . . . . . . . . . . . . . 200.00
Volume 2, any, except #5 . . . . . 200.00
5 Pope Pius XII . . . . . . . . . . . . . 250.00
Volume 3, any . . . . . . . . . . . . . 200.00
Volume 4, any . . . . . . . . . . . . . 175.00
Volume 5, any, except #12 . . . . 150.00
12 Life of Christ . . . . . . . . . . . . 175.00
Volume 6, any . . . . . . . . . . . . . 125.00
Volume 7, any . . . . . . . . . . . . . 100.00
Volume 8, any #4 . . . . . . . . . . . 150.00

4 Dagwood Splits Atom . . . . . . . 150.00
Volume 9, any, except #12 . . . . . 100.00
12 Christmas issue . . . . . . . . . . 100.00
Volume 10, any . . . . . . . . . . . . . 100.00

## TOP LOVE STORIES
**Star Publications, May, 1951**
3 LbC(c) . . . . . . . . . . . . . . . . . 300.00
4 LbC(c) . . . . . . . . . . . . . . . . . 200.00
5 LbC(c) . . . . . . . . . . . . . . . . . 200.00
6 LbC(c),WW . . . . . . . . . . . . . . 300.00
7 LbC(c), WW . . . . . . . . . . . . . . 250.00
8 LbC(c), WW Story . . . . . . . . . 275.00
9 LbC(c) . . . . . . . . . . . . . . . . . 250.00
10 thru 16 LbC(c) . . . . . . . . @250.00
17 LbC(c),WW . . . . . . . . . . . . . 275.00
18 LbC(c) . . . . . . . . . . . . . . . . 250.00
19 LbC(c),JyD . . . . . . . . . . . . . 250.00

## TOP-NOTCH COMICS
**MLJ Magazines, Dec., 1939**
1 JaB,JCo,B&O:The Wizard,
    B:Kandak,Swift of the Secret
    Service,The Westpointer,
    Mystic, Air Patrol,Scott
    Rand, Manhunter . . . . . . 12,000.00
2 JaB,JCo,B:Dick Storm,
    E:Mystic, B:Stacy Knight . . 7,600.00
3 JaB,JCo,EA(c),E:Swift of the
    Secret Service,Scott Rand  4,000.00
4 JCo,EA(c),MMe,O&I:Streak,
    Chandler . . . . . . . . . . . . . 3,500.00
5 Ea(c),MMe,O&I:Galahad,
    B:Shanghai Sheridan . . . . 3,500.00
6 Ea(c),MMe,A:The Shield . . . 3,000.00
7 Ea(c),MMe,N:The Wizard . . 3,800.00
8 E:Dick Sorm,B&O:Roy The1
    Super Boy,The Firefly . . . 3,500.00
9 O&I:Black Hood,
    B:Fran Frazier . . . . . . . . 10,000.00
10 A:Black Hood . . . . . . . . . . . 3,500.00
11 . . . . . . . . . . . . . . . . . . . . 2,800.00
12 . . . . . . . . . . . . . . . . . . . . 2,800.00
13 . . . . . . . . . . . . . . . . . . . . 2,800.00
14 Bondage(c) . . . . . . . . . . . . 2,800.00
15 MMe . . . . . . . . . . . . . . . . . 2,800.00
16 . . . . . . . . . . . . . . . . . . . . 2,500.00
17 Bondage(c) . . . . . . . . . . . . 2,800.00
18 . . . . . . . . . . . . . . . . . . . . 2,500.00
19 Bondage(c) . . . . . . . . . . . . 2,800.00
20 . . . . . . . . . . . . . . . . . . . . 2,500.00
21 . . . . . . . . . . . . . . . . . . . . 2,000.00

22 . . . . . . . . . . . . . . . . . . . . 2,000.00
23 Bondage(c) . . . . . . . . . . . . 2,200.00
24 Black Hood Smashes
    Murder Ring . . . . . . . . . . 2,000.00
25 E:Bob Phantom . . . . . . . . . 2,000.00
26 . . . . . . . . . . . . . . . . . . . . 2,000.00
27 E:The Firefly . . . . . . . . . . . 2,000.00
28 B:Suzie,Pokey Okay,
    Gag Oriented . . . . . . . . . 2,000.00
29 E:Kandak . . . . . . . . . . . . . 2,000.00
30 . . . . . . . . . . . . . . . . . . . . 2,000.00
31 . . . . . . . . . . . . . . . . . . . . . 900.00
32 . . . . . . . . . . . . . . . . . . . . . 900.00
33 BWo,B:Dotty&Ditto . . . . . . . 900.00
34 BWo . . . . . . . . . . . . . . . . . . 900.00
35 BWo . . . . . . . . . . . . . . . . . . 900.00
36 BWo . . . . . . . . . . . . . . . . . . 900.00
37 thru 40 BWo . . . . . . . . . @900.00
41 . . . . . . . . . . . . . . . . . . . . . 900.00
42 BWo . . . . . . . . . . . . . . . . . . 900.00
43 . . . . . . . . . . . . . . . . . . . . . 900.00
44 EW:Black Hood,I:Suzie . . . . . 900.00
45 Suzie(c) . . . . . . . . . . . . . . 1,000.00
**Becomes:**

### LAUGH COMIX
**Summer, 1944**
46 Suzie & Wilbur . . . . . . . . . . 500.00
47 Suzie & Wilbur . . . . . . . . . . 400.00
48 Suzie & Wilbur . . . . . . . . . . 400.00
**Becomes:**

### SUZIE COMICS
**Spring, 1945**
49 B:Ginger . . . . . . . . . . . . . . 600.00
50 AFy(c) . . . . . . . . . . . . . . . . 400.00
51 AFy(c) . . . . . . . . . . . . . . . . 400.00
52 AFy(c) . . . . . . . . . . . . . . . . 400.00
53 AFy(c) . . . . . . . . . . . . . . . . 400.00
54 AFy(c) . . . . . . . . . . . . . . . . 500.00
55 AFy(c) . . . . . . . . . . . . . . . . 500.00
56 BWo,B;Katie Keene . . . . . . . 300.00
57 thru 70 BWo . . . . . . . . . @300.00
71 thru 79 BWo . . . . . . . . . @200.00
80 thru 99 BWo . . . . . . . . . @200.00
100 Aug., 1954, BWo . . . . . . . . 200.00

### TOPS
**Tops Mag. Inc. (Lev Gleason), July, 1949**
1 RC&BLb,GT,DBa,CBi(c),I'll Buy
    That Girl,Our Explosive
    Children . . . . . . . . . . . . . 1,500.00
2 FGu,BF,CBi(c),RC&BLb . . . . 1,400.00

To

*Top Secrets #8*
*© Street & Smith Publications*

*Torchy #3*
*© Quality Comics Group*

*Trapped N#*
*© Harvey Publications*

## TOPS COMICS
**Consolidated Book Publishers, 1944**
2000 Don on the Farm. . . . . . . . 400.00
2001 The Jack of Spades
V:The Hawkman . . . . . . . . . 300.00
2002 Rip Raiders . . . . . . . . . . . 250.00
2003 Red Birch . . . . . . . . . . . . 200.00

## TOP SECRET
**Hillman Publications, Jan., 1952**
1 The Tricks of the Secret
Agent Revealed . . . . . . . . . 250.00

## TOP SECRETS
**Street & Smith Publ., Nov., 1947**
1 BP,BP(c),Of the Men Who
Guard the U.S. Mail . . . . . . 400.00
2 BP,BP(c),True Story of Jim
the Penman . . . . . . . . . . . . 350.00
3 BP,BP(c),Crime Solved by
Mental Telepathy . . . . . . . . 300.00
4 Highway Pirates. . . . . . . . . . 300.00
5 BP,BP(c),Can Music Kill . . . . . 300.00
6 BP,BP(c),The Clue of the
Forgotten Film . . . . . . . . . . 300.00
7 BP,BP(c),Train For Sale. . . . . 375.00
8 BP,BP(c) . . . . . . . . . . . . . . . 300.00
9 BP,BP(c) . . . . . . . . . . . . . . . 300.00
10 BP,BP(c),July–Aug., 1949. . . . 375.00

## TOPS IN ADVENTURE
**Approved Comics (Ziff-Davis), Autumn, 1952**
1 BP,Crusaders From Mars . . . . 600.00

## TOP SPOT COMICS
**Top Spot Publishing Co., 1945**
1 The Duke Of Darkness . . . . . . 450.00

## TOPSY-TURVY
**R.B. Leffingwell Publ., April, 1945**
1 I:Cookie . . . . . . . . . . . . . . . . 200.00

## TOR
**St. John Publishing Co., Sept., 1953**
1 JKu,JKu(c),O;Tor,One Million
Years Ago . . . . . . . . . . . . . 150.00
2 JKu,JKu(c),3-D Issue . . . . . . 100.00
3 JKu,JKu(c),ATh,historic life . . 125.00
4 JKu,JKu(c),ATh . . . . . . . . . . . 125.00
5 JKu,JKu(c),ATh,Oct., 1954 . . . 125.00

## TORCHY
**Quality Comics Group, Nov., 1949**
1 GFx,BWa(c),The Blonde
Bombshell . . . . . . . . . . . . 2,200.00
2 GFx(a&c),Beauty at Its Best . 1,100.00
3 GFx,GFx(c),You Can't
Beat Nature . . . . . . . . . . . 1,100.00
4 GFx,GFx(c),The Girl to
Keep Your Eye On . . . . . . . 1,400.00
5 BWa,GFx,BWa(c),At the
Masquerade Party . . . . . . . 1,800.00
6 Sept., 1950,BWa,GFx,
BWa(c),The Libido Driven
Boy Scout. . . . . . . . . . . . . 1,800.00

## TORMENTED, THE
**Sterling Comics, July, 1954**
1 Buried Alive . . . . . . . . . . . . . 400.00
2 Sept., 1954,The Devils Circus 250.00
**Becomes:**

## SURPRISE ADVENTURES
**Sterling Comics, 1955**
3 MSy . . . . . . . . . . . . . . . . . . . 250.00
4 . . . . . . . . . . . . . . . . . . . . . . 150.00
5 MSy . . . . . . . . . . . . . . . . . . . 200.00

## TOUGH KID SQUAD COMICS
**Marvel Timely, March, 1942**
1 AAv,SSh,O:The Human Top,
Tough Kid Squad,A:The Flying
Flame, V:Doctor Klutch . . 15,000.00

## TOYLAND COMICS
**Fiction House Magazines, Jan., 1947**
1 Wizard of the Moon . . . . . . . . 400.00
2 Buddy Bruin & Stu Rabbit . . . . 200.00
3 GT,The Candy Maker . . . . . . . 250.00
4 July, 1947 . . . . . . . . . . . . . . . 200.00

## TOY TOWN COMICS
**Toytown Publ./Orbit Publ., Feb., 1945**
1 LbC,LbC(c)(fa) . . . . . . . . . . . 500.00
2 LbC,(fa) . . . . . . . . . . . . . . . . 300.00
3 LbC,LbC(c),(fa) . . . . . . . . . . . 250.00
4 thru 7 LbC,(fa) May, 1947 . . @250.00

## TRAIL BLAZERS
**See: RED DRAGON COMICS**

## TRAPPED
**Harvey Publications, 1951**
N# . . . . . . . . . . . . . . . . . . . . . 150.00

## TRAPPED!
**Periodical Magazines (Ace Magazines), 1954**
1 . . . . . . . . . . . . . . . . . . . . . . 125.00
2 and 3 . . . . . . . . . . . . . . . . . @60.00

## TREASURE CHEST
**George A Pflaum Publ., Inc., 1946**
1 . . . . . . . . . . . . . . . . . . . . . . 300.00
2 thru 4 . . . . . . . . . . . . . . . . . @150.00
5 Dr Styx. . . . . . . . . . . . . . . . . 160.00
6 . . . . . . . . . . . . . . . . . . . . . . 150.00
Vol 2, 1 thru 20 . . . . . . . . . . . @150.00
Vol 3, 1 thru 5 (1947–48) . . . . . @150.00
Vol 3, #6 Verne,Voyage to Moon, 135.00
Vol 3, 7 thru 20 . . . . . . . . . . . @110.00
Vol 4, 1 thru 20 (1948–49) . . . . @135.00
Vol 5, 1 thru 20 (1949–50) . . . . @125.00
Vol 6, 1 thru 20 (1950–51) . . . . @125.00
Vol 7, 1 thru 20 (1951–52) . . . . @125.00
Vol 8, 1 thru 20 (1952–53) . . . . @125.00
Vol 9, 1 thru 20 (1953–54) . . . . @100.00
Vol 10, 1 thru 10 (1954–55) . . . @100.00
Vol 10, #11 BP . . . . . . . . . . . . . 100.00
Vol 10, 12 thru 20 . . . . . . . . . @100.00
Vol 11, 1 thru 20 (1955–56) . . . @100.00
Vol 12, 1 thru 20 (1956–57) . . . @100.00
Vol 13, 1 thru 20 (1957–58) . . . @75.00
Vol 14, 1 thru 20 (1958–59) . . . @75.00
Vol 15, 1 thru 20 (1959–60) . . . @75.00
Vol 16, 1 thru 20 (1960–61) . . . @75.00
Vol 17, 1 thru 20 (1962–63)
odd #s . . . . . . . . . . . . . . . @75.00
even #s "Godless Communism"

Treasure Comics #4
© Prize Publications

True Aviation Picture Stories #1
© Parent's Institute

True Comics #14
© Parents' Magazine Press

2 RC . . . . . . . . . . . . . . . . . 275.00
4 and 6 . . . . . . . . . . . . . @275.00
8 thru 14 Stalin, WWII . . . . @275.00
14 thru 20 Kruschev . . . . . @225.00

## TREASURE COMICS
**Prize Comics Group, 1943**
1 S&K,Reprints of Prize Comics
  #7 through #11 . . . . . . . . 3,000.00

## TREASURE COMICS
**American Boys Comics
(Prize Publications),
June–July, 1945**
1 HcK,B:PaulBunyan,MarcoPolo 500.00
2 HcK(a&c),B:Arabian Knight,
  Gorilla King,Dr.Styx . . . . . . 300.00
3 HcK . . . . . . . . . . . . . . . . . 250.00
4 HcK . . . . . . . . . . . . . . . . . 250.00
5 HcK,JK, Marco Polo . . . . . . 300.00
6 BK,HcK(a&c) . . . . . . . . . . . 250.00
7 FF,HcK(a&c),Capt.Kidd, Jr. . . 500.00
8 HcK,FF . . . . . . . . . . . . . . . 500.00
9 HcK,DBa . . . . . . . . . . . . . . 250.00
10 JK,DBa,JK(c) . . . . . . . . . . 400.00
11 BK,HcK,DBa,The Weird
  Adventures of Mr. Bottle . . 300.00
12 DBa,DBa(c),Autumn, 1947 . . 250.00

## TREASURY OF COMICS
**St. John Publishing Co., 1947**
1 RvB,RvB(c),Abbie an' Slats . . 150.00
2 Jim Hardy . . . . . . . . . . . . . 125.00
3 Bill Bimlin . . . . . . . . . . . . . 125.00
4 RvB,RvB(c),Abbie an' Slats . . 125.00
5 Jim Hardy,Jan., 1948 . . . . . . 100.00

## TREASURY OF COMICS
**St. John Publishing Co., 1948**
1 Abbott & Costello,
  Little Audrey. . . . . . . . . . . . 250.00
2 . . . . . . . . . . . . . . . . . . . . 125.00
3 thru 5 . . . . . . . . . . . . . . . @110.00

## TRIPLE THREAT
**Gerona Publications,
Winter, 1945**
1 F:King O'Leary,The Duke of
  Darkness,Beau Brummell . . . 350.00

## TRUE ADVENTURES
### See: TRUE WESTERN

## TRUE ANIMAL
## PICTURE STORIES
**True Comics Press, 1947**
1 . . . . . . . . . . . . . . . . . . . . 125.00
2 . . . . . . . . . . . . . . . . . . . . 125.00

## TRUE AVIATION
## PICTURE STORIES
**Parents' Institute/P.M.I.,
Aug., 1942**
1 How Jimmy Doolittle
  Bombed Tokyo . . . . . . . . . . 300.00
2 Knight of the Air Mail . . . . . . 250.00
3 The Amazing One-Man
  Air Force . . . . . . . . . . . . . . 200.00
4 Joe Foss America's No. 1
  Air Force . . . . . . . . . . . . . . 200.00
5 Bombs over Germany . . . . . . 200.00
6 Flight Lt. Richard
  Hillary R.A.F. . . . . . . . . . . . 200.00
7 "Fatty" Chow China's
  Sky Champ . . . . . . . . . . . . . 200.00
8 Blitz over Burma . . . . . . . . . 200.00
9 Off the Beam . . . . . . . . . . . 200.00
10 "Pappy" Boyington . . . . . . . 200.00
11 Ph(c) . . . . . . . . . . . . . . . . 200.00
12 . . . . . . . . . . . . . . . . . . . . 200.00
13 Ph(c),Flying Facts. . . . . . . . 200.00
14 . . . . . . . . . . . . . . . . . . . . 200.00
15 True Aviation Adventures . . . 200.00
**Becomes:**

## AVIATION AND MODEL
## BUILDING
**Dec., 1946**
16 . . . . . . . . . . . . . . . . . . . . 125.00
17 Feb., 1947. . . . . . . . . . . . . 150.00

## TRUE BRIDES'
## EXPERIENCES
### See: TEEN-AGE BRIDES

## TRUE BRIDE-TO-BE
## ROMANCES
### See: TEEN-AGE BRIDES

## TRUE COMICS
**True Comics/
Parents' Magazine Press,
April, 1941–Aug., 1950**
1 My Greatest Adventure-by
  Lowell Thomas, Churchill . . . 450.00
2 BEv,The Story of the
  Red Cross . . . . . . . . . . . . . 200.00
3 Baseball Hall of Fame . . . . . . 225.00
4 Danger in the Artic . . . . . . . . 150.00
5 Father Duffy-the Fighting
  Chaplain, Joe Louis. . . . . . . . 165.00
6 The Capture of Aquinaldo . . . . 175.00
7 JKa,Wilderness Adventures of
  George Washington . . . . . . . 165.00
8 U.S. Army Wings . . . . . . . . . 125.00
9 A Pig that Made History . . . . . 125.00
10 Adrift on an Ice Pan . . . . . . . 125.00
11 Gen. Douglas MacArthur. . . . 110.00
12 Mackenzie-King of Cananda. . 110.00
13 The Real Robinson Crusoe. . . 110.00
14 Australia war base of
  the South Pacific . . . . . . . . . 110.00
15 The Story of West Point . . . . 125.00
16 How Jimmy Doolittle
  Bombed Tokyo. . . . . . . . . . . 120.00
17 The Ghost of Captain Blig,
  B.Feller . . . . . . . . . . . . . . . 125.00
18 Battling Bill of the
  Merchant Marine . . . . . . . . . 135.00
19 Secret Message Codes. . . . . 110.00
20 The Story of India . . . . . . . . 100.00
21 Timoshenko the Blitz Buster . . 110.00
22 Gen. Bernard L. Montgomery. 100.00
23 The Story of Steel. . . . . . . . . 100.00
24 Gen. Henri Giraud-Master
  of Escape . . . . . . . . . . . . . . 100.00
25 Medicine's Miracle Men . . . . 100.00
26 Hero of the Bismarck Sea. . . . 100.00
27 Leathernecks have Landed. . . 110.00
28 The Story of Radar . . . . . . . . 100.00
29 The Fighting Seabees. . . . . . 100.00
30 Dr. Norman Bethune-Blood
  Bank Founder . . . . . . . . . . . 100.00
31 Our Good Neighbor Bolivia,
  Red Grange. . . . . . . . . . . . . 110.00
32 Men against the Desert . . . . . 125.00
33 Gen.Clark and his Fighting 5th 150.00
34 Angel of the Battlefield . . . . . 125.00
35 Carlson's Marine Raiders . . . . 125.00
36 Canada's Sub-Busters . . . . . 125.00
37 Commander of the Crocodile
  Fleet. . . . . . . . . . . . . . . . . . 125.00
38 Oregon Trailblazer . . . . . . . . 125.00
39 Saved by Sub, FBI . . . . . . . . 125.00

**Tr**

*True Comics #84*
*© Parents Magazine Press*

*True Crime Comics #3*
*© Magazine Village, Inc.*

*True Love Problems and Advice*
*Illustrated #40 © Harvey Publications*

40 Sea Furies . . . . . . . . . . . . . . 125.00
41 Cavalcade of England. . . . . . . 100.00
42 Gen. Jaques Le Clerc-Hero
   of Paris . . . . . . . . . . . . . . . . 100.00
43 Unsinkable Ship . . . . . . . . . . 100.00
44 El Senor Goofy, Truman . . . . 100.00
45 Tokyo Express . . . . . . . . . . . 100.00
46 The Magnificent Runt . . . . . . 100.00
47 Atoms Unleashed,
   Atomic Bomb. . . . . . . . . . . . 175.00
48 Pirate Patriot. . . . . . . . . . . . . 100.00
49 Smoking Fists . . . . . . . . . . . . 100.00
50 Lumber Pirates . . . . . . . . . . . 100.00
51 Exercise Musk-Ox. . . . . . . . . 100.00
52 King of the Buckaneers . . . . . 100.00
53 Baseline Booby. . . . . . . . . . . 100.00
54 Santa Fe Sailor. . . . . . . . . . . 100.00
55 Sea Going Santa . . . . . . . . . 100.00
56 End of a Terror . . . . . . . . . . . 100.00
57 Newfangled Machines . . . . . . 100.00
58 Leonardo da Vinci-500 years
   too Soon, Houdini . . . . . . . . 100.00
59 Pursuit Pirates, Bob Hope . . . 100.00
60 Emmett Kelly-The World's
   Funniest Clown . . . . . . . . . . 100.00
61 Peter Le Grand-
   Bold Buckaneer. . . . . . . . . . 100.00
62 Sutter's Gold. . . . . . . . . . . . . 100.00
63 Outboard Outcome . . . . . . . . 100.00
64 Man-Eater at Large. . . . . . . . 100.00
65 The Story of Scotland Yard . . 100.00
66 Easy Guide to Football
   Formations, Will Rogers . . . . 100.00
67 The Changing Zebra. . . . . . . . 100.00
68 Admiral Byrd . . . . . . . . . . . . . 100.00
69 FBI Special Agent Steve
   Saunders, Jack Benny . . . . . 100.00
70 The Case of the Seven
   Hunted Men. . . . . . . . . . . . . 100.00
71 Story of Joe DiMaggio . . . . . . 150.00
72 FBI,Jackie Robinson. . . . . . . . 100.00
73 The 26 Mile Dash-Story of
   the Marathon, Walt Disney . . 100.00
74 A Famous Coach's Special
   Football Tips, Amos & Andy . 100.00
75 King of Reporters . . . . . . . . . 100.00
76 Story of a Buried Treasure . . . 100.00
77 France's Greatest Detective . . 100.00
78 Cagliostro-Master Rogue . . . . 100.00
79 Ralph Bunche-Hero of Peace. 100.00
80 Rocket Trip to the Moon . . . . 200.00
81 Red Grange . . . . . . . . . . . . . 200.00
82 Marie Celeste Ship of
   Mystery . . . . . . . . . . . . . . . . 175.00
83 Bullfighter from Brooklyn. . . . . 175.00
84 King of the Buckaneers . . . . . 175.00

## TRUE COMPLETE MYSTERY
### See: COMPLETE MYSTERY

## TRUE CONFIDENCES
**Fawcett Publications,**
**Autumn, 1949**
1 . . . . . . . . . . . . . . . . . . . . . . . 200.00
2 and 3 . . . . . . . . . . . . . . . . @125.00
4 DP . . . . . . . . . . . . . . . . . . . . . 125.00

## TRUE CRIME COMICS
**Magazine Village, Inc.,**
**May, 1947**
2 JCo(c),James Kent-Crook,
   Murderer,Escaped Convict;
   Drug . . . . . . . . . . . . . . . . . 2,000.00
3 JCo(a&c),Benny Dickson-
   Killer;Drug. . . . . . . . . . . . . 1,500.00
4 JCo(a&c),Little Jake-
   Big Shot . . . . . . . . . . . . . . 1,400.00
5 JCo(c),The Rat & the Blond
   Gun Moll;Drug . . . . . . . . . 1,000.00
6 Joseph Metley-Swindler,
   Jailbird, Killer . . . . . . . . . . . 800.00
2-1(7) ATh,WW,Ph(c),Phil
   Coppolla,Sept., 1949 . . . . . 1,200.00

## TRUE LIFE ROMANCES
**Ajax/Farrell Publications,**
**Dec., 1955**
1 . . . . . . . . . . . . . . . . . . . . . . . 125.00
2 and 3 . . . . . . . . . . . . . . . . . @75.00

## TRUE LIFE SECRETS
**Romantic Love Stories/**
**Charlton Comics,**
**March–April, 1951**
1 Ph(c) . . . . . . . . . . . . . . . . . . 150.00
2 . . . . . . . . . . . . . . . . . . . . . . . . 75.00
3 thru 11 . . . . . . . . . . . . . . . . @60.00
12 Escort Girl . . . . . . . . . . . . . . 65.00
13 thru 20 . . . . . . . . . . . . . . . @60.00
21 thru 25 . . . . . . . . . . . . . . . @50.00
26 thru 29 . . . . . . . . . . . . . . . @40.00

## TRUE LIFE TALES
**Marvel Comics, 1949**
1 (8) Ph(c). . . . . . . . . . . . . . . . 125.00

2 Ph(c) . . . . . . . . . . . . . . . . . . 125.00

## TRUE LOVE CONFESSIONS
**Premier Magazines, 1954**
1 Marijuana . . . . . . . . . . . . . . . 135.00
2 . . . . . . . . . . . . . . . . . . . . . . . . 65.00
3 thru 11 . . . . . . . . . . . . . . . . @50.00

## TRUE LOVE PICTORIAL
**St. John Publishing Co., 1952**
1 Ph(c) . . . . . . . . . . . . . . . . . . 350.00
2 MB . . . . . . . . . . . . . . . . . . . . 450.00
3 MB(c),MB,JKu . . . . . . . . . . . 750.00
4 MB(c),MB,JKu . . . . . . . . . . . 750.00
5 MB(c),MB,JKu . . . . . . . . . . . 750.00
6 MB(c) . . . . . . . . . . . . . . . . . . 350.00
7 MB(c) . . . . . . . . . . . . . . . . . . 350.00
8 MB(c) . . . . . . . . . . . . . . . . . . 300.00
9 MB(c) . . . . . . . . . . . . . . . . . . 300.00
10 MB(c),MB . . . . . . . . . . . . . . 300.00
11 MB(c),MB . . . . . . . . . . . . . . 300.00

## TRUE LOVE PROBLEMS AND ADVICE ILLUSTRATED
**Harvey Publications, 1949–57**
1 . . . . . . . . . . . . . . . . . . . . . . . 150.00
2 . . . . . . . . . . . . . . . . . . . . . . . 125.00
3 thru 10 . . . . . . . . . . . . . . . . @100.00
11 thru 20 . . . . . . . . . . . . . . . @100.00
21 thru 37 . . . . . . . . . . . . . . . @100.00
38 S&K(c). . . . . . . . . . . . . . . . 125.00
39 thru 44. . . . . . . . . . . . . . . . @100.00
Becomes:

## ROMANCE STORIES OF TRUE LOVE
**Harvey Publications, 1957–58**
45 thru 51 . . . . . . . . . . . . . . . . 100.00
52 . . . . . . . . . . . . . . . . . . . . . . 125.00

## TRUE MOVIE AND TELEVISION
**Toby Press, Aug., 1950**
1 Liz Taylor, Ph(c) . . . . . . . . . . 650.00
2 FF,Ph(c),John Wayne,
   L.Taylor . . . . . . . . . . . . . . . . 500.00
3 June Allyson,Ph(c) . . . . . . . . 350.00
4 Jane Powell,Ph(c),Jan.,1951 . 200.00

*True Sport Picture Stories #10*
*© Street & Smith Publications*

*True Sport Picture Stories*
*Volume 3, #11 © Street & Smith Publ.*

*True-To-Life Romances #22*
*© Star Publications*

## TRUE SECRETS
### Marvel Atlas, 1950–56
*Previously LOVE DIARY or OUR LOVE,*
*depending on who you believe.*

| | |
|---|---|
| 3 | 150.00 |
| 4 | 125.00 |
| 5 | 125.00 |
| 6 BEv | 135.00 |
| 7 | 125.00 |
| 8 | 125.00 |
| 9 | 125.00 |
| 10 | 125.00 |
| 11 thru 21 | @110.00 |
| 22 BEv | 125.00 |
| 23 | 110.00 |
| 24 ViC | 125.00 |
| 25 thru 28 | @110.00 |
| 29 thru 39 | @100.00 |
| 40 Sept., 1956 | 100.00 |

## SPORT COMICS
### Street & Smith Publ., Oct., 1940

| | |
|---|---|
| 1 F:Lou Gehrig | 700.00 |
| 2 F:Gene Tunney | 400.00 |
| 3 F:Phil Rizzuto | 450.00 |
| 4 F:Frank Leahy | 300.00 |

**Becomes:**

## TRUE SPORT PICTURE STORIES
### Street & Smith Publ., Feb., 1942–July-Aug., 1949

| | |
|---|---|
| 5 Joe DiMaggio | 400.00 |
| 6 Billy Confidence | 250.00 |
| 7 Mel Ott | 275.00 |
| 8 Lou Ambers | 250.00 |
| 9 Pete Reiser | 250.00 |
| 10 Frankie Sinkwich | 250.00 |
| 11 Marty Serfo | 250.00 |
| 12 JaB(c),Jack Dempsey | 265.00 |
| 2-1 JaB(c),Willie Pep | 250.00 |
| 2-2 JaB(c) | 250.00 |
| 2-3 JaB(c),Carl Hubbell | 265.00 |
| 2-4 Advs. in Football & Battle | 275.00 |
| 2-5 Don Hutson | 250.00 |
| 2-6 Dixie Walker | 275.00 |
| 2-7 Stan Musial | 300.00 |
| 2-8 Famous Ring Champions of All Time | 275.00 |
| 2-9 List of War Year Rookies | 300.00 |
| 2-10 Connie Mack | 275.00 |
| 2-11 Winning Basketball Plays | 250.00 |
| 2-12 Eddie Gottlieb | 250.00 |
| 3-1 Bill Conn | 250.00 |

| | |
|---|---|
| 3-2 Philadelphia Athletics | 200.00 |
| 3-3 Leo Durocher | 250.00 |
| 3-4 Rudy Dusek | 200.00 |
| 3-5 Ernie Pyle | 200.00 |
| 3-6 Bowling with Ned Day | 200.00 |
| 3-7 Return of the Mighty (Home from War);Joe DiMaggio(c) | 400.00 |
| 3-8 Conn V:Louis | 300.00 |
| 3-9 Reuben Shark | 200.00 |
| 3-10 BP,BP(c),Don "Dopey" Dillock | 200.00 |
| 3-11 BP,BP(c),Death Scores a Touchdown | 200.00 |
| 3-12 Red Sox V:Senators | 200.00 |
| 4-1 Spring Training in Full Spring | 200.00 |
| 4-2 BP,BP(c),How to Pitch 'Em Where They Can't Hit 'Em | 200.00 |
| 4-3 BP,BP(c),1947 Super Stars | 235.00 |
| 4-4 BP,BP(c),Get Ready for the Olympics | 235.00 |
| 4-5 BP,BP,(c),Hugh Casey | 200.00 |
| 4-6 BP,BP(c),Phantom Phil Hergesheimer | 200.00 |
| 4-7 BP,BP(c),How to Bowl Better | 200.00 |
| 4-8 Tips on the Big Fight | 235.00 |
| 4-9 BP,BP(c),Bill McCahan | 200.00 |
| 4-10 BP,BP(c),Great Football Plays | 200.00 |
| 4-11 BP,BP(c),Football | 200.00 |
| 4-12 BP,BP(c),Basketball | 200.00 |
| 5-1 Satchel Paige | 250.00 |
| 5-2 History of Boxing | 200.00 |

## TRUE STORIES OF ROMANCE
### Fawcett Publications, 1950

| | |
|---|---|
| 1 Ph(c) | 150.00 |
| 2 Ph(c) | 100.00 |
| 3 Ph(c) | 100.00 |

## TRUE SWEETHEART SECRETS
### Fawcett Publications, May, 1950

| | |
|---|---|
| 1 Debbie Reynolds,Ph(c) | 150.00 |
| 2 WW | 250.00 |
| 3 BD | 125.00 |
| 4 BD | 125.00 |
| 5 BD | 125.00 |
| 6 thru 11 | @125.00 |

## TRUE TALES OF ROMANCE
### Fawcett Publications

| | |
|---|---|
| 4 Ph(c) | 100.00 |

## TRUE-TO-LIFE ROMANCES
### Star Publications, Nov.–Dec., 1949

| | |
|---|---|
| 3 LbC(c),GlennFord/JanetLeigh | 300.00 |
| 4 LbC(c) | 200.00 |
| 5 LbC(c) | 200.00 |
| 6 LbC(c) | 200.00 |
| 7 LbC(c) | 200.00 |
| 8 LbC(c) | 200.00 |
| 9 LbC(c) | 200.00 |
| 10 LbC(c) | 200.00 |
| 11 LbC(c) | 200.00 |
| 12 LbC(c) | 200.00 |
| 13 LbC(c),JyD | 200.00 |
| 14 LbC(c),JyD | 200.00 |
| 15 LbC(c),WW,JyD | 250.00 |
| 16 LbC(c),WW,JyD | 250.00 |
| 17 LbC(c),JyD | 175.00 |
| 18 LbC(c),JyD | 175.00 |
| 19 LbC(c),JyD | 175.00 |
| 20 LbC(c),JyD | 175.00 |
| 21 LbC(c),JyD | 175.00 |
| 22 LbC(c) | 175.00 |
| 23 LbC(c) | 175.00 |

## TRUE WAR EXPERIENCES
### Harvey Publications, 1952

| | |
|---|---|
| 1 | 150.00 |
| 2 thru 4 | @100.00 |

## TRUE WAR ROMANCES
### Comic Magazines, Inc. (Quality Comics), Sept., 1952

| | |
|---|---|
| 1 Ph(c) | 150.00 |
| 2 | 125.00 |
| 3 thru 10 | @100.00 |
| 11 thru 20 | @100.00 |
| 21 Comics Code | 100.00 |

**Becomes:**

## EXOTIC ROMANCES
### Oct., 1955

| | |
|---|---|
| 22 | 125.00 |
| 23 thru 26 | @100.00 |
| 27 MB | 150.00 |

**Tr**

True Western #1
© Marvel Comics Group

Turok, Son of Stone #15
© Dell Publishing Co.

Two-Fisted Tales #18
© E.C. Comics

28 MB. . . . . . . . . . . . . . . . . . . . . . 125.00
29 . . . . . . . . . . . . . . . . . . . . . . . . . 100.00
30 MB. . . . . . . . . . . . . . . . . . . . . . 125.00
31 MB. . . . . . . . . . . . . . . . . . . . . . 150.00

## TRUE WESTERN
### Marvel, Dec., 1949
1 Ph(c),Billy the Kid . . . . . . . . . 200.00
2 Ph(c),Alan Ladd,Badmen vs.
   Lawmen . . . . . . . . . . . . . . . . 250.00
Becomes:

## TRUE ADVENTURES
3 BP,MSy,Boss of Black Devil . . 200.00
Becomes:

## MEN'S ADVENTURES
4 AvB,He Called me a Coward . . 400.00
5 AvB,Brother Act . . . . . . . . . . . 225.00
6 AvB,Heat of Battle . . . . . . . . . 200.00
7 AvB,The Walking Death . . . . . 200.00
8 AvB,RH,Journey Into Death . . 200.00
9 AvB,Bullets,Blades and Death 125.00
10 BEv,The Education of Thomas
   Dillon . . . . . . . . . . . . . . . . . . 125.00
11 Death of A Soldier . . . . . . . . . 125.00
12 Firing Squad . . . . . . . . . . . . . 125.00
13 RH(c),The Three Stripes. . . . . 125.00
14 GC,BEv,Steel Coffin . . . . . . . . 125.00
15 JMn(c). . . . . . . . . . . . . . . . . . . 125.00
16 . . . . . . . . . . . . . . . . . . . . . . . . 125.00
17 . . . . . . . . . . . . . . . . . . . . . . . . 125.00
18 . . . . . . . . . . . . . . . . . . . . . . . . 125.00
19 JRo . . . . . . . . . . . . . . . . . . . . . 125.00
20 GC,RH(c) . . . . . . . . . . . . . . . . 125.00
21 BEv(c),JSt,The Eye of Man . . 225.00
22 BEv,JR,Mark of the Witch. . . . 225.00
23 BEv(c),RC,The Wrong Body. . 225.00
24 RH,JMn,GT,Torture Master . . . 225.00
25 SSh(c),Who Shrinks My Head 400.00
26 Midnight in the Morgue. . . . . . 225.00
27 BP,CBu(c),A:Capt.America,
   Human Torch,Sub-Mariner . 1,400.00
28 BEv,A:Capt.America,Human Torch,
   Sub-Mariner,July, 1954. . . . 1,300.00

## TUBBY
### See: MARGE'S TUBBY

## TUFFY
### Best Books, Inc.
### (Standard Comics) 1949
5 . . . . . . . . . . . . . . . . . . . . . . . . . 125.00
6 true 9 . . . . . . . . . . . . . . . . . @100.00

## TUROK, SON OF STONE
### Dell Publishing Co.,
### Dec., 1954
(1) see Dell Four Color #596
(2) see Dell Four Color #656
3 Cavemen . . . . . . . . . . . . . . . . 350.00
4 & 5 . . . . . . . . . . . . . . . . . . . @300.00
6 & 7 . . . . . . . . . . . . . . . . . . . @250.00
8 Dinosaur, Lost Valley . . . . . . . 275.00
9 thru 16 . . . . . . . . . . . . . . . . @150.00
17 Prehistoric Pigmies . . . . . . . . 175.00
18 thru 29 . . . . . . . . . . . . . . . @125.00

## TV SCREEN CARTOONS
### (see REAL SCREEN COMICS)

## TV TEENS
### Charlton Comics, 1954
1 Ozzie & Babs. . . . . . . . . . . . . . 125.00
2 . . . . . . . . . . . . . . . . . . . . . . . . 100.00
3 . . . . . . . . . . . . . . . . . . . . . . . . 100.00
4 . . . . . . . . . . . . . . . . . . . . . . . . 100.00
5 . . . . . . . . . . . . . . . . . . . . . . . . 100.00
6 Don Winslow . . . . . . . . . . . . . 100.00
7 B:Mopsy. . . . . . . . . . . . . . . . . . 100.00
8 . . . . . . . . . . . . . . . . . . . . . . . . 100.00
9 . . . . . . . . . . . . . . . . . . . . . . . . 100.00
10 . . . . . . . . . . . . . . . . . . . . . . . . 100.00
11 thru 13 . . . . . . . . . . . . . . . @100.00

## TWEETY AND SYLVESTER
### Dell Publishing Co.,
### June, 1952
(1) see Dell Four Color #406
(2) see Dell Four Color #489
(3) see Dell Four Color #524
4 thru 20 . . . . . . . . . . . . . . . @125.00
21 thru 37 . . . . . . . . . . . . . . . @100.00

## TWINKLE COMICS
### Spotlight Publications,
### May, 1945
1 Humor Format . . . . . . . . . . . . 300.00

## TWO-BIT WACKY WOODPECKER
### Toby Press, 1952
1 . . . . . . . . . . . . . . . . . . . . . . . . 150.00
2 . . . . . . . . . . . . . . . . . . . . . . . . 120.00
3 . . . . . . . . . . . . . . . . . . . . . . . . 120.00

## TWO-FISTED TALES
### Fables Publications
### (E.C. Comics),
### Nov.–Dec., 1950–March, 1955
18 JCr,WW,JSe,HK(a&c) . . . . . 2,000.00
19 JCr,WW,JSe,HK(a&c) . . . . . 1,500.00
20 JDa,WW,JSe,HK(a&c) . . . . . 900.00
21 JDa,WW,JSe,HK(a&c) . . . . . 800.00
22 JDa,WW,JSe,HK(a&c) . . . . . 800.00
23 JDa,WW,JSe,HK(a&c) . . . . . 600.00
24 JDa,WW,JSe,HK(a&c) . . . . . 500.00
25 JDa,WW,JSe,HK(a&c) . . . . . 500.00
26 JDa,JSe,HK(c),Action at
   the Changing Reservoir. . . . 400.00
27 JDa,JSe,HK(c) . . . . . . . . . . . 400.00
28 JDa,JSe,HK(c) . . . . . . . . . . . 400.00
29 JDa,JSe,HK(c) . . . . . . . . . . . 450.00
30 JSe,JDa(a&c) . . . . . . . . . . . . 450.00
31 JDa,JSe,HK(c),Civil
   War Story. . . . . . . . . . . . . . . 400.00
32 JDa,JKu,WW(c) . . . . . . . . . . 400.00
33 JDa,JKu,WW(c),A-Bomb . . . 500.00
34 JSe,JDa(a&c) . . . . . . . . . . . . 400.00
35 JSe,JDa(a&c),Civil
   War Story. . . . . . . . . . . . . . . 400.00
36 JDa,JSe(a&c),A
   Difference of Opinion. . . . . . 500.00
37 JSe(a&c),Bugles &
   Battle Cries . . . . . . . . . . . . . 500.00
38 JSe(a&c). . . . . . . . . . . . . . . . . 500.00
39 JSe(a&c). . . . . . . . . . . . . . . . . 500.00
40 JDa,JSe,GE(a&c) . . . . . . . . . 550.00
41 JSe,GE,JDa(c) . . . . . . . . . . . 500.00
Ann. 1952 (#1) . . . . . . . . . . . 1,750.00
Ann. 1953 (#2) JDa(c) . . . . . . 1,400.00

## 2-GUN KID
### See: BILLY BUCKSKIN

## TWO-GUN KID
### Marvel Atlas, March, 1948
1 SSh,B:Two-Gun Kid,The
   Sheriff . . . . . . . . . . . . . . . . 1,400.00
2 Killers of Outlaw City . . . . . . . 600.00
3 RH,SSh,A:Annie Oakley . . . . . 400.00
4 RH,A:Black Rider . . . . . . . . . . 400.00
5 RH . . . . . . . . . . . . . . . . . . . . . 500.00
6 . . . . . . . . . . . . . . . . . . . . . . . . 400.00
7 RH,Brand of a Killer . . . . . . . . 400.00
8 Secret of the Castle of Slaves 400.00
9 JSe,SSh,Trapped in Hidden
   Valley, A:Black Rider . . . . . . 400.00

Tr

*Two-Gun Kid #52*
© Marvel Comics Group

*Uncanny Tales #48*
© Marvel Comics Group

*Uncle Scrooge #4*
© Walt Disney

10 JK(c),The Horrible Hermit
  of Hidden Mesa . . . . . . . . . . 400.00
11 JMn(c),GT,A:Black Rider. . . . 250.00
12 JMn(c),GT,A:Black Rider . . . . 250.00
13 . . . . . . . . . . . . . . . . . . . . . . . 225.00
14 . . . . . . . . . . . . . . . . . . . . . . . 225.00
15 thru 24 . . . . . . . . . . . . . . . @225.00
25 AW,JMn . . . . . . . . . . . . . . . . 225.00
26 DAy,JMn . . . . . . . . . . . . . . . . 150.00
27 DAy,JMn . . . . . . . . . . . . . . . . 150.00
28 JMn . . . . . . . . . . . . . . . . . . . 150.00
29 . . . . . . . . . . . . . . . . . . . . . . . 150.00
30 AW . . . . . . . . . . . . . . . . . . . . 150.00
31 thru 44 . . . . . . . . . . . . . . . @125.00
45 JDa . . . . . . . . . . . . . . . . . . . . 100.00
46 JDa . . . . . . . . . . . . . . . . . . . . 100.00
47 JDa . . . . . . . . . . . . . . . . . . . . 100.00
48 . . . . . . . . . . . . . . . . . . . . . . . 100.00
49 JMn . . . . . . . . . . . . . . . . . . . 100.00
50 . . . . . . . . . . . . . . . . . . . . . . . 100.00
51 AW . . . . . . . . . . . . . . . . . . . . 100.00
52 thru 59 . . . . . . . . . . . . . . . @100.00
60 DAy,New O:Two-Gun Kid . . . 125.00

## TWO GUN WESTERN
### See: CASEY–CRIME PHOTOGRAPHER

## TWO-GUN WESTERN
### See: BILLY BUCKSKIN

## UNCANNY TALES
### Marvel Atlas, June, 1952
1 RH,While the City Sleeps . . 1,200.00
2 JMn,BEv . . . . . . . . . . . . . . . . . 600.00
3 Escape to What . . . . . . . . . . . 500.00
4 JMn,Nobody's Fool . . . . . . . . . 500.00
5 Fear . . . . . . . . . . . . . . . . . . . . 500.00
6 He Lurks in the Shadows . . . . . 550.00
7 BEv,Kill,Clown,Kill . . . . . . . . . . 550.00
8 JMn,Bring Back My Face. . . . . 450.00
9 BEv,RC,The Executioner . . . . . 450.00
10 JMn,RH(c),JR,The Man Who
  Came Back To Life . . . . . . . . 450.00
11 GC,The Man Who Changed . . 350.00
12 BP,BEv,Bertha Gets Buried . . 350.00
13 RH,Scared Out of His Skin . . . 350.00
14 RH,TLw,Victims of Vonntor . . . 350.00
15 RA,JSt,The Man Who
  Saw Death . . . . . . . . . . . . . . 350.00
16 JMn,GC,Zombie at Large . . . . 350.00
17 GC,TLw,I Live With Corpses . 350.00

18 JF,BP,Clock Face(c) . . . . . . . 350.00
19 DBr,RKr,TLw,The Man Who
  Died Again . . . . . . . . . . . . . . 350.00
20 DBr,Ted's Head . . . . . . . . . . . 350.00
21 . . . . . . . . . . . . . . . . . . . . . . . 300.00
22 DAy . . . . . . . . . . . . . . . . . . . . 300.00
23 TLw . . . . . . . . . . . . . . . . . . . . 300.00
24 . . . . . . . . . . . . . . . . . . . . . . . 300.00
25 MSy . . . . . . . . . . . . . . . . . . . . 300.00
26 Spider-Man prototype story . . 400.00
27 RA,TLw . . . . . . . . . . . . . . . . . 275.00
28 TLw . . . . . . . . . . . . . . . . . . . . 275.00
29 JMn . . . . . . . . . . . . . . . . . . . 200.00
30 . . . . . . . . . . . . . . . . . . . . . . . 200.00
31 . . . . . . . . . . . . . . . . . . . . . . . 200.00
32 BEv . . . . . . . . . . . . . . . . . . . . 200.00
33 . . . . . . . . . . . . . . . . . . . . . . . 200.00
34 BP . . . . . . . . . . . . . . . . . . . . . 200.00
35 TLw,JMn . . . . . . . . . . . . . . . . 200.00
36 BP,BEv . . . . . . . . . . . . . . . . . 200.00
37 MD . . . . . . . . . . . . . . . . . . . . 200.00
38 BP . . . . . . . . . . . . . . . . . . . . . 200.00
39 BEv . . . . . . . . . . . . . . . . . . . . 200.00
40 . . . . . . . . . . . . . . . . . . . . . . . 200.00
41 . . . . . . . . . . . . . . . . . . . . . . . 200.00
42 MD . . . . . . . . . . . . . . . . . . . . 225.00
43 . . . . . . . . . . . . . . . . . . . . . . . 200.00
44 . . . . . . . . . . . . . . . . . . . . . . . 200.00
45 MD . . . . . . . . . . . . . . . . . . . . 200.00
46 GM . . . . . . . . . . . . . . . . . . . . 200.00
47 TSe . . . . . . . . . . . . . . . . . . . . 200.00
48 BEv . . . . . . . . . . . . . . . . . . . . 200.00
49 JO . . . . . . . . . . . . . . . . . . . . . 200.00
50 JO . . . . . . . . . . . . . . . . . . . . . 200.00
51 GM . . . . . . . . . . . . . . . . . . . . 225.00
52 GC . . . . . . . . . . . . . . . . . . . . 200.00
53 JO,AT . . . . . . . . . . . . . . . . . . 200.00
54 . . . . . . . . . . . . . . . . . . . . . . . 220.00
55 . . . . . . . . . . . . . . . . . . . . . . . 200.00
56 Sept., 1957 . . . . . . . . . . . . . . 225.00

## UNCLE CHARLIE'S FABLES
### Lev Gleason Publications, Jan., 1952
1 CBi(c),Ph(c) . . . . . . . . . . . . . . 200.00
2 BF,CBi(c),Ph(c) . . . . . . . . . . . 125.00
3 CBi(c),Ph(c) . . . . . . . . . . . . . . 135.00
4 CBi(c),Ph(c) . . . . . . . . . . . . . . 135.00
5 CBi,Ph(c),Sept., 1952 . . . . . . 135.00

## UNCLE JOE'S FUNNIES
### Centaur Publications, 1938
1 BEv,Puzzles & Comics . . . . . . 650.00

## UNCLE MILTY
### Victoria Publications (True Cross Comic), 1950
1 Milton Berle . . . . . . . . . . . . . . 600.00
2 . . . . . . . . . . . . . . . . . . . . . . . . 400.00
3 . . . . . . . . . . . . . . . . . . . . . . . . 350.00
4 . . . . . . . . . . . . . . . . . . . . . . . . 325.00

## UNCLE SAM
### See: BLACKHAWK

## UNCLE SCROOGE
### Dell Publishing Co., March, 1952
(1) *see Dell Four Color #386*
(2) *see Dell Four Color #456*
(3) *see Dell Four Color #495*
4 Gladstone Album #11 . . . . . . . 600.00
5 Gladstone Special . . . . . . . . . 450.00
6 . . . . . . . . . . . . . . . . . . . . . . . . 350.00
7 CB, Seven Cities of Cibola . . . 325.00
8 thru 10 . . . . . . . . . . . . . . . . @300.00
11 thru 23 . . . . . . . . . . . . . . . . @275.00
24 Christmas issue . . . . . . . . . . . 275.00
25 thru 30 . . . . . . . . . . . . . . . . @250.00
31 thru 39 . . . . . . . . . . . . . . . . @200.00

## UNDERWORLD
### D.S. Publishing Co., Feb.–March, 1948
1 SMo(c),Violence . . . . . . . . . . . 600.00
2 SMo(c),Electrocution . . . . . . . 600.00
3 AMc,AMc(c),The Ancient Club 500.00
4 Grl,The Beer Baron Murder . . 450.00
5 Grl,The Postal Clue . . . . . . . . 300.00
6 The Polka Dot Gang . . . . . . . . 250.00
7 Mono-The Master . . . . . . . . . . 250.00
8 The Double Tenth . . . . . . . . . . 250.00
9 Thrilling Stories of the Fight
  against Crime,June, 1953 . . 250.00

## UNDERWORLD CRIME
### Fawcett Publications, June, 1952
1 The Crime Army . . . . . . . . . . . 500.00
2 Jailbreak . . . . . . . . . . . . . . . . . 350.00
3 Microscope Murder . . . . . . . . 300.00
4 Death on the Docks . . . . . . . . 300.00
5 River of Blood . . . . . . . . . . . . . 300.00
6 The Sky Pirates . . . . . . . . . . . 300.00
7 Bondage & Torture(c) . . . . . . . 500.00
8 and 9 June, 1953 . . . . . . . . @300.00

United States Marines #3
© Magazine Enterprises

Unusual Tales #1
© Charlton Comics

U. S. A. Comics #4
© Marvel Comics Group

## UNITED COMICS
### See: FRITZI RITZ

## UNITED STATES FIGHTING AIR FORCE
**Superior Comics, Ltd., Sept., 1952**
1 Coward's Courage . . . . . . . . . 150.00
2 Clouds that Killed . . . . . . . . . . 125.00
3 Operation Decoy . . . . . . . . . . . 100.00
4 thru 28 . . . . . . . . . . . . . . . . @100.00
29 Oct., 1959 . . . . . . . . . . . . . 100.00

## UNITED STATES MARINES
**Wm. H. Wise/Magazine Ent/ Toby Press, 1943–52**
N# MBi,MBi(c),Hellcat out
of Heaven . . . . . . . . . . . . . . . 200.00
2 MBi,Drama of Wake
Island, Tojo . . . . . . . . . . . . . 450.00
3 A Leatherneck Flame
Thrower, Tojo . . . . . . . . . . 350.00
4 MBi . . . . . . . . . . . . . . . . . . . 125.00
5 BP . . . . . . . . . . . . . . . . . . . . 100.00
6 BP . . . . . . . . . . . . . . . . . . . . 100.00
7 BP . . . . . . . . . . . . . . . . . . . . 100.00
8 thru 11 . . . . . . . . . . . . . . . . @100.00

## UNKEPT PROMISE
**Legion of Truth, 1949**
1 Anti:Alcoholic Drinking . . . . . . 100.00

## UNKNOWN WORLDS
### See: STRANGE STORIES FROM ANOTHER WORLD

## UNSANE
### See: HOLIDAY COMICS

## UNSEEN, THE
**Visual Editions (Standard Comics), 1952**
5 ATh,The Hungry Lodger . . . . 500.00
6 JKa,MSy,Bayou Vengeance . . 350.00
7 JKz,MSy,Time is the Killer . . . 350.00
8 JKz,MSy,The Vengeance Vat . 300.00
9 JKz,MSy,Your Grave is Ready 350.00

10 JKz,MSy . . . . . . . . . . . . . . . . 350.00
11 JKz,MSy . . . . . . . . . . . . . . . . 300.00
12 ATh,GT,Till Death Do Us Part . 350.00
13 . . . . . . . . . . . . . . . . . . . . . . 250.00
14 . . . . . . . . . . . . . . . . . . . . . . 250.00
15 ATh,The Curse of the
Undead!, July, 1954. . . . . . . 350.00

## UNTAMED LOVE
**Comic Magazines (Quality Comics Group), Jan., 1950**
1 BWa(c),PGv . . . . . . . . . . . . . 300.00
2 Ph(c) . . . . . . . . . . . . . . . . . . 175.00
3 PGv, Ph(c) . . . . . . . . . . . . . . 200.00
4 Ph(c) . . . . . . . . . . . . . . . . . . 175.00
5 PGv, Ph(c) . . . . . . . . . . . . . . 200.00

## UNUSUAL TALES
**Charlton Comics, 1955–65**
1 . . . . . . . . . . . . . . . . . . . . . . . 300.00
2 . . . . . . . . . . . . . . . . . . . . . . . 150.00
3 thru 5 . . . . . . . . . . . . . . . . @100.00
6 SD,SD(c) . . . . . . . . . . . . . . . 225.00
7 SD,SD(c) . . . . . . . . . . . . . . . 275.00
8 SD,SD(c) . . . . . . . . . . . . . . . 275.00
9 SD,SD(c) . . . . . . . . . . . . . . . 300.00
10 SD,SD(c). . . . . . . . . . . . . . . 325.00
11 SD . . . . . . . . . . . . . . . . . . . 300.00
12 SD . . . . . . . . . . . . . . . . . . . 200.00
13 . . . . . . . . . . . . . . . . . . . . . . 125.00
14 SD . . . . . . . . . . . . . . . . . . . 200.00
15 SD,SD(c) . . . . . . . . . . . . . . . 225.00
16 thru 20 . . . . . . . . . . . . . . @125.00
21 . . . . . . . . . . . . . . . . . . . . . . 100.00
22 SD . . . . . . . . . . . . . . . . . . . 150.00
23 . . . . . . . . . . . . . . . . . . . . . . 100.00
24 . . . . . . . . . . . . . . . . . . . . . . 100.00
25 thru 27 SD . . . . . . . . . . . . @135.00
28 . . . . . . . . . . . . . . . . . . . . . . 100.00
29 SD . . . . . . . . . . . . . . . . . . . 125.00
30 thru 49 . . . . . . . . . . . . . . @100.00

## U.S.A. COMICS
**Marvel Timely, Aug., 1941**
1 S&K(c),BW,AAv,SSh,Bondage(c),
The Defender(c) . . . . . . . 20,000.00
2 S&K(c),BW,SSh, Capt.
Terror(c) . . . . . . . . . . . . . 6,000.00
3 S&K(c),SSh,Capt.Terror(c) . . 4,000.00
4 SSh,Major Liberty . . . . . . . 3,500.00
5 Hitler(c),O:AmericanAvenger 3,800.00
6 ASh(c),Capt.America(c) . . . . 4,000.00

7 BW,O:Marvel Boy . . . . . . . . 3,800.00
8 ASh(c),Capt.America (c). . . . 3,500.00
9 ASh(c),Bondage(c), Captain
America . . . . . . . . . . . . . . 3,500.00
10 ASh(c),Bondage(c), Captain
America . . . . . . . . . . . . . . 3,500.00
11 SSh(c),Bondage(c), Captain
America . . . . . . . . . . . . . . 2,000.00
12 ASh(c),Capt.America . . . . . . 2,000.00
13 ASh(c),Capt.America . . . . . . 2,000.00
14 AyB(c),Capt.America . . . . . . 1,500.00
15 Capt.America . . . . . . . . . . . 1,500.00
16 ASh(c),Bondage(c),
Capt.America . . . . . . . . . . 1,500.00
17 Bondage(c),Capt.America . . 1,500.00

## USA IS READY
**Dell Publishing Co., 1941**
1 Propaganda WWII . . . . . . . . . 500.00

## U.S. JONES
**Fox Features Syndicate, Nov., 1941**
1 Death Over the Airways . . . . 1,900.00
2 Nazi (c),Jan., 1942 . . . . . . . 1,400.00

## U.S. MARINES
### See: A-1 COMICS

## U.S. MARINES IN ACTION!
**Avon Periodicals, Aug.–Dec., 1952**
1 On Land,Sea & in the Air . . . . 125.00
2 The Killer Patrol . . . . . . . . . . . 100.00
3 EK(c),Death Ridge. . . . . . . . . 100.00

## U.S. PARATROOPS
**Avon Periodicals, 1951**
1 WW . . . . . . . . . . . . . . . . . . . 200.00
2 EK . . . . . . . . . . . . . . . . . . . . 125.00
3 . . . . . . . . . . . . . . . . . . . . . . . 100.00
4 thru 6 EK . . . . . . . . . . . . . . @125.00

## U.S. TANK COMMANDOS
**Avon Periodicals, June, 1952**
1 EK(c),Fighting Daredevils
of the USA . . . . . . . . . . . . . 150.00

Un

All comics prices listed are for *Near Mint* condition.

*V... Comics #2*
© Fox Features Syndicate

*Venus #6*
© Marvel Comics Group

*Victory Comics #2*
© Hillman Periodicals

2 EK(c) . . . . . . . . . . . . . . . . . . 100.00
3 EK,EK(c),Robot Armanda . . . . 100.00
4 EK,EK(c),March, 1953 . . . . . . 100.00

## VALOR
**E.C. Comics, March, 1955**
1 AW,AT,WW,WW(c),Grl,BK . . . . 800.00
2 AW(c),AW,WWGrl,BK . . . . . . . 700.00
3 AW,RC,BK,JOc(c) . . . . . . . . . 500.00
4 WW(c),RC,Grl,BK,JO . . . . . . . 500.00
5 WW(c),WW,AW,GE,Grl,BK . . . 450.00

## VARIETY COMICS
**Rural Home Publ./
Croyden Publ. Co., 1944**
1 MvS,MvS(c),O:Capt, Valiant . . 300.00
2 MvS,MvS(c) . . . . . . . . . . . . . 250.00
3 MvS,MvS(c) . . . . . . . . . . . . . 200.00
4 . . . . . . . . . . . . . . . . . . . . . . 150.00
5 1946 . . . . . . . . . . . . . . . . . . 150.00

## VAULT OF HORROR
## See: WAR AGAINST
## CRIME

## V...COMICS
**Fox Features Syndicate,
Jan., 1942**
1 V:V-Man, Nazi(c) . . . . . . . . 1,800.00
2 The Horror of the
Dungeons, March, 1942 . . 1,400.00

## VENUS
**Marvel Atlas, Aug., 1948**
1 B:Venus,Hedy Devine,HK,Hey
Look . . . . . . . . . . . . . . . . 2,000.00
2 Venus(c) . . . . . . . . . . . . . . 1,300.00
3 Carnival(c) . . . . . . . . . . . . . 1,400.00
4 Cupid(c).HK,Hey Look . . . . . 1,400.00
5 Serenade(c) . . . . . . . . . . . . 1,400.00
6 SSh(c),Wrath of a Goddess,
A:Loki . . . . . . . . . . . . . . . 1,000.00
7 Romance that Could Not Be. 1,000.00
8 The Love Trap . . . . . . . . . . 1,000.00
9 Whom the Gods Destroy . . . 1,000.00
10 JMn,B:Science Fiction/Horror,
Trapped On the Moon . . . . 1,300.00
11 RH,The End of the World. . . 1,500.00
12 GC,The Lost World . . . . . . . 1,300.00
13 BEv,King o/t Living Dead . . . 1,300.00
14 BEv,The Fountain of Death . 1,300.00

15 BEv,The Empty Grave . . . . 1,300.00
16 BEv,Where Gargoyles Dwell 1,500.00
17 BEv,Tower of Death,
Bondage(c) . . . . . . . . . . . 1,300.00
18 BEv,Terror in the Tunnel . . . 1,300.00
19 BEv,PMo, Kiss Of Death . . . 1,300.00

## VERI BEST
## SURE FIRE COMICS
**Holyoke Publishing Co., 1945**
1 . . . . . . . . . . . . . . . . . . . . . . 250.00

## VERI BEST
## SURE SHOT COMICS
**Holyoke Publishing Co., 1945**
1 reprint Holyoke One-Shots . . . 500.00

## VIC FLINT
**St. John Publishing Co.,
Aug., 1948**
1 ...Crime Buster . . . . . . . . . . . 200.00
2 . . . . . . . . . . . . . . . . . . . . . . 175.00
3 . . . . . . . . . . . . . . . . . . . . . . 150.00
4 . . . . . . . . . . . . . . . . . . . . . . 150.00
5 April, 1949 . . . . . . . . . . . . . . 150.00

## VIC FLINT
**Argo Publ., 1956**
1 . . . . . . . . . . . . . . . . . . . . . . 125.00
2 . . . . . . . . . . . . . . . . . . . . . . 100.00

## VIC JORDAN
**Civil Service Publications,
April, 1945**
1 Escape From a Nazi Prison . . 150.00

## VICKY
**Ace Magazines, 1948**
N# Teenage . . . . . . . . . . . . . . . 150.00
2 . . . . . . . . . . . . . . . . . . . . . . 125.00
3 . . . . . . . . . . . . . . . . . . . . . . 125.00
4 . . . . . . . . . . . . . . . . . . . . . . 125.00
5 A:Dotty . . . . . . . . . . . . . . . . . 125.00

## VIC TORRY AND HIS
## FLYING SAUCER
**Fawcett Publications, 1950**
1 Ph(c),Revealed at Last . . . . . 1,000.00

## VICTORY COMICS
**Hillman Periodicals,
Aug., 1941**
1 BEv,BEv(c),F:TheConqueror 4,200.00
2 BEv,BEv(c) . . . . . . . . . . . . 1,900.00
3 The Conqueror(c) . . . . . . . . 1,200.00
4 Dec., 1941 . . . . . . . . . . . . . 1,100.00

## VIC VERITY MAGAZINE
**Vic Verity Publications,
1945**
1 CCB,CCB(c),B:Vic Verity,Hot-
Shot Galvan, Tom Travis . . . 250.00
2 CCB,CCB(c),Annual Classic
Dance Recital . . . . . . . . . . . 150.00
3 CCB . . . . . . . . . . . . . . . . . . 125.00
4 CCB,I:Boomer Young;The
Bee-U-TiFul Weekend . . . . . 125.00
5 CCB,Championship Baseball
Game . . . . . . . . . . . . . . . . 125.00
6 CCB,High School Hero . . . . . 125.00
7 CCB,CCB(c),F:Rocket Rex . . 125.00

## VOODOO
**Four Star Publ./Farrell/
Ajax Comics, May, 1952**
1 MB,South Sea Girl . . . . . . . . 800.00
2 MB . . . . . . . . . . . . . . . . . . . 600.00
3 Face Stabbing . . . . . . . . . . . 500.00
4 MB,Rendezvous . . . . . . . . . . 500.00
5 Ghoul For A Day,Nazi . . . . . . 350.00
6 The Weird Dead,
Severed Head . . . . . . . . . . . 400.00
7 Goodbye World . . . . . . . . . . 350.00
8 MB, Revenge . . . . . . . . . . . . 450.00
9 Will this thing Never Stew? . . 350.00
10 Land of Shadows & Screams. 350.00
11 Human Harvest . . . . . . . . . . 300.00
12 The Wazen Taper . . . . . . . . 300.00
13 Bondage(c),Caskets to
Fit Everybody . . . . . . . . . . . 325.00
14 Death Judges the
Beauty Contest, Zombies . . . 300.00
15 Loose their Heads, Opium . . . 325.00
16 Fog Was Her Shroud . . . . . . 300.00
17 Apes Laughter,Electric Chair . 325.00
18 Astounding Fantasy . . . . . . . 300.00
19 MB,Bondage(c);
Destination Congo. . . . . . . . 450.00
Ann.#1 100-pg. . . . . . . . . . . . 1,250.00
Becomes:

Voodoo #12
© Ferrell Publications

Walt Disney's Comics and Stories #38
© Walt Disney

Walt Disney's Comics and Stories #100
© Walt Disney

## VOODA
### April, 1955
20 MB,MB(c),Echoes of
  an A-Bomb. . . . . . . . . . . . . 500.00
21 MB,MB(c),Trek of Danger. . . . 400.00
22 MB,MB(c),The Sun Blew
  Away, Aug., 1955. . . . . . . . . 400.00

## WACKY DUCK
## See: DOPEY DUCK

## WALT DISNEY'S
## COMICS & STORIES
### Dell Publishing Co.
N# 1943 dpt.store giveway . . . . . 750.00
N# 1945 X-mas giveaway. . . . . . 350.00

## WALT DISNEY'S
## COMICS & STORIES
### Dell Publishing Co.,
### Oct., 1940
1 (1940)FGu,Donald Duck &
  Mickey Mouse . . . . . . . . . 25,000.00
2 . . . . . . . . . . . . . . . . . . . . . . 9,000.00
3 . . . . . . . . . . . . . . . . . . . . . . 3,000.00
4 1st Huey, Dewey & Louie
  Christmas(c) . . . . . . . . . . . . 2,500.00
4a Promo issue . . . . . . . . . . . 3,500.00
5 Goofy(c) . . . . . . . . . . . . . . 1,700.00
6 . . . . . . . . . . . . . . . . . . . . . . 1,500.00
7 . . . . . . . . . . . . . . . . . . . . . . 1,500.00
8 Clarabelle Cow(c). . . . . . . . . 1,500.00
9 . . . . . . . . . . . . . . . . . . . . . . 1,500.00
10 . . . . . . . . . . . . . . . . . . . . . 1,500.00
11 2nd Huey,Louie,Dewey(c) . . 1,500.00
12 . . . . . . . . . . . . . . . . . . . . . 1,200.00
13 . . . . . . . . . . . . . . . . . . . . . 1,100.00
14 . . . . . . . . . . . . . . . . . . . . . 1,100.00
15 3 Little Kittens . . . . . . . . . . . 1,000.00
16 3 Little Pigs . . . . . . . . . . . . . 1,000.00
17 The Ugly Ducklings . . . . . . . 1,000.00
18 . . . . . . . . . . . . . . . . . . . . . . . 850.00
19 . . . . . . . . . . . . . . . . . . . . . . . 800.00
20 . . . . . . . . . . . . . . . . . . . . . . . 800.00
21 . . . . . . . . . . . . . . . . . . . . . . . 850.00
22 . . . . . . . . . . . . . . . . . . . . . . . 750.00
23 . . . . . . . . . . . . . . . . . . . . . . . 750.00
24 Flying Gauchito. . . . . . . . . . . . 700.00
25 . . . . . . . . . . . . . . . . . . . . . . . 700.00
26 . . . . . . . . . . . . . . . . . . . . . . . 700.00
27 Jose Carioca. . . . . . . . . . . . . . 700.00
28 . . . . . . . . . . . . . . . . . . . . . . . 750.00

29 . . . . . . . . . . . . . . . . . . . . . . . 700.00
30 . . . . . . . . . . . . . . . . . . . . . . . 700.00
31 CB; Donald Duck . . . . . . . . . 6,000.00
32 CB . . . . . . . . . . . . . . . . . . . 2,500.00
33 CB . . . . . . . . . . . . . . . . . . . 1,700.00
34 CB;WK; Gremlins. . . . . . . . . 1,500.00
35 CB;WK; Gremlins . . . . . . . . . 1,500.00
36 CB;WK; Gremlins . . . . . . . . . 1,500.00
37 CB;WK; Gremlins . . . . . . . . . . 800.00
38 CB;WK; Gremlins. . . . . . . . . 1,000.00
39 CB;WK; Gremlins, X-mas . . 1,000.00
40 CB;WK; Gremlins. . . . . . . . . 1,000.00
41 CB;WK; Gremlins . . . . . . . . . . 900.00
42 CB . . . . . . . . . . . . . . . . . . . . . 800.00
43 CB,Seven Dwarfs . . . . . . . . . . 800.00
44 CB . . . . . . . . . . . . . . . . . . . . . 800.00
45 CB,Nazis in stories . . . . . . . . . 800.00
46 CB,Nazis in stories . . . . . . . . . 800.00
47 CB,Nazis in stories . . . . . . . . . 800.00
48 CB,Nazis in stories . . . . . . . . . 800.00
49 CB,Nazis in stories . . . . . . . . . 800.00
50 CB,Nazis in stories . . . . . . . . . 800.00
51 CB,Christmas . . . . . . . . . . . . . 700.00
52 CB; Li'l Bad Wolf begins. . . . . 700.00
53 CB . . . . . . . . . . . . . . . . . . . . . 700.00
54 CB . . . . . . . . . . . . . . . . . . . . . 700.00
55 CB . . . . . . . . . . . . . . . . . . . . . 700.00
56 CB . . . . . . . . . . . . . . . . . . . . . 700.00
57 CB . . . . . . . . . . . . . . . . . . . . . 700.00
58 CB . . . . . . . . . . . . . . . . . . . . . 700.00
59 CB . . . . . . . . . . . . . . . . . . . . . 700.00
60 CB . . . . . . . . . . . . . . . . . . . . . 700.00
61 CB; Dumbo . . . . . . . . . . . . . . 600.00
62 CB . . . . . . . . . . . . . . . . . . . . . 600.00
63 CB; Pinocchio . . . . . . . . . . . . . 600.00
64 CB; Pinocchio, X-mas. . . . . . . 600.00
65 CB; Pluto. . . . . . . . . . . . . . . . . 600.00
66 CB . . . . . . . . . . . . . . . . . . . . . 600.00
67 CB . . . . . . . . . . . . . . . . . . . . . 600.00
68 CB, Mickey Mouse . . . . . . . . . 600.00
69 CB . . . . . . . . . . . . . . . . . . . . . 600.00
70 CB . . . . . . . . . . . . . . . . . . . . . 600.00
71 CB . . . . . . . . . . . . . . . . . . . . . 500.00
72 CB . . . . . . . . . . . . . . . . . . . . . 500.00
73 CB . . . . . . . . . . . . . . . . . . . . . 500.00
74 CB . . . . . . . . . . . . . . . . . . . . . 500.00
75 CB; Brer Rabbit. . . . . . . . . . . . 500.00
76 CB; Brer Rabbit, X-mas . . . . . 500.00
77 CB; Brer Rabbit. . . . . . . . . . . . 500.00
78 CB . . . . . . . . . . . . . . . . . . . . . 500.00
79 CB . . . . . . . . . . . . . . . . . . . . . 500.00
80 CB . . . . . . . . . . . . . . . . . . . . . 500.00
81 CB . . . . . . . . . . . . . . . . . . . . . 500.00
82 CB;Bongo,Googy . . . . . . . . . . 500.00
83 CB;Bongo . . . . . . . . . . . . . . . . 500.00
84 CB;Bongo . . . . . . . . . . . . . . . . 500.00

85 CB. . . . . . . . . . . . . . . . . . . . . 500.00
86 CB;Goofy & Agnes . . . . . . . . 500.00
87 CB;Goofy & Agnes . . . . . . . . 375.00
88 CB;Goofy & Agnes,
  I:Gladstone Gander. . . . . . . 500.00
89 CB;Goofy&Agnes,Chip'n'Dale 375.00
90 CB;Goofy & Agnes . . . . . . . . 375.00
91 CB. . . . . . . . . . . . . . . . . . . . . 300.00
92 CB. . . . . . . . . . . . . . . . . . . . . 300.00
93 CB . . . . . . . . . . . . . . . . . . . . 300.00
94 CB. . . . . . . . . . . . . . . . . . . . . 300.00
95 CB(c). . . . . . . . . . . . . . . . . . . 300.00
96 Little Toot . . . . . . . . . . . . . . . 300.00
97 CB; Little Toot . . . . . . . . . . . . 300.00
98 CB; Uncle Scrooge. . . . . . . . . 600.00
99 CB. . . . . . . . . . . . . . . . . . . . . 300.00
100 CB . . . . . . . . . . . . . . . . . . . . 400.00
101 CB. . . . . . . . . . . . . . . . . . . . 300.00
102 CB . . . . . . . . . . . . . . . . . . . . 300.00
103 CB . . . . . . . . . . . . . . . . . . . . 275.00
104 . . . . . . . . . . . . . . . . . . . . . . 275.00
105 CB . . . . . . . . . . . . . . . . . . . . 300.00
106 CB . . . . . . . . . . . . . . . . . . . . 300.00
107 CB, Donald super-powers . . 500.00
108 . . . . . . . . . . . . . . . . . . . . . . 275.00
109 . . . . . . . . . . . . . . . . . . . . . . 275.00
110 CB . . . . . . . . . . . . . . . . . . . . 300.00
111 CB . . . . . . . . . . . . . . . . . . . . 300.00
112 CB; drugs . . . . . . . . . . . . . . 400.00
113 CB . . . . . . . . . . . . . . . . . . . . 300.00
114 CB . . . . . . . . . . . . . . . . . . . . 300.00
115 WK(c) . . . . . . . . . . . . . . . . . 300.00
116 Dumbo . . . . . . . . . . . . . . . . . 150.00
117 . . . . . . . . . . . . . . . . . . . . . . 150.00
118 . . . . . . . . . . . . . . . . . . . . . . 150.00
119 . . . . . . . . . . . . . . . . . . . . . . 150.00
120 . . . . . . . . . . . . . . . . . . . . . . 150.00
121 Grandma Duck begins . . . . . 150.00
122 . . . . . . . . . . . . . . . . . . . . . . 150.00
123 . . . . . . . . . . . . . . . . . . . . . . 300.00
124 CB,Christmas . . . . . . . . . . . 250.00
125 CB;I:Junior Woodchucks . . . 400.00
126 CB . . . . . . . . . . . . . . . . . . . . 450.00
127 CB . . . . . . . . . . . . . . . . . . . . 250.00
128 CB . . . . . . . . . . . . . . . . . . . . 250.00
129 CB . . . . . . . . . . . . . . . . . . . . 250.00
130 CB . . . . . . . . . . . . . . . . . . . . 250.00
131 CB . . . . . . . . . . . . . . . . . . . . 250.00
132 CB A:Grandma Duck . . . . . . 250.00
133 CB . . . . . . . . . . . . . . . . . . . . 250.00
134 I:The Beagle Boys . . . . . . . . 500.00
135 CB . . . . . . . . . . . . . . . . . . . . 250.00
136 CB . . . . . . . . . . . . . . . . . . . . 250.00
137 CB . . . . . . . . . . . . . . . . . . . . 250.00
138 CB,Scrooge & Money. . . . . . 350.00
139 CB . . . . . . . . . . . . . . . . . . . . 250.00

**Vo**

*Walt Disney's Comics and Stories #146*
*© Walt Disney*

*Walt Disney's Dell Giant Silly*
*Symphonies #1 © Walt Disney*

*Wambi Jungle Boy #1*
*© Fiction House*

140 CB; I:Gyro Gearloose . . . . . . 500.00
141 CB. . . . . . . . . . . . . . . . . . . 200.00
142 CB. . . . . . . . . . . . . . . . . . . 200.00
143 CB; Little Hiawatha . . . . . . . . 200.00
144 CB; Little Hiawatha . . . . . . . . 200.00
145 CB; Little Hiawatha . . . . . . . . 200.00
146 CB; Little Hiawatha . . . . . . . . 200.00
147 CB; Little Hiawatha . . . . . . . . 200.00
148 CB; Little Hiawatha . . . . . . . . 200.00
149 CB; Little Hiawatha . . . . . . . . 200.00
150 CB; Little Hiawatha . . . . . . . . 200.00
151 CB; Little Hiawatha . . . . . . . . 200.00
152 thru 200 CB. . . . . . . . . . . @150.00
201 thru 203 CB. . . . . . . . . . . @125.00
204 CB, Chip 'n' Dale & Scamp. . 125.00
205 thru 240 CB. . . . . . . . . . . @125.00
241 CB; Dumbo x-over . . . . . . . . 125.00
242 CB. . . . . . . . . . . . . . . . . . . 125.00
243 CB. . . . . . . . . . . . . . . . . . . 125.00
244 CB. . . . . . . . . . . . . . . . . . . 125.00
245 CB. . . . . . . . . . . . . . . . . . . 125.00
246 CB. . . . . . . . . . . . . . . . . . . 125.00
247 thru 255 CB;GyroGearloose . . . . . .
@125.00
256 thru 263 CB;Ludwig Von
Drake & Gearloose . . . . . . @125.00

## WALT DISNEY'S
## DELL GIANT EDITIONS
### Dell Publishing Co.
1 CB,W.Disney'sXmas
Parade('49) . . . . . . . . . . . . . 1,200.00
2 CB,W.Disney'sXmas
Parade('50). . . . . . . . . . . . . 1,000.00
3 W.Disney'sXmas Parade('51) . 300.00
4 W.Disney'sXmas Parade('52) . 250.00
5 W.Disney'sXmas Parade('53) . 250.00
6 W.Disney'sXmas Parade('54) . 250.00
7 W.Disney'sXmas Parade('55) . 250.00
8 CB,W.Disney'sXmas
Parade('56) . . . . . . . . . . . . . 500.00
9 CB,W.Disney'sXmas
Parade('57) . . . . . . . . . . . . . 500.00
1 CB,W.Disney's Christmas in
Disneyland (1957) . . . . . . . . 600.00
1 CB,W.Disney's Disneyland
Birthday Party (1958) . . . . . . 600.00
1 W.Disney's Donald and Mickey
in Disneyland (1958) . . . . . . . 250.00
1 W.Disney's Donald Duck
Beach Party (1954) . . . . . . . . 300.00
2 W.Disney's Donald Duck
Beach Party (1955) . . . . . . . 250.00

3 W.Disney's Donald Duck
Beach Party (1956) . . . . . . . 250.00
4 W.Disney's Donald Duck
Beach Party (1957) . . . . . . . 250.00
5 W.Disney's Donald Duck
Beach Party (1958) . . . . . . . 250.00
6 W.Disney's Donald Duck
Beach Party (1959) . . . . . . . 250.00
1 W.Disney's Donald Duck
Fun Book (1954). . . . . . . . 1,200.00
2 W.Disney's Donald Duck
Fun Book (1954). . . . . . . . 1,100.00
1 W.Disney's Donald Duck
in Disneyland (1955) . . . . . . 275.00
1 W.Disney's Huey, Dewey
and Louie (1958) . . . . . . . . 175.00
1 W.Disney's DavyCrockett('55) . 350.00
1 W.Disney's Lady and the
Tramp (1955) . . . . . . . . . . . 400.00
1 CB,W.Disney's Mickey Mouse
Almanac (1957) . . . . . . . . . . 600.00
1 W.Disney's Mickey Mouse
Birthday Party (1953) . . . . . . 700.00
1 W.Disney's Mickey Mouse
Club Parade (1955) . . . . . . . 600.00
1 W.Disney's Mickey Mouse
in Fantasyland (1957) . . . . . . 275.00
1 W.Disney's Mickey Mouse
in Frontierland (1956) . . . . . . 275.00
1 W.Disney's Summer Fun('58) . 275.00
2 CB,W.Disney'sSummer
Fun('59). . . . . . . . . . . . . . . . 275.00
1 W.Disney's Peter Pan
Treasure Chest (1953) . . . . 2,200.00
1 Disney Silly Symphonies('52) . 600.00
2 Disney Silly Symphonies('53) . 500.00
3 Disney Silly Symphonies('54) . 450.00
4 Disney Silly Symphonies('54) . 450.00
5 Disney Silly Symphonies('55) . 400.00
6 Disney Silly Symphonies('56) . 400.00
7 Disney Silly Symphonies('57) . 400.00
8 Disney Silly Symphonies('58) . 400.00
9 Disney Silly Symphonies('59) . 400.00
1 Disney SleepingBeauty('59) . . 600.00
1 CB,W.Disney's Uncle Scrooge
Goes to Disneyland (1957) . . 550.00
1 W.Disney's Vacation in
Disneyland (1958) . . . . . . . . 250.00
1 CB,Disney's Vacation
Parade('50). . . . . . . . . . . . 1,700.00
2 Disney'sVacation Parade('51) . 600.00
3 Disney'sVacation Parade('52) . 300.00
4 Disney'sVacation Parade('53) . 300.00
5 Disney'sVacation Parade('54) . 300.00
6 Disney's Picnic Party (1955) . 250.00
7 Disney's Picnic Party (1956) . 250.00

8 CB,Disney's Picnic
Party (1957). . . . . . . . . . . . . 500.00

## WALT DISNEY'S
## DELL JUNIOR TREASURY
1 W.Disney's Alice in Wonderland
(1955) . . . . . . . . . . . . . . . . . 250.00

## WALT DISNEY
## PRESENTS
### Dell Publishing Co.,
### June–Aug., 1952
1 Ph(c), Four Color. . . . . . . . . . 200.00
2 Ph(c) . . . . . . . . . . . . . . . . . . 150.00
3 Ph(c) . . . . . . . . . . . . . . . . . . 150.00
4 Ph(c) . . . . . . . . . . . . . . . . . . 150.00
5 and 6 Ph(c) . . . . . . . . . . . . . @150.00

## WAMBI
## JUNGLE BOY
### Fiction House Magazines,
### Spring, 1942–Winter, 1952
1 HcK,HcK(c),Vengence of
the Beasts . . . . . . . . . . . . . 1,200.00
2 HcK,HcK(c),Lair of the
Killer Rajah . . . . . . . . . . . . . . 650.00
3 HcK,HcK(c) . . . . . . . . . . . . . . 500.00
4 HcK,HcK(c),The Valley of
the Whispering Drums . . . . . 250.00
5 HcK,HcK(c),SwamplandSafari. 250.00
6 Taming of the Tigress . . . . . . . 225.00
7 Duel of the Congo Kings . . . . 225.00
8 AB(c),Friend of the Animals . . 225.00
9 Quest of the Devils Juju . . . . . 225.00
10 Friend of the Animals . . . . . . . 200.00
11 . . . . . . . . . . . . . . . . . . . . . . . 200.00
12 Curse of the Jungle Jewels . . 200.00
13 New Adventures of Wambi . . . 175.00
14 . . . . . . . . . . . . . . . . . . . . . . . 175.00
15 The Leopard Legions . . . . . . . 175.00
16 . . . . . . . . . . . . . . . . . . . . . . . 175.00
17 Beware Bwana! . . . . . . . . . . . 175.00
18 Ogg the Great Bull Ape. . . . . . 175.00

## WANTED COMICS
### Toytown Comics/
### Orbit Publications,
### Sept.–Oct., 1947
9 Victor Everhart. . . . . . . . . . . . 250.00
10 Carlo Banone . . . . . . . . . . . . . 150.00
11 Dwight Band . . . . . . . . . . . . . 150.00
12 Ralph Roe. . . . . . . . . . . . . . . 165.00

---

All comics prices listed are for *Near Mint* condition.

*Wanted Comics #16*
© *Toytown Comics*

*War Against Crime #9*
© *E. C. Comics*

*The Vault of Horror #35*
© *E. C. Comics*

13 James Spencer;Drug . . . . . . . 175.00
14 John "Jiggs" Sullivan;Drug . . . 175.00
15 Harry Dunlap;Drug . . . . . . . . . 125.00
16 Jack Parisi;Drug . . . . . . . . . . . 135.00
17 Herber Ayers;Drug . . . . . . . . . 135.00
18 Satan's Cigarettes;Drug . . . . . 250.00
19 Jackson Stringer . . . . . . . . . . . 125.00
20 George Morgan . . . . . . . . . . . 125.00
21 BK,Paul Wilson . . . . . . . . . . . 135.00
22 Strong violence . . . . . . . . . . . . 135.00
23 George Elmo Wells . . . . . . . . . 125.00
24 BK,Bruce Cornett;Drug . . . . . . 135.00
25 Henry Anger . . . . . . . . . . . . . . 125.00
26 John Wormly . . . . . . . . . . . . . . 125.00
27 Death Always Knocks Twice . . 125.00
28 Paul H. Payton . . . . . . . . . . . . 125.00
29 Hangmans Holiday . . . . . . . . . 125.00
30 George Lee . . . . . . . . . . . . . . . 125.00
31 M Consolo . . . . . . . . . . . . . . . . 125.00
32 William Davis . . . . . . . . . . . . . 125.00
33 The Web of Davis . . . . . . . . . . 125.00
34 Dead End . . . . . . . . . . . . . . . . 125.00
35 Glen Roy Wright . . . . . . . . . . . 125.00
36 SSh,SSh(c),Bernard Lee
   Thomas . . . . . . . . . . . . . . . . 100.00
37 SSh,SSh(c),Joseph M. Moore 100.00
38 SSh,SSh(c) . . . . . . . . . . . . . . 100.00
39 The Horror Weed;Drug . . . . . . 175.00
40 . . . . . . . . . . . . . . . . . . . . . . . . 100.00
41 . . . . . . . . . . . . . . . . . . . . . . . . 100.00
42 . . . . . . . . . . . . . . . . . . . . . . . . 100.00
43 . . . . . . . . . . . . . . . . . . . . . . . . 100.00
44 . . . . . . . . . . . . . . . . . . . . . . . . 100.00
45 Killers on the Loose;Drug . . . . 125.00
46 Charles Edward Crews . . . . . . 100.00
47 . . . . . . . . . . . . . . . . . . . . . . . . 100.00
48 SSh,SSh(c) . . . . . . . . . . . . . . 100.00
49 . . . . . . . . . . . . . . . . . . . . . . . . 100.00
50 JB(c),Make Way for Murder . . 150.00
51 JB(c),Dope Addict on a
   Holiday of Murder;Drug . . . . . 135.00
52 The Cult of Killers;
   Classic Drug . . . . . . . . . . . . 135.00
53 April, 1953 . . . . . . . . . . . . . . . 100.00

## WAR ACTION
### Marvel Atlas, April, 1952
1 JMn,RH,War Stories, Six Dead
  Men . . . . . . . . . . . . . . . . . . . 250.00
2 GT . . . . . . . . . . . . . . . . . . . . . . 125.00
3 Invasion in Korea . . . . . . . . . . 100.00
4 thru 10 . . . . . . . . . . . . . . . . @100.00
11 and 12 . . . . . . . . . . . . . . . . @125.00
13 BK . . . . . . . . . . . . . . . . . . . . . . 125.00
14 Rangers Strike,June, 1953 . . . 100.00

## WAR ADVENTURES
### Marvel Atlas, Jan., 1952
1 GT,Battle Fatigue . . . . . . . . . . 200.00
2 The Story of a Slaughter . . . . . 125.00
3 JRo . . . . . . . . . . . . . . . . . . . . . 100.00
4 RH(c) . . . . . . . . . . . . . . . . . . . . 100.00
5 RH,Violent(c) . . . . . . . . . . . . . . 100.00
6 Stand or Die . . . . . . . . . . . . . . 100.00
7 JMn(c) . . . . . . . . . . . . . . . . . . . 100.00
8 BK . . . . . . . . . . . . . . . . . . . . . . 125.00
9 RH(c) . . . . . . . . . . . . . . . . . . . . 100.00
10 JRo(c),Attack at Dawn . . . . . . 100.00
11 Red Trap . . . . . . . . . . . . . . . . 100.00
12 . . . . . . . . . . . . . . . . . . . . . . . . 100.00
13 RH(c),The Commies Strike
   Feb., 1953 . . . . . . . . . . . . . . 100.00

## WAR AGAINST CRIME
### L.L. Publishing Co.
### (E.C. Comics), Spring, 1948
1 Grl, Stories from Police . . . . 1,000.00
2 Grl,Guilty of Murder . . . . . . . . 700.00
3 JCr(c) . . . . . . . . . . . . . . . . . . . 700.00
4 AF,JCr(c) . . . . . . . . . . . . . . . . 600.00
5 JCr(c) . . . . . . . . . . . . . . . . . . . 600.00
6 AF,JCr(c) . . . . . . . . . . . . . . . . 600.00
7 AF,JCr(c) . . . . . . . . . . . . . . . . 600.00
8 AF,JCr(c) . . . . . . . . . . . . . . . . 600.00
9 AF,JCr(c),The Kid . . . . . . . . . 600.00
10 JCr(c),I:Vault Keeper . . . . . 2,800.00
11 JCr(c) . . . . . . . . . . . . . . . . . 1,600.00
**Becomes:**

## VAULT OF HORROR, THE
### April–May, 1950–Jan., 1955
12 AF,JCr(a&c),Wax Museum . . 6,700.00
13 AF,WW,JCr(c),Grl,Drug . . . . 2,500.00
14 AF,WW,JCr(c),Grl. . . . . . . . 2,500.00
15 AF,JCr(a&c),Grl,JKa. . . . . . 2,500.00
16 Grl,JKa,JCr(a&c) . . . . . . . . 1,800.00
17 JDa,Grl,JKa,JCr(a&c) . . . . . 1,800.00
18 JDa,Grl,JKa,JCr(a&c) . . . . . 1,500.00
19 JDa,Grl,JKa,JCr(a&c) . . . . . 1,500.00
20 JDa,Grl,JKa,JCr(a&c) . . . . . 1,600.00
21 JDa,Grl,JKa,JCr(a&c) . . . . . 1,600.00
22 JDa,JKa,JCr(a&c) . . . . . . . . 1,600.00
23 JDa,Grl,JCr(a&c) . . . . . . . . . 1,600.00
24 JDa,Grl,JO,JCr(a&c) . . . . . . 1,600.00
25 JDa,Grl,JKa,JCr(a&c) . . . . . 1,600.00
26 JDa,Grl,JCr(a&c) . . . . . . . . . 1,200.00
27 JDa,Grl,GE,JCr(a&c) . . . . . . 1,500.00
28 JDa,Grl,JCr(a&c) . . . . . . . . . 1,500.00
29 JDa,Grl,JKa,JCr(a&c),
   Bradbury Adapt. . . . . . . . . . 1,500.00
30 JDa,Grl,JCr(a&c) . . . . . . . . . 1,500.00

31 JDa,Grl,JCr(a&c),
   Bradbury Adapt. . . . . . . . . . 1,200.00
32 JDa,Grl,JCr(a&c) . . . . . . . . . 1,200.00
33 JDa,Grl,RC,JCr(c) . . . . . . . . 1,200.00
34 JDa,Grl,RC,JCr(a&c) . . . . . . 1,200.00
35 JDa,Grl,JCr(a&c),X-mas . . . 1,200.00
36 JDa,Grl,BK,JCr(a&c),Drug. . 1,200.00
37 JDa,Grl,AW,JCr(a&c)
   Hanging . . . . . . . . . . . . . . . 1,200.00
38 JDa,Grl,BK,JCr(a&c) . . . . . . 1,200.00
39 Grl,BK,RC,JCr(a&c)
   Bondage(c). . . . . . . . . . . . . 1,200.00
40 Grl,BK,JO,JCr(a&c) . . . . . . . 1,400.00

## WAR BATTLES
### Harvey Publications,
### Feb., 1952
1 BP,Devils of the Deep . . . . . . . 175.00
2 BP,A Present From Benny . . . . 125.00
3 BP . . . . . . . . . . . . . . . . . . . . . . 100.00
4 . . . . . . . . . . . . . . . . . . . . . . . . . 100.00
5 . . . . . . . . . . . . . . . . . . . . . . . . . 100.00
6 HN . . . . . . . . . . . . . . . . . . . . . . 100.00
7 BP . . . . . . . . . . . . . . . . . . . . . . 125.00
8 . . . . . . . . . . . . . . . . . . . . . . . . . 100.00
9 Dec., 1953 . . . . . . . . . . . . . . . . 100.00

## WAR BIRDS
### Fiction House Magazines, 1952
1 Willie the Washout . . . . . . . . . 175.00
2 Mystery MIGs of Kwanjamu . . 110.00
3 thru 6 . . . . . . . . . . . . . . . . . @100.00
7 Winter, 1953,Across the
  Wild Yalu . . . . . . . . . . . . . . . 100.00

## WAR COMBAT
### Marvel Atlas, March, 1952
1 JMn,Death of Platoon Leader . 175.00
2 . . . . . . . . . . . . . . . . . . . . . . . . . 125.00
3 JMn(c) . . . . . . . . . . . . . . . . . . . 100.00
4 JMn(c) . . . . . . . . . . . . . . . . . . . 100.00
5 The Red Hordes . . . . . . . . . . . 100.00
**Becomes:**

## COMBAT CASEY
6 BEv,Combat Casey cont . . . . . 175.00
7 . . . . . . . . . . . . . . . . . . . . . . . . . 125.00
8 JMn(c) . . . . . . . . . . . . . . . . . . . 100.00
9 . . . . . . . . . . . . . . . . . . . . . . . . . 100.00
10 RH(c). . . . . . . . . . . . . . . . . . . 125.00
11 . . . . . . . . . . . . . . . . . . . . . . . . 100.00
12 . . . . . . . . . . . . . . . . . . . . . . . . 100.00
13 thru 19 . . . . . . . . . . . . . . . @125.00
20 . . . . . . . . . . . . . . . . . . . . . . . . 100.00

All comics prices listed are for *Near Mint* condition.

*War Comics #2*
© Marvel Comics Group

*War Heroes #5*
© Ace Magazines

*Wartime Romances #16*
© St. John Publishing Co.

| | | |
|---|---|---|
| 21 thru 33 | @100.00 | |
| 34 July, 1957 | 100.00 | |

| | |
|---|---|
| 34 JK | 100.00 |
| 35 | 100.00 |

| | |
|---|---|
| 3 | 125.00 |
| 4 | 125.00 |
| 5 | 125.00 |

## WAR COMICS
### Dell Publishing Co., May, 1940

| | |
|---|---|
| 1 AMc,Sky Hawk | 800.00 |
| 2 O:Greg Gildam | 450.00 |
| 3 | 350.00 |
| 4 O:Night Devils | 400.00 |

## WAR COMICS
### Marvel Atlas, Dec., 1950

| | |
|---|---|
| 1 You Only Die Twice | 300.00 |
| 2 Infantry's War | 150.00 |
| 3 | 125.00 |
| 4 GC,The General Said Nuts | 125.00 |
| 5 | 125.00 |
| 6 The Deadly Decision of General Kwang | 125.00 |
| 7 RH,JMn | 125.00 |
| 8 RH,No Survivors | 125.00 |
| 9 RH,JMn | 125.00 |
| 10 | 125.00 |
| 11 Flame thrower | 135.00 |
| 12 thru 21 | @100.00 |
| 22 | 100.00 |
| 23 thru 37 | @100.00 |
| 38 JKu | 125.00 |
| 39 | 100.00 |
| 40 | 100.00 |
| 41 | 100.00 |
| 42 JO | 100.00 |
| 43 AT,MD | 125.00 |
| 44 | 100.00 |
| 45 | 100.00 |
| 46 RC | 125.00 |
| 47 | 100.00 |
| 48 MD,JO | 100.00 |
| 49 Sept., 1957 | 125.00 |

## WARFRONT
### Fighting Forces Publ./ Harvey Publications

| | |
|---|---|
| 1 Korean War | 200.00 |
| 2 | 150.00 |
| 3 | 125.00 |
| 4 | 125.00 |
| 5 | 125.00 |
| 6 thru 10 | @125.00 |
| 11 thru 21 | @100.00 |
| 22 HN | 125.00 |
| 23 thru 33 | @100.00 |

## WAR FURY
### Comic Media/Harwell, 1952

| | |
|---|---|
| 1 DH,RP,hole in head | 300.00 |
| 2 Violent | 150.00 |
| 3 Violent | 150.00 |
| 4 PMo,Violent | 150.00 |

## WAR HEROES
### Dell Publishing Co., July–Sept., 1942

| | |
|---|---|
| 1 Gen. Douglas MacArthur (c) | 400.00 |
| 2 | 300.00 |
| 3 Pro-Soviet | 250.00 |
| 4 A:Gremlins | 350.00 |
| 5 | 250.00 |
| 6 | 200.00 |
| 7 | 200.00 |
| 8 thru 11 | @200.00 |

## WAR HEROES
### Ace Magazines, May, 1952

| | |
|---|---|
| 1 Always Comin' | 150.00 |
| 2 LC,The Last Red Tank | 125.00 |
| 3 You Got it | 100.00 |
| 4 A Red Patrol | 100.00 |
| 5 Hustle it Up | 100.00 |
| 6 LC,Hang on Pal | 125.00 |
| 7 LC | 125.00 |
| 8 LC, April, 1953 | 125.00 |

## WARPATH
### Key Publications/ Stanmore, Nov., 1954

| | |
|---|---|
| 1 Red Men Raid | 125.00 |
| 2 AH(c),Braves Battle | 100.00 |
| 3 April, 1955 | 100.00 |

## WARRIOR COMICS
### H.C. Blackerby, 1944

| | |
|---|---|
| 1 Ironman wing Brady | 400.00 |

## WAR REPORT
### Excellent Publ. (Ajax/Farrell Publ.), 1952

| | |
|---|---|
| 1 | 150.00 |
| 2 Burning bodies | 250.00 |

## WAR SHIPS
### Dell Publishing Co., 1942

| | |
|---|---|
| 1 AMc | 200.00 |

## WAR STORIES
### Dell Publishing Co., 1942

| | |
|---|---|
| 5 O:The Whistler | 300.00 |
| 6 A:Night Devils | 250.00 |
| 7 A:Night Devils | 250.00 |
| 8 A:Night Devils | 250.00 |

## WARTIME ROMANCES
### St. John Publishing Co., July, 1951

| | |
|---|---|
| 1 MB(c),MB | 400.00 |
| 2 MB(c),MB | 300.00 |
| 3 MB(c),MB | 250.00 |
| 4 MB(c),MB | 250.00 |
| 5 MB(c),MB | 225.00 |
| 6 MB(c),MB | 250.00 |
| 7 MB(c),MB | 225.00 |
| 8 MB(c),MB | 225.00 |
| 9 MB(c),MB | 200.00 |
| 10 MB(c),MB | 200.00 |
| 11 MB(c),MB | 200.00 |
| 12 MB(c),MB | 200.00 |
| 13 MB(c) | 100.00 |
| 14 MB(c) | 100.00 |
| 15 MB(c) | 100.00 |
| 16 MB(c),MB | 175.00 |
| 17 MB(c) | 100.00 |
| 18 MB(c),MB | 175.00 |

## WAR VICTORY COMICS
### U.S. Treasury/War Victory/ Harvey Publ., Summer, 1942

| | |
|---|---|
| 1 Savings Bond Promo with Top Syndicated Cartoonists, benefit USO | 500.00 |

Becomes:

## WAR VICTORY ADVENTURES
### Summer, 1942

| | |
|---|---|
| 2 BP,2nd Front Comics | 300.00 |
| 3 BP,F:Capt Cross of the Red Cross | 250.00 |

# STANDARD GUIDE TO GOLDEN AGE COMICS

*Web of Mystery #7*
*© Ace Magazines*

*The Weekender, Vol. 2 #1*
*© Rucker Publishing Co.*

*Weird Comics #20*
*© Fox Features Syndicate*

## WASHABLE JONES AND THE SHMOO

**Toby Press Publ., 1953**
1 Super Shmoo. . . . . . . . . . . . . 225.00

## WEB OF EVIL

**Comic Magazines, Inc.
(Quality Comics Group),
Nov., 1952**
1 Custodian of the Dead . . . . . . 750.00
2 JCo,Hangmans Horror . . . . . . 500.00
3 JCo . . . . . . . . . . . . . . . . . . . 500.00
4 JCo(a&c),Monsters of
   the Mist . . . . . . . . . . . . . . . . 500.00
5 JCo(a&c),The Man who Died
   Twice,Electric Chair(c). . . . . . 600.00
6 JCo(a&c),Orgy of Death . . . . . 500.00
7 JCo(a&c),The Strangling
   Hands . . . . . . . . . . . . . . . . . 500.00
8 JCo,Flaming Vengeance . . . . 450.00
9 JCo,The Monster in Flesh . . . 450.00
10 JCo,Brain that Wouldn't Die . . 450.00
11 JCo,Buried Alive . . . . . . . . . . 450.00
12 Phantom Killer . . . . . . . . . . . . 300.00
13 Demon Inferno . . . . . . . . . . . . 300.00
14 RC(c),The Monster Genie. . . . 300.00
15 Crypts of Horror . . . . . . . . . . . 300.00
16 Hamlet of Horror . . . . . . . . . . . 300.00
17 Terror in Chinatown, Drug. . . . 325.00
18 Scared to Death,Acid Face. . . 300.00
19 Demon of the Pit. . . . . . . . . . . 275.00
20 Man Made Terror . . . . . . . . . . 275.00
21 Dec., 1954, Death's Ambush . 275.00

## WEB OF MYSTERY

**A.A. Wyn Publ.
(Ace Magazines), Feb., 1951**
1 MSy,Venom of the Vampires . 700.00
2 MSy,Legacy of the Accursed . 350.00
3 MSy,The Violin Curse . . . . . . 300.00
4 GC . . . . . . . . . . . . . . . . . . . . 300.00
5 . . . . . . . . . . . . . . . . . . . . . . 300.00
6 LC . . . . . . . . . . . . . . . . . . . . 300.00
7 MSy . . . . . . . . . . . . . . . . . . . 300.00
8 LC,LC(c),MSy,The Haunt of
   Death Lake . . . . . . . . . . . . . . 300.00
9 LC,LC(c) . . . . . . . . . . . . . . . . 300.00
10 . . . . . . . . . . . . . . . . . . . . . . 300.00
11 MSy. . . . . . . . . . . . . . . . . . . . 300.00
12 LC . . . . . . . . . . . . . . . . . . . . 275.00
13 LC,LC(c)Surrealist . . . . . . . . . 275.00
14 MSy. . . . . . . . . . . . . . . . . . . . 275.00
15 . . . . . . . . . . . . . . . . . . . . . . 275.00

16 . . . . . . . . . . . . . . . . . . . . . . 275.00
17 LC,LC(c) . . . . . . . . . . . . . . . . 275.00
18 LC . . . . . . . . . . . . . . . . . . . . 275.00
19 LC . . . . . . . . . . . . . . . . . . . . 275.00
20 LC, Beyond . . . . . . . . . . . . . . 275.00
21 MSy. . . . . . . . . . . . . . . . . . . . 275.00
22 . . . . . . . . . . . . . . . . . . . . . . 275.00
23 . . . . . . . . . . . . . . . . . . . . . . 275.00
24 LC . . . . . . . . . . . . . . . . . . . . 275.00
25 LC . . . . . . . . . . . . . . . . . . . . 275.00
26 . . . . . . . . . . . . . . . . . . . . . . 275.00
27 LC, Beyond. . . . . . . . . . . . . . . 275.00
28 RP,1st Comics Code issue . . . 200.00
29 MSy,Sept., 1955 . . . . . . . . . . 200.00

## WEDDING BELLS

**Quality Comics Group,
Feb., 1954**
1 OW. . . . . . . . . . . . . . . . . . . . 175.00
2 . . . . . . . . . . . . . . . . . . . . . . 125.00
3 . . . . . . . . . . . . . . . . . . . . . . 125.00
4 . . . . . . . . . . . . . . . . . . . . . . 125.00
5 . . . . . . . . . . . . . . . . . . . . . . 125.00
6 . . . . . . . . . . . . . . . . . . . . . . 125.00
7 . . . . . . . . . . . . . . . . . . . . . . 125.00
8 . . . . . . . . . . . . . . . . . . . . . . 125.00
9 Comics Code . . . . . . . . . . . . 125.00
10 BWa . . . . . . . . . . . . . . . . . . . 200.00
11 . . . . . . . . . . . . . . . . . . . . . . 100.00
12 . . . . . . . . . . . . . . . . . . . . . . 100.00
13 . . . . . . . . . . . . . . . . . . . . . . 100.00
14 . . . . . . . . . . . . . . . . . . . . . . 100.00
15 MB(c) . . . . . . . . . . . . . . . . . . 100.00
16 MB(c),MB . . . . . . . . . . . . . . . 150.00
17 . . . . . . . . . . . . . . . . . . . . . . 100.00
18 MB. . . . . . . . . . . . . . . . . . . . 125.00
19 MB. . . . . . . . . . . . . . . . . . . . 125.00

## WEEKENDER, THE

**Rucker Publishing Co.,
Sept., 1945**
1-1 rep.(c), As Zip . . . . . . . . . . . 175.00
1-2 thru 1-4 . . . . . . . . . . . . . . @175.00
2-1 rep.(c), As Dynamic . . . . . . . 200.00
2-2 Jco,rep.(c), As Dynamic . . . . 175.00
2-3 WMc,Jan., 1946 . . . . . . . . . 175.00

## WEIRD ADVENTURES

**P.L. Publishing,
May, 1951–Oct., 1951**
1 MB,Missing Diamonds . . . . . . 700.00
2 Puppet Peril . . . . . . . . . . . . . 600.00
3 Blood Vengeance. . . . . . . . . . 500.00

## WEIRD ADVENTURES

**Approved Comics
(Ziff-Davis),
July–Aug., 1951**
10 P(c),Seeker from Beyond . . . . 500.00

## WEIRD CHILLS

**Key Publications,
July, 1954**
1 MBi(c),BW . . . . . . . . . . . . . . 1,100.00
2 Eye Torture(c) . . . . . . . . . . . . 1,000.00
3 Bondage(c),Nov., 1954 . . . . . . 600.00

## WEIRD COMICS

**Fox Features Syndicate,
April, 1940**
1 LF(c),Bondage(c),B:Birdman,
   Thor,Sorceress of Doom,
   BlastBennett,Typhon,Voodoo
   Man, Dr.Mortal . . . . . . . . . 7,000.00
2 LF(c),Mummy(c) . . . . . . . . . 3,000.00
3 JSm(c) . . . . . . . . . . . . . . . . 1,500.00
4 JSm(c) . . . . . . . . . . . . . . . . 1,500.00
5 Bondage(c),I:Dart,Ace;
   E:Thor . . . . . . . . . . . . . . . . 1,700.00
6 Dart & Ace(c) . . . . . . . . . . . . 1,400.00
7 Battle of Kooba . . . . . . . . . . . 1,400.00
8 B:Panther Woman,Dynamo,
   The Eagle . . . . . . . . . . . . . 1,400.00
9 V:Pirates . . . . . . . . . . . . . . . 1,000.00
10 A:Navy Jones. . . . . . . . . . . . . 1,000.00
11 Dart & Ace(c). . . . . . . . . . . . . 800.00
12 Dart & Ace(c) . . . . . . . . . . . . 800.00
13 Dart & Ace(c) . . . . . . . . . . . . 800.00
14 The Rage(c) . . . . . . . . . . . . . 800.00
15 Dart & Ace (c). . . . . . . . . . . . 800.00
16 Flag,The Encore(c). . . . . . . . . 800.00
17 O:Black Rider . . . . . . . . . . . . 775.00
18 . . . . . . . . . . . . . . . . . . . . . . 750.00
19 . . . . . . . . . . . . . . . . . . . . . . 750.00
20 Jan., 1941,I'm The Master
   of Life and Death. . . . . . . . . 950.00

## WEIRD FANTASY

**I.C. Publishing Co.
(E.C. Comics),
May–June, 1950**
13(1)AF,HK,JKa,WW,AF(c),
   Roger Harvey's Brain . . . . . 3,500.00
14(2)AF,HK,JKa,WW,AF(c),Cosmic
   Ray Brain Explosion. . . . . . 2,500.00
15(3)AF,HK,JKa,WW,AF(c),Your
   Destination is the Moon . . . 1,800.00

**Wa**

*Weird Fantasy #17*
© E. C. Comics

*Weird Science #19*
© E. C. Comics

*Weird Science-Fantasy #23*
© E. C. Comics

16(4)AF,HK,JKa,WW,AF(c) . . . 1,800.00
17(5)AF,HK,JKa,WW,AF(c),Not
  Made by Human Hands . . . 1,600.00
6 AF,HK,JKa,WW,AF(c),Robot. 1,500.00
7 AF,JKa,WW,AF(c) . . . . . . . . 1,500.00
8 JKa,WW,AF(c) . . . . . . . . . . 1,500.00
9 AF,Jka,WW,JO,AF(c) . . . . . . 1,500.00
10 AF,Jka,WW,JO,AF(c) . . . . . . . 900.00
11 AF,Jka,WW,JO,AF(c) . . . . . . 1,500.00
12 AF,Jka,WW,JO,AF(c) . . . . . . 1,500.00
13 AF,Jka,WW,JO,AF(c) . . . . . . 1,500.00
14 AF,JKa,WW,JO,AW&FF,
  AF(c). . . . . . . . . . . . . . . . . 1,200.00
15 AF,JKa,JO,AW&RKr,AF(c),
  Bondage(c). . . . . . . . . . . . 1,500.00
16 AF,Jka,JO,AW&RKr,AF(c) . . 2,000.00
17 AF,JOP,JKa,AF(c),Bradbury 1,500.00
18 AF,JO,JKa,AF(c),Bradbury. . 1,500.00
19 JO,JKa,JO(c),Bradbury . . . . 1,500.00
20 JO,JKa,FF,AF(c) . . . . . . . . 1,500.00
21 JO,JKa,AW&FF(c) . . . . . . . . 1,800.00
22 JO,JKa,JO(c),Nov.,1953 . . . 1,100.00
**With Weird Science, Becomes:**

## WEIRD SCIENCE FANTASY

## WEIRD HORRORS
**St. John Publishing Co.,**
**June, 1952**
1 GT,Dungeon of the Doomed . . 750.00
2 Strangest Music Ever . . . . . . . 400.00
3 PMo,Strange Fakir From
  the Orient, Drug . . . . . . . . . 400.00
4 Murderers Knoll . . . . . . . . . . 350.00
5 Phantom Bowman . . . . . . . . . 350.00
6 Monsters from Outer Space . . 600.00
7 LC,Deadly Double . . . . . . . . 700.00
8 JKu,JKu(c),Bloody Yesterday . 500.00
9 JKu,JKu(c),Map Of Doom . . . . 500.00
**Becomes:**

## NIGHTMARE
**Dec., 1953**
10 JKu(c),The Murderer's Mask . 800.00
11 BK,Ph(c),Fangs of Death . . . 600.00
12 JKu(c),The Forgotten Mask . . 500.00
13 BP,Princess of the Sea . . . . . 350.00
**Becomes:**

## AMAZING GHOST STORIES
**Oct., 1954**
14 EK,MB(c),Pit & Pendulum. . . . 400.00
15 BP,Weird Thrillers . . . . . . . . . . 300.00
16 Feb., 1955, EK,JKu. . . . . . . . 350.00

## WEIRD JUNGLE TALES
**Star Publications, 1953**
202 . . . . . . . . . . . . . . . . . . . . . 150.00

## WEIRD MYSTERIES
**Gilmore Publications,**
**Oct., 1952**
1 BW(c) . . . . . . . . . . . . . . . . 1,100.00
2 BWi, Robot Woman . . . . . . . 1,500.00
3 Severed Heads(c) . . . . . . . . . 750.00
4 BW,Human headed ants(c) . 1,300.00
5 BW,Brains From Head(c) . . . 1,500.00
6 Severed Head(c) . . . . . . . . . . 750.00
7 Used in "Seduction" . . . . . . . 1,100.00
8 The One That Got Away . . . . . 800.00
9 Epitaph,Cyclops, Violence. . . . 750.00
10 The Ruby . . . . . . . . . . . . . . 600.00
11 Voodoo Dolls . . . . . . . . . . . . 550.00
12 Sept., 1954 . . . . . . . . . . . . . 550.00

## WEIRD SCIENCE
**E.C. Comics, 1950**
1 AF(a&c),JKu,HK,WW . . . . . . 6,000.00
2 AF(a&c),JKu,HK,WW,Flying
  Saucers(c) . . . . . . . . . . . . 3,000.00
3 AF(a&c),JKu,HK . . . . . . . . . 2,000.00
4 AF(a&c),JKu,HK . . . . . . . . . 2,000.00
5 AF(a&c),JKu,HK,WW,
  Atomic Bomb(c) . . . . . . . . 2,000.00
6 AF(a&c),JKu,HK . . . . . . . . . 2,000.00
7 AF(a&c),JKu,HK,Classic(c). . 2,000.00
8 AF(a&c),JKu . . . . . . . . . . . 2,000.00
9 WW(c),JKu,Classic(c). . . . . 2,200.00
10 WW(c),JKu,JO,Classic(c) . . 2,000.00
11 AF,JKu,Space war . . . . . . . 1,200.00
12 WW(c),JKu,JO,Classic(c) . . 1,200.00
13 WW(c),JKu,JO, . . . . . . . . . 1,200.00
14 WW(a&c),JO . . . . . . . . . . . 1,500.00
15 WW(a&c),JO,Grl,AW,
  RKr,JKa . . . . . . . . . . . . . 1,500.00
16 WW(a&c),JO,AW,RKr,JKa . . 1,400.00
17 WW(a&c),JO,AW,RKr,JKa . . 1,400.00
18 WW(a&c),JO,AW,RKr,
  JKa,Atomic Bomb. . . . . . . 1,400.00
19 WW(a&c),JO,AW,
  FF,Horror(c) . . . . . . . . . . 1,500.00
20 WW(a&c),JO,AW,FF,JKa . . . 1,500.00
21 WW(a&c),JO,AW,FF,JKa . . . 1,500.00
22 WW(a&c),JO,AW,FF . . . . . . 1,500.00
**Becomes:**

## WEIRD SCIENCE FANTASY
**March, 1954**
23 WW(a&c),AW,BK . . . . . . . . 1,300.00
24 WW,AW,BK,Classic(c) . . . . . 1,300.00
25 WW,AW,BK,Classic(c) . . . . . 1,400.00
26 AF(c),WW,RC,
  Flying Saucer(c) . . . . . . . . . 1,200.00
27 WW(a&c),RC . . . . . . . . . . . 1,200.00
28 AF(c),WW . . . . . . . . . . . . . 1,400.00
29 AF(c),WW,Classic(c) . . . . . . 3,500.00
**Becomes:**

## INCREDIBLE SCIENCE FANTASY
**July–Aug., 1955**
30 WW,JDa(c),BK,AW,RKr,JO . . 600.00
31 WW,JDa(c),BK,AW,RKr . . . . . 750.00
32 JDa(c),BK,WW,JO . . . . . . . . 750.00
33 WW(c),BK,WW,JO . . . . . . . . 750.00

## WEIRD TALES OF THE FUTURE
**S.P.M. Publ./**
**Aragon Publications,**
**March, 1952**
1 RA . . . . . . . . . . . . . . . . . . 2,000.00
2 BW,BW(c), Jumpin Jupiter . . 3,000.00
3 BW,BW(c) . . . . . . . . . . . . . 3,000.00
4 BW,BW(c) . . . . . . . . . . . . . 2,000.00
5 BW,BW(c),Jumpin' Jupiter
  Lingerie(c) . . . . . . . . . . . . 3,000.00
6 Bondage(c) . . . . . . . . . . . . 1,500.00
7 BW,Devil(c) . . . . . . . . . . . . . 2,000.00
8 July–Aug., 1953 . . . . . . . . . 2,500.00

## WEIRD TERROR
**Allen Hardy Associates**
**(Comic Media), Sept., 1952**
1 RP,DH,DH(c),Dungeon of the
  Doomed;Hitler . . . . . . . . . . . 750.00
2 HcK(c),PMo, Torture . . . . . . . 600.00
3 PMo,DH,DH(c),Strong
  Violence. . . . . . . . . . . . . . . 600.00
4 PMo,DH,DH(c),Severed Head. 600.00
5 PMo,DH,RP,DH(c),Hanging(c). 550.00
6 DH,RP,DH(c),Step into
  My Parlour, Severed Head . . 550.00
7 DH,PMo,DH(c),Blood o/t Bats . 500.00
8 DH,RP,DH(c),Step into
  My Parlour, Severed Head . . 550.00
9 DH,PMo,DH(c),The Fleabite . . 450.00

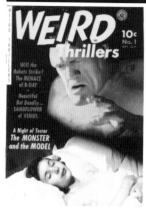

Weird Thrillers #1
© Ziff-Davis Publications

Western Comics #23
© DC Comics

Western Crime Busters #9
© Trojan Magazines

10 DH,BP,RP,DH(c) . . . . . . . . . . 450.00
11 DH,DH(c),Satan's Love Call . . 500.00
12 DH,DH(c),King Whitey . . . . . . 450.00
13 DH,DH(c),Wings of Death,
 Severed Head, Sept. 1954 . . 450.00

## WEIRD THRILLERS
### Approved Comics
### (Ziff-Davis),
### Sept.–Oct., 1951
1 Ph(c),Monsters & The Model 1,200.00
2 AW,P(c),The Last Man . . . . . . 850.00
3 AW,P(c),Princess o/t Sea . . 1,100.00
4 AW,P(c),The Widows Lover. . . 800.00
5 BP,Oct., 1952,AW,P(c),
 Wings of Death . . . . . . . . . . 800.00

## WENDY PARKER COMICS
### Marvel Atlas, 1953
1 . . . . . . . . . . . . . . . . . . . . . . . . 150.00
2 . . . . . . . . . . . . . . . . . . . . . . . . 100.00
3 . . . . . . . . . . . . . . . . . . . . . . . . 125.00
4 . . . . . . . . . . . . . . . . . . . . . . . . 125.00
5 . . . . . . . . . . . . . . . . . . . . . . . . 125.00
6 . . . . . . . . . . . . . . . . . . . . . . . . 125.00
7 . . . . . . . . . . . . . . . . . . . . . . . . 125.00
8 . . . . . . . . . . . . . . . . . . . . . . . . 125.00

## WESTERN ACTION
## THRILLERS
### Dell Publishing Co.,
### April, 1937
1 Buffalo Bill, Texas Kid . . . . . . 1,200.00

## WESTERN ADVENTURES
## COMICS
### A.A. Wyn, Inc.
### (Ace Magazines), Oct., 1948
N#(1)Injun Gun Bait . . . . . . . . . 275.00
N#(2)Cross-Draw Kid . . . . . . . . . 150.00
N#(3)Outlaw Mesa . . . . . . . . . 150.00
4 Sheriff, Sal . . . . . . . . . . . . . . 125.00
5 . . . . . . . . . . . . . . . . . . . . . . . . 125.00
6 Rip Roaring Adventure . . . . . . 125.00
Becomes:

## WESTERN LOVE TRAILS
### Nov., 1949
7 . . . . . . . . . . . . . . . . . . . . . . . . 150.00
8 Maverick Love . . . . . . . . . . . 125.00
9 March, 1950 . . . . . . . . . . . . . 100.00

## WESTERN BANDIT
## TRAILS
### St. John Publishing Co.,
### Jan., 1949
1 GT,MB(c), Blue Monk . . . . . . 300.00
2 GT,MB(c) . . . . . . . . . . . . . . . 250.00
3 GT,MB,MB(c),Gingham Fury . 275.00

## WESTERN COMICS
### DC Comics, Jan.–Feb., 1948
1 MMe,B:Vigilante,Rodeo Rick,
 Wyoming Kid, Cowboy
 Marshal . . . . . . . . . . . . . . 1,500.00
2 MMe,Vigilante vs. Dirk Bigger . 600.00
3 MMe,Vigilante vs. Pecos Kid . 700.00
4 MMe,Vigilante as Pecos Kid . . 700.00
5 I:Nighthawk . . . . . . . . . . . . . . 500.00
6 Wyoming Kid vs. The
 Murder Mustang . . . . . . . . . 300.00
7 Wyoming Kid in The Town
 That Was Never Robbed. . . . 300.00
8 O:Wyoming Kid . . . . . . . . . . . 500.00
9 Wyoming Kid vs. Jack
 Slaughter . . . . . . . . . . . . . . . 300.00
10 Nighthawk in Tunnel ofTerror . 300.00
11 Wyoming Kid vs. Mayor Brock 275.00
12 Wyoming Kid vs. Baldy Ryan . 275.00
13 I:Running Eagle . . . . . . . . . . 275.00
14 Wyoming Kid in The Siege
 of Prairie City . . . . . . . . . . . . 275.00
15 Nighthawk in Silver, Salt
 and Pepper . . . . . . . . . . . . . 275.00
16 Wyoming Kid vs. Smilin' Jim. . 275.00
17 BP,Wyoming Kid vs. Prof.
 Penny . . . . . . . . . . . . . . . . . 275.00
18 LSt on Nighthawk,Wyoming Kid
 in Challenge of the Chiefs . . . 275.00
19 LSt,Nighthawk in The
 Invisible Rustlers . . . . . . . . . 275.00
20 LSt,Nighthawk in The Mystery
 Mail From Defender Dip . . . . 250.00
21 LSt,Nighthawk in Rattlesnake
 Hollow . . . . . . . . . . . . . . . . . 250.00
22 LSt,I:Jim Pegton . . . . . . . . . . 250.00
23 LSt,Nighthawk reveals
 ID to Jim . . . . . . . . . . . . . . . 250.00
24 The $100,000 Impersonation . 250.00
25 V:Souix Invaders. . . . . . . . . . 250.00
26 The Storming of the Sante
 Fe Trail . . . . . . . . . . . . . . . . 250.00
27 The Looters of Lost Valley . . . 250.00
28 The Thunder Creek Rebellion. 250.00
29 Six Guns of the Wyoming Kid. 250.00
30 V:Green Haired Killer . . . . . . . 250.00

31 The Sky Riding Lawman. . . . . 250.00
32 Death Rides the Stage Coach 250.00
33 . . . . . . . . . . . . . . . . . . . . . . 250.00
34 Prescription For Killers . . . . . . 250.00
35 The River of Rogues. . . . . . . . 250.00
36 Nighthawk,Duel in the Dark 200.00
37 The Death Dancer . . . . . . . . . 200.00
38 Warpath in the Sky . . . . . . . . 200.00
39 Death to Fort Danger . . . . . . . 200.00
40 Blind Man's Bluff. . . . . . . . . . 200.00
41 thru 60. . . . . . . . . . . . . . . @175.00
61 thru 85. . . . . . . . . . . . . . . @150.00

## WESTERN CRIME
## BUSTERS
### Trojan Magazines,
### Sept., 1950–April, 1952
1 Gunslingin' Galoots . . . . . . . . 400.00
2 K-Bar Kate . . . . . . . . . . . . . . 250.00
3 Wilma West . . . . . . . . . . . . . 250.00
4 Bob Dale . . . . . . . . . . . . . . . 250.00
5 Six-Gun Smith . . . . . . . . . . . 250.00
6 WW . . . . . . . . . . . . . . . . . . 400.00
7 WW,Wells Fargo Robbery . . . 400.00
8 . . . . . . . . . . . . . . . . . . . . . . 250.00
9 WW,Lariat Lucy . . . . . . . . . . 400.00
10 WW,Tex Gordon . . . . . . . . . . 400.00

## WESTERN CRIME CASES
## See: OUTLAWS, THE

## WESTERNER, THE
### Wanted Comics Group/
### Toytown Publ.,
### June, 1948
14 F:Jack McCall . . . . . . . . . . . . 250.00
15 F:Bill Jamett . . . . . . . . . . . . . 200.00
16 F:Tom McLowery . . . . . . . . . . 200.00
17 F:Black Bill Desmond . . . . . . 200.00
18 BK,F:Silver Dollar Dalton . . . 250.00
19 MMe,F:Jess Meeton . . . . . . . 150.00
20 . . . . . . . . . . . . . . . . . . . . . . 150.00
21 BK,MMe . . . . . . . . . . . . . . . 200.00
22 BK,MMe . . . . . . . . . . . . . . . 200.00
23 BK,MMe . . . . . . . . . . . . . . . 200.00
24 BK,MMe . . . . . . . . . . . . . . . 200.00
25 O,I,B:Calamity Jane . . . . . . . 200.00
26 BK,F:The Widowmaker. . . . . . 250.00
27 BK . . . . . . . . . . . . . . . . . . . . 250.00
28 thru 31 . . . . . . . . . . . . . . . @125.00
32 E:Calamity Jane . . . . . . . . . . 125.00
33 A:Quest. . . . . . . . . . . . . . . . . 125.00
34 . . . . . . . . . . . . . . . . . . . . . . 125.00

*Western Fighters #1*
© Hillman Periodicals

*Western Killers N#*
© Fox Features Syndicate

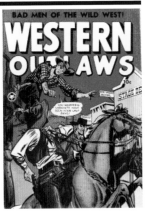

*Western Outlaws #19*
© Marvel Comics Group

| | |
|---|---|
| 35 SSh(c) | 125.00 |
| 36 | 125.00 |
| 37 Lobo-Wolf Boy | 125.00 |
| 38 | 125.00 |
| 39 | 125.00 |
| 40 SSh(c) | 125.00 |
| 41 Dec., 1951 | 125.00 |

## WESTERN FIGHTERS
**Hillman Periodicals,
April–May, 1948**

| | |
|---|---|
| 1 S&K(c) | 450.00 |
| 2 BF(c) | 200.00 |
| 3 BF(c) | 150.00 |
| 4 BK,BF | 175.00 |
| 5 | 125.00 |
| 6 | 125.00 |
| 7 BK | 150.00 |
| 8 | 125.00 |
| 9 | 125.00 |
| 10 BK | 150.00 |
| 11 AMC&FF | 400.00 |
| 2-1 BK | 150.00 |
| 2-2 BP | 125.00 |
| 2-3 thru 2-12 | @100.00 |
| 3-1 thru 3-11 | @100.00 |
| 3-12 BK | 125.00 |
| 4-1 | 100.00 |
| 4-2 BK | 150.00 |
| 4-3 BK | 150.00 |
| 4-4 BK | 150.00 |
| 4-5 BK | 150.00 |
| 4-6 BK | 150.00 |
| 4-7 March–April, 1953 | 100.00 |

## WESTERN FRONTIER
**P.L. Publishers
(Approved Comics),
May, 1951**

| | |
|---|---|
| 1 Flaming Vengeance | 150.00 |
| 2 | 125.00 |
| 3 Death Rides the Iron Horse | 100.00 |
| 4 thru 6 | @100.00 |
| 7 1952 | 100.00 |

## WESTERN GUNFIGHTERS
### See: APACHE KID

## WESTERN HEARTS
**Standard Magazine, Inc.,
Dec., 1949**

| | |
|---|---|
| 1 JSe, Whip Wilson, Ph(c) | 275.00 |

| | |
|---|---|
| 2 AW,FF, Palomino, Ph(c) | 275.00 |
| 3 Rex Allen, Ph(c) | 150.00 |
| 4 JSe,BE, Ph(c) | 150.00 |
| 5 JSe,BE,Ray Milland, Ph(c) | 150.00 |
| 6 JSe,BE,Irene Dunn, Ph(c) | 150.00 |
| 7 JSe,BE,Jock Mahoney Ph(c) | 150.00 |
| 8 Randolph Scott, Ph(c) | 150.00 |
| 9 JSe,BE, Whip Wilson, Ph(c) | 150.00 |
| 10 JSe,BE, Bill Williams,Ph(c) | 150.00 |

## WESTERN HERO
### See: WOW COMICS

## WESTERN KID
**Marvel, [1st Series] Dec., 1954**

| | |
|---|---|
| 1 JR,B:Western Kid,O:Western Kid (Tex Dawson) | 250.00 |
| 2 JMn,JR,Western Adventure | 125.00 |
| 3 JMn(c),JR,Gunfight(c) | 100.00 |
| 4 JMn(c),JR,The Badlands | 100.00 |
| 5 JR | 100.00 |
| 6 JR | 100.00 |
| 7 JR | 100.00 |
| 8 JR | 100.00 |
| 9 JR,AW | 125.00 |
| 10 JR,AW,Man in the Middle | 125.00 |
| 11 thru 16 | @100.00 |
| 17 Aug., 1957 | 100.00 |

## WESTERN KILLERS
**Fox Features Syndicate, 1948**

| | |
|---|---|
| N# Lingerie | 280.00 |
| 60 Violence | 300.00 |
| 61 JCo,LSe | 250.00 |
| 62 | 225.00 |
| 63 | 225.00 |
| 64 | 225.00 |

## WESTERN LIFE ROMANCES
### See: MY FRIEND IRMA

## WESTERN LOVE
**Feature Publications
(Prize Comics Group),
July–Aug., 1949**

| | |
|---|---|
| 1 S&K, Randolph Scott | 350.00 |
| 2 S&K, Whip Wilson | 250.00 |
| 3 JSe,BE, Reno Brown | 200.00 |
| 4 JSe,BE | 200.00 |
| 5 JSe,BE, Dale Robertson | 250.00 |

## WESTERN LOVE TRAILS
### See: WESTERN ADVENTURE COMICS

## WESTERN OUTLAWS
**Marvel Atlas,
Feb., 1954—Aug., 1957**

| | |
|---|---|
| 1 JMn(c),RH,BP,The Greenville Gallows,Hanging(c) | 250.00 |
| 2 | 125.00 |
| 3 thru 10 | @100.00 |
| 11 AW,MD | 125.00 |
| 12 JMn | 100.00 |
| 13 MB,JMn | 125.00 |
| 14 AW | 125.00 |
| 15 AT,GT | 100.00 |
| 16 BP,JMn,JSe,AW | 100.00 |
| 17 JMn,AW | 100.00 |
| 18 JSe | 100.00 |
| 19 JMn,JSe,RC | 100.00 |
| 20 and 21 JSe | @100.00 |

## WESTERN OUTLAWS & SHERIFFS
### See: BEST WESTERN

## WESTERN PICTURE STORIES
**Comics Magazine Co.,
Feb., 1937–June, 1937**

| | |
|---|---|
| 1 WE,Treachery Trail, 1st Western | 2,500.00 |
| 2 WE,Weapons of the West | 1,500.00 |
| 3 WE,Dragon Pass | 1,200.00 |
| 4 CavemanCowboy | 1,200.00 |

## WESTERN ROUGH RIDERS
**Stanmor Publ.
(Gilmore Magazines), 1954**

| | |
|---|---|
| 1 | 125.00 |
| 2 | 125.00 |
| 3 | 125.00 |
| 4 | 125.00 |

## WESTERN TALES
### See: WITCHCRAFT

---

*Western Thrillers #5*
*© Fox Features Syndicate*

*Western True Crime #2 (#16)*
*© Fox Features Syndicate*

*White Princess of the Jungle #3*
*© Avon Periodicals*

## WESTERN TALES OF BLACK RIDER
### See: ALL WINNERS COMICS

## WESTERN THRILLERS
**Fox Features Syndicate, Aug., 1948**

| | |
|---|---|
| 1 Velvet Rose | 600.00 |
| 2 | 250.00 |
| 3 GT,RH(c) | 225.00 |
| 4 | 250.00 |
| 5 Butch Cassidy | 250.00 |
| 6 June, 1949 | 225.00 |

**Becomes:**

## MY PAST CONFESSIONS
**Aug., 1949**

| | |
|---|---|
| 7 | 225.00 |
| 8 | 150.00 |
| 9 | 150.00 |
| 10 | 150.00 |
| 11 WW | 300.00 |
| 12 Crimes Inc. | 125.00 |

## WESTERN THRILLERS
**Marvel, Nov., 1954**

| | |
|---|---|
| 1 JMn,Western tales | 175.00 |
| 2 | 100.00 |
| 3 | 100.00 |
| 4 | 100.00 |

**Becomes:**

## COWBOY ACTION
**Marvel, March, 1955–March, 1956**

| | |
|---|---|
| 5 JMn(c),The Prairie Kid | 150.00 |
| 6 | 100.00 |
| 7 | 100.00 |
| 9 | 100.00 |
| 10 | 100.00 |
| 11 MN,AW,The Manhunter | 125.00 |

**Becomes:**

## QUICK-TRIGGER WESTERN
**Marvel, May, 1956–Sept., 1957**

| | |
|---|---|
| 12 Bill Larson Strikes | 175.00 |
| 13 AW,The Man From Cheyenne | 175.00 |
| 14 BEv,RH(c) | 175.00 |
| 15 AT,RC | 150.00 |
| 16 JK,JD | 125.00 |

| | |
|---|---|
| 17 GT | 125.00 |
| 18 GM | 125.00 |
| 19 JSe | 100.00 |

## WESTERN TRAILS
**Marvel Atlas, 1957**

| | |
|---|---|
| 1 MMe,FBe,JSe(c),Ringo Kid | 165.00 |
| 2 MMe,FBe,JSe(c) | 100.00 |

## WESTERN TRUE CRIME
**Fox Features Syndicate, Aug., 1948**

| | |
|---|---|
| 1 (#15) JKa, Zoot 14. | 450.00 |
| 2 (#16) JKa, Violence | 300.00 |
| 3 JKa. | 250.00 |
| 4 JCr | 300.00 |
| 5 | 200.00 |
| 6 | 200.00 |

**Becomes:**

## MY CONFESSION
**Aug., 1949–Feb., 1950**

| | |
|---|---|
| 7 WW | 400.00 |
| 8 WW,My Tarnished Reputation | 350.00 |
| 9 I:Tormented Men | 150.00 |
| 10 I Am Damaged Goods | 150.00 |

## WESTERN WINNERS
### See: ALL WINNERS COMICS

## WHACK
**St. John Publishing Co., Dec., 1953**

| | |
|---|---|
| 1 3-D | 400.00 |
| 2 Steve Crevice,Flush Jordan V:Bing (Crosby)The Merciful | 300.00 |
| 3 F:Little Awful Fannie | 200.00 |

## WHAM COMICS
**Centaur Publications, Nov., 1940**

| | |
|---|---|
| 1 PG,The Sparkler & His Disappearing Suit | 2,400.00 |
| 2 Dec., 1940,PG,PG(C), Men Turn into Icicles | 1,500.00 |

## WHIP WILSON
### See: BLAZE CARSON

## WHIRLWIND COMICS
**Nita Publications, June, 1940**

| | |
|---|---|
| 1 F:The Cyclone | 2,500.00 |
| 2 A:Scoops Hanlon,Cyclone(c) | 1,500.00 |
| 3 Sept., 1940,A:Magic Mandarin,Cyclone(c) | 1,400.00 |

## WHITE INDIAN
### See: A-1 COMICS

## WHITE PRINCESS OF THE JUNGLE
**Avon Periodicals, July, 1951**

| | |
|---|---|
| 1 EK(c),Terror Fangs | 750.00 |
| 2 EK,EK(c),Jungle Vengeance | 500.00 |
| 3 EK,EK(c),The Blue Gorilla | 450.00 |
| 4 Fangs of the Swamp Beast | 400.00 |
| 5 EK,Coils of the Tree Snake Nov., 1952 | 400.00 |

## WHITE RIDER AND SUPER HORSE
### See: OUTLAWS, THE

## WHIZ COMICS
**Fawcett Publications, Feb., 1940**

| | |
|---|---|
| 1 O:Captain Marvel, B:Spy Smasher, Golden Arrow,Dan Dare, Scoop Smith, Ibis the Invincible, Sivana | 125,000.00 |
| 2 | 15,000.00 |
| 3 Make way for Captain Marvel | 10,000.00 |
| 4 Captain Marvel Crashes Through | 7,500.00 |
| 5 Captain Marvel Scores Again! | 7,000.00 |
| 6 Circus of Death | 4,800.00 |
| 7 B:Dr Voodoo,Squadron of Death | 4,800.00 |
| 8 Saved by Captain Marvel! | 4,800.00 |
| 9 MRa,Captain Marvel on the Job. | 4,800.00 |
| 10 Battles the Winged Death | 4,800.00 |
| 11 Hurray for Captain Marvel | 3,000.00 |
| 12 Captain Marvel rides the Engine of Doom | 3,000.00 |
| 13 Worlds Most Powerful Man!. | 3,000.00 |
| 14 Boomerangs the Torpedo | 3,000.00 |

*Whiz Comics #19*
© Fawcett Publications

*Whiz Comics #88*
© Fawcett Publications

*Wilbur Comics #7*
© Archie Publications

15 O:Sivana . . . . . . . . . . . . . 2,500.00
16 Dr. Voodoo . . . . . . . . . . . 2,500.00
17 Knocks out a Tank . . . . . . . 2,500.00
18 V:Spy Smasher . . . . . . . . . 2,500.00
19 Crushes the Tiger Shark . . . 2,200.00
20 V:Sivana . . . . . . . . . . . . . 2,200.00
21 O:Lt. Marvels . . . . . . . . . . 2,300.00
22 Mayan Temple . . . . . . . . . . 1,500.00
23 GT,A:Dr. Voodoo . . . . . . . . 1,500.00
24 . . . . . . . . . . . . . . . . . . . 1,500.00
25 O&I:Captain Marvel Jr., Stops
    the Turbine of Death. . . . . 12,000.00
26 . . . . . . . . . . . . . . . . . . . 1,400.00
27 V:Death God of the
    Katonkas. . . . . . . . . . . . . 1,500.00
28 V:Mad Dervish of Ank-Har . . 1,500.00
29 Three Lt. Marvels (c), Pan
    American Olympics . . . . . . 1,500.00
30 CCB(c) . . . . . . . . . . . . . . 1,400.00
31 Douglass MacArthur
    & Spy Smasher(c) . . . . . . . 1,300.00
32 Spy Smasher(c) . . . . . . . . . 1,300.00
33 Spy Smasher(c) . . . . . . . . . 1,600.00
34 Three Lt. Marvels (c) . . . . . . 1,000.00
35 Capt. Marvel and the
    Three Fates . . . . . . . . . . . 1,200.00
36 Haunted Hallowe'en Hotel . . 1,000.00
37 Return of the Trolls . . . . . . 1,000.00
38 Grand Steeplechase . . . . . . 1,000.00
39 A Nazi Utopia . . . . . . . . . . 1,000.00
40 A:Three Lt. Marvels, The
    Earth's 4 Corners . . . . . . . 1,000.00
41 Captain Marvel 1,000 years
    from Now . . . . . . . . . . . . . . 800.00
42 Returns in Time Chair . . . . . . 800.00
43 V:Sinister Spies,
    Spy Smasher(c) . . . . . . . . . . 800.00
44 Life Story of Captain Marvel . . 900.00
45 Cures His Critics . . . . . . . . . . 800.00
46 . . . . . . . . . . . . . . . . . . . . . 800.00
47 Captain Marvel needs
    a Birthday . . . . . . . . . . . . . . 800.00
48 . . . . . . . . . . . . . . . . . . . . . 800.00
49 Writes a Victory song . . . . . . 800.00
50 Captain Marvel's most
    embarrassing moment . . . . . 800.00
51 Judges the Ugly-
    Beauty Contest . . . . . . . . . . 700.00
52 V:Sivana, Chooses
    His Birthday . . . . . . . . . . . . . 700.00
53 Captain Marvel fights
    Billy Batson . . . . . . . . . . . . . 700.00
54 Jack of all Trades . . . . . . . . . 700.00
55 Family Tree . . . . . . . . . . . . . 700.00
56 Tells what the Future Will Be . 700.00

57 A:Spy Smasher,Golden Arrow,
    Ibis . . . . . . . . . . . . . . . . . . 700.00
58 . . . . . . . . . . . . . . . . . . . . . 700.00
59 V:Sivana's Twin . . . . . . . . . . 700.00
60 Missing Person's Machine . . . 700.00
61 Gets a first name . . . . . . . . . 650.00
62 Plays in a Band . . . . . . . . . . 650.00
63 Great Indian Rope Trick . . . . . 650.00
64 Suspected of Murder . . . . . . . 650.00
65 Lamp of Diogenes . . . . . . . . . 650.00
66 The Trial of Mr. Morris! . . . . . 650.00
67 . . . . . . . . . . . . . . . . . . . . . 650.00
68 Laugh Lotion, V:Sivana . . . . . 650.00
69 Mission to Mercury . . . . . . 1,000.00
70 Climbs the World's Mightiest
    Mountain . . . . . . . . . . . . . . 650.00
71 Strange Magician . . . . . . . . . 600.00
72 V:The Man of the Future . . . . 600.00
73 In Ogre Land . . . . . . . . . . . . 600.00
74 Old Man River . . . . . . . . . . . 600.00
75 The City Olympics . . . . . . . . 600.00
76 Spy Smasher become
    Crime Smasher . . . . . . . . . . 600.00
77 . . . . . . . . . . . . . . . . . . . . . 600.00
78 Golden Arrow . . . . . . . . . . . 600.00
79 . . . . . . . . . . . . . . . . . . . . . 600.00
80 . . . . . . . . . . . . . . . . . . . . . 600.00
81 . . . . . . . . . . . . . . . . . . . . . 600.00
82 The Atomic Ship . . . . . . . . . 600.00
83 Magic Locket . . . . . . . . . . . . 600.00
84 . . . . . . . . . . . . . . . . . . . . . 600.00
85 The Clock of San Lojardo . . . 600.00
86 V:Sinister Sivanas . . . . . . . . . 600.00
87 The War on Olympia . . . . . . . 600.00
88 The Wonderful Magic Carpet . 600.00
89 Webs of Crime . . . . . . . . . . . 600.00
90 . . . . . . . . . . . . . . . . . . . . . 600.00
91 Infinity (c) . . . . . . . . . . . . . . 600.00
92 . . . . . . . . . . . . . . . . . . . . . 600.00
93 Captain America become
    a Hobo? . . . . . . . . . . . . . . . 600.00
94 V:Sivana . . . . . . . . . . . . . . . 600.00
95 Captain Marvel is grounded . . 600.00
96 The Battle Between Buildings . 600.00
97 Visits Mirage City . . . . . . . . . 600.00
98 . . . . . . . . . . . . . . . . . . . . . 600.00
99 V:Menace in the Mountains . . 600.00
100 Anniversary Issue . . . . . . . . 700.00
101 . . . . . . . . . . . . . . . . . . . . 600.00
102 A:Commando Yank . . . . . . . 600.00
103 . . . . . . . . . . . . . . . . . . . . 600.00
104 Flag(c) . . . . . . . . . . . . . . . 600.00
105 . . . . . . . . . . . . . . . . . . . . 600.00
106 A:Bulletman . . . . . . . . . . . . 600.00
107 The Great Experiment . . . . . 700.00

108 thru 114 . . . . . . . . . . . . . @500.00
115 The Marine Invasion . . . . . . . 500.00
116 . . . . . . . . . . . . . . . . . . . . 500.00
117 V:Sivana . . . . . . . . . . . . . . 500.00
118 thru 121 . . . . . . . . . . . . . @500.00
122 V:Sivana . . . . . . . . . . . . . . 500.00
123 . . . . . . . . . . . . . . . . . . . . 500.00
124 . . . . . . . . . . . . . . . . . . . . 500.00
125 Olympic Games of the Gods 500.00
126 . . . . . . . . . . . . . . . . . . . . 500.00
127 . . . . . . . . . . . . . . . . . . . . 500.00
128 . . . . . . . . . . . . . . . . . . . . 500.00
129 . . . . . . . . . . . . . . . . . . . . 400.00
130 . . . . . . . . . . . . . . . . . . . . 400.00
131 The Television Trap . . . . . . . 400.00
132 thru 142 . . . . . . . . . . . . . @400.00
143 Mystery of the Flying Studio . 400.00
144 V:The Disaster Master . . . . . 400.00
145 . . . . . . . . . . . . . . . . . . . . 400.00
146 . . . . . . . . . . . . . . . . . . . . 400.00
147 . . . . . . . . . . . . . . . . . . . . 400.00
148 . . . . . . . . . . . . . . . . . . . . 400.00
149 . . . . . . . . . . . . . . . . . . . . 400.00
150 V:Bug Bombs . . . . . . . . . . . 450.00
151 . . . . . . . . . . . . . . . . . . . . 450.00
152 . . . . . . . . . . . . . . . . . . . . 450.00
153 V:The Death Horror . . . . . . . 700.00
154 Horror Tale, I:Dr.Death . . . . . 700.00
155 V:Legend Horror,Dr.Death . . 750.00

## WHODUNIT?
### D.S. Publishing Co.,
### Aug.–Sept., 1948
1 MB,Weeping Widow . . . . . . . . 300.00
2 Diploma For Death . . . . . . . . . 150.00
3 Dec.–Jan., 1949 . . . . . . . . . . 150.00

## WHO IS NEXT?
### Standard Comics,
### Jan., 1953
5 ATh,RA,Don't Let Me Kill . . . . 250.00

## WILBUR COMICS
### MLJ Magazines
### (Archie Publications),
### Summer, 1944
1 F:Wilbur Wilkin-America's Song
    of Fun . . . . . . . . . . . . . . . . 700.00
2 . . . . . . . . . . . . . . . . . . . . . 350.00
3 . . . . . . . . . . . . . . . . . . . . . 250.00
4 . . . . . . . . . . . . . . . . . . . . . 200.00
5 I:Katy Keene . . . . . . . . . . . 1,200.00
6 F:Katy Keene . . . . . . . . . . . . 350.00

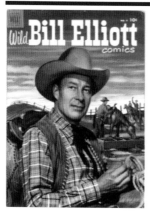

*Wild Bill Elliot #9*
© Dell Publishing Co.

*Wild Boy of the Congo #11*
© Ziff-Davis Publications

*Wild Western #3*
© Marvel Comics Group

7 F:Katy Keene . . . . . . . . . . . . . 350.00
8 F:Katy Keene . . . . . . . . . . . . . 350.00
9 F:Katy Keene . . . . . . . . . . . . . 350.00
10 F:Katy Keene . . . . . . . . . . . . 350.00
11 thru 20 F:Katy Keene . . . . @300.00
21 thru 30 F:Katy Keene . . . . @250.00
31 thru 40 F:Katy Keene . . . . @150.00
41 thru 56 F:Katy Keene . . . . @125.00
57 thru 89 . . . . . . . . . . . . . . . @100.00
90 Oct., 1965 . . . . . . . . . . . . . . 100.00

## WILD
### Marvel Atlas, Feb., 1954
1 BEv,JMn,Charlie Chan
Parody . . . . . . . . . . . . . . . . . 300.00
2 BEv,RH,JMn,Witches(c). . . . . 175.00
3 CBu(c),BEv,RH,JMn, . . . . . . . . 150.00
4 GC,Didja Ever See a Cannon
Brawl . . . . . . . . . . . . . . . . . 150.00
5 RH,JMn,Aug., 1954 . . . . . . . . 150.00

## WILD BILL ELLIOT
### Dell Publishing Co., May, 1950
(1) *see Dell Four Color #278*
2 . . . . . . . . . . . . . . . . . . . . . . . . 125.00
3 thru 5 . . . . . . . . . . . . . . . . . @100.00
6 thru 10 . . . . . . . . . . . . . . . . @100.00
(11-12) *see Four Color #472, 520*
13 thru 17 . . . . . . . . . . . . . . . . @100.00

## WILD BILL HICKOK
## AND JINGLES
## See: YELLOWJACKET
## COMICS

## WILD BILL HICKOK
### Avon Periodicals, Sept.–Oct., 1949
1 Grl(c),Frontier Fighter . . . . . . . 275.00
2 Ph(c),Gambler's Guns . . . . . . 150.00
3 Ph(c),Great Stage Robbery . . 100.00
4 Ph(c),Guerilla Gunmen . . . . . . 100.00
5 Ph(c),Return of the Renegade 100.00
6 EK,EK(c),Along the Apache
Trail . . . . . . . . . . . . . . . . . . 100.00
7 EK,EK(c)Outlaws of
Hell's Bend . . . . . . . . . . . . . 100.00
8 Ph(c),The Border Outlaws . . . 100.00
9 PH(c),Killers From Texas . . . . 100.00
10 Ph(c) . . . . . . . . . . . . . . . . . . 100.00

11 EK,EK(c),The Hell Riders . . . . 100.00
12 EK,EK(c),The Lost Gold Mine 100.00
13 EK,EK(c),Bloody Canyon
Massacre . . . . . . . . . . . . . . . 125.00
14 . . . . . . . . . . . . . . . . . . . . . . . 125.00
15 . . . . . . . . . . . . . . . . . . . . . . . 100.00
16 JKa,Bad Men of Deadwood . . 100.00
17 JKa . . . . . . . . . . . . . . . . . . . 100.00
18 JKa,Kit West . . . . . . . . . . . . . 100.00
19 thru 23 . . . . . . . . . . . . . . . @100.00
24 EK,EK(c) . . . . . . . . . . . . . . . 100.00
25 EK,EK(c) . . . . . . . . . . . . . . . 100.00
26 EK,EK(c) . . . . . . . . . . . . . . . 100.00
27 EK,EK(c) . . . . . . . . . . . . . . . 100.00
28 EK,EK(c),May–June, 1956 . . . 100.00

## WILD BOY OF
## THE CONGO
### Approved(Ziff-Davis)/ St. John Publ. Co., Feb.–March, 1951
10(1)NS,PH(c),Bondage(c),The
Gorilla God . . . . . . . . . . . . . 500.00
11(2)NS,Ph(c),Star of the Jungle . 250.00
12(3)NS,Ph(c),Ice-Age Men. . . . . 250.00
4 NS,Ph(c),Tyrant of the Jungle 350.00
5 NS,Ph(c),The White Robe
of Courage . . . . . . . . . . . . . 200.00
6 NS,Ph(c) . . . . . . . . . . . . . . . . 200.00
7 MB,EK.Ph(c) . . . . . . . . . . . . . 250.00
8 Ph(c),Man-Eater . . . . . . . . . . . 200.00
9 Ph(c),Killer Leopard . . . . . . . . 200.00
10 . . . . . . . . . . . . . . . . . . . . . . . 200.00
11 MB(c). . . . . . . . . . . . . . . . . . 250.00
12 MB(c) . . . . . . . . . . . . . . . . . . 250.00
13 MB(c) . . . . . . . . . . . . . . . . . . 250.00
14 MB(c) . . . . . . . . . . . . . . . . . . 250.00
15 June, 1955 . . . . . . . . . . . . . . 200.00

## WILD FRONTIER
### Charlton Comics, 1955
1 Davy Crockett . . . . . . . . . . . . . 125.00
2 same . . . . . . . . . . . . . . . . . . . 100.00
3 same . . . . . . . . . . . . . . . . . . . 100.00
4 same . . . . . . . . . . . . . . . . . . . 100.00
5 same . . . . . . . . . . . . . . . . . . . 100.00
6 same . . . . . . . . . . . . . . . . . . . 100.00
7 O:Cheyenne Kid . . . . . . . . . . . 100.00
Becomes:

## CHEYENNE KID
8 . . . . . . . . . . . . . . . . . . . . . . . 125.00
9 . . . . . . . . . . . . . . . . . . . . . . . 100.00
10 AW,AT,SD(c) . . . . . . . . . . . . . 125.00

11 Giant,Geronimo. . . . . . . . . . . 125.00
12 AW,AT . . . . . . . . . . . . . . . . . 125.00
13 AW,AT . . . . . . . . . . . . . . . . . 125.00
14 AW . . . . . . . . . . . . . . . . . . . . 125.00
15 . . . . . . . . . . . . . . . . . . . . . . . 125.00
16 . . . . . . . . . . . . . . . . . . . . . . . 100.00
17 . . . . . . . . . . . . . . . . . . . . . . . 100.00
18 . . . . . . . . . . . . . . . . . . . . . . . 100.00
19 . . . . . . . . . . . . . . . . . . . . . . . 100.00
20 JSe . . . . . . . . . . . . . . . . . . . 100.00
21 JSe . . . . . . . . . . . . . . . . . . . 125.00
22 JSe . . . . . . . . . . . . . . . . . . . 125.00
23 . . . . . . . . . . . . . . . . . . . . . . . . 75.00
24 JSe . . . . . . . . . . . . . . . . . . . 100.00
25 JSe . . . . . . . . . . . . . . . . . . . 100.00
26 JSe . . . . . . . . . . . . . . . . . . . 100.00
27 . . . . . . . . . . . . . . . . . . . . . . . . 75.00
28 . . . . . . . . . . . . . . . . . . . . . . . . 75.00
29 . . . . . . . . . . . . . . . . . . . . . . . . 75.00
30 JSe . . . . . . . . . . . . . . . . . . . 100.00

## WILD WEST
### Marvel, Spring, 1948
1 SSh(c),B:Two Gun Kids,Tex
Taylor,Arizona Annie . . . . . . 400.00
2 SSh(c),CCb, Captain Tootsie. . 250.00
Becomes:

## WILD WESTERN
### Marvel, 1948
3 SSh(c),B:Tex Morgan,Two Gun
Kid,Tex Taylor,Arizona Annie 350.00
4 Rh,SSh,CCB,Capt. Tootsie.
A:Kid Colt,E:Arizona Annie . . 250.00
5 RH,CCB,SSh,Captain Tootsie
A;Black Rider,Blaze Carson . 250.00
6 A:Blaze Carson,Kid Colt . . . . . 200.00
7 Two-Gun Kid . . . . . . . . . . . . . 200.00
8 RH . . . . . . . . . . . . . . . . . . . . . 200.00
9 Ph(c),B:Black Rider,
Tex Morgan . . . . . . . . . . . . . 225.00
10 Ph(c), Black Rider. . . . . . . . . 250.00
11 Black Rider . . . . . . . . . . . . . . 200.00
12 Black Rider . . . . . . . . . . . . . . 200.00
13 Black Rider . . . . . . . . . . . . . . 200.00
14 Prairie Kid,Black Rider . . . . . . 175.00
15 Black Rider . . . . . . . . . . . . . . 175.00
16 thru 18 Black Rider . . . . . . @175.00
19 Black Rider . . . . . . . . . . . . . . 185.00
20 thru 29 Kid Colt . . . . . . . . . @150.00
30 JKa, Kid Colt. . . . . . . . . . . . . 150.00
31 thru 40 . . . . . . . . . . . . . . . . @100.00
41 thru 47 . . . . . . . . . . . . . . . . @100.00
48 AW . . . . . . . . . . . . . . . . . . . . 125.00
49 thru 53 . . . . . . . . . . . . . . . . @100.00

All comics prices listed are for *Near Mint* condition.

Will Rogers Western #2
© Fox Features Syndicate

Wings Comics #6
© Fiction House Magazines

Wings Comics #80
© Fiction House Magazines

54 AW . . . . . . . . . . . . . . . . . . 125.00
55 AW . . . . . . . . . . . . . . . . . . 125.00
56 and 57 Sept., 1957 . . . . . . @100.00

## WILLIE COMICS
### See: IDEAL COMICS

## WILLIE THE PENGUIN
### Animated Cartoons
### (Standard Comics), 1951
1 Funny animal . . . . . . . . . . . . . 125.00
2 . . . . . . . . . . . . . . . . . . . . . . . 100.00
3 . . . . . . . . . . . . . . . . . . . . . . . 100.00
4 . . . . . . . . . . . . . . . . . . . . . . . 100.00
5 . . . . . . . . . . . . . . . . . . . . . . . 100.00
6 . . . . . . . . . . . . . . . . . . . . . . . 100.00

## WILLIE THE WISE-GUY
### Marvel Atlas, 1957
1 MMe . . . . . . . . . . . . . . . . . . . 125.00

## WILL ROGERS WESTERN
### Fox Features Syndicate, 1950
1 (5) . . . . . . . . . . . . . . . . . . . . 400.00
2 Ph(c) . . . . . . . . . . . . . . . . . . 350.00

## WIN A PRIZE COMICS
### Charlton Comics, 1955
1 S&K,Edgar Allen Poe adapt. . . 900.00
2 S&K . . . . . . . . . . . . . . . . . . . 600.00
Becomes:

## TIMMY THE TIMID GHOST
### Charlton Comics, 1957
3 . . . . . . . . . . . . . . . . . . . . . . . 150.00
4 . . . . . . . . . . . . . . . . . . . . . . . 125.00
5 . . . . . . . . . . . . . . . . . . . . . . . 125.00
6 . . . . . . . . . . . . . . . . . . . . . . . 100.00
7 . . . . . . . . . . . . . . . . . . . . . . . 100.00
8 . . . . . . . . . . . . . . . . . . . . . . . 100.00
9 . . . . . . . . . . . . . . . . . . . . . . . 100.00
10 . . . . . . . . . . . . . . . . . . . . . . 100.00
11 giant . . . . . . . . . . . . . . . . . . 125.00
12 giant . . . . . . . . . . . . . . . . . . 125.00
13 . . . . . . . . . . . . . . . . . . . . . . 100.00
14 . . . . . . . . . . . . . . . . . . . . . . 100.00
15 . . . . . . . . . . . . . . . . . . . . . . 100.00
16 . . . . . . . . . . . . . . . . . . . . . . 100.00
17 . . . . . . . . . . . . . . . . . . . . . . 100.00
18 . . . . . . . . . . . . . . . . . . . . . . 100.00
19 . . . . . . . . . . . . . . . . . . . . . . 100.00
20 thru 25 . . . . . . . . . . . . . . . @100.00

## WINGS COMICS
### Wings Publ.
### (Fiction House Magazines),
### Sept., 1940
1 HcK,AB,GT,Ph(c),B:Skull Squad,
  Clipper Kirk,Suicide Smith,
  War Nurse,Phantom Falcons,
  GreasemonkeyGriffin,Parachute
  Patrol,Powder Burns . . . . . 6,000.00
2 HcK,AB,GT,Bomber Patrol . . 3,000.00
3 HcK,AB,GT . . . . . . . . . . . . . 1,700.00
4 HcK,AB,GT,B:Spitfire Ace . . . 1,700.00
5 HcK,AB,GT,Torpedo Patrol . 1,700.00
6 HcK,AB,GT,Bombs for Berlin 1,500.00
7 HcK,AB . . . . . . . . . . . . . . . . 1,500.00
8 HcK,AB,The Wings of Doom 1,500.00
9 Sky-Wolf . . . . . . . . . . . . . . 1,400.00
10 The Upside Down . . . . . . . . 1,400.00
11 . . . . . . . . . . . . . . . . . . . . . 1,300.00
12 Fury of the fire Boards . . . . . 1,300.00
13 Coffin Slugs For The
  Luftwaffe . . . . . . . . . . . . . . 1,300.00
14 Stuka Buster . . . . . . . . . . . . 1,300.00
15 Boomerang Blitz . . . . . . . . . 1,300.00
16 O:Capt.Wings . . . . . . . . . . . 1,500.00
17 Skyway to Death . . . . . . . . . 1,200.00
18 Horsemen of the Sky . . . . . . 1,200.00
19 Nazi Spy Trap . . . . . . . . . . . 1,200.00
20 The One Eyed Devil . . . . . . 1,200.00
21 Chute Troop Tornado . . . . . . 1,000.00
22 TNT for Tokyo . . . . . . . . . . . 1,000.00
23 RP,Battling Eagles of Bataan 1,000.00
24 RP,The Death of a Hero . . . 1,000.00
25 RP,Suicide Squeeze . . . . . . 1,000.00
26 Tojo's Eagle Trap . . . . . . . . 1,000.00
27 BLb,Mile High Gauntlet . . . . 1,000.00
28 BLb,Tail Gun Tornado . . . . . 1,000.00
29 BLb,Buzzards from Berlin . . 1,000.00
30 BLb,Monsters of the
  Stratosphere . . . . . . . . . . . . 950.00
31 BLb,Sea Hawks away . . . . . . 950.00
32 BLb,Sky Mammoth . . . . . . . . 950.00
33 BLb,Roll Call of the Yankee
  Eagles . . . . . . . . . . . . . . . . . 950.00
34 BLb,So Sorry,Mr Tojo . . . . . . 950.00
35 BLb,RWb,Hell's Lightning . . . 950.00
36 RWb,The Crash-Master . . . . . 950.00
37 RWb,Sneak Blitz . . . . . . . . . . 950.00
38 RWb,Rescue Raid of the
  Yank Eagle . . . . . . . . . . . . . 950.00
39 RWb,Sky Hell/Pigboat Patrol . 950.00
40 RWb,Luftwaffe Gamble . . . . . 950.00
41 RWb,.50 Caliber Justice . . . . . 900.00
42 RWb,PanzerMeat forMosquito 900.00
43 RWb,Suicide Sentinels . . . . . . 900.00

44 RWb,Berlin Bombs Away . . . . 900.00
45 RWb,Hells Cargo . . . . . . . . . . 900.00
46 RWb,Sea-Hawk Patrol . . . . . . 900.00
47 RWb,Tojo's Tin Gibraltar . . . . . 900.00
48 RWb . . . . . . . . . . . . . . . . . . . 900.00
49 RWb,Rockets Away . . . . . . . . 900.00
50 RWb,Mission For a Madman . 900.00
51 RWb,Toll for a Typhoon . . . . 800.00
52 MB,Madam Marauder . . . . . . . 800.00
53 MB,Robot Death Over
  Manhattan . . . . . . . . . . . . . . 800.00
54 MB,Juggernauts of Death . . . . 800.00
55 MB . . . . . . . . . . . . . . . . . . . . 800.00
56 MB,Sea Raiders Grave . . . . . . 800.00
57 MB,Yankee Warbirds over
  Tokyo . . . . . . . . . . . . . . . . . . 800.00
58 MB . . . . . . . . . . . . . . . . . . . . 800.00
59 MB,Prey of the Night Hawks . . 800.00
60 MB,E:Skull Squad,
  Hell's Eyes . . . . . . . . . . . . . . 800.00
61 MB,Raiders o/t Purple Dawn . 750.00
62 Twilight of the Gods . . . . . . . 750.00
63 Hara Kiri Rides the Skyways . 750.00
64 Taps For Tokyo . . . . . . . . . . . 750.00
65 AB,Warhawk for the Kill . . . . . 750.00
66 AB,B:Ghost Patrol . . . . . . . . . 750.00
67 AB . . . . . . . . . . . . . . . . . . . . . 750.00
68 AB,ClipperKirkBecomesPhantom
  Falcon;O:Phantom Falcon . . . 750.00
69 AB,O:cont,Phantom Falcon . . 750.00
70 AB,N:Phantom Falcon;
  O:Final Phantom Falcon . . . . 750.00
71 Ghost Patrol becomes
  Ghost Squadron . . . . . . . . . . 750.00
72 V:Capt. Kamikaze . . . . . . . . . 750.00
73 Hell & Stormoviks . . . . . . . . . 750.00
74 BLb(c),Loot is What She
  Lived For . . . . . . . . . . . . . . . 750.00
75 BLb(c),The Sky Hag . . . . . . . 750.00
76 BLb(c),Temple of the Dead . . 750.00
77 BLb(c),Sky Express to Hell . . 750.00
78 BLb(c),Loot Queen of
  Satan's Skyway . . . . . . . . . . . 750.00
79 BLb(c),Buzzards of
  Plunder Sky . . . . . . . . . . . . . 750.00
80 BLb(c),Port of Missing Pilots . 750.00
81 BLb(c),Sky Trail of the
  Terror Tong . . . . . . . . . . . . . . 750.00
82 BLb(c),Bondage(c),Spider &
  The Fly Guy . . . . . . . . . . . . . . 800.00
83 BLb(c),GE,Deep Six For
  Capt. Wings . . . . . . . . . . . . . 750.00
84 BLb(c),GE,Sky Sharks to
  the Kill . . . . . . . . . . . . . . . . . 750.00
85 BLb(c),GE . . . . . . . . . . . . . . . 750.00
86 BLb(c),GE,Moon Raiders . . . . 750.00

Wi

*Winnie Winkle #1*
© Dell Publishing Co.

*Witchcraft #2*
© Avon Periodicals

*Witty Comics #1*
© Irwin H. Rubin

87 BLb(c),GE . . . . . . . . . . . . . . 750.00
88 BLb(c),GE,Madmans Mission . 750.00
89 BLb(c),GE,Bondage(c),
  Rockets Away . . . . . . . . . . . 900.00
90 BLb(c),GE,Bondage(c),The
  Radar Rocketeers . . . . . . . . 900.00
91 BLb(c),GT,Bondage(c),V-9 for
  Vengeance . . . . . . . . . . . . . 900.00
92 BLb(c),GE,Death's red Rocket 750.00
93 BLb(c),GE,Kidnap Cargo . . . 1,100.00
94 BLb(c),GE,Bondage(c),Ace
  of the A-Bomb Patrol . . . . . 1,200.00
95 BLb(c),GE,The Ace of
  the Assassins . . . . . . . . . . . 750.00
96 BLb(c),GE . . . . . . . . . . . . . . 750.00
97 BLb(c),GE,The Sky Octopus . 750.00
98 BLb(c),GE,The Witch Queen
  of Satan's Skyways . . . . . . . 750.00
99 BLb(c),GE,The Spy Circus . . . 750.00
100 BLb(c),GE,King o/t Congo . . 800.00
101 BLb(c),GE,Trator of
  the Cockpit . . . . . . . . . . . . 700.00
102 BLb(c),GE,Doves of Doom . . 700.00
103 BLb(c),GE . . . . . . . . . . . . . 700.00
104 BLb(c),GE,Fireflies of Fury . . 700.00
105 BLb(c),GE . . . . . . . . . . . . . 700.00
106 BLb(c),GE,Six Aces & A
  Firing Squad . . . . . . . . . . . 700.00
107 BLb(c),GE,Operation Satan . 700.00
108 BLb(c),GE,The Phantom
  of Berlin . . . . . . . . . . . . . . 700.00
109 GE,Vultures of
  Vengeance Sky . . . . . . . . . . 700.00
110 GE,The Red Ray Vortex . . . 700.00
111 GE,E:Jane Martin . . . . . . . . 500.00
112 The Flight of the
  Silver Saucers . . . . . . . . . . . 500.00
113 Suicide Skyways . . . . . . . . . 500.00
114 D-Day for Death Rays . . . . . 500.00
115 Ace of Space . . . . . . . . . . . . 500.00
116 Jet Aces of Korea . . . . . . . . 500.00
117 Reap the Red Wind . . . . . . 500.00
118 Vengeance Flies Blind . . . . 500.00
119 The Whistling Death . . . . . 500.00
120 Doomsday Mission . . . . . . . 500.00
121 Ace of the Spyways . . . . . . 500.00
122 Last Kill Korea . . . . . . . . . 500.00
123 The Cat & the Canaries . . . 500.00
124 Summer, 1954, Death
  Below Zero . . . . . . . . . . . . 500.00

## WINNIE WINKLE
### Dell Publishing Co., 1941
1 . . . . . . . . . . . . . . . . . . . . . . 250.00

2 . . . . . . . . . . . . . . . . . . . . . . 200.00
3 thru 7 . . . . . . . . . . . . . . . . @200.00

## WITCHCRAFT
### Avon Periodicals, March–April, 1952
1 SC,JKu,Heritage of Horror . . . 900.00
2 SC,JKu,The Death Tattoo . . . . 700.00
3 EK,Better off Dead . . . . . . . . 500.00
4 Claws of the Cat,
  Boiling Humans . . . . . . . . . . 525.00
5 Ph(c),Where Zombies Walk . . 550.00
6 March, 1953 Mysteries of the
  Moaning Statue . . . . . . . . . . 500.00

## WITCHES TALES
### Harvey Publications, Jan., 1951
1 RP,Bondage(c),Weird Yarns
  of Unseen Terror . . . . . . . . . 900.00
2 RP,AAv,We Dare You . . . . . . 600.00
3 RP,Bondage(c)Forest of
  Skeletons . . . . . . . . . . . . . . 400.00
4 BP . . . . . . . . . . . . . . . . . . . 400.00
5 BP,Bondage(c),Share
  My Coffin . . . . . . . . . . . . . . 450.00
6 BP,Bondage(c),Servants of
  the Tomb . . . . . . . . . . . . . . 400.00
7 BP,Screaming City . . . . . . . . . 400.00
8 Bondage(c) . . . . . . . . . . . . . . 450.00
9 Fatal Steps . . . . . . . . . . . . . . 400.00
10 BP,.....,IT! . . . . . . . . . . . . . 400.00
11 BP,Monster Maker . . . . . . . . 350.00
12 Bondage(c);The Web
  of the Spider . . . . . . . . . . . . 350.00
13 The Torture Jar . . . . . . . . . . 350.00
14 AAv,Transformation . . . . . . . 350.00
15 Drooling Zombie . . . . . . . . . 350.00
16 Revenge of a Witch . . . . . . . 350.00
17 Dimension IV . . . . . . . . . . . 350.00
18 HN,Bird of Prey . . . . . . . . . 400.00
19 HN,The Pact . . . . . . . . . . . . 400.00
20 HN,Kiss & Tell . . . . . . . . . . 400.00
21 HN,The Invasion . . . . . . . . . 400.00
22 HN,A Day of Panic . . . . . . . 400.00
23 HN,The Wig Maker . . . . . . . 400.00
24 HN,The Undertaker . . . . . . . 425.00
25 What Happens at 8:30 PM?
  Severed Heads(c) . . . . . . . . 500.00
26 Up There . . . . . . . . . . . . . . 350.00
27 The Thing That Grew . . . . . 350.00
28 AAv,Demon Flies . . . . . . . . . 350.00
Becomes:

## WITCHES WESTERN TALES
### Feb., 1955
29 S&K(a&c),F:Davy Crockett . . . 450.00
30 S&K(a&c) . . . . . . . . . . . . . . 400.00
Becomes:

## WESTERN TALES
### Oct., 1955
31 S&K(a&c),F:Davy Crockett . . . 250.00
32 S&K(a&c),F:Davy Crockett . . . 250.00
33 S&K(a&c),July–Sept.,1956 . . . 250.00

## WITH THE MARINES ON THE BATTLEFRONTS OF THE WORLD
### Toby Press, June, 1953
1 Flaming Soul, John
  Wayne, Ph(c) . . . . . . . . . . . 325.00
2 Mar., 1954, Monty Hall, Ph(c) . 100.00

## WITNESS, THE
### Marvel, Sept., 1948
1 . . . . . . . . . . . . . . . . . . . . 2,200.00

## WITTY COMICS
### Irwin H. Rubin/Chicago Nite Life News, 1945
1 Pioneer, Jr. Patrol . . . . . . . . . 325.00
2 1945 . . . . . . . . . . . . . . . . . . 150.00
3 thru 7 . . . . . . . . . . . . . . . . @125.00

## WOMEN IN LOVE
### Fox Features Synd./ Hero Books/ Ziff-Davis, Aug., 1949
1 . . . . . . . . . . . . . . . . . . . . . . 700.00
2 . . . . . . . . . . . . . . . . . . . . . . 400.00
3 . . . . . . . . . . . . . . . . . . . . . . 250.00
4 WW . . . . . . . . . . . . . . . . . . 300.00

## WOMEN OUTLAWS
### Fox Features Syndicate, July, 1948
1 . . . . . . . . . . . . . . . . . . . . 1,000.00
2 . . . . . . . . . . . . . . . . . . . . . . 800.00
3 . . . . . . . . . . . . . . . . . . . . . . 800.00
4 . . . . . . . . . . . . . . . . . . . . . . 700.00
5 thru 8 . . . . . . . . . . . . . . . . @550.00
N# Cody of the Pony Express . . . 400.00

All comics prices listed are for *Near Mint* condition.

*Wonder Comics #10*
© Better Publications

*Wonderworld #32*
© Fox Features Syndicate

*Wonder Woman #17*
© DC Comics

**Becomes:**

## MY LOVE MEMORIES
**Fox Features Syndicate, Nov., 1949**
| | |
|---|---|
| 9 | 250.00 |
| 10 | 150.00 |
| 11 | 175.00 |
| 12 WW | 200.00 |

## WONDERBOY
**See: HORRIFIC**

## WONDER COMICS
**Great Publ./Nedor/ Better Publications, May, 1944**
| | |
|---|---|
| 1 SSh(c),B:Grim Reaper, Spectro Hitler(c) | 2,500.00 |
| 2 ASh(c),O:Grim Reaper,B:Super Sleuths,Grim Reaper(c) | 1,800.00 |
| 3 ASh(c),Grim Reaper(c) | 1,500.00 |
| 4 ASh(c),Grim Reaper(c) | 1,000.00 |
| 5 ASh(c),Grim Reaper(c) | 1,000.00 |
| 6 ASh(c),Grim Reaper(c) | 900.00 |
| 7 ASh(c),Grim Reaper(c) | 900.00 |
| 8 ASh(c),E:Super Sleuths, Spectro | 900.00 |
| 9 ASh(c),B:Wonderman | 900.00 |
| 10 ASh(c),Wonderman(c) | 950.00 |
| 11 Grl(c),B:Dick Devins | 1,000.00 |
| 12 Grl(c),Bondage(c) | 1,000.00 |
| 13 ASh(c),Bondage(c). | 1,000.00 |
| 14 ASh(c),Bondage(c) E:Dick Devins | 1,000.00 |
| 15 ASh(c),Bondage(c),B:Tara | 1,700.00 |
| 16 ASh(c),A:Spectro, E:Grim Reaper | 1,000.00 |
| 17 FF,ASh(c),A:Super Sleuth | 1,600.00 |
| 18 ASh(c),B:Silver Knight | 1,500.00 |
| 19 ASh(c),FF | 1,500.00 |
| 20 FF,ASh(c),Oct., 1948 | 1,700.00 |

## WONDER COMICS
**Fox Features Syndicate, May, 1939**
| | |
|---|---|
| 1 BKa,WE,WE(c),B:Wonderman, DR.Kung,K-51 | 28,000.00 |
| 2 WE,BKa,LF(c),B:Yarko the Great,A:Spark Stevens | 9,000.00 |
| **Becomes:** | |

## WONDERWORLD COMICS
**Fox Features Syndicate, July, 1939–Jan., 1942**
| | |
|---|---|
| 3 WE,LF,BP,LF&WE,I:Flame | 14,000.00 |
| 4 WE,LF,BP,LF(c) | 7,000.00 |
| 5 WE,LF,BP,GT,LF(c),Flame | 4,000.00 |
| 6 WE,LF,BP,GT,LF(c),Flame | 4,000.00 |
| 7 WE,LF,BP,GT,LF(c),Flame | 5,000.00 |
| 8 WE,LF,BP,GT,LF(c),Flame | 5,000.00 |
| 9 WE,LF,BP,GT,LF(c),Flame | 3,800.00 |
| 10 WE,LF,BP,LF(c),Flame | 3,800.00 |
| 11 WE,LF,BP,LF(c),O:Flame | 3,800.00 |
| 12 BP,LF(c),Bondage(c),Flame | 3,500.00 |
| 13 LF(c),E:Dr Fung,Flame | 3,500.00 |
| 14 JoS,Bondage(c),Flame | 3,000.00 |
| 15 JoS&LF(c),Flame | 2,200.00 |
| 16 Flame(c) | 1,600.00 |
| 17 Flame(c) | 1,600.00 |
| 18 Flame(c) | 1,600.00 |
| 19 Male Bondage(c),Flame | 1,800.00 |
| 20 Flame(c) | 1,500.00 |
| 21 O:Black Club &Lion,Flame. | 1,400.00 |
| 22 Flame(c) | 1,200.00 |
| 23 Flame(c) | 1,000.00 |
| 24 Flame(c) | 1,000.00 |
| 25 A:Dr Fung,Flame | 1,000.00 |
| 26 Flame(c) | 1,000.00 |
| 27 Flame(c) | 1,000.00 |
| 28 Bondage(c)I&O:US Jones, B:Lu-nar,Flame | 1,600.00 |
| 29 Bondage(c),Flame | 1,000.00 |
| 30 O:Flame(c),Flame | 1,700.00 |
| 31 Bondage(c),Flame | 1,000.00 |
| 32 Hitler(c),Flame | 1,100.00 |
| 33 Male Bondage(c) | 1,000.00 |

## WONDER DUCK
**Marvel, Sept., 1949**
| | |
|---|---|
| 1 Whale(c) | 175.00 |
| 2 | 125.00 |
| 3 March, 1950 | 125.00 |

## WONDERLAND COMICS
**Feature Publications (Prize Comics Group), Summer, 1945**
| | |
|---|---|
| 1 (fa),B:Alex in Wonderland | 250.00 |
| 2 | 150.00 |
| 3 thru 8 | @125.00 |
| 9 1947 | 125.00 |

## WONDER WOMAN
**DC Comics, 1942**
| | |
|---|---|
| 1 O:Wonder Woman,A:Paula Von Gunther | 40,000.00 |
| 2 I:Earl of Greed,Duke of Deception and Lord Conquest. | 7,500.00 |
| 3 Paula Von Gunther reforms | 3,500.00 |
| 4 A:Paula Von Gunther | 2,600.00 |
| 5 I:Dr. Psycho,A:Mars | 2,600.00 |
| 6 I:Cheetah | 2,000.00 |
| 7 | 2,000.00 |
| 8 I:Queen Clea. | 2,000.00 |
| 9 I:Giganto | 2,000.00 |
| 10 I:Duke Mephisto Saturno | 2,400.00 |
| 11 I:Hypnoto | 1,700.00 |
| 12 I:Queen Desira. | 1,700.00 |
| 13 V:King Rigor & the Seal Men | 1,700.00 |
| 14 I:Gentleman Killer | 1,700.00 |
| 15 I:Solo | 1,700.00 |
| 16 I:King Pluto | 1,700.00 |
| 17 Wonder Woman goes to Ancient Rome. | 1,700.00 |
| 18 V:Dr. Psycho | 1,700.00 |
| 19 V:Blitz. | 1,700.00 |
| 20 V:Nifty and the Air Pirates | 1,700.00 |
| 21 I:Queen Atomia | 1,500.00 |
| 22 V:Saturno. | 1,500.00 |
| 23 V:Odin and the Valkyries | 1,500.00 |
| 24 I:Mask | 1,500.00 |
| 25 V:Purple Priestess | 1,500.00 |
| 26 I:Queen Celerita. | 1,500.00 |
| 27 V:Pik Socket. | 1,500.00 |
| 28 V:Cheetah,Clea,Dr. Poison, Giganta,Hypnata,Snowman, Zara (Villainy,Inc.). | 2,000.00 |
| 29 V:Paddy Gypso | 2,000.00 |
| 30 The Secret of the Limestone Caves | 2,000.00 |
| 31 V:Solo | 1,000.00 |
| 32 V:Uvo | 1,000.00 |
| 33 V:Inventa | 1,000.00 |
| 34 V:Duke of Deception | 1,000.00 |
| 35 Jaxo,Master of Thoughts | 1,000.00 |
| 36 V:Lord Cruello | 1,000.00 |
| 37 A:Circe | 1,000.00 |
| 38 V:Brutex | 1,000.00 |
| 39 The Unmasking of Wonder Woman | 1,000.00 |
| 40 Hollywood Goes To Paradise Island | 1,000.00 |
| 41 Wonder Woman,Romance Editor | 900.00 |
| 42 V:General Vertigo | 900.00 |
| 43 The Amazing Spy Ring Mystery | 900.00 |

*Wonder Woman #49*
© DC Comics

*Wonder Woman #98*
© DC Comics

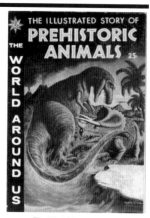

*The World Around Us #15*
© Gilberton Publications

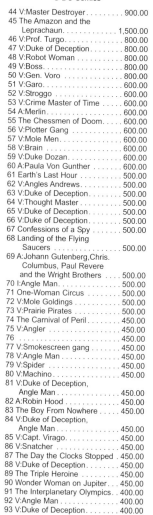

44 V:Master Destroyer . . . . . . . . 900.00
45 The Amazon and the
    Leprachaun. . . . . . . . . . . . 1,500.00
46 V:Prof. Turgo. . . . . . . . . . . . . . 800.00
47 V:Duke of Deception . . . . . . . 800.00
48 V:Robot Woman . . . . . . . . . . . 800.00
49 V:Boss. . . . . . . . . . . . . . . . . . . 800.00
50 V:Gen. Voro . . . . . . . . . . . . . . 800.00
51 V:Garo. . . . . . . . . . . . . . . . . . . 600.00
52 V:Stroggo . . . . . . . . . . . . . . . . 600.00
53 V:Crime Master of Time . . . . 600.00
54 A:Merlin. . . . . . . . . . . . . . . . . . 600.00
55 The Chessmen of Doom. . . . . 600.00
56 V:Plotter Gang . . . . . . . . . . . . 600.00
57 V:Mole Men. . . . . . . . . . . . . . . 600.00
58 V:Brain . . . . . . . . . . . . . . . . . . 600.00
59 V:Duke Dozan. . . . . . . . . . . . . 600.00
60 A:Paula Von Gunther . . . . . . . 600.00
61 Earth's Last Hour . . . . . . . . . . 500.00
62 V:Angles Andrews. . . . . . . . . . 500.00
63 V:Duke of Deception. . . . . . . . 500.00
64 V:Thought Master . . . . . . . . . . 500.00
65 V:Duke of Deception. . . . . . . . 500.00
66 V:Duke of Deception. . . . . . . . 500.00
67 Confessions of a Spy . . . . . . . 500.00
68 Landing of the Flying
    Saucers . . . . . . . . . . . . . . . . . 500.00
69 A:Johann Gutenberg,Chris.
    Columbus, Paul Revere
    and the Wright Brothers . . . . 500.00
70 I:Angle Man. . . . . . . . . . . . . . . 500.00
71 One-Woman Circus . . . . . . . . 500.00
72 V:Mole Goldings . . . . . . . . . . . 500.00
73 V:Prairie Pirates . . . . . . . . . . . 500.00
74 The Carnival of Peril. . . . . . . . 450.00
75 V:Angler . . . . . . . . . . . . . . . . . 450.00
76 . . . . . . . . . . . . . . . . . . . . . . . . . 450.00
77 V:Smokescreen gang . . . . . . . 450.00
78 V:Angle Man . . . . . . . . . . . . . . 450.00
79 V:Spider . . . . . . . . . . . . . . . . . 450.00
80 V:Machino . . . . . . . . . . . . . . . . 450.00
81 V:Duke of Deception,
    Angle Man . . . . . . . . . . . . . . 450.00
82 A:Robin Hood . . . . . . . . . . . . . 450.00
83 The Boy From Nowhere . . . . . 450.00
84 V:Duke of Deception,
    Angle Man . . . . . . . . . . . . . . 450.00
85 V:Capt. Virago. . . . . . . . . . . . . 450.00
86 V:Snatcher . . . . . . . . . . . . . . . 450.00
87 The Day the Clocks Stopped . 450.00
88 V:Duke of Deception. . . . . . . . 450.00
89 The Triple Heroine . . . . . . . . . 450.00
90 Wonder Woman on Jupiter . . . 450.00
91 The Interplanetary Olympics. . 400.00
92 V:Angle Man . . . . . . . . . . . . . . 400.00
93 V:Duke of Deception . . . . . . . 400.00

94 V:Duke of Deception,
    A:Robin Hood . . . . . . . . . . . 400.00
95 O:Wonder Woman's Tiara. . . . 400.00
96 V:Angle Man . . . . . . . . . . . . . . 400.00
97 The Runaway Time Express. . 400.00
98 . . . . . . . . . . . . . . . . . . . . . . . . . 400.00
99 V:Silicons . . . . . . . . . . . . . . . . 400.00
100 Anniversary Issue . . . . . . . . . 450.00
101 V:Time Master. . . . . . . . . . . . 350.00
102 F:Steve Trevor . . . . . . . . . . . 350.00
103 V:Gadget-Maker . . . . . . . . . . 350.00
104 A:Duke of Deception . . . . . . . 350.00
105 O,I:Wonder Woman . . . . . . 1,500.00
106 W.Woman space adventure . 350.00
107 Battles space cowboys . . . . 350.00
108 Honored by U.S. Post Off. . . 350.00
109 V:Slicker . . . . . . . . . . . . . . . . 350.00
110 I:Princess 1003 . . . . . . . . . . 350.00
111 I:Prof. Menace. . . . . . . . . . . . 350.00
112 V:Chest of Monsters . . . . . . . 300.00
113 A:Queen Mikra . . . . . . . . . . . 300.00
114 V:Flying Saucers . . . . . . . . . 300.00
115 A:Angle Man . . . . . . . . . . . . . 300.00
116 A:Professor Andro . . . . . . . . . 300.00
117 A:Etta Candy . . . . . . . . . . . . . 300.00
118 A:Merman . . . . . . . . . . . . . . . 300.00
119 A:Mer Boy . . . . . . . . . . . . . . . 300.00
120 A:Hot & Cold Alien . . . . . . . . 300.00
121 A:Wonder Woman Family . . . 250.00
122 I:Wonder Tot . . . . . . . . . . . . . 250.00
123 A:Wonder Girl,Wonder Tot . . 250.00
124 A:Wonder Girl,Wonder Tot . . 250.00
125 WW-Battle Prize . . . . . . . . . . 250.00
126 I:Mr.Genie . . . . . . . . . . . . . . . 250.00

## WONDERWORLD
## See: WONDER COMICS

## WOOLWORTH'S
## CHRISTMAS STORY BOOK
### Western Printing Co., 1954
N# . . . . . . . . . . . . . . . . . . . . . . . . 100.00

## THE WORLD AROUND US
### Gilberton Publications, 1958
1 GE,Dogs . . . . . . . . . . . . . . . . 125.00
2 SC,Indians . . . . . . . . . . . . . . . 125.00
3 LbC,Horses . . . . . . . . . . . . . . 125.00
4 LbC,Railroads . . . . . . . . . . . . 100.00
5 Grl,Space . . . . . . . . . . . . . . . . 125.00
6 GE,The FBI . . . . . . . . . . . . . . 125.00
7 Grl,Pirates . . . . . . . . . . . . . . . 100.00
8 GE,Grl,Flight . . . . . . . . . . . . . 100.00

9 Grl,EK,Army. . . . . . . . . . . . . . 100.00
10 EK,Navy . . . . . . . . . . . . . . . . 100.00
11 Marines . . . . . . . . . . . . . . . . . 100.00
12 Grl,Coast Guard . . . . . . . . . . 100.00
13 JCo,Air Force . . . . . . . . . . . . 100.00
14 GE,EK,The French Revolution 125.00
15 AW,GM,EK,Prehistoric
    Animals . . . . . . . . . . . . . . . 135.00
16 EK,The Crusades . . . . . . . . . 100.00
17 GE,RC,Festivals . . . . . . . . . . 100.00
18 GE,RC,Great Scientists . . . . 100.00
19 AW,GM,The Jungle . . . . . . . . 125.00
20 RC,GE,AT,Communications . . 125.00
21 RC,GE,GM,American
    Presidents . . . . . . . . . . . . . 125.00
22 GE,Boating . . . . . . . . . . . . . . 100.00
23 RC,GE,Great Explorers . . . . 100.00
24 GM,GE,Ghosts . . . . . . . . . . . 125.00
25 GM,GE,Magic . . . . . . . . . . . . 125.00
26 The Civil War . . . . . . . . . . . . . 150.00
27 RC,GE,CM,AT,High Adventure 100.00
28 RC,GE,GM,AT,LbC(c),Whaling 110.00
29 RC,GE,AT,GM,Vikings . . . . . 125.00
30 RC,GE,JK,AT,Undersea
    Adventures . . . . . . . . . . . . . 125.00
31 RC,GE,Grl,EK,JK,Hunting . . . 100.00
32 GM,JK,RC,GE,For Gold
    and Glory . . . . . . . . . . . . . . 100.00
33 AT,GE,RC,Famous Teens . . . . 110.00
34 RC,GE,Fishing . . . . . . . . . . . . 100.00
35 LcM,JK,GM,GE,Spies . . . . . . . 110.00
36 JK,Fight For Life . . . . . . . . . . 100.00

## WORLD FAMOUS
## HEROES MAGAZINE
### Comic Corp. of America
### (Centaur) Oct., 1941
1 BLb,Paul Revere . . . . . . . . . 1,600.00
2 BLb,Andrew Jackson,V:
    Dickinson, Lou Gehrig . . . . . 750.00
3 BLb,Juarez-Mexican patriot . . 600.00
4 BLb,Canadian Mounties . . . . . 600.00

## WORLD FAMOUS
## STORIES
### Croyden Publ., 1945
1 Rip Van Winkle,Ali Baba . . . . . 150.00

## THE WORLD
## IS HIS PARISH
### George A. Pflaum, 1953
N# Pope Pius XII . . . . . . . . . . . . . 75.00

*World of Fantasy #11*
© Marvel Comics Group

*World's Best Comics #1*
© DC Comics

*World's Finest Comics #35*
© DC Comics

## WORLD OF FANTASY

### Marvel Atlas, May, 1956

1 The Secret of the Mountain . . . 600.00
2 JMn,AW,Inside the Tunnel. . . . 400.00
3 DAy,SC, The Man in the Cave. 350.00
4 BEv(c),BP,JF,Back to the
   Lost City . . . . . . . . . . . . . . . . 250.00
5 BEv(c),BP,In the Swamp . . . . . 250.00
6 BEv(c),BP,The Strange Wife
   of Henry Johnson . . . . . . . . . 250.00
7 BEv(c),GM,Man in Grey . . . . . 250.00
8 GM,JO,MF,The Secret of the
   Black Cloud . . . . . . . . . . . . . 275.00
9 BEv,BK. . . . . . . . . . . . . . . . . . 250.00
10 . . . . . . . . . . . . . . . . . . . . . . . 200.00
11 AT . . . . . . . . . . . . . . . . . . . . . 200.00
12 BEv(c) . . . . . . . . . . . . . . . . . . 200.00
13 BEv,JO . . . . . . . . . . . . . . . . . 200.00
14 JMn(c),GM,JO,CI,JM . . . . . . . 200.00
15 JK(c) . . . . . . . . . . . . . . . . . . . 200.00
16 AW,SD,JK . . . . . . . . . . . . . . . 275.00
17 JK(c),SD . . . . . . . . . . . . . . . . 275.00
18 JK(c) . . . . . . . . . . . . . . . . . . . 275.00
19 JK(c),SD,Aug., 1959. . . . . . . 275.00

## WORLD OF MYSTERY

### Marvel Atlas, 1956–57

1 BEv(c),AT,JO,The Long Wait . 600.00
2 BEv(c),The Man From
   Nowhere . . . . . . . . . . . . . . . 225.00
3 SD,AT,JDa, The Bugs . . . . . . . 300.00
4 SD(c),BP,What Happened in
   the Basement . . . . . . . . . . . 300.00
5 JO,She Stands in Shadows . . 225.00
6 AW,SD,GC,Sinking Man . . . . . 300.00
7 GC,JSe,Pick A Door . . . . . . . . 225.00

## WORLD OF SUSPENSE

### Marvel Atlas, April, 1956

1 JO,BEv,JMn,A Stranger
   Among Us . . . . . . . . . . . . . . . 500.00
2 SD,LC,JMN(c),When Walks
   the Scarecrow . . . . . . . . . . . 300.00
3 AW,JMN(c),The Man Who
   Couldn't Be Touched . . . . . . . 300.00
4 Something is in This House . . 225.00
5 BEv,DH,JO. . . . . . . . . . . . . . . 225.00
6 BEv(c),BP . . . . . . . . . . . . . . . . 225.00
7 AW,The Face . . . . . . . . . . . . . 300.00
8 Prisoner of the Ghost Ship . . . 225.00

## WORLD'S BEST COMICS

### DC Comics, Spring, 1941

1 Superman vs. the Rainmaker,
   Batman vs. Wright . . . . . . 27,000.00

**Becomes:**

## WORLD'S FINEST COMICS

### DC Comics, 1941

2 Superman V:The Unknown X,
   Batman V:Ambrose Taylor 12,000.00
3 I&O:Scarecrow . . . . . . . . . . 9,000.00
4 Superman V:Dan Brandon,
   Batman V:Ghost Gang . . . . 7,000.00
5 Superman V:Lemuel P.Potts,
   Batman V:Brains Kelly . . . . 6,500.00
6 Superman V:Metalo,Batman
   meets Scoop Scanlon . . . . 5,200.00
7 Superman V:Jenkins,Batman
   V:Snow Man Bandits . . . . . 5,200.00
8 Superman:Talent Unlimited
   Batman V:Little Nap Boyd,
   B:Boy Commandos . . . . . . 5,000.00
9 Superman:One Second to
   Live,Batman V:Bramwell B.
   Bramwell. . . . . . . . . . . . . . . 5,200.00
10 Superman V:The Insect Master,
   Batman reforms OliverHunt 5,000.00
11 Superman V:Charlie Frost,
   Batman V:Rob Calendar . . 4,200.00
12 Superman V:Lynx,Batman:
   Alfred Gets His Man . . . . . . 4,200.00
13 Superman V:Dice Dimant,
   Batman V:Swami Pravhoz . 4,200.00
14 Superman V:Al Bandar,Batman
   V:Jib Buckler. . . . . . . . . . . . 4,200.00
15 Superman V:Derby Bowser,
   Batman V:Mennekin . . . . . . 4,200.00
16 Superman:Music for the Masses,
   Batman V:Nocky Johnson . 4,200.00
17 Superman:The Great Godini,
   Batman V:Dr.Dreemo . . . . . 4,200.00
18 Superman:The Junior Reporters,
   Batman V:Prof.Brane . . . . . 4,000.00
19 A:The Joker . . . . . . . . . . . . . . 4,000.00
20 A:Toyman . . . . . . . . . . . . . . . 4,000.00
21 Superman:Swindle in
   Sweethearts!. . . . . . . . . . . . 3,000.00
22 Batman V:Nails Finney . . . . 3,000.00
23 Superman:The Colossus
   of Metropolis. . . . . . . . . . . . 3,000.00
24 . . . . . . . . . . . . . . . . . . . . . . . 3,000.00
25 Superman V:Ed Rook,Batman:
   The Famous First Crimes. . 3,000.00
26 Confessions of Superman . . 3,000.00

27 The Man Who Out-Supered
   Superman. . . . . . . . . . . . . . 3,000.00
28 A:Lex Luther,Batman V:Glass
   Man. . . . . . . . . . . . . . . . . . . 3,000.00
29 Superman:The Books that
   Couldn't Be Bound . . . . . . . 3,000.00
30 Superman:Sheriff Clark Kent,
   Batman V:Joe Coyne . . . . . 3,000.00
31 Superman's Super-Rival,Batman:
   Man with the X-Ray Eyes. . 2,700.00
32 Superman Visits
   Ancient Egypt . . . . . . . . . . 2,700.00
33 Superman Press, Inc.,
   Batman V:James Harmon . 2,700.00
34 The Un-Super Superman. . . 2,700.00
35 Daddy Superman,A:Penguin 2,700.00
36 Lois Lane,Sleeping Beauty . 2,700.00
37 The Superman Story,Batman
   V:T-Gun Jones . . . . . . . . . . 2,700.00
38 If There were No Superman 2,700.00
39 Superman V:Big Jim Martin,
   Batman V:J.J.Jason . . . . . . 2,700.00
40 Superman V:Check,Batman:4
   Killers Against Fate! . . . . . 2,700.00
41 I:Supermanium,
   E:Boy Commandos . . . . . . 2,000.00
42 Superman goes to Uranus,
   A:Marco Polo & Kubla Khan 2,000.00
43 A:J.Wilbur Wolfingham. . . . . 2,000.00
44 Superman:The Revolt of the
   Thought Machine . . . . . . . . 2,000.00
45 Superman:Lois Lane and Clark
   Kent,Private Detectives . . . 2,000.00
46 Superman V:Mr. 7 . . . . . . . . 2,000.00
47 Superman:The Girl Who
   Hated Reporters . . . . . . . . . 2,000.00
48 A:Joker. . . . . . . . . . . . . . . . . 2,000.00
49 Superman Meets the
   Metropolis Shutterbug
   Society, A:Penguin . . . . . . . 2,000.00
50 Superman Super Wrecker . 2,000.00
51 Superman:The Amazing
   Talents of Lois Lane . . . . . . 2,000.00
52 A:J.Wilbur Wolfingham. . . . . 2,000.00
53 Superman V:Elias Toomey . 2,000.00
54 The Superman Who Avoided
   Danger!. . . . . . . . . . . . . . . . 2,000.00
55 A:Penguin. . . . . . . . . . . . . . . 2,000.00
56 Superman V:Dr.Vallin,Batman
   V:Big Dan Hooker. . . . . . . . 2,000.00
57 The Artificial Superman . . . . 2,000.00
58 Superman V:Mr.Fenton . . . . 2,000.00
59 A:Lex Luthor,Joker. . . . . . . . 2,000.00
60 A:J.Wilbur Wolfingham. . . . . 2,000.00
61 A:Joker,Superman's
   Blackout . . . . . . . . . . . . . . . 1,500.00

*World's Finest Comics #88*
© DC Comics

*Worlds of Fear #5*
© Fawcett Publications

*World War III #1*
© Ace Periodicals

62 A:Lex Luthor. . . . . . . . . . . . 1,500.00
63 Superman:Clark Kent,
    Gangster. . . . . . . . . . . . . . 1,500.00
64 Superman:The Death of Lois
    Lane,Batman:Bruce Wayne...
    Amateur Detective . . . . . . . 1,500.00
65 The Confessions of Superman,
    Batman V:The Blaster . . . . 2,500.00
66 Superman,Ex-Crimebuster;
    Batman V:Brass Haley . . . . 1,500.00
67 Superman:Metropolis-Crime
    Center! . . . . . . . . . . . . . . . 1,500.00
68 Batman V:The Crimesmith. . 1,500.00
69 A:Jor-El,Batman
    V:Tom Becket . . . . . . . . . . . 1,500.00
70 The Two Faces of Superman,
    Batman:Crime Consultant . 1,500.00
71 B:Superman/Batman
    team-ups. . . . . . . . . . . . . . 3,000.00
72 V:Heavy Weapon gang . . . . 2,000.00
73 V:Fang . . . . . . . . . . . . . . . . 2,000.00
74 The Contest of Heroes . . . . 1,600.00
75 V:The Purple Mask Mob . . . 1,500.00
76 When Gotham City
    Challenged Metropolis . . . . 1,200.00
77 V:Prof.Pender . . . . . . . . . 1,200.00
78 V:Varrel mob . . . . . . . . . . . 1,200.00
79 A:Aladdin . . . . . . . . . . . . . . 1,200.00
80 V:Mole . . . . . . . . . . . . . . . 1,200.00
81 Meet Ka Thar from future . . . 900.00
82 A:Three Musketeers . . . . . . . 900.00
83 The Case of the Mother
    Goose Mystery . . . . . . . . . . 900.00
84 V:Thad Linnis Gang . . . . . . . 900.00
85 Meet Princess Varina . . . . . . 900.00
86 V:Henry Bartle. . . . . . . . . . . 900.00
87 V:Elton Craig. . . . . . . . . . . . 900.00
88 1st team-up Luthor & Joker . . 950.00
89 I:Club of Heroes . . . . . . . . . 900.00
90 A:Batwoman . . . . . . . . . . . . 900.00
91 V:Rohtul,Descendent of Lex
    Luthor . . . . . . . . . . . . . . . . . 700.00
92 1st & only A:Skyboy. . . . . . . 700.00
93 V:Victor Danning . . . . . . . . . 700.00
94 O:Superman/Batman team,
    A:Lex Luthor. . . . . . . . . . . 1,200.00
95 Battle o/t Super Heroes . . . . 700.00
96 Super-Foes from Planet X . . . 700.00
97 V:Condor Gang. . . . . . . . . . . 700.00
98 I:Moonman . . . . . . . . . . . . . 700.00
99 JK,V:Carl Verril . . . . . . . . . . 700.00
100 A:Kandor, Lex Luthor . . . . . 1,200.00
101 A:Atom Master . . . . . . . . . . 450.00
102 V:Jo-Jo Groff gang,
    B:Tommy Tomorrow. . . . . . . 450.00

103 The Secrets of the
    Sorcerer's Treasure. . . . . . . 450.00
104 A:Lex Luthor . . . . . . . . . . . 450.00
105 V:Khalex . . . . . . . . . . . . . . 450.00
106 V:Duplicate Man . . . . . . . . 450.00
107 The Secret of the Time
    Creature. . . . . . . . . . . . . . . 450.00
108 The Star Creatures . . . . . . . 450.00
109 V:Fangan . . . . . . . . . . . . . . 450.00
110 The Alien Who Doomed
    Robin! . . . . . . . . . . . . . . . . 450.00
111 V:Floyd Frisby . . . . . . . . . . 450.00
112 . . . . . . . . . . . . . . . . . . . . . 450.00
113 1st Bat-Mite/Mr.Mxyzptlk
    team-up . . . . . . . . . . . . . . . 450.00
114 Captives o/t Space Globes . . 450.00
115 The Curse That Doomed
    Superman . . . . . . . . . . . . . 350.00
116 V:Vance Collins . . . . . . . . . 350.00
117 A:Batwoman,Lex Luthor . . . 350.00
118 V:Vath-Gar. . . . . . . . . . . . . 350.00
119 V:General Grambly . . . . . . . 350.00
120 V:Faceless Creature . . . . . . 350.00
121 I:Miss Arrowette . . . . . . . . . 350.00

## WORLD'S GREATEST SONGS
**Marvel Atlas, 1954**
1 Eddie Fisher, Frank Sinatra. . . 500.00

## WORLD'S GREATEST STORIES
**Jubilee Publications Jan., 1949**
1 F:Alice in Wonderland . . . . . . 450.00
2 F:Pinocchio . . . . . . . . . . . . . . 400.00

## WORLDS BEYOND
**Fawcett Publications, 1951**
1 BP,BBa. . . . . . . . . . . . . . . . . . 500.00
Becomes:
## WORLDS OF FEAR
**Fawcett Publications, 1952**
2 BP. . . . . . . . . . . . . . . . . . . . 1,200.00
3 GE . . . . . . . . . . . . . . . . . . . . 900.00
4 BP,MSy . . . . . . . . . . . . . . . . 750.00
5 BP,MSy . . . . . . . . . . . . . . . . 750.00
6 . . . . . . . . . . . . . . . . . . . . . . . 750.00
7 . . . . . . . . . . . . . . . . . . . . . . . 750.00
8 . . . . . . . . . . . . . . . . . . . . . . . 750.00
9 . . . . . . . . . . . . . . . . . . . . . . . 750.00
10 no-eyed man, eyeballs(c) . . 2,200.00

## WORLD WAR III
**Ace Periodicals, March–May, 1953**
1 Atomic Bomb (c) . . . . . . . . . 1,000.00
2 The War That Will Never
    Happen . . . . . . . . . . . . . . . 750.00

## WOTALIFE COMICS
## See: PHANTOM LADY

## WOW COMICS
**David McKay/Henle Publ., July, 1936–Nov., 1936**
1 WE,DBr(c),Fu Manchu,
    Buck Jones. . . . . . . . . . . . 3,800.00
2 WE,Little King . . . . . . . . . . . 2,800.00
3 WE,WE(c), Popeye. . . . . . . . 2,500.00
4 WE,BKa,AR,DBr(c),Popeye,
    Flash Gordon . . . . . . . . . . 3,000.00

## WOW COMICS
**Fawcett Publications, Winter, 1940**
N#(1)S&K,CCB(c),B&O:Mr Scarlett;
    B:Atom Blake,Jim Dolan,Rick
    O'Shay,Bondage(c) . . . . . 27,000.00
2 B:Hunchback . . . . . . . . . . . 4,500.00
3 V:Mummy Ray Gun . . . . . . . 3,000.00
4 O:Pinky . . . . . . . . . . . . . . . 3,200.00
5 F:Pinky the Whiz Kid . . . . . . 2,000.00
6 O:Phantom Eagle;
    B:Commando Yank . . . . . . 2,000.00
7 Spearhead of Invasion . . . . . 1,500.00
8 All Three Heroes . . . . . . . . . 1,500.00
9 A:Capt Marvel,Capt MarvelJr.
    Shazam;Mary Marvel . . . 3,200.00
10 The Sinister Secret of
    Hotel Hideaway . . . . . . . . . 1,500.00
11 . . . . . . . . . . . . . . . . . . . . . 1,400.00
12 Rocketing adventures . . . . . 1,400.00
13 Thrill Show . . . . . . . . . . . . . 1,400.00
14 V:Mr Night . . . . . . . . . . . . . 1,400.00
15 Shazam Girl of America . . . 1,200.00
16 Ride to the Moon . . . . . . . . 1,200.00
17 V:Mary Batson,Alter Ego
    Goes Berserk . . . . . . . . . . 1,200.00
18 I:Uncle Marvel,Infinity(c)
    V is For Victory. . . . . . . . . 1,200.00
19 A Whirlwind Fantasy . . . . . . 1,200.00
20 Mary Marvel's Magic Carpet 1,200.00
21 Word That Shook the World . . 500.00

*Wow Comics #38*
© *Fawcett Publications*

*Real Western Hero #75*
© *Fawcett Publications*

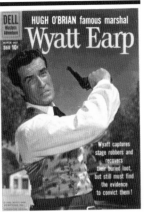

*Wyatt Earp #10*
© *Dell Publishing Co.*

22 Come on Boys-
Everybody Sing . . . . . . . . . . 500.00
23 Trapped by the Terror of
the Future . . . . . . . . . . . . . . 500.00
24 Mary Marvel . . . . . . . . . . . . . 500.00
25 Mary Marvel Crushes Crime. . 500.00
26 Smashing Star-
Studded Stories . . . . . . . . . . 400.00
27 War Stamp Plea(c) . . . . . . . . 400.00
28 Pinky . . . . . . . . . . . . . . . . . . . 400.00
29 . . . . . . . . . . . . . . . . . . . . . . . 400.00
30 In Mirror Land . . . . . . . . . . . . 400.00
31 Stars of Action . . . . . . . . . . . 350.00
32 The Millinery Marauders . . . . 350.00
33 Mary Marvel(c) . . . . . . . . . . . 350.00
34 A:Uncle Marvel . . . . . . . . . . . 350.00
35 I:Freckles Marvel . . . . . . . . . 500.00
36 Secret of the Buried City. . . . 350.00
37 7th War loan plea . . . . . . . . . 350.00
38 Pictures That Came to Life . . . 350.00
39 The Perilous Packages . . . . . 350.00
40 The Quarrel of the Gnomes . . 350.00
41 Hazardous Adventures . . . . . 300.00
42 . . . . . . . . . . . . . . . . . . . . . . . 300.00
43 Curtain Time . . . . . . . . . . . . . 300.00
44 Volcanic Adventure . . . . . . . . 300.00
45 . . . . . . . . . . . . . . . . . . . . . . . 300.00
46 . . . . . . . . . . . . . . . . . . . . . . . 300.00
47 . . . . . . . . . . . . . . . . . . . . . . . 300.00
48 . . . . . . . . . . . . . . . . . . . . . . . 300.00
49 . . . . . . . . . . . . . . . . . . . . . . . 300.00
50 Mary Marvel/Commando Yank 300.00
51 Command Yank . . . . . . . . . . . 250.00
52 . . . . . . . . . . . . . . . . . . . . . . . 250.00
53 Murder in the Tall Timbers . . . 250.00
54 Flaming Adventure . . . . . . . . . 250.00
55 Earthquake!. . . . . . . . . . . . . . 250.00
56 Sacred Pearls of Comatesh . . 250.00
57 . . . . . . . . . . . . . . . . . . . . . . . 250.00
58 E:Mary Marvel;The Curse
of the Keys . . . . . . . . . . . . . . 250.00
59 B:Ozzie the Hilarious
Teenager . . . . . . . . . . . . . . . 250.00
60 thru 64 . . . . . . . . . . . . . . . . @250.00
65 A:Tom Mix . . . . . . . . . . . . . . . 250.00
66 A:Tom Mix . . . . . . . . . . . . . . . 250.00
67 A:Tom Mix . . . . . . . . . . . . . . . 250.00
68 A:Tom Mix . . . . . . . . . . . . . . . 250.00
69 A:Tom Mix,Baseball . . . . . . . 250.00
Becomes:

## REAL WESTERN HERO
### Sept., 1948
70 It's Round-up Time . . . . . . . . 500.00
71 CCB,P(c),A Rip
Roaring Rodeo . . . . . . . . . . 325.00

72 w/Gabby Hayes . . . . . . . . . . 325.00
73 thru 75 . . . . . . . . . . . . . . . . @325.00
Becomes:

## WESTERN HERO
### March, 1949
76 Partial Ph(c)&P(c) . . . . . . . . . 350.00
77 Partial Ph(c)&P(c) . . . . . . . . . 200.00
78 Partial Ph(c)&P(c) . . . . . . . . . 200.00
79 Partial Ph(c)&P(c),
Shadow of Death . . . . . . . . . 175.00
80 Partial Ph(c)&P(c) . . . . . . . . . 200.00
81 CCB,Partial Ph(c)&P(c),
F:Tootsie . . . . . . . . . . . . . . . 200.00
82 Partial Ph(c)&P(c),
A:Hopalong Cassidy . . . . . . . 200.00
83 Partial Ph(c)&P(c) . . . . . . . . . 200.00
84 Ph(c) . . . . . . . . . . . . . . . . . . . 175.00
85 Ph(c) . . . . . . . . . . . . . . . . . . . 175.00
86 Ph(c),The Case of the
Extra Buddy, giant . . . . . . . . 175.00
87 Ph(c),The Strange Lands . . . . 175.00
88 Ph(c),A:Senor Diablo . . . . . . . 175.00
89 Ph(c),The Hypnotist . . . . . . . . 175.00
90 Ph(c),The Menace of
the Cougar, giant . . . . . . . . . 150.00
91 Ph(c),Song of Death . . . . . . . 150.00
92 Ph(c),The Fatal Hide-out,
giant. . . . . . . . . . . . . . . . . . . 150.00
93 Ph(c),Treachery at
Triple T, giant . . . . . . . . . . . 150.00
94 Ph(c),Bank Busters,giant . . . . 150.00
95 Ph(c),Rampaging River . . . . . 150.00
96 Ph(c),Range Robbers,giant . . 150.00
97 Ph(c),Death on the
Hook,giant . . . . . . . . . . . . . . 150.00
98 Ph(c),Web of Death,giant . . . . 150.00
99 Ph(c),The Hidden Evidence . . 150.00
100 Ph(c),A:Red Eagle,Giant . . . 150.00
101 Red Eagle, Ph(c) . . . . . . . . . 150.00
102 thru 111 Ph(c) . . . . . . . . . . @150.00
112 Ph(c),March, 1952 . . . . . . . . 175.00

## WYATT EARP
### Marvel Atlas, Nov., 1955
1 JMn,F:Wyatt Earp . . . . . . . . . . 250.00
2 AW,Saloon(c) . . . . . . . . . . . . . 150.00
3 JMn(c),The Showdown,
A:Black Bart . . . . . . . . . . . . . 125.00
4 Ph(c),Hugh O'Brian,JSe,
India Sundown . . . . . . . . . . . 125.00
5 Ph(c),Hugh O'Brian,DW,
Gun Wild Fever . . . . . . . . . . 125.00
6 BEv(c) . . . . . . . . . . . . . . . . . . 125.00
7 AW . . . . . . . . . . . . . . . . . . . . 125.00

8 JMn,Wild Bill Hickok . . . . . . . . 125.00
9 and 10 . . . . . . . . . . . . . . . . @125.00
11 . . . . . . . . . . . . . . . . . . . . . . . 125.00
12 AW,JMn . . . . . . . . . . . . . . . . . 125.00
13 . . . . . . . . . . . . . . . . . . . . . . . 100.00
14 . . . . . . . . . . . . . . . . . . . . . . . 100.00
15 thru 20 . . . . . . . . . . . . . . . . @100.00
21 JDa(c) . . . . . . . . . . . . . . . . . . 100.00
22 thru 29 . . . . . . . . . . . . . . . . @100.00

## WYATT EARP
### Dell Publishing Co., 1957
1 RsM . . . . . . . . . . . . . . . . . . . . 175.00
2 RsM . . . . . . . . . . . . . . . . . . . . 125.00
3 RsM . . . . . . . . . . . . . . . . . . . . 110.00
4 . . . . . . . . . . . . . . . . . . . . . . . . 100.00
5 Ph(c) . . . . . . . . . . . . . . . . . . . 100.00
6 . . . . . . . . . . . . . . . . . . . . . . . . 100.00
7 . . . . . . . . . . . . . . . . . . . . . . . . 100.00
8 . . . . . . . . . . . . . . . . . . . . . . . . 100.00
9 . . . . . . . . . . . . . . . . . . . . . . . . 100.00
10 . . . . . . . . . . . . . . . . . . . . . . . 100.00
11 . . . . . . . . . . . . . . . . . . . . . . . 100.00
12 RsM . . . . . . . . . . . . . . . . . . . . 100.00
13 AT . . . . . . . . . . . . . . . . . . . . . 100.00

## XMAS COMICS
### Fawcett Publications, 1941
1 Whiz #21 . . . . . . . . . . . . . . . 5,500.00
2 Capt. Marvel . . . . . . . . . . . . 2,200.00
7 Hoppy, Funny Animal . . . . . . . 900.00
### Second Series, 1949–52
4 Whiz, Capt. Marvel, Nyoka . . . 900.00
5 . . . . . . . . . . . . . . . . . . . . . . . . 700.00
6 . . . . . . . . . . . . . . . . . . . . . . . . 700.00
7 Bill Boyd . . . . . . . . . . . . . . . . . 700.00

## X-VENTURE
### Victory Magazines, 1947
1 Mystery Shadow, Atom
Wizard . . . . . . . . . . . . . . . . 1,500.00
2 same . . . . . . . . . . . . . . . . . . . 750.00

## YANKEE COMICS
### Chesler Publications
### (Harry A. Chesler),
### Sept., 1941–March, 1942
1 F:Yankee Doodle Jones . . . 2,400.00
2 The Spirit of '41 . . . . . . . . . 1,100.00
3 Yankee Doodle Jones . . . . . . . 800.00
4 JCo,Yankee Doodle Jones . . . 800.00

**Ya**

*Cowboy Western Comics #27*
*© Charlton Comics*

*Space Western Comics #43*
*© Charlton Comics*

*Young Allies #1*
*© Marvel Comics Group*

## YANKS IN BATTLE
### Comic Magazine, Inc.
### (Quality Comics Group), 1956
1 CCv . . . . . . . . . . . . . . . 125.00
2 CCv . . . . . . . . . . . . . . . 100.00
3 CCv . . . . . . . . . . . . . . . 100.00
4 CCv . . . . . . . . . . . . . . . 100.00

## THE YARDBIRDS
### Ziff-Davis Publishing Co., 1952
1 . . . . . . . . . . . . . . . . . . 125.00

## YELLOW CLAW
### Marvel Atlas, 1956
1 MMe . . . . . . . . . . . . . 1,300.00
2 JK,JSe . . . . . . . . . . . . 1,000.00
3 BEv . . . . . . . . . . . . . . . 975.00
4 JK,JSe . . . . . . . . . . . . . 975.00

## YELLOWJACKET
## COMICS
### Levy Publ./Frank Comunale/
### Charlton, Sept., 1944
1 O&B:Yellowjackets,B:Diana
   the Huntress . . . . . . . . . . 1,500.00
2 Rosita &The Filipino Kid . . . . . 750.00
3 . . . . . . . . . . . . . . . . . . 700.00
4 Fall of the House of Usher. . . . 750.00
5 King of Beasts . . . . . . . . . . . 750.00
6 . . . . . . . . . . . . . . . . . . 800.00
7 I:Diane Carter;The
   Lonely Guy . . . . . . . . . . . 2,000.00
8 The Buzzing Bee Code . . . . . 800.00
9 . . . . . . . . . . . . . . . . . . 750.00
10 Capt Grim V:The Salvage
   Pirates . . . . . . . . . . . . . . . . . 800.00
Becomes:

## JACK IN THE BOX
### Charlton, Feb., 1946
11 Funny Animal,Yellow Jacket . . 300.00
12 Funny Animal . . . . . . . . . . 200.00
13 BW,Funny Animal . . . . . . . . . 300.00
14 thru 16 Funny Animal . . . . . @200.00
Becomes:

## COWBOY WESTERN
## COMICS
### Charlton, July, 1948
17 Annie Oakley,Jesse James. . . 250.00
18 JO,JO(c) . . . . . . . . . . . . . . . 200.00

19 JO,JO(c),Legends of Paul
   Bunyan . . . . . . . . . . . . . . . . 200.00
20 JO(c),Jesse James. . . . . . . . 125.00
21 Annie Oakley VisitsDryGulch . 125.00
22 Story of the Texas Rangers . . 125.00
23 . . . . . . . . . . . . . . . . . . 125.00
24 Ph(c),F:James Craig. . . . . . . 125.00
25 Ph(c),F:Sunset Carson . . . . . 125.00
26 Ph(c) . . . . . . . . . . . . . . . . 150.00
27 Ph(c),Sunset Carson movie . . 750.00
28 Ph(c),Sunset Carson movie . . 400.00
29 Ph(c),Sunset Carson movie . . 400.00
30 Ph(c),Sunset Carson movie . . 400.00
31 Ph(c) . . . . . . . . . . . . . . . . 100.00
32 thru 34 Ph(c) . . . . . . . . . . @100.00
35 thru 37 Sunset Carson . . . @350.00
38 and 39 . . . . . . . . . . . . . @100.00
Becomes:

## SPACE WESTERN
## COMICS
### Charlton Comics, Oct., 1952
40 Spurs Jackson,V:The
   Saucer Men . . . . . . . . . . . 1,100.00
41 StC(c),Space Vigilantes . . . . . 750.00
42 StC(c),Atomic Bomb . . . . . . . 900.00
43 StC(c),Battle of
   Spacemans Gulch . . . . . . . . 800.00
44 StC(c),The Madman of Mars . 750.00
45 StC(c),The Moon Bat,Hitler. . . 775.00
Becomes:

## COWBOY WESTERN
## COMICS
### Oct., 1953
46 . . . . . . . . . . . . . . . . . . . 250.00
Becomes:

## COWBOY WESTERN
## HEROES
### Dec., 1953
47 . . . . . . . . . . . . . . . . . . . 150.00
48 . . . . . . . . . . . . . . . . . . . 150.00
Becomes:

## COWBOY WESTERN
### May–June, 1954
49 . . . . . . . . . . . . . . . . . . . 125.00
50 F:Jesse James . . . . . . . . . . . 125.00
51 thru 57. . . . . . . . . . . . . . @100.00
58, Wild Bill Hickock, giant . . . . . 125.00
59 thru 66 . . . . . . . . . . . . . @100.00
67 AW&AT . . . . . . . . . . . . . . . 150.00
Becomes:

## WILD BILL HICKOK
## AND JINGLES
### Aug., 1958
68 AW . . . . . . . . . . . . . . . . . 125.00
69 AW . . . . . . . . . . . . . . . . . 100.00
70 AW . . . . . . . . . . . . . . . . . 100.00
71 thru 73. . . . . . . . . . . . . . @100.00
74 1960 . . . . . . . . . . . . . . . . 100.00

## YOGI BERRA
### Fawcett, 1957
1 Ph(c). . . . . . . . . . . . . . . . 1,000.00

## YOUNG ALLIES COMICS
### Marvel Timely,
### Summer, 1941—Oct., 1946
1 S&K,SSh,Hitler(c),I&O:Young Allies
   1st meeting Capt. America &
   Human Torch 45,000.00
2 S&K,A;Capt.America,Human
   Torch. . . . . . . . . . . . . . . . 9,000.00
3 Remember Pearl Harbor(c) . 8,000.00
4 A;Capt. America,Torch,Red Skull
   ASh(c),Horror In Hollywood
   A:Capt.America,Torch. . . . . 9,000.00
5 ASh(c),AAv,Capt.America. . . 3,500.00
6 ASh(c) . . . . . . . . . . . . . . 2,800.00
7 ASh(c),SSh . . . . . . . . . . . 2,800.00
8 ASh(c),WW2,Bondage . . . . . 2,800.00
9 ASh(c),Axis leaders(c),
   B:Tommy Type,Hitler . . . . . 3,000.00
10 ASh(c),O:Tommy Type. . . . . 2,800.00
11 ASh(c) . . . . . . . . . . . . . . 2,000.00
12 ASh(c),Decapitation . . . . . . 2,000.00
13 ASh(c) . . . . . . . . . . . . . . 2,000.00
14 ASh(c) . . . . . . . . . . . . . . 2,000.00
15 ASh(c),AAv. . . . . . . . . . . . 2,000.00
16 ASh(c) . . . . . . . . . . . . . . 2,000.00
17 ASh(c),SSh . . . . . . . . . . . 2,000.00
18 ASh(c) . . . . . . . . . . . . . . 1,800.00
19 ASh(c),E:Tommy Type . . . . . 1,800.00
20 SSh . . . . . . . . . . . . . . . . 1,800.00

## YOUNG BRIDES
### Feature Publications (Prize
### Comics), Sept.–Oct., 1952
1 S&K,Ph(c) . . . . . . . . . . . . . 400.00
2 S&K,Ph(c) . . . . . . . . . . . . . 225.00
3 S&K,Ph(c) . . . . . . . . . . . . . 200.00
4 S&K . . . . . . . . . . . . . . . . 200.00
5 S&K . . . . . . . . . . . . . . . . 200.00
6 S&K . . . . . . . . . . . . . . . . 200.00

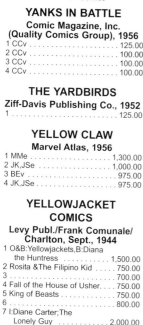

**Ya**

All comics prices listed are for *Near Mint* condition.

| | | |
|---|---|---|
| *Young Eagle #1* | *Young King Cole Vol 2 #5* | *Young Love #2* |
| © Fawcett Publications | © Novelty Press | © Prize Publications |

| | | |
|---|---|---|
| 2-1 S&K . . . . . . . . . . . . . . . . . 175.00 | 1-4 . . . . . . . . . . . . . . . . . . . . . 200.00 | 2-7 S&K(c),S&K . . . . . . . . . . . 200.00 |
| 2-2 S&K . . . . . . . . . . . . . . . . . 100.00 | 2-1 . . . . . . . . . . . . . . . . . . . . . 150.00 | 2-8 S&K . . . . . . . . . . . . . . . . . 200.00 |
| 2-3 S&K . . . . . . . . . . . . . . . . . 175.00 | 2-2 . . . . . . . . . . . . . . . . . . . . . 150.00 | 2-9 S&K(c),S&K . . . . . . . . . . . 200.00 |
| 2-4 S&K . . . . . . . . . . . . . . . . . 175.00 | 2-3 . . . . . . . . . . . . . . . . . . . . . 150.00 | 2-10 S&K(c),S&K . . . . . . . . . . 200.00 |
| 2-5 S&K . . . . . . . . . . . . . . . . . 175.00 | 2-4 . . . . . . . . . . . . . . . . . . . . . 150.00 | 2-11 S&K(c),S&K . . . . . . . . . . 200.00 |
| 2-6 S&K . . . . . . . . . . . . . . . . . 175.00 | 2-5 . . . . . . . . . . . . . . . . . . . . . 150.00 | 2-12 S&K(c),S&K . . . . . . . . . . 200.00 |
| 2-7 S&K . . . . . . . . . . . . . . . . . 175.00 | 2-6 . . . . . . . . . . . . . . . . . . . . . 150.00 | 3-1 S&K(c),S&K . . . . . . . . . . . 200.00 |
| 2-8 S&K . . . . . . . . . . . . . . . . . 100.00 | 2-7 . . . . . . . . . . . . . . . . . . . . . 150.00 | 3-2 S&K(c),S&K . . . . . . . . . . . 200.00 |
| 2-9 S&K . . . . . . . . . . . . . . . . . 100.00 | 3-1 . . . . . . . . . . . . . . . . . . . . . 175.00 | 3-3 S&K(c),S&K . . . . . . . . . . . 200.00 |
| 2-10 S&K . . . . . . . . . . . . . . . . 175.00 | 3-2 LbC . . . . . . . . . . . . . . . . . 250.00 | 3-4 S&K(c),S&K . . . . . . . . . . . 200.00 |
| 2-11 S&K. . . . . . . . . . . . . . . . 175.00 | 3-3 The Killer With The Hat . . . . 150.00 | 3-5 Ph(c) . . . . . . . . . . . . . . . . 175.00 |
| 2-12 S&K . . . . . . . . . . . . . . . . 175.00 | 3-4 The Fierce Tiger . . . . . . . . . 150.00 | 3-6 BP,Ph(c). . . . . . . . . . . . . . 175.00 |
| 3-1 thru 4-1 . . . . . . . . . . . . . @100.00 | 3-5 AMc . . . . . . . . . . . . . . . . . 150.00 | 3-7 Ph(c) . . . . . . . . . . . . . . . . 175.00 |
| 4-2 S&K . . . . . . . . . . . . . . . . . 150.00 | 3-6 . . . . . . . . . . . . . . . . . . . . . 175.00 | 3-8 Ph(c) . . . . . . . . . . . . . . . . 175.00 |
| 4-3 . . . . . . . . . . . . . . . . . . . . . 100.00 | 3-7 LbC(c),Case of the | 3-9 MMe,Ph(c) . . . . . . . . . . . 175.00 |
| 4-4 S&K . . . . . . . . . . . . . . . . . 150.00 | Devil's Twin . . . . . . . . . . . . . 250.00 | 3-10 Ph(c) . . . . . . . . . . . . . . . 175.00 |
| 4-5 . . . . . . . . . . . . . . . . . . . . . 100.00 | 3-8 . . . . . . . . . . . . . . . . . . . . . 150.00 | 3-11 Ph(c) . . . . . . . . . . . . . . . 175.00 |
| | 3-9 The Crime Fighting King . . . 150.00 | 3-12 Ph(c) . . . . . . . . . . . . . . . 175.00 |
| | 3-10 LbC(c) . . . . . . . . . . . . . . 250.00 | 4-1 S&K . . . . . . . . . . . . . . . . . 175.00 |
| **YOUNG EAGLE** | 3-11 LbC(c) . . . . . . . . . . . . . . 250.00 | 4-2 Ph(c) . . . . . . . . . . . . . . . . 150.00 |
| **Fawcett Publications/** | 3-12 July, 1948,AMc(c) . . . . . . . 150.00 | 4-3 Ph(c) . . . . . . . . . . . . . . . . 150.00 |
| **Charlton Comics, Dec., 1950** | | 4-4 Ph(c) . . . . . . . . . . . . . . . . 150.00 |
| 1 Ph(c) . . . . . . . . . . . . . . . . . 200.00 | **YOUNG LIFE** | 4-5 Ph(c) . . . . . . . . . . . . . . . . 150.00 |
| 2 Ph(c),Mystery of Thunder | **New Age Publications,** | 4-5 Ph(c) . . . . . . . . . . . . . . . . 150.00 |
| Canyon . . . . . . . . . . . . . . . 125.00 | **Summer, 1945** | 4-6 S&K,Ph(c) . . . . . . . . . . . . 150.00 |
| 3 Ph(c),Death at Dawn . . . . . . 100.00 | 1 Partial Ph(c),Louis Prima . . . . 175.00 | 4-7 thru 4-12 Ph(c). . . . . . . . @125.00 |
| 4 Ph(c) . . . . . . . . . . . . . . . . . 100.00 | 2 Partial Ph(c),Frank Sinatra . . . 200.00 | 5-1 thru 5-12 Ph(c). . . . . . . . @125.00 |
| 5 Ph(c),The Golden Flood . . . . 100.00 | **Becomes:** | 6-1 thru 6-9 . . . . . . . . . . . . . @100.00 |
| 6 Ph(c),The Nightmare Empire. . 100.00 | | 6-10 thru 6-12 . . . . . . . . . . . @100.00 |
| 7 Ph(c),Vigilante Vengeance . . . 100.00 | **TEEN LIFE** | 7-1 thru 7-7 . . . . . . . . . . . . . @100.00 |
| 8 Ph(c),The Rogues Rodeo . . . . 100.00 | **Winter, 1945** | 7-8 thru 7-11 . . . . . . . . . . . . @100.00 |
| 9 Ph(c),The Great Railroad | 3 Partial Ph(c),Croon without | 7-12 thru 8-5 . . . . . . . . . . . . @100.00 |
| Swindle . . . . . . . . . . . . . . . 100.00 | Tricks,June Allyson(c) . . . . . . 150.00 | 8-6 thru 8-12 . . . . . . . . . . . . @100.00 |
| 10 June, 1952, Ph(c),Thunder Rides | 4 Partial Ph(c),Atom Smasher | |
| the Trail,O:Thunder . . . . . . . 100.00 | Blueprints,Duke Ellington(c) . 125.00 | **YOUNG MARRIAGE** |
| | 5 Partial Ph(c), Build Your Own | **Fawcett Publications, 1950** |
| **YOUNG HEARTS** | Pocket Radio, Jackie | 1 BP,Romance,Ph(c) . . . . . . . . . 150.00 |
| **Marvel, Nov., 1949—Feb., 1950** | Robinson(c). . . . . . . . . . . . . 150.00 | |
| 1 . . . . . . . . . . . . . . . . . . . . . . 150.00 | | **YOUNG MEN** |
| 2 Feb., 1950 . . . . . . . . . . . . . 100.00 | **YOUNG LOVE** | **See: COWBOY** |
| | **Feature Publ.** | **ROMANCES** |
| **YOUNG HEROES** | **(Prize Comics Group),** | |
| **Titan Publ. (American** | **Feb.–March, 1949** | **YOUNG ROMANCE** |
| **Comics Group), 1955** | 1 S&K,S&K(c) . . . . . . . . . . . . . 600.00 | **COMICS** |
| 35 Frontier Scout . . . . . . . . . . . 125.00 | 2 S&K,Ph(c) . . . . . . . . . . . . . . 300.00 | **Feature Publ./Headline/** |
| 36 . . . . . . . . . . . . . . . . . . . . . 125.00 | 3 S&K,JSe,BE,Ph(c) . . . . . . . . . 250.00 | **Prize Publ., Sept.–Oct., 1947** |
| 37 . . . . . . . . . . . . . . . . . . . . . 125.00 | 4 S&K,Ph(c) . . . . . . . . . . . . . . 150.00 | 1 S&K(c),S&K . . . . . . . . . . . . . 650.00 |
| | 5 S&K,Ph(c) . . . . . . . . . . . . . . 150.00 | 2 S&K(c),S&K . . . . . . . . . . . . . 350.00 |
| **YOUNG KING COLE** | 2-1 S&K,Ph(c) . . . . . . . . . . . . . 250.00 | 3 S&K(c),S&K . . . . . . . . . . . . . 300.00 |
| **Novelty Press/Premium** | 2-2 Ph(c) . . . . . . . . . . . . . . . . 135.00 | 4 S&K(c),S&K . . . . . . . . . . . . . 300.00 |
| **Svcs. Co., Autumn, 1945** | 2-3 Ph(c) . . . . . . . . . . . . . . . . 135.00 | 5 S&K(c),S&K . . . . . . . . . . . . . 300.00 |
| 1-1 Detective Toni Gayle . . . . . . 400.00 | 2-4 Ph(c) . . . . . . . . . . . . . . . . 135.00 | 6 S&K(c),S&K . . . . . . . . . . . . . 300.00 |
| 1-2 . . . . . . . . . . . . . . . . . . . . . 250.00 | 2-5 Ph(c) . . . . . . . . . . . . . . . . 135.00 | |
| 1-3 . . . . . . . . . . . . . . . . . . . . . 200.00 | 2-6 S&K(c) . . . . . . . . . . . . . . . 200.00 | |

**Yo**

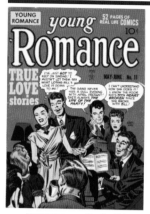

*Young Romance Comics #11*
© Prize Publications

*Zago, Jungle Prince #2*
© Fox Features Syndicate

*Zegra, Jungle Empress #2*
© Fox Features Syndicate

2-1 S&K(c),S&K . . . . . . . . . . . . 275.00
2-2 S&K(c),S&K . . . . . . . . . . . . 275.00
2-3 S&K(c),S&K . . . . . . . . . . . . 275.00
2-4 S&K(c),S&K . . . . . . . . . . . . 275.00
2-5 S&K(c),S&K . . . . . . . . . . . . 275.00
2-6 S&K(c),S&K . . . . . . . . . . . . 250.00
3-1 thru 3-12 S&K(c),S&K . . . . @250.00
4-1 thru 4-12 S&K . . . . . . . . . @250.00
5-1 ATh,S&K . . . . . . . . . . . . . . 250.00
5-2 . . . . . . . . . . . . . . . . . . . . . . 250.00
5-3 . . . . . . . . . . . . . . . . . . . . . . 225.00
5-4 thru 5-12 S&K . . . . . . . . . @225.00
6-1 . . . . . . . . . . . . . . . . . . . . . . 100.00
6-2 . . . . . . . . . . . . . . . . . . . . . . 100.00
6-3 . . . . . . . . . . . . . . . . . . . . . . 100.00

## YOUR UNITED STATES
### Lloyd Jacquet Studios, 1946
1N# Teeming Nation of Nations . 300.00

## YOUTHFUL HEARTS
### Youthful Magazines, May, 1952
1 Frankie Lane(c) . . . . . . . . . . . 350.00
2 Vic Damone . . . . . . . . . . . . . . 250.00
3 Johnnie Ray . . . . . . . . . . . . . . 250.00
Becomes:
### DARING CONFESSIONS
#### Nov., 1952
4 DW,Tony Curtis . . . . . . . . . . . 175.00
5 Ray Anthony . . . . . . . . . . . . . 125.00
6 DW . . . . . . . . . . . . . . . . . . . . 135.00
7 . . . . . . . . . . . . . . . . . . . . . . . 125.00
8 DW . . . . . . . . . . . . . . . . . . . . 125.00

## YOUTHFUL ROMANCES
### Pix Parade/Ribage/ Trojan, Aug.–Sept., 1949
1 . . . . . . . . . . . . . . . . . . . . . . . 300.00
2 Walter Johnson . . . . . . . . . . . 200.00
3 Tex Beneke . . . . . . . . . . . . . . 150.00
4 . . . . . . . . . . . . . . . . . . . . . . . 150.00
5 . . . . . . . . . . . . . . . . . . . . . . . 150.00
6 . . . . . . . . . . . . . . . . . . . . . . . 125.00
7 Tony Martin(c) . . . . . . . . . . . . 150.00
8 WW(c), Frank Sinatra . . . . . . . 250.00
9 . . . . . . . . . . . . . . . . . . . . . . . 125.00
10 Mel Torme . . . . . . . . . . . . . . 135.00
11 . . . . . . . . . . . . . . . . . . . . . . 125.00
12 Tony Benett . . . . . . . . . . . . . 135.00
13 Richard Hays . . . . . . . . . . . . 125.00
14 . . . . . . . . . . . . . . . . . . . . . . 125.00
Becomes:

## DARLING LOVE
### Oct.–Nov., 1949
15 WD,Spike Jones, Ph(c) . . . . . 125.00
16 Tony Bavaar, Ph(c) . . . . . . . . 125.00
17 DW,Ph(c) . . . . . . . . . . . . . . . 125.00
also continues as
## YOUTHFUL ROMANCES
### Ribage/Trojan 1953
15 (1) Ph(c),Spike Jones . . . . . . 125.00
16 (2) Ph(c) . . . . . . . . . . . . . . . 125.00
17 (3) Ph(c) . . . . . . . . . . . . . . . 125.00
18 (4) . . . . . . . . . . . . . . . . . . . 125.00
5 Les Paul & Mary Ford . . . . . . . 110.00
6 Debbie Reynolds . . . . . . . . . . 100.00
7 Tony Martin . . . . . . . . . . . . . . 100.00
8 Aydrey Hepburn . . . . . . . . . . . 100.00

## ZAGO, JUNGLE PRINCE
### Fox Features Syndicate, Sept., 1948
1 A:Blue Beetle . . . . . . . . . . . . . 900.00
2 JKa . . . . . . . . . . . . . . . . . . . . 750.00
3 JKa . . . . . . . . . . . . . . . . . . . . 600.00
4 MB(c) . . . . . . . . . . . . . . . . . . 600.00
Becomes:
## MY STORY
### May, 1949
5 JKa,Too Young To Fall in Love 250.00
6 I Was A She-Wolf . . . . . . . . . . 125.00
7 I Lost My Reputation . . . . . . . . 125.00
8 My Words Condemned Me . . . 125.00
9 WW,Wayward Bride . . . . . . . . 250.00
10 WW,March, 1950,Second
   Rate Girl . . . . . . . . . . . . . . . . 250.00
11 . . . . . . . . . . . . . . . . . . . . . . 125.00
12 Ph(c) . . . . . . . . . . . . . . . . . . 125.00

## ZAZA THE MYSTIC
### See: CHARLIE CHAN

## TEGRA, JUNGLE EMPRESS
### Fox Features Syndicate Aug., 1948
1 Blue Bettle,Rocket Kelly . . . . . 750.00
Becomes:

## ZEGRA, JUNGLE EMPRESS
### Oct., 1948
2 JKa . . . . . . . . . . . . . . . . . . . . 750.00
3 . . . . . . . . . . . . . . . . . . . . . . . 600.00
4 . . . . . . . . . . . . . . . . . . . . . . . 600.00
5 . . . . . . . . . . . . . . . . . . . . . . . 600.00
Becomes:

## MY LOVE LIFE
### June, 1949–Aug., 1950
6 I Put A Price Tag On Love . . . 175.00
7 An Old Man's Fancy . . . . . . . . 125.00
8 My Forbidden Affair . . . . . . . . 125.00
9 I Loved too Often . . . . . . . . . . 125.00
10 My Secret Torture . . . . . . . . . 125.00
11 I Broke My Own Heart . . . . . . 125.00
12 I Was An Untamed Filly . . . . . 125.00
13 I Can Never Marry You . . . . . . 100.00

## ZIGGY PIG, SILLY SEAL
### Marvel Timely, 1944
1 Funny Animals vs. Japs . . . . . . 300.00
2 . . . . . . . . . . . . . . . . . . . . . . . 150.00
3 . . . . . . . . . . . . . . . . . . . . . . . 125.00
4 . . . . . . . . . . . . . . . . . . . . . . . 125.00
5 . . . . . . . . . . . . . . . . . . . . . . . 125.00
6 . . . . . . . . . . . . . . . . . . . . . . . 150.00

## ZIP COMICS
### MLJ Magazines, Feb., 1940–Summer, 1944
1 MMe,O&B:Kalathar,The Scarlet
   Avenger,Steel Sterling,B:Mr
   Satan,Nevada Jones,War Eagle
   Captain Valor . . . . . . . . . . 7,500.00
2 MMe,CBi(c)B:Steel
   Sterling(c) . . . . . . . . . . . . 3,000.00
3 MMe, CBi(a&c) . . . . . . . . . . 2,500.00
4 MMe,CBi(a&c) . . . . . . . . . . 2,000.00
5 MMe,CBi(a&c) . . . . . . . . . . 2,000.00
6 MMe,CBi(a&c) . . . . . . . . . . 1,700.00
7 MMe,CBi(a&c) . . . . . . . . . . 1,700.00
8 MMe,CBi(a&c),Bondage(c) . 1,700.00
9 CMMe,CBi(a&c),E:Kalathar,
   Mr Satan;Bondage(c) . . . . 2,000.00
10 MMe,CBi(a&c),B:Inferno . . 1,800.00
11 MMe,CBi(a&c) . . . . . . . . . . 1,500.00
12 MMe,CBi(a&c),Bondage(c) . 1,500.00
13 MMe,CBi(a&c),E:Inferno,
   Bondage(c),Woman in
   Electric Chair . . . . . . . . . . 1,600.00
14 MMe,CBi(a&c),Bondage(c) . 1,500.00

All comics prices listed are for *Near Mint* condition.

*Zip-Jet 1*
*© St. John Publishing Co.*

*Zoo Funnies 1st Series #2*
*© Charlton Comics*

*Rulah, Jungle Goddess #17*
*© Fox Features Syndicate*

15 MMe,CBi(a&c),Bondage(c) . 1,600.00
16 MMe,CBi(a&c),Bondage(c) . 1,500.00
17 CBI(a&c),E:Scarlet
Avenger Bondage(c). . . . . 1,500.00
18 IN(c),B:Wilbur. . . . . . . . . . 1,500.00
19 IN(c),Steel Sterling(c). . . . . 1,500.00
20 IN(c),O&I:Black Jack
Hitler(c). . . . . . . . . . . . . . 2,400.00
21 IN(c),V:Nazis . . . . . . . . . . . 1,200.00
22 IN(c). . . . . . . . . . . . . . . . . 1,200.00
23 IN(c),Flying Fortress . . . . . 1,200.00
24 IN(c),China Town Exploit . . . 1,200.00
25 IN(c),E:Nevada Jones . . . . . 1,200.00
26 IN(c),B:Black Witch,
E:Capt Valor . . . . . . . . . . . 1,200.00
27 IN(c),I:Web,V:Japanese . . . . 2,000.00
28 IN(C),O:Web,Bondage(c). . . 1,600.00
29 Steel Sterling & Web. . . . . . . 750.00
30 V:Nazis . . . . . . . . . . . . . . . . . 750.00
31 IN(c) . . . . . . . . . . . . . . . . . . 650.00
32 Nazi Skeleton, WWII. . . . . . . 800.00
33 Bondage(c) . . . . . . . . . . . . . . 700.00
34 I:Applejack;Bondage(c). . . . . 700.00
35 E:Zambini . . . . . . . . . . . . . . 650.00
36 I:Senor Banana. . . . . . . . . . . 650.00
37 . . . . . . . . . . . . . . . . . . . . . . 650.00
38 E:Web . . . . . . . . . . . . . . . . . 650.00
39 O&B:Red Rube . . . . . . . . . . 650.00
40 . . . . . . . . . . . . . . . . . . . . . . 550.00
41 . . . . . . . . . . . . . . . . . . . . . . 550.00
42 . . . . . . . . . . . . . . . . . . . . . . 550.00
43 . . . . . . . . . . . . . . . . . . . . . . 550.00
44 Red Rube . . . . . . . . . . . . . . 550.00
45 E:Wilbur . . . . . . . . . . . . . . . 550.00
46 Red Rube . . . . . . . . . . . . . . 550.00
47 Crooks Can't Win . . . . . . . . . 550.00

## ZIP-JET
### St. John Publishing Co., Feb., 1953
1 Rocketman . . . . . . . . . . . . . 1,000.00
2 April–May, 1953, Assassin
of the Airlanes . . . . . . . . . . 650.00

## ZIPPY THE CHIMP
### Pines Comics, 1957
50 . . . . . . . . . . . . . . . . . . . . . . . 70.00
51 . . . . . . . . . . . . . . . . . . . . . . . 70.00

## ZOO FUNNIES
### Charlton Magazines, 1945
1 Funny Animals (1st Charlton) . 250.00
2 . . . . . . . . . . . . . . . . . . . . . . 125.00

3 . . . . . . . . . . . . . . . . . . . . . . 125.00
4 . . . . . . . . . . . . . . . . . . . . . . 125.00
5 . . . . . . . . . . . . . . . . . . . . . . 125.00
6 . . . . . . . . . . . . . . . . . . . . . . 100.00
7 . . . . . . . . . . . . . . . . . . . . . . 100.00
8 Diana the Huntress . . . . . . . 100.00
9 . . . . . . . . . . . . . . . . . . . . . . 100.00
10 . . . . . . . . . . . . . . . . . . . . . . 100.00
11 thru 15 . . . . . . . . . . . . . . @100.00
Becomes:

## TIM MCCOY
### Charlton Comics, 1948
16 Western Movie Stories,
John Wayne. . . . . . . . . . . . 600.00
17 Rocky Lane. . . . . . . . . . . . . 500.00
18 Rod Cameron . . . . . . . . . . . 500.00
19 Jessie James . . . . . . . . . . . 500.00
20 Jimmy Wakley. . . . . . . . . . . 500.00
21 Johnny Mack Brown . . . . . . . 500.00
Becomes:

## PICTORIAL LOVE STORIES
### Charlton Comics, 1949
22 B:Me-Dan Cupid . . . . . . . . . 225.00
23 . . . . . . . . . . . . . . . . . . . . . . 225.00
24 Fred Astaire . . . . . . . . . . . . 250.00
25 . . . . . . . . . . . . . . . . . . . . . . 225.00
26 . . . . . . . . . . . . . . . . . . . . . . 225.00

## ZOO FUNNIES
### Charlton Comics, 1953–55
1 Timothy the Ghost . . . . . . . . . 150.00
2 Leo the Lyin' Lion. . . . . . . . . . 100.00
3 thru 7 . . . . . . . . . . . . . . . . @125.00
8 Nyoka. . . . . . . . . . . . . . . . . . 150.00
9 Nyoka. . . . . . . . . . . . . . . . . . 150.00
10 Nyoka . . . . . . . . . . . . . . . . . 150.00
11 Nyoka . . . . . . . . . . . . . . . . . 150.00
12 Nyoka . . . . . . . . . . . . . . . . . 150.00
13 Nyoka . . . . . . . . . . . . . . . . . 150.00

## ZOOM COMICS
### Carlton Publishing Co., Dec., 1945
N# O:Captain Milksop. . . . . . . . 600.00

## ZOOT COMICS
### Fox Features Syndicate, Spring, 1946
N#(1)(fa) . . . . . . . . . . . . . . . . . 250.00
2 A:Jaguar(fa) . . . . . . . . . . . . . 250.00

3 (fa) . . . . . . . . . . . . . . . . . . . 150.00
4 (fa) . . . . . . . . . . . . . . . . . . . 150.00
5 (fa) . . . . . . . . . . . . . . . . . . . 125.00
6 (fa) . . . . . . . . . . . . . . . . . . . 125.00
7 B:Rulah . . . . . . . . . . . . . . . 1,300.00
8 JKa(c),Fangs of Stone . . . . . . 850.00
9 JKa(c),Fangs of Black Fury . . 850.00
10 JKa(c),Inferno Land . . . . . . . 850.00
11 JKa,The Purple Plague,
Bondage(c) . . . . . . . . . . . . 900.00
12 JKa(c),The Thirsty Stone,
Bondage(c) . . . . . . . . . . . . 800.00
13 Bloody Moon . . . . . . . . . . . . 650.00
14 Pearls of Pathos,Woman
Carried off by Bird . . . . . . . . 850.00
15 Death Dancers . . . . . . . . . . 650.00
16 . . . . . . . . . . . . . . . . . . . . . . 650.00
Becomes:

## RULAH, JUNGLE GODDESS
### Aug., 1948
17 JKa(c),Wolf Doctor. . . . . . . 1,300.00
18 JKa(c),Vampire Garden . . . . 900.00
19 JKa(c) . . . . . . . . . . . . . . . . . 850.00
20 . . . . . . . . . . . . . . . . . . . . . . 850.00
21 JKa(c) . . . . . . . . . . . . . . . . . 850.00
22 JKa(c) . . . . . . . . . . . . . . . . . 850.00
23 . . . . . . . . . . . . . . . . . . . . . . 750.00
24 . . . . . . . . . . . . . . . . . . . . . . 650.00
25 . . . . . . . . . . . . . . . . . . . . . . 650.00
26 . . . . . . . . . . . . . . . . . . . . . . 650.00
27 . . . . . . . . . . . . . . . . . . . . . . 700.00
Becomes:

## I LOVED
### July, 1949–March, 1950
28 . . . . . . . . . . . . . . . . . . . . . . 150.00
29 thru 31 . . . . . . . . . . . . . . @100.00
32 My Poison Love . . . . . . . . . . 100.00

## ZORRO
### Dell Publ. Co., 1959–61
*1 thru 8, see Dell 4-Color*
8 . . . . . . . . . . . . . . . . . . . . . . 125.00
9 . . . . . . . . . . . . . . . . . . . . . . 150.00
10 . . . . . . . . . . . . . . . . . . . . . . 110.00
11 . . . . . . . . . . . . . . . . . . . . . . 110.00
12 ATh . . . . . . . . . . . . . . . . . . . 150.00
13 . . . . . . . . . . . . . . . . . . . . . . 100.00
14 . . . . . . . . . . . . . . . . . . . . . . 100.00
15 . . . . . . . . . . . . . . . . . . . . . . 100.00

# GRADING/PRICE GUIDE

Grading comics is an objective art. This grading guide outlines the many conditions you should look for when purchasing comics, from the highest grade and top condition to the lowest collectible grade and condition. Your own comics will fall into one of these categories. A more complete description and our comments on comics grades can be found inside. We would like to point out, however, that no reader or advertiser is required to follow this or any other standard. All prices in this guide are for comics in Near Mint condition. Happy collecting!

**Mint:** Perfect, pristine, devoid of any trace of wear or printing or handling flaws. Covers must be fully lustrous with sharply pointed corners. No color fading. Must be well centered. Many "rack" comics are not "Mint" even when new.

**Near Mint:** Almost perfect with virtually no wear. No significant printing flaws. Covers must be essentially lustrous with sharp corners. Spine is as tight as new. In older comics, minimal color fading is acceptable, as is slight aging of the paper. Most price guides, including this one, quote prices in this grade.

**Very Fine:** Well preserved, still pleasing in appearance. Small signs of wear, most particularly around the staples. Most luster is readily visible. Corners may no longer be sharp, but are not rounded. Typical of a comic read only a few times and then properly stored.

**Fine:** Clean, presentable, with noticeable signs of wear. Some white may show through enamel around staples, and moderate rounding of corners. No tape or writing damage. Book still lies flat.

**Very Good:** A well worn reading copy with some minor damage such as creasing, small tears or cover flaking. Some discoloration may be evident, with obvious wear around the staples. Little luster remains, and some rolling of the spine may be seen when comic is laid flat on the table.

**Good:** A fully intact comic with very heavy wear. Tears, cover creases and flaking, and rolled spine will all be evident. No tape repairs present. Only very scarce or valuable issues are collected in this state.

The adjoining price table shows the prices for the other collectible grades which correspond to any "near mint" price given in this book.

| Mint | Near Mint | Very Fine | Fine | Very Good |
|---|---|---|---|---|
| $60,000 | $50,000 | $35,000 | $20,000 | $10,000 |
| 48,000 | 40,000 | 28,000 | 16,000 | 8,000 |
| 36,000 | 30,000 | 21,000 | 12,000 | 6,000 |
| 24,000 | 20,000 | 14,000 | 8,000 | 4,000 |
| 18,000 | 15,000 | 10,500 | 6,000 | 3,000 |
| 12,000 | 10,000 | 7,000 | 4,000 | 2,000 |
| 10,800 | 9,000 | 6,300 | 3,600 | 1,800 |
| 9,600 | 8,000 | 5,600 | 3,200 | 1,600 |
| 9,000 | 7,500 | 5,250 | 3,000 | 1,500 |
| 8,400 | 7,000 | 4,900 | 2,800 | 1,400 |
| 7,800 | 6,500 | 4,550 | 2,600 | 1,300 |
| 7,200 | 6,000 | 4,200 | 2,400 | 1,200 |
| 6,600 | 5,500 | 3,850 | 2,200 | 1,100 |
| 6,000 | 5,000 | 3,500 | 2,000 | 1,000 |
| 4,800 | 4,000 | 2,800 | 1,600 | 800 |
| 3,600 | 3,000 | 2,100 | 1,200 | 600 |
| 2,400 | 2,000 | 1,400 | 800 | 400 |
| 1,800 | 1,500 | 1,050 | 600 | 300 |
| 1,200 | 1,000 | 700 | 400 | 200 |
| 1,080 | 900 | 630 | 360 | 180 |
| 960 | 800 | 560 | 320 | 160 |
| 900 | 750 | 525 | 300 | 150 |
| 840 | 700 | 490 | 280 | 140 |
| 780 | 650 | 455 | 260 | 130 |
| 720 | 600 | 420 | 240 | 120 |
| 660 | 550 | 385 | 220 | 110 |
| 600 | 500 | 350 | 200 | 100 |
| 570 | 475 | 332 | 190 | 95 |
| 540 | 450 | 315 | 180 | 90 |
| 510 | 425 | 297 | 170 | 85 |
| 480 | 400 | 280 | 160 | 80 |
| 450 | 375 | 262 | 150 | 75 |
| 420 | 350 | 245 | 140 | 70 |
| 390 | 325 | 227 | 130 | 65 |
| 360 | 300 | 210 | 120 | 60 |
| 330 | 275 | 192 | 110 | 55 |
| 300 | 250 | 175 | 100 | 50 |
| 270 | 225 | 157 | 90 | 45 |
| 240 | 200 | 140 | 80 | 40 |
| 210 | 175 | 122 | 70 | 35 |
| 180 | 150 | 105 | 60 | 30 |
| 150 | 125 | 87 | 50 | 25 |
| 120 | 100 | 70 | 40 | 20 |
| 114 | 95 | 66 | 38 | 19 |
| 108 | 90 | 63 | 36 | 18 |
| 102 | 85 | 59 | 32 | 17 |
| 96 | 80 | 56 | 32 | 16 |
| 90 | 75 | 52 | 30 | 15 |
| 84 | 70 | 49 | 28 | 14 |
| 78 | 65 | 45 | 26 | 13 |
| 72 | 60 | 42 | 24 | 12 |
| 66 | 55 | 38 | 22 | 11 |
| 60 | 50 | 35 | 20 | 10 |